ELEVENTH EDITI

The Bedford Reader

X. J. Kennedy · Dorothy M. Kennedy · Jane E. Aaron

What do you need for class today?

We want to make sure you're the first to hear about the things we provide to help teachers: resources for professional development and the classroom, workshops, and symposia.

Sign up for updates, and we'll send you these professional resources:

- *Writing and Community Engagement: A Critical Sourcebook,* by Thomas Deans, Barbara Roswell, and Adrian J. Wurr

- *How Has Composition Changed?,* a report based on a survey of over 3,000 writing teachers

Help make our resources better. We want to hear your feedback on new projects, ideas, revisions, and media. Tell us what kind of projects you're interested in reviewing.

Sign up for news and opportunities to review at bedfordstmartins.com/englishupdates.

"Year after year, *The Bedford Reader* provides the coverage and scope to **engage students' critical thinking**, which is the essential desired outcome of any freshman composition class. . . . The selections in each section really **open students' eyes to the power of the written word**." — Joseph Couch, *Montgomery College*

Methods for Achieving Your Purpose in Writing

The Bedford Reader centers on common ways of thinking and writing about all kinds of subjects, from everyday experiences to complex scientific theories. Whatever your purpose in writing, one or more of these ways of thinking—or methods of development—can help you discover and shape your ideas in individual paragraphs or entire papers.

The following list connects various purposes you may have for writing and the methods for achieving those purposes. The blue boxes along the right edge of the page correspond to tabs on later pages where each method is explained.

PURPOSE	METHOD
To tell a story about your subject, possibly to enlighten readers or to explain something to them	**Narration**
To help readers understand your subject through the evidence of their senses—sight, hearing, touch, smell, taste	**Description**
To explain your subject with instances that show readers its nature or character	**Example**
To explain or evaluate your subject by helping readers see the similarities and differences between it and another subject	**Comparison and Contrast**
To inform readers how to do something or how something works—how a sequence of actions leads to a particular result	**Process Analysis**
To explain a conclusion about your subject by showing readers the subject's parts or elements	**Division or Analysis**
To help readers see order in your subject by understanding the kinds or groups it can be sorted into	**Classification**
To tell readers the reasons for or consequences of your subject, explaining why or what if	**Cause and Effect**
To show readers the meaning of your subject—its boundaries and its distinctions from other subjects	**Definition**
To have readers consider your opinion about your subject or your proposal for it	**Argument and Persuasion**

THE BEDFORD READER

Eleventh Edition

X. J. Kennedy

Dorothy M. Kennedy

Jane E. Aaron

BEDFORD/ST. MARTIN'S   BOSTON ◆ NEW YORK

FOR BEDFORD/ST. MARTIN'S

Associate Developmental Editor: Sarah Macomber
Senior Production Editor: Lori Chong Roncka
Senior Production Supervisor: Jennifer L. Peterson
Senior Marketing Manager: Molly Parke
Editorial Assistant: Allie Goldstein
Production Assistants: Lidia MacDonald-Carr and David Ayers
Copy Editor: Mary Lou Wilshaw-Watts
Indexer: Leoni Z. McVey
Photo Researcher: Naomi Kornhauser
Permissions Manager: Kalina Ingham Hintz
Senior Art Director: Anna Palchik
Text Design: Anna Palchik, Dorothy Bungert/EriBen Graphics, and Jean Hammond
Cover Design: Donna Lee Dennison
Cover Art: Dmitri Cavander, *Cherry Blossoms in Dining Room*, oil on canvas, 40" × 54", 2004.
    http://www.dcavander.com
Composition: Achorn International, Inc.
Printing and Binding: RR Donnelley and Sons

President: Joan E. Feinberg
Editorial Director: Denise B. Wydra
Editor in Chief: Karen S. Henry
Director of Marketing: Karen R. Soeltz
Director of Production: Susan W. Brown
Associate Director, Editorial Production: Elise S. Kaiser
Managing Editor: Elizabeth M. Schaaf

Library of Congress Control Number: 2010928980

Manufactured in the United States of America.

1 2 3 4 5 6   15 14 13 12 11

For information, write: Bedford/St. Martin's, 75 Arlington Street, Boston, MA 02116
(617-399-4000)

ISBN-10: 0–312–60969–8   ISBN-13: 978–0–312–60969–6
ISBN-10: 0–312–65779–X   ISBN-13: 978–0–312–65779–6 (High School edition)

PREFACE FOR INSTRUCTORS

"A writer" says Saul Bellow, "is a reader moved to emulate." In a nutshell, the aim of *The Bedford Reader* is to move students to be writers, through reading and emulating the good writing of others.

Like its predecessor, this eleventh edition of *The Bedford Reader* works toward its aim both rhetorically and thematically. We present the rhetorical methods realistically, as we ourselves use them—as natural forms that assist invention and fruition and as flexible forms that mix easily for any purpose a writer may have. Further, we forge scores of thematic connections among selections, both in paired essays in each rhetorical chapter and in writing topics after all the selections.

Filling in this outline is a wealth of features, new and old.

NEW FEATURES

ENGAGING NEW READINGS BY REMARKABLE WRITERS.   As always, we have been engrossed in freshening the book's selections. Exceptional rhetorical models that also compel students' interest, the twenty-three new selections include pieces by established favorites such as John Updike, Barbara Ehrenreich, and William Least Heat-Moon as well as contemporary voices such as Firoozeh Dumas and Michael Pollan. Four new selections are illustrated; three are based on sources and serve as models of the documented essays students are assigned in college courses. And three new student essays add to the strong collection of models by college writers.

MORE HELP WITH REVISING AND EDITING. *The Bedford Reader* now does more to guide students through revising and editing their work for an academic audience, helping them move from rough draft to polished essay.

- **New detailed coverage of key topics.** In Chapter 2 on writing, we have added concise explanations and clear examples of common revision and editing challenges, from reshaping for overall purpose to ensuring paragraph coherence to correcting sentence grammar. These discussions give new context to a favorite feature of previous editions: the "Focus" boxes in the rhetorical chapters that highlight relevant revision or editing concerns, such as verbs in narration or tone in argument and persuasion.
- **New revision and editing boxes.** Two checklists summarize the major goals of revising and editing and provide a convenient reference.

UNIQUE EMPHASIS ON GENRE. *The Bedford Reader* is now the only rhetorical reader to show students how they can apply the methods to various genres of writing. New instruction and examples show, for instance, how narration can help build a case study or how argument and persuasion are essential in a proposal.

- **New focus on writing situations.** Integrated discussions throughout Part One now introduce students to the concept of genre and help them understand how purpose, audience, and convention affect a writer's choices.
- **New annotated examples.** In each rhetorical chapter in Part Two, an annotated sample of an academic or work-related document—such as a business case study, a field observation, a lab report, or a résumé—demonstrates a specific application of method to genre.

CLOSER ATTENTION TO CRITICAL READING AND ACADEMIC WRITING. We have revised the three chapters in Part One—on critical reading, the writing process, and academic writing—to give students more help with key skills.

- **Newly annotated essays.** Each chapter in Part One now includes an annotated essay to help students hone their critical-reading skills. Complementing the sample analysis of an essay, new marginal notes alongside the text of Nancy Mairs's "Disability" show the strategies the author uses to achieve her purpose. Similarly, updated annotations for the two student essays inspired by "Disability" highlight the features of a critical response to reading and a research paper.
- **New student Writer on Writing.** The author of Part One's two student essays, Rosie Anaya, has provided us with a new extended commentary,

with examples, in which she reflects on the multiple revisions that took her from personal experience to source-based academic writing.

- **Expanded discussion of synthesis.** Because students often have difficulty maintaining their voices when working with sources, Chapter 3 now clarifies the key distinction between summarizing and analyzing a text and offers annotated paragraphs to demonstrate the uses of each approach.
- **Updated MLA style.** Reflecting the 2009 revision of the *MLA Handbook*, the documentation section of Chapter 3 includes seventy-one current models — and a new directory to help students find the ones they need.

TRADEMARK FEATURES

VARIED SELECTIONS BY WELL-KNOWN AUTHORS.   The selections in *The Bedford Reader* vary in authorship, topics, even length. We offer clear models of the methods of development by noted writers such as Annie Dillard, Amy Tan, E. B. White, and Brent Staples. Half the selections are by women, and a third touch on cultural diversity. They range in subject from family to science, from language to disability, from food to international politics.

EXCITING VISUAL DIMENSION.   *The Bedford Reader* emphasizes the visual as well as the verbal. Chapter 1 on reading provides a short course in thinking critically about images, with a photograph serving as a case study. Each rhetorical chapter then opens with a striking image — an ad, a cartoon, a photograph, a painting, a chart. With accompanying text and questions, these openers invite students' own critical reading and show how the rhetorical methods work visually. Finally, several of the book's selections either take images as their starting points or use illustrations to explain or highlight key ideas.

REALISTIC TREATMENT OF THE RHETORICAL METHODS.   *The Bedford Reader* treats the methods of development not as boxes to be stuffed full of verbiage but as tools for inventing, for shaping, and, ultimately, for accomplishing a purpose. Clear, practical chapter introductions link the methods to the range of purposes they can serve and give step-by-step guidance for writing and revising in the method. (For quick reference, the purpose–method links also appear inside the front cover, where they are keyed to the marginal page tabs in each chapter introduction.) The new annotated genre examples in the rhetorical chapters emphasize the practical applications of the methods as well.

Taking the realistic approach to the methods even further, we show how writers freely combine the methods to achieve their purposes: Each rhetorical introduction discusses how that method might work with others, and at least one "Other Methods" question after every selection helps students analyze how methods work together. Most significantly, Part Three provides an anthology of works by well-known writers that specifically illustrate mixed methods. The headnotes for these selections point to where each method comes into play.

A FOUNDATION IN CRITICAL READING AND ACADEMIC WRITING.   Providing the context and support students need to succeed as readers and writers, Part One of *The Bedford Reader* gives concrete advice on critical reading, the writing process, and academic writing. Chapter 1 includes a sample of a student's annotations on a text and practical guidelines for summarizing, analyzing, and interpreting texts and visual images. Chapter 2 takes students through the writing process and includes a student work-in-progress. And Chapter 3 introduces the features of college writing, focusing on both responding to a text and drawing on multiple sources, with emphases on synthesis, integrating and evaluating sources, avoiding plagiarism, and documenting sources.

Both response writing and researched writing are illustrated by an annotated student essay—written by the same student on related subjects—to show how reading can expand and refine ideas. Ten additional examples of documented writing, spread throughout the book, give students a taste for work that draws on and acknowledges sources.

EXTENSIVE THEMATIC CONNECTIONS.   *The Bedford Reader* provides substantial topics for class discussion and writing. A pair of essays in each rhetorical chapter addresses the same subject, from the ordinary (housekeeping) to the controversial (immigration), and the chapter on argument includes two essay pairs (one new) and a casebook of four essays (two new). At least one "Connections" writing topic after every selection suggests links to other selections. And an alternate thematic table of contents arranges the book's selections under more than two dozen topics (three new).

UNIQUE COMMENTS BY WRITERS ON WRITING.   After their essays, fifty-two of the book's writers offer comments on everything from grammar to revision to how they developed the reprinted piece. Besides providing rock-solid advice, these comments also prove that for the pros, too, writing is usually a challenge. Writers on Writing new to this edition include those by William Least Heat-Moon, David Foster Wallace, Firoozeh Dumas, and Judy Brady.

For easy access, the Writers on Writing are listed in the book's index under the topics they address. Look up *Revision,* for instance, and find that Annie Dillard, Dave Barry, Bruce Catton, and Russell Baker, among others, have something to say about this crucial stage of the writing process.

ABUNDANT EDITORIAL APPARATUS.   As always, we've surrounded the selections with a wealth of material designed to get students reading, thinking, and writing. To help structure students' critical approach to the selections, each one is preceded by headnotes on the author and on the selection itself that outline the selection's cultural and historical contexts, and each is followed by three sets of questions (on meaning, writing strategy, and language) and at least five writing topics. One writing topic encourages students to explore their responses in their journals; another suggests how to develop the journal writing into an essay; and others emphasize critical writing, research, and connections among selections.

Besides the aids with every selection, the book also includes additional writing topics for every rhetorical chapter, a glossary ("Useful Terms") that defines all terms used in the book (including all those printed in SMALL CAPITAL LETTERS), and an index that alphabetizes authors and titles and important topics (including the elements of composition and, as noted earlier, those covered in the Writers on Writing).

EXTENSIVE INSTRUCTOR'S MANUAL.   Available as a separate manual, bound into the instructor's edition, or online, *Notes and Resources for Teaching The Bedford Reader* suggests ways to integrate journal writing and collaboration into writing classes and ways to use the book's opening chapters on critical reading, the writing process, and academic writing. In addition, *Notes and Resources* discusses every method, every selection (with possible answers to all questions), and every Writer on Writing.

COMPREHENSIVE SUPPLEMENTS.   Bedford/St. Martin's offers several additional resources to help students and instructors get the most out of *The Bedford Reader.*

A free companion Web site (*bedfordstmartins.com/thebedfordreader*) links to a broad range of resources for both students and instructors.

- **For students:** an interactive reading quiz for each selection; access to editorially selected Web links for major authors and topics; *Exercise Central,* the largest online collection of grammar, usage, and writing exercises; *Research and Documentation Online,* providing extra help and additional documentation models; *The Bedford Bibliographer,* a tool for collecting source information and making a bibliography in MLA, APA, and Chicago styles; and *Re:Writing*, the largest, most comprehensive collection of free resources for the writing class.

• **For instructors:** the complete text of the instructor's manual, sample syllabi, and classroom activities; *Teaching Central*, a rich library of bibliographies, teaching advice, classroom materials, adjunct support, and more; *Bits*, a collection of creative ideas for teaching in an easily searchable blog; and *The Bedford Bibliography for Teachers of Writing*.

The Bedford Reader can also be packaged with innovative resources at a significant discount. *VideoCentral: English* is a growing collection of videos that capture real-world, academic, and student writers talking about how and why they write. And the *i-series* on CD-ROM offers interactive exercises on key rhetorical and visual concepts (*ix visual exercises*), multimedia argument tutorials (*i-claim: Visualizing Argument*), and hands-on practice with research and source citation (*i-cite: Visualizing Sources*).

Finally, content cartridges for the most common course-management systems — *Blackboard, WebCT, Angel,* and *Desire2Learn* — make it easy to download digital materials for *The Bedford Reader* and use them in an online teaching environment.

TWO VERSIONS.   *The Bedford Reader* has a sibling. A shorter edition, *The Brief Bedford Reader*, features fifty-one selections instead of seventy-two, including five essays (rather than twelve) in Part Three.

ACKNOWLEDGMENTS

Hundreds of the teachers and students using *The Bedford Reader* over the years have helped us shape the book. For this edition, the following teachers offered insights from their experiences that encouraged worthy changes: James E. Allen, College of DuPage; David Bockoven, Linn-Benton Community College; Wyatt Bonikowski, Suffolk University; Eugenia P. Bryan, Georgia Southwestern State University; Thomas F. Connolly, Suffolk University; Joseph Couch, Montgomery College; Darren DeFrain, Wichita State University; Kathleen Dixon, University of North Dakota; Roger Robin Elkins, Butte College; Natalie Katerina Eschenbaum, University of Wisconsin, La Crosse; Africa Fine, Palm Beach Community College; Annie Fuller, Lenoir Community College; Kim D. Gainer, Radford University; Timothy D. Giles, Georgia Southern University; Roy Neil Graves, University of Tennessee, Martin; J. Bartholomay Grier, Wilkes University; Michael Helfen, Cape Cod Community College; Michael Hricik, Westmoreland County Community College; S. L. Jackson, County College of Morris; Tamara Kuzmenkov, Tacoma Community College; Jim LaBate, Hudson Valley Community College; Linda LaPointe, St. Petersburg College; Mike Matthews, Central Texas College; Stephen Monroe, University of Mississippi; Julie A. Myatt, Middle Tennessee State University; Katherine P. Simpson, Lord Fairfax Community College; Michele Singletary, Nashville State Community College; Jeff Larsen, Lowell High School; and Jason Webb, Columbine High School.

We were delighted by the initiative and thoughtfulness demonstrated by a group of Advanced Placement students at Columbus High School in Columbus, Wisconsin, who compared Martin Luther King's "I Have a Dream" (p. 643) line-by-line against a film of King delivering the speech in 1963. They wrote to tell us of their discoveries, and we have taken note of them in the headnote to the selection and in the instructor's manual. Many thanks to Shane Bartow, Rachael Bublitz, Lindsay Bursaw, Marie Busse, Melina Droessler, Darcie First, Sarah Kikkert, Kelsey Mook, Cortney Netzel, Michelle Skalitzy, Meagan Stettnisch, Lindsey Torowski, and Teddy Whitman.

We are as ever deeply in debt to the creative people at and around Bedford/ St. Martin's. Joan Feinberg, Denise Wydra, Steve Scipione, Maura Shea, and especially Karen Henry contributed insight and support. Sarah Macomber, developing the book, suggested and directed the revisions and new features with imagination, determination, and a teacher's keen sense for what does and doesn't work. Her assistant, Allie Goldstein, cheerfully hunted down readings, helped to draft the headnotes and writers on writing, and rescued us several times over. Jeff Ousbourne helped us develop the new genre feature. Ellen Kuhl Repetto was all-around indispensable as she found new selections and shaped new materials, reading apparatus, and the instructor's manual. Donna Dennison created the striking cover. Jennifer Peterson planned and oversaw the production of the book. And Lori Chong Roncka worked with grace and aplomb to transform the raw manuscript into the book you hold.

CONTENTS

A writer with multiple sclerosis thinks she knows why the media carry so few images of
people like herself with disabilities: Viewers might conclude, correctly, that "there is
something ordinary about disability itself."

    Writing while reading • Summarizing • Thinking critically

ROSIE ANAYA   The Best Kept Secret on Campus (*annotated essay*)   86

When college students suffer psychological problems—and the number who do is "staggering"—they seldom seek or receive the help they need. Drawing on sources, the student author of the response essay in Chapter 2 probes more deeply into the subject of psychological disability.

PART TWO
THE METHODS   95

4   NARRATION: Telling a Story   97

Visual Image: *How Joe's Body Brought Him Fame instead of Shame,* advertisement for Charles Atlas

DIFFERENCE

MAYA ANGELOU   Champion of the World   110

She didn't dare ring up a sale while that epic battle was on. A noted African American writer remembers from her early childhood the night when a people's fate hung on a pair of boxing gloves.

PAIRED
SELECTIONS

AMY TAN   Fish Cheeks   116

The writer remembers her teenage angst when the minister and his cute blond son attended her family's Christmas Eve dinner, an elaborate Chinese feast.

PERSONALITIES

SUZANNE BRITT   Neat People vs. Sloppy People   255

"Neat people are lazier and meaner than sloppy people," asserts the writer. As she compares and contrasts, she takes up a cudgel and chooses sides.

Suzanne Britt on Writing   259

**PAIRED
SELECTIONS**

DAVE BARRY   Batting Clean-Up and Striking Out   261

An expert at comedic observation takes a humorous swing at the difference between the sexes. It hinges on the importance each sex gives to dirt and baseball.

Dave Barry on Writing   265

BRUCE CATTON   Grant and Lee: A Study in Contrasts   267

The great Civil War generals Ulysses S. Grant and Robert E. Lee clearly personified their opposing traditions. But what they had in common was more vital by far.

Bruce Catton on Writing   272

DAVID SEDARIS   Remembering My Childhood on the Continent
                  of Africa   274

A popular essayist complains about his "unspeakably dull" childhood, when he might have grown up like his partner, Hugh, amid monkeys and machete-wielding guards.

David Sedaris on Writing   280

FATEMA MERNISSI   Size 6: The Western Women's Harem   282

Trying to buy a skirt in a US department store leads the author, a Moroccan Muslim, to compare the relative disadvantages of women in Western and Muslim countries. Who's actually better off?

GEORGE CHAUNCEY   The Legacy of Antigay Discrimination   290

Whatever today's prejudice against gays and lesbians, the "systematic and powerful" discrimination of fifty years ago was much worse. A historian explains the difference.

ADDITIONAL WRITING TOPICS   297

THEMATIC CONTENTS

CHILDHOOD AND FAMILY

CLASS

COMMUNICATION

COMMUNITY

CULTURAL DIVERSITY

DEATH

ENVIRONMENT

ETHICS

FOOD

GLOBALIZATION AND ECONOMICS

MEDIA

MEMORY

MINORITY EXPERIENCE

MYTH AND BELIEF

THE NATURAL WORLD

OTHER PEOPLES, OTHER CULTURES

PLACE AND PLACES

POPULAR CULTURE

PSYCHOLOGY AND BEHAVIOR

READING, WRITING, AND LANGUAGE

SPORTS AND LEISURE

VIOLENCE

WAR AND NATIONAL SECURITY

WOMEN AND MEN

WORK

INTRODUCTION

WHY READ? WHY WRITE?

Many prophets have predicted the doom of the word on paper, and they may yet be proved correct. We may soon be reading books and magazines mainly on pocket computers and communicating exclusively by e-mail and text message. But even if we do discard paper and pens, the basic aims and methods of writing will not fundamentally change. Whether on paper or on screen, we will need to explain our thoughts to others plainly and forcefully.

In almost any career or profession you may enter, you will be expected to read continually and also to write. This book assumes that reading and writing are a unity. Deepen your mastery of one, and you deepen your mastery of the other. The experience of carefully reading an excellent writer, noticing not only what the writer has to say but also the quality of its saying, rubs off (if you are patient and perceptive) on your own writing. "We go to college," said the poet Robert Frost, "to be given one more chance to learn to read in case we haven't learned in high school. Once we have learned to read, the rest can be trusted to add itself *unto us*."

For any writer, reading is indispensable. It turns up fresh ideas; it stocks the mind with information, understanding, examples, and illustrations;

1

it instills critical awareness of one's surroundings. When you have a well-stocked and girded mental storehouse, you tell truths, even small and ordinary truths. Instead of building shimmering spires of words in an attempt to make a reader think, "Wow, what a grade A writer," you write what most readers will find worth reading. Thornton Wilder, playwright and novelist, put this advice memorably: "If you write to *impress* it will always be bad, but if you write to *express* it will be good."

USING *THE BEDFORD READER*

The Selections

In this book, we trust, you'll find at least a few selections you will enjoy and care to remember. *The Bedford Reader* features work by many of the finest nonfiction writers and even a few sterling literary figures.

The selections deal with more than just writing and literature and such usual concerns of English courses; they cut broadly across a college curriculum. You'll find writings on science, history, business, popular culture, sociology, food, education, communication, the environment, technology, sports, politics, health, and minority experience. Some writers recall their childhoods, their families, their problems and challenges. Some explore matters likely to spark debate: global warming, gay rights, sex roles, race relations, immigration. Some writers are intently serious; others, funny. In all, these seventy-one selections — including a short story and a poem — reveal kinds of reading you will meet in other college courses. Such reading is the usual diet of well-informed people with lively minds — who, to be sure, aren't found only on campuses.

We have chosen the selections with one main purpose in mind: to show you how good writers write. Don't feel glum if at first you find an immense gap in quality between E. B. White's writing and yours. Of course there's a gap: White is an immortal with a unique style that he perfected over half a century. You don't have to judge your efforts by comparison. The idea is to gain whatever writing techniques you can. If you're going to learn from other writers, why not go to the best of them? Do you want to know how to compare and contrast two subjects so that each becomes vividly clear? Read Bruce Catton's "Grant and Lee." Do you want to know how to tell a story about your childhood and make it stick in someone's memory? Read Maya Angelou's "Champion of the World." Incidentally, not all the selections in this book are the work of professional writers: Students, too, write essays worth studying, as proved by Rosie Anaya, Bradley Philbert, Brad Manning, Linnea Saukko,

Laila Ayad, Marie Javdani, Christine Leong, Colleen Wenke, Peter F. Martin, and Rodrigo Villagomez.

Not all the selections in this book are solely verbal, either, for much of what we "read" in the world is visual information, such as in photographs and paintings, or visual-with-verbal information, such as in advertisements, films, and Web sites. In all, we include sixteen visual works. Some of them are subjects of writing, as when a writer analyzes a photograph. Other visual works stand free, offering themselves to be understood, interpreted, and perhaps enjoyed, just as prose and poetry do.

We combine visual material with written texts to further a key aim of *The Bedford Reader*: to encourage you to think critically about what you see, hear, and read, that is, to think with an open, questioning mind. Like everyone else, you face a daily barrage of words and pictures—from the media, from your courses, from relatives and friends. Mulling over the views of the writers, artists, and others represented in this book—figuring out their motives and strategies, agreeing or disagreeing with their ideas—will help you learn to manage, digest, and use, in your own writing, what you read, see, and hear.

The Organization

As a glance over the table of contents will show, the selections in *The Bedford Reader* fall into two parts. In Part Two each of the ten chapters explains a familiar method of developing ideas, such as NARRATION, DESCRIPTION, EXAMPLE, CAUSE AND EFFECT, and DEFINITION. The selections in the chapter illustrate the method. Then Part Three offers an anthology of selections by well-known writers that illustrate how, most often, the methods work together.

These methods of development aren't empty jugs to pour full of any old, dull words. Neither are they straitjackets woven by fiendish English teachers to pin your writing arm to your side and keep you from expressing yourself naturally. The methods are tools for achieving your PURPOSE in writing, whatever that purpose may be. They can help you discover what you know, what you need to know, how to think critically about your subject, and how to shape your writing.

Suppose, for example, that you set out to explain what makes a certain popular singer unique. You want to discuss her voice, her music, her lyrics, her style. While putting your ideas down on paper, it strikes you that you can best illustrate the singer's distinctions by showing the differences between her and another popular singer, one she is often compared with. To achieve your purpose, then, you draw on the method of COMPARISON AND CONTRAST, and as you proceed the method prompts you to notice differences between the two singers that you hadn't dreamed of noticing. With the methods, such little miracles of focusing and creating take place with heartening regularity. Give the methods a try. See how they help you reach your writing goals by giving you more to say, more that you think is worth saying.

Examining *The Bedford Reader*'s selections, you'll discover two important facts about the methods of development. First, they are flexible: Two people can use the same method for quite different ends, and just about any method can point a way into just about any subject in any medium. This flexibility is apparent in every method chapter:

- A photograph, advertisement, cartoon, or other image shows how the method can contribute to visual representation of an idea.
- Two sample paragraphs—one about television, one from a college textbook—illustrate the method's useful range.
- An excerpt from an academic genre—such as a lab report or an essay exam—demonstrates the method's potential applications in college writing.
- A pair of essays shows authors using the same method to focus on the same general subject but with different purposes and results.

In addition, three annotated essays show how the methods operate in practice, highlighting the writers' choices and strategies and revealing the rewards of critical reading.

The second point about the methods of development is this: A writer never sticks to just one method all the way through a piece of writing. Even when one method predominates, as in all the essays in Part Two, you'll see the writer pick up another method, let it shape a paragraph or more, and then move on to yet another method—all to achieve some overriding aim. In "The Best Pizza in the World," Elizabeth Gilbert depends heavily on description to capture the delight of eating the cheesy treat in the Italian city that invented it. But Gilbert also uses narration to tell a story, examples to illustrate her points, and comparison and contrast to explain why the experience made such an impression.

So the methods are like oxygen, iron, and other elements that make up substances in nature: all around us, indispensable to us, but seldom found alone and isolated, in laboratory-pure states. When you read an essay in a chapter called "Description" or "Classification," don't expect it to describe or classify in every line, but do notice how the method is central to the writer's purpose. Then, when you read the selections in Part Three, notice how the "elements" of description, example, comparison, definition, and so on rise to prominence and recede as the writer's need dictates.

The Journal Prompts, Questions, Writing Topics, and Glossary

After every selection you'll find a suggestion for responding in your journal to what you've just read. (See p. 37 for more on journal writing.) Then you'll find questions on meaning, writing strategy, and language that can help you analyze the selection and learn from it. (You can see a sample of how these questions work when we analyze Nancy Mairs's "Disability," starting on p. 24). After these questions are at least four suggestions for writing, including one that proposes turning your journal entry into an essay, one that links the selection with one or two others in the book, and one that asks you to read the selection and write about it with your critical faculties alert (more on this in Chap. 1). More writing topics conclude each chapter.

In this introduction and throughout the following chapters, certain terms appear in CAPITAL LETTERS. These are words helpful in discussing both the selections in this book and the reading and writing you do. If you'd like to see such a term defined and illustrated, you can find it in the glossary, Useful Terms, at the back of this book. This section offers more than just brief definitions. It is there to provide you with further information and support.

Writers on Writing

We have tried to give this book another dimension. We want to show that the writers represented here do not produce their readable and informative text on the first try, as if by magic, leaving the rest of us to cope with writer's block, awkward sentences, and all the other difficulties of writing. Take comfort and cheer: These writers, too, struggled to make themselves interesting and clear. In proof, we visit their workshops littered with crumpled paper and forgotten coffee cups. In Chapter 2, an essay by a student, Rosie Anaya, illustrates the writing process, and we include Anaya's thoughts about her drafts. In Chapter 3, another essay by Anaya illustrates researched academic writing, and we provide her thoughts about using sources. Then following most of the other selections are statements by the writers, revealing how they write (or wrote), offering their tricks, setting forth things they admire about good writing.

No doubt you'll soon notice some contradictions in these statements: The writers disagree about when and how to think about their readers, about whether outlines have any value, about whether style follows subject or vice versa. The reason for the difference of opinion is, simply, that no two writers follow the same path to finished work. Even the same writer may take the left instead of the customary right fork if the writing situation demands a change.

A key aim of providing Anaya's drafts and comments and the other writers' statements on writing, then, is to suggest the sheer variety of routes open to you, the many approaches to writing and strategies for succeeding at it. At the very end of the book, an index points you toward the writers' comments on such practical matters as drafting, finding your point, and revising sentences.

PART ONE

READING, WRITING, AND RESEARCH

1

CRITICAL READING

Whatever career you enter, much of the reading you will do—for business, not for pleasure—will probably be hasty. You'll skim: glance at words here and there, find essential facts, catch the drift of an argument. To cross oceans of print, you won't have time to paddle: You'll need to hop a jet. By skimming, you'll be able to tear through screens full of electronic mail or quickly locate the useful parts of a long report.

But other reading that you do for work, most that you do in college, and all that you do in this book call for closer attention. You may be trying to understand a new company policy, seeking the truth in a campaign ad, researching a complicated historical treaty, or (in using this book) looking for pointers to sharpen your reading and writing skills. To learn from the selections here how to write better yourself, expect to spend an hour or two in the company of each one. Does the essay assigned for today remain unread, and does class start in five minutes? "I'll just breeze through this little item," you might tell yourself. But no, give up. You're a goner.

Good writing, as every writer knows, demands toil, and so does CRITICAL READING—reading that looks beneath the surface of a work, whether written or visual, seeking to understand the creator's intentions, the strategies for achieving them, and their worthiness. Never try to gulp down a rich and potent work without chewing; all it will give you is indigestion. When you're going to

read an essay or study a visual image in depth, seek out some quiet place—
a library, a study cubicle, your room (provided it doesn't also hold a cranky
baby or two roommates playing poker). Flick off the radio, stereo, or television.
The fewer the distractions, the easier your task will be and the more you'll enjoy it.

How do you read critically? Exactly how, that is, do you see beneath the
surface of a work, master its complexities, gauge its intentions and techniques,
judge its value? To find out, we'll model critical-thinking processes that you
can apply to the selections in this book, taking a close look at an essay, Nancy
Mairs's "Disability" (p. 13), and at a photograph (p. 29).

READING AN ESSAY
The Preliminaries

Critical reading starts before you read the first word of a piece of writing.
Like a pilot circling an airfield, you take stock of what's before you, locating
clues to the work's content and the writer's biases.

The Title

Often the title will tell you the writer's subject, as in Suzanne Britt's "Neat
People vs. Sloppy People" or Stephanie Ericsson's "The Ways We Lie." Sometimes the title immediately states the THESIS, the main point the writer will
make: "I Want a Wife." Some titles spell out the method a writer proposes to
follow: "Grant and Lee: A Study in Contrasts." The TONE of the title may also
reveal the writer's attitude toward the material, as "The Plot against People"
or "Live Free and Starve" does.

Whatever it does, a title sits atop its essay like a neon sign. It tells you
what's inside or makes you want to venture in. To pick an alluring title for an
essay of your own is a skill worth cultivating.

The Author

Whatever you know about a writer—background, special training, previous works, outlook, or ideology—often will help you guess something about
the essay before you read a word of it. Is the writer on new taxes a political
conservative? Expect an argument against added "revenue enhancement." Is
the writer a liberal? Expect an argument that new social programs are worth
the price. Is the writer a feminist? an athlete? an internationally renowned

philosopher? a popular television comedian? By knowing something about a writer's background or beliefs, you may know beforehand a little of what he or she will say. To help provide such knowledge, this book supplies biographical notes, such as the one about Nancy Mairs on page 13.

The Genre

Identifying the type, or GENRE, of a written work can tell you much about the writer's intentions and likely strategies. The works in a particular genre typically follow distinctive conventions for content, format, and other features; and we readers, whether consciously or not, expect those features from that genre. For instance, we expect that a scholarly article will take a serious, academic tone, lay out its arguments carefully, provide substantial evidence, and cite other published works. If we encountered the same approach in a personal narrative about a life-changing event, however, we'd be surprised—and probably annoyed.

The best way to learn about genres and their conventions is to read widely. To that end, the selections in this book represent many different kinds of writing: personal reflections, critical analyses, business writing, works of literature, humor pieces, researched essays, arguments, and more. In addition, the introductions to Chapters 4–13 provide annotated examples of ten academic genres—such as a field observation, a lab report, and a proposal—to show how they work with the methods of development and to preview the kinds of writing you may be assigned in your classes.

Where the Work Was Published

Clearly, it matters to a writer's credibility whether an article called "Creatures of the Dark Oceans" appears in *Scientific American*, a magazine for scientists and interested nonscientists, or in a popular tabloid weekly, sold at supermarket checkout counters, that is full of eye-popping sensations. But no less important, examining where a work appears can tell you for whom the writer was writing.

In this book we'll strongly urge you as a writer to think of your AUDIENCE, your readers, and to try looking at what you write as if through their eyes. To help you develop this ability, we tell you something about the sources and thus the original readers of each essay you study, in a note just before the essay. (Such a note precedes "Disability" on page 13.) After you have read the sample essay, we'll further consider how having a sense of your readers helps you write.

When the Work Was Published

Knowing in what year a work appeared may give you another key to understanding it. A 2010 article on ocean creatures will contain statements of fact more recent and more reliable than an essay printed in 1700—although the older essay might contain valuable information, too, and perhaps some delectable language, folklore, and poetry. In *The Bedford Reader* the introductory note on every essay tells you not only where but also when the essay was originally printed. If you're reading an essay elsewhere—say, in one of the writer's books—you can usually find this information on the copyright page.

The First Reading

On first reading an essay, you don't want to bog down in every troublesome particular. When you run into an unfamiliar word or name, see if you can figure it out from its surroundings. If a word stops you cold and you feel lost, circle it in pencil; you can always look it up later. (In a little while we'll come back to the helpful habit of reading with a pencil. Indeed, some readers feel more confident with pencil in hand from the start.)

The first time you read an essay, size up the forest; later, you can squint at the acorns all you like. Try this approach now, reading Nancy Mairs's "Disability."

NANCY MAIRS

A self-described "radical feminist, pacifist, and cripple," Nancy Mairs aims to "speak the 'unspeakable.'" Her poetry, memoirs, and essays deal with many sensitive subjects, including her struggles with the debilitating disease of multiple sclerosis. Born in Long Beach, California, in 1943, Mairs grew up in New Hampshire and Massachusetts. She received a BA from Wheaton College in Massachusetts (1964) and an MFA in creative writing (1975) and a PhD in English literature (1984) from the University of Arizona. While working on her advanced degrees, Mairs taught high school and college writing courses. Her second book of poetry, *In All the Rooms of the Yellow House* (1984), received a Western States Arts Foundation book award. Her essays are published in *Plaintext* (1986), *Remembering the Bone-House* (1988), *Carnal Acts* (1990), *Ordinary Time* (1993), *Waist High in the World: A Life among the Nondisabled* (1996), and *A Troubled Guest* (2001). Her most recent book, *A Dynamic God* (2007), explores her spiritual experience as a convert to Catholicism.

Disability

As a writer afflicted with multiple sclerosis, Nancy Mairs is in a unique position to examine how the culture responds to people with disabilities. In this essay from *Carnal Acts*, she examines the media's depiction of disability and argues with her usual unsentimental candor that the media must treat disability as normal. The essay was first published in 1987 in the *New York Times*. To what extent is Mairs's critique of the media still valid today?

For months now I've been consciously searching for representation of myself in the media, especially television. I know I'd recognize this self because of certain distinctive, though not unique, features: I am a forty-three-year-old woman crippled with multiple sclerosis; although I can still totter short distances with the aid of a brace and a cane, more and more of the time I ride in a wheelchair. Because of these appliances and my peculiar gait, I'm easy to spot even in a crowd. So when I tell you I haven't noticed any women like me on television, you can believe me.

Actually, last summer I did see a woman with multiple sclerosis portrayed on one of those medical dramas that offer an illness-of-the-week like the daily special at your local diner. In fact, that was the whole point of the show: that this poor young woman had MS. She was terribly upset (understandably, I assure you) by the diagnosis, and her response was to plan a trip to Kenya while she was still physically capable of making it, against the advice of the young, fit, handsome doctor who had fallen in love with her. And she almost did it.

At least, she got as far as a taxi to the airport, hotly pursued by the doctor. But at the last she succumbed to his blandishments and fled the taxi into his manly protective embrace. No escape to Kenya for this cripple.

Capitulation into the arms of a man who uses his medical powers to strip 3 one of even the urge toward independence is hardly the sort of representation I had in mind. But even if the situation had been sensitively handled, according to the woman her right to her own adventures, it wouldn't have been what I'm looking for. Such a television show, as well as films like *Duet for One* and *Children of a Lesser God*, in taking disability as its major premise, excludes the complexities that round out a character and make her whole. It's not about a woman who happens to be physically disabled; it's about physical disability as the determining factor of a woman's existence.

Take it from me, physical disability looms pretty large in one's life. But it 4 doesn't devour one wholly. I'm not, for instance, Ms. MS, a walking, talking embodiment of a chronic incurable degenerative disease. In most ways I'm just like every other woman of my age, nationality, and socioeconomic background. I menstruate, so I have to buy tampons. I worry about smoker's breath, so I buy mouthwash. I smear my wrinkling skin with lotions. I put bleach in the washer so my family's undies won't be dingy. I drive a car, talk on the telephone, get runs in my pantyhose, eat pizza. In most ways, that is, I'm the advertisers' dream: Ms. Great American Consumer. And yet the advertisers, who determine nowadays who will get represented publicly and who will not, deny the existence of me and my kind absolutely.

I once asked a local advertiser why he didn't include disabled people in 5 his spots. His response seemed direct enough: "We don't want to give people the idea that our product is just for the handicapped." But tell me truly now: If you saw me pouring out puppy biscuits, would you think these kibbles were only for the puppies of the cripples? If you saw my blind niece ordering a Coke, would you switch to Pepsi lest you be struck sightless? No, I think the advertiser's excuse masked a deeper and more anxious rationale: To depict disabled people in the ordinary activities of daily life is to admit that there is something ordinary about disability itself, that it may enter anybody's life. If it is effaced completely, or at least isolated as a separate "problem," so that it remains at a safe distance from other human issues, then the viewer won't feel threatened by her or his own physical vulnerability.

This kind of effacement or isolation has painful, even dangerous conse- 6 quences, however. For the disabled person, these include self-degradation and a subtle kind of self-alienation not unlike that experienced by other minorities. Socialized human beings love to conform, to study others and then mold themselves to the contours of those whose images, for good reasons or bad, they come to love. Imagine a life in which feasible others — others you can hope to be like—don't exist. At the least you might conclude that there is something queer about you, something ugly or foolish or shameful. In the extreme, you might feel as though you don't exist, in any meaningful social sense, at all. Everyone else is "there," sucking breath mints and splashing cologne and swigging wine coolers. You're "not there." And if not there, nowhere.

But this denial of disability imperils even you who are able-bodied, and   7
not just by shrinking your insight into the physically and emotionally complex world you live in. Some disabled people call you TAPs, or Temporarily Abled Persons. The fact is that ours is the only minority you can join involuntarily, without warning, at any time. And if you live long enough, as you're increasingly likely to do, you may well join it. The transition will probably be difficult from a physical point of view no matter what. But it will be a good bit easier psychologically if you are accustomed to seeing disability as a normal characteristic, one that complicates but does not ruin human existence. Achieving this integration, for disabled and able-bodied people alike, requires that we insert disability daily into our field of vision: quietly, naturally, in the small and common scenes of our ordinary lives.

Writing while Reading

In giving an essay a going-over, many readers find a pencil in hand as good as a currycomb for a horse's coat. The pencil (or pen or computer keyboard) concentrates the attention wonderfully, and, as often happens with writing, it can lead you to unexpected questions and connections. (Some readers favor markers that roll pink or yellow ink over a word or line, making the eye jump to that spot, but you can't use a highlighter to note *why* a word or an idea is important.) You can annotate your own printed material, underlining essential ideas, scoring key passages with vertical lines, writing questions in the margins about difficult words or concepts, venting feelings ("Bull!" "Yes!" "Says who?"). Here, as an example, are the jottings of one student, Rosie Anaya, on a paragraph of Mairs's essay:

> This kind of (effacement) or isolation has painful, even dangerous consequences, however. For the disabled person, these include (self-)degradation and a subtle kind of (self-)alienation not unlike that experienced by other minorities. Socialized human beings love to conform, to study others and then mold themselves to the contours of those whose images, for good reasons or bad, they come to love. Imagine a life in which feasible others — others you can hope to be like — don't exist. At the least you might conclude that there is something queer about you, something ugly or foolish or shameful. In the extreme, you might feel as though you don't exist, in any meaningful social sense, at all. Everyone else is "there," sucking breath mints and splashing cologne and swigging wine coolers. You're "not there." And if not there, nowhere.

Margin notes:
- ? (at top)
- IMPORTANT
- Why "self"?
- True? What about individuality?
- ✔ emotions
- examples are insignificant, but that's the point

If you can't annotate what you're reading — because it's borrowed or it appears on a screen — make your notes on a separate sheet of paper or in a separate file on your computer.

Apart from specific notes about the text, you'll also need a place for the longer summaries, detailed analyses, and evaluations discussed below and on the following pages. For such responses, you may find a JOURNAL handy. It can be a repository of your ideas, a comfortable place to record meandering or direct thoughts about what you read. You may be surprised to find that the more you write in an unstructured way, the more you'll have to say when it's time to write a structured essay. (For more on journals, see p. 37.)

Writing while reading helps you behold the very spine of an essay, as if in an X-ray view, so that you, as much as any expert, can judge its curves and connections. You'll develop an opinion about what you read, and you'll want to express it. While reading this way, you're being a writer. Your pencil tracks or keystrokes will jog your memory, too, when you review for a test, when you take part in class discussion, or write about what you've read.

Summarizing

It's usually good practice, especially with more difficult essays, to SUMMA-RIZE the content in writing to be sure you understand it or, as often happens, to come to understand it. (We're suggesting that you write summaries for yourself, but the technique is also useful when you discuss other people's works in your writing, as shown on p. 64.) In summarizing a work of writing, you digest, *in your own words*, what the author says: You take the essence of the author's meaning, without the supporting evidence and other details that make that gist convincing or interesting. When you are practicing reading and the work is short (the case with the reading you do in this book), you may want to make this a two-step procedure: First write a summary sentence for every paragraph or related group of paragraphs; then summarize those sentences in two or three others that capture the heart of the author's meaning.

Here is a two-step summary of "Disability." (The numbers in parentheses refer to paragraph numbers in the essay.) First, the longer version:

(1) Mairs searches the media in vain for depictions of women like herself with disabilities. (2) One TV movie showed a woman recently diagnosed with multiple sclerosis, but she chose dependence over independence. (3) Such shows oversimplify people with disabilities by making disability central to their lives. (4) People with disabilities live lives and consume goods like everyone else, but the media ignore them. (5) Showing disability as ordinary would remind nondisabled viewers that they are vulnerable. (6) The media's exclusion of others like themselves deprives people with disabilities of role models and makes them feel undesirable or invisible. (7) Nondisabled viewers lose an understanding that could enrich them and would help them adjust to disability of their own.

Now the short summary:

Mairs believes that the media, by failing to depict disability as ordinary, both marginalize viewers with disabilities and impair the outlook and coping skills of the "temporarily abled."

Thinking Critically

Summarizing will start you toward understanding the author's meaning, but it won't take you as far as you're capable of going, or as far as you'll need to go in school or work or just to live well in our demanding Information Age.

Passive, rote learning (such as memorizing the times tables in arithmetic) won't do. You require techniques for comprehending what you encounter. But more: You need tools for discovering the meaning and intentions of an essay or case study or business letter or political message. You need ways to discriminate between the trustworthy and the not so and to apply what's valid in your own work and life.

We're talking here about critical thinking—not "negative," the common conception of *critical*, but "thorough, thoughtful, question asking, judgment forming." When you approach something critically, you harness your faculties, your fund of knowledge, and your experiences to understand, appreciate, and evaluate the object. Using this book—guided by questions on meaning, writing strategy, and language—you'll read an essay and ask what the author's purpose and main idea are, how clear they are, and how well supported. You'll isolate which writing techniques the author has used to special advantage, what hits you as particularly fresh, clever, or wise—and what *doesn't* work, too. You'll discover exactly what the writer is saying, how he or she says it, and whether, in the end, it was worth saying. In class discussions and in writing, you'll tell others what you think and why.

Critical thinking is a process involving several overlapping operations: analysis, inference, synthesis, and evaluation.

Analysis

Say you're listening to a new album by a band called Domix. Without thinking much about it, you isolate melodies, song lyrics, and instrumentals—in other words, you ANALYZE the album by separating it into its parts. Analysis is a way of thinking so basic to us that it has its own chapter (9) in this book. For reading in this book, you'll consciously analyze essays by looking at the author's main idea, support for the idea, special writing strategies, and other elements. To show you how the beginnings of such an analysis might look, we annotate these elements in "Disability" later in this chapter.

Analysis underlies many of the other methods of development discussed in this book, so that while you are analyzing a subject you might also (even unconsciously) begin classifying it, or comparing it with something else, or figuring out what caused it. For instance, you might compare Domix's new instrumentals with those on the band's earlier albums, or you might notice that the lyrics seem to be influenced by another band's. Similarly, in analyzing a poem you might compare several images of water, or in analyzing a journal article in psychology you might consider how the theories of the author affect her interpretations of behavior.

Inference

Say that after listening to Domix's new album, you conclude that it reveals a preoccupation with traditional blues music and themes. Now you are using INFERENCE, drawing conclusions about a work based on your store of information and experience, your knowledge of the creator's background and biases, and your analysis. When you infer, you add to the work, making explicit what was only implicit.

In critical thinking, inference is especially important in discovering a writer's ASSUMPTIONS: opinions or beliefs, often unstated, that direct the writer's choices of ideas, support, writing strategies, and language. A writer who favors gun control may assume without saying so that some individual rights (such as the right to bear arms) may be infringed for the good of the community. A writer who opposes gun control may assume the opposite — that in this case the individual's right is superior to the community's.

Synthesis

What is Domix trying to accomplish with its new album? Is it different from the band's previous album in its understanding of the blues? Answering such questions leads you into SYNTHESIS, using your perspective to link elements into a whole or to link two or more wholes. During synthesis, you use your special aptitudes, interests, and training to reconstitute the work so that it now contains not just the original elements but also your sense of their underpinnings, relationships, and implications.

Synthesis is the core of much academic writing, as Chapter 3 shows. Sometimes you'll respond directly to a work, or you'll use it as a springboard to another subject. Sometimes you'll show how two or more works resemble each other or how they differ. Sometimes you'll draw on many works to answer a question. In all these cases, you'll be putting your critical reading to use for your own ideas.

Evaluation

Not all critical thinking involves EVALUATION, or judging the quality of the work. You'll probably form a judgment of Domix's new album (Is the band getting better or just standing still?), but often you (and your teachers) will be satisfied with a nonjudgmental reading of a work. ("Nonjudgmental" does not mean "uncritical": You will still be expected to analyze, infer, and synthesize.) When you *do* evaluate, you determine adequacy, significance, value.

You answer a question such as whether an essay moves you as it was intended to, or whether the author has proved a case, or whether the argument is even worthwhile.

ANALYZING AN ESSAY

To help you in your critical reading, questions after every selection in this book direct your attention to specific elements of the writer's work. We introduce the types of questions below and on the following pages: The headings "Meaning," "Writing Strategy," and "Language" are the same as those organizing the end-of-essay questions. And then on pages 23–26 we show what focusing on these elements can reveal about Nancy Mairs's "Disability."

Meaning

By *meaning*, we intend what the author's words say literally, of course, but also what they imply and, more generally, what the author's aims are.

Thesis   Every essay has—or should have—a point, a main idea the writer wants to communicate. Many writers come right out and sum up this idea in a sentence or two, a THESIS STATEMENT. They may provide it in the first or second paragraph, give it somewhere in the middle of the essay, or hold it for the end. Sometimes a writer will not state his or her thesis outright at all, although it remains in the background controlling the work and can be inferred by a critical reader.

You may occasionally be confused by a writer's point—"What *is* this about?"—and sometimes your confusion won't yield to repeated careful readings. That's when you'll want to toss the work aside, but you won't always have the choice: A school or work assignment or just an urge to understand the writer's problem may keep you at it. Then it will be up to you to figure out what the author is trying to say—in essence, to clarify what's unclear. It may help to outline the text so that you can see its structure and main points at a glance.

Purpose   When you read an essay, you'll find it rewarding to ask, "What is this writer's PURPOSE?" By purpose, we mean the writer's apparent reason for writing: what he or she was trying to achieve with readers. A purpose is as essential to a good, pointed essay as a destination is to a trip. It affects every choice or decision the writer makes. (On vacation, of course, people sometimes wander without a specific goal. A writer may ramble like that in an early draft, too, with good results. But in a final draft such wandering will leave the reader pleading, "Let me out!")

In making a simple statement of a writer's purpose, we might say that the writer writes *to entertain* readers, or *to explain* something to them, or *to persuade* them. To state a purpose more fully, we might say that a writer writes not just to entertain but "to tell a horror story to make chills shoot down readers' spines," not just to persuade but "to tell readers a story to illustrate the point that when you are being cheated it's a good idea to complain" or "to motivate readers to take action by writing their representatives and urging more federal spending for the rehabilitation of criminals."

Analyzing writers' purposes and whether those purposes succeed can make you an alert and critical reader. Applied to your own writing, this analysis also gives you a decided advantage, for when you write with a clear-cut purpose in mind, you head toward a goal. Of course, sometimes you just can't know what you are going to say until you say it, to echo the English novelist E. M. Forster. In such a situation, your purpose emerges as you write. But the earlier and more exactly you define your purpose, the easier you'll find it to fulfill.

Writing Strategy

To the extent that writers hold our interest, make us think, and convince us to accept a thesis, it pays to ask, "How do they succeed?" (When writers bore or anger us, we ask why they fail.) Conscious writers make choices intended to get their audience on their side so that they can achieve their purpose. These choices are what we mean by STRATEGY in writing.

Audience   Almost all writing is a *transaction* between a writer and an audience, maybe one reader, maybe millions. The success or failure of writing depends on the extent to which the writer achieves his or her purpose with the intended audience.

We can tell much about a writer's intended audience from the context in which the piece was first published. For instance, if an essay first appeared in the *New York Times*, we can assume that the writer was addressing an audience of educated readers with diverse interests. If an essay first appeared in the *Journal of the American Medical Association*, we can assume that the writer was addressing readers with a special interest in medicine and knowledge of its terms and research methods. When we know something of the intended audience, we can better analyze the writer's decisions, from the choice of supporting information to the use of a particular tone.

Seeing how other writers consider their audiences can help you become more aware of audience in your own writing. To help you build this kind of awareness, we tell you a little bit about the publication context for each selection in *The Bedford Reader*, and in the follow-up questions we ask you to examine how assumptions about intended readers seem to have influenced the writer's choices.

Evidence   A crucial part of writing strategy is how the author supports ideas, making them concrete and convincing. For this EVIDENCE, the writer may use facts, examples, reasons, expert opinions—whatever best delivers the point.

This is one place the methods of development come in—DESCRIPTION, DEFINITION, and the other ways of finding and presenting evidence around which this book is organized. Typically, each method benefits from—and lends itself to—different kinds of support. In a NARRATION, for instance, a writer might rely on personal experience for evidence, drawing on memory to fill in the parts of the story so that readers can imagine the author's experience for themselves. But to analyze a local issue of CAUSE AND EFFECT, most writers would find that they need more objective information—such as verifiable facts from reliable sources—to back up their claims and bring readers around to their way of thinking.

The introductions to each method in Part Two discuss types of evidence writers may find particularly helpful. We also have more to say about evidence when discussing argument in detail (see pp. 550–51, 557).

Structure   Aside from considering an audience's needs and attitudes and choosing the methods for developing ideas, probably no writing strategy is as crucial to success as finding an appropriate structure. Writing that we find interesting and clear and convincing almost always has UNITY (everything relates to the main idea) and COHERENCE (the relations between parts are clear). When we find an essay wanting, it may be because the writer got lost in digressions or couldn't make the parts fit together.

Sometimes structure almost takes care of itself. In NARRATION, for instance, events usually follow a chronological sequence, as they occurred in time. But when neither subject nor method dictates a structure, then the writer must mold and arrange ideas to pique, hold, and direct our interest.

Decisions about structure come out of the writer's purpose and GENRE: What is the aim? What arrangement will readers expect? What do I want them to think or feel? What's the best way to achieve that? For instance, anyone writing a proposal to solve a problem wants to cover all the reasonable solutions and make a case for one or more. But one writer might bring readers gradually to his favored solution by first discussing and rejecting the alternatives, while another writer might grab readers' attention by focusing right away on her own solution, dispensing with alternatives only near the end.

In either case, the choices aren't random but depend on the writer's understanding of his or her readers—their assumptions, their biases, and their own purposes for reading.

Language

To examine the element of language is often to go even more deeply into an essay and how it was made. Language not only expresses meaning but also conveys the writer's attitudes and elicits those attitudes from readers. It creates a TONE, the equivalent of tone of voice in speaking, whether angry, sarcastic, or sad, joking or serious. Tone comes in part from sentence structures—the distinction, for instance, between the informal "Everyone involved seems to have a different opinion" and the more formal "This is a dispute in which every participant seems to have an opinion that is unique." Tone also comes from the CONNOTATIONS of words—their implied meanings, their associations. When one writer calls the homeless "society's downtrodden" and another calls them "human refuse," we know something of both writers' attitudes and can use that knowledge to analyze and evaluate their assertions about homelessness.

One other use of language is worth noting: FIGURES OF SPEECH, bits of colorful language not meant to be taken literally. The most common figures are the *simile*, which states that one thing is *like* another ("Deer leaped around the meadow like a troupe of dancers"), and the *metaphor*, which states that one thing *is* another ("He is an ogre when he's tired"). Such figures can give writing flavor and force, often capturing meaning or attitude better than literal words can. (Examples of these and other figures of speech appear in Useful Terms, p. 733.)

Many questions in this book point to figures of speech, to oddities of tone, or to troublesome or unfamiliar words. As a writer, you can have no traits more valuable to you than a fondness and respect for words and a yen to experiment with them.

A Close Look at Nancy Mairs's "Disability"

To see how an analysis of meaning, writing strategy, and language can work, we've printed Nancy Mairs's "Disability" on pages 24–26 with marginal notes that highlight its elements. Notice especially how Mairs combines various strategies to put forth her thesis, establish her purpose for writing, and strike a compelling and appropriate tone.

Disability

For months now I've been consciously searching for representation of myself in the media, especially television. I know I'd recognize this self because of certain distinctive, though not unique, features: I am a forty-three-year-old woman crippled with multiple sclerosis; although I can still totter short distances with the aid of a brace and a cane, more and more of the time I ride in a wheelchair. Because of these appliances and my peculiar gait, I'm easy to spot even in a crowd. So when I tell you I haven't noticed any women like me on television, you can believe me.

Actually, last summer I did see a woman with multiple sclerosis portrayed on one of those medical dramas that offer an illness-of-the-week like the daily special at your local diner. In fact, that was the whole point of the show: that this poor young woman had MS. She was terribly upset (understandably, I assure you) by the diagnosis, and her response was to plan a trip to Kenya while she was still physically capable of making it, against the advice of the young, fit, handsome doctor who had fallen in love with her. And she almost did it. At least, she got as far as a taxi to the airport, hotly pursued by the doctor. But at the last she succumbed to his blandishments and fled the taxi into his manly protective embrace. No escape to Kenya for this cripple.

Capitulation into the arms of a man who uses his medical powers to strip one of even the urge toward independence is hardly the sort of representation I had in mind. But even if the situation had been sensitively handled, according to the woman her right to her own adventures, it wouldn't have been what I'm looking for. Such a television show, as well as films like *Duet for One* and *Children of a Lesser God*, in taking disability as its

Straightforward title suggests subject of impairment.

Par. 1: Mairs introduces herself and her complaint that the media do not show people with disabilities.

Description portrays the author's disability. This description and others indicate that Mairs assumes most readers do not have disabilities.

Par. 2: Mairs uses example to dismiss a TV show that doesn't satisfy her.

A *simile* (shaded) equates medical dramas and unimaginative meals.

Description shows the helplessness of the woman in the TV drama.

Throughout, Mairs's tone mixes seriousness (underlined words) with naturalness and humor (boxed words).

"Cripple," a word with strong connotations, reinforces Mairs's bluntness about her own condition and suggests that old insensitivities persist.

Par. 3: Mairs explains why the TV drama and similar films are inadequate.

With examples, Mairs clarifies her point and establishes that she knows popular culture.

major premise, excludes the complexities that round out a character and make her whole. It's not about a woman who happens to be physically disabled; it's about physical disability as the determining factor of a woman's existence.

> Comparison shows similarities and differences between Mairs and characters with disabilities on TV and in films.

Take it from me, physical disability looms pretty large in one's life. But it doesn't devour one wholly. I'm not, for instance, Ms. MS, a walking, talking embodiment of a chronic incurable degenerative disease. In most ways I'm just like every other woman of my age, nationality, and socioeconomic background. I menstruate, so I have to buy tampons. I worry about smoker's breath, so I buy mouthwash. I smear my wrinkling skin with lotions. I put bleach in the washer so my family's undies won't be dingy. I drive a car, talk on the telephone, get runs in my pantyhose, eat pizza. In most ways, that is, I'm the advertisers' dream: Ms. Great American Consumer. And yet the advertisers, who determine nowadays who will get represented publicly and who will not, deny the existence of me and my kind absolutely.

> Par. 4: Mairs establishes that she is someone advertisers *should* be appealing to.

> Comparison shows how Mairs resembles people without disabilities.

> Description and examples convey the flavor of Mairs's own daily life.

> A blend of plain talk, humor, and insistence gives readers the facts they need, wins them over with common humanity and lightness, and conveys the gravity of the problem.

I once asked a local advertiser why he didn't include disabled people in his spots. His response seemed direct enough: "We don't want to give people the idea that our product is just for the handicapped." But tell me truly now: If you saw me pouring out puppy biscuits, would you think these kibbles were only for the puppies of the cripples? If you saw my blind niece ordering a Coke, would you switch to Pepsi lest you be struck sightless? No, I think the advertiser's excuse masked a deeper and more anxious rationale: To depict disabled people in the ordinary activities of daily life is to admit that there is something ordinary about disability itself, that it may enter anybody's life. If it is effaced completely, or at least isolated as a separate "problem," so that it remains

> Par. 5: Mairs takes issue with an advertiser's view and suggests her own.

> Mairs engages readers by addressing them directly.

> Examples of ads in which people with disabilities might appear.

> Irony (shaded) underscores the absurdity of the advertiser's view.

> Cause and effect explains why disability is effaced (or rubbed out) from the media.

at a safe distance from other human issues, then the viewer won't feel threatened by her or his own physical vulnerability.

This kind of effacement or isolation has painful, even dangerous consequences, however. For the disabled person, these include self-degradation and a subtle kind of self-alienation not unlike that experienced by other minorities. Socialized human beings love to conform, to study others and then mold themselves to the contours of those whose images, for good reasons or bad, they come to love. Imagine a life in which feasible others—others you can hope to be like—don't exist. At the least you might conclude that there is something queer about you, something ugly or foolish or shameful. In the extreme, you might feel as though you don't exist, in any meaningful social sense, at all. Everyone else is "there," sucking breath mints and splashing cologne and swigging wine coolers. You're "not there." And if not there, nowhere.

But this denial of disability imperils even you who are able-bodied, and not just by shrinking your insight into the physically and emotionally complex world you live in. Some disabled people call you TAPs, or Temporarily Abled Persons. The fact is that ours is the only minority you can join involuntarily, without warning, at any time. And if you live long enough, as you're increasingly likely to do, you may well join it. The transition will probably be difficult from a physical point of view no matter what. But it will be a good bit easier psychologically if you are accustomed to seeing disability as a normal characteristic, one that complicates but does not ruin human existence. Achieving this integration, for disabled and able-bodied people alike, requires that we insert disability daily into our field of vision: quietly, naturally, in the small and common scenes of our ordinary lives.

Par. 6: Mairs uses several methods to reveal the negative effects of effacement on people with and without disabilities.

Description

Cause-and-effect analysis

A *metaphor* (shaded) equates behavioral change and physical change.

"You" forces readers to imagine themselves with disabilities.

Comparison and contrast

Par. 7: Mairs concludes by presenting the positive effects of normalizing disability.

With cause-and-effect analysis, Mairs explains why treating disability as ordinary could help those without disabilities.

Overall, Mairs's essay is an argument meant to convince readers that the media hurt people without disabilities as much as they do people with disabilities.

Mairs saves her main idea, her thesis, for the very end, perhaps because she thinks readers may not accept it at the outset.

THINKING CRITICALLY ABOUT VISUAL IMAGES

Does a particular billboard always catch your eye when you drive by it? Does a certain television commercial irritate you or make you smile? Do you look at the pictures in a magazine before you read the articles? If so, you're like everyone else in that you are subject to the visual representations coming at you continually, unbidden, from all around.

Much of the flood of visual information just washes over us, like noise to the eyes. Sometimes we do focus on an image or a whole sequence that interests us—maybe it tweaks our emotions or tells us something we want to know. But even then we aren't always thinking that an image, just as much as a sentence of words, was created by somebody for a reason. No matter what it is—Web advertisement, TV commercial, painting, music video, photograph, cartoon—a visual image originated with a creator or creators who had a purpose, an intention for how the image should look and how we, the viewers, should respond to it.

In their purposefulness, then, visual images are not much different from written texts, and they are no less open to critical thinking that will uncover their meanings and effects. To a great extent, the method for critically "reading" visuals parallels the one for essays outlined on pages 10–12 and 16–20. In short:

- *Get the big picture:* As when scoping out a written work, survey the image or sequence for a view of the whole and clues about its origins and purposes.
- *Analyze:* Discern the elements of the image or sequence.
- *Infer:* Interpret the underlying meanings of the elements and the ASSUMP-TIONS and intentions of the work's creators.
- *Synthesize:* Form an idea about how the elements function together to produce a whole and to deliver a message.
- Often, *evaluate:* Judge the quality, significance, or value of the work.

One other important parallel with critical reading of written works: Always write while examining a visual image or images. Jotting down responses, questions, and other notes will not only help you remember what you were thinking but also jog further thoughts into being.

To show the critical method in action, we'll look closely at the photograph by Erik S. Lesser on page 29. Further examples of analyzing visual works appear elsewhere in *The Bedford Reader* as well: See pages 195 (a painting); 134, 388, and 448 (photographs); and 714–19 (drawings). In addition, Chapters 4–13 each open with a visual image that gives you a chance to try out the method yourself.

The Big Picture

To examine any visual representation, it helps first to get an overview, a sense of the whole. Try making some inquiries of the work:

- What is the source of the work? Who created it—for instance, a painter, a teacher, an advertiser—and when?
- What does the work show overall? What appears to be happening?
- At a glance, why was the work created—for instance, to educate, to sell, to shock, to entertain?

The photograph on the facing page was taken by Erik S. Lesser at Fort Benning, Georgia, and was used by *US News & World Report* to illustrate an article on the deployment of troops to Iraq and Afghanistan. The picture shows a young girl and a man in military uniform holding hands, with other soldiers in the background. Evidently, the main figures are father and daughter. Given the context, the father is probably being sent to war.

Analysis

After you've gained an overview of the visual work, begin focusing on the elements that contribute to the whole—not just the people, animals, or objects depicted but the background and what might be called the artistic elements of lighting, color, shape, and balance.

- Which elements of the image stand out? What is distinctive about each one?
- What does the composition of the image emphasize?
- If spoken or written words accompany the work, what do they say? How are they sized and placed in relation to the visual elements?

In Lesser's photograph, the dominant elements are the soldier and the girl, presumably father and daughter, holding hands and facing a brick building in the background. Other soldiers are also evident, particularly in a large rectangular door in the background building. The girl wears light-colored clothing, and she carries an umbrella, which indicates that it is raining. The father wears a camouflage uniform and helmet and carries a rifle across his back, which suggest that he is prepared to fight. He is walking (his left heel is raised), apparently headed toward the door. The daughter seems to be playfully hopping or skipping.

Inference

Identifying the elements of the visual representation leads you to consider what they mean and how the image's creator has selected and arranged them

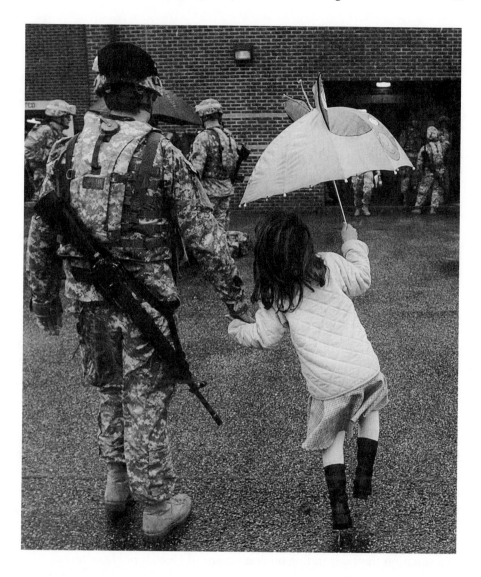

so that viewers will respond in certain ways. As when reading a written text critically, you make explicit what may only be implicit in the work.

- What do the elements of the work say about the creator's intentions and assumptions? In particular, what does the creator seem to assume about viewers' backgrounds, needs, interests, and values?
- If the work includes written or spoken words, how do they interact with the visual components?

We can guess Erik Lesser's intentions for the photograph. He seems to assume that we viewers will instantly recognize the main figures as a soldier going off to war and his daughter coming to say good-bye. He may assume more as well: that whatever viewers think about US military actions, they will sympathize with this couple. The large father's steady gait, uniform, and rifle portray him as determined and courageous in going to war. The girl's brighter clothes and jaunty step show her as excited, perhaps unaware of what lies in store for her father. Lesser may see these opposites as reflecting the controversy over the war.

Synthesis

Linking the elements and your inferences about them, you'll move into a new conception of the visual representation: your own conclusions about its overall intentions and effect.

- What general appeal does the work make to viewers? For instance, does it emphasize logical argument, emotion, or the creator's or subject's worthiness?
- What feelings, memories, moods, or ideas does the work seem intended to summon from viewers' own store of experiences? Why, given the purpose of the work, would its creator try to establish these associations?

As we see it, Lesser's photograph represents Americans' mixed feelings about the wars in Iraq and Afghanistan. The apparent rain and the yawning door are ominous, suggesting the danger facing the father and also the United States as a whole. The determination of the father despite the risk evokes our appreciation and pride; his connection with his daughter evokes our sympathy and approval as it also intensifies our anxiety for his safety. At the same time, the buoyant daughter is both sweetly supportive and sadly innocent, because she may not realize what her father's departure means. In a larger sense, these two figures could represent the joining of the armed forces and the home front in a situation that, depending on one's point of view, is noble or tragic.

When using synthesis, you may often go outside the work itself to explore its cultural context. For instance, Lesser's photograph might be compared with other photographs that depict soldiers on their way to war, or it might be analyzed in the context of one or more written opinions about US military actions.

Evaluation

Often in criticizing visual works, you'll take one step beyond synthesis to evaluate success or significance or value.

- Does the work seem to fulfill its creator's intentions? Does it do what the creator wanted?
- Apart from the creator's intentions, how does the work affect you? Does it move you? amuse you? bore you? offend you?
- Was the work worth creating?

Erik Lesser's photograph seems to us masterful as concise storytelling with a big message. As Lesser seems to have intended, he distills strong and even contradictory feelings about war into a deceptively simple image of a father and his daughter.

2

THE WRITING PROCESS

The CRITICAL THINKING discussed in the previous chapter will serve you in just about every role you'll play in life—consumer, voter, friend, parent. As a student and a worker, though, you'll find critical thinking especially important as the foundation for writing. Whether to demonstrate your competence or to contribute to discussions and projects, writing will be the main way you communicate with teachers, supervisors, and peers.

Like critical thinking, writing is no snap: As this book's Writers on Writing attest, even professionals do not produce thoughtful, detailed, attention-getting prose in a single draft. Writing well demands, and rewards, a willingness to work recursively—to begin tentatively, perhaps, and then to double back, to welcome change and endure frustration, to recognize and exploit progress.

This recursive writing process is not really a single process at all, not even for an individual writer. Some people work out meticulous plans before beginning to compose sentences; others find plans stifling and prefer to just start writing; still others will work one way for one project and a different way for another. Generally, though, writers do move through five rough stages between assignment or initial idea and finished work: analysis of the writing situation, discovery, drafting, revising, and editing.

In examining these stages, we'll have the help of a student, Rosie Anaya, who wrote an essay for *The Bedford Reader* responding to Nancy Mairs's essay

"Disability." Along with the final draft of her essay (pp. 57–59), Anaya also provided her notes and earlier drafts and her comments on her progress at each stage.

ANALYZING THE WRITING SITUATION

Any writing you do will occur in a specific situation: What are you writing about? Whom are you writing for? Why are you writing about this subject to these people? What will they expect of you? Subject, audience, and purpose are the main components in the writing situation, discussed in detail on these pages. We also touch on another component, genre (or type of writing), which relates to audience and purpose.

Subject

Your subject may be specified or at least suggested in the writing assignment you receive. "Discuss one of the works we've read this semester in its historical and social context," reads a literature assignment; "Can you draw me up a proposal for holiday staffing?" asks your boss. If you're left to your own devices and nothing occurs to you, try the discovery techniques explained on pages 37–39 to find a subject that interests you.

In *The Bedford Reader* we've provided ideas for writing about the selections that will also give you practice in working with writing assignments. Immediately after each selection, a "Journal Writing" prompt encourages you to respond to the selection just for yourself. (See p. 37 for a discussion of journal writing.) Then, in "Suggestions for Writing," one assignment proposes turning that journal writing into an essay for others to read. Of the three or four other suggestions, one labeled "Critical Writing" asks you to take a deliberate, critical look at the selection, and another labeled "Connections" helps you relate the selection to one or two others in the book. You may not wish to take any of our suggestions as worded; they may merely urge your own thoughts toward what you want to say.

To give you an idea of the writing suggestions we provide, here are possibilities for Nancy Mairs's "Disability," the essay reprinted in the preceding chapter (p. 13):

Journal Writing

Do you agree that many people respond with discomfort to people with disabilities? What do you feel when you see a stranger using a wheelchair: pity? sympathy? curiosity? uncertainty? admiration? fear? something else? In your journal, set down your answers to these questions as honestly as you can. What do you think causes these feelings? Consider how they are colored by your experiences with disability—whether you are disabled yourself, know someone who is disabled, or have no firsthand experience with disability.

Suggestions for Writing

1. **FROM JOURNAL TO ESSAY**   Based on your journal reflections, write an essay that explains how your own responses to people with disabilities lead you to accept or dispute Mairs's call for depicting "disabled people in the ordinary activities of daily life."

2. Have media depictions of people with disabilities changed since Mairs wrote her essay in 1987? If so, how? If not, why? Write an essay in which you ANALYZE current media representations of disability, using specific examples to support your ideas.

3. Choose another group you think has been "effaced" in television advertising and programming—a racial, ethnic, or religious group, for instance. Write an essay detailing how and why that group is overlooked. How could representations of the group be incorporated into the media? What effects might such representation have?

4. **CRITICAL WRITING**   Reread this essay carefully. Mairs tells us about herself through details and through TONE (for example, through IRONY, intensity, and humor). Write an essay on how Mairs's self-revelations do or do not help further her THESIS.

5. **CONNECTIONS**   In "On Compassion" (p. 211), Barbara Lazear Ascher writes about the way people who are comfortable tend to respond to homeless people on the street, and she suggests that compassion must be "learned by having adversity at our window." Does what Ascher asks in relation to homeless people resemble what Mairs asks in relation to people with disabilities? In an essay, discuss the similarities and differences between these two writers' views of how people's attitudes could or should change.

Audience and Purpose

We looked at AUDIENCE and PURPOSE in the previous chapter as concerns of writers that can help us readers analyze their works. When you are *doing* the writing, considering audience and purpose moves from informative to necessary: Knowing whom you're addressing and why tells you what approach to take, what EVIDENCE to gather, how to arrange ideas, even what words to use.

You can conceive of your audience generally—for instance, your classmates, the readers of a particular newspaper, or members of the city council. Usually, though, you'll want to think about the characteristics of readers that will affect how they respond to you:

- What do readers need to know if they are to understand you or agree with you? How much background should you provide? How thoroughly should you support your ideas? What kinds of evidence will be most effective?
- What in readers' own makeup will influence their responses? How old are they? Are they educated? Do they share your values? Are they likely to have some misconceptions about your subject?

While you are considering readers' backgrounds and inclinations, you'll also be refining your purpose. You may know early on whether you want to explain something about your subject or argue something about it—a general purpose. To be most helpful, though, your idea of purpose should include what you want readers to think or do as a result of reading your writing. For instance:

> To explain two treatments for autism in young children so that readers clearly understand the similarities and differences

> To defend term limits for state legislators so that readers who are now undecided on the issue will support limits

> To analyze Shakespeare's *Macbeth* so that readers see the strengths as well as the flaws of the title character

> To propose an online system for scheduling work shifts so that company managers decide to explore the options

We have more to say about audience and purpose in the introduction to each rhetorical method (Chaps. 4–13).

Genre

Closely tied to audience and purpose is the type of writing, the GENRE, that you will use to shape your ideas. Your assignment might specify the genre: Have you been asked to write a personal narrative? a critical analysis? an argumentative response? These and other genres have distinctive features—such as organization, kinds of evidence, and even tone—that readers expect. If you're not already familiar with the expectations for an assigned genre, ask your instructor for guidance and seek out examples.

You will find many examples of different genres in this book. In a sense each method of development (NARRATION, COMPARISON, and so on) is itself a genre, and its conventions and strategies are covered in the introduction to the method (Chaps. 4–13). Each introduction also shows the method at work in a specific academic genre, such as a case study or a review. And the book's selections illustrate a range of genres, from personal reflection and memoir to objective reporting and critical evaluation.

DISCOVERING IDEAS

During the second phase of the writing process, DISCOVERY, you'll feel your way into an assignment. This is the time when you critically examine any text or image that is part of the assignment and begin to generate ideas for writing. When writing about selections in this book, you'll be reading and rereading and writing, coming to understand the work, figuring out what you think of it, figuring out what you have to *say* about it. From notes during reading to jotted phrases, lists, or half-finished paragraphs after reading, this stage should always be a writing stage. You may even produce a rough draft. The important thing is to let yourself go: Do not, above all, concern yourself with making beautiful sentences or correcting errors. Such self-consciousness at this stage will only jam the flow of thoughts. If your idea of "audience" is "teacher with sharp pencil" (not, by the way, a fair picture), then temporarily blank out your audience, too.

Several techniques can help you let go and open up during the discovery stage, among them writing in a journal, freewriting, and using the methods of development.

Journal Writing

A JOURNAL is a notebook or tablet or computer file in which you record your thoughts *for yourself*. (Teachers sometimes assign journals and periodically collect them to see how students are doing, but even in these situations the journal is for you.) In keeping a journal, you don't have to worry about being understood by a reader or making mistakes: You are free to write however you want to get your thoughts down.

Kept faithfully—say, for ten or fifteen minutes a day—a journal can limber up your writing muscles, giving you more confidence and flexibility as a writer. It can also provide a place to work out personal difficulties, explore half-formed ideas, make connections between courses, or respond to reading. Here, for instance, is Rosie Anaya's initial journal entry on Nancy Mairs's "Disability":

> I think Mairs is right that disability makes a lot of people uncomfortable. I know that when I see someone in a wheelchair or on crutches I can feel anxious, but that's usually because I don't know whether I should offer to help or just pretend I don't notice the disability. Honestly, I'm more afraid of the strange woman mumbling to herself on the corner, or the man on the subway rocking back and forth in his seat. But why? It's not like they're contagious. I guess I just worry that they might lash out without warning.

Freewriting

Another technique for limbering up, but more in response to specific writing assignments than as a regular habit, is *freewriting*. When freewriting, you write without stopping for ten or fifteen minutes, not halting to reread, criticize, edit, or admire. You can use partial sentences, abbreviations, question marks for uncertain words. If you can't think of anything to write about, jot "can't think" over and over until new words come. (They will.)

You can use this technique to find a subject for writing or to explore ideas on a subject you already have. Of course, when you've finished, you'll need to separate the promising passages from the dead ends, using those promising bits as the starting place for more freewriting or perhaps a freely written first draft.

The Methods of Development

Since each method of development provides a different perspective on your subject, you can use the methods singly or together to discover direction, ideas, and support for the ideas. Say you already have a sense of your purpose for writing: Then you can search the methods for one or more that will help you achieve that purpose by revealing and focusing your ideas. Or say you're still in the dark about your purpose: Then you can apply each method of development systematically to throw light on your subject, as a headlight illuminates a midnight road, so that you see its possible angles.

The introductions to Chapters 4–13 suggest the purposes each method is suited for and some specific ways the method can open up your subject. For now, we've given some examples of how the methods can reveal responses, either direct or indirect, to Mairs's "Disability."

- *Narration:* Tell a story about the subject, possibly to enlighten or entertain readers or to explain something to them. Answer the journalist's questions: who, what, when, where, why, how? For instance, relate a day in the life of a person with a disability.
- *Description:* To explain or evoke the subject, focus on its look, sound, feel, smell, taste—the evidence of the senses. For instance, describe Mairs's feelings about her subject as revealed in her use of language.
- *Example:* Point to instances, or illustrations, of the subject that clarify and support your idea about it. For instance, give examples that illustrate the media's current representation of people with disabilities.
- *Comparison and contrast:* Set the subject beside something else, noting similarities or differences or both, for the purpose of either explaining or

evaluating. For instance, compare and contrast characters with disabilities in two movies or TV shows.

- *Process analysis:* Explain step by step how to do something or how something works—in other words, how a sequence of actions leads to a particular result. For instance, explain a process for convincing advertisers to use people with disabilities in TV commercials.
- *Division or analysis:* Slice the subject into its parts or elements in order to show how they relate and to explain your conclusions about the subject. For instance, analyze Mairs's tone and its relation to her purpose.
- *Classification:* To show resemblances and differences among many related subjects, or the many forms of a subject, sort them into kinds or groups. For example, classify attitudes toward people with disabilities, physical and mental.
- *Cause and effect:* Explain why or what if, showing reasons for or consequences of the subject. For instance, explain how someone's life changed and didn't change, as a result of disability.
- *Definition:* Trace a boundary around the subject to pin down its meaning. For instance, define *disability*.
- *Argument and persuasion:* Formulate an opinion or make a proposal about the subject. For instance, argue for a change in grocery or department stores to accommodate people who use wheelchairs.

FOCUSING ON THE THESIS AND THE THESIS STATEMENT

Your finished essay will need to center on a THESIS, a core idea to which everything relates. You may start a project with an idea already in mind, but more often your idea will take shape as you proceed through the writing process. Sometimes you may have to write one or more drafts to know exactly what your core idea is.

Writers often express the thesis in a sentence or two, called a THESIS STATEMENT, like these from essays in this book:

> These were two strong men, these oddly different generals [Ulysses S. Grant and Robert E. Lee], and they represented the strengths of two conflicting currents that, through them, had come into final collision.
> —Bruce Catton, "Grant and Lee: A Study in Contrasts"

> Inanimate objects are classified into three major categories—those that don't work, those that break down and those that get lost.
> —Russell Baker, "The Plot against People"

A bill [to prohibit import of goods produced with children's labor] is of no use unless it goes hand in hand with programs that will offer a new life to these newly released children.

—Chitra Divakaruni, "Live Free and Starve"

These diverse examples share a few important qualities:

- The authors assert opinions, taking positions on their subjects. They do not merely state facts, as in "Grant and Lee both signed the document ending the Civil War" or "Grant and Lee were different men."
- Each thesis statement projects a single idea. The thesis may have parts (such as Baker's three categories of objects), but the parts fit under a single umbrella idea.
- As you will see when you read the essays themselves, each thesis statement accurately forecasts the scope of its essay, neither taking on too much nor leaving out essential parts.
- Each thesis statement hints about the writer's purpose—we can tell that Catton and Baker want to explain, whereas Divakaruni wants mainly to persuade. (Explaining and persuading overlap a great deal; we're talking here about the writer's *primary* purpose.)

Every single essay in this book has a *thesis* because a central, controlling idea is a requirement of good writing. But we can give no rock-hard rules about the *thesis statement*—how long it must be or where it must appear in an essay or even whether it must appear. Indeed, the essays in this book demonstrate that writers have great flexibility in these areas, even within a given method. For your own writing, we advise stating your thesis explicitly and putting it near the beginning of your essay—at least until you've gained experience as a writer. The stated thesis will help you check that you have that necessary focus, and the early placement will tell your readers what to expect from your writing.

DRAFTING

Sooner or later, the discovery stage yields to DRAFTING: writing out sentences and paragraphs, linking ideas, focusing them. For most writers, drafting is the occasion for exploring the relations among ideas, filling in the details to support them, beginning to work out the shape and aim of the whole. During drafting, you may clarify or even discover your purpose and your thesis, try out different arrangements of material, or experiment with tone. Sometimes, though, you may find that just spelling out thoughts into complete sentences is challenge enough for a first draft, and you'll leave issues of purpose, thesis, structure, and tone for another round.

A few suggestions for drafting:

- Give yourself time, at least a couple of hours.
- Work in a place where you won't be disturbed.
- Stay loose so that you can wander down intriguing avenues or consider changing direction altogether.
- Don't feel compelled to follow a straight path from beginning to end. If the introduction is giving you fits, skip it until later.
- Keep your eyes on what's ahead, not on the pebbles underfoot—the possible mistakes, "wrong" words, and bumpy sentences that you can attend to later. This is an important message that many inexperienced writers miss: It's okay to make mistakes. You can fix them later.

REVISING

If it helps you produce writing, you may want to view your draft as a kind of dialog with readers, fulfilling their expectations, answering the questions you imagine they would ask. But some writers save this kind of thinking for the next stage, REVISION. Literally "re-seeing," revision is the price you pay for the freedom to experiment and explore. Initially the work centers on you and your material, but gradually it shifts into that transaction we spoke of earlier between you and your reader. And that means stepping outside the intense circle of you-and-the-material to see the work as a reader will, with whatever qualities you imagine that reader to have. Questions after most essays in this book ask you to analyze how the writers' ideas about their readers have influenced their writing strategies, and how you as a reader react to the writers' choices. These analyses will teach you much about responding to your own readers.

The first task of revising is to step back and view your draft as a whole, looking at the big picture and ignoring pesky little details like grammar and spelling. It's always a good idea to let a draft sit for a while before you come back to revise it: at least a few hours, ideally a day or more. When you return with fresh eyes and a refreshed mind, you'll be in a better position to see what works, what doesn't, and what needs your attention. The checklist on page 42 and the ensuing discussion can guide you to the big-picture view. Specific revision guidelines for the methods of development appear in the introductions to Chapters 4–13.

Purpose and Genre

Earlier we looked at PURPOSE and GENRE as important considerations in planning an essay. They are even more important in revision. Like many writers,

---

QUESTIONS FOR REVISION

✔ Will my purpose be clear to readers? Have I achieved it?

✔ Have I met readers' expectations for this genre, this kind of writing?

✔ What is my thesis? Have I supported it for readers?

✔ Is the essay unified so that readers can see how all parts relate to the thesis?

✔ Have I developed my points with enough details, examples, and other specifics so that readers can understand me and follow my reasoning?

✔ Is the essay coherent so that readers can see how the parts relate?

✔ Will readers be able to follow the organization?

---

in the discovery and experimentation of drafting you may lose track of your original direction. Did you set out to write a critical analysis of a reading but end up with a summary? Did you rely too heavily on personal experience when you were supposed to use evidence from sources? Did you set out to persuade readers but not get beyond explanation? That's okay. You've jumped the first hurdle simply by putting your thoughts into words. Now you can add, delete, and reorganize until your purpose will be clear to readers and you meet their expectations for how it should be fulfilled.

Thesis

As you've developed your ideas and your draft, you've also been developing your THESIS, the main idea that you want to get across to readers. The thesis may be stated up front or just hover in the background, but it should be clear to readers and the rest of the essay should in fact support it. You may find that you need to revise your thesis statement to reflect what you ended up writing in your draft, or you may need to rework your supporting ideas so that they develop your thesis. We have more to say about theses and thesis statements in the introduction to every method chapter in Part Two and in "Focus on the Thesis Statement" on page 356.

Unity

Drafting freely, as we encourage you to do, can easily take you into some of the byways of your topic. A goal of revision, then, is to deal with digressions so that your essay has UNITY, with every paragraph relating to the thesis and every sentence in a paragraph relating to a single idea, often expressed in a TOPIC SEN-TENCE. You may choose to cut a digression altogether or to rework it so that it connects to the main idea. Sometimes you may find that a digression is really what you want to write about and then opt to recast your thesis instead. For more help, see "Focus on Paragraph and Essay Unity" on page 512.

Development

While some points in your draft may have to be sacrificed for the sake of unity, others will probably want more attention. Be sure that any general statements you make are backed up with evidence: details, examples, analysis, information from sources, whatever it takes to show readers that your point is valid. The introduction to each method in Chapters 4–13 offers suggestions for developing specific kinds of essays; take a look, too, at "Focus on Paragraph Development" on page 403.

Coherence

Drafting ideas into sentences can be halting work, and a first draft can seem jumbled as a result. In revision, you want to help readers follow your thoughts with COHERENCE: the clear flow and relation of parts. You can achieve coherence through your use of paragraphs, transitions, and organization.

PARAGRAPHS help readers grasp related information in an essay by developing one supporting point at a time: All of the sentences hang together, defining, explaining, illustrating, or supporting one central idea. Check all your paragraphs to be sure that each sentence connects with the one preceding and that readers will see the connection without having to stop and reread. One way to clarify such connections is with TRANSITIONS: linking words and phrases such as *in addition, moreover,* and *at the same time.* We have more to say about transitions in "Focus on Paragraph Coherence" on page 250.

Some methods of development lend themselves to familiar patterns of ORGANIZATION, which we discuss in the introductions to Chapters 4–13. In a NARRATIVE or a PROCESS ANALYSIS, for instance, you might naturally put events in chronological order. No matter your method, however, be sure that each point follows logically from those before it and leads clearly to those that follow. Constructing an outline of what you've written can help you see the scaffolding that holds your thoughts together: It may look sturdy and square, or it may tilt and teeter. Expect to experiment, moving paragraphs around, deleting some and adding others, before everything clicks into place.

EDITING

Like many writers, you may find that you produce better work when you approach revision as at least a two-step process. First revise, focusing on fundamental, whole-essay matters such as purpose and organization. Only then turn to editing, focusing on surface issues such as grammar and word choice. This two-step process is like inspecting a ship before it sails: First check below the waterline for holes to make sure the boat will stay afloat; then look above the waterline at what will move the boat and please the passengers, such as intact sails, sparkling hardware, and gleaming decks.

EDITING gives you a chance to improve the flow of your writing and to fix the grammatical mistakes that tend to get in the way of readers' understanding. The checklist below covers the most common opportunities and problems, which are explained on the pages following. Because some challenges tend to pop up more often when writing with a particular method, we also give additional help in the introductions to Chapters 4–13, in boxes labeled "Focus on . . ." that highlight specific issues and provide tips for solving them.

QUESTIONS FOR EDITING

✔ Are my language and tone appropriate for my purpose, audience, and genre?

✔ Do my words say what I mean, and are they as vivid as I can make them?

✔ Are my sentences smooth and concise? Do they use emphasis, parallelism, variety, and other techniques to clarify meaning and hold readers' interest?

✔ Are my sentences grammatically correct? In particular, have I avoided sentence fragments, run-on sentences, comma splices, mismatched subjects and verbs, unclear pronouns, unclear modifiers, and inconsistencies?

✔ Are any words misspelled?

Effective Language

Many of us, when we draft, fall back on the familiar language we use when chatting with friends in person or online: We might rely on COLLOQUIAL EXPRESSIONS such as *get into* and *freak out* or slip into texting shortcuts such as *u* for "you," *cuz* for "because," and *L8R* for "later." The strategy can be a good one because it lets us put our ideas together without getting sidetracked by details. But the informal patterns of casual communication are usually too imprecise for college writing, where word choices can dramatically affect how readers understand your ideas, perceive your attitude, and respond to your thesis. As you edit, you'll adapt your general language and your specific words to reflect your purpose, your meaning, and your audience.

A few guidelines:

- *Adopt a relatively formal voice.* Replace overly casual or emotional language with standard English DICTION and a neutral TONE. (Refer to pp. 737 and 746 of Useful Terms and to "Focus on Tone" on p. 558.)

- *Choose an appropriate point of view.* In most academic writing, you should prefer the more objective third PERSON (*he, she, it, they*) over the first person *I* or second person *you*. There are exceptions, of course: A personal NARRATIVE written without *I* would ring strange to most ears, and a how-to PROCESS ANALYSIS often addresses readers as *you*.

- *Check that words have the meanings you intend.* The DENOTATION of a word is its dictionary meaning, as *affection* means "caring regard." A CONNOTATION is an emotional association that a word produces in readers, as *passion* evokes intensity or *obsession* evokes compulsion. Using a word with the wrong denotation muddies meaning, while using words with strong connotations can shape readers' responses to your ideas—for good or for ill.

- *Use concrete and specific words.* Effective writing balances ABSTRACT and GENERAL words, which provide outlines of ideas and things, with CONCRETE and SPECIFIC words, which limit and sharpen. You need abstract and general words such as *old* and *transportation* for broad statements that set the course for your writing, conveying concepts or referring to entire groups. But you also need concrete and specific words such as *crumbling* and *streetcar line* to make meaning precise and vivid by appealing to readers' senses and experiences. See "Focus on Specific and Concrete Language" on page 158.

- *Be creative.* You can make your writing more lively and forceful with FIGURES OF SPEECH, expressions that imply meanings beyond or different from their literal meanings, such as *curled tight like a rosebud* or *a suit worn to threads*. By briefly translating experiences and qualities into vividly concrete images, figures of speech can be economical and powerful when used sparingly. Be careful not to resort to CLICHÉS, worn phrases that have lost their power (*hour of need, thin as a rail, goes on forever*), or to combine figures of speech into confusing or absurd images, such as *The players flooded the soccer field like pit bulls ready for a fight.*

Clear and Engaging Sentences

When you read the selections in this book, you may notice that each writer's sentences have a certain flow, with one idea moving seamlessly into the next. Although the result may seem effortless, we promise you that it was not: Effective sentences are the product of a writer's careful attention to meaning and readability. Editing for emphasis, parallelism, and variety will ensure that readers can follow your ideas without difficulty and stay interested in what you have to say.

Emphasis

While we're drafting, simply getting ideas down in sentence form can be challenge enough. But once the ideas are down, we can see that some are more important than others. Editing offers an opportunity to clarify those relationships for readers. To edit for emphasis, focus on the following changes:

- **Put verbs in the active voice.** A verb in the *active voice* expresses action by the subject (*He recorded a new song*), whereas a verb in the *passive voice* expresses action done to the subject (*A new song was recorded*, or, adding who did the action, *A new song was recorded by him*). The active voice is usually more emphatic and therefore easier to follow. See "Focus on Verbs" on page 104.

- **Simplify wordy sentences.** Unnecessary padding puzzles readers and loses their interest. Weed out any empty phrases or meaningless repetition:

  WORDY   The nature of social-networking sites is such that they reconnect lost and distant friends but can also for all intents and purposes dredge up old relationships that were better left forgotten.

  CONCISE   Social-networking sites reconnect lost and distant friends but can also dredge up old relationships that were better left forgotten.

  WORDY   Many older adults who use the sites have been surprised and shocked to hear from high-school classmates, classmates they had never considered friends in the first place.

  CONCISE   Many adults who use the sites have been surprised to hear from high-school classmates they had never considered friends.

  See also "Focus on Clarity and Conciseness" on page 461.

- **Combine sentences.** You can clarify the importance of ideas by merging sentences to emphasize relationships. Use *coordination* to combine and balance equally important ideas, joining them with *and, but, or, nor, for, so,* or *yet*:

Unemphatic   Many restaurant meals are high in fat. Their sodium content is also high. To diners they seem harmless.

Emphatic   Many restaurant meals are high in fat <u>and</u> sodium, <u>but</u> to diners they seem harmless.

Use *subordination* to de-emphasize less important ideas, placing minor information in modifying words or word groups:

Unemphatic   Restaurant menus sometimes label certain options. They use the label "healthy." These options are lower in fat and sodium.

Emphatic   Restaurant menus sometimes label <u>as "healthy"</u> the options <u>that are lower in fat and sodium.</u>

Parallelism

Another way to clarify the relationship among ideas is to give parallel structure to related words, phrases, and sentences. Parallelism is the use of similar grammatical forms for elements of similar importance, either within or among sentences.

Parallelism within a sentence   Binge drinking can <u>worsen heart disease</u> and <u>cause liver failure.</u>

Parallelism among sentences   Binge drinking has less well-known effects, too. <u>It can cause</u> brain damage. <u>It can raise</u> blood sugar to diabetic levels. And <u>it can reduce</u> the body's ability to fight off infections.

Readers tend to stumble over elements that seem equally important but are not in parallel form. As you edit, look for groups of related ideas and make a point of expressing them consistently:

Nonparallel   Even occasional binges can cause serious problems, from <u>the experience of blackouts</u> to <u>getting arrested</u> to <u>injury.</u>

Parallel   Even occasional binges can cause serious problems, from <u>black-outs</u> to <u>arrests</u> to <u>injuries.</u>

Sentence Variety

Sentence after sentence with the same length and structure can be stiff and dull, like soldiers marching down the page. By varying sentences, you can hold readers' interest while also achieving the emphasis you want. The techniques to achieve variety include adjusting the lengths of sentences and varying their beginnings. For examples and specifics, see "Focus on Sentence Variety" on page 207.

Correct Grammar

Students sometimes think of grammar as a set of rigid rules that exist solely to give nitpickers a chance to point out mistakes. But errors can actually undermine an otherwise excellent piece of writing because they are unclear or distracting. The guidelines here can help you catch some of the most common problems.

Sentence Fragments

A sentence fragment is a word group that, although punctuated like a sentence, is not a complete sentence. Experienced writers sometimes use fragments deliberately and effectively, but readers usually stumble over fragments and view them as errors. For the sake of clarity, make sure every sentence has a subject and a verb and expresses a complete thought:

FRAGMENT   Snowboarding a relatively young sport.

COMPLETE   Snowboarding is a relatively young sport.

FRAGMENT   Many ski resorts banned snowboards at first. Believing they were dangerous and destructive.

COMPLETE   Many ski resorts banned snowboards at first, believing they were dangerous and destructive.

Run-on Sentences and Comma Splices

Complete sentences need clear separation from each other. When two or more sentences run together with no punctuation between them, they create a *run-on sentence.* When they run together with only a comma between them, they create a *comma splice.* Writers usually correct these errors with a period, with a semicolon, or with a comma along with *and, but, or, nor, for, so,* or *yet*:

RUN-ON   Snowboarding has become a mainstream sport riders are now as common as skiers on the slopes.

COMMA SPLICE   Snowboarding has become a mainstream sport, riders are now as common as skiers on the slopes.

EDITED   Snowboarding has become a mainstream sport. Riders are now as common as skiers on the slopes.

EDITED   Snowboarding has become a mainstream sport; riders are now as common as skiers on the slopes.

EDITED   Snowboarding has become a mainstream sport, and riders are now as common as skiers on the slopes.

Subject-Verb Agreement

Most writers know to use singular verbs with singular subjects and plural verbs with plural subjects, but matching subjects and verbs can sometimes be tricky. Watch especially for these situations:

- **Don't mistake a noun that follows the subject for the actual subject.** In the examples below, the subject is *appearance*, not *snowboarders* or *Olympics*:

  MISMATCHED   The <u>appearance</u> of snowboarders in the Olympics <u>prove</u> their status as true athletes.

  MATCHED   The appearance of snowboarders in the Olympics <u>proves</u> their status as true athletes.

- **With subjects joined by and, use a plural verb.** Compound word groups are treated as plural even if the word closest to the verb is singular:

  MISMATCHED   <u>The cross course and the half-pipe</u> <u>shows</u> the sport's versatility.

  MATCHED   The cross course and the half-pipe <u>show</u> the sport's versatility.

Pronouns

We tend to use pronouns without thinking much about them. Problems occur when usage that feels natural in speech causes confusion in writing:

- **Check that each pronoun refers clearly to an appropriate noun.** Rewrite sentences in which the reference is vague or only implied:

  VAGUE   Students asked the administration to add more parking spaces, but <u>it</u> had no effect.

  CLEAR   Students asked the administration to add more parking spaces, but <u>their pleas</u> had no effect.

  IMPLIED   Although commuter parking is hard to find, <u>they</u> keep driving to campus.

  CLEAR   Although <u>commuters know that</u> parking is hard to find, they keep driving to campus.

- **Take care with indefinite pronouns.** We often use singular indefinite pronouns—such as *anybody, anyone, everyone,* and *somebody*—to mean "many" or "all" and then mistakenly refer to them with plural pronouns:

  MISMATCHED   <u>Everyone</u> should change <u>their</u> passwords frequently.

  MATCHED   <u>Everyone</u> should change <u>his or her</u> passwords frequently.

  MATCHED   <u>All computer users</u> should change <u>their</u> passwords frequently.

Misplaced and Dangling Modifiers

A *modifier* describes another word or group of words in a sentence. Make sure that modifiers clearly describe the intended words. Misplaced and dangling modifiers can be awkward or even unintentionally amusing:

MISPLACED   I swam away as the jellyfish approached <u>in fear of being stung</u>.

CLEAR   <u>In fear of being stung</u>, I swam away as the jellyfish approached.

DANGLING   <u>Floating in the ocean, the clouds</u> drifted by.

CLEAR   Floating in the ocean, <u>I</u> watched as the clouds drifted by.

Shifts

Be consistent in your use of verb tense (past, present, and so on), person (*I, you, he/she/it, they*), and voice (active or passive). Unnecessary shifts can confuse readers. For details, see "Focus on Verbs" on page 104 and "Focus on Consistency" on page 303.

COLLABORATING

Your writing teacher may ask you to spend some time talking with your classmates, as a whole class or in small groups or pairs. You may analyze the essays in this book (perhaps answering the end-of-essay questions), read each other's journals or drafts, or plot revision strategies. Such conversation and collaboration—voicing, listening to, and arguing about ideas—can help you develop more confidence in your writing and give you a clearer sense of audience. One classmate may show you that your introduction, which you thought was weak, really worked to get her involved in your essay. Another classmate may question you in a way that helps you see how the introduction sets up expectations in the reader, expectations you're obliged to fulfill. Rosie Anaya received classmates' comments on the first draft of her paper responding to Nancy Mairs's "Disability" (see p. 53).

You may at first be anxious about collaboration: How can I judge others' writing? How can I stand others' criticism of my own writing? These are natural worries, and your teacher will try to help you with both of them—for instance, by providing a checklist to guide your critique of your classmates' writing. (The revision checklist on p. 41 works for reading others' drafts as well as your own.) With practice and plentiful feedback, you'll soon appreciate how much you're learning about writing and what a good effect that knowledge has on your work. You're writing for an audience, after all, and you can't beat the immediate feedback of a live one.

AN ESSAY-IN-PROGRESS

In the following pages, you have a chance to watch Rosie Anaya as she develops an essay through journal notes and several drafts. Her topic is the third of the writing suggestions given on page 35—about a group that has been "effaced" by the media—which she had already started exploring in her journal (p. 37). Anaya's journal notes through each stage enlighten us about her thinking as she proceeds through the writing process.

Reading and Drafting

Journal Notes on Reading

"For months now I've been consciously searching for representation of myself in the media" (¶ 1)

- "representation of myself" = a person who just happens to have a disability (Mairs has multiple sclerosis) living a full, normal life
- Media shows disability consuming a character's life or doesn't show disability at all

Haven't the media gotten a little better about showing people with disabilities since Mairs wrote in 1987? Lots of TV shows have characters who just happen to use canes or wheelchairs.

"Effaced" (¶ 5) means to erase, or to make something disappear. I see why Mairs has a problem with this: I would be bothered, too, if I didn't see people like me represented in the media. I would feel left out, probably hurt, maybe angry.

Mairs is doing more: Invisibility is a problem for healthy people too — anybody could become disabled and wouldn't know that people with disabilities live full, normal lives (¶ 7).

Interesting that Mairs mentions emotional health more than once:

- "self-degradation and a subtle kind of self-alienation" (¶ 6)
- "you might feel as though you don't exist, in any meaningful social sense" (¶ 6)
- "the physically and emotionally complex world you live in" (¶ 7)
- "it will be a good bit easier psychologically if . . ." (¶ 7)

References to feelings and psychology raise a question about people with mental disabilities, like depression or autism or schizophrenia. How are *they* represented by the media?

- Definitely *not* as regular people with "a normal characteristic, one that complicates but does not ruin human existence" (¶ 7)
- Stories in the news about emotionally disturbed people who go over the edge and hurt or even kill people. And *CSI*, *Law and Order*, etc., always

using some kind of psychological disorder to explain why someone committed a crime.

I think I have a start for an essay that answers question 3, about other minority
groups that are "effaced" in the media. Except the problem with mental illness
isn't just invisibility — it's also negative stereotyping. What if you're either not
being represented at all or you're represented as a danger to yourself and others?
That's got to be even worse.

First Draft

Nancy Mairs is upset with television and movies that don't show physical
disability as a feature of normal life. She says the media shows disability consuming a character's life or it doesn't show disability at all, and she wants to see
"representation of myself in the media, especially television" (p. no.).

Mairs makes a convincing argument that the media should portray physical disability as part of everyday life because "effacement" leaves the rest of
us unprepared to cope in the case that we should eventually become disabled
ourselves. As she explains it, anybody could become disabled, but because we
rarely see people with disabilities living full, normal lives on tv, we assume that
becoming disabled means life is pretty much over (p. no.). It's been more than
two decades since Mairs wrote her essay, and she seems to have gotten her wish.
Plenty of characters on television today who have a disability are not defined by
it. But psychological disabilities are disabilities too, and they have never been
shown "as a normal characteristic, one that complicates but does not ruin human
existence" (p. no.).

Television routinely portrays people with mental illness as threats to themselves and to others. Think about all those stories on the evening news about a
man suffering from anxiety who went on a shooting spree before turning his gun
on himself, or a mother who drowned her own children in the throes of postpartum depression, or a bipolar teenager who commits suicide. Such events are
tragic, no doubt, but although the vast majority of people with these illnesses
hurt nobody, the news implies that they're all potential killers.

Fictional shows, too, are always using some kind of psychological disorder
to explain why someone committed a crime. On *Law and Order* an Iraq war veteran
committed murder because he couldn't cope with his memories of the war and
lashed out at a homeless person. And an entire season of *CSI* kept coming back
to a story about the "miniature killer." Over several episodes, Gil Grissom, Sara
Seidel, Catherine Willows, and Nick Stokes found perfect miniature replicas of
crime scenes and tried to figure out who was so obsessive/compulsive that they

would go to so much trouble to re-create their crime scenes in elaborately crafted dollhouses. After chasing down a few false leads, they were surprised to discover that the serial killer was a woman whose father had rejected her because she pushed her little sister out of a treehouse and killed her when she was only six years old. She spent her childhood being shunted around between foster homes, where nobody wanted her either. She was even described by one former foster parent as "broken"! Meanwhile, the father projected his love for his dead daughter onto his ventriloquism dummy, making him seem more than a little mentally ill himself.

It is my belief that the presentation of psychological disability may do worse than the "effacement" of disability that bothered Mairs. People with mental illness are discouraged from seeking help and are sent deeper into isolation and despair. This negative stereotype hurts us all.

Revising

Peer Responses to First Draft

Your essay is fascinating. I never really thought about how mental illness is treated on TV before! But your introduction is pretty abrupt, and what is your thesis? I don't see it anywhere. Also, the essay seems to kind of fizzle out at the end.

—Liz Kingham

You do a good job showing how TV shows stereotype people with mental illness, but the *CSI* example goes on a bit long — it's hard to see how it all relates. Also, can you give some examples of the characters with physical disabilities you mention in paragraph 2? All the ones I can think of are from shows that have been canceled, so I wonder if the problem has really improved after all.

—Hahlil Jones

Your idea is really original, but I'm having trouble following how it connects to Mairs's argument. Could you tie the two issues together more clearly?

—Maria Child

Journal Notes on First Draft

I thought I did a good job explaining myself, but Maria's right: I assume that other people interpreted Mairs the same way I did, and that's not necessarily true. I'm supposed to be responding to Mairs and building on what she says, so I need to go through my essay and spell out what her ideas are — and then show how the problems she identified are even more important in the case of mental illness.

Hahlil's right about the *CSI* example — I got carried away with it. I only need to make the point that the show emphasizes the killer's mental disturbance.

The introduction and conclusion need a lot of work: a less abrupt start, a thesis statement, and a fuller conclusion that says why the media should improve the way psychological disability is portrayed — more with Mairs's point about the impact of "effacement" on "Temporarily Abled People" might help with that.

Also need to add page numbers from Mairs and works cited at end.

Revised Draft

Mental Illness on Television

In her essay "Disability" Nancy Mairs ~~is upset with~~ argues that television and movies ~~that don't~~ fail to show physical disability as a feature of normal life. Instead, Mairs ~~She~~ says, the media shows disability consuming a character's life or it doesn't show disability at all~~, and she wants to see "representation of myself in the media, especially television"~~ (~~p. no.~~ 13-14). But Mairs wrote her essay in 1987. Since then the situation has actually improved for physical disability. At the same time, another group — those with mental illness — have come to suffer even worse representation.

~~Mairs makes a convincing argument~~ Mairs's purpose in writing her essay was to persuade her readers that the media should portray physical disability as part of everyday life because ~~"effacement"~~ otherwise it denies or misrepresents disability, and it leaves ~~the rest of us~~ "Temporarily Abled Persons" (those without disability for now) unprepared to cope in the case that ~~we~~ they should eventually become disabled ~~ourselves~~ themselves (14-15). ~~As she explains it, anybody could become disabled, but because we rarely see people with disabilities living full, normal lives on tv, we assume that becoming disabled means life is pretty much over (p. no.). It's been more than two decades since Mairs wrote her essay, and~~ Two decades later, Mairs ~~she~~ seems to have gotten her wish. Plenty of characters on television today who have a disability are not defined by it. The title character on *House* walks with a cane, and Artie Abrams of *Glee*, a paraplegic who uses a wheelchair, sings and dances with a show choir. Joe Swanson of *Family Guy* is also paraplegic. Jimmy on *South Park* uses crutches. The medical examiner on *CSI*, Al Robbins, has prosthetic legs.

However, the media depiction of one type of disability is, if anything, worse than it was two decades ago. Although Mairs doesn't address mental illness in "Disability," mental illness falls squarely into the misrepresentation she criticizes. ~~But p~~Psychological disabilities are disabilities too, ~~and~~ but they have never been shown "as a normal characteristic, one that complicates but does not ruin human existence" (p. no. 15). People who cope with a disability such as depression, bipolar disorder, or obsessive-compulsive disorder as parts of their lives do not see themselves in the media; those who don't have a psychological disability now but may someday do not see that mental illness is usually a condition they can live with.

The depictions of mental illness actually go beyond Mairs's concerns, as the media actually exploits it. Television routinely portrays people with mental illness as threats to themselves and to others. Think about all those stories on the evening news about a man suffering from anxiety who went on a shooting spree before turning his gun on himself, or a mother who drowned her own children in the throes of postpartum depression, or a bipolar teenager who commits suicide. ~~Such events are tragic, no doubt, but although the vast majority of people with these illnesses hurt nobody, the news implies that they're all potential killers.~~ Fictional shows, too, are always using some kind of psychological disorder to explain why someone committed a crime. On *Law and Order* an Iraq war veteran commited murder because he couldn't cope with his memories of the war and lashed out at a homeless person. And after an entire season of *CSI*, ~~kept coming back to a story about the "miniature killer." Over several episodes, Gil Grissom, Sara Seidel, Catherine Willows, and Nick Stokes found perfect miniature replicas of crime scenes and tried to figure out who was so obsessive/compulsive that they would go to so much trouble to re-create their crime scenes in elaborately crafted dollhouses. After chasing down a few false leads, they were surprised to discover that the~~ a serial killer ~~was~~ turns out to be a deranged woman who had been driven by delusions since childhood. ~~whose father had rejected her because she pushed her little sister out of a treehouse and killed her when she was only six years old. She spent her childhood being shunted around between foster homes, where nobody wanted her either.~~ She was even described by one former foster parent as "broken."~~! Meanwhile, the father projected his love for his dead daughter onto his ventriloquism dummy, making him seem more than a little mentally ill himself.~~

These programs highlight mental illness to get viewers' attention. But the media is also telling us that the proper response to people with mental illness is to be afraid of them. Mairs argues that invisibility in the media can cause people with disabilities to feel unattractive or inappropriate (14-15). It is my belief that the presentation of psychological disability may do worse. ~~than the "effacement" of disability that bothered Mairs.~~ People with mental illness are discouraged from seeking help and are sent deeper into isolation and despair. Those feelings are often cited as the fuel for violent outbursts, but ironically the media portrays such violence as inevitable with mental illness. ~~This negative stereotype hurts us all.~~

More complex and varied depictions of all kinds of impairments, both physical and mental, will weaken the negative stereotypes that are harmful to all of us. With mental illness especially, we would all be better served if psychological disability was portrayed by the media as a part of everyday life. It's not a crime.

Works Cited

"Built to Kill," "Built to Kill, Part 2," "Post Mortem," "Loco Motives," "Monster in a Box," "Lab Rats," "Living Doll," and "Dead Doll." *CSI: Crime Scene Investigation*. 2006-07. CBS, 2007. DVD.

Mairs, Nancy. "Disability." *The Bedford Reader*. Ed. X. J. Kennedy, Dorothy M. Kennedy, and Jane E. Aaron. 11th ed. Boston: Bedford, 2012. 13-15. Print.

"Over Here." *Law and Order*. 11 May 2007. NBC, 2008. DVD.

Editing

Journal Notes on Revised Draft

This is much better now that I've clarified my thesis and connected my argument better with Mairs's. She adds more authority to my own point. The examples of mental illness on TV are much tighter. And the conclusion explains why this topic is important — much needed.

There's still some work to do, though. Need to fix some errors ("media" is plural) and do something about awkward sentences. Maybe give a little more explanation in a couple of places too.

Edited Paragraph

Mairs's purpose in ~~writing her essay~~ "Disability" ~~was~~ is to persuade ~~her~~ readers that the media should portray physical disability as part of everyday life because otherwise ~~it~~ they ~~denies~~ deny or misrepresents disability~~,~~ and ~~it~~ leaves "Temporarily Abled Persons" (those without disability, for now) unprepared to cope ~~in the case that they should eventually~~ if they become disabled ~~themselves~~ (14-15). Two decades later, Mairs seems to have gotten her wish~~. Plenty of~~ for characters ~~on television today~~ who have a disability but are not defined by it. The title character on *House*, for example, walks with a cane~~,~~. Artie Abrams of *Glee,* ~~a~~

~~paraplegic who~~ uses a wheelchair~~,~~ and also sings and dances with a show choir. Joe Swanson of *Family Guy* is also paraplegic. Jimmy on *South Park* uses crutches. ~~The m~~Medical examiner Al Robbins on *CSI*~~, Al Robbins,~~ has prosthetic legs. The media still have a long way to go in representing physical disability, but they have made progress.

Final Draft

Rosie Anaya

Professor DeBeer

English 102A

2 February 2010

Mental Illness on Television

In her essay "Disability," Nancy Mairs argues that the media, such as television and movies, fail to show physical disability as a feature of normal life. Instead, Mairs says, they show disability consuming a character's life or they don't show disability at all. Mairs wrote her essay in 1987, and since then the situation has actually improved for depiction of physical disability. At the same time, another group — those with mental illness — has come to suffer even worse representation.

Mairs's purpose in "Disability" is to persuade readers that the media should portray physical disability as part of everyday life because otherwise they deny or misrepresent disability and leave "Temporarily Abled Persons" (those without disability, for now) unprepared to cope if they become disabled (14-15). Two decades later, Mairs seems to have gotten her wish for characters who have a disability but are not defined by it. The title character on *House*, for example, walks with a cane. Artie Abrams of *Glee* uses a wheelchair and also sings and dances with a show choir. Joe Swanson of *Family Guy* is also paraplegic. Jimmy on *South Park* uses crutches. Medical examiner Al Robbins on *CSI* has prosthetic legs. The media still have a long way to go in representing physical disability, but they have made progress.

However, in depicting one type of disability, the media are, if anything, worse than they were two decades ago. Mairs doesn't address mental illness, but it falls squarely into the

Introduction summarizes Mairs's essay and sets up Anaya's thesis.

Thesis statement establishes Anaya's main idea.

Page numbers in parentheses refer to "Works Cited" at end of paper. (See also p. 73.)

Examples provide support for Anaya's analysis.

Comparison and contrast extends Mairs's idea to Anaya's new subject.

misrepresentation she criticizes. It has never been shown, in Mairs's words, "as a normal characteristic, one that complicates but does not ruin human existence" (15). Thus people who cope with a psychological disability such as depression, bipolar disorder, or obsessive-compulsive disorder as part of their lives do not see themselves in the media. And those who don't have a psychological disability now but may someday do not see that mental illness is usually a condition one can live with.

> Follow-up comments explain what the quotation contributes to Anaya's thesis. (See also p. 63.)

Unfortunately, the depictions of mental illness also go beyond Mairs's concerns, because the media actually exploit it. Television routinely portrays people with mental illness as threats to themselves and to others. TV news features stories about a man suffering from anxiety who goes on a shooting spree before turning his gun on himself, a mother with postpartum depression who drowns her own children, and a teenager with bipolar disorder who commits suicide. Fictional programs, especially crime dramas, regularly use mental illness to develop their plots. On *Law and Order* an Iraq war veteran with post-traumatic stress disorder commits murder, and on *CSI* a serial killer turns out to be a deranged woman — described by a former foster parent as "broken" — who had been driven by delusions since childhood.

> Topic sentence introduces new idea.

> Examples provide evidence for Anaya's point.

These programs and many others like them highlight mental illness to get viewers' attention, and they strongly imply that the proper response is fear. Mairs argues that the invisibility of physical disability in the media can cause people with disabilities to feel unattractive or inappropriate (14-15), but the presentation of psychological disability may do worse. It can prevent people with mental illness from seeking help and send them deeper into isolation and despair. Those feelings are often cited as the fuel for violent outbursts, but ironically the media portray such violence as inevitable with mental illness.

> Paraphrase explains one of Mairs's points in Anaya's own words. (See also p. 65.)

> Cause and effect applies Mairs's idea to Anaya's thesis.

Seeing more complex and varied depictions of people living with all kinds of impairments, physical and mental, can weaken the negative stereotypes that are harmful to all of us. With mental illness especially, we would all be better served if the media would make an effort to portray psychological disability as a part of everyday life, not a crime.

> Conclusion reasserts thesis and explains the broader implications of the subject.

Works Cited

"Built to Kill," "Built to Kill Part 2," "Post Mortem," "Loco Motives," "Monster in a Box," "Lab Rats," "Living Doll," and
"Dead Doll." *CSI: Crime Scene Investigation*. 2006-07. CBS,
2007. DVD.

Mairs, Nancy. "Disability." *The Bedford Reader*. Ed. X. J. Kennedy, Dorothy M. Kennedy, and Jane E. Aaron. 11th ed.
Boston: Bedford, 2012. 13-15. Print.

"Over Here." *Law and Order*. 11 May 2007. NBC, 2008. DVD.

"Works Cited" begins on a new page and gives complete publication information for Anaya's sources. (See also p. 76.)

3

ACADEMIC WRITING

In college you will write in many disciplines—history, psychology, chemistry, and so on—each with its own subjects and approaches and GENRES for shaping ideas and information. As varied as your writing projects may be, however, they will share the goals and requirements of ACADEMIC WRITING: They will ask you to build and exchange knowledge by thinking critically (Chap. 1) and writing effectively (Chap. 2) about what you read, see, hear, or do.

For a taste of academic knowledge building, you can take a look at the examples of academic genres that appear in the introductions to Chapters 4–13, such as the case study on pages 107–09 and the proposal on pages 561–63. You can also examine any of the essays in this book that use and document sources, such as Rosie Anaya's "The Best Kept Secret on Campus" at the end of this chapter, George Chauncey's "The Legacy of Antigay Discrimination" (p. 290), Bella DePaulo's "The Myth of Doomed Kids" (p. 379), Laila Ayad's "The Capricious Camera" (p. 387), Dacher Keltner's "A Vocabulary of Smiles" (p. 445), Marie Javdani's "*Plata o Plomo*: Silver or Lead" (p. 472), Colleen Wenke's "Too Much Pressure" (p. 564), Rodrigo Villagomez's "The Designer Player" (p. 586), and Barbara Ehrenreich's "The Menace of Negative People" (p. 634). You may notice that these essays have in common certain features of academic writing:

- Each writer attempts to gain readers' agreement with his or her debatable idea — or THESIS — about the subject.
- To support their theses, the writers provide EVIDENCE from one or more other TEXTS, or sources that can be examined or interpreted. (Ayad's subject, a photograph, is a kind of text; so is a written document, an experiment, a conversation, or any form of creative expression.)
- The writers do not merely SUMMARIZE their sources; they grapple with them. They ANALYZE meaning, infer ASSUMPTIONS, and SYNTHESIZE the texts' and their own views — in short, they read and write critically.
- The writers acknowledge their use of sources with documentation that is appropriate for the discipline each is writing in — footnotes in some cases, parenthetical citations and a bibliography in other cases.
- Each writer assumes an educated audience — one that can be counted on to read critically in turn. The writers state their ideas clearly, provide information readers need to analyze those ideas, and organize ideas and evidence effectively. Further, they approach their subjects seriously and discuss evidence and opposing views fairly.

This chapter will help you achieve such academic writing yourself by responding directly to what you read (below), integrating textual evidence into your ideas (p. 64), orchestrating multiple sources to develop and support your ideas (p. 67), avoiding plagiarism (p. 71), and documenting sources (p. 73). The chapter concludes with a sample research paper (p. 86) and comments by the student writer on her writing process (p. 91).

RESPONDING TO A TEXT

The essay by Rosie Anaya in the previous chapter (p. 57) illustrates one kind of academic writing, the critical response: Anaya summarizes Nancy Mairs's essay "Disability" (p. 13), explores its implications, and uses it as a springboard to her own related subject, which she supports with personal observation and experience. Just as Anaya responds to Mairs's essay, so you can respond to any essay in this book or for that matter to any text you read, see, or hear. (A response of this type relies heavily on ANALYSIS, a skill so central to academic writing that we devote an entire chapter to it; see pp. 351–57.) Using evidence from the text, from your own experiences, and sometimes from additional sources, you can take a variety of approaches:

- Like Anaya, agree with and extend the author's ideas, providing additional examples or exploring related ideas.
- Agree with the author on some points, but disagree on others.
- Disagree with the author on one of his or her key points.

- Explain how the author achieves a particular EFFECT, such as enlisting your sympathy or sparking your anger.
- Judge the overall effectiveness of the essay—for instance, how well the writer supports the thesis, whether the argument is convincing, or whether the author succeeds in his or her stated or unstated purpose.

These suggestions and this discussion assume that you are responding to a single work, but of course you may take on two or even more works at the same time. You might, for instance, use the method of COMPARISON AND CONTRAST to show how two stories are alike or different or to find your own way between two arguments on the same issue.

Forming a Response

Some works you analyze will spark an immediate reaction, maybe because you disagree or agree strongly right from the start. Other works may require a more gradual entry into the author's meaning and what you think about it. At the same time, you may have an assignment that narrows the scope of your response—for instance, by asking you to look at TONE or some other element of the work or by asking you to agree or disagree with the author's thesis.

Whatever your initial reaction or your assignment, you can use the tools discussed in Chapter 1 to generate and structure your response: summary, analysis, inference, synthesis, evaluation. (See pp. 17–20.) Your first goal is to understand the work thoroughly, both what it says outright and what it assumes and implies. For this step, you'll certainly need to make notes of some sort: For instance, those by Rosie Anaya on pages 51–52 include summaries of Mairs's essay, key quotations from it, interpretations of its meaning, and the beginnings of Anaya's ideas in response. Such notes may grow increasingly focused as you refine your response and return to the work to interpret it further and gather additional passages to discuss.

Synthesizing Your Own and Another's Views

Synthesis, as we note in Chapter 1, is the core of academic writing: Knowledge builds as writers bring their own perspectives to bear on what others have written, making their own contributions to what has come before.

When you write about a text, your perspective on it will be your thesis—the main point you have in response to the text or (if you take off in another direction) as a result of examining the text. As you develop the thesis, always keep your ideas front and center, pulling in material from the text as needed for support. In each paragraph, your idea should come first and, usually, last:

State the idea, use evidence from the reading to support it, and then interpret the evidence. (As a way to encourage this final interpretation, some writing teachers ask students not to end paragraphs with source citations.)

You can see a paragraph structured like this in Rosie Anaya's essay "Mental Illness on Television" in the previous chapter:

SYNTHESIS

However, in depicting one type of disability, the media are, if anything, worse than they were two decades ago. Mairs doesn't address mental illness, but it falls squarely into the misrepresentation she criticizes. It has never been shown, in Mairs's words, "as a normal characteristic, one that complicates but does not ruin human existence" (15). Thus people who cope with a psychological disability such as depression, bipolar disorder, or obsessive-compulsive disorder as part of their lives do not see themselves in the media. And those who don't have a psychological disability now but may someday do not see that mental illness is usually a condition one can live with.

Anaya's idea

Evidence from Mairs

Anaya's interpretation of Mairs's idea

Remember that synthesis is more than SUMMARY, which just distills what the text says or shows. Summary has its uses, especially in understanding a writer's ideas (p. 17) and in presenting evidence from source material (below), but it should not substitute for your own ideas. Contrast the preceding paragraph from Anaya's essay with the following draft passage in which Anaya uses summary to present evidence:

SUMMARY

Mairs argues that media misrepresentation of disability hurts not only viewers with disabilities but also those without disabilities. The media either ignore disability altogether or present it as the defining characteristic of a person's life (13-14). In doing so, they deny "Temporarily Abled Persons" the opportunity to see disability as something common that may be difficult to adjust to but does not destroy one's life (15).

Mairs's idea

Mairs's idea

Mairs's idea

INTEGRATING SOURCE MATERIAL

Key to synthesis are first deciding how to present evidence from your reading and then working the evidence into your own text.

Summary, Paraphrase, and Quotation

When you summarize or paraphrase a source, you express its ideas in your own words. When you quote, you use the source's exact words, in quotation marks. *All summaries, paraphrases, and quotations must be acknowledged in source citations.* See pages 71–73 on avoiding plagiarism and pages 73–86 on MLA documentation.

Summary

With SUMMARY you use your own words to condense a paragraph, an entire article, or even a book into a few lines that convey the source's essential meaning. We discuss summary as a reading technique on page 17, and the advice and examples there apply here as well. When responding to a text, you may use brief summaries to catch readers up on the gist of the author's argument or a significant point in the argument. Here, for example, is a summary of Barbara Lazear Ascher's "On Compassion," which appears on pages 211–13:

> SUMMARY   Ascher shows how contact with the homeless can be unsettling and depressing. Yet she also suggests that these encounters are useful because they can teach others to be more compassionate (211–13).

Notice how the summary identifies the source author and page numbers and uses words that are *not* the author's. (Any of Ascher's distinctive phrasing would have to be placed in quotation marks.)

Paraphrase

When you PARAPHRASE, you restate a specific passage in your own words. Paraphrase adheres more closely than summary to the source author's line of thought, so it's useful to present an author's ideas or data in detail. Generally, use paraphrase rather than quotation for this purpose, since paraphrase shows that you're in command of your evidence and lets your own voice come through. (See below for when to use quotations.) Here is a quotation from Ascher's essay and a paraphrase of it:

> ORIGINAL QUOTATION   "Could it be that the homeless, like [Greek dramatists], are reminding us of our common humanity? Of course, there is a difference. This play doesn't end—and the players can't go home."
>
> PARAPHRASE   Ascher points out an important distinction between the New York City homeless and the characters in Greek tragedies: The homeless are living real lives, not performing on a stage (213).

As with a summary, note that a paraphrase cites the original author and page number. Here is another example of paraphrase, this from an essay about immigration by David Cole:

ORIGINAL QUOTATION   "We stand to be collectively judged by our treatment of immigrants, who may appear to be 'other' now but in a generation will be 'us.'"

PARAPHRASE   Cole argues that the way the United States deals with immigrants now will come back to haunt it when those immigrants eventually become part of mainstream society (110).

Quotation

Quotations from sources can both support and enliven your own ideas—*if* you choose them well. When analyzing a primary source, such as a work of literature or a historical document, you may need to quote many passages in order to give the flavor of the author's words and evidence for your analysis. With secondary sources, however, too many quotations will clutter an essay and detract from your voice. Select quotations that are relevant to the point you are making, that are concise and pithy, and that use lively, bold, or original language. Sentences that lack distinction—for example, a statement providing statistics on economic growth—should be paraphrased.

Always enclose quotations in quotation marks and cite the source author and page number.

Introduction of Source Material

With synthesis, you're always making it clear to readers what your idea is and how the evidence from your reading supports that idea. To achieve this clarity, you want to fit summaries, paraphrases, and quotations into your sentences and show what you make of them.

In the passage below, the writer drops a quotation awkwardly into her sentence and doesn't clarify how the quotation relates to her idea:

NOT INTRODUCED   The problem of homelessness is not decreasing, and "It is impossible to insulate ourselves against what is at our very doorstep" (Ascher 213).

In the following revision, however, the writer indicates with "As Ascher says" that she is using the quotation to reinforce her point. This SIGNAL PHRASE also links the quotation to the writer's sentence.

INTRODUCED   The problem of homelessness is not decreasing, nor is our awareness of it, however much we wish otherwise. As Ascher says, "It is impossible to insulate ourselves against what is at our very doorstep" (213).

You can introduce source material into your sentence by interpreting it and by mentioning the author in your text—both techniques illustrated in the previous example. The signal phrase "As Ascher says" has a number of variations:

> According to one authority . . .
>
> John Eng maintains that . . .
>
> The author of an important study, Hilda Brown, observes that . . .
>
> Barbara Lazear Ascher, the author of "On Compassion," has a different view, claiming . . .

For variety, such a phrase can also fall elsewhere in the quotation:

> "It is impossible," Ascher says, "to insulate ourselves against what is at our very doorstep" (213).

When you omit something from a quotation, signal the omission with the three spaced periods of an ellipsis mark as shown:

> "It is impossible to insulate ourselves . . . ," says Ascher (213).
>
> In Ascher's view, "Compassion . . . must be learned . . ." (213).

WRITING FROM RESEARCH

Responding to a reading—thinking critically about it and synthesizing its ideas into your own—prepares you for the source-based writing that will occupy you for much of your academic career. In this kind of writing, you test and support your thesis by exploring and orchestrating a range of opinions and evidence found in multiple sources. The writing is source *based* but not source *dominated*: As when responding to a single work, your critical reading and your views set the direction and govern the final presentation.

Evaluating Sources

When examining multiple works for possible use in your paper, you of course want each one to be relevant to your subject and to your thesis. But you also want it to be reliable—that is, based on good evidence, carefully reasoned. To evaluate relevance and reliability, you'll depend on your critical-reading skills of analysis, inference, and synthesis to answer a series of questions:

- What is the PURPOSE of the source, and who is the source's intended AUDIENCE?
- Is the material a primary or a secondary source?
- Is the author an expert? What are his or her credentials?
- Does the author's bias affect the reliability of his or her argument?

- Does the author support his or her argument with EVIDENCE that is complete and up to date?

Purpose and Audience

The potential sources you find may have been written for a variety of reasons—for instance, to inform the public, to publish new research, to promote a product or service, to influence readers' opinions about a particular issue. While the first two of these purposes might lead to a balanced approach to the subject, the second two should raise yellow caution flags: Watch for bias that undermines the source's reliability.

A source's intended audience can suggest relevance. Was the work written for general readers? Then it may provide a helpful overview but not much detail. Was the work written for specialists? Then it will probably cover the topic in depth, but it may be difficult to understand.

Primary versus Secondary Sources

Primary sources are works by people who conducted or saw events firsthand. They include research reports, eyewitness accounts, diaries, and personal essays as well as novels, poems, and other works of literature. Secondary sources, in contrast, present and analyze the information in primary sources and include histories, reviews, and surveys of a field. Both types of source can be useful in research writing. For example, if you were writing about the debate over the assassination of President John F. Kennedy, you might seek an overview in books that discuss the evidence and propose theories about what happened—secondary sources. But you would be remiss not to read eyewitness accounts and law-enforcement documents—the primary sources.

Author's Credentials and Bias

Before you use a source to support your ideas, investigate the author's background to be sure that he or she is trustworthy. Look for biographical information in the introduction or preface of a book or in a note at the beginning or end of an article. Is the author an expert on the topic? Do other writers cite the author of your source in their work?

Investigating the author's background and credentials will probably uncover any bias as well—that is, the author's preference for a particular view of an issue. Actually, bias itself is not a problem: Everyone has a unique outlook created by experience, training, and even research techniques. What does matter is whether the author deals frankly with his or her bias and argues reasonably despite it. (See Chap. 13 for a discussion of reasoning.)

Evidence

Look for strong and convincing evidence to support the ideas in a source: facts, examples, reported experience, expert opinions. A source that doesn't muster convincing evidence, or much evidence at all, is not a reliable source. For very current topics, such as in medicine or technology, the source's ideas and evidence should be as up to date as possible.

Working with Online Sources

You have two paths to online sources: the Web site of your school's library and a public search engine such as *Google* or *Yahoo!* Always start with the library path: It leads to scholarly journals, reputable newspapers, and other sources that you can trust because they have passed through filters of verification, editing, and library review. The same is not necessarily true of online sources you reach directly. Anyone can put anything on the Internet, so you're as likely to find the rantings of an extremist or an advertisement posing as science as you are to find reasonable opinions and scholarly research.

Use the criteria discussed above—gauging purpose, audience, bias, and other factors—for all online sources, including those found through the library. But broaden your evaluation when considering sources you reach directly.

Authorship or Sponsorship

Often you won't be able to tell easily, or at all, who put a potential source on the Internet and thus whether that author or sponsor is credible and reliable. Sometimes an abbreviation in an electronic address contains a clue to the origin of a source: *edu* for educational institution, *gov* for government body, *org* for nonprofit organization, *com* for commercial organization. More specific background on the author or sponsor may require digging. On Web sites look for pages that have information about the author or sponsor or links to such information on other sites. On blogs and in discussion groups, ask anonymous authors for information about themselves. If you can't identify an author or a sponsor at all, you probably should not use the source.

Links or References to Sources

Most reliable sources will acknowledge borrowed evidence and ideas and tell you where you can find them. Some but not all online sources will do the same: A Web site, for instance, may provide links to its sources. Check out source citations that you find to be sure they represent a range of views. Be suspicious of any online work that doesn't acknowledge sources at all.

Currency

Online sources tend to be more current than print sources, which can actually be a disadvantage: The most current information may not have been tested by others and so may not be reliable. Always seek to verify recent information in other online sources or in print sources.

If they aren't tended regularly by their authors or sponsors, online sources can also be deceptive — that is, they may seem current but actually be out of date. Look for a date of copyright, publication, or last revision to gauge currency. If you don't find a date (and often you won't), compare the source with others you know to be recent before using its information.

Synthesizing Multiple Sources

In research writing as in response writing, your views should predominate over those of others. You decide which sources to use, how to treat them, and what conclusions to draw from them in order to test and support your thesis. In your writing, this thinking about sources' merits and relevance should be evident to readers. Here, for example, is a paragraph from Rosie Anaya's research paper at the end of this chapter. Notice how Anaya states her idea at the outset, guides us through the presentation of evidence from sources, and finally concludes by tying the evidence back to her idea.

> Despite the prevalence of depression and related disorders on campus, however, most students avoid seeking help when they need it. The American Psychiatric Association maintains that most mental health issues — depression especially — can be managed or overcome with treatment by therapy and/or medication. But among students with diagnosed depression, according to the American College Health Association, a mere 25% get therapy and only 36% take medication (484). One reason for such low numbers can be found in a study published in *Medical Care Research and Review*: Three in four American students would be unwilling to ask for help even if they were certain they needed it, because they perceive mental illness as embarrassing or shameful (Eisenberg et al. 524). Thus students who need help suffer additional pain — and no treatment — because they fear the stigma of mental illness.

This paragraph also illustrates other techniques of synthesis discussed in the previous section:

- In her own words, Anaya paraphrases the data and ideas of the sources, stressing her own voice and her mastery of the source material. (See p. 64.)
- Anaya integrates each paraphrase into her sentences with a signal phrase that names the source author and tells readers how the borrowed material relates to her idea. (See p. 64.)

Notice one other important feature of Anaya's paragraph as well: It clearly indicates what material Anaya has borrowed and where she borrowed it from. Such source citation is crucial to avoid plagiarism, the subject of the next section. The MLA citation style that Anaya uses is discussed on pages 73–86.

AVOIDING PLAGIARISM

Academic knowledge building depends on the integrity and trust of its participants. When you write in college, your readers expect you to distinguish your own contributions from those of others, honestly acknowledging material that originated elsewhere. If you do otherwise — if you copy another's idea, data, or even wording without acknowledgment — then you steal that person's intellectual property. Called PLAGIARISM, this theft is a serious and often punishable offense.

Examples and Revisions

For a blatant example of plagiarism, look at the following use of a quotation from Barbara Lazear Ascher's essay "On Compassion":

ORIGINAL QUOTATION "Could it be that the homeless, like [Greek dramatists], are reminding us of our common humanity? Of course, there is a difference. This play doesn't end — and the players can't go home."

PLAGIARISM The homeless are like the Greek dramatists in that they remind us of our common humanity, but of course now the players can't go home.

By not acknowledging Ascher at all, the plagiarizing writer takes claim for her idea and for much of her wording. A source citation would help — at least the idea would be credited — but still the expression of the idea would be stolen because there's no indication that it's Ascher's. Here is an acceptable revision:

CITATION AND QUOTATION MARKS Ascher suggests that "the homeless, like [Greek dramatists], are reminding us of our common humanity," although now "the players can't go home" (213).

Plagiarism can be more subtle, too, as in the following attempt to paraphrase a quotation by David Cole:

ORIGINAL QUOTATION   "We stand to be collectively judged by our treatment of immigrants, who may appear to be 'other' now but in a generation will be 'us.'"

PLAGIARISM   Cole argues that we will be judged as a group by how we treat immigrants, who seem to be different now but eventually will be the same (110).

Even though the writer identifies Cole as the source of the information, much of the language and the sentence structure are also Cole's. In a paraphrase or summary, it's not enough to change a few words—"collectively" to "as a group," "they may appear to be 'other'" to "they may seem different," "in a generation" to "eventually." A paraphrase or summary must express the original idea in an entirely new way, both in word choice and in sentence structure, as in this acceptable paraphrase seen earlier in the chapter:

PARAPHRASE   Cole argues that the way the United States deals with immigrants now will come back to haunt it when those immigrants are eventually integrated into mainstream society (110).

Plagiarism and the Internet

The Internet has made plagiarism both easier and riskier. Whether accidentally or deliberately, you can download source material directly into your own document with a few clicks of a mouse. And you can buy complete papers from term-paper sites. *Using downloaded material without credit, even accidentally, or turning in someone else's work as your own, even if you paid for it, is plagiarism.*

The chances of being caught plagiarizing from the Internet have also increased. Teachers can use search engines and plagiarism-detection programs to match phrases in students' papers with the same words anywhere on the Internet.

Common Knowledge

Not all information from sources must be cited. Some falls under the category of common knowledge—facts so widely known or agreed upon that they are not attributable to a specific source. The statement "World War II ended after the United States dropped atomic bombs on Hiroshima and Nagasaki, Japan" is an obvious example: Most people recognize this statement as true. But some lesser-known information is also common knowledge. You may not know that President Dwight Eisenhower coined the term *military-industrial complex* during his 1961 farewell address; still, you could easily discover the information in encyclopedias, in books and articles about Eisenhower, and in contemporary newspaper accounts. The prevalence of the information and the fact that it is used elsewhere without source citation tell you that it's common knowledge.

In contrast, a scholar's argument that Eisenhower waited too long to criticize the defense industry, or the president's own comments on the subject in his diary, or an opinion from a Defense Department report in 1959—any of these needs to be credited. Unlike common knowledge, each of them remains the property of its author.

SOURCE CITATION USING MLA STYLE

On the following pages we explain the documentation style of the Modern Language Association, as described in the *MLA Handbook for Writers of Research Papers*, 7th edition (2009). This style—used in English, foreign languages, and some other humanities—involves a brief parenthetical citation in the text that refers to an entry in a list of works cited at the end of the text:

PARENTHETICAL TEXT CITATION

The homeless may be to us what tragic heroes were to the ancient Greeks (Ascher 213).

ENTRY IN LIST OF WORKS CITED

Ascher, Barbara Lazear. "On Compassion." *The Bedford Reader*. Ed. X. J. Kennedy, Dorothy M. Kennedy, and Jane E. Aaron. 11th ed. Boston: Bedford, 2012. 211-13. Print.

By providing the author's name and page number in your text citation, you give the reader just enough information to find the source in the list of works cited and then find the place in the source where the borrowed material appears.

MLA Parenthetical Citations

When citing sources in your text, you have two options:

- You can identify both the author and the page number within parentheses, as in the Ascher example above.

- You can introduce the author's name into your own sentence and use the parentheses only for the page number, as here:

Wilson points out that sharks, which have existed for 350 million years, are now more diverse than ever (301).

A work with two or three authors

More than 90% of the hazardous waste produced in the United States comes from seven major industries, all energy-intensive (Romm and Curtis 70).

A work with more than three authors

With more than three authors, name all the authors, or name only the first author followed by "et al." ("and others"). Use the same form in your list of works cited.

Gilman herself created the misconception that doctors tried to ban her story "The Yellow Wallpaper" when it appeared in 1892 (Dock, Allen, Palais, and Tracy 61).

Gilman herself created the misconception that doctors tried to ban her story "The Yellow Wallpaper" when it appeared in 1892 (Dock et al. 61).

An entire work or a work with no page or other reference numbers

Omit page numbers when you cite an entire work or cite a work that does not number pages, paragraphs, or other parts.

Postman argues that television is destructive because of the nature of the medium itself.

MLA Parenthetical Citations

A nonprint source

Cite a nonprint source, such as a Web document or a DVD, just as you would a print source: by author's name or, if there is no author, by title. If a source numbers screens or paragraphs instead of pages, give the reference number as in the following model, after "par." (one paragraph), "pars." (more than one paragraph), "screen," or "screens." For a source with no reference numbers at all, use the preceding model for an entire work.

> One nurse questions whether doctors are adequately trained in tending patients' feelings (Van Eijk, pars. 6-7).

A work in more than one volume

If you cite two or more volumes of the same work, identify the volume number before the page number. Separate volume number and page number with a colon.

> According to Gibbon, during the reign of Gallienus "every province of the Roman world was afflicted by barbarous invaders and military tyrants" (1: 133).

Two or more works by the same author(s)

If you cite more than one work by the same author or authors, include the work's title. If the title is long, shorten it to the first one or two main words. (The full title for the first citation below is *Death at an Early Age*.)

> In the 1960s Kozol was reprimanded by his principal for teaching the poetry of Langston Hughes (*Death* 83).

> Kozol believes that most people do not understand the effect that tax and revenue policies have on the quality of urban public schools (*Savage Inequalities* 207).

An unsigned work

Cite an unsigned work by using a full or shortened version of the title.

> In 1995 concern about Taiwan's relationship with China caused investors to transfer capital to the United States ("How the Missiles Help" 45).

An indirect source

Use "qtd. in" ("quoted in") to indicate that you found the source you quote within another source.

> Despite his tendency to view human existence as an unfulfilling struggle, Schopenhauer disparaged suicide as "a vain and foolish act" (qtd. in Durant 248).

A literary work

Because novels, poems, and plays may be published in various editions, the page number may not be enough to lead readers to the quoted line or passage. For a novel, specify the chapter number after the page number and a semicolon.

> Among South Pacific islanders, the hero of Conrad's *Lord Jim* found "a totally new set of conditions for his imaginative faculty to work upon" (160; ch. 21).

For a verse play or a poem, omit the page number in favor of line numbers.

> In "Dulce et Decorum Est," Wilfred Owen undercuts the heroic image of warfare by comparing suffering soldiers to "beggars" and "hags" (lines 1-2) and describing a man dying in a poison-gas attack as "guttering, choking, drowning" (17).

If the work has parts, acts, or scenes, cite those as well (below: act 1, scene 5, lines 16–17).

> Lady Macbeth worries about her husband's ambition: "Yet I do fear thy nature; / It is too full o' the milk of human kindness" (1.5.16-17).

More than one work

> In the post-Watergate era, journalists have often employed aggressive reporting techniques not for the good of the public but simply to advance their careers (Gopnik 92; Fallows 64).

MLA List of Works Cited

Your list of works cited is a complete record of your sources. Follow these guidelines for the list:

- Title the list "Works Cited." (Do not enclose the title in quotation marks.)
- Double-space the entire list.
- Arrange the sources alphabetically by the last name of the first author.
- Begin the first line of each entry at the left margin. Indent the subsequent lines of the entry one-half inch or five spaces.

MLA List of Works Cited

Print Books

A book with one author 78
A book with two or three
 authors 78
A book with more than three
 authors 78
More than one work by the same
 author(s) 78
A book with an editor 79
A book with an author and an
 editor 79
A later edition 79
A work in a series 79
An anthology 79
A selection from an anthology 79
A reference work 80

*Print Periodicals: Journals,
Magazines, and Newspapers*

An article in a journal 80
An article in a journal that numbers
 only issues 80
An article in a monthly or bimonthly
 magazine 80
An article in a weekly
 magazine 80
An article in a newspaper 80
An unsigned article 81
A review 81

Online Sources

Nonperiodical Web publications
A short work on a Web site 81
An entire Web site 81

A newspaper or magazine on the
 Web 82
A government publication on the
 Web 82
A book on the Web 82
A wiki 82
A television or radio program on the
 Web 82
An image on the Web 82
A video recording on the Web 82
A sound recording or podcast on the
 Web 83
A posting to a blog 83

Periodical Web publications
An article in a scholarly journal on
 the Web 83
A periodical article in an online
 database 83

Other online sources
E-mail 84
A posting to a discussion group 84

Other Sources

A publication on CD-ROM or
 DVD-ROM 84
A photograph, painting, sculpture, or
 other work of art 84
A map or chart 85
An advertisement 85
A television or radio program 85
A sound recording 85
A film, video, or DVD 85
A letter 85
An interview 86

Following are the essentials of a works-cited entry:

- Reverse the names of the author, last name first, with a comma between. If there is more than one author, give the others' names in normal order.
- Give the full title of the work, capitalizing all important words. Italicize the titles of books, periodicals, and Web sites; use quotation marks for the titles of parts of books, articles in periodicals, and pages on Web sites.

- Give publication information. For books, this information includes city of publication, publisher, date of publication. For periodicals, this information includes volume number, issue number, date of publication, and page numbers for the article you cite. For online sources such as Web sites, this information includes the sponsor and date of the site and the date you consulted the source. (See pp. 81–84 for more on electronic sources.)
- Give the medium of publication. Use a designation such as "Print," "Web," "DVD," "Lecture," "Performance," "Radio," "Television," or "E-mail."
- Use periods between parts of each entry.

You may need to combine the models below for a given source—for instance, combine "A book with two or three authors" and "An article in an online journal" for an online article with two or three authors.

Print Books

A book with one author

Gladwell, Malcolm. *Outliers: The Story of Success*. New York: Little, 2008.
    Print.

A book with two or three authors

Silverstein, Olga, and Beth Rashbaum. *The Courage to Raise Good Men*. New
    York: Viking, 2004. Print.
Trevor, Sylvia, Joan Hapgood, and William Leumi. *Women Writers of the
    1920s*. New York: Columbia UP, 1998. Print.

A book with more than three authors

You may list all authors or only the first author followed by "et al." ("and others"). Use the same form in your parenthetical text citation.

Kippax, Susan, R. W. Connel, G. W. Dowsett, and June Crawford. *Gay Commu-
    nities Respond to Change*. London: Falmer, 2004. Print.
Kippax, Susan, et al. *Gay Communities Respond to Change*. London: Falmer,
    2004. Print.

More than one work by the same author(s)

Kozol, Jonathan. *Letters to a Young Teacher*. New York: Crown, 2007. Print.
---. *Savage Inequalities: Children in America's Schools*. New York: Crown, 1991.
    Print.

A book with an editor

Gwaltney, John Langston, ed. *Drylongso: A Self-Portrait of Black America*.
New York: Random, 2000. Print.

A book with an author and an editor

Emerson, Ralph Waldo. *The Essential Writings of Ralph Waldo Emerson*. Ed.
Brooks Atkinson. New York: Modern, 2000. Print.

A later edition

Bordo, Susan. *Unbearable Weight: Feminism, Western Culture, and the Body*.
2nd ed. Berkeley: U of California P, 2004. Print.

A work in a series

Hall, Donald. *Poetry and Ambition*. Ann Arbor: U of Michigan P, 1998. Print.
Poets on Poetry.

An anthology

Glantz, Michael H., ed. *Societal Responses to Regional Climatic Change*.
London: Westview, 2007. Print.

Cite an entire anthology only when you are citing the work of the editor
or you are cross-referencing it, as in the Brady and Quindlen models below.

A selection from an anthology

The numbers near the end of the following entry are the page numbers on
which the entire cited selection appears.

Kellog, William D. "Human Impact on Climate: The Evolution of an Awareness." *Societal Responses to Regional Climatic Change*. Ed. Michael H.
Glantz. London: Westview, 2007. 283-96. Print.

If you cite more than one selection from the same anthology, you may
give the anthology as a separate entry and cross-reference it by the editor's
or editors' last names in the selection entries. Place each entry in its proper
alphabetical place in the list of works cited.

Brady, Judy. "I Want a Wife." Kennedy, Kennedy, and Aaron.
Kennedy, X. J., Dorothy M. Kennedy, and Jane E. Aaron, eds. *The Bedford
Reader*. 11th ed. Boston: Bedford, 2012. Print.
Quindlen, Anna. "Homeless." Kennedy, Kennedy, and Aaron 216-18.

A reference work

Cheney, Ralph Holt. "Coffee." *Collier's Encyclopedia*. 2007 ed. Print.

"Versailles, Treaty of." *The New Encyclopaedia Britannica: Macropaedia*. 15th
ed. 1996. Print.

Print Periodicals: Journals, Magazines, and Newspapers

An article in a journal

After the journal title, give the volume and issue numbers separated by a
period, the year of publication in parentheses, a colon, the page numbers of
the article, a period, and the medium of publication.

Spencer, Renée, and Belle Liang. "'She Gives Me a Break from the World': Formal Youth Mentoring Relationships between Adolescent Girls and Adult
Women." *Journal of Primary Prevention* 30.2 (2009): 109-30. Print.

An article in a journal that numbers only issues

If a journal numbers issues but not annual volumes, give just the issue
number after the title.

Williams, Jeanne. "Evocations of Enigma in the Work of Ivar Shevtsov."
Review of Poetry 31 (2006): 21-29. Print.

An article in a monthly or bimonthly magazine

Fallows, James. "Why Americans Hate the Media." *Atlantic Monthly* Feb. 2007:
45-64. Print.

An article in a weekly magazine

MacFarquhar, Larissa. "Busted: The Investigators Who Try to Keep City
Employees Honest." *New Yorker* 1 Feb. 2010: 50-57. Print.

An article in a newspaper

McNeil, Donald G. "Gates Group to Double Spending on Vaccines." *New York
Times* 30 Jan. 2010, natl. ed.: A1+. Print.

The page number "A1+" means that the article begins on page 1 of section A and continues on a later page. If the newspaper has an edition, such as
"natl. ed." in the example, it will be labeled at the top of the first page.

An unsigned article

"How the Missiles Help California." *Time* 1 Apr. 2005: 45. Print.

A review

Iyer, Pico. "Secret Love of the Lost City." Rev. of *The Museum of Innocence,*
    by Orhan Pamuk. *New York Review of Books* 19 Nov. 2009: 38-40. Print.

Online Sources

Online sources vary greatly, and they may be and often are updated. Your
aim in citing such a source should be to tell what version you used and how
readers can find it for themselves. If you don't see a model for the type of source
you used, follow a model that comes close. If you can't find all the information
shown in a model, give what you can find. Substitute an abbreviation for missing information: "N.p." for "no publisher" and "n.d." for "no date."

Nonperiodical Web publications Nonperiodical Web publications include most of what you'll find on the open Web: works that are not published
on a schedule but just once or irregularly. This definition encompasses online
newspapers and magazines as well, because their content is changeable. Thus
the Web versions of the *New York Times* and *Newsweek* magazine are considered nonperiodical publications.

A short work on a Web site

The following model includes the basic information for a nonperiodical
Web publication: (1) author's name, (2) title of the short work, (3) title of
the site, (4) sponsor or publisher of the site, (5) date of the electronic publication or last update, (6) medium of publication, and (7) date the source was
consulted.

          ①   ②   ③ ④
Speer, Cindy Lynn. "Neil Gaiman's Film Work." *Neil Gaiman.* Harper,
       ⑤   ⑥   ⑦
    Aug. 2007. Web. 28 Apr. 2011.

An entire Web site

Center for Social Innovation. Stanford Graduate School of Business,
    4 Apr. 2009. Web. 13 Jan. 2010.

A newspaper or magazine on the Web

Jacobs, Andrew. "China Turns Drug Rehab into a Punishing Ordeal." *New York Times*. New York Times, 8 Jan. 2010. Web. 26 Nov. 2010.

Schulman, Candy. "The Vocabulary of Love." *Salon*. Salon, 5 Jan. 2010. Web. 12 Feb. 2010.

A government publication on the Web

United States. Dept. of Educ. "Teaching Literacy in English to K-5 English Learners." *Doing What Works: Research-Based Education Practices Online*. US Dept. of Educ., Feb. 2010. Web. 2 Mar. 2010.

A book on the Web

Addington, H. Bruce. *Historic Ghosts and Ghost Hunters*. New York: Moffat, 1908. *Internet Archive*. Web. 28 Apr. 2010.

A wiki

"Daguerreotype." *Wikipedia*. Wikimedia, 2 Feb. 2010. Web. 24 Feb. 2010.

A television or radio program on the Web

Murphy, Patricia. "For Veterans with Burns, a Virtual Reality Aid." *All Things Considered*. Natl. Public Radio, 4 Jan. 2010. Web. 8 Feb. 2010.

An image on the Web

Doble, Rick. *Spring Rain Abstraction*. 2009. *Digital Art Photography*. Rick Doble, 2010. Web. 12 Jan. 2010.

If the image originally or simultaneously appeared in another medium, you may provide the information for the other medium before the Web information:

Matisse, Henri. *La Musique*. 1939. Albright-Knox Gallery, Buffalo. *WebMuseum*. Web. 3 Mar. 2011.

A video recording on the Web

Jardin, Xeni. *Mardi Gras 1956: Through My Father's Lens*. *YouTube*. YouTube, 2010. Web. 15 Apr. 2010.

If the video originally or simultaneously appeared in another medium, you may provide the information for the other medium before the Web information:

> *San Francisco Earthquake and Fire*. 18 Apr. 1906. *American Memory*. Lib. of
> Congress, n.d. Web. 22 Sept. 2010.

In the example above, "n.d." means "no date" of publication or posting.

A sound recording or podcast on the Web

> Roosevelt, Eleanor. Address at the AFL-CIO Unity Convention. 9 Dec. 1955.
> *Vincent Voice Lib*. Michigan State U, 11 Oct. 2005. Web. 5 Oct. 2011.
> Wismer, George, narr. "Winter White." By Rose Adkins. *The Atlantic*. Atlantic
> Monthly, 2010. Web. 16 May 2010.

A posting to a blog

> Anderson, Brett. "Just Moderate Warming Can Lead to Large-Scale Melting
> of Ice Sheets." *AccuWeather.com Climate Change Blog*. AccuWeather, 29
> Dec. 2009. Web. 12 Jan. 2010.

Periodical Web publications

An article in a scholarly journal on the Web

Base an entry for an online journal article on one of the models on page 80 for a print journal article, changing the medium to "Web" and adding your access date. Use "n. pag." if the journal does not number pages.

> Sjostrand, Odile. "Law Philosophy in *Mansfield Park*." *Jane Austen Quarterly*
> 33.1 (1999): n. pag. Web. 12 Oct. 2010.

A periodical article in an online database

For an article that you obtain from a library or other database, provide print publication information using the models for journals, magazines, and newspapers on pages 80–81. Add the database title, the medium, and your access date.

> Conway, Daniel W. "Reading Henry James as a Critic of Modern Moral Life."
> *Inquiry* 45.3 (2002): 319-30. *Academic Search Elite*. Web. 20 Apr.
> 2011.

Other online sources

E-mail

Dove, Chris. "Re: Bishop's Poems." Message to the author. 7 May 2011.
    E-mail.

A posting to a discussion group

Riffenburgh, Audrey. "Learning about Health Literacy — Front Line Experience
    Crucial." *Health Literacy Discussion List*. Natl. Inst. for Literacy, 7 Jan.
    2010. Web. 13 Jan. 2010.

If the posting has no title, give "Online posting" (without quotation
marks) instead.

Other Sources

A publication on CD-ROM or DVD-ROM

The format for citing a publication on CD-ROM or DVD-ROM depends
on whether the publication is a periodical or not. Periodicals usually have
print versions as well, so start with the print information and end with the CD
or DVD medium, title, vendor, and publication date.

Rausch, Janet. "So Late in the Day." *Daily Sun* 10 Dec. 2006, late ed.: C1.
    CD-ROM. *Daily Disk*. Cybernews. Jan. 2007.

For a nonperiodical disk, adapt the format for a print book (p. 78), changing the medium to "CD-ROM" or "DVD-ROM" as appropriate:

"China." *Concise Columbia Encyclopedia*. 2009-10 ed. Redmond: Microsoft,
    2009. CD-ROM.

If the disk is available in print as well, it may have both a publisher and
a vendor. In that case, after the medium add the vendor's city and name and
the disk publication date.

A photograph, painting, sculpture, or other work of art

For a work of art that you see in the original, follow this format:

van Gogh, Vincent. *The Starry Night*. 1889. Oil on canvas. Museum of Mod.
    Art, New York.

For a work of art that you see in a reproduction, provide the publication information for the source you used:

> Hockney, David. *Nichols Canyon*. 1980. Private collection. *David Hockney: A Retrospective*. Ed. Maurice Tuchman and Stephanie Barron. Los Angeles: Los Angeles County Museum of Art, 1988. 205. Print.

A map or chart

> "Annual Rainfall in Las Vegas, 1950-2009." Chart. *The Development of Las Vegas*. By Sarah G. Murphy. Las Vegas: SynthEdge, 2010. 94. Print.

An advertisement

> IBM. Advertisement. *New Yorker* 8 Feb. 2010: 4-5. Print.

A television or radio program

> Nass, Clifford, guest. "Multitasking May Not Mean Higher Productivity." *Talk of the Nation*. Natl. Public Radio. KQED, San Francisco, 28 Aug. 2009. Radio.

A sound recording

> Mendelssohn, Felix. *A Midsummer Night's Dream*. Cond. Erich Leinsdorf. Boston Symphony Orch. RCA, 1982. LP.

A film, video, or DVD

> Achbar, Mark, and Peter Wintonick, dirs. *Manufacturing Consent: Noam Chomsky and the Media*. Zeitgeist, 1992. DVD.

A letter

List a published letter under the author's name, and provide full publication information.

> Hemingway, Ernest. Letter to Grace Hemingway. 15 Jan. 1920. In *Ernest Hemingway: Selected Letters*. Ed. Carlos Baker. New York: Scribner's, 1981. 44. Print.

For a letter that you receive, list the source under the writer's name, add "to the author," provide the date of the correspondence, and end with the medium (use "MS" for a manuscript, a letter written by hand, or "TS" for a typescript, a letter composed on a machine).

> Dove, Chris. Letter to the author. 7 May 2011. TS.

An interview

> Macedo, Donaldo. Personal interview. 13 May 2011.
> Smith, Patti. Interview by David Marchese. *Spin*. Spin Media, 27 Aug. 2008.
> Web. 26 Sep. 2008.

SAMPLE RESEARCH PAPER

In the previous chapter we saw Rosie Anaya respond to Nancy Mairs's "Disability" with her own essay on television portrayals of psychological disabilities (pp. 57–59). After completing that paper, Anaya began to wonder about some of the disturbing news stories she had seen that linked campus violence with mental illness. For a research assignment, she decided to delve further into the subject and was surprised by what she found. We reprint her research paper for three reasons: It illustrates many techniques of using and documenting sources, which are highlighted in the marginal comments; it shows a writer working with a topic that interests her in a way that arouses the readers' interest as well; and it explores a problem that affects most college students, often profoundly.

Rosie Anaya

Professor DeBeer

English 102A

5 May 2010

The Best Kept Secret on Campus

The college experience, as depicted in advertising and the movies, consists of happy scenes: students engrossed in class discussions, partying with friends, walking in small groups across campus. Such images insist that college is a great time of learning and friendship, but some students have a very different experience of emotional and psychological problems, ranging from anxiety to depression to acute bipolar disorder. These students endure social stigma and barriers to treatment that their colleges and universities must do more to help them surmount.

Title arouses readers' curiosity.

Images establish contrast between expectations and experiences of college students. No source citation needed for Anaya's generalization.

Thesis statement.

The numbers of college students suffering from psychological problems are staggering. A 2008 survey conducted by the American College Health Association found that 62% of students have experienced feelings of hopelessness, more than 90% have felt overwhelmed or emotionally exhausted, nearly 50% have been so depressed that they had trouble functioning, 15% have been formally diagnosed with depression, and almost 10% have contemplated suicide (484-85, 487). The simple fact, unknown to many, is that a college student is more likely than not to experience a severe psychological problem at least once. In other words, such problems are a common aspect of college life.

Despite the prevalence of depression and related disorders on campus, however, most students avoid seeking help when they need it. The American Psychiatric Association maintains that most mental-health issues — depression especially — can be managed or overcome with treatment by therapy and/or medication. But among students with diagnosed depression, according to the American College Health Association, a mere 25% get therapy and only 36% take medication (484). One reason for such low numbers can be found in a study published in *Medical Care Research and Review:* Three in four American students would be unwilling to ask for help even if they were certain they needed it, because they perceive mental illness as embarrassing or shameful (Eisenberg et al. 524). Thus students who need help suffer additional pain — and no treatment — because they fear the stigma of mental illness.

We've all heard the horror stories about what happens when a college student's mental illness goes untreated. The news media have been reporting such incidents with regularity since a sniper gunned down sixteen classmates at the University of Texas in 1966. In the past few years alone, a student at Virginia Tech killed thirty-two people before turning his gun on himself, a former Northern Illinois University graduate student killed five people and himself in a campus shooting spree, a failing student killed three professors and himself at Arizona Nursing College, a student at Louisiana Technical College fatally shot two classmates and herself, and a UCLA undergraduate stabbed a lab partner during class. After repeated exposure to these kinds

---

Statistics establish the scope of the problem.

Citation of a paraphrase. Citation includes only page numbers because author (American College Health Association) is named in the text.

Follow-up comments give Anaya's interpretation of the evidence.

Students' reluctance to seek help for psychological problems.

No parenthetical citation because author (American Psychiatric Association) is named in the text and online source has no page numbers.

In parenthetical citation, "et al." ("and others") indicates more than three authors.

Paragraph integrates information from three sources to support Anaya's own idea.

Perceived consequences of untreated mental illness.

No source citations in this paragraph because it relies on common knowledge: facts available in several sources, not attributable to any one source.

of stories, fear seems like a natural — and reasonable — response to mental illness on campus.

The news stories are misleading, however. Richard A. Friedman, a psychiatrist and professor at Cornell University, explains that journalists tend to emphasize mental illness in reports of violent crime even though the connection is rare — accounting for less than 5% of all incidents of violence. Friedman warns that this tendency feeds harmful stereotypes:

> Popular media affect not just how the public views people with psychiatric illness but how the public thinks about the disorders themselves. . . . In fact, major mental disorders are quite treatable and have response rates to psychosocial and biological treatments that are on par with, if not better than, common nonpsychiatric medical illnesses. But the public has little sense from stories in the popular media that mentally ill people can get better with treatment, recover, and go on to lead productive lives.

Although there is little reason to fear people with mental disorders, we are bombarded with the message that they are dangerous and incurable. No wonder, then, that most college students hide their emotional problems from people who could help them, never guessing that half of their peers are struggling with the same issues.

As unfortunate as it is, social stigma is not the only barrier to treatment faced by students with mental illness. The uncertain availability of on-campus psychological care poses another obstacle. As Richard Kadison and Theresa Foy DiGeronimo point out in a standard work on college mental-health care, creating and running a mental-health system is expensive, and only some schools can afford to offer comprehensive mental-health programming that ranges from outreach to counseling to follow-up treatment. Other schools have minimal resources and can do little more than react to a crisis, while still others offer no counseling or treatment at all (162–66). Struggling students who finally accept that they need help and work up the courage to ask for it may discover that they can't obtain it, at least not easily. It's not hard to imagine that most students — especially those in the grip of depression — would give up.

Margin notes:

Refutation of common perception of mental illness.

No parenthetical citation for summary, statistic, or block quotation because author (Friedman) is named in the text and online source has no page numbers.

Ellipsis mark indicates deletion of words from original passage.

Quotation of more than four typed lines is set off and indented one inch.

Long quotation is followed by Anaya's interpretation and explanation of its significance for her thesis.

Mental-health care on college campuses.

Authors' names and parenthetical page numbers clearly indicate the beginning and end of borrowed material.

Anaya's interpretation of the evidence.

Even at schools that do offer mental-health services, legal restrictions can make psychiatric intervention difficult or impossible. Tamar Lewin, an education specialist with the *New York Times*, points out that the Americans with Disabilities Act protects people with mental illness from discrimination, so schools cannot screen for psychological disorders or force students to obtain treatment unless a court declares them to be a threat. And because nearly all college students are adults, confidentiality rules prevent schools from notifying parents or teachers of potential problems without the student's written consent ("Laws" A1). This combination of social stigma and legal obstacle creates an awkward dilemma: Students suffering from mental illness are reluctant to ask for help, yet the very people who can help are prevented from reaching out. The burden of treatment rests squarely on those who are suffering.

So what should concerned colleges and universities do? Perhaps the best solution is for them to take active steps to remove the stigma associated with mental illness. Just being open about the extent of depression and related disorders among college students is a start, and it doesn't have to cost a lot of money. For example, a simple poster campaign announcing the basic statistics of mental illness and assuring students that there is no reason to be ashamed of their feelings might reduce reluctance to seek help. Even if a campus has limited mental-health facilities, prominently displaying links to good Web resources on bulletin boards and on the school's Web site is an inexpensive and easy way both to normalize mental illness and to offer help. Two excellent sites are *Half of Us*, which offers, among other things, a self-evaluation test for common psychological disorders and advice on where to go for help, and the American Psychiatric Association's *Healthy Minds*, which offers mental-health information geared to college students, video testimonials, and explanations of available treatments.

Students themselves can also take the lead in addressing mental-health issues. At the University of Pennsylvania, junior Alison Malmon started the 226-chapter student support group Active Minds after her brother's suicide jolted her into the conviction that "students [need] to talk about what they're going through, and share their experiences" (qtd. in Lewin, "From

Legal issues related to psychiatric care for college students.

Lewin's name above and the parenthetical citation below clearly indicate the beginning and end of borrowed material.

Citation includes shortened version of title to distinguish source from another one by the same author.

Anaya's interpretation of Lewin's article.

Anaya's own suggestions for solving the problem.

No parenthetical citations needed for entire Web sites named in the text.

Other students' efforts to solve the problem.

Brackets indicate word added by Anaya to clarify original quotation.

Brother's Death"). At a smaller college, a freshman who was successfully treated for depression told her story in the school paper and helped dozens of other students to recognize and seek help for their illnesses (Kadison and DiGeronimo 214-17). As these examples show, students everywhere can make an enormous difference simply by sharing their feelings.

Students are in a unique position to help each other through mental illness, but they should not be left to do this important work on their own. Colleges and universities need to collaborate with students to erase the stigma associated with mental illness, to encourage students to get help when they need it, and to prevent the kinds of sensational violence that dominate the news.

Works Cited

Amer. College Health Assn. "American College Health Association National College Health Assessment: Spring 2008 Reference Group Data Report (Abridged)." *Journal of American College Health* 57.5 (2009): 477-88. Web. 4 Apr. 2010.

Amer. Psychiatric Assn. *Healthy Minds.* Amer. Psychiatric Assn., 2010. Web. 8 Apr. 2010.

Eisenberg, Daniel, et al. "Stigma and Help Seeking for Mental Health among College Students." *Medical Care Research and Review* 66.5 (2009): 522-41. Print.

Friedman, Richard A. "Media and Madness." *American Prospect.* The American Prospect, July-Aug. 2008. Web. 20 Mar. 2010.

Half of Us. MTV Networks, 2010. Web. 6 Apr. 2010.

Kadison, Richard, and Theresa Foy DiGeronimo. *College of the Overwhelmed: The Campus Mental Health Crisis and What to Do about It.* San Francisco: Jossey, 2004. Print.

Lewin, Tamar. "From Brother's Death, a Crusade." *New York Times* 25 Apr. 2007, late ed.: B8. *Academic Search Elite.* Web. 26 Apr. 2010.

---. "Laws Limit Options When a Student Is Mentally Ill." *New York Times* 19 Apr. 2007, late ed.: A1+. *Academic Search Elite.* Web. 26 Mar. 2010.

Margin annotations:

Citation of quotation from an indirect source. Citation includes shortened version of title to distinguish source from another one by the same author.

Anaya's own conclusion.

Conclusion summarizes Anaya's main points and restates her thesis.

"Works Cited" begins on a new page.

An article in a scholarly journal posted on the Web.

An entire Web site.

An article in a print journal. "Et al." ("and others") indicates more than three authors.

An article in the Web version of a magazine.

An entire Web site.

A book with two authors.

A newspaper article in an online database.

The second of two works by the same author.

Rosie Anaya on Writing

We asked Rosie Anaya to tell us about her experience writing "The Best Kept Secret on Campus." She focused on the challenges of working with sources and maintaining her own perspective.

Writing "The Best Kept Secret on Campus" started off as a very personal process. I had a tough time adjusting to college and was diagnosed with a mild depression about halfway through my first semester. My experience with depression made me more aware of how the media show mental illness, which I wrote about in one of my composition papers. [See pp. 57–59.] When it came time to write a research paper, I was still thinking about the topic and decided to research mental illness among college students.

The research fascinated me. In fact, I got too absorbed. I spent hours on the Internet, reading blogs and magazine articles and psychology sites. I was surprised to learn how common my experience of depression was! It was a huge revelation, especially when I stumbled across the study that said most college students struggle with psychological problems of one sort or another.

I wound up with more material than I could possibly use—and yet not enough, either. I had dozens of stories and examples to work with, but most of it seemed either too personal or too focused on diagnosis. I had to force myself to look for more authoritative sources. I'm glad I did, because the scholarly article on stigma helped me pull everything together. Why should anyone feel too embarrassed to get help when mental illness is so common? Once I had that question in mind, it was easier to toss out all of the personal stories and medical details I had collected and focus on the idea that people should never feel ashamed to ask for psychological help if they need it.

Once I started my first draft, I faced another problem: I somehow didn't feel right adding my own thoughts to what the experts had to say. Really, who am I to argue with them? My first draft more or less compiled summaries and quotations from my sources. Here's an example:

> A survey conducted by the National Alliance for the Mentally Ill reports that "one in three students report having experienced prolonged periods of depression; one in four students report having suicidal thoughts or feelings; one in seven students report engaging in abnormally reckless behavior; and one in seven students report difficulty functioning at school due to mental illness" (82). An annual nationwide study noted a rise since 1985 in the number of first-year students struggling with emotional health (Shea), and

the American College Health Association announced that more than 90% of college students have felt overwhelmed or emotionally exhausted (484). The Web site *Half of Us*, created by and for college students and sponsored by MTV, takes its name from the claim that "nearly half of all college students reported feeling so depressed that they couldn't function during the last school year." One-tenth of college students in the US have seriously considered suicide (Shute).

This patchwork of summaries and quotations didn't work. But then another student in my class pointed out that I didn't have to argue with the experts, I just had to interact with them. I had my own perspectives on this subject after all, and I could use them. I tried describing my personal struggles with depression and using the sources to fill in the blanks:

> I felt alone in my sadness, so I was shocked to find out how many people cope with psychological disabilities. Would you believe that 15% of college students share my formal diagnosis of depression? According to the American College Health Association, that's only a small part of the problem: More than 90% of us have felt overwhelmed or emotionally exhausted, and nearly half of all college students have been so depressed that we had trouble functioning (484). Given numbers like these, there was no reason for me to be embarrassed about my feelings, and yet I couldn't bring myself to go to the school's counseling office.

But that didn't feel right either. I had to step back and think about what I wanted to accomplish with this paper, and I realized it wasn't all about me. I had a lot of goals, but mainly I wanted to correct stereotypes about students with psychological problems so that readers would view such students fairly and support improved mental-health services at colleges and universities. To get my point across, I went back to a more objective approach, focusing on what I had learned but letting my personal perspective shape it:

> The numbers of college students suffering from psychological problems are staggering. A 2008 survey conducted by the American College Health Association found that 62% of students have experienced feelings of hopelessness, more than 90% have felt overwhelmed or emotionally exhausted, nearly 50% have been so depressed that they had trouble functioning, 15% have been formally diagnosed with depression, and almost 10% have contemplated suicide (484–85, 487). The simple fact, unknown to many, is that a college student is more likely than not to experience a severe psychological problem at least once. In other words, such problems are a common aspect of college life.

In the end, I rewrote the paper three times before I was happy with it. And in case anyone is wondering, I've been going to talk therapy to help manage my depression, and it has helped. Writing this paper was a big step toward healing.

For Discussion

1. In her comments, Anaya reveals a very personal fact about herself. Based on your reading of "The Best Kept Secret on Campus," why do you think she tells us that she struggles with depression?

2. Anaya says of her initial research that she had "more material than [she] could possibly use—and yet not enough, either." What does she mean? Have you encountered a similar dilemma in any of your research projects?

3. Why was Anaya dissatisfied with her first two attempts to provide information from her sources? Why didn't they work or "feel right"? How does her final draft resolve those problems?

PART TWO

THE METHODS

4

NARRATION

Telling a Story

THE METHOD

"What happened?" you ask a friend who sports a luminous black eye. Unless he merely grunts "A golf ball," he may answer you with a narrative — a story, true or fictional.

"Okay," he sighs, "you know The Tenth Round? That nightclub down by the docks that smells of formaldehyde? Last night I heard they were giving away $500 to anybody who could stand up for three minutes against this karate expert, the Masked Samurai. And so . . ."

You lean forward. At least, you lean forward *if* you love a story. Most of us do, particularly if the story tells us of people in action or in conflict, and if it is told briskly, vividly, and with insight into the human heart. NARRATION, or storytelling, is therefore a powerful method by which to engage and hold the attention of listeners — readers as well. A little of its tremendous power flows to the public speaker who starts off with a joke, even a stale joke ("A funny thing happened to me on my way over here . . ."), and to the preacher who at the beginning of a sermon tells of some funny or touching incident.

The term *narrative* takes in abundant territory. A narrative may be short or long, factual or imagined, as artless as a tale told in a locker room or as artful as a novel by Henry James. A narrative may instruct and inform, or simply divert and regale. It may set forth some point or message, or it may be no more significant than a horror tale that aims to curdle your blood.

At least a hundred times a year, you probably resort to narration, not always for the purpose of telling an entertaining story, but often to report information or to illustrate a point. In academic writing, you will use mainly brief narratives, or ANECDOTES, that recount single incidents as a way of supporting an explanation or an ARGUMENT with the flesh and blood of real life. Early in the twentieth century, President Woodrow Wilson used an anecdote to explain why he had appointed his harshest critic to a cabinet post. He told of an acquaintance who spied a strange man urinating through her picket fence into her flower garden. She promptly invited the offender into her yard because, as she explained to him, "I'd a whole lot rather have you inside pissing out than have you outside pissing in." By telling this story, Wilson made clear his situation in regard to his political enemy more succinctly and pointedly than if he had given a more abstract explanation.

Anecdotes add color and specifics to writing, and they can be deeply revealing. In a biography of Samuel Johnson, the great eighteenth-century critic and scholar, W. Jackson Bate uses an anecdote to show that his subject was human and lovable. As Bate tells us, Dr. Johnson, a portly and imposing gentleman of fifty-five, had walked with some friends to the crest of a hill, where the great man, delighted by its steepness, said he wanted to "take a roll down." They tried to stop him. But he said he "had not had a roll for a long time," and taking out of his pockets his keys, a pencil, a purse, and other objects, lay down parallel at the edge of the hill, and rolled down its full length, "turning himself over and over till he came to the bottom."

However small the event it relates, this anecdote is memorable—partly because of its attention to detail, such as the exact list of the contents of Johnson's pockets. In such a brief story, a superhuman figure comes down to human size. In one stroke, Bate reveals an essential part of Johnson: his bois-terous, hearty, and boyish sense of fun.

THE PROCESS

Purpose and Shape

Every good story has a purpose, and we've suggested several in the preced-ing section. A narrative without a purpose is bound to irritate readers, as a young child's rambling can vex an unsympathetic adult.

Whatever its length or the reason for its telling, an effective narrative holds the attention of readers. Say you're writing about therapies for autism and you want readers to see how one particular method works. In a paragraph or so, you can narrate a session you observed between an autistic child and his teacher. Your purpose will determine which of the session's events you relate—not every action and exchange but the ones that, in your eyes, convey the essence of the therapy and make it interesting for readers.

The Thesis

In writing a news story, a reporter often begins with the conclusion, plac-ing the main event in the opening paragraph (called the *lead*) so that readers get the essentials up front. Similarly, in using an anecdote to explain something or to argue a point, you'll want to tell readers directly what you think the story demonstrates. But in most other kinds of narration, whether fiction or nonfic-tion, whether to entertain or to make an idea clear, the storyteller refrains from revealing the gist of the story, its point, right at the beginning. In fact, many narratives do not contain a THESIS STATEMENT, an assertion of the idea behind the story, because such a statement can rob the reader of the very plea-sure of narration, the excitement of seeing a story build. That doesn't mean the story lacks a thesis, however—far from it. The writer has every obligation to construct the narrative as if a thesis statement showed the way at the start, even when it didn't.

By the end of the story, that thesis should become obvious, as the writer builds toward a memorable CONCLUSION. In a story Mark Twain liked to tell aloud, a woman's ghost returns to claim her artificial arm made of gold, which she wore in life and which her greedy husband had unscrewed from her corpse. Carefully, Twain would build up suspense as the ghost pursued the husband upstairs to his bedroom, stood by his bed, breathed her cold breath on him, and intoned, "*Who's got my golden arm?*" Twain used to end his story by suddenly yelling at a member of the audience, "*You've* got it!" — and enjoying the victim's shriek of surprise. That final punctuating shriek may be a technique that will work only in oral storytelling, yet, like Twain, most storytellers end with a bang if they can. For another example, take specific notice in this chapter of Shirley Jackson's ending for "The Lottery" (*after* you've read the whole story, that is). The final impact need not be as dramatic as Twain's or Jackson's, either. As Maya Angelou demonstrates in her narrative in this chapter, you can achieve a lot just by leading to your point, stating your thesis at the very end. You can sometimes make your point just by saving the best incident — the most dramatic or the funniest — for last.

The Narrator in the Story

Narratives often report personal experience, whether in reality or in fiction. The NARRATOR (or teller) of such a personal experience is the speaker, the one who was there. (Four of the selections in this chapter tell of such experiences. All use the first-PERSON *I*.) The telling is usually SUBJECTIVE, with details and language chosen to express the writer's feelings. Of course, a personal experience told in the first person can use some artful telling and some structuring. (In the course of this discussion, we'll offer advice on telling stories of different kinds.)

When a story isn't your own experience but a recital of someone else's, or of events that are public knowledge, then you proceed differently as narrator. Without expressing opinions, you step back and report, content to stay invisible. Instead of saying, "I did this; I did that," you use the third person, *he, she, it,* or *they*: "The experimenter did this; she did that." You may have been on the scene; if so, you will probably write as a spectator, from your own POINT OF VIEW (or angle of seeing). If you put together what happened from the testimony of others, you tell the story from the point of view of a nonparticipant (a witness who didn't take part). Generally, a nonparticipant is OBJECTIVE in setting forth events: unbiased, as accurate and dispassionate as possible.

When you narrate a story in the third person, you aren't a character central in the eyes of your audience. Unlike the first-person writer of a personal experience, you aren't the main actor; you are the camera operator, whose job is to focus on what transpires. Most history books and news stories are third-person narratives, and so is much fiction. (In this chapter, the essay by Howard Markel and the story by Shirley Jackson illustrate third-person narration.) In telling of actual events, writers stick to the facts and do not invent the thoughts of participants (historical novels, though, do mingle fact and fancy in this way.) And even writers of fiction and anecdote imagine the thoughts of their characters only if they want to explore psychology. Look back at the anecdote by Woodrow Wilson on page 98, and notice how much would be lost if Wilson had gone into the thoughts of his characters: "The woman was angry and embarrassed at seeing the stranger. . . ."

A final element of the narrator's place in the story is verb tense, whether present (*I stare, he stares*) or past (*I stared, he stared*). The present tense is often tempting because it gives events a sense of immediacy. Told as though everything were happening right now, Wilson's story might have begun, "Peering out her window, a woman spies a strange man. . . ." But the present tense can seem artificial because we're used to reading stories in the past tense, and it can be difficult to sustain throughout an entire narrative. (See p. 105 on consistency in tenses.) The past tense may be more removed, but it is still powerful: Just look at Maya Angelou's gripping "Champion of the World," beginning on page 110.

What to Emphasize

Discovery of Details

Whether you tell of your own experience or of someone else's, even if it is brief, you need a whole story to tell. If the story is complex, do some searching and discovering in writing. One trusty method to test your memory (or to make sure you have all the necessary elements of a story) is that of a news reporter. Ask yourself:

1. *What* happened?
2. *Who* took part?
3. *When?*
4. *Where?*
5. *Why* did this event (or these events) take place?
6. *How* did it (or they) happen?

Journalists call this handy list of questions "the five *W*'s and the *H*." The *H*—*how*—isn't merely another way of asking what happened. It means: In exactly what way or under what circumstances? If the event was a murder, how was it done—with an ax or with a bulldozer?

Scene versus Summary

If you have prepared well—searching your memory or doing some research—you'll have far more information on hand than you can use in your narrative. You'll need to choose carefully, to pick out just those events and details that will accomplish your purpose with your readers.

A key decision is to choose between the two main strategies of narration: to tell a story by SCENE or to tell it by SUMMARY. When you tell a story in a scene, or in scenes, you visualize each event as vividly and precisely as if you were there—as though it were a scene in a film, and your reader sat before the screen. This is the strategy of most fine novels and short stories—and of much excellent nonfiction as well. Instead of just mentioning people, you portray them. You recall dialog as best you can, or you invent some that could have been spoken. You include DESCRIPTION (a mode of writing to be dealt with fully in our next chapter).

For a lively example of a well-drawn scene, see Maya Angelou's account of a tense crowd's behavior as, jammed into a small-town store, they listen to a fight broadcast (in "Champion of the World"). Angelou prolongs one scene for almost her entire essay. Sometimes, though, a writer will draw a scene in only two or three sentences. This is the brevity we find in W. Jackson Bate's glimpse of the hill-rolling Johnson (pp. 98–99). Unlike Angelou, Bate evidently seeks not to weave a tapestry of detail but to show, in telling of one brief event, a trait of his hero's character.

When, in contrast, you tell a story by the method of summary, you relate events concisely. Instead of depicting people and their surroundings in great detail, you set down just the essentials of what happened. Such is the strategy Howard Markel uses, in "Mary Ellen's Story" (p. 133), to tell of the first time child abuse was recognized by the courts. Most of us employ this method in most stories we tell, for it takes less time and fewer words. A summary is to a scene, then, as a simple stick figure is to a portrait in oils. This is not to dismiss simple stick figures as inferior. The economy of a story told in summary may be as effective as the lavish detail of a story told in scenes.

Again, your choice of a method depends on your answer to the questions you ask yourself: What is my purpose? Who is my audience? How fully to flesh out a scene, how much detail to include—these choices depend on what you seek to do and on how much your audience needs to know to follow you. Read the life of some famous person in an encyclopedia, and you will find the article telling its story in summary form. Its writer's purpose, evidently, is to recount the main events of a whole life in a short space. But glance through a book-length biography of the same person, and you will probably find scenes in it. A biographer writes with a different purpose: to present a detailed portrait roundly and thoroughly, bringing the subject vividly to life.

To be sure, you can use both methods in telling a single story. Often, summary will serve a writer who passes briskly from one scene to the next or hurries over events of lesser importance. Were you to write, let's say, the story of your grandfather's immigration to the United States from Cuba, you might just summarize his decision to leave Cuba and his settlement in Florida. These summaries could frame and emphasize a detailed telling of the events that you consider essential and most interesting—his nighttime escape, his harrowing voyage in a small boat, his surprising welcome by immigration authorities.

In *The Bedford Reader* we are concerned with the kind of writing you do every day in college: nonfiction writing in which you generally explain ideas, organize information you have learned, analyze other people's ideas, or argue a case. In fiction, though, we find an enormously popular and appealing use of narration and certain devices of storytelling from which all storytellers can learn. For these reasons, this chapter includes one celebrated short story by a master storyteller, Shirley Jackson. But fiction and fact barely separate Jackson's tale and the equally compelling true stories in this chapter. All of the authors strive to make people and events come alive for us. All of them also use a tool that academic writers generally do not: dialog. Reported speech, in quotation marks, is invaluable for revealing characters' feelings.

Organization

In any kind of narration, the simplest approach is to set down events in CHRONOLOGICAL ORDER, the way they happened. To do so is to have your story already organized for you. A chronological order is therefore an excellent sequence to follow unless you can see some special advantage in violating it. Ask: What am I trying to do? If you are trying to capture your readers' attention right away, you might begin in medias res (Latin, "in the middle of things") and open with a colorful, dramatic event, even though it took place late in the chronology. If trying for dramatic effect, you might save the most exciting or impressive event for last, even though it actually happened early. By this means, you can keep your readers in suspense for as long as possible. (You can return to earlier events by a FLASHBACK, an earlier scene recalled.) Let your purpose be your guide.

The writer Calvin Trillin has recalled why, in a narrative titled "The Tunica Treasure," he deliberately chose not to follow a chronology:

> I wrote a story on the discovery of the Tunica treasure which I couldn't begin by saying, "Here is a man who works as a prison guard in Angola State Prison, and on his weekends he sometimes looks for buried treasure that is rumored to be around the Indian village." Because the real point of the story centered around the problems caused when an amateur wanders onto

professional territory, I thought it would be much better to open with how momentous the discovery was, that it was the most important archeological discovery about Indian contact with the European settlers to date, and *then* to say that it was discovered by a prison guard. So I made a conscious choice *not* to start with Leonard Charrier working as a prison guard, not to go back to his boyhood in Bunkie, Louisiana, not to talk about how he'd always been interested in treasure hunting—hoping that the reader would assume I was about to say that the treasure was found by an archeologist from the Peabody Museum at Harvard.

Trillin, by saving the fact that a prison guard made the earthshaking discovery, effectively took his reader by surprise.

No matter what order you choose, either following chronology or departing from it, make sure your audience can follow it. The sequence of events has to be clear. This calls for TRANSITIONS of time, whether they are brief phrases that point out exactly when each event happened ("Seven years later," "A moment earlier"), or whole sentences that announce an event and clearly locate it in time ("If you had known Leonard Charrier ten years earlier, you would have found him voraciously poring over every archeology text he could lay his hands on in the public library"). See *Transitions* in Useful Terms for a list of possibilities.

FOCUS ON VERBS

Narration depends heavily on verbs to clarify and enliven events. Strong verbs sharpen meaning and encourage you to add other informative details:

> WEAK   The wind made an awful noise.

> STRONG   The wind roared around the house and rattled the trees.

Forms of *make* (as in the example above) and forms of *be* (as in the next example) can sap the life from narration:

> WEAK   The noises were alarming to us.

> STRONG   The noises alarmed us.

Verbs in the ACTIVE VOICE (the subject does the action) usually pack more power into fewer words than verbs in the PASSIVE VOICE (the subject is acted upon):

> WEAK PASSIVE   We were besieged in the basement by the wind, as the water at our feet was swelled by the rain.

> STRONG ACTIVE   The wind besieged us in the basement, as the rain swelled the water at our feet.

Narration

While strengthening verbs, also ensure that they're consistent in tense. The tense you choose for relating events, present or past, should not shift unnecessarily.

INCONSISTENT TENSES   We <u>held</u> a frantic conference to consider our options. It <u>takes</u> only a minute to decide to stay put.

CONSISTENT TENSE   We <u>held</u> a frantic conference to consider our options. It <u>took</u> only a minute to decide to stay put.

*For exercises on verbs, visit Exercise Central at **bedfordstmartins.com/ thebedfordreader**.*

CHECKLIST FOR REVISING A NARRATIVE

✔ **THESIS**   What is the point of your narrative? Will it be clear to readers by the end? Even if you don't provide a thesis statement, your story should focus on a central idea. If you can't risk readers' misunderstanding—if, for instance, you're using narration to support an argument or explain a concept—then have you stated your thesis outright?

✔ **POINT OF VIEW**   Is your narrator's position in the story appropriate for your purpose and consistent throughout? Check for awkward or confusing shifts in point of view (participant or nonparticipant; first, second, or third person) and in the tenses of verbs (present to past or vice versa).

✔ **SELECTION OF EVENTS**   Have you selected and emphasized events to suit your audience and fulfill your purpose? Tell the important parts of the story in the greatest detail. Summarize the less important, connective events.

✔ **ORGANIZATION**   If your organization is not strictly chronological (first event to last), do you have a compelling reason for altering it? If you start somewhere other than the beginning of the story or use flashbacks at any point, will your readers benefit from your creativity?

✔ **TRANSITIONS**   Have you used transitions to help clarify the order of events and their duration?

✔ **DIALOG**   If you have used dialog, quoting participants in the story, is it appropriate for your purpose? Is it concise, telling only the important, revealing lines? Does the language sound like spoken English?

✔ **VERBS**   Do strong, active verbs move your narrative from event to event? Are verb tenses consistent?

NARRATION IN PARAGRAPHS
Writing about Television

The following paragraph was written for *The Bedford Reader* as a kind of mini-essay. But it is easy to see how it might have worked in the context of a full essay about, say, the emotional effects of television on children. Recounting events vividly, moment by moment, the writer gives evidence for a rather dramatic effect on one little girl.

Oozing menace from beyond the stars or from the deeps, televised horror powerfully stimulates a child's already frisky imagination. As parents know, a "Creature Double Feature" has an impact that lasts long after the click of the *off* button. Recently a neighbor reported the strange case of her eight-year-old. Discovered late at night in the game room watching *The Exorcist*, the girl was promptly sent to bed. An hour later, her parents could hear her chanting something in the darkness of her bedroom. On tiptoe, they stole to her door to listen. The creak of springs told them that their daughter was swaying rhythmically to and fro, and the smell of acrid smoke warned them that something was burning. At once, they shoved open the door to find the room flickering with shadows cast by a lighted candle. Their daughter was sitting in bed, rocking back and forth as she intoned over and over, "Fiend in human form . . . Fiend in human form . . ." This case may be unique; still, it seems likely that similar events take place each night all over the screen-watching world.

> Claim to be supported by narrative
>
> Transitions (underlined) clarify sequence and pace of events
>
> Anecdote builds suspense:
>
>   Mystery
>
>   Warnings
>
>   Crisis
>
> Conclusion broadens claim

Writing in an Academic Discipline

In this paragraph from a geology textbook, the authors use narration to illustrate a powerful geological occurrence. Following another paragraph that explains landslides more generally, the narrative places the reader at an actual event.

The news media periodically relate the terrifying and often grim details of landslides. On May 31, 1970, one such event occurred when a gigantic rock avalanche buried more than 20,000 people in Yungay and Ranrahirca, Peru. There was little warning of the impending disaster; it began and ended in just a matter of a few minutes. The avalanche started 14 kilometers from Yungay, near the summit of 6,700-meter-high Nevados Huascaran, the loftiest peak in the Peruvian Andes. Triggered by the ground motion from a strong offshore earthquake, a huge mass of rock and ice broke free from the precipitous north face of the mountain. After plunging nearly one kilometer, the material pulverized on impact and imme-

> Generalization illustrated by narrative
>
> Anecdote helps explain landslides:
>
>   Sudden beginning

diately began rushing down the mountainside, made fluid by trapped air and melted ice. The initial mass ripped loose additional millions of tons of debris <u>as it roared downhill</u>. The shock waves produced by the event created <u>thunderlike noise</u> and stripped nearby hillsides of vegetation. Although the material followed a previously eroded gorge, a portion of the debris jumped a 200–300-meter-high bedrock ridge that had protected Yungay from past rock avalanches and buried the entire city. <u>After inundating another town in its path,</u> Ranrahirca, the mass of debris <u>finally</u> reached the bottom of the valley where its momentum carried it across the Rio Santa and tens of meters up the opposite bank.

—Edward J. Tarbuck and Frederick K. Lutgens,
The Earth: An Introducton to Physical Geology

Fast movement

Irresistible force

Transitions (underlined) clarify sequence and pace of events

NARRATION IN A CASE STUDY

Why did one company survive a scandal while its main competitor folded? How did a small, local business solve a marketing problem? What did a company's management do to increase productivity? These questions are typical of those asked by business analysts and students as they read and write case studies. A research method in all the social sciences, the case study examines a particular group, situation, or individual to discover what happened and why.

A business case study often consists of a narrative, telling the story of its subject to establish the background and facts of the case: what happened, who was involved, where and when events took place, and why a problem is relevant. A case study may then proceed to CAUSE AND EFFECT, explaining why this one EXAMPLE happened as it did, and it may draw conclusions about the principles or lessons to be learned from the case.

Emily Thibodeau wrote a case study for an introductory class in business management. Intrigued by the popularity of Tesla Motors, a manufacturer of luxury electric cars based in California, she wondered how other automobile start-ups had fared in difficult economic climates. Her preliminary research led her to Owen Motors, a builder of luxury cars in the early twentieth century. In the introduction to her case study, below, Thibodeau narrates Owen's story.

Company History

The history of Owen Motors goes back to April of 1909, when Robert and Joseph Owen built a car for themselves in Robert Owen's Detroit, Michigan, garage. The entrepreneurial brothers secured the backing of five investors <u>in January 1910</u>

Narrative opens with the company's beginnings

Chronological order

with a design for a luxury automobile <u>and immediately</u> resigned from their jobs at the Packard Motor Car Company. The first automobile manufactured by Owen Motors rolled off the assembly line <u>in 1912</u>. The cars were notable not only for the quality of their interior leather and wood but also for their high-performing multivalve engines and their innovative safety features, including the first padded dashboard. <u>By 1917</u> the company was producing almost four thousand cars annually.

During America's involvement in World War I (1917-18), Owen Motors did not attempt to secure design or manufacturing contracts with the military, as the Ford Motor Company and other car manufacturers did. <u>In the years after the war,</u> however, Robert Owen came to see this decision as a missed opportunity and wanted the company to diversify its products and expand into new markets. Joseph, in contrast, preferred to keep the company's focus on luxury cars, believing that the market would continue to grow. <u>Consequently</u>, Joseph bought out Robert's share of the company <u>in 1921</u> and assumed sole leadership. Owen Motors expanded its manufacturing facilities to produce additional models of luxury cars, which continued to be profitable <u>throughout the boom of the 1920s</u> even though the price of an Owen automobile never fell below $3,000. <u>In 1928</u> Owen Motors cleared $2 million in profits.

<u>In 1929 and 1930, with the onset of the Great Depression,</u> overall car sales in the United States declined rapidly. <u>As the Depression continued</u>, US salaries and wages plummeted and unemployment rose, exceeding 22% in 1933. Larger car companies, such as General Motors and Ford, were able to absorb losses and weather the long economic downturn, but smaller, independent companies like Owen often could not. Consumers <u>now</u> focused almost exclusively on inexpensive cars, which Owen had never made, and its sales had declined almost 50% <u>by 1933</u>. Joseph Owen focused on maintaining quality with just his most popular models and worked with his engineers to make the assembly line more efficient with technological innovations such as an early welding robot.

The company did survive the Depression, "limping along," as Joseph Owen himself put it. Despite some pressure from his

Transitions (<u>underlined</u>) clarify sequence and pace of events

Explanation of the company's changes in response to key historic events:

World War I

The economic boom of the 1920s

The Great Depression

board to sell to a larger company, Owen rejected at least two offers between 1934 and 1938. Then the United States began sup-
plying its allies with arms and supplies in the build-up to World   World War II
War II, and Owen saw the opportunity that his brother, Robert,
had seen with World War I. Trading on the company's reputation for advanced technology and efficient manufacturing, Owen
obtained a few small but lucrative contracts to produce trucks.
Within two years, the company had abandoned auto manufacturing. In February of 1941 Joseph Owen was severely injured in a
car accident and he lost control of the company. It was sold to   Narrative concludes
General Motors later that year.   with the company's
                                                                         sale.

MAYA ANGELOU

Maya Angelou was born Marguerite Johnson in Saint Louis in 1928. After an unpleasantly eventful youth by her account ("from a broken family, raped at eight, unwed mother at sixteen"), she went on to join a dance company, act in the off-Broadway play *The Blacks* and the television series *Roots,* write several books of poetry, produce a TV series on Africa, serve as a coordinator for the Southern Christian Leadership Conference, win the Presidential Medal of Arts, write and deliver the inaugural poem ("On the Pulse of Morning") for President Clinton, and secure lifetime membership in the National Women's Hall of Fame. Angelou is the author of thirty best-selling titles but is probably best known for the six books of her searching, frank, and joyful autobiography—from *I Know Why the Caged Bird Sings* (1970) through *A Song Flung Up to Heaven* (2002). Her most recent book, *Letter to My Daughter* (2008), addresses the daughter she never had. Angelou is Reynolds Professor of American Studies at Wake Forest University.

Champion of the World

"Champion of the World" is the nineteenth chapter in *I Know Why the Caged Bird Sings;* the title is a phrase taken from the chapter. Remembering her childhood, the writer tells how she and her older brother, Bailey, grew up in a town in Arkansas. The center of their lives was Grandmother and Uncle Willie's store. On the night of this story, in the late 1930s, the African American community gathers in the store to listen to a boxing match on the radio. Joe Louis, the "Brown Bomber," who was a hero to black people, is defending his heavyweight title against a white contender. (Louis successfully defended his title twenty-five times, a record that stands today.) Angelou's telling of the event both entertains us and explains what it was like to be African American in a certain time and place.

Amy Tan's "Fish Cheeks," following Angelou's essay, also explores the experience of growing up an outsider in America.

The last inch of space was filled, yet people continued to wedge themselves along the walls of the Store. Uncle Willie had turned the radio up to its last notch so that youngsters on the porch wouldn't miss a word. Women sat on kitchen chairs, dining-room chairs, stools, and upturned wooden boxes. Small children and babies perched on every lap available and men leaned on the shelves or on each other.

The apprehensive mood was shot through with shafts of gaiety, as a black   2
sky is streaked with lightning.

"I ain't worried 'bout this fight. Joe's gonna whip that cracker like it's   3
open season."

"He gone whip him till that white boy call him Momma."   4

At last the talking finished and the string-along songs about razor blades   5
were over and the fight began.

"A quick jab to the head." In the Store the crowd grunted. "A left to the   6
head and a right and another left." One of the listeners cackled like a hen and
was quieted.

"They're in a clinch, Louis is trying to fight his way out."   7

Some bitter comedian on the porch said, "That white man don't mind   8
hugging that niggah now, I betcha."

"The referee is moving in to break them up, but Louis finally pushed the   9
contender away and it's an uppercut to the chin. The contender is hanging
on, now he's backing away. Louis catches him with a short left to the jaw."

A tide of murmuring assent poured out the door and into the yard.   10

"Another left and another left. Louis is saving that mighty right . . ."   11
The mutter in the Store had grown into a baby roar and it was pierced by the
clang of a bell and the announcer's "That's the bell for round three, ladies and
gentlemen."

As I pushed my way into the Store I wondered if the announcer gave any   12
thought to the fact that he was addressing as "ladies and gentlemen" all the
Negroes around the world who sat sweating and praying, glued to their "Master's voice."[1]

There were only a few calls for RC Colas, Dr Peppers, and Hires root beer.   13
The real festivities would begin after the fight. Then even the old Christian
ladies who taught their children and tried themselves to practice turning the
other cheek would buy soft drinks, and if the Brown Bomber's victory was a
particularly bloody one they would order peanut patties and Baby Ruths also.

Bailey and I laid the coins on top of the cash register. Uncle Willie didn't   14
allow us to ring up sales during a fight. It was too noisy and might shake up the
atmosphere. When the gong rang for the next round we pushed through the
near-sacred quiet to the herd of children outside.

"He's got Louis against the ropes and now it's a left to the body and a right   15
to the ribs. Another right to the body, it looks like it was low . . . Yes, ladies and
gentlemen, the referee is signaling but the contender keeps raining the blows
on Louis. It's another to the body, and it looks like Louis is going down."

---

[1] "His master's voice," accompanied by a picture of a little dog listening to a phonograph,
was a familiar advertising slogan. (The picture still appears on some RCA recordings.) —Eds.

My race groaned. It was our people falling. It was another lynching, yet   16
another Black man hanging on a tree. One more woman ambushed and raped.
A Black boy whipped and maimed. It was hounds on the trail of a man running through slimy swamps. It was a white woman slapping her maid for being
forgetful.

The men in the Store stood away from the walls and at attention. Women   17
greedily clutched the babes on their laps while on the porch the shufflings and
smiles, flirtings and pinching of a few minutes before were gone. This might
be the end of the world. If Joe lost we were back in slavery and beyond help. It
would all be true, the accusations that we were lower types of human beings.
Only a little higher than apes. True that we were stupid and ugly and lazy and
dirty and, unlucky and worst of all, that God Himself hated us and ordained
us to be hewers of wood and drawers of water, forever and ever, world without
end.

We didn't breathe. We didn't hope. We waited.   18

"He's off the ropes, ladies and gentlemen. He's moving towards the center   19
of the ring." There was no time to be relieved. The worst might still happen.

"And now it looks like Joe is mad. He's caught Carnera with a left hook   20
to the head and a right to the head. It's a left jab to the body and another left
to the head. There's a left cross and a right to the head. The contender's right
eye is bleeding and he can't seem to keep his block up. Louis is penetrating
every block. The referee is moving in, but Louis sends a left to the body and
it's an uppercut to the chin and the contender is dropping. He's on the canvas,
ladies and gentlemen."

Babies slid to the floor as women stood up and men leaned toward the   21
radio.

"Here's the referee. He's counting. One, two, three, four, five, six,   22
seven . . . Is the contender trying to get up again?"

All the men in the store shouted, "NO."   23

"—eight, nine, ten." There were a few sounds from the audience, but   24
they seemed to be holding themselves in against tremendous pressure.

"The fight is all over, ladies and gentlemen. Let's get the microphone over   25
to the referee . . . Here he is. He's got the Brown Bomber's hand, he's holding
it up . . . Here he is . . ."

Then the voice, husky and familiar, came to wash over us—"The win-   26
nah, and still heavyweight champeen of the world . . . Joe Louis."

Champion of the world. A Black boy. Some Black mother's son. He was   27
the strongest man in the world. People drank Coca-Colas like ambrosia and
ate candy bars like Christmas. Some of the men went behind the Store and
poured white lightning in their soft-drink bottles, and a few of the bigger boys

followed them. Those who were not chased away came back blowing their breath in front of themselves like proud smokers.

It would take an hour or more before the people would leave the Store 28 and head for home. Those who lived too far had made arrangements to stay in town. It wouldn't do for a Black man and his family to be caught on a lonely country road on a night when Joe Louis had proved that we were the strongest people in the world.

---

*For a reading quiz, sources on Maya Angelou, and annotated links to further readings on Joe Louis and the history of segregation in the South, visit **bedfordstmartins.com/ thebedfordreader**.*

Journal Writing

How do you respond to the group identification and solidarity that Angelou writes about in this essay? What groups do you belong to, and how do you know you're a member? Consider groups based on race, ethnic background, religion, sports, hobbies, politics, friendship, kinship, or any other ties. (To take your journal writing further, see "From Journal to Essay" on the next page.)

Questions on Meaning

1. What do you take to be the author's PURPOSE in telling this story?
2. What connection does Angelou make between the outcome of the fight and the pride of African Americans? To what degree do you think the author's view is shared by the others in the store listening to the broadcast?
3. To what extent are the statements in paragraphs 16 and 17 to be taken literally? What function do they serve in Angelou's narrative?
4. Primo Carnera was probably *not* the Brown Bomber's opponent on the night Maya Angelou recalls. Louis fought Carnera only once, on June 25, 1935, and it was not a title match. Does the author's apparent error detract from her story?

Questions on Writing Strategy

1. What details in the opening paragraphs indicate that an event of crucial importance is about to take place?
2. How does Angelou build up SUSPENSE in her account of the fight? At what point were you able to predict the winner?

3. Comment on the IRONY in Angelou's final paragraph.
4. What EFFECT does the author's use of direct quotation have on her narrative?
5. **OTHER METHODS**   Besides narration, Angelou also relies heavily on the method of DESCRIPTION. Analyze how narration depends on description in paragraph 27 alone.

Questions on Language

1. Explain what the author means by "string-along songs about razor blades" (par. 5).
2. Point to some examples in the essay of Angelou's use of strong verbs.
3. How does Angelou's use of NONSTANDARD ENGLISH contribute to her narrative?
4. Be sure you know the meanings of these words: apprehensive (par. 2); assent (10); ambushed, maimed (16); ordained (17); ambrosia, white lightning (27).

Suggestions for Writing

1. **FROM JOURNAL TO ESSAY**   From your journal entry, choose one of the groups you belong to and explore your sense of membership through a narrative that tells of an incident that occurred when that sense was strong. Try to make the incident come alive for your readers with vivid details, dialog, and tight sequencing of events.
2. Write an essay based on some childhood experience of your own, still vivid in your memory.
3. Do some research about the boxing career of Joe Louis. Then write an essay in which you discuss popular attitudes toward the Brown Bomber in his day.
4. **CRITICAL WRITING**   Angelou does not directly describe relations between African Americans and whites, yet her essay implies quite a lot. Write a brief essay about what you can INFER from the exaggeration of paragraphs 16–17 and the obliqueness of paragraph 28. Focus on Angelou's details and the language she uses to present them.
5. **CONNECTIONS**   Angelou's "Champion of the World" and the next essay, Amy Tan's "Fish Cheeks," both tell stories of children who felt like outsiders in predominantly white America. COMPARE AND CONTRAST the two writers' perceptions of what sets them apart from the dominant culture. How does the event each reports affect that sense of difference? Use specific examples from both essays as your EVIDENCE.

Maya Angelou on Writing

Maya Angelou's writings have shown great variety: She has done notable work as an autobiographer, poet, short-story writer, screenwriter, journalist, and song lyricist. Asked by interviewer Sheila Weller, "Do you start each project with a specific idea?" Angelou replied:

It starts with a definite subject, but it might end with something entirely different. When I start a project, the first thing I do is write down, in longhand, everything I know about the subject, every thought I've ever had on it. This may be twelve or fourteen pages. Then I read it back through, for quite a few days, and find — given that subject — what its rhythm is. 'Cause everything in the universe has a rhythm. So if it's free form, it still has a rhythm. And once I hear the rhythm of the piece, then I try to find out what are the salient points that I must make. And then it begins to take shape.

I try to set myself up in each chapter by saying: "This is what I want to go from — from B to, say, G-sharp. Or from D to L." And then I find the hook. It's like the knitting, where, after you knit a certain amount, there's one thread that begins to pull. You know, you can see it right along the cloth. Well, in writing, I think: "Now where is that one hook, that one little thread?" It may be a sentence. If I can catch that, then I'm home free. It's the one that tells me where I'm going. It may not even turn out to be in the final chapter. I may throw it out later or change it. But if I follow it through, it leads me right out.

For Discussion

1. How would you define the word *rhythm* as Maya Angelou uses it?
2. What response would you give a student who said, "Doesn't Angelou's approach to writing waste more time and thought than it's worth?"

AMY TAN

Amy Tan is a gifted storyteller whose first novel, *The Joy Luck Club* (1989), met with critical acclaim and huge success. The relationships it details between immigrant Chinese mothers and their Chinese American daughters came from Tan's firsthand experience. She was born in 1952 in Oakland, California, the daughter of immigrants who had fled China's civil war in the late 1940s. She majored in English and linguistics at San Jose State University, where she received a BA in 1973 and an MA in 1974. After two more years of graduate work, Tan became a consultant in language development for disabled children and then started her own company writing reports and speeches for business corporations. Tan began writing fiction to explore her ethnic ambivalence and to find her voice. Since *The Joy Luck Club*, she has published four more novels—most recently *Saving Fish from Drowning* (2005)—as well as children's books and *The Opposite of Fate* (2003), a collection of autobiographical essays. She sometimes sings with the Rock Bottom Remainders, a "literary garage band" that also includes Dave Barry (p. 261) and Barbara Kingsolver (p. 534).

Fish Cheeks

In Tan's novel *The Bonesetter's Daughter* (2001), one of the characters says, "Good manners are not enough. . . . They are not the same as a good heart." Much of Tan's writing explores the tensions between keeping up appearances and having true intentions. In the brief narrative that follows, the author deftly portrays the contradictory feelings and the advantages of a girl with feet in different cultures. The essay first appeared in *Seventeen*, a magazine for teenage girls and young women, in 1987.

For a complementary view of growing up "different," read the preceding essay, Maya Angelou's "Champion of the World."

I fell in love with the minister's son the winter I turned fourteen. He was not Chinese, but as white as Mary in the manger. For Christmas I prayed for this blond-haired boy, Robert, and a slim new American nose.

When I found out that my parents had invited the minister's family over for Christmas Eve dinner, I cried. What would Robert think of our shabby Chinese Christmas? What would he think of our noisy Chinese relatives who lacked proper American manners? What terrible disappointment would he feel upon seeing not a roasted turkey and sweet potatoes but Chinese food?

On Christmas Eve I saw that my mother had outdone herself in creating   3
a strange menu. She was pulling black veins out of the backs of fleshy prawns.
The kitchen was littered with appalling mounds of raw food: A slimy rock cod
with bulging eyes that pleaded not to be thrown into a pan of hot oil. Tofu,
which looked like stacked wedges of rubbery white sponges. A bowl soaking
dried fungus back to life. A plate of squid, their backs crisscrossed with knife
markings so they resembled bicycle tires.

And then they arrived—the minister's family and all my relatives in a   4
clamor of doorbells and rumpled Christmas packages. Robert grunted hello,
and I pretended he was not worthy of existence.

Dinner threw me deeper into despair. My relatives licked the ends of their   5
chopsticks and reached across the table, dipping them into the dozen or so
plates of food. Robert and his family waited patiently for platters to be passed
to them. My relatives murmured with pleasure when my mother brought out
the whole steamed fish. Robert grimaced. Then my father poked his chopsticks
just below the fish eye and plucked out the soft meat. "Amy, your favorite," he
said, offering me the tender fish cheek. I wanted to disappear.

At the end of the meal my father leaned back and belched loudly, thank-   6
ing my mother for her fine cooking. "It's a polite Chinese custom to show you
are satisfied," explained my father to our astonished guests. Robert was looking down at his plate with a reddened face. The minister managed to muster
up a quiet burp. I was stunned into silence for the rest of the night.

After everyone had gone, my mother said to me, "You want to be the   7
same as American girls on the outside." She handed me an early gift. It was a
miniskirt in beige tweed. "But inside you must always be Chinese. You must
be proud you are different. Your only shame is to have shame."

And even though I didn't agree with her then, I knew that she understood   8
how much I had suffered during the evening's dinner. It wasn't until many
years later—long after I had gotten over my crush on Robert—that I was able
to fully appreciate her lesson and the true purpose behind our particular menu.
For Christmas Eve that year, she had chosen all my favorite foods.

*For a reading quiz, sources on Amy Tan, and annotated links to further readings on Chinese Americans, visit **bedfordstmartins.com/thebedfordreader**.*

Journal Writing

Do you sympathize with the shame Tan feels because of her family's differences from their non-Chinese guests? Or do you think she should have been more proud to share her family's customs? Think of an occasion when, for whatever reason, you were acutely aware of being different. How did you react? Did you try to hide your difference in order to fit in, or did you reveal or celebrate your uniqueness? (To take your journal writing further, see "From Journal to Essay" below.)

Questions on Meaning

1. Why does Tan cry when she finds out that the boy she is in love with is coming to dinner?
2. Why does Tan's mother go out of her way to prepare a disturbingly traditional Chinese dinner for her daughter and guests? What one sentence best sums up the lesson Tan was not able to understand until years later?
3. How does the fourteen-year-old Tan feel about her Chinese background? about her mother?
4. What is Tan's PURPOSE in writing this essay? Does she just want to entertain readers, or might she have a weightier goal?

Questions on Writing Strategy

1. How does Tan draw the reader into her story right from the beginning?
2. How does Tan use TRANSITIONS both to drive and to clarify her narrative?
3. What is the IRONY of the last sentence of the essay?
4. **OTHER METHODS**   Paragraph 3 is a passage of pure DESCRIPTION. Why does Tan linger over the food? What is the EFFECT of this paragraph?

Questions on Language

1. The simile about Mary in the second sentence of the essay is surprising. Why? Why is it amusing? (See *Figures of speech* in Useful Terms for a definition of *simile*.)
2. How does the narrator's age affect the TONE of this essay? Give EXAMPLES of language particularly appropriate to a fourteen-year-old.
3. In which paragraph does Tan use strong verbs most effectively?
4. Make sure you know the meanings of the following words: prawns, tofu (par. 3); clamor (4); grimaced (5); muster (6).

Suggestions for Writing

1. **FROM JOURNAL TO ESSAY**   Using Tan's essay as a model, write a brief narrative based on your journal sketch about a time when you felt different from others. Try to imitate the way Tan integrates the external events of the dinner with her

own feelings about what is going on. Your story may be humorous, like Tan's, or more serious.

2. Take a perspective like that of the minister's son, Robert: Write a narrative essay about a time when you had to adjust to participating in a culture different from your own. It could be a meal, a wedding or other rite of passage, a religious ceremony, a trip to another country. What did you learn from your experience, about yourself and others?

3. **CRITICAL WRITING** From this essay one can INFER two very different sets of ASSUMPTIONS about the extent to which immigrants should seek to integrate themselves into the culture of their adopted country. Take either of these positions, in favor of or against assimilation (cultural integration), and make an ARGUMENT for your case.

4. **CONNECTIONS** Both Tan and Maya Angelou, in "Champion of the World" (p. 110), write about difference from white Americans, but their POINTS OF VIEW are not the same: Tan's is a teenager's lament about not fitting in; Angelou's is an oppressed child's excitement about proving the injustice of oppression. In an essay, ANALYZE the two authors' uses of narration to convey their perspectives. What details do they focus on? What internal thoughts do they report? Is one essay more effective than the other? Why, or why not?

Amy Tan on Writing

In 1989 Amy Tan delivered a lecture titled "Mother Tongue" at the State of the Language Symposium in San Francisco. The lecture, later published in *The Threepenny Review* in 1990, addresses Tan's own experience as a bilingual child speaking both Chinese and English. "I do think that the language spoken in the family, especially in immigrant families, which are more insular, plays a large role in shaping the language of the child. And I believe that it affected my results on achievement tests, IQ tests, and the SAT. While my English skills were never judged as poor, compared to math English could not be considered my strong suit. . . . This was understandable. Math is precise; there is only one correct answer. Whereas, for me at least, the answers on English tests were always a judgment call, a matter of opinion and personal experience."

Tan goes on to say that the necessity of adapting to different styles of expression may affect other children from bilingual households. "I've been asked, as a writer, why there are not more Asian-Americans represented in American literature? Why are there few Asian-Americans enrolled in creative-writing programs? Why do so many Chinese students go into engineering? Well, these are broad sociological questions I can't begin to answer. But I have noticed in surveys . . . that Asian students, as a whole, always do significantly better on math achievements tests than in English. And this makes me think that there are other Asian-American students whose English spoken in the home might also be described as 'broken' or 'limited.' And perhaps they also have teachers who are steering them away from writing and into math and science, which is what happened to me."

Tan admits that when she first began writing fiction, she wrote "what I thought to be wittily crafted sentences, sentences that would finally prove I had mastery over the English language." But they were awkward and self-conscious, so she changed her tactic. "I later decided I should envision a reader for the stories I would write. And the reader I decided upon was my mother, because these were stories about mothers. So with this reader in mind—and in fact, she did read my early drafts—I began to write stories using all the Englishes I grew up with: the English I spoke to my mother, . . . the English she used with me, . . . my translation of her Chinese, . . . and what I imagined to be her translation of her Chinese if she could speak in perfect English, her internal language, and for that I sought to preserve the essence, but not either an English or a Chinese structure. I wanted to capture what language ability tests can never reveal: her intent, her passion, her imagery, the rhythms of her speech and the nature of her thoughts.

"Apart from what any critic had to say about my writing, I knew I had succeeded where it counted when my mother finished reading my book and gave me her vedict: 'So easy to read.'"

For Discussion

1. How could growing up in a household of "broken" English be a handicap for a student taking an achievement test?
2. What does the author suggest is the reason why more Asian Americans major in engineering than major in writing?
3. Why did Amy Tan's mother make a good reader?

ANNIE DILLARD

Annie Dillard is accomplished as a prose writer, poet, and literary critic. Born in 1945, she earned a BA (1967) and an MA (1968) from Hollins College in Virginia. Dillard's first published prose, *Pilgrim at Tinker Creek* (1974), attracted notice for its close, intense, and poetic descriptions of the natural world. It won her a Pulitzer Prize and comparison with Thoreau. Since then, Dillard's entranced and entrancing writing has appeared regularly in *Harper's, The Atlantic Monthly*, and other magazines and in her wide-ranging books, including *Holy the Firm* (1978), a prose poem; *Living by Fiction* (1982), literary criticism; *Teaching a Stone to Talk* (1982), nonfiction; *An American Childhood* (1987), autobiography; *The Writing Life* (1989), anecdotes and metaphors about writing; *For the Time Being* (1999), an exploration of how God and meaninglessness can co-exist; and *The Maytrees* (2007), a novel. In 1999 Dillard was inducted into the American Academy of Arts and Letters.

The Chase

Dillard's autobiography, *An American Childhood*, views experience with the sharply perceptive eyes of a child. In this chapter from the book, Dillard leads us running desperately through snow-filled backyards. Like all of her writing, this romp shows unparalleled enthusiasm for life and skill at expressing it.

Some boys taught me to play football. This was fine sport. You thought up a 1 new strategy for every play and whispered it to the others. You went out for a pass, fooling everyone. Best, you got to throw yourself mightily at someone's running legs. Either you brought him down or you hit the ground flat on your chin, with your arms empty before you. It was all or nothing. If you hesitated in fear, you would miss and get hurt: you would take a hard fall while the kid got away, or you would get kicked in the face while the kid got away. But if you flung yourself wholeheartedly at the back of his knees—if you gathered and joined body and soul and pointed them diving fearlessly—then you likely wouldn't get hurt, and you'd stop the ball. Your fate, and your team's score, depended on your concentration and courage. Nothing girls did could compare with it.

Boys welcomed me at baseball, too, for I had, through enthusiastic prac- 2 tice, what was weirdly known as a boy's arm. In winter, in the snow, there was neither baseball nor football, so the boys and I threw snowballs at passing cars. I got in trouble throwing snowballs, and have seldom been happier since.

On one weekday morning after Christmas, six inches of new snow had 3
just fallen. We were standing up to our boot tops in snow on a front yard on
trafficked Reynolds Street, waiting for cars. The cars traveled Reynolds Street
slowly and evenly; they were targets all but wrapped in red ribbons, cream
puffs. We couldn't miss.

I was seven; the boys were eight, nine, and ten. The oldest two Fahey boys 4
were there — Mikey and Peter — polite blond boys who lived near me on Lloyd
Street, and who already had four brothers and sisters. My parents approved
Mikey and Peter Fahey. Chickie McBride was there, a tough kid, and Billy
Paul and Mackie Kean too, from across Reynolds, where the boys grew up dark
and furious, grew up skinny, knowing, and skilled. We had all drifted from our
houses that morning looking for action, and had found it here on Reynolds
Street.

It was cloudy but cold. The cars' tires laid behind them on the snowy street 5
a complex trail of beige chunks like crenellated castle walls. I had stepped on
some earlier; they squeaked. We could have wished for more traffic. When a
car came, we all popped it one. In the intervals between cars we reverted to
the natural solitude of children.

I started making an iceball — a perfect iceball, from perfectly white snow, 6
perfectly spherical, and squeezed perfectly translucent so no snow remained
all the way through. (The Fahey boys and I considered it unfair actually to
throw an iceball at somebody, but it had been known to happen.)

I had just embarked on the iceball project when we heard tire chains come 7
clanking from afar. A black Buick was moving toward us down the street. We
all spread out, banged together some regular snowballs, took aim, and, when
the Buick drew nigh, fired.

A soft snowball hit the driver's windshield right before the driver's face. It 8
made a smashed star with a hump in the middle.

Often, of course, we hit our target, but this time, the only time in all of 9
life, the car pulled over and stopped. Its wide black door opened; a man got
out of it, running. He didn't even close the car door.

He ran after us, and we ran away from him, up the snowy Reynolds side- 10
walk. At the corner, I looked back; incredibly, he was still after us. He was in
city clothes: a suit and tie, street shoes. Any normal adult would have quit,
having sprung us into flight and made his point. This man was gaining on us.
He was a thin man, all action. All of a sudden, we were running for our lives.

Wordless, we split up. We were on our turf; we could lose ourselves in the 11
neighborhood backyards, everyone for himself. I paused and considered. Everyone had vanished except Mikey Fahey, who was just rounding the corner of a
yellow brick house. Poor Mikey, I trailed him. The driver of the Buick sensibly
picked the two of us to follow. The man apparently had all day.

He chased Mikey and me around the yellow house and up a backyard path   12
we knew by heart: under a low tree, up a bank, through a hedge, down some
snowy steps, and across the grocery store's delivery driveway. We smashed
through a gap in another hedge, entered a scruffy backyard and ran around
its back porch and tight between houses to Edgerton Avenue; we ran across
Edgerton to an alley and up our own sliding woodpile to the Halls' front yard;
he kept coming. We ran up Lloyd Street and wound through mazy backyards
toward the steep hilltop at Willard and Lang.

He chased us silently, block after block. He chased us silently over picket   13
fences, through thorny hedges, between houses, around garbage cans, and
across streets. Every time I glanced back, choking for breath, I expected he
would have quit. He must have been as breathless as we were. His jacket
strained over his body. It was an immense discovery, pounding into my hot head
with every sliding, joyous step, that this ordinary adult evidently knew what
I thought only children who trained at football knew: that you have to fling
yourself at what you're doing, you have to point yourself, forget yourself, aim,
dive.

Mikey and I had nowhere to go, in our own neighborhood or out of it, but   14
away from this man who was chasing us. He impelled us forward; we compelled
him to follow our route. The air was cold; every breath tore my throat. We
kept running, block after block; we kept improvising, backyard after backyard,
running a frantic course and choosing it simultaneously, failing always to find
small places or hard places to slow him down, and discovering always, exhilarated, dismayed, that only bare speed could save us—for he would never give
up, this man—and we were losing speed.

He chased us through the backyard labyrinths of ten blocks before he   15
caught us by our jackets. He caught us and we all stopped.

We three stood staggering, half blinded, coughing, in an obscure hilltop   16
backyard: a man in his twenties, a boy, a girl. He had released our jackets,
our pursuer, our captor, our hero: He knew we weren't going anywhere.
We all played by the rules. Mikey and I unzipped our jackets. I pulled off
my sopping mittens. Our tracks multiplied in the backyard's new snow. We
had been breaking new snow all morning. We didn't look at each other. I
was cherishing my excitement. The man's lower pants legs were wet; his
cuffs were full of snow, and there was a prow of snow beneath them on his
shoes and socks. Some trees bordered the little flat backyard, some messy
winter trees. There was no one around: a clearing in a grove, and we the only
players.

It was a long time before he could speak. I had some difficulty at first   17
recalling why we were there. My lips felt swollen; I couldn't see out of the
sides of my eyes; I kept coughing.

"You stupid kids," he began perfunctorily.   18

We listened perfunctorily indeed, if we listened at all, for the chewing out   19
was redundant, a mere formality, and beside the point. The point was that he
had chased us passionately without giving up, and so he had caught us. Now
he came down to earth. I wanted the glory to last forever.

But how could the glory have lasted forever? We could have run through   20
every backyard in North America until we got to Panama. But when he trapped
us at the lip of the Panama Canal, what precisely could he have done to prolong the drama of the chase and cap its glory? I brooded about this for the next
few years. He could only have fried Mikey Fahey and me in boiling oil, say,
or dismembered us piecemeal, or staked us to anthills. None of which I really
wanted, and none of which any adult was likely to do, even in the spirit of
fun. He could only chew us out there in the Panamanian jungle, after months
or years of exalting pursuit. He could only begin, "You stupid kids," and continue in his ordinary Pittsburgh accent with his normal righteous anger and
the usual common sense.

If in that snowy backyard the driver of the black Buick had cut off our   21
heads, Mikey's and mine, I would have died happy, for nothing has required
so much of me since as being chased all over Pittsburgh in the middle of
winter—running terrified, exhausted—by this sainted, skinny, furious redheaded man who wished to have a word with us. I don't know how he found
his way back to his car.

---

*For a reading quiz, sources on Annie Dillard, and annotated links to further readings
on play for children and adults, visit **bedfordstmartins.com/thebedfordreader**.*

Journal Writing

Why do you suppose Dillard remembers in such vivid detail the rather insignificant
event she describes? What incidents from your childhood seem momentous even now?
List these incidents, along with some notes about their importance. (To take your
journal writing further, see "From Journal to Essay" on the facing page.)

Questions on Meaning

1. What is Dillard's PURPOSE in this essay? Obviously, she wants to entertain readers,
   but does she have another purpose as well?
2. Does the persistence of the pursuer seem reasonable to you, given the children's
   prank?

3. What does the pursuer represent for the narrator? How do her feelings about him change after the chase is over, and why?
4. Why does Dillard describe the "chewing out," seemingly the object of the chase, as "redundant, a mere formality, and beside the point" (par. 19)?

Questions on Writing Strategy

1. Why does Dillard open her story with a discussion of football? In what way does the game of football serve as a metaphor in the story? (Hint: Look at par. 13, as well as the sentence "It was all or nothing" in par. 1.) (See *Figures of speech* in Useful Terms for a definition of *metaphor*.)
2. Identify the two rapid TRANSITIONS in paragraph 2. Do they contribute to or detract from the COHERENCE of the essay?
3. Why does Dillard interrupt the story of the chase with an "immense discovery" (par. 13)? Does this interruption weaken the narrative?
4. Discuss Dillard's POINT OF VIEW. Is her perspective that of a seven-year-old girl or that of an adult writer reflecting on her childhood experience?
5. **OTHER METHODS**   Dillard's story implicitly COMPARES AND CONTRASTS a child's and an adult's way of looking at life. What are some of the differences that Dillard implies?

Questions on Language

1. Look up the meaning of any of the following words you don't already know: crenellated (par. 5); translucent (6); nigh (7); impelled, compelled (14); prow (16); perfunctorily (18); redundant (19); piecemeal, exalting, righteous (20).
2. Explain the contradiction in this statement: "I got in trouble throwing snowballs, and have seldom been happier since" (par. 2). Can you find other examples of paradox in what the narrator says? How is this paradox related to the narrator's apparent view of children? (See *Figures of speech* in Useful Terms for a definition of *paradox*.)
3. Why are the strong verbs Dillard uses in paragraph 20 especially appropriate?
4. What is the EFFECT of the last sentence of the essay?

Suggestions for Writing

1. **FROM JOURNAL TO ESSAY**   Choose one significant incident from the list of childhood experiences you wrote in your journal, and narrate the incident as vividly as you can. Include the details: Where did the event take place? What did people say? How were they dressed? What was the weather like? Follow Dillard's model in putting CONCRETE IMAGES to work for an idea, in this case an idea about the significance of the incident to you then and now.
2. From what you have seen of children and adults, do you agree with Dillard's characterization of the two groups (see "Writing Strategy" question 5)? Write an essay comparing and contrasting children's and adults' attitudes toward play. (You will have to GENERALIZE, of course, but try to keep your broad statements grounded in a reality your readers will share.)

3. **CRITICAL WRITING**   Dillard's narration of the chase is only six paragraphs long (pars. 10–15), but it seems longer, as if almost in real time. What techniques does Dillard use in these paragraphs to hold our attention and re-create the breathlessness of the chase? Look at concrete details, repetition, PARALLELISM, and the near absence of time-marking transitions. In ANALYZING Dillard's techniques, use plenty of quotations from the essay.

4. **CONNECTIONS**   Dillard's essay and Brad Manning's "Arm Wrestling with My Father" (p. 163) both deal with childhood values and how they are transformed as one grows older. In an essay, compare and contrast the two writers' treatment of this subject. How does the TONE of each essay contribute to its effect?

Annie Dillard on Writing

Writing for *The Bedford Reader*, Dillard has testified to her work habits. Rarely satisfied with an essay until it has gone through many drafts, she sometimes goes on correcting and improving it even after it has been published. "I always have to condense or toss openings," she affirms; "I suspect most writers do. When you begin something, you're so grateful to have begun you'll write down anything, just to prolong the sensation. Later, when you've learned what the writing is really about, you go back and throw away the beginning and start over."

Often she replaces a phrase or sentence with a shorter one. In one essay, to tell how a drop of pond water began to evaporate on a microscope slide, she first wrote, "Its contours pulled together." But that sentence seemed to suffer from "tortured abstraction." She made the sentence read instead, "Its edges shrank." Dillard observes, "I like short sentences. They're forceful, and they can get you out of big trouble."

For Discussion

1. Why, according to Dillard, is it usually necessary for writers to revise the opening paragraphs of what they write?

2. Dillard says that short sentences "can get you out of big trouble." What kinds of "big trouble" do you suppose she means?

BRADLEY PHILBERT

Bradley Philbert was born in Santa Rosa, California, in 1986. After high school, he moved to San Francisco, where he studied film, reviewed video games for the Web site *GamerNode*, and worked as a section editor for *No Cover* magazine. Philbert switched coasts to continue his education at Fairleigh Dickinson University in New Jersey, where he edited and wrote for *Knightscapes*, an undergraduate magazine that publishes writing and art by students. He earned a BA in English in 2009. Philbert is currently working as a writing tutor.

Good

Philbert first wrote "Good" for a writing class and, after significant revision, published it in the fall 2008 issue of *Knightscapes*. With unflinching honesty, Philbert tells the story of putting his dog, George, to sleep — an experience that is at once clinical, nostalgic, and dislocating.

There's an uneven strip in the new sod in my backyard, no more than an inch wide and a few inches long, where the roots sit on a rock or a clump of dirt. It's the spot where, this summer, I had my dog, George, killed. It seems an odd way to put it, but it's the truth: I contacted and arranged for a veterinarian to come into my home — to this small patch of sparse grass, in fact — and stick a syringe full of candy-pink barbiturates into George's leg. I paid extra for sedation, for the dog and for myself. (My sedation came later, hours and days after his, straight up and served in a leaded crystal tumbler, in darkened silence. Like a good Irish-Latino, I knew only celebrations were held in public view. Sorrow was for the dark and the quiet, after phone calls that contained the words "malignant carcinoma" and "inoperable.") George got his sedatives while sitting on my lap on the patio, an injection right above his tail. The vet told me to scratch around the injection site as she did it and George wouldn't feel any pain, but he did. He yelped. He never was good with pain.

Maybe that's what made him such a lovable dog. I never saw him bite anything in anger. He would fetch tennis balls mostly by licking them back toward me. He might have growled at a burglar, pulled his floppy, chestnut ears back and showed a little tooth, but he would have drawn the line before biting. So perhaps he wasn't a good guard dog — eleven pound Shih-Tzus rarely are — but by every other measure as a companion, he did well. Though as he aged — age is relative, he was only twelve — he defecated in the house a few times. As he got sicker, silently and almost invisibly, he must have felt uncomfortable or vulnerable going outside on a leash. Normally, he'd have the full backyard to run around in, but the summer was swallowed by land-scaping projects. As the cancer grew in George's body, in the cavity between his heart and lungs, I spent my time at the windows or in the backyard, watch-ing plants move from hole to hole, repositioning cloth umbrellas, arranging patio chairs, all until everything was just right from every angle. Very precise and attentive. George had to watch from the sliding glass door as the project spread from the backyard to the front, down the driveway, to the mailbox. I never heard him cry to go out.

My family could tell earlier—June, July—that George was showing his   3 age. We would talk about it. We would discuss, in short bursts, how his energy had dimmed, but without acknowledging any uncomfortable truths. "He's just not that active anymore, with the backyard torn up. I bet he can't wait to go outside again." He was in the hospital the day the landscapers finished. After the months of work and flux, George couldn't enjoy the new yard. All I wanted was for him to live long enough to run in the grass again, to pee on one of the new trees, or even on one of the overpriced art pieces from Mali. I prayed for that—ridiculous, yes, not just praying for the dog, but praying for a dog to get to enjoy something he couldn't comprehend, an investment of time and money, a beautification catering to human tastes. I doubt George wanted to run, in the end.

The tumor in his chest filled his lungs with fluid. He had to be tapped   4 and drained with a long needle every few hours. The nurses gave him opi-ates, which one would hope might lend him a who-cares attitude, but they said he cried with each tap all the same. He leaked, too. A thin, yellow fluid seeped from the pinpricks on his sides. I've never been more broken than when I saw George in the hospital, all gauze and tubes, wrapped in a towel and stuck inside a Plexiglas cage pumped full of oxygen. The fluid and the stress were hard on George's lungs. After we admitted him, they told us he couldn't breathe comfortably without oxygen for more than a few minutes. He'd been in a cage for two days when I visited him for the first, and only, time. The first day, I thought it was pneumonia. On day two, the vet called personally. I got the news on my cell phone, between classes. *The* news. I went in to see him after visiting hours: The hospital was huge and mostly quiet, and one of the nurses let me in the room where George slept behind a sheet of Plexiglas, like Magneto in X-Men. He saw me and sat up, one crooked front leg jutting out in defiance of the rest. Over the noise of the oxygen pump, like a small vacuum, I could hear his tail thumping against the side of his enclosure, and the cry I, after twelve years, understood to mean, "Please, I don't like this. I want to go." George pushed his nose against the clear wall between us. I put the back of my right hand on the same spot, but I couldn't feel anything. Just plastic, amid noise of the crying, the thumping tail, and the whirring oxygen.

I wanted to stay, to sleep in the room, on the chance I could hear him stop crying, as if to say "I'm okay. Everything's going to be okay." But he didn't stop, the sound just faded as I left the room, then the hallway, then the waiting room, and then the entry foyer. One of the nurses returned his tags. They jingled in my pocket.

The next morning, a Saturday, I called another vet. One who would be willing to come to the house, do everything there. I decided on doing it outside, because I knew that dogs, like humans, sometimes evacuate when they die. The only thing more painful than losing George might have been losing him and having to clean up his last mess in the house after he was gone. So I chose a spot in the backyard, on the lawn. And then we brought George home. I didn't have to see him in that plastic cage: The vet brought him right into the exam room, said she was sorry, and left. I held George on my lap on the ride home. The fluid leaking from his sides left dots on my pants. I didn't care about the stains.

It felt like a conspiracy, a betrayal, taking George home, knowing that twenty minutes after we arrived, a woman carrying a tackle box full of poison would be coming to end his life. I carried George inside the house first, so the assembled family could say goodbye and tell him he was a good dog, and he wagged his tail for them. Then everybody left me alone with him, so I could tell him the same and he could wag his tail for me. I knew he couldn't understand, so I rubbed his ears and gave him the piece of jerky I couldn't give him when he was in the hospital.

George got one last opportunity to go outside, in the backyard, on his own. He lasted a few minutes, sniffing the air and smelling the new foliage, before he stopped and sat down, his chest rising rapidly, then falling, exposing his ribs through thin skin. I knew it was time. I took him in my lap on the patio—he left more spots—and the vet gave him his first cocktail, the sedative. I rubbed his ears more until he slumped over, his breathing slow, virtually asleep with his eyes open. I carried him to the grass for the last shot, placed him in the uneven patch near the patio, and rubbed his ears some more, while the vet stuck the syringe in his leg. She nodded to me and I kissed the top of George's head and told him he was a good dog. And then he was gone.

The vet gave me a moment before she stood and hugged me. Then she asked me to leave the backyard, explained that I didn't want to see what came next—the body bag, the freezer, the crematorium, the cherry-wood box. So I stood up and I left him on the patch of grass, then I left the lawn, then the patio, then the family room. Like leaving the hospital, a set of small departures that, together, meant something had changed, something fundamental. Inside, I walked from room to room, his tags still jangling in my pocket. George had left. Good dogs do.

For a reading quiz and annotated links to further readings on death and dying, visit **bedfordstmartins.com/thebedfordreader.**

Journal Writing

How do you respond to Philbert's apparent guilt over having his dog "killed"? Was his choice cruel, as he worries in paragraph 6, or was it the right thing to do? In your journal, explore how you feel about putting companion animals to sleep. Under what circumstances is destroying a pet necessary, or at least understandable? Under what circumstances is it inexcusable? (To take your journal writing further, see "From Journal to Essay" on the facing page.)

Questions on Meaning

1. Why, in Philbert's mind, was George a good dog? Might other pet owners disagree with his assessment?
2. In his first paragraph, Philbert writes, "Like a good Irish-Latino, I knew only celebrations were held in public view." What does he mean? How does this statement preview the FOCUS of his essay?
3. Does Philbert have a THESIS? In which sentence or sentences does he state the point of his story most directly?
4. What would you say is Philbert's PURPOSE in this essay? Is it primarily to inform readers about the death of a pet, or does he seem to have another purpose as well?

Questions on Writing Strategy

1. What is the EFFECT of Philbert's opening paragraph? Why does he begin the story at its end?
2. How would you describe Philbert's use of DETAIL in this essay? Where are events compressed, and where are they expanded with more detail? What events receive the most detail, and why?
3. Identify some of the TRANSITIONS throughout the essay. How do they create COHERENCE among the different episodes that Philbert narrates?
4. **OTHER METHODS** How does Philbert use CAUSE AND EFFECT to explain his actions, both to readers and himself?

Questions on Language

1. Why do you think Philbert chose "Good" for his title? Why not "Good Dog"?
2. Paragraphs 4 and 8 both contain sentences that use the same construction ("then

the . . . then the . . . then the . . ."). What is the effect of these sentences? Why does Philbert repeat the pattern?

3. Twice in paragraph 4, Philbert translates his dog's cries into words. What do these translations contribute to his essay?

4. Be sure you know how to define the following words: barbiturates, sedation, malignant, carcinoma (par. 1); defeated (2); flux (3); tapped, opiates (4); evacuate (5); crematorium (8).

Suggestions for Writing

1. **FROM JOURNAL TO ESSAY**   Working from your journal entry, write an essay about the ethics of euthanasia, the controversial act of speeding the death of a terminally ill animal or person. Like Philbert, you may structure your essay around a single extended EXAMPLE, or you may prefer to arrange your thoughts into an ARGUMENT for or against the practice.

2. Using Philbert's essay as a model, write a narrative essay about a difficult or painful choice you had to make. What events led to the need to make a choice? How did you feel about the situation, and what did you do? Do you think you made the right decision?

3. **CRITICAL WRITING**   Write an essay in which you ANALYZE Philbert's TONE in this essay. You might consider how Philbert manages to invoke readers' empathy, even tears, for a dog and a person they don't know.

4. **CONNECTIONS**   Although Philbert takes an active role in his dog's death, the veterinarian shields him from seeing the artifacts of burial—"the body bag, the freezer, the crematorium, the cherry-wood box" (par. 8). Jessica Mitford, in "Behind the Formaldehyde Curtain" (p. 326), also writes about mortuary practices most of us would rather not view too closely. Taking these two essays as a starting point, write an essay of your own that considers, instead, the benefits of observing funeral rituals. Why *shouldn't* Philbert, for example, see his dog's ashes? What purposes might the practice of embalming and displaying dead bodies serve for those who attend wakes? In what ways might facing death help the living?

Bradley Philbert on Writing

In comments he wrote for *The Bedford Reader*, Bradley Philbert discusses the challenge of starting a draft and explains what, to his mind, makes a narrative stand out.

I don't think I'm at all different from most writers. Either I'll get an idea and experience that distinct moment of "I wonder," in which case a first draft starts smoothly—or the thought (and ensuing first draft) will clamp itself to the substrate of my mind. "Good" fell into the second category. In its early drafts, I was not hopeful, and I became less sure of its potential as I revised. It took a good deal of effort to develop a distinct, consistent voice.

I would contend that narratives are as dependent on an interesting and compelling voice as they are on an interesting and compelling story. This has mostly to do with the ubiquity of narratives themselves; they form the foundation of almost every sort of creative writing. The manner of the tell-ing matters, too, and a nonlinear structure—like that of "Good"—does help counter some of the banality inherent in a narrative. But there's a reason nar-ratives are so common—when they're done well, no other form of discourse is as satisfying.

For Discussion

1. Philbert describes two different ways of moving from idea to first draft: one a casual flow and the other a rougher "clamp." What are the advantages of each form of inspiration? How might the process affect the resulting piece of writing?
2. What does Philbert mean when he says that banality is "inherent in a narrative"? Do you agree with him?

HOWARD MARKEL

Howard Markel is a physician and writer known internationally for his work as a pediatrician, professor, and historian of medicine. Born in Detroit, Michigan, in 1960, he earned degrees in literature and medicine from the University of Michigan and took a PhD in the history of science, medicine, and technology at Johns Hopkins University. Markel began writing between the round-the-clock shifts of his medical residency and found that his work as a writer inspired his work as a doctor and vice versa. Markel's many books include *When Germs Travel: Six Major Epidemics That Have Invaded America since 1900 and the Fears They Have Unleashed* (2004) and *William and Sigmund: How the Brilliant Drs. Halsted and Freud Discovered Cocaine, Struggled to Break Free of Its Addiction Grip, and Changed the World* (2010). Markel was named a Centennial Historian of the City of New York in 1998 and became a member of the Institute of Medicine of the National Academy of Science in 2008. A frequent contributor to the *New York Times*, he teaches and practices medicine at the University of Michigan Medical School.

Mary Ellen's Story

In this essay Markel relates the story of Mary Ellen McCormack, an orphan who was neglected and routinely beaten by her adoptive mother in the 1870s. Strangely, it was the New York Society for the Prevention of Cruelty to Animals that came to Mary Ellen's rescue. Weaving together trial testimony and newspaper reports, Markel reveals why that was — and reminds us that this nineteenth-century legal case is still very relevant today. "Mary Ellen's Story" (editors' title) first appeared in the *New York Times* in 2009.

"Mamma has been in the habit of whipping and beating me almost every day," the little girl testified. "She used to whip me with a twisted whip — a rawhide. I have now on my head two black-and-blue marks which were made by Mamma with the whip, and a cut on the left side of my forehead which was made by a pair of scissors in Mamma's hand; she struck me with the scissors and cut me. . . . I never dared speak to anybody, because if I did I would get whipped."

If the words sound depressingly familiar, it is because they could have come from any number of recent news accounts — or, for that matter, popular

Mary Ellen McCormack

entertainment, like the . . . movie *Precious,* which depicts the emotional and
sexual abuse of a Harlem girl.

In fact, though, the quotation is from the 1874 case of Mary Ellen McCor-   3
mack, a self-possessed ten-year-old who lived on West 41st Street, in the Hell's
Kitchen section of Manhattan. It was Mary Ellen who finally put a human
face on child abuse — and prompted a reformers' crusade to prevent it and to
protect its victims, an effort that continues to this day.

Tellingly, the case was brought by the American Society for the Preven-   4
tion of Cruelty to Animals. In 1874, there were no laws protecting children
from physical abuse from their parents. It was an era of "spare the rod and spoil
the child," and parents routinely meted out painful and damaging punishment
without comment or penalty.

Mary Ellen had been orphaned as a baby. Her father, Thomas Wilson, was   5
a Union soldier who died in the Second Battle of Cold Harbor, in Virginia. Her
mother, Frances, boarded the baby with a woman living on Mulberry Bend,
on the Lower East Side, while working double shifts as a laundress at the St.
Nicholas Hotel. This arrangement cost two dollars a week, consuming her
entire widow's pension. When she lost her job, she could no longer afford

to care for her daughter and was forced to send her to the city orphanage on Blackwell's Island.

A few years later, Mary Ellen was adopted by a Manhattan couple, Thomas   6
and Mary McCormack. But Thomas died soon after the adoption, and his widow married Francis Connolly. Unhappy and overburdened, the adoptive mother took to physically abusing Mary Ellen. Sometime in late 1873, the severely battered and neglected child attracted the attention of her neighbors. They complained to the Department of Public Charities and Correction, which administered the city's almshouse, workhouse, insane asylums, orphanages, jails and public hospitals. Even the hard-boiled investigator assigned to Mary Ellen's case, Etta Angell Wheeler, was shocked and became inspired to do something.

Frustrated by the lack of child-protection laws, Wheeler approached the   7
ASPCA. It proved to be a shrewd move. Mary Ellen's plight captured the imagination of the society's founder, Henry Bergh, who saw the girl—like the horses he routinely saved from violent stable owners—as a vulnerable member of the animal kingdom needing the protection of the state. Bergh recruited a prominent lawyer, Elbridge Gerry (grandson of the politician who gave his name to gerrymandering), who took the case to the New York State Supreme Court. Applying a novel use of habeas corpus,[1] Gerry argued there was good reason to believe that Mary Ellen would be subjected to irreparable harm unless she was removed from her home.

Judge Abraham R. Lawrence ordered the child brought into the court-   8
room. Her heart-wrenching testimony was featured in the *New York Times* the next day, April 10, 1874, under the subheading "Inhuman Treatment of a Little Waif." "She is a bright little girl," the article said, "with features indicating unusual mental capacity, but with a careworn, stunted and prematurely old look. Her apparent condition of health, as well as her scanty wardrobe, indicated that no change of custody or condition could be much for the worse."

Ms. Connolly was charged and found guilty of several counts of assault   9
and battery. Mary Ellen never returned to her adoptive home, but her temporary placement in a home for delinquent teenagers was not much of an improvement. In a lifesaving act of kindness, Etta Wheeler, her mother, and her sister volunteered to raise Mary Ellen in bucolic North Chili, New York, outside Rochester.

At twenty-four, Mary Ellen married Louis Schutt. The couple had two   10
children of their own, along with three children of Schutt's from a previous marriage, and Mary Ellen passed on her good fortune by adopting an orphan

---

[1]Latin for "you have the body," *habeas corpus* is a legal term for unlawful imprisonment. —Eds.

girl. By all accounts, she was a superb and caring mother. She died in 1956, at ninety-two.

Mary Ellen's case led Bergh, Gerry, and the philanthropist John D. Wright   11
to found the New York Society for the Prevention of Cruelty to Children in December 1874. It was believed to be the first child protective agency in the world. In the years since, the society has helped rescue thousands of battered children, created shelters to care for them and, working with similar groups and agencies in cities across the nation, instituted laws that punish abusive parents.

Gone are the days when beasts of burden enjoyed more legal protection   12
than children. In recent years, a broad spectrum of programs, diagnostic and reporting protocols, safe houses, and legal protections have been developed to protect physically or sexually abused children. But every day, at least three children die in the United States as a result of parental mistreatment. Many more remain out of sight and in harm's way. Mary Ellen's story reminds us of a simple equation: How much our society values its children can be measured by how well they are treated and protected.

For a reading quiz and annotated links to further readings on child abuse, visit **bedfordstmartins.com/thebedfordreader**.

Journal Writing

Markel writes in his conclusion that "every day, at least three children die in the United States as a result of parental mistreatment" (par. 12). How do you react to this statement? Why would any parent hurt a child? And why don't families, neighbors, or authority figures (such as teachers or doctors) step in to stop abuse? Explore your thoughts on these questions in your journal. (To take your journal writing further, see "From Journal to Essay" on the facing page.)

Questions on Meaning

1. Why, in 1874, would a child-abuse case have been brought forward by the American Society for the Prevention of Cruelty to Animals?
2. In paragraph 4 Markel comments, "It was an era of 'spare the rod and spoil the child.'" What does he mean?

3. Why does Markel ALLUDE to the 2009 movie *Precious*? What does the film have to do with a story about a legal case from more than a century ago?
4. What seems to be Markel's primary PURPOSE in this essay?
5. Where does Markel state his THESIS? Is any part of his main idea left unsaid?

Questions on Writing Strategy

1. Markel starts his story in the middle. Why do you suppose he opens with the trial rather than, say, the early years of Mary Ellen McCormack's life?
2. What POINT OF VIEW does Markel take as a NARRATOR? Why was his choice appropriate, given his subject?
3. Take a close look at the photograph on page 134. Why does Markel include it? What does it reveal about the abuse inflicted on the child?
4. "Mary Ellen's Story" originally appeared in the *New York Times*. What evidence in the text reveals that Markel was writing for an audience of New York City residents? How does he ensure that readers with no firsthand knowledge of the city can follow his ideas?
5. **OTHER METHODS** What CAUSE AND EFFECT relationship does Markel draw between the 1874 case of Mary Ellen McCormack and current child-protection laws?

Questions on Language

1. Why does Markel quote Mary Ellen McCormack's testimony from the trial?
2. Consult a dictionary if you need help defining the following: meted (par. 4); boarded, laundress (5); almshouse, workhouse (6); gerrymandering (7); waif (8); bucolic (9); philanthropist (11); spectrum, protocols (12).
3. How would you characterize Markel's TONE? How does it differ from the tone of the earlier *New York Times* article on the same subject that he quotes in paragraph 8?

Suggestions for Writing

1. **FROM JOURNAL TO ESSAY** Building on your journal entry (p. 136), compose an essay that examines one of the CAUSES AND EFFECTS of child abuse. If you have had some experience with abuse (as a counselor, a bystander, a victim, or an abuser) and you care to write about it, you might develop your THESIS based on your experience and observation; otherwise draw on information you have gleaned from the media and your reading, being sure to acknowledge any sources you use.
2. Research the history of Blackwell's Island in New York or a similar public institution in the late nineteenth century, such as the "almshouse[s], workhouse[s], insane asylums, orphanages, jails and public hospitals" Markel mentions in paragraph 6. What ASSUMPTIONS did reformers make about poverty, personal responsibility, and charity? Was there any practical difference between a workhouse and a jail, for instance, or between an almshouse and a hospital? To what extent did charitable organizations exist to punish, rather than to help, those who sought assistance? Do such assumptions still hold?

3. **CRITICAL WRITING**   Using the *New York Times Index* and your school's microfilm collection or the newspaper's digital archive online, track down and read the article Markel quotes in paragraph 8. ANALYZE Markel's use of this source: How much of his information is taken from it? What does the original article add to your understanding of the story Markel relates? Should he have acknowledged any other sources?

4. **CONNECTIONS**   Chitra Divakaruni, in "Live Free and Starve" (p. 466), also writes about mistreatment of children and the need to protect them, but her focus is on modern-day child labor. Based on what Markel and Divakaruni have to say, what parallels can you draw between attitudes toward children in nineteenth-century America and contemporary "Third World" countries? How are definitions of childhood shaped by culture?

SHIRLEY JACKSON

Shirley Jackson was a fiction writer best known for horror stories that probe the dark side of human nature and social behavior. But she also wrote humorously about domestic life, a subject she knew well as a wife and the mother of four children. Born in 1919 in California, Jackson moved as a teenager to upstate New York, and graduated from Syracuse University in 1940. She started writing as a young girl and was highly disciplined and productive all her life. She began publishing stories in 1941, and eventually her fiction appeared in *The New Yorker, Harper's, Good Housekeeping,* and many other magazines. Her tales of family life appeared in two books, *Life among the Savages* (1953) and *Raising Demons* (1957). Her suspense novels, which were more significant to her, included *The Haunting of Hill House* (1959) and *We Have Always Lived in the Castle* (1962). After Jackson died in 1965, her husband, the literary critic Stanley Edgar Hyman, published two volumes of her stories, novels, and lectures: *The Magic of Shirley Jackson* (1966) and *Come Along with Me* (1968).

The Lottery

By far Jackson's best-known work and indeed one of the best-known short stories ever written, "The Lottery" first appeared in *The New Yorker* in 1948 to loud applause and louder cries of outrage. The time was just after World War II, when Nazi concentration camps and the dropping of atomic bombs had revealed horrors of organized human cruelty. Jackson's husband, denying that her work purveyed "neurotic fantasies," argued instead that it was fitting "for our distressing world." Is the story still relevant today?

The morning of June 27th was clear and sunny, with the fresh warmth of a full-summer day; the flowers were blossoming profusely and the grass was richly green. The people of the village began to gather in the square, between the post office and the bank, around ten o'clock; in some towns there were so many people that the lottery took two days and had to be started on June 26th, but in this village, where there were only about three hundred people, the whole lottery took less than two hours, so it could begin at ten o'clock in the morning and still be through in time to allow the villagers to get home for noon dinner.

The children assembled first, of course. School was recently over for the summer, and the feeling of liberty sat uneasily on most of them; they tended to gather together quietly for a while before they broke into boisterous play, and their talk was still of the classroom and the teacher, of books and reprimands. Bobby Martin had already stuffed his pockets full of stones, and the other boys soon followed his example, selecting the smoothest and round-est stones; Bobby and Harry Jones and Dickie Delacroix—the villagers pro-nounced this name "Dellacroy"—eventually made a great pile of stones in one corner of the square and guarded it against the raids of the other boys. The girls stood aside, talking among themselves, looking over their shoulders at the boys, and the very small children rolled in the dust or clung to the hands of their older brothers or sisters.

Soon the men began to gather, surveying their own children, speaking of   3
planting and rain, tractors and taxes. They stood together, away from the pile of stones in the corner, and their jokes were quiet and they smiled rather than laughed. The women, wearing faded house dresses and sweaters, came shortly after their menfolk. They greeted one another and exchanged bits of gossip as they went to join their husbands. Soon the women, standing by their hus-bands, began to call to their children, and the children came reluctantly, hav-ing to be called four or five times. Bobby Martin ducked under his mother's grasping hand and ran, laughing, back to the pile of stones. His father spoke up sharply, and Bobby came quickly and took his place between his father and his oldest brother.

The lottery was conducted—as were the square dances, the teenage   4
club, the Halloween program—by Mr. Summers, who had time and energy to devote to civic activities. He was a round-faced, jovial man and he ran the coal business, and people were sorry for him, because he had no children and his wife was a scold. When he arrived in the square, carrying the black wooden box, there was a murmur of conversation among the villagers, and he waved and called, "Little late today, folks." The postmaster, Mr. Graves, fol-lowed him, carrying a three-legged stool, and the stool was put in the center of the square and Mr. Summers set the black box down on it. The villagers kept their distance, leaving a space between themselves and the stool, and when Mr. Summers said, "Some of you fellows want to give me a hand?" there was a hesitation before two men, Mr. Martin and his oldest son, Baxter, came forward to hold the box steady on the stool while Mr. Summers stirred up the papers inside it.

The original paraphernalia for the lottery had been lost long ago, and the   5
black box now resting on the stool had been put into use even before Old Man Warner, the oldest man in town, was born. Mr. Summers spoke frequently to the villagers about making a new box, but no one liked to upset even as much tradition as was represented by the black box. There was a story that the pres-ent box had been made with some pieces of the box that had preceded it, the one that had been constructed when the first people settled down to make a village here. Every year, after the lottery, Mr. Summers began talking again about a new box, but every year the subject was allowed to fade off without

anything's being done. The black box grew shabbier each year; by now it was no longer completely black but splintered badly along one side to show the original wood color, and in some places faded or stained.

Mr. Martin and his oldest son, Baxter, held the black box securely on 6
the stool until Mr. Summers had stirred the papers thoroughly with his hand. Because so much of the ritual had been forgotten or discarded, Mr. Summers had been successful in having slips of paper substituted for the chips of wood that had been used for generations. Chips of wood, Mr. Summers had argued, had been all very well when the village was tiny, but now that the population was more than three hundred and likely to keep on growing, it was necessary to use something that would fit more easily into the black box. The night before the lottery, Mr. Summers and Mr. Graves made up the slips of paper and put them in the box, and it was then taken to the safe of Mr. Summers's coal company and locked up until Mr. Summers was ready to take it to the square next morning. The rest of the year, the box was put away, sometimes one place, sometimes another; it had spent one year in Mr. Graves's barn and another year underfoot in the post office, and sometimes it was set on a shelf in the Martin grocery and left there.

There was a great deal of fussing to be done before Mr. Summers declared 7
the lottery open. There were the lists to make up — of heads of families, heads of households in each family, members of each household in each family. There was the proper swearing-in of Mr. Summers by the postmaster, as the official of the lottery; at one time, some people remembered, there had been a recital of some sort, performed by the official of the lottery, a perfunctory, tuneless chant that had been rattled off duly each year; some people believed that the official of the lottery used to stand just so when he said or sang it, others believed that he was supposed to walk among the people, but years and years ago this part of the ritual had been allowed to lapse. There had been, also, a ritual salute, which the official of the lottery had had to use in addressing each person who came up to draw from the box, but this also had changed with time, until now it was felt necessary only for the official to speak to each person approaching. Mr. Summers was very good at all this; in his clean white shirt and blue jeans, with one hand resting carelessly on the black box, he seemed very proper and important as he talked interminably to Mr. Graves and the Martins.

Just as Mr. Summers finally left off talking and turned to the assembled 8
villagers, Mrs. Hutchinson came hurriedly along the path to the square, her sweater thrown over her shoulders, and slid into place in the back of the crowd. "Clean forgot what day it was," she said to Mrs. Delacroix, who stood next to her, and they both laughed softly. "Thought my old man was out back stacking wood," Mrs. Hutchinson went on, "and then I looked out the window

and the kids was gone, and then I remembered it was the twenty-seventh and came a-running." She dried her hands on her apron, and Mrs. Delacroix said, "You're in time, though. They're still talking away up there."

Mrs. Hutchinson craned her neck to see through the crowd and found   9
her husband and children standing near the front. She tapped Mrs. Delacroix on the arm as a farewell and began to make her way through the crowd. The people separated good-humoredly to let her through; two or three people said, in voices just loud enough to be heard across the crowd, "Here comes your Missus, Hutchinson," and "Bill, she made it after all." Mrs. Hutchinson reached her husband, and Mr. Summers, who had been waiting, said cheerfully, "Thought we were going to have to get on without you, Tessie." Mrs. Hutchinson said, grinning, "Wouldn't have me leave m'dishes in the sink, now, would you, Joe?" and soft laughter ran through the crowd as the people stirred back into position after Mrs. Hutchinson's arrival.

"Well now," Mr. Summers said soberly, "guess we better get started, get   10
this over with, so's we can go back to work. Anybody ain't here?"

"Dunbar," several people said. "Dunbar, Dunbar."   11

Mr. Summers consulted his list. "Clyde Dunbar," he said. "That's right.   12
He's broke his leg, hasn't he? Who's drawing for him?"

"Me, I guess," a woman said, and Mr. Summers turned to look at her.   13
"Wife draws for her husband," Mrs. Summers said. "Don't you have a grown boy to do it for you, Janey?" Although Mr. Summers and everyone else in the village knew the answer perfectly well, it was the business of the official of the lottery to ask such questions formally. Mr. Summers waited with an expression of polite interest while Mrs. Dunbar answered.

"Horace's not but sixteen yet," Mrs. Dunbar said regretfully. "Guess I gotta   14
fill in for the old man this year."

"Right," Mr. Summers said. He made a note on the list he was holding.   15
Then he asked, "Watson boy drawing this year?"

A tall boy in the crowd raised his hand. "Here," he said. "I'm drawing for   16
m'mother and me." He blinked his eyes nervously and ducked his head as several voices in the crowd said things like "Good fellow, Jack," and "Glad to see your mother's got a man to do it."

"Well," Mr. Summers said, "guess that's everyone. Old Man Warner   17
make it?"

"Here," a voice said, and Mr. Summers nodded.   18

A sudden hush fell on the crowd as Mr. Summers cleared his throat and   19
looked at the list. "All ready?" he called. "Now, I'll read the names—heads of families first—and the men come up and take a paper out of the box. Keep

the paper folded in your hand without looking at it until everyone has had a turn. Everything clear?"

The people had done it so many times that they only half listened to the directions, most of them were quiet, wetting their lips, not looking around. Then Mr. Summers raised one hand high and said, "Adams." A man disengaged himself from the crowd and came forward. "Hi, Steve," Mr. Summers said, and Mr. Adams said, "Hi, Joe." They grinned at one another humorlessly and nervously. Then Mr. Adams reached into the black box and took out a folded paper. He held it firmly by one corner as he turned and went hastily back to his place in the crowd, where he stood a little apart from his family, not looking down at his hand.

"Allen," Mr. Summers said, "Anderson. . . . Bentham."

"Seems like there's no time at all between lotteries anymore," Mrs. Delacroix said to Mrs. Graves in the back row. "Seems like we got through with the last one only last week."

"Time sure goes fast," Mrs. Graves said.

"Clark. . . . Delacroix."

"There goes my old man," Mrs. Delacroix said. She held her breath while her husband went forward.

"Dunbar," Mr. Summers said, and Mrs. Dunbar went steadily to the box while one of the women said, "Go on, Janey," and another said, "There she goes."

"We're next," Mrs. Graves said. She watched while Mr. Graves came around from the side of the box, greeted Mr. Summers gravely, and selected a slip of paper from the box. By now, all through the crowd there were men holding the small folded papers in their large hands, turning them over and over nervously. Mrs. Dunbar and her two sons stood together, Mrs. Dunbar holding the slip of paper.

"Harburt. . . . Hutchinson."

"Get up there, Bill," Mrs. Hutchinson said, and the people near her laughed.

"Jones."

"They do say," Mr. Adams said to Old Man Warner, who stood next to him, "that over in the north village they're talking of giving up the lottery."

Old Man Warner snorted. "Pack of crazy fools," he said. "Listening to the young folks, nothing's good enough for *them.* Next thing you know, they'll be wanting to go back to living in caves, nobody work anymore, live *that* way for a while. Used to be a saying about 'Lottery in June, corn be heavy soon.' First thing you know, we'd all be eating stewed chickweed and acorns. There's *always* been a lottery," he added petulantly. "Bad enough to see young Joe Summers up there joking with everybody."

"Some places have already quit lotteries," Mrs. Adams said. 33

"Nothing but trouble in *that*," Old Man Warner said stoutly. "Pack of 34
young fools."

"Martin." And Bobby Martin watched his father go forward. "Overdyke.... 35
Percy."

"I wish they'd hurry," Mrs. Dunbar said to her older son. "I wish they'd 36
hurry."

"They're almost through," her son said. 37

"You get ready to run tell Dad," Mrs. Dunbar said. 38

Mr. Summers called his own name and then stepped forward precisely and 39
selected a slip from the box. Then he called, "Warner."

"Seventy-seventh year I been in the lottery," Old Man Warner said as he 40
went through the crowd. "Seventy-seventh time."

"Watson." The tall boy came awkwardly through the crowd. Someone 41
said, "Don't be nervous, Jack," and Mr. Summers said, "Take your time, son."

"Zanini." 42

After that, there was a long pause, a breathless pause, until Mr. Summers 43
holding his slip of paper in the air, said, "All right, fellows." For a minute,
no one moved, and then all the slips of paper were opened. Suddenly, all the
women began to speak at once, saying, "Who is it?" "Who's got it?" "Is it the
Dunbars?" "Is it the Watsons?" Then the voices began to say, "It's Hutchinson.
It's Bill," "Bill Hutchinson's got it."

"Go tell your father," Mrs. Dunbar said to her older son. 44

People began to look around to see the Hutchinsons. Bill Hutchinson 45
was standing quiet, staring down at the paper in his hand. Suddenly, Tessie
Hutchinson shouted to Mrs. Summers, "You didn't give him time enough to
take any paper he wanted. I saw you. It wasn't fair!"

"Be a good sport, Tessie," Mrs. Delacroix called, and Mrs. Graves said, "All 46
of us took the same chance."

"Shut up, Tessie," Bill Hutchinson said. 47

"Well, everyone," Mr. Summers said, "that was done pretty fast, and now 48
we've got to be hurrying a little more to get done in time." He consulted his
next list. "Bill," he said, "you draw for the Hutchinson family. You got any
other households in the Hutchinsons?"

"There's Don and Eva," Mrs. Hutchinson yelled. "Make *them* take their 49
chance!"

"Daughters drew with their husband's families, Tessie," Mr. Summers said 50
gently. "You know that as well as anyone else."

"It wasn't *fair*," Tessie said. 51

"I guess not, Joe," Bill Hutchinson said regretfully. "My daughter draws 52 with her husband's family, that's only fair. And I've got no other family except the kids."

"Then, as far as drawing for families is concerned, it's you," Mr. Summers   53
said in explanation, "and as far as drawing for households is concerned, that's you, too. Right?"

"Right," Bill Hutchinson said.   54

"How many kids, Bill?" Mr. Summers asked formally.   55

"Three," Bill Hutchinson said. "There's Bill, Jr., and Nancy, and little   56
Dave. And Tessie and me."

"All right, then," Mr. Summers said. "Harry, you got their tickets back?"   57

Mr. Graves nodded and held up the slips of paper. "Put them in the box,   58
then," Mr. Summers directed. "Take Bill's and put it in."

"I think we ought to start over," Mrs. Hutchinson said, as quietly as she   59
could. "I tell you it wasn't *fair*. You didn't give him time enough to choose. *Everybody* saw that."

Mr. Graves had selected the five slips and put them in the box, and he   60
dropped all the papers but those onto the ground, where the breeze caught them and lifted them off.

"Listen, everybody," Mrs. Hutchinson was saying to the people around   61
her.

"Ready, Bill?" Mr. Summers asked, and Bill Hutchinson, with one quick   62
glance around at his wife and children, nodded.

"Remember," Mr. Summers said, "take the slips and keep them folded   63
until each person has taken one. Harry, you help little Dave." Mr. Graves took the hand of the little boy, who came willingly with him up to the box. "Take a paper out of the box, Davy," Mr. Summers said. Davy put his hand into the box and laughed. "Take just *one* paper," Mrs. Summers said. "Harry, you hold it for him." Mr. Graves took the child's hand and removed the folded paper from the tight fist and held it while little Dave stood next to him and looked up at him wonderingly.

"Nancy next," Mr. Summers said. Nancy was twelve, and her school   64
friends breathed heavily as she went forward, switching her skirt, and took a slip daintily from the box. "Bill, Jr.," Mr. Summers said, and Billy, his face red and his feet overlarge, nearly knocked the box over as he got a paper out. "Tessie," Mr. Summers said. She hesitated for a minute, looking around defiantly, and then set her lips and went up to the box. She snatched a paper out and held it behind her.

"Bill," Mr. Summers said, and Bill Hutchinson reached into the box and   65
felt around, bringing his hand out at last with the slip of paper in it.

The crowd was quiet. A girl whispered, "I hope it's not Nancy," and the   66
sound of the whisper reached the edges of the crowd.

"It's not the way it used to be," Old Man Warner said clearly. "People ain't   67
the way they used to be."

"All right," Mr. Summers said. "Open the papers. Harry, you open little   68
Dave's."

Mr. Graves opened the slip of paper and there was a general sigh through   69
the crowd as he held it up and everyone could see that it was blank. Nancy and
Bill, Jr., opened theirs at the same time, and both beamed and laughed, turning around to the crowd and holding their slips of paper above their heads.

"Tessie," Mr. Summers said. There was a pause, and then Mr. Summers   70
looked at Bill Hutchinson, and Bill unfolded his paper and showed it. It was
blank.

"It's Tessie," Mr. Summers said, and his voice was hushed. "Show us her   71
paper, Bill."

Bill Hutchinson went over to his wife and forced the slip of paper out of   72
her hand. It had a black spot on it, the black spot Mr. Summers had made the
night before with the heavy pencil in the coal-company office. Bill Hutchinson held it up and there was a stir in the crowd.

"All right, folks," Mr. Summers said. "Let's finish quickly."   73

Although the villagers had forgotten the ritual and lost the original black   74
box, they still remembered to use stones. The pile of stones the boys had made
earlier was ready; there were stones on the ground with the blowing scraps of
paper that had come out of the box. Mrs. Delacroix selected a stone so large
she had to pick it up with both hands and turned to Mrs. Dunbar. "Come on,"
she said. "Hurry up."

Mrs. Dunbar had small stones in both hands, and she said, gasping for   75
breath, "I can't run at all. You'll have to go ahead and I'll catch up with you."

The children had stones already, and someone gave little Davy Hutchin-   76
son a few pebbles.

Tessie Hutchinson was in the center of a cleared space by now, and she   77
held her hands out desperately as the villagers moved in on her. "It isn't fair,"
she said. A stone hit her on the side of the head.

Old Man Warner was saying, "Come on, come on, everyone." Steve   78
Adams was in front of the crowd of villagers, with Mrs. Graves beside him.

"It isn't fair, it isn't right," Mrs. Hutchinson screamed and then they were   79
upon her.

---

*For a reading quiz, sources on Shirley Jackson, and annotated links to further read-
ings on the psychology of conformity, visit bedfordstmartins.com/thebedfordreader.*

Journal Writing

Think about rituals in which you participate, such as those involving holidays, meals, religious observances, family vacations, sporting events—anything that is repeated and traditional. List some of these in your journal and write about their significance to you. (To take your writing further, see "From Journal to Essay" on the next page.)

Questions on Meaning

1. The PURPOSE of all fiction might be taken as entertainment or self-expression. Does Jackson have any other purpose in "The Lottery"?
2. When does the reader know what is actually going to occur?
3. Describe this story's community on the basis of what Jackson says of it.
4. What do the villagers' attitudes toward the black box indicate about their feelings toward the lottery?

Questions on Writing Strategy

1. Jackson uses the third PERSON (*he, she, it, they*) to narrate the story, and she does not enter the minds of her characters. Why do you think she keeps this distant POINT OF VIEW?
2. On your first reading of the story, what did you make of the references to rocks in paragraphs 2–3? Do you think they effectively forecast the ending?
3. Jackson has a character introduce a controversial notion in paragraph 31. Why does she do this?
4. **OTHER METHODS**   Jackson is exploring—or inviting us to explore—CAUSES AND EFFECTS. Why do the villagers participate in the lottery every year? What does paragraph 32 hint might have been the original reason for it?

Questions on Language

1. Dialog provides much information not stated elsewhere in the story. Give three examples of such information about the community and its interactions.
2. Check a dictionary for definitions of the following words: profusely (par. 1); boisterous, reprimand (2); jovial, scold, paraphernalia (4); perfunctory, duly, interminably (7); petulantly (32).
3. In paragraph 64 we read that Mrs. Hutchinson "snatched" the paper out of the box. What does this verb suggest about her attitude?
4. Jackson admits to setting the story in her Vermont village in the present time (that is, 1948). Judging from the names of the villagers, where did these people's ancestors originally come from? What do you make of the names Delacroix and Zanini? What is their significance?
5. Unlike much fiction, "The Lottery" contains few FIGURES OF SPEECH. Why do you think this is?

Suggestions for Writing

1. **FROM JOURNAL TO ESSAY**   Choose one of the rituals you wrote about in your journal, and compose a narrative about the last time you participated in this ritual. Use DESCRIPTION and dialog to convey the significance of the ritual and your own and other participants' attitudes toward it.

2. Write an imaginary narrative, perhaps set in the future, of a ritual that demonstrates something about the people who participate in it. The ritual can be, but need not be, as sinister as Jackson's lottery; yours could concern bathing, eating, dating, going to school, driving, growing older.

3. In his 1974 book *Obedience to Authority*, the psychologist Stanley Milgram reported and analyzed the results of a study he had conducted that caused a furor among psychologists and the general public. Under orders from white-coated "experimenters," many subjects administered what they believed to be life-threatening electric shocks to other people whom they could hear but not see. In fact, the "victims" were actors and received no shocks, but the subjects thought otherwise and many continued to administer stronger and stronger "shocks" when ordered to do so. Find *Obedience to Authority* in the library and compare and contrast the circumstances of Milgram's experiment with those of Jackson's lottery. For instance, who or what is the order-giving authority in the lottery? What is the significance of seeing or not seeing one's victim?

4. **CRITICAL WRITING**   In a 1960 lecture (which we quote more from in "Shirley Jackson on Writing"), Jackson said that a common response she received to "The Lottery" was "What does this story mean?" (She never answered the question.) In an essay, interpret the meaning of the story as *you* understand it. (What does it say, for instance, about social customs, conformity, guilt, obliviousness, or good and evil?) You will have to INFER meaning from such features as Jackson's own TONE as narrator, the tone of the villagers' dialog, and, of course, the events of the story. Your essay should be supported with specific EVIDENCE from the story.

5. **CONNECTIONS**   Although very different from Jackson's story, Firoozeh Dumas's "Sweet, Sour, and Resentful" (p. 320) also focuses on observing a tradition. Taken together, what do Dumas's essay and Jackson's story say about both the benefits and the dangers of adhering to tradition? Write an essay in which you explore the pros and cons of maintaining rituals and traditions, giving examples from these selections and from your own experience and reading.

Shirley Jackson on Writing

Come Along with Me, a posthumous collection of her work, contains a lecture by Shirley Jackson titled "Biography of a Story"—specifically a biography of "The Lottery." Far from being born in cruelty or cynicism, the story had quite benign origins. Jackson wrote the story, she recalled, "on a bright June morning when summer seemed to have come at last, with blue skies and warm sun and no heavenly signs to warn me that my morning's work was anything but just another story. The idea had come to me while I was pushing my daughter up the hill in her stroller—it was, as I say, a warm morning, and the hill was steep, and beside my daughter the stroller held the day's groceries—and perhaps the effort of that last fifty yards up the hill put an edge on the story; at any rate, I had the idea fairly clearly in my mind when I put my daughter in her playpen and the frozen vegetables in the refrigerator, and, writing the story, I found that it went quickly and easily, moving from beginning to end without pause. As a matter of fact, when I read it over later I decided that except for one or two minor corrections, it needed no changes, and the story I finally typed up and sent off to my agent the next day was almost word for word the original draft. This, as any writer of stories can tell you, is not a usual thing. All I know is that when I came to read the story over I felt strongly that I didn't want to fuss with it. I didn't think it was perfect, but I didn't want to fuss with it. It was, I thought, a serious, straightforward story, and I was pleased and a little surprised at the ease with which it had been written; I was reasonably proud of it, and hoped that my agent would sell it to some magazine and I would have the gratification of seeing it in print."

After the story was published, however, Jackson was surprised to find both it and herself the subject of "bewilderment, speculation, and plain old-fashioned abuse." She wrote that "one of the most terrifying aspects of publishing stories and books is the realization that they are going to be read, and read by strangers. I had never fully realized this before, although I had of course in my imagination dwelt lovingly upon the thought of the millions and millions of people who were going to be uplifted and enriched and delighted by the stories I wrote. It had simply never occurred to me that these millions and millions of people might be so far from being uplifted that they would sit down and write me letters I was downright scared to open; of the three-hundred-odd letters that I received that summer I can count only thirteen that spoke kindly to me, and they were mostly from friends."

Jackson's favorite letter was one concluding, "Our brothers feel that Miss Jackson is a true prophet and disciple of the true gospel of the redeeming light. When will the next revelation be published?" Jackson's answer: "Never. I am out of the lottery business for good."

For Discussion

1. What lesson can we draw about creative inspiration from Jackson's anecdote about the origins of "The Lottery"?
2. What seems to have alarmed Jackson about readers' reactions to her story? Do you think she was naive in expecting otherwise?

ADDITIONAL WRITING TOPICS

Narration

1. Write a narrative with one of the following as your subject. It may be (as your instructor may advise) either a first-PERSON memoir or a story written in the third person, observing the experience of someone else. Decide before you begin what your PURPOSE is and whether you are writing (1) an anecdote; (2) an essay consisting mainly of a single narrative; or (3) an essay that includes more than one story.

   A memorable experience from your early life
   A lesson you learned the hard way
   A trip into unfamiliar territory
   An embarrassing moment that taught you something
   A monumental misunderstanding
   An accident
   An unexpected encounter
   A story about a famous person or someone close to you
   A conflict or contest
   A destructive storm
   An assassination attempt
   A historical event of significance

2. Tell a true story of your early or recent school days, either humorous or serious, relating a struggle you experienced (or still experience) in school.

Note: Writing topics combining narration and description appear on page 201.

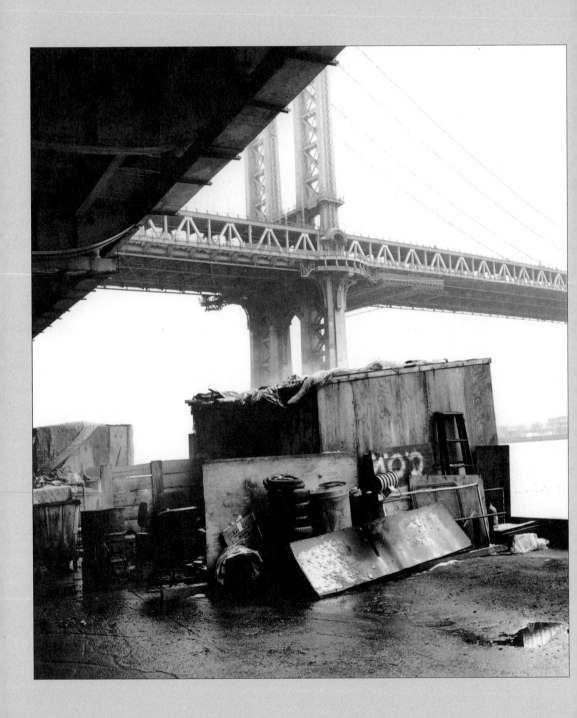

5

DESCRIPTION

Writing with Your Senses

◀ **Description in a photograph**

Margaret Morton photographs homeless communities in New York City. This photograph, titled *Doug and Mizan's House, East River*, depicts a makeshift dwelling on a Manhattan riverbank. Consider Morton's photograph as a work of description—revealing a thing through the perceptions of the senses. What do you see through her eyes? What is the house made of? What do the overhanging structure on the upper left and the bridge behind the house add to the impression of the house? If you were standing in the picture, in front of the house, what might you hear or smell? If you touched the house, what textures might you feel? What main idea do you think Morton wants this photograph to convey?

THE METHOD

Like narration, DESCRIPTION is a familiar method of expression, already a working part of you. In any talk-fest with friends, you probably do your share of describing. You depict in words someone you've met by describing her clothes, the look on her face, the way she walks. You describe somewhere you've been, something you admire, something you just can't abide. In a diary or in e-mail to a friend, you describe your college (cast concrete building, crowded walks, pigeons rattling their wings); or perhaps you describe your brand-new second-hand car, from the snakelike glitter of its hubcaps to the odd antiques in its trunk, bequeathed by its previous owner. You hardly can live a day without describing (or hearing described) some person, place, or thing. Small wonder that, in written discourse, description is almost as indispensable as words.

Description reports the testimony of your senses. It invites your readers to imagine that they, too, not only see but perhaps also hear, taste, smell, and touch the subject you describe. Usually, you write a description for either of two PURPOSES: (1) to convey information without bias or emotion; or (2) to convey it with feeling.

In writing with the first purpose in mind, you write an OBJECTIVE (or *impartial*, *public*, or *functional*) description. You describe your subject so clearly and exactly that your reader will understand it or recognize it, and you leave your emotions out. The description in academic writing is usually objective: A biology report on a particular species of frog, for instance, might detail the animal's appearance (four-inch-wide body, bright orange skin with light brown spots), its sounds (hoarse clucks), and its feel (smooth, slippery). You also write this kind of description in sending a friend directions for finding your house: "Look for the green shutters on the windows and a new garbage can at the front door." Although in a personal letter describing a frog or your house you might very well become emotionally involved with it (perhaps calling one "weird" and the other a "fleabag"), in writing an objective description your purpose is not to convey your feelings. You are trying to make the frog or the house easily recognized.

The other type of descriptive writing is SUBJECTIVE (or *emotional*, *personal*, or *impressionistic*). This is the kind included in a magazine advertisement for a new car. It's what you write in your e-mail to a friend setting forth what your college is like—whether you are pleased or displeased with it. In this kind of description, you may use biases and personal feelings—in fact, they are essential. Let us consider a splendid example: a subjective description of a storm at sea. Charles Dickens, in his memoir *American Notes*, conveys his passenger's-eye view of an Atlantic steamship on a morning when the ocean is wild:

> Imagine the ship herself, with every pulse and artery of her huge body swollen and bursting . . . sworn to go on or die. Imagine the wind howling, the

sea roaring, the rain beating; all in furious array against her. Picture the sky both dark and wild, and the clouds in fearful sympathy with the waves, making another ocean in the air. Add to all this the clattering on deck and down below; the tread of hurried feet; the loud hoarse shouts of seamen; the gurgling in and out of water through the scuppers; with every now and then the striking of a heavy sea upon the planks above, with the deep, dead, heavy sound of thunder heard within a vault; and there is the head wind of that January morning.

I say nothing of what may be called the domestic noises of the ship; such as the breaking of glass and crockery, the tumbling down of stewards, the gambols, overhead, of loose casks and truant dozens of bottled porter, and the very remarkable and far from exhilarating sounds raised in their various staterooms by the seventy passengers who were too ill to get up to breakfast.

Notice how many *sounds* are included in this primarily ear-minded description. We can infer how Dickens feels about the storm. It is a terrifying event that reduces the interior of the vessel to chaos; and yet the writer (in hearing the loose barrel and beer bottles merrily gambol, in finding humor in the seasick passengers' plight) apparently delights in it. Writing subjectively, he intrudes his feelings. Think of what a starkly different description of the very same storm the captain might set down—objectively—in the ship's log: "At 0600 hours, watch reported a wind from due north of 70 knots. Whitecaps were noticed, in height two ells above the bow. Below deck much gear was reported adrift, and ten casks of ale were broken and their staves strewn about. Mr. Liam Jones, chief steward, suffered a compound fracture of the left leg. . . ." But Dickens, not content simply to record information, strives to ensure that the mind's eye is dazzled and the mind's ear regaled.

Description is usually found in the company of other methods of writing. Often, for instance, it will enliven NARRATION and make the people in the story and the setting unmistakably clear. Writing an ARGUMENT in her essay "Not Your Homeland" (p. 598), Edwidge Danticat begins with a description of a Florida hotel that turns out to serve as a prison for families who are trying to immigrate to the United States. Description will help a writer in examining the EFFECTS of a flood or in COMPARING AND CONTRASTING two paintings. Keep the method of description in mind when you come to try expository and argumentative writing.

THE PROCESS

Purpose and Audience

Understand, first of all, why you are writing about your subject and thus what kind of description is called for. Is it appropriate to perceive and report without emotion or bias—and thus write an objective description? Or is it appropriate to express your personal feelings as well as your perceptions—and thus write a subjective description?

Give a little thought to your AUDIENCE. What do your readers need to be told, if they are to share the perceptions you would have them share, if they are clearly to behold what you want them to? If, let's say, you are describing a downtown street on a Saturday night for an audience of fellow students who live in the same city and know it well, then you need not dwell on the street's familiar geography. What must you tell? Only those details that make the place different on a Saturday night. But if you are remembering your home city, and writing for readers who don't know it, you'll need to establish a few central landmarks to sketch (in their minds) an unfamiliar street on a Saturday night.

Before you begin to write a description, go look at your subject. If that is not possible, your next best course is to spend a few minutes imagining the subject until, in your mind's eye, you can see every flyspeck on it. Then, having fixed your subject in mind, ask yourself which of its features you'll need to report to your particular audience, for your particular purpose. Ask, "What am I out to accomplish?"

Dominant Impression and Thesis

When you consider your aim in describing, you'll begin to see what impression you intend your subject to make on readers. Let your description, as a whole, convey this one DOMINANT IMPRESSION. If you plan to write a subjective description of an old house, laying weight on its spooky atmosphere for readers you wish to make shiver, then you might mention its squeaking bats and its shadowy halls. If, however, you are describing the house in a classified ad, for an audience of possible buyers, you might focus instead on its eat-in kitchen, working fireplace, and proximity to public transportation. Details have to be carefully selected. Feel no grim duty to include every perceptible detail. To do so would only invite chaos—or perhaps, for the reader, mere tedium. Pick out the features that matter most.

Your dominant impression is like the THESIS of your description—the main idea about your subject that you want readers to take away with them. When you use description to explain or to argue, it's usually a good strategy to state that dominant impression outright, tying it to your essay's thesis or a part of it. In the biology report on a species of frog, for instance, you might preface your description with a statement like this one:

A number of unique features distinguish this frog from others in the order Anura.

Or in an argument in favor of cleaning a local toxic-waste site, you might begin with a description of the site and then state your point about it:

> This landscape is as poisonous as it looks, for underneath its barren crust are enough toxic chemicals to sicken a small village.

When you use subjective description more for its own sake — to show the reader a place or a person, to evoke feelings — you needn't always state your dominant impression as a THESIS STATEMENT, as long as the impression is there dictating the details.

Organization

You can organize a description in several ways. In depicting the storm at sea — a subjective description — Charles Dickens sorts out the pandemonium for us. He groups the various sounds into two classes: those of sea and sailors, and the "domestic noises" of the ship's passengers — their smashing dishes, their rolling bottles, the crashing of stewards who wait on them.

Other writers of description rely on their POINT OF VIEW to help them arrange details — the physical angle from which they're perceiving and describing. In the previous chapter, on narration, we spoke of point of view: how essential it is for a story to have a narrator — one who, from a certain position, reports what takes place. A description, too, needs a consistent point of view: that of an observer who stays put and observes steadily. From this point of view, you can make a carefully planned inspection tour of your subject, moving spatially (from left to right, from near to far, from top to bottom, from center to periphery), or perhaps moving from prominent objects to tiny ones, from dull to bright, from commonplace to extraordinary — or vice versa.

The plan for you is the one that best fulfills your purpose, arranging details so that the reader firmly receives the impression you mean to convey. If you were to describe, for instance, a chapel in the middle of a desert, you might begin with the details of the lonely terrain. Then, as if approaching the chapel with the aid of a zoom lens, you might detail its exterior before going on inside. That might be a workable method to write a description *if* you wanted to create the dominant impression of the chapel as an island of beauty and feeling in the midst of desolation. Say, however, that you had a different impression in mind: to emphasize the spirituality of the chapel's interior. You might then begin your description inside the structure, perhaps with its most prominent feature, the stained glass windows. You might mention the surrounding desert later in your description, but only incidentally.

Whatever method you follow in arranging details, stick with it all the way through so that your arrangement causes no difficulty for the reader. In describing the chapel in the desert, you wouldn't necessarily proceed in the way you explored the structure, first noting its isolation, then entering and studying its windows and some of its artwork, then going outside again to see what the walls were made of, then moving back inside to finish looking at the artwork, and so on. Instead, you would lead the reader around and through (or through and around) the structure in an organized manner. Look again at Charles Dickens's description of a storm-battered ship: The scene is chaotic, but the prose is orderly.

Details

Luckily, to write a memorable description, you don't need a storm at sea or any other awe-inspiring subject. As Sarah Vowell demonstrates in "Shooting Dad" later in this chapter, you can write about your family as effectively as you write about a tornado. The secret is in the vividness, the evocativeness of the details. Like most good describers, Vowell uses many IMAGES (language calling up concrete sensory experiences), including FIGURES OF SPEECH (expressions that do not mean literally what they say, often describing one thing in terms of another). For instance, using *metaphor* Vowell writes that "the respective work spaces governed by my father and me were jealously guarded totalitarian states in which each of us declared ourselves dictator." Using *similes*, Vowell describes shooting a pistol as a six-year-old: "The sound it made was as big as God. It kicked little me back to the ground like a bully, like a foe."

FOCUS ON SPECIFIC AND CONCRETE LANGUAGE

When you write effective description, you'll convey your experience as exactly as possible. You may use figures of speech, as discussed above, and you'll definitely rely on language that is specific (tied to actual things) and concrete (tied to the senses of sight, hearing, touch, smell, and taste). Specific and concrete language enables readers to behold with the mind's eye—and to feel with the mind's fingertips.

The first sentence below shows a writer's first-draft attempt to describe something she saw. After editing, the second sentence is much more vivid.

VAGUE   Beautiful, scented wildflowers were in the field.

CONCRETE AND SPECIFIC   Backlighted by the sun and smelling faintly sweet, an acre of tiny lavender flowers spread away from me.

When editing your description, keep a sharp eye out for vague words such as *delicious, handsome, loud,* and *short* that force readers to create their own impressions or, worse, leave them with no impression at all. Using details that call on readers' sensory experiences, say why *delicious* or why *handsome*, how *loud* or how *short*. When stuck for a word, conjure up your subject and see it, hear it, touch it, smell it, taste it.

Note that *concrete* and *specific* do not mean "fancy": Good description does not demand five-dollar words when nickel equivalents are just as informative. The writer who uses *rubiginous* instead of *rusty red* actually says less because fewer readers will understand the less common word and all readers will sense a writer showing off.

> For exercises on language, visit Exercise Central at **bedfordstmartins.com/ thebedfordreader.**

CHECKLIST FOR REVISING A DESCRIPTION

✔ **SUBJECTIVE OR OBJECTIVE**   Given your purpose and audience, is your description appropriately subjective (emphasizing feelings) or objective (unemotional)?

✔ **DOMINANT IMPRESSION**   What is the dominant impression of your subject? If you haven't stated it, will your readers be able to express it accurately to themselves?

✔ **POINT OF VIEW AND ORGANIZATION**   Do your point of view and organization work together to make your subject clear in readers' minds? Are they consistent?

✔ **DETAILS**   Have you provided all the details—and just those—needed to convey your dominant impression? What needs expanding? What needs condensing or cutting?

✔ **SPECIFIC AND CONCRETE LANGUAGE**   Have you used words that pin down your meaning exactly and appeal to the senses of sight, hearing, touch, taste, and smell?

DESCRIPTION IN PARAGRAPHS

Writing about Television

In the following paragraph written especially for *The Bedford Reader*, description works with narration to create suspense. Without even knowing the cause of the suspense, we gather tension from the details. Such a paragraph might pull us into an essay on the subject that is finally revealed only in the last sentence.

At 7:59 this Thursday night, a thick hush settles like fog inside the sweat-scented TV room of Harris Hall. First to arrive, freshman Lee Ann squashes down into the catbird seat in front of the screen. Soon she is flanked by roommates Lisa and Kate, silent, their mouths straight lines, their upturned faces lit by the nervous flicker of a car ad. To the left and right of the couch, Pete and Anse crouch on the floor, leaning forward like runners awaiting a starting gun. Behind them, stiff standees line up at attention. Farther back still, English majors and jocks compete for an unobstructed view. Fresh from class, shirttail flapping, arm crooking a bundle of books, Dave barges into the room demanding, "Has it started? Has it started yet?" He is shushed. Somebody shushes a popped-open can of Dr Pepper whose fizz is distractingly loud. What do these students so intently look forward to? At last it starts—TV's hottest reality show.

Dominant impression (not stated): tense expectation of something vital

Details (underlined) contribute to dominant impression

Organization proceeds from front of room (at TV) to back

Writing in an Academic Discipline

Description interprets a familiar painting in the following paragraph from a text on art history. The details "translate" the painting, creating a bridge between the reader and the text's reproduction of the great work.

While working on *The Battle of Anghiari*, Leonardo painted his most famous portrait, the *Mona Lisa*. The delicate *sfumato* already noted in the *Madonna of the Rocks* is here so perfected that it seemed miraculous to the artist's contemporaries. The forms are built from layers of glazes so gossamer-thin that the entire panel seems to glow with a gentle light from within. But the fame of the *Mona Lisa* comes not from this pictorial subtlety alone; even more intriguing is the psychological fascination of the sitter's personality. Why, among all the smiling faces ever painted, has this particular one been singled out as "mysterious"? Perhaps the reason is that, as a portrait, the picture does not fit our expectations. The features are too individual for Leonardo to have simply depicted an ideal type, yet the element of idealization is so strong that it blurs the sitter's character. Once again the artist has brought two opposites into harmonious balance. The smile, too, may be read in two ways: as the echo of a momentary mood, and as a timeless, symbolic expression (somewhat like the "Archaic smile" of the Greeks . . .). Clearly, the *Mona Lisa* embodies a quality of maternal tenderness which was to Leonardo the essence of womanhood. Even the landscape in the background, composed mainly of rocks and water, suggests elemental generative forces.

—H. W. Janson, *History of Art*

(Sfumato: soft gradations of light and dark)

Main idea (topic sentence) of the paragraph, supported by description of "pictorial subtlety" (above) and "psychological fascination" (below)

Details (underlined) contribute to dominant impression

DESCRIPTION IN A FIELD OBSERVATION

In many of your classes, particularly those in the social sciences, you will be asked to observe people or phenomena in particular settings and to describe what your senses perceive. A systematic observation may produce evidence for an ARGUMENT, as when a writer observes and describes the listlessness of kittens in an animal shelter to encourage support for a citywide spay-and-neuter program. Just as often, however, an observation results in an objective report from which readers draw their own conclusions from the information provided. Like any description, such a field report emphasizes details and uses concrete language to convey the writer's perceptions. Because the writer's purpose is to inform, the report takes a neutral, third-PERSON (*he, she, they*) point of view, uses unemotional language, and refrains from interpretation or opinion—or withholds such analysis for a separate section near the end.

For a psychology class in child development, Nick Fiorelli spent a morning in a local private preschool, observing the teachers' techniques and the children's behaviors and taking note of how they interacted with one another. The paragraphs below, excerpted from his final written report, describe both the classroom itself and some of the activities Fiorelli witnessed while he was there. The full report goes on to outline the educational philosophies and developmental theories that inform the school's approach, with additional examples and descriptions from Fiorelli's visit.

The preschool's Web site explains that it draws on elements of Waldorf, Montessori, Reggio Emillia, and other educational models. This background was evident in the large and colorful classroom, which included separate interest areas for different activities. The room was also open and well lit, with long windows that opened to a playground and an open lawn. The walls of the room were decorated with students' paintings and drawings. Colored rugs, floor tiles, or rubber mats indicated the boundaries of each activity area.

Background information sets the stage

Organization moves from the periphery to the center, then around the room's distinct areas

At first, the general atmosphere appeared noisy and unstructured, but a sense of order emerged within a few minutes of observation. At a large wooden art table, two students used safety scissors to cut shapes from large sheets of red construction paper. Behind them, a child in a red smock stood at a small wooden easel and painted with a large brush. Another strung multicolored beads on a string. Next to the art table, two children at a sensory station poured wet sand and rocks through

Dominant impression: structured creativity

a large funnel into a miniature sandbox, while a third filled a small glass tank with water from a blue enameled pail. A teacher moved between the two tables, encouraging the students and asking questions about their play. In the back of the room, at a literacy area with a thick blue rug and low yellow bookshelves, six students lolled on beanbag chairs, pillows, and a low brown couch, listening to a teacher read a story from an illustrated children's book. She paused on each page to help the children connect the pictures with the story.

Concrete details contribute to the dominant impression

BRAD MANNING

Brad Manning was born in Little Rock, Arkansas, in 1967 and grew up near Charlottesville, Virginia. He attended Harvard University, graduating in 1990 with a BA in history and religion. At Harvard he played intramural sports and wrote articles and reviews for the *Harvard Independent*. After graduation Manning wrote features and news stories for the *Charlotte Observer* and then studied law and medicine at the University of Virginia, graduating from law school in 1995 and completing his residency in psychiatry in 2007. He also studied child and family psychotherapy at the Tavistock Center in London. Now living in Charlottesville, Manning is a psychiatrist specializing in the treatment of children and adolescents.

Arm Wrestling with My Father

In this essay written for his freshman composition course, Manning explores his physical contact with his father over the years, perceiving gradual changes that are, he realizes, inevitable. For Manning, description provides a way to express his feelings about his father and to comment on relations between sons and fathers. In the essay after Manning's, Sarah Vowell uses description for similar ends, but her subject is the relationship between a daughter and her father.

Manning's essay has been published in a Harvard collection of students' writing; in *Student Writers at Work: The Bedford Prizes*; and in *Montage*, a collection of Russian and American stories published in Russian.

"Now you say when" is what he always said before an arm-wrestling match. 1 He liked to put the responsibility on me, knowing that he would always control the outcome. "When!" I'd shout, and it would start. And I would tense up, concentrating and straining and trying to push his wrist down to the carpet with all my weight and strength. But Dad would always win; I always had to lose. "Want to try it again?" he would ask, grinning. He would see my downcast eyes, my reddened, sweating face, and sense my intensity. And with squinting eyes he would laugh at me, a high laugh, through his perfect white teeth. Too bitter to smile, I would not answer or look at him, but I would just roll over on my back and frown at the ceiling. I never thought it was funny at all.

That was the way I felt for a number of years during my teens, after I 2 had lost my enjoyment of arm wrestling and before I had given up that same intense desire to beat my father. Ours had always been a physical relationship,

I suppose, one determined by athleticism and strength. We never communicated as well in speech or in writing as in a strong hug, battling to make the other gasp for breath. I could never find him at one of my orchestra concerts. But at my lacrosse games, he would be there in the stands, with an angry look, ready to coach me after the game on how I could do better. He never helped me write a paper or a poem. Instead, he would take me outside and show me a new move for my game, in the hope that I would score a couple of goals and gain confidence in my ability. Dad knew almost nothing about lacrosse and his movements were all wrong and sad to watch. But at those times I could just feel how hard he was trying to communicate, to help me, to show the love he had for me, the love I could only assume was there.

His words were physical. The truth is, I have never read a card or a letter   3
written in his hand because he never wrote to me. Never. Mom wrote me all the cards and letters when I was away from home. The closest my father ever came, that I recall, was in a newspaper clipping Mom had sent with a letter. He had gone through and underlined all the important words about the dangers of not wearing a bicycle helmet. Our communication was physical, and that is why we did things like arm wrestle. To get down on the floor and grapple, arm against arm, was like having a conversation.

This ritual of father-son competition in fact had started early in my life,   4
back when Dad started the matches with his arm almost horizontal, his wrist an inch from defeat, and still won. I remember in those battles how my tiny shoulders would press over our locked hands, my whole upper body pushing down in hope of winning that single inch from his calm, unmoving forearm. "Say when," he'd repeat, killing my concentration and causing me to squeal, "I did, I did!" And so he'd grin with his eyes fixed on me, not seeming to notice his own arm, which would begin to rise slowly from its starting position. My greatest efforts could not slow it down. As soon as my hopes had disappeared I'd start to cheat and use both hands. But the arm would continue to move steadily along its arc toward the carpet. My brother, if he was watching, would sometimes join in against the arm. He once even wrapped his little legs around our embattled wrists and pulled back with everything he had. But he did not have much and, regardless of the opposition, the man would win. My arm would lie at rest, pressed into the carpet beneath a solid, immovable arm. In that pinned position, I could only giggle, happy to have such a strong father.

My feelings have changed, though. I don't giggle anymore, at least not   5
around my father. And I don't feel pressured to compete with him the way I thought necessary for years. Now my father is not really so strong as he used to be and I am getting stronger. This change in strength comes at a time when I am growing faster mentally than at any time before. I am becoming less my father and more myself. And as a result, there is less of a need to be set apart

from him and his command. I am no longer a rebel in the household, wanting to stand up against the master with clenched fists and tensing jaws, trying to impress him with my education or my views on religion. I am no longer a challenger, quick to correct his verbal mistakes, determined to beat him whenever possible in physical competition.

I am not sure when it was that I began to feel less competitive with my father, but it all became clearer to me one day this past January. I was home in Virginia for a week between exams, and Dad had stayed home from work because the house was snowed in deep. It was then that I learned something I never could have guessed.   6

I don't recall who suggested arm wrestling that day. We hadn't done it for a long time, for months. But there we were, lying flat on the carpet, face to face, extending our right arms. Our arms were different. His still resembled a fat tree branch, one which had leveled my wrist to the ground countless times before. It was hairy and white with some pink moles scattered about. It looked strong, to be sure, though not so strong as it had in past years. I expect that back in his youth it had looked even stronger. In high school he had played halfback and had been voted "best-built body" of the senior class. Between college semesters he had worked on road crews and on Louisiana dredges. I admired him for that. I had begun to row crew in college and that accounted for some small buildup along the muscle lines, but it did not seem to be enough. The arm I extended was lanky and featureless. Even so, he insisted that he would lose the match, that he was certain I'd win. I had to ignore this, however, because it was something he always said, whether or not he believed it himself.   7

Our warm palms came together, much the same way we had shaken hands the day before at the airport. Fingers twisted and wrapped about once again, testing for a better grip. Elbows slid up and back making their little indentations on the itchy carpet. My eyes pinched closed in concentration as I tried to center as much of my thought as possible on the match. Arm wrestling, I knew, was a competition that depended less on talent and experience than on one's mental control and confidence. I looked up into his eyes and was ready. He looked back, smiled at me, and said softly (did he sound nervous?), "You say when."   8

It was not a long match. I had expected him to be stronger, faster. I was conditioned to lose and would have accepted defeat easily. However, after some struggle, his arm yielded to my efforts and began to move unsteadily toward the carpet. I worked against his arm with all the strength I could find. He was working hard as well, straining, breathing heavily. It seemed that this time was different, that I was going to win. Then something occurred to me, something unexpected. I discovered that I was feeling sorry for my father. I wanted to win but I did not want to see him lose.   9

It was like the thrill I had once experienced as a young boy at my grand-   10
father's lake house in Louisiana when I hooked my first big fish. There was
that sudden tug that made me leap. The red bobber was sucked down beneath
the surface and I pulled back against it, reeling it in excitedly. But when my
cousin caught sight of the fish and shouted out, "It's a keeper," I realized that
I would be happier for the fish if it were let go rather than grilled for dinner.
Arm wrestling my father was now like this, like hooking "Big Joe," the old fish
that Lake Quachita holds but you can never catch, and when you finally think
you've got him, you want to let him go, cut the line, keep the legend alive.

Perhaps at that point I could have given up, letting my father win. But it   11
was so fast and absorbing. How could I have learned so quickly how it would
feel to have overpowered the arm that had protected and provided for me all
of my life? His arms have always protected me and the family. Whenever I
am near him I am unafraid, knowing his arms are ready to catch me and keep
me safe, the way they caught my mother one time when she fainted halfway
across the room, the way he carried me, full grown, up and down the stairs
when I had mononucleosis, the way he once held my feet as I stood on his
shoulders to put up a new basketball net. My mother may have had the words
or the touch that sustained our family, but his were the arms that protected
us. And his were the arms now that I had pushed to the carpet, first the right
arm, then the left.

I might have preferred him to be always the stronger, the one who carries   12
me. But this wish is impossible now; our roles have begun to switch. I do not
know if I will ever physically carry my father as he has carried me, though I
fear that someday I may have that responsibility. More than once this year I
have hesitated before answering the phone late at night, fearing my mother's
voice calling me back to help carry his wood coffin. When I am home with
him and he mentions a sharp pain in his chest, I imagine him collapsing onto
the floor. And in that second vision I see me rushing to him, lifting him onto
my shoulders, and running.

A week after our match, we parted at the airport. The arm-wrestling   13
match was by that time mostly forgotten. My thoughts were on school. I had
been awake most of the night studying for my last exam, and by that morning I
was already back into my college-student manner of reserve and detachment.
To say goodbye, I kissed and hugged my mother and I prepared to shake my
father's hand. A handshake had always seemed easier to handle than a hug. His
hugs had always been powerful ones, intended I suppose to give me strength.
They made me suck in my breath and struggle for control, and the way he
would pound his hand on my back made rumbles in my ears. So I offered a
handshake; but he offered a hug. I accepted it, bracing myself for the impact.
Once our arms were wrapped around each other, however, I sensed a differ-

ent message. His embrace was softer, longer than before. I remember how it surprised me and how I gave an embarrassed laugh as if to apologize to anyone watching.

I got on the airplane and my father and mother were gone. But as the   14
plane lifted my throat was hurting with sadness. I realized then that Dad must have learned something as well, and what he had said to me in that last hug was that he loved me. Love was a rare expression between us, so I had denied it at first. As the plane turned north, I had a sudden wish to go back to Dad and embrace his arms with all the love I felt for him. I wanted to hold him for a long time and to speak with him silently, telling him how happy I was, telling him all my feelings, in that language we shared.

In his hug, Dad had tried to tell me something he himself had discovered.   15
I hope he tries again. Maybe this spring, when he sees his first crew match, he'll advise me on how to improve my stroke. Maybe he has started doing pushups to rebuild his strength and challenge me to another match—if this were true, I know I would feel less challenged than loved. Or maybe, rather than any of this, he'll just send me a card.

For a reading quiz and annotated links to further readings on fathers and sons, visit **bedfordstmartins.com/thebedfordreader**.

Journal Writing

Manning expresses conflicting feelings about his father. How do you respond to his conflict? When have you felt strongly conflicting emotions about a person or an event, such as a relative, friend, breakup, ceremony, move? Write a paragraph or two exploring your feelings. (To take your journal writing further, see "From Journal to Essay" on the next page.)

Questions on Meaning

1. In paragraph 3 Manning says that his father's "words were physical." What does this mean?
2. After his most recent trip home, Manning says, "I realized then that Dad must have learned something as well" (par. 14). What is it that father and son have each learned?

3. Manning says in the last paragraph that he "would feel less challenged than loved" if his father challenged him to a rematch. Does this statement suggest that he did not feel loved earlier? Why, or why not?
4. What do you think is Manning's PURPOSE in this essay? Does he want to express love for his father, or is there something more as well?

Questions on Writing Strategy

1. Why does Manning start his essay with a match that leaves him "too bitter to smile" and then move backward to earlier bouts of arm wrestling?
2. In the last paragraph Manning suggests that his father might work harder at competing with him and pushing him to be competitive, or he might just send his son a card. Why does Manning present both of these options? Are we supposed to know which will happen?
3. Explain the fishing ANALOGY Manning uses in paragraph 10.
4. **OTHER METHODS**   Manning's essay is as much a NARRATIVE as a description: The author gives brief stories, like video clips, to show the dynamic of his relationship with his father. Look at the story in paragraph 4. How does Manning mix elements of both methods to convey his powerlessness?

Questions on Language

1. Manning uses the word *competition* throughout this essay. Why is this a more accurate word than *conflict* to describe Manning's relationship with his father?
2. What is the EFFECT of "the arm" in this line from paragraph 4: "But the arm would continue to move steadily along its arc toward the carpet"?
3. In paragraph 9 Manning writes, "I wanted to win but I did not want to see him lose." What does this apparent contradiction mean?
4. If any of these words is unfamiliar, look it up in a dictionary: embattled (par. 4); dredges, crew (7); conditioned (9); mononucleosis (11).

Suggestions for Writing

1. **FROM JOURNAL TO ESSAY**   Expand your journal entry into a descriptive essay that brings to life your mixed feelings about a person or an event. Focus less on the circumstances and events than on emotions, both positive and negative.
2. Write an essay that describes your relationship with a parent or another close adult. You may want to focus on just one aspect of your relationship, or one especially vivid moment, in order to give yourself the space and time to build many sensory details into your description.
3. Arm wrestling is a highly competitive sport with a long history. Research the sport in the library or on the Internet. Then write a brief essay that traces its history and explains its current standing.
4. **CRITICAL WRITING**   In paragraph 12 Manning writes, "our roles have begun to switch." Does this seem like an inevitable switch, or one that this father and son have been working to achieve? Use EVIDENCE from Manning's essay to support

your answer. Also consider whether Manning and his father would respond the same way to this question.

5. **CONNECTIONS** Like "Arm Wrestling with My Father," the next essay, Sarah Vowell's "Shooting Dad," depicts a struggle for communication between child and parent. In an essay, COMPARE AND CONTRAST the two essays on this point. What impedes positive communication between the two authors and their fathers? In what circumstances are they able to communicate?

Brad Manning on Writing

For *The Bedford Reader,* Brad Manning offered some valuable concrete advice on writing as a student.

You hear this a lot, but writing takes a long time. For me, this is especially true. The only difference between the "Arm Wrestling" essay and all the other essays I wrote in college (and the only reason it's in this book and not thrown away) is that I rewrote it six or seven times over a period of weeks.

If I have something to write, I need to start early. In college, I had a bad habit of putting off papers until 10 PM the night before they were due and spending a desperate night typing whatever ideas the coffee inspired. But putting off papers didn't just lower my writing quality; it robbed me of a good time.

I like starting early because I can jot down notes over a stretch of days; then I type them up fast, ignoring typos; I print the notes with narrow margins, cut them up, and divide them into piles that seem to fit together; then it helps to get away for a day and come back all fresh so I can throw away the corny ideas. Finally, I sit on the floor and make an outline with all the cutouts of paper, trying at the same time to work out some clear purpose for the essay.

When the writing starts, I often get hung up most on trying to "sound" like a good writer. If you're like me and came to college from a shy family that never discussed much over dinner, you might think your best shot is to sound like a famous writer like T. S. Eliot and you might try to sneak in words that aren't really your own like *ephemeral* or *the lilacs smelled like springtime.* But the last thing you really want a reader thinking is how good or bad a writer you are.

Also, in the essay on arm wrestling, I got hung up thinking I had to make my conflict with my father somehow "universal." So in an early draft I wrote in a classical allusion—Aeneas lifting his old father up onto his shoulders and carrying him out of the burning city of Troy.[1] I'd read that story in high school and guessed one classical allusion might make the reader think I knew a lot more. But Aeneas didn't help the essay much, and I'm glad my teacher warned me off trying to universalize. He told me to write just what was true for me.

But that was hard, too, and still is—especially in the first draft. I don't know anyone who enjoys the first draft. If you do, I envy you. But in my early drafts, I always get this sensation like I have to impress somebody and I end up overanalyzing the effects of every word I am about to write. This self-consciousness may be unavoidable (I get self-conscious calling L. L. Bean to order a shirt), but, in this respect, writing is great for shy people because you can edit all you want, all day long, until it finally sounds right. I never feel that I am being myself until the third or fourth draft, and it's only then that it gets personal and starts to be fun.

When I said that putting off papers robbed me of a good time, I really meant it. Writing the essay about my father turned out to be a high point in my life. And on top of having a good time with it, I now have a record of what happened. And my ten-month-old son, when he grows up, can read things about his grandfather and father that he'd probably not have learned any other way.

For Discussion

1. What did Manning miss by writing his college papers at the last minute?
2. Why does Manning say that "writing is great for shy people"? Have you ever felt that you could express yourself in writing better than in speech?

---

[1] In the *Aeneid*, by the Roman poet Vergil (70–19 BC), the mythic hero Aeneas escapes from the city of Troy when it is sacked by the Greeks and goes on to found Rome.—EDS.

SARAH VOWELL

Sarah Vowell is best known for the smart, witty spoken essays she delivers on public radio. Born in Muskogee, Oklahoma, in 1969, Vowell grew up in Oklahoma and Montana. After graduating from Montana State University, she earned an MA in art history and criticism from the School of the Art Institute of Chicago. Radio has played a large part in Vowell's life: She was a DJ for her college station in Montana; published a day-by-day diary of one year spent listening to the radio, *Radio On: A Listener's Diary* (1996); and worked as a contributing editor for *This American Life* on Public Radio International from 1996 to 2008. She has appeared on television talk shows as well, including David Letterman's and Jon Stewart's. Many of Vowell's essays from *This American Life* appear in her book *Take the Cannoli: Stories from the New World* (2000). Her books *Partly Cloudy Patriot* (2002), *Assassination Vacation* (2005), and *The Wordy Shipmates* (2008) all adopt a witty, unexpected perspective on American history. Vowell also works with 826NYC, a nonprofit writing center for children and teenagers, and she was the voice of the young superhero Violet in the animated film *The Incredibles* (2004). She lives in New York City and occasionally writes guest columns for *Salon, Time, San Francisco Weekly,* and the *New York Times.*

Shooting Dad

Vowell read "Shooting Dad," in slightly different form, on *This American Life* and then included it in *Take the Cannoli.* Like the previous essay, Brad Manning's "Arm Wrestling with My Father," this one explores the relationship between child and father. Engaged in a lifelong opposition to her father, Vowell sees their differences in terms of the Constitution: She cherishes the First Amendment's guarantee of freedom of religion, speech, and assembly, while he holds fast to the Second Amendment's guarantee of the right to bear arms. Then one day, with a jolt, Vowell realizes how much they have in common.

If you were passing by the house where I grew up during my teenage years 1 and it happened to be before Election Day, you wouldn't have needed to come inside to see that it was a house divided. You could have looked at the Democratic campaign poster in the upstairs window and the Republican one in the downstairs window and seen our home for the Civil War battleground it was. I'm not saying who was the Democrat or who was the Republican — my father or I — but I will tell you that I have never subscribed to *Guns & Ammo,* that

I did not plaster the family vehicle with National Rifle Association stickers, and that hunter's orange was never my color.

About the only thing my father and I agree on is the Constitution, though I'm partial to the First Amendment, while he's always favored the Second.

I am a gunsmith's daughter. I like to call my parents' house, located on a quiet residential street in Bozeman, Montana, the United States of Firearms. Guns were everywhere: the so-called pretty ones like the circa 1850 walnut muzzleloader hanging on the wall, Dad's clients' fixer-uppers leaning into corners, an entire rack right next to the TV. I had to move revolvers out of my way to make room for a bowl of Rice Krispies on the kitchen table.

I was eleven when we moved into that Bozeman house. We had never lived in town before, and this was a college town at that. We came from Oklahoma—a dusty little Muskogee County nowhere called Braggs. My parents' property there included an orchard, a horse pasture, and a couple of acres of woods. I knew our lives had changed one morning not long after we moved to Montana when, during breakfast, my father heard a noise and jumped out of his chair. Grabbing a BB gun, he rushed out the front door. Standing in the yard, he started shooting at crows. My mother sprinted after him screaming, "Pat, you might ought to check, but I don't think they do that up here!" From the look on his face, she might as well have told him that his American citizenship had been revoked. He shook his head, mumbling, "Why, shooting crows is a national pastime, like baseball and apple pie." Personally, I preferred baseball and apple pie. I looked up at those crows flying away and thought, I'm going to like it here.

Dad and I started bickering in earnest when I was fourteen, after the 1984 Democratic National Convention. I was so excited when Walter Mondale chose Geraldine Ferraro as his running mate that I taped the front page of the newspaper with her picture on it to the refrigerator door. But there was some sort of mysterious gravity surge in the kitchen. Somehow, that picture ended up in the trash all the way across the room.

Nowadays, I giggle when Dad calls me on Election Day to cheerfully inform me that he has once again canceled out my vote, but I was not always so mature. There were times when I found the fact that he was a gunsmith horrifying. And just *weird*. All he ever cared about were guns. All I ever cared about was art. There were years and years when he hid out by himself in the garage making rifle barrels and I holed up in my room reading Allen Ginsberg poems, and we were incapable of having a conversation that didn't end in an argument.

Our house was partitioned off into territories. While the kitchen and the living room were well within the DMZ,[1] the respective work spaces governed

---

[1] Abbreviation for *demilitarized zone*, an area off-limits to war making. —Eds.

by my father and me were jealously guarded totalitarian states in which each of us declared ourselves dictator. Dad's shop was a messy disaster area, a labyrinth of lathes. Its walls were hung with the mounted antlers of deer he'd bagged, forming a makeshift museum of death. The available flat surfaces were buried under a million scraps of paper on which he sketched his mechanical inventions in blue ballpoint pen. And the floor, carpeted with spiky metal shavings, was a tetanus shot waiting to happen. My domain was the cramped, cold space known as the music room. It was also a messy disaster area, an obstacle course of musical instruments—piano, trumpet, baritone horn, valve trombone, various percussion doodads (bells!), and recorders. A framed portrait of the French composer Claude Debussy was nailed to the wall. The available flat surfaces were buried under piles of staff paper, on which I penciled in the pompous orchestra music given titles like "Prelude to the Green Door" (named after an O. Henry short story by the way, not the watershed porn flick *Behind the Green Door*) I started writing in junior high.

It has been my experience that in order to impress potential suitors, skip   8 the teen Debussy anecdotes and stick with the always attention-getting line "My dad makes guns." Though it won't cause the guy to like me any better, it will make him handle the inevitable breakup with diplomacy—just in case I happen to have any loaded family heirlooms lying around the house.

But the fact is, I have only shot a gun once and once was plenty. My twin   9 sister, Amy, and I were six years old—six—when Dad decided that it was high time we learned how to shoot. Amy remembers the day he handed us the gun for the first time differently. She liked it.

Amy shared our father's enthusiasm for firearms and the quick-draw   10 cowboy mythology surrounding them. I tended to daydream through Dad's activities—the car trip to Dodge City's Boot Hill, his beloved John Wayne Westerns on TV. My sister, on the other hand, turned into Rooster Cogburn Jr., devouring Duke movies with Dad. In fact, she named her teddy bear Duke, hung a colossal John Wayne portrait next to her bed, and took to wearing one of those John Wayne shirts that button on the side. So when Dad led us out to the backyard when we were six and, to Amy's delight, put the gun in her hand, she says she felt it meant that Daddy trusted us and that he thought of us as "big girls."

But I remember holding the pistol only made me feel small. It was so heavy   11 in my hand. I stretched out my arm and pointed it away and winced. It was a very long time before I had the nerve to pull the trigger and I was so scared I had to close my eyes. It felt like it just went off by itself, as if I had no say in the matter, as if the gun just had this *need*. The sound it made was as big as God. It kicked little me back to the ground like a bully, like a foe. It hurt. I don't know if I dropped it or just handed it back over to my dad, but I do know that I never wanted to touch another one again. And, because I believed in the devil, I did what my mother told me to do every time I felt an evil presence. I looked at the smoke and whispered under my breath, "Satan, I rebuke thee."

It's not like I'm saying I was traumatized. It's more like I was decided. Guns: 12 Not For Me. Luckily, both my parents grew up in exasperating households where children were considered puppets and/or slaves. My mom and dad were hell-bent on letting my sister and me make our own choices. So if I decided that I didn't want my father's little death sticks to kick me to the ground again, that was fine with him. He would go hunting with my sister, who started calling herself "the loneliest twin in history" because of my reluctance to engage in family activities.

Of course, the fact that I was allowed to voice my opinions did not mean 13 that my father would silence his own. Some things were said during the Reagan administration that cannot be taken back. Let's just say that I blamed Dad for nuclear proliferation and Contra aid. He believed that if I had my way, all the guns would be confiscated and it would take the commies about fifteen minutes to parachute in and assume control.

We're older now, my dad and I. The older I get, the more I'm interested in 14 becoming a better daughter. First on my list: Figure out the whole gun thing.

Not long ago, my dad finished his most elaborate tool of death yet. A can- 15 non. He built a nineteenth-century cannon. From scratch. It took two years.

My father's cannon is a smaller replica of a cannon called the Big Horn 16 Gun in front of Bozeman's Pioneer Museum. The barrel of the original has been filled with concrete ever since some high school kids in the '50s pointed it at the school across the street and shot out its windows one night as a prank. According to Dad's historical source, a man known to scholars as A Guy at the Museum, the cannon was brought to Bozeman around 1870, and was used by local white merchants to fire at the Sioux and Cheyenne Indians who blocked their trade access to the East in 1874.

"Bozeman was founded on greed," Dad says. The courthouse cannon, he 17 continues, "definitely killed Indians. The merchants filled it full of nuts, bolts, and chopped-up horseshoes. Sitting Bull could have been part of these engagements. They definitely ticked off the Indians, because a couple of years later, Custer wanders into them at Little Bighorn. The Bozeman merchants were out to cause trouble. They left fresh baked bread with cyanide in it on the trail to poison a few Indians."

Because my father's sarcastic American history yarns rarely go on for long 18 before he trots out some nefarious ancestor of ours — I come from a long line of moonshiners, Confederate soldiers, murderers, even Democrats — he cracks that the merchants hired some "community-minded Southern soldiers from North Texas." These soldiers had, like my great-great-grandfather John Vowell, fought under pro-slavery guerrilla William C. Quantrill. Quantrill is most famous for riding into Lawrence, Kansas, in 1863 flying a black flag and commanding his men pharaohlike to "kill every male and burn down every house."

"John Vowell," Dad says, "had a little rep for killing people." And since 19 he abandoned my great-grandfather Charles, whose mother died giving birth to him in 1870, and wasn't seen again until 1912, Dad doesn't rule out the possibility that John Vowell could have been one of the hired guns on the Bozeman Trail. So the cannon isn't just another gun to my dad. It's a map of all his obsessions—firearms, certainly, but also American history and family history, subjects he's never bothered separating from each other.

After tooling a million guns, after inventing and building a rifle barrel 20 boring machine, after setting up that complicated shop filled with lathes and blueing tanks and outmoded blacksmithing tools, the cannon is his most ambitious project ever. I thought that if I was ever going to understand the ballistic bee in his bonnet, this was my chance. It was the biggest gun he ever made and I could experience it and spend time with it with the added bonus of not having to actually pull a trigger myself.

I called Dad and said that I wanted to come to Montana and watch him 21 shoot off the cannon. He was immediately suspicious. But I had never taken much interest in his work before and he would take what he could get. He loaded the cannon into the back of his truck and we drove up into the Bridger Mountains. I was a little worried that the National Forest Service would object to us lobbing fiery balls of metal onto its property. Dad laughed, assuring me that "you cannot shoot fireworks, but this is considered a firearm."

It is a small cannon, about as long as a baseball bat and as wide as a coffee 22 can. But it's heavy—110 pounds. We park near the side of the hill. Dad takes his gunpowder and other tools out of this adorable wooden box on which he has stenciled "PAT G. VOWELL CANNONWORKS." Cannonworks: So that's what NRA members call a metal-strewn garage.

Dad plunges his homemade bullets into the barrel, points it at an embank- 23 ment just to be safe, and lights the fuse. When the fuse is lit, it resembles a cartoon. So does the sound, which warrants Ben Day dot[2] words along the lines of ker-pow! There's so much Fourth of July smoke everywhere I feel compelled to sing the national anthem.

I've given this a lot of thought—how to convey the giddiness I felt when 24 the cannon shot off. But there isn't a sophisticated way to say this. It's just really, really cool. My dad thought so, too.

---

[2] Ben Day dots are colored dots in various sizes, used in comics to intensify words for actions and loud sounds. —EDS.

Sometimes, I put together stories about the more eccentric corners of the   25
American experience for public radio. So I happen to have my tape recorder
with me, and I've never seen levels like these. Every time the cannon goes off,
the delicate needles which keep track of the sound quality lurch into the bad,
red zone so fast and so hard I'm surprised they don't break.

The cannon was so loud and so painful, I had to touch my head to make   26
sure my skull hadn't cracked open. One thing that my dad and I share is that
we're both a little hard of hearing—me from Aerosmith, him from gunsmith.

He lights the fuse again. The bullet knocks over the log he was aiming at.   27
I instantly utter a sentence I never in my entire life thought I would say. I tell
him, "Good shot, Dad."

Just as I'm wondering what's coming over me, two hikers walk by. Appar-   28
ently, they have never seen a man set off a homemade cannon in the middle
of the wilderness while his daughter holds a foot-long microphone up into the
air recording its terrorist boom. One hiker gives me a puzzled look and asks,
"So you work for the radio and that's your dad?"

Dad shoots the cannon again so that they can see how it works. The   29
other hiker says, "That's quite the machine you got there." But he isn't talking about the cannon. He's talking about my tape recorder and my microphone—which is called a *shotgun* mike. I stare back at him, then I look over
at my father's cannon, then down at my microphone, and I think, Oh. My.
God. My dad and I are the same person. We're both smart-alecky loners with
goofy projects and weird equipment. And since this whole target practice out-
ing was my idea, I was no longer his adversary. I was his accomplice. What's
worse, I was liking it.

I haven't changed my mind about guns. I can get behind the cannon   30
because it is a completely ceremonial object. It's unwieldy and impractical,
just like everything else I care about. Try to rob a convenience store with
this 110-pound Saturday night special, you'd still be dragging it in the door
Sunday afternoon.

I love noise. As a music fan, I'm always waiting for that moment in a song   31
when something just flies out of it and explodes in the air. My dad is a one-
man garage band, the kind of rock 'n' roller who slaves away at his art for
no reason other than to make his own sound. My dad is an artist—a pretty
driven, idiosyncratic one, too. He's got his last *Gesamtkunstwerk*[3] all planned
out. It's a performance piece. We're all in it—my mom, the loneliest twin in
history, and me.

When my father dies, take a wild guess what he wants done with his ashes.   32
Here's a hint: It requires a cannon.

---

[3] German, "total work of art," specifically a work that seeks to unify all the arts.—Eds.

"You guys are going to love this," he smirks, eyeballing the cannon. "You   33
get to drag this thing up on top of the Gravellies on opening day of hunting
season. And looking off at Sphinx Mountain, you get to put me in little paper
bags. I can take my last hunting trip on opening morning."

I'll do it, too. I will have my father's body burned into ashes. I will pack   34
these ashes into paper bags. I will go to the mountains with my mother, my
sister, and the cannon. I will plunge his remains into the barrel and point it
into a hill so that he doesn't take anyone with him. I will light the fuse. But I
will not cover my ears. Because when I blow what used to be my dad into the
earth, I want it to hurt.

---

*For a reading quiz, sources on Sarah Vowell, and annotated links to further readings
on fathers and daughters, visit **bedfordstmartins.com/thebedfordreader**.*

Journal Writing

How do you respond to Vowell's eccentric, even obsessive, father? Do you basically
come to sympathize with him or not? Who in your life has quirky behavior that you
find charming or annoying or a little of both? Write a paragraph or two about this
person, focusing on his or her particular habits or obsessions. (To take your journal
writing further, see "From Journal to Essay" on the next page.)

Questions on Meaning

1. In her opening sentence, Vowell describes growing up in "a house divided." What
   does she mean? Where in the essay does she make the divisions in her household
   explicit?
2. Why, given Vowell's father's love of guns, was it "fine" with him that his daughter decided as a young child that she wanted nothing to do with guns (par. 12)?
   What does this attitude suggest about his character?
3. What motivated Vowell to come home to watch her father shoot off his homemade cannon? Why, given her aversion to guns, does she regard this cannon
   positively?
4. What do paragraphs 18–19, about her father's family history, contribute to Vowell's
   portrait of him?
5. What seems to be Vowell's PURPOSE in writing here? What DOMINANT IMPRESSION
   of her father does she create?

Questions on Writing Strategy

1. Why is the anecdote Vowell relates in paragraph 4 an effective introduction both to her father and to their relationship?
2. Paragraph 8 is sort of an aside in this essay—not entirely on the main topic. What purpose does it serve?
3. What does Vowell's final sentence mean? Do you find it a satisfying conclusion to her essay? Why, or why not?
4. **OTHER METHODS**   Throughout her essay, Vowell relies on COMPARISON AND CONTRAST to express her relationship with her father (and with her twin sister in pars. 9–12). Find examples of comparison and contrast. Why is the method important to the essay? How does the method help reinforce Vowell's main point about her relationship with her father?

Questions on Language

1. In paragraph 4 Vowell shows her father "mumbling" that "shooting crows is a national pastime, like baseball and apple pie," while she notes that she herself "preferred baseball and apple pie." How does the language here illustrate IRONY?
2. Pick out five or six concrete and specific words in paragraph 7. What do they accomplish?
3. In paragraph 9 Vowell writes, "My twin sister, Amy, and I were six years old— six—when Dad decided that it was high time we learned how to shoot. Amy remembers the day he handed us the gun for the first time differently. She liked it." What are the EFFECTS of the repetition of the word *six* in the first sentence and of the three-word final sentence?
4. Study the FIGURES OF SPEECH Vowell uses in paragraph 11 to describe the gun she shot. What is their effect?
5. Consult a dictionary if you need help in defining the following: muzzleloader (par. 3); revoked (4); bickering (5); partitioned, respective, totalitarian, labyrinth, lathes, pompous (7); colossal (10); traumatized (12); proliferation, confiscated (13); cyanide (17); nefarious, moonshiners, guerrilla, pharaohlike (18); ballistic (20); giddiness (24); adversary, accomplice (29); unwieldy (30); idiosyncratic (31).

Suggestions for Writing

1. **FROM JOURNAL TO ESSAY**   Based on your journal writing, compose an essay that uses description to portray your subject and his or her personal quirks. Be sure to include specific incidents you've witnessed and specific details to create a vivid dominant impression of the person. You may, like Vowell, focus on the evolution of your relationship with this person—whether mainly positive or mainly negative.
2. Conflict between generations is common in many families—whether over music, clothing, hairstyles, friends, or larger issues of politics, values, and religion. Write an essay about generational conflicts you have experienced in your family or that

you have witnessed in other families. Are such conflicts inevitable? How can they be resolved?

3. Gun ownership is a divisive issue in the United States. Research and explain the main arguments for and against gun control. Whatever your own position, strive for an objective presentation, neither pro nor con.

4. **CRITICAL WRITING**   Vowell's essay divides into several fairly distinct sections: paragraphs 1–4, 5–7, 8, 9–12, 13, 14–31 (which includes an aside in pars. 17–19), and 32–34. In an essay, analyze what happens in each of these sections. How do they fit together to help develop Vowell's dominant impression? How does the relative length of each section contribute to your understanding of her evolving relationship with her father?

5. **CONNECTIONS**   Both Vowell and Brad Manning, in "Arm Wrestling with My Father" (p. 163), describe their fathers. In an essay, examine words Manning and Vowell use to convey their feelings of distance from their fathers and also their feelings of closeness. Use quotations from both essays to support your analysis.

Sarah Vowell on Writing

Writing for both radio and print, Sarah Vowell has discovered differences in listening and reading audiences. On *Transom.org*'s Internet discussion board, she explained how she writes differently for the two media.

[S]ometimes I feel like I'm so much more manipulative on the radio. I know how to use my voice to make you feel a certain way. And that's not writing — that's acting. I get tired of acting sometimes. Which is why it's nice to be able to go back to the cold old page. Also, real time is an unforgiving medium. I still maintain a little academic streak, and any time I read something on the air or out loud, I have to cut back on the abstract, thinky bits. I have to read a story out loud in front of an audience this week and I had to lop it off by half, to prune it of its dull information and, sometimes, its very point. Those things for you the listener, are bonuses — the listener doesn't get as much filler, the listener gets to feel more. Readers are more patient. . . .

The only real drawback I think from moving between verbal and print media is punctuation. I'm working on another book right now, and there are so many things I want to say that I have to normalize on the page because I do not think in complete, fluid sentences. I seem to think in stopgaps and asides. Which the listener doesn't notice. But the reader, I think, becomes antsy when there are too many dashes and parentheses. So that is a constant battle — (dash!) trying to retain my casual, late twentieth-century (it's where I'm from), American-girl cadences, but without driving the reader crazy with a bunch of marks all over the place. Also, I love the word *and*. And I start too many sentences with *and*. Again, no one notices out loud because that's normative speech. But do that too much on the page and it's distracting and stupid.

For Discussion

1. What does Vowell mean by having to "normalize [her thoughts] on the page"?
2. What difficulties or rewards have you encountered trying to put ideas into written words for others to read?
3. In your experience as a speaker and a writer, what are the advantages of each form of communication? What are the disadvantages of each?

ELIZABETH GILBERT

Elizabeth Gilbert was born in Waterbury, Connecticut, in 1969 and grew up on her family's Christmas-tree farm. She studied political science at New York University and, after graduating in 1991, took up travel, odd jobs, and constant writing. Many of her experiences on the road found their way into *Pilgrims* (1997), Gilbert's debut collection of short stories. She also wrote a coming-of-age novel, *Stern Men* (2000); a biography of adventurer Eustace Conway, *The Last American Man* (2002); and a *GQ* article about working in a Manhattan bar that became the basis for the movie *Coyote Ugly*. She is best known, however, for her travel memoir *Eat, Pray, Love: One Woman's Search for Everything across Italy, India, and Indonesia* (2006). The book—which chronicles a year-long quest for indulgence, spirituality, and romance—was translated into thirty languages, earned Gilbert a spot on *Time* magazine's list of the most influential people in the world, and was made into a motion picture. In Gilbert's most recent work, *Committed: A Skeptic Makes Peace with Marriage* (2010), the once-divorced author grapples with the institution of marriage as she prepares to wed a man she met in Indonesia. She lives and writes in rural New Jersey.

The Best Pizza in the World

In this excerpt from *Eat, Pray, Love*, Gilbert depicts an urge to travel that compels her—even while she's already living abroad—to embark on a day trip to Naples, Italy. With her trademark humor and affability, Gilbert describes the "dangerous and cheerful nuthouse" of the city in vivid detail, through a series of impressions, observations, and imagined dialog. As she does throughout her book, Gilbert gives a sense of the disorienting but thrilling experience of stepping outside the familiar.

I met a young Australian girl last week who was backpacking through Europe for the first time in her life. I gave her directions to the train station. She was heading up to Slovenia, just to check it out. When I heard her plans, I was stricken with such a dumb spasm of jealousy, thinking, *I want to go to Slovenia! How come I never get to travel anywhere?* 1

Now, to the innocent eye it might appear that I already *am* traveling. And longing to travel while you are already traveling is, I admit, a kind of greedy madness. It's kind of like fantasizing about having sex with your favorite movie star while you're having sex with your *other* favorite movie star. But the fact that this girl asked directions from me (clearly, in her mind, a civilian) suggests that I am not technically traveling in Rome, but living here. However temporary it may be, I am a civilian. When I ran into the girl, in fact, I was 2 just on my way to pay my electricity bill, which is not something travelers worry about. Traveling-to-a-place energy and living-in-a-place energy are two fundamentally different energies, and something about meeting this Australian girl on her way to Slovenia just gave me such a jones to hit the road.

And that's why I called my friend Sofie and said, "Let's go down to Naples   3
for the day and eat some pizza!"

Immediately, just a few hours later, we are on the train, and then—like   4
magic—we are there. I instantly love Naples. Wild, raucous, noisy, dirty, balls-out Naples. An anthill inside a rabbit warren, with all the exoticism of a Middle Eastern bazaar and a touch of New Orleans voodoo. A tripped-out, dangerous and cheerful nuthouse. My friend Wade came to Naples in the 1970s and was mugged . . . in a *museum*. The city is all decorated with the laundry that hangs from every window and dangles across every street; everybody's fresh-washed undershirts and brassieres flapping in the wind like Tibetan prayer flags. There is not a street in Naples in which some tough little kid in shorts and mismatched socks is not screaming up from the sidewalk to some other tough little kid on a rooftop nearby. Nor is there a building in this town that doesn't have at least one crooked old woman seated at her window, peering suspiciously down at the activity below.

The people here are so insanely psyched to be from Naples, and why   5
shouldn't they be? This is a city that gave the world pizza *and* ice cream. The Neapolitan women in particular are such a gang of tough-voiced, loud-mouthed, generous, nosy dames, all bossy and annoyed and right up in your face and just trying to friggin' *help* you for chrissake, you dope—*why they gotta do everything around here?* The accent in Naples is like a friendly cuff on the ear. It's like walking through a city of short-order cooks, everybody hollering at the same time. They still have their own dialect here, and an ever-changing liquid dictionary of local slang, but somehow I find that the Neapolitans are the easiest people for me to understand in Italy. Why? Because they *want* you to understand, damn it. They talk loud and emphatically, and if you can't understand what they're actually saying out of their mouths, you can usually pick up the inference from the gesture. Like that punk little grammar-school girl on the back of her older cousin's motorbike, who flipped me the finger *and* a charming smile as she drove by, just to make me understand, "Hey, no hard feelings, lady. But I'm only seven, and I can already tell you're a complete moron, but that's cool—I think you're halfway OK despite yourself and I kinda like your dumb-ass face. We both know you would love to be me, but sorry—you can't. Anyhow, here's my middle finger, enjoy your stay in Naples, and *ciao!*"

As in every public space in Italy, there are always boys, teenagers and   6
grown men playing soccer, but here in Naples there's something extra, too. For

instance, today I found kids—I mean, a group of eight-year-old boys—who had gathered up some old chicken crates to create makeshift chairs and a table, and they were playing *poker* in the piazza with such intensity I feared one of them might get shot.

[My friends] Giovanni and Dario . . . are originally from Naples. I cannot   7
picture it. I cannot imagine shy, studious, sympathetic Giovanni as a young boy amongst this—and I don't use the word lightly—mob. But he is Neapolitan, no question about it, because before I left Rome he gave me the name of a pizzeria in Naples that I had to try, because, Giovanni informed me, it sold the best pizza in Naples. I found this a wildly exciting prospect, given that the best pizza in Italy is from Naples, and the best pizza in the world is from Italy, which means that this pizzeria must offer . . . I'm almost too superstitious to say it . . . *the best pizza in the world?* Giovanni passed along the name of the place with such seriousness and intensity, I almost felt I was being inducted into a secret society. He pressed the address into the palm of my hand and said, in gravest confidence, "Please go to this pizzeria. Order the margherita pizza with double mozzarella. If you do not eat this pizza when you are in Naples, please lie to me later and tell me that you did."

So Sofie and I have come to Pizzeria da Michele, and these pies we have   8
just ordered—one for each of us—are making us lose our minds. I love my pizza so much, in fact, that I have come to believe in my delirium that my pizza might actually love me, in return. I am having a relationship with this pizza, almost an affair. Meanwhile, Sofie is practically in tears over hers, she's having a metaphysical crisis about it, she's begging me, "Why do they even *bother* trying to make pizza in Stockholm? Why do we even bother eating food at *all* in Stockholm?"

Pizzeria da Michele is a small place with only two rooms and one non-   9
stop oven. It's about a fifteen-minute walk from the train station in the rain, don't even worry about it, just go. You need to get there fairly early in the day because sometimes they run out of dough, which will break your heart. By 1:00 PM, the streets outside the pizzeria have become jammed with Neapolitans trying to get into the place, shoving for access like they're trying to get space on a lifeboat. There's not a menu. They have only two varieties of pizza here—regular and extra cheese. None of this new age southern California olives-and-sun-dried-tomato wannabe pizza twaddle. The dough, it takes me half my meal to figure out, tastes more like Indian *nan* than like any pizza dough I ever tried. It's soft and chewy and yielding, but incredibly thin. I always thought we only had two choices in our lives when it came to pizza crust—thin and crispy, or thick and doughy. How was I to have known there could be a crust in this world that was thin *and* doughy? Holy of holies! Thin,

doughy, strong, gummy, yummy, chewy, salty pizza paradise. On top, there is a sweet tomato sauce that foams up all bubbly and creamy when it melts the fresh buffalo mozzarella, and the one sprig of basil in the middle of the whole deal somehow infuses the entire pizza with herbal radiance, much the same way one shimmering movie star in the middle of a party brings a contact high of glamour to everyone around her. It's technically impossible to eat this thing, of course. You try to take a bite off your slice and the gummy crust folds, and the hot cheese runs away like topsoil in a landslide, makes a mess of you and your surroundings, but just deal with it.

The guys who make this miracle happen are shoveling the pizzas in and out   10
of the wood-burning oven, looking for all the world like the boilermen in the belly of a great ship who shovel coal into the raging furnaces. Their sleeves are rolled up over their sweaty forearms, their faces red with exertion, one eye squinted against the heat of the fire and a cigarette dangling from the lips. Sofie and I each order another pie—another whole pizza each—and Sofie tries to pull herself together, but really, the pizza is so good we can barely cope.

A word about my body. I am gaining weight every day, of course. I am doing   11
rude things to my body here in Italy, taking in such ghastly amounts of cheese and pasta and bread and wine and chocolate and pizza dough. (Elsewhere in Naples, I'd been told, you can actually get something called chocolate pizza. What kind of nonsense is that? I mean, later I did go find some, and it's delicious, but honestly—*chocolate pizza*?) I'm not exercising, I'm not eating enough fiber, I'm not taking any vitamins. In my real life, I have been known to eat organic goat's milk yoghurt sprinkled with wheat germ for breakfast. My real-life days are long gone. Back in America, my friend Susan is telling people I'm on a "No Carb Left Behind" tour. But my body is being such a good sport about all this. My body is turning a blind eye to my misdoings and my over-indulgences, as if to say, "OK, kid, live it up, I recognize that this is just temporary. Let me know when your little experiment with pure pleasure is over, and I'll see what I can do about damage control."

Still, when I look at myself in the mirror of the best pizzeria in Naples, I   12
see a bright-eyed, clear-skinned, happy and healthy face. I haven't seen a face like that on me for a long time.

"Thank you," I whisper. Then Sofie and I run out in the rain to look for   13
pastries.

*For a reading quiz and annotated links to further readings on Italian food and culture, visit **bedfordstmartins.com/thebedfordreader**.*

Journal Writing

What food or drink holds a special place in your memory? In your journal, write down as many sensory details about this food or drink as you can. (To take your journal writing further, see "From Journal to Essay" on the next page.)

Questions on Meaning

1. What DOMINANT IMPRESSION does Gilbert create of Naples and of the pizza she ate there? Does she state this impression in a THESIS STATEMENT or is it implied?
2. What would you say is Gilbert's PURPOSE in this essay?
3. What distinction does Gilbert make between traveling to a new place and living somewhere temporarily? Into which category does she put herself, and why?
4. In paragraph 8, Gilbert comments that her friend Sofie is "having a metaphysical crisis" over her pizza. What does she mean? How does Sofie's reaction mirror the point of Gilbert's essay?
5. In what ways does pizza serve as a SYMBOL for Gilbert?

Questions on Writing Strategy

1. Most of Gilbert's essay moves in spatial order, from the streets of Naples to a particular pizzeria to the table at which she and her companion ate. Paragraph 7, however, jumps to another city, where Gilbert explains that a friend gave her the name of the pizzeria and begged her to go there. Why do you think Gilbert placed this paragraph in the middle of her essay, instead of at the beginning?
2. Comment on the IRONY in the last three paragraphs of the essay.
3. As the essay's headnote mentions, Gilbert included this piece in a travel memoir titled *Eat, Pray, Love*. What ASSUMPTIONS does she seem to make about the interests of her readers and their knowledge of Italian culture? Where in the essay do you see EVIDENCE of these assumptions?
4. **OTHER METHODS** Where does Gilbert use CAUSE AND EFFECT to explain something to readers? What does the method contribute to her essay?

Questions on Language

1. Gilbert uses an abundance of FIGURES OF SPEECH in this essay, most notably *metaphor* and *simile*, but also *hyperbole*. Find at least two or three examples of each and comment on their effectiveness.
2. How would you characterize Gilbert's DICTION and TONE? Is her language appropriate? Why, or why not?
3. What is the EFFECT of the imagined dialog in paragraph 5? Why do you suppose Gilbert places quotation marks around the young girl's words but not the women's?

4. Consult a dictionary if you need help defining the following words: jones (par. 2); raucous, warren, exoticism, bazaar (4); Neapolitan, cuff, inference (5); piazza (6); inducted, gravest (7); delirium (8); twaddle, *nan* (9); ghastly (11).

Suggestions for Writing

1. **FROM JOURNAL TO ESSAY**   In an essay, describe the food or drink you wrote about in your journal, but also do more: Like Gilbert, focus not just on the food or beverage itself but also on its larger context. Why is it so special? What does it represent to you? Be sure to infuse your writing with vivid IMAGES evoking concrete sensory experiences.

2. In an essay that combines NARRATION and description, write about a memorable experience you have had in your travels. What prompted you to take the trip? Was the place anything like you expected? What about it stands out in your memory, and why? Try to use colorful FIGURES OF SPEECH and specific details to help readers share in your experience.

3. **CRITICAL WRITING**   Closely examine how Gilbert appeals to each of the five senses in her descriptions of Naples and its pizza. In an essay, choose three to five particularly effective sensory IMAGES and explain both their purpose and their effect.

4. **CONNECTIONS**   Both Gilbert and Amy Tan, in "Fish Cheeks" (p. 116), write about the emotions they felt while consuming a particular meal. Write an essay in which you COMPARE AND CONTRAST the ways the two writers describe food and how each writer uses food to make a larger point about desire.

WILLIAM LEAST HEAT-MOON

Born William Lewis Trogdon in 1939, William Least Heat-Moon grew up in Kansas City, Missouri, and changed his name to honor his father's Osage ancestry. He studied literature and photojournalism at the University of Missouri, earning two bachelor's degrees, a master's, and a doctorate between 1961 and 1978. Shortly after completing his studies, Heat-Moon indulged a whim and set off on a three-month journey along the back roads of America. The result was *Blue Highways: A Journey into America* (1982), a travelog based on his journals and interviews with hundreds of locals. Heat-Moon went on to write *PrairyErth* (1991), an examination of the history and people of Chase County, Kansas; *River-Horse: The Logbook of a Boat across America* (1999), his chronicle of a long river voyage; *Columbus in the Americas* (2002), a critical biography of the explorer; and, most recently, *Roads to Quoz: An American Mosey* (2008), a quest for out-of-the-ordinary sights and experiences. Often compared with Jack Kerouac, John Steinbeck, and Henry David Thoreau, Heat-Moon is known for his sharp descriptions of the natural world and his portraiture of small-town America. He lives in Columbia, Missouri, on an old tobacco farm.

Dance of the Hobs

During their travels, Heat-Moon and his wife (whom he calls "Q") sought to witness the Quapaw Ghost Light—a mysterious glow that reportedly hovers above a local highway between Missouri and Oklahoma. Popular explanations for the apparition include, as Heat-Moon puts it, "yarns of a vicious, captured Civil War sergeant—vengefully decapitated by being stood in front of a cannon—who spends eternity hunting his head; of a lady walking moonless nights with a ball of fire where her noddle should be; of a miner following his shaking carbide lamp in quest of a lost you-name-it." Given such fanciful folklore, Heat-Moon didn't expect to find anything. In "Dance of the Hobs," abridged from a chapter in *Roads to Quoz,* he conveys his delight in being wrong.

Perhaps somewhere in Missouri or Oklahoma exists a local newspaper or 1 magazine never to have carried an item about the Quapaw Light, more commonly known in the old mining area . . . as the Hornet Spook Light. . . . Reports, both in print and from people I spoke to, claimed the phantasm sometimes appeared briefly or not at all, and on other occasions would shine till dawn. Generally, it had a constancy rather alien in the realm of ghosts. "It's reliable enough, especially on cloudy nights," a librarian told me, "and I never heard of it harming anybody, unless scaring the dickens out of you is harmful—you know, out there in the dark, getting a whack put on your ticker."

In both Jasper and Ottawa counties, I came upon nobody unaware of the   2
thing, about half saying they'd seen it, and most of them believing it not yet
properly explained by science. But one fellow, ignoring the many photographs
of it, called it "the Hornet Spoof Light." I asked had he seen it, and he replied,
"How does a sane person see what isn't there?"

Based upon no physical evidence except declarations written and spoken,   3
and in spite of the sanity question, I still believed in the possibility of something spectral: not a specter perhaps but maybe a manifestation of a spectrum out on the wooded slope above the Spring River on the western edge of
the Ozark Plateau. I further believed Q and I would encounter nothing, yet
we nevertheless went forth, interested not so much in debunking as merely
observing. . . . [We] headed south as the sky was clearing just enough to reveal
a frail, crescent moon setting beyond the prairie of eastern Oklahoma. The
Devil's Promenade . . . was a wooded vale dropping down to the Spring River
to the west. The lane was less forested than formerly but yet woodsy and
remote enough, despite a couple of tumbledown dwellings and a farm near the
river, to create good darkness for a light show. Still, steady electrification had
recently caused a few visitors — those managing to find the proper lane — to
watch some electrical radiant and entirely miss the Ghost Light. Or so we
were told.

The customary accounts concurred on the phenomenon earlier appearing   4
in another location not far distant, but for the past half century it had taken
its shine to E-50. "She jiggles around a little, but she don't go straggling across
the county," said an old fellow tottering through the library. "She's a homebody. You just got to sit real quiet like you was in Granny's parlor."

At Halloween, he'd often known the road to be lined with cars, but on   5
the March evening Q and I drove to the hollow, no one else was around, and
our expectation was tempered only by a sense we'd not be lucky enough to
glimpse the whatever. I rolled us along slowly over the new asphalt running as
straight west as a surveyor's transit can lay a lane down, the engineered perfection having relief only in its rise and fall over low hills of blackjack oaks.
Melodious calls of toads roused the darkness, and the damp air smelled of
spring. . . .

Right after we crossed the Missouri line and entered the Promenade, a   6
small light appeared in the distance on the left of the road. My anticipation
apparently got the better of me, and I blurted out something to which Q said,
"You're seeing some kind of vehicle way ahead of us," and a pickup did pass by
soon after. I pulled to the side, shut off the engine, got out of the car. In a darkness so deep I could see down only to my knees, I began walking as if I were
wading the night. When I returned, my sudden emergence from the thick ob-
scurity caused Q to jump.

In a whisper, as if the Powers of Spectral Illumination have ears, she asked   7
for explanations I'd read that afternoon: ball lightning, will-o'-the-wisp, marsh
gas mine gas, fox fire, Saint Elmo's fire, sunspots, glowing minerals, static electricity, ionized plasma; headlights from automobiles, billboards, a water tower,
a landing field, a farm; and, of course, those ectoplasmic souls in search of
craniums—theirs or yours. . . .

Thirty minutes passed, and no emanation of any sort appeared, so I drove   8
back eastward to a higher spot with a longer view. A van had arrived, with
four intent faces staring into the west. I stopped far enough away not to block
their view, then walked to them. A woman of middle years and three teenage
girls glanced at me only to ascertain I was possessed of a more or less standard
head lacking any luminescence and in the accustomed location.

Had they seen it? Without looking my way, the woman murmured slowly,   9
uneasily, "It's there right now."

I turned to the west. Blackness. Soot, pitch, ebony, the inside of a crow.   10
Otherwise, zilch. She whispered, eyes still fixed forward, "In thirty years, this
is the best I've ever seen it." I looked again. Nothing. Spoof Light.

Then, as if I'd suddenly regained lost vision, the dark got punctured—a   11
white-hot poker thrust through a black tent. The whiteness rose above the distant road, waxed brighter, dimmed, then again brighter, its edge tinged blood-
red. A not-of-this-Earth gleaming seemed to float a mile or two away, slightly
shifting laterally, like an animal moving its head side to side as it fixes on its
quarry. Great Caesar's Ghost!

. . . I was at last seeing the Quapaw Light! I started off down the black   12
road to tell Q, but I couldn't keep from turning around to assure that nothing
was coming up from behind. Holy Willie! A Nodgort[1] had found a crack in
my rationality, and the pesky hob was dancing, mocking. I forced myself to
stand still for a moment to prove reason yet prevailed, even if a bit equivocally. *There*, I thought, *that's a moment, that's enough.* But I had to restrain an
impulse to quickstep back to the safety of the car. (Oh, reader, do you shake
your head? Well, consider this: A jokester jumping out of the scrub at that
moment could have put a whack on my ticker.)

"What's wrong?" Q asked, and I nodded westward, and she looked that   13
way. "What am I supposed to be seeing?" The road was black again. "I don't
see any—oh! Is that it?" It was it: waxing, pendulating, waning, throwing out
a bubble of redness, sucking it back in, vanishing only to show itself again,
making a tiny zig to set up a zag. . . .

The thing glimmered and shimmered, twinkled and blinked, flickered   14
and fluttered, glistened and winked. We stared so long I began to believe our

---

[1] "Trogdon," the author's former last name, spelled backward.—Eds.

eyes were playing tricks, so we corroborated what the little dazzler was doing: Tell me what you're seeing, I said, and Q answered, "It just moved left." Yes. "Coming back the other way." Yes. "Getting reddish again." Yep. "Oops, just disappeared—no, it's back—and brighter." Exactly.

It was doing the pixy peekaboo. "The thing's playful," Q said. "No wonder   15 people are fond of it—it's a Tinker Bell." In my satanic voice I rasped, No, my pretty—mistake not a tool of the Devil. Then, changing to a falsetto, I repeated the librarian's wisecrack: "Around here, we take it lightly."

Spooky, as it's sometimes called, resembled an evening star low in the sky   16 on a clear night, but it upended astrophysics in its shifting from a red dwarf to a white giant, although it was never bigger than a bright planet seen with moderate-power binoculars.

A farm truck came from behind and passed, and we watched to see whether   17 it would spook the Light, but the globe bravely continued its performance. I started the engine and went slowly forward to get closer; I was an infant reaching out to touch the first star he ever sees. At our approach, the gleaming kept its distance as does a rainbow or mirage, then it winked out. We turned around to go back to where we'd been, and again there it was, hanging above the lane. If we couldn't close the distance on it, then that eliminated explanations like will-o'-the-wisp or lights from a tower—anything with a fixed location. Q: "It's not a figment of the imagination. It's actually there—or somewhere. Something's somewhere. It's real as a rainbow. Maybe not as beautiful, but a lot more lively."

We gaped at it for nearly two hours because it was what we had wanted   18 to find: an authentic optical phenomenon reportedly unexplained by science. A merry spectral puzzle. Observing it was like stepping back into the Dark Ages when nature was full of phantasmagoria, when mysteries overwhelmed explications and ignorance transcended illumination, a time when superstition could extinguish enlightenment, when priestly obfuscations manipulated folk into blind faiths where charms and potions, spells and incantations, holy relics and amulets, were defenses against hobgoblins going thumpity-bump in the night or rising in the woods to flicker their mischief. . . .

The Light was less spectacular than suggested by the most fanciful claims,   19 so much so that had someone not initially observed it prior to the electrification of the county, the phenomenon might not be noticed today. In fact, when we arrived, I *had* seen it, only to be convinced by Q that it was a moving vehicle. As we were leaving, she said, "It's my first UFO," adding before I could cavil, "Unexplained Flickering Orb."

The Quapaw Ghost Light is remarkable but not incredible, modest but   20 worth its myth, possessed of the power of the peculiar, and among the many phantasms of the Ozarks, Spooky is one of the few to come forth predictably and allow examination. You can't hear, touch, smell, or taste it, but you can't doubt seeing it if your patience allows.

> For a reading quiz and annotated links to further readings on ghost lights and other urban legends, visit **bedfordstmartins.com/thebedfordreader**.

Journal Writing

Every region of the United States has its share of mysteries and urban legends like the flickering orb Heat-Moon seeks out: gravity hills, hitchhiking ghosts, buried treasures, and so forth. Think of one such local story you've heard. Do you believe it? Why, or why not? Why do you think people tell such tales? (To take your journal writing further, see "From Journal to Essay" on the next page.)

Questions on Meaning

1. Why is Heat-Moon fascinated by the idea of the Quapaw Light? What does it represent to him?
2. What does Heat-Moon mean when he says he hoped to see "not a specter perhaps but maybe a manifestation of a spectrum" (par. 3)?
3. What do you think the light looks like, based on Heat-Moon's description? What DOMINANT IMPRESSION of the phenomenon does he create?
4. How would you describe Heat-Moon's PURPOSE in this essay?
5. Does "Dance of the Hobs" have a THESIS? What is Heat-Moon's point?

Questions on Writing Strategy

1. Does Heat-Moon ASSUME that his readers believe in ghosts and apparitions, or does he expect that they will be skeptical? How does he ensure that readers won't write him off as crazy?
2. In paragraph 3, Heat-Moon says that he was "interested not so much in debunking as merely observing," suggesting that he will describe his experience with the objectivity of a scientist. Is this, in fact, what he does? Would you say that his description is mainly OBJECTIVE or SUBJECTIVE? Why?
3. Point to a few sentences in the essay that make particularly effective use of CONCRETE details and FIGURES OF SPEECH to describe Heat-Moon's experience of searching for and seeing the light.
4. In his first paragraph, Heat-Moon quotes a librarian, who warns of "getting a whack put on your ticker." What does that mean? Where in his essay does Heat-Moon return to this notion, and what is the effect of the repetition?

5. **OTHER METHODS** "Dance of the Hobs" is as much NARRATION as it is description. How does Heat-Moon use dialog to structure his story and add interest?

Questions on Language

1. Consult a dictionary if you are unsure of the meaning of any of the following: phantasm, constancy (par. 1); spoof (2); spectral, promenade, vale (3); concurred (4); tempered, surveyor (5); ectoplasmic, craniums (7); emanation, ascertain, luminescence (8); pitch (10); waxed, laterally, quarry (11); hob, equivocally, scrub (12); pendulating, waning (13); corroborated (14); falsetto (15); will-o'-the-wisp (17); gaped, phantasmagoria, explications, transcended, extinguish, enlightenment, obfuscations, amulets, hobgoblins (18); cavil (19). Why do you suppose Heat-Moon uses so many difficult words in paragraph 18 in particular?
2. How would you describe Heat-Moon's DICTION? What does his language contribute to the overall effectiveness of his essay?
3. Why do you suppose Heat-Moon chose to capitalize "Powers of Spectral Illumination" (par. 7) and "Light" (19)?
4. What is the effect of the first sentence of paragraph 14?

Suggestions for Writing

1. **FROM JOURNAL TO ESSAY** Building on your journal entry and using Heat-Moon's essay and your own experiences as EVIDENCE, write an essay that explores the function of urban legends. Where do they come from? What purpose do they serve in contemporary American culture? How do they compare to other forms of mythology?
2. Answer the question posed by Heat-Moon's informant in paragraph 2: "How does a sane person see what isn't there?" Have you ever seen something you couldn't explain? In an essay, consider how expectation and context might shape a person's perception of reality. Draw on Heat-Moon's experience as well as your own.
3. In paragraph 7, Heat-Moon lists many explanations for ghost lights — "ball lightning, will-o'-the-wisp, marsh gas, mine gas, fox fire, Saint Elmo's fire, sunspots, glowing minerals, static electricity, ionized plasma; headlights from automobiles, billboards, a water tower, a landing field, a farm; and, of course, those ectoplasmic souls in search of craniums." Choose three or four of these explanations and learn a little about the theories they represent. Then, write a CAUSE-AND-EFFECT analysis that considers the plausibility of each explanation in turn, concluding with the one you find most reasonable or, if none of them satisfy you, proposing a theory of your own.
4. **CRITICAL WRITING** Although a nonfiction essay, "Dance of the Hobs" is told like a ghost story. ANALYZE how Heat-Moon crafts his tale. How does he move from one stage of his quest to the next? Does the story seem to build in a particular way? What strategies does the author use to build suspense?
5. **CONNECTIONS** Heat-Moon is clearly exhilarated by the sight of the Quapaw Light. Annie Dillard, in "The Chase" (p. 121), also writes about the thrill of an unexpected encounter. In an essay, COMPARE the strategies these writers use to

convey a sense of excitement and joy. How is the narrative voice, pace, and TONE of each essay suitable for the story being told?

William Least Heat-Moon on Writing

As a seasoned interviewer, William Least Heat-Moon has developed a careful ear for narrative. In a 1991 conversation with Daniel Bourne for *Artful Dodge*, he describes the creative challenges he faced while writing *PrairyErth*, a nonfiction study of one Midwestern county based on extensive interviews and research.

I had all the agonies and problems of the novelist as well as all the agonies and problems of the writer of nonfiction. I had continually to be truthful and accurate, the fundamental problem of the nonfiction writer, but I also had to create characters who had a dimension—who had three dimensions to them—the problem of the novelist. I also had to find issues that would carry a "plot" in a book in which there is no plot other than perhaps the motif of the continuing journey. I had to keep the reader moving in a plotless land. . . . Like a novelist, I had to create setting, introduce people, make them alive, and pull the reader into it all. I also felt I had the problems of a poet: to compress and evoke. All those challenges nearly did me in. Whether I met them or not, I'm not the one to say, but I tried to meet them all. . . .

There was also this: I went into a land where I was a stranger, an outsider, knew nothing about it, and I had to become something of an authority on each topic I faced. What did I know about breeding Herefords? I had to learn. What did I know about the root system of big bluestem, a prairie grass? I had to find out. What did I know about the father of the county, Sam Wood? Every topic I took, I had to become the master of, I thought, before I could write it. At least I tried to become the master of it.

For Discussion

1. According to Heat-Moon, in what ways is writing nonfiction similar to writing novels or poetry?
2. Have you ever had the experience of having to "become the master of" an unfamiliar topic in order to write about it? If so, what advantages and disadvantages did you encounter in the process of tackling the unknown?

JOYCE CAROL OATES

One of America's most respected and prolific contemporary authors, Joyce Carol Oates was born in 1938 in Lockport, New York. After graduating from Syracuse University in 1960, she earned a master's degree from the University of Wisconsin. In 1963 she published her first book, a collection of short stories, and she has published an average of two books a year since then. (To the charge that she publishes too much, Oates replies that her critics may be "secretly afraid that someone will accuse them of having done too little with their lives.") With the novel *them* (1969), Oates became one of the youngest writers to receive the National Book Award for fiction. Other notable novels include *Wonderland* (1971), *Black Water* (1992), *Blonde* (2000), and, most recently, *A Fair Maiden* (2010). Oates has also written more than a dozen volumes of poetry, a score of plays, and many works of nonfiction, including literary criticism and a study of boxing. In almost every novel, short story, poem, play, literary analysis, or essay, Oates remains, she says, "concerned with only one thing: the moral and social conditions of my generation." Since 1978 Oates has taught writing and literature at Princeton University.

Edward Hopper's *Nighthawks*, 1942

First published in Oates's poetry collection *The Time Traveler* (1989), this poem responds to a well-known painting by the American artist Edward Hopper (1882–1967). The painting, *Nighthawks*, is reproduced on the facing page, both in full view and in detail.

> The three men are fully clothed, long sleeves,
> even hats, though it's indoors, and brightly lit,
> and there's a woman. The woman is wearing
> a short-sleeved red dress cut to expose her arms,
> a curve of her creamy chest; she's contemplating   5
> a cigarette in her right hand, thinking that
> her companion has finally left his wife but
> can she trust him? Her heavy-lidded eyes,
> pouty lipsticked mouth, she has the redhead's
> true pallor like skim milk, damned good-looking   10
> and she guesses she knows it but what exactly
> has it gotten her so far, and where?—he'll start
> to feel guilty in a few days, she knows
> the signs, an actual smell, sweaty, rancid, like
> dirty socks; he'll slip away to make telephone calls   15

Edward Hopper, American, 1882–1967, *Nighthawks* (full painting and detail), 1942, oil on canvas, 84.1 × 152.4 cm, Friends of American Art Collection, 1942.51. The Art Institute of Chicago. Photography © The Art Institute of Chicago.

and she swears she isn't going to go through that
again, isn't going to break down crying or begging
nor is she going to scream at him, she's finished
with all that. And he's silent beside her,
not the kind to talk much but he's thinking   20
thank God he made the right move at last,
he's a little dazed like a man in a dream—
is this a dream?—so much that's wide, still,
mute, horizontal, and the counterman in white,
stooped as he is and unmoving, and the man   25
on the other stool unmoving except to sip
his coffee; but he's feeling pretty good,
it's primarily relief, this time he's sure
as hell going to make it work, he owes it to her
and to himself, Christ's sake. And she's thinking   30
the light in this place is too bright, probably
not very flattering, she hates it when her lipstick
wears off and her makeup gets caked, she'd like
to use a ladies' room but there isn't one here
and Jesus how long before a gas station opens?—   35
it's the middle of the night and she has a feeling
time is never going to budge. This time
though she isn't going to demean herself—
he starts in about his wife, his kids, how
he let them down, they trusted him and he let   40
them down, she'll slam out of the goddamned room
and if he calls her *Sugar* or *Baby* in that voice,
running his hands over her like he has the right,
she'll slap his face hard, *You know I hate that: Stop!*
And he'll stop. He'd better. The angrier   45
she gets the stiller she is, hasn't said a word
for the past ten minutes, not a strand
of her hair stirs, and it smells a little like ashes
or like the henna she uses to brighten it, but
the smell is faint or anyway, crazy for her   50
like he is, he doesn't notice, or mind—
burying his hot face in her neck, between her cool
breasts, or her legs—wherever she'll have him,
and whenever. She's still contemplating
the cigarette burning in her hand,   55

the counterman is still stooped gaping
at her, and he doesn't mind that, why not,
as long as she doesn't look back, in fact
he's thinking he's the luckiest man in the world
so why isn't he happier?   60

For a reading quiz, sources on Joyce Carol Oates, and annotated links to further readings on Edward Hopper and reproductions of his paintings, visit bedfordstmartins.com/thebedfordreader.

Journal Writing

In this poem Oates describes what she sees in Hopper's painting and also what she imagines, particularly about the woman. Most of us have unobtrusively observed strangers in a public place and imagined what they were thinking or what was going on between them. Write a paragraph or two on why such observation can be interesting or what it can (or can't) reveal. (To take your journal writing further, see "From Journal to Essay" on the next page.)

Questions on Meaning

1. What story does Oates imagine about the couple in *Nighthawks*? How are the man's and the woman's thoughts different?
2. Line 23 of the poem asks, "*is* this a dream?" Who is posing this question? What about the painting is dreamlike?
3. Throughout the poem, Oates emphasizes the silence and stillness of the scene in the coffee shop—for instance, "The angrier / she gets the stiller she is, hasn't said a word / for the past ten minutes" (lines 45–47). What meanings about the painting and the people in it might Oates be emphasizing?

Questions on Writing Strategy

1. Where in the poem does Oates use CONCRETE language to describe what can actually be seen in the painting, as opposed to what she imagines? How does she use the former to support the latter? What does the mixture suggest about Oates's PURPOSE?
2. The thoughts of the woman include some vivid sensory images. What are some examples? How do these thoughts contrast with the man's?

3. What techniques of sentence structure does Oates use in lines 12–19 and 30–45 to suggest the woman's rising anger?
4. **OTHER METHODS** Where does Oates use NARRATION in the poem? Where does she imply a narrative? Why is narration important to her analysis of Hopper's painting?

Questions on Language

1. Oates uses just a few words that might be unfamiliar. Make sure you know the meanings of contemplating (line 5); rancid (14); budge (37); demean (38); henna (49).
2. The man's and woman's thoughts are peppered with strong language that some might find offensive. What does this suggest about how Oates sees the characters?
3. In lines 27–28 Oates writes that the man is "feeling pretty good, / primarily relief." How does the word "relief" undercut the notion of "feeling pretty good"?

Suggestions for Writing

1. **FROM JOURNAL TO ESSAY** Find a public place where you can observe strangers unobtrusively from a distance—a park, for example, or a plaza, campus quad, dining hall, restaurant, bus, train. Take notes about what you observe—what your subject or subjects look like, how they behave, how they interact with each other. Then write an essay based on your notes that incorporates both actual description of your subjects and what the details lead you to imagine the subjects are thinking to themselves and saying to each other. Make sure the link between actual and imaginary is clear to your readers.
2. In a local gallery or museum, in a library art book, or on a Web site such as *WebMuseum* (*ibiblio.org/wm/paint*), find a painting that seems to you particularly intriguing or appealing. Then write a prose essay or a poem that expresses the painting's appeal to you. You may but need not imitate Oates by focusing on the thoughts of any figures in the painting. Describe the details of the painting and how they work together to create meaning for you. If you write a poem, don't worry about the technical aspects of poetry (meter, rhyme, and the rest). Think instead about your choice of words and IMAGES, building the poem through description.
3. **CRITICAL WRITING** Throughout her poem, Oates interweaves description of the painting and its figures with what she imagines the figures are thinking. Mark each kind of material in the poem, and then analyze the shifts from one to the other. How does Oates make readers aware that she is moving from one to the other? Are the shifts always clear? If not, are the blurrings deliberate or a mistake? What do you think of this technique overall?
4. **CONNECTIONS** In "But What Do You Mean?" (p. 435), Deborah Tannen outlines differences in the ways women and men communicate. Read that essay, and ANALYZE which of the differences seem to apply to Hopper's woman and man, either as Oates imagines them or as you see them. In an essay, explain how Tannen might view each as typifying his or her gender.

Joyce Carol Oates on Writing

For a 1997 book titled *Introspections: American Poets on One of Their Own Poems,* Joyce Carol Oates did us the valuable service of writing an essay about her poem "Edward Hopper's *Nighthawks,* 1942." She tells us why and how the painting sparked her own work of imagination.

The attempt to give concrete expression to a very amorphous impression is the insurmountable difficulty in painting.

These words of Edward Hopper's apply to all forms of art, of course. Certainly to poetry. How to evoke, in mere words, the powerful, inchoate flood of emotions that constitute "real life"? How to take the reader into the poet's innermost self, where the poet's language becomes the reader's, if only for a quicksilver moment? This is the great challenge of art, which even to fail in requires faith.

Insomniac nights began for me when I was a young teenager. Those long, lonely stretches of time when no one else in the house was awake (so far as I knew); the romance of solitude and self-sufficiency in which time seems not to pass or passes so slowly it will never bring dawn.

Always there was an air of mystery in the insomniac night. What profound thoughts and visions came to me! How strangely detached from the day-self I became! Dawn brought the familiar world, and the familiar self; a "self" that was obliged to accommodate others' expectations, and was, indeed, defined by others, predominantly adults. *Yes but you don't know me,* I would think by day, in adolescent secrecy and defiance. *You don't really know me!*

Many of Edward Hopper's paintings evoke the insomniac's uncanny vision, none more forcefully than *Nighthawks,* which both portrays insomniacs and evokes their solitude in the viewer. In this famous painting, "reality" has undergone some sort of subtle yet drastic alteration. The immense field of detail that would strike the eye has been reduced to smooth, streamlined surfaces; people and objects are enhanced, as on a lighted stage; not life but a nostalgia for life, a memory of life, is the true subject. Men and women in Hopper's paintings are somnambulists, if not mannequins, stiffly posed, with faces of the kind that populate our dreams, at which we dare not look too closely for fear of seeing the faces dissolve.

Here is, not the world, but a memory of it. For all dreams are memory: cobbled-together sights, sounds, impressions, snatches of previous experience.

The dream-vision is the perpetual present, yet its contents relate only to the past.

There is little of Eros in Hopper's puritanical vision, *Nighthawks* being the rare exception. The poem enters the painting as a way of animating what cannot be animated; a way of delving into the painting's mystery. *Who are these people, what has brought them together, are they in fact together?* At the time of writing the poem I hadn't read Gail Levin's definitive biography of Hopper, and did not know how Hopper had made himself into the most methodical and premeditated of artists, continuously seeking, with his wife Jo (who would have posed for the redheaded nighthawk), scenes and tableaux to paint. Many of Hopper's canvases are elaborately posed, and their suggestion of movie stills is not accidental. This is a visual art purposefully evoking narrative, or at least the opening strategies of narrative, in which a scene is "set," "characters" are presented, often in ambiguous relationships.

Nighthawks is a work of silence. Here is an Eros of stasis, and of melancholy. It is an uncommonly beautiful painting of stark, separate, sculpted forms, in heightened juxtapositions, brightly lit and yet infinitely mysterious. The poem slips into it with no transition, as we "wake" in a dream, yearning to make the frozen narrative come alive; but finally thwarted by the painting's measured void of a world, in which silence outweighs the human voice, and the barriers between human beings are impenetrable. So the poem ends as it begins, circling upon its lovers' obsessions, achieving no crisis, no confrontation, no epiphany, no release, time forever frozen in the insomniac night.

For Discussion

1. For Oates, as well as for Hopper, what is the "great challenge of art"?
2. Why, according to Oates, did she write a poem about Hopper's painting?
3. Why is the poem circular, ending where it began?

ADDITIONAL WRITING TOPICS

Description

1. This is an in-class writing experiment. Describe another person in the room so clearly and unmistakably that when you read your description aloud, your subject will be recognized. (Be OBJECTIVE. No insulting descriptions, please!)
2. Write a paragraph describing one subject from *each* of the following categories. It will be up to you to make the general subject refer to a particular person, place, or thing. Write at least one paragraph as an objective description and at least one as a SUBJECTIVE description.

PERSON

A friend or roommate
A typical hip-hop, jazz, or
   country musician
One of your parents
An elderly person you know
A prominent politician
A historical figure

THING

A car
A dentist's drill
A painting or photograph
A foggy day
A season of the year
A musical instrument

PLACE

An office
A classroom
A college campus
A vacation spot
A hospital emergency room
A forest

3. In a brief essay, describe your ideal place—perhaps an apartment, a dorm room, a vacation spot, a restaurant, a gym, a store, a garden, a dance club or other kind of club. With concrete details, try to make the ideal seem actual.

Narration and Description

4. Use a combination of NARRATION and description to develop any one of the following topics:

Your first day on the job
Your first day at college
Returning to an old neighborhood
Getting lost
A brush with a celebrity
Delivering bad (or good) news

LOW-ENERGY DRINKS

LeLIEVRE

6

EXAMPLE

Pointing to Instances

◀ **Examples in a cartoon**

This cartoon by Glen Le Lievre, first published in *The New Yorker*, uses the method of example in a complex way. Most simply, the drawings propose instances of the general category stated in the title—imaginary "low-energy drinks." At the same time, the humor of the examples comes from their contrast with real caffeine-laced high-energy drinks such as Xtreme Shock Fruit Punch, Jolt Cola, Zippfizz Liquid Shot, and AMP High Energy Overdrive. Whom are these drinks marketed to? (Consider visiting a grocery store or gas station minimart to see some samples up close.) Whom does their marketing ignore? How would you express Le Lievre's general idea in this cartoon?

THE METHOD

"There have been many women runners of distinction," a writer begins, and quickly goes on, "among them Joan Benoit, Grete Waitz, Florence Griffith Joyner, and Marion Jones."

You have just seen examples at work. An EXAMPLE (from the Latin *exemplum*: "one thing selected from among many") is an instance that reveals a whole type. By selecting an example, a writer shows the nature or character of the group from which it is taken. In a written essay, examples will often serve to illustrate a general statement, or GENERALIZATION. Here, for instance, the writer Linda Wolfe makes a point about the food fetishes of Roman emperors (Domitian and Claudius ruled in the first century AD).

> The emperors used their gastronomical concerns to indicate their contempt of the country and the whole task of governing it. Domitian humiliated his cabinet by forcing them to attend him at his villa to help solve a serious problem. When they arrived he kept them waiting for hours. The problem, it finally appeared, was that the emperor had just purchased a giant fish, too large for any dish he owned, and he needed the learned brains of his ministers to decide whether the fish should be minced or whether a larger pot should be sought. The emperor Claudius one day rode hurriedly to the Senate and demanded they deliberate the importance of a life without pork. Another time he sat in his tribunal ostensibly administering justice but actually allowing the litigants to argue and orate while he grew dreamy, interrupting the discussions only to announce, "Meat pies are wonderful. We shall have them for dinner."

Wolfe might have allowed the opening sentence of her paragraph—the TOPIC SENTENCE—to remain a vague generalization. Instead, she supports it with three examples, each a brief story of an emperor's contemptuous behavior. With these examples, Wolfe not only explains and supports her generalization but also animates it.

The method of giving examples—of illustrating what you're saying with a "for instance"—is not merely helpful to all kinds of writing; it is indispensable. Writers who bore us, or lose us completely, often have an ample supply of ideas; their trouble is that they never pull their ideas down out of the clouds. A dull writer, for instance, might declare, "The emperors used food to humiliate their governments," and then, instead of giving examples, go on, "They also manipulated their families," or something—adding still another large, unillustrated idea. Specific examples are *needed* elements in effective prose. Not only do they make ideas understandable, but they also keep readers awake. (The previous paragraphs have tried—by giving examples from Linda Wolfe and from "a dull writer"—to illustrate this point.)

THE PROCESS

The Generalization and the Thesis

Examples illustrate a generalization, such as Linda Wolfe's opening statement about the Roman emperors. Any example essay is bound to have such a generalization as its THESIS, expressed in a THESIS STATEMENT. Here are two examples from the essays in this chapter:

> Sometimes I think we would be better off [in dealing with social problems] if we forgot about the broad strokes and concentrated on the details.
> —Anna Quindlen, "Homeless"

> That first encounter, and those that followed, signified that a vast, unnerving gulf lay between nighttime pedestrians—particularly women—and me.
> —Brent Staples, "Black Men and Public Space"

The thesis statement establishes the backbone, the central idea, of an essay developed by example. Then the specifics bring the idea down to earth for readers.

The Examples

An essay developed by example will often start with an example or two. That is, you'll see something—a man pilfering a quarter for bus fare from a child's Kool-Aid stand, a friend dating another friend's fiancé (or fiancée)—and your observation will suggest a generalization (perhaps a statement about how people mishandle ethical dilemmas). But a mere example or two probably won't demonstrate your generalization for readers and thus won't achieve your PURPOSE. For that you'll need a range of instances.

Where do you find more? In anything you know—or care to learn. Start close to home. Seek examples in your own immediate knowledge and experience. Explore your conversations with others, your studies, and the storehouse of information you have gathered from books, newspapers, radio, TV, and the Internet as well as from popular hearsay: proverbs and sayings, popular songs, bits of wisdom you've heard voiced in your family.

Now and again, you may feel an irresistible temptation to make up an example out of thin air. This procedure is risky, but with imagination it can work wonderfully. When Henry David Thoreau, in *Walden*, attacked Americans' smug pride in the achievements of nineteenth-century science and industry, he wanted to illustrate that kind of invention or discovery "which distracts our attention from serious things." Two decades before the invention of the telephone, Thoreau made up the example of a transatlantic speaking tube and what it might convey: "We are eager to tunnel under the Atlantic and bring the Old World some weeks nearer to the New; but perchance the first news that will leak through into the broad, flapping American ear will be that the Princess Adelaide has the whooping cough." (Thoreau would be appalled at what we know of the British Royal Family via just the sort of communication he imagined.)

A hypothetical example can work if, like Thoreau's, it is fresh and apt; but an example from fact or experience is likely to carry more weight. Suppose you have to write about the benefits—any benefits—that recent science has conferred upon the nation. You might imagine one such benefit: the prospect of one day being able to vacation in outer space and drift about in free-fall like a soap bubble. That imagined benefit would be all right, but it is obviously a conjecture that you dreamed up without going to the library. Do a little digging on the Internet or in recent books and magazines. Your reader will feel better informed to be told that science—specifically, the NASA space program—has produced useful inventions. You add:

> Among these are the smoke detector, originally developed as Skylab equipment; the inflatable air bag to protect drivers and pilots, designed to cushion astronauts in splashdowns; a walking chair that enables paraplegics to mount stairs and travel over uneven ground, derived from the moonwalkers' surface buggy; the technique of cryosurgery, the removal of cancerous tissue by fast freezing.

By using specific examples like these, you render the idea of "benefits to society" more concrete and more definite. Such examples are not prettifications of your essay; they are necessary if you are to hold your readers' attention and convince them that you are worth listening to.

When giving examples, you'll find other methods useful. Sometimes, as in the paragraph by Linda Wolfe, an example takes the form of a NARRATIVE (Chap. 4): an ANECDOTE or a case history. Sometimes an example embodies a vivid DESCRIPTION of a person, place, or thing (Chap. 5).

Lazy writers think, "Oh well, I can't come up with any example here—I'll just leave it to the reader to find one." The flaw in this ASSUMPTION is that the reader may be as lazy as the writer. As a result, a perfectly good idea may be left suspended in the stratosphere. The linguist and writer S. I. Hayakawa tells the story of a professor who, in teaching a philosophy course, spent a whole semester on the theory of beauty. When students asked him for a few examples of beautiful paintings, symphonies, or works of nature, he refused, saying, "We are interested in principles, not in particulars." The professor himself may well have been interested in principles, but it is a safe bet that his classroom resounded with snores. In written EXPOSITION, it is undoubtedly the particulars—the pertinent examples—that keep a reader awake and having a good time, and taking in the principles besides.

Example   **207**

> ### FOCUS ON SENTENCE VARIETY

While accumulating and detailing examples during drafting, you may find yourself writing strings of similar sentences:

> UNVARIED   One example of a movie about a disease is *In the Forest*. Another example is *The Beating Heart*. Another is *Tree of Life*. These three movies treat misunderstood or little-known diseases in a way that increases the viewer's sympathy and understanding. *In the Forest* deals with a little boy who suffers from cystic fibrosis. *The Beating Heart* deals with a middle-aged woman who is weakening from multiple sclerosis. *Tree of Life* deals with a father of four who is dying from AIDS. All three movies show complex, struggling human beings caught blamelessly in desperate circumstances.

The writer of this paragraph was clearly pushing to add examples and to expand them—both essential tasks—but the resulting passage needs editing so that the writer's labor isn't so obvious. In the more readable and interesting revision, the sentences vary in structure, group similar details, and distinguish the specifics from the generalizations:

> VARIED   Three movies dealing with disease are *In the Forest, The Beating Heart,* and *Tree of Life*. In these movies people with little-known or misunderstood diseases become subjects for the viewer's sympathy and understanding. A little boy suffering from cystic fibrosis, a middle-aged woman weakening from multiple sclerosis, a father of four dying from AIDS—these complex, struggling human beings are caught blamelessly in desperate circumstances.

*For exercises on sentence variety, visit Exercise Central at **bedfordstmartins.com/thebedfordreader**.*

> ### CHECKLIST FOR REVISING AN EXAMPLE ESSAY
>
> ✔ **GENERALIZATION**   What general statement do your examples illustrate? Will it be clear to readers what ties the examples together?
>
> ✔ **SUPPORT**   Do you have enough examples to establish your generalization, or will readers be left needing more?
>
> ✔ **SPECIFICS**   Are your examples detailed? Does each capture some aspects of the generalization?
>
> ✔ **RELEVANCE**   Do all your examples relate to your generalization? Should any be cut because they go off track?
>
> ✔ **SENTENCE VARIETY**   Have you varied sentence structures for clarity and interest?

Example

EXAMPLES IN PARAGRAPHS

Writing about Television

This paragraph appears in an essay maintaining that television merely simulates, or imitates, real problems, events, activities, and institutions. The essay offers many examples of programming that only seem to represent what's real, such as morning news shows, small-claims courts, and wrestling. (Although the essay predates the recent explosion of "reality" TV, from *Survivor* to *The Biggest Loser*, it would apply to those shows as well.) Here the author uses specific examples of TV wrestling to show how it simulates televised football, basketball, and other sports.

To sustain the simulation, wrestling must construct and maintain a little universe of the simulated. To do this, its discourse refers ⎤ Generalization to in its every enunciation to the apparatus used to broadcast conven- ⎦ be illustrated tional sport. Wrestling features the same style of ringside commentary, the same interpolation of interviews, the same mystification of sporting expertise, the same freeze-frame and instant replay formats, ⎱ Six examples the same faintly prurient interest in the wrestlers' private lives (not to mention parts), the same cults of personality, and so on. This system of understanding, however, is marshaled in the service of an event which is a parody of its originating source: "real" sport.

—Michael Sorkin, "Faking It,"
in *Watching Television*, ed. Todd Gitlin

Writing in an Academic Discipline

The following paragraph from an economics textbook appears amid the author's explanation of how markets work. To dispel what might seem like clouds of theory, the author here brings an abstract principle down to earth with a concrete and detailed example.

The primary function of the market is to bring together suppliers and demanders so that they can trade with one another. Buyers ⎤ and sellers do not necessarily have to be in face-to-face contact; ⎬ Generalization to they can signal their desires and intentions through various inter- ⎦ be illustrated mediaries. For example, the demand for green beans in California is not expressed directly by the green bean consumers to the green bean growers. People who want green beans buy them at a grocery store; the store orders them from a vegetable wholesaler; the wholesaler buys them from a bean cooperative, whose manager tells local ⎱ Single extended farmers of the size of the current demand for green beans. The ⎰ example demanders of green beans are able to signal their demand schedule to the original suppliers, the farmers who raise the beans, without any personal communication between the two parties.

—Lewis C. Solmon, *Microeconomics*

Example   209

EXAMPLES IN A JOB-APPLICATION LETTER

To obtain the kinds of jobs a college education prepares you for, you'll submit a résumé that presents your previous work experience, your education, and your qualifications for a specific career field. To capture the prospective employer's interest, you'll introduce yourself and your résumé with a cover letter.

Rather than merely repeat or summarize the contents of a résumé, a job-application letter highlights the connections between your background and the employer's needs for someone with particular training and skills. Typically brief and tightly focused on the job in question, an application letter aims to persuade the reader to look at the accompanying résumé and then to follow up with an interview.

When college sophomore Kharron Reid was applying for a summer internship implementing computer networks for businesses, he put together a résumé tailored for a specific opportunity posted at his school's placement office. (See the résumé on p. 407.) His cover letter, below, pulls out examples from the résumé to support the statement (in the second-to-last paragraph) that "my education and my hands-on experience with network development have prepared me for the opening you have."

137 Chester St., Apt. E
Allston, MA 02134
February 23, 2010

Ms. Dolores Jackson
Human Resources Director
E-line Systems
75 Arondale Avenue
Boston, MA 02114

Dear Ms. Jackson:

I am applying for the network development internship in your information technology department, advertised in the career services office of Boston University.

Introduction states purpose of letter

I have considerable experience in network development from summer internships at NBS Systems and at Pioneer Networking. At NBS I planned and laid the physical platforms and configured the software for seven WANs on Windows Server 2008. At Pioneer, I laid the physical platforms and configured the software

Generalization about experience

Two examples of experience

to connect eight workstations into a LAN. Both internships gave me experience in every stage of network development.

In my two years in Boston University's School of Management, I have concentrated on developing skills in business administration and information systems. I have completed courses in organizational behavior, computer science (including programming), and networking and data communications. At the same time, I have become proficient in Unix, Windows 7/Vista/XP/2003, Windows Server 2008/2003, and Red Hat Enterprise Linux.

Generalization about education and skills

Two sets of examples about education and skills

As the enclosed résumé indicates, my education and my hands-on experience with network development have prepared me for the opening you have.

Concluding paragraphs summarize qualifications, refer reader to résumé, and invite a response

I am available for an interview at your convenience. Please call me at (617) 555-4009 or e-mail me at kreid@bu.edu.

Sincerely,

Kharron Reid

Kharron Reid

BARBARA LAZEAR ASCHER

Barbara Lazear Ascher was born in 1946 and educated at Bennington College and Cardozo School of Law. She practiced law for two years in a private firm, where she found herself part of a power structure in which those on top resembled "the two-year-old with the biggest plastic pail and shovel on the beach." Ascher quit law to devote herself to writing, to explore, as she says, "what really matters." She became a frequent contributor to the "Hers" column in the *New York Times*, a forum for women writers in the 1980s; her writing has also appeared in the *Yale Review, Vogue,* and other periodicals. Ascher's essays have been collected in *Playing after Dark* (1986), *The Habit of Loving* (1989), and *Dancing in the Dark* (1999). She has also published *Landscape without Gravity: A Memoir of Grief* (1993), about her brother's death from AIDS. Ascher has worked as an editor at several magazines and at a book publisher. She periodically teaches writing at Bennington.

On Compassion

Ascher often writes about life in New York City, where human problems sometimes seem larger and more stubborn than in other places. In this essay Ascher uses examples from the city to address a universal need: compassion for those who require help. In New York and elsewhere in the United States, the problem of homelessness has not abated since Ascher's essay first appeared in *Elle* magazine in 1988. Using government data, the National Alliance to End Homelessness estimates that more than 700,000 Americans are currently homeless on any given day. The essay following this one, Anna Quindlen's "Homeless," addresses the same issue.

The man's grin is less the result of circumstance than dreams or madness. His buttonless shirt, with one sleeve missing, hangs outside the waist of his baggy trousers. Carefully plaited dreadlocks bespeak a better time, long ago. As he crosses Manhattan's Seventy-ninth Street, his gait is the shuffle of the forgotten ones held in place by gravity rather than plans. On the corner of Madison Avenue, he stops before a blond baby in an Aprica stroller. The baby's mother waits for the light to change and her hands close tighter on the stroller's handle as she sees the man approach. 1

The others on the corner, five men and women waiting for the crosstown bus, look away. They daydream a bit and gaze into the weak rays of November 2 light. A man with a briefcase lifts and lowers the shiny toe of his right shoe, watching the light reflect, trying to catch and balance it, as if he could hold and make it his, to ease the heavy gray of coming January, February, and March. The winter months that will send snow around the feet, calves, and knees of the grinning man as he heads for the shelter of Grand Central or Pennsylvania Station.

But for now, in this last gasp of autumn warmth, he is still. His eyes fix 3 on the baby. The mother removes her purse from her shoulder and rummages through its contents: lipstick, a lace handkerchief, an address book. She finds what she's looking for and passes a folded dollar over her child's head to the man who stands and stares even though the light has changed and traffic navigates about his hips.

His hands continue to dangle at his sides. He does not know his part. He 4 does not know that acceptance of the gift and gratitude are what make this transaction complete. The baby, weary of the unwavering stare, pulls its blanket over its head. The man does not look away. Like a bridegroom waiting at the altar, his eyes pierce the white veil.

The mother grows impatient and pushes the stroller before her, bearing 5 the dollar like a cross. Finally, a black hand rises and closes around green.

Was it fear or compassion that motivated the gift? 6

Up the avenue, at Ninety-first Street, there is a small French bread shop 7 where you can sit and eat a buttery, overpriced croissant and wash it down with rich cappuccino. Twice when I have stopped here to stave hunger or stay the cold, twice as I have sat and read and felt the warm rush of hot coffee and milk, an old man has wandered in and stood inside the entrance. He wears a stained blanket pulled up to his chin, and a woolen hood pulled down to his gray, bushy eyebrows. As he stands, the scent of stale cigarettes and urine fills the small, overheated room.

The owner of the shop, a moody French woman, emerges from the kitchen 8 with steaming coffee in a Styrofoam cup, and a small paper bag of . . . of what? Yesterday's bread? Today's croissant? He accepts the offering as silently as he came, and is gone.

Twice I have witnessed this, and twice I have wondered, what compels 9 this woman to feed this man? Pity? Care? Compassion? Or does she simply want to rid her shop of his troublesome presence? If expulsion were her motivation she would not reward his arrival with gifts of food. Most proprietors do not. They chase the homeless from their midst with expletives and threats.

As winter approaches, the mayor of New York City is moving the home- 10 less off the streets and into Bellevue Hospital. The New York Civil Liberties Union is watchful. They question whether the rights of these people who live in our parks and doorways are being violated by involuntary hospitalization.

I think the mayor's notion is humane, but I fear it is something else as   11
well. Raw humanity offends our sensibilities. We want to protect ourselves
from an awareness of rags with voices that make no sense and scream forth in
inarticulate rage. We do not wish to be reminded of the tentative state of our
own well-being and sanity. And so, the troublesome presence is removed from
the awareness of the electorate.

Like other cities, there is much about Manhattan now that resembles   12
Dickensian London. Ladies in high-heeled shoes pick their way through poverty and madness. You hear more cocktail party complaints than usual, "I just
can't take New York anymore." Our citizens dream of the open spaces of Wyoming, the manicured exclusivity of Hobe Sound.

And yet, it may be that these are the conditions that finally give birth to   13
empathy, the mother of compassion. We cannot deny the existence of the
helpless as their presence grows. It is impossible to insulate ourselves against
what is at our very doorstep. I don't believe that one is born compassionate.
Compassion is not a character trait like a sunny disposition. It must be learned,
and it is learned by having adversity at our windows, coming through the gates
of our yards, the walls of our towns, adversity that becomes so familiar that we
begin to identify and empathize with it.

For the ancient Greeks, drama taught and reinforced compassion within   14
a society. The object of Greek tragedy was to inspire empathy in the audience so that the common response to the hero's fall was: "There, but for the
grace of God, go I." Could it be that this was the response of the mother who
offered the dollar, the French woman who gave the food? Could it be that the
homeless, like those ancients, are reminding us of our common humanity? Of
course, there is a difference. This play doesn't end—and the players can't go
home.

*For a reading quiz, sources on Barbara Lazear Ascher, and annotated links to further
readings on homelessness, visit **bedfordstmartins.com/thebedfordreader**.*

Journal Writing

Using Ascher's essay as a springboard, consider a personal experience that involved
misfortune. Have you ever needed to beg on the street, been evicted from an apartment, or had to scrounge for food? Have you ever been asked for money by beggars,

worked in a soup kitchen, or volunteered at a shelter or public hospital? Write about such an experience in your journal. (To take your journal writing further, see "From Journal to Essay" below.)

Questions on Meaning

1. What do the two men in Ascher's essay exemplify?
2. What is Ascher's THESIS? What is her PURPOSE?
3. What solution to homelessness is introduced in paragraph 10? What does Ascher think of this possibility?
4. How do you interpret Ascher's last sentence? Is she optimistic or pessimistic about whether people will learn compassion?

Questions on Writing Strategy

1. Which comes first, the GENERALIZATIONS or the supporting examples? Why has Ascher chosen this order?
2. What assumptions does the author make about her AUDIENCE?
3. Why do the other people at the bus stop look away (par. 2)? What does Ascher's DESCRIPTION of their activities say about them?
4. Look at the sentences in paragraph 13. How does the variety in their structure reinforce Ascher's meaning?
5. **OTHER METHODS**   Ascher explores CAUSES AND EFFECTS. Do you agree with her that exposure to others' helplessness increases our compassion? Why, or why not?

Questions on Language

1. What is the difference between empathy and compassion? Why does Ascher say that "empathy [is] the mother of compassion" (par. 13)?
2. Find definitions for the following words: plaited, dreadlocks, bespeak (par. 1); stave, stay (7); expletives (9); inarticulate, electorate (11).
3. What are the implications of Ascher's ALLUSION to "Dickensian London" (par. 12)?
4. Examine the language Ascher uses to describe the two homeless men. Is it OBJECTIVE? sympathetic? negative?

Suggestions for Writing

1. **FROM JOURNAL TO ESSAY**   Write an essay on the experience you explored in your journal, using examples to convey the effect the experience had on you.
2. Write an essay on the problem of homelessness in your town or city. Use examples to support your view of the problem and a possible solution.
3. In paragraph 10 Ascher refers to the involuntary hospitalization of homeless people and the concerns such government action raises among supporters of individual rights, such as the American Civil Liberties Union. What is your opinion of the rights of homeless people to live on the streets? How do you distinguish

among the individual's rights, the community's responsibilities to the individual, and the community's rights? (For instance, what if a homeless person seems sick? What if he or she seems unstable, if not violent?) You may work solo on this assignment—stating your ideas and supporting them with EVIDENCE from your own observations and experience—or you may conduct research to discover legal and other arguments and data to support your ideas.

4. **CRITICAL WRITING**   In her last paragraph, Ascher mentions but does not address another key difference between the characters in Greek tragedy and the homeless on today's streets: The former were "heroes"—gods and goddesses, kings and queens—whereas the latter are placeless, poor, anonymous, even reviled. Does this difference negate Ascher's comparison between Greek theatergoers and ourselves or her larger point about how compassion is learned? Answer in a brief essay, saying why, or why not.

5. **CONNECTIONS**   The next essay, Anna Quindlen's "Homeless," also uses examples to make a point about homelessness. What are some of the differences in the examples each writer uses? In a brief essay, explore whether and how these differences create different TONES in the two works.

Barbara Lazear Ascher on Writing

A lawyer before she was a full-time writer, Barbara Lazear Ascher thinks that her legal training helped her become a stronger writer.

"I believe there is a kind of legal thinking that becomes part of your own thinking," she told Jean W. Ross of *Contemporary Authors*. "What it did for me was help me to become quite a tight writer. My pieces are very short, and I think a lot of that has to do with the training in law, which is to tell the facts and the theories, and then put it all together and close it up. I might have been a more excessive writer if I hadn't had the legal training."

For Ascher, the essay is the ideal form of expression. "I'm quite impatient, so it's very satisfying to have a small space in which to tell what it was you wanted to tell. You get to the point right away instead of having to drag it out and slowly reveal it."

For Discussion

1. How did her legal training help Ascher when she became a writer? How does a "tight writer" help readers as well?
2. How might an "excessive writer" have trouble with the essay form? What, in your view, is "excessive" writing?

ANNA QUINDLEN

Anna Quindlen was born in 1953 and graduated from Barnard College in 1974. She worked as a reporter for the *New York Post* and the *New York Times* before taking over the *Times*'s "About New York" column, serving as the paper's deputy metropolitan editor, and in 1986 creating her own weekly column, "Life in the Thirties." In the early 1990s Quindlen wrote a twice-weekly op-ed column for the *Times* on social and political issues, earning a Pulitzer Prize in 1992. In 1999 she began writing "The Last Word," a biweekly column for *Newsweek* magazine. Her essays and columns are collected in *Living Out Loud* (1988), *Thinking Out Loud* (1993), and *Loud and Clear* (2004). Much of Quindlen's popular nonfiction—*How Reading Changed My Life* (1998), *A Short Guide to a Happy Life* (2000), and *Being Perfect* (2005)—takes a how-to bent. She has also published two books for children and six successful novels: *Object Lessons* (1991), *One True Thing* (1994), *Black and Blue: A Novel* (1998), *Blessings* (2002), *Rise and Shine* (2006), and *Every Last One* (2010).

Homeless

In this essay from *Living Out Loud,* Quindlen mingles a reporter's respect for details with a keen sense of empathy. She uses examples to explore the same topic as Barbara Lazear Ascher (p. 211) from a different slant. Both essays date from the late 1980s, but both also remain fresh because of the persistence of homelessness as a social problem.

Her name was Ann, and we met in the Port Authority Bus Terminal several Januarys ago. I was doing a story on homeless people. She said I was wasting my time talking to her; she was just passing through, although she'd been passing through for more than two weeks. To prove to me that this was true, she rummaged through a tote bag and a manila envelope and finally unfolded a sheet of typing paper and brought out her photographs.

They were not pictures of family, or friends, or even a dog or cat, its eyes brown-red in the flashbulb's light. They were pictures of a house. It was like a thousand houses in a hundred towns, not suburb, not city, but somewhere in between, with aluminum siding and a chain-link fence, a narrow driveway running up to a one-car garage and a patch of backyard. The house was yellow. I looked on the back for a date or a name, but neither was there. There was no need for discussion. I knew what she was trying to tell me, for it was something

I had often felt. She was not adrift, alone, anonymous, although her bags and her raincoat with the grime shadowing its creases had made me believe she was. She had a house, or at least once upon a time had had one. Inside were curtains, a couch, a stove, potholders. You are where you live. She was somebody.

I've never been very good at looking at the big picture, taking the global view, and I've always been a person with an overactive sense of place, the legacy of an Irish grandfather. So it is natural that the thing that seems most wrong with the world to me right now is that there are so many people with no homes. I'm not simply talking about shelter from the elements, or three square meals a day or a mailing address to which the welfare people can send the check—although I know that all these are important for survival. I'm talking about a home, about precisely those kinds of feelings that have wound up in cross-stitch and French knots on samplers over the years.

Home is where the heart is. There's no place like it. I love my home with a ferocity totally out of proportion to its appearance or location. I love dumb things about it: the hot-water heater, the plastic rack you drain dishes in, the roof over my head, which occasionally leaks. And yet it is precisely those dumb things that make it what it is—a place of certainty, stability, predictability, privacy, for me and for my family. It is where I live. What more can you say about a place than that? That is everything.

Yet it is something that we have been edging away from gradually during my lifetime and the lifetimes of my parents and grandparents. There was a time when where you lived often was where you worked and where you grew the food you ate and even where you were buried. When that era passed, where you lived at least was where your parents had lived and where you would live with your children when you became enfeebled. Then, suddenly where you lived was where you lived for three years, until you could move on to something else and something else again.

And so we have come to something else again, to children who do not understand what it means to go to their rooms because they have never had a room, to men and women whose fantasy is a wall they can paint a color of their own choosing, to old people reduced to sitting on molded plastic chairs, their skin blue-white in the lights of a bus station, who pull pictures of houses out of their bags. Homes have stopped being homes. Now they are real estate.

People find it curious that those without homes would rather sleep sitting up on benches or huddled in doorways than go to shelters. Certainly some prefer to do so because they are emotionally ill, because they have been locked in before and they are damned if they will be locked in again. Others are afraid of the violence and trouble they may find there. But some seem to want something that is not available in shelters, and they will not compromise, not for a cot, or oatmeal, or a shower with special soap that kills the bugs. "One room," a woman with a baby who was sleeping on her sister's floor, once told me, "painted blue." That was the crux of it; not size or location, but pride of ownership. Painted blue.

This is a difficult problem, and some wise and compassionate people are 8 working hard at it. But in the main I think we work around it, just as we walk around it when it is lying on the sidewalk or sitting in the bus terminal—the problem, that is. It has been customary to take people's pain and lessen our own participation in it by turning it into an issue, not a collection of human beings. We turn an adjective into a noun: the poor, not poor people; the homeless, not Ann or the man who lives in the box or the woman who sleeps on the subway grate.

Sometimes I think we would be better off if we forgot about the broad 9 strokes and concentrated on the details. Here is a woman without a bureau. There is a man with no mirror, no wall to hang it on. They are not the homeless. They are people who have no homes. No drawer that holds the spoons. No window to look out upon the world. My God. That is everything.

For a reading quiz, sources on Anna Quindlen, and annotated links to further readings on homelessness, visit **bedfordstmartins.com/thebedfordreader**.

Journal Writing

What does the word *home* mean to you? Does it involve material things, privacy, family, a sense of permanence? In your journal, explore your ideas about this word. (To take your journal writing further, see "From Journal to Essay" on the facing page.)

Questions on Meaning

1. What is Quindlen's THESIS?
2. What distinction is Quindlen making in her CONCLUSION with the sentences "They are not the homeless. They are people who have no homes"?
3. Why does Quindlen believe that having a home is important?

Questions on Writing Strategy

1. Why do you think Quindlen begins with the story of Ann? How else might Quindlen have begun her essay?

2. What is the EFFECT of Quindlen's examples of her own home?
3. What key ASSUMPTIONS does the author make about her AUDIENCE? Are the assumptions reasonable? Where does she specifically address an assumption that might undermine her view?
4. How does Quindlen vary the sentences in paragraph 7 that give examples of why homeless people avoid shelters?
5. **OTHER METHODS**   Quindlen uses examples to support an ARGUMENT. What position does she want readers to recognize and accept?

Questions on Language

1. What is the effect of "My God" in the last paragraph?
2. How might Quindlen be said to give new meaning to the old CLICHÉ "Home is where the heart is" (par. 4)?
3. What is meant by "crux" (par. 7)? Where does the word come from?

Suggestions for Writing

1. **FROM JOURNAL TO ESSAY**   Write an essay that gives a detailed DEFINITION of *home* by using your own home(s), hometown(s), or experiences with home(s) as supporting examples. (See Chap. 12 if you need help with definition.)
2. Have you ever moved from one place to another? What sort of experience was it? Write an essay about leaving an old home and moving to a new one. Was there an activity or a piece of furniture that helped ease the transition?
3. Estimates of the number of homeless people in the United States vary widely. Research the numbers, and then write an essay in which you present your findings and propose reasons for the variations.
4. **CRITICAL WRITING**   Write a brief essay in which you agree or disagree with Quindlen's assertion that a home is "everything." Can one, for instance, be a fulfilled person without a home? In your answer, take account of the values that might underlie an attachment to home; Quindlen mentions "certainty, stability, predictability, privacy" (par. 4), but there are others, including some (such as fear) that are less positive.
5. **CONNECTIONS**   COMPARE AND CONTRAST the views of homelessness and its solution in Quindlen's "Homeless" and Barbara Lazear Ascher's "On Compassion" (p. 211). Use specific passages from each essay to support your comparison.

Anna Quindlen on Writing

Anna Quindlen started her writing career as a newspaper reporter. "I had wanted to be a writer for most of my life," she recalls in the introduction to her book *Living Out Loud*, "and in the service of the writing I became a reporter.

For many years I was able to observe, even to feel, life vividly, but at second-hand. I was able to stand over the chalk outline of a body on a sidewalk dappled with black blood; to stand behind the glass and look down into an operating theater where one man was placing a heart in the yawning chest of another; to sit in the park on the first day of summer and find myself professionally obligated to record all the glories of it. Every day I found answers: who, what, when, where, and why."

Quindlen was a good reporter, but the business of finding answers did not satisfy her personally. "In my own life," she continues, "I had only questions." Then she switched from reporter to columnist at the *New York Times*. It was "exhilarating," she says, that "my work became a reflection of my life. After years of being a professional observer of other people's lives, I was given the opportunity to be a professional observer of my own. I was permitted—and permitted myself—to write a column, not about my answers, but about my questions. Never did I make so much sense of my life as I did then, for it was inevitable that as a writer I would find out most clearly what I thought, and what I only thought I thought, when I saw it written down. . . . After years of feeling secondhand, of feeling the pain of the widow, the joy of the winner, I was able to allow myself to feel those emotions for myself."

For Discussion

1. What were the advantages and disadvantages of news reporting, according to Quindlen?
2. What did Quindlen feel she could accomplish in a column that she could not accomplish in a news report? What evidence of this difference do you see in her essay "Homeless"?

SHARMAN APT RUSSELL

Sharman Apt Russell was born in 1954 at Edwards Air Force Base in California and has lived most of her life in the Southwest. She earned a BA in conservation and natural resources from the University of California at Berkeley and an MFA in creative writing from the University of Montana. Russell has published her work in *Threepenny Review, North American Review,* the *New York Times,* and *Nature Conservancy*; she won the Pushcart Prize in 1990. Her nonfiction books include *When the Land Was Young: Reflections on American Archaeology* (1996), *Hunger: An Unnatural History* (2005), and *Standing in the Light: My Life as a Pantheist* (2008). Though often dubbed a nature writer, Russell notes that a writer's life is "also about being in the world of politics and social change." She teaches writing at Western New Mexico University and Antioch University and is the founder of Alimento para el Niño (Nourishment for the Child), a program that provides backpacks filled with snacks for hungry schoolchildren in her community.

The Adored, Buzzing around Us

Russell is known for crafting prose that is simultaneously scientific and poetic. In this 2009 essay from *Orion* magazine, she ponders the glories of insects and, with a series of startling examples, makes a case for realigning our view of the natural world.

1   I am fortunate to live in an area where the stink bug, also called the darkling, pinacate, or clown beetle, is common. About an inch long, with a jet-black carapace and long walking legs, the stink bug is nothing out of the ordinary — except when startled. Then the insect bends its front legs, extends its rear legs, raises its posterior almost vertically, and emits a powerful odor. It is meant to be the scariest headstand in the world.

2   A pinacate beetle can brighten my day. I connect to something nonhuman and am knocked happily out of myself. Many of us have this experience when we see a charismatic mammal like a deer or bear, raccoon or moose. Birds can have the same effect. Hawks, cranes, ravens, hummingbirds — they give us a thrill. They say: Stop! Look at how beautiful I am, how different from you. They make us feel grateful for being on such an interesting planet.

3   Insects can do this, too, if we shift our attitude — and spatial perspective. Insects are also wild creatures and have the advantage of being everywhere. If you are a lover of insects, you have many opportunities to love, and you will feel less lonely and discouraged than if you have chosen only to adore the vanishing Siberian tiger or your local threatened predator. You may become

a connoisseur of anthills—or intrigued by spiders. Even the most familiar or seemingly insignificant insect can surprise you. (Viewed up close—I promise—the oak treehopper will make you gasp.)

Another beetle example (as the naturalist J. B. S. Haldane noted, God must 4 have had an inordinate fondness for beetles since he made so many different kinds): Tiger beetles are often brightly patterned and look like small jewels. An Australian species is the fastest running insect in the world, going nine kilometers per hour or 170 body lengths per second. After a successful chase, tiger beetles cover their victims in a corrosive liquid that begins the process of digestion. Tiger beetle larvae are equally ferocious; these white grubs have horns on their backs, which they anchor to the sides of their tunnels, allowing them to lunge out and pull in prey with a single powerful motion.

In their way, tiger beetles are as charismatic as their mammalian coun- 5 terpart. *In their way*. That's the rub. The truth is that insects usually inspire repulsion more than admiration. They scurry away with an unpleasant sound. They have disgusting eating habits. That compound eye gives us the creeps. All those reflections. And all those legs! Mouthparts that drink blood? Hairy distended abdomens? Not before eating, please.

For most of us, insects are just too far outside the human aesthetic—alien, 6 brutal, and uncuddly. This is also good. Because this is nature, too. I have learned (somewhat slowly) that if I want to have a relationship with the natural world, it can't just be with the parts I pick and choose. The gorgeous mountain view makes my lover's heart ache. But I also have to admire the rejuvenating after-math of a forest fire, as "ugly" a landscape as any on Earth. I have to get to know the parts of nature that make me wince and turn away. Because turning away is not really what good lovers do.

So I'm paying more attention to insects. It usually requires getting down 7 on my knees, much lower to the ground. A new perspective. And, inevitably, another beetle—this time, the giant North American rhinoceros beetle, with its jaunty horn and ability to lift its own weight hundreds of times over! Right here on my front porch! I feel that thrill of gratitude. I live on such an inter-esting planet.

*For a reading quiz, sources on Sharman Apt Russell, and annotated links to further readings on nature and the environment, visit **bedfordstmartins.com/ thebedfordreader**.*

Journal Writing

Russell says that "insects usually inspire repulsion more than admiration" (par. 5). How do you respond to this statement? In your experience is it true of people generally, or are some people more predisposed to such feelings than others? What is your own reaction to crawling insects? Write a journal entry in which you consider these questions. (To take your journal writing further, see "From Journal to Essay" on the next page.)

Questions on Meaning

1. In what two sentences does Russell state her THESIS most explicitly? How does she use metaphor to reveal her PURPOSE? (See *Figures of speech* in Useful Terms for a definition of *metaphor*.)
2. Why does Russell admire beetles as much as she does? Which of their attributes does she find especially interesting? Does she succeed in getting you to share her fascination?
3. To what environmental concern does Russell ALLUDE in paragraph 3? Why do you suppose she glosses over such a serious issue? What does it have to do with her point?

Questions on Writing Strategy

1. This essay originally appeared in *Orion*, a magazine devoted to nature, the environment, and grassroots activism. In what ways are environmentalists the perfect AUDIENCE for Russell's reflections? What does she seem to ASSUME about her readers' interests and inclinations?
2. What three examples does Russell give to illustrate her GENERALIZATION about insects? How does she make those examples concrete and vivid?
3. In paragraph 3, Russell uses the second-PERSON *you*. Everywhere else she uses a combination of the first person (*I, we, us*) and the third person (*it, they*) to share her experiences and to describe some of her favorite insects. What is the EFFECT of the use of the second person in paragraph 3?
4. **OTHER METHODS**   Where does Russell use COMPARISON AND CONTRAST? What do these passages contribute to the essay?

Questions on Language

1. What are the CONNOTATIONS of "stink bug"? Why do you suppose Russell opens with that insect name, rather than "darkling, pinacate, or clown beetle" (par. 1)?
2. How would you describe Russell's overall TONE? Why is this tone appropriate for her purpose?
3. Why does Russell repeat and italicize the phrase "in their way" in paragraph 5? What does she mean by it?

4. Consult a dictionary if you are unsure of the meanings of any of the following: carapace, posterior (par. 1); charismatic (2); connoisseur (3); inordinate, corrosive, larvae (4); mammalian, compound, distended (5); aesthetic, rejuvenating (6); jaunty (7).

Suggestions for Writing

1. **FROM JOURNAL TO ESSAY**   Based on your journal entry, write an essay that examines people's reactions to insects, especially the creepy crawly kind. Does everyone respond the same way, in your experience? If you see variation, what do you think accounts for it: upbringing? gender? heredity? personality? Use EXAMPLES from your experience to illustrate and support your ideas.
2. Russell writes of being "knocked happily out of [her]self" when she sees a pinacate beetle, and observes that "[m]any of us have this experience when we see a charismatic mammal" or a beautiful bird (par. 2). Have you had such an experience? In an essay that combines NARRATION and DESCRIPTION, write about a time when observing a wild animal filled you with awe and made you feel connected to the natural world.
3. **CRITICAL WRITING**   In an essay, ANALYZE Russell's use of romantic language and IMAGES. How does the concept of love inform and complicate the writer's "relationship with the natural world" (par. 6)? Use specific examples of the language she uses and of the scenes she describes.
4. **CONNECTIONS**   John Updike, in "Extreme Dinosaurs" (p. 713), also uses EXAMPLES and DESCRIPTION to express his admiration for unusual creatures. In an essay of your own, COMPARE AND CONTRAST Updike's purpose and method with Russell's. What similarities and differences do you find in each writer's approach to his or her subject? Are either writer's strategies more effective than the other's? Why, or why not?

Sharman Apt Russell on Writing

In an interview with Susan J. Tweit of Story Circle Network, Sharman Apt Russell responded to the questions "How do you pick your subjects? Or do they pick you?"

When I teach creative writing, I talk about what I call "fruitful questions." For me, a fruitful question must be real, not rhetorical. There must be a real moment of wonder and mystery before possible answers rush in. The question must also energize me in some way. And the question must be possible for me to pursue. All my books and essays are driven by a fruitful question. For archaeology, the question was, "What makes me get so excited about finding a piece of clay on the ground—a simple and relatively unimportant pot shard? What is *my* link to the past?" For flowers, the question was, "What would it be like living in this almost unimaginable nonhuman world of flowers and pollinators, with these nonhuman smells and colors and motivations?"

As I answer that fruitful question, writing becomes an act of discovery and exploration. I think this desire for discovery and "quest" is often true for people, whether they are writing or studying or just living their daily life. But why do certain questions energize us? In my experience, they often connect to something essential to our childhood or to our nature. Sometimes they act like important metaphors. For me, uncovering the secret world of flowers and butterflies was like opening the door into Narnia.[1] Here was another world of magic—with magic a metaphor for my spirituality.

For Discussion

1. Russell answers a question about choosing her *subjects* by explaining how she chooses her *questions*. To what extent is picking a topic really about asking a question?
2. What does Russell mean when she says that a fruitful question must be "real"?
3. Do you agree with Russell that the questions that most "energize" us are ones that relate to "something essential to our childhood or to our nature"?

---

[1] A fantasy world created by C. S. Lewis in his series of children's books, *The Chronicles of Narnia* (1950–56).—Eds.

BRENT STAPLES

Brent Staples is a member of the editorial board of the *New York Times*. Born in 1951 in Chester, Pennsylvania, Staples has a BA in behavioral science from Widener University in Chester and a PhD in psychology from the University of Chicago. Before joining the *New York Times* in 1985, he worked for the *Chicago Sun-Times*, the *Chicago Reader, Chicago* magazine, and *Down Beat* magazine. At the *Times,* Staples writes on culture, politics, reading, and special education, advocating for children with learning disabilities. He has also contributed to the *New York Times Magazine, New York Woman, Ms., Harper's,* and other magazines. His memoir, *Parallel Time: Growing Up in Black and White,* appeared in 1994.

Black Men and Public Space

"Black Men and Public Space" appeared in the December 1986 issue of *Harper's* magazine and was then published, in a slightly different version, in Staples's memoir, *Parallel Time.* To explain a recurring experience of African American men, Staples relates incidents when he has been "a night walker in the urban landscape." Sometimes his only defense against others' stereotypes is to whistle.

My first victim was a woman—white, well dressed, probably in her late 1
twenties. I came upon her late one evening on a deserted street in Hyde Park, a relatively affluent neighborhood in an otherwise mean, impoverished section of Chicago. As I swung onto the avenue behind her, there seemed to be a discreet, uninflammatory distance between us. Not so. She cast back a worried glance. To her, the youngish black man—a broad six feet two inches with a beard and billowing hair, both hands shoved into the pockets of a bulky military jacket—seemed menacingly close. After a few more quick glimpses, she picked up her pace and was soon running in earnest. Within seconds she disappeared into a cross street.

That was more than a decade ago. I was twenty-two years old, a graduate 2
student newly arrived at the University of Chicago. It was in the echo of that terrified woman's footfalls that I first began to know the unwieldy inheritance I'd come into—the ability to alter public space in ugly ways. It was clear that she thought herself the quarry of a mugger, a rapist, or worse. Suffering a bout of insomnia, however, I was stalking sleep, not defenseless wayfarers. As a softy who is scarcely able to take a knife to a raw chicken—let alone hold one to a person's throat—I was surprised, embarrassed, and dismayed all at once. Her flight made me feel like an accomplice in tyranny. It also made it clear

that I was indistinguishable from the muggers who occasionally seeped into the area from the surrounding ghetto. That first encounter, and those that followed, signified that a vast, unnerving gulf lay between nighttime pedestrians—particularly women—and me. And I soon gathered that being perceived as dangerous is a hazard in itself. I only needed to turn a corner into a dicey situation, or crowd some frightened, armed person in a foyer somewhere, or make an errant move after being pulled over by a policeman. Where fear and weapons meet—and they often do in urban America—there is always the possibility of death.

In that first year, my first away from my hometown, I was to become thoroughly familiar with the language of fear. At dark, shadowy intersections, I could cross in front of a car stopped at a traffic light and elicit the *thunk, thunk, thunk, thunk* of the driver—black, white, male, or female—hammering down the door locks. On less traveled streets after dark, I grew accustomed to but never comfortable with people crossing to the other side of the street rather than pass me. Then there were the standard unpleasantries with policemen, doormen, bouncers, cabdrivers, and others whose business it is to screen out troublesome individuals *before* there is any nastiness.

I moved to New York nearly two years ago and I have remained an avid night walker. In central Manhattan, the near-constant crowd cover minimizes tense one-on-one street encounters. Elsewhere—in SoHo, for example, where sidewalks are narrow and tightly spaced buildings shut out the sky—things can get very taut indeed.

After dark, on the warrenlike streets of Brooklyn where I live, I often see women who fear the worst from me. They seem to have set their faces on neutral, and with their purse straps strung across their chests bandolier-style, they forge ahead as though bracing themselves against being tackled. I understand, of course, that the danger they perceive is not a hallucination. Women are particularly vulnerable to street violence, and young black males are drastically overrepresented among the perpetrators of that violence. Yet these truths are no solace against the kind of alienation that comes of being ever the suspect, a fearsome entity with whom pedestrians avoid making eye contact.

It is not altogether clear to me how I reached the ripe old age of twenty-two without being conscious of the lethality nighttime pedestrians attributed to me. Perhaps it was because in Chester, Pennsylvania, the small, angry industrial town where I came of age in the 1960s, I was scarcely noticeable against a backdrop of gang warfare, street knifings, and murders. I grew up one of the good boys, had perhaps a half-dozen fistfights. In retrospect, my shyness of combat has clear sources.

As a boy, I saw countless tough guys locked away; I have since buried several, too. They were babies, really—a teenage cousin, a brother of twenty-two, a childhood friend in his mid-twenties — all gone down in episodes of bravado played out in the streets. I came to doubt the virtues of intimidation early on. I chose, perhaps unconsciously, to remain a shadow — timid, but a survivor.

The fearsomeness mistakenly attributed to me in public places often has a perilous flavor. The most frightening of these confusions occurred in the late 1970s and early 1980s, when I worked as a journalist in Chicago. One day, rushing into the office of a magazine I was writing for with a deadline story in hand, I was mistaken for a burglar. The office manager called security and, with an ad hoc posse, pursued me through the labyrinthine halls, nearly to my editor's door. I had no way of proving who I was. I could only move briskly toward the company of someone who knew me. 8

Another time I was on assignment for a local paper and killing time before an interview. I entered a jewelry store on the city's affluent Near North Side. The proprietor excused herself and returned with an enormous red Doberman pinscher straining at the end of a leash. She stood, the dog extended toward me, silent to my questions, her eyes bulging nearly out of her head. I took a cursory look around, nodded, and bade her good night. 9

Relatively speaking, however, I never fared as badly as another black male journalist. He went to nearby Waukegan, Illinois, a couple of summers ago to work on a story about a murderer who was born there. Mistaking the reporter for the killer, police officers hauled him from his car at gunpoint and but for his press credentials would probably have tried to book him. Such episodes are not uncommon. Black men trade tales like this all the time. 10

Over the years, I learned to smother the rage I felt at so often being taken for a criminal. Not to do so would surely have led to madness. I now take precautions to make myself less threatening. I move about with care, particularly late in the evening. I give a wide berth to nervous people on subway platforms during the wee hours, particularly when I have exchanged business clothes for jeans. If I happen to be entering a building behind some people who appear skittish, I may walk by, letting them clear the lobby before I return, so as not to seem to be following them. I have been calm and extremely congenial on those rare occasions when I've been pulled over by the police. 11

And on late-evening constitutionals I employ what has proved to be an excellent tension-reducing measure: I whistle melodies from Beethoven and Vivaldi and the more popular classical composers. Even steely New Yorkers hunching toward nighttime destinations seem to relax, and occasionally they even join in the tune. Virtually everybody seems to sense that a mugger wouldn't be warbling bright, sunny selections from Vivaldi's *Four Seasons*. It is my equivalent of the cowbell that hikers wear when they know they are in bear country. 12

*For a reading quiz, sources on Brent Staples, and annotated links to further readings on racial stereotyping, visit **bedfordstmartins.com/thebedfordreader**.*

Journal Writing

Staples explains how he perceives himself altering public space. Write in your journal about a time when you felt as if *you* altered public space—in other words, you changed people's attitudes or behavior just by being in a place or entering a situation. If you haven't had this experience, write about a time when you saw someone else alter public space in this way. (To take your journal writing further, see "From Journal to Essay" on the following page.)

Questions on Meaning

1. What is the PURPOSE of this essay? Do you think Staples believes that he (or other African American men) will cease "to alter public space in ugly ways" in the near future? Does he suggest any long-term solution for "the kind of alienation that comes of being ever the suspect" (par. 5)?
2. In paragraph 5 Staples says he understands that the danger women fear when they see him "is not a hallucination." Do you take this to mean that Staples perceives himself to be dangerous? Explain.
3. Staples says, "I chose, perhaps unconsciously, to remain a shadow—timid, but a survivor" (par. 7). What are the usual CONNOTATIONS of the word *survivor*? Is "timid" one of them? How can you explain this apparent discrepancy?

Questions on Writing Strategy

1. The concept of altering public space is relatively abstract. How does Staples convince you that this phenomenon really takes place?
2. Staples employs a large number of examples in a fairly small space. How does he avoid having the piece sound like a list? How does he establish COHERENCE among all these examples? (Look, for example, at details and TRANSITIONS.)
3. **OTHER METHODS**   Many of Staples's examples are actually ANECDOTES—brief NARRATIVES. The opening paragraph is especially notable. Why is it so effective?

Questions on Language

1. What does the author accomplish by using the word *victim* in the essay's first paragraph? Is the word used literally? What TONE does it set for the essay?

2. Be sure you know how to define the following words, as used in this essay: affluent, uninflammatory (par. 1); unwieldy, tyranny, pedestrians (2); intimidation (7); congenial (11); constitutionals (12).
3. The word *dicey* (par. 2) comes from British slang. Without looking it up in your dictionary, can you figure out its meaning from the context in which it appears?

Suggestions for Writing

1. **FROM JOURNAL TO ESSAY**   Write an essay narrating your experience of either altering public space yourself or being a witness when someone else altered public space. What changes did you observe in people's behavior? Was your behavior similarly affected? In retrospect, do you think your reactions were justified?
2. Write an essay using examples to show how a trait of your own or of someone you know well always seems to affect people, whether positively or negatively.
3. The ironic term *DWB* (driving while black) expresses the common perception that African American drivers are more likely than white drivers to be pulled over by authorities for minor infractions—or no infraction at all. Research and write an essay about the accuracy of this perception in one state or municipality: Is there truth to it? If African Americans have been discriminated against, what if anything have the appropriate governments done to address the problem?
4. **CRITICAL WRITING**   Consider, more broadly than Staples does, what it means to alter public space. Staples would rather not have the power to do so, but it *is* a power, and it could perhaps be positive in some circumstances (wielded by a street performer, for instance, or the architect of a beautiful new building on campus). Write an essay expanding on Staples's essay in which you examine the pros and cons of altering public space. Use specific examples as your EVIDENCE.
5. **CONNECTIONS**   Like Staples, Barbara Lazear Ascher, in "On Compassion" (p. 211), considers how people regard and respond to "the Other," the one who is viewed as different. In an essay, COMPARE AND CONTRAST the POINTS OF VIEW of these two authors. How does point of view affect each author's selection of details and tone?

Brent Staples on Writing

In comments written especially for *The Bedford Reader*, Brent Staples talks about the writing of "Black Men and Public Space": "I was only partly aware of how I felt when I began this essay. I knew only that I had this collection of experiences (facts) and that I felt uneasy with them. I sketched out the experiences one by one and strung them together. The bridge to the essay—what I wanted to say, but did not know when I started—sprang into life quite unexpectedly as I sat looking over these experiences. The crucial sentence comes right after the opening anecdote, in which my first 'victim' runs away from me: 'It was in the echo of that terrified woman's footfalls that I first began to know the unwieldy inheritance I'd come into—the ability to alter public space in ugly ways.' 'Aha!' I said. 'This is why I feel bothered and hurt and frustrated when this happens. I don't want people to think I'm stalking them. I want some fresh air. I want to stretch my legs. I want to be as anonymous as any other person out for a walk in the night.' "

A news reporter and editor by training and trade, Staples sees much similarity between the writing of a personal essay like "Black Men and Public Space" and the writing of, say, a murder story for a daily newspaper. "The newspaper murder," he says, "begins with standard newspaper information: the fact that the man was found dead in an alley in such-and-such a section of the city; his name, occupation, and where he lived; that he died of gunshot wounds to such-and-such a part of his body; that arrests were or were not made; that such-and-such a weapon was found at the scene; that the police have established no motive; etc.

"Personal essays take a different tack, but they, too, begin as assemblies of facts. In 'Black Men and Public Space,' I start out with an anecdote that crystallizes the issue I want to discuss—what it is like to be viewed as a criminal all the time. I devise a sentence that serves this purpose and also catches the reader's attention: 'My first victim was a woman—white, well dressed, probably in her late twenties.' The piece gives examples that are meant to illustrate the same point and discusses what those examples mean.

"The newspaper story stacks its details in a specified way, with each piece taking a prescribed place in a prescribed order. The personal essay begins often with a flourish, an anecdote, or the recounting of a crucial experience, then goes off to consider related experiences and their meanings. But both pieces rely on reporting. Both are built of facts. Reporting is the act of finding and analyzing facts.

"A fact can be a state of the world—a date, the color of someone's eyes, the arc of a body that flies through the air after having been struck by a car. A fact can also be a feeling—sorrow, grief, confusion, the sense of being pleased, offended, or frustrated. 'Black Men and Public Space' explores the relationship between two sets of facts: (1) the way people cast worried glances at me and sometimes run away from me on the streets after dark, and (2) the frustration and anger I feel at being made an object of fear as I try to go about my business in the city."

Personal essays and news stories share one other quality as well, Staples thinks: They affect the writer even when the writing is finished. "The discoveries I made in 'Black Men and Public Space' continued long after the essay was published. Writing about the experiences gave me access to a whole range of internal concerns and ideas, much the way a well-reported news story opens the door onto a given neighborhood, situation, or set of issues."

For Discussion

1. In recounting how his essay developed, what does Staples reveal about his writing process?
2. How, according to Staples, are essay writing and news writing similar? How are they different?
3. What does Staples mean when he says that "writing about the experiences gave me access to a whole range of internal concerns and ideas"?

DAVID FOSTER WALLACE

Often described as a literary hero, David Foster Wallace defied boundaries of style and subject matter. Born in 1962 in Ithaca, New York, to a philosopher and an English teacher, Wallace graduated from Amherst College in 1985 and completed his MFA at the University of Arizona in 1987. His senior thesis became his first novel, *The Broom of the System* (1987), about a woman who fears that she is a fictional character. A frequent contributor to *The New Yorker* and *Harper's* magazine, Wallace published three collections of short fiction, two collections of essays, a history of infinity, and the ambitiously unconventional novel *Infinite Jest* (1996). He also taught at Illinois State University and Pomona College. After struggling with severe depression for more than two decades, Wallace committed suicide in 2008. He left behind hundreds of pages of a meticulously researched novel about IRS employees and the idea that bliss "lies on the other side of crushing, crushing boredom." The unfinished work, titled *The Pale King,* is scheduled for publication in 2011.

This Is Water

"This Is Water" transcribes the commencement address that Wallace gave to Kenyon College graduates in 2005; it was later published in *Best American Non-required Reading* and as a book. In the speech, Wallace invokes a long example to urge his listeners to reset their human "default setting" of self-centeredness.

There are these two young fish swimming along, and they happen to meet an 1
older fish swimming the other way, who nods at them and says, "Morning, boys, how's the water?" And the two young fish swim on for a bit, and then eventually one of them looks over at the other and goes, "What the hell is water?"

If at this moment, you're worried that I plan to present myself here as the 2
wise old fish explaining what water is to you younger fish, please don't be. I am not the wise old fish. The immediate point of the fish story is that the most obvious, ubiquitous, important realities are often the ones that are the hardest to see and talk about. Stated as an English sentence, of course, this is just a banal platitude — but the fact is that, in the day-to-day trenches of adult existence, banal platitudes can have life-or-death importance. That may sound like hyperbole, or abstract nonsense.

A huge percentage of the stuff that I tend to be automatically certain of is, 3
it turns out, totally wrong and deluded. Here's one example of the utter wrongness of something I tend to be automatically sure of: Everything in my own immediate experience supports my deep belief that I am the absolute center of the universe, the realest, most vivid and important person in existence. We

rarely talk about this sort of natural, basic self-centeredness, because it's so socially repulsive, but it's pretty much the same for all of us, deep down. It is our default setting, hardwired into our boards at birth. Think about it: There is no experience you've had that you were not at the absolute center of. The world as you experience it is right there in front of you, or behind you, to the left or right of you, on your TV, or your monitor, or whatever. Other people's thoughts and feelings have to be communicated to you somehow, but your own are so immediate, urgent, *real*—you get the idea. But please don't worry that I'm getting ready to preach to you about compassion or other-directedness or the so-called virtues. This is not a matter of virtue—it's a matter of my choosing to do the work of somehow altering or getting free of my natural, hardwired default setting, which is to be deeply and literally self-centered, and to see and interpret everything through this lens of self.

People who can adjust their natural default setting this way are often de-   4
scribed as being "well adjusted," which I suggest to you is not an accidental term.

Given the triumphal academic setting here, an obvious question is how   5
much of this work of adjusting our default setting involves actual knowledge or intellect. This question gets tricky. Probably the most dangerous thing about college education, at least in my own case, is that it enables my tendency to overintellectualize stuff, to get lost in abstract arguments inside my head instead of simply paying attention to what's going on right in front of me. Paying attention to what's going on inside me. As I'm sure you guys know by now, it is extremely difficult to stay alert and attentive instead of getting hypnotized by the constant monologue inside your own head. Twenty years after my own graduation, I have come gradually to understand that the liberal-arts cliché about "teaching you how to think" is actually shorthand for a much deeper, more serious idea: "Learning how to think" really means learning how to exercise some control over how and what you think. It means being conscious and aware enough to choose what you pay attention to and to choose how you construct meaning from experience. Because if you cannot exercise this kind of choice in adult life, you will be totally hosed. Think of the old cliché about "the mind being an excellent servant but a terrible master." This, like many clichés, so lame and unexciting on the surface, actually expresses a great and terrible truth. It is not the least bit coincidental that adults who commit suicide with firearms almost always shoot themselves in the head. And the truth is that most of these suicides are actually dead long before they pull the trigger. And I submit that this is what the real, no-bull value of your liberal-arts education is supposed to be about: How to keep from going through your comfortable, prosperous, respectable adult life dead, unconscious, a slave to

your head and to your natural default setting of being uniquely, completely, imperially alone, day in and day out.

That may sound like hyperbole, or abstract nonsense. So let's get concrete. The plain fact is that you graduating seniors do not yet have any clue what "day in, day out" really means. There happen to be whole large parts of adult American life that nobody talks about in commencement speeches. One such part involves boredom, routine, and petty frustration. The parents and older folks here will know all too well what I'm talking about.

By way of example, let's say it's an average day, and you get up in the morning, go to your challenging job, and you work hard for nine or ten hours, and at the end of the day you're tired, and you're stressed out, and all you want is to go home and have a good supper and maybe unwind for a couple of hours and then hit the rack early because you have to get up the next day and do it all again. But then you remember there's no food at home — you haven't had time to shop this week, because of your challenging job — and so now after work you have to get in your car and drive to the supermarket. It's the end of the workday, and the traffic's very bad, so getting to the store takes way longer than it should, and when you finally get there the supermarket is very crowded, because of course it's the time of day when all the other people with jobs also try to squeeze in some grocery shopping, and the store's hideously, fluorescently lit, and infused with soul-killing Muzak or corporate pop, and it's pretty much the last place you want to be, but you can't just get in and quickly out: You have to wander all over the huge, overlit store's crowded aisles to find the stuff you want, and you have to maneuver your junky cart through all these other tired, hurried people with carts, and of course there are also the glacially slow old people and the spacey people and the ADHD kids who all block the aisle and you have to grit your teeth and try to be polite as you ask them to let you by, and eventually, finally, you get all your supper supplies, except now it turns out there aren't enough checkout lanes open even though it's the end-of-the-day rush, so the checkout line is incredibly long, which is stupid and infuriating, but you can't take your fury out on the frantic lady working the register.

Anyway, you finally get to the checkout line's front, and pay for your food, and wait to get your check or card authenticated by a machine, and then get told to "Have a nice day" in a voice that is the absolute voice of *death*, and then you have to take your creepy flimsy plastic bags of groceries in your cart through the crowded, bumpy, littery parking lot, and try to load the bags in your car in such a way that everything doesn't fall out of the bags and roll around in the trunk on the way home, and then you have to drive all the way home through slow, heavy, SUV-intensive rush-hour traffic, etcetera, etcetera.

The point is that petty, frustrating crap like this is exactly where the work 9
of choosing comes in. Because the traffic jams and crowded aisles and long
checkout lines give me time to think, and if I don't make a conscious decision
about how to think and what to pay attention to, I'm going to be pissed and
miserable every time I have to food-shop, because my natural default setting
is the certainty that situations like this are really all about *me*, about my hun-
griness and my fatigue and my desire to just get home, and it's going to seem,
for all the world, like everybody else is just *in my way*, and who are all these
people in my way? And look at how repulsive most of them are and how stupid
and cow-like and dead-eyed and nonhuman they seem here in the checkout
line, or at how annoying and rude it is that people are talking loudly on cell
phones in the middle of the line, and look at how deeply unfair this is: I've
worked really hard all day and I'm starved and tired and I can't even get home
to eat and unwind because of all these stupid g——d—— *people.*

Or, of course, if I'm in a more socially conscious form of my default set- 10
ting, I can spend time in the end-of-the-day traffic jam being angry and disgusted at all the huge, stupid, lane-blocking SUVs and Hummers and V-12
pickup trucks burning their wasteful, selfish, forty-gallon tanks of gas, and I can
dwell on the fact that the patriotic or religious bumper stickers always seem
to be on the biggest, most disgustingly selfish vehicles driven by the ugliest,
most inconsiderate and aggressive drivers, who are usually talking on cell
phones as they cut people off in order to get just twenty stupid feet ahead in a
traffic jam, and I can think about how our children's children will despise us
for wasting all the future's fuel and probably screwing up the climate, and how
spoiled and stupid and disgusting we all are, and how it all just *sucks*, and so
on and so forth . . .

Look, if I choose to think this way, fine, lots of us do—except that think- 11
ing this way tends to be so easy and automatic it doesn't *have* to be a choice.
Thinking this way is my natural default setting. It's the automatic, unconscious way that I experience the boring, frustrating, crowded parts of adult
life when I'm operating on the automatic, unconscious belief that I am the
center of the world and that my immediate needs and feelings are what should
determine the world's priorities. The thing is that there are obviously different
ways to think about these kinds of situations. In this traffic, all these vehicles
stuck and idling in my way: It's not impossible that some of these people in
SUVs have been in horrible auto accidents in the past and now find driving
so traumatic that their therapist has all but ordered them to get a huge, heavy
SUV so they can feel safe enough to drive; or that the Hummer that just cut
me off is maybe being driven by a father whose little child is hurt or sick in
the seat next to him, and he's trying to rush to the hospital, and he's in a way
bigger, more legitimate hurry than I am—it is actually *I* who am in *his* way.

Or I can choose to force myself to consider the likelihood that everyone else in the supermarket's checkout line is just as bored and frustrated as I am, and that some of these people probably have much harder, more tedious or painful lives than I do, overall.

Again, please don't think that I'm giving you moral advice, or that I'm saying you're "supposed to" think this way, or that anyone expects you to just automatically do it, because it's hard, it takes will and mental effort, and if you're like me, some days you won't be able to do it, or you just flat-out won't want to. But most days, if you're aware enough to give yourself a choice, you can choose to look differently at this fat, dead-eyed, over-made lady who just screamed at her little child in the checkout line — maybe she's not usually like this; maybe she's been up three straight nights holding the hand of her husband who's dying of bone cancer, or maybe this very lady is the low-wage clerk at the Motor Vehicles Department who just yesterday helped your spouse resolve a nightmarish red-tape problem through some small act of bureaucratic kindness. Of course, none of this is likely, but it's also not impossible — it just depends on what you want to consider. If you're automatically sure that you know what reality is and who and what is really important — if you want to operate on your default setting — then you, like me, will not consider possibilities that aren't pointless and annoying. But if you've really learned how to think, how to pay attention, then you will know you have other options. It will actually be within your power to experience a crowded, loud, slow, consumer-hell-type situation as not only meaningful but sacred, on fire with the same force that lit the stars — compassion, love, the subsurface unity of all things. Not that that mystical stuff's necessarily true: The only thing that's capital-T True is that you get to *decide* how you're going to try to see it. You get to consciously decide what has meaning and what doesn't. You get to decide what to worship.

Because here's something else that's true. In the day-to-day trenches of adult life, there is actually no such thing as atheism. There is no such thing as not worshipping. Everybody worships. The only choice we get is *what* to worship. And an outstanding reason for choosing some sort of God or spiritual-type thing to worship — be it JC or Allah, be it Yahweh or the Wiccan mother-goddess or the Four Noble Truths or some infrangible set of ethical principles — is that pretty much anything else you worship will eat you alive. If you worship money and things — if they are where you tap real meaning in life — then you will never have enough. Never feel you have enough. It's the truth. Worship your own body and beauty and sexual allure and you will always feel ugly, and when time and age start showing, you will die a million deaths before they finally plant you. On one level, we all know this stuff already — it's been codified as myths, proverbs, clichés, bromides, epigrams, parables: the skeleton of

12

13

every great story. The trick is keeping the truth up-front in daily conscious-ness. Worship power—you will feel weak and afraid, and you will need ever more power over others to keep the fear at bay. Worship your intellect, being seen as smart—you will end up feeling stupid, a fraud, always on the verge of being found out. And so on.

Look, the insidious thing about these forms of worship is not that they're evil or sinful; it is that they are *unconscious*. They are default settings. They're the kind of worship you just gradually slip into, day after day, getting more and more selective about what you see and how you measure value without ever being fully aware that that's what you're doing. And the world will not dis-courage you from operating on your default settings, because the world of men and money and power hums along quite nicely on the fuel of fear and con-tempt and frustration and craving and the worship of self. Our own present culture has harnessed these forces in ways that have yielded extraordinary wealth and comfort and personal freedom. The freedom to be lords of our own tiny skull-sized kingdoms, alone at the center of all creation. This kind of freedom has much to recommend it. But of course there are all different kinds of freedom, and the kind that is most precious you will not hear much talked about in the great outside world of winning and achieving and displaying. The really important kind of freedom involves attention, and awareness, and discipline, and effort, and being able truly to care about other people and to sacrifice for them, over and over, in myriad petty little unsexy ways, every day. That is real freedom. The alternative is unconsciousness, the default set-ting, the "rat race"—the constant gnawing sense of having had and lost some infinite thing. 14

I know that this stuff probably doesn't sound fun and breezy or grandly inspirational. What it is, so far as I can see, is the truth with a whole lot of rhetorical bull pared away. Obviously, you can think of it whatever you wish. But please don't dismiss it as some finger-wagging Dr. Laura sermon. None of this is about morality, or religion, or dogma, or big fancy questions of life after death. The capital-T Truth is about life *before* death. It is about making it to thirty, or maybe fifty, without wanting to shoot yourself in the head. It is about simple awareness—awareness of what is so real and essential, so hidden in plain sight all around us, that we have to keep reminding ourselves, over and over: "This is water, this is water." 15

For a reading quiz, sources on David Foster Wallace, and annotated links to other famous commencement speeches, visit **bedfordstmartins.com/thebedfordreader**.

Journal Writing

Think of a time when a stranger's behavior left you feeling frustrated, irritated, or angry. Then, taking Wallace's advice, try to imagine a background for the other person's action that would make the action forgivable. Set down the scenario of background and action in your journal. (To take your journal writing further, see "From Journal to Essay" on the next page.)

Questions on Meaning

1. What is the PURPOSE of Wallace's speech? What is the THESIS? In your own words, summarize the central idea in "This Is Water."
2. What, according to Wallace, are the true purpose and value of a liberal-arts college education?
3. What are the consequences of indulging a self-centered view of the world, as Wallace sees it? Explain the IRONY of his position.
4. In paragraph 13, Wallace says, "There is no such thing as not worshipping. Everybody worships. The only choice we get is *what* to worship." What does he mean? Is he referring to religion or to something else entirely? Explain your answer.
5. Repeatedly throughout the speech, Wallace accuses himself of sloppy thinking, referring to his points as "banal platitude," "cliché," "hyperbole," or "abstract nonsense." Find instances of each. Does Wallace truly believe that his ideas are weak? Do you? Use EVIDENCE from the text to support your answer.

Questions on Writing Strategy

1. "This Is Water" was directed at a very specific AUDIENCE. Who were Wallace's intended listeners? What ASSUMPTIONS does he make about them, and what strategies does he use to capture and hold their attention?
2. Wallace uses a single extended example to set up his philosophy of life. Where does the example begin and end? What does it illustrate?
3. Paragraphs 8 and 10 each consist of one long sentence. Find other examples of extraordinarily long sentences in the speech. What is their EFFECT?
4. Wallace begins and ends his speech with an ANECDOTE about fish. What GENERALIZATION is the story meant to illustrate?
5. **OTHER METHODS** What does Wallace COMPARE AND CONTRAST in paragraphs 9 and 12 and in paragraphs 10 and 11? What point is he making with the comparison?

Questions on Language

1. How would you describe Wallace's DICTION? Is it appropriate for a commencement speech? Is it effective? Why, or why not?

2. Wallace returns several times to the concept of a "default setting, hardwired into our boards at birth" (par. 3). What exactly is this "setting," as Wallace understands it? What does the metaphor suggest about the author's view of humanity? (See *Figures of speech* in Useful Terms for a definition of *metaphor*.)

3. Look up any of the following words you don't already know: ubiquitous, banal, platitude (par. 2); triumphal, imperially (5); infrangible, codified, bromides, epigrams (13); dogma (15).

Suggestions for Writing

1. **FROM JOURNAL TO ESSAY** Building on the scenario you imagined for your journal entry, write a NARRATIVE essay that interprets the situation and your reaction to it from the other person's point of view.

2. How do you respond to petty inconveniences and frustrations of the sort Wallace describes? Are you quick to become annoyed, even angry? Or do you take things in stride? Why do you think you respond the way you do? Are your reactions a matter of habit or of choice? Write an essay about the importance (or unimportance) of self-awareness and conscious decision making, using concrete examples or a single extended example to support your point. You may refer to some of Wallace's ideas if you wish, but be sure to develop a unique THESIS of your own.

3. Using Wallace's speech as a model, try your hand at writing a commencement address, perhaps for the next graduating class of your high school. What is your philosophy of life? What advice would you give to students about to move on to college or into the workforce?

4. **CRITICAL WRITING** "This Is Water" contains several off-hand mentions of suicide. Tragically, Wallace took his own life three years after delivering the speech. How, if at all, does that knowledge affect your interpretation of what he has to say? Does Wallace's own suicide undermine the value of his advice or change his meaning? Look up the causes and symptoms of clinical depression, and then write an essay that ANALYZES "This Is Water" as a personal meditation on battling depression, rather than as a conventional commencement speech.

5. **CONNECTIONS** Wallace's "This Is Water" and Martin Luther King's "I Have a Dream" (p. 643) were both written as persuasive speeches to be delivered to live audiences, yet they take very different approaches to influencing their listeners. COMPARE AND CONTRAST the authors' strategies, considering especially their effectiveness for the situation each spoke in and the audience each addressed. Consider as well how successfully each speech translates into a text for reading. What is lost (or gained) when an address that was intended to be heard is instead read in silence?

David Foster Wallace on Writing

As an author who grew up watching a "daily megadose" of television, David Foster Wallace used his writing to push back against the effects of the screen. In a 1991 interview with Larry McCaffery, Wallace identified his imagined readership as "people more or less like me"—twenty- and thirty-somethings who have "been raised with US commercial culture and are engaged with it and informed by it and fascinated with it but still hungry for something commercial art can't provide." He explained that young Americans, as a result of spending too many "slack-jawed, spittle-chinned, formative hours" in front of the television, have come to believe that the purpose of art is to entertain: "TV promulgates the idea that good art is just art which makes people like and depend on the vehicle that brings them the art."

According to Wallace, the expectation that art amuses is a "poisonous lesson for a would-be artist to grow up with," since it places all of the power with the audience, sometimes breeding resentment on the part of the author. "I can see it in myself and in other young writers," he told McCaffery: "this desperate desire to please coupled with a kind of hostility to the reader." Wallace expressed his "hostility" by writing unwieldy sentences, refusing to fulfill readers' expectations, and "bludgeoning the reader with data"—all strategies he used to wrestle back some of the power held by modern audiences.

Though Wallace admitted to annoying his readers on purpose, his overriding goal was to restore the relationship between artist and audience: Television's "biggest hook is that it's figured out ways to 'reward' passive spectation. A certain amount of the form-conscious stuff I write," he explained, "is trying—with whatever success—to do the opposite." Wallace's prose often switches suddenly between scenes or digresses from chronology, techniques that "prohibit the reader from forgetting that . . . this process is a relationship between the writer's consciousness and her own, and that in order for it to be anything like a full human relationship, she's going to have to put in her share of the linguistic work."

For Discussion

1. How does television affect viewers' expectations about the purpose of any type of art?
2. Why did Wallace say that he sometimes felt "hostility" toward his readers? As a reader, how do you respond?

ADDITIONAL WRITING TOPICS

Example

1. Select one of the following general statements, or set forth a general statement of your own that one of these inspires. Making it your central idea (or THESIS), support it in an essay full of examples. Draw your examples from your reading, your studies, your conversation, or your own experience.

> Compared to voice phone, text messaging has many advantages (or many disadvantages).
> Individual consumers can help slow down global warming.
> People one comes to admire don't always at first seem likable.
> Good (or bad) habits are necessary to the nation's economy.
> Each family has its distinctive lifestyle.
> Certain song lyrics, closely inspected, promote violence.
> Comic books are going to the dogs.
> At some point in life, most people triumph over crushing difficulties.
> Churchgoers aren't perfect.
> TV commercials suggest that buying the advertised product will improve your love life.
> Home cooking can't win over fast food (or vice versa).
> Ordinary lives sometimes give rise to legends.
> Some people I know are born winners (or losers).
> Books can change our lives.
> Certain machines *do* have personalities.
> Some road signs lead drivers astray.

2. In a brief essay, make a GENERALIZATION about the fears, joys, or contradictions that members of minority groups seem to share. To illustrate your generalization, draw examples from personal experience, from outside reading, or from two or three of the essays in this book by the following authors: Nancy Mairs (p. 13), Maya Angelou (p. 110), Amy Tan (p. 116), Brent Staples (p. 226), Firoozeh Dumas (p. 320), Gloria Naylor (p. 517), Christine Leong (p. 523), Linda Chavez (p. 605), Sandra Cisneros (p. 620), Martin Luther King, Jr. (p. 643), and Richard Rodriguez (p. 681).

American Gothic, 1930, painting by Grant Wood, American, 1891–1942. Oil on beaverboard, 30 11/16 × 25 11/16 in. (78 × 65.3 cm) unframed, Friends of American Art Collection, 1930.934, The Art Institute of Chicago. Photography © The Art Institute of Chicago. Art © Figge Art Museum, successors to the Estate of Nan Wood Graham / Licensed by VAGA, New York, NY.

Rural Rehabilitation Client, photograph by Ben Shahn. © CORBIS. Reprinted by permission.

7

COMPARISON AND CONTRAST

Setting Things Side by Side

◀ **Comparison and contrast in a painting and a photograph**

Created just five years apart, these works relate in time as well as subject. On the top, the painting *American Gothic,* by the Iowan Grant Wood (1892–1942), depicts farmers in 1930, before the Great Depression was fully under way. On the bottom, the photograph *Rural Rehabilitation Client,* by the Lithuanian-born New Jerseyan Ben Shahn (1899–1969), depicts recipients of a federal aid program in Arkansas in 1935, at the Depression's low point. Closely examine the people in each image (clothes, postures, expressions) and their settings. What striking and not-so-striking similarities do you notice? What is the most obvious difference? What are some more subtle differences? What does the medium of each work (painting versus photography) contribute to the differences? How would you summarize the visions of rural folk conveyed by Wood and Shahn?

THE METHOD

Should we pass laws to regulate pornography or just let pornography run wild? Which team do you place your money on, the Cowboys or the Forty-Niners? To go to school full-time or part-time: What are the rewards and drawbacks of each way of life? How do the Republican and the Democratic platforms stack up against each other? How is the work of Picasso like or unlike that of Matisse? These are questions that may be addressed by the dual method of COMPARISON AND CONTRAST. In comparing, you point to similar features of the subjects; in contrasting, to different features. (The features themselves you identify by the method of DIVISION or ANALYSIS; see Chap. 9.)

With the aid of comparison and contrast, you can show why you prefer one thing to another, one course of action to another, one idea to another. In an argument in which you support one of two possible choices, a careful and detailed comparison and contrast of the choices may be extremely convincing. In an expository essay, it can demonstrate that you understand your subjects thoroughly. That is why, on exams that call for essay answers, often you will be asked to compare and contrast. Sometimes the examiner will come right out and say, "Compare and contrast nineteenth-century methods of treating drug addiction with those of the present day." Sometimes, however, comparison and contrast won't even be mentioned by name; instead, the examiner will ask, "What resemblances and differences do you find between John Updike's short story 'A & P' and the Grimm fairy tale 'Godfather Death'?" Or, "Explain the relative desirability of holding a franchise as against going into business as an independent proprietor." But those—as you realize when you begin to plan your reply—are just other ways of asking you to compare and contrast.

In practice, the two methods are usually inseparable because two subjects are generally neither entirely alike nor entirely unlike. When Bruce Catton sets out to portray the Civil War generals Ulysses S. Grant and Robert E. Lee (p. 267), he considers both their similarities and their differences. Often, as in this case, the similarities make the subjects comparable at all and the differences make comparison worthwhile.

A good essay in comparing and contrasting serves a PURPOSE. Most of the time, the writer of such an essay has one of two purposes in mind:

1. *The purpose of showing each of two subjects distinctly by considering both, side by side.* Writing with such a purpose, the writer doesn't necessarily find one of the subjects better than the other. In his essay on Grant and Lee, Bruce Catton does not favor either general but concludes that each reflected strong currents of American history.

2. *The purpose of choosing between two things.* To EVALUATE subjects, a writer shows how one is better than the other on the basis of some standard:

Which of two short stories more convincingly captures the experience of being a teenager? Which of two chemical processes works better to clean waste water? To answer either question, the writer has to consider the features of both subjects—both the positive and the negative—and then choose the subject whose positive features more clearly predominate.

THE PROCESS

Subjects for Comparison

When you find yourself considering two subjects side by side or preferring one subject over another, you have already embarked on comparison and contrast. Just be sure that your two subjects display a clear basis for comparison. In other words, they should have something significant in common. Comparison usually works best with two of a kind: two means of reading for the visually impaired, two Civil War generals, two short stories on the same subject, two processes for cleaning waste water, two mystery writers, two schools of political thought.

It can sometimes be effective to find similarities between evidently unlike subjects—a city and a country town, say—and a special form of comparison, ANALOGY, always equates two very unlike things, explaining one in terms of the other. (In an analogy you might explain how the human eye works by comparing it to a simple camera, or you might explain the forces in a thunderstorm by comparing them to armies in battle.) In any comparison of unlike things, you must have a valid reason for bringing the two together—that is, the similarities must be significant. In a comparison of a city and a country town, for instance, the likenesses must extend beyond the obvious ones that people live in both places, both have streets and shops, and so on.

Basis for Comparison and Thesis

Beginning to identify the shared and dissimilar features of your subjects will get you started, but the comparison won't be manageable for you or interesting to your readers unless you also limit it. You would be overly ambitious to try to compare and contrast the Russian way of life with the American way of life in five hundred words; you couldn't include all the important similarities and differences. In a brief paper, you would be wise to select a single basis for comparison: to show, for instance, how day-care centers in Russia and the United States are both like and unlike each other.

This basis for comparison will eventually underpin the THESIS of your essay—the claim you have to make about the similarities and dissimilarities of two things or about one thing's superiority over another. Here, from essays in this chapter, are THESIS STATEMENTS that clearly lay out what's being compared and why:

> Neat people are lazier and meaner than sloppy people.
> —Suzanne Britt, "Neat People vs. Sloppy People"

> These were two strong men, these oddly different generals, and they represented the strengths of two conflicting currents that, through them, had come into collision.
> —Bruce Catton, "Grant and Lee: A Study in Contrasts"

Notice that each author not only identifies his or her subjects (neat and sloppy people, two generals) but also previews the purpose of the comparison, whether to evaluate (Britt) or to explain (Catton).

Organization

Even with a limited basis for comparison, the method of comparison and contrast can be tricky without some planning. We suggest that you make an outline (preferably in writing), using one of two organizations described below. Say you're writing an essay on two banjo-pickers, Jed and Jake. Your purpose is to explain the distinctive identities of the two players, and your thesis statement might be the following:

> Jed and Jake are both excellent banjo-pickers whose differences reflect their training.

Here are the two ways you might arrange your comparison:

1. *Subject by subject.* Set forth all your facts about Jed, then do the same for Jake. Next, sum up their similarities and differences. In your conclusion, state what you think you have shown.

   1. *Jed*
      Training
      Choice of material
      Technical dexterity
      Playing style

   2. *Jake*
      Training
      Choice of material
      Technical dexterity
      Playing style

SUMMARY
CONCLUSION

This procedure works for a paper of a few paragraphs, but for a longer one, it has a built-in disadvantage: Readers need to remember all the facts about subject 1 while they read about subject 2. If the essay is long and lists many facts, this procedure may be burdensome.

2. *Point by point.* Usually more workable in writing a long paper than the first method, the second scheme is to compare and contrast as you go. You consider one point at a time, taking up your two subjects alternately. In this way, you continually bring the subjects together, perhaps in every paragraph. Notice the differences in the outline:

1. *Training*
   Jed: studied under Earl Scruggs
   Jake: studied under Bela Fleck

2. *Choice of material*
   Jed: bluegrass
   Jake: jazz-oriented

3. *Technical dexterity*
   Jed: highly skilled
   Jake: highly skilled

4. *Playing style*
   Jed: rapid-fire
   Jake: impressionistic
   SUMMARY
   CONCLUSION

For either the subject-by-subject or the point-by-point scheme, your conclusion might be: Although similar in skills, the two differ greatly in aims and in personalities. Jed is better suited to the Grand Ol' Opry and Jake to a concert hall.

No matter how you group your points, they have to balance; you can't discuss Jed's on-stage manner without discussing Jake's, too. If you have nothing to say about Jake's on-stage manner, then you might as well omit the point. A surefire loser is the paper that proposes to compare and contrast two subjects but then proceeds to discuss quite different elements in each: Jed's playing style and Jake's choice of material, Jed's fondness for Italian food and Jake's hobby of antique-car collecting. The writer of such a paper doesn't compare and contrast the two musicians at all, but provides two quite separate discussions.

By the way, a subject-by-subject organization works most efficiently for a *pair* of subjects. If you want to write about *three* banjo-pickers, you might first consider Jed and Jake, then Jake and Josh, then Josh and Jed — but it would probably be easiest to compare and contrast all three point by point.

Flexibility

As you write, an outline will help you see the shape of your paper and keep your procedure in mind. But don't be the simple tool of your outline. Few essays are more boring to read than the long comparison and contrast written mechanically. The reader comes to feel like a weary tennis spectator whose head has to swivel from side to side: now Jed, now Jake; now Jed again, now back to Jake. You need to mention the same features of both subjects, it is true, but no law decrees *how* you must mention them. You need not follow your outline in lockstep order, or cover similarities and differences at precisely the same length, or spend a hundred words on Jed's banjo-picking skill just because you spend a hundred words on Jake's. Your essay, remember, doesn't need to be as symmetrical as a pair of salt and pepper shakers. What is your outline but a simple means to organize your account of a complicated reality? As you write, keep casting your thoughts upon a living, particular world—not twisting and squeezing that world into a rigid scheme, but moving through it with open senses, being patient and faithful and exact in your telling of it.

FOCUS ON PARAGRAPH COHERENCE

With several points of comparison and alternating subjects, a comparison will be easy for your readers to follow only if you frequently clarify what subject and what point you are discussing. Two techniques, especially, can help you guide readers through your comparison: transitions and repetition or restatement.

- Use TRANSITIONS as signposts to tell readers where you, and they, are headed. Some transitions indicate that you are shifting between subjects, either finding resemblances between them (*also, like, likewise, similarly*) or finding differences (*but, however, in contrast, instead, unlike, whereas, yet*). Other transitions indicate that you are moving on to a new point (*in addition, also, furthermore, moreover*).

  > Traditional public schools depend for financing, of course, on tax receipts and on other public money like bonds, and as a result they generally open enrollment to all students without regard to background, skills, or special needs. Magnet schools are similarly funded by public money. But they often require prospective students to pass a test or other hurdle for admission. In addition, whereas traditional public schools usually offer a general curriculum, magnet schools often focus on a specialized program emphasizing an area of knowledge or competence, such as science and technology or performing arts.

- Use repetition or restatement of subjects and points of comparison to clarify and link sentences. Here is the same passage on schools with its repetitions and restatements underlined:

Traditional public schools depend for financing, of course, on tax receipts and on other public money like bonds, and as a result they generally open enrollment to all students without regard to background, skills, or special needs. Magnet schools are similarly funded by public money. But they often require prospective students to pass a test or other hurdle for admission. In addition, whereas traditional public schools usually offer a general curriculum, magnet schools often focus on a specialized program emphasizing an area of knowledge or competence, such as science and technology or performing arts.

*For exercises on transitions, visit Exercise Central at **bedfordstmartins.com/ thebedfordreader**.*

CHECKLIST FOR REVISING A COMPARISON AND CONTRAST

✔ **PURPOSE**   What is the aim of your comparison: to explain two subjects or to evaluate them? Will the purpose be clear to readers from the start?

✔ **SUBJECTS**   Are the subjects enough alike, sharing enough features, to make comparison worthwhile?

✔ **THESIS**   Does your thesis establish a limited basis for comparison so that you have room and time to cover all the relevant similarities and differences?

✔ **ORGANIZATION**   Does your arrangement of material, whether subject by subject or point by point, do justice to your subjects and help readers follow the comparison?

✔ **BALANCE AND FLEXIBILITY**   Have you covered the same features of both subjects? At the same time, have you avoided a rigid back-and-forth movement that could bore or exhaust a reader?

✔ **COHERENCE**   Have you used transitions and repetition or restatement to clarify which subjects and which points you are discussing?

COMPARISON AND CONTRAST IN PARAGRAPHS

Writing about Television

The following example, written especially for *The Bedford Reader*, uses point-by-point comparison for a clear purpose: to evaluate television drama, then and now, and to express a preference for one over the other. Notice that the writer is fair—acknowledging (toward the end) that today's dramas also have none of the primitiveness of yesterday's dramas.

Though written to be freestanding, this paragraph on drama might do good work in a full essay about, say, the chief differences between TV programming in the medium's early days and programming now.

Seen on aged 16-millimeter film, the original production of Paddy Chayevsky's *Marty* makes clear the differences between television drama of 1953 and that of today. Today there's no weekly Goodyear Playhouse to showcase original one-hour plays by important authors; most scriptwriters collaborate, all but anonymously, on serials about familiar characters. *Marty* features no bodice ripping, no drug busts, no deadly illness, no laugh track. Instead, it simply shows the awakening of love between a heavyset butcher and a mousy high-school teacher: both single, lonely, and shy, never twice dating the same person. Unlike the writer of today, Chayevsky couldn't set scenes outdoors or on location. In one small studio, in slow lingering takes (some five minutes long—not eight to twelve seconds, as we now expect), the camera probes the faces of two seated characters as Marty and his pal Angie plan Saturday night ("What do you want to do?"—"I dunno. What do *you* want to do?"). Oddly, the effect is spellbinding. To bring such scenes to life, the actors must project with vigor; and like the finer actors of today, Rod Steiger as Marty exploits each moment. In 1953, plays were telecast live. Today, editing may eliminate blown lines, but a chill slickness prevails. Technically, *Marty* is primitive, yet it probes souls. Most televised drama today displays a physically larger world—only to nail a box around it.

Marginal notes:

Point-by-point comparison supporting this topic sentence

1. Original plays vs. serials

2. Simple love story vs. violence and sex

3. Studio sets with long takes vs. locations with short takes

4. Good acting vs. good acting

5. Live vs. recorded

6. Primitive and probing vs. big and limited

Transitions (underlined) clarify the comparison

Writing in an Academic Discipline

Taken from a textbook on architectural history, the following subject-by-subject comparison explains the differences between two competing theories of architecture in Russia in the 1920s and 1930s. The paragraph is one of several in which the author demonstrates how modernist architects divided into those concerned mainly with form and those concerned mainly with social progress.

In Russia, too, modernists fell into two camps. They squared off against each other in public debate and in Vkhutemas, a school of architecture organized in 1920 along lines parallel to the Bauhaus. "The measure of architecture is architecture," went the motto of one camp. They believed in an unfettered experimentalism of form.

Marginal notes:

Subject-by-subject comparison supporting this topic sentence

1. First camp: experimental

The rival camp had a problem-solving orientation. The architect's main mission, in their view, was to share in the common task of achieving the transformation of society promised by the October Revolution [of 1917]. They were keen on standardization, user interviews, and ideological prompting. They worked on new building programs that would consolidate the social order of communism. These they referred to as "social condensers."

—Spiro Kostof, A History of Architecture

2. Second camp: problem solving (receives more attention because it eventually prevailed)

COMPARISON AND CONTRAST IN A REVIEW

If you browse the Web or flip through a newspaper, a magazine, or an academic journal, you're bound to spot a review: a writer's assessment of anything from a restaurant to a scholarly book. Reviews are a common assignment in college courses, too, because they require writers to examine a subject carefully, form considered judgments, and express them convincingly.

Reviews rely most heavily on ANALYSIS, identifying and interpreting the elements of a subject. But because a review EVALUATES quality or value, writers naturally turn to comparison and contrast as well, weighing two or more products, works, or ideas to determine their relative worth. Such a comparison takes its evidence from the subjects themselves, such as descriptions of the paintings in an exhibition or quotations from written works.

For a course in popular culture, Charlotte Pak wrote a lengthy review of singer Beyoncé Knowles's solo career. Pak chose her subject after Beyoncé's enormously successful "Single Ladies (Put a Ring on It)" won song of the year at the 2010 Grammy Awards. Although Pak enjoyed the song, she found herself bothered by some of the implications in its lyrics, and she decided to investigate the singer's work for similar themes. In the paragraphs below, excerpted from her full review, Pak compares "Single Ladies" with a popular song from the 1960s, with unexpected results.

Critics and fans often view Beyoncé as one of the leaders in the "strong woman" style that encourages female independence, equality, and self-worth. These listeners offer Beyoncé's 2009 hit "Single Ladies (Put a Ring on It)" as a symbol of how far women have come since the 1950s and 1960s. But this and other songs by Beyoncé just seem strong when in fact they present women who are no more independent than the ones portrayed half a century ago.

Basis for comparison: portrayals of women's strength

Subject-by-subject organization supporting this claim

A classic example of the older style is the Dixie Cups' 1964 hit "Chapel of Love." The refrain of the song is familiar even

1. Representative older song: "Chapel of Love" by the Dixie Cups

Comparison and Contrast

today: "Goin' to the chapel and we're / Gonna get married / . . . Goin' to the chapel of love." The song itself seems sentimental and even naive on the surface. In a sweet, dreamy voice, the female singer imagines marital bliss, as "Birds all sing as if they knew / Today's the day we'll say 'I do.'" She sings of marriage as the fulfillment of her life, implying her dependence on a man. Yet despite the tone and the sentimentality, the song also suggests equality between the singer and her husband-to-be within the bounds of traditional marriage: "I'll be his and he'll be mine." The possession is mutual. Two independent individuals will say "I do."

    In contrast, the singer in Beyoncé's "Single Ladies" seems pleased to be free from an ex-boyfriend. She dances with another man in a club while her ex jealously watches: "Don't pay him any attention / 'Cause you had your turn and now you're gonna learn / What it really feels like to miss me." Her tone is feisty and no-nonsense, the voice of a sophisticated and independent woman. Yet she remains preoccupied with her ex-boyfriend and still sees herself through his eyes. In the song's chorus — "If you like it then you shoulda put a ring on it" — the "it" suggests that she has a sense of herself as an object to be possessed rather than an independent being. That suggestion is explicit in the lines "Pull me into your arms, / Say I'm the one you own." The wimpy "Chapel of Love" at least offers an image of equality. "Single Ladies" misleads by casting dependency as strength.

Margin notes:

Quotations from song

Interpretation

2. Representative Beyoncé song: "Single Ladies (Put a Ring on It)"

Quotations from song

Interpretation

Concluding sentences express judgment

SUZANNE BRITT

Suzanne Britt was born in Winston-Salem, North Carolina, and studied at Salem College and Washington University, where she earned an MA in English. Britt has written for *Sky Magazine*, the *New York Times*, *Newsweek*, the *Boston Globe*, and many other publications. Her poems have been published in the *Denver Quarterly*, the *Southern Poetry Review*, and other literary magazines. Britt teaches English at Meredith College in North Carolina and has published a history of the college and two English textbooks. Her other books are collections of her essays: *Skinny People Are Dull and Crunchy like Carrots* (1982) and *Show and Tell* (1983).

Neat People
vs.
Sloppy People

"Neat People vs. Sloppy People" appears in Britt's collection *Show and Tell*. Mingling humor with seriousness (as she often does), Britt has called the book a report on her journey into "the awful cave of self: You shout your name and voices come back in exultant response, telling you their names." In this essay, Britt uses comparison mainly to entertain by showing us aspects of our own selves, awful or not. For another approach to a similar subject, see the next essay, by Dave Barry.

I've finally figured out the difference between neat people and sloppy people. The distinction is, as always, moral. Neat people are lazier and meaner than sloppy people.

Sloppy people, you see, are not really sloppy. Their sloppiness is merely the unfortunate consequence of their extreme moral rectitude. Sloppy people carry in their mind's eye a heavenly vision, a precise plan, that is so stupendous, so perfect, it can't be achieved in this world or the next.

Sloppy people live in Never-Never Land. Someday is their métier. Someday they are planning to alphabetize all their books and set up home catalogs. Someday they will go through their wardrobes and mark certain items for tentative mending and certain items for passing on to relatives of similar shape and size. Someday sloppy people will make family scrapbooks into which they will put newspaper clippings, postcards, locks of hair, and the dried corsage from their senior prom. Someday they will file everything on the surface of their desks, including the cash receipts from coffee purchases at the snack shop. Someday they will sit down and read all the back issues of *The New Yorker*.

For all these noble reasons and more, sloppy people never get neat. They aim too high and wide. They save everything, planning someday to file, order, and straighten out the world. But while these ambitious plans take clearer and clearer shape in their heads, the books spill from the shelves onto the floor, the clothes pile up in the hamper and closet, the family mementos accumulate in every drawer, the surface of the desk is buried under mounds of paper, and the unread magazines threaten to reach the ceiling. 4

Sloppy people can't bear to part with anything. They give loving attention to every detail. When sloppy people say they're going to tackle the surface of a desk, they really mean it. Not a paper will go unturned; not a rubber band will go unboxed. Four hours or two weeks into the excavation, the desk looks exactly the same, primarily because the sloppy person is meticulously creating new piles of papers with new headings and scrupulously stopping to read all the old book catalogs before he throws them away. A neat person would just bulldoze the desk. 5

Neat people are bums and clods at heart. They have cavalier attitudes toward possessions, including family heirlooms. Everything is just another dust-catcher to them. If anything collects dust, it's got to go and that's that. Neat people will toy with the idea of throwing the children out of the house just to cut down on the clutter. 6

Neat people don't care about process. They like results. What they want to do is get the whole thing over with so they can sit down and watch the rasslin' on TV. Neat people operate on two unvarying principles: Never handle any item twice, and throw everything away. 7

The only thing messy in a neat person's house is the trash can. The minute something comes to a neat person's hand, he will look at it, try to decide if it has immediate use and, finding none, throw it in the trash. 8

Neat people are especially vicious with mail. They never go through their mail unless they are standing directly over a trash can. If the trash can is beside the mailbox, even better. All ads, catalogs, pleas for charitable contributions, church bulletins, and money-saving coupons go straight into the trash can without being opened. All letters from home, postcards from Europe, bills, and paychecks are opened, immediately responded to, then dropped in the trash can. Neat people keep their receipts only for tax purposes. That's it. No sentimental salvaging of birthday cards or the last letter a dying relative ever wrote. Into the trash it goes. 9

Neat people place neatness above everything, even economics. They are incredibly wasteful. Neat people throw away several toys every time they 10 walk through the den. I knew a neat person once who threw away a perfectly good dish drainer because it had mold on it. The drainer was too much trouble to wash. And neat people sell their furniture when they move. They will sell a La-Z-Boy recliner while you are reclining in it.

Neat people are no good to borrow from. Neat people buy everything in   11
expensive little single portions. They get their flour and sugar in two-pound bags. They wouldn't consider clipping a coupon, saving a leftover, reusing plastic nondairy whipped cream containers, or rinsing off tin foil and draping it over the unmoldy dish drainer. You can never borrow a neat person's newspaper to see what's playing at the movies. Neat people have the paper all wadded up and in the trash by 7:05 AM.

Neat people cut a clean swath through the organic as well as the inorganic   12
world. People, animals, and things are all one to them. They are so insensitive. After they've finished with the pantry, the medicine cabinet, and the attic, they will throw out the red geranium (too many leaves), sell the dog (too many fleas), and send the children off to boarding school (too many scuff-marks on the hardwood floors).

For a reading quiz, sources on Suzanne Britt, and annotated links to further readings on personality traits, visit **bedfordstmartins.com/thebedfordreader**.

Journal Writing

Britt suggests that grouping people according to oppositions, such as neat versus sloppy, reveals other things about them. Write about the oppositions you use to evaluate people. Smart versus dumb? Fit versus out of shape? Hip versus clueless? Rich versus poor? Outgoing versus shy? Open-minded versus narrow-minded? (To take your journal writing further, see "From Journal to Essay" on the next page.)

Questions on Meaning

1. "Suzanne Britt believes that neat people are lazy, mean, petty, callous, wasteful, and insensitive." How would you respond to this statement?
2. Is the author's main PURPOSE to make fun of neat people, to assess the habits of neat and sloppy people, to help neat and sloppy people get along better, to defend

sloppy people, to amuse and entertain, or to prove that neat people are morally inferior to sloppy people? Discuss.

3. What is meant by "as always" in the sentence "The distinction is, as always, moral" (par. 1)? Does the author seem to be suggesting that any and all distinctions between people are moral?

Questions on Writing Strategy

1. What is the general TONE of this essay? What words and phrases help you determine that tone?
2. Britt mentions no similarities between neat and sloppy people. Does that mean this is not a good comparison and contrast essay? Why might a writer deliberately focus on differences and give very little or no time to similarities?
3. Consider the following GENERALIZATIONS: "For all these noble reasons and more, sloppy people never get neat" (par. 4) and "The only thing messy in a neat person's house is the trash can" (8). How can you tell that these statements are generalizations? Look for other generalizations in the essay. What is the EFFECT of using so many?
4. How does Britt use repetition to clarify her comparison?
5. **OTHER METHODS**   Although filled with generalizations, Britt's essay does not lack for EXAMPLES. Study the examples in paragraph 11, and explain how they do and don't work the way examples should: to bring the generalizations about people down to earth.

Questions on Language

1. Consult your dictionary for definitions of these words: rectitude (par. 2); métier, tentative (3); accumulate (4); excavation, meticulously, scrupulously (5); salvaging (9).
2. How do you understand the use of the word *noble* in the first sentence of paragraph 4? Is it meant literally? Are there other words in the essay that appear to be written in a similar tone?

Suggestions for Writing

1. **FROM JOURNAL TO ESSAY**   From your journal entry, choose your favorite opposition for evaluating people, and write an essay in which you compare and contrast those who pass your "test" with those who fail it. You may choose to write a tongue-in-cheek essay, as Britt does, or a serious one.
2. Write an essay in which you compare and contrast two apparently dissimilar groups of people: for example, blue-collar workers and white-collar workers, people who write a lot of e-mail and people who don't bother with it, runners and football players, readers and TV watchers, or any other variation you choose. Your approach may be either lighthearted or serious, but make sure you come to some conclusion about your subjects. Which group do you favor? Why?

3. ANALYZE the similarities and differences between two characters in your favorite novel, story, film, or television show. Which aspects of their personalities make them work well together, within the context in which they appear? Which characteristics work against each other, and therefore provide the necessary conflict to hold the reader's or viewer's attention?

4. **CRITICAL WRITING** Britt's essay is remarkable for its exaggeration of the two types. Write a brief essay analyzing and contrasting the ways Britt characterizes sloppy people and neat people. Be sure to consider the CONNOTATIONS of the words, such as "moral rectitude" for sloppy people (par. 2) and "cavalier" for neat people (6).

5. **CONNECTIONS** Neither Suzanne Britt nor the author of the next essay, Dave Barry, seems to have much sympathy for neat people. Write a brief essay in which you explain why neatness matters. Or if you haven't a clue why, then write a brief essay in which you explain the benefits of dirt and disorder.

Suzanne Britt on Writing

Asked to tell how she writes, Suzanne Britt contributed the following comment to *The Bedford Reader.*

The question "How do you write?" gets a snappy, snappish response from me. The first commandment is "Live!" And the second is like unto it: "Pay attention!" I don't mean that you have to live high or fast or deep or wise or broad. And I certainly don't mean you have to live true and upright. I just mean that you have to suck out all the marrow of whatever you do, whether it's picking the lint off the navy-blue suit you'll be wearing to Cousin Ione's funeral or popping an Aunt Jemimah frozen waffle into the toaster oven or lying between sand dunes, watching the way the sea oats slice the azure sky. The ominous question put to me by students on all occasions of possible accountability is "Will this count?" My answer is rock bottom and hard: "Everything counts," I say, and silence falls like prayers across the room.

The same is true of writing. Everything counts. Despair is good. Numbness can be excellent. Misery is fine. Ecstasy will work — or pain or sorrow or passion. The only thing that won't work is indifference. A writer refuses to be shocked and appalled by anything going or coming, rising or falling, singing or soundless. The only thing that shocks me, truth to tell, is indifference. How dare you not fight for the right to the crispy end piece on the standing-rib roast? How dare you let the fragrance of Joy go by without taking a whiff of it? How dare you not see the old woman in the snap-front housedress and the rolled-down socks, carrying her Polident and Charmin in a canvas tote that says, simply, elegantly, Le Bag?

After you have lived, paid attention, seen connections, felt the harmony, writhed under the dissonance, fixed a Diet Coke, popped a big stick of Juicy Fruit in your mouth, gathered your life around you as a mother hen gathers her brood, as a queen settles the folds in her purple robes, you are ready to write. And what you will write about, even if you have one of those teachers who makes you write about, say, Guatemala, will be something very exclusive and intimate — something just between you and Guatemala. All you have to find out is what that small intimacy might be. It is there. And having found it, you have to make it count.

There is no rest for a writer. But there is no boredom either. A Sunday morning with a bottle of extra-strength aspirin within easy reach and an ice bag on your head can serve you very well in writing. So can a fly buzzing at your ear or a heart-stopping siren in the night or an interminable afternoon in a biology lab in front of a frog's innards.

All you need, really, is the audacity to believe, with your whole being, that if you tell it right, tell it truly, tell it so we can all see it, the "it" will play in Peoria, Poughkeepsie, Pompeii, or Podunk. In the South we call that conviction, that audacity, an act of faith. But you can call it writing.

For Discussion

1. What advice does Britt offer a student assigned to write a paper about, say, Guatemala? If you were that student, how would you go about taking her advice?
2. Where in her comment does the author use colorful and effective FIGURES OF SPEECH?
3. What is the TONE of Britt's remarks? Sum up her attitude toward her subject, writing.

DAVE BARRY

Dave Barry is a humorist whom the *New York Times* has called "the funniest man in America." Barry was born in 1947 in Armonk, New York, and graduated from Haverford College in 1969. He worked as a reporter for five years and lectured businesspeople on writing for eight years while he began to establish himself. As a columnist for the *Miami Herald* for two decades, Barry published humor writing that was syndicated in several hundred newspapers nationwide. He retired from his weekly column in 2005 but still writes occasional essays as well as a blog. He also has published thirty books, including *Bad Habits: A 100% Fact Free Book* (1985), *The World According to Dave Barry* (1994), *Dave Barry in Cyberspace* (1996), and *Dave Barry's Money Secrets* (2006), the last offering funny advice on everything from buying a new car to filing taxes to talking to children about money. In 1988 Barry received the Pulitzer Prize for "distinguished commentary," although, he says, "nothing I've ever written fits the definition." (He thinks he won because his columns stood out from the "earthshakingly important" competition.) Barry lives in Miami.

Batting Clean-Up and Striking Out

This essay from *Dave Barry's Greatest Hits* (1988) illustrates Barry's gift, in the words of critic Alison Teal, "for taking things at face value and rendering them funny on those grounds alone, for rendering every ounce of humor out of a perfectly ordinary experience." Like Suzanne Britt in the previous essay, Barry contrasts two styles of dealing with a mess.

The primary difference between men and women is that women can see [1] extremely small quantities of dirt. Not when they're babies, of course. Babies of both sexes have a very low awareness of dirt, other than to think it tastes better than food.

But somewhere during the growth process, a hormonal secretion takes [2] place in women that enables them to see dirt that men cannot see, dirt at the level of *molecules*, whereas men don't generally notice it until it forms clumps large enough to support agriculture. This can lead to tragedy, as it did in the ill-fated ancient city of Pompeii, where the residents all got killed when the local volcano erupted and covered them with a layer of ash twenty feet deep.[1]

---

[1] Pompeii, in what is now southern Italy, was buried in the eruption of Mount Vesuvius in AD 79. —EDS.

Modern people often ask, "How come, when the ashes started falling, the Pompeii people didn't just *leave?*" The answer is that in Pompeii, it was the custom for the men to do the housework. They never even *noticed* the ash until it had for the most part covered the children. "Hey!" the men said (in Latin). "It's mighty quiet around here!" This is one major historical reason why, to this very day, men tend to do extremely little in the way of useful housework.

What often happens in my specific family unit is that my wife will say   3 to me: "Could you clean Robert's bathroom? It's filthy." So I'll gather up the Standard Male Cleaning Implements, namely a spray bottle of Windex and a wad of paper towels, and I'll go into Robert's bathroom, and it *always looks perfectly fine*. I mean, when I hear the word "filthy" used to describe a bathroom, I think about this bar where I used to hang out called Joe's Sportsman's Lounge, where the men's room had bacteria you could enter in a rodeo.

Nevertheless, because I am a sensitive and caring kind of guy, I "clean"   4 the bathroom, spraying Windex all over everything including the six hundred action figures each sold separately that God forbid Robert should ever take a bath without, and then I wipe it back off with the paper towels, and I go back to whatever activity I had been engaged in, such as doing an important project on the Etch-a-Sketch, and a little while later my wife will say: "I hate to rush you, but could you do Robert's bathroom? It's really *filthy*." She is in there looking at the very walls I *just Windexed*, and she is seeing *dirt! Everywhere!* And if I tell her I already *cleaned* the bathroom, she gives me this look that she has perfected, the same look she used on me the time I selected Robert's outfit for school and part of it turned out to be pajamas.

The opposite side of the dirt coin, of course, is sports. This is an area   5 where men tend to feel very sensitive and women tend to be extremely callous. I have written about this before and I always get irate letters from women who say they are the heavyweight racquetball champion of someplace like Iowa and are sensitive to sports to the point where they could crush my skull like a ripe grape, but I feel these women are the exception.

A more representative woman is my friend Maddy, who once invited   6 some people, including my wife and me, over to her house for an evening of stimulating conversation and jovial companionship, which sounds fine except that this particular evening occurred *during a World Series game*. If you can imagine such a social gaffe.

We sat around the living room and Maddy tried to stimulate a conversa-   7 tion, but we males could not focus our attention on the various suggested topics because we could actually *feel* the World Series television and radio broadcast rays zinging through the air, penetrating right into our bodies, causing our dental fillings to vibrate, and all the while the women were behaving *as though nothing were wrong*. It was exactly like that story by Edgar Allan Poe where the murderer can hear the victim's heart beating louder and louder even though he (the murder victim) is dead, until finally he (the murderer) can't stand it anymore, and he just *has* to watch the World Series on television.[2] That was how we felt.

Maddy's husband made the first move, coming up with an absolutely brilliant means of escape: *He used their baby.* He picked up Justine, their seven-month-old daughter, who was fussing a little, and announced: "What this child needs is to have her bottle and watch the World Series." And just like that he was off to the family room, moving very quickly for a big man holding a baby. A second male escaped by pretending to clear the dessert plates. Soon all four of us were in there, watching the Annual Fall Classic, while the women prattled away about human relationships or something. It turned out to be an extremely pivotal game.

8

*For a reading quiz, sources on Dave Barry, and annotated links to further readings on gender differences, visit **bedfordstmartins.com/thebedfordreader**.*

Journal Writing

Are you ever baffled by the behavior of members of the opposite sex — or members of your own sex, if you often find yourself behaving differently from most of them? List traits of men or women that you find foreign or bewildering, such as that they do or do not want to talk about their feelings or that they can spend countless hours watching sports on television or shopping. (To take your journal writing further, see "From Journal to Essay" on the next page.)

Questions on Meaning

1. What is the PURPOSE of Barry's essay? How do you know?
2. How OBJECTIVE is Barry's portrayal of men and women? Does he seem to understand one sex better than the other? Does he seek to justify and excuse male sloppiness and antisocial behavior?
3. What can you INFER about Barry's attitude toward the differences between the sexes? Does he see a way out?

---

[2] Except for the World Series ending, Barry refers to Poe's story "The Tell-Tale Heart" (1843). — EDS.

Questions on Writing Strategy

1. Barry's comparison is organized point by point—differences in sensitivity to dirt, then differences in sensitivity to sports. What is the EFFECT of this organization? Or, from another angle, what would have been the effect of a subject-by-subject organization—just men, then just women (or vice versa)?
2. How does Barry set the TONE of this piece from the very first paragraph?
3. The first sentence looks like a THESIS STATEMENT but turns out not to be complete. Where does Barry finish his statement of the essay's thesis? Does it hurt or help the essay that the thesis is divided? Why?
4. How does Barry's ALLUSION to Poe's "The Tell-Tale Heart" (par. 7) enhance Barry's own story?
5. In paragraph 5, how does Barry indicate that he's changing points of comparison?
6. **OTHER METHODS** How persuasive is the historical EXAMPLE cited in paragraph 2 as EVIDENCE for Barry's claims about men's and women's differing abilities to perceive dirt? Must examples always be persuasive?

Questions on Language

1. Define these words: hormonal (par. 2); implements (3); callous, irate (5); jovial, gaffe (6); prattled, pivotal (8).
2. Paragraph 4 begins with a textbook example of a run-on sentence. Does Barry need a better copy editor, or is he going for an effect here? If so, what is it?
3. What effect does Barry achieve with frequent italics (for example, *"just Windexed,"* par. 4) and capital letters ("Standard Male Cleaning Implements," 3)?
4. Why does Barry use the word *males* instead of *men* in paragraphs 7 and 8?

Suggestions for Writing

1. **FROM JOURNAL TO ESSAY** From the list you compiled in your journal, choose the trait of men or women that seems to have the most potential for humor. Write an essay similar to Barry's, exaggerating the difference to the point where it becomes the defining distinction between men and women.
2. How well do you conform to Barry's GENERALIZATIONS about your gender? In what ways are you stereotypically male or female? Do such generalizations amuse or merely annoy you? Why?
3. Considerable research has examined whether the differences between women and men are caused by heredity or by the environment. Explore some of this research, and write an essay ANALYZING what you discover. Based on your reading, do you think gender differences result primarily from biology or from social conditioning?
4. **CRITICAL WRITING** Barry is obviously not afraid of offending women: He claims to have already done so (par. 5), and yet he persists. Do you take offense at any of this essay's stereotypes of women and men? If so, explain the nature of the offense as coolly as you can. Whether you take offense or not, can you see any virtue in using such stereotypes for humor? For instance, does the humor help undermine

the stereotypes or merely strengthen them? Write an essay in which you address these questions, using quotations from Barry as examples and evidence.

5. **CONNECTIONS** Write an essay about the humor gained from exaggeration, relying on Barry's essay and Suzanne Britt's "Neat People vs. Sloppy People" (p. 255). Why is exaggeration often funny? What qualities does humorous exaggeration have? Quote and PARAPHRASE from Barry's and Britt's essays for your support.

Dave Barry on Writing

For Dave Barry, coming up with ideas for humorous writing is no problem. "Just about anything's a topic for a humor column," he told an interviewer for *Contemporary Authors* in 1990, "any event that occurs in the news, anything that happens in daily life—driving, shopping, reading, eating. You can look at just about anything and see humor in it somewhere."

Writing challenges, for Barry, occur after he has his idea. "Writing has always been hard for me," he says. "The hard part is getting the jokes to come, and it never happens all at once for me. I very rarely have any idea where a column is going to go when it starts. It's a matter of piling a little piece here and a little piece there, fitting them together, going on to the next part, then going back and gradually shaping the whole piece into something. I know what I want in terms of reaction, and I want it to have a certain feel. I know when it does and when it doesn't. But I'm never sure when it's going to get there. That's what writing is. That's why it's so painful and slow. But that's more technique than anything else. You don't rely on inspiration—I don't, anyway, and I don't think most writers do. The creative process is just not an inspirational one for most people. There's a little bit of that and a whole lot of polishing."

A humor writer must be sensitive to readers, trying to make them smile, but Barry warns against catering to an audience. "I think it's a big mistake to write humor for anybody but yourself, to try to adopt any persona other than your own. If I don't at some point think something is funny, then I'm not going to write it." Not that his own sense of humor will always make a piece fly. "Thinking of it in rough form is one thing," Barry confesses, "and shaping and polishing it so that you like the way it reads is so agonizingly slow that by the time you're done, you don't think anything is funny. You think this is something you might use to console a widow."

More often, though, the shaping and polishing—the constant revision—do work. "Since I know how to do that," Barry says, "since I do it every day of the week and have for years and years, I'm confident that if I keep at it I'll get something."

For Discussion

1. Do you agree with Barry that "[y]ou can look at just about anything and see humor in it somewhere"? What topics might be off-limits for humor?
2. What does successful writing depend on, according to Barry? What role does inspiration play?
3. How might Barry's views on writing be relevant to your own experiences as a writer? What can a humor writer teach a college writer?

BRUCE CATTON

Bruce Catton (1899–1978) was one of America's best-known historians of the American Civil War. As a boy in Benzonia, Michigan, Catton acted out historical battles on local playing fields. In his memoir *Waiting for the Morning Train* (1972), he recalls how he would listen by the hour to the memories of Union army veterans. His studies at Oberlin College interrupted by service in World War I, Catton never finished his bachelor's degree. Instead, he worked as a reporter, columnist, and editorial writer for the *Cleveland Plain Dealer* and other newspapers, then became a speechwriter and information director for government agencies. Of Catton's eighteen books, seventeen were written after his fiftieth year. *A Stillness at Appomattox* (1953) won him both a Pulitzer Prize for history and a National Book Award; other notable works include *This Hallowed Ground* (1956) and *Gettysburg: The Final Fury* (1974). From 1954 until his death, Catton edited *American Heritage*, a magazine of history. President Gerald Ford awarded him a Medal of Freedom for his life's accomplishment.

Grant and Lee:
A Study in Contrasts

"Grant and Lee: A Study in Contrasts" first appeared in *The American Story,* a book of essays written by eminent historians for interested general readers. Ulysses S. Grant and Robert E. Lee were opposing generals of the Civil War, Grant commanding forces of the North and Lee commanding forces of the South (called the Confederacy). The war lasted from 1861 to 1865, ending with Lee's surrender to Grant at the meeting Catton describes. Contrasting the two great generals allows Catton to portray not only two very different men but also the conflicting traditions they represented. Catton's essay builds toward the conclusion that, in one outstanding way, the two leaders were more than a little alike.

When Ulysses S. Grant and Robert E. Lee met in the parlor of a modest house at Appomattox Court House, Virginia, on April 9, 1865, to work out the terms for the surrender of Lee's Army of Northern Virginia, a great chapter in American life came to a close, and a great new chapter began. 1

These men were bringing the Civil War to its virtual finish. To be sure, other armies had yet to surrender, and for a few days the fugitive confederate government would struggle desperately and vainly, trying to find some way to go on living now that its chief support was gone. But in effect it was all over when Grant and Lee signed the papers. And the little room where they wrote out the terms was the scene of one of the poignant, dramatic contrasts in American history. 2

They were two strong men, these oddly different generals, and they repre-   3
sented the strengths of two conflicting currents that, through them, had come
into final collision.

Back of Robert E. Lee was the notion that the old aristocratic concept   4
might somehow survive and be dominant in American life.

Lee was tidewater Virginia, and in his background were family, culture,   5
and tradition . . . the age of chivalry transplanted to a New World which was
making its own legends and its own myths. He embodied a way of life that had
come down through the age of knighthood and the English country squire.
America was a land that was beginning all over again, dedicated to nothing
much more complicated than the rather hazy belief that all men had equal
rights, and should have an equal chance in the world. In such a land Lee stood
for the feeling that it was somehow of advantage to human society to have a
pronounced inequality in the social structure. There should be a leisure class,
backed by ownership of land; in turn, society itself should be keyed to the land
as the chief source of wealth and influence. It would bring forth (according to
this ideal) a class of men with a strong sense of obligation to the community;
men who lived not to gain advantage for themselves, but to meet the solemn
obligations which had been laid on them by the very fact that they were privileged. From them the country would get its leadership; to them it could look
for the higher values—of thought, of conduct, of personal deportment—to
give it strength and virtue.

Lee embodied the noblest elements of this aristocratic ideal. Through   6
him, the landed nobility justified itself. For four years, the Southern states had
fought a desperate war to uphold the ideals for which Lee stood. In the end,
it almost seemed as if the Confederacy fought for Lee; as if he himself was the
Confederacy . . . the best thing that the way of life for which the Confederacy
stood could ever have to offer. He had passed into legend before Appomattox.
Thousands of tired, underfed, poorly clothed Confederate soldiers, long since
past the simple enthusiasm of the early days of the struggle, somehow considered Lee the symbol of everything for which they had been willing to die. But
they could not quite put this feeling into words. If the Lost Cause, sanctified
by so much heroism and so many deaths, had a living justification, its justification was General Lee.

Grant, the son of a tanner on the Western frontier, was everything Lee   7
was not. He had come up the hard way, and embodied nothing in particular
except the eternal toughness and sinewy fiber of the men who grew up beyond
the mountains. He was one of a body of men who owed reverence and obeisance to no one, who were self-reliant to a fault, who cared hardly anything
for the past but who had a sharp eye for the future.

These frontier men were the precise opposites of the tidewater aristocrats.   8
Back of them, in the great surge that had taken people over the Alleghenies
and into the opening Western country, there was a deep, implicit dissatisfaction with a past that had settled into grooves. They stood for democracy, not
from any reasoned conclusion about the proper ordering of human society, but
simply because they had grown up in the middle of democracy and knew how
it worked. Their society might have privileges, but they would be privileges
each man had won for himself. Forms and patterns meant nothing. No man
was born to anything, except perhaps to a chance to show how far he could
rise. Life was competition.

Yet along with this feeling had come a deep sense of belonging to a   9
national community. The Westerner who developed a farm, opened a shop,
or set up in business as a trader could hope to prosper only as his own community prospered—and his community ran from the Atlantic to the Pacific
and from Canada down to Mexico. If the land was settled, with towns and
highways and accessible markets, he could better himself. He saw his fate in
terms of the nation's own destiny. As its horizons expanded, so did his. He
had, in other words, an acute dollars-and-cents stake in the continued growth
and development of his country.

And that, perhaps, is where the contrast between Grant and Lee becomes   10
most striking. The Virginia aristocrat, inevitably, saw himself in relation to
his own region. He lived in a static society which could endure almost anything except change. Instinctively, his first loyalty would go to the locality in
which that society existed. He would fight to the limit of endurance to defend
it, because in defending it he was defending everything that gave his own life
its deepest meaning.

The Westerner, on the other hand, would fight with an equal tenacity   11
for the broader concept of society. He fought so because everything he lived
by was tied to growth, expansion, and a constantly widening horizon. What
he lived by would survive or fall with the nation itself. He could not possibly
stand by unmoved in the face of an attempt to destroy the Union. He would
combat it with everything he had, because he could only see it as an effort to
cut the ground out from under his feet.

So Grant and Lee were in complete contrast, representing two diametri-   12
cally opposed elements in American life. Grant was the modern man emerging; beyond him, ready to come on the stage, was the great age of steel and
machinery, of crowded cities and a restless, burgeoning vitality. Lee might
have ridden down from the old age of chivalry, lance in hand, silken banner
fluttering over his head. Each man was the perfect champion of his cause,
drawing both his strengths and his weaknesses from the people he led.

Yet it was not all contrast, after all. Different as they were — in back-   13
ground, in personality, in underlying aspiration — these two great soldiers
had much in common. Under everything else, they were marvelous fighters.
Furthermore, their fighting qualities were really very much alike.

Each man had, to begin with, the great virtue of utter tenacity and fidel-   14
ity. Grant fought his way down the Mississippi Valley in spite of acute personal discouragement and profound military handicaps. Lee hung on in the
trenches at Petersburg after hope itself had died. In each man there was an
indomitable quality . . . the born fighter's refusal to give up as long as he can
still remain on his feet and lift his two fists.

Daring and resourcefulness they had, too; the ability to think faster and   15
move faster than the enemy. These were the qualities which gave Lee the dazzling campaigns of Second Manassas and Chancellorsville and won Vicksburg
for Grant.

Lastly, and perhaps greatest of all, there was the ability, at the end, to   16
turn quickly from war to peace once the fighting was over. Out of the way
these two men behaved at Appomattox came the possibility of a peace of reconciliation. It was a possibility not wholly realized, in the years to come, but
which did, in the end, help the two sections to become one nation again . . .
after a war whose bitterness might have seemed to make such a reunion wholly
impossible. No part of either man's life became him more than the part he
played in their brief meeting in the McLean house at Appomattox. Their
behavior there put all succeeding generations of Americans in their debt. Two
great Americans, Grant and Lee — very different, yet under everything very
much alike. Their encounter at Appomattox was one of the great moments of
American history.

For a reading quiz, sources on Bruce Catton, and annotated links to further readings on the American Civil War, Ulysses S. Grant, and Robert E. Lee, visit
bedfordstmartins.com/thebedfordreader.

Journal Writing

How do you respond to the opposing political beliefs represented by Grant and Lee?
During the American Civil War, nearly every citizen had an opinion and chose sides.
Do you think Americans today commit themselves as strongly to political and social

causes? In your journal, explain why, or why not. (To take your journal writing further, see "From Journal to Essay" on the next page.)

Questions on Meaning

1. What is Bruce Catton's PURPOSE in writing: to describe the meeting of two generals at a famous moment in history; to explain how the two men stood for opposing social forces in America; or to show how the two differed in personality?
2. SUMMARIZE the background and the way of life that produced Robert E. Lee; then do the same for Ulysses S. Grant. According to Catton, what ideals did each man represent?
3. In the historian's view, what essential traits did the two men have in common? Which trait does Catton think most important of all? For what reason?
4. How does this essay help you understand why Grant and Lee were such determined fighters?

Questions on Writing Strategy

1. From the content of this essay, and from knowing where it first appeared, what can you infer about Catton's original AUDIENCE? At what places in "Grant and Lee: A Study in Contrasts" does the writer expect of his readers a familiarity with US history?
2. What EFFECT does the writer achieve by setting both his INTRODUCTION and his CONCLUSION in Appomattox?
3. For what reasons does Catton contrast the two generals *before* he compares them? Suppose he had reversed his outline, and had dealt first with Grant's and Lee's mutual resemblances. Why would his essay have been less effective?
4. Closely read the first sentence of every paragraph and underline each word or phrase in it that serves as a TRANSITION. Then review your underlinings. How much COHERENCE has Catton given his essay?
5. What is the TONE of this essay — that is, what is the writer's attitude toward his two subjects? Is Catton poking fun at Lee by imagining the Confederate general as a knight of the Middle Ages, "lance in hand, silken banner fluttering over his head" (par. 12)?
6. **OTHER METHODS** In identifying "two conflicting currents," Catton uses CLASSIFICATION to sort Civil War–era Americans into two groups represented by Lee and Grant. Catton then uses ANALYSIS to tease out the characteristics of each current, each type. How do classification and analysis serve Catton's comparison and contrast?

Questions on Language

1. In his opening paragraph, Catton uses a metaphor: American life is a book containing chapters. Find other FIGURES OF SPEECH in his essay (consulting Useful Terms if you need help). What do the figures of speech contribute?
2. Look up *poignant* in the dictionary. Why is it such a fitting word in paragraph 2? Why wouldn't *touching*, *sad*, or *teary* have been as good?

3. What information do you glean from the sentence "Lee was tidewater Virginia" (par. 5)?
4. Define *aristocratic* as Catton uses it in paragraphs 4 and 6.
5. Define *obeisance* (par. 7) and *indomitable* (14).

Suggestions for Writing

1. **FROM JOURNAL TO ESSAY** Using your journal entry as a starting point, write an essay that offers an explanation for public participation in or commitment to political and social causes today. What fires people up or turns them off? To help focus your essay, zero in on a specific issue, such as education, government spending, health insurance, or gun control.
2. In a brief essay full of specific examples, discuss: Do the "two diametrically opposed elements in American life" (as Catton calls them) still exist in the country today? Are there still any "landed nobility"?
3. In your thinking and your attitudes, whom do you more closely resemble—Grant or Lee? Compare and contrast your outlook with that of one famous American or the other. (A serious tone for this topic isn't required.)
4. **CRITICAL WRITING** Although slavery, along with other issues, helped precipitate the Civil War, Catton in this particular essay does not deal with it. Perhaps he assumes that his readers will supply the missing context themselves. Is this a fair ASSUMPTION? If Catton had recalled the facts of slavery, would he have undermined any of his assertions about Lee? (Though the general of the pro-slavery Confederacy, Lee was personally opposed to slavery.) In a brief essay, judge whether or not the omission of slavery weakens the essay, and explain why.
5. **CONNECTIONS** In paragraph 3 Catton writes that Grant and Lee signified "two conflicting currents" in American society. In "Safety through Immigration Control" (p. 593) and "Not Your Homeland" (p. 598), Mark Krikorian and Edwidge Danticat present opposing viewpoints on an issue currently causing a divide in American society: immigration. Do some research into pro-immigration and anti-immigration opinions, and write an essay in which you compare and contrast the ideals and beliefs that underlie each side's position. Like Catton, make your purpose explanation, not evaluation: Treat the two positions impartially.

Bruce Catton on Writing

Most of Bruce Catton's comments on writing, those that have been preserved, refer to the work of others. As editor of *American Heritage*, he was known for his blunt, succinct comments on unsuccessful manuscripts: "This article can't be repaired and wouldn't be much good if it were." Or: "The high-water mark of this piece comes at the bottom of page one, where the naked Indian nymph offers the hero strawberries. Unfortunately, this level is not maintained."

In a memoir published in *Bruce Catton's America* (1979), Catton's associate Oliver Jensen marvels that, besides editing *American Heritage* for twenty-four years (and contributing to nearly every issue), Catton managed to produce so many substantial books. "Concentration was no doubt the secret, that and getting an early start. For many years Catton was always the first person in the office, so early that most of the staff never knew when he did arrive. On his desk the little piles of yellow sheets grew slowly, with much larger piles in the wastebasket. A neat and orderly man, he preferred to type a new page than correct very much in pencil."

His whole purpose as a writer, Catton once said, was "to reexamine [our] debt to the past."

For Discussion

1. To which of Catton's traits does Oliver Jensen attribute the historian's impressive output?
2. Which characteristics of Catton the editor would you expect to have served him well as a writer?

DAVID SEDARIS

Named Humorist of the Year 2001 by *Time* magazine, David Sedaris was born in 1957 and grew up in North Carolina. After graduating from the School of the Art Institute of Chicago in 1987, Sedaris taught writing there part-time and then moved to New York City, where he took various odd jobs. One of these jobs — a stint as a department-store Christmas elf — provided Sedaris with material for "The Santaland Diaries," the essay that launched his career as a humorist after he read it on National Public Radio's *Morning Edition* in 1993. Since then, Sedaris has contributed numerous commentaries to public radio's *Morning Edition* and *This American Life*, and his work appears frequently in *The New Yorker, Esquire*, and other magazines. He has published six collections of essays and short fiction: *Barrel Fever* (1994), *Naked* (1997), *Holidays on Ice* (1997), *Me Talk Pretty One Day* (2000), *Dress Your Family in Corduroy and Denim* (2004), and *When You Are Engulfed in Flames* (2008). In 2001 Sedaris received the Thurber Prize for American Humor. He lives in France and in New York City.

Remembering My Childhood on the Continent of Africa

Many of Sedaris's essays locate comedy in his basically normal North Carolina childhood. In this essay from *Me Talk Pretty One Day*, Sedaris highlights that normality by contrasting it with the distinctly unusual childhood of his partner.

When Hugh was in the fifth grade, his class took a field trip to an Ethiopian 1 slaughterhouse. He was living in Addis Ababa at the time, and the slaughterhouse was chosen because, he says, "it was convenient."

This was a school system in which the matter of proximity outweighed 2 such petty concerns as what may or may not be appropriate for a busload of eleven-year-olds. "What?" I asked. "Were there no autopsies scheduled at the local morgue? Was the federal prison just a bit too far out of the way?"

Hugh defends his former school, saying, "Well, isn't that the whole point 3 of a field trip? To see something new?"

"Technically yes, but . . ." 4

"All right then," he says. "So we saw some new things." 5

One of his field trips was literally a trip to a field where the class watched 6 a wrinkled man fill his mouth with rotten goat meat and feed it to a pack of waiting hyenas. On another occasion they were taken to examine the bloodied bedroom curtains hanging in the palace of the former dictator. There were tamer trips, to textile factories and sugar refineries, but my favorite is always the slaughterhouse. It wasn't a big company, just a small rural enterprise run by a couple of brothers operating out of a low-ceilinged concrete building. Following a brief lecture on the importance of proper sanitation, a small white piglet was herded into the room, its dainty hooves clicking against the concrete floor. The class gathered in a circle to get a better look at the animal, who seemed delighted with the attention he was getting. He turned from face to face and was looking up at Hugh when one of the brothers drew a pistol from his back pocket, held it against the animal's temple, and shot the piglet, execution-style. Blood spattered, frightened children wept, and the man with the gun offered the teacher and bus driver some meat from a freshly slaughtered goat.

When I'm told such stories, it's all I can do to hold back my feelings of   7
jealousy. An Ethiopian slaughterhouse. Some people have all the luck. When I was in elementary school, the best we ever got was a trip to Old Salem or Colonial Williamsburg, one of those preserved brick villages where time supposedly stands still and someone earns his living as a town crier. There was always a blacksmith, a group of wandering patriots, and a collection of bonneted women hawking corn bread or gingersnaps made "the ol'-fashioned way." Every now and then you might come across a doer of bad deed serving time in the stocks, but that was generally as exciting as it got.

Certain events are parallel, but compared with Hugh's, my childhood was   8
unspeakably dull. When I was seven years old, my family moved to North Carolina. When he was seven years old, Hugh's family moved to the Congo. We had a collie and a house cat. They had a monkey and two horses named Charlie Brown and Satan. I threw stones at stop signs. Hugh threw stones at crocodiles. The verbs are the same, but he definitely wins the prize when it comes to nouns and objects. An eventful day for my mother might have involved a trip to the dry cleaner or a conversation with the potato-chip deliveryman. Asked one ordinary Congo afternoon what she'd done with her day, Hugh's mother answered that she and a fellow member of the Ladies' Club had visited a leper colony on the outskirts of Kinshasa. No reason was given for the expedition, though chances are she was staking it out for a future field trip.

Due to his upbringing, Hugh sits through inane movies never realizing   9
that they're often based on inane television shows. There were no poker-faced sitcom martians in his part of Africa, no oil-rich hillbillies or aproned brides trying to wean themselves from the practice of witchcraft. From time to time a movie would arrive packed in a dented canister, the film scratched and faded from its slow trip around the world. The theater consisted of a few dozen folding chairs arranged before a bedsheet or the blank wall of a vacant hangar out near the airstrip. Occasionally a man would sell warm soft drinks out of a cardboard box, but that was it in terms of concessions.

When I was young, I went to the theater at the nearby shopping center   10
and watched a movie about a talking Volkswagen. I believe the little car had
a taste for mischief but I can't be certain, as both the movie and the afternoon
proved unremarkable and have faded from my memory. Hugh saw the same
movie a few years after it was released. His family had left the Congo by this
time and were living in Ethiopia. Like me, Hugh saw the movie by himself on
a weekend afternoon. Unlike me, he left the theater two hours later, to find a
dead man hanging from a telephone pole at the far end of the unpaved parking lot. None of the people who'd seen the movie seemed to care about the
dead man. They stared at him for a moment or two and then headed home,
saying they'd never seen anything as crazy as that talking Volkswagen. His
father was late picking him up, so Hugh just stood there for an hour, watching
the dead man dangle and turn in the breeze. The death was not reported in
the newspaper, and when Hugh related the story to his friends, they said, "You
saw the movie about the talking car?"

I could have done without the flies and the primitive theaters, but I   11
wouldn't have minded growing up with a houseful of servants. In North Carolina it wasn't unusual to have a once-a-week maid, but Hugh's family had
houseboys, a word that never fails to charge my imagination. They had cooks
and drivers, and guards who occupied a gatehouse, armed with machetes. Seeing as I had regularly petitioned my parents for an electric fence, the business
with the guards strikes me as the last word in quiet sophistication. Having
protection suggests that you are important. Having that protection paid for
by the government is even better, as it suggests your safety is of interest to
someone other than yourself.

Hugh's father was a career officer with the US State Department, and   12
every morning a black sedan carried him off to the embassy. I'm told it's not
as glamorous as it sounds, but in terms of fun for the entire family, I'm fairly
confident that it beats the sack race at the annual IBM picnic. By the age of
three, Hugh was already carrying a diplomatic passport. The rules that applied
to others did not apply to him. No tickets, no arrests, no luggage search: He
was officially licensed to act like a brat. Being an American, it was expected of
him, and who was he to deny the world an occasional tantrum?

They weren't rich, but what Hugh's family lacked financially they more   13
than made up for with the sort of exoticism that works wonders at cocktail parties, leading always to the remark "That sounds fascinating." It's a compliment
one rarely receives when describing an adolescence spent drinking Icees at
the North Hills Mall. No fifteen-foot python ever wandered onto my school's
basketball court. I begged, I prayed nightly, but it just never happened. Neither did I get to witness a military coup in which forces sympathetic to the

colonel arrived late at night to assassinate my next-door neighbor. Hugh had been at the Addis Ababa teen club when the electricity was cut off and soldiers arrived to evacuate the building. He and his friends had to hide in the back of a jeep and cover themselves with blankets during the ride home. It's something that sticks in his mind for one reason or another.

Among my personal highlights is the memory of having my picture taken   14
with Uncle Paul, the legally blind host of a Raleigh children's television show. Among Hugh's is the memory of having his picture taken with Buzz Aldrin on the last leg of the astronaut's world tour. The man who had walked on the moon placed his hand on Hugh's shoulder and offered to sign his autograph book. The man who led Wake County schoolchildren in afternoon song turned at the sound of my voice and asked, "So what's your name, princess?"

When I was fourteen years old, I was sent to spend ten days with my   15
maternal grandmother in western New York State. She was a small and private woman named Billie, and though she never came right out and asked, I had the distinct impression she had no idea who I was. It was the way she looked at me, squinting through her glasses while chewing on her lower lip. That, coupled with the fact that she never once called me by name. "Oh," she'd say, "are you still here?" She was just beginning her long struggle with Alzheimer's disease, and each time I entered the room, I felt the need to reintroduce myself and set her at ease. "Hi, it's me. Sharon's boy, David. I was just in the kitchen admiring your collection of ceramic toads." Aside from a few trips to summer camp, this was the longest I'd ever been away from home and I like to think I was toughened by the experience.

About the same time I was frightening my grandmother, Hugh and his   16
family were packing their belongings for a move to Somalia. There were no English-speaking schools in Mogadishu, so, after a few months spent lying around the family compound with his pet monkey, Hugh was sent back to Ethiopia to live with a beer enthusiast his father had met at a cocktail party. Mr. Hoyt installed security systems in foreign embassies. He and his family gave Hugh a room. They invited him to join them at the table, but that was as far as they extended themselves. No one ever asked him when his birthday was, so when the day came, he kept it to himself. There was no telephone service between Ethiopia and Somalia, and letters to his parents were sent to Washington and then forwarded on to Mogadishu, meaning that his news was more than a month old by the time they got it. I suppose it wasn't much different than living as a foreign-exchange student. Young people do it all the time, but to me it sounds awful. The Hoyts had two sons about Hugh's age who were always saying things like "Hey that's *our* sofa you're sitting on" and "Hands off that ornamental stein. It doesn't belong to you."

He'd been living with these people for a year when he overheard   17
Mr. Hoyt tell a friend that he and his family would soon be moving to Munich,
Germany, the beer capital of the world.

"And that worried me," Hugh said, "because it meant I'd have to find   18
some other place to live."

Where I come from, finding shelter is a problem the average teenager   19
might confidently leave to his parents. It was just something that came with
having a mom and a dad. Worried that he might be sent to live with his
grandparents in Kentucky, Hugh turned to the school's guidance counselor,
who knew of a family whose son had recently left for college. And so he spent
another year living with strangers and not mentioning his birthday. While I
wouldn't have wanted to do it myself, I can't help but envy the sense of fortitude he gained from the experience. After graduating from college, he moved
to France knowing only the phrase "Do you speak French?" — a question guaranteed to get you nowhere unless you also speak the language.

While living in Africa, Hugh and his family took frequent vacations,   20
often in the company of their monkey. The Nairobi Hilton, some suite of
high-ceilinged rooms in Cairo or Kharoum: These are the places his people
recall when gathered at a common table. "Was that the summer we spent in
Beirut or, no, I'm thinking of the time we sailed from Cyprus and took the
Orient Express to Istanbul."

Theirs was the life I dreamt about during my vacations in eastern North   21
Carolina. Hugh's family was hobnobbing with chiefs and sultans while I ate
hush puppies at the Sanitary Fish Market in Morehead City, a beach towel
wrapped like a hijab[1] around my head. Someone unknown to me was very
likely standing in a muddy ditch and dreaming of an evening spent sitting in
a clean family restaurant, drinking iced tea and working his way through an
extra-large seaman's platter, but that did not concern me, as it meant I should
have been happy with what I had. Rather than surrender to my bitterness,
I have learned to take satisfaction in the life that Hugh has led. His stories
have, over time, become my own. I say this with no trace of a kumbaya.[2]
There is no spiritual symbiosis; I'm just a petty thief who lifts his memories
the same way I'll take a handful of change left on his dresser. When my own
experiences fall short of the mark, I just go out and spend some of his. It is
with pleasure that I sometimes recall the dead man's purpled face or the report
of the handgun ringing in my ears as I studied the blood pooling beneath the

---

[1] A headscarf worn by Muslim women. — EDS.

[2] From the gospel-folk song with the line "Kumbaya, my Lord, kumbaya," meaning "Come
by here." Probably because of its popularity in folk music, the word now also has negative connotations of passivity or touchy-feely spiritualism. — EDS.

dead white piglet. On the way back from the slaughterhouse, we stopped for Cokes in the village of Mojo, where the gas-station owner had arranged a few tables and chairs beneath a dying canopy of vines. It was late afternoon by the time we returned to school, where a second bus carried me to the foot of Coffeeboard Road. Once there, I walked through a grove of eucalyptus trees and alongside a bald pasture of starving cattle, past the guard napping in his gatehouse, and into the waiting arms of my monkey.

---

*For a reading quiz, sources on David Sedaris, and annotated links to further readings on Americans' experiences among other cultures, visit **bedfordstmartins.com/ thebedfordreader**.*

Journal Writing

When have you envied the life of a friend or relative? Write about what was attractive to you in that person's life. Was it family relationships? educational or employment opportunities? travel experiences? something else? (To take your journal writing further, see "From Journal to Essay" on the next page.)

Questions on Meaning

1. What is the subject of Sedaris's comparison and contrast in this essay?
2. What do you think is the THESIS of this essay? Take into account both Sedaris's obvious envy of Hugh's childhood and Sedaris's awareness that Hugh's life was often lonely and insecure. Is the thesis stated or only implied?
3. There is a certain amount of IRONY in Sedaris's envy of Hugh's childhood. What is this irony? How does Sedaris make this irony explicit in paragraph 21?

Questions on Writing Strategy

1. Does Sedaris develop his comparison and contrast subject by subject or point by point? Briefly outline the essay to explain your answer.
2. Point to some of the TRANSITIONS Sedaris uses in moving between his and Hugh's lives.
3. Sedaris refers to Hugh's monkey in paragraphs 8, 20, and 21. In what sense does he use the monkey as a SYMBOL?
4. The first five paragraphs of the essay include a conversation between Sedaris and Hugh about Hugh's childhood. Why do you think the author opened the essay this way?

5. **OTHER METHODS**   How does Sedaris use NARRATION to develop his comparison and contrast?

Questions on Language

1. How does Sedaris use PARALLEL STRUCTURE in paragraph 8 to highlight the contrast between himself and Hugh? How does he then point up this parallelism?
2. Sedaris offers the image of himself as a "petty thief" in paragraph 21. What is the effect of this IMAGE?
3. Sedaris's language in this essay is notably SPECIFIC and CONCRETE. Point to examples of such language just in paragraph 6.
4. Consult a dictionary if necessary to learn the meanings of the following words: proximity, petty, autopsies, morgue (par. 2); hyenas (6); hawking, stocks (7); leper (8); hangar (9); machetes (11); diplomatic (12); exoticism, coup, evacuate (13); ornamental, stein (16); fortitude (19); hobnobbing, symbiosis, report, canopy, eucalyptus (21).

Suggestions for Writing

1. **FROM JOURNAL TO ESSAY**   Starting from your journal entry, write an essay in which you compare and contrast your own experiences with those of someone whose life you've envied. Have your feelings changed over time? Why, or why not?
2. Hugh's experiences living with strangers gave him a "sense of fortitude" (par. 19), according to Sedaris. When have you ever gone through a difficult experience that left you somehow stronger? Write an essay about such an experience that shows how you were different before and after.
3. In your library or on the Internet, locate and read reviews of Sedaris's book *Me Talk Pretty One Day*, the source of "Remembering My Childhood," or of another essay collection by Sedaris. Write an essay in which you SYNTHESIZE the reviewers' responses to Sedaris's work.
4. **CRITICAL WRITING**   How seriously does Sedaris want the readers of his essay to take him? Write an essay in which you analyze his TONE, citing specific passages from the text to support your conclusions.
5. **CONNECTIONS**   Gloria Naylor, in "The Meanings of a Word" (p. 517), writes about a childhood very different from either Sedaris's or Hugh's. In an essay, consider how Sedaris and Naylor might view each other's childhoods.

David Sedaris on Writing

Most of us are contented users of word processors, but not David Sedaris. In "Nutcracker.com," an essay in *Me Talk Pretty One Day*, Sedaris explains why he refuses to give up his typewriter.

I hate computers for any number of reasons, but I despise them most for what they've done to my friend the typewriter. In a democratic country you'd think there would be room for both of them, but computers won't rest until I'm making my ribbons from torn shirts and brewing Wite-Out in my bathtub. Their goal is to place the IBM Selectric II beside the feather quill and chisel in the museum of antiquated writing implements. They're power hungry, and someone needs to stop them.

When told I'm like the guy still pining for his eight-track tapes, I say, "You have eight-tracks? Where?" In reality I know nothing about them, yet I feel it's important to express some solidarity with others who have had the rug pulled out from beneath them. I don't care if it can count words or rearrange paragraphs at the push of a button, I don't want a computer. Unlike the faint scurry raised by fingers against a plastic computer keyboard, the smack and clatter of a typewriter suggests that you're actually building something. At the end of a miserable day, instead of grieving my virtual nothing, I can always look at my loaded wastepaper basket and tell myself that if I failed, at least I took a few trees down with me.

For Discussion

1. Why does Sedaris prefer writing with a typewriter instead of with a computer?
2. Defend the computerized word processor from Sedaris's attack. What are some advantages of the newer technology?

FATEMA MERNISSI

A teacher, writer, and feminist sociologist, Fatema Mernissi was born in 1940 in Fez, Morocco, and educated at the University of Mohammed V in Rabat, the Sorbonne in Paris, and Brandeis University in Massachusetts, from which she earned a PhD. Mernissi soon established herself as both a scholar and a lively writer on women's studies, religion, history, and sociology. She writes in French, English, and Arabic, and her books have been translated into several other languages. Her English titles include *Beyond the Veil: Male-Female Dynamics in Modern Muslim Society* (1975, revised in 1987), *Islam and Democracy: Fear of the Modern World* (1992, revised in 2002), *Dreams of Trespass: Tales of a Harem Girlhood* (1994), and *Women's Rebellion and Islamic Memory* (1996). Mernissi is a professor and research scholar at the University of Mohammed V. She is currently studying how the Internet and other communications technologies affect Muslim societies.

Size 6: The Western Women's Harem

Mernissi was raised in a harem, an enclave of women and children within a traditional Muslim household, off-limits to men. Traveling outside the Middle East, she encounters common Western misconceptions of a harem as either a "peaceful pleasure-garden" or an "orgiastic feast" in which "men reign supreme over obedient women"—when in fact Muslim men and women both acknowledge the inequality of the harem and women resist men in any way they can. In *Scheherazade Goes West: Different Cultures, Different Harems* (2001), Mernissi explores the "mystery of the Western harem," trying to understand why outsiders imagine harem women as totally compliant and unthreatening to men. In this last chapter from the book, Mernissi finds her answer.

Note that Mernissi provides source citations for the book she quotes in paragraph 20. The citations are in the format of *The Chicago Manual of Style*.

It was during my unsuccessful attempt to buy a cotton skirt in an American department store that I was told my hips were too large to fit into a size 6. That distressing experience made me realize how the image of beauty in the West can hurt and humiliate a woman as much as the veil does when enforced by the state police in extremist nations such as Iran, Afghanistan, or Saudi Arabia. Yes, that day I stumbled onto one of the keys to the enigma of passive beauty in Western harem fantasies. The elegant saleslady in the American store looked at me without moving from her desk and said that she had no skirt my size. "In this whole big store, there is no skirt for me?" I said. "You are joking." I felt very suspicious and thought that she just might be too tired to help me. I could understand that. But then the saleswoman added a condescending judgment, which sounded to me like an imam's fatwa.[1] It left no room for discussion:

"You are too big!" she said.   2

"I am too big compared to what?" I asked, looking at her intently, because   3
I realized that I was facing a critical cultural gap here.

"Compared to a size 6," came the saleslady's reply.   4

Her voice had a clear-cut edge to it that is typical of those who enforce   5
religious laws. "Size 4 and 6 are the norm," she went on, encouraged by my bewildered look. "Deviant sizes such as the one you need can be bought in special stores."

That was the first time that I had ever heard such nonsense about my size.   6
In the Moroccan streets, men's flattering comments regarding my particularly generous hips have for decades led me to believe that the entire planet shared their convictions. It is true that with advancing age, I have been hearing fewer and fewer flattering comments when walking in the medina, and sometimes the silence around me in the bazaars is deafening. But since my face has never met with the local beauty standards, and I have often had to defend myself against remarks such as *zirafa* (giraffe), because of my long neck, I learned long ago not to rely too much on the outside world for my sense of self-worth. In fact, paradoxically, as I discovered when I went to Rabat as a student, it was the self-reliance that I had developed to protect myself against "beauty black-mail" that made me attractive to others. My male fellow students could not believe that I did not give a damn about what they thought about my body. "You know, my dear," I would say in response to one of them, "all I need to survive is bread, olives, and sardines. That you think my neck is too long is your problem, not mine."

In any case, when it comes to beauty and compliments, nothing is too   7
serious or definite in the medina, where everything can be negotiated. But things seemed to be different in that American department store. In fact, I have to confess that I lost my usual self-confidence in that New York envi-ronment. Not that I am always sure of myself, but I don't walk around the Moroccan streets or down the university corridors wondering what people are thinking about me. Of course, when I hear a compliment, my ego expands like a cheese soufflé, but on the whole, I don't expect to hear much from others. Some mornings, I feel ugly because I am sick or tired; others, I feel wonderful because it is sunny out or I have written a good paragraph. But sud-denly, in that peaceful American store that I had entered so triumphantly, as

---

[1] An *imam* is a Muslim leader. A *fatwa* is a Muslim legal opinion or ruling. — EDS.

a sovereign consumer ready to spend money, I felt savagely attacked. My hips, until then the sign of a relaxed and uninhibited maturity, were suddenly being condemned as a deformity. . . .

"And who says that everyone must be a size 6?" I joked to the saleslady   8
that day, deliberately neglecting to mention size 4, which is the size of my skinny twelve-year-old niece.

At that point, the saleslady suddenly gave me an anxious look. "The norm   9
is everywhere, my dear," she said. "It's all over, in the magazines, on television, in the ads. You can't escape it. There is Calvin Klein, Ralph Lauren, Gianni Versace, Giorgio Armani, Mario Valentino, Salvatore Ferragamo, Christian Dior, Yves Saint-Laurent, Christian Lacroix, and Jean-Paul Gaultier. Big department stores go by the norm." She paused and then concluded, "If they sold size 14 or 16, which is probably what you need, they would go bankrupt."

She stopped for a minute and then stared at me, intrigued. "Where on   10
earth do you come from? I am sorry I can't help you. Really, I am." And she looked it too. She seemed, all of a sudden, interested, and brushed off another woman who was seeking her attention with a cutting, "Get someone else to help you, I'm busy." Only then did I notice that she was probably my age, in her late fifties. But unlike me, she had the thin body of an adolescent girl. Her knee-length, navy blue, Chanel dress had a white silk collar reminiscent of the subdued elegance of aristocratic French Catholic schoolgirls at the turn of the century. A pearl-studded belt emphasized the slimness of her waist. With her meticulously styled short hair and sophisticated makeup, she looked half my age at first glance.

"I come from a country where there is no size for women's clothes," I told   11
her. "I buy my own material and the neighborhood seamstress or craftsman makes me the silk or leather skirt I want. They just take my measurements each time I see them. Neither the seamstress nor I know exactly what size my new skirt is. We discover it together in the making. No one cares about my size in Morocco as long as I pay taxes on time. Actually, I don't know what my size is, to tell you the truth."

The saleswoman laughed merrily and said that I should advertise my   12
country as a paradise for stressed working women. "You mean you don't watch your weight?" she inquired, with a tinge of disbelief in her voice. And then, after a brief moment of silence, she added in a lower register, as if talking to herself: "Many women working in highly paid fashion-related jobs could lose their positions if they didn't keep to a strict diet."

Her words sounded so simple, but the threat they implied was so cruel   13
that I realized for the first time that maybe "size 6" is a more violent restriction imposed on women than is the Muslim veil. Quickly I said good-bye so as not

to make any more demands on the saleslady's time or involve her in any more unwelcome, confidential exchanges about age-discriminating salary cuts. A surveillance camera was probably watching us both.

Yes, I thought as I wandered off, I have finally found the answer to my   14
harem enigma. Unlike the Muslim man, who uses space to establish male domination by excluding women from the public arena, the Western man manipulates time and light. He declares that in order to be beautiful, a woman must look fourteen years old. If she dares to look fifty, or worse, sixty, she is beyond the pale. By putting the spotlight on the female child and framing her as the ideal of beauty, he condemns the mature woman to invisibility. In fact, the modern Western man enforces Immanuel Kant's nineteenth-century theories:[2] To be beautiful, women have to appear childish and brainless. When a woman looks mature and self-assertive, or allows her hips to expand, she is condemned as ugly. Thus, the walls of the European harem separate youthful beauty from ugly maturity.

These Western attitudes, I thought, are even more dangerous and cun-   15
ning than the Muslim ones because the weapon used against women is time. Time is less visible, more fluid than space. The Western man uses images and spotlights to freeze female beauty within an idealized childhood, and forces women to perceive aging — that normal unfolding of the years — as a shameful devaluation. "Here I am, transformed into a dinosaur," I caught myself saying aloud as I went up and down the rows of skirts in the store, hoping to prove the saleslady wrong — to no avail. This Western time-defined veil is even crazier than the space-defined one enforced by the ayatollahs.[3]

The violence embodied in the Western harem is less visible than in the   16
Eastern harem because aging is not attacked directly, but rather masked as an aesthetic choice. Yes, I suddenly felt not only very ugly but also quite useless in that store, where, if you had big hips, you were simply out of the picture. You drifted into the fringes of nothingness. By putting the spotlight on the prepubescent female, the Western man veils the older, more mature woman, wrapping her in shrouds of ugliness. This idea gives me the chills because it tattoos the invisible harem directly onto a woman's skin. Chinese footbinding worked the same way: Men declared beautiful only those women who had small, childlike feet. Chinese men did not force women to bandage their feet to keep them from developing normally — all they did was to define the beauty ideal. In feudal China, a beautiful woman was the one who voluntarily sacrificed her right to unhindered physical movement by mutilating her own feet, and thereby proving that her main goal in life was to please men. Similarly, in

[2] Kant (1724–1804) was a German philosopher. — Eds.
[3] Among Shiite Muslims, the authorities who interpret religious law. — Eds.

the Western world, I was expected to shrink my hips into a size 6 if I wanted to find a decent skirt tailored for a beautiful woman. We Muslim women have only one month of fasting, Ramadan, but the poor Western woman who diets has to fast twelve months out of the year. "*Quelle horreur*,"[4] I kept repeating to myself, while looking around at the American women shopping. All those my age looked like youthful teenagers. . . .

Now, at last, the mystery of my Western harem made sense. Framing youth as beauty and condemning maturity is the weapon used against women in the West just as limiting access to public space is the weapon used in the East. The objective remains identical in both cultures: to make women feel unwelcome, inadequate, and ugly.   17

The power of the Western man resides in dictating what women should wear and how they should look. He controls the whole fashion industry, from cosmetics to underwear. The West, I realized, was the only part of the world where women's fashion is a man's business. In places like Morocco, where you design your own clothes and discuss them with craftsmen and -women, fashion is your own business. Not so in the West. . . .   18

But how does the system function? I wondered. Why do women accept it?   19

Of all the possible explanations, I like that of the French sociologist Pierre Bourdieu the best. In his latest book, *La Domination Masculine*, he proposes something he calls "*la violence symbolique*": "Symbolic violence is a form of power which is hammered directly on the body, and as if by magic, without any apparent physical constraint. But this magic operates only because it activates the codes pounded in the deepest layers of the body."[5] Reading Bourdieu, I had the impression that I finally understood Western man's psyche better. The cosmetic and fashion industries are only the tip of the iceberg, he states, which is why women are so ready to adhere to their dictates. Something else is going on on a far deeper level. Otherwise, why would women belittle themselves spontaneously? Why, argues Bourdieu, would women make their lives more difficult, for example, by preferring men who are taller or older than they are? "The majority of French women wish to have a husband who is older and also, which seems consistent, bigger as far as size is concerned," writes Bourdieu.[6] Caught in the enchanted submission characteristic of the symbolic violence inscribed in the mysterious layers of the flesh, women relinquish what he calls "les signes ordinaires de la hiérarchie sexuelle," the ordinary signs of sexual hierarchy, such as old age and a larger body. By so doing,   20

---

[4] French, "What a horror."—Eds.
[5] Pierre Bourdieu, *La Domination Masculine* (Paris: Editions du Seuil, 1998), p. 44.
[6] Ibid., p. 41.

explains Bourdieu, women spontaneously accept the subservient position. It is this spontaneity Bourdieu describes as magic enchantment.[7]

Once I understood how this magic submission worked, I became very   21
happy that the conservative ayatollahs do not know about it yet. If they did, they would readily switch to its sophisticated methods, because they are so much more effective. To deprive me of food is definitely the best way to paralyze my thinking capabilities. . . .

"I thank you, Allah, for sparing me the tyranny of the 'size 6 harem,' " I   22
repeatedly said to myself while seated on the Paris-Casablanca flight, on my way back home at last. "I am so happy that the conservative male elite does not know about it. Imagine the fundamentalists switching from the veil to forcing women to fit size 6."

How can you stage a credible political demonstration and shout in the   23
streets that your human rights have been violated when you cannot find the right skirt?

---

*For a reading quiz, sources on Fatema Mernissi, and annotated links to further readings on harems and on cultural ideals of attractiveness, visit **bedfordstmartins.com/thebedfordreader**.*

Journal Writing

Within your peer group, what constitutes the norm of physical attractiveness for women and for men? (Don't focus on the ideal here, but on what is expected for a person not to be considered *un*attractive.) Are the norms similar for women and for men? (To take your journal writing further, see "From Journal to Essay" on the next page.)

Questions on Meaning

1. What two subjects does Mernissi compare? Where does she state her THESIS initially, and where later does she restate and expand on it? What does Mernissi conclude is the same about the two subjects?
2. What is the saleswoman's initial attitude toward Mernissi? How does her attitude seem to change, and how does this change contribute to Mernissi's point?

[7] Ibid., p. 42.

3. Why does Mernissi believe Western attitudes toward women are "more danger-ous and cunning" than Muslim attitudes (par. 15)?

Questions on Writing Strategy

1. What is the PURPOSE of paragraphs 6–7? What do these paragraphs contribute to Mernissi's larger point?
2. What two further comparisons does Mernissi make in paragraph 16? What TRAN-SITIONS does she use to signal the shift of subject within these comparisons?
3. **OTHER METHODS** Mernissi devotes considerable attention to a NARRATIVE of her adventure in the department store. Why does she tell this story in such detail? What does it contribute to the essay?

Questions on Language

1. What are the CONNOTATIONS of the saleswoman's word *deviant* (par. 5)?
2. Why is the metaphor of the veil in paragraph 16 especially appropriate? (See *Figures of speech* in Useful Terms if you need a definition of *metaphor*.)
3. Consult a dictionary if you are unsure of the meaning of any of the following: enigma (par. 1); generous, medina, bazaars, paradoxically (6); soufflé, sovereign (7); subdued (10); cunning, devaluation (15); aesthetic, prepubescent, unhin-dered, mutilating (16).

Suggestions for Writing

1. **FROM JOURNAL TO ESSAY** Based on your journal entry, draft an essay in which you compare and contrast standards of attractiveness for women and men within your peer group. Be sure to consider how strictly the standards are applied to each gender.
2. Write an essay about a time when your self-confidence was shaken because of how someone else treated or spoke to you. Like Mernissi, explain why you had been confident of yourself before this encounter and what effect it had on you.
3. Mernissi comes from the country of Morocco. Put her essay in context by research-ing the history and culture of Morocco. Then write an essay in which you discuss what you have learned about the country. How is Morocco different from the more "extremist nations" Mernissi refers to in her first paragraph?
4. **CRITICAL WRITING** Respond to Mernissi's essay. Do you agree with her views about "the tyranny of the 'size 6 harem'"? Does Mernissi provide enough EVIDENCE to convince you of her views? Even if you agree with her take on her department-store experience, do you think her conclusions apply across the board, as she implies: For instance, do they apply among the poor and working class as well as among the affluent? Write an essay that ANALYZES and EVALUATES Mernissi's thesis and the support for it.
5. **CONNECTIONS** When Mernissi asks who declared size 6 to be the norm in the United States, the sales clerk implicates the media: "The norm is everywhere, my

dear. . . . It's all over, in the magazines, on television, in the ads. You can't escape it" (par. 9). In "The Squeeze" (p. 487), Charles Fishman also touches on the power of marketing, describing how Wal-Mart enticed customers to purchase more pickles than they could eat. Using examples from both essays as well as from your own experience and observations, write an essay exploring a positive or a negative EFFECT of advertising and marketing on consumers. You might do some library or Internet research to further support your point.

GEORGE CHAUNCEY

George Chauncey is a professor of history at Yale University, specializing in gay and lesbian history and twentieth-century American history. He was born in 1954 in Tennessee and grew up there and in Arkansas, Kentucky, Georgia, and Virginia. He received a BA, an MA, and a PhD from Yale, where he became active in groups championing gay and lesbian rights. His PhD dissertation received an award from Yale's history department for being "a pioneering work of scholarship." It became his first book, also an award winner: *Gay New York: Gender, Urban Culture, and the Making of the Gay Male World, 1890–1940* (1994). As an expert in the history of gay rights, Chauncey has testified in several landmark court cases. He is currently working on *The Strange Career of the Closet*, which examines issues of class and race among homosexuals after World War II.

The Legacy of Antigay Discrimination

As a history student and a gay-rights activist in college, Chauncey discovered that history "is important politically: Historical analysis is required to understand present social arrangements and how they can be changed." This essay is the opening chapter in Chauncey's second book, *Why Marriage? The History Shaping Today's Debate over Gay Equality* (2004). The essay makes a historical contrast: In nine sentences beginning "Fifty years ago," Chauncey sets out aspects of current gay life or gay rights that did not exist half a century ago, and he then details the situation of discrimination that did exist. In the rest of his book, Chauncey shows how this contrast explains and strengthens the case for equal rights for homosexuals, including marriage rights.

As a scholarly work, Chauncey's essay includes acknowledgments of the author's sources. The footnotes follow the format of *The Chicago Manual of Style*, generally used in history.

The place of lesbians and gay men in American society has dramatically changed in the last half century. The change has been so profound that the harsh discrimination once faced by gay people has virtually disappeared from popular memory. That history bears repeating, since its legacy shapes today's debate over marriage.

Although most people recognize that gay life was difficult before the growth of the gay movement in the 1970s, they often have only the vaguest sense of why: that gay people were scorned and ridiculed, made to feel ashamed, afraid, and alone. But antigay discrimination was much more systematic and powerful than this.

Fifty years ago, there was no *Will & Grace* or *Ellen*, no *Queer Eye for the Straight Guy*, no *Philadelphia* or *The Hours*, no annual Lesbian, Gay, Bisexual, and Transgender (LGBT) film festival. In fact, Hollywood films were *prohibited* from including lesbian or gay characters, discussing gay themes, or even infer-ring the existence of homosexuality. The Hollywood studios established these rules (popularly known as the Hays Code) in the 1930s under pressure from a censorship movement led by Catholic and other religious leaders, who threat-ened them with mass boycotts and restrictive federal legislation. The absolute ban on gay representation, vigorously enforced by Hollywood's own censorship board, remained in effect for some thirty years and effectively prohibited the discussion of homosexuality in the most important medium of the midtwenti-eth century, even though some film makers found subtle ways to subvert it.

Censorship extended to the stage as well. In 1927, after a serious les-   4
bian drama opened on Broadway to critical acclaim—and after Mae West announced that she planned to open a play called *The Drag*—New York State passed a "padlock law" that threatened to shut down for a year any theater that dared to stage a play with lesbian or gay characters. Given Broadway's national importance as a staging ground for new plays, this law had dramatic effects on American theater for a generation.[1]

Fifty years ago, no openly gay people worked for the federal government.   5
In fact, shortly after he became president in 1953, Dwight Eisenhower issued an executive order that banned homosexuals from government employ-ment, civilian as well as military, and required companies with government contracts to ferret out and fire their gay employees. At the height of the McCarthy witch-hunt,[2] the US State Department fired more homosexuals than Communists. In the 1950s and 1960s literally thousands of men and women were discharged or forced to resign from civilian positions in the fed-eral government because they were suspected of being gay or lesbian.[3] It was only in 1975 that the ban on gay federal employees was lifted, and it took until the late 1990s before such discrimination in federal hiring was prohibited.

Fifty years ago, countless teachers, hospital workers, and other state and   6
municipal employees also lost their jobs as a result of official policy. Beginning in 1958, for instance, the Florida Legislative Investigation Committee, which had been established by the legislature in 1956 to investigate and discredit

---

[1] Kaier Curtin, *"We Can Always Call Them Bulgarians": The Emergence of Lesbians and Gay Men on the American Stage* (Boston: Alyson, 1987). George Chauncey, *Gay New York: Gender, Urban Culture, and the Making of the Gay Male World, 1890–1940* (New York: Basic Books, 1994), 311–13.

[2] US Senator Joseph McCarthy (1908–57) spearheaded aggressive investigations of sus-pected Communists in the 1940s and 1950s. —Eds.

[3] David K. Johnson, *The Lavender Scare: The Cold War Persecution of Gays and Lesbians in the Federal Government* (Chicago: University of Chicago Press, 2004), 166 and passim; Robert D. Dean, *Imperial Brotherhood: Gender and the Making of Cold War Foreign Policy* (Amherst: University of Massachusetts Press, 2001).

civil rights activists, turned its attention to homosexuals working in the state's universities and public schools. Its initial investigation of the University of Florida resulted in the dismissal of fourteen faculty and staff members, and in the next five years it interrogated some 320 suspected gay men and lesbians. Under pressure from the committee, numerous teachers gave up their jobs and countless students were forced to drop out of college.[4]

Fifty years ago, there were no gay business associations or gay bars adver-   7
tising in newspapers. In fact, many gay-oriented businesses were illegal and gay people had no right to public assembly. In many states, following the repeal of Prohibition in 1933, it even became illegal for restaurants and bars to serve lesbians or gay men. The New York State Liquor Authority, for instance, issued regulations prohibiting bars, restaurants, cabarets, and other establishments with liquor licenses from employing or serving homosexuals or allowing homosexuals to congregate on their premises.[5] The authority's rationale was that the mere presence of homosexuals made an establishment "disorderly," and when the courts rejected that argument the authority began using evidence gathered by plainclothes investigators of one man trying to pick up another or of patrons' unconventional gender behavior to provide proof of a bar's disorderly character.[6] . . .

Fifty years ago, elected officials did not court the gay vote and the nation's   8
mayors did not proclaim LGBT Pride Week. Instead, many mayors periodically declared war on homosexuals — or sex deviates, as they were usually called. In many cities, gay residents knew that if the mayor needed to show he was tough on crime and vice just before an election, he would order a crackdown on gay bars. Hundreds of people would be arrested. Their names put in the paper. Their meeting places closed. This did not just happen once or twice, or just in smaller cities. Rather, it happened regularly in every major city, from New York and Miami to Chicago, San Francisco, and LA. After his administration's commitment to suppressing gay life became an issue in his 1959 re-election campaign, San Francisco's mayor launched a two-year-long crackdown on the city's gay bars and other meeting places. Forty to sixty men and women were arrested every week in bar sweeps, and within two years almost a third of the city's gay bars had been closed.[7] Miami's gay scene was relentlessly attacked by the police and press in 1954. New York launched major crackdowns on gay

[4] Stacy Braukman, " 'Nothing Else Matters But Sex': Cold War Narratives of Deviance and the Search for Lesbian Teachers in Florida, 1959–1963," *Feminist Studies* 27 (2001): 553, 555. See also 553–57, 573, and n. 3.

[5] Chauncey, *Gay New York*, 173, 337.

[6] Chauncey, *Gay New York*, 377.

[7] John D'Emilio, *Sexual Politics, Sexual Communities: The Making of a Homosexual Minority, 1940–1970* (Chicago: University of Chicago Press, 1981), 182–84.

bars as part of its campaign to "clean up the city" before both the 1939 and 1964 World's Fairs. During the course of a 1955 investigation of the gay scene in Boise, Idaho, 1,400 people were interrogated and coerced into identifying the names of other gay residents.[8] Across America, homosexuals were an easy target, with few allies.

Fifty years ago, there was no mass LGBT movement. In fact, the hand-ful of early gay activists risked everything to speak up for their rights. When the police learned of the country's earliest known gay political group, which had been established by a postal worker in Chicago in 1924, they raided his home and seized his group's files and membership list. A quarter century later, when the first national gay rights group, the Mattachine Society, was founded, it repeatedly had to reassure its anxious members that the police would not seize its membership list. The US Post Office banned its newspaper from the mails in 1954, and in some cities the police shut down newsstands that dared to carry it. In 1959, a few weeks after Mattachine held its first press confer-ence during a national convention in Denver, the police raided the homes of three of its Denver organizers; one lost his job and spent sixty days in jail. Such harassment and censorship of free speech made it difficult for people to organize or speak on their own behalf and for all Americans to debate and learn about gay issues.[9]

Fifty years ago, no state had a gay rights law. Rather, every state had a sodomy law and other laws penalizing homosexual conduct. Beginning in the late nineteenth century, municipal police forces began using misdemeanor charges such as disorderly conduct, vagrancy, lewdness, and loitering to harass gay men.[10] In 1923, the New York State legislature tailored its statutes to specify for the first time that a man's "frequent[ing] or loiter[ing] about any public place soliciting men for the purpose of committing a crime against nature or other lewdness" was punishable as a form of disorderly conduct.[11]

---

[8] D'Emilio, *Sexual Politics*, 51; Chauncey, *Gay New York*, 340; Chauncey, *The Strange Career of the Closet: Gay Culture, Consciousness, and Politics from the Second World War to the Gay Liberation Era* (New York, Basic Books, forthcoming); John Gerassi, *The Boys of Boise: Furor, Vice, and Folly in an American City* (New York: Macmillan, 1966); Fred Fejes, "Murder, Perversion, and Moral Panic: The 1954 Media Campaign Against Miami's Homosexuals and the Discourse of Civic Betterment," *Journal of the History of Sexuality* 9 (2000): 305–47.

[9] On the Chicago group, see Jonathan Ned Katz, *Gay American History: Lesbians and Gay Men in the U.S.A.* (New York: Crowell, 1976), 385–89; Katz, *The Gay/Lesbian Almanac* (New York: Morrow, 1983), 554–61; on Mattachine, see D'Emilio, *Sexual Politics*, 115, 120–21.

[10] See John D'Emilio and Estelle B. Freedman, *Intimate Matters: A History of Sexuality in America* (San Francisco/New York: Harper and Row, 1988), 150–56, 202–15; Chauncey, *Gay New York*, 137–41, 183–86, 197–98, 249–50; Paul Boyer, *Urban Masses and Moral Order in America, 1820–1920* (Cambridge: Harvard University Press, 1978), 191–219.

[11] Chauncey, *Gay New York*, 172.

Many more men were arrested and prosecuted under this misdemeanor charge than for the felony charge of sodomy, since misdemeanor laws carried fewer procedural protections for defendants. Between 1923 and 1966, when Mayor John Lindsay ordered the police to stop using entrapment by plainclothes officers to secure arrests of gay men, more than 50,000 men had been arrested on this charge in New York City alone.[12] The number of arrests escalated dramatically after the Second World War. More than 3,000 New Yorkers were arrested every year on this charge in the late 1940s. By 1950, Philadelphia's six-man "morals squad" was arresting more gay men than the courts knew how to handle, some 200 a month. In the District of Columbia, there were more than a thousand arrests every year.[13]

Fifty years ago, more than half of the nation's states, including New York, 11 Michigan, and California, enacted laws authorizing the police to force persons who were convicted of certain sexual offenses, including sodomy—or, in some states, merely suspected of being "sexual deviants"—to undergo psychiatric examinations. Many of these laws authorized the indefinite confinement of homosexuals in mental institutions, from which they were to be released only if they were cured of their homosexuality, something prison doctors soon began to complain was impossible. The medical director of a state hospital in California argued, "Whenever a doubt arises in the judge's mind" that a suspect "might be a sexual deviate, maybe by his mannerisms or his dress, something to attract the attention, I think he should immediately call for a psychiatric examination." Detroit's prosecuting attorney demanded the authority to arrest, examine, and possibly confine indefinitely "anyone who exhibited abnormal sexual behavior, whether or not dangerous."[14]

Fifty years ago, in other words, homosexuals were not just ridiculed and 12 scorned. They were systematically denied their civil rights: their right to free assembly, to patronize public accommodations, to free speech, to a free press, to a form of intimacy of their own choosing. And they confronted a degree of policing and harassment that is almost unimaginable to us today.

---

[12] Chauncey, "A Gay World, Vibrant and Forgotten," *New York Times*, 26 June 1994, E17.

[13] John D'Emilio, "The Homosexual Menace: The Politics of Sexuality in Cold War America," in *Passion and Power: Sexuality in History*, eds. Kathy Peiss and Christina Simmons, with Robert A. Padgug (Philadelphia: Temple University Press, 1989), 231; Chauncey, "The Postwar Sex Crime Panic," in *True Stories from the American Past*, ed. William Graebner (New York: McGraw-Hill, 1993), 160–78.

[14] Estelle B. Freedman, " 'Uncontrolled Desires': The Response to the Sexual Psychopath, 1920–1960," *Journal of American History* 74 (1987): 83–106; Chauncey, "Postwar Sex Crime Panic."

*For a reading quiz, sources on George Chauncey, and annotated links to further readings on lesbian and gay rights, visit **bedfordstmartins.com/thebedfordreader**.*

Journal Writing

When have you either witnessed or been the object of unfair treatment based on race, ethnicity, language, religion, gender, age, sexual preference, economic background, or some other factor? What happened, and what was your reaction? (To take your journal writing further, see "From Journal to Essay" on the next page.)

Questions on Meaning

1. What is Chauncey's THESIS? Where does he state it?
2. What seems to be Chauncey's PURPOSE in this essay?
3. In paragraph 2, Chauncey says that antigay discrimination fifty years ago was "much more systematic" than most people realize. What does he mean by this?

Questions on Writing Strategy

1. Chauncey organizes his essay point by point. What are the main points of comparison?
2. Why does Chauncey spend more time discussing the treatment of gays and lesbians fifty years ago than discussing their treatment today? What ASSUMPTIONS does he make about his reader's knowledge of gay rights?
3. Discuss Chauncey's use of TRANSITIONS and REPETITION. What is the EFFECT of these devices?
4. Throughout his essay, Chauncey cites a number of statistics, or facts expressed numerically (see, for example, par. 10). What do these statistics accomplish?
5. **OTHER METHODS**   Discuss how Chauncey uses EXAMPLE to develop his comparison and contrast. What is the effect of his use of numerous examples?

Questions on Language

1. How would you describe the overall TONE of this essay: serious? detached? passionate? angry? astonished? Point to some words and phrases that support your answer.
2. In paragraph 5, Chauncey says that companies with government contracts were required to "ferret out and fire their gay employees." What is the CONNOTATION of the verb *ferret*? (If necessary, look up *ferret* in a dictionary.) Given Chauncey's purpose, why is this a better verb than *search out* or *find*?

3. Why does Chauncey use quotation marks around the phrases *morals squad* (par. 10) and *sexual deviants* (11)?

4. Consult a dictionary if necessary to learn the meanings of the following words: profound (par. 1); scorned (2); boycotts, subtle, subvert (3); discredit (6); repeal, cabarets (7); deviates, vice, coerced, allies (8); sodomy, vagrancy, lewdness, statutes, soliciting, procedural, entrapment, escalated (10); enacted (11); patronize (12).

Suggestions for Writing

1. **FROM JOURNAL TO ESSAY**   Write a narrative essay about the unfair treatment you recorded in your journal. Use vivid detail to re-create the incident and your reaction to it, but also reflect on its larger significance. Do you view the incident as fairly unusual, or do you think it is symptomatic of widespread prejudice? What are the causes of this prejudice, and how does it affect the people it is directed against?

2. Choose a subject that has seen significant change in the past fifty years or so—for example, gender roles, fashion, manners, a particular sport, ideals of beauty, or the rights of another group such as women, African Americans, or immigrants. Do some research on the topic and then write an essay in which you compare and contrast the situation then and now. Support your essay with specific EVIDENCE from your experience, observation, and research.

3. Although the entertainment media have clearly come a long way in the portrayal of gay and lesbian characters in the past fifty years, some critics complain that there is still much progress to be made. Write an essay in which you EVALUATE the representation of gays and lesbians in the media, considering examples of your own choosing or those mentioned by Chauncey (par. 3). Overall, do you find the portrayals to be negative or positive? What messages do these portrayals send to audiences? How might the portrayals be improved?

4. **CRITICAL WRITING**   Evaluate the effectiveness of Chauncey's essay. What do you think of the use of evidence? How successful is the author's attempt to convince readers that gays and lesbians "confronted a degree of policing and harassment that is almost unimaginable to us today" (par. 12)? Is the essay weakened by the fact that Chauncey doesn't mention prejudice and discrimination that gays and lesbians still face today? Why, or why not?

5. **CONNECTIONS**   Both Chauncey and Martin Luther King, Jr., in "I Have a Dream" (p. 643), defend the rights of a group that has faced harsh discrimination in American society, but their techniques are very different. Write an essay in which you compare and contrast Chauncey's essay with King's speech, focusing on the two writers' purposes, tones, points of view, persuasive appeals, and use of repetition and parallelism. What gives each selection its power? What makes each writer's piece particularly effective for his writing situation?

ADDITIONAL WRITING TOPICS
Comparison and Contrast

1. In an essay replete with EXAMPLES, compare and contrast the two subjects in any one of the following pairs:

   The main characters of two films, stories, or novels
   Women and men as consumers
   The styles of two runners
   Liberals and conservatives: their opposing views of the role of government
   How city dwellers and country dwellers spend their leisure time
   The presentation styles of two television news commentators

2. Approach a comparison and contrast essay on one of the following general subjects by explaining why you prefer one thing to the other:

   Vehicles: hybrids and conventional engines; sedans and SUVs; American and Asian; Asian and European
   Computers: Macs and PCs
   Two buildings on campus or in town
   Two football teams
   Two horror movies
   Television when you were a child and television today
   City life and small-town or rural life
   Malls and main streets
   Two neighborhoods
   Two sports

3. Write an essay in which you compare a reality (what actually exists) with an ideal (what should exist). Some possible topics:

   The affordable car
   Available living quarters
   A job
   The college curriculum
   Public transportation
   Financial aid for college students

8

PROCESS ANALYSIS

Explaining Step by Step

◀ **Process analysis in a photograph**

In a factory in Shenzhen, China, workers create dolls for export to the United States. The single image catches several steps in the doll-making process. At the very back of the assembly line, flat, unstuffed dolls begin the journey past the ranks of workers who stuff the body parts, using material prepared by other workers on the sides. A supervisor, hands behind his or her back, oversees the process. What do you think the photographer, Wally McNamee, wants viewers to understand about this process? What do you imagine the workers themselves think about it?

THE METHOD

A chemist working for a soft-drink firm is asked to improve on a competitor's product, Green Tea Tonic. First, she chemically tests a sample to figure out what's in the drink. This is the method of DIVISION or ANALYSIS, the separation of something into its parts in order to understand it (see the following chapter). Then the chemist writes a report telling her boss how to make a drink like Green Tea Tonic, but better. This recipe is a special kind of analysis, called PROCESS ANALYSIS: explaining step by step how to do something or how something is done.

Like any type of analysis, process analysis divides a subject into its components: It divides a continuous action into stages. Processes much larger and more involved than the making of a green tea drink also may be analyzed. When geologists explain how a formation such as the Grand Canyon occurred—a process taking several hundred million years—they describe the successive layers of sediment deposited by oceans, floods, and wind; then the great uplift of the entire region by underground forces; and then the erosion, visible to us today, by the Colorado River and its tributaries, by little streams and flash floods, by crumbling and falling rock, and by wind. Exactly what are the geologists doing in this explanation? They are taking a complicated event (or process) and dividing it into parts. They are telling us what happened first, second, and third, and what is still happening today.

Because it is useful in explaining what is complicated, process analysis is a favorite method of scientists such as geologists. The method, however, may be useful to anybody. Two PURPOSES of process analysis are very familiar to you:

- A *directive process analysis* explains how to do something or make something. You meet it when you read a set of instructions for taking an exam or for conducting a chemistry experiment ("From a 5-milliliter burette, add hydrochloride to a 20-milliliter beaker of water . . .").
- An *informative process analysis* explains how something is done or how it takes place. You see it in textbook descriptions of how atoms behave when they split, how lions hunt, and how a fertilized egg develops into a child.

In this chapter, you will find examples of both kinds of process analysis— both the "how to" and the "how." For instance, Linnea Saukko offers a directive for destroying the environment (not to be taken literally), while Jessica Mitford spellbindingly informs us of how corpses are embalmed.

Sometimes process analysis is used very imaginatively. Foreseeing that eventually the sun will burn out and all life on Earth will perish, an astronomer who cannot possibly behold the end of the world nevertheless can write a process analysis of it. An exercise in learned guesswork, such an essay divides a vast and almost inconceivable event into stages that, taken one at a time, become clearer and more readily imaginable.

Whether it is useful or useless (but fun or scary to imagine), an effective process analysis can grip readers and even hold them fascinated. Say you were proposing a change in the procedures for course registration at your school. You could argue your point until you were out of words, but you would get nowhere if you failed to tell your readers exactly how the new process would work: That's what makes your proposal sing. Leaf through a current issue of a newsstand magazine, and you will find that process analysis abounds. You may meet, for instance, articles telling you how to tenderize cuts of meat, sew homemade designer jeans, lose fat, cut hair, arouse a bored mate, and score at Internet stock trading. Less practical, but not necessarily less interesting, are the informative articles: how brain surgeons work, how diamonds are formed, how cities fight crime. Readers, it seems, have an unslakable thirst for process analysis. In every issue of the *New York Times Book Review*, we find an entire best-seller list devoted to "Advice, How-to, and Miscellaneous," including books on how to make money in real estate, how to lose weight, how to find a good mate, and how to lose a bad one. Evidently, if anything will still make an American crack open a book, it is a step-by-step explanation of how he or she, too, can be a success at living.

THE PROCESS

Here are suggestions for writing an effective process analysis of your own. (In fact, what you are about to read is itself a process analysis.)

1. *Understand clearly the process you are about to analyze.* Think it through. This preliminary survey will make the task of writing far easier for you.
2. *Consider your thesis.* What is the point of your process analysis: Why are you bothering to tell readers about it? The THESIS STATEMENT for a process analysis need do no more than say what the subject is and maybe outline its essential stages. For instance:

   The main stages in writing a process analysis are listing the steps in the process, drafting to explain the steps, and revising to clarify the steps.

   But your readers will surely appreciate something livelier and more pointed, something that says "You can use this" or "This may surprise you" or "Listen up." Here are two thesis statements from essays in this chapter:

   [In a mortuary the body] is in short order sprayed, sliced, pierced, pickled, trussed, trimmed, creamed, waxed, painted, rouged, and neatly dressed— transformed from a common corpse into a Beautiful Memory Picture.
   —Jessica Mitford, "Behind the Formaldehyde Curtain"

Poisoning the earth can be difficult because the earth is always trying to cleanse and renew itself.   —Linnea Saukko, "How to Poison the Earth"

3. *Think about preparatory steps.* If the reader should do something before beginning the process, list these steps. For instance, you might begin, "Assemble the needed equipment: a 20-milliliter beaker, a 5-milliliter burette, safety gloves, and safety goggles."

4. *List the steps or stages in the process.* Try setting them down in chronological order, one at a time—if this is possible. Some processes, however, do not happen in an orderly sequence, but occur all at once. If, for instance, you are writing an account of a typical earthquake, what do you mention first? The shifting of underground rock strata? Cracks in the earth? Falling houses? Bursting water mains? Toppling trees? Mangled cars? Casualties? Here is a subject for which the method of CLASSIFICATION (Chap. 10) may come to your aid. You might sort out apparently simultaneous events into categories: injury to people; damage to homes, to land, to public property.

5. *Check the completeness and order of the steps.* Make sure your list includes *all* the steps in the right order. Sometimes a stage of a process may contain a number of smaller stages. Make sure none has been left out. If any seems particularly tricky or complicated, underline it on your list to remind yourself when you write your essay to slow down and detail it with extra care.

6. *Define your terms.* Ask yourself, "Do I need any specialized or technical terms?" If so, be sure to define them. You'll sympathize with your reader if you have ever tried to assemble a bicycle according to a directive that begins, "Position sleeve casing on wheel center in fork with shaft in tong groove, and gently but forcibly tap in medium pal nut head."

7. *Use time-markers or TRANSITIONS.* These words or phrases indicate *when* one stage of a process stops and the next begins, and they greatly aid your reader in following you. Here, for example, is a paragraph of plain medical prose that makes good use of helpful time-markers (underlined). (The paragraph is adapted from Alan Frank Guttmacher's *Pregnancy and Birth: A Book for Expectant Parents.*)

In the human, thirty-six hours after the egg is fertilized, a two-cell egg appears. A twelve-cell development takes place in seventy-two hours. The egg is still round and has increased little in diameter. In this respect it is like a real estate development. At first a road bisects the whole area, then a cross road divides it into quarters, and later other roads divide it into eighths and twelfths. This happens without the taking of any more land, simply by subdivision of the original tract. On the third or fourth day, the egg passes from the Fallopian tube into the uterus. By the fifth

<u>day</u> the original single large cell has subdivided into sixty small cells and floats about the slitlike uterine cavity <u>a day or two longer,</u> <u>then</u> adheres to the cavity's inner lining. <u>By the twelfth day</u> the human egg is already firmly implanted. Impregnation is <u>now</u> completed, <u>as yet</u> unbeknown to the woman. <u>At present,</u> she has not even had time to miss her first menstrual period, and other symptoms of pregnancy are <u>still several days distant.</u>

Brief as these time-markers are, they define each stage of the human egg's journey. Note how the writer, after declaring in the second sentence that the egg forms twelve cells, backtracks for a moment and retraces the process by which the egg has subdivided, comparing it (by a brief ANALOGY) to a piece of real estate. When using time-markers, vary them so that they won't seem mechanical. If you can, avoid the monotonous repetition of a fixed phrase (*In the fourteenth stage . . . , In the fifteenth stage . . .*). Even boring time-markers, though, are better than none at all. As in any chronological NARRATIVE, words and phrases such as *in the beginning, first, second, next, then, after that, three seconds later, at the same time,* and *finally* can help a process to move smoothly in the telling and lodge firmly in the reader's mind.

8. *Be specific.* When you write a first draft, state your analysis in generous detail, even at the risk of being wordy. When you revise, it will be easier to delete than to amplify.

9. *Revise.* When your essay is finished, reread it carefully against the checklist on the next page. You might also enlist a friend's help. If your process analysis is a directive ("How to Eat an Ice-Cream Cone without Dribbling"), see if the friend can follow your instructions without difficulty. If your process analysis is informative ("How a New Word Enters the Dictionary"), ask the friend whether the process unfolds as clearly in his or her mind as it does in yours.

FOCUS ON CONSISTENCY

While drafting a process analysis, you may start off with subjects or verbs in one form and then shift to another form because the original choice feels awkward. In directive analyses, shifts occur most often with the subjects *a person* and *one*:

INCONSISTENT   To keep the car from rolling while changing the tire, <u>one</u> should first set the car's emergency brake. Then <u>you</u> should block the three other tires with objects like rocks or chunks of wood.

In informative analyses, shifts usually occur from singular to plural as a way to get around *he* when the meaning includes males and females:

INCONSISTENT   The poll worker first checks each voter against the registration list. Then they ask the voter to sign another list.

To repair inconsistencies, start with a subject that is both comfortable and sustainable:

CONSISTENT   To keep the car from rolling while changing the tire, you should set the car's emergency brake. Then you should block the three other tires with objects like rocks or chunks of wood.

CONSISTENT   Poll workers first check each voter against the registration list. Then they ask the voter to sign another list.

Sometimes, writers try to avoid naming or shifting subjects by using PASSIVE verbs that don't require actors:

INCONSISTENT   To keep the car from rolling while changing the tire, one should first set the car's emergency brake. Then the three other tires should be blocked with objects like rocks or chunks of wood.

INCONSISTENT   First each voter is checked against the registration list. Then the voter is asked to sign another list.

In directive analyses, avoid passive verbs by using *you*, as shown in the consistent example above, or use the commanding form of verbs, in which *you* is understood as the subject:

CONSISTENT   To keep the car from rolling while changing the tire, first set the car's emergency brake. Then block the three other tires with objects like rocks or chunks of wood.

In informative analyses, passive verbs may be necessary if you don't know who the actor is or want to emphasize the action over the actor. But identifying the actor is generally clearer and more concise:

CONSISTENT   Poll workers first check each voter against the registration list. Then they ask the voter to sign another list.

For exercises on consistency and passive verbs, visit Exercise Central at **bedfordstmartins.com/thebedfordreader.**

CHECKLIST FOR REVISING A PROCESS ANALYSIS

✔ **THESIS**   Does your process analysis have a point? Have you made sure readers know what it is?

✔ **ORGANIZATION**   Have you arranged the steps of your process in a clear chronological order? If steps occur simultaneously, have you grouped them so that readers perceive some order?

✔ **COMPLETENESS** Have you included all the necessary steps and explained each one fully? Is it clear how each one contributes to the result?

✔ **DEFINITIONS** Have you explained the meanings of any terms your readers may not know?

✔ **TRANSITIONS** Do time-markers distinguish the steps of your process and clarify their sequence?

✔ **CONSISTENCY** Have you maintained comfortable, consistent, and clear subjects and verb forms?

PROCESS ANALYSIS IN PARAGRAPHS

Writing about Television

The following paragraph, written especially for *The Bedford Reader*, explains the process of setting a digital video recorder to record a television program. Though composed to be freestanding, the paragraph (ideally with an accompanying illustration) could easily be dropped into a complete set of instructions on how to operate the DVR.

Your DVR allows you to schedule recording of any television programming up to two weeks in advance. Start at the on-screen command center (CMND on the DVR remote) and use the remote's arrow and "Select" keys to move around on screens and to make choices. At the command center, select "Record" and then, at the next screen, "Choose title." Using the alphabet that appears, spell out the program title. When the title is complete, select "Done." At the program screen following, select "Choose episodes." A list of available episodes then appears, and you can select the particular ones you want to record. When you're finished, press "TV" on the remote to view live television.

Margin notes:
Process to be explained with directive analysis
General instruction for all steps
Step 1, Step 2
Step 3
Step 4
Step 5
Step 6
Step 7
Transitions (underlined) clarify steps

Writing in an Academic Discipline

This paragraph on our descent into sleep comes from a psychology textbook's section on "the most perplexing of our biological rhythms." Before this paragraph the authors review the history of sleep research; after it they continue to analyze the night-long process that follows this initial descent.

When you first climb into bed, close your eyes, and relax, your brain emits bursts of *alpha waves* in a regular, high-amplitude, low-frequency rhythm of 8–12 cycles per second. Alpha is associated

Margin note:
Steps preceding process

Side text: Process Analysis

with relaxing or not concentrating on anything in particular. Grad- ⎤ Process to be
ually these waves slow down even further and you drift into the ⎬ explained with
Land of Nod, passing through four stages, each deeper than the pre- ⎟ informative analysis
vious one. ⎦

1. *Stage 1.* Your brain waves become small and irregular, indi-   Step 1
cating activity with low voltage and mixed frequencies. You
feel yourself drifting on the edge of consciousness, in a state of
light sleep. If awakened, you may recall fantasies or a few visual
images.
2. *Stage 2.* Your brain emits occasional short bursts of rapid, high-   Step 2
peaking waves called *sleep spindles.* Light sounds or minor noises
probably won't disturb you.
3. *Stage 3.* In addition to the waves characteristic of stage 2, your   Step 3
brain occasionally emits very slow waves of about 1–3 cycles
per second, with very high peaks. These *delta waves* are a sure
sign that you will be hard to arouse. Your breathing and pulse
have slowed down, your temperature has dropped, and your
muscles are relaxed.
4. *Stage 4.* Delta waves have now largely taken over, and you   Step 4
are in deep sleep. It will take vigorous shaking or a loud noise
to awaken you, and you won't be very happy about it. Oddly
enough, though, if you talk or walk in your sleep, this is when
you are likely to do so.
—Carole Wade and Carol Tavris, *Psychology*

PROCESS ANALYSIS IN A LAB REPORT

When scientists conduct experiments to test their hypotheses, or theories, they almost always write reports outlining the processes they followed so
that other researchers can attempt to duplicate the outcome. These laboratory
reports are straightforward and objective accounts of procedures and results.
They are generally organized under standardized headings, such as *Purpose,
Materials, Procedure,* and *Results*; and they often include tables, figures, and cal-
culations pertaining to the experiment. Most writers of lab reports strengthen
the focus on the experiment by keeping themselves in the background: They
avoid *I* or *we* and use the PASSIVE VOICE of verbs (*the solution was heated,* as
opposed to *we heated the solution*). The passive voice is not universal, however.
Most lab assignments you receive in college will include detailed instructions
for writing up the experiment and its results, so the best writing strategy is to
follow those instructions to the letter.

For a first-year chemistry experiment, Victor Khoury used mostly household materials to extract and isolate deoxyribonucleic acid (DNA) from an

onion. Found in all plants and animals, DNA is the molecule that holds the genetic information needed to create and direct living organisms. Khoury's instructor intended the experiment to teach students basic techniques and interactions in chemistry and to help them understand genetics at a molecular level. In the following excerpt from his lab report, Khoury explains the procedure and the main result.

Procedure

A small onion was coarsely chopped and placed in a 1000 ml measuring cup along with 100 ml of a solution consisting of 10 ml of liquid dishwashing detergent, 1.5 g of table salt, and distilled water. The solution was intended to dissolve the proteins and lipids binding the cell membranes of the onion. The onion pieces were next pressed with the back of a spoon for 30 seconds to break the onion structure down into a mash.

Step 1

Reason for step
Step 2

Reason for step

The measuring cup was then placed in a pan of preheated 58°C water for 13 minutes to further separate the DNA from the walls of the onion cells. For the first 7 minutes the onion was continuously pressed with a spoon. After 13 minutes of heating, the cup of mixture was then placed in a pan of ice water and the mixture was pressed and stirred for 5 minutes to cool it and to slow enzyme activity that would otherwise break down the DNA. The onion mixture was then placed in a coffee filter over a lab beaker and stored for 1 hour in a 4°C refrigerator in order to filter and further cool the solution.

Step 3
Reason for step

Step 4

Reason for step

Step 5
Reason for step

After refrigeration, the filtered solution was stirred for 30 seconds and 10 ml were poured into a clean vial. A toothpick dipped in meat tenderizer was placed into the onion solution so that the enzymes in the tenderizer would further separate any remaining proteins from the DNA. Then refrigerated ethyl alcohol was poured into the vial until it formed a 1 cm layer on top of the onion solution.

Steps 6, 7, and 8

Reason for steps
Step 9

Results

After the solution sat for 2 minutes, the DNA precipitated into the alcohol layer. The DNA was long, white, and stringy, with a gelatinous texture. This experiment demonstrated that DNA can be extracted and isolated using a process of homogenization and deproteinization. . . .

Discussion of results

LINNEA SAUKKO

Linnea Saukko was born in Warren, Ohio, in 1956. After receiving a degree in environmental quality control from Muskingum Area Technical College, she spent three years as an environmental technician, developing hazardous waste programs and acting as adviser on chemical safety at a large corporation. Concerned about the lack of safe methods for disposing of hazardous waste, Saukko went back to school to earn a BA in geology (Ohio State University, 1985) so that she could help address this issue. She currently lives in Hilliard, Ohio, and works as a groundwater manager at the Ohio Environmental Protection Agency, evaluating various sites for possible contamination of the groundwater.

How to Poison the Earth

"How to Poison the Earth" was written in response to an assignment given in a freshman composition class and was awarded a Bedford Prize in Student Writing. It was subsequently published in *Student Writers at Work: The Bedford Prizes.* Saukko's essay is largely a directive process analysis, but it is also a SATIRE: By outwardly showing us one way to guarantee the fate of the earth, the author implicitly urges us not to do it.

Saukko focuses in this essay on the toxins, or poisons, that make earth, air, and water dangerous for life. The actions and risks she addresses have not abated, but in recent years they have been eclipsed by public concern about global warming. The next essay, Gretel Ehrlich's "Chronicles of Ice," takes on that environmental problem.

Poisoning the earth can be difficult because the earth is always trying to cleanse and renew itself. Keeping this in mind, we should generate as much waste as possible from substances such as uranium-238, which has a half-life (the time it takes for half of the substance to decay) of one million years, or plutonium, which has a half-life of only 0.5 million years but is so toxic that if distributed evenly, ten pounds of it could kill every person on the earth. Because the United States generates about eighteen tons of plutonium per year, it is about the best substance for long-term poisoning of the earth. It would help if we would build more nuclear power plants because each one generates only 500 pounds of plutonium each year. Of course, we must include persistent toxic chemicals such as polychlorinated biphenyl (PCB) and dichlorodiphenyl trichloroethane (DDT) to make sure we have enough toxins to poison the earth from the core to the outer atmosphere. First, we must develop many different ways of putting the waste from these nuclear and chemical substances in, on, and around the earth.

Putting these substances in the earth is a most important step in the poisoning process. With deep-well injection we can ensure that the earth is poisoned all the way to the core. Deep-well injection involves drilling a hole that is a few thousand feet deep and injecting toxic substances at extremely high pressures so they will penetrate deep into the earth. According to the Environmental Protection Agency (EPA), there are about 360 such deep injection wells in the United States. We cannot forget the groundwater aquifers that are closer to the surface. These must also be contaminated. This is easily done by shallow-well injection, which operates on the same principle as deep-well injection, only closer to the surface. The groundwater that has been injected with toxins will spread contamination beneath the earth. The EPA estimates that there are approximately 500,000 shallow injection wells in the United States.

Burying the toxins in the earth is the next best method. The toxins from landfills, dumps, and lagoons slowly seep into the earth, guaranteeing that contamination will last a long time. Because the EPA estimates there are only about 50,000 of these dumps in the United States, they should be located in areas where they will leak to the surrounding ground and surface water.

Applying pesticides and other poisons on the earth is another part of the poisoning process. This is good for coating the earth's surface so that the poisons will be absorbed by plants, will seep into the ground, and will run off into surface water.

Surface water is very important to contaminate because it will transport the poisons to places that cannot be contaminated directly. Lakes are good for long-term storage of pollutants while they release some of their contamination to rivers. The only trouble with rivers is that they act as a natural cleansing system for the earth. No matter how much poison is dumped into them, they will try to transport it away to reach the ocean eventually.

The ocean is very hard to contaminate because it has such a large volume and a natural buffering capacity that tends to neutralize some of the contamination. So in addition to the pollution from rivers, we must use the ocean as a dumping place for as many toxins as possible. The ocean currents will help transport the pollution to places that cannot otherwise be reached.

Now make sure that the air around the earth is very polluted. Combustion and evaporation are major mechanisms for doing this. We must continuously pollute because the wind will disperse the toxins while rain washes them from the air. But this is good because a few lakes are stripped of all living animals each year from acid rain. Because the lower atmosphere can cleanse itself fairly easily, we must explode nuclear test bombs that shoot radioactive particles high into the upper atmosphere where they will circle the earth for years. Gravity must pull some of the particles to earth, so we must continue exploding these bombs.

So it is that easy. Just be sure to generate as many poisonous substances as   8 possible and be sure they are distributed in, on, and around the entire earth at a greater rate than it can cleanse itself. By following these easy steps we can guarantee the poisoning of the earth.

For a reading quiz and annotated links to further readings on pollution, visit **bedfordstmartins.com/thebedfordreader**.

Journal Writing

Saukko's essay is SATIRE — that is, an indirect attack on human follies or flaws, using IRONY to urge behavior exactly opposite what is really desired. In your journal, explore when you have proposed satirical solutions to problems that seem ridiculous or overwhelming — for example, suggesting breaking all the dishes so that they don't have to be washed again or barring pedestrians from city streets so that they don't interfere with cars. What kinds of situations might lead you to make suggestions like these? (To take your journal writing further, see "From Journal to Essay" on the facing page.)

Questions on Meaning

1. Is the author's main PURPOSE to amuse and entertain, to inform readers of ways they can make better use of natural resources, to warn readers about threats to the future of our planet, or to make fun of scientists? Support your answer with EVIDENCE from the essay.
2. Describe at least three of the earth's mechanisms for cleansing its land, water, and atmosphere, as presented in this essay.
3. According to Saukko, many of our actions are detrimental, if not outright destructive, to our environment. Identify these practices and discuss them. If these activities are harmful to the earth, why are they permitted? Do they serve some other important goal or purpose? If so, what? Are there other ways that these goals might be reached?

Questions on Writing Strategy

1. How detailed and specific are Saukko's instructions for poisoning the earth? Which steps in this process would you be able to carry out, once you finished reading the essay? In what instances might an author choose not to provide concrete, comprehensive instructions for a procedure? Relate your answer to the TONE and purpose of this essay.
2. How is Saukko's essay organized? Follow the process carefully to determine whether it happens chronologically, with each step depending on the one before it, or whether it follows another order. How effective is this method of organization and presentation?
3. For what AUDIENCE is this essay intended? How can you tell?
4. What is the tone of this essay? Consider especially the title and the last paragraph as well as examples from the body of the essay. How does the tone contribute to Saukko's satire?
5. What consistent sentence subject does Saukko use in explaining "how to poison the earth"? Who is to perform the process?
6. **OTHER METHODS**   Saukko doesn't mention every possible pollutant but instead focuses on certain EXAMPLES. Why do you think she chooses these particular examples? What serious pollutants can you think of that Saukko doesn't mention specifically?

Questions on Language

1. How do the phrases "next best method" (par. 3), "another part of the poisoning process" (4), and "[l]akes are good for long-term storage of pollutants" (5) signal the tone of this essay? Should they be read literally, ironically, metaphorically, or some other way?
2. Be sure you know how to define the following words: generate, nuclear, toxins (par. 1); lagoons, contamination (3); buffering, neutralize (6); combustion (7).

Suggestions for Writing

1. **FROM JOURNAL TO ESSAY**   Choose one of the solutions you wrote about in your journal, or propose a solution to a problem that your journal entry has suggested. Write an essay detailing this satirical solution, paying careful attention to explaining each step of the process and to maintaining your satiric tone throughout.
2. Write an essay defending and justifying the use of nuclear power plants, pesticides, or another pollutant Saukko mentions. This essay will require some research because you will need to argue that the benefits of these methods outweigh their hazardous and destructive effects. Be sure to support your claims with factual information and statistics. Or approach the issue from the same point of view that Saukko did and argue against the use of nuclear power plants or pesticides. Substantiate your argument with data and facts, and be sure to propose alternative sources of power or alternative methods of insect control.
3. **CRITICAL WRITING**   What does Saukko gain or lose by using satire and irony to make her point? What would be the comparative strengths and weaknesses of

an essay that approached the same pollution problems straightforwardly and sincerely, perhaps urging or pleading with readers to stop polluting?

4. **CONNECTIONS** In the next essay, "Chronicles of Ice," Gretel Ehrlich explores
an environmental problem that Saukko doesn't address: global warming. Using
evidence from Ehrlich's piece and from research, write a satirical essay loosely
based on Saukko's entitled "How to Warm Up the Earth." Like Saukko, use irony
to persuade readers to do the opposite of what you suggest. Your purpose should
be to warn readers about the dangers of global warming.

Linnea Saukko on Writing

"After I have chosen a topic," says Linnea Saukko, "the easiest thing for
me to do is to write about how I really feel about it. The goal of 'How to Poison the Earth' was to inform people, or, more specifically, to open their eyes.

"As soon as I decided on my topic, I made a list of all the types of pollution
and I sat down and basically wrote the paper in less than two hours. The information seemed to pour from me onto the page. Of course I did a lot of editing
afterward, but I never changed the idea and the tone that I started with."

For Discussion

When have you had the experience of writing on a subject that compelled your words
to pour forth with little effort? What was the subject? What did you learn from this
experience?

GRETEL EHRLICH

Gretel Ehrlich is a writer known for her affinity with nature at its chilliest. She was born in Santa Barbara, California, in 1946 and attended Bennington College and the film school at the University of California, Los Angeles. She worked as a documentary filmmaker for ten years and then settled in Wyoming to learn sheepherding and to write. Her first nonfiction book, *The Solace of Open Spaces* (1985), tells of life on the plains of Wyoming and won an award from the American Academy and Institute of Arts and Letters. Ehrlich has also published three books of poetry; several books of fiction, including the novel *Heart Mountain* (1988) and the story collection *Drinking Dry Clouds* (1991, reissued 2005); and six other nonfiction works, ranging from memoir (*A Match to the Heart: One Woman's Story of Being Struck by Lightning*, 1994) to biography (*John Muir: Nature's Visionary*, 2000) to travel (*This Cold Heaven: Seven Seasons in Greenland*, 2001). Her most recent book, *In the Empire of Ice: Encounters in a Changing Landscape* (2010), relates the struggles of indigenous peoples living around the Arctic Circle as they adjust to the effects of climate change.

Chronicles of Ice

"Chronicles of Ice" was excerpted in *Orion* magazine from Ehrlich's book *The Future of Ice: A Journey into Cold* (2004), which recounts the author's travels to some of the world's remotest places. Like Linnea Saukko in the previous essay, Ehrlich is worried about the effects that human activity—what Ehrlich elsewhere calls "the democracy of gratification"—is having on the environment. In this essay she visits the Perito Moreno glacier in southern Argentina, part of an ice field that is second only to Antarctica in size. Using process analysis, she explains both how glaciers form and how, with human help, they decline.

A trapped turbulence—as if wind had solidified. Then noise: timpani and 1
a hard crack, the glacier's internal heat spilling out as an ice stream far below.
I've come on a bus from El Calafate, Argentina, to visit the World Heritage
glacier Perito Moreno, to see its bowls, lips, wombs, fenders, gravelly elbows,
ponds, and ice streams, and to learn whatever lessons a glacier has to teach.

Some glaciers retreat, some surge, some do both, advancing and retreating 2
even as the climate warms. Perito Moreno is 257 square kilometers[1] across. It

---

[1] About ninety-nine square miles.—EDS.

advances two meters a day at the center. From where I'm standing, I can look directly down on the glacier's snout. Two spires tilt forward, their lips touching. They meet head to head, but their bodies are hollow. Sun scours them as they twist toward light.

I walk down stairs to a platform that gives me a more intimate view. A row   3
of ice teeth is bent sideways, indicating basal movement. Out of the corner of my eye I see something fall. A spectator gasps. An icy cheekbone crumbles. People come here to see only the falling and failings, not the power it takes for the glacier to stay unified.

A glacier is not static. Snow falls, accretes, and settles until finally its own   4
weight presses it down. The flakes become deformed. They lose coherence and pattern, become something crystalline called *firn* which then turns to ice. As an ice mountain grows, its weight displaces its bulk and it spreads outward, filling whole valleys, hanging off mountains, running toward seas.

There are warm glaciers and cold glaciers, depending on latitude and alti-   5
tude. Cold glaciers don't slide easily; they're fixed and frozen to rock. They move like men on stilts—all awkwardness, broken bones of sheared rock. Internal deformation affects flow patterns; melting occurs faster at the margins than in the center. Warm glaciers have internal melt-streams at every level and torrents of water flow out from under the ice at the glacier's foot. The "sole" of the glacier is close to the melting point and slides easily over rock. Friction creates heat, heat increases sole-melt, slipperiness, and speed. The quasi-liquid surface that results is a disordered layer, a complicated boundary where heat and cold, melting and freezing, play off each other and are inextricably bound, the way madness and sanity, cacophony and stillness, are.

Because ice melts as it moves and moves as it melts, a glacier is always   6
undermining itself. It lives by giving itself away.

A glacier balances its gains and losses like a banker. Accumulation has to   7
exceed ablation[2] for a glacier to grow. At the top, snow stacks up and does not melt. Midway down, the area of "mass balance" is where the profits and losses of snow can go either way. Surface melting can mean that water percolates down, refreezes, melts, and freezes again, creating a lens of ice. Below this region of equilibrium, ablation occurs. Profits are lost when the rate of melting exceeds the rate of accumulation. But a glacier will still advance if enough snow falls at the top and stays. . . .

A glacier is an archivist and historian. It registers every fluctuation of   8
weather. It saves everything no matter how small or big, including pollen,

---

[2] Reduction by melting, erosion, and other means. —EDS.

dust, heavy metals, bugs, and minerals. As snow becomes firn and then ice, oxygen bubbles are trapped in the glacier, providing samples of ancient atmosphere: carbon dioxide and methane. Records of temperatures and levels of atmospheric gases from before industrialization can be compared with those after — a mere 150 years. We can now see that the steady gains in greenhouse gases and air and water temperatures have occurred only since the rise of our smokestack and tailpipe society.

A glacier is time incarnate. When we lose a glacier — and we are losing most of them — we lose history, an eye into the past; we lose stories of how living beings evolved, how weather vacillated, why plants and animals died. The retreat and disappearance of glaciers — there are only 160,000 left — means we're burning libraries and damaging the planet, possibly beyond repair. Bit by bit, glacier by glacier, rib by rib, we're living the Fall. . . .   9

Twenty thousand years ago temperatures plummeted and ice grew from the top of the world like vines and ground covers. Glaciers sprouted and surged, covering 10 million square miles — more than thirteen times what they cover now. As a result of their worldwide retreat and a global decrease in winter snow cover, the albedo effect — the ability of ice and snow to deflect heat back into space — is quickly diminishing. Snow and ice are the Earth's built-in air conditioner — crucial to the health of the planet. Without winter's white mantle, Earth will become a heat sponge. As heat escalates, all our sources of fresh water will disappear.   10

Already, warmer temperatures are causing meltwater to stream into oceans, changing temperature and salinity; sea ice and permafrost are thawing, pulsing methane into the air; seawater is expanding, causing floods and intrusions. Islands are disappearing, and vast human populations in places like Bangladesh are in grave danger. The high-mountain peoples of Peru, Chile, and Bolivia who depend on meltwater from snowpack are at risk; the Inuit cultures in Alaska, Arctic Canada, Siberia, and Greenland that depend on ice for transportation, and live on a diet of marine mammals, could disappear.   11

In temperate climates everywhere, the early onset of spring and the late arrival of winter are creating ecosystem pandemonium. It is not unreasonable to think that a whole season can become extinct, at least for a time. Winter might last only one day — minor punctuation in a long sentence of heat. Mirages rising from shimmering heat waves would be the only storms. . . .   12

The bus takes me back to town. I get out near a grove of trees where loose horses wander. It's good to be in a place where there are such freedoms. All over the world the life of rocks, ice, mountains, snow, oceans, islands, albatross,   13 sooty gulls, whales, crabs, limpets, and guanaco once flowed up into the bodies of the people who lived in small hunting groups and villages, and out came killer-whale prayers, condor chants, crab feasts, and guanaco songs. Life went where there was food. Food occurred in places of great beauty, and the act of living directly fueled people's movements, thoughts, and lives.

Everything spoke. Everything made a sound—birds, ghosts, animals, oceans, bogs, rocks, humans, trees, flowers, and rivers—and when they passed each other a third sound occurred. That's why weather, mountains, and each passing season were so noisy. Song and dance, sex and gratitude, were the season-sensitive ceremonies linking the human psyche to the larger, wild, weather-ridden world.   14

Now, the enterprise we human beings in the "developed world" have engaged in is almost too darkly insane to contemplate. Our bent has been to "improve" on nature and local culture, which has meant that we've reduced the parallel worlds of spirit, imagination, and daily life to a single secularized pile. The process of empire-building is a kind of denigration. Nothing that's not nuts and bolts and money-making is allowed in. Our can-do optimism and our head-in-the-sand approach to economics—one that takes only profit, and not the biological health of our planet, into account—has left us one-sided.   15

When did we begin thinking that weather was something to be rescued from? Why did we trade in our ceremonial lives for the workplace? Is this a natural progression or a hiccup in human civilization that we'll soon renounce?   16

I eat at a rustic bar with other travelers. It's late when night comes, maybe 10:30. In the darkness, Perito Moreno is still calving and moving, grabbing snowflakes, stirring weather, spitting out ice water, and it makes me smile.   17

*For a reading quiz, sources on Gretel Ehrlich, and annotated links to further readings on glaciers and global warming, visit **bedfordstmartins.com/thebedfordreader**.*

Journal Writing

In your journal, write about a powerful natural phenomenon that you have witnessed—for example, a thunderstorm, a blizzard, an earthquake, a hurricane, a tornado, or a fire. What was your emotional response to the experience? (To take your journal writing further, see "From Journal to Essay" on the next page.)

Questions on Meaning

1. What does Ehrlich mean by "our smokestack and tailpipe society" (par. 8)? What point is she making here?
2. How is destroying glaciers similar to "burning libraries" (par. 9)?
3. According to Ehrlich's last paragraphs, what does the disappearance of glaciers suggest about humans' changing relationship to nature?
4. What do you think is Ehrlich's PURPOSE in explaining the life cycle of a glacier? What does she seem to want readers to take away from the essay? Where do you first see evidence of this purpose in the essay?
5. What would you say is Ehrlich's implied THESIS?

Questions on Writing Strategy

1. Examine the organization of the essay. What major sections does it fall into? Why do you think Ehrlich chose to order the essay as she did?
2. Where in the essay does Ehrlich use process analysis? What does this method contribute to her overall purpose in the essay?
3. This essay originally appeared in the nature magazine *Orion*. How can you tell that the magazine is intended for general readers, not for a specialized AUDIENCE of professional geologists or ecologists? What else can you assume about the magazine's audience?
4. **OTHER METHODS** Examine Ehrlich's use of CAUSE AND EFFECT in paragraphs 10–11. How does she organize the effects here?

Questions on Language

1. Identify some places in the essay where Ehrlich gives human qualities to the glacier. What is the effect of these uses of PERSONIFICATION?
2. What does Ehrlich ALLUDE to with the sentence "Bit by bit, glacier by glacier, rib by rib, we're living the Fall" (par. 9)?
3. Consult a dictionary if any of the following words are unfamiliar: turbulence, timpani, gravelly (par. 1); scours (2); basal (3); static, accretes, crystalline (4); torrents, inextricably, cacophony (5); percolates, equilibrium (7); archivist, fluctuation (8); incarnate, vacillated (9); mantle (10); meltwater, salinity, permafrost (11); temperate, pandemonium (12); albatross, limpets, guanaco (13); psyche (14); enterprise, bent, secularized, denigration (15); rustic, calving (17).

Suggestions for Writing

1. **FROM JOURNAL TO ESSAY** Write an essay exploring the natural phenomenon that you wrote about in your journal. Like Ehrlich, you might begin and end your essay by grounding the phenomenon in your personal experience of it, but focus on analyzing the general process by which it occurs and reflecting on its significance. What makes this force of nature so impressive? What impact does it have on people and on the environment? Use vivid IMAGES that will make the process come to life for your readers.

2. Scientists believe that glaciers are shrinking because of rising temperatures caused in large part by carbon dioxide emissions. Use a carbon calculator on the Internet, such as the one provided by the Nature Conservancy at *nature.org /initiatives/ climatechange/calculator*, to measure your impact on climate change. What can you do in your daily life to reduce carbon emissions? Do further research, if necessary, and then write a process analysis laying out the steps by which you personally will help stem global warming.

3. **CRITICAL WRITING** EVALUATE Ehrlich's success in making a complicated geologic process clear and engaging for a nonspecialist audience. Consider, in particular, her use of concrete images, personification, and ANALOGY. What do these techniques contribute to the essay?

4. **CONNECTIONS** In the previous essay, "How to Poison the Earth" (p. 308), Linnea Saukko also attempts to inspire readers to care more about the future of the earth. The two writers use very different techniques to achieve this purpose, however. COMPARE AND CONTRAST Saukko's approach with Ehrlich's. Do you find one essay more effective than the other? Why?

Gretel Ehrlich on Writing

In a wide-ranging interview with Jonathan White, Gretel Ehrlich answered the question "Does writing serve as a tool to bring you closer to nature?"

I wouldn't say my writing brings me closer to nature — maybe it brings the people who read what I write closer to nature. It's tough to bring yourself to the truths that result from experience. I take all my cues about writing from the images around me. In writing, you work to find a language that actually embodies the life of what you are writing about. Wallace Stevens[1] calls this "the palm at the end of the mind." I'm not saying I have succeeded, but as with any form of expression, whether it's writing, painting, or dance, you try to go directly from the gut.

The Navajo talk about the land as if it were parts of the body and soul. I sometimes think of landscape that way. It's a matter of transposing identities and seeing how that makes you feel and think. You can easily spend a day noticing the human aspects of a tree or the treeness inside you. I don't mean to trivialize it; allowing the life of other beings to enter yours is an important and valuable skill for a writer and for all humans. When you surrender like that, you can't write from the ego, which is so dominant in our culture. I like the word *inter-living*, because in order to express something well you need to

---

[1] American poet (1879–1955). —EDS.

have observed the details of it so closely that the boundary between its life and yours becomes blurred. . . .

When our cows were pregnant in the spring, they would lie down in the snow and groan in the late afternoon sun. I'd go out and sit with them for hours — just hang out with them. I learned a lot from doing that. The more I gave myself over to being with them, the more equality I felt between us. They have a kingdom of their own consciousness, and you can enter into as much of that as you want. I think that's what writers have to do. When you write fiction, you give yourself over to the characters; when you write nonfiction, it's the same. Emerson[2] said, "You must treat the days respectfully, you must be a day yourself. And not interrogate life like a college professor. Everything in the universe goes by indirection. There are no straight lines."

For Discussion

1. What do you make of the Wallace Stevens line "the palm at the end of the mind"? How might this line relate to Ehrlich's goal of finding "a language that actually embodies the life of what you are writing about"?
2. Ehrlich says that writing comes "from the gut," from having "observed the details of [the subject] so closely that the boundary between its life and yours becomes blurred." To what extent does this view apply to writing as you've experienced it? Are there stages of the writing process or types of writing in which letting go works well and other stages or types in which it doesn't?

[2] Ralph Waldo Emerson (1803–82), American philosopher, poet, and essayist. — Eds.

FIROOZEH DUMAS

Born in Abadan, Iran, in 1966, Firoozeh Dumas immigrated with her family to Whittier, California, at the age of seven, moved back to Iran two years later, then finally settled for good in the United States two years after that. She earned her bachelor's degree from the University of California at Berkeley in 1988. Dumas, who has said that the worst misconception about Iranians is "that we are completely humorless," took up writing partly to correct such assumptions. Her popular first book, *Funny in Farsi: A Memoir of Growing Up Iranian in America* (2003), portrays the humor in her family's experiences as Middle Eastern immigrants. Her second book, *Laughing without an Accent: Adventures of an Iranian American, at Home and Abroad* (2008), continues the theme with essays about trying to sell a cross-shaped potato on eBay and taking a cruise with fifty-one family members, among other topics. The two books are the basis for an upcoming television sitcom. Dumas contributes to several periodicals—including the *New York Times*, the *Wall Street Journal*, the *Los Angeles Times*, and *Lifetime*—and is an occasional commentator on National Public Radio.

Sweet, Sour, and Resentful

In this 2009 essay from *Gourmet* magazine, Dumas outlines her mother's painstaking process of preparing a traditional Persian meal for the dozens of distant relatives and friends of friends who descended on her family's California condo every weekend. Through her mother's weekly routine—from hunting down ingredients to chopping herbs to refusing praise—Dumas reveals much about family, culture, and humility.

My mother's main ingredient in cooking was resentment—not that I can [1] blame her. In 1979, my family was living temporarily in Newport Beach, California. Our real home was in Abadan, a city in the southwest of Iran. Despite its desert location and ubiquitous refineries, Abadan was the quintessential small town. Everybody's father (including my own) worked for the National Iranian Oil Company, and almost all the moms stayed home. The employees' kids attended the same schools. No one locked their doors. Whenever I hear John Mellencamp's "Small Town," I think of Abadan, although I'm guessing John Mellencamp was thinking of somewhere else when he wrote that song.

By the time of the Iranian revolution,[1] we had adjusted to life in Califor- 2
nia. We said "Hello" and "Have a nice day" to perfect strangers, wore flip-
flops, and grilled cheeseburgers next to our kebabs. We never understood why
Americans put ice in tea or bought shampoo that smelled like strawberries,
but other than that, America felt like home.

When the revolution happened, thousands left Iran for Southern Califor- 3
nia. Since we were one of the few Iranian families already there, our phone did
not stop ringing. Relatives, friends, friends of relatives, friends of friends, and
people whose connection we never quite figured out called us with questions
about settling into this new land. Displaying the hospitality that Iranians so
cherish, my father extended a dinner invitation to everyone who called. As a
result, we found ourselves feeding dozens of people every weekend.

The marathon started on Monday, with my mother planning the menu 4
while letting us know that she was already tired. Fortunately, our rice dishes
were made to be shared; our dilemma, however, was space. Our condo was
small. Our guests squeezed onto the sofa, sat on the floor, or overflowed onto
the patio. We eventually had to explain to our American neighbors why there
were so many cars parked in front of our place every weekend. My mother, her
diplomatic skills in full swing, had me deliver plates of Persian food, decorated
with radish roses and mint sprigs, to them. In time, we learned not to share
fesenjan, pomegranate stew with ground walnuts. "Yes, now that you mention
it, it does look like mud, but it's really good," I'd explain, convincing no one.

Because my mother did not drive, my father took her to buy ingredients 5
every Tuesday after work. In Abadan, my mother and I had started most days
in the market, going from vendor to vendor looking for herbs, vegetables,
and fruits. The fish came from the Karun and Arvand (Shatt al Arab) rivers,
the *lavash* and the *sangak* breads were freshly baked, and the chickens were
still alive. We were locavores by necessity and foodies without knowing it.
In America, I learned that the time my parents spent shopping was in direct
correlation to the degree of my mother's bad mood. An extra-long trip meant
that my mother could not find everything she needed, a point she would make
loud and clear when she got home: "Why don't they let fruit ripen here?"
"Why are the chickens so huge and flavorless?" "I couldn't find fresh herbs."
"My feet hurt." "How am I supposed to get everything done?"

The first step was preparing the herbs. My mother insisted that the parsley, 6
cilantro, and chives for *qormeh sabzi*, herb stew, had to be finely chopped by

---

[1] In 1979 fundamentalist rebels led by Ayatollah Ruhollah Khomeini overthrew the Iranian monarchy and established the Islamic Republic of Iran, a theocratic dictatorship. —Eds.

hand. The food processor, she explained, squished them. As she and my father sat across the table wielding huge knives, they argued incessantly. My father did his best to help her. It wasn't enough. As soon as the mountain of herbs was chopped, my mother started frying them. At any given time, my mother was also frying onions. Every few days, while my father was watching the six o'clock news, my mother would hand him a dozen onions, a cutting board, and a knife. No words were exchanged. Much to my father's relief, I once volunteered for this task, but apparently my slices were neither thin enough nor even. It took my father's precision as an engineer to slice correctly.

While all four burners were in use, my mother mixed the ground beef, rice, split peas, scallions, and herbs for stuffed grape leaves. I chopped the stems of the grape leaves. I had tried stuffing them once, but my rolls, deemed not tight enough, were promptly unrolled and then rerolled by my mother. 7

In between cooking, my mother made yogurt — the thick, sour variety that we couldn't find in America. She soaked walnuts and almonds in water to plump them up; fried eggplants for *kashk-e bademjan*, a popular appetizer with garlic, turmeric, mint, and whey; made *torshi-e limo*, a sour lemon condiment; and slivered orange peels. I had been fired from this task also, having left on far too much pith. 8

By the time our guests arrived, my mother was exhausted. But the work was not finished. Rice, the foundation of the Persian meal, the litmus test of the cook's ability, cannot be prepared ahead of time. To wit, one day in Abadan, the phone rang when my mother was about to drain the rice. During the time it took her to answer the phone and tell her sister that she would call her back, the rice overcooked. Almost forty years later, I still remember my mother's disappointment and her explaining to my father that her sister had time to talk because my aunt's maid did all the cooking. My aunt did not even drain her own rice. 9

We certainly did not have a table big enough to set, so we simply stacked dishes and utensils, buffet-style. As the guest list grew, we added paper plates and plastic utensils. It was always my job to announce that dinner was ready. As people entered the dining room, they gasped at the sight of my mother's table. Her *zereshk polow*, barberry rice, made many emotional. There are no fresh barberries in America (my mother had brought dried berries from Iran in her suitcase), and the sight of that dish, with its distinct deep red hue, was a reminder of the life our guests had left behind. 10

Our dinners took days to cook and disappeared in twenty minutes. As our guests heaped their plates and looked for a place to sit, they lavished praise on my mother, who, according to tradition, deflected it all. "It's nothing," she 11 said. "I wish I could've done more." When they told her how lucky she was to have me to help her, my mother politely nodded, while my father added, "Firoozeh's good at math."

On Sundays, my mother lay on the sofa, her swollen feet elevated, field-   12
ing thank-you phone calls from our guests. She had the same conversation a dozen times; each one ended with, "Of course you can give our name to your cousins." As I watched my mother experience the same draining routine week after week, I decided that tradition is good only if it brings joy to all involved. This includes the hostess. Sometimes, even our most cherished beliefs must evolve. Evolution, thy name is potluck.

For a reading quiz, sources on Firoozeh Dumas, and annotated links to further readings on Iranians in America, visit ***bedfordstmartins.com/thebedfordreader***.

Journal Writing

Many people have unique rituals, like Dumas's parents' practice of serving elaborate Persian meals to distant acquaintances every weekend. List some rituals that are unique to your family, to another group you belong to, or to you alone—for instance, a holiday celebration, a vacation activity, a way of decompressing after a stressful week. (To take your journal writing further, see "From Journal to Essay" on the next page.)

Questions on Meaning

1. Why were weekend dinners so important to the author's parents and their guests? Consider not just the meals themselves but the larger context that prompted them.
2. In which sentence or sentences does Dumas state her THESIS most directly?
3. What would you say is Dumas's PURPOSE in this essay? Is it primarily to entertain readers by describing her family's weekly routine, or does she seem to have another purpose in mind?
4. What solution to her mother's exhausting role as hostess does Dumas propose in paragraph 12? Do you think her mother would have agreed to it? Why, or why not?

Questions on Writing Strategy

1. Why does Dumas begin her essay with an overview of life in Abadan and an ALLUSION to the Iranian revolution (pars. 1–3)? What purpose does this opening serve?
2. How does Dumas seem to imagine her AUDIENCE? To what extent could she ASSUME that readers would appreciate her mother's situation?
3. What steps does Dumas identify in the process of hosting Iranian guests every weekend? How does she ensure that her analysis has COHERENCE?
4. **OTHER METHODS** What role does COMPARISON AND CONTRAST play in paragraph 5?

Questions on Language

1. Explain how Dumas's TONE contributes to the humor in her essay.
2. Where in this essay does Dumas use Persian words? What is their EFFECT?
3. In paragraph 9, Dumas says that rice is "the litmus test" for Iranian cooks. What does she mean? What is a litmus test, and how does the phrase connect to the focus (and title) of Dumas's essay?
4. Be sure you know the meanings of the following words: ubiquitous, quintessential (par. 1); Persian (4); locavores, correlation (5); pith (8); lavished, deflected (11); potluck (12).

Suggestions for Writing

1. **FROM JOURNAL TO ESSAY** Write an essay explaining one of the rituals you listed in your journal. Focus on the details and steps of the ritual itself as well as on the significance it holds for you and for any others who participate in it with you.
2. Research the influx of Iranian families into California during the 1970s. What prompted this migration? What quality of life did newcomers face on arrival? What tensions did their arrival create? In an essay, consider these questions and others your research may lead you to. You may prefer to focus on a different migration—such as those during the nineteenth and twentieth centuries of Irish to the eastern United States, Chinese to the western United States, or African Americans from the southern to the northern United States.
3. **CRITICAL WRITING** What impression of herself does Dumas create in this essay? What adjectives would you use to describe the writer as she reveals herself on the page? Cite specific language from the essay to support your ANALYSIS.
4. **CONNECTIONS** Several other writers in this book focus on the struggle to adjust to mainstream American culture while maintaining one's ethnic ties: for example, Amy Tan in "Fish Cheeks" (p. 116), Christine Leong in "Being a Chink" (p. 523), Linda Chavez in "Supporting Family Values" (p. 605), Sandra Cisneros in "Only Daughter" (p. 620), and Richard Rodriguez in "Aria: A Memoir of a Bilingual Childhood" (p. 681). Based on "Sweet, Sour, and Resentful" and one or more of the other essays, write an essay of your own that considers one aspect of the immigrant experience in the United States, such as the challenges of assimilation, the effects of prejudice, or the role of family ties and cultural loyalty.

Firoozeh Dumas on Writing

In a 2004 interview with Khaled Hosseini (author of *The Kite Runner* and *A Thousand Splendid Suns*), Firoozeh Dumas explained how writing awakens her memory. As a girl growing up in Iran and the United States, Dumas says she "was always that quiet kid in a room full of adults" who carefully "listened and observed." When she started writing as an adult, her collected observations "just flooded back." Unlike those who experience writer's block, Dumas was easily inspired: "Every time I finished a story, another popped up in its place. It was like using a vending machine: the candy falls down and is immediately replaced by another."

In order to keep up with her vending machine of ideas—and to accommodate her busy family life—Dumas writes "in spurts," often waking at four in the morning. "Once a story is in my head, I'm possessed, and the only thing I can do is write like mad," she told Hosseini. "This means the house gets very messy and dinner is something frozen. I do not read or go to the movies when I am writing, because I can't concentrate on anything else. I also keep writing in my head when I'm not actually writing, which means that I become a terrible listener."

For Discussion

1. Have you ever found that the act of writing triggers your memory?
2. What does Dumas mean when she says "I . . . keep writing in my head when I'm not actually writing"?
3. For Dumas, what is the relationship between listening and writing?

JESSICA MITFORD

Born in Batsford Mansion, England, in 1917, the daughter of Lord and Lady Redesdale, Jessica Mitford devoted much of her early life to defying her aristocratic upbringing. In her autobiography *Daughters and Rebels* (1960), she tells how she received a genteel schooling at home, then as a young woman moved to Loyalist Spain during the violent Spanish Civil War. Later she immigrated to the United States, where for a time she worked in Miami as a bartender. She became one of her adopted country's most noted reporters: *Time* called her "Queen of the Muckrakers." Exposing with her typewriter what she regarded as corruption, abuse, and absurdity, Mitford wrote *The American Way of Death* (1963, revised as *The American Way of Death Revisited* in 1998), *Kind and Unusual Punishment: The Prison Business* (1973), and *The American Way of Birth* (1992). *Poison Penmanship* (1979) collects articles from *The Atlantic Monthly, Harper's,* and other magazines. *A Fine Old Conflict* (1976) is the second volume of Mitford's autobiography. And a novel, *Grace Had an English Heart* (1989), examines how the media transform ordinary people into celebrities. Jessica Mitford died in 1996.

Behind the Formaldehyde Curtain

The most famous (or infamous) thing Jessica Mitford wrote is *The American Way of Death,* a critique of the funeral industry. In this selection from the book, Mitford analyzes the twin processes of embalming and restoring a corpse, the practices she finds most objectionable. You may need a stable stomach to enjoy the selection, but in it you'll find a clear, painstaking process analysis, written with masterly style and outrageous wit. (For those who want to know, Mitford herself was cremated after her death.)

The drama begins to unfold with the arrival of the corpse at the mortuary.   1

Alas, poor Yorick! How surprised he would be to see how his counterpart   2
of today is whisked off to a funeral parlor and is in short order sprayed, sliced, pierced, pickled, trussed, trimmed, creamed, waxed, painted, rouged, and neatly dressed — transformed from a common corpse into a Beautiful Memory Picture. This process is known in the trade as embalming and restorative art, and is so universally employed in the United States and Canada that the funeral director does it routinely, without consulting corpse or kin. He regards as eccentric those few who are hardy enough to suggest that it might be dispensed with. Yet no law requires embalming, no religious doctrine commends it, nor is it dictated by considerations of health, sanitation, or even of personal

daintiness. In no part of the world but in Northern America is it widely used. The purpose of embalming is to make the corpse presentable for viewing in a suitably costly container; and here too the funeral director routinely, without first consulting the family, prepares the body for public display.

Is all this legal? The processes to which a dead body may be subjected are   3
after all to some extent circumscribed by law. In most states, for instance, the signature of next of kin must be obtained before an autopsy may be performed, before the deceased may be cremated, before the body may be turned over to a medical school for research purposes; or such provision must be made in the decedent's will. In the case of embalming, no such permission is required nor is it ever sought.[1] A textbook, *The Principles and Practices of Embalming,* comments on this: "There is some question regarding the legality of much that is done within the preparation room." The author points out that it would be most unusual for a responsible member of a bereaved family to instruct the mortician, in so many words, to "embalm" the body of a deceased relative. The very term *embalming* is so seldom used that the mortician must rely upon custom in the matter. The author concludes that unless the family specifies otherwise, the act of entrusting the body to the care of a funeral establishment carries with it an implied permission to go ahead and embalm.

Embalming is indeed a most extraordinary procedure, and one must won-   4
der at the docility of Americans who each year pay hundreds of millions of dollars for its perpetuation, blissfully ignorant of what it is all about, what is done, how it is done. Not one in ten thousand has any idea of what actually takes place. Books on the subject are extremely hard to come by. They are not to be found in most libraries or bookshops.

In an era when huge television audiences watch surgical operations in   5
the comfort of their living rooms, when, thanks to the animated cartoon, the geography of the digestive system has become familiar territory even to the nursery school set, in a land where the satisfaction of curiosity about almost all matters is a national pastime, the secrecy surrounding embalming can, surely, hardly be attributed to the inherent gruesomeness of the subject. Custom in this regard has within this century suffered a complete reversal. In the early days of American embalming, when it was performed in the home of the deceased, it was almost mandatory for some relative to stay by the embalmer's side and witness the procedure. Today, family members who might wish to be

---

[1] Partly because of Mitford's attack, the Federal Trade Commission now requires the funeral industry to provide families with itemized price lists, including the price of embalming, to state that embalming is not required, and to obtain the family's consent to embalming before charging for it. Shortly before her death, however, Mitford observed that the FTC had "watered down" the regulations and "routinely ignored" consumer complaints about the funeral industry. —Eds.

in attendance would certainly be dissuaded by the funeral director. All others, except apprentices, are excluded by law from the preparation room.

A close look at what does actually take place may explain in large measure the undertaker's intractable reticence concerning a procedure that has become his major *raison d'être*. Is it possible he fears that public information about embalming might lead patrons to wonder if they really want this service? If the funeral men are loath to discuss the subject outside the trade, the reader may, understandably, be equally loath to go on reading at this point. For those who have the stomach for it, let us part the formaldehyde curtain. . . . 6

The body is first laid out in the undertaker's morgue — or rather, Mr. Jones is reposing in the preparation room — to be readied to bid the world farewell. 7

The preparation room in any of the better funeral establishments has the tiled and sterile look of a surgery, and indeed the embalmer–restorative artist who does his chores there is beginning to adopt the term *dermasurgeon* (appropriately corrupted by some mortician-writers as "demi-surgeon") to describe his calling. His equipment, consisting of scalpels, scissors, augers, forceps, clamps, needles, pumps, tubes, bowls, and basins, is crudely imitative of the surgeon's, as is his technique, acquired in a nine- or twelve-month post-high-school course in an embalming school. He is supplied by an advanced chemical industry with a bewildering array of fluids, sprays, pastes, oils, powders, creams, to fix or soften tissue, shrink or distend it as needed, dry it here, restore the moisture there. There are cosmetics, waxes, and paints to fill and cover features, even plaster of Paris to replace entire limbs. There are ingenious aids to prop and stabilize the cadaver: a Vari-Pose Head Rest, the Edwards Arm and Hand Positioner, the Repose Block (to support the shoulders during the embalming), and the Throop Foot Positioner, which resembles an old-fashioned stocks. 8

Mr. John H. Eckels, president of the Eckels College of Mortuary Science, thus describes the first part of the embalming procedure: "In the hands of a skilled practitioner, this work may be done in a comparatively short time and without mutilating the body other than by slight incision — so slight that it scarcely would cause serious inconvenience if made upon a living person. It is necessary to remove the blood, and doing this not only helps in the disinfecting, but removes the principal cause of disfigurements due to discoloration." 9

Another textbook discusses the all-important time element: "The earlier this is done, the better, for every hour that elapses between death and embalming will add to the problems and complications encountered. . . ." Just how soon should one get going on the embalming? The author tells us, "On the basis of such scanty information made available to this profession through its rudimentary and haphazard system of technical research, we must conclude that the best results are to be obtained if the subject is embalmed before life is 10 completely extinct—that is, before cellular death has occurred. In the average case, this would mean within an hour after somatic death." For those who feel that there is something a little rudimentary, not to say haphazard, about this advice, a comforting thought is offered by another writer. Speaking of fears entertained in early days of premature burial, he points out, "One of the effects of embalming by chemical injection, however, has been to dispel fears of live burial." How true; once the blood is removed, chances of live burial are indeed remote.

To return to Mr. Jones, the blood is drained out through the veins and   11
replaced by embalming fluid pumped in through the arteries. As noted in *The Principles and Practices of Embalming*, "every operator has a favorite injection and drainage point—a fact which becomes a handicap only if he fails or refuses to forsake his favorites when conditions demand it." Typical favorites are the carotid artery, femoral artery, jugular vein, subclavian vein. There are various choices of embalming fluid. If Flextone is used, it will produce a "mild, flexible rigidity. The skin retains a velvety softness, the tissues are rubbery and pliable. Ideal for women and children." It may be blended with B. and G. Products Company's Lyf-Lyk tint, which is guaranteed to reproduce "nature's own skin texture . . . the velvety appearance of living tissue." Sun-tone comes in three separate tints: Suntan; Special Cosmetic Tint, a pink shade "especially indicated for female subjects"; and Regular Cosmetic Tint, moderately pink.

About three to six gallons of a dyed and perfumed solution of formalde-   12
hyde, glycerin, borax, phenol, alcohol, and water is soon circulating through Mr. Jones, whose mouth has been sewn together with a "needle directed upward between the upper lip and gum and brought out through the left nostril," with the corners raised slightly "for a more pleasant expression." If he should be bucktoothed, his teeth are cleaned with Bon Ami and coated with colorless nail polish. His eyes, meanwhile, are closed with flesh-tinted eye caps and eye cement.

The next step is to have at Mr. Jones with a thing called a trocar. This is   13
a long, hollow needle attached to a tube. It is jabbed into the abdomen, poked around the entrails and chest cavity, the contents of which are pumped out and replaced with "cavity fluid." This done, and the hole in the abdomen sewn up, Mr. Jones's face is heavily creamed (to protect the skin from burns which may be caused by leakage of the chemicals), and he is covered with a sheet and left unmolested for a while. But not for long—there is more, much more, in store for him. He has been embalmed, but not yet restored, and the best time to start the restorative work is eight to ten hours after embalming, when the tissues have become firm and dry.

The object of all this attention to the corpse, it must be remembered,   14
is to make it presentable for viewing in an attitude of healthy repose. "Our

customs require the presentation of our dead in the semblance of normality . . . unmarred by the ravages of illness, disease, or mutilation," says Mr. J.
Sheridan Mayer in his *Restorative Art*. This is rather a large order since few
people die in the full bloom of health, unravaged by illness and unmarked
by some disfigurement. The funeral industry is equal to the challenge: "In
some cases the gruesome appearance of a mutilated or disease-ridden subject
may be quite discouraging. The task of restoration may seem impossible and
shake the confidence of the embalmer. This is the time for intestinal fortitude
and determination. Once the formative work is begun and affected tissues are
cleaned or removed, all doubts of success vanish. It is surprising and gratifying
to discover the results which may be obtained."

The embalmer, having allowed an appropriate interval to elapse, returns   15
to the attack, but now he brings into play the skill and equipment of sculptor
and cosmetician. Is a hand missing? Casting one in plaster of Paris is a simple
matter. "For replacement purposes, only a cast of the back of the hand is necessary; this is within the ability of the average operator and is quite adequate."
If a lip or two, a nose, or an ear should be missing, the embalmer has at hand a
variety of restorative waxes with which to model replacements. Pores and skin
texture are simulated by stippling with a little brush, and over this cosmetics
are laid on. Head off? Decapitation cases are rather routinely handled. Ragged
edges are trimmed, and head joined to torso with a series of splints, wires, and
sutures. It is a good idea to have a little something at the neck—a scarf or a
high collar—when time for viewing comes. Swollen mouth? Cut out tissue
as needed from inside the lips. If too much is removed, the surface contour
can easily be restored by padding with cotton. Swollen necks and cheeks are
reduced by removing tissue through vertical incisions made down each side
of the neck. "When the deceased is casketed, the pillow will hide the suture
incisions . . . as an extra precaution against leakage, the suture may be painted
with liquid sealer."

The opposite condition is more likely to present itself—that of emacia-   16
tion. His hypodermic syringe now loaded with massage cream, the embalmer
seeks out and fills the hollowed and sunken areas by injection. In this procedure the backs of the hands and fingers and the under-chin area should not
be neglected.

Positioning the lips is a problem that recurrently challenges the ingenuity   17
of the embalmer. Closed too tightly, they tend to give a stern, even disapprov-
ing expression. Ideally, embalmers feel, the lips should give the impression
of being ever so slightly parted, the upper lip protruding slightly for a more
youthful appearance. This takes some engineering, however, as the lips tend
to drift apart. Lip drift can sometimes be remedied by pushing one or two
straight pins through the inner margin of the lower lip and then inserting

them between the two front upper teeth. If Mr. Jones happens to have no teeth, the pins can just as easily be anchored in his Armstrong Face Former and Denture Replacer. Another method to maintain lip closure is to dislocate the lower jaw, which is then held in its new position by a wire run through holes which have been drilled through the upper and lower jaws at the midline. As the French are fond of saying, *il faut souffrir pour être belle*.[2]

If Mr. Jones has died of jaundice, the embalming fluid will very likely turn   18
him green. Does this deter the embalmer? Not if he has intestinal fortitude. Masking pastes and cosmetics are heavily laid on, burial garments and casket interiors are color-correlated with particular care, and Jones is displayed beneath rose-colored lights. Friends will say "How *well* he looks." Death by carbon monoxide, on the other hand, can be rather a good thing from the embalmer's viewpoint: "One advantage is the fact that this type of discoloration is an exaggerated form of a natural pink coloration." This is nice because the healthy glow is already present and needs but little attention.

The patching and filling completed, Mr. Jones is now shaved, washed,   19
and dressed. Cream-based cosmetic, available in pink, flesh, suntan, brunette, and blond, is applied to his hands and face, his hair is shampooed and combed (and, in the case of Mrs. Jones, set), his hands manicured. For the horny-handed son of toil special care must be taken; cream should be applied to remove ingrained grime, and the nails cleaned. "If he were not in the habit of having them manicured in life, trimming and shaping is advised for better appearance — never questioned by kin."

Jones is now ready for casketing (this is the present participle of the verb   20
"to casket"). In this operation his right shoulder should be depressed slightly "to turn the body a bit to the right and soften the appearance of lying flat on the back." Positioning the hands is a matter of importance, and special rubber positioning blocks may be used. The hands should be cupped slightly for a more lifelike, relaxed appearance. Proper placement of the body requires a delicate sense of balance. It should lie as high as possible in the casket, yet not so high that the lid, when lowered, will hit the nose. On the other hand, we are cautioned, placing the body too low "creates the impression that the body is in a box."

Jones is next wheeled into the appointed slumber room where a few last   21
touches may be added — his favorite pipe placed in his hand or, if he was a great reader, a book propped into position. (In the case of little Master Jones a Teddy bear may be clutched.) Here he will hold open house for a few days, visiting hours 10 AM to 9 PM.

---

[2] You have to suffer to be beautiful. — EDS.

All now being in readiness, the funeral director calls a staff conference   22
to make sure that each assistant knows his precise duties. Mr. Wilber Kriege
writes: "This makes your staff feel that they are a part of the team, with a
definite assignment that must be properly carried out if the whole plan is to
succeed. You never heard of a football coach who failed to talk to his entire
team before they go on the field. They have drilled on the plays they are to
execute for hours and days, and yet the successful coach knows the importance of making even the benchwarming third-string substitute feel that he
is important if the game is to be won." The winning of *this* game is predicated
upon glass-smooth handling of the logistics. The funeral director has notified
the pallbearers whose names were furnished by the family, has arranged for the
presence of clergyman, organist, and soloist, has provided transportation for
everybody, has organized and listed the flowers sent by friends. In *Psychology
of Funeral Service* Mr. Edward A. Martin points out, "He may not always do as
much as the family thinks he is doing, but it is his helpful guidance that they
appreciate in knowing they are proceeding as they should. . . . The important
thing is how well his services can be used to make the family believe they are
giving unlimited expression to their own sentiment."

The religious service may be held in a church or in the chapel of the   23
funeral home; the funeral director vastly prefers the latter arrangement, for
not only is it more convenient for him but it affords him the opportunity to
show off his beautiful facilities to the gathered mourners. After the clergyman
has had his say, the mourners queue up to file past the casket for a last look
at the deceased. The family is *never* asked whether they want an open-casket
ceremony; in the absence of their instruction to the contrary, this is taken for
granted. Consequently well over 90 percent of all American funerals feature
the open casket—a custom unknown in other parts of the world. Foreigners
are astonished by it. An English woman living in San Francisco described her
reaction in a letter to the writer:

> I myself have attended only one funeral here—that of an elderly fellow
> worker of mine. After the service I could not understand why everyone was
> walking towards the coffin (sorry, I mean casket), but thought I had better
> follow the crowd. It shook me rigid to get there and find the casket open and
> poor old Oscar lying there in his brown tweed suit, wearing a sun-tan makeup
> and just the wrong shade of lipstick. If I had not been extremely fond of the
> old boy, I have a horrible feeling that I might have giggled. Then and there I
> decided that I could never face another American funeral—even dead.

The casket (which has been resting throughout the service on a Classic   24
Beauty Ultra Metal Casket Bier) is now transferred by a hydraulically operated
device called Porto-Lift to a balloon-tired, Glide Easy casket carriage which

will wheel it to yet another conveyance, the Cadillac Funeral Coach. This may be lavender, cream, light green — anything but black. Interiors, of course, are color-correlated, "for the man who cannot stop short of perfection."

At graveside, the casket is lowered into the earth. This office, once the prerogative of friends of the deceased, is now performed by a patented mechanical lowering device. A "Lifetime Green" artificial grass mat is at the ready to conceal the sere earth, and overhead, to conceal the sky, is a portable Steril Chapel Tent ("resists the intense heat and humidity of summer and the terrific storms of winter . . . available in Silver Gray, Rose, or Evergreen"). Now is the time for the ritual scattering of earth over the coffin, as the solemn words "earth to earth, ashes to ashes, dust to dust" are pronounced by the officiating cleric. This can today be accomplished "with a mere flick of the wrist with the Gordon Leak-Proof Earth Dispenser. No grasping of a handful of dirt, no soiled fingers. Simple, dignified, beautiful, reverent! The modern way!" The Gordon Earth Dispenser (at $5) is of nickel-plated brass construction. It is not only "attractive to the eye and long wearing"; it is also "one of the 'tools' for building better public relations" if presented as "an appropriate noncommercial gift" to the clergyman. It is shaped something like a saltshaker.   25

Untouched by human hand, the coffin and the earth are now united.   26

It is in the function of directing the participants through this maze of gadgetry that the funeral director has assigned to himself his relatively new role of "grief therapist." He has relieved the family of every detail, he has revamped the corpse to look like a living doll, he has arranged for it to nap for a few days in a slumber room, he has put on a well-oiled performance in which the concept of *death* has played no part whatsoever — unless it was inconsiderately mentioned by the clergyman who conducted the religious service. He has done everything in his power to make the funeral a real pleasure for everybody concerned. He and his team have given their all to score an upset victory over death.   27

For a reading quiz, sources on Jessica Mitford, and annotated links to further readings on customs related to death, visit **bedfordstmartins.com/thebedfordreader.**

Journal Writing

Presumably, morticians embalm and restore corpses, and survivors support the work, because the practices are thought to ease the shock of death. Now that you know what goes on behind the scenes, how do you feel about a loved one's undergoing these procedures? (To take your journal writing further, see "From Journal to Essay" on the facing page.)

Questions on Meaning

1. What was your emotional response to this essay? Can you analyze your feelings?
2. To what does the author attribute the secrecy surrounding the embalming process?
3. What, according to Mitford, is the mortician's intent? What common obstacles to fulfilling it must be surmounted?
4. What do you understand from Mitford's remark in paragraph 10, on dispelling fears of live burial: "How true; once the blood is removed, chances of live burial are indeed remote"?
5. Do you find any implied PURPOSE in this essay? Does Mitford seem primarily out to rake muck, or does she offer any positive suggestions to Americans?

Questions on Writing Strategy

1. What is Mitford's TONE? In her opening two paragraphs, exactly what shows her attitude toward her subject?
2. Why do you think Mitford goes into so much grisly detail in analyzing the processes of embalming and restoration? How does the detail serve her purpose?
3. What is the EFFECT of calling the body Mr. Jones (or Master Jones)?
4. Paragraph by paragraph, what TRANSITIONS does the author employ? (If you need a refresher on this point, see the discussion of transitions on p. 747.)
5. To whom does Mitford address her process analysis? How do you know she isn't writing for an AUDIENCE of professional morticians?
6. Consider one of the quotations from the journals and textbooks of professionals and explain how it serves the author's general purpose.
7. Why do you think Mitford often uses PASSIVE verbs to describe the actions of embalmers—for instance, "the blood is drained," "If Flextone is used," and "It may be blended" in paragraph 11? Are the passive verbs effective or ineffective? Why?
8. **OTHER METHODS** In paragraph 8, Mitford uses CLASSIFICATION in listing the embalmer's equipment and supplies. What groups does she identify, and why does she bother sorting the items at all?

Questions on Language

1. Explain the ALLUSION to Yorick in paragraph 2.
2. What IRONY do you find in this statement in paragraph 7: "The body is first laid out in the undertaker's morgue—or rather, Mr. Jones is reposing in the preparation

room"? Pick out any other words or phrases in the essay that seem ironic. Comment especially on those you find in the essay's last two sentences.

3. Why is it useful to Mitford's purpose that she cites the brand names of morticians' equipment and supplies (the Edwards Arm and Hand Positioner, Lyf-Lyk tint)? List all the brand names in the essay that are memorable.

4. Define the following words or terms: counterpart (par. 2); circumscribed, autopsy, cremated, decedent, bereaved (3); docility, perpetuation (4); inherent, mandatory (5); intractable, reticence, *raison d'être,* formaldehyde (6); "derma-" (in *dermasurgeon*), augers, forceps, distend, stocks (8); somatic (10); carotid artery, femoral artery, jugular vein, subclavian vein, pliable (11); glycerin, borax, phenol, bucktoothed (12); trocar, entrails (13); stippling, sutures (15); emaciation (16); jaundice (18); predicated (22); queue (23); hydraulically (24); cleric, sere (25); therapist (27).

Suggestions for Writing

1. **FROM JOURNAL TO ESSAY** Drawing on your personal response to Mitford's essay in your journal, write a brief essay that ARGUES either for or against embalming and restoration. Consider the purposes served by these practices, both for the mortician and for the dead person's relatives and friends, as well as their costs and effects.

2. Search the Web or consult a periodical index for sources of information about the phenomenon of quick-freezing the dead. Set forth this process, including its hoped-for result of being able to revive the corpses in the far future.

3. ANALYZE some other process whose operations may not be familiar to everyone. (Have you ever held a job, or helped out in a family business, that has taken you behind the scenes? How is fast food prepared? How are cars serviced? How is a baby sat? How is a house constructed?) Detail it step by step, including transitions to clarify the steps.

4. **CRITICAL WRITING** In attacking the funeral industry, Mitford also, implicitly, attacks the people who pay for and comply with the industry's attitudes and practices. What ASSUMPTIONS does Mitford seem to make about how we ought to deal with death and the dead? (Consider, for instance, her statements about the "docility of Americans, . . . blissfully ignorant" [par. 4] and the funeral director's making "the funeral a real pleasure for everybody concerned" [27].) Write an essay in which you interpret Mitford's assumptions and agree or disagree with them, based on your own reading and experience. If you like, defend the ritual of the funeral, or the mortician's profession, against Mitford's attack.

5. **CONNECTIONS** In "Vampires Never Die" (p. 372), Guillermo del Toro and Chuck Hogan also comment on fears of death, noting that "we have no true jurisdiction over our bodies." Taken together, what do Mitford's and del Toro and Hogan's essays say about the importance of the body in Western culture? Write an essay either defending or criticizing the desire for physical immortality, whether real or imagined.

Jessica Mitford on Writing

"Choice of subject is of cardinal importance," declared Jessica Mitford in *Poison Penmanship*. "One does by far one's best work when besotted by and absorbed in the matter at hand." After *The American Way of Death* was published, Mitford received hundreds of letters suggesting alleged rackets that ought to be exposed, and to her surprise, an overwhelming majority of these letters complained about defective and overpriced hearing aids. But Mitford never wrote a book blasting the hearing aid industry. "Somehow, although there may well be need for such an exposé, I could not warm up to hearing aids as a subject for the kind of thorough, intensive, long-range research that would be needed to do an effective job." She once taught a course at Yale on muckraking, with each student choosing a subject to investigate. "Those who tackled hot issues on campus, such as violations of academic freedom or failure to implement affirmative-action hiring policies, turned in some excellent work; but the lad who decided to investigate 'waste in the Yale dining halls' was predictably unable to make much of this trivial topic." (The editors interject: We aren't sure that the topic is necessarily trivial, but obviously not everyone would burn to write about it!)

The hardest problem Mitford faced in writing *The American Way of Death*, she recalled, was doing her factual, step-by-step account of the embalming process. She felt "determined to describe it in all its revolting details, but how to make this subject palatable to the reader?" Her solution was to cast the whole process analysis in the official JARGON of the mortuary industry, drawing on lists of taboo words and their EUPHEMISMS (or acceptable synonyms), as published in the trade journal *Casket & Sunnyside:* "Mr., Mrs., Miss Blank, not corpse or body; preparation room, not morgue; reposing room, not laying-out room. . . ." The story of Mr. Jones thus took shape, and Mitford's use of jargon, she found, added macabre humor to the proceedings.

For Discussion

1. What seem to be Mitford's criteria for an effective essay or book?
2. What is muckraking? Why do you suppose anyone would want to do it?

MICHAEL POLLAN

Journalist Michael Pollan is best known for bringing attention to exactly what it is that Americans put on their dinner tables. Born in 1955 in New York, Pollan studied at Bennington College and Columbia University. He worked as a reporter and a producer before serving as executive editor at *Harper's* magazine for nearly a decade. Pollan's eye-opening books include *Second Nature: A Gardener's Education* (1991) and *The Botany of Desire: A Plant's Eye View of the World* (2001), but the award-winning *The Omnivore's Dilemma: A Natural History of Four Meals* (2006) earned him a position as one of America's most influential writers. He followed it with *In Defense of Food: An Eater's Manifesto* (2008) and *Food Rules: An Eater's Manual* (2009), both of which expand on his mantra: "Eat food. Not too much. Mostly plants." Pollan is the Knight Professor of Journalism at the University of California at Berkeley and a contributing writer for the *New York Times Magazine*.

Corn's Conquest

In *The Omnivore's Dilemma*, Pollan uncovers the origins of four dinners—one bought at McDonald's, one compiled from the bins at Whole Foods, one prepared with products from an organic farm, and one hunted and gathered himself. He devotes the early chapters to examining "industrial corn," a substance that has insinuated itself into a surprising number of the products available in a typical supermarket. Too much of what we eat, he says, contains corn in one form or another. In this excerpt, Pollan explains the plant's role in the modern food chain and what the abundance of corn in American foodstuffs has done to our bodies.

A Naturalist in the Supermarket

Air-conditioned, odorless, illuminated by buzzing fluorescent tubes, the 1 American supermarket doesn't present itself as having very much to do with Nature. And yet what is this place if not a landscape (manmade, it's true) teeming with plants and animals?

I'm not just talking about the produce section or the meat counter, 2 either—the supermarket's flora and fauna. Ecologically speaking, these are this landscape's most legible zones, the places where it doesn't take a field guide to identify the resident species. Over there's your eggplant, onion, potato, and leek; here your apple, banana, and orange. Spritzed with morning dew every few minutes, produce is the only corner of the supermarket where we're apt to think "Ah, yes, the bounty of Nature!" Which probably explains why such a garden of fruits and vegetables (sometimes flowers, too) is what usually greets the shopper coming through the automatic doors.

Keep rolling, back to the mirrored rear wall behind which the butchers   3
toil, and you encounter a set of species only slightly harder to identify—there's chicken and turkey, lamb and cow and pig. Though in Meat the creaturely character of the species on display does seem to be fading, as the cows and pigs increasingly come subdivided into boneless and bloodless geometrical cuts. In recent years some of this supermarket euphemism has seeped into Produce, where you'll now find formerly soil-encrusted potatoes cubed pristine white, and "baby" carrots machine-lathed into neatly tapered torpedoes. But in general here in flora and fauna you don't need to be a naturalist, much less a food scientist, to know what species you're tossing into your cart.

Venture farther, though, and you come to regions of the supermarket   4
where the very notion of species seems increasingly obscure: the canyons of breakfast cereals and condiments; the freezer cases stacked with "home meal replacements" and bagged platonic peas; the broad expanses of soft drinks and towering cliffs of snacks; the unclassifiable Pop-Tarts and Lunchables; the frankly synthetic coffee whiteners and the Linnaeus-defying[1] Twinkie. Plants? Animals?! Though it might not always seem that way, even the deathless Twinkie is constructed out of . . . well, precisely *what* I don't know offhand, but ultimately some sort of formerly living creature, i.e., a *species*. We haven't yet begun to synthesize our foods from petroleum, at least not directly.

If you do manage to regard the supermarket through the eyes of a natural-   5
ist, your first impression is apt to be of its astounding biodiversity. Look how many different plants and animals (and fungi) are represented on this single acre of land! What forest or prairie could hope to match it? There must be a hundred different species in the produce section alone, a handful more in the meat counter. And this diversity appears only to be increasing: When I was a kid, you never saw radicchio in the produce section, or a half dozen differ-ent kinds of mushrooms, or kiwis and passion fruit and durians and mangoes. Indeed, in the last few years a whole catalog of exotic species from the tropics has colonized, and considerably enlivened, the produce department. Over in fauna, on a good day you're apt to find—beyond beef—ostrich and quail and even bison, while in Fish you can catch not just salmon and shrimp but catfish and tilapia, too. Naturalists regard biodiversity as a measure of a land-scape's health, and the modern supermarket's devotion to variety and choice

---

[1] Carl Linnaeus (1707–78) created the system of classifying plants and animals that is still in use today.—EDS.

would seem to reflect, perhaps even promote, precisely that sort of ecological vigor.

Except for the salt and a handful of synthetic food additives, every edible   6
item in the supermarket is a link in a food chain that begins with a particular plant growing in a specific patch of soil (or, more seldom, stretch of sea) somewhere on earth. Sometimes, as in the produce section, that chain is fairly short and easy to follow: As the netted bag says, this potato was grown in Idaho, that onion came from a farm in Texas. Move over to Meat, though, and the chain grows longer and less comprehensible: The label doesn't mention that the rib-eye steak came from a steer born in South Dakota and fattened in a Kansas feedlot on grain grown in Iowa. Once you get into the processed foods you have to be a fairly determined ecological detective to follow the intricate and increasingly obscure lines of connection linking the Twinkie, or the nondairy creamer, to a plant growing in the earth some place, but it can be done.

So what exactly would an ecological detective set loose in an American   7
supermarket discover, were he to trace the items in his shopping cart all the way back to the soil? The notion began to occupy me a few years ago, after I realized that the straightforward question "What should I eat?" could no longer be answered without first addressing two other even more straightforward questions: "What *am* I eating? And where in the world did it come from?" Not very long ago an eater didn't need a journalist to answer these questions. The fact that today one so often does suggests a pretty good start on a working definition of industrial food: Any food whose provenance is so complex or obscure that it requires expert help to ascertain.

When I started trying to follow the industrial food chain—the one that   8
now feeds most of us most of the time and typically culminates either in a supermarket or fast-food meal—I expected that my investigations would lead me to a wide variety of places. And though my journeys did take me to a great many states, and covered a great many miles, at the very end of these food chains (which is to say, at the very beginning), I invariably found myself in almost exactly the same place: a farm field in the American Corn Belt. The great edifice of variety and choice that is an American supermarket turns out to rest on a remarkably narrow biological foundation comprised of a tiny group of plants that is dominated by a single species: *Zea mays*, the giant tropical grass most Americans know as corn.

Corn is what feeds the steer that becomes the steak. Corn feeds the   9
chicken and the pig, the turkey and the lamb, the catfish and the tilapia and, increasingly, even the salmon, a carnivore by nature that the fish farmers are reengineering to tolerate corn. The eggs are made of corn. The milk and

cheese and yogurt, which once came from dairy cows that grazed on grass, now typically come from Holsteins that spend their working lives indoors tethered to machines, eating corn.

Head over to the processed foods and you find ever more intricate mani-   10
festations of corn. A chicken nugget, for example, piles corn upon corn: What chicken it contains consists of corn, of course, but so do most of a nugget's other constituents, including the modified corn starch that glues the thing together, the corn flour in the batter that coats it, and the corn oil in which it gets fried. Much less obviously, the leavenings and lecithin, the mono-, di-, and triglycerides, the attractive golden coloring, and even the citric acid that keeps the nugget "fresh" can all be derived from corn.

To wash down your chicken nuggets with virtually any soft drink in the   11
supermarket is to have some corn with your corn. Since the 1980s virtually all the sodas and most of the fruit drinks sold in the supermarket have been sweetened with high-fructose corn syrup (HFCS)—after water, corn sweetener is their principal ingredient. Grab a beer for your beverage instead and you'd still be drinking corn, in the form of alcohol fermented from glucose refined from corn. Read the ingredients on the label of any processed food and, provided you know the chemical names it travels under, corn is what you will find. For modified or unmodified starch, for glucose syrup and maltodextrin, for crystalline fructose and ascorbic acid, for lecithin and dextrose, lactic acid and lysine, for maltose and HFCS, for MSG and polyols, for the caramel color and xanthan gum, read: corn. Corn is in the coffee whitener and Cheez Whiz, the frozen yogurt and TV dinner, the canned fruit and ketchup and candies, the soups and snacks and cake mixes, the frosting and gravy and frozen waffles, the syrups and hot sauces, the mayonnaise and mustard, the hot dogs and the bologna, the margarine and shortening, the salad dressings and the relishes and even the vitamins. (Yes, it's in the Twinkie, too.) There are some forty-five thousand items in the average American supermarket and more than a quarter of them now contain corn. This goes for the nonfood items as well: Everything from the toothpaste and cosmetics to the disposable diapers, trash bags, cleansers, charcoal briquettes, matches, and batteries, right down to the shine on the cover of the magazine that catches your eye by the checkout: corn. Even in Produce on a day when there's ostensibly no corn for sale you'll nevertheless find plenty of corn: in the vegetable wax that gives the cucumbers their sheen, in the pesticide responsible for the produce's perfection, even in the coating on the cardboard it was shipped in. Indeed, the supermarket itself—the wallboard and joint compound, the linoleum and fiberglass and adhesives out of which the building itself has been built—is in no small measure a manifestation of corn.

And us?   12

Corn Walking

Descendents of the Maya living in Mexico still sometimes refer to themselves as "the corn people." The phrase is not intended as metaphor. Rather, it's meant to acknowledge their abiding dependence on this miraculous grass, the staple of their diet for almost nine thousand years. Forty percent of the calories a Mexican eats in a day comes directly from corn, most of it in the form of tortillas. So when a Mexican says "I am maize" or "corn walking," it is simply a statement of fact: The very substance of the Mexican's body is to a considerable extent a manifestation of this plant.

For an American like me, growing up linked to a very different food chain, yet one that is also rooted in a field of corn, *not* to think of himself as a corn person suggests either a failure of imagination or a triumph of capitalism. Or perhaps a little of both. It does take some imagination to recognize the ear of corn in the Coke bottle or the Big Mac. At the same time, the food industry has done a good job of persuading us that the forty-five thousand different items or SKUs (stock keeping units) in the supermarket—seventeen thousand new ones every year—represent genuine variety rather than so many clever rearrangements of molecules extracted from the same plant.

You are what you eat, it's often said, and if this is true, then what we mostly are is corn—or, more precisely, processed corn. This proposition is susceptible to scientific proof: The same scientists who glean the composition of ancient diets from mummified human remains can do the same for you or me, using a snip of hair or fingernail. The science works by identifying stable isotopes of carbon in human tissue that bear the signatures, in effect, of the different types of plants that originally took them from the air and introduced them into the food chain. The intricacies of this process are worth following, since they go some distance toward explaining how corn could have conquered our diet and, in turn, more of the earth's surface than virtually any other domesticated species, our own included.

Carbon is the most common element in our bodies—indeed, in all living things on earth. We earthlings are, as they say, a carbon life form. (As one scientist put it, carbon supplies life's quantity, since it is the main structural element in living matter, while much scarcer nitrogen supplies its quality—but more on that later.) Originally, the atoms of carbon from which we're made were floating in the air, part of a carbon dioxide molecule. The only way to recruit these carbon atoms for the molecules necessary to support life—the carbohydrates, amino acids, proteins, and lipids—is by means of photosynthesis. Using sunlight as a catalyst the green cells of plants combine carbon atoms taken from the air with water and elements drawn from the soil to form the simple organic compounds that stand at the base of every food chain. It is more than a figure of speech to say that plants create life out of thin air.

But corn goes about this procedure a little differently than most other   17
plants, a difference that not only renders the plant more efficient than most,
but happens also to preserve the identity of the carbon atoms it recruits, even
after they've been transformed into things like Gatorade and Ring Dings and
hamburgers, not to mention the human bodies nourished on those things.
Where most plants during photosynthesis create compounds that have three
carbon atoms, corn (along with a small handful of other species) make compounds that have four: hence "C-4," the botanical nickname for this gifted
group of plants, which wasn't identified until the 1970s.

The C-4 trick represents an important economy for a plant, giving it an   18
advantage, especially in areas where water is scarce and temperatures high.
In order to gather carbon atoms from the air, a plant has to open its stomata,
the microscopic orifices in the leaves through which plants both take in and
exhaust gases. Every time a stoma opens to admit carbon dioxide precious
molecules of water escape. It's as though every time you opened your mouth to
eat you lost a quantity of blood. Ideally, you would open your mouth as seldom
as possible, ingesting as much food as you could with every bite. This is essentially what a C-4 plant does. By recruiting extra atoms of carbon during each
instance of photosynthesis, the corn plant is able to limit its loss of water and
"fix"—that is, take from the atmosphere and link in a useful molecule—significantly more carbon than other plants.

At its most basic, the story of life on earth is the competition among spe-   19
cies to capture and store as much energy as possible—either directly from the
sun, in the case of plants, or, in the case of animals, by eating plants and plant
eaters. The energy is stored in the form of carbon molecules and measured in
calories. The calories we eat, whether in an ear of corn or a steak, represent
packets of energy once captured by a plant. The C-4 trick helps explain the
corn plant's success in this competition: Few plants can manufacture quite as
much organic matter (and calories) from the same quantities of sunlight and
water and basic elements as corn. (Ninety-seven percent of what a corn plant
is comes from the air, three percent from the ground.)

The trick doesn't yet, however, explain how a scientist could tell that a   20
given carbon atom in a human bone owes its presence there to a photosynthetic
event that occurred in the leaf of one kind of plant and not another—in corn,
say, instead of lettuce or wheat. The scientist can do this because all carbon
is not created equal. Some carbon atoms, called isotopes, have more than the
usual complement of six protons and six neutrons, giving them a slightly different atomic weight. C-13, for example, has six protons and seven neutrons.
(Hence "C-13.") For whatever reason, when a C-4 plant goes scavenging for its
four-packs of carbon, it takes in more carbon 13 than ordinary—C-3—plants,
which exhibit a marked preference for the more common carbon 12. Greedy

for carbon, C-4 plants can't afford to discriminate among isotopes, and so end up with relatively more carbon 13. The higher the ratio of carbon 13 to carbon 12 in a person's flesh, the more corn has been in his diet—or in the diet of the animals he or she ate. (As far as we're concerned, it makes little difference whether we consume relatively more or less carbon 13.)

One would expect to find a comparatively high proportion of carbon 13   21 in the flesh of people whose staple food of choice is corn—Mexicans, most famously. Americans eat much more wheat than corn—114 pounds of wheat flour per person per year, compared to 11 pounds of corn flour. The Europeans who colonized America regarded themselves as wheat people, in contrast to the native corn people they encountered; wheat in the West has always been considered the most refined, or civilized, grain. If asked to choose, most of us would probably still consider ourselves wheat people (except perhaps the proud corn-fed Midwesterners, and they don't know the half of it), though by now the whole idea of identifying with a plant at all strikes us as a little old-fashioned. Beef people sounds more like it, though nowadays chicken people, which sounds not nearly so good, is probably closer to the truth of the matter. But carbon 13 doesn't lie, and researchers who have compared the isotopes in the flesh or hair of North Americans to those in the same tissues of Mexicans report that it is now we in the North who are the true people of corn. "When you look at the isotope ratios," Todd Dawson, a Berkeley biologist who's done this sort of research, told me, "we North Americans look like corn chips with legs." Compared to us, Mexicans today consume a far more varied carbon diet: the animals they eat still eat grass (until recently, Mexicans regarded feeding corn to livestock as a sacrilege); much of their protein comes from legumes; and they still sweeten their beverages with cane sugar.

So that's us: processed corn, walking.   22

Sources

In addition to the printed sources below, I learned a great deal about the natural and social history of *Zea mays* from my conversations with Ricardo Salvador at Iowa State (*www.public.iastate.edu/~rjsalvad/home.html*) and Ignacio Chapela at the University of California at Berkeley. Ignacio introduced me to his colleague Todd Dawson, who not only helped me understand what a C-4 plant is, but generously tested various foods and hair samples for corn content using his department's mass spectrometer.

The two indispensable books on the history of corn are:

Fussell, Betty. *The Story of Corn* (New York: Knopf, 1994). . . . The statistics on wheat versus corn consumption are on page 215.

Warman, Arturo. *Corn & Capitalism: How a Botanical Bastard Grew to Global Dominance*. Trans. Nancy L. Westrate (Chapel Hill: University of North Carolina Press, 2003).

Other helpful works touching on the history of corn include:

Anderson, Edgar. *Plants, Man and Life* (Berkeley: University of California Press, 1952).
Crosby, Alfred W. *Germs, Seeds & Animals: Studies in Ecological History* (Armonk, NY: M. E. Sharpe, 1994).
————. *Ecological Imperialism: The Biological Expansion of Europe, 900–1900* (Cambridge, UK: Cambridge University Press, 1986).
Mann, Charles C. *1494: New Revelations of the Americas before Columbus* (New York: Alfred A. Knopf, 2005). Excellent on the evolutionary origins of the plant and pre-Columbian maize agriculture.
Sargent, Frederick. *Corn Plants: Their Uses and Ways of Life* (Boston: Houghton Mifflin, 1901).
Wallace, H. A., and E. N. Bressman. *Corn and Corn Growing* (New York: John Wiley & Sons, 1949).
Weatherford, Jack. *Indian Givers: How the Indians of the Americas Transformed the World* (New York: Crown, 1988).
Will, George F. and George E. Hyde. *Corn among the Indians of the Upper Missouri* (Lincoln: University of Nebraska Press, 1917).

For a reading quiz, sources on Michael Pollan, and annotated links to further readings on nutrition, visit **bedfordstmartins.com/thebedfordreader**.

Journal Writing

How do you react to the idea that the molecules in your body have been fundamentally altered by the prevalence of corn in your diet? Are you surprised? Concerned? In your journal, contemplate the personal and biological implications of the information Pollan provides in "Corn's Conquest." Has he changed the way you look at food? (To take your journal writing further, see "From Journal to Essay" on the facing page.)

Questions on Meaning

1. What do you take to be Pollan's PURPOSE in writing this selection? How well does he accomplish it?
2. What is "the C-4 trick," as Pollan explains it in paragraph 18? Why is it significant?
3. What does Pollan mean by "wheat people" and "corn people" (par. 21)? Who belongs to these two groups, and what distinguishes them?
4. In what ways does the IMAGE of "corn walking," in both the second heading and the final sentence, SUMMARIZE Pollan's main point?

Questions on Writing Strategy

1. What parts of this essay illustrate process analysis? What processes does Pollan analyze, and how are they related?
2. Why does Pollan mention Twinkies and nondairy creamer as often as he does? What do they have to do with his subject?
3. Pollan provides a list of sources at the end of his essay, but he doesn't cite them within the text. Why do you suppose he does this? Does it matter to you that the author doesn't indicate which information came from which source? Why, or why not?
4. **OTHER METHODS**   What principle of CLASSIFICATION does Pollan use to categorize the contents of a typical supermarket in paragraphs 1–12? Why does he devote the first part of his essay to examining modern food products in such detail?

Questions on Language

1. How would you characterize Pollan's DICTION in this essay? What does his diction suggest about his intended AUDIENCE? Does he assume that readers are scientists, for instance?
2. Pollan uses the word *corn* twenty seven times in the space of three paragraphs (9–11). Why? What is the EFFECT of this repetition?
3. In paragraph 11, Pollan rattles off several chemical terms, such as *maltodextrin*, *ascorbic acid*, and *polyols*. Why do you suppose he uses these terms without explaining them? Do you need to know the meanings of the words to follow his point?
4. Consult a dictionary if any of the following words are unfamiliar: teeming (par. 1); flora, fauna (2); pristine, lathed, tapered (3); platonic (4); culminates, edifice, comprised (8); manifestations, constituents, leavenings (10); ostensibly (11); glean, stable, isotopes, intricacies (15); catalyst, organic (16); renders (17); stomata, orifices (18); complement, protons, neutrons, atomic weight (20); sacrilege, legumes (21).

Suggestions for Writing

1. **FROM JOURNAL TO ESSAY**   Based on your journal writing, draft an essay in which you explain your attitude toward processed foods. To what extent do you see

yourself as part of an "industrial food chain" (par. 8)? Why should the origins and chemical composition of your food matter?

2. In recent years, the Corn Refiners Association has mounted a publicity campaign in defense of high-fructose corn syrup, or HFCS. (The television ads typically feature a person stumped for a response when challenged for warning "You know what they say about high-fructose corn syrup.") Visit the association's Web site (*www.sweetsurprise.com*) and critically examine the advertisements provided there. Then, using the Web site's information and Pollan's essay for EVIDENCE, write an essay of your own that explains why people should (or should not) limit their consumption of HFCS. You may search for more information in additional sources, if you wish.

3. **CRITICAL WRITING**   ANALYZE Pollan's use of FIGURES OF SPEECH in this essay. How does the author combine *personification, metaphor, simile, understatement,* and similar devices to add life to his explanation of scientific processes and to make the information more accessible to general readers? In your analysis, pay particular attention to those figures of speech you find especially fresh or compelling.

4. **CONNECTIONS**   "Chronicles of Ice," by Gretel Ehrlich (p. 313), is another essay about a natural process written for a nonspecialist audience. In an essay COMPARE AND CONTRAST Pollan's essay with Ehrlich's. Do both writers succeed equally well in presenting complex concepts in ways that most readers can understand? Use quotations and PARAPHRASES from both essays to support your ideas.

Michael Pollan on Writing

Although a journalist by trade, Michael Pollan has been praised for the highly polished, literary quality of his writing. In a 2006 interview with Pamela Demory for *Writing on the Edge*, he detailed his writing process to explain how he achieves that quality.

Well, there are two phases; obviously, there's the research phase and the writing phase. The whole time I'm researching I'm keeping one file open on my computer all the time, which is, essentially, my notebook. . . . I type into the file any ideas that occur to me. Anything interesting I read, . . . highlights from interviews I do, I'll copy it in, and I'll try out sentences and I'll try out leads and I'll try out conclusions and I'll make lists of points and reading lists and it's kind of a big mess. Usually there are about fifty single-spaced pages of this. . . . Somewhere in there is my lead, usually, and when I find it, I'll start writing. Research is easier than the writing and more fun—it gets you out in the world and you get to read books and it doesn't quite feel like work. But there's a gathering sense of anxiety that you're not really working and that it's time to start working.

Once I start writing I'm pretty disciplined, and I'll sit down every day and do it from about 8:30 or 9:00 until lunch, and then maybe a couple of hours after that, depending on how well the morning's gone. I finish the writing day by printing out what I've done that day, from the beginning again. And then I start the [next] writing day editing all that, from the beginning, with a pen, going through it, marking it up, fixing it, and then putting the changes on. And as I get deep into . . . a piece, that editing process can take up a good chunk of the morning. I get to the end of that and then I push forward another couple thousand words and start the process all over again. So the beginnings are edited, revised, rewritten countless times, but as I get deeper into the piece of course they've gotten less rewritten because I haven't had as many days with the latter stages.

. . . [It] might make sense to write a messier draft through, and I know a lot of writers who do that, who just don't stop; they keep going and they feel a real tension between their creative and their critical side. I find that revision and writing is very much of a piece and I like to warm up by revising my sentences. That gets me back in the rhythm of it, reminds me where I am. I have a very poor memory, so the process of going back to the beginning every time reminds me of where I am, where I need to be. And I also do that old Hemingway[1] trick at the end of any writing day of making a couple of notes about exactly where I'm going, never stopping at a hard place. So the beginning of the day is a kind of fun bit to write or a clear bit to write. There are parts of pieces you look forward to writing and there are parts of pieces you dread, so I always stop at a fun bit. That's basically the routine until I get to the end, and by the time I get to the end I have a very clean draft.

For Discussion

1. Do you agree with Pollan that "[r]esearch is easier than the writing and more fun"? Why do you think writing feels more like "work" to him?
2. Is your writing strategy similar to Pollan's, or do you prefer to complete a full first draft before going back to revise?
3. What are the advantages of never stopping at a "hard place" when writing?

---

[1] Ernest Hemingway (1899–1961), American novelist and short story writer. —EDS.

ADDITIONAL WRITING TOPICS

Process Analysis

1. Write a *directive* process analysis (a "how-to" essay) in which, drawing on your own knowledge, you instruct someone in doing or making something. Divide the process into steps, and be sure to detail each step thoroughly. Some possible subjects (any of which may be modified or narrowed):

How to create a Web site or a blog
How to post a video on *YouTube*
How to enlist people's confidence
How to bake bread
How to meditate
How to teach a child to swim
How to select a science fiction novel
How to drive a car in snow or rain
How to prepare yourself to take an intelligence test
How to compose a photograph
How to judge cattle
How to buy a used motorcycle
How to enjoy an opera
How to organize your own rock group
How to eat an artichoke
How to groom a horse
How to belly dance
How to build (or fly) a kite
How to start weight training
How to aid a person who is choking
How to behave on a first date
How to get your own way
How to kick a habit
How to lose weight
How to win at poker
How to make an effective protest or complaint

Or, if you don't like any of those topics, what else do you know that others might care to learn from you?

2. Step by step, working in chronological order, write a careful *informative* analysis of any one of the following processes. (This is not to be a "how-to" essay, but an essay that explains how something works or happens.) Make use of DESCRIPTION wherever necessary, and be sure to include frequent TRANSITIONS. If one of these topics gives you a better idea for a paper, go with your own subject.

How a student is processed during orientation or registration
How the student newspaper gets published
How a particular Web search engine works
How a stereo amplifier or an MP3 player works

How a professional umpire (or an acupuncturist, or some other professional) does his or her job

How an air conditioner (or other household appliance) works

How birds teach their young (or some other process in the natural world: how sharks feed, how a snake swallows an egg, how the human liver works)

How police control crowds

How people usually make up their minds when shopping for new cars (or new clothes)

3. Write a directive process analysis in which you use a light TONE. Although you need not take your subject in deadly earnest, your humor will probably be effective only if you take the method of process analysis seriously. Make clear each stage of the process and explain it in sufficient detail. Possible topics:

How to get through the month of November (or March)

How to flunk out of college swiftly and efficiently

How to outwit a pinball machine

How to choose a mate

How to go broke

How to sell something that nobody wants

DECONSTRUCTING LUNCH

① IT'S A SANDWICH:

That, in itself, means you are a _normal_ child from a _normal_ family.

② IT'S ON WHOLE-WHEAT BREAD:

O.K., so we're liberal, big-city Democrats.

③ BUT IT'S THE BIG-BRAND, EASY-TO-CHEW KIND:

I didn't say "radical." I said "liberal."

④ BOLOGNA AND MAYO:

People _always_ mistake us for Republicans!

⑤ IT'S KOSHER BOLOGNA:

It's not about religion—it's about _taste_.

⑥ LETTUCE:

Other parents may not care about their kids' health, but _I_ do.

⑦ LOOK, THERE'S A SLICE OF AMERICAN CHEESE IN THERE:

If you want to become a Mormon, I'll love you anyway. I just want you to be happy.

R. Chast

9

DIVISION OR ANALYSIS

Slicing into Parts

◀ **Division or analysis in a cartoon**

The cartoonist Roz Chast is well known for witty and perceptive comments on the everyday, made through words and simple, almost childlike drawings. Dividing or analyzing, this cartoon identifies the elements of a boy's sandwich to discover what the elements can tell about the values and politics of the parent who made the sandwich. The title, *Deconstructing Lunch*, refers to a type of analysis that focuses on the multiple meanings of the subject and especially its internal contradictions. Summarize what the sandwich reveals about the boy's parent. What contradictions do you spot in his or her values or politics? What might Chast be saying more generally about food choices?

THE METHOD

A chemist working for a soft-drink company is asked to improve on a competitor's product, Green Tea Tonic. (In Chap. 8, the same chemist was working on a different part of the same problem.) To do the job, the chemist first has to figure out what's in the drink. She smells the stuff and tastes it. Then she tests a sample chemically to discover the actual ingredients: water, green tea, corn syrup, citric acid, sodium benzoate, coloring. Methodically, the chemist has performed DIVISION or ANALYSIS: She has separated the beverage into its components. Green Tea Tonic stands revealed, understood, ready to be bettered.

Division or analysis (the terms are interchangeable) is a key skill in learning and in life. It is an instrument allowing you to slice a large and complicated subject into smaller parts that you can grasp and relate to one another. With analysis you comprehend — and communicate — the structure of things. And when it works, you find in the parts an idea or conclusion about the subject that makes it clearer, truer, more comprehensive, or more vivid than before you started.

If you have worked with the previous two chapters, you have already used division or analysis in explaining a process (Chap. 8) and in comparing and contrasting (Chap. 7). To make a better Green Tea Tonic (a process), the chemist might prepare a recipe that divides the process into separate steps or actions ("First, boil a gallon of water . . ."). When the batch is done, she might taste-test the two drinks, analyzing and then comparing their green tea flavor, sweetness, and acidity. As you'll see in following chapters, too, division or analysis figures in all the other methods of developing ideas, for it is basic to any concerted thought, explanation, or evaluation.

Kinds of Division or Analysis

Although division or analysis always works the same way — separating a whole, singular subject into its elements, slicing it into parts — the method can be more or less difficult depending on how unfamiliar, complex, and abstract the subject is. Obviously, it's going to be much easier to analyze a chicken (wings, legs, thighs . . .) than a poem by T. S. Eliot (this image, that allusion . . .), easier to analyze the structure of a small business than that of a multinational conglomerate. Just about any subject *can* be analyzed and will be the clearer for it. In "I Want a Wife," an essay in this chapter, Judy Brady divides the role of a wife into its various functions or services. In an essay called "Teacher" from his book *Pot Shots at Poetry* (1980), Robert Francis divides the knowledge of poetry he imparted to his class into six pie sections. The first slice is what he told his students that they knew already.

> The second slice is what I told them that they could have found out just as well or better from books. What, for instance, is a sestina?
> The third slice is what I told them that they refused to accept. I could see it on their faces, and later I saw the evidence in their writing.
> The fourth slice is what I told them that they were willing to accept and may have thought they accepted but couldn't accept since they couldn't fully understand. This also I saw in their faces and in their work. Here, no doubt, I was mostly to blame.
> The fifth slice is what I told them that they discounted as whimsy or something simply to fill up time. After all, I was being paid to talk.
> The sixth slice is what I didn't tell them, for I didn't try to tell them all I knew. Deliberately I kept back something—a few professional secrets, a magic formula or two.

There are always multiple ways to divide or analyze a subject, just as there are many ways to slice a pie. Francis could have divided his knowledge of poetry into knowledge of rhyme, knowledge of meter, knowledge of imagery, and so forth—basically following the components of a poem. In other words, the outcome of an analysis depends on the rule or principle used to do the slicing. This fact accounts for some of the differences among academic disciplines: A psychologist, say, may look at the individual person primarily as a bundle of drives and needs, whereas a sociologist may emphasize the individual's roles in society. Even within disciplines, different factions analyze differently, using different principles of division or analysis. Some psychologists are interested mainly in thought, others mainly in behavior; some psychologists focus mainly on emotional development, others mainly on moral development.

Analysis and Critical Thinking

Analysis plays a fundamental role in CRITICAL THINKING, READING, and WRITING, topics discussed in Chapters 1 and 3. In fact, *analysis* and *criticism* are deeply related: The first comes from a Greek word meaning "to undo," the second from a Greek word meaning "to separate."

Critical thinking, reading, and writing go beneath the surface of the object, word, image, or whatever the subject is. When you work critically, you divide the subject into its elements, INFER the buried meanings and ASSUMPTIONS that define its essence, and SYNTHESIZE the parts into a new whole that is now informed by your perspective. Say a campaign brochure quotes a candidate as favoring "reasonable government expenditures on reasonable highway projects." The candidate will support new roads, right? Wrong. As a critical reader of the brochure, you quickly sense something fishy in the use (twice) of *reasonable*. As an informed reader, you know (or find out) that the candidate has consistently opposed new roads, so the chances of her finding a highway project "reasonable" are slim. At the same time, her stand has been unpopular, so of course she wants to seem "reasonable" on the issue. Read critically, then, a campaign statement that seems to offer mild support for highways is actually a slippery evasion of any such commitment.

Analysis (a convenient term for the overlapping operations of analysis, inference, and synthesis) is very useful for exposing such evasiveness, but that isn't its only function. If you've read this far in this book, you've already done quite a bit of analytical/critical thinking as you read and analyzed the selections. The method will also help you understand a sculpture, perceive the importance of a case study in sociology, or form a response to an environmental impact report. And the method can be invaluable for straight thinking about popular culture, from TV to toys.

THE PROCESS

Subjects and Theses

Keep an eye out for writing assignments requiring division or analysis — in college and work, they won't be few or hard to find. They will probably include the word *analyze* or a word implying analysis such as *evaluate, examine, explore, interpret, discuss,* or *criticize*. Any time you spot such a term, you know your job is to separate the subject into its elements, to infer their meanings, to explore the relations among them, and to draw a conclusion about the subject.

Almost any coherent entity — object, person, place, concept — is a fit subject for analysis *if* the analysis will add to the subject's meaning or significance. Little is deadlier than the rote analytical exercise that leaves the parts neatly dissected and the subject comatose on the page. As a writer, you have to animate the subject, and that means finding your interest. What about your subject seems curious? What's appealing? or mysterious? or awful? And what will be your PURPOSE in writing about the subject: Do you simply want to explain it, or do you want to argue for or against it?

Such questions can help you find the principle or framework you will use to divide the subject into parts. (As we mentioned before, there's more than one way to slice most subjects.) Say you've got an assignment to write about a sculpture in a nearby park. Why do you like the sculpture, or why don't you? What elements of its creation and physical form make it art? What is the point of such public art? What does this sculpture do to this park, or vice versa? Any of these questions could suggest a slant on the subject, a framework for analysis, and a purpose for writing, getting your analysis moving.

Finding your principle of analysis will lead you to your essay's THESIS as well—the main point you want to make about your subject. Expressed in a THESIS STATEMENT, this idea will help keep you focused and help your readers see your subject as a whole rather than as a bundle of parts. Here is the thesis statement in one of this chapter's selections:

> In the face of what we know, it is altogether unreasonable to deny the biological basis for distinctive male and female preferences and abilities.
> —Christina Hoff Sommers, "Men—It's in Their Nature"

See the next page for more on the thesis statement in analysis.

In developing an essay by analysis, having an outline at your elbow can be a help. You don't want to overlook any parts or elements that should be included in your framework. (You needn't mention every feature in your final essay or give them all equal treatment, but any omissions or variations should be conscious.) And you want to use your framework consistently, not switching carelessly (and confusingly) from, say, the form of the sculpture to the cost of public art. In writing her brief essay "I Want a Wife," Judy Brady must have needed an outline to work out carefully the different activities of a wife, so that she covered them all and clearly distinguished them.

Evidence

Making a valid analysis is chiefly a matter of giving your subject thought, but for the result to seem useful and convincing to your readers, it will have to refer to the concrete world. The method requires not only cogitation, but open eyes and a willingness to provide EVIDENCE. The nature of the evidence will depend entirely on what you are analyzing—physical details for a sculpture, quotations for a poem, financial data for a business case study, statistics for a psychology case study, and so forth. The idea is to supply enough evidence to justify and support your particular slant on the subject.

A final caution: It's possible to get carried away with one's own analysis, to become so enamored of the details that the subject itself becomes dim or distorted. You can avoid this danger by keeping the subject literally in front of you as you work (or at least imagining it vividly) and by maintaining an outline. It often helps to reassemble your subject at the end of the essay, placing it in a larger context, speculating on its influence, or affirming its significance.

By the end of the essay, your subject must be a coherent whole truly represented by your analysis, not twisted, inflated, or obliterated. The reader should be intrigued by your subject, yes, but also able to recognize it on the street.

FOCUS ON THE THESIS STATEMENT

Readers will have an easier time following your analysis—and will more likely appreciate it—if they have a hook on which to hang the details. Your thesis statement can be that hook if you use it to establish your framework, your principle of analysis.

In each of the following pairs, the first statement is too vague to work as a hook: It conveys the writer's general opinion but not its basis. Each revised statement clarifies the point.

VAGUE   The sculpture is a beautiful piece of work.

REVISED   Although it may not be obvious at first, this smooth bronze sculpture unites urban and natural elements to represent the city dweller's relationship with nature.

VAGUE   The sculpture is a waste of money.

REVISED   The huge bronze sculpture in the middle of McBean Park demonstrates that so-called public art may actually undermine the public interest.

A well-focused thesis statement can help you as well, because it gives you a yardstick to judge how complete, consistent, and supportive your analysis is. Don't be discouraged, though, if your thesis statement doesn't come to you until *after* you've written a first draft and had a chance to discover your interest. Writing about your subject may be the best way for you to find its meaning and significance.

CHECKLIST FOR REVISING A DIVISION OR ANALYSIS ESSAY

✔ **PRINCIPLE OF ANALYSIS AND THESIS**   What is your particular slant on your subject, the rule or principle you have used to divide your subject into its elements? Do you specify it in your thesis statement?

✔ **COMPLETENESS**   Have you considered all the subject's elements required by your principle of analysis?

✔ **CONSISTENCY**   Have you applied your principle of analysis consistently, viewing your subject from a definite slant?

✔ **EVIDENCE** Is your division or analysis well supported with concrete details, quotations, data, or statistics, as appropriate?

✔ **SIGNIFICANCE** Why should readers care about your analysis? Have you told them something about your subject that wasn't obvious on its surface?

✔ **TRUTH TO SUBJECT** Is your analysis faithful to the subject, not distorted, exaggerated, deflated?

DIVISION OR ANALYSIS IN PARAGRAPHS

Writing about Television

The following paragraph analyzes the components of a television laugh track, the recorded chorus that tells us when a comedy is funny. Though written especially for *The Bedford Reader*, not as part of an essay, this brief analysis could itself be one component in an examination of TV comedy. Or, with the related paragraph on pages 404–05, illustrating CLASSIFICATION, it could contribute to an essay on, say, how the producers of TV comedies manipulate the viewers.

Many television comedies, even some that boast live audiences, rely on laugh tracks to fill too-quiet moments. The effect of a canned laugh comes from its four overlapping elements. The first is style, from titter to belly laugh. The second is intensity, the volume, ranging from mild to medium to earsplitting. The third ingredient is duration, the length of the laugh, whether quick, medium, or extended. And finally, there's the number of laughers, from a lone giggler to a roaring throng. According to rumor (for the exact workings are still a secret), the laugh-track editor draws from a bank of hundreds of prerecorded laugh files. Playing them singly or in combination, the editor blends the four ingredients as a maestro weaves a symphony out of brass, woodwinds, percussion, and strings.

Principle of analysis: elements creating the effect of a canned laugh

1. Style
2. Intensity
3. Duration
4. Number

Details and examples clarify elements

Writing in an Academic Discipline

The next paragraph appeared first in a scholarly journal and then in a textbook on medical ethics. The author discusses four possible models for the doctor-patient relationship, ending with the one detailed in this paragraph. The careful analysis supports his preference for this model over the others.

Division or Analysis

The model of social relationship which fits these conditions [of realistic equality between patient and doctor] is that of the contract or covenant. The notion of contract should not be loaded with legalistic implications, but taken in its more symbolic form as in the traditional religious or marriage "contract" or "covenant." Here two individuals or groups are interacting in a way where there are obligations and expected benefits for both parties. The obligations and benefits are limited in scope, though, even if they are expressed in somewhat vague terms. The basic norms of freedom, dignity, truth-telling, promise-keeping, and justice are essential to a contractual relationship. The premise is trust and confidence even though it is recognized that there is not a full mutuality of interests. Social sanctions institutionalize and stand behind the relationship, in case there is a violation of the contract, but for the most part the assumption is that there will be a faithful fulfillment of the obligations.

—Robert M. Veatch,
"Models for Medicine in a Revolutionary Age"

Principle of analysis: elements of a contract between doctor and patient

1. Obligations and benefits for both parties
2. Obligations and benefits limited
3. Freedom, dignity, and other norms
4. Trust and confidence
5. Support of social sanctions (meaning that society upholds the relationship)

DIVISION OR ANALYSIS IN AN ANNOTATED BIBLIOGRAPHY

As a college student, you are likely to write research papers in many of your courses. Whether on your own or as part of the research-writing assignment, preparing an annotated bibliography during research can help you keep track of your sources and use them effectively.

A common form of annotated bibliography contains a two-part entry for every potential source: (1) full publication information for the source, so that you can find it again and cite it accurately in your paper; and (2) your own comments on the source, including a brief summary and a brief analysis that addresses its value in its field, its usefulness to you, and other matters. If you include an annotation along with the publication information in your final paper, the two together can help readers locate and assess the source for themselves.

For a course in American literature, sophomore Lauren Soto researched and wrote a literary analysis about revenge in the works of Edgar Allan Poe, focusing on the parallels in Poe's life and fiction. Soto read and reread several of Poe's short stories and then searched her library and the Internet for critical analyses of the author's work. At her instructor's request, she compiled an annotated bibliography that listed and commented on the sources she thought would be most helpful in writing her paper, using MLA style (p. 73) to format the publication information. Here are two of Soto's entries:

Allen, Brooke. "The Tell-Tale Artist: Edgar Allan Poe Turns 200."
    Weekly Standard 28 Sept. 2009: 28-31. Print.

Source: magazine
article

A literary critic's view of Poe's place in literary history and
popular culture on the 200th anniversary of his birth. Allen
claims that Poe essentially invented horror fiction, science
fiction, and the detective story. She also sees parallels between
Poe himself and the characters in his fiction. Allen's focus
on Poe's mental instability and its effects on his creativity is
helpful in understanding some themes in his work, particularly
revenge. Poe's sensitivity to insults, for example, connects to
Montressor in "The Cask of Amontillado," who kills to avenge an
unnamed slight.

Elements of article
1. Poe's influence

2. Parallels between
   Poe's life and work
Potential use of source

Edgar Allan Poe Society of Baltimore. Edgar Allan Poe Society
    of Baltimore, 2010. Web. 26 Feb. 2010.

Source: Web site

A comprehensive online collection of all of Poe's works,
including letters and other documents, as well as links to critical articles from the journal *Poe Studies/Dark Romanticism*. The
site's most useful features are essays by scholars that address
common misconceptions about Poe, particularly that his poems
and stories about anger, loss, fear, and vengeance mirror events
and relationships in his own life. This perspective is valuable to
balance Allen and other writers who make a great deal of the
connections between Poe's life and work. At the same time, the
site seems somewhat defensive about Poe and protective of him,
so information about Poe and his life needs to be verified in
other sources.

Elements of Web site
1. Collection of Poe's
   works

2. Scholarly criticism

3. Balancing
   perspectives
Potential use of source

Division or Analysis

JUDY BRADY

Judy Brady, born in 1937 in San Francisco, where she now lives, earned a BFA in painting from the University of Iowa in 1962. Drawn into political action by her work in the feminist movement, she went to Cuba in 1973, where she studied class relationships as a way of understanding change in a society. When she was diagnosed with cancer in 1980, Brady became an activist against what she calls "the cancer establishment." ("Cancer is, after all, a multibillion dollar business," she says.) In 1991 she published *1 in 3: Women with Cancer Confront an Epidemic,* an anthology of writings by women. She is a board member of Greenaction, an environmental justice organization, and a founding member of the Toxic Links Coalition. She provided a chapter for the book *Sweeping the Earth: Women Taking Action for a Healthy Planet,* and she writes articles for Breast Cancer Action in San Francisco.

I Want a Wife

After reading "I Want a Wife" aloud at a 1970 women's meeting in San Francisco, Brady submitted the essay for the Spring 1972 issue of *Ms.* magazine, which had started the year before as a vehicle for the modern feminist movement, then in its first decade. "I Want a Wife" became one of the best-known manifestos in popular feminist writing. In the essay, Brady trenchantly divides the work of a wife into its multiple duties and functions, leading to an inescapable conclusion. If you find that Brady stereotypes men, read the essay after hers, Christina Hoff Sommers's "Men—It's in Their Nature," for a different view.

I belong to that classification of people known as wives. I am A Wife. And, not altogether incidentally, I am a mother.

Not too long ago a male friend of mine appeared on the scene fresh from a recent divorce. He had one child, who is, of course, with his ex-wife. He is looking for another wife. As I thought about him while I was ironing one evening, it suddenly occurred to me that I, too, would like to have a wife. Why do I want a wife?

I would like to go back to school so that I can become economically independent, support myself, and, if need be, support those dependent upon me. I want a wife who will work and send me to school. And while I am going to school I want a wife to take care of my children. I want a wife to keep track of the children's doctor and dentist appointments. And to keep track of mine, too.

I want a wife to make sure my children eat properly and are kept clean. I want a wife who will wash the children's clothes and keep them mended. I want a wife who is a good nurturant attendant to my children, who arranges for their schooling, makes sure that they have an adequate social life with their peers, takes them to the park, the zoo, etc. I want a wife who takes care of the children when they are sick, a wife who arranges to be around when the children need special care, because, of course, I cannot miss classes at school. My wife must arrange to lose time at work and not lose the job. It may mean a small cut in my wife's income from time to time, but I guess I can tolerate that. Needless to say, my wife will arrange and pay for the care of the children while my wife is working.

I want a wife who will take care of *my* physical needs. I want a wife who   4
will keep my house clean. A wife who will pick up after my children, a wife who will pick up after me. I want a wife who will keep my clothes clean, ironed, mended, replaced when need be, and who will see to it that my personal things are kept in their proper place so that I can find what I need the minute I need it. I want a wife who cooks the meals, a wife who is a *good* cook. I want a wife who will plan the menus, do the necessary grocery shopping, prepare the meals, serve them pleasantly, and then do the cleaning up while I do my studying. I want a wife who will care for me when I am sick and sympathize with my pain and loss of time from school. I want a wife to go along when our family takes vacation so that someone can continue to care for me and my children when I need a rest and change of scene.

I want a wife who will not bother me with rambling complaints about a   5
wife's duties. But I want a wife who will listen to me when I feel the need to explain a rather difficult point I have come across in my course of studies. And I want a wife who will type my papers for me when I have written them.

I want a wife who will take care of the details of my social life. When my   6
wife and I are invited out by my friends, I want a wife who will take care of the babysitting arrangements. When I meet people at school that I like and want to entertain, I want a wife who will have the house clean, will prepare a special meal, serve it to me and my friends, and not interrupt when I talk about things that interest me and my friends. I want a wife who will have arranged that the children are fed and ready for bed before my guests arrive so that the children do not bother us. I want a wife who takes care of the needs of my guests so that they feel comfortable, who makes sure that they have an ashtray, that they are passed the hors d'oeuvres, that they are offered a second helping of the food, that their wine glasses are replenished when necessary, that their coffee is served to them as they like it. And I want a wife who knows that sometimes I need a night out by myself.

I want a wife who is sensitive to my sexual needs, a wife who makes love   7
passionately and eagerly when I feel like it, a wife who makes sure that I am

satisfied. And, of course, I want a wife who will not demand sexual attention when I am not in the mood for it. I want a wife who assumes the complete responsibility for birth control, because I do not want more children. I want a wife who will remain sexually faithful to me so that I do not have to clutter up my intellectual life with jealousies. And I want a wife who understands that *my* sexual needs may entail more than strict adherence to monogamy. I must, after all, be able to relate to people as fully as possible.

If, by chance, I find another person more suitable as a wife than the wife I   8
already have, I want the liberty to replace my present wife with another one. Naturally, I will expect a fresh, new life; my wife will take the children and be solely responsible for them so that I am left free.

When I am through with school and have a job, I want my wife to quit   9
working and remain at home so that my wife can more fully and completely take care of a wife's duties.

My God, who *wouldn't* want a wife?   10

---

*For a reading quiz, sources on Judy Brady, and annotated links to further readings on feminism and on gender roles, visit **bedfordstmartins.com/thebedfordreader**.*

Journal Writing

Brady addresses the traditional obligations of a wife and mother. In your journal, jot down parallel obligations of a husband and father. (To take your journal writing further, see "From Journal to Essay" on the facing page.)

Questions on Meaning

1. Sum up the duties of a wife as Brady sees them.
2. To what inequities in the roles traditionally assigned to men and to women does "I Want a Wife" call attention?
3. What is the THESIS of this essay? Is it stated or implied?
4. Is Brady unfair to men?

Questions on Writing Strategy

1. What EFFECT does Brady obtain with the title "I Want a Wife"?
2. What do the first two paragraphs accomplish?

3. What is the TONE of this essay?
4. How do you explain the fact that Brady never uses the pronoun *she* to refer to a wife? Does this make her prose unnecessarily awkward?
5. What principle does Brady use to analyze the role of wife? Can you think of some other principle for analyzing the job?
6. Knowing that this essay was first published in *Ms.* magazine in 1972, what can you guess about its intended readers? Does "I Want a Wife" strike a college AUDIENCE today as revolutionary?
7. **OTHER METHODS**   Although she mainly divides or analyzes the role of wife, Brady also creates a DEFINITION by using CLASSIFICATION to sort the many duties and responsibilities into manageable groups. What are the groups?

Questions on Language

1. What is achieved by the author's frequent repetition of the phrase "I want a wife"?
2. Be sure you know how to define the following words as Brady uses them: nurturant (par. 3); replenished (6); adherence, monogamy (7).
3. In general, how would you describe the DICTION of this essay? How well does it suit the essay's intended audience?

Suggestions for Writing

1. **FROM JOURNAL TO ESSAY**   Working from your journal entry, write an essay titled "I Want a Husband" in which, using examples as Brady does, you enumerate the roles traditionally assigned to men in our society.
2. Imagining that you want to employ someone to do a specific job, divide the task into its duties and functions. Then, guided by your analysis, write an accurate job description in essay form.
3. **CRITICAL WRITING**   As indicated in the note introducing it, Brady's essay was first published in 1972 in *Ms.*, a feminist magazine. Do some research about the evolving role of women between, say, 1970 and today. How have women's expectations, opportunities, and positions changed? One approach is to locate statistics for then and now about women in higher education (studying and teaching), in medicine and other professions, in the workforce, as wives and mothers, as home-makers, and so on. Based on your research, write an essay in which you SUMMARIZE Brady's view as you understand it and then EVALUATE her essay. Consider: Is Brady fair? If not, is unfairness justified? Is the essay relevant today? If not, what has changed? Provide specific EVIDENCE from your experience, observation, and research.
4. **CONNECTIONS**   Both "I Want a Wife" and the next essay, Christina Hoff Sommers's "Men — It's in Their Nature," challenge traditional ideas about men's and women's roles and expected behaviors. However, Brady's STYLE is fast paced and her tone is sarcastic, while Sommers is more methodical and earnest. Which method of addressing these issues do you find more effective? Why? Write an essay that COMPARES AND CONTRASTS the essays' tones, styles, POINTS OF VIEW, and OBJECTIVE versus SUBJECTIVE language. What conclusions can you draw about the connection between the writers' strategies and their messages?

Judy Brady on Writing

Before Judy Brady penned "I Want a Wife" in 1970, she had never considered being a writer. In a 2007 interview with Dick Gordon on American Public Media, Brady recalled that the idea of writing the essay was planted at a women's movement gathering at Glide Memorial Church in San Francisco: "Well, I was complaining at one of the consciousness-raising group meetings and somebody just said, 'Why don't you write it?' Which hadn't occurred to me. And I went home and did."

Brady says that although writing the essay took her only a couple of hours, its inspiration had been brewing for the decade of marriage and motherhood that preceded it. Brady remembers feeling spitefully awakened when she began to speak with other women about their position in the home and in society: "There was tremendous anger when I began to understand how I had been . . . how can I say this? . . . how I had been *molded* by forces about which I was totally unconscious."

At a rally celebrating the fiftieth anniversary of American women's right to vote, Brady read "I Want a Wife" aloud (and "totally terrified") to a gathering of both supporters and hecklers. Her now ex-husband bought her flowers after the event, a gesture that Brady describes as "bizarre." "He meant it well, but he sort of didn't get it," she says.

Inspired by the response to her essay, Brady became an active supporter of social and political causes, volunteering in Cuba, advocating for cancer patients, and getting involved in the environmental movement while continuing to work for women's rights. Reflecting on the impact of "I Want a Wife" forty years later, Brady is still frustrated by what she sees as a lack of meaningful change for women and for underprivileged people in general. Writing the essay did, however, affect her personally: "I've had a much more interesting life than I would have had had I not found the women's movement and not . . . done this essay."

For Discussion

1. What sparked Brady to write "I Want a Wife"? Why does she say that it was the work of ten years rather than just a couple of hours?
2. What did Brady's husband not "get" about her essay? Why do you think he may have failed to grasp its point?

CHRISTINA HOFF SOMMERS

Christina Hoff Sommers is a former philosophy professor who studies feminism in American culture. Born in 1950 in Petaluma, California, she earned a PhD from Brandeis University in 1979 and went on to teach ethics at the University of Massachusetts and Clark University. Sommers is best known for her 1994 book *Who Stole Feminism?: How Women Have Betrayed Women*, a critique of the contemporary feminist movement. She has also published *The War against Boys: How Misguided Feminism Is Harming Our Young Men* (2000), *One Nation under Therapy: How the Helping Culture Is Eroding Self-Reliance* (2005), and *The Science on Women and Science* (2009). Sommers is a resident scholar at the American Enterprise Institute for Public Policy Research and lectures widely at businesses and schools.

Men — It's in Their Nature

Sommers wrote "Men — It's in Their Nature" as a guest columnist for *The American Enterprise* in 2003. Like Judy Brady in the previous selection, Sommers analyzes the distinct roles of men and women and takes issue with cultural assumptions, particularly as they apply to raising boys. Unlike Brady, Sommers concludes that the gender divide can be a positive force in society.

This past spring, my son spent a month in Israel with his senior class. Only one activity disappointed him. While camping in the Negev Desert, special counselors from a progressive-socialist kibbutz paid a visit and led the students through a sensitivity exercise. The students were told to walk out into the desert until they were completely alone. The counselors (mostly American-born) supplied them with a pencil, paper, matches, and a candle and instructed them to absorb the quiet calm of the desert, to record their feelings, and to "find themselves."

The girls happily complied. Most of the boys did not. They scattered into the desert, quickly became bored, and sought out each other's company. Then they threw the pencils and paper into a pile, and used the candles and matches to start a little bonfire. The boys loved it; the sensitivity trainers were horrified. They viewed the boys' behavior as an expression of primitive violence — a lethal masculinity straight from *The Lord of the Flies*.[1]

---

[1] A novel by William Golding (1911–93) that details the warlike society established by a group of young boys who are stranded on an island. — EDS.

Later in the evening, the students sat in a circle while the girls read their   3
impassioned reactions to the "haunting loneliness" of the desert; the boys
could barely suppress laughter—confirming once again the worst fears of the
sensitivity trainers. Gender equity experts in America's schools, universities,
government agencies, and major women's groups would share the distress of
the kibbutz counselors, having spent more than a decade trying to resocialize
boys away from "toxic masculinity."

In a great number of American schools, gender reformers have succeeded   4
in expunging many activities that young boys enjoy: dodge ball, cops and robbers, reading or listening to stories about battles and war heroes. A daycare
center in North Carolina was censured by the State Division of Child Development for letting boys play with two-inch green Army men. The division
director described the toys as "potentially dangerous if children use them to
act out violent themes."

Activities deemed "safe" by the gender equity experts and the teachers   5
they inspire include quilting, games without scores, and stories about brave
girls and boys who learn to cry. The goal is to resocialize boys, freeing them
from male stereotypes, and, ultimately, to promote genuine equality between
the sexes—which for the reformers means sameness.

But decades of research in neuroscience, endocrinology, genetics, and   6
developmental psychology, strongly suggest that masculine traits are hardwired. There are exceptions, but here are the rules: Males have better spatial reasoning skills, females better verbal skills. Males are greater risk takers,
females are more nurturing. Boys like action, competitive roughhousing, and
inanimate objects, and they are the one group of Americans who do not spend
a lot of time talking about their feelings.

Try as they may, parents, teachers, and gender facilitators have not been   7
successful in rooting out male behavior they regard as harmful. An "equity
facilitator" tried to persuade a group of nine-year-old boys in a Baltimore public school to accept the idea of playing with baby dolls. According to one
observer, "Their reaction was so hostile, the teacher had trouble keeping
order." And then there was Jimmy. At age eleven, this San Francisco sixth
grader was made to contribute a square to a class quilt "celebrating women
we admire." He chose to honor tennis player Monica Seles who, in 1993,
was stabbed on the court by a deranged fan of Steffi Graf. Jimmy handed in a
muslin square festooned with a tennis racket and a bloody dagger. His square
may be unique in the history of quilting, but his teacher did not appreciate its
originality and rejected it. American classrooms are full of Jimmys.

Efforts to change boys like Jimmy or my son and his bonfire compan-   8
ions will be difficult if not impossible. Nature is obdurate on some matters.
While environment and socialization do play a significant role, scientists are

beginning to pinpoint the precise biological correlates to many typical gender differences. A 2001 special issue of *Scientific American* reviewed the growing evidence that children's play preferences are, in large part, hormonally determined. Researchers confirmed what parents experience all the time: Even with counterconditioning, boys and girls gravitate toward very different toys.

The entire anthropological record offers not a single example of a society where females have better spatial reasoning skills and males better verbal skills, where females are fixated on objects and men on feelings, or where males are physically docile and females aggressive. In the face of what we know, it is altogether unreasonable to deny the biological basis for distinctive male and female preferences and abilities.

Does this mean biology is destiny? As anthropologist Lionel Tiger says, "biology is not destiny, but it is good statistical probability." There is still room for equity. A fair and just society offers equality of opportunity to all. But it cannot promise, and should not try to enforce, sameness. The natural differences between men and women suggest there will never be mathematical parity in all fields; far more men than women will choose to be mechanics, engineers, or soldiers. Early childhood education, family medicine, and social work will continue to be dominated by women.

Boys will prefer bonfires to diaries and any teacher who requires them to contribute squares to a quilt should brace herself for insensitive images of monsters, dangerous animals, and weaponry. The male tendency to be competitive, risk-loving, more narrowly focused, and less concerned with feelings has consequences in the real world. It could explain why there are more males at the extremes of success and failure: more male CEOs, more males in maximum security prisons.

Of course, boys' natural masculinity must be tempered. Social theorist Hannah Arendt is believed to have said that every year civilization is invaded by millions of tiny barbarians—they are called children. All societies confront the problem of civilizing their children, particularly the male ones. History teaches that masculinity constrained by morality is powerful and constructive; it also teaches that masculinity without ethics is dangerous and destructive.

We have a set of proven social practices for raising young men. The traditional approach is through character education to develop a young man's sense of honor and help him become a considerate, conscientious human being. Sociologists make an important distinction between pathological and healthy masculinity. Boys who exhibit aberrational masculinity define their manhood through antisocial and destructive acts; instead of protecting the vulnerable, they exploit them. Healthy masculinity is the opposite. Males who possess it—the vast majority of American boys and men—strive to be helpful and to achieve. They sublimate their natural aggression into sports, hobbies, and work. They build rather than destroy. And they do not exploit women and children, they protect them.

Efforts to civilize boys with honor codes, character education, manners, and rules of good sportsmanship are necessary and effective, and fully consistent with their masculine natures. Efforts to feminize them with dolls, quilts, noncompetitive games, girl-centered books, and feelings exercises will fail; though they will succeed in making millions of boys quite unhappy.   14

Dissident feminist Camille Paglia is one of the few scholars who values maleness: "Masculinity is aggressive, unstable, combustible. It is also the most creative cultural force in history. When I cross . . . any of America's great bridges, I think—men have done this. Construction is a sublime male poetry."   15

This sublime poetry has been unappreciated in American society for more than a quarter of a century. But that appears to be changing. The awesome display of masculine courage shown by the firefighters and policemen at Ground Zero [and] the heroic soldiers fighting in Afghanistan and Iraq . . . have rekindled in Americans an appreciation for masculine virtues. Many courageous and even heroic women took part in all these endeavors. But fighting enemies and protecting the nation are overwhelmingly male projects.   16

The gender activists who fill our schools and government agencies will continue with their efforts to make boys more docile and emotional. But fewer and fewer Americans will support them. Maleness is back in fashion. And one reason is that Americans are increasingly aware that traditional male traits such as aggression, competitiveness, risk taking, and stoicism—constrained by virtues of valor, honor, and self-sacrifice—are essential to the well-being and safety of our society.   17

For a reading quiz, sources on Christina Hoff Sommers, and annotated links to further readings on gender roles and the debate over nature versus nurture, visit **bedfordstmartins.com/thebedfordreader**.

Journal Writing

How do you respond to Sommers's assertion that gender differences are "hardwired" from birth, that boys and girls are inherently and unalterably different? Take her point about biology down to the level of the individual: To what extent were you born with a genetic predisposition to your characteristics—kindness, aggressiveness, athleticism, intelligence, shyness, and so on? (To take your journal writing further, see "From Journal to Essay" below.)

Questions on Meaning

1. What is Sommers's PURPOSE in this essay? How can you tell?
2. What does Sommers seem to ASSUME about her AUDIENCE? To what extent do you fit her assumptions?
3. Sommers makes a distinction between "resocializing" boys and "civilizing" them. What is this distinction, and why is it important?

Questions on Writing Strategy

1. What, according to Sommers, are the elements of maleness—both positive and negative? What principle of analysis does she apply to her subject?
2. What EVIDENCE does Sommers offer to support her assertions? Are you satisfied that her evidence sufficiently supports her thesis? Why, or why not?
3. Where in the essay does Sommers relate stories about reformers' efforts to encourage sensitivity in boys? What do these ANECDOTES contribute to her point?
4. Sommers states her THESIS near the middle of her essay. What is it? How do her points before and after her thesis statement differ?
5. **OTHER METHODS**   How does Sommers use COMPARISON AND CONTRAST to characterize men and women throughout her essay, particularly in paragraphs 6 and 9? What is the purpose of her comparisons?

Questions on Language

1. How would you analyze Sommers's TONE? Is it consistent throughout?
2. Why does Sommers use quotation marks around the words *toxic masculinity* (par. 3) and *safe* (5)? Does she use this strategy anywhere else?
3. Sommers uses a number of words that might be unfamiliar to you. Consult a dictionary if you need help defining any of the following: kibbutz (par. 1); complied (2); suppress, equity (3); expunging, censured (4); neuroscience, endocrinology (6); muslin, festooned (7); obdurate (8); anthropological, fixated, docile (9); parity (10); tempered (12); pathological, aberrational, sublimate (13); dissident, sublime (15); rekindled (16); stoicism, valor (17).

Suggestions for Writing

1. **FROM JOURNAL TO ESSAY**   Working from your journal entry, write an essay that explores the debate about heredity versus environment, nature versus nurture, as it applies to you. Using specific EXAMPLES, discuss the extent to which you think your gender or your upbringing have shaped who you are.
2. Think about the virtues Sommers cites in her conclusion: "valor, honor, and self-sacrifice." Choose one of these words, or another of the values Sommers

mentions in the essay, and write a DEFINITION essay that explains its meanings for you. Use examples from your own experience, observations, and reading to make your definition concrete.

3. **CRITICAL WRITING**   Based on this essay, ANALYZE Sommers's apparent attitude toward the feminist movement. How does she characterize attempts to shift cultural assumptions about men and women? Does she believe that gender equity is possible or even desirable? What does she suggest have been (or will be) the effects of feminism? Support your ideas with EVIDENCE from the essay.

4. **CONNECTIONS**   Look over Judy Brady's "I Want a Wife" (p. 360) and make a list of her implied complaints about the traditional responsibilities of women. Now make a list of the responsibilities that Sommers implies a good man is happy to take on. How could Sommers's essay be viewed as a sort of response or solution to some of the problems Brady raises? Taking "I Want a Wife" and "Men—It's in Their Nature" together, write an essay explaining how attitudes toward traditional gender roles have changed over the last four decades. Are such changes good, or have they raised new problems? Why do you think so?

―――――――――――

Christina Hoff Sommers on Writing

When she published *Who Stole Feminism?*—a book that disputes the idea that American women as a group are disadvantaged by gender—Christina Hoff Sommers found herself "excommunicated" from the feminist academic community to which she belonged. As a result, she has closely examined and affirmed her reasons for writing.

In a lecture delivered at Hamilton College in 2008, Sommers explained why she pursues her research despite facing harsh criticism. Characterizing herself as a writer "with a respect for logic, clear thinking, rules of evidence and—I hope—a strong sense of fairness," she asserts that "most—not all—but most of the victim statistics are, at best, misleading—at worst, completely inaccurate." She then asks, "Does it matter that much that there is a large body of factually challenged information at the heart of contemporary feminism? Does it matter that feminist leaders in the United States think and say a lot of intemperate things?" For Sommers, "the answer is an emphatic yes." As a researcher and a writer, she insists on accuracy and levelheadedness and cautions that "misrepresentation almost always clouds the true causes of suffering and provides obstacles to genuine ways of preventing it. . . ."

Sommers emphasizes that she doesn't believe "we should reject contemporary feminism." She has a more ambitious goal in mind: "We should reform it, correct its excesses, insist that moderate and conservative feminists be given a voice, and then set about helping to write the next great chapter in the history of women's quest for freedom."

For Discussion

1. Why does Sommers continue to research and write despite critical reactions to her work? What are her goals?
2. Describe a time when you wrote something controversial. Why did you write it? Were there any repercussions? If so, how did you deal with them?

GUILLERMO DEL TORO AND CHUCK HOGAN

Guillermo del Toro and Chuck Hogan are coauthors of *The Strain* (2009) and *The Fall* (2010), the first two installments of a planned trilogy of vampire novels. Although they share an interest in telling a new kind of story about vampires, the authors arrived at their collaboration from very different backgrounds. Born in Guadalajara, Mexico, Guillermo del Toro began his career as a cinematic makeup artist. His debut as a director, with the 1992 film *Cronos,* caught the attention of Hollywood and allowed him to go on to direct *The Devil's Backbone* (2001), *Blade II* (2002), both *Hellboy* films (2004, 2008), and *Pan's Labyrinth* (2006), which won three Academy Awards. Chuck Hogan, by contrast, is a Boston-based thriller novelist who was working as a video-store manager when he made his breakthrough with *The Standoff* (1995), a story about a tense hostage negotiation. Hogan has since published *The Blood Artists* (1998), *Prince of Thieves* (2004), *The Killing Moon* (2007), and *Devils in Exile* (2010). *Prince of Thieves* won the 2005 Hammett Award for literary crime writing and was the basis for the 2010 motion picture *The Town.*

Vampires Never Die

The filmmaker del Toro and the novelist Hogan bonded over their fascination with how ancient myths about vampires have been adapted and readapted into popular culture. In a 2009 essay published in the *New York Times,* del Toro and Hogan trace the perpetual craving for vampire stories back to its historical, literary, and scientific roots.

Tonight, you or someone you love will likely be visited by a vampire — on cable television or the big screen, or in the bookstore. Our own novel describes a modern-day epidemic that spreads across New York City.

It all started nearly two hundred years ago. It was the "Year Without a Summer" of 1816, when ash from volcanic eruptions lowered temperatures around the globe, giving rise to widespread famine. A few friends gathered at the Villa Diodati on Lake Geneva and decided to engage in a small competition to see who could come up with the most terrifying tale — and the two great monsters of the modern age were born.

One was created by Mary Godwin, soon to become Mary Shelley, whose Dr. Frankenstein gave life to a desolate creature. The other monster was less created than fused. John William Polidori stitched together folklore, personal resentment and erotic anxieties into "The Vampyre," a story that is the basis for vampires as they are understood today.

With "The Vampyre," Polidori gave birth to the two main branches of vampiric fiction: the vampire as romantic hero, and the vampire as undead monster. This ambivalence may reflect Polidori's own, as it is widely accepted that Lord Ruthven, the titular creature, was based upon Lord Byron — literary superstar of the era and another resident of the lakeside villa that fateful summer. Polidori tended to Byron day and night, both as his doctor and most devoted groupie. But Polidori resented him as well: Byron was dashing and brilliant, while the poor doctor had a rather drab talent and unremarkable physique.

But this was just a new twist to a very old idea. The myth, established well before the invention of the word "vampire," seems to cross every culture, language and era. The Indian Baital, the Ch'ing Shih in China, and the Romanian Strigoi are but a few of its names. The creature seems to be as old as Babylonia and Sumer.[1] Or even older.

The vampire may originate from a repressed memory we had as primates. Perhaps at some point we were — out of necessity — cannibalistic. As soon as we became sedentary, agricultural tribes with social boundaries, one seminal myth might have featured our ancestors as primitive beasts who slept in the cold loam of the earth and fed off the salty blood of the living.

Monsters, like angels, are invoked by our individual and collective needs. Today, much as during that gloomy summer in 1816, we feel the need to seek their cold embrace.

Herein lies an important clue: In contrast to timeless creatures like the dragon, the vampire does not seek to obliterate us, but instead offers a peculiar brand of blood alchemy. For as his contagion bestows its nocturnal gift, the vampire transforms our vile, mortal selves into the gold of eternal youth and instills in us something that every social construct seeks to quash: primal lust. If youth is desire married with unending possibility, then vampire lust creates within us a delicious void, one we long to fulfill.

In other words, whereas other monsters emphasize what is mortal in us, the vampire emphasizes the eternal in us. Through the panacea of its blood it turns the lead of our toxic flesh into golden matter.

In a society that moves as fast as ours, where every week a new "blockbuster" must be enthroned at the box office, or where idols are fabricated by

---

[1] Countries from ancient Mesopotamia (in the vicinity of modern-day Iraq), dating back to approximately 4000 BCE and 2000 BCE, respectively. They are generally considered the origins of Western civilization. — EDS.

consensus every new television season, the promise of something everlasting, something truly eternal, holds a special allure. As a seductive figure, the
vampire is as flexible and polyvalent as ever. Witness its slow mutation from
the pansexual, decadent Anne Rice[2] creatures to the current permutations—
promising anything from chaste eternal love to wild nocturnal escapades—and
there you will find the true essence of immortality: adaptability.

Vampires find their niche and mutate at an accelerated rate now—in the   11
past one would see, for decades, the same variety of fiend, repeated in multiple
storylines. Now, vampires simultaneously occur in all forms and tap into our
every need: soap opera storylines, sexual liberation, noir detective fiction, etc.
The myth seems to be twittering promiscuously to serve all avenues of life,
from cereal boxes to romantic fiction. The fast pace of technology accelerates
its viral dispersion in our culture.

But if Polidori remains the roots in the genealogy of our creature, the most   12
widely known vampire was birthed by Bram Stoker in 1897.

Part of the reason for the great success of his "Dracula" is generally ac-   13
knowledged to be its appearance at a time of great technological revolution.
The narrative is full of new gadgets (telegraphs, typing machines), various
forms of communication (diaries, ship logs), and cutting-edge science (blood
transfusions)—a mash-up of ancient myth in conflict with the world of the
present.

Today as well, we stand at the rich uncertain dawn of a new level of sci-   14
entific innovation. The wireless technology we carry in our pockets today
was the stuff of the science fiction in our youth. Our technological arrogance
mirrors more and more the Wellsian[3] dystopia of dissatisfaction, while allowing us to feel safe and connected at all times. We can call, see or hear almost
anything and anyone no matter where we are. For most people then, the only
remote place remains within. "Know thyself" we do not.

Despite our obsessive harnessing of information, we are still ultimately vul-   15
nerable to our fates and our nightmares. We enthrone the deadly virus in the
very same way that "Dracula" allowed the British public to believe in monsters:
through science. Science becomes the modern man's superstition. It allows him
to experience fear and awe again, and to believe in the things he cannot see.

And through awe, we once again regain spiritual humility. The current   16
vampire pandemic serves to remind us that we have no true jurisdiction over
our bodies, our climate or our very souls. Monsters will always provide the

---

[2] Anne Rice (born 1941) is a novelist best known for *Interview with the Vampire* (1976),
The Vampire Lestat (1985), and *The Queen of the Damned* (1988). —Eds.

[3] H. G. Wells (1866–1946) was an influential science fiction writer whose works include *The Time Machine* (1895), *The Island of Doctor Moreau* (1896), and *War of the Worlds*
(1898). —Eds.

possibility of mystery in our mundane "reality show" lives, hinting at a larger spiritual world; for if there are demons in our midst, there surely must be angels lurking nearby as well. In the vampire we find Eros and Thanatos[4] fused together in archetypal embrace, spiraling through the ages, undying.

Forever.   17

> *For a reading quiz, sources on Guillermo del Toro and Chuck Hogan, and annotated links to further readings on vampire legends and fiction, visit* **bedfordstmartins.com/ thebedfordreader.**

Journal Writing

Do you enjoy vampire stories, whether in books, in movies, or on television? Of the vampire characters in popular culture (past or present), who is your favorite? Why do you think this character appeals to you? In your journal, explore what vampires mean to you. If you don't care for vampire fiction, consider why it leaves you cold. (To take your journal writing further, see "From Journal to Essay" on the next page.)

Questions on Meaning

1. Why do you suppose del Toro and Hogan wrote this essay? Are they merely promoting their novels, or do they have a more serious PURPOSE as well?
2. What is the THESIS of "Vampires Never Die"? Where, if at all, is it stated succinctly?
3. How do del Toro and Hogan explain the appeal of vampires in contemporary culture? In what ways has that appeal changed across time and geography? In what ways has it remained consistent?
4. What is a "social construct" (par. 8)? How is the concept central to the authors' interpretation of vampires?
5. In paragraph 15, del Toro and Hogan say, "Science becomes the modern man's superstition." What do they mean? How do you explain the PARADOX in that statement?

Questions on Writing Strategy

1. "Vampires Never Die" uses advanced academic vocabulary and contains several literary, historical, scientific, and psychological references. How, then, do

---

[4]Greek gods of love (Eros) and death (Thanatos). —Eds.

the authors imagine their AUDIENCE? Are their ASSUMPTIONS reasonable in your case?

2. What principle of analysis do del Toro and Hogan use in examining vampire stories? What enduring elements do they perceive in the characters?

3. Why do del Toro and Hogan speculate in their introduction about the "resentment and erotic anxieties" (par. 3) felt by John William Polidori, the author of the first modern vampire story? What do his personal conflicts have to do with how we think about vampires even today?

4. What is the effect of the essay's final paragraph?

5. **OTHER METHODS**   Del Toro and Hogan COMPARE AND CONTRAST new technologies from the late nineteenth and early twenty-first centuries. What similarities do they find?

Questions on Language

1. Make sure you know the meanings of the following words: desolate (par. 3); ambivalence, titular, dashing (4); repressed, sedentary, seminal, loam (6); invoked (7); obliterate, primal (8); panacea (9); consensus, polyvalent, pansexual, permutations, chaste (10); noir, promiscuously, dispersion (11); mash-up (13); dystopia (14); pandemic, mundane, archetypal (16).

2. Explain the double meaning of "twittering" in paragraph 11. Why do you think del Toro and Hogan chose this particular word?

3. What do the authors mean by "a peculiar brand of blood alchemy" (par. 8)? Where else do they use this metaphor? Why is it particularly appropriate for their subject? (For a definition of *metaphor*, see *Figures of speech* in Useful Terms.)

Suggestions for Writing

1. **FROM JOURNAL TO ESSAY**   Expanding on your journal entry, write an essay that ANALYZES one vampire character from popular culture—such as Bram Stoker's Dracula, Edward from the *Twilight* series, Yvette from Anne Rice's novels, Bill Compton from *True Blood*, or The Master from del Toro and Hogan's trilogy. Break the character down into his (or her) elements, considering backstory as well as personality, and reassemble the parts into a new whole of your understanding.

2. Write an essay that analyzes several examples of another type of writing by examining their shared characteristics and hidden meanings. You may choose any narrowly defined GENRE that's familiar to you: food blog, parenting-advice column, amateur film review, gay romance, alternative-history science fiction, and so on. Be sure to make your principle of analysis clear to your readers.

3. Some cultural analysts have said that the resurgence of vampire stories in the last quarter century can be attributed to the AIDS epidemic that emerged in the 1980s. In your library's database of scholarly journal articles, conduct a keyword search for "vampires" and "AIDS" and read one or two of the arguments in favor of this theory. (If you wish, you may search for other academic analyses of vampire lore.) How do you respond to them? Do alternate interpretations undermine del Toro and Hogan's analysis, or do they simply complicate it?

4. **CRITICAL WRITING**   Del Toro and Hogan explore CAUSES AND EFFECTS to explain the prevalence of vampires in popular culture. How persuasive is their analysis? Do you agree with them that vampire legends fill psychological and spiritual voids that have been created by advances in science and technology? Why, or why not?

5. **CONNECTIONS**   William Least Heat-Moon, in "Dance of the Hobs" (p. 187) also writes about folklore and legend, albeit from a very different perspective. In an essay, COMPARE AND CONTRAST Heat-Moon's and del Toro and Hogan's ASSUMPTIONS about the sources and functions of contemporary mythologies. Consider, as well, your own thoughts about the value of such interpretations: Are rumors and popular culture worthy of serious inquiry?

Guillermo del Toro and Chuck Hogan on Writing

"Vampires Never Die" was by no means Guillermo del Toro and Chuck Hogan's first experience working together as writers. In 2006, they began collaborating on a trilogy of horror novels about vampires. The project started when Hogan's literary agent sent him a twelve-page outline of del Toro's story idea, originally conceived for the small screen, and told him the director was thinking about trying a novel. "I got a page and a half in before calling [my agent] back and essentially telling him that I would do anything to be involved," Hogan gushes in a 2009 interview with blogger Sarah Weinman. In lieu of a publishing deal or any kind of contract, the authors made a pact on a handshake — "actually more of a bro-hug," according to Hogan — and agreed to join forces. They finished the first installment of the trilogy, *The Strain*, after three years.

Hogan admits to being apprehensive about writing with del Toro, whom he calls "a god of the genre," especially since the storyline was the director's. However, he says that del Toro "completely opened up his story," giving Hogan the freedom to expand and change the narrative in the drafting stage. In a separate interview with Rick Kleffel on KUSP Central Coast Public Radio, del Toro praises Hogan's contributions to the shape of the story: "The book is full of intimate moments of terror that come from personal experience, and others that Chuck created. . . . Some of the best, most disturbing moments in the book come from his imagination, curiously enough."

Both authors note that, though their drafting processes were loose, revising the book was "rigorous." Exchanging drafts by e-mail, they commented extensively on each other's chapters, a practice that del Toro calls "riffing." As he explains, "I was merciless with his chapters; he was merciless with my chapters." Revisions involved moving or cutting large portions of text. Del Toro often rearranged chapters, and Hogan sometimes scrapped entire sections. Speaking of Hogan's editing style, del Toro jokes that some changes were made "subverticiously" (a word of his own invention): "All of a sudden I would get the manuscript and it was missing one chapter I wrote or half a chapter I wrote." However, it was this kind of harsh revision that in the end made for the "seamless blending" of two writers' talents.

For Discussion

1. Why do you think Guillermo del Toro and Chuck Hogan write freely but revise rigorously?
2. Have you ever worked collaboratively on a writing project? What were some of the advantages or frustrations of working together?

BELLA DePAULO

Bella DePaulo is a social scientist who specializes in lying and lie detection and in the ways single people are perceived in US society. Born in 1953 in Scranton, Pennsylvania, she earned a BA from Vassar College in 1975 and received a PhD in psychology from Harvard University in 1979. She has published over a hundred scholarly articles, and her research has been supported by the National Science Foundation, the National Institute of Mental Health, and the National Academy of Education. DePaulo writes a blog for *Psychology Today* and contributes to the *Huffington Post,* the *New York Times,* the *Chronicle of Higher Education,* and other periodicals. Her essays on "the stereotyping and stigmatizing of people who are single" are collected in *Single with Attitude* (2009). She is also the author of two books on lying: *Behind the Door of Deceit* and *The Lies We Tell and the Clues We Miss* (both 2009). DePaulo is currently a visiting professor at the University of California at Santa Barbara.

The Myth of Doomed Kids

In her book *Singled Out: How Singles Are Stereotyped, Stigmatized, and Ignored, and Still Live Happily Ever After* (2006), DePaulo challenges myths about unmarried people. "The Myth of Doomed Kids" (editors' title) is an excerpt from the book. The opening paragraph refers to the early 1980s, when debates over public-assistance programs sometimes reduced single mothers to the stereotype of the welfare recipient who neglects her children and scams the system for her own benefit. Recent discussion may have become less blatantly hostile to single parents, but the idea persists that their children are at great risk for psychological problems.

Parents who are single get pummeled in the public discourse—especially [1] if they are poor. President Ronald Reagan seared a scathing image onto the national psyche when he described the Welfare Queen in her welfare Cadillac, who only pretended to have an array of dead husbands so she could bilk the public assistance system for even more ill-gotten gains. The queen had a short life—not because she was single but because she never existed. She was fabricated.[1] Her legacy, though, has been enduring.

---

[1] Reporters tried to find the Welfare Queen to interview her, but they never did find anyone who met Reagan's description. The closest they came was a woman from Chicago who was in fact charged with welfare fraud. Reagan claimed that the Welfare Queen used eighty names; the Chicago woman used four. Reagan also claimed that the queen had bilked the system for more than $150,000; the fraud alleged to have been committed by the Chicago woman amounted to $8,000. See "'Welfare Queen' Becomes Issue in Reagan Campaign," *New York Times,* February 15, 1980, and David Zucchino, *The Myth of the Welfare Queen* (New York: Simon & Schuster, 1999), 65.

As insulting as single parents must find such apocryphal morality tales, 2 they seethe even more, I think, when it is their children who are chided. True, their kids are rarely branded as bastards anymore, but often they are still described as illegitimate or as products of "broken" homes. Then there are those ominous prognostications of lives filled with delinquency, failure, and despair, emanating like black smoke from the labs of evil scientists. . . .

I want some numbers. Don't worry, I'm not going to plow through every 3 study linking the fate of children to whether they live with one or both parents. I'm just going to choose one. And since I'm going to present just one, it had better be good, and it is. First, it documents drug use, one of the most widely heralded "risks" of growing up with just one parent. Second, the results are drawn from "the principal source of data about drug use in the United States." I'll call it the National Drug Abuse Survey.[2] The people who were sampled for the research represent the population of the United States, ages twelve and older. The report focused on the subgroup often believed to be the most worrisome—adolescents ages twelve to seventeen. More than 22,000 participated.

The fear for the children of single parents is not just that they will try 4 drugs or alcohol but that the use will become a problem. The substance abuse might result in symptoms such as anxiety, irritability, or depression. The abusers might be unable to use less often, even if they try, and may need more and more of the substance to achieve the same high. Abusers might also get less work done than they had before they became so taken with the alcohol or the drug. To be classified as having a problem with drugs or alcohol, the adolescent had to report at least two such troublesome experiences in the past year.

The numbers in the table show the percentage of adolescents in each 5 family type who had a substance-abuse problem. The family types included single-mother and single-father families, mother-and-father families, and two other two-parent families: mother and stepfather, and father and stepmother.

Substance-Abuse Problems Among Twelve- to Seventeen-Year-Olds	
%	Family Type
4.5	Mother plus father
5.3	Mother plus stepfather
5.7	Mother only
11.0	Father only
11.8	Father plus stepmother

[2] John P. Hoffman and Robert A. Johnson, "A National Portrait of Family Structure and Adolescent Drug Use," *Journal of Marriage and Family* 60 (1998): 633–45.

The first thing to notice is the overall rates of substance abuse. In every   6
type of family, at least 88% of the adolescents do *not* have a problem with
drugs or alcohol. Second, what the pro-marriage advocates have claimed all
along is that kids raised by their own mom and dad should do better than all
the others. They do. And not because two is a magic number. Adolescents
living with a father and stepmother had more drug-abuse problems than all
the rest.

The most important comparison, I think, is the one the culture has ob-   7
sessed about the most: How do the kids raised by a single mom compare with
the kids raised by their mother and father? Again, the adolescents living
with their own two parents do better: 4.5% of them have substance-abuse
problems, compared with 5.7% of the adolescents living with only their mom.
It is a difference, but not much of one.

In the preceding table, I list only some of the family types included in   8
the National Drug Abuse Survey. I wanted to highlight the single-parent and
two-parent homes, since those are the ones that have most often been subject
to debate. . . . Here now is the full list of family types described in the report,
and the corresponding rates of substance-abuse problems.

Substance-Abuse Problems Among Twelve- to Seventeen-Year-Olds	
%	Family Type
3.4	Mother plus father plus other relative
4.5	Mother plus father
5.3	Mother plus stepfather
5.7	Mother only
6.0	Mother plus other relative
7.2	Other relative only
8.1	Other family type
11.0	Father only
11.8	Father plus stepmother

"Other relative" included relatives other than a mother or father. Typically, they were grandparents, aunts, or uncles.
"Other family types" included miscellaneous combinations of adults, including adults to whom the children were not related.

The mom-plus-dad family has been knocked off its perch. Kids are even   9
less likely to have substance-abuse problems if they live with Mom, Dad, and
another relative—typically a grandparent, aunt, or uncle. Notice also that

there are two new family types that do not include Mom or Dad: other relatives only, and other family types. (In the latter, the kids live with miscellaneous combinations of people, including adults to whom they are not related.) The rate of substance abuse is only a few percentage points higher in the families in which neither a mother nor a father is present than in the families that include both Mom and Dad. . . .

I want to return now to the two family types that set off so much of the   10
sound and fury about mothers who need to be stigmatized, children who need to have their suffering acknowledged, and monsters in the making. They are the single-mother families, in which 5.7% of the kids had substance-abuse problems, and the mom-plus-dad families, in which 4.5% did. Here's the question that bothers me: Why is this difference so small?

Think about it this way. If you had a town with a hundred adolescents   11
living with their mother and father, and another hundred living just with their mothers, there would be four or five substance-abusing kids in the former group, and maybe six in the latter. Think about all the advantages that adolescents supposedly have when they live with Mom and Dad rather than just Mom. There are two adults in the home to help them, care about them, and spend time with them. The adults can also support each other, and that, too, can redound to the benefit of the kids. There are two sources of income. And there is no source of stigma or shame attached to growing up in a home with your own mother and father.

For double the money, time, love, and attention, the kids of mom-plus-   12
dad families did not seem to be doing all that much better than the kids of single moms. There must be something wrong with my blather about all that emotional goodness that kids in nuclear families get that children living with just their moms do not.

If it really were true that the children of single mothers had only one adult   13
in their lives to care for them, love them, spend time with them, and contribute to their well-being and that their moms had no adults in their lives to help them, and if it were also true that the children in nuclear families had two fully devoted adults in their lives, loving them and each other—well, then it would be astounding that there could be so little difference in the problem behaviors of the two sets of adolescents.

I think there are several ways around this dilemma. The first is to let go   14
of the fantasy that all children living in nuclear families have two totally engaged parents who lavish their love and attention on all their children, and on each other, in a home free of anger, conflict, or recriminations. The second is to grab onto a different sort of possibility—that many children living with single mothers have other important adults in their lives, too. . . . I also mean

all the kids who have grandparents, aunts, uncles, neighbors, teachers, family friends, and others who care about them and make sure they know it.

It is true that the other important adults in the lives of the children of   15 single parents do not always live in the same home as the children. That means that they are not always on the scene to help with homework or cover for Mom while she runs to the store. Again, though, it is important to remember that two-parent homes are not always homes with two continually available parents. And something else is important: Although mutual love and support is what adults hope to enjoy when they live together and raise children, sometimes what they get instead is chaos, strife, and even abuse.

*For a reading quiz, sources on Bella DePaulo, and annotated links to further readings on children in single-parent families and substance abuse, visit **bedfordstmartins.com/ thebedfordreader.***

Journal Writing

In what kind of family did you grow up? Did you live with both of your parents in one household? with a parent and a stepparent? with a single mother? with a single father? with a large extended family? How do you respond to DePaulo's characterization of your particular family structure? Based on your experience, is she fair? (To take your journal writing further, see "From Journal to Essay" on the next page.)

Questions on Meaning

1. Is Ronald Reagan's "Welfare Queen" real or imaginary? Why does DePaulo open her discussion with a description of this person?
2. What do you think is the THESIS of this selection? Where, if at all, does DePaulo state it?
3. What ASSUMPTIONS does DePaulo make about the love and support provided by a traditional two-parent family versus that provided by nontraditional families?
4. How do the rates of drug abuse among teenagers living with both parents compare with those among teenagers living with a single mother?
5. What does the author think of "those ominous prognostications of lives filled with delinquency, failure, and despair, emanating like black smoke from the labs of evil scientists" (par. 2)?

Questions on Writing Strategy

1. This excerpt from DePaulo's book *Singled Out* started the chapter titled "Myth #7: Attention, Single Parents: Your Kids Are Doomed." Based on this information, what can you INFER about the author's intended AUDIENCE and her PURPOSE in writing?
2. What is DePaulo analyzing in this selection? What principle does she use to dissect her subject, and how does she reassemble the parts into a new whole?
3. What do the two tables contribute to DePaulo's analysis? Why does she use two tables? How do they differ?
4. **OTHER METHODS** DePaulo disputes one claim of CAUSE AND EFFECT and makes another. What are the two claims?

Questions on Language

1. Locate several examples of COLLOQUIAL language in this selection, and explain how such language sets DePaulo's TONE. Why is—or isn't—this tone appropriate for her subject and her audience?
2. What are the CONNOTATIONS of the words *mom* and *dad*? Why do you think the author chose these words over the more formal *mother* and *father* in some spots?
3. The phrase "sound and fury" in paragraph 10 is an ALLUSION to a famous line in Shakespeare's *Macbeth*, act 5, scene 5:

> Life's but a walking shadow; a poor player,
> That struts and frets his hour upon the stage,
> And then is heard no more. It is a tale
> Told by an idiot, full of sound and fury,
> Signifying nothing.

How does this allusion serve DePaulo?
4. Consult your dictionary if any of the following words are unfamiliar: scathing, bilk, fabricated (par. 1); apocryphal, seethe, chided, ominous, prognostications (2); heralded (3); stigmatized (10); redound (11); blather (12); recriminations (14); strife (15).

Suggestions for Writing

1. **FROM JOURNAL TO ESSAY** Drawing on your journal entry, write an essay that analyzes DePaulo's characterization of one of the types of families she describes in her essay. Explain why her assumptions about that family structure are or are not accurate, and offer your own characterizations as appropriate. Alternatively, you may want to describe a type of family that DePaulo leaves out of her discussion, explaining why she should have considered it in her analysis.
2. Despite significant changes in the 1990s, welfare reform is an ongoing battle in the United States. Research the main arguments for and against requiring single mothers to find work outside the home after a limited time on public assistance. Then write an essay in which you SUMMARIZE your findings. If your research—or your own experience—leads you to form an opinion favoring one side of the issue, present and support that as well.

3. **CRITICAL WRITING** Using the information in footnote 2, locate the research study by Hoffman and Johnson and read it critically yourself. In an essay, weigh DePaulo's use of the study: Does she represent it accurately and fairly? Why, or why not?

4. **CONNECTIONS** In his essay "Needs" (p. 530), Thomas Sowell argues that most of what we think is necessary for a happy life is not really necessary at all. In an essay, apply Sowell's evaluation of *need* to DePaulo's examination of social concerns for children raised in nontraditional families. Do children need two parents to become well-adjusted adults? Why, or why not?

Bella DePaulo on Writing

Bella DePaulo spent more than two decades studying deception and then switched topics to explore the misperceptions of singlehood. On her Web site (*belladepaulo.com*), she discusses how the change—and the sometimes negative responses to it—affected her.

It has been an absolutely exhilarating experience. I am passionate about the topic. Even though I had lived as a singleton my entire life, the study of singlehood was entirely new to me. I read voraciously, on topics I knew nothing about previously. I constantly examined the claims that were made about singles in the media, and even in scientific journals, and again and again found them misleading or totally inaccurate. I thought about why this was happening, talked to lots of people, and read some more. Before I began writing about singles, I had an area of academic expertise, on deception. I had written more than one hundred scholarly papers on the topic. None of that writing was anything like the experiences I have had writing about singles.

I was interested in deception; I'm passionate about singles. When I sat down to write about deception, I already knew what I was going to say; when I sat down to write about singles, I learned something new almost every time. I still do. The cultural discourse on singlehood is stuck in a rut, and has been for decades. In writing *Singled Out*, I was blasting my way outside of that narrow box, and loving every step of the way.

OK, not every step. There were times when people read what I had written and did not exactly bubble over with enthusiasm. Those were difficult times. But now, even some of the very negative reactions are heartening. For example, when people totally disagree with my point of view, and are angered by my position, I know I have struck a nerve. I do not enjoy their ire—effusive praise is much more fun—but I love it when they are engaged by my arguments and examples. More than just about anything else, I want people to think—no, to rethink what they thought they already knew. Even if they cycle back to their original position, it will be a more informed position.

For Discussion

1. What does DePaulo appreciate about negative reactions to her work?
2. When have you learned something by writing? Was the experience unexpected, or did you seek discovery?

LAILA AYAD

Born in 1981, Laila Ayad grew up in Columbia, Maryland, a planned community based on ideals of racial, social, and economic diversity and balance. "Being exposed at an early age to such a diverse community and coming from a multiethnic family have given me great insight into different cultures and perspectives," says Ayad. After graduating from New York University in 2003 with a degree in theater and English literature, Ayad embarked on an acting career. She is a founding member of two theater companies: Apple Girl Productions in New York, which promotes new works by female playwrights and directors, and IAMA in Los Angeles, which produces original independent theater. Ayad has accrued dozens of theater credits, including a ten-month national tour with a musical theater company and a lead role in IAMA's 2008 production of *Bachelorette*. When not on stage, Ayad paints and draws and continues to write.

The Capricious Camera

Ayad began college as an art major and produced this essay for a writing class in her sophomore year. The essay first appeared in 2001 in *Mercer Street,* a journal of writing by New York University students. With an artist's eye for detail, Ayad explores the elements of a photograph to find its meaning. The analysis takes her to Nazi Germany before and during World War II.

In the years between 1933 and 1945, Germany was engulfed by the rise 1 of a powerful new regime and the eventual spoils of war. During this period, Hitler's quest for racial purification turned Germany not only at odds with itself, but with the rest of the world. Photography as an art and as a business became a regulated and potent force in the fight for Aryan domination, Nazi influence, and anti-Semitism. Whether such images were used to promote Nazi ideology, document the Holocaust, or scare Germany's citizens into accepting their own changing country, the effect of this photography provides enormous insight into the true stories and lives of the people most affected by Hitler's racism. In fact, this photography has become so widespread in our understanding and teaching of the Holocaust that often other factors involved in the Nazis' racial policy have been undervalued in our history textbooks—especially the attempt by Nazi Germany to establish the Nordic Aryans as a master race through the *Lebensborn* experiment, a breeding and adoption program designed to eliminate racial imperfections. It is not merely people of other persecuted races who can become victims in a racial war, but also those we would least expect—the persecuting race itself.

To understand the importance of this often shrouded side of Nazi Ger- 2 many we might look at the photograph captioned "Mounted Nazi troops on

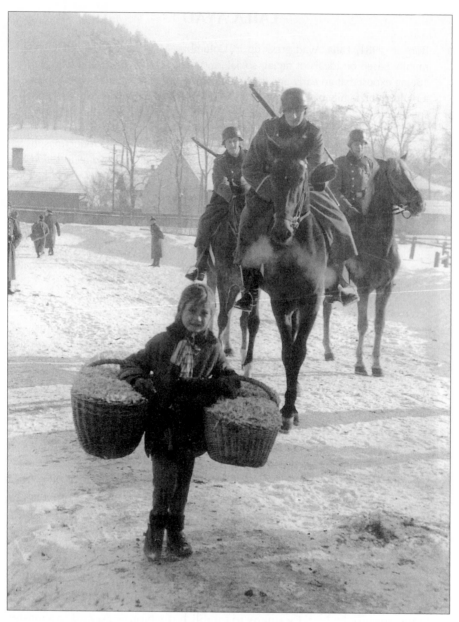

Mounted Nazi troops on the lookout for likely Polish children.

the lookout for likely Polish children." Archived by Catrine Clay and Michael Leapman, this black-and-white photo depicts a young girl in the foreground, carrying two large baskets and treading across a rural and snow-covered countryside, while three mounted and armed Nazi soldiers follow closely behind her. In the distance, we can see farmhouses and a wooden fence, as well as four other uniformed soldiers or guards. Though the photograph accompanies the text without the name of the photographer, year, or information as to where it was found, Clay and Leapman suggest that the photo was taken in Poland between 1943 and 1945.

Who is this young white girl surrounded by armed soldiers? Is she being   3 protected, watched, persecuted? It would be easy enough to assume that she is Jewish, but unlike photos documenting the Holocaust, with *this* image the intent is uncertain. In our general ignorance of the events surrounding this photo, the picture can be deceiving, and yet it is the picture that can also be used to shed light on the story.

Looking just at the photo, and ignoring the descriptive caption, there are   4 some interesting visual and artistic effects that help a viewer better understand the circumstances surrounding the image. One of its most prominent features is the way the photographer decides to focus on only one young child in the foreground, while including seven Nazi soldiers behind her. The effect is overwhelming, and in gazing at the image, one is struck by the magnitude and force of the oppressing men in sharp contrast to the innocence and helplessness of the lone girl. By juxtaposing one child with seven men, the image comes across strongly as both cruel and terribly frightening. In addition, the child in the foreground is a young girl, which only adds to the potency of the image. The photographer makes the soldiers appear far more menacing and unjust, in that there appears to be no physical way in which a young girl could possibly defend herself against these men.

What is additionally interesting about this particular aspect of the photo   5 is that the seven men are not grouped together, or in any way concentrated right next to the child. There are three directly behind the girl, one a little farther behind and to the left, one even slightly farther behind and to the right, and two very far off in the distance, walking in the opposite direction. This placement of the soldiers not only gives the photo an excellent sense of depth, but also conveys to the viewer a sense that the entire surroundings, not just the little girl, are being controlled and surveyed. It allows the viewer to imagine and wonder in what way other children, or perhaps just the other parts of the village, are being similarly restricted. For the young girl, and the viewer, it allows no way out; all angles and directions of the photo are covered by symbols of oppression, producing an eerily suffocating effect.

The child is the only person in the photo looking directly at the photog-   6
rapher. Whether this technique was manipulated on purpose remains to be
seen, but it goes without saying that the effect is dramatic. Her gaze is wistful
and innocent. In contrast, the men occupying the rest of the photo, and most
prominently the three mounted ones in the foreground, are gazing either away
or down. While it is uncertain what the soldiers behind the child are staring at,
their downward stare causes their heads to hang in almost shameful disgrace.
They do not look at the child, and yet they do not look at the photographer,
who is quite obviously standing in front of them. Is this because they do not see
that there is a picture being taken, or perhaps the photographer is another soldier, and this picture is simply routine in recording the progress of their work?

If not a Nazi soldier, the photographer could be a Polish citizen; if this   7
were the case, it might change our interpretation of the photo. Suddenly, the
girl's facial expression and direct gaze seem pleading, while, for fear of being
caught, the photographer snaps the picture quickly, in the exact moment the
soldiers are looking away. Perhaps the soldiers did not mind having their picture taken. Many Polish were considered, after all, their racial equals, and
maybe they would have respected and appreciated an amateur photographer's
interest in their work.

While all of these scenarios are seemingly plausible, the purpose of the pho-   8
tograph is still uncertain. There are also several possibilities. One is that the
Nazis commissioned the photograph, as they did others at the time, to properly
record the events surrounding the development of their plan. In an article
entitled "The Camera as Weapon: Documentary Photography and the Holocaust," Sybil Milton describes the ways in which Nazi photographers worked:

> Nazi professional photographers produced in excess of one-quarter million
> images. Their work was officially regulated and licensed. . . . All photos were
> screened by military censors subservient to official directives of the Pro-
> paganda Ministry. . . . Press photographers of World War II rarely showed
> atrocities and seldom published prints unfavorable to their own side. (1)

However, while the evidence is compelling, Milton recognizes another possibility that significantly changes the motive for the photo: "Portable cameras,
and other technical innovations like interchangeable lenses and multiple
exposure film, meant that nonprofessionals owned and used cameras with
ease. Many soldiers carried small Leica or Ermanox cameras in their rucksacks
or pillaged optical equipment from the towns they occupied" (2). While it is
possible that the photograph was taken by a soldier seeking to document the
work in Poland for his own interests, this probability, against the numerous
commissioned photographs and the nature of the subject matter being
documented, is unlikely. The photo alone, while intriguing in its image, tells

only half of the story, and without a definitive context can become akin to a "choose your own adventure" novel. In other words, the possibilities for a photographic purpose are all laid out, but the true meaning or end remains undetermined. Unlike hand-made art, which in its very purpose begs to be viewed through various interpretations, photography, and particularly photo-journalism, captures a certain moment in time, featuring specific subject matter, under a genuine set of circumstances. The picture is not invented, it is real life, and in being so demands to be viewed alongside its agenda, for without this context, it may never be fully understood.

When we turn to the caption describing the photograph, "Mounted Nazi troops on the lookout for likely Polish children," the book *Master Race* and its accompanying story can now properly be discussed. Instead of typically dealing with the issues of a racist Nazi Germany as it relates to the Holocaust, and the other forms of racial extermination and discrimination that were subsequently involved, Clay and Leapman's book looks at the other side of the coin. It is important in dealing with and understanding the concept of racism to realize that racists are not simply those who dislike others; they are also those who worship themselves. In *Mein Kampf* Hitler outlined the inspiration for his racial tyranny by saying, "The products of human culture, the achievements in art, science and technology . . . are almost exclusively the creative product of the Aryan." He was heavily influenced by the work of racially charged popular science writers, such as H. F. K. Gunther, who in his *Ethnology of the German Nation* wrote: "The man of Nordic race is not only the most gifted but also the most beautiful. . . . The man's face is hard and chiseled, the woman's tender, with rose-pink skin and bright triumphant eyes" (qtd. in Clay and Leapman 17). Through the course of the book, the topic of racism in Nazi Germany focuses intently on the concept of racial purification. By following the work of the carefully selected (meaning those of impeccable Aryan ancestry) members of Himmler's elite SS corps, Clay and Leapman introduce the history of Germany's failed *Lebensborn* experiment and the homes that were created by the Third Reich to breed and raise "perfect Aryans" (ix).

In a disturbing segment on Hitler's racial utopia, Clay and Leapman de-scribe the practice of eugenics, improving humankind by eliminating unde-sirable genetic traits and breeding those that were considered superior. The SS soldiers who are commonly known for forcing the Jews into concentration camps are mentioned, but this time they are discussed as the same men who were ordered to father white babies with volunteer German and Norwegian mothers. However, it is the final fact, the story of the SS soldiers who occupied surrounding countries and then stole children "who looked as if they might further improve the breed," that becomes the focus and ultimate subject mat-ter of the photograph (ix).

Looking at the photograph in this context, the soldier no longer appears   11
to be protecting the Polish children, but hunting them. The word "likely"
in the caption denotes this. Children who possessed strong Nordic or Aryan
qualities were systematically taken from their native countries, adopted by
German parents (who were paid by the Nazi regime), taught to forget their
families and former lives, and raised to breed not only many children of their
own but, above all, families that would uphold Nazi ideology. For Hitler and
Heinrich Himmler, who was appointed Commissar for Consolidating German
Nationhood, exterminating the racially impure was merely preparation. It was
the process of breeding and stealing children that Himmler considered central
and key in the ultimate goal for racial purification:

> Obviously in such a mixture of peoples there will always be some racially
> good types. Therefore I think that it is our duty to take their children with
> us, to remove them from their environment, if necessary by robbing or steal-
> ing them. . . . My aim has always been the same, to attract all the Nordic
> blood in the world and take it for ourselves. (qtd. in Clay and Leapman 91)

Additionally, Himmler's objective in targeting children, rather than adults,
was a planned and strategic tool. Through teachings at school, children were
used to control their parents by being encouraged to report what they did and
said. Himmler realized that older people would be less enthusiastic about his
ideas, so he made every effort to win the minds of the next generation.

What is perhaps most compelling about the *Lebensborn* experiment and   12
thus most poignant when viewing the photograph is the reminder that for
every child that was stolen from nations like Poland, his or her family was
being equally betrayed. One Polish girl recounted the events of her kidnap-
ping years later, describing both her and her father's reaction to the incident:

> Three SS men came into the room and put us up against a wall. . . . They
> immediately picked out the fair children with blue eyes — seven altogether,
> including me. . . . My father, who tried to stop my being taken away, was
> threatened by the soldiers. They even said he would be taken to a concen-
> tration camp. But I have no idea what happened to him later. (qtd. in Clay
> and Leapman 95)

The girl who spoke above just as easily could have been the young girl being
followed by soldiers in the photograph, only moments after she was taken.
Such incidents force us to broaden our sense of whom the Nazis victimized.
While there is no mistaking the victimization of the Jewish population and
other races in Germany, amidst these better-known hate crimes the Nazis
were also perpetrating a horrific exploitation of the so-called "white" race.

The complexities surrounding this photograph remind us that the story of   13
any photograph is liable to contain ambiguity. As an art, photography relies

on the imagination of the viewer; not *knowing* provides the viewer with a realm of interesting possibilities. Context matters even with art, and playing with possible contexts gives a photograph diverse meanings. It is in these various viewpoints that we find pleasure, amusement, fear, or wonder. It is perhaps in the shift to photojournalism that determining a particular context becomes even more important. In fact, even if the original photographer saw the image as artistic, subsequent events compel us to try to see the image of the Polish girl with Nazis as journalism. In this endeavor, we must uncover as much as possible about the surrounding context. As much as we can, we need to know this girl's particular story. Without a name, date, place, or relevant data, this girl would fall even further backwards into the chapters of unrecorded history.

Works Cited

"Mounted Nazi Troops on the Lookout for Likely Polish Children." Clay and Leapman 87.

Clay, Catrine, and Michael Leapman. *Master Race: The Lebensborn Experiment in Nazi Germany*. London: Hodder, 1995. Print.

Hitler, Adolf. *Mein Kampf*. Vol. 2, chap. 3. *Hitler Historical Museum*. 1996–2000. Web. 1 Dec. 2000.

Milton, Sybil. "The Camera as Weapon: Documentary Photography and the Holocaust." 1970. *The Museum of Tolerance*. Simon Wiesenthal Center, 2000. Web. 6 Dec. 2000.

For a reading quiz and annotated links to further readings on the Holocaust and on the Lebensborn *experiment, visit **bedfordstmartins.com/thebedfordreader**.*

Journal Writing

Ayad uncovers an aspect of Nazi history that is not well known and may seem startling. Think of a time when you learned something that surprised you about history, science, or culture—either in a class or through independent research. In your journal, write about your discovery and how it affected you. (To take your journal writing further, see "From Journal to Essay" on the next page.)

Questions on Meaning

1. Ayad's essay pursues two threads: certain events in German history and certain characteristics of photography, especially photojournalism. Each thread in essence has its own THESIS, stated in paragraphs 1 and 8. What are these theses? Where in the essay does Ayad bring them together?
2. Ayad writes about events in history that she thinks some readers do not know about. What are these events?
3. What do you see as Ayad's PURPOSE in this essay?

Questions on Writing Strategy

1. Why does Ayad devote so much of her essay to discussing the photograph? What is the EFFECT of her speculations about the content and the creation of the photograph?
2. Ayad's AUDIENCE was originally the teacher and students in her writing class. What does she ASSUME readers already know about Nazi Germany? What does she assume they may not know?
3. What is the effect of Ayad's last two sentences? Why does Ayad end this way?
4. **OTHER METHODS** Where in the essay does Ayad draw on DESCRIPTION? Why is description crucial to Ayad's analysis?

Questions on Language

1. What words and phrases does Ayad use in paragraphs 4–6 to communicate her own feelings about the photograph? What are those feelings?
2. Why does Ayad quote Adolf Hitler and H. F. K. Gunther (par. 9), Heinrich Himmler (11), and the Polish woman who was kidnapped as a child (12)? What does Ayad achieve with these quotations?
3. What is the effect of the word *targeting* in paragraph 11?
4. Consult a dictionary if you are unsure of the meaning of any of the following: capricious (title); Aryan, anti-Semitism, ideology, Nordic (par. 1); shrouded, elucidate (2); juxtaposing (4); suffocating (5); scenarios, plausible, commissioned, pillaged, definitive (8); extermination, tyranny, impeccable (9); poignant (12); ambiguity, subsequent (13).

Suggestions for Writing

1. **FROM JOURNAL TO ESSAY** Using your journal writing as a starting point, draft an essay about a surprising discovery you made in a class or on your own. If it will be helpful, do some research to extend your knowledge of the subject. Involve your readers in the essay by distinguishing general knowledge—that is, what they probably know already—from the new information.
2. Locate a photograph that you find especially striking, perhaps in a library book or through an online photo collection such as Corbis (*pro.corbis.com*). Write an essay that describes and analyzes the image, using a thesis statement and vivid language to make your interpretation clear.

3. **CRITICAL WRITING**   Some of Ayad's paragraphs are long, especially 1, 8, 9, and 11. How COHERENT are these long paragraphs? Write a brief essay in which you analyze two of them in terms of their organization, the TRANSITIONS or other devices that connect sentences, and any problems with coherence that you see.
4. **CONNECTIONS**   In "Shooting an Elephant" (p. 663), George Orwell writes about the actions of an occupying government from the perspective of an official uncomfortable with his role and reluctant to perform his duties. Write an essay in which you imagine how one of the mounted soldiers in Ayad's photograph may have felt about his role in Germany's *Lebensborn* experiment, whether enthusiastic or, like Orwell, doubtful.

ADDITIONAL WRITING TOPICS
Division or Analysis

Write an essay by the method of division or analysis using one of the following sub-jects (or choose your own subject). In your essay, make sure your purpose and your principle of division or analysis are clear to your readers. Explain the parts of your subject so that readers know how each relates to the others and contributes to the whole.

1. The slang or technical terminology of a group such as stand-up comedians or computer hackers
2. An especially bad movie, television show, or book
3. A doll, game, or other toy from childhood
4. A typical TV commercial for a product such as laundry soap, deodorant, beer, a luxury car, or an economy car
5. An appliance or a machine, such as a stereo speaker, a motorcycle, a microwave oven, or a camera
6. An organization or association, such as a social club, a sports league, or a support group
7. The characteristic appearance of a rock singer or a classical violinist
8. A year in the life of a student
9. Your favorite poem
10. A short story, an essay, or another work that made you think
11. The government of your community
12. The most popular restaurant (or other place of business) in town
13. The Bible
14. A band or an orchestra
15. A painting or statue

Please Recycle:		**Yes** (acceptable)		**No** (not acceptable)
	Newspaper	Newspapers with flyers		No hardcover books
	Cardboard	Corrugate, boxboard, brown paper, manila envelopes *Please flatten and cut to fit in bag		No milk cartons, waxed or soiled cardboard No large (over 3x2') or unflattened cardboard
	Cans: Tin & Aluminum	Clean cans, aluminum, metal lids and milk cartons.		No large metal objects
USED BAG	**Plastic**	Use clear bags. Insert squashed and clean plastic milk jugs, yogurt cups, bottles, detergent, etc. All plastic numbered:		**No styrofoam or plastics numbered 3, 6 or 7**
	Office Papers Magazines	Office paper envelopes, glossy magazines, catalogues, phone books		No paper towel, carbon, waxed or tissue paper
	Glass Bottles & Jars	Clean glass bottles and jars, orange bag, phone books		No light bulbs, dishes or mirrors

10

CLASSIFICATION

Sorting into Kinds

◀ **Classification in a chart**

Most communities support recycling, and many require it, but the guidelines for recycling vary by municipality. This chart was provided to residents of a small town that offers curbside pickup of recyclable materials. Like similar flyers distributed throughout North America, it groups household waste into categories to clarify both what materials can be recycled and how they should be sorted. The images in the first column indicate the containers participants should use for each kind of material, and the drawings and photographs in the second and third columns give clear examples of those items that will be accepted for recycling—as well as those that won't be. Why do you suppose some materials are acceptable for recycling, while closely related materials are not? How might charts like this help to encourage, or discourage, recycling?

THE METHOD

To CLASSIFY is to make sense of the world by arranging many units—trucks, chemical elements, wasps, students—into more manageable groups. Zoologists classify animals, botanists classify plants—and their classifications help us understand a vast and complex subject: life on earth. To help us find books in a library, librarians classify books into categories: fiction, biography, history, psychology, and so forth. For the convenience of readers, newspapers run classified advertising, grouping many small ads into categories such as Help Wanted and Cars for Sale.

Subjects and Reasons for Classification

The subject of a classification is always a number of things, such as peaches or political systems. (In contrast, DIVISION or ANALYSIS, the topic of the preceding chapter, usually deals with a solitary subject, a coherent whole, such as *a* peach or *a* political system.) The job of classification is to sort the things into groups or classes based on their similarities and differences. Say, for instance, you're going to write an essay about how people write. After interviewing a lot of writers, you determine that writers' processes differ widely, mainly in the amount of planning and rewriting they entail. (Notice that this determination involves analyzing the process of writing, separating it into steps. See Chap. 8.) On the basis of your findings, you create groups for planners, one-drafters, and rewriters. Once your groups are defined (and assuming they are valid), your subjects (the writers) almost sort themselves out.

Classification is done for a PURPOSE. In a New York City guidebook, Joan Hamburg and Norma Ketay discuss low-priced hotels. (Notice that already they are examining the members of a group: low-priced as opposed to medium- and high-priced hotels.) They cast the low-priced hotels into categories: Rooms for Singles and Students, Rooms for Families, Rooms for Service-people, and Rooms for General Occupancy. Always their purpose is evident: to match up the visitor with a suitable kind of room. When a classification has no purpose, it seems a silly and hollow exercise.

Just as you can ANALYZE a subject (or divide a pie) in many ways, you can classify a subject according to many principles. A different New York guidebook might classify all hotels according to price: grand luxury, luxury, moderate, low-priced (Hamburg and Ketay's category), fleabag, and flophouse. The purpose of this classification would be to match visitors to hotels fitting their pocketbooks. The principle you use in classifying things depends on your purpose. A linguist might explain the languages of the world by classifying them according to their origins (Romance languages, Germanic languages, Coptic languages . . .), but a student battling with a college language requirement might try to entertain fellow students by classifying languages into three groups: hard to learn, harder to learn, and unlearnable.

Kinds of Classification

The simplest classification is binary (or two-part), in which you sort things out into (1) those with a certain distinguishing feature and (2) those without it. You might classify a number of persons, let's say, into smokers and nonsmokers, heavy metal fans and nonfans, runners and nonrunners, believers and nonbelievers. Binary classification is most useful when your subject is easily divisible into positive and negative categories.

Classification can be complex as well. As we are reminded by the English writer Jonathan Swift (1667–1745),

> So, naturalists observe, a flea
> Hath smaller fleas that on him prey,
> And these have smaller yet to bite 'em.
> And so proceed *ad infinitum*.

In being faithful to reality, you will sometimes find that you have to sort out the members of categories into subcategories. Hamburg and Ketay did something of the kind when they subclassified the class of low-priced New York hotels. Writing about the varieties of one Germanic language, such as English, a writer could identify the subclasses of British English, North American English, Australian English, and so on.

As readers, we all enjoy watching a clever writer sort things into categories. We like to meet classifications that strike us as true and familiar. This pleasure may account for the appeal of magazine articles that classify things ("The Seven Common Garden Varieties of Moocher," "Five Embarrassing Types of Social Blunder"). Usefulness as well as pleasure may explain the popularity of classifications that EVALUATE things. The magazine *Consumer Reports* sorts products as varied as computer monitors and canned tuna into groups based on quality (excellent, good, fair, poor, and not acceptable), and then, using DESCRIPTION, discusses each product. (Of a frozen pot pie: "Bottom crust gummy, meat spongy when chewed, with nondescript old-poultry and stale-flour flavor.")

THE PROCESS

Purposes and Theses

Classification will usually come into play when you want to impose order on a complex subject that includes many items. In one essay in this chapter, for instance, Stephanie Ericsson tackles the lies people tell one another.

Sometimes you may use classification humorously, as Russell Baker does in another essay in this chapter, to give a charge to familiar experiences. Whichever use you make of classification, though, do it for a reason. The files of composition instructors are littered with student essays in which nothing was ventured and nothing gained by classification.

Things can be classified into categories that reveal truth or into categories that don't tell us a thing. To sort out ten US cities according to their relative freedom from air pollution or their cost of living or the degree of progress they have made in civil rights might prove highly informative and useful. Such a classification might even tell us where we'd want to live. But to sort out the cities according to a superficial feature such as the relative size of their cat and dog populations wouldn't interest anyone, probably, except a veterinarian looking for a job.

Your purpose, your THESIS, and your principle of classification will all overlap at the point where you find your interest in your subject. Say you're curious about how other students write. Is your interest primarily in the materials they use (computer, felt-tip pen, pencil), in where and when they write, or in how much planning and rewriting they do? Any of these could lead to a principle for sorting the students into groups. And that principle should be revealed in your THESIS STATEMENT, letting readers know why you are classifying. Here, from the essays in this chapter, are two examples of classification thesis statements:

> Inanimate objects are classified into three major categories—those that don't work, those that break down and those that get lost.
>   —Russell Baker, "The Plot against People"

> [I]t's not easy to entirely eliminate lies from our lives. No matter how pious we may try to be, we will still embellish, hedge, and omit to lubricate the daily machinery of living. But . . . acceptance of lies becomes a cultural cancer that eventually shrouds and reorders reality until moral garbage becomes as invisible to us as water is to a fish.
>   —Stephanie Ericsson, "The Ways We Lie"

Categories

For a workable classification, make sure that the categories you choose don't overlap. If you were writing a survey of popular magazines for adults and you were sorting your subject into categories that included women's magazines and sports magazines, you might soon run into trouble. Into which category would you place *Women's Sports*? The trouble is that both categories take in the same item. To avoid this problem, you'll need to reorganize your classification on a different principle. You might sort out the magazines by their audiences: magazines mainly for women, magazines mainly for men, magazines for both women and men. Or you might group them according to subject matter: sports magazines, literary magazines, astrology magazines, fashion magazines, celebrity magazines, trade journals, and so on. *Women's Sports* would fit into either of those classification schemes, but into only *one* category in each scheme.

When you draw up a scheme of classification, be sure also that you include all essential categories. Omitting an important category can weaken the effect of your essay, no matter how well written it is. It would be a major oversight, for example, if you were to classify the residents of a dormitory according to their religious affiliations and not include a category for the numerous non-affiliated. Your reader might wonder if your carelessness in forgetting a category extended to your thinking about the topic as well.

Some form of outline can be helpful to keep the classes and their members straight as you develop and draft ideas. You might experiment with a diagram in which you jot down headings for the groups, with plenty of space around them, and then let each heading accumulate members as you think of them, the way a magnet attracts paper clips. This kind of diagram offers more flexibility than a vertical list or an outline, and it may be a better aid for keeping categories from overlapping or disappearing.

FOCUS ON PARAGRAPH DEVELOPMENT

A crucial aim of classification is to make sure each group is clear: what's counted in, what's counted out, and why. You'll provide the examples and other details that make the groups clear as you develop the paragraph(s) devoted to each group.

The following paragraph barely outlines one group in a four-part classification of ex-smokers into zealots, evangelists, the elect, and the serene:

> The second group, evangelists, does not condemn smokers but encourages them to quit. Evangelists think quitting is easy, and they preach this message, often earning the resentment of potential converts.

Contrast this bare-bones adaptation with the actual paragraphs written by Franklin E. Zimring in his essay "Confessions of a Former Smoker":

> By contrast, the antismoking evangelist does not condemn smokers. Unlike the zealot, he regards smoking as an easily curable condition, as a social disease, and not a sin. The evangelist spends an enormous amount of time seeking and preaching to the unconverted. He argues that kicking the habit is not *that* difficult. After all, *he* did it; moreover, as he describes it, the benefits of quitting are beyond measure and the disadvantages are nil.

The hallmark of the evangelist is his insistence that he never misses tobacco. Though he is less hostile to smokers than the zealot, he is resented more. Friends and loved ones who have been the targets of his preachments frequently greet the resumption of smoking by the evangelist as an occasion for unmitigated glee.

In the second sentence of each paragraph, Zimring explicitly contrasts evangelists with zealots, the group he previously defined. And he does more as well: He provides specific examples of the evangelist's message (first paragraph) and of others' reactions to him (second paragraph). These details pin down the group, making it distinct from other groups and clear in itself.

CHECKLIST FOR REVISING A CLASSIFICATION

✔ **PURPOSE** Have you classified for a reason? Will readers see why you bothered?

✔ **PRINCIPLE OF CLASSIFICATION** Will readers also see what rule or principle you have used for sorting individuals into groups? Is this principle apparent in your thesis sentence?

✔ **CONSISTENCY** Does each representative of your subject fall into one category only, so that categories don't overlap?

✔ **COMPLETENESS** Have you mentioned all the essential categories suggested by your principle of classification?

✔ **PARAGRAPH DEVELOPMENT** Have you provided enough examples and other details so that readers can easily distinguish each category from the others?

CLASSIFICATION IN PARAGRAPHS

Writing about Television

Written for *The Bedford Reader*, the following paragraph uses classification to explain how a TV comedy's laugh track combines various laughs to sound like an actual rib-tickled audience. With the related paragraph on page 357, which ANALYZES the elements of any particular kind of laugh, this paragraph could be part of a full behind-the-scenes essay on how TV comedies make us laugh, even despite ourselves.

Most canned laughs produced by laugh machines fall into one of five reliable sounds. There are *titters*, light vocal laughs with which an imaginary audience responds to a comedian's least wriggle or grimace. Some laugh-track editors rely heavily on *chuckles*,

Topic sentence names principle of classification

Categories:

1. Titters

2. Chuckles

deeper, more chesty responses. Most profound of all, *belly laughs* are summoned to acclaim broader jokes and sexual innuendos. When provided at full level of sound and in longest duration, the belly laugh becomes the Big Boffola, the ultimate proof of successful humor. There are also *wild howls* or *screamers*, extreme responses used not more than three times per show, lest they seem fake. These are crowd laughs, and yet the tracks also offer *freaky laughs*, the piercing, eccentric screeches of solitary kooks. With them, a laugh editor affirms that even a canned audience may include one thorny individualist.

3. Belly laughs

4. Wild howls or screamers

5. Freaky laughs

Examples clearly distinguish categories

Writing in an Academic Discipline

This paragraph comes from a textbook on human physical and cultural evolution. The author offers a standard classification of hand grips in order to explain one of several important differences between human beings and their nearest relatives, apes and monkeys.

There are two distinct ways of holding and using tools: the *power grip* and the *precision grip,* as John Napier termed them. Human infants and children begin with the power grip and progress to the precision grip. Think of how a child holds a spoon: first in the power grip, in its fist or between its fingers and palm, and later between the tips of the thumb and first two fingers, in the precision grip. Many primates have the power grip also. It is the way they get firm hold of a tree branch. But neither a monkey nor an ape has a thumb long enough or flexible enough to be completely *opposable* through rotation at the wrist, able to reach comfortably to the tips of all the other fingers, as is required for our delicate yet strong precision grip. It is the opposability of our thumb and the independent control of our fingers that make possible nearly all the movements necessary to handle tools, to make clothing, to write with a pencil, to play a flute.   —Bernard Campbell, *Humankind Emerging*

Topic sentence names principle of classification

Two categories explained side by side

Second category explained in greater detail

Classification

CLASSIFICATION IN A RÉSUMÉ

Sooner or later, every college student needs a résumé: a one-page overview of skills and experiences that will appeal to a potential employer. Part of the challenge in drafting a résumé is to bring order to what seems a complex and unwieldy subject, a life. The main solution is to classify activities and interests into clearly defined groups: typically work experience, education, and special skills.

The group that poses the biggest challenge is usually work experience: Some résumés list jobs with the most recent first, detailing the specifics of each one; others sort experience into skills (such as computer skills, administrative skills, and communication skills) and then list job specifics under each subcategory. The first arrangement tends to be more straightforward and potentially less confusing to readers. However, college students and recent graduates with few previous jobs often find the second arrangement preferable because it downplays experience and showcases abilities.

The résumé on the facing page was prepared by Kharron Reid, who was seeking an internship in computer networking for the summer between his sophomore and junior years of college. After experimenting with organizational strategies, he decided to put the category of work experience first because it related directly to the internships he sought. And he chose to organize his work experience by jobs rather than skills because the companies he had worked for were similar to the companies he was applying to.

For the cover letter Reid wrote to go with the résumé, see pages 209–10.

Kharron Reid
137 Chester Street, Apt. E
Allston, MA 02134
(617) 555-4009
kreid@bu.edu

OBJECTIVE

An internship that offers experience in information systems

EXPERIENCE

Pioneer Networking, Damani, MI, May-September 2009

As an intern, worked as a LAN specialist using a
Unix-based server

- Connected eight workstations onto a LAN by laying
  physical platform and configuring software
- Assisted network engineer in monitoring operations
  of LAN

NBS Systems Corp., Denniston, MI, June-September 2008

As an intern, helped install seven WANs using Windows
Server 2008

- Planned layout for WANs
- Installed physical platform and configured servers

SPECIAL SKILLS

Computer proficiency:

Windows 7/Vista/XP/2003	QuarkXPress	HTML
Unix	Adobe Photoshop	XML
Red Hat Enterprise Linux	Adobe InDesign	JavaScript

Internet research

EDUCATION

Boston University, School of Management, 2008 to present

Double major: business administration and information
systems

Courses: organizational behavior, computer science, advanced
programming, networking and data communications

Lahser High School, Bloomfield Hills, MI, 2004-2008

Similar to a thesis statement, an objective expresses the applicant's purpose

First major category: work experience

A subcategory for each job includes summaries and specific details

Second major category: special skills

Specific skills

Third major category: education

Specific information relevant to job objective

Classification

STEPHANIE ERICSSON

Stephanie Ericsson is an insightful and frank writer who composes out of her own life. Her book on loss, *Companion through the Darkness: Inner Dialogues on Grief* (1993), grew out of journal entries and extensive research into the grieving process following the sudden death of her husband while she was pregnant. Ericsson was born in 1953, grew up in San Francisco, and began writing at the age of fifteen. After studying filmmaking in college, she became a screenwriter's assistant and later a writer of situation comedies and advertising. During these years she struggled with substance abuse; after her recovery in 1980 she published *Shame Faced* and *Womansafe: The Women of Alcoholics Anonymous* (both 1986). *Companion into the Dawn: Inner Dialogues on Loving* was published in 1997. Ericsson lives in Saint Paul, Minnesota, where she continues to write.

The Ways We Lie

Psychologists have claimed that most people lie at least once a day, and one recent study found that college students lied in half of their conversations with their mothers. In this essay from the *Utne Reader* in 1992, Ericsson classifies the kinds of lies we all tell at one time or another. Lying, she finds, may be unavoidable and even sometimes beneficial. But then how do we know when to stop?

William Lutz's "The World of Doublespeak," the essay following Ericsson's, also uses classification to examine types of lies, specifically the verbal substitutions that make "the bad seem good, the negative appear positive."

The bank called today and I told them my deposit was in the mail, even 1 though I hadn't written a check yet. It'd been a rough day. The baby I'm pregnant with decided to do aerobics on my lungs for two hours, our three-year-old daughter painted the living-room couch with lipstick, the IRS put me on hold for an hour, and I was late to a business meeting because I was tired.

I told my client that traffic had been bad. When my partner came home, 2 his haggard face told me his day hadn't gone any better than mine, so when he asked, "How was your day?" I said, "Oh, fine," knowing that one more straw might break his back. A friend called and wanted to take me to lunch. I said I was busy. Four lies in the course of a day, none of which I felt the least bit guilty about.

We lie. We all do. We exaggerate, we minimize, we avoid confrontation, 3 we spare people's feelings, we conveniently forget, we keep secrets, we justify lying to the big-guy institutions. Like most people, I indulge in small false-hoods and still think of myself as an honest person. Sure I lie, but it doesn't hurt anything. Or does it?

I once tried going a whole week without telling a lie, and it was paralyzing.   4
I discovered that telling the truth all the time is nearly impossible. It means living with some serious consequences: The bank charges me $60 in overdraft fees, my partner keels over when I tell him about my travails, my client fires me for telling her I didn't feel like being on time, and my friend takes it personally when I say I'm not hungry. There must be some merit to lying.

But if I justify lying, what makes me any different from slick politicians or   5
the corporate robbers who raided the S&L industry? Saying it's okay to lie one way and not another is hedging. I cannot seem to escape the voice deep inside me that tells me: When someone lies, someone loses.

What far-reaching consequences will I, or others, pay as a result of my lie?   6
Will someone's trust be destroyed? Will someone else pay *my* penance because I ducked out? We must consider the *meaning of our actions*. Deception, lies, capital crimes, and misdemeanors all carry meanings. *Webster's* definition of *lie* is specific:

> 1: a false statement or action especially made with the intent to deceive;
>
> 2: anything that gives or is meant to give a false impression.

A definition like this implies that there are many, many ways to tell a lie.   7
Here are just a few.

The White Lie

A man who won't lie to a woman has very little consideration for her feelings.
—Bergen Evans

The white lie assumes that the truth will cause more damage than a simple,   8
harmless untruth. Telling a friend he looks great when he looks like hell can be based on a decision that the friend needs a compliment more than a frank opinion. But, in effect, it is the liar deciding what is best for the lied to. Ultimately, it is a vote of no confidence. It is an act of subtle arrogance for anyone to decide what is best for someone else.

Yet not all circumstances are quite so cut-and-dried. Take, for instance,   9
the sergeant in Vietnam who knew one of his men was killed in action but listed him as missing so that the man's family would receive indefinite compensation instead of the lump-sum pittance the military gives widows and children. His intent was honorable. Yet for twenty years this family kept their hopes alive, unable to move on to a new life.

Façades

Et tu, Brute?
—Caesar

We all put up façades to one degree or another. When I put on a suit to   10
go to see a client, I feel as though I am putting on another face, obeying the
expectation that serious businesspeople wear suits rather than sweatpants. But
I'm a writer. Normally, I get up, get the kid off to school, and sit at my computer in my pajamas until four in the afternoon. When I answer the phone,
the caller thinks I'm wearing a suit (though the UPS man knows better).

But façades can be destructive because they are used to seduce others into   11
an illusion. For instance, I recently realized that a former friend was a liar.
He presented himself with all the right looks and the right words and offered
lots of new consciousness theories, fabulous books to read, and fascinating
insights. Then I did some business with him, and the time came for him to pay
me. He turned out to be all talk and no walk. I heard a plethora of reasonable
excuses, including in-depth descriptions of the big break around the corner. In
six months of work, I saw less than a hundred bucks. When I confronted him,
he raised both eyebrows and tried to convince me that I'd heard him wrong,
that he'd made no commitment to me. A simple investigation into his past
revealed a crowded graveyard of disenchanted former friends.

Ignoring the Plain Facts

Well, you must understand that Father Porter is only human.
—A Massachusetts priest

In the '60s, the Catholic Church in Massachusetts began hearing com-   12
plaints that Father James Porter was sexually molesting children. Rather than
relieving him of his duties, the ecclesiastical authorities simply moved him
from one parish to another between 1960 and 1967, actually providing him
with a fresh supply of unsuspecting families and innocent children to abuse.
After treatment in 1967 for pedophilia, he went back to work, this time in
Minnesota. The new diocese was aware of Father Porter's obsession with children, but they needed priests and recklessly believed treatment had cured
him. More children were abused until he was relieved of his duties a year
later. By his own admission, Porter may have abused as many as a hundred
children.

Ignoring the facts may not in and of itself be a form of lying, but con-   13
sider the context of this situation. If a lie is *a false action done with the intent
to deceive*, then the Catholic Church's conscious covering for Porter created
irreparable consequences. The church became a co-perpetrator with Porter.

Deflecting

When you have no basis for an argument, abuse the plaintiff.
—Cicero

I've discovered that I can keep anyone from seeing the true me by being   14
selectively blatant. I set a precedent of being up-front about intimate issues,
but I never bring up the things I truly want to hide; I just let people assume
I'm revealing everything. It's an effective way of hiding.

Any good liar knows that the way to perpetuate an untruth is to deflect   15
attention from it. When Clarence Thomas exploded with accusations that
the Senate hearings were a "high-tech lynching," he simply switched the focus
from a highly charged subject to a radioactive subject.[1] Rather than defending
himself, he took the offensive and accused the country of racism. It was a brilliant maneuver. Racism is now politically incorrect in official circles—unlike
sexual harassment, which still rewards those who can get away with it.

Some of the most skilled deflectors are passive-aggressive people who,   16
when accused of inappropriate behavior, refuse to respond to the accusations. This you-don't-exist stance infuriates the accuser, who, understandably,
screams something obscene out of frustration. The trap is sprung and the act
of deflection successful, because now the passive-aggressive person can indig-
nantly say, "Who can talk to someone as unreasonable as you?" The real issue
is forgotten and the sins of the original victim become the focus. Feeling guilty
of name-calling, the victim is fully tamed and crawls into a hole, ashamed.
I have watched this fighting technique work thousands of times in disputes
between men and women, and what I've learned is that the real culprit is not
necessarily the one who swears the loudest.

Omission

The cruelest lies are often told in silence.
—R. L. Stevenson

Omission involves telling most of the truth minus one or two key facts   17
whose absence changes the story completely. You break a pair of glasses that
are guaranteed under normal use and get a new pair, without mentioning that
the first pair broke during a rowdy game of basketball. Who hasn't tried something like that? But what about omission of information that could make a
difference in how a person lives his or her life?

---

[1] Ericsson refers to the 1991 hearings to confirm Thomas for the Supreme Court, at which
Thomas was accused by Anita Hill of sexual harassment.—Eds.

For instance, one day I found out that rabbinical legends tell of another   18
woman in the Garden of Eden before Eve. I was stunned. The omission of
the Sumerian goddess Lilith from Genesis—as well as her demonization by
ancient misogynists as an embodiment of female evil—felt like spiritual robbery. I felt like I'd just found out my mother was really my stepmother. To
take seriously the tradition that Adam was created out of the same mud as his
equal counterpart, Lilith, redefines all of Judeo-Christian history.

Some renegade Catholic feminists introduced me to a view of Lilith that   19
had been suppressed during the many centuries when this strong goddess was
seen only as a spirit of evil. Lilith was a proud goddess who defied Adam's
need to control her, attempted negotiations, and when this failed, said adios
and left the Garden of Eden.

This omission of Lilith from the Bible was a patriarchal strategy to keep   20
women weak. Omitting the strong-woman archetype of Lilith from Western religions and starting the story with Eve the Rib has helped keep Christian and Jewish women believing they were the lesser sex for thousands of
years.

Stereotypes and Clichés

Where opinion does not exist, the status quo becomes stereotyped and all
originality is discouraged.   —Bertrand Russell

Stereotype and cliché serve a purpose as a form of shorthand. Our need for   21
vast amounts of information in nanoseconds has made the stereotype vital to
modern communication. Unfortunately, it often shuts down original thinking, giving those hungry for the truth a candy bar of misinformation instead
of a balanced meal. The stereotype explains a situation with just enough truth
to seem unquestionable.

All the "isms"—racism, sexism, ageism, et al.—are founded on and fueled   22
by the stereotype and the cliché, which are lies of exaggeration, omission, and
ignorance. They are always dangerous. They take a single tree and make it a
landscape. They destroy curiosity. They close minds and separate people. The
single mother on welfare is assumed to be cheating. Any black male could tell
you how much of his identity is obliterated daily by stereotypes. Fat people,
ugly people, beautiful people, old people, large-breasted women, short men,
the mentally ill, and the homeless all could tell you how much more they are
like us than we want to think. I once admitted to a group of people that I had a
mouth like a truck driver. Much to my surprise, a man stood up and said, "I'm
a truck driver, and I never cuss." Needless to say, I was humbled.

Groupthink

Who is more foolish, the child afraid of the dark, or the man afraid
of the light?   —Maurice Freehill

Irving Janis, in *Victims of Group Think,* defines this sort of lie as a psy-   23
chological phenomenon within decision-making groups in which loyalty to
the group has become more important than any other value, with the result
that dissent and the appraisal of alternatives are suppressed. If you've ever
worked on a committee or in a corporation, you've encountered groupthink.
It requires a combination of other forms of lying—ignoring facts, selective
memory, omission, and denial, to name a few.

The textbook example of groupthink came on December 7, 1941. From as   24
early as the fall of 1941, the warnings came in, one after another, that Japan
was preparing for a massive military operation. The navy command in Hawaii
assumed Pearl Harbor was invulnerable—the Japanese weren't stupid enough
to attack the United States' most important base. On the other hand, racist
stereotypes said the Japanese weren't smart enough to invent a torpedo effective in less than 60 feet of water (the fleet was docked in 30 feet); after all, US
technology hadn't been able to do it.

On Friday, December 5, normal weekend leave was granted to all the   25
commanders at Pearl Harbor, even though the Japanese consulate in Hawaii
was busy burning papers. Within the tight, good-ole-boy cohesiveness of the
US command in Hawaii, the myth of invulnerability stayed well entrenched.
No one in the group considered the alternatives. The rest is history.

Out-and-Out Lies

The only form of lying that is beyond reproach is lying for its
own sake.   —Oscar Wilde

Of all the ways to lie, I like this one the best, probably because I get tired   26
of trying to figure out the real meanings behind things. At least I can trust the
bald-faced lie. I once asked my five-year-old nephew, "Who broke the fence?"
(I had seen him do it.) He answered, "The murderers." Who could argue?

At least when this sort of lie is told it can be easily confronted. As the per-   27
son who is lied to, I know where I stand. The bald-faced lie doesn't toy with
my perceptions—it argues with them. It doesn't try to refashion reality, it
tries to refute it. *Read my lips.* . . . No sleight of hand. No guessing. If this were
the only form of lying, there would be no such things as floating anxiety or the
adult-children-of-alcoholics movement.

Dismissal

Pay no attention to that man behind the curtain!
I am the Great Oz! — The Wizard of Oz

Dismissal is perhaps the slipperiest of all lies. Dismissing feelings, percep-   28
tions, or even the raw facts of a situation ranks as a kind of lie that can do as
much damage to a person as any other kind of lie.

The roots of many mental disorders can be traced back to the dismissal of   29
reality. Imagine that a person is told from the time she is a tot that her perceptions are inaccurate. *"Mommy, I'm scared."* "No you're not, darling." *"I don't
like that man next door, he makes me feel icky."* "Johnny, that's a terrible thing to
say, of course you like him. You go over there right now and be nice to him."

I've often mused over the idea that madness is actually a sane reaction to   30
an insane world. Psychologist R. D. Laing supports this hypothesis in *Sanity,
Madness and the Family*, an account of his investigation into the families of
schizophrenics. The common thread that ran through all of the families he
studied was a deliberate, staunch dismissal of the patient's perceptions from
a very early age. Each of the patients started out with an accurate grasp of
reality, which, through meticulous and methodical dismissal, was demolished
until the only reality the patient could trust was catatonia.

Dismissal runs the gamut. Mild dismissal can be quite handy for forgiving   31
the foibles of others in our day-to-day lives. Toddlers who have just learned to
manipulate their parents' attention sometimes are dismissed out of necessity.
Absolute attention from the parents would require so much energy that no
one would get to eat dinner. But we must be careful and attentive about how
far we take our "necessary" dismissals. Dismissal is a dangerous tool, because
it's nothing less than a lie.

Delusion

We lie loudest when we lie to ourselves.
—Eric Hoffer

I could write the book on this one. Delusion, a cousin of dismissal, is the   32
tendency to see excuses as facts. It's a powerful lying tool because it filters out
information that contradicts what we want to believe. Alcoholics who believe
that the problems in their lives are legitimate reasons for drinking rather than
results of the drinking offer the classic example of deluded thinking. Delusion
uses the mind's ability to see things in myriad ways to support what it wants
to be the truth.

But delusion is also a survival mechanism we all use. If we were to fully   33
contemplate the consequences of our stockpiles of nuclear weapons or global

warming, we could hardly function on a day-to-day level. We don't want to incorporate that much reality into our lives because to do so would be paralyzing.

Delusion acts as an adhesive to keep the status quo intact. It shamelessly   34
employs dismissal, omission, and amnesia, among other sorts of lies. Its most cunning defense is that it cannot see itself.

The liar's punishment . . . is that he cannot believe anyone else.
—George Bernard Shaw

These are only a few of the ways we lie. Or are lied to. As I said earlier, it's   35
not easy to entirely eliminate lies from our lives. No matter how pious we may try to be, we will still embellish, hedge, and omit to lubricate the daily machinery of living. But there is a world of difference between telling functional lies and living a lie. Martin Buber once said, "The lie is the spirit committing treason against itself." Our acceptance of lies becomes a cultural cancer that eventually shrouds and reorders reality until moral garbage becomes as invisible to us as water is to a fish.

How much do we tolerate before we become sick and tired of being sick   36
and tired? When will we stand up and declare our *right* to trust? When do we stop accepting that the real truth is in the fine print? Whose lips do we read this year when we vote for president? When will we stop being so reticent about making judgments? When do we stop turning over our personal power and responsibility to liars?

Maybe if I don't tell the bank the check's in the mail I'll be less tolerant   37
of the lies told me every day. A country song I once heard said it all for me: "You've got to stand for something or you'll fall for anything."

---

*For a reading quiz, sources on Stephanie Ericsson, and annotated links to further readings on lying, visit **bedfordstmartins.com/thebedfordreader**.*

Journal Writing

Ericsson says, "We lie. We all do" (par. 3)—and that must mean you, too. In your journal, write about lies you have told. When is the last time you remember lying? What was the most significant lie you ever told? What circumstances have justified lying? Have you ever been ashamed of a lie or faced consequences for lying? (To take your journal writing further, see "From Journal to Essay" below.)

Questions on Meaning

1. What is Ericsson's THESIS?
2. Does Ericsson think it's possible to eliminate lies from our lives? What EVIDENCE does she offer?
3. If it were possible to eliminate lies from our lives, why would that be desirable?
4. What is this essay's PURPOSE?

Questions on Writing Strategy

1. Ericsson starts out by recounting her own four-lie day (pars. 1–2). What is the EFFECT of this INTRODUCTION?
2. At the beginning of each kind of lie, Ericsson provides an epigraph, a short quotation that forecasts a theme. Which of these epigraphs work best, do you think? What are your criteria for judgment?
3. How does Ericsson develop her discussion of delusion in paragraphs 32–34?
4. What is the message of Ericsson's CONCLUSION? Does the conclusion work well? Why, or why not?
5. **OTHER METHODS**   Examine the way Ericsson uses DEFINITION and EXAMPLE to support her classification. Which definitions are clearest? Which examples are the most effective? Why?

Questions on Language

1. In paragraph 35 Ericsson writes, "Our acceptance of lies becomes a cultural cancer that eventually shrouds and reorders reality until moral garbage becomes as invisible to us as water is to a fish." How do the two FIGURES OF SPEECH in this sentence—cancer and garbage—relate to each other?
2. Occasionally Ericsson's anger shows through, as in paragraphs 12–13 and 18–20. Is the TONE appropriate in these cases? Why, or why not?
3. Look up any of these words you do not know: haggard (par. 2); travails (4); façades (10); plethora (11); ecclesiastical, pedophilia (12); irreparable, co-perpetrator (13); patriarchal, archetype (20); gamut (31); myriad (32); reticent (36).
4. Ericsson uses several words and phrases from the fields of psychology and sociology. Define: passive-aggressive (par. 16); floating anxiety, adult-children-of-alcoholics movement (27); schizophrenics, catatonia (30).

Suggestions for Writing

1. **FROM JOURNAL TO ESSAY**   Develop one or more of the lies you recalled in your journal into an essay. You may choose to elaborate on your lies by classifying according to some principle or by NARRATING the story of a particular lie and its outcome. Give your reader a sense of your motivation for lying in the first place.

2. Ericsson writes, "All the 'isms'—racism, sexism, ageism, et al.—are founded on and fueled by the stereotype and the cliché, which are lies of exaggeration, omission, and ignorance. They are always dangerous. They take a single tree and make it a landscape" (par. 22). Write an essay discussing stereotypes and how they work to encourage prejudice. Use Ericsson's definition as a base, and expand it to include stereotypes you find particularly injurious. How do these stereotypes oversimplify? How are they "dangerous"?

3. Research pathological liars—that is, people who because of a psychological disorder are compelled to tell lies. In an essay, develop an extended definition of the pathological liar.

4. **CRITICAL WRITING** EVALUATE the success of Ericsson's essay, considering especially how well her evidence supports her GENERALIZATIONS. Are there important categories she overlooks, exceptions she does not account for, gaps in definitions? Offer specific evidence for your own view, whether positive or negative.

5. **CONNECTIONS** Ericsson begins her essay by acknowledging her own lies, and she often uses the first-person *I* or *we* in explaining her categories. In contrast, the author of the following essay, William Lutz, takes a more distant approach in classifying the dishonest language called *doublespeak*. Which of these two approaches, confessional or more distant, do you find more effective, and why? When, in your view, is it appropriate to inject yourself into your writing, and when is it not?

Stephanie Ericsson on Writing

In an interview on the *Amazon.com* Web site, Stephanie Ericsson discussed when and why she began writing. At first, she said, she did not write to communicate but to find and express herself.

I was fifteen in the year 1968, in the heart of hippie-saturated San Francisco, and like the world, I, too, underwent a major transformation. These spiritual awakenings tend to sound lofty, but the truth is that they are always messy. I began writing regularly then, when I lost my family. There was no one to tell my feelings to, so I turned to the blank white page. The page will never contradict you, never ignore you, and never judge you. I could put the chaos outside of me, and move on. It was a survival tool that I became attached to.

For Discussion

1. Do you agree with Ericsson's assessment of the "blank white page" as benevolent and nonjudgmental?

2. In the passage above, Ericsson is talking about writing for oneself. Is it merely the absence of an audience that makes such writing potentially therapeutic? Why does articulating her thoughts—if only for herself—help Ericsson "move on"?

WILLIAM LUTZ

William Lutz was born in 1940 in Racine, Wisconsin. He received a BA from Dominican College, an MA from Marquette University, a PhD from the University of Nevada at Reno, and a JD from Rutgers School of Law. Since 1971 Lutz has taught at Rutgers University in Camden, New Jersey. For much of his career, Lutz's interest in words and composition has made him an active campaigner against misleading and irresponsible language. For fourteen years he edited the *Quarterly Journal of Doublespeak,* and he has written three popular books on such language: *Doublespeak: From Revenue Enhancement to Terminal Living* (1989), *The New Doublespeak: Why No One Knows What Anyone's Saying Anymore* (1996), and *Doublespeak Defined: Cut through the Bull**** and Get to the Point!* (1999). In 1996 Lutz received the George Orwell Award for Distinguished Contribution to Honesty and Clarity in Public Language. He continues to publish articles on language in newspapers and magazines. Most recently, Lutz has been working as a consultant with the US Securities and Exchange Commission and several large corporations to develop plain English guidelines for financial and legal documents.

The World of Doublespeak

In the previous essay, Stephanie Ericsson examines the damage caused by the deliberate lies we tell each other every day. But what if our language doesn't lie, exactly, and instead just obscures meanings we'd rather not admit to? Such intentional fudging, or *doublespeak,* is the sort of language Lutz specializes in, and here he uses classification to expose its many guises. "The World of Doublespeak" abridges the first chapter in Lutz's book *Doublespeak;* the essay's title is the chapter's subtitle.

There are no potholes in the streets of Tucson, Arizona, just "pavement   1
deficiencies." The Reagan Administration didn't propose any new taxes, just "revenue enhancement" through new "user's fees." Those aren't bums on the street, just "non–goal oriented members of society." There are no more poor people, just "fiscal underachievers." There was no robbery of an automatic teller machine, just an "unauthorized withdrawal." The patient didn't die because of medical malpractice, it was just a "diagnostic misadventure of a high magnitude." The US Army doesn't kill the enemy anymore, it just "services the target." And the doublespeak goes on.

Doublespeak is language that pretends to communicate but really doesn't.   2
It is language that makes the bad seem good, the negative appear positive,
the unpleasant appear attractive or at least tolerable. Doublespeak is language
that avoids or shifts responsibility, language that is at variance with its real or
purported meaning. It is language that conceals or prevents thought; rather
than extending thought, doublespeak limits it.

Doublespeak is not a matter of subjects and verbs agreeing; it is a matter   3
of words and facts agreeing. Basic to doublespeak is incongruity, the incongruity between what is said or left unsaid, and what really is. It is the incongruity between the word and the referent, between seem and be, between
the essential function of language—communication—and what doublespeak
does—mislead, distort, deceive, inflate, circumvent, obfuscate.

How to Spot Doublespeak

How can you spot doublespeak? Most of the time you will recognize double-   4
speak when you see or hear it. But, if you have any doubts, you can identify
doublespeak just by answering these questions: Who is saying what to whom,
under what conditions and circumstances, with what intent, and with what
results? Answering these questions will usually help you identify as doublespeak language that appears to be legitimate or that at first glance doesn't even
appear to be doublespeak.

First Kind of Doublespeak

There are at least four kinds of doublespeak. The first is the euphemism,   5
an inoffensive or positive word or phrase used to avoid a harsh, unpleasant, or
distasteful reality. But a euphemism can also be a tactful word or phrase which
avoids directly mentioning a painful reality, or it can be an expression used
out of concern for the feelings of someone else, or to avoid directly discussing
a topic subject to a social or cultural taboo.

When you use a euphemism because of your sensitivity for someone's   6
feelings or out of concern for a recognized social or cultural taboo, it is not
doublespeak. For example, you express your condolences that someone has
"passed away" because you do not want to say to a grieving person, "I'm sorry
your father is dead." When you use the euphemism "passed away," no one is
misled. Moreover, the euphemism functions here not just to protect the feelings of another person, but to communicate also your concern for that person's feelings during a period of mourning. When you excuse yourself to go to
the "restroom," or you mention that someone is "sleeping with" or "involved
with" someone else, you do not mislead anyone about your meaning, but you

do respect the social taboos about discussing bodily functions and sex in direct terms. You also indicate your sensitivity to the feelings of your audience, which is usually considered a mark of courtesy and good manners.

However, when a euphemism is used to mislead or deceive, it becomes doublespeak. For example, in 1984 the US State Department announced that it would no longer use the word "killing" in its annual report on the status of human rights in countries around the world. Instead, it would use the phrase "unlawful or arbitrary deprivation of life," which the department claimed was more accurate. Its real purpose for using this phrase was simply to avoid discussing the embarrassing situation of government-sanctioned killings in countries that are supported by the United States and have been certified by the United States as respecting the human rights of their citizens. This use of a euphemism constitutes doublespeak, since it is designed to mislead, to cover up the unpleasant. Its real intent is at variance with its apparent intent. It is language designed to alter our perception of reality.

The Pentagon, too, avoids discussing unpleasant realities when it refers to bombs and artillery shells that fall on civilian targets as "incontinent ordnance." And in 1977 the Pentagon tried to slip funding for the neutron bomb unnoticed into an appropriations bill by calling it a "radiation enhancement device."

Second Kind of Doublespeak

A second kind of doublespeak is jargon, the specialized language of a trade, profession, or similar group, such as that used by doctors, lawyers, engineers, educators, or car mechanics. Jargon can serve an important and useful function. Within a group, jargon functions as a kind of verbal shorthand that allows members of the group to communicate with each other clearly, efficiently, and quickly. Indeed, it is a mark of membership in the group to be able to use and understand the group's jargon.

But jargon, like the euphemism, can also be doublespeak. It can be—and often is—pretentious, obscure, and esoteric terminology used to give an air of profundity, authority, and prestige to speakers and their subject matter. Jargon as doublespeak often makes the simple appear complex, the ordinary profound, the obvious insightful. In this sense it is used not to express but impress. With such doublespeak, the act of smelling something becomes "organoleptic analysis," glass becomes "fused silicate," a crack in a metal support beam becomes a "discontinuity," conservative economic policies become "distributionally conservative notions."

Lawyers, for example, speak of an "involuntary conversion" of property when discussing the loss or destruction of property through theft, accident, or condemnation. If your house burns down or if your car is stolen, you have suffered an involuntary conversion of your property. When used by lawyers in a legal situation, such jargon is a legitimate use of language, since lawyers can be expected to understand the term.

However, when a member of a specialized group uses its jargon to commu-   12
nicate with a person outside the group, and uses it knowing that the non-member does not understand such language, then there is doublespeak. For example, on May 9, 1978, a National Airlines 727 airplane crashed while attempting to land at the Pensacola, Florida, airport. Three of the fifty-two passengers aboard the airplane were killed. As a result of the crash, National made an after-tax insurance benefit of $1.7 million, or an extra 18¢ a share dividend for its stockholders. Now National Airlines had two problems: It did not want to talk about one of its airplanes crashing, and it had to account for the $1.7 million when it issued its annual report to its stockholders. National solved the problem by inserting a footnote in its annual report which explained that the $1.7 million income was due to "the involuntary conversion of a 727." National thus acknowledged the crash of its airplane and the subsequent profit it made from the crash, without once mentioning the accident or the deaths. However, because airline officials knew that most stockholders in the company, and indeed most of the general public, were not familiar with legal jargon, the use of such jargon constituted doublespeak.

Third Kind of Doublespeak

A third kind of doublespeak is gobbledygook or bureaucratese. Basically,   13
such doublespeak is simply a matter of piling on words, of overwhelming the audience with words, the bigger the words and the longer the sentences the better. Alan Greenspan, then chair of President Nixon's Council of Economic Advisors, was quoted in *The Philadelphia Inquirer* in 1974 as having testified before a Senate committee that "It is a tricky problem to find the particular calibration in timing that would be appropriate to stem the acceleration in risk premiums created by falling incomes without prematurely aborting the decline in the inflation-generated risk premiums."

Nor has Mr. Greenspan's language changed since then. Speaking to the   14
meeting of the Economic Club of New York in 1988, Mr. Greenspan, now Federal Reserve chair, said, "I guess I should warn you, if I turn out to be particularly clear, you've probably misunderstood what I've said." Mr. Greenspan's doublespeak doesn't seem to have held back his career.

Sometimes gobbledygook may sound impressive, but when the quote is   15
later examined in print it doesn't even make sense. During the 1988 presidential campaign, vice-presidential candidate Senator Dan Quayle explained the need for a strategic-defense initiative by saying, "Why wouldn't an

enhanced deterrent, a more stable peace, a better prospect to denying the ones who enter conflict in the first place to have a reduction of offensive systems and an introduction to defense capability? I believe this is the route the country will eventually go."

The investigation into the *Challenger* disaster in 1986 revealed the doublespeak of gobbledygook and bureaucratese used by too many involved in the shuttle program. When Jesse Moore, NASA's associate administrator, was asked if the performance of the shuttle program had improved with each launch or if it had remained the same, he answered, "I think our performance in terms of the liftoff performance and in terms of the orbital performance, we knew more about the envelope we were operating under, and we have been pretty accurately staying in that. And so I would say the performance has not by design drastically improved. I think we have been able to characterize the performance more as a function of our launch experience as opposed to it improving as a function of time." While this language may appear to be jargon, a close look will reveal that it is really just gobbledygook laced with jargon. But you really have to wonder if Mr. Moore had any idea what he was saying.   16

Fourth Kind of Doublespeak

The fourth kind of doublespeak is inflated language that is designed to make the ordinary seem extraordinary; to make everyday things seem impressive; to give an air of importance to people, situations, or things that would not normally be considered important; to make the simple seem complex. Often this kind of doublespeak isn't hard to spot, and it is usually pretty funny. While car mechanics may be called "automotive internists," elevator operators members of the "vertical transportation corps," used cars "pre-owned" or "experienced cars," and black-and-white television sets described as having "non-multicolor capability," you really aren't misled all that much by such language.   17

However, you may have trouble figuring out that, when Chrysler "initiates a career alternative enhancement program," it is really laying off five thousand workers; or that "negative patient-care outcome" means the patient died; or that "rapid oxidation" means a fire in a nuclear power plant.   18

The doublespeak of inflated language can have serious consequences. In Pentagon doublespeak, "pre-emptive counterattack" means that American forces attacked first; "engaged the enemy on all sides" means American troops were ambushed; "backloading of augmentation personnel" means a retreat by American troops. In the doublespeak of the military, the 1983 invasion of Grenada was conducted not by the US Army, Navy, Air Force, and Marines,   19 but by the "Caribbean Peace Keeping Forces." But then, according to the Pentagon, it wasn't an invasion, it was a "predawn vertical insertion." . . .

The Dangers of Doublespeak

Doublespeak is not the product of carelessness or sloppy thinking. Indeed, [20] most doublespeak is the product of clear thinking and is carefully designed and constructed to appear to communicate when in fact it doesn't. It is language designed not to lead but mislead. It is language designed to distort reality and corrupt thought. . . . In the world created by doublespeak, if it's not a tax increase, but rather "revenue enhancement" or "tax base broadening," how can you complain about higher taxes? If it's not acid rain, but rather "poorly buffered precipitation," how can you worry about all those dead trees? If that isn't the Mafia in Atlantic City, but just "members of a career-offender cartel," why worry about the influence of organized crime in the city? If Supreme Court Justice William Rehnquist wasn't addicted to the pain-killing drug his doctor prescribed, but instead it was just that the drug had "established an interrelationship with the body, such that if the drug is removed precipitously, there is a reaction," you needn't question that his decisions might have been influenced by his drug addiction. If it's not a Titan II nuclear-armed intercontinental ballistic missile with a warhead 630 times more powerful than the atomic bomb dropped on Hiroshima, but instead, according to air force colonel Frank Horton, it's just a "very large, potentially disruptive reentry system," why be concerned about the threat of nuclear destruction? Why worry about the neutron bomb escalating the arms race if it's just a "radiation enhancement weapon"? If it's not an invasion, but a "rescue mission" or a "predawn vertical insertion," you won't need to think about any violations of US or international law.

Doublespeak has become so common in everyday living that many people [21] fail to notice it. Even worse, when they do notice doublespeak being used on them, they don't react, they don't protest. Do you protest when you are asked to check your packages at the desk "for your convenience," when it's not for your convenience at all but for someone else's? You see advertisements for "genuine imitation leather," "virgin vinyl," or "real counterfeit diamonds," but do you question the language or the supposed quality of the product? Do you question politicians who don't speak of slums or ghettos but of the "inner city" or "substandard housing" where the "disadvantaged" live and thus avoid talking about the poor who have to live in filthy, poorly heated, ramshackle apartments or houses? Aren't you amazed that patients don't die in the hospital anymore, it's just "negative patient-care outcome"?

Doublespeak such as that noted earlier that defines cab drivers as "urban [22] transportation specialists," elevator operators as members of the "vertical transportation corps," and automobile mechanics as "automotive internists" can be considered humorous and relatively harmless. However, when a fire in a nuclear reactor building is called "rapid oxidation," an explosion in a nuclear power plant is called an "energetic disassembly," the illegal overthrow of a legitimate government is termed "destabilizing a government," and lies are seen as "inoperative statements," we are hearing doublespeak that attempts to avoid responsibility and make the bad seem good, the negative appear positive, something unpleasant appear attractive; and which seems to communicate but doesn't. It is language designed to alter our perception of reality and corrupt our thinking. Such language does not provide us with the tools we need to develop, advance, and preserve our culture and our civilization. Such language breeds suspicion, cynicism, distrust, and, ultimately, hostility.

Doublespeak is insidious because it can infect and eventually destroy the function of language, which is communication between people and social groups. This corruption of the function of language can have serious and far-reaching consequences. We live in a country that depends upon an informed electorate to make decisions in selecting candidates for office and deciding issues of public policy. The use of doublespeak can become so pervasive that it becomes the coin of the political realm, with speakers and listeners convinced that they really understand such language. After a while we may really believe that politicians don't lie but only "misspeak," that illegal acts are merely "inappropriate actions," that fraud and criminal conspiracy are just "miscertification." President Jimmy Carter in April of 1980 could call the aborted raid to free the American hostages in Teheran an "incomplete success" and really believe that he had made a statement that clearly communicated with the American public. So, too, could President Ronald Reagan say in 1985 that "ultimately our security and our hopes for success at the arms reduction talks hinge on the determination that we show here to continue our program to rebuild and refortify our defenses" and really believe that greatly increasing the amount of money spent building new weapons would lead to a reduction in the number of weapons in the world. If we really believe that we understand such language and that such language communicates and promotes clear thought, then the world of 1984,[1] with its control of reality through language, is upon us.

---

[1] In a section omitted from this abridgement of his chapter, Lutz discusses *Nineteen Eighty-Four*, the 1949 novel by George Orwell in which a frightening totalitarian state devises a language, called *newspeak*, to shape and control thought in politically acceptable forms. (For an example of Orwell's writing, see p. 663.) — EDS.

*For a reading quiz, sources on William Lutz, and annotated links to further readings on doublespeak, visit **bedfordstmartins.com/thebedfordreader**.*

Journal Writing

Now that you know the name for it, when have you read or heard examples of double-speak? Over the next few days, jot down examples of doublespeak that you recall or that you read and hear—from politicians or news commentators; in the lease for your dwelling or your car; in advertising and catalogs; from bosses, teachers, or other figures of authority; in overheard conversations. (To take your journal writing further, see "From Journal to Essay" on the following page.)

Questions on Meaning

1. What is Lutz's THESIS? Where does he state it?
2. According to Lutz, four questions can help us identify doublespeak. What are they? How can they help us distinguish between truthful language and double-speak?
3. What, according to Lutz, are "the dangers of doublespeak"?
4. What ASSUMPTIONS does the author make about his readers' educational back-grounds and familiarity with his subject?

Questions on Writing Strategy

1. What principle does Lutz use for creating his four kinds of doublespeak—that is, what mainly distinguishes the groups?
2. How does Lutz develop the discussion of euphemism in paragraphs 5–8?
3. Lutz quotes Alan Greenspan twice in paragraphs 13–14. What is surprising about the comment in paragraph 14? Why does Lutz include this second quotation?
4. Lutz uses many quotations that were quite current when he first published this piece in 1989 but that now may seem dated—for instance, references to Presidents Carter and Reagan or to the nuclear arms race. Do these EXAMPLES under-mine Lutz's essay in any way? Is his discussion of doublespeak still valid today? Explain your answers.
5. **OTHER METHODS**   Lutz's essay is not only a classification but also a DEFINITION of *doublespeak* and an examination of CAUSE AND EFFECT. Where are these other methods used most prominently? What do they contribute to the essay?

Questions on Language

1. How does Lutz's own language compare with the language he quotes as double-speak? Do you find his language clear and easy to understand?

2. ANALYZE Lutz's language in paragraphs 22 and 23. How do the CONNOTATIONS of words such as "corrupt," "hostility," "insidious," and "control" strengthen the author's message?

3. The following list of possibly unfamiliar words includes only those found in Lutz's own sentences, not those in the doublespeak he quotes. Be sure you can define variance (par. 2); incongruity, referent (3); taboo (5); condolences (6); esoteric, profundity (10); condemnation (11); ramshackle (21); cynicism (22); insidious (23).

Suggestions for Writing

1. **FROM JOURNAL TO ESSAY**   Choose at least one of the examples of doublespeak noted in your journal, and write an essay explaining why it qualifies as doublespeak. Which of Lutz's categories does it fit under? How did you recognize it? Can you understand what it means?

2. Just about all of us have resorted to doublespeak at one time or another — when making an excuse, when trying to conceal the fact that we're unprepared for an exam, when trying to impress a supervisor or potential employer. Write a NARRATIVE about a time you used deliberately unclear language, perhaps language that you yourself didn't understand. What were the circumstances? Did you consciously decide to use unclear language, or did it just leak out? How did others react to your use of this language?

3. The National Council of Teachers of English has posted a number of articles from the *Quarterly Review of Doublespeak*, which Lutz once edited, on its Web site at *ncte.org*. (Your library may also subscribe to the journal.) Read a few related articles from the journal, and based on them write an essay in which you challenge, expand, or add more examples to Lutz's categories.

4. **CRITICAL WRITING**   Can you determine from his essay who Lutz believes is responsible for the proliferation of doublespeak? Whose responsibility is it to curtail the use of doublespeak: just those who use it? the schools? the government? the media? we who hear it? Write an essay that considers these questions, citing specific passages from the essay and incorporating your own ideas.

5. **CONNECTIONS**   Read Stephanie Ericsson's "The Ways We Lie" (p. 408), which classifies the lies we tell in our daily lives. In what way, if any, do doublespeakers also lie? How, if at all, do the intentions of Ericsson's liars and Lutz's doublespeakers differ? How, if at all, are their intentions the same? Are the results of lying and doublespeak, according to each author, different or the same? Write an essay that answers these questions and that points out any other similarities or differences you notice between liars and doublespeakers. Use EVIDENCE from the two essays or from your own experience to support your thesis.

William Lutz on Writing

In 1989 C-SPAN aired an interview between Brian Lamb and William Lutz. Lamb asked Lutz about his writing process. "I have a rule about writing,"

Lutz answered, "which I discovered when I wrote my dissertation: You never write a book, you write three pages, or you write five pages. I put off writing my dissertation for a year, because I could not think of writing this whole thing. . . . I had put off doing this book [*Doublespeak*] for quite a while, and my wife said, 'You've got to do the book.' And I said, 'Yes, I am going to, just as soon as I . . . ,' and, of course, I did every other thing I could possibly think of before that, and then I realized one day that she was right, I had to start writing. . . . So one day, I sit down and say, 'I am going to write five pages—that's all—and when I am done with five pages, I'll reward myself.' So I do the five pages, or the next time I will do ten pages or whatever number of pages, but I set a number of pages."

Perhaps wondering just how high Lutz's daily page count might go, Lamb asked Lutz how much he wrote at one time. "It depends," Lutz admitted. "I always begin a writing session by sitting down and rewriting what I wrote the previous day—and that is the first thing, and it does two things. First of all, it makes your writing a little bit better, because rewriting is the essential part of writing. And the second thing is to get you flowing again, get back into the mainstream. Truman Capote[1] once gave the best piece of advice for writers ever given. He said, 'Never pump the well dry; always leave a bucket there.' So, I never stop writing when I run out of ideas. I always stop when I have something more to write about, and write a note to myself, 'This is what I am going to do next,' and then I stop. The worst feeling in the world is to have written yourself dry and have to come back the next day, knowing that you are dry and not knowing where you are going to pick up at this point."

For Discussion

1. Though his work is devoted to words and writing, William Lutz once spent a great deal of time avoiding writing. What finally got him to stop procrastinating? When you are avoiding a writing assignment, is it the length of the project or something else that prevents you from getting to work?
2. Lutz always rewrites before he starts writing about the idea that he didn't develop on the previous day. How come? Do you think Lutz's strategy is a good one?

---

[1] Truman Capote (1924–84) was an American journalist and fiction writer. —EDS.

RUSSELL BAKER

Russell Baker is one of America's notable humorists and political satirists. Born in 1925 in Virginia, Baker was raised in New Jersey and Maryland by his widowed mother. After serving in the navy during World War II, he earned a BA from Johns Hopkins University in 1947. He became a reporter for the *Baltimore Sun* that year and then joined the *New York Times* in 1954, covering the State Department, the White House, and Congress. From 1962 until his retirement from the *Times* in 1998, he wrote a popular column that ranged over the merely bothersome (unreadable menus) and the serious (the Cold War). Many of Baker's columns and essays have been collected in books, such as *There's a Country in My Cellar* (1990). Baker has twice received the Pulitzer Prize, once for distinguished commentary and again for the first volume of his autobiography, *Growing Up* (1982). He has also written fiction and children's books, edited *Russell Baker's Book of American Humor* (1993), and served as host of *Masterpiece Theatre* on public television.

The Plot against People

The critic R. Z. Sheppard has commented that Baker can "best be appreciated for doing what a good humorist has always done: writing to preserve his sanity for at least one more day." In this piece from the *New York Times* in 1968, Baker uses classification for that purpose, taking aim, as he has often done, at inanimate objects. In the decades since this piece was written, the proliferation of electronic gadgets has, if anything, intensified the plot Baker imagines.

Inanimate objects are classified into three major categories—those that don't work, those that break down and those that get lost.

The goal of all inanimate objects is to resist man and ultimately to defeat him, and the three major classifications are based on the method each object uses to achieve its purpose. As a general rule, any object capable of breaking down at the moment when it is most needed will do so. The automobile is typical of the category.

With the cunning typical of its breed, the automobile never breaks down while entering a filling station with a large staff of idle mechanics. It waits until it reaches a downtown intersection in the middle of the rush hour, or until it is fully loaded with family and luggage on the Ohio Turnpike.

Thus it creates maximum misery, inconvenience, frustration and irritability among its human cargo, thereby reducing its owner's life span.

Washing machines, garbage disposals, lawn mowers, light bulbs, automatic   5
laundry dryers, water pipes, furnaces, electrical fuses, television tubes, hose
nozzles, tape recorders, slide projectors—all are in league with the automobile
to take their turn at breaking down whenever life threatens to flow smoothly
for their human enemies.

Many inanimate objects, of course, find it extremely difficult to break down.   6
Pliers, for example, and gloves and keys are almost totally incapable of breaking down. Therefore, they have had to evolve a different technique for resisting man.

They get lost. Science has still not solved the mystery of how they do it,   7
and no man has ever caught one of them in the act of getting lost. The most
plausible theory is that they have developed a secret method of locomotion
which they are able to conceal the instant a human eye falls upon them.

It is not uncommon for a pair of pliers to climb all the way from the cellar   8
to the attic in its single-minded determination to raise its owner's blood pressure. Keys have been known to burrow three feet under mattresses. Women's
purses, despite their great weight, frequently travel through six or seven rooms
to find hiding space under a couch.

Scientists have been struck by the fact that things that break down virtu-   9
ally never get lost, while things that get lost hardly ever break down.

A furnace, for example, will invariably break down at the depth of the   10
first winter cold wave, but it will never get lost. A woman's purse, which after
all does have some inherent capacity for breaking down, hardly ever does; it
almost invariably chooses to get lost.

Some persons believe this constitutes evidence that inanimate objects are   11
not entirely hostile to man, and that a negotiated peace is possible. After all,
they point out, a furnace could infuriate a man even more thoroughly by getting lost than by breaking down, just as a glove could upset him far more by
breaking down than by getting lost.

Not everyone agrees, however, that this indicates a conciliatory attitude   12
among inanimate objects. Many say it merely proves that furnaces, gloves and
pliers are incredibly stupid.

The third class of objects—those that don't work—is the most curious   13
of all. These include such objects as barometers, car clocks, cigarette lighters,
flashlights and toy-train locomotives. It is inaccurate, of course, to say that
they never work. They work once, usually for the first few hours after being
brought home, and then quit. Thereafter, they never work again.

In fact, it is widely assumed that they are built for the purpose of not work-   14
ing. Some people have reached advanced ages without ever seeing some of
these objects—barometers, for example—in working order.

Science is utterly baffled by the entire category. There are many theories   15
about it. The most interesting holds that the things that don't work have

attained the highest state possible for an inanimate object, the state to which things that break down and things that get lost can still only aspire.

They have truly defeated man by conditioning him never to expect any- 16 thing of them, and in return they have given man the only peace he receives from inanimate society. He does not expect his barometer to work, his electric locomotive to run, his cigarette lighter to light or his flashlight to illuminate, and when they don't it does not raise his blood pressure.

He cannot attain that peace with furnaces and keys and cars and women's 17 purses as long as he demands that they work for their keep.

*For a reading quiz, sources on Russell Baker, and annotated links to additional humor writing, visit **bedfordstmartins.com/thebedfordreader**.*

Journal Writing

What other ways can you think of to classify inanimate objects? In your journal, try expanding on Baker's categories, or create new categories of your own based on a different principle—for example, objects no student can live without or objects no student would want to be caught dead with. (To take your journal writing further, see "From Journal to Essay" on the facing page.)

Questions on Meaning

1. What is Baker's THESIS?
2. Why don't things that break down get lost, and vice versa?
3. Does Baker have any PURPOSE other than to make his readers smile?
4. How have inanimate objects "defeated man"?

Questions on Writing Strategy

1. What is the EFFECT of Baker's principle of classification? What categories are omitted here, and why?
2. In paragraphs 6–10, how does Baker develop the category of things that get lost? Itemize the strategies he uses to make the category clear.
3. Find three places where Baker uses hyperbole. (See *Figures of speech* in Useful Terms if you need a definition.) What is the effect of the hyperbole?
4. How does the essay's INTRODUCTION help set its TONE? How does the CONCLUSION reinforce the tone?

5. **OTHER METHODS**   How does Baker use NARRATION to portray inanimate objects in the act of "resisting" people? Discuss how these mini-narratives make his classification more persuasive.

Questions on Language

1. Look up any of these words that are unfamiliar: plausible, locomotion (par. 7); invariably, inherent (10); conciliatory (12).
2. What are the CONNOTATIONS of the word "cunning" (par. 3)? What is its effect in this context?
3. Why does Baker use such expressions as "man," "some people," and "their human enemies" rather than *I* to describe those who come into conflict with inanimate objects? How might the essay have been different if Baker had relied on *I*?

Suggestions for Writing

1. **FROM JOURNAL TO ESSAY**   Write a brief, humorous essay based on one classification system from your journal entry. It may be helpful to use narration or DESCRIPTION in your classification. FIGURES OF SPEECH, especially hyperbole and understatement, can help you establish a comic tone.
2. Think of a topic that would not generally be considered appropriate for a serious classification (some examples: game-show winners, body odors, stupid pet tricks, knock-knock jokes). Select a principle of classification and write a brief essay sorting the subject into categories. You may want to use a humorous tone; then again, you may want to approach the topic "seriously," counting on the contrast between subject and treatment to make your IRONY clear.
3. **CRITICAL WRITING**   In a short essay, discuss the likely AUDIENCE for "The Plot against People." (Recall that it was first published in the *New York Times*.) What can you INFER from his EXAMPLES about Baker's own age and economic status? Does he ASSUME his audience is similar? How do the connections between author and audience help establish the essay's humor? Could this humor be seen as excluding some readers?
4. **CONNECTIONS**   Baker's essay bears comparison with "Remembering My Childhood on the Continent of Africa" by another humorist, David Sedaris (p. 274). Each man writes about himself with a self-deprecating, mock-serious tone. Read both works closely, and write an essay in which you COMPARE AND CONTRAST the words the authors use to present themselves and their situations.

Russell Baker on Writing

In "Computer Fallout," an essay from the October 11, 1987, *New York Times Magazine,* Baker sets out to prove that computers make a writer's life easier, but he ends up somewhere else entirely. Although Baker wrote this piece when word processors were still fairly new on the writing scene, those who share his affliction will recognize the experience even today.

The wonderful thing about writing with a computer instead of a typewriter or a lead pencil is that it's so easy to rewrite that you can make each sentence almost perfect before moving on to the next sentence.

An impressive aspect of using a computer to write with

One of the plusses about a computer on which to write

Happily, the computer is a marked improvement over both the typewriter and the lead pencil for purposes of literary composition, due to the ease with which rewriting can be effectuated, thus enabling

What a marked improvement the computer is for the writer over the typewriter and lead pencil

The typewriter and lead pencil were good enough in their day, but if Shakespeare had been able to access a computer with a good writing program

If writing friends scoff when you sit down at the computer and say, "The lead pencil was good enough for Shakespeare

One of the drawbacks of having a computer on which to write is the ease and rapidity with which the writing can be done, thus leading to the inclusion of many superfluous terms like "lead pencil," when the single word "pencil" would be completely, entirely and utterly adequate.

The ease with which one can rewrite on a computer gives it an advantage over such writing instruments as the pencil and typewriter by enabling the writer to turn an awkward and graceless sentence into one that is practically perfect, although it

The writer's eternal quest for the practically perfect sentence may be ending at last, thanks to the computer's gift of editing ease and swiftness to those confronting awkward, formless, nasty, illiterate sentences such as

Man's quest is eternal, but what specifically is it that he quests, and why does he

Mankind's quest is

Man's and woman's quest

Mankind's and womankind's quest

Humanity's quest for the perfect writing device

Eternal has been humanity's quest

Eternal have been many of humanity's quests

From the earliest cave writing, eternal has been the quest for a device that will forever prevent writers from using the word "quest," particularly when modified by such adjectives as "eternal," "endless," "tireless" and

Many people are amazed at the ease

Many persons are amazed by the ease

Lots of people are astounded when they see the nearly perfect sentences I write since upgrading my writing instrumentation from pencil and typewriter to

Listen, folks, there's nothing to writing almost perfect sentences with ease and rapidity provided you've given up the old horse-and-buggy writing mentality that says Shakespeare couldn't have written those great plays if he had enjoyed the convenience of electronic compositional instrumentation.

Folks, have you ever realized that there's nothing to writing almost

Have you ever stopped to think, folks, that maybe Shakespeare could have written even better if

To be or not to be, that is the central focus of the inquiry.

In the intrapersonal relationships played out within the mind as to the relative merits of continuing to exist as opposed to not continuing to exist

Live or die, a choice as ancient as humanities' eternal quest, is a tough choice which has confounded mankind as well as womankind ever since the option of dreaming was first perceived as a potentially negating effect of the quiescence assumed to be obtainable through the latter course of action.

I'm sick and tired of Luddites saying pencils and typewriters are just as good as computers for writing nearly perfect sentences when they—the Luddites, that is—have never experienced the swiftness and ease of computer writing which makes it possible to compose almost perfect sentences in practically no time at

Folks, are you sick and tired of

Are you, dear reader

Good reader, are you

A lot of you nice folks out there are probably just as sick and tired as I am of hearing people say they are sick and tired of this and that and

Listen, people, I'm just as sick and tired as you are of having writers and TV commercial performers who oil me in cornpone politician prose addressed to "you nice folks out

A curious feature of computers, as opposed to pencils and typewriters, is that when you ought to be writing something more interesting than a nearly perfect sentence

Since it is easier to revise and edit with a computer than with a typewriter or pencil, this amazing machine makes it very hard to stop editing and revising long enough to write a readable sentence, much less an entire newspaper column.

For Discussion

1. What is Baker's unstated THESIS? Does he convince you?
2. Do you find yourself ever having the problem Baker finally admits to in the last paragraph?

DEBORAH TANNEN

Deborah Tannen is a linguist who is best known for her popular studies of communication between men and women. Born and raised in New York City, Tannen earned a BA from Harpur College (now the State University of New York at Binghamton); MAs from Wayne State University and the University of California at Berkeley; and a PhD in linguistics from Berkeley. She is University Professor at Georgetown University, has published many scholarly articles and books, and has lectured on linguistics all over the world. But her renown is more than academic: With television talk-show appearances, speeches to businesspeople and senators, and best-selling books, Tannen has become, in the words of one reviewer, "America's conversational therapist." The books include *You Just Don't Understand* (1990), *The Argument Culture* (1998), *I Only Say This Because I Love You* (2001), and *You Were Always Mom's Favorite!* (2009), the last about communication between sisters.

But What Do You Mean?

Why do men and women so often communicate badly, if at all? This question has motivated much of Tannen's research and writing, including the essay here. Excerpted in *Redbook* magazine from Tannen's book *Talking from 9 to 5* (1994), "But What Do You Mean?" classifies the conversational areas where men and women have the most difficulty communicating in the workplace.

Conversation is a ritual. We say things that seem obviously the thing to say, without thinking of the literal meaning of our words, any more than we expect the question "How are you?" to call forth a detailed account of aches and pains.

Unfortunately, women and men often have different ideas about what's appropriate, different ways of speaking. Many of the conversational rituals common among women are designed to take the other person's feelings into account, while many of the conversational rituals common among men are designed to maintain the one-up position, or at least avoid appearing one-down. As a result, when men and women interact — especially at work — it's often women who are at the disadvantage. Because women are not trying to avoid the one-down position, that is unfortunately where they may end up.

Here, the biggest areas of miscommunication.

1. Apologies

Women are often told they apologize too much. The reason they're told to stop doing it is that, to many men, apologizing seems synonymous with putting oneself down. But there are many times when "I'm sorry" isn't self-deprecating, or even an apology; it's an automatic way of keeping both speakers on an equal footing. For example, a well-known columnist once interviewed me and gave me her phone number in case I needed to call her back. I misplaced the number and had to go through the newspaper's main switchboard. When our conversation was winding down and we'd both made ending-type remarks, I added, "Oh, I almost forgot—I lost your direct number, can I get it again?" "Oh, I'm sorry," she came back instantly, even though she had done nothing wrong and *I* was the one who'd lost the number. But I understood she wasn't really apologizing; she was just automatically reassuring me she had no intention of denying me her number.

Even when "I'm sorry" *is* an apology, women often assume it will be the first step in a two-step ritual: I say "I'm sorry" and take half the blame, then you take the other half. At work, it might go something like this: 5

> A: When you typed this letter, you missed this phrase I inserted.
>
> B: Oh, I'm sorry. I'll fix it.
>
> A: Well, I wrote it so small it was easy to miss.

When both parties share blame, it's a mutual face-saving device. But if one person, usually the woman, utters frequent apologies and the other doesn't, she ends up looking as if she's taking the blame for mishaps that aren't her fault. When she's only partially to blame, she looks entirely in the wrong.   6

I recently sat in on a meeting at an insurance company where the sole woman, Helen, said "I'm sorry" or "I apologize" repeatedly. At one point she said, "I'm thinking out loud. I apologize." Yet the meeting was intended to be an informal brainstorming session, and *everyone* was thinking out loud.   7

The reason Helen's apologies stood out was that she was the only person in the room making so many. And the reason I was concerned was that Helen felt the annual bonus she had received was unfair. When I interviewed her colleagues, they said that Helen was one of the best and most productive workers—yet she got one of the smallest bonuses. Although the problem might have been outright sexism, I suspect her speech style, which differs from that of her male colleagues, masks her competence.   8

Unfortunately, not apologizing can have its price too. Since so many women use ritual apologies, those who don't may be seen as hard-edged. What's important is to be aware of how often you say you're sorry (and why), and to monitor your speech based on the reaction you get.   9

2. Criticism

A woman who cowrote a report with a male colleague was hurt when she read a rough draft to him and he leapt into a critical response—"Oh, that's   10 too dry! You have to make it snappier!" She herself would have been more likely to say, "That's a really good start. Of course, you'll want to make it a little snappier when you revise."

Whether criticism is given straight or softened is often a matter of convention. In general, women use more softeners. I noticed this difference when talking to an editor about an essay I'd written. While going over changes she wanted to make, she said, "There's one more thing. I know you may not agree with me. The reason I noticed the problem is that your other points are so lucid and elegant." She went on hedging for several more sentences until I put her out of her misery: "Do you want to cut that part?" I asked—and of course she did. But I appreciated her tentativeness. In contrast, another editor (a man) I once called summarily rejected my idea for an article by barking, "Call me when you have something new to say."

Those who are used to ways of talking that soften the impact of criticism may find it hard to deal with the right-between-the-eyes style. It has its own logic, however, and neither style is intrinsically better. People who prefer criticism given straight are operating on an assumption that feelings aren't involved: "Here's the dope. I know you're good; you can take it."

3. Thank-Yous

A woman manager I know starts meetings by thanking everyone for coming, even though it's clearly their job to do so. Her "thank-you" is simply a ritual.

A novelist received a fax from an assistant in her publisher's office; it contained suggested catalog copy for her book. She immediately faxed him her suggested changes and said, "Thanks for running this by me," even though her contract gave her the right to approve all copy. When she thanked the assistant, she fully expected him to reciprocate: "Thanks for giving me such a quick response." Instead, he said, "You're welcome." Suddenly, rather than an equal exchange of pleasantries, she found herself positioned as the recipient of a favor. This made her feel like responding, "Thanks for nothing!"

Many women use "thanks" as an automatic conversation starter and closer; there's nothing literally to say thank you for. Like many rituals typical of women's conversation, it depends on the goodwill of the other to restore the balance. When the other speaker doesn't reciprocate, a woman may feel like someone on a seesaw whose partner abandoned his end. Instead of balancing in the air, she has plopped to the ground, wondering how she got there.

4. Fighting

Many men expect the discussion of ideas to be a ritual fight — explored   16
through verbal opposition. They state their ideas in the strongest possible
terms, thinking that if there are weaknesses someone will point them out, and
by trying to argue against those objections, they will see how well their ideas
hold up.

Those who expect their own ideas to be challenged will respond to anoth-   17
er's ideas by trying to poke holes and find weak links — as a way *of helping*. The
logic is that when you are challenged you will rise to the occasion: Adrenaline makes your mind sharper; you get ideas and insights you would not have
thought of without the spur of battle.

But many women take this approach as a personal attack. Worse, they   18
find it impossible to do their best work in such a contentious environment. If
you're not used to ritual fighting, you begin to hear criticism of your ideas as
soon as they are formed. Rather than making you think more clearly, it makes
you doubt what you know. When you state your ideas, you hedge in order to
fend off potential attacks. Ironically, this is more likely to *invite* attack because
it makes you look weak.

Although you may never enjoy verbal sparring, some women find it help-   19
ful to learn how to do it. An engineer who was the only woman among four
men in a small company found that as soon as she learned to argue she was
accepted and taken seriously. A doctor attending a hospital staff meeting
made a similar discovery. She was becoming more and more angry with a male
colleague who'd loudly disagreed with a point she'd made. Her better judgment told her to hold her tongue, to avoid making an enemy of this powerful
senior colleague. But finally she couldn't hold it in any longer, and she rose
to her feet and delivered an impassioned attack on his position. She sat down
in a panic, certain she had permanently damaged her relationship with him.
To her amazement, he came up to her afterward and said, "That was a great
rebuttal. I'm really impressed. Let's go out for a beer after work and hash out
our approaches to this problem."

5. Praise

A manager I'll call Lester had been on his new job six months when he   20
heard that the women reporting to him were deeply dissatisfied. When he
talked to them about it, their feelings erupted; two said they were on the verge
of quitting because he didn't appreciate their work, and they didn't want to
wait to be fired. Lester was dumbfounded: He believed they were doing a fine
job. Surely, he thought, he had said nothing to give them the impression he
didn't like their work. And indeed he hadn't. That was the problem. He had

said *nothing*—and the women assumed he was following the adage "If you can't say something nice, don't say anything." He thought he was showing confidence in them by leaving them alone.

Men and women have different habits in regard to giving praise. For 21 example, Deirdre and her colleague William both gave presentations at a conference. Afterward, Deirdre told William, "That was a great talk!" He thanked her. Then she asked, "What did you think of mine?" and he gave her a lengthy and detailed critique. She found it uncomfortable to listen to his comments. But she assured herself that he meant well, and that his honesty was a signal that she, too, should be honest when he asked for a critique of his performance. As a matter of fact, she had noticed quite a few ways in which he could have improved his presentation. But she never got a chance to tell him because he never asked—and she felt put down. The worst part was that it seemed she had only herself to blame, since she *had* asked what he thought of her talk.

But had she really asked for his critique? The truth is, when she asked 22 for his opinion, she was expecting a compliment, which she felt was more or less required following anyone's talk. When he responded with criticism, she figured, "Oh, he's playing 'Let's critique each other'"—not a game she'd initiated, but one which she was willing to play. Had she realized he was going to criticize her and not ask her to reciprocate, she would never have asked in the first place.

It would be easy to assume that Deirdre was insecure, whether she was 23 fishing for a compliment or soliciting a critique. But she was simply talking automatically, performing one of the many conversational rituals that allow us to get through the day. William may have sincerely misunderstood Deirdre's intention—or may have been unable to pass up a chance to one-up her when given the opportunity.

6. Complaints

"Troubles talk" can be a way to establish rapport with a colleague. You 24 complain about a problem (which shows that you are just folks) and the other person responds with a similar problem (which puts you on equal footing). But while such commiserating is common among women, men are likely to hear it as a request to *solve* the problem.

One woman told me she would frequently initiate what she thought would 25 be pleasant complaint-airing sessions at work. She'd talk about situations that bothered her just to talk about them, maybe to understand them better. But her male office mate would quickly tell her how she could improve the situation. This left her feeling condescended to and frustrated. She was delighted to see this very impasse in a section in my book *You Just Don't Understand*, and showed it to him. "Oh," he said, "I see the problem. How can we solve it?" Then they both laughed, because it had happened again: He short-circuited the detailed discussion she'd hoped for and cut to the chase of finding a solution.

Sometimes the consequences of complaining are more serious: A man might take a woman's lighthearted griping literally, and she can get a reputation as a chronic malcontent. Furthermore, she may be seen as not up to solving the problems that arise on the job.   26

7. Jokes

I heard a man call in to a talk show and say, "I've worked for two women and neither one had a sense of humor. You know, when you work with men, there's a lot of joking and teasing." The show's host and the guest (both women) took his comment at face value and assumed the women this man worked for were humorless. The guest said, "Isn't it sad that women don't feel comfortable enough with authority to see the humor?" The host said, "Maybe when more women are in authority roles, they'll be more comfortable with power." But although the women this man worked for *may* have taken themselves too seriously, it's just as likely that they each had a terrific sense of humor, but maybe the humor wasn't the type he was used to. They may have been like the woman who wrote to me: "When I'm with men, my wit or cleverness seems inappropriate (or lost!) so I don't bother. When I'm with my women friends, however, there's no hold on puns or cracks and my humor is fully appreciated."   27

The types of humor women and men tend to prefer differ. Research has shown that the most common form of humor among men is razzing, teasing, and mock-hostile attacks, while among women it's self-mocking. Women often mistake men's teasing as genuinely hostile. Men often mistake women's mock self-deprecation as truly putting themselves down.   28

Women have told me they were taken more seriously when they learned to joke the way the guys did. For example, a teacher who went to a national conference with seven other teachers (mostly women) and a group of administrators (mostly men) was annoyed that the administrators always found reasons to leave boring seminars, while the teachers felt they had to stay and take notes. One evening, when the group met at a bar in the hotel, the principal asked her how one such seminar had turned out. She retorted, "As soon as you left, it got much better." He laughed out loud at her response. The playful insult appealed to the men—but there was a trade-off. The women seemed to back off from her after this. (Perhaps they were put off by her using joking to align herself with the bosses.)   29

There is no "right" way to talk. When problems arise, the culprit may be   30
style differences—and *all* styles will at times fail with others who don't share
or understand them, just as English won't do you much good if you try to speak
to someone who knows only French. If you want to get your message across,
it's not a question of being "right"; it's a question of using language that's
shared—or at least understood.

For a reading quiz, sources on Deborah Tannen, and annotated links to further read-
ings on gender differences in communication, visit **bedfordstmartins.com/**
thebedfordreader.

Journal Writing

Tannen's ANECDOTE about the newspaper columnist (par. 4) illustrates that much of
what we say is purely automatic. Do you excuse yourself when you bump into inanimate objects? When someone says, "Have a good trip," do you answer, "You, too," even if
the other person isn't going anywhere? Do you find yourself overusing certain words or
phrases such as "like" or "you know"? Pay close attention to these kinds of verbal tics
in your own and others' speech. Over the course of a few days, note as many of them
as you can in your journal. (To take your journal writing further, see "From Journal to
Essay" on the following page.)

Questions on Meaning

1. What is Tannen's PURPOSE in writing this essay? What does she hope it will
   accomplish?
2. What does Tannen mean when she writes, "Conversation is a ritual" (par. 1)?
3. What does Tannen see as the fundamental difference between men's and
   women's conversational strategies?
4. Why is "You're welcome" not always an appropriate response to "Thank you"?

Questions on Writing Strategy

1. This essay has a large cast of characters: twenty-three to be exact. What function
   do these characters serve? How does Tannen introduce them to the reader? Does
   she describe them in sufficient detail?
2. Whom does Tannen see as her primary AUDIENCE? ANALYZE her use of the pronoun *you* in paragraphs 9 and 19. Whom does she seem to be addressing here?
   Why?

3. Analyze how Tannen develops the category of apologies in paragraphs 4–9. Where does she use EXAMPLE, DEFINITION, and COMPARISON AND CONTRAST?
4. How does Tannen's DESCRIPTION of a columnist as "well-known" (par. 4) contribute to the effectiveness of her example?
5. **OTHER METHODS** For each of her seven areas of miscommunication, Tannen compares and contrasts male and female communication styles and strategies. SUMMARIZE the main source of misunderstanding in each area.

Questions on Language

1. What is the EFFECT of "I put her out of her misery" (par. 11)? What does this phrase usually mean?
2. What does Tannen mean by a "right-between-the-eyes style" (par. 12)? What is the FIGURE OF SPEECH involved here?
3. What is the effect of Tannen's use of figurative verbs, such as "barking" (par. 11) and "erupted" (20)? Find at least one other example of the use of a verb in a non-literal sense.
4. Look up any of the following words whose meanings you are unsure of: synonymous, self-deprecating (par. 4); lucid, tentativeness (11); intrinsically (12); reciprocate (14); adrenaline, spur (17); contentious, hedge (18); sparring, rebuttal (19); adage (20); soliciting (23); commiserating (24); initiate, condescended, impasse (25); chronic, malcontent (26); razzing (28); retorted (29).

Suggestions for Writing

1. **FROM JOURNAL TO ESSAY** Write an essay classifying the examples from your journal entry into categories of your own devising. You might sort out the examples by context ("phone blunders," "faulty farewells"), by purpose ("nervous tics," "space fillers"), or by some other principle of classification. Given your subject matter, you might want to adopt a humorous TONE.
2. How well does your style of communication conform to that of your gender as described by Tannen? Write a short essay about a specific communication problem or misunderstanding you have had with someone of the opposite sex (sibling, friend, parent, significant other). How well does Tannen's differentiation of male and female communication styles account for your particular problem?
3. How true do you find Tannen's assessment of miscommunication between the sexes? Consider the conflicts you have observed between your parents, among fellow students or coworkers, in fictional portrayals in books and movies. You could also go beyond your personal experiences and observations by researching the opinions of other experts (linguists, psychologists, sociologists, and so on). Write an essay confirming or questioning Tannen's GENERALIZATIONS, backing up your (and perhaps others') views with your own examples.
4. **CRITICAL WRITING** Tannen insists that "neither [communication] style is intrinsically better" (par. 12), that "There is no 'right' way to talk" (30). What do you make of this refusal to take sides in the battle of the sexes? Is Tannen always successful? Is absolute neutrality possible, or even desirable, when it comes to such divisive issues?

5. **CONNECTIONS**   What pictures of men and women emerge from Tannen's essay and from Dave Barry's "Batting Clean-Up and Striking Out" (p. 261)? In an essay, DEFINE each sex as portrayed by these two authors, and then agree or disagree with the definitions. Support your opinions with examples from your own observations and experience.

Deborah Tannen on Writing

Though Deborah Tannen's "But What Do You Mean?" is written for a general audience, Tannen is a linguistics scholar who does considerable academic writing. One debate among scholarly writers is whether it is appropriate to incorporate one's experiences and biases into academic writing, especially given the goal of objectivity in conducting and reporting research. The October 1996 *PMLA (Publications of the Modern Language Association)* printed a discussion of the academic uses of the personal, with contributions from more than two dozen scholars. Tannen's comments, excerpted here, focused on the first-person *I*.

When I write academic prose, I use the first person, and I instruct my students to do the same. The principle that researchers should acknowledge their participation in their work is an outgrowth of a humanistic approach to linguistic analysis. . . . Understanding discourse is not a passive act of decoding but a creative act of imagining a scene (composed of people engaged in culturally recognizable activities) within which the ideas being talked about have meaning. The listener's active participation in sense making both results from and creates interpersonal involvement. For researchers to deny their involvement in their interpreting of discourse would be a logical and ethical violation of this framework. . . .

[O]bjectivity in the analysis of interactions is impossible anyway. Whether they took part in the interaction or not, researchers identify with one or another speaker, are put off or charmed by the styles of participants. This one reminds you of a cousin you adore; that one sounds like a neighbor you despise. Researchers are human beings, not atomic particles or chemical elements. . . .

Another danger of claiming objectivity rather than acknowledging and correcting for subjectivity is that scholars who don't reveal their participation in interactions they analyze risk the appearance of hiding it. "Following is an exchange that occurred between a professor and a student," I have read in articles in my field. The speakers are identified as "A" and "B." The reader is not told that the professor, A (of course the professor is A and the student

B), is the author. Yet that knowledge is crucial to contextualizing the author's interpretation. Furthermore, the impersonal designations A and B are another means of constructing a false objectivity. They obscure the fact that human interaction is being analyzed, and they interfere with the reader's understanding. The letters replace what in the author's mind are names and voices and personas that are the basis for understanding the discourse. Readers, given only initials, are left to scramble for understanding by imagining people in place of letters.

Avoiding self-reference by using the third person also results in the depersonalization of knowledge. Knowledge and understanding do not occur in abstract isolation. They always and only occur among people. . . . Denying that scholarship is a personal endeavor entails a failure to understand and correct for the inevitable bias that human beings bring to all their enterprises.

For Discussion

1. In arguing for the use of the first-person *I* in academic prose, Tannen is speaking primarily about its use in her own field, linguistics. From your experience with academic writing, is Tannen's argument applicable to other disciplines as well, such as history, biology, psychology, or government? Why, or why not? What have your teachers in various courses advised you about writing in the first person?

2. Try this experiment on the effects of the first person and third person (*he, she, they*): Write a passage of academic prose in one person or the other. (Tannen's example of professor A and student B can perhaps suggest a direction for your passage, or you may have one already written in a paper you've submitted.) Rewrite the passage in the other person, and ANALYZE the two versions. Does one sound more academic than the other? What are the advantages and disadvantages of each one?

DACHER KELTNER

Dacher Keltner is a social psychologist who studies power, morality, and emotion. He earned a BA from the University of California at Santa Barbara in 1984 and a PhD from Stanford University in 1989. Keltner teaches psychology at the University of California at Berkeley, where he directs the Berkeley Social Interaction Laboratory. In 2001 he founded the Greater Good Research Center, which combines interdisciplinary research with community outreach to help people apply the science of positive emotions to their lives. Keltner is executive editor of the center's magazine, *Greater Good*, and coeditor (with Jeremy Adam Smith and Jason Marsh) of *The Compassionate Instinct: The Science of Human Goodness* (2010), a collection of articles from the magazine. At the forefront of the positive psychology movement, Keltner has presented his research to diverse audiences, including the Dalai Lama. He publishes widely in scientific journals and has received awards for his research and his teaching.

A Vocabulary of Smiles

Keltner is known for his accessible but carefully researched explanations of how and why humans express emotion. His popular book *Born to Be Good* (2009) explores how positivity and altruism, which exist across all cultures, make evolutionary sense. In "A Vocabulary of Smiles," a section from that book, Keltner explains in human and scientific terms how emotion is revealed in two distinct kinds of facial expression: the "service industry" smile and the genuine smile.

Most of Keltner's observations are based on experiments and published studies. Accordingly, he documents each of his sources in a footnote.

During the summer following my freshman year in college, I decided to teach myself classical guitar while living at home in Penryn, California, a tiny rural backwater named after an island in Wales. Two weeks into thick-fingered attempts at "Classical Gas," my mother had had enough. A week later I found myself donning the brown polyester and golden arches insignia of the McDonald's uniform, serving burgers, fries, Chicken McNuggets, and gooey sundaes to sunburned revelers on their way to underaged drinking and debauchery at the rocky rivers in the foothills of the Sierras or the noisy waterskiing lakes. Each and every day at 11:10 AM a middle-aged man arrived, strode to the counter in shoes that made a strange clicking sound, and, with somber brown eyes and Lincolnesque sideburns, placed the same order: four plain hamburgers, with nothing on the gray patties and buns that dissolved upon touch, and a cup of black coffee, which I had to refill a dozen or so times in the span of the thirty-six minutes he reliably took to finish his lunch. He became a Sisyphus-like[1] commentary on my fate: the minimum-wage under-mining of my musical career and the missed opportunities for summertime rev-elry. My manager, a good-hearted, optimistic soul, recognized my deep despair and offered managerial guidance straight out of some McDonald's handbook: Just smile. I felt deeply oppressed, filling the regular customer's Styrofoam cup with another round of coffee, smiling as I delivered his cup of joe.

I can assure you that I was not smiling the smile that evolution has pro-duced, and which we will soon dissect, and which promotes goodwill between individuals. Much more likely, I was emitting the service industry smile, the one that signals that the customer is always right, that the sale should always come first. Sociologist Arlie Hochschild has argued that this smile is part of the emotional labor required of so many service-oriented jobs and the tip of the iceberg of alienation from the fruits of human labor. Research shows that when workers smile in the service industry, for example when greeting customers at a 7-11 counter, customers are more satisfied and actually more likely to consume.[2] As the bottom line is enhanced, however, workers expe-rience a problematic disconnect, Hochschild argues, between the emotions they display to the outer world and the feelings they experience within.[3] This disconnect has parallels to recent studies by my colleague Ann Kring of schizo-phrenics.[4] Contrary to long-standing assumptions about schizophrenia and flat affect, schizophrenics have been shown to feel the emotions that you and I feel but not to express them in the face. Service industry jobs produce a form of schizophrenia: We may experience feelings of emptiness and quiet frustra-tion, or a deep ennui, but we display to the world the smile of satisfaction.

How then can we provide a coherent analysis of a category of behav-iors—smiles—that includes my McD smile as well as the loving smiles of old friends and parents and children? At first glance, the empirical literature on the smile yields similarly paradoxical findings:[5] People have been shown to smile when winning, losing, watching a film of an amputation, eating sweets,

[1] In Greek mythology, Sisyphus is a former king condemned for eternity to roll a boulder up a hill, only to have it roll down again just before reaching the top. —EDS.

[2] For a review of the role of emotion in the workplace, see M. W. Morris and D. Keltner, "How Emotions Work: An Analysis of the Social Functions of Emotional Expression in Nego-tiations," *Review of Organizational Behavior* 22 (2000): 1–50.

[3] A. R. Hochschild, *The Managed Heart: Commercialization of Human Feeling* (Berkeley: University of California Press, 1983).

[4] A. M. Kring, S. L. Kerr, A. D. Smith, and J. M. Neale, "Flat Affect in Schizophrenia Does Not Reflect Diminished Subjective Experience of Emotion," *Journal of Abnormal Psychology* 102 (1993): 507–17; Kring and Neale, "Do Schizophrenics Show a Disjunctive Relationship among Expressive, Experiential, and Psychophysiological Components of Emotion?" *Journal of Abnormal Psychology* 105 (1996): 249–57.

[5] D. Keltner et al., "Facial Expression of Emotion," in *Handbook of Affective Sciences*, ed. R. Davidson, K. Scherer, and H. H. Goldsmith (London: Oxford University Press, 2003), 415–32.

facing adversaries, experiencing pain, feeling affection toward loved ones. The answer is provided by Paul Ekman, and it involves looking away from the lip corners to that wellspring of the soul—the eyes.[6]

A vocabulary of smiles comes sharply into focus when we consider the activity of the happiness muscle, the orbicularis oculi. This muscle surrounds the eyes and when contracted leads to the raising of the cheek, the pouching of the lower eyelid, and the appearance of those dreaded crow's-feet—the most visible sign of happiness—which the Botox industry is trying to wipe out of the vocabulary of human expression. People may think they look prettier following Botox injections, but their partners will receive fewer clues to their joy, love, and devotion.

Ekman has called smiles that involve the activation of the zygomatic major muscle and the orbicularis oculi the Duchenne or D smile, in honor of the French neuroanatomist Guillaume Benjamin Amand Duchenne (1806–1875), who first discovered the visible traces of the activity of orbicularis oculi. Smiles that do not involve the activity of the happiness muscle, the orbicularis oculi, are sensibly known as non-Duchenne or non-D smiles. To try your hand at this subtle distinction between Duchenne and non-Duchenne smiles, see if you can detect which is which in the photographs on the next page (answers provided on page 450).

Dozens of scientific studies speak to the importance of parsing the heterogeneous category of smiles according to the activity of the orbicularis oculi muscle. Duchenne smiles differ morphologically in many ways from the many other smiles that do not involve the action of the orbicularis oculi muscle.[7] They tend to last between one and five seconds, and the lip corners tend to be raised to equal degrees on both sides of the face. Smiles missing the action of the orbicularis oculi and likely masking negative states can be on the face for very brief periods (250 milliseconds) or very long periods (a lifetime of polite smiling by oppressed airline stewardesses and fast-food servers). Non-D smiles are more likely to be asymmetrical in the intensity of muscle firing on the two sides of the face.

D smiles tend to be associated with activity in the left anterior portion of the frontal lobes, a region of the brain preferentially activated during positive emotional experiences.[8] Non-D smiles, in contrast, are associated with activity

---

[6] M. Frank, P. Ekman, and W. V. Friesen, "Behavioral Markers and Recognizability of the Smile of Enjoyment," *Journal of Personality and Social Psychology* 64 (1993): 83–93.

[7] Ibid., 83.

[8] Neuroscientist Richard Davidson has made the persuasive case that positive emotions tend to activate regions of the brain on the left side of the frontal lobes, because these regions enable the individual to approach rewards. P. Ekman, R. Davidson, and W. V. Friesen, "The Duchenne Smile: Emotional Expression and Brain Physiology II," *Journal of Personality and Social Psychology* 58 (1996): 342–53.

Smile Quiz: Examples of Duchenne and non-Duchenne smiles

in the right anterior portion of the brain—a region associated with the activation of negative emotion. When a ten-month-old is approached by his or her mother, the face lights up with the D smile; when a stranger approaches, the same infant greets the approaching adult with a wary non-D smile.[9]

And importantly, several studies have found that Duchenne and non-Duchenne smiles, brief two- to three-second displays differing only in the activation of the orbicularis oculi muscle, map onto entirely different emotional experiences. For example, in a long-standing collaboration with my

[9]R. Davidson and N. A. Fox, "Frontal Brain Asymmetry Predicts Infants' Response to Maternal Separation," *Journal of Abnormal Psychology* 98 (1989): 127–31.

friend George Bonanno, a pioneer in the study of trauma . . . we interviewed middle-aged adults six months after their deceased spouse had passed away.[10] These individuals were asked to describe their relationship with their deceased spouse for six minutes. I spent a summer coding the occurrence of Duchenne and non-Duchenne smiles from videotapes of these narratives. We then related measures of bereaved participants' D and non-D smiles to their reports of how much enjoyment, anger, distress, and fear they felt during the interview, which we gathered immediately after the participants had finished talking about their deceased spouse.

Portrayed in the table below are the correlations between how much participants showed these brief Duchenne and non-Duchenne smiles and their ensuing self-reports of emotion gathered moments later. Positive scores indicate that the more they showed the particular smile during the six-minute interview, the more they subsequently felt the particular emotion listed on the left. Negative correlation values reveal the opposite, that the more the participant smiled in Duchenne or non-Duchenne fashion, the less of the emotion they felt. Asterisks indicate that the observed correlation was statistically significant, and not likely produced by chance.

9

	Duchenne Smiles	Non-Duchenne Smiles
Enjoyment	.35*	−.25*
Anger	−.28*	.09
Distress	−.49*	−.16
Fear	−.31*	.04

What is impressive about these data is that very brief Duchenne smiles involving the activity of the orbicularis oculi were associated with increased feelings of enjoyment during the conversation, and reduced feelings of anger, distress, and fear. Non-Duchenne smiles were associated with the opposite pattern of experience — reduced feelings of enjoyment and none of the negative emotions.

10

The Duchenne/non-Duchenne distinction is the first big distinction in a taxonomy of different smiles. One kind of smile involves the orbicularis oculi muscle, and accompanies high spirits and goodwill. When other movements are added to the D smile, people can communicate different positive states like love, awe, and desire. A second kind of smile is the non-D smile,

11

[10] D. Keltner and G. A. Bonanno, "A Study of Laughter and Dissociation: The Distinct Correlates of Laughter and Smiling during Bereavement," *Journal of Personality and Social Psychology* 73 (1997): 687–702.

which reflects the attempt to mask some underlying negative state. In *Emotions Revealed*, Ekman deconstructed the non-D smile into a dizzying array of smiles, including pained smiles, fearful smiles, contemptuous smiles, and submissive smiles.[11]

Twenty-five summers ago, as I served that reliable customer his four burgers and coffee, I am absolutely confident that not a trace of orbicularis oculi activity was to be seen on my late-pubescent face. I would have been an easy case study for Ekman; it would have been simple for him to reveal which negative states—despair, frustration, contempt—I was attempting to hide with my halfhearted McD smile. Off work, and at last with friends jumping off rocks into alpine rivers, I am sure the D smiles would have washed over my face. Studies inspired by Ekman's analysis would reveal that these D smiles are a glue of social life, and a provenance of the camaraderie that make me nostalgic for those carefree times.

12

Answers to the smile quiz on page 448: For the first gentleman, the D smile is on the right; for the second, it's on the left.

For a reading quiz, sources on Dacher Keltner, and annotated links to further readings on emotional intelligence, visit bedfordstmartins.com/thebedfordreader.

Journal Writing

How did you do on the photo quiz on page 448? Could you tell the difference between a Duchenne and a non-Duchenne smile? Did you need Keltner's explanations to solve the puzzle? Why, or why not? Write in your journal about your ability to interpret facial expressions. How skilled are you in general at reading other people's emotions? How do you explain your ability? (To take your journal writing further, see "From Journal to Essay" on the facing page.)

Questions on Meaning

1. What is Keltner's reason for distinguishing between different kinds of smiles? What does he hope readers will learn from his research?

[11]P. Ekman, *Emotions Revealed* (New York: Owl, 2004).

2. What is an "orbicularis oculi" (par. 4)? Why is it significant to Keltner's classification scheme?
3. Interpret the table on page 449. What point does Keltner make with these data?
4. How would you summarize Keltner's THESIS? Where in the essay does he state it most directly?

Questions on Writing Strategy

1. Why does Keltner begin and end with a personal ANECDOTE about a job he had at McDonald's during college? What is the EFFECT of these paragraphs?
2. "A Vocabulary of Smiles" presents a binary classification (see p. 401). In your own words, explain the distinction between Duchenne smiles and non-Duchenne smiles.
3. Take a close look at Keltner's list of sources. From what discipline, or disciplines, does he take most of his information? Why do you suppose he cites several of his own previous publications? Do his sources seem appropriate? Why, or why not?
4. **OTHER METHODS** What is a "service industry smile"? Why does Keltner discuss its CAUSES AND EFFECTS at such length?

Questions on Language

1. How would you describe Keltner's DICTION? What do his word choices reveal about the way he imagines his AUDIENCE?
2. What does Keltner mean by "alienation from the fruits of human labor" (par. 2)? Do you recognize the ALLUSION he is making with this phrase?
3. Look up any of the following words whose meanings you are unsure of: backwater, insignia, revelers, debauchery (par. 1); schizophrenia, ennui (2); empirical, paradoxical (3); zygomatic, neuroanatomist (5); parsing, heterogeneous, morphologically (6); anterior (7); bereaved (8); correlations, ensuing (9); taxonomy, deconstructed, contemptuous (11); pubescent, provenance, camaraderie (12).

Suggestions for Writing

1. **FROM JOURNAL TO ESSAY** In your favorite magazine, select a half dozen or so photographs of smiling faces, from both the advertisements and any article illustrations. Considering the context of each smile—for instance, are the people working? playing? eating? arguing? flirting?—determine what emotions they suggest to you. Then, drawing on your journal entry, write an essay that classifies them by expanding on Keltner's classification system. Which smiles seem sincere, and which do not? What subcategories might you propose? How does the context of each smile determine your categorization and affect your interpretations of the images?
2. The ability to read other people's moods is a key element of emotional intelligence, a relatively new concept that is often evoked in the fields of psychology and education to help people improve their work and life skills. Search your library catalog and databases for books and articles about emotional intelligence;

then write a brief DEFINITION of the concept. Consider as well how developed your own emotional intelligence skills are and how you could improve them.

3. Like other social scientists, psychologists work under a code of ethics that specifies how they may and may not treat the people they are studying. Read about this subject, perhaps starting with the Human Research Protections page of the American Psychological Association (*apa.org/research/responsible/human/index.aspx*) or with the psychology department or Institutional Review Board (IRB) at your school. Then write an essay in which you explain the ethical obligations of research psychologists.

4. **CRITICAL WRITING** Write an essay that examines the paragraph development in Keltner's essay. How thoroughly does Keltner explain each category of his classification? What kinds of EVIDENCE and detail does he offer to support his ideas? Has he provided enough information to help readers clearly see the distinctions between the two kinds of smiles he identifies? Use specific EXAMPLES from the essay to support your conclusions.

5. **CONNECTIONS** Both Keltner and Bella DePaulo, in "The Myth of Doomed Kids" (p. 379), SYNTHESIZE information from scholarly studies to discover new meaning in their subjects, but their approaches are markedly different. Write an essay in which you analyze how each author adapts his or her TONE for both AUDIENCE and PURPOSE, using quotations from both essays to support your analysis. Which essay, in your opinion, is more successful? Why?

ADDITIONAL WRITING TOPICS
Classification

Write an essay by the method of classification, in which you sort one of the following subjects into categories of your own. Make clear your PURPOSE in classifying and the basis of your classification. Explain each class with DEFINITIONS and EXAMPLES (you may find it helpful to make up a name for each group). Check your classes to be sure they neither gap nor overlap.

1. Commuters, or people who use public transportation
2. Environmental problems or environmental solutions
3. Web sites
4. Vegetarians
5. Talk shows
6. The ills or benefits of city life
7. The recordings you own
8. Families
9. Stand-up comedians
10. Present-day styles of marriage
11. Vacations
12. College students today
13. Movies for teenagers or men or women
14. Waiters you'd never tip
15. Comic strips
16. Movie monsters
17. Sports announcers
18. Inconsiderate people
19. Radio stations
20. Mall millers (people who mill around malls)

11

CAUSE AND EFFECT

Asking Why

◀ **Cause and effect in a cartoon**

With simple drawings and perhaps a few words, editorial car-
toonists often make striking comments on events and trends. This
cartoon by Mike Luckovich, published in the *Atlanta Journal
Constitution*, proposes a disturbing effect of a common cause.
What is the cause? What, according to Luckovich, is the effect?
How does the content of both text messages in the cartoon
reinforce Luckovich's position? What other effects might result
from the cause depicted here? Do you agree or disagree with
Luckovich's view? Why?

THE METHOD

Press the button of a doorbell and, inside the house or apartment, chimes sound. Why? Because the touch of your finger on the button closed an electrical circuit. But why did you ring the doorbell? Because you were sent by your dispatcher: You are a bill collector calling on a customer whose payments are three months overdue.

The touch of your finger on the button is the *immediate cause* of the chimes: the event that precipitates another. That you were ordered by your dispatcher to go ring the doorbell is a *remote cause:* an underlying, more basic reason for the event, not apparent to an observer. Probably, ringing the doorbell will lead to some results: The door will open, and you may be given a check—or have the door slammed in your face.

To figure out reasons and results is to use the method of CAUSE AND EFFECT. Either to explain events or to argue for one version of them, you try to answer the question "Why did something happen?" or "What were the consequences?" or "What might be the consequences?" As part of answering such a question, you use DIVISION or ANALYSIS (Chap. 9) to separate the flow of events into causes.

Seeking causes, you can ask, for example, "Why do birds migrate?" "What has caused sales of Detroit-made cars to pick up (or decline) lately?" "What were the principal causes of America's involvement in the war in Vietnam?" Looking for effects, you can ask, "What have been the effects of the birth-control pill on the typical American family?" "What impact have handheld computers had on the nursing profession?" You can look to a possible future and ask, "Of what use might a course in psychology be to me if I become an office manager?" "Suppose an asteroid the size of a sofa were to strike Philadelphia—what would be the probable consequences?"

Don't, by the way, confuse cause and effect with the method of PROCESS ANALYSIS (Chap. 8). Some process analysis essays, too, deal with happenings; but they focus more on repeatable events (rather than unique ones) and they explain *how* (rather than why) something happened. If you were explaining the process by which the doorbell rings, you might break the happening into stages—(1) the finger presses the button; (2) the circuit closes; (3) the current travels the wire; (4) the chimes make music—and you'd set forth the process in detail. But why did the finger press the button? What happened because the doorbell rang? To answer those questions, you need cause and effect.

In trying to explain why things happen, you can expect to find a whole array of causes—interconnected, perhaps, like the strands of a spiderweb. You'll want to do an honest job of unraveling, and this may take time. For a jury to acquit or convict an accused slayer, weeks of testimony from witnesses, detectives, and psychiatrists may be required, then days of deliberation. It took a great historian, Jakob Burckhardt, most of his lifetime to set forth a few reasons for the dawn of the Italian Renaissance. To be sure, juries must take great care when a life hangs in the balance; and Burckhardt, after all, was writing an immense book. To produce a college essay, you don't have forty years; but before you start to write, you will need to devote extra time and thought to seeing which facts are the causes, and which matter most.

To answer the questions "Why?" and "What followed as a result?" may sometimes be hard, but it can be satisfying—even illuminating. Indeed, to seek causes and effects is one way for the mind to discover order in a reality that otherwise might seem random and pointless.

THE PROCESS

Subjects, Purposes, and Theses

The method of cause and effect tends to suggest itself: If you have a subject and soon start thinking "Why?" or "What results?" or "What if?" then you are on the way to analyzing causation. Your subject may be impersonal—like a change in voting patterns or the failure or success of a business—or it may be quite personal. Indeed, an excellent cause-and-effect paper may be written on a subject very near to you. You can ask yourself why you behaved in a certain way at a certain moment. You can examine the reasons for your current beliefs and attitudes. Writing such a paper, you might happen upon a truth you hadn't realized before.

Whether your subject is personal or impersonal, make sure it is manageable: You should be able to get to the bottom of it, given the time and information available. For a 500-word essay due Thursday, the causes of teenage rebellion would be a less feasible topic than why a certain thirteen-year-old you know ran away from home.

Before rushing to list causes or effects, stop a moment to consider what your PURPOSE might be in writing. Much of the time you'll seek simply to explain what did or might occur, discovering and laying out the connections as clearly and accurately as you can. But when reasonable people could disagree over causes or effects, you will want to go further, arguing for one interpretation over others. You'll still need to be clear and accurate in presenting your interpretation, but you'll also need to treat the others fairly. (See Chap. 13 on argument and persuasion.)

When you have a grip on your subject and your purpose, you can draft a tentative THESIS STATEMENT to express the main point of your analysis. The statement may be hypothetical at this stage, before you have gathered

EVIDENCE and sorted out the complexity of causes and effects. Still, a statement framed early can help direct your later thinking and research.

The essays in this chapter provide good examples of thesis statements that put across, concisely, the author's central finding about causes and effects. Here are a few examples:

> A bill like the one we've just passed [to ban imports from factories that use child labor] is of no use unless it goes hand in hand with programs that will offer a new life to these newly released children.
>
> —Chitra Divakaruni, "Live Free and Starve"

> To begin to solve the problem [of the illegal drug trade], we need to understand what's happening in drug-source countries, how the United States can and can't help there, and what, instead, can be done at home.
>
> —Marie Javdani, "*Plata o Plomo:* Silver or Lead"

> [Because of the Internet,] we are abandoning the tyranny of the top [media producers] and becoming a niche nation again, defined not by our geography but by our interests.
>
> —Chris Anderson, "The Rise and Fall of the Hit"

Causal Relations

Your toughest job in writing a cause-and-effect essay may be figuring out what caused what. Sometimes one event will appear to trigger another, and it in turn will trigger yet another, and another still, in an order we call a *causal chain*. A classic example of such a chain is set forth in a Mother Goose rhyme:

> For want of a nail the shoe was lost,
> For want of a shoe the horse was lost,
> For want of a horse the rider was lost,
> For want of a rider the battle was lost,
> For want of a battle the kingdom was lost—
> And all for the want of a nail.

In reality, causes are seldom so easy to find as that missing nail: They tend to be many and complicated. A battle may be lost for more than one reason. Perhaps the losing general had fewer soldiers and had a blinding hangover the morning he mapped out his battle strategy. Perhaps winter set in, expected reinforcements failed to arrive, and a Joan of Arc inspired the winning army. The downfall of a kingdom is not to be explained as though it were the toppling of the last domino in a file. Still, one event precedes another in time, and in discerning causes you don't ignore chronological order; you pay attention to it.

When you can see a number of apparent causes, weigh them and assign each a relative importance. Which do you find matter most? Often, you will see that causes are more important or less so: major or minor. If you seek to explain why your small town has fallen on hard times, you might note that two businesses shut down: a factory employing three hundred and a drug-store employing six. The factory's closing is a *major cause*, leading to significant unemployment in the town, while the drugstore's closing is perhaps a *minor cause* — or not a cause at all but an effect. In writing about the causes, you would emphasize the factory and mention the drugstore only briefly if at all.

When seeking remote causes, look only as far back as necessary. Explaining your town's misfortunes, you might see the factory's closing as the immediate cause. You could show what caused the shutdown: a dispute between union and management. You might even go back to the cause of the dispute (announced firings) and the cause of the firings (loss of sales to a competitor). A paper showing effects might work in the other direction, moving from the factory closing to its impact on the town: unemployment, the closing of stores (including the drugstore), people packing up and moving away.

Two cautions about causal relations are in order here. One is to beware of confusing coincidence with cause. In the logical FALLACY called *post hoc* (short for the Latin *post hoc, ergo propter hoc,* "after this, therefore because of this"), one assumes, erroneously, that because A happened before B, A must have caused B. This is the error of the superstitious man who decides that he lost his job because a black cat walked in front of him. Another error is to oversimplify causes by failing to recognize their full number and complexity — claiming, say, that violent crime is simply a result of "all those gangster shows on TV." Avoid such wrong turns in reasoning by patiently looking for evidence before you write, and by giving it careful thought. (For a fuller list of such fallacies, or errors in reasoning, see pp. 554–56.)

Discovery of Causes

To help find causes of actions and events, you can ask yourself a few searching questions. These have been suggested by the work of the literary critic Kenneth Burke:

1. *What act am I trying to explain?*
2. *What is the character, personality, or mental state of whoever acted?*
3. *In what scene or location did the act take place, and in what circumstances?*
4. *What instruments or means did the person use?*
5. *For what purpose did the person act?*

Burke calls these elements a *pentad* (or set of five): the *act*, the *actor*, the *scene*, the *agency*, and the *purpose*. If you were a detective trying to explain why a liquor store burned down, you might ask these questions:

1. *Act:* Was the fire deliberately set by someone, or was there an accident?
2. *Actors:* If the fire was arson, who set it: the store's worried, debt-ridden owner? a mentally disturbed anti-alcohol crusader? a drunk who had been denied a purchase?
3. *Scene:* Was the shop near a church? a mental hospital? a fireworks factory?
4. *Agency, or means of the act:* Was the fire caused by faulty electrical wiring? a carelessly tossed cigarette butt? a flaming torch? rags soaked in kerosene?
5. *Purpose:* If the fire wasn't accidental, was it set to collect insurance? to punish drinkers? to get revenge?

You can further deepen your inquiry by seeing relationships between the terms of the pentad. Ask, for instance, what does the actor have to do with this scene? (Is he or she the neighbor across the street, who has been staring at the liquor shop resentfully for years?)

Don't worry if not all the questions apply, if not all the answers are immediately forthcoming. Burke's pentad isn't meant to be a grim rigmarole; it is a means of discovery, to generate a lot of possible material for you—insights, observations, hunches to pursue. It won't solve each and every human mystery, but sometimes it will helpfully deepen your thought.

Final Word

In stating what you believe to be causes and effects, don't be afraid to voice a well-considered hunch. Your instructor doesn't expect you to write, in a short time, a definitive account of the causes of an event or a belief or a phenomenon—only to write a coherent and reasonable one. To discern all causes—including remote ones—and all effects is beyond the power of any one human mind. Still, admirable and well-informed writers on matters such as politics, economics, and world and national affairs are often canny guessers and brave drawers of inferences. At times, even the most cautious and responsible writer has to leap boldly over a void to strike firm ground on the far side. Consider your evidence. Focus your thinking. Look well before leaping. Then take off.

FOCUS ON CLARITY AND CONCISENESS

While drafting a cause-and-effect analysis, you may need to grope a bit to discover just what you think about the sequence and relative importance of reasons and consequences. Your sentences may grope a bit, too, reflecting your initial confusion or your need to circle around your ideas in order to find them. The following draft passage reveals such difficulties:

> WORDY AND UNCLEAR   Employees often worry about suggestive comments from others. The employee may not only worry but feel the need to discuss the situation with coworkers. One thing that is an effect of sexual harassment, even verbal harassment, in the workplace is that productivity is lost. Plans also need to be made to figure out how to deal with future comments. Engaging in these activities is sure to take time and concentration from work.

Drafting this passage, the writer seems to have built up to the idea about lost productivity (third sentence) after providing support for it in the first two sentences. The fourth sentence then adds more support. And sentences 2–4 all show a writer working out his ideas: Sentence subjects and verbs do not focus on the main actors and actions of the sentences, words repeat unnecessarily, and word groups run longer than needed for clarity.

These problems disappear from the edited version below, which moves the idea of the passage up front, uses subjects and verbs to state what the sentences are about (underlined), and cuts unneeded words.

> CONCISE AND CLEAR   Even verbal sexual <u>harassment</u> in the workplace <u>causes</u> a loss of productivity. Worrying about suggestive comments from others, discussing those comments with coworkers, planning how to deal with future comments—these <u>activities</u> <u>consume</u> time and concentration that a harassed employee could spend on work.

For exercises on clarity and conciseness, visit Exercise Central at
bedfordstmartins.com/thebedfordreader.

CHECKLIST FOR REVISING A CAUSE-AND-EFFECT ESSAY

✔ **SUBJECT**   Have you been able to cover your subject adequately in the time and space available? Should you perhaps narrow the subject so that you can fairly address the important causes and/or effects?

✔ **THESIS**   For your readers' benefit, have you focused your analysis by stating your main idea succinctly in a thesis statement?

✔ **COMPLETENESS**   Have you included all relevant causes or effects? Does your analysis reach back to locate remote causes or forward to locate remote effects?

✔ **CAUSAL RELATIONS**   Have you presented a clear pattern of causes or effects? Have you distinguished the remote from the immediate, the major from the minor?

✔ **ACCURACY AND FAIRNESS**   Have you avoided the *post hoc* fallacy, assuming that A caused B just because it preceded B? Have you also avoided over-simplifying and instead covered causes or effects in all their complexity?

✔ **CLARITY AND CONCISENESS**   Have you edited your draft to foreground your main points and tighten your sentences?

CAUSE AND EFFECT IN PARAGRAPHS

Writing about Television

In the following paragraph, the writer poses and concisely answers a question about the near-absence of soccer from mainstream American TV. The paragraph was written especially for *The Bedford Reader*, but it could serve as a component of a full essay, perhaps one analyzing how television affects sports in general.

Why is it that, despite a growing interest in soccer among American athletes, and despite its ranking as the most popular sport in the world, the major US television networks all but ignore it? Granted, soccer sometimes makes it to the all-sports channels, but mostly it's shut out. The reason stems partly from the basic nature of commercial television, which exists not to inform and entertain but to sell. During most major sporting events on television—football, baseball, basketball, boxing—producers can take advantage of natural interruptions in the action to broadcast sales pitches; or, if the natural breaks occur too infrequently, the producers can contrive time-outs for the sole purpose of airing lucrative commercials. But soccer is played in two solid halves of forty-five minutes each; not even injury to a player is cause for a time-out. How, then, to insert the requisite number of commercial breaks without resorting to false fouls or other questionable tactics? After CBS aired a soccer match in 1967, players reported, according to Stanley Frank, that before the game the referee had instructed them "to stay down every nine minutes." The resulting hue and cry rose all the way to the House Communications Subcommittee. From that day to this, no one has been able to figure out how to screen advertising jingles during a televised soccer game. The result is that most commercial television has treated soccer as if it didn't exist.

Margin notes:

Topic sentence: question to be answered

Analysis of causes

Commercial TV requires commercial breaks

Soccer is played with only one break

Example of failed attempt to adapt soccer to TV

Result: little soccer on TV

Writing in an Academic Discipline

This paragraph from a textbook on American history explains the causes of a "fateful decision" in the 1960s—fateful because, as the authors' text goes on to explain, the decision had grave and far-reaching consequences for the United States.

Many factors played a role in [President Lyndon] Johnson's fateful decision [to escalate the Vietnam War]. But the most obvious explanation is that the new president faced many pressures to expand the American involvement and only a very few to limit it. As the untested successor to a revered and martyred president, he felt obliged to prove his worthiness for the office by continuing the policies of his predecessor. Aid to South Vietnam had been one of the most prominent of those policies. Johnson also felt it necessary to retain in his administration many of the important figures of the Kennedy years. In doing so, he surrounded himself with a group of foreign-policy advisers—Secretary of State Dean Rusk, Secretary of Defense Robert McNamara, National Security Adviser McGeorge Bundy—who strongly believed not only that the United States had an important obligation to resist communism in Vietnam, but that it possessed the ability and resources to make that resistance successful. As a result, Johnson seldom had access to information making clear how difficult the new commitment might become. A compliant Congress raised little protest to, and indeed at one point openly endorsed, Johnson's use of executive powers to lead the nation into war. And for several years at least, public opinion remained firmly behind him—in part because Barry Goldwater's bellicose remarks about the war during the 1964 campaign made Johnson seem by comparison to be a moderate on the issue. Above all, intervention in South Vietnam was fully consistent with nearly twenty years of American foreign policy. An anti-Communist ally was appealing to the United States for assistance; all the assumptions of the containment doctrine seemed to require the nation to oblige. Johnson seemed unconcerned that the government of South Vietnam existed only because the United States had put it there, and that the regime had never succeeded in acquiring the loyalty of its people. Vietnam, he believed, provided a test of American willingness to fight Communist aggression, a test he was determined not to fail.

—Richard N. Current et al., *American History: A Survey*

Topic sentence: summary of causes to be discussed

Causes:
  Need to prove worthiness

Advisers urging involvement and shutting off alternative views

Congressional cooperation

Support of public opinion

Consistency with American foreign policy against Communism

CAUSE AND EFFECT IN A LETTER TO THE EDITOR

As you develop your skills in critical reading, you may find yourself getting particularly involved with at least some of what you read: disagreeing with an author, finding flaws in a writer's reasoning, or wanting to expand on an idea. Many publications give you an opportunity to do just that in a public forum. Most newspapers, magazines, and journals as well as some Web sites solicit and publish letters to the editor.

Unlike the anonymous comments readers may attach to news and opinion articles online, letters to the editor are signed by their authors and screened by editors. To be published, such letters generally must take a calm tone and express ideas rationally. In most cases, the writer refers to the original article or other piece that prompted the letter and responds by agreeing or disagreeing (or a little of both). The point is to add a new perspective and move a conversation forward.

An ardent supporter of her school's track team, Kate Krueger was a sophomore during the team's first winning season in many years. At the end of the season, the student newspaper published a sports column crediting the successes to a new coach. Krueger found this explanation inadequate and wrote her own cause-and-effect analysis in the following letter to the newspaper's editor. Notice that because Krueger actually agreed with the original writer that the coach had helped the team, she acknowledged the coach's contributions while also detailing the other causes she saw at work.

May 2, 2010

To the Editor:

I take issue with Tom Boatz's column that was printed in the April 30 *Weekly*. Boatz attributes the success of this year's track team solely to the new coach, John Barak. I have several close friends who are athletes on the track team, so as an interested observer and fan I believe that Boatz oversimplified the causes of the team's recent success.

> Reason for writing: Original author over-simplified cause-and-effect relationship

To be sure, Coach Barak did improve the training regimen and overall morale, and these have certainly contributed to the winning season. Both Coach Barak and the team members themselves can share credit for an impressive work ethic and a sense of camaraderie unequaled in previous years. However, several factors outside Coach Barak's control were also influential.

> Point of agreement: The new coach was one cause of the team's success

> Thesis statement: Other causes played a role

This year's team gained several phenomenal freshman athletes, such as Kristin Hall, who anchored the 4x400 and 4x800 relays and played

> Other causes:
>   Talented new team members

an integral part in setting several school records, and Eric Asper, who was undefeated in the shot put.

Even more important, and also unmentioned by Tom Boatz, is the college's increased funding for the track program. Last year the school allotted fifty percent more for equipment, and the results have been dramatic. For example, the new vaulting poles are now the correct length and correspond to the weights of the individual athletes, giving them more power and height. Some vaulters have been able to vault as much as a foot higher than their previous records. Similarly, new starting blocks have allowed the team's sprinters to drop valuable seconds off their times.

I agree with Tom Boatz that Coach Barak deserves much credit for the track team's successes. But the athletes do, too, and so does the college for at last supporting its track program.

—KATE KRUEGER '12

Financial support from the college

Examples of positive effects:

Improved vaulting performance

Improved sprinting times

Conclusion summarizes Krueger's analysis

CHITRA DIVAKARUNI

Born in 1956 in Calcutta, India, Chitra Banerjee Divakaruni spent nineteen years in her homeland before immigrating to the United States. She holds a BA from Calcutta University, an MA from Wright State University, and a PhD from the University of California at Berkeley. Her books, often addressing the immigrant experience in America, include the novels *The Mistress of Spice* (1997), *Sister of My Heart* (1999), *The Vine of Desire* (2002), *Queen of Dreams* (2004), and *The Palace of Illusions* (2008); the story collections *Arranged Marriage* (1995) and *The Unknown Errors of Our Lives* (2001); and the poetry collections *Leaving Yuba City* (1997) and *Black Candle* (1991, revised 2000). Divakaruni has received a number of awards for her work, including the Before Columbus Foundation's 1996 American Book Award. She teaches creative writing at the University of Houston and serves on the boards of several organizations that help women and children.

Live Free and Starve

Many of the consumer goods sold in the United States—shoes, clothing, toys, rugs—are made in countries whose labor practices do not meet US standards for safety and fairness. Americans have been horrified at tales of children put to work by force or under contracts (called *indentures*) with the children's parents. Some in the United States government have tried to stop or at least discourage such practices: For instance, the bill Divakaruni cites in her first paragraph, which was signed into law, requires the US Customs Service to issue a detention order on goods that are suspected of having been produced by forced or indentured child labor; and a bill to ban goods made with any kind of child labor has been introduced in Congress every year since 1993. In this essay from *Salon* magazine in 1997, Divakaruni argues that these efforts, however well intentioned they are, mean dreadful consequences for the very people they are designed to protect.

For a different perspective on the effects of globalization, see the next essay, Marie Javdani's "*Plata o Plomo:* Silver or Lead."

Some days back, the House passed a bill that stated that the United States would no longer permit the import of goods from factories where forced or indentured child labor was used. My liberal friends applauded the bill. It was a triumphant advance in the field of human rights. Now children in Third

World countries wouldn't have to spend their days chained to their posts in factories manufacturing goods for other people to enjoy while their childhoods slipped by them. They could be free and happy, like American children.

I am not so sure.   2

It is true that child labor is a terrible thing, especially for those children   3
who are sold to employers by their parents at the age of five or six and have no way to protect themselves from abuse. In many cases it will be decades—perhaps a lifetime, due to the fines heaped upon them whenever they make mistakes—before they can buy back their freedom. Meanwhile these children, mostly employed by rug-makers, spend their days in dark, ill-ventilated rooms doing work that damages their eyes and lungs. They aren't even allowed to stand up and stretch. Each time they go to the bathroom, they suffer a pay cut.

But is this bill, which, if it passes the Senate and is signed by President   4
Clinton, will lead to the unemployment of almost a million children, the answer? If the children themselves were asked whether they would rather work under such harsh conditions or enjoy a leisure that comes without the benefit of food or clothing or shelter, I wonder what their response would be.

It is easy for us in America to make the error of evaluating situations in   5
the rest of the world as though they were happening in this country and propose solutions that make excellent sense—in the context of our society. Even we immigrants, who should know better, have wiped from our minds the memory of what it is to live under the kind of desperate conditions that force a parent to sell his or her child. Looking down from the heights of Maslow's pyramid,[1] it seems inconceivable to us that someone could actually prefer bread to freedom.

When I was growing up in Calcutta, there was a boy who used to work in   6
our house. His name was Nimai, and when he came to us, he must have been about ten or so, just a little older than my brother and I. He'd been brought to our home by his uncle, who lived in our ancestral village and was a field laborer for my grandfather. The uncle explained to my mother that Nimai's parents were too poor to feed their several children, and while his older brothers were already working in the fields and earning their keep, Nimai was too frail to do so. My mother was reluctant to take on a sickly child who might prove more of a burden than a help, but finally she agreed, and Nimai lived and worked in our home for six or seven years. My mother was a good employer—Nimai

---

[1] The psychologist Abraham Maslow (1908–70) proposed a "hierarchy of needs" in the shape of a five-level pyramid with survival needs at the bottom and "self-actualization" and "self-transcendence" at the top. According to Maslow, one must satisfy the needs at each level before moving up to the next. —Eds.

ate the same food that we children did and was given new clothes during Indian New Year, just as we were. In the time between his chores—dusting and sweeping and pumping water from the tube-well and running to the market—my mother encouraged him to learn to read and write. Still, I would not disagree with anyone who says that it was hardly a desirable existence for a child.

But what would life have been like for Nimai if an anti–child-labor law   7 had prohibited my mother from hiring him? Every year, when we went to visit our grandfather in the village, we were struck by the many children we saw by the mud roads, their ribs sticking out through the rags they wore. They trailed after us, begging for a few paise.[2] When the hunger was too much to bear, they stole into the neighbors' fields and ate whatever they could find—raw potatoes, cauliflower, green sugar cane and corn torn from the stalk—even though they knew they'd be beaten for it. Whenever Nimai passed these children, he always walked a little taller. And when he handed the bulk of his earnings over to his father, there was a certain pride in his eye. Exploitation, you might be thinking. But he thought he was a responsible member of his family.

A bill like the one we've just passed is of no use unless it goes hand in   8 hand with programs that will offer a new life to these newly released children. But where are the schools in which they are to be educated? Where is the money to buy them food and clothing and medication, so that they don't return home to become the extra weight that capsizes the already shaky raft of their family's finances? Their own governments, mired in countless other problems, seem incapable of bringing these services to them. Are we in America who, with one blithe stroke of our congressional pen, rendered these children jobless, willing to shoulder that burden? And when many of these children turn to the streets, to survival through thievery and violence and begging and prostitution—as surely in the absence of other options they must—are we willing to shoulder that responsibility?

*For a reading quiz, sources on Chitra Divakaruni, and annotated links to further readings on globalization and its effects on workers, visit **bedfordstmartins.com/ thebedfordreader**.*

---

[2] *Paise* (pronounced "pie-say") are the smallest unit of Indian currency, worth a fraction of an American penny.—EDS.

Journal Writing

Write a journal response to Divakaruni's argument against legislation that bans goods produced by forced or indentured child laborers. Do you basically agree or disagree with the author? Why? (To take your journal writing further, see "From Journal to Essay" below.)

Questions on Meaning

1. What do you take to be Divakaruni's PURPOSE in this essay? At what point did it become clear?
2. What is Divakaruni's THESIS? Where is it stated?
3. What are "Third World countries" (par. 1)?
4. From the further information given in the footnote on page 467, what does it mean to be "[l]ooking down from the heights of Maslow's pyramid" (par. 5)? What point is Divakaruni making here?
5. In paragraph 8 Divakaruni suggests some of the reasons that children in other countries may be forced or sold into labor. What are they?

Questions on Writing Strategy

1. In her last paragraph, Divakaruni asks a series of RHETORICAL QUESTIONS. What is the EFFECT of this strategy?
2. How does the structure of paragraph 3 clarify causes and effects?
3. **OTHER METHODS** What does the extended EXAMPLE of Nimai (pars. 6–7) contribute to Divakaruni's argument? What, if anything, does it add to Divakaruni's authority? What does it tell us about child labor abroad?

Questions on Language

1. Divakaruni says that laboring children could otherwise be "the extra weight that capsizes the already shaky raft of their family's finances" (par. 8). How does this metaphor capture the problem of children in poor families? (See *Figures of speech* in Useful Terms for a definition of *metaphor*.)
2. What do the words in paragraph 7 tell you about Divakaruni's attitude toward the village children? Is it disdain? pity? compassion? horror?
3. Consult a dictionary if you need help in defining the following: indentured (par. 1); inconceivable (5); exploitation (7); mired, blithe (8).

Suggestions for Writing

1. **FROM JOURNAL TO ESSAY** Starting from your journal entry, write a letter to your congressional representative or one of your senators who takes a position for or against laws such as that opposed by Divakaruni. You can use quotations from

Divakaruni's essay if they serve your purpose, but the letter should center on your own views of the issue. When you've finished your letter, send it. (You can find your representative's and your senators' names and addresses on the Web at *house.gov/writerep* and *senate.gov*.)

2. David Parker, a photographer and doctor, has documented child laborers in a series of powerful photographs (*hsph.harvard.edu/gallery/intro.html*). He asks viewers, "Under what circumstances and conditions should children work?" Look at Parker's photographs, and answer his question in an essay. What kind of paid work, for how many hours a week, is appropriate for, say, a ten- or twelve-year-old child? Consider: What about children working in their family's business? Where do you draw the line between occasional babysitting or lawn mowing and full-time factory work?

3. Research the history of child labor in the United States, including the development of child-labor laws. Then write an essay in which you explain how and why the laws evolved and what the current laws are.

4. **CRITICAL WRITING** Divakaruni's essay depends significantly on appeals to readers' emotions (see p. 466). Locate one emotional appeal that either helps to convince you of the author's point or, in your mind, weakens the argument. What does the appeal ASSUME about the reader's (your) feelings or values? Why are the assumptions correct or incorrect in your case? How, specifically, does the appeal strengthen or undermine Divakaruni's argument?

5. **CONNECTIONS** In the next essay, *"Plata o Plomo:* Silver or Lead" (p. 472), Marie Javdani examines another global relationship that can harm children: the international traffic in cocaine, heroin, and other drugs. To what extent do you think the people in one country are responsible for what happens in other countries as a result of their actions? Write a brief essay that answers this question, explaining clearly the beliefs and values that guide your answer.

Chitra Divakaruni on Writing

Chitra Divakaruni is both a writer and a community worker, reaching out to immigrants and other groups through organizations such as Maitri, a refuge for abused women that Divakaruni helped to found. In a 1998 interview in *Atlantic Unbound* (the online version of *The Atlantic Monthly*), Katie Bolick asked Divakaruni how her activism and writing affected each other. Here is Divakaruni's response.

Being helpful where I can has always been an important value for me. I did community work in India, and I continue to do it in America, because being involved in my community is something I feel I need to do. Activism has given me enormous satisfaction—not just as a person, but also as a writer. The lives of people I would have only known from the outside, or had stereotyped notions of, have been opened up to me. My hotline work with Maitri has certainly influenced both my life and my writing immensely. Overall, I have a great deal of sensitivity that I did not have before, and a lot of my preconceptions have changed. I hope that translates into my writing and reaches my readers.

For Discussion

1. What evidence does "Live Free and Starve" give to support Divakaruni's statement about how her activist work has affected her writing?
2. What does Divakaruni mean when she speaks of lives that she "would have only known from the outside"? Of what use is "insider's" knowledge to an activist? to a writer?
3. Do you have a project or an activity—comparable to Divakaruni's activism—that you believe positively affects your writing? What is it? How does it help you as you write?

MARIE JAVDANI

Marie Javdani was born in Albuquerque, New Mexico, and attended the University of Oregon, where she earned a BA and an MA in geography and was published in *Harvest*, the university's annual writing publication. As an undergraduate Javdani became interested in international development. She worked as a research assistant for Harvard's Center for International Development and traveled to Malawi to conduct research for her master's thesis, which examines the connection between fertilizer subsidies and food security. She speaks Swahili and plans to pursue a PhD in African studies. Always an avid reader, Javdani cites her father and the children's authors Shel Silverstein and Roald Dahl as her early inspirations to write. She is also a musician whose instrument of choice is currently the marimba, an African percussion device similar to the xylophone.

Plata o Plomo: Silver or Lead

Like Chitra Divakaruni in the previous selection, Javdani is concerned in this essay with how actions taken in the United States can affect people in other countries, often without our realizing it. To make her argument concrete, Javdani tells the stories of two boys, Eric, an American, and Miguel, a Colombian. (Colombia is a country in South America.) Reminding us that global problems start and end with people, the boys represent cause and effect at their most specific. Javdani wrote this paper for her freshman writing course and revised it for *The Bedford Reader* in 2004. It is documented in MLA style, described on pages 73–86.

At 8:00 on a Friday night, Eric walks down the street in his American 1 hometown whistling. Tonight, for the first time in almost a week, Eric does not have to do homework or chores. Tonight Eric is a free spirit. Best of all, tonight Eric has scored some drugs. He and his friends will trade their bland, controlled existence for some action and a little bit of fun.

At 8:00 on a Friday night, Miguel creeps down the road in his Colombian 2 village praying. Tonight, for the last time in his life, Miguel will have to watch where he is going and listen anxiously for distant gunshots. Tonight Miguel will die. The guerillas who have been threatening him and his father will end his life for some coca and a lot of money.

Eric and Miguel represent opposite poles in what the United States gov-   3
ernment refers to as the "war on drugs." Miguel's home is where it starts. In
his little village, drug production is the only possible way of life. Eric's home
is where it ends. In his suburban paradise, the stress of homework and ex-
girlfriends requires weekend breaks for drugs. All but ignoring both youths,
congresspeople, governors, and presidents talk about how their actions will
combat the flow of drugs into our homeland. In an attempt to find the quickest route around a complicated problem, the United States sends billions in
aid dollars every year to the governments of Latin American "drug-source"
countries such as Colombia, Ecuador, Bolivia, and Peru (Carpenter 205). But
the solution isn't working: Political turmoil and violence continue to plague
the countries to which we are sending aid, and illegal drug use in the United
States remains fairly constant (Vásquez 571–75). To begin to solve the problem, we need to understand what's happening in drug-source countries, how
the United States can and can't help there, and what, instead, can be done
at home.

Miguel's country, Colombia, is one of the top recipients of US money and   4
military weaponry and equipment. According to the US Department of State,
Colombia produces nearly 80% of the world's cocaine as well as a significant
amount of the US heroin supply. Drug production has become a way of life
for Colombians. Some call it the *plata o plomo* mentality. As Gonzalo Sanchez
explains it, *plata o plomo* is literally translated as "silver or lead" and means
that one can either take the money—drug money, bribe money, and so on—
or take a bullet (7). Since 1964, the country has been essentially run by drug
lords and leftist extremists, mainly the FARC (the military wing of the Colombian Communist Party), whose guerilla presence is much stronger and
more threatening than that of the actual government. In response, extreme
right-wing paramilitary forces act in an equally deadly manner. Both of these
groups raid villages continually, looking to root out "traitors" and executing
whomever they please (Sanchez 12–15).

According to the humanitarian organization Human Rights Watch, US   5
aid money has helped fund, supply, and train Colombian military units that
maintain close alliances with paramilitary groups. Although Colombia has
recently taken a tougher stance toward the paramilitaries and peace negotiations are in progress, the US State Department, major human rights organizations, and the United Nations claim that the Colombian government is still
linked to illicit paramilitary activities. For example, government forces have
often invaded, emptied, and then left a guerilla-held area, clearing the way for
paramilitary fighters to take control (Carpenter 162). Human rights groups
also criticize what Adam Isacson calls a "forgive and forget" government
policy toward paramilitary leaders accused of crimes, including promises of

amnesty in return for gradual demobilization (251–52). Although the US has threatened to suspend aid if Colombia does not break such ties with paramilitary groups, the full amount of promised aid continues to be granted (Human Rights Watch).

For the past forty years, the people of Colombia have found themselves   6
between a rock and a hard place over the production of coca, the plant used for making cocaine and heroin. Under threats from the rebel drug lords, who now control many areas, civilians must either allow their land to be cultivated for the growth of coca or put themselves and their families at deadly risk. At the same time, however, the consequence of "cooperation" with the rebels is execution by paramilitary groups or even by the Colombian government. Some coca farmers, fearful of the government, willingly form alliances with rebels who offer to protect their farms for a fee (Vásquez 572).

Entire villages get caught in the crossfire between paramilitaries and rebels.   7
els. In the past ten years, over 35,000 civilians have lost their lives in the conflict and hundreds of thousands have been forced from their homes (Carpenter 215). A terrible incident in the town of Bellavista was reported in the *New York Times* in 2002 (Forero, "Colombian War"). Paramilitary forces took over the town in an attempt to gain control of jungle smuggling routes. When leftist rebels arrived ready to fight a battle, the paramilitaries fled, leaving the civilians trapped and defenseless. Most of the villagers huddled together in their church, and 117 were killed when a stray rocket destroyed the church.

What is to be done to prevent such atrocities? The United States rushes   8
aid to Colombia, hoping to stop the violence and the drugs. Unfortunately, the solutions attempted so far have had their own bad results. For instance, eradicating coca fields has alienated peasants, who then turn to the rebels for support, and it has also escalated violence over the reduced coca supply (Vásquez 575). Money intended to help peasants establish alternative crops has ended up buying weapons for branches of the military that support paramilitary operations (Human Rights Watch). Not long ago $2 million intended for the Colombian police just disappeared (Forero, "Two Million").

Obviously, the United States needs to monitor how its dollars are used   9
in Colombia. It can continue to discourage the Colombian government from supporting the paramilitaries and encourage it to seek peace among the warring factions. But ultimately the United States is limited in what it can do by international law and by the tolerance of the US people for foreign intervention.

Instead, the United States should be looking to its home front and should   10
focus on cutting the demand for drugs. Any economist will affirm that where there is demand, there will be supply. A report by the United Nations Office on Drugs and Crime connects this basic economic principle to illegal drugs:

> Production of illicit drugs is market driven. In the United States alone, illicit
> drugs are an $80 billion market. More than $70 billion of that amount goes

to traffickers, those who bring the drugs to market. Stopping the demand would stop their business. (26)

The United States should reduce demand by dramatically increasing both treatment and education. The first will help people stop using drugs. The second will make users aware of the consequences of their choices.

The war on drugs is not fought just in the jungles of some distant country.   11 It takes place daily at our schools, in our homes, and on our streets. People my age who justify their use of illegal drugs by saying "It's my life, and I can do with it what I please" should be made aware that they are funding drug lords and contributing to the suffering of people across the globe, including in Colombia. Eric's "little bit of fun" is costing Miguel his life.

Works Cited

Carpenter, Ted Galen. *Peace and Freedom: Foreign Policy for a Constitutional Republic.* Washington: Cato, 2002. Print.

Forero, Juan. "Colombian War Brings Carnage to Village Altar." *New York Times* 9 May 2002. *LexisNexis Academic.* Web. 18 Mar. 2004.

---. "Two Million in US Aid to Colombia Missing from Colombian Police Fund." *New York Times* 11 May 2002. *LexisNexis Academic.* Web. 18 Mar. 2004.

Human Rights Watch. *World Report 2003.* Human Rights Watch. 2004. Web. 9 Mar. 2004.

Isacson, Adam. "Optimism, Pessimism, and Terrorism: The United States and Colombia in 2003." *Brown Journal of World Affairs* 10.2 (2004): 245–55. Print.

Sanchez, Gonzalo. *Violence in Colombia.* Wilmington: Scholarly Resources, 1992. Print.

United Nations. Office on Drugs and Crime. *Drug Consumption Stimulates Cultivation and Trade.* UNODC, 3 Dec. 2003. Web. 18 Mar. 2004.

United States. Dept. of State. *International Narcotics Control Strategy Report, 2003.* US State Dept., 1 Mar. 2004. Web. 12 Mar. 2004.

Vásquez, Ian. "The International War on Drugs." *Cato Handbook for Congress: Policy Recommendations for the 108th Congress.* Ed. Edward H. Crane and David Boaz. Washington: Cato, 2003. 567–76. *Cato Institute.* 2003. Web. 18 Mar. 2004.

*For a reading quiz and annotated links to further readings on the causes and effects of the illegal drug trade, visit **bedfordstmartins.com/thebedfordreader**.*

Journal Writing

What do you think about Javdani's solution to the twin problems of violence in drug-producing countries and drug use in the United States (pars. 10–11)? Do you think her solution would work? Why, or why not? (To take your journal writing further, see "From Journal to Essay" below.)

Questions on Meaning

1. Where does Javdani state her THESIS? How does she develop the thesis?
2. Why do the Colombian peasants often support the Communist rebels rather than the government?
3. What, according to Javdani, are the problems caused by the US government's sending "billions in aid dollars every year to the governments of Latin American 'drug-source' countries" (par. 3)? What does Javdani offer as a solution?

Questions on Writing Strategy

1. Who seems to be Javdani's intended AUDIENCE for this essay? How does she appeal to this audience?
2. With whom do Javdani's sympathies lie? What EVIDENCE in the essay supports your answer?
3. Javdani cites a variety of outside sources throughout the essay. What is the EFFECT of her use of these sources?
4. **OTHER METHODS** Why does Javdani use COMPARISON AND CONTRAST in her opening paragraphs? What is the effect of her returning to this comparison in her conclusion?

Questions on Language

1. In paragraph 6 Javdani describes the people of Colombia as "between a rock and a hard place over the production of coca." What does she mean?
2. How and why does Javdani use IRONY to describe Eric in paragraph 3?
3. Why does Javdani use quotation marks around *traitors* (par. 4) and *cooperation* (6)?
4. Consult a dictionary if you are unsure of the meanings of any of the following words: guerillas (par. 2); turmoil, plague (3); paramilitary (4); humanitarian, amnesty, demobilization (5); atrocities, eradicating, alienated (8).

Suggestions for Writing

1. **FROM JOURNAL TO ESSAY** Working from your journal writing and, like Javdani, drawing on research, develop an essay that lays out your view of the most effective ways to curtail either the production or the consumption of illegal drugs.

Which current US government efforts are successful, and which fall short? What more could be done?

2. Write a report on the use of illegal drugs by US adolescents, focusing on an aspect of the problem that interests you, such as how widespread it is, what groups it affects most and least, or what drugs are involved. An excellent starting place for your research is Monitoring the Future, a long-term study of "the behavior, attitudes, and values" of students and young adults. Its 2009 report, *National Results on Adolescent Drug Use*, is available at *monitoringthefuture.org/pubs/monographs/overview2009.pdf*.

3. **CRITICAL WRITING**   Is Javdani's essay an effective ARGUMENT? Consider the thesis development, the organization, the evidence, and the clarity of the presentation. What would you say are the strengths and weaknesses of this argument?

4. **CONNECTIONS**   Javdani's essay and Chitra Divakaruni's "Live Free and Starve" (p. 466) both look at effects of globalization, the increasing economic, cultural, and political connections among nations and their people. Write a brief essay discussing what you see as the main advantages and the main disadvantages of globalization. For instance, advantages might include the availability in this country of varied ethnic foods or of relatively inexpensive consumer goods that were produced elsewhere, while disadvantages might include the loss of American manufacturing jobs to foreign factories or the strong international drug trade.

Marie Javdani on Writing

In an interview for *The Bedford Reader,* we asked Marie Javdani to describe her writing process.

Depending on my writing topic, it can often take a while to get a good start. If it's a topic I chose myself and am interested in or am at least somewhat knowledgeable about, the first steps are usually much easier. I usually start by brainstorming an outline by just writing things as I think of them. What questions do I want to answer? How does this topic actually affect people? Once I get a start, the writing process usually goes fairly quickly. I try to write in a way that I would speak if I were, for instance, teaching on the subject. That tends to make my work more readable. As for the introduction, I try to stay away from prescribed formats. I try to think of what would make me want to read more about a topic or to put a spin on it that makes it stand out. Also, I tend to write my introduction last. I've found that if I write it first it typically doesn't match what I write once I get "on a roll." If I plan ahead properly, I don't usually have to do more than two drafts unless I come upon new research that makes me need to rearrange my arguments. I try to write early enough to leave it alone for a few days before I go back and proofread it.

Javdani also offered suggestions for college writers based on her own experiences as a student.

From a student's perspective, the best thing you can do to improve your
writing is to be interested in your topic. On the same note, however, don't soapbox. Just say what you want to say, support it, and move on. If you're writing
for an assignment for which you weren't able to choose the topic, try to take
an angle that you think no one else will take. . . . Do take the time to spell-check
and edit your writing. The spelling checker on the computer is not sufficient.
You're (not *your*) in college and you know (not *no*) better. Try reading your
writing out loud to yourself. If it doesn't sound good when you say it, it doesn't
sound good on paper either.

For Discussion

1. Do you share Javdani's experience that it's usually easier to write when you're
   interested in your topic? How does your writing process differ when you're interested beforehand from when you're not?
2. Why do you think Javdani advises "don't soapbox"? (If you aren't sure what *soapbox* means, look it up in a dictionary.)

HELEN PILCHER

Helen Pilcher is a molecular neurobiologist and a stand-up comedian. While studying for her PhD at the Institute of Psychiatry in London, Pilcher spent five years going back and forth between the laboratory and the comedy club. After completing her degree, she decided that her roles of scientist and comedian didn't have to be so separate. She earned a science communication diploma from London's Birkbeck University and began writing and producing humorous science shows for Einstein TV. She also managed the Science in Society team for the Royal Society (the United Kingdom's national academy of science). In an effort to prove the hypothesis that "science can be funny," Pilcher and her friend Timandra Harkness founded the Comedy Research Project, a two-woman comedy show that performs skits on DNA, brain chemistry, and notable developments in science. Pilcher's writing is frequently published in *Nature* online and in other magazines. She lives in London.

The New Witch Doctors: How Belief Can Kill

The word *voodoo* comes with all kinds of occult connotations, but there are ways in which modern physicians' practices resemble those of so-called witch doctors. In this 2009 article for *New Scientist* magazine, Pilcher explains how negative diagnoses can affect patients physically. She finds that science, not just dark magic, can explain the connection between belief and illness.

1   Late one night in a small Alabama cemetery, Vance Vanders had a run-in with the local witch doctor, who wafted a bottle of unpleasant-smelling liquid in front of his face, and told him he was about to die and that no one could save him.

2   Back home, Vanders took to his bed and began to deteriorate. Some weeks later, emaciated and near death, he was admitted to the local hospital, where doctors were unable to find a cause for his symptoms or slow his decline. Only then did his wife tell one of the doctors, Drayton Doherty, of the hex.

3   Doherty thought long and hard. The next morning, he called Vanders's family to his bedside. He told them that the previous night he had lured the witch doctor back to the cemetery, where he had choked him against a tree until he explained how the curse worked. The medicine man had, he said, rubbed lizard eggs into Vanders's stomach, which had hatched inside his body. One reptile remained, which was eating Vanders from the inside out.

4   Doherty then summoned a nurse who had, by prior arrangement, filled a large syringe with a powerful emetic. With great ceremony, he inspected the

instrument and injected its contents into Vanders's arm. A few minutes later, Vanders began to gag and vomit uncontrollably. In the midst of it all, unnoticed by everyone in the room, Doherty produced his pièce de résistance[1]—a green lizard he had stashed in his black bag. "Look what has come out of you, Vance," he cried. "The voodoo curse is lifted."

Vanders did a double take, lurched backwards to the head of the bed, then   5
drifted into a deep sleep. When he woke next day he was alert and ravenous. He quickly regained his strength and was discharged a week later.

The facts of this case from eighty years ago were corroborated by four med-   6
ical professionals. Perhaps the most remarkable thing about it is that Vanders survived. There are numerous documented instances from many parts of the globe of people dying after being cursed.

With no medical records and no autopsy results, there's no way to be sure   7
exactly how these people met their end. The common thread in these cases, however, is that a respected figure puts a curse on someone, perhaps by chanting or pointing a bone at them. Soon afterwards, the victim dies, apparently of natural causes.

Voodoo Nouveau[2]

You might think this sort of thing is increasingly rare, and limited to   8
remote tribes. But according to Clifton Meador, a doctor at Vanderbilt School of Medicine in Nashville, Tennessee, who has documented cases like Vanders's, the curse has taken on a new form.

Take Sam Shoeman, who was diagnosed with end-stage liver cancer in   9
the 1970s and given just months to live. Shoeman duly died in the allotted time frame—yet the autopsy revealed that his doctors had got it wrong. The tumor was tiny and had not spread. "He didn't die from cancer, but from believing he was dying of cancer," says Meador. "If everyone treats you as if you are dying, you buy into it. Everything in your whole being becomes about dying."

Cases such as Shoeman's may be extreme examples of a far more widespread   10
phenomenon. Many patients who suffer harmful side effects, for instance, may do so only because they have been told to expect them. What's more, people who believe they have a high risk of certain diseases are more likely to get them than people with the same risk factors who believe they have a low risk. It seems modern witch doctors wear white coats and carry stethoscopes.

---

[1]Colloquial French for the showcase piece of a collection or the main dish of a meal.—Eds.
[2]French, meaning "new voodoo."—Eds.

The idea that believing you are ill can make you ill may seem far-fetched,   11
yet rigorous trials have established beyond doubt that the converse is true—
that the power of suggestion can improve health. This is the well-known placebo effect. Placebos cannot produce miracles, but they do produce measurable physical effects.

The placebo effect has an evil twin: the nocebo effect, in which dummy   12
pills and negative expectations can produce harmful effects. The term *nocebo*,
which means "I will harm," was not coined until the 1960s, and the phenomenon has been far less studied than the placebo effect. It's not easy, after all, to
get ethical approval for studies designed to make people feel worse.

What we do know suggests the impact of nocebo is far-reaching. "Voodoo   13
death, if it exists, may represent an extreme form of the nocebo phenomenon,"
says anthropologist Robert Hahn of the US Centers for Disease Control and
Prevention in Atlanta, Georgia, who has studied the nocebo effect.

In clinical trials, around a quarter of patients in control groups—those   14
given supposedly inert therapies—experience negative side effects. The severity of these side effects sometimes matches those associated with real drugs. A
retrospective study of fifteen trials involving thousands of patients prescribed
either beta blockers or a control showed that both groups reported comparable levels of side effects, including fatigue, depressive symptoms and sexual
dysfunction. A similar number had to withdraw from the studies because of
them.

Occasionally, the effects can be life-threatening (see "The Overdose").   15
"Beliefs and expectations are not only conscious, logical phenomena, they also
have physical consequences," says Hahn.

The Overdose

Depressed after splitting up with his girlfriend, Derek Adams took all his
pills . . . then regretted it. Fearing he might die, he asked a neighbor to take him to
the hospital, where he collapsed. Shaky, pale and drowsy, his blood pressure
dropped and his breaths came quickly.

Yet lab tests and toxicology screening came back clear. Over the next four
hours Adams received six liters of saline, but improved little.

Then a doctor arrived from the clinical trial of an antidepressant in which
Adams had been taking part. Adams had enrolled in the study about a month earlier. Initially he had felt his mood buoyed, but an argument with his ex-girlfriend
saw him swallow the twenty-nine remaining tablets.

The doctor revealed that Adams was in the control group. The pills he had
"overdosed" on were harmless. Hearing this, Adams was surprised and tearfully
relieved. Within fifteen minutes he was fully alert, and his blood pressure and
heart rate had returned to normal.

Nocebo effects are also seen in normal medical practice. Around sixty   16
percent of patients undergoing chemotherapy start feeling sick before their
treatment. "It can happen days before, or on the journey on the way in," says
clinical psychologist Guy Montgomery from Mount Sinai School of Medicine
in New York. Sometimes the mere thought of treatment or the doctor's voice is
enough to make patients feel unwell. This "anticipatory nausea" may be partly
due to conditioning—when patients subconsciously link some part of their
experience with nausea—and partly due to expectation.

Alarmingly, the nocebo effect can even be catching. Cases where symp-   17
toms without an identifiable cause spread through groups of people have been
around for centuries, a phenomenon known as mass psychogenic illness. One
outbreak (see "It's Catching") inspired a recent study by psychologists Irving
Kirsch and Giuliana Mazzoni of the University of Hull in the UK.

They asked some of a group of students to inhale a sample of normal air,   18
which all participants were told contained "a suspected environmental toxin"
linked to headache, nausea, itchy skin and drowsiness. Half of the participants
also watched a woman inhale the sample and apparently develop these symptoms. Students who inhaled were more likely to report these symptoms than
those who did not. Symptoms were also more pronounced in women, particularly those who had seen another apparently become ill—a bias also seen in
mass psychogenic illness.

It's Catching

In November 1998, a teacher at a Tennessee high school noticed a "gasoline-
like" smell, and began complaining of headache, nausea, shortness of breath and
dizziness. The school was evacuated and over the next week more than one hundred staff and students were admitted to the local emergency room complaining of
similar symptoms.

After extensive tests, no medical explanation for the reported illnesses could
be found. A questionnaire a month later revealed that the people who reported
symptoms were more likely to be female, and to have known or seen a classmate
who was ill. It was the nocebo effect on a grand scale, says psychologist Irving
Kirsch at the University of Hull in the UK. "There was, as far as we can tell, no
environmental toxin, but people began to feel ill."

Kirsch thinks that seeing a classmate develop symptoms shaped expectancies
of illness in other children, triggering mass psychogenic illness. Outbreaks occur
all over the world. In Jordan in 1998, 800 children apparently suffered side effects
after a vaccination and 122 were admitted to the hospital, but no problem was
found with the vaccine.

The study shows that if you hear of or observe a possible side effect, you 19
are more likely to develop it yourself. That puts doctors in a tricky situation.
"On the one hand people have the right to be informed about what to expect,
but this makes it more likely they will experience these effects," says Mazzoni.

This means doctors need to choose their words carefully so as to minimize 20
negative expectations, says Montgomery. "It's all about how you say it."

Hypnosis might also help. "Hypnosis changes expectancies, which de- 21
creases anxiety and stress, which improves the outcome," Montgomery says.
"I think hypnosis could be applied to a wide variety of symptoms where expectancy plays a role."

Is the scale of the nocebo problem serious enough to justify such counter- 22
measures? We just don't know, because so many questions remain unanswered.
In what circumstances do nocebo effects occur? And how long do the symptoms last?

It appears that, as with the placebo response, nocebo effects vary widely, 23
and may depend heavily on context. Placebo effects in clinical settings are often
much more potent than those induced in the laboratory, says Paul Enck, a psychologist at the University Hospital in Tübingen, Germany, which suggests
the nocebo problem may have profound effects in the real world. For obvious
reasons, though, lab experiments are designed to induce only mild and temporary nocebo symptoms.

Real Consequences

It is also unclear who is susceptible. A person's optimism or pessimism may 24
play a role, but there are no consistent personality predictors. Both sexes can
succumb to mass psychogenic illness, though women report more symptoms
than men. Enck has shown that in men, expectancy rather than conditioning
is more likely to influence nocebo symptoms. For women, the opposite is true.
"Women tend to operate more on past experiences, whereas men seem more
reluctant to take history into a situation," he says.

What is becoming clear is that these apparently psychological phenom- 25
ena have very real consequences in the brain. Using PET scans to peer into
the brains of people given a placebo or nocebo, Jon-Kar Zubieta of the University of Michigan, Ann Arbor, showed last year that nocebo effects were
linked with a decrease in dopamine and opioid activity. This would explain
how nocebos can increase pain. Placebos, unsurprisingly, produced the opposite response.

Meanwhile, Fabrizio Benedetti of the University of Turin Medical School 26
in Italy has found that nocebo-induced pain can be suppressed by a drug called
proglumide, which blocks receptors for a hormone called cholecystokinin

(CCK). Normally, expectations of pain induce anxiety, which activates CCK receptors, enhancing pain.

The ultimate cause of the nocebo effect, however, is not neurochemistry but belief. According to Hahn, surgeons are often wary of operating on people who think they will die—because such patients often do. And the mere belief that one is susceptible to a heart attack is itself a risk factor. One study found that women who believed they are particularly prone to heart attack are nearly four times as likely to die from coronary conditions than other women with the same risk factors. 27

Despite the growing evidence that the nocebo effect is all too real, it is hard in this rational age to accept that people's beliefs can kill them. After all, most of us would laugh if a strangely attired man leapt about waving a bone and told us we were going to die. But imagine how you would feel if you were told the same thing by a smartly dressed doctor with a wallful of medical degrees and a computerful of your scans and test results. The social and cultural background is crucial, says Enck. 28

Meador argues that Shoeman's misdiagnosis and subsequent death shares many of the crucial elements found in hex death. A powerful doctor pronounces a death sentence, which is accepted unquestioningly by the "victim" and his family, who then start to act upon that belief. Shoeman, his family and his doctors all believed he was dying from cancer. It became a self-fulfilling prophecy. 29

"Bad news promotes bad physiology. I think you can persuade people that they're going to die and have it happen," Meador says. "I don't think there's anything mystical about it. We're uncomfortable with the idea that words or symbolic actions can cause death because it challenges our biomolecular model of the world." 30

Perhaps when the biomedical basis of voodoo death is revealed in detail we will find it easier to accept that it is real—and that it can affect any one of us. 31

---

*For a reading quiz, sources on Helen Pilcher, and annotated links to further readings on medicine, visit **bedfordstmartins.com/thebedfordreader**.*

Journal Writing

Pilcher offers several examples of perfectly healthy people becoming ill with no known physical cause. Can you think of any such instances in your own experience, perhaps a family member, a friend, a neighbor, or an acquaintance who became sick for no apparent reason or a time when you seemed to develop symptoms because someone close to you had something contagious, only to discover that you were fine? In your journal, describe what happened, to the best of your knowledge. (To take your journal writing further, see "From Journal to Essay" on the next page.)

Questions on Meaning

1. What do you take to be Pilcher's main PURPOSE in writing this essay? How well does she accomplish it?
2. What is Pilcher's THESIS? Does she state it anywhere, or is it implied?
3. What is the "nocebo effect," as Pilcher explains it? How is it related to the "placebo effect"?
4. What does Pilcher mean by a "self-fulfilling prophecy" (par. 29)? In what ways might the phrase serve as a SUMMARY of her analysis?

Questions on Writing Strategy

1. Why do you think Pilcher opens her essay as she does? What is the EFFECT of this opening?
2. For whom does Pilcher seem to be writing: victims of voodoo curses, doctors, patients, research scientists, drug-study subjects, another group? How can you tell?
3. Does Pilcher seem more interested in causes or in effects? Why do you think she focuses on the one, instead of the other?
4. What function is served by the two headings in this essay?
5. **OTHER METHODS**   Pilcher's cause-and-effect analysis relies heavily on EXAMPLES. How are the two examples presented in boxes different from the others? Why do you suppose Pilcher highlights them?

Questions on Language

1. What CONNOTATIONS do you associate with the word *voodoo*? How does Pilcher seem to define it?
2. Pilcher is both a trained neurobiologist and a comedian. What attempts at humor, if any, do you detect in her essay? Do such attempts undermine her credibility as a science writer? Why, or why not?
3. Consult a dictionary for definitions of the following words: wafted (par. 1); emetic (4); corroborated (6); converse (11); inert, retrospective, dysfunction (14); anticipatory (16); psychogenic (17); induced (23); susceptible (24); dopamine, opioid (25); suppressed, receptors (26); neurochemistry, coronary (27); physiology, biomolecular (30).

Suggestions for Writing

1. **FROM JOURNAL TO ESSAY** Building on your journal entry, write an essay that responds to Pilcher's claim that mere belief can make a person sick, even to the point of death. How do her examples compare to similar instances from your own experience? Is her analysis sufficient to explain why some people seem susceptible to suggestion while others do not? To what extent, if any, can Pilcher be accused of blaming the victim? What other causes can you think of to explain the phenomenon Pilcher examines?

2. As Pilcher suggests, curses, hexes, and spells continue to play a role in many world cultures, from Creole to Italian to Romanian to Chinese. Do some research about a particular facet of "black magic," such as voodoo dolls, the evil eye, or love potions. Then report on it, explaining how it works and discussing its history as well as its place in modern society. Or write a similarly researched essay on a particular superstition. For example, why is the number 13 thought to be unlucky? Why is it considered bad luck for a black cat to cross your path? Why is a four-leaf clover or a rabbit's foot believed to bring good luck?

3. **CRITICAL WRITING** Take a close look at Pilcher's use of SUMMARY, PARAPHRASE, and direct QUOTATION. In an essay, analyze the ways she SYNTHESIZES and integrates information and ideas from her sources. Why does she quote directly where she does? How effective are her summaries and paraphrases? How does she combine source materials to create an argument of her own?

4. **CONNECTIONS** While Pilcher suggests that negative thinking can prove fatal, Barbara Ehrenreich, in "The Menace of Negative People" (p. 634), argues that negative thinking can benefit a person's mental health. What assumptions do the writers seem to share, and where do they diverge? How might the apparent contradiction between their two perspectives be resolved?

CHARLES FISHMAN

Born in 1961 in Miami, Florida, Charles Fishman earned a BA from Harvard University before launching his career in investigative journalism. His first assignment was at the *Washington Post,* where he investigated the tragic explosion of the space shuttle *Challenger,* which killed seven astronauts in 1986. From the *Post* he went on to work at the *Orlando Sentinel,* where he edited the Sunday magazine, and then at the *News & Observer* in Raleigh, North Carolina, where he edited features, culture, sports, and business. Fishman now lives in Philadelphia, Pennsylvania, and has been a senior writer at *Fast Company* magazine since 1996. He is known for his ability to gain access to sources that elude other journalists: He was the first reporter ever allowed inside a Tupperware factory and the first reporter in thirty years to set foot in the United States' only bomb factory. Fishman has won awards for his business journalism, including the New York Press Club Award in 2004 and the Gerald Loeb Award in 2005. He is working on a book about how water scarcity will reshape global economics.

The Squeeze

Charles Fishman's first book, *The Wal-Mart Effect* (2006), is an inside portrait of the most powerful company in the world. In "The Squeeze," excerpted from a chapter of the same name, Fishman details what happened when Wal-Mart began selling pickles in unprecedented quantities, at an unprecedented price. The story shows how the company is able to "defy the laws of supply, demand, and competition" and thus, on a massive scale, affect suppliers, consumers, and whole economies.

A gallon-sized jar of whole pickles is something to behold. The jar itself 1
is the size of a small aquarium. The fat green pickles, floating in swampy juice, look reptilian, their shapes exaggerated by the glass of the jar. The jar weighs twelve pounds, too big to carry with one hand.

The gallon jar of pickles is a display of abundance and excess. It is entranc- 2
ing, and also vaguely unsettling. Wal-Mart fell in love with Vlasic's gallon jar of pickles.

Wal-Mart priced it at $2.97—a year's supply of pickles for less than $3! 3
"They were using it as a 'statement' item," says Pat Hunn, who calls himself the mad scientist of the gallon jar of pickles at Vlasic. "Wal-Mart was putting it before consumers, saying this represents what Wal-Mart's about: *You can buy a stinkin' gallon of pickles for $2.97.* And it's the nation's number-one brand."

Because of Wal-Mart's scale, the Wal-Mart effect isn't just about deliver- 4
ing "always low prices." It's also about how Wal-Mart gets those low prices,

and what impact the low prices have far beyond Wal-Mart's shelves, and beyond our own wallets: the cost of low prices to the companies that supply Wal-Mart, and to the people who work for those companies. That story can be found floating in Vlasic's gallon jar of pickles, the tale of how that gallon jar came to be sold at Wal-Mart.

Back in the late 1990s, Vlasic wasn't looking to build its brand on a gallon   5
of whole pickles. Pickle companies make money on "the cut," slicing cucumbers into specialty items like spears and hamburger chips. "Cucumbers in the jar, you don't make a whole lot of money there," says Steve Young, who was then vice president of marketing for pickles at Vlasic, but has since left the company. But a Wal-Mart buyer saw the gallon jar at some point in the late 1990s, and started talking to Pat Hunn about it. Hunn, who has also since left Vlasic, was then head of Vlasic's Wal-Mart sales team, based in Dallas.

The gallon intrigued the buyer. For Vlasic, it was a niche product aimed   6
at small businesses and people having large events. Still, in sales tests in Wal-Mart stores, priced somewhere over $3, "the gallon sold like crazy," says Hunn, "surprising us all." The Wal-Mart pickle buyer had a brainstorm: What would happen to the gallon if they offered it nationwide, and got it below $3? Hunn was skeptical, but his job was to look for ways to sell pickles at Wal-Mart. Why not?

And so in 1998, Vlasic's gallon jar of pickles went into every Wal-Mart,   7
2,500 stores, at $2.97, a price so low that Vlasic and Wal-Mart were only making a penny or two on a jar, if that. The gallon was showcased on a big, freestanding pallet display near the front of stores. It was an abundance of abundance.

"They went through the roof," says Hunn.   8

Says Young, "It was selling eighty jars a week, on average, in every store."   9
Doesn't sound like much until you do the math: That's 200,000 gallons of pickles, just in gallon jars, just at Wal-Mart, every week. Whole fields of cucumbers were heading out the door.

The gallon jar of pickles became what you might call a "devastating suc-   10
cess" for Vlasic. "Quickly, it started cannibalizing our non–Wal-Mart business," says Young. "We saw consumers who used to buy the spears and the chips in supermarkets"—where a small quart jar of Vlasic pickles cost $2.49—"buying the Wal-Mart gallons. They'd eat a quarter of a jar and throw the thing away when they got moldy. A family can't eat them fast enough."

The gallon jar reshaped Vlasic's pickle business: It chewed up the profit   11
margin of the business with Wal-Mart, and of pickles generally; procurement had to scramble to find enough pickles to fill the gallons. The volume also gave Vlasic strong sales numbers, strong growth numbers, and a powerful place in the world of pickles at Wal-Mart.

The gallon was hoisting Vlasic and hurting it at the same time. Indeed,   12
Steve Young, Vlasic's marketing guy, and Pat Hunn, Vlasic's Wal-Mart sales
guy, agree on the details of the gallon, but years later they disagree over
whether it was good or bad for Vlasic.

Hunn remembers cutting a deal with Wal-Mart whereby the retailer could   13
only increase its sales of gallons if it increased its sales of the more profitable
spears and chips in lockstep. The gallon was good.

Young remembers begging Wal-Mart for relief. "They said, 'No way,'" says   14
Young. "We said we'll increase the price"—even $3.49 would have helped
tremendously—"and they said, 'If you do that, all the other products of yours
we buy, we'll stop buying.' It was a clear threat."

Hunn remembers the conversations differently. Things were more com-   15
plicated, more subtle. "They did not put a gun to our head and say, 'It's $2.97
or you're out of here,'" says Hunn. "They said, 'We want the $2.97 gallon of
pickles. If you don't do it, we'll see if someone else might.' I knew our competi-
tors were saying to Wal-Mart, 'We'll do the $2.97 gallons if you give us your
other business.'

"We're all big boys," Hunn says. "We all make decisions."   16

Wal-Mart's business was so indispensable to Vlasic, and the gallon so cen-   17
tral to the Wal-Mart relationship, that decisions about the future of the gallon
were made at the CEO level. "One option was to call their bluff," says Young.
But Vlasic was struggling as an independent spin-off of Campbell Soup Company, and couldn't afford to risk the Wal-Mart business. The pain didn't continue for weeks or months—the $2.97 gallon of Vlasic dills was on the shelves
at Wal-Mart for two and a half years.

Finally, Wal-Mart let Vlasic up for air. "The Wal-Mart guy's response was   18
classic," says Young. "He said, 'Well, we've done to pickles what we did to
orange juice. We've killed it. We can back off.'"

Vlasic got to take the product down to half a gallon of pickles, for $2.49.   19
By that point, Young says, profits in pickles had been cut by 50 percent—
millions of dollars in lost profit, even as the business itself grew. Devastating
success, indeed.

The meaning of the Vlasic story is complicated, but it cuts to the heart   20
of how Wal-Mart does business. It shows the impact of Wal-Mart's scale and
power in what we all think is a market economy. Wal-Mart's focus on pricing,
and its ability to hold a supplier's business hostage to its own agenda, distorts
markets in ways that consumers don't see, and ways the suppliers can't effectively counter. Wal-Mart is so large that it can often defy the laws of supply,
demand, and competition.

That's the scary part of the Vlasic story: The market didn't create   21
the $2.97 gallon of pickles, nor did waning consumer demand or a wild

abundance of cucumbers. Wal-Mart created the $2.97 gallon jar of pickles. The price—a number that is a critical piece of information to buyers, sellers, and competitors about the state of the pickle market—the price was a lie. It was unrelated to either the supply of cucumbers or the demand for pickles. The price was a fiction imposed on the pickle market in Bentonville. Consumers saw a bargain; Vlasic saw no way out. Both were responding not to real market forces, but to a pickle price gimmick imposed by Wal-Mart as a way of making a statement.

*For a reading quiz, sources on Charles Fishman, and annotated links to further readings on Wal-Mart, visit **bedfordstmartins.com/thebedfordreader**.*

Journal Writing

Fifty-seven percent of American adults shop at Wal-Mart every week, but even those who don't are affected by the retail giant. How do you feel about Wal-Mart? Are you a fan of Sam Walton's store, do you shop there reluctantly, or do you go out of your way to avoid the place? Have you or has somebody you know ever worked there? In your journal, write a few paragraphs about your experiences with Wal-Mart, whether good or bad. (To take your journal writing further, see "From Journal to Essay" on the facing page.)

Questions on Meaning

1. What seems to be Fishman's primary PURPOSE in this piece? Does he want to express his opinion about Wal-Mart's business practices? persuade shoppers to boycott the store? educate his readers? How can you tell?
2. Why, according to Fishman, did Wal-Mart want to sell a gallon jar of pickles for under three dollars? What was the store trying to accomplish by offering such a low price, and what was the actual result?
3. What is a "devastating success" (pars. 10, 19)? How does the Vlasic story illustrate this concept?
4. What does Fishman mean when he says that "the price was a lie" (par. 21)? Is he accusing Wal-Mart of being unethical, or is he saying something else? Put the idea in your own words.

Questions on Writing Strategy

1. To whom does Fishman seem to be writing here? Why do you think so?
2. How well does cause-and-effect analysis suit Fishman's subject? In what way does this method provide an effective means of achieving his purpose?

3. Summarize the causal chain Fishman identifies in paragraphs 5–11.
4. Do you think Fishman oversimplifies the cause-and-effect relationship between Wal-Mart's pricing and Vlasic's profit losses? Why, or why not?
5. **OTHER METHODS** Aside from cause-and-effect analysis, what other method does Fishman use extensively to show how Wal-Mart affects its suppliers? Why does he use it?

Questions on Language

1. Fishman introduces his essay by using a metaphor to describe a gallon jar of pickles. What is the metaphor, and how effective is it? Why do you think the author chose to start this way? (For a definition of *metaphor*, refer to *Figures of speech* in Useful Terms.)
2. Fishman uses the word *abundance* several times in this essay. How does repetition of this key word emphasize the author's point? In what ways does context affect the word's meaning?
3. How would you characterize Fishman's TONE? Is it appropriate, given his purpose and his AUDIENCE?
4. If any of the following words are new to you, look them up in a dictionary: reptilian (par. 1); entrancing (2); niche (6); procurement (11); hoisting (12); lockstep (13); waning (21).

Suggestions for Writing

1. **FROM JOURNAL TO ESSAY** Use your journal entry as the starting point for an essay that takes a position on the ongoing debate over Wal-Mart's impact on America and the rest of the world. Is the chain good or bad for the economy? In what ways might the store's overwhelming success affect our way of life? Why do you think so? (If you wish, you may research and quote expert opinion to support your argument, as Fishman does in his consideration of the subject.)
2. Although he is interested primarily in Wal-Mart's and Vlasic's business choices, Fishman's essay can also be read as an illustration of the Latin phrase *caveat emptor*, or "buyer beware." Many of the pickles in a gallon jar, after all, end up in the trash. Look back on your own experience and think of another example of a consumer product or service that isn't as good as it seems. (For example, you might consider a digital music service whose files won't transfer between players, an "as-seen-on-TV" gadget that didn't deliver on its promises, or low-fat convenience foods that are loaded with salt or high fructose corn syrup.) In an essay that provides plenty of details to clarify your reasoning, explain to readers why they shouldn't buy the item or use the service.
3. As Fishman's pickle example suggests, Americans are notorious for snapping up products they don't need in quantities that border on the absurd. Many cultures, however, actively discourage this kind of behavior, prizing thrift and generosity over personal acquisition. Write an essay that defends or argues against consumption for its own sake, making a point of explaining what, in your mind, constitutes a necessity and what is a luxury. Do we have a right—or even an obligation—to spend money on things we don't need? Why, or why not?

4. **CRITICAL WRITING** In a brief essay, evaluate Fishman's EVIDENCE, which consists largely of quotations from interviews with former Wal-Mart executives and suppliers. How convincing do you find this evidence? Do you think Fishman's analysis would have been weaker or stronger if he had talked to current employees? Why?

5. **CONNECTIONS** Fishman argues that a large commercial industry (in his case, Wal-Mart) has the power to create artificial demand for products that people wouldn't otherwise want or need. Read Jessica Mitford's "Behind the Formaldehyde Curtain" (p. 326), and then write an essay analyzing embalming and restoration—which Mitford notes are widely practiced only in North America—as a consumer product. How do funeral industry expectations and assumptions influence these practices? What is the consumer really buying?

Charles Fishman on Writing

Charles Fishman wrote *The Wal-Mart Effect* with a purpose familiar to many writers: to advance a conversation that was otherwise "stuck." As he explains in an interview with his publisher, Penguin Books, "One group of people shouts, 'Wal-Mart is horrible! evil! hurtful!' The other group of people shouts, 'Wal-Mart is great! brilliant! wonderful!' That's not a constructive shouting match. No one is learning anything. No new information is offered. No one's mind is changed. It's just people with strong opinions—and sometimes, opinions not too well grounded in facts—insisting they are right." Fishman decided that people on both sides of the dispute needed better information to ground—and perhaps challenge—their opinions. As an investigative journalist, he was in a position to conduct the interviews and uncover the data.

Fishman's two-year research process for *The Wal-Mart Effect* was extensive and innovative. In the afterword of the book, he describes the lengths he went to in his reporting: "I did everything I could think of to get a full understanding of Wal-Mart—the statistics and the scale, the impact and the spirit. I talked to hundreds of people with experience working either for the company or for suppliers to the company. I read thousands of pages about Wal-Mart—books, reports, academic studies, hundreds of newspaper stories. I visited dozens of Wal-Mart stores, often traveling miles out of my way to check out one I hadn't been to before." At one point, Fishman even arranged to fly in a small plane over Wal-Mart's headquarters in Bentonville, Arkansas, but the flight was rained out. He says he persevered with the research despite such obstacles because he firmly believes that communicating the truth about the company will become even more important in the coming years.

For Discussion

1. Why did Fishman characterize the conversation about Wal-Mart as "stuck"? Why aren't "strong opinions" enough to make an ARGUMENT productive?
2. What were Fishman's various sources of information for writing *The Wal-Mart Effect*? How might the information he gleaned from, say, an interview be different from the information he collected from an academic study?

CHRIS ANDERSON

Chris Anderson was born in England in 1961 and moved with his family to Washington, DC, where he attended high school and obtained a BS degree from George Washington University. Anderson did research at Los Alamos National Laboratory and then held editorial positions at *Nature, Science,* and *The Economist* magazines. Anderson is now editor-in-chief of *Wired* magazine, which has received five National Magazine awards under his editorship. In 2005 he was named editor of the year by *Advertising Age.* Anderson's book *The Long Tail: Why the Future of Business Is Selling Less of More* (2006) attracted wide notice for proposing a significant shift in the way business works in the Internet age. He followed that book with *Free: The Future of a Radical Price* (2009), about how businesses can profit by giving products away. Anderson lives in Berkeley, California, with his wife and their four children.

The Rise and Fall of the Hit

In *The Long Tail* Anderson argues that the Internet allows businesses to target small groups of customers that previously could not be reached because of limited shelves in stores, movie screens in cineplexes, pages in newspapers, and air time on the radio. Now, instead of aiming for blockbusters—selling vast quantities of a few items—businesses can do even better by selling small quantities of a vast number of items. The result, Anderson says, is maximum choice for consumers. In "The Rise and Fall of the Hit," which Anderson adapted from his book for *Wired* magazine, he applies this new model to the music landscape.

On March 21, 2000, Jive Records released *No Strings Attached*, the much-anticipated second album from NSync. The album debuted strong. It sold 1.1 million copies its first day and 2.4 million in the first week, making it the fastest-selling album ever. It went on to top the charts for eight weeks, moving 10 million copies by the end of the year. The music industry had cracked the commercial code. With NSync, a pop-idol boy band fronted by the charismatic Justin Timberlake, Jive had perfected the elusive formula for making a hit. In retrospect it was so obvious: What worked for the Monkees could now be replicated on an industrial scale. It was all about looks and scripted personalities. The music itself, which was outsourced to a small army of professionals (there are sixty people credited with creating *No Strings Attached*), hardly mattered.

Labels were on a roll. Between 1990 and 2000, album sales had doubled, the fastest growth rate in the history of the industry. Half of the top-grossing 100 albums ever were sold during that decade.

But even as NSync was celebrating its huge launch, the ground was shift- 3 ing. Total music sales fell during 2000, for only the second time in a decade. Over the next few years, even after the economy recovered, the music industry continued to suffer. Something fundamental had changed. Sales fell 2.5% in 2001, 6.8% in 2002, and just kept dropping. By the end of 2005 (down an- other 8.3%), album sales in the United States had declined 20% from their 1999 peak. Twenty-one of the all-time top 100 albums were released in the five-year period between 1996 and 2000. The next five years produced only two—Norah Jones's *Come Away With Me* and OutKast's *Speakerboxxx/The Love Below*—ranking 79 and 91, respectively.

It's altogether possible that NSync's first-week record may never be bro- 4 ken. The band could go down in history not just for launching Timberlake but also for marking the peak of the hit bubble—the last bit of manufactured pop to use the twentieth century's fine-tuned marketing machine to its fullest before the gears were stripped and the wheels fell off.

Music itself hasn't gone out of favor—just the opposite. There has never 5 been a better time to be an artist or a fan, and there has never been more music made or listened to. But the traditional model of marketing and selling music no longer works. The big players in the distribution system—major record labels, retail giants—depend on huge, platinum hits. These days, though, there are not nearly enough of those to support the industry in the style to which it has become accustomed. We are witnessing the end of an era.

What caused a generation of the industry's best customers—fans in their 6 teens and twenties—to abandon the record store? The labels cried piracy: *Napster* and other online file-sharing networks, along with CD burning and trading, had given rise to an underground economy of stolen music. Of course, there's something to that. Despite countless record-industry lawsuits, traffic on the peer-to-peer file-trading networks has continued to grow, and about 10 million users now share music files each day.

But technology didn't just allow fans to sidestep the cash register. It also 7 offered massive, unprecedented choice in terms of what they could hear. The average file-trading network has more songs than any music store—by a fac- tor of more than 100. Music fans had the opportunity for limitless choice, and they took it. Today, listeners have not only stopped buying as many CDs, they're also losing their taste for the blockbuster hits that used to bring throngs into record stores on release days. If they have to choose between a packaged act and something new, more and more people are opting for exploration.

Technology also gave consumers a new way to buy music. Rather than 8 having to purchase an entire album to get a couple of good tracks, they can buy songs à la carte for 99 cents each. The online music industry is primarily a singles business, which depresses album sales further. Meanwhile, the music marketing machine has lost its power. When consumers were buying mainly from record stores, prominent in-store displays could drive tremendous demand, which is why the labels paid so much for them. But now most of the largest record store chains, from Tower Records to Sam Goody, are either in bankruptcy or emerging from it with greatly diminished clout.[1] MTV doesn't play much music anymore, and money-losing *Spin* magazine was just, well, spun off for a fire-sale sum.

When it comes to lost marketing power, nothing compares to the decline of rock radio. In 1993, Americans spent an average of 23 hours and 15 minutes per week tuned to a local station. As of summer 2005, that figure had dropped to 19 hours and 15 minutes. Time spent listening to the radio is now at a twelve-year low, and rock music is among the formats suffering the most. Since 1998, the rock radio audience has dropped 26%. What's killing rock radio? A perfect storm of competition. Start with the 1996 Telecommunications Act, which added more than 700 FM stations to the dial. This fragmented the market and depressed the economics of the incumbents. At the same time, the limits of ownership in each market were relaxed, which led to a nationwide roll up by Clear Channel and Infinity, whose operating efficiencies included bringing cookie-cutter playlists to once-distinctive local stations.

Then came the cell phone, which gave people something else to do during their commutes. And finally, the iPod, the ultimate personal radio. With 10,000 of your favorite songs on tap, who needs FM? . . .

Before you shed too many tears for the declining hit, remember that the era of the blockbuster was an anomaly. Before the Industrial Revolution,[2] culture was mostly local—niches were geographic. The economy was agrarian, which distributed populations as broadly as the land. Distance divided people, giving rise to such diversity as regional accents and folk music, and the lack of rapid transportation and communications limited the mixing of cultures and the propagation of ideas and trends.

Influences varied from town to town, because the vehicles for carrying common culture were so limited. There was a reason the church was the main

---

[1] In 2006 and 2007 Tower Records and Sam Goody stores all but disappeared. Tower is now only a music-download Web site, and most of the remaining Sam Goody stores were renamed FYE.—EDS.

[2] *Industrial Revolution* refers to the sweeping social, economic, and technological changes during the late eighteenth and early nineteenth centuries, caused by the use of machines rather than manual labor for production.—EDS.

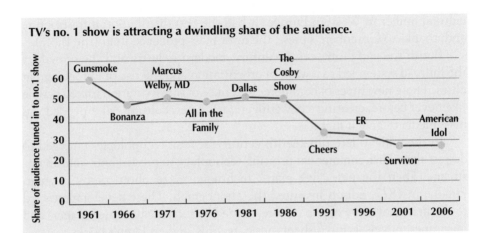

TV's no. 1 show is attracting a dwindling share of the audience.

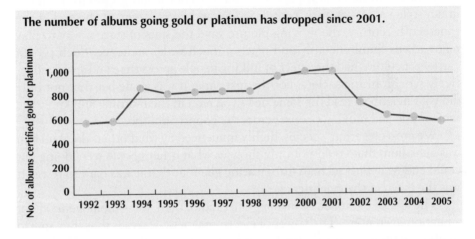

The number of albums going gold or platinum has dropped since 2001.

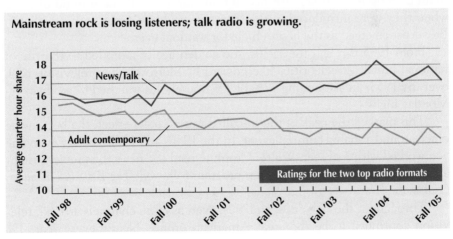

Mainstream rock is losing listeners; talk radio is growing.

cultural unifier in Western Europe: It had the best distribution infrastructure and, thanks to Gutenberg's press, the most mass-produced item (the Bible).

But in the early nineteenth century, modern industry and the growth of the railroad system led to a wave of urbanization and the rise of Europe's great cities. These new hives of commerce and hubs of transportation mixed people like never before, creating a powerful engine of new culture. All it needed was mass media to give it flight.   13

In the mid- to late nineteenth century, several technologies emerged to do just that. First commercial printing technology improved and went mainstream. Then the new "wet plate" technique made photography popular. Finally, in 1877, Edison invented the phonograph. These developments led to the first great wave of pop culture, carried by such media as newspapers and magazines, novels, printed sheet music, records, and children's books.   14

Along with news, newspapers spread word of the latest fashions from the urban style centers of New York, London, and Paris. Then, at the end of the nineteenth century, the moving picture gave the stars of stage a way to play many towns simultaneously and reach a much wider audience. Such potent carriers of culture had the effect of linking people across time and space, effectively synchronizing society. For the first time, it was a safe bet that not only did your neighbors read the same news you read in the morning and know the same music and movies, people across the country did too.   15

We are a gregarious species, highly influenced by what others do. And film was a medium that could not only show us what other people were doing but could endow it with such an intoxicating glamour that it was hard to resist. It was the dawn of the celebrity age.   16

The arrival of broadcast media—first radio, then TV—homogenized our adulation even more. The power of electromagnetic waves is that they spread in all directions essentially for *free*, a trait that made them as mind-blowing when they were introduced as the Internet would be some sixty years later. Broadcast emerged as the best vehicle for stardom ever.   17

From 1935 through the 1950s, the golden age of radio led to the rise of national broadcast celebrities like Edward R. Murrow. Then television took over. By 1953, an astounding 72% of TV households watched *I Love Lucy* on Monday night.   18

This marked the peak of the so-called water-cooler effect, the buzz in the office around a shared cultural event. In the 1950s and 1960s, nearly everyone you worked with had seen Walter Cronkite read the news the previous night and then tuned in to whatever top program followed: *The Beverly Hillbillies, Gunsmoke, The Andy Griffith Show*.   19

Throughout the '70s, '80s, and '90s, even as more channels arrived, television continued to be the great American unifier. Nearly every year, TV   20 advertising set a new record as companies paid more and more for prime time. And why not? Prime-time TV defined the mainstream.

Then came the great unraveling. A new medium arose, one even more 21 powerful than broadcast, and its distribution economics favored infinite niches, not one-size-fits-all fare. The Internet's peer-to-peer architecture is optimized for a symmetrical traffic load, with as many senders as receivers and data transmissions spread out over geography and time. In other words, it's the opposite of broadcast. . . . We are abandoning the tyranny of the top and becoming a niche nation again, defined not by our geography but by our interests. Instead of the weak connections of the office water cooler, we're increasingly forming our own tribes, groups bound together more by affinity and shared interests than by broadcast schedules. These days our water coolers are increasingly virtual — there are many different ones, and the people who gather around them are self-selected.

The mass market is yielding to a million minimarkets. Hits will always be 22 with us, but they have lost their monopoly. Blockbusters must now compete with an infinite number of niche offerings, which can be distributed just as easily. Justin Timberlake still makes albums, but today he has thousands of bands on *MySpace* as rivals. The hierarchy of attention has inverted — credibility now rises from below. MTV and Tower Records no longer decide who will win. You do.

*For a reading quiz, sources on Chris Anderson, and annotated links to further readings on the effects of the Internet on popular culture, visit **bedfordstmartins.com/ thebedfordreader**.*

Journal Writing

How are you likely to access various kinds of popular culture? Make a list of what you've seen or heard over the past six months and what the medium was — whether the Internet or more traditional channels such as TV, radio, movie theaters, magazines, and books. (To take your journal writing further, see "From Journal to Essay" on the next page.)

Questions on Meaning

1. Where does Anderson fully state his THESIS? Restate it in your own words.
2. What is Anderson's point in paragraphs 11–20? How does the causal chain he describes here relate to his thesis?
3. What does Anderson mean by the "water-cooler effect" (par. 19)? And what does he mean by "These days our water coolers are increasingly virtual" (21)? What has changed?
4. How do you suppose Anderson expected readers to respond to this essay? What do you think he hoped they would take away from their reading? What in the essay supports your answer?

Questions on Writing Strategy

1. Why does Anderson open by detailing the sales figures for NSync's *No Strings Attached*? How does this introduction lead into his first major point?
2. Anderson analyzes a number of cause-and-effect relationships. What are they, specifically? How does he tie them together?
3. In his two concluding paragraphs, Anderson uses the pronouns *we/us* and *you*. What does this suggest about his view of his AUDIENCE?
4. **OTHER METHODS** Where in the essay does Anderson use EXAMPLES? What do these examples contribute to his explanation of the "rise and fall of the hit"?

Questions on Language

1. ANALYZE the language Anderson uses to describe the mass marketing of popular culture. What do his words suggest about his attitude toward such mass marketing?
2. Why does Anderson italicize the word *free* in paragraph 17?
3. Notice Anderson's uses of *culture, cultural,* and words suggesting *culture* throughout paragraphs 11–20. How do these repetitions and restatements help to clarify the changes Anderson describes?
4. Consult a dictionary if you are unsure of the meanings of any of the following words: throngs (par. 7); à la carte (8); fragmented, incumbents (9); anomaly, agrarian, propagation (11); synchronizing (15); gregarious (16); homogenized, adulation (17); symmetrical, niches, tyranny, affinity (21); monopoly (22).

Suggestions for Writing

1. **FROM JOURNAL TO ESSAY** Write an essay in which you explain your own relationship with the media of popular culture—Internet, TV, books, radio, and so on. Which media do you prefer, and why? Have your preferences changed in the past year or two? Give specific examples to support your explanation.
2. Anderson writes of popular music, "There has never been a better time to be an artist or a fan, and there has never been more music made or listened to" (par. 5). Do you agree? Write an essay in which you analyze the state of popular music in the United States today. Base your analysis on your own and others' experiences

with popular music, on your reading about it, and, if possible, on the experiences of musicians.

3. Contemporary culture seems obsessed with celebrities, as evidenced by the popularity of magazines, tabloids, television programs, and Internet sites that track the slightest comings and goings of actors, musicians, models, and even those who are famous simply for being famous. Write an essay in which you speculate about the causes of this obsession with celebrities. What is it about the lives of ordinary people that makes them so interested in the lives of famous people?

4. **CRITICAL WRITING** Some observers believe that the "niche nation" Anderson promotes (par. 21) may have a downside because the more we congregate with people like ourselves, the less we learn about the world outside. What is your view of this issue in the context of Anderson's essay? Could traditional mass marketing of popular culture have an advantage in introducing us to works we might not select ourselves? Or is such a consideration outweighed by the freedom to make our own culture?

5. **CONNECTIONS** In "The Squeeze" (p. 487), Charles Fishman describes how mass-market distribution led to "devastating success" for one of Wal-Mart's suppliers. How might Fishman's cautionary tale apply to the products of popular culture that Anderson discusses? In what ways could "niche" marketing and scattered delivery channels prove a boon not only to consumers but to the music industry as well?

Chris Anderson on Writing

In an interview in *Reason* magazine, Nick Gillespie asked Chris Anderson whether the Internet fosters individual talent as well as it does consumer choice. Anderson's response should encourage anyone who has dreamed of being heard but despaired at the obstacles to reaching an audience.

What we're realizing is that talent and expertise and knowledge and writing ability are much more broadly distributed than our previous forms of identifying it revealed. The old model was if you want to make a movie, you have to get your foot in the door in Hollywood. If you want an audience for your music, you've got to get signed by a label. If you want to write a book, you've got to have a publisher.

The old model said: We control the factory, and you have to go through us. Now everyone's got a factory, and we find that there are more people who have talent and, more important, they're making things that our filters haven't previously recognized as having appeal. They're making stuff because they want to make stuff and because they can. Most of it's crap, but a surprising amount of it is not crap, and you're getting these grassroots, bottoms-up hits that are resonating with subcultures that we traditional gatekeepers would never have bothered with.

For Discussion

1. Who are the "gatekeepers" Anderson refers to? Why does he include himself in that group?
2. If the old "filters" are no longer useful, how can Internet users sift the good work from the bad?
3. Have you written on a blog, posted music or video on *YouTube*, or otherwise contributed to the Internet culture Anderson describes? What was the response?

ADDITIONAL WRITING TOPICS
Cause and Effect

1. In a short essay, explain *either* the causes *or* the effects of a situation that concerns you. Narrow your topic enough to treat it in some detail, and provide more than a mere list of causes or effects. If seeking causes, you will have to decide carefully how far back to go in your search for remote causes. If stating effects, fill your essay with examples. Here are some topics to consider:

    Labor strikes in professional sports
    Minors encountering pornography on the Internet
    State laws mandating the use of seat belts in cars (or the wearing of helmets on motorcycles)
    Friction between two roommates, or two friends
    The pressure on students to get good grades
    Some quirk in your personality, or a friend's
    The increasing need for more than one breadwinner per family
    The temptation to do something dishonest to get ahead
    The popularity of a particular television program, comic strip, rock group, or pop singer
    The steady increase in college costs
    The scarcity of people in training for employment as skilled workers: plumbers, tool and die makers, electricians, masons, carpenters, to name a few
    A decision to enter the ministry or a religious order
    The fact that cigarette advertising is banned from television
    The absence of a military draft
    The fact that more couples are choosing to have only one child, or none
    The growing popularity of private elementary and high schools
    Being "born again"
    The fact that women increasingly get jobs formerly regarded as being for men only
    The pressure on young people to conform to the standards of their peers
    The emphasis on competitive sports in high school and college

2. In *Blue Highways* (1982), an account of his rambles around America, William Least Heat-Moon explains why Americans, and not the British, settled the vast tract of northern land that lies between the Mississippi and the Rockies. He traces what he believes to be the major cause in this paragraph:

    > Were it not for a web-footed rodent and a haberdashery fad in eighteenth-century Europe, Minnesota might be a Canadian province today. The beaver, almost as much as the horse, helped shape the course of early American history. Some *Mayflower* colonists paid their passage with beaver pelts; and a good fur could bring an Indian three steel knives or a five-foot stack could bring a musket. But even more influential were the trappers and fur traders penetrating the great Northern wilderness between the Mississippi River and the Rocky Mountains, since it was

their presence that helped hold the Near West against British expansion from the north; and it was their explorations that opened the heart of the nation to white settlement. These men, by making pelts the currency of the wilds, laid the base for a new economy that quickly overwhelmed the old. And all because European men of mode simply had to wear a beaver hat.

In a Heat-Moon–like paragraph of your own, explain how a small cause produced a large effect. You might generate ideas by browsing in a history book—where you might find, for instance, that a cow belonging to Mrs. Patrick O'Leary is believed to have started the Great Chicago Fire of 1871 by kicking over a lighted lantern—or in a collection of *Ripley's Believe It or Not.* If some small event in your life has had large consequences, you might care to write instead from personal experience. (To read more about and by Heat-Moon, see p. 187.)

Notes and Resources for Teaching

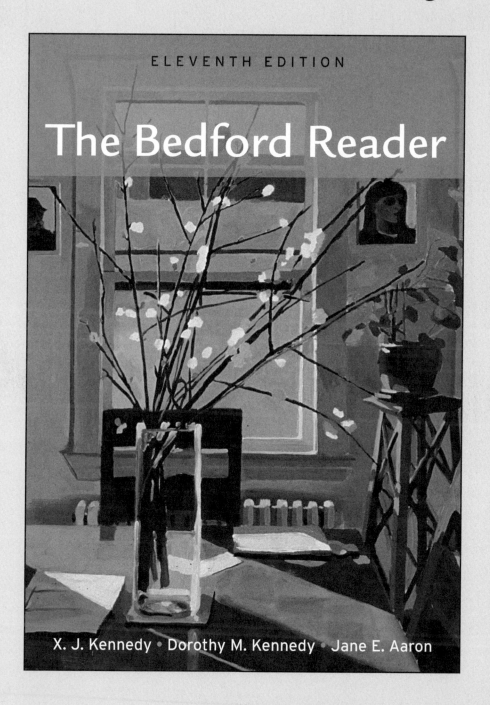

ELEVENTH EDITION

The Bedford Reader

X. J. Kennedy • Dorothy M. Kennedy • Jane E. Aaron

NOTES AND RESOURCES
FOR TEACHING

THE
BEDFORD
READER

ELEVENTH EDITION

X. J. Kennedy • Dorothy M. Kennedy

Jane E. Aaron

Bedford/St. Martin's   Boston   ◆   New York

Manufactured in the United States of America.

6   5   4   3   2   1
f   e   d   c   b   a

For information, write: Bedford/St. Martin's, 75 Arlington Street, Boston, MA 02116 (617-399-4000)

ISBN-10: 0–312–67829–0
ISBN-13: 978–0–312–67829–6

PREFACE

In finding your way to this preface, you may already have discovered the innovations in the eleventh edition of *The Bedford Reader*. (If not, they are summed up in the text's own preface.) Here we describe the various resources for teachers provided in this manual.

"Teaching with Journals and Collaboration" (p. 1). *The Bedford Reader* includes quite a bit on journal writing and small-group collaboration, and here we support the text with background on these popular techniques — benefits, pitfalls, suggestions.

"Teaching Visual Literacy" (p. 4). We suggest ways to use an exciting feature of *The Bedford Reader*: the introductory material on critical reading of visual images and the many images appearing throughout the book.

"Part One: Reading, Writing, and Research" (p. 7). This section gives an overview of the text's crucial chapters on critical reading, the writing process, and academic writing.

Chapter introductions. For each rhetorical chapter, we preview the method, predicting difficulties that students may have with it and suggesting various uses for the selections that illustrate the method.

Selection introductions. For each selection, we highlight what students may like (or dislike) about the piece, suggest topics for discussion and collaboration, and mark connections to other selections.

Answers to questions. For each selection, we also give answers to the questions on meaning, writing strategy, and language that follow the selection in the text.

Comments on the "Writers on Writing." For each comment by a selection author on his or her process, we suggest how the author's reported experience may be instructive for students. Note that the index at the end of the text lists each of these comments under the topic it addresses, such as choosing a subject or outlining or revising.

As always, these resources are intended not as a pedagogic *CliffsNotes* but as the notes of colleagues with whom you might care to hold a dialog. The question answers, especially, are necessarily brief, and undoubtedly you and your students will find much to disagree with. We hope you will also find views to test and enlarge your own questions to prompt better answers.

CONTENTS

TEACHING WITH JOURNALS AND COLLABORATION

Our users report that they often employ journal writing and small-group collaboration in their writing classes. *The Bedford Reader* and this instructor's manual support these techniques in several ways.

JOURNALS

The Bedford Reader includes a discussion of journal writing in Chapter 2 (see p. 37) and a journal-writing assignment just after every selection (for example, pp. 34–35).

More and more instructors use the journal as a teaching tool because it offers students a place to experiment with their ideas without the pressure of producing a crafted, polished essay. This opportunity for creative thinking can also lead to more provocative classroom discussions and formal essays.

One advantage of journals from the teacher's perspective is that they encourage students to share the responsibility of preparing for discussion. You can require a journal entry as part of every assignment, as the first step of writing a paper, or as an integrated part of class discussion. You can allow students to keep their entries on loose paper for easy submission or ask them to keep a notebook so they (and you) have all their entries in one place. You can use the structured journal questions we've suggested at the end of each selection, or you can allow students to write anything at all, in any direction, as long as they write something. Most instructors find that journal writing, like any other teaching technique, requires trial and error in the classroom. One teacher's pleasure is another's pain, after all; and some classes will sit slack-jawed before the same assignment that fires others into animated participation. Following are some general guidelines for those who do or want to use journals.

However often or seldom you require journal entries, try to present them in the context of other writing and discussion in the course; the danger of using journals in an unstructured way is that they can become busywork. Explain to students that it's in their best interest to use their journals as idea notebooks: safe places to record notes and impressions, grapple with difficult issues, respond to the essays in *The Bedford Reader*, and generate ideas for more formal writing assignments. They'll find that papers, discussions, and tests are easier because of the time they spend responding to what they read. Your promise not to grade the entries will guarantee more experimentation.

1

However, you may need scheduled or surprise checks to ensure that writing is actually being committed to paper, and of course some students will be disappointed if you don't personally respond to their personal entries. One productive system is to schedule one or two submissions — emphasizing that they're just for a check in the gradebook toward a discussion grade — while encouraging unscheduled submissions for your comments on a particular entry whenever a student wants them. A student who is worried about a paper can get your early feedback, or a student who prefers writing to speaking can have a conversation with you.

Many students will be unfamiliar, even uncomfortable, with required writing that is informal and ungraded, so you may want to coax and guide them into writing. For those who are anxious about your expectations, emphasize that journals provide a free space where there are no right answers and where organization and sentence structure may simply reflect the student's train of thought. For everyone, make use of the open-ended journal assignment after every selection in the book: It asks students for personal recollections or gut responses to the selection, in an effort to help them recognize their own connection to it. Farther on, a "From Journal to Essay" writing topic asks students to hone their personal responses into structured essays, sometimes personal, often critical. You can use the journal prompt by itself to get students writing and talking. Even if you don't build journals into your course, you might find some of the prompts useful as in-class freewriting prompts or as remedies for dull discussions. Try assigning a journal entry for a particular selection and then asking volunteers to read theirs aloud and lead a discussion for five minutes or so. Try asking pairs of students to trade journals, read each other's entries on a given topic, and write responses. Try giving the journal assignments as starting points for small-group discussions.

Some students will have strong responses to the essays in *The Bedford Reader* and will not need any prompting to come up with "something to write about." Definitely encourage students to stray from our suggested avenues of response if they have another idea to explore. The main purpose of journals, after all, is to challenge students to articulate their own ideas more fully.

COLLABORATION

Working in small groups creates unique opportunities for students to examine the concepts of a course and the process of writing. Like journals, small groups are a useful testing ground for ideas and a means for exploring the nuances of issues. Often less intimidating than a whole-class discussion, a small group can provide students with a more collaborative forum for voicing their opinions. In fact, many teachers find that a major benefit of small groups is that they require all students to participate actively both as talkers and as listeners.

Small groups can augment learning in a variety of ways. Discussions might center on an opinion presented in a selection on writing style or rhetorical strategy or on solving a problem raised by an author. (This manual's introduction to each selection suggests possible directions.) The result could be a collaborative written response that you collect or a series of brief presentations in which groups explain their responses to the rest of the class. Or, keeping it more informal, you may choose simply to roam and eavesdrop throughout the group sessions to see that groups stay focused and to discover what kinds of conclusions they are reaching.

Groups can also enhance whole-class discussions. Try having small groups spend the first fifteen minutes of class brainstorming answers to difficult questions as a precursor to a whole-class discussion. Have groups do outside research related to upcoming essays and report their findings to the class as a whole. Toward the end of the semester, you may feel confident enough in your groups to allow them to take turns planning and running class discussions.

Small groups can also be invaluable as writing workshops, to help students learn to become better readers and revisers of their own essays. Once students get to know members of their group well, they will begin to trust the feedback they receive. From brainstorming on an essay topic to providing suggestions on drafts, peer readers are often uniquely able to point out what works in an essay, what is confusing, what needs expanding, and so on.

You may have to teach students how to give this kind of feedback. Toward that end, Chapter 2 sets the stage with some words of encouragement (see p. 50) and includes sample peer responses to the student essay-in-progress (p. 53). For further encouragement, try modeling a workshop process for the class, beginning with a conversation about what *constructive criticism* means. Ask a volunteer to bring copies of a draft paper to class, or copy a paper from a previous term, or even copy something of your own. Distribute copies to the class. Have the author read the paper aloud, as would occur in the small group. (If the author isn't present, ask a volunteer to read.) Ask the author to explain his or her main concerns about the essay (introduction doesn't seem to fit rest of paper, organization feels choppy, transitions awkward, and so on) — or if there is no author, take this role yourself. Then lead the whole class in a discussion of the essay, starting with what works particularly well and moving to what doesn't work. (Often students will shy away from criticizing a peer, and you may need to get the discussion going.) Give the author (you, if you're role-playing) plenty of opportunities to respond to people's comments. During the discussion, point out what works in workshopping and what doesn't. The most useful feedback will reflect the reader's understanding of the essay ("I got confused when you . . ." or "I wish you would give more details so I could see this place better" or "I don't follow your logic in paragraph 3"). *Discussion* of how to solve such problems will be more fruitful than blunt suggestions like "This passage should be cut" or "You should just rewrite this sentence like this."

Of course, negotiating personality conflicts and overcoming shyness and other qualities that can silence a small group can sometimes be tricky. To minimize these problems, have students compose a "personals" ad on an index card at the beginning of the term, explaining that they're searching for their workshop soul mates. Write a few questions on the board, such as what their strengths and weaknesses are as writers, readers, and talkers or how they respond to constructive criticism. Such self-portraits may not be entirely accurate, but they can help you group students according to complementary abilities and attitudes: You can group some who like to do research with others who like to talk in front of a large group; some who struggle to organize essays with others who feel that organizing is their biggest strength; some who are experienced in collaboration with others who aren't.

Small groups give students a chance to practice the ideas and strategies gleaned from lectures and reading. And such collaborative learning eases some of the burden on you, too: Students will not only gain a great sense of authority over their learning but also share the hot seat at the front of the room.

TEACHING VISUAL LITERACY

Throughout *The Bedford Reader*, we provide many opportunities to incorporate the visual into writing classes: A section in Chapter 1 extends critical thinking from texts to illustrations; every rhetorical chapter opens with an image or related images, along with a caption that prompts students' critical responses; and a few of the written selections center on illustrations that we also reprint.

THINKING CRITICALLY ABOUT VISUAL IMAGES

In Chapter 1 on reading, we offer a detailed approach to thinking critically about visuals (pp. 27–31). Paralleling the method for evaluating written texts, the approach involves five steps: getting the big picture, analyzing, inferring, synthesizing, and evaluating. A photograph provides a rich opportunity to apply the method.

Students generally like looking at images, and they often form immediate, almost visceral responses to what they see. The challenge, then, may be to guide their responses along critical pathways. For instance, they may need coaching to perceive the value of information about artists or advertisers or historical and cultural contexts — and they may need help gathering such information. In analyzing an image, they often benefit from small-group discussions in which they hear several points of view. Similarly, in the inference phase they can listen to the meanings attributed by others with different backgrounds and outlooks. Finally, as they evaluate images they may need encouragement to step back from their natural emotional responses and judge the worthiness of the image's purpose and its success in fulfilling that purpose.

CHAPTER-OPENING IMAGES

Each rhetorical chapter in Part Two opens with a visual representation of the chapter's method at work, accompanied by background information and questions about the image or images.

- An advertisement tells the story of a former "weakling" who decided to try a bodybuilding program (narration, Chap. 4)
- A photograph depicts a riverside shanty (description, Chap. 5)
- A cartoon proposes "low-energy drinks" that could counteract today's trendy jolters (example, Chap. 6)
- A well-known painting and a contemporaneous photograph play off each other (comparison and contrast, Chap. 7)

4

- A photograph makes a telling comment on a doll-making factory (process analysis, Chap. 8)
- A cartoon deconstructs a kid's bologna sandwich (division or analysis, Chap. 9)
- A chart illustrates a typical community's recycling guidelines (classification, Chap. 10)
- A cartoon examines the effects of texting while driving (cause and effect, Chap. 11)
- An Army advertisement probes the meaning of *strong* (definition, Chap. 12)
- An alternative version of America's Stars and Stripes makes a strong argument about the United States (argument and persuasion, Chap. 13)

We anticipate that these images will inspire you and your students in several possible ways:

- Because each chapter opener shows a rhetorical method at work, it provides an additional way to introduce the method. The images may especially help students who resist or struggle with reading.
- The caption accompanying each chapter opener provides background on the image so that students have essential information for a critical response. The questions in each caption encourage reflection and discourage snap judgments such as "I like it" or "I don't like it" or "I don't get it," and they can serve as journal or discussion prompts. Using the caption questions or your own assignments, you can devise various class or small-group projects centered on the chapter openers. For instance, the Grant Wood painting and the Ben Shahn photograph in Chapter 7 open up worlds to investigate — the backgrounds and interests of the artists, the effects of the Great Depression on farmers, the effect of medium on perception. For another example, the cartoon in Chapter 11 practically begs for a more detailed and substantiated examination of the problem of distracted driving. (At the same time, the cartoon has an undeniable punch. What are the advantages of simplifying causes and effects?)

ILLUSTRATIONS ACCOMPANYING TEXT SELECTIONS

Seven of *The Bedford Reader*'s text selections include illustrations. In each case, the juxtaposition deepens the meaning of both the written text and the illustration.

- Howard Markel, in "Mary Ellen's Story" (p. 133), includes a photograph of his subject, a nineteenth-century victim of child abuse, to reveal the nature of her injuries.
- Joyce Carol Oates's poem "Edward Hopper's *Nighthawks*, 1942" (p. 194) describes and interprets Hopper's famous urban scene, which we show in full view and in a detail. "Joyce Carol Oates on Writing" comments on the making of the poem and further interprets the painting.
- In "The Myth of Doomed Kids" (p. 379), Bella DePaulo analyzes the data presented in tables, demonstrating the careful reading needed to get at the truth of statistics.
- Student Laila Ayad's "The Capricious Camera" (p. 387) models the close analysis of a photograph. Examining an arresting image from World War II, Ayad makes a point about the Nazis' agenda of racial purification and about the ambiguities of photography.

- In "A Vocabulary of Smiles" (p. 445), psychologist Dacher Keltner presents four facial photographs to test readers' ability to apply his classification system in their own lives.
- In "The Rise and Fall of the Hit" (p. 494), Chris Anderson uses three line graphs to visually reinforce his point about the effects of niche media on the entertainment industry.
- John Updike's "Extreme Dinosaurs" (p. 713) includes artists' renderings of several unusual prehistoric creatures to show the oddities of evolution.

PART ONE

READING, WRITING, AND RESEARCH

Part One of *The Bedford Reader* provides a substantial and well-illustrated discussion of critical reading, the writing process, and academic writing (including research and documentation). The outline of Part One (below) is followed by a description of the contents.

Chapter 3: Academic Writing (p. 61)

Chapter 1 gives step-by-step instructions on attentive, critical reading, including examples of annotating a text, summarizing, and using analysis, interpretation, synthesis, and evaluation. A sample essay by Nancy Mairs and our commentary and marginal annotations illustrate the steps. Then a section shows students, again by example, how to apply their faculties for critical thinking to visual images. (For more on this topic, see p. 4 of this manual.)

Chapter 2 then details the stages of the writing process, including aids to discovery (journals, freewriting, and the rhetorical methods themselves), a stress on the thesis statement, detailed advice for and examples of revising and editing, and encouragement for collaboration. This section also includes the stages of a student's response to Mairs's essay, from first journal entry through annotated final draft. This paper also serves the next chapter as an example of response writing.

Chapter 3, "Academic Writing," aims to help students surmount one of their biggest hurdles: learning to write critically about what they have read. The chapter focuses on response writing and research writing, emphasizing synthesis in both cases. The research-writing help includes extensive sections on evaluating sources, avoiding plagiarism, and documenting sources in MLA style. Concluding the chapter is an annotated research paper by the same student who wrote the response paper in Chapter 2. She also writes on the same subject, modeling the way reading can expand and refine ideas, and reflects on the process in a writers-on-writing commentary.

You can use Chapters 1–3 in various ways, depending on your students' needs and, of course, your own inclinations. Many instructors teach directly from this material, especially when students are unfamiliar with the processes of critical reading and writing, have little experience with academic writing or with research, or have no other text to rely on. Other instructors ask their students to read the material on their own — it does not assume previous knowledge and so can be self-teaching. Still others select for classwork the parts they wish to stress (summary, say, or the thesis statement) and ask students to cover the remaining sections on their own.

PART TWO

THE METHODS

4
NARRATION
Telling a Story

To write a short account of a personal experience is, for many freshmen, a first assignment that looks reassuring and possible to fulfill. Instructors who wish to begin in this way may assign for reading one or more of this chapter's essays by Angelou, Tan, Dillard, Philbert, and Markel. Four of the writers give students a sense of what a good writer can do with material perhaps much like their own: recollections and observations of ordinary experience from childhood and college days. The fifth writer, Markel, reflects on information gathered from research to weight and broaden what another person experienced in another time. Angelou's and Tan's essays — both recalling experiences of "outsider" children in a predominantly white culture — can be paired for discussion and writing.

Not all freshmen feel comfortable writing in the first person. Some may writhe under a burden of self-consciousness. Some may feel guilty about not following the doctrine of a high-school teacher who once urged them to avoid *I*. A few members of the composition staff at Chapel Hill reported encountering this problem and, because of it, some preferred to begin their courses with *The Bedford Reader*'s chapter on description. Writing in the third person seems to give such students greater assurance about constructing that crucial first paper in which they're trying hard to please.

Chapter 4 ends with a short story. By juxtaposing Jackson's "The Lottery" with the nonfictional narratives of the others, this chapter gives you a chance to ask, "How does fiction differ from nonfiction?"

MAYA ANGELOU

Champion of the World

A story within a story, Maya Angelou's suspenseful narrative invites attention to both its method and its matter. Inside the story of what happens in the general store (told in the first person, as Angelou looks back to her childhood), we follow the story of the Louis-Carnera fight. Suspense builds from the beginning, in the introductory glimpse of the people crowding in eagerly, in the "apprehensive mood" compared to a sky "streaked with lightning" (par. 2), and in the scraps of conversation. Larger events of the history of civil rights form a background to this narrative — for example, the fact that African Americans were not safe at night, although we learn this only at the end of the story.

You might begin by asking students what they know of the career of Joe Louis. (In some classes no one may know of him.) You could break the class into groups of three or four and have them research what it meant in the 1930s for an African American to become a prominent and universally admired athlete. Come up with a few contextual categories: Louis's career overall; other firsthand reminiscences of boxing in the 1930s; African American life in the 1930s. Each group could then present its findings for five to ten minutes, ending with a whole-class discussion of Angelou's memoir. (Note: If this sort of background research is something you'd like to have students do fairly regularly, you might consider rotating the responsibility so that just one group works and reports on any given essay.)

Audio aids: Angelou reads excerpts from *I Know Why the Caged Bird Sings* on a set of CDs with the same title, produced by Random House Audiobooks. The recordings may be ordered from *Amazon.com*.

QUESTIONS ON MEANING

1. Like the rest of the autobiography from which this selection is taken, "Champion of the World" seems written for a dual purpose: to recall vivid and significant moments of the author's life and to reveal the ironic situation of African Americans in America in the 1930s: able to become world champions but not able to walk a country road at night. This irony is given great weight by being placed at the end of the story.

2–3. As Angelou indicates in much of her story, and especially in paragraphs 16 and 17, the pride of the race depends on the fight. Not only pride but a whole future rides on the outcome: "If Joe lost we were back in slavery. . . ." Everyone in the store believes this, but the author's view is not so simple. Obviously she doesn't share the notion that if Joe Louis lost it would be clear that "God Himself hated us"; she is exaggerating the assumptions of the people in the store to emphasize the ideological importance of the fight.

4. The error makes untrue a small corner of the story (and might distract people who recognize it), but the fact that Angelou mixed up Louis's fights does not discredit what she reports experiencing.

QUESTIONS ON WRITING STRATEGY

1. Every sentence in the first paragraph contributes to our sense of the importance of the coming events. Note that, with space inside the store at such a premium, children (except infants and toddlers who could fit on a lap) are banished to the porch outside.

2. From paragraph 1 we feel anticipation and a tension that mounts to a crisis in paragraph 15, when the contender rains blows on Louis and staggers him. Short, punchy sentences add speed and force to Angelou's account: "We didn't breathe. We didn't hope. We waited" (par. 18 — and, incidentally, a good example of parallelism). The whole device of telling the story of the fight through a radio announcer's spiel is particularly effective because, as Angelou makes clear, the listeners in the store hang on the announcer's every word. Using radio as a medium in storytelling can increase suspense by leaving much to the imagination.

   Anyone familiar with the history of boxing will predict the winner as soon as the name of Joe Louis emerges; others may not be sure until Louis rallies in paragraph 20.

3. Students who sense the irony will probably express it in any of several ways. Some will say that despite all the hopes and dreams bound up in the fight, Louis's victory hasn't delivered his people. Maybe Louis is the strongest man in the ring, but African Americans in rural Arkansas are still vulnerable. Angelou's irony in the final line is so strong that it is practically sarcasm. Isn't there a suggestion, too, that on this particular night some whites, resenting the Louis victory, will be out to punish any African Americans they can find alone or in small numbers?

4. Here, as everywhere, direct quotation lends immediacy to any scene an author creates.

5. The descriptive details in paragraph 27 — drinking Coke "like ambrosia," eating candy "like Christmas," boys "blowing their breath in front of themselves like proud smokers" — move the story ahead and re-create the special joy and pride of the occasion.

QUESTIONS ON LANGUAGE

1. Singing commercials for razor blades; sales pitches designed to "string" the listener along. It is possible that Angelou finds irony in the sponsor's product, too, since a racist, stereotypical view of poor African Americans might have them fighting with razors or razor blades.

2. Examples of strong verbs include "perched" (par. 1); "grunted" (6); "poured" (10); "pushed" (12); "groaned," "ambushed," "raped," "whipped," "maimed," "slapping" (16); "clutched" (17); "slid" (21); and "shouted" (23).

3. Nonstandard English here makes the people gathered in the store come alive for us. (This story offers a great opportunity to point out the occasional high value of nonstandard English. The comments in pars. 4 and 8 are so well put that they're hard to forget.)

4. The definition of *white lightning* is hard to find in standard dictionaries. *The Dictionary of American Slang* defines it as "cheap, inferior, home-made, or bootleg whisky, usually uncolored corn whisky."

MAYA ANGELOU ON WRITING

Here are some responses to the questions for discussion.

1. What Angelou means by rhythm won't be easily defined, but for her, finding the rhythm of a subject is that early stage all writers go through when first preparing to write. It means (we'd guess) getting a sense of the size and shape of a subject — or perhaps working up some feeling for it.
2. Writing twelve or fourteen pages of longhand notes, setting down all she knows about the subject, may seem to some students an excessive amount of toil. But Angelou invites the observation that the more work you do before you write, the easier it is to write.

AMY TAN

Fish Cheeks

Amy Tan remains one of the best-known Chinese American writers on the current scene. This brief, amusing piece about a shock between two cultures is a good example of how much can be accomplished in very little space. Every detail contributes to the contrast between the two families and their cultures.

We have paired "Fish Cheeks" with Maya Angelou's "Champion of the World." Both essays illuminate the experience of being an outsider in America and the ways family can ameliorate or exacerbate a child's grappling with social identity.

Some students may take offense at Tan's use of stereotypes for humor, while others may see her Asian Americanness as exempting her from criticism on those grounds. If this issue is controversial in your class, consider setting up small-group debates on the "political correctness" of the essay.

Students who enjoy Tan's story should be encouraged to look further into Tan's works — *The Joy Luck Club* (1989), *The Kitchen God's Wife* (1991), *The Hundred Secret Senses* (1995), *The Bonesetter's Daughter* (2001), and *The Opposite of Fate* (2003). Another valuable look at the Chinese American experience is Maxine Hong Kingston's *The Woman Warrior* (1976), a portion of which is reprinted on page 649.

QUESTIONS ON MEANING

1. Tan believes that her family will embarrass her.
2. Tan's mother wants to teach her not to be ashamed of her Chineseness, not to become completely Americanized. "Your only shame is to have shame" (par. 7).
3. Tan is ashamed of her background, referring to her family's "shabby Chinese Christmas" and "noisy Chinese relatives who lacked proper American manners" (par. 2). She resents her mother at the time, but eventually learns to appreciate the lesson she has taught her.

4. Tan's purpose is to amuse and entertain, yes, but possibly also to thank her mother and to impart her lesson to the reader.

QUESTIONS ON WRITING STRATEGY

1. Tan sets us up for a story right away. We know immediately that we're going to hear an anecdote about the minister's cute son — and an ethnic conflict.
2. The narrative progression is straightforward; each paragraph starts with a transition that places us in time: "the winter I turned fourteen" (par. 1); "When I found out" (2); "On Christmas Eve" (3); "And then" (4); "Dinner" (5); "At the end of the meal" (6); "After everyone had gone" (7); "And even though I didn't agree with her then" (8). This gives a sense of constant forward momentum to the story.
3. The irony lies in the narrator's inability to acknowledge or realize that the dishes she has described with such disgust in paragraph 3 are in fact her favorites. The Chinese Tan and the American Tan conflict with each other.
4. The descriptive paragraph is meant to be humorous and entertaining, and it will probably have the desired effect on non-Chinese readers: to make clear the culture shock the narrator thinks the minister's family will experience. (Some readers, though, may relish the description.)

QUESTIONS ON LANGUAGE

1. The comparison is amusing because the minister's son is compared to a chaste female figure even though it's a first crush and the narrator is "in love"; it also underscores both the cultural and nonsexual nature of her love.
2. Tan's language is typical of a young adolescent girl: "my mother had outdone herself" (par. 3); "Robert grunted hello, and I pretended he was not worthy of existence" (4); "Dinner threw me deeper into despair," "I wanted to disappear" (5).
3. Students' opinions may differ, but Tan's use of verbs in paragraph 5 is especially strong.
4. Tofu (a curd of soybean milk) comes from the Chinese *dòu*, "bean," and *fu*, "curdled." Once exotic in the United States, tofu is now a staple of many American diets.

AMY TAN ON WRITING

Tan provides a lesson in turning a negative into a positive, from her initial difficulties with language to her acceptance of the richness her many Englishes give her voice. Many readers have been consistently impressed with her ear for dialog. If you have second-generation students in your classroom, they may have strong opinions on the fairness of standardized testing and the reasons why more children of immigrants enter the precise scientific fields than the subjective field of English. Incidentally, Tan's comments bear comparison with Richard Rodriguez's "Aria" (p. 681). Both deal with the conflicts for bilingual children between the private and public realms.

ANNIE DILLARD

The Chase

This portrait of childhood beautifully captures the energy and idealism of youth. It originally appeared as a chapter in *An American Childhood* (1987), which one reviewer described as being "less about a coming-to-age than about a coming-to-consciousness, a consciousness so heightened by what appears to be an overactive autonomic nervous system that one sometimes fears her nerves will burst through her skin."

The narration of the chase itself (pars. 10–15) is an excellent model for students' own narrative writing. Point out the rhetorical devices Dillard uses to vary the narration and to make the chase seem endless (such as asyndeton, repetition, use of the plural in par. 13).

The story is also a good example of how narration can be used in the service of a larger theme, with implications that go beyond the events recounted. Dillard does more than simply tell a story; she makes an interesting observation about the death of enthusiasm.

Students might want to share in small groups their reactions to Dillard's contrast between a child's and an adult's point of view. Some may find Dillard's description of adulthood overly cynical and her portrait of childhood romanticized. Others may recall a time when they themselves expected more from life, when their own senses of joy were greater. (Or they may have experienced moments when they suddenly caught themselves thinking or speaking like their parents.) Encourage students to discuss their reactions to this theme and to come up with other examples of it from literature and movies.

QUESTIONS ON MEANING

1. Dillard wants to show how a harmless chase can take on epic proportions in the mind of a child. She wants to point out valuable qualities of childhood lost in adulthood: energy and wholeheartedness.
2. No. This driver is exceptional, the only one who has ever left his car (par. 9).
3. The pursuer is the only adult the narrator has encountered who "knew what I thought only children who trained at football knew: that you have to fling yourself at what you're doing, you have to point yourself, forget yourself, aim, dive" (par. 13). At the end of the chase he comes "down to earth" (19), addressing the children in the banal, perfunctory tones of an ordinary adult. Dillard is disillusioned because of the gap between her ideals and reality.
4. Nothing can live up to the glorious moment that was the chase. The pursuer has resumed the role of just another adult, parroting the words all adults are required to say at such moments.

QUESTIONS ON WRITING STRATEGY

1. Football serves as a metaphor for life in the story: Everything you do, you have to tackle, giving 100% of yourself.

2. From football to baseball, from baseball to snowball throwing: These transitions contribute to the essay's coherence. Baseball is a logical link between football (another boys' sport) and snowball throwing, in which the throwing arm is all-important. The lesson Dillard has learned from playing sports is carried over to a more general lesson about life.

3. Far from weakening the narrative, this is the story's epiphany, where Dillard explains the larger meaning the chase was to take on.

4. Dillard's narration seamlessly combines the articulateness and sophistication of an adult interpreter with a child's view of the events taking place.

5. Adults are lazy and take shortcuts. ("Any normal adult would have quit, having sprung us into flight and made his point," par. 10.) Unlike children playing football, adults are unwilling to fling themselves "wholeheartedly" (1) into things. With their "normal righteous anger" and "usual common sense" (20), they are victims of habit and routine. Children are willing to go all out; they know that life is "all or nothing" (1). (See also the second writing suggestion.)

QUESTIONS ON LANGUAGE

1. Dillard uses language with religious connotations to describe her pursuer. Besides "exalting" and "righteous," she also uses "glory" (par. 19) and "sainted" (21).

2. The children, though playing together, exhibit a "natural solitude" (par. 5). While being chased they are at once "exhilarated" and "dismayed" (14). The man chasing them is referred to as "our pursuer, our captor" and "our hero" (16). Dillard portrays childhood as a time of confusion and contradiction.

3. Dillard is imagining what the pursuer might have done if he had "trapped" her and her companion in crime: "fried" them in boiling oil, "dismembered" them, "staked" them to anthills; but his only option, disappointingly to her, is to "chew [them] out."

4. The sentence indicates how long and complicated the chase was and helps to bring the pursuer back down to earth. It is also anticlimactic after the imaginative digression about the Panama Canal and the lyrical tribute to the pursuer that precede it. It is a typically banal, "adult" question.

ANNIE DILLARD ON WRITING

Any student who has ever become tangled in a long, complicated sentence and gone around in circles, losing track of an idea, will find sense in Dillard's remark that short sentences "can get you out of big trouble." If we teach sentence combining, we sometimes risk creating monsters; some students — often the best ones — may try to make a sentence carry too much weight. But Dillard's advice shouldn't be construed as urging us to write in nothing but short, simple sentences, sounding like a first-grade reader as a result. A good point to suggest: Mix up your sentences; vary them in length. And don't worry at all about your sentences while you write a draft; deal with them when you edit.

BRADLEY PHILBERT

Good

For anybody who has ever lost a pet, or loved one dearly, "Good" is nothing short of heartbreaking. Even readers who have no affinity for dogs will almost certainly choke up as they read Bradley Philbert's raw, emotional account of putting his beloved George to death while trying to come to terms with his loss.

One way to begin discussion might be to focus on the third writing suggestion. Begin by asking your students for a show of hands: Who cried? Then ask them how Philbert manages to elicit readers' empathy so effectively. What is the difference between empathy and sympathy? Is it appropriate for a writer to expose emotions so nakedly? What elements of Philbert's very personal story touch on universal human experience?

Film aficionados might detect some parallels between "Good" and the classic 1957 tear-jerker *Old Yeller*. For students who are particularly moved by Philbert's story, you might encourage them to watch the Disney film — available in many public libraries — and write an essay comparing the strategies used in the movie and the essay to manipulate the audiences' emotions.

QUESTIONS ON MEANING

1. Although George was squeamish, useless as a guard dog, small, old, and incontinent, he was also a playful, complacent, unthreatening, and loving companion. For Philbert, the good qualities clearly outweighed those that some (but certainly not all) dog enthusiasts might consider shortcomings.
2. That Philbert is Irish *and* Latino suggests that he is probably Catholic; according to Philbert, his cultural tradition holds that mourning is to be done in private. The religious implication, as well as the allusion to wakes, suggests that the essay will serve for Philbert as both a confession and a eulogy. Rather than celebrate George's life, Philbert focuses on the dog's decline and his own conflicted feelings over having to euthanize it.
3. Philbert does not state his thesis directly, but he hints at it in paragraph 8: ". . . I left him on the patch of grass, then I left the lawn, then the patio, then the family room. Like leaving the hospital, a set of small departures that, together, meant something had changed, something fundamental." That "something" is not just the loss of his dog, apparently, but also Philbert's attitude toward his own life.
4. Philbert intends to reflect on the meaning of his loss, perhaps to assuage his own feelings of guilt or to persuade readers to cherish living things over their possessions.

QUESTIONS ON WRITING STRATEGY

1. By opening with George's death and his own complicity in it, Philbert grounds his subject and hints at his purpose for writing (see question 5

under "Meaning"). Because he is writing to reflect on the meaning of his dog's death, he establishes the painful fact that it happened (and how) from the start. To save the death for the end would have created a sense of suspense, or maybe even of hope for a positive outcome — which would have conflicted with Philbert's overwhelmingly mournful and guilt-ridden tone.

2. Philbert glosses over most of George's life, giving only a few sentences to his playful days (par. 2). He devotes two paragraphs (2 and 3) to the dog's decline, but even there Philbert limits the details, focusing more on the landscaping project than he does on George's health, much as he did when those events were taking place and he couldn't bring himself to face the fact that the dog was "getting sicker, silently and almost invisibly" (2). Philbert spends the most time on the grueling experience of George's last days, when he finally had to accept "[t]he news" (4) and do something about it. The details in paragraphs 4 and 7, where Philbert describes George's physical condition, are painfully forceful and concrete, rendering it almost impossible for readers not to feel the dog's — and the writer's — agony.

3. The transitions in the first third of the essay reflect Philbert's focus on past events and the dog's gradual, almost imperceptible, decline: "as he aged" (par. 2), "[a]s he got sicker" (2), "[a]s the cancer grew" (2), "[m]y family could tell earlier" (3), "[a]fter the months of work and flux" (3). Beginning with the dog's hospitalization in paragraph 4, the transitions shift to a more urgent, rapid sense: almost always some variation on "and then" (4, 5, 6, 7, 8). The immediacy and lack of variation in the later transitions mimic what the writer must have been feeling as the events transpired: overwhelmed, disoriented, unable to control what happens.

4. He establishes the cause of George's condition — inoperable cancer — in the introductory paragraphs but details the effects in paragraph 4: The dog's lungs filled with fluids that had to be surgically drained, and he couldn't breathe on his own; at the same time, he suffered from pain that couldn't be controlled, and the medical interventions not only weren't helping but also were causing additional discomfort and, apparently, infection. Given those effects, very few people would fault Philbert for deciding to put the animal out of its misery.

QUESTIONS ON LANGUAGE

1. Philbert's purpose goes beyond praising the dog. In many ways, he's examining the events that led to a very difficult choice and trying to justify an action that felt to him like "a conspiracy, a betrayal" (par. 6). His final judgment, "Good," applies to himself as much as to his dog: Although it pained him, Philbert seems to conclude that he made the right choice.

2. The pattern creates an irresistible rhythm and suggests both emotional numbness and small steps toward acceptance. By using the construction to describe himself leaving the hospital, and then the scene of his dog's death, Philbert ties the two momentous events together and gives them significance: each "set of small departures" (par. 8) indicated a "fundamental" (8) change that was painful, but inevitable and right.

3. The translations underscore how deeply Philbert loved the dog and considered him a member of the family (even his name, George, is one usually associated with humans). By translating George's cries into sen-

tences, Philbert empathizes with his pet and tries to mentally communicate with him, even though he "knew he couldn't understand" (par. 6).

4. Philbert uses slightly euphemistic clinical terms to try to distance himself from his feelings at key points in his narrative. Notice "barbiturates," "sedation," and "malignant carcinoma" (par. 1) in his initial description of the moment the dog is euthanized. Tellingly, Philbert abandons most of the clinical language in his conclusion, preferring instead to describe the dog's death, and his role in it, with unflinching honesty.

BRADLEY PHILBERT ON WRITING

Philbert makes a good point that the success of a narrative is in the telling. Students who insist that they don't have anything to write about might be reminded that many of the best narratives revolve around small moments, not major events. Whether they realize it or not, readers can be captivated by voice and style more than by subject matter.

HOWARD MARKEL
Mary Ellen's Story

In this straightforward but compelling historical narrative, Howard Markel relates the story of the first time a parent (adoptive or otherwise) was tried for and convicted of child abuse. Students will likely be surprised to learn that, until the end of the nineteenth century, no laws existed to prevent or punish violence toward children. Some will latch onto Markel's underlying point — that child abuse continues to be a serious problem — while others may miss it at first. You might wish, then, to begin discussion with the question of Markel's purpose (question 4 under "Meaning"). His essay is not an exercise in shocking readers with images of violence, but rather it is a plea for stronger protections for children today.

Students who choose to take on the research suggested for the second writing topic might start with any of the following sources:

On Blackwell's Island

Dickens, Charles. *American Notes*. New York: D. Appleton and Co., 1868. Chapter 6. (Available online at *gutenberg.org/dirs/etext96/amnts10.txt*.)

McCabe, James D., Jr. *Lights and Shadows of New York Life*. Philadelphia: National Publishing Co., 1872. (Available online at *correctionhistory.org/html/chronicl/nycdoc/html/blakwel3.html*.)

On Nineteenth-Century Institutions

Boyer, Paul. *Urban Masses and Moral Order in America, 1820–1920*. Cambridge: Harvard UP, 1978.

Freedman, Estelle B. *Their Sister's Keepers: Women's Prison Reform in America, 1830–1930*. Ann Arbor: U of Michigan P, 1984.

Katz, Michael B. *In the Shadow of the Poorhouse: A Social History of Welfare in America*. New York: Basic, 1996.

Mandler, Peter, ed. *The Uses of Charity: The Poor on Relief in the Nineteenth-Century Metropolis*. Philadelphia: U of Pennsylvania P, 1990.

Stansell, Christine. *City of Women*. Urbana: U of Illinois P, 1982.

Those who wish to learn more about the history of child abuse will find an excellent resource in Linda Gordon's *Heroes of Their Own Lives: The Politics and History of Family Violence* (U of Illinois P, 1988).

QUESTIONS ON MEANING

1. As Markel explains, "In 1874, there were no laws protecting children from physical abuse from their parents" (par. 4). He further implies, but does not state, that children were thought of more as property, small adults, or "beasts of burden" (12) than as innocent, vulnerable beings requiring nurturance (that assumption developed in the early twentieth century). For those who wished to protect Mary Ellen McCormack, and others like her, the ASPCA offered the closest available models of legal arguments against abuse. Students might be shocked to read that Henry Bergh "saw the girl . . . as a vulnerable member of the animal kingdom" (7), but at the time, his perspective was unusually compassionate.

2. The adage, which originated in the Bible (Prov. 13.24), was — and often still is — used to justify corporal punishment. The "rod" refers to a switch, or wooden stick, used to spank children. The idea is that without discipline, children will become unruly and unproductive members of society. The line also reinforces Markel's implication (see question 1, above) that children were not thought of as especially vulnerable or in need of protection: quite the opposite, in fact.

3. For readers who aren't familiar with the film, Markel offers a brief synopsis, noting that *Precious* "depicts the emotional and sexual abuse of a Harlem girl" (par. 2). He refers to the film, which garnered a lot of attention (both positive and negative) when it was released, to emphasize that abuse of children has not stopped. Worse still, it now serves as a form of popular entertainment. By alluding to contemporary news and movies, Markel establishes the continuing relevance of a historical subject.

4. Markel's purpose becomes clear in the last two paragraphs: He is writing to explain why (and how) the Society for the Prevention of Cruelty to Children was established and to remind readers that its services are still sorely needed.

5. Markel concludes with his thesis statement: "Mary Ellen's story reminds us of a simple equation: How much our society values its children can be measured by how well they are treated and protected" (par. 12). Implied in this statement is the writer's wish that readers will take action to help children and support the organizations that do protective work.

QUESTIONS ON WRITING STRATEGY

1. The trial is the most dramatic part of the story, and a good hook to grab readers' interest. It also lets Markel establish the significance of the story before he turns back to its origins.

2. Markel writes in the third person, as an objective nonparticipant. The choice is not only appropriate, since he was writing a historical narrative for a newspaper, but also necessary, given that he wasn't involved in the events and could learn of them only through sources.

3. The photograph provides physical evidence of the cuts on Mary Ellen's face and legs, her tattered dress and lack of shoes, and her diminutive size. It also appeals to viewers' pathos by showing the girl's vacant, faraway expression. To use Markel's words, the picture "put[s] a human face on child abuse" (par. 3). You may need to point out to students that family photos were expensive and rare (and usually very formal) at the time; the picture was almost certainly taken by the prosecutors as evidence for the trial and carefully staged (notice the scissors on the floor) for its melodramatic quality.

4. Markel makes several references to local neighborhoods, landmarks, and political figures, including "the Hell's Kitchen section of Manhattan" (par. 3); "the Lower East Side," "St. Nicholas Hotel," and "Blackwell's Island" (5); and Henry Bergh and Elbridge Gerry (7). In each case, though, he offers contextualizing information for readers unfamiliar with New York City, such as street addresses ("West 41st Street," [3]), brief descriptions of institutions ("the city orphanage," [5]), and relationships ("grandson of the politician who gave his name to gerrymandering," [7]).

5. As Markel explains it, Mary Ellen's case revealed a need for child protection laws, and the people who stepped in to help her later worked together to found the New York Society for the Prevention of Cruelty to Children, presumably to better help future children in need of protection. The NYSPCC, in turn, has "helped rescue thousands of battered children, created shelters to care for them, and working with similar groups and agencies in cities across the nation, instituted laws that punish abusive parents" (par. 11). In other words, Mary Ellen McCormack did not suffer in vain: Her experience was the catalyst for a system of supports and laws meant to protect children from similar abuse.

QUESTIONS ON LANGUAGE

1. McCormack's testimony is primary-source evidence. By quoting her extensively, Markel personally introduces the subject of his narrative, lends immediacy and life to a historical account, and proves that the story he is about to tell is true.

2. The senior Elbridge Gerry, vice president under James Madison, was governor of Massachusetts from 1810 to 1812. In the last year of his governorship, the Gerry administration redrew the boundaries of several electoral districts to favor their own party. The word *gerrymander* combines the statesman's name with the word *salamander* (such was the shape of one of the districts created) to characterize the practice of redistricting for political gain.

3. Markel's tone is (mostly) dispassionate. Modern newspaper writers are expected to report objectively, with no emotion or judgment. This was not, of course, the case in the nineteenth century, when reporters were much more likely to appeal to pathos and inject their personal opinions, such as "no change of custody or condition could be much for the worse" (par. 8).

SHIRLEY JACKSON
The Lottery

"The Biography of a Story" by Shirley Jackson appeared in *Come Along with Me* (1968), a posthumous collection of sixteen stories, part of a novel, and three lectures, edited by Jackson's husband, S. E. Hyman. In the lecture, Jackson discusses the writing and publishing of, and the public reaction to, "The Lottery." We have used excerpts in "Shirley Jackson on Writing," but you may find the entire lecture worth investigating.

Some students may know of Stanley Milgram's psychological experiments in obedience to authority. (We've directed students to Milgram's book in writing suggestion 3.) For the skeptics in your class, a brief discussion of Milgram's work could make Jackson's fiction more worthy of serious discussion.

Jackson reads "The Lottery" (and "The Demon Lover") on a Folkways recording made in 1963. Carol Jordan Stewart reads "The Lottery" on an Audio Partners cassette made in 1998. You can purchase and download the latter recording from *audible.com.*

QUESTIONS ON MEANING

1. "The Lottery" makes sharp statements on human nature and the nature of society. It attempts to warn about the consequences of unthinking conformity to social practices.
2. The reader senses a problem in paragraph 45, when Mrs. Hutchinson objects. Full knowledge comes in paragraph 74 and is confirmed when Tessie is hit in paragraph 77.
3. It is a close-knit, rural community of farmers (pars. 3, 4). The villagers know each other well — all questions and instructions are mere formalities (13, 20, 50). It is a hardworking community — the lottery is rushed so that people can get back to work (10).
4. Villagers hesitate before touching the box (par. 4). They won't replace it, no matter how shabby it is (5). It is ignored throughout the year (6). And Mr. Summers gains in importance by resting his hand on it (7). It seems that the villagers respect their tradition but also fear it and feel ashamed of it.

QUESTIONS ON WRITING STRATEGY

1. By keeping her distance, Jackson heightens the suspense, for relating even one character's thoughts would doubtless reveal the lottery's nature. This point of view also emphasizes the complacency and hypocrisy of the townspeople — we mostly see and hear only their cheerful, bland interaction — and it intensifies the mystery of the lottery itself.
2. The references to rocks are puzzling but not the least alarming because of the conviviality and playfulness — the normalcy — surrounding them. By the end of the story, the reader has forgotten all about the rocks until he or she is suddenly reminded in paragraph 74.

3. Through the characters' discussion of giving up the lottery, we get a hint that not everyone likes the ritual (some villages have stopped it), and we hear the most vehement defense of the practice from Old Man Warner.

4. The lottery is now merely tradition. It may have originated as a superstition to ensure a good corn harvest (par. 32), but it has long since lost that meaning even for its staunchest supporters.

QUESTIONS ON LANGUAGE

1. We would not know that the lottery is losing ground in some places or the more conservative defense of the ritual (pars. 31–34, 67); how Tessie Hutchinson feels about her fate (45, 49, 51, 59, 79) and how others feel (46, 47, 50, 67, 75). Other examples are possible.

2. The vocabulary in this story should not present much of a stumbling block to students. Even if they don't know all the words, contextual clues are numerous, and the suspense pulls the reader through any barriers.

3. "Snatched" suggests Mrs. Hutchinson's anger that her family has been chosen. She is following the rules but at the same time showing her defiance.

4. All the names seem British except for Delacroix and Zanini: Evidently, we are to think this is a British town or an American New England town. The non-British names indicate perhaps that immigrants have settled in the town, have been accepted (though the pronunciation of the Delacroix name has been altered in par. 2), and have in turn accepted the tradition. "Zanini," of course, gives a clear signal that the alphabet has ended (par. 42).

5. Figurative writing might have contradicted the plainness of the people and would certainly have mitigated the distance that Jackson establishes between herself and the story.

SHIRLEY JACKSON ON WRITING

We heartily recommend the rest of "Biography of a Story" for the grace and humor of its author and for the numerous quotations from hostile readers.

Students should be interested to learn that the inspiration for such a story struck Jackson on her way home from grocery shopping. As writers frequently observe, inspiration often comes when least expected — in the shower, while driving, in a dream. Students should note, though, that Jackson didn't wait for inspiration to actually *write* the story: She sat right down and began work.

Is Jackson's surprise at readers' reactions naive or even disingenuous? Perhaps. Some students, even many, will think she asked for a harsh response.

5
DESCRIPTION
Writing with Your Senses

Because most instructors make much of descriptive writing, this chapter offers an ample choice of illustrations. Students tend to think of descriptive writing as a kind of still-life painting in words: An apple or a banana sits on a table and you write about it. In this chapter, we strive to demonstrate that, on the contrary, description can involve the testimony of all the senses. All the writers employ description in fresh and engaging ways. And the poet — Joyce Carol Oates — examines with careful eyes the smallest details of a painting, Edward Hopper's *Nighthawks* (reproduced along with the poem).

For our pairing in this chapter, we have chosen Brad Manning's "Arm Wrestling with My Father" (Manning wrote the essay as a college freshman) and Sarah Vowell's "Shooting Dad." Both authors look at their fathers, but otherwise their views (and their descriptions) are quite different. Note that each essay is followed by a "Connections" writing suggestion involving the other.

BRAD MANNING

Arm Wrestling with My Father

Manning's essay specifically addresses the male experience by exploring how masculine ideals (such as strong, silent, athletic) can affect father-son relations. Most students will have something to say about the general difficulties of parent-child communication, and you may want to extend discussion to how Manning's personal experience represents larger issues. That men communicate nonverbally and women verbally is a commonly held belief. Ask students whether they agree with this gender generalization. Is it easier, more common, or more acceptable for mothers to talk openly with their daughters than for fathers to do so with their sons? What about for mothers and sons, for fathers and daughters? (For a take on the latter relationship, see Sarah Vowell's "Shooting Dad," the essay following this one.) Students may need encouragement to complicate their answers to these questions with specific reasons for their generalizations.

To enhance class discussion, small groups could initially be asked to spend ten to fifteen minutes brainstorming stereotypes about a particular gendered parent/child relationship: one group working with fathers and sons, one with mothers and daughters, and so on (you could even throw stepparents into the mix). When the class reassembles, groups should both respond to each other's ideas and connect their claims to the relationship and standard of communication that Manning describes with his father.

QUESTIONS ON MEANING

1. Manning's father communicates through gestures rather than words.
2. They have learned primarily that they don't have to compete to express affection and that there are many different kinds of communication.
3. Clearly Manning has always felt loved, but he recognizes that these challenges *show* that his father loves him.
4. His purpose is definitely to express love for his father. In a larger context, he also wants to suggest the strength of a nonverbal relationship between fathers and sons.

QUESTIONS ON WRITING STRATEGY

1. Manning begins with his bitterness to set us up for the emotional progress of the essay, which moves from frustration and anger to acceptance (all responses to various arm-wrestling competitions).
2. These options suggest that he believes they have both learned something about new avenues of communication. We aren't supposed to predict anything; just knowing options exist shows progress is being made.
3. Manning compares the thrill of hooking his first big fish (par. 10) to the sense of accomplishment he initially felt when he realized that he was going to win his first arm-wrestling match with his father. Although both events are exciting firsts that suggest the approach toward manhood, Manning is a little sorry in both cases to know that he can defeat (kill?) a worthy and longtime foe: "I wanted to win but I did not want to see him lose" (9); "when you finally think you've got him, you want to let him go, cut the line, keep the legend alive" (10). Still, these poetic and self-sacrificing impulses stand in contrast to the end of this wrestling match, which Manning, despite his regrets, won't lose on purpose (11).
4. The narrative progresses through events that demonstrate Manning's boyish powerlessness: his "whole upper body pushing down in hope of winning," his father would "grin with his eyes fixed on me," Manning would "start to cheat and use both hands," his brother once even tried to help, and yet "the man would win." The description emphasizes the contrast between the boy and the man in terms of size ("tiny shoulders" and "little legs" are no match for the man's "calm, unmoving forearm"); effort (the father "not seeming to notice his own arm" while the boy's "greatest efforts" were useless); and power (the father's arm moves "steadily . . . regardless of the opposition").

QUESTIONS ON LANGUAGE

1. *Competition* suggests sportsmanship, organized rivalry with a goal, rather than the discordant clash of wills that *conflict* suggests.

2. This reduces the father to just the arm, giving the reader a greater sense of how large a role the father's arms play in characterizing the man as a whole. The image of him as "the arm" suggests both his competitiveness and his protectiveness (par. 4).
3. Manning still feels competitive with his father but is loath to sacrifice his sense of being protected by a father who is stronger than he is.
4. *Mononucleosis* is a disease involving a high white-blood-cell count, causing fever, weakness, swollen lymph nodes, and a sore throat.

BRAD MANNING ON WRITING

Manning has some good advice for college writers, especially about taking the time to plan and revise and working for one's own voice. Students who struggle to write may dispute Manning's implication that writing can be a better means of self-expression than speaking. You might reinforce Manning's message that writing, unlike speaking, provides a chance to build and shape thought.

SARAH VOWELL

Shooting Dad

To begin discussion of this essay, consider the particular cleverness of Vowell's title: Her father is literally a "shooting dad" (a dad whose pastime is shooting firearms), and, in her conclusion, Vowell says that after his death the family will fulfill his request to bag his ashes and shoot them from his cannon (thus, the family will be literally "shooting Dad").

If you pair this with the previous essay, Brad Manning's "Arm Wrestling with My Father," consider asking students to compare and contrast the father-child relationships these two writers present. One interesting difference is that Manning focuses much more overtly on the love he feels for his father and his father's love for him than Vowell does in describing her relationship with her father. Why might this be less of an issue for Vowell? How would students characterize Vowell's feelings for her father and his feelings for her? Her portrait is for the most part quite affectionate, but she also treats her father with considerable humor, poking fun at his various foibles. Despite their differences, as Vowell has grown older she and her father seem to have developed an easygoing relationship, with little if any of the unspoken baggage Manning describes between himself and his father. Do students think this a reflection more of gender, age, or basic family dynamics? (Note that Vowell's family seems far less "shy" than the family Manning describes.)

Another focus of discussion might be Vowell's highly polished comic tone, her delightful way of casually tossing in a verbal joke — having "to move revolvers out of my way to make room for a bowl of Rice Krispies" (par. 3), for example, or referring to her father's shop as "a tetanus shot waiting to happen" (7). You could divide students into groups, have each group analyze

Vowell's essay for further examples, and then report on their findings and how the examples contribute to the persona Vowell presents in this essay. What relationship does she establish with her readers?

QUESTIONS ON MEANING

1. Throughout their lives, Vowell and her father have been at odds over political issues and divided in their interests — she the liberal, he the conservative; she antigun, he progun; she artistic, he mechanical. The division is made explicit in paragraphs 1–2, 5, 7–8, and 13.
2. Vowell writes that both her parents grew up in controlling households "where children were considered puppets and/or slaves" (par. 12). In reaction to the rigidity of his own parents, her father wanted his children to have the freedom to make their own choices. We see him, then, as fundamentally open-minded.
3. Vowell had reached a point in adulthood where she wanted to connect more closely with her father and decided that sharing in this major project of his was a good place to start — particularly since it represents "a map of all his obsessions" (par. 19). She isn't bothered by her father's cannon as she is by other guns because "it is a completely ceremonial object" (30), not a weapon that could readily be used to harm others. Also, she enjoys the noise it makes and the way its smoke fills the air.
4. Vowell's father is proud to be the descendant of reactionaries and renegades and enjoys recalling tales of his "nefarious" ancestors. His slyly ornery streak helps explain his outspoken individualism.
5. Vowell's purpose seems to be to trace her evolving view of her father, from seeing him as her polar opposite to realizing that they have more in common — in terms of being "smart-alecky loners with goofy projects and weird equipment" (par. 29) — than she ever expected. She creates the impression of a man who is exasperating, obsessive in his beliefs and habits, but somehow endearing, finally, because of his idiosyncratic devotion to "his art" (31).

QUESTIONS ON WRITING STRATEGY

1. The anecdote demonstrates in a nutshell her father's penchant for guns and his tendency to behave as he sees fit. It also shows that, even at eleven, Vowell saw things completely differently and welcomed the restrictions that town life would place on her father's behavior.
2. The paragraph provides a bit of humor with its suggestion that boyfriends feared Vowell just might shoot them if they betrayed her. It also acts as a transition into the following paragraph, where Vowell admits that she has only shot a gun once in her life. While this aside doesn't contribute directly to the portrait of Vowell's father, it does bring in outsiders' views of her father's guns.
3. The final sentence suggests the depth of Vowell's feelings for her father: When he dies, she will and wants to feel pain. The double meaning of "hurt" — the pain of the cannon noise and the pain of loss — ties together the threads of guns and father and sharply etches Vowell's love for her father.
4. Comparison and contrast is found in paragraphs 1–2, 6–7, 13, and 29. The method is important to show how different Vowell believed herself and her father to be until she came to share one of his pleasures and realized that they were surprisingly alike.

QUESTIONS ON LANGUAGE

1. Shooting crows is clearly not "a national pastime, like baseball and apple pie." Vowell points up the irony of her father's statement by stating her own preference.
2. Our favorite concrete and specific words: *labyrinth, bagged, blue ballpoint pen, spiky, cramped,* the list of musical instruments, *penciled, pompous.* The words create two vividly real spaces, down to the writing on paper.
3. Repeating the word *six* asks the reader to focus on the young age of the twins when they were first allowed to shoot a gun. The short final sentence neatly summarizes, by contrast, Vowell's own bad experience with shooting.
4. In personification and similes, Vowell says the gun "kicked little me back to the ground like a bully, like a foe." It's not just big and heavy and dangerous to others but malevolent to her, "an evil presence."
5. *Pharaohlike* (par. 18) will not show up in students' dictionaries, though of course *pharaoh* will ("a king of ancient Egypt; a tyrant"). Vowell alludes to the biblical story of Moses, in which the ruler of Egypt ordered all Hebrew boy babies killed.

SARAH VOWELL ON WRITING

Most students won't share Vowell's experience of writing for radio and print, but they will know some frustrations of getting thoughts into writing and they may, like Vowell, have experienced distinct advantages and disadvantages in speaking and in writing. For instance, in speaking, as Vowell says, you can leave some things unsaid and can be a bit slapdash. But in writing you don't have to face your audience and can take time to work out your ideas.

ELIZABETH GILBERT

The Best Pizza in the World

An excerpt from one of the most widely read memoirs in recent memory, "The Best Pizza in the World" is great fun to read. Most of us have, at one point or another, experienced gastronomic delight of the kind Gilbert describes, but few could express it as forcefully or with as much originality as she does. Students should enjoy both Gilbert's infectious enthusiasm for her subject and her strikingly fresh figures of speech, many of which are irresistible.

You may want to spend some time considering Gilbert's overwhelmingly colloquial language (see question 2 under "Language"). Such casual, everyday usage is normally frowned upon in formal writing, but in Gilbert's case it works quite well, creating a strong writer's voice, infusing a sense of intimacy with her readers, and forging an unmistakably clear emotional image of her joy at being in Naples.

QUESTIONS ON MEANING

1. The essay does not include an explicit thesis statement, but the dominant impression is of a breathless joy, even ecstasy, in the experience of chaos and sensory overload.
2. Gilbert means to entertain her readers, no doubt, but also, it seems, to persuade them to seek out pleasure for themselves. She appeals to readers directly in paragraph 9, enjoining them to not "even worry about it, just go," to "get there fairly early," and when "[y]ou try to take a bite off your slice and the gummy crust folds, and the hot cheese runs away like topsoil in a landslide . . . just deal with it." The suggestion is that readers should undertake the same journey Gilbert describes.
3. As Gilbert sees it, "[t]raveling-to-a-place energy and living-in-a-place energy are two fundamentally different energies" (par. 2). Travelers seek out new places "just to check [them] out" (1) and focus on novel experiences; temporary civilians necessarily get caught up in the mundane aspects of real life, such as paying utility bills. Gilbert places herself in both categories: She's temporarily living in Rome but travels to Naples to reignite a traveler's sense of newness and wonder.
4. *Metaphysics* is the philosophical study of reality and being. The pizza is so good, and so beyond the realm of anything she's ever experienced, that it causes Sofie to question everything she ever knew — about pizza, about eating, about her place in the world, and perhaps even the meaning of life. The same is true for Gilbert.
5. The pizza represents everything that is good and special about Naples and serves as the embodiment of the "pure pleasure" (par. 11) Gilbert sought as a visitor to Italy.

QUESTIONS ON WRITING STRATEGY

1. Gilbert didn't go to Naples for the pizza, but it turned out to be the defining moment of her trip. The jump back to Rome serves as a transition between the two halves of Gilbert's essay: her description of Naples and her description of the pizza.
2. The irony is that, although Gilbert thinks she is abusing her body, she feels better than she has in a very long time. She seems to conclude that sometimes the healthiest thing a person can do is abandon all concerns about health and focus, instead, on pleasure.
3. Readers of a book titled *Eat, Pray, Love* would presumably expect and appreciate ecstatic descriptions of food that holds a special significance for the writer. Gilbert assumes that her readers are interested in traveling to new places and that, if they haven't done so themselves, they've at least read about exotic destinations (notice, for instance, her casual reference to "Tibetan prayer flags" in par. 4). She also assumes that they have some general idea of what Italy is like, yet she is careful to describe the specific experience of Naples with vivid and unforgettable images, such as a "crooked old woman seated at her window, peering suspiciously down at the activity below" (4) and pizza makers whose "sleeves are rolled up over their sweaty forearms, their faces red with exertion, one eye squinted against the heat of the fire and a cigarette dangling from the lips" (10).
4. The first two paragraphs explain that Gilbert met somebody who was traveling for pleasure, and the encounter made her jealous, sparking a desire for adventure. The introduction establishes Gilbert's reasons for traveling to Naples and puts her experience in a broader context.

QUESTIONS ON LANGUAGE

1. *Similes*: "undershirts and brassieres flapping in the wind like Tibetan prayer flags" (par. 4); "The accent in Naples is like a friendly cuff on the ear," "It's like walking through a city of short-order cooks . . ." (5); "shoving for access like they're trying to get space on a lifeboat," "much the same way one shimmering movie star . . . ," "hot cheese runs away like topsoil in a landslide" (9); "looking for all the world like the boilermen in the belly of a great ship . . ." (10). *Metaphors*: "longing to travel while you are already traveling is . . . a kind of greedy madness," "a jones to hit the road" (2); "An anthill inside a rabbit warren . . . ," "A tripped-out, dangerous and cheerful nuthouse" (4); "I almost felt I was being inducted into a secret society" (7); "contact high of glamour" (9). *Hyperbole*: "There is not a street in Naples in which some tough little kid in shorts and mismatched socks is not screaming up from the sidewalk . . . ," "Nor is there a building in this town that doesn't have at least one crooked old woman seated at her window . . ." (4); "I feared one of them might get shot" (6). We also particularly enjoy the writer's *personification* of her pizza in paragraph 8, where she imagines that it loves her back. Every one of Gilbert's figures of speech is fresh, imaginative, and highly evocative.
2. Gilbert's diction is profoundly colloquial. Just a few examples include "gave me such a jones to hit the road" (par. 2); "tripped-out" (4); "so insanely psyched," "right up in your face," "flipped me the finger" (5); "don't even worry about it," "wannabe pizza twaddle," "deal with it" (9); "can barely cope" (10). Piled one on top of the next, her colloquialisms build a tone that is breathless and exuberant. She is utterly thrilled by Naples and can't contain her excitement, which she wants to share with her readers. Her choice of language therefore strikes us as not only appropriate but also effective.
3. The effect is one of intensity and immediacy. Students may have trouble finding a reason for the inconsistent use of quotation marks, but it seems that the girl's thoughts are directed at Gilbert, whereas the women's (in italics) are more general, meant for everyone, and possibly muttered to themselves.
4. Students may have difficulty finding *nan* (sometimes spelled *naan*) in a general dictionary, but recipes abound online. The slightly sweet and aromatic leavened flat bread, similar to pita bread but fluffier and more flavorful, is common in south Asian cuisine.

WILLIAM LEAST HEAT-MOON

Dance of the Hobs

Students should enjoy Heat-Moon's entertaining and engagingly descriptive tale of his encounter with a mysterious, luminous apparition in the Ozarks. Structured as a ghost story (see the writing suggestion labeled "Critical Writing"), "Dance of the Hobs" reads like something Edgar Allan Poe might have written — if he had a contemporary sense of humor and an ear for southwestern backcountry dialect.

A good way to begin discussion is to focus on the journal prompt. What similar tales have students heard in their hometowns or at school? Campus folklore can be especially evocative: If a popular legend or rumor circulates at your school, encourage students to investigate it, perhaps visiting the site involved or searching the campus newpaper's archives for details, and then report on what they learn.

Readers especially taken by Heat-Moon's essay will also enjoy the Weird US series. An outgrowth of a self-published New Jersey 'zine (*Weird NJ*), the books are edited by self-taught folklorists Mark Sceurman and Mark Moran and share readers' experiences with urban legends and quirky sites in at least twenty states and several regions. Visit *weirdus.com* for more information.

QUESTIONS ON MEANING

1. Heat-Moon is drawn to the light and the stories surrounding it because the apparition is a mystery, "an authentic optical phenomenon reportedly unexplained by science" (par. 18). For Heat-Moon, observing the light is a mystical, almost religious, experience, "like stepping back into the Dark Ages . . . , when mysteries overwhelmed explications and ignorance transcended illumination, a time when superstition could extinguish enlightenment, when priestly obfuscations manipulated folk into blind faiths" (18).

2. Heat-Moon didn't expect to see a ghost, per se, but rather something ghostlike. "Manifestation of a spectrum" is a pun: The word *spectrum* suggests specter, or ghost, but in physics refers to radiating energy forms, specifically light.

3. Heat-Moon is both puzzled and delighted by the light, which he describes as a small, flickering white ball that sometimes fades into red and then back to white while darting through the air. The dominant impression is that of a sprightly, playful, and mischievous living thing.

4. The writer means to entertain. As we suggest in the writing suggestion labeled "Critical Writing," Heat-Moon is essentially telling a ghost story, engaging his readers' imaginations yet emphasizing that the spook in question is harmless, if indeed it is even real.

5. Heat-Moon's straightforward thesis appears in his last paragraph: "The Quapaw Ghost Light is remarkable but not incredible, modest but worth its myth, possessed of the power of the peculiar" (par. 20). Put succinctly, one might say that his point is simply that mysteries are fun.

QUESTIONS ON WRITING STRATEGY

1. Heat-Moon expects that his readers will be as skeptical as he was, but he also recognizes that most people enjoy a good ghost story. He repeatedly stresses that the light is a mystery, that several people in the area (whom he quotes) have seen it, that even those who have seen it aren't sure what to make of it. He softens his readers' doubts by acknowledging the validity of "the sanity question" (par. 3) and insisting that he was driven mostly by curiosity, not by a real expectation of seeing anything. He also offers several possible rational explanations for the phenomenon (in par. 7 especially) to assure readers that he doesn't necessarily accept that the light is a specter of some sort; there may indeed be some physical cause. (For readers interested in Heat-Moon's analysis of that cause,

we encourage them to find a copy of *Roads to Quoz* and read chapter 10.)

2. Although Heat-Moon assumes the persona of an impersonal "observer," his description is subjective, invested with emotions. Throughout, the description conveys both his doubt about and his delight over what he anticipates as well as what he sees.

3. The majority of Heat-Moon's details take the form of figures of speech, and most of them are delightful. We especially like the metaphors in "[m]elodious calls of toads roused the darkness" (par. 5) and "a white-hot poker thrust through a black tent" (11); the similes in "I began walking as if I were wading the night" (6) and "like an animal moving its head side to side as it fixes on its quarry" (11); the hyperbole of "it upended astrophysics in its shifting from a red dwarf to a white giant" (16); and the personification of the light itself, most notable in the name "Spooky" (16) and comments like "She's a homebody" (4).

4. Heat-Moon refers back to the librarian's line — simply a colorful way of describing a fright-induced heart attack — in paragraph 12 to stress how jittery he was. The repetition is funny for its regional twang and sense of irony, but it also effectively circles back to an earlier point and validates what others have said to the author. Some readers might notice that Heat-Moon uses the same device when he repeats, in paragraph 10, the words "Spoof Light," originally uttered by the man who asks, "How does a sane person see what isn't there?" (par. 2).

5. The dialog builds suspense and previews what's to come. By quoting locals, in particular, Heat-Moon also invokes the rumored, whispery nature of much folklore. And the exchange between Heat-Moon and his wife creates a sense of immediacy, encouraging readers to imagine themselves there with the couple as they witness the light's movements.

QUESTIONS ON LANGUAGE

1. The string of difficult words in paragraph 18 re-creates for readers the sense of ignorance and confusion Heat-Moon imagines mysterious phenomena created for people in the Dark Ages. *Obfuscations* (from the Latin *fucare*, to darken) refers to deliberately muddied meanings and seems especially appropriate in this context.

2. Heat-Moon combines formal, academic vocabulary with an abundance of regional dialect and colloquialisms. The mixture of objective, almost scientific language — such as "[b]ased upon no physical evidence except declarations written and spoken" (par. 3) — with colorful phrases and exclamations (our favorites are the nonsensical "Nodgort" and the exuberant "Holy Willie!" [12]) underscores the conflict between the writer's desire to be rational and his love of the weird.

3. The capital letters impart a comic sense of formality and ironic distance between himself and his subject (which, of course, many readers might dismiss as silly).

4. The line — "The thing glimmered and shimmered, twinkled and blinked, flickered and fluttered, glistened and winked" — reads like a nursery rhyme and perfectly captures Heat-Moon's unrestrained childish glee.

WILLIAM LEAST HEAT-MOON ON WRITING

Students have probably heard the adage "Write what you know." Heat-Moon might revise this advice to "Write what you know, and if you don't know it, *learn*." He becomes a "master" of his topics by observing, meeting new people, and asking lots of questions. Remind students that they can do the same.

JOYCE CAROL OATES

Edward Hopper's *Nighthawks*, 1942

When assigning this poem, also ask students to look carefully at the reproduction and detail of Hopper's painting that accompanies it. You might even ask students to complete a variation of the "Journal Writing" suggestion in which they jot down their own responses to the painting before reading the poem.

In class discussion, a central question for students is what they see as Oates's larger theme in the poem. Oates goes well beyond simply describing the scene of the painting and those peopling it — and even beyond imagining its characters' thoughts and feelings (although these are presented quite vividly). Implicitly, she is contemplating the painting as a work of art in which "time is never going to budge" (line 37), in which the word *still* has the connotations both of "not moving" and of "not changing," even being trapped in the moment the artist has created. In Oates's hands the image could be a metaphor for the human condition ("so why isn't he happier?" [60]).

Your library can probably provide you with other works by Hopper either in books about the artist or on slides, and numerous online links to Hopper images can be found at *The Bedford Reader*'s Web site (*bedfordstmartins.com/thebedfordreader*). You may also want to bring to class a color reproduction of *Nighthawks* to share with students.

QUESTIONS ON MEANING

1. The couple are in the midst of an extramarital affair. The man has apparently left his wife (line 7), but he's done that before and gone back (15–19, 28–30, 39–41). He's relieved but, in the end, not happy (60). The woman's thoughts dwell on her mistrust of the man (7–8) as she works herself up not to be hurt by him again (37–41, 45–47).
2. Various interpretations are possible, of course. Perhaps the poem's speaker poses the question about the painting itself; none of the figures in the painting would seem to have this wider perspective. The setting of the picture seems to have the characteristics of a dream — "so much that's wide, still, mute, horizontal" (lines 23–24).
3. Two possible interpretations stand out. The figures in any painting are caught forever in a particular moment, still and silent, so Oates could be urging her readers to contemplate the larger idea of art and its permanency. And Oates also pictures a relationship that is stagnant, going

nowhere (although the man is blind to this fact at the moment), which may be interpreted as a fact of the human condition.

QUESTIONS ON WRITING STRATEGY

1. Oates uses concrete language to describe the painting in lines 1–6, 8–10, 22–27, and 54–56. She uses these specific details as a springboard, imagining what they reveal about the characters or how the characters respond to them: for instance, "And she's thinking / the light in this place is too bright, probably / not very flattering, she hates it when her lipstick / wears off and her makeup gets caked" (30–34). Oates's purpose is not so much to render the physical details of the painting as to describe the situation those details could be illuminating, as well as to parallel the situation with the idea of artistic creation.

2. In lines 14–15 the woman thinks of her lover's guilt as "an actual smell, sweaty, rancid, like / dirty socks," and in lines 52–53 she recalls him "burying his hot face in her neck, between her cool / breasts." The man, in contrast, is "not the kind to talk much" (20), and his thoughts lack imagery: "he's thinking / thank God he made the right move at last" (20–21), "he's feeling pretty good, . . . this time he's sure / as hell going to make it work, he owes it to her / and to himself" (27–30), "he's thinking he's the luckiest man in the world" (59).

3. Oates runs sentences and phrases together with few pauses, in a stream of consciousness that builds to the italicized sentence ending line 44.

4. The man's thoughts and, particularly, the woman's thoughts are essentially narrative, and through them the reader can infer the larger narrative of their past relationship. The painting suggests a story to Oates, so she needs narration to relate it.

QUESTIONS ON LANGUAGE

1. *Rancid*, from the Latin *rancēre* ("to have a rank, unpleasant smell"), is a particularly effective word, its sound mimicking its meaning. One almost curls one's lip when saying it.

2. Oates clearly sees these two as a couple of tough characters, not at all refined or even admirable. Who else would be sitting in a coffee shop on a deserted street in the middle of the night?

3. "Relief" implies escape from a bad situation, whether from his unhappy home life or from his girlfriend's anger. It suggests looking back at something unpleasant rather than looking forward to something good.

JOYCE CAROL OATES ON WRITING

Both the prolific and the protean Joyce Carol Oates reveal themselves in her essay about her poem about a painting: Oates likes to communicate, and she has much to say in many different ways. This explicit analysis illuminates the painting and also Oates's description of it in her poem. Some students may at first have difficulty penetrating Oates's brief essay, but they should get the point that she wrote the poem for just the reason that most people write anything: to find meaning ("The poem enters the painting as a way of animating what cannot be animated; a way of delving into the painting's mystery").

6
EXAMPLE
Pointing to Instances

Some essays in this chapter use only a few examples; others use many. They all show the ways examples can pin down and give meaning to generalizations.

Barbara Lazear Ascher's and Anna Quindlen's essays are connected by theme as well as by method: Both treat homelessness — what it means and how to confront it. "The Adored, Buzzing around Us," by naturalist Sharman Apt Russell, explores through unexpected examples the glories of the natural world. Brent Staples's personal memoir, "Black Men and Public Space," provides instances when the author aroused suspicion simply because of his skin color — anecdotes that generally arouse keen interest and lively discussion. And David Foster Wallace's "This Is Water" ekes a meaningful lesson from the irritations of daily life.

Some students find difficulty in seeing the difference between giving an example and giving evidence to support a general statement. The latter is a larger concern, in which example is only one strategy. It may help to explain that, usually, an example backs up a general statement ("There have been many fine woman runners: Grete Waitz . . ."), but not everything supporting a general statement is an example. Statistics and other data, factual statements, expert opinions, and quotations also serve as evidence. The distinction may not be worth losing sleep over, but if a class has trouble seeing it, ask them to take a more painstaking look at "The Method" at the beginning of this chapter.

BARBARA LAZEAR ASCHER

On Compassion

Ascher's essay on responding compassionately to human desperation forms a pair with the next essay, Anna Quindlen's "Homeless." Both concern the prevalent and disturbing condition of homelessness. The headnote to Ascher's essay anticipates students' possible objections that Ascher's essay is just a "New York story." Are what we think of as big-city problems really national problems?

The third writing suggestion gives students a chance to do research into and write about the rights of the homeless — to supplement the evidence of their own experience with facts, expert opinions, and so on. Students could research collaboratively, with small groups focusing on each of the following questions to cover more ground: How widespread is homelessness in your area? What are local attitudes toward the homeless? What provisions are made for the homeless? Are the homeless thought of differently on the national level? Each group could report its findings back to the class. (If this sort of research is something you'd like to have students do fairly regularly, you might consider rotating the responsibility so that just one group works and reports on any given essay.)

QUESTIONS ON MEANING

1. They are examples of poor, unkempt, somewhat frightening, and probably homeless human beings.
2. Ascher's thesis is stated at the end of paragraph 13: "[Compassion] must be learned, and it is learned by having adversity at our windows, . . . adversity that becomes so familiar that we begin to identify and empathize with it." Ascher's purpose is to heighten readers' awareness of this point, perhaps to make them more tolerant.
3. The homeless may be moved off the streets into hospitals and shelters. To Ascher, the humanity of the idea is mitigated by its less noble goal of burying the problem.
4. She is, shall we say, cautiously optimistic. Exposure to "There but" situations worked for the Greeks, but then they could walk away when the play was over. We, Ascher implies, must stay and deal with the problem.

QUESTIONS ON WRITING STRATEGY

1. Examples precede generalizations, probably because the examples are dramatic and draw the reader into the essay.
2. The author assumes readers who are economically comfortable: "We" are the bystanders with nice clothes, enough food, and homes to live in.
3. Ascher says charitably, or perhaps ironically, that the bystanders "daydream"; one man plays with his shoe. The people seem to represent all those who "look away" from the homeless to anywhere else.
4. After the opening transitional sentence, Ascher emphasizes her points in four short, almost staccato sentences. Breaking with this pattern, Ascher spins out a long, structurally complicated sentence that states her thesis.
5. Students' answers will vary.

QUESTIONS ON LANGUAGE

1. According to *The American Heritage Dictionary*, compassion is "the deep feeling of sharing the suffering of another, together with the inclination to give aid or support or to show mercy" (from Latin *com* + *pati*, "to bear with"). Empathy is "identification with and understanding of another's situation, feelings, and motives" (from Greek *empatheia*, "passion"). Empathy is thus the first half of compassion, which goes further to involve aid, support, or mercy.

2. Ascher uses *stay* as a transitive verb ("stay the cold"), whereas students may know it only as an intransitive verb ("stay in school") or even as a noun ("stay of execution"). The word comes from the Latin *stare*, "to stand."
3. London during Charles Dickens's time (he lived 1812–70) was a city of sharp contrasts between rich and poor.
4. Ascher's description is mainly objective, although she indicates sympathy for the first man (he has "carefully plaited dreadlocks," he walks with "the shuffle of the forgotten ones," he resembles "a bridegroom waiting at the altar"), and the unsparing detail in the description of both men is obviously intended to push us close to them.

BARBARA LAZEAR ASCHER ON WRITING

Ascher's comments on writing "tight" reinforce our own advice about coming to a point and writing concisely. The questions for discussion encourage students to explore in more detail just what makes writing tight, versus Ascher's opposing term "excessive," and how the former benefits readers.

ANNA QUINDLEN

Homeless

In this direct, personal essay, Quindlen uses detailed examples to explore what it is to be without a home. The third question on meaning provides a likely occasion for class discussion of the importance of a home and what a home is.

Barbara Lazear Ascher's "On Compassion" complements Quindlen's essay. A "Connections" writing suggestion after each essay helps students compare them. The collaborative research suggestion we provide for Ascher's essay (p. 36 of this manual) could be equally useful for Quindlen's, if you are not planning to use the essays together and you think your students may need more background on the issue of homelessness. If they already have this background, you might use Quindlen's essay as a springboard for discussing practical measures to help solve the problem. Working in groups of three or four, students could discuss the practicalities of Quindlen's claim that nothing but a home will solve the problems of the homeless: With this as a premise, what can be done to achieve this goal? Fifteen minutes of collaborative brainstorming on this question should give students enough time to prepare for a whole-class discussion of the issues Quindlen raises.

QUESTIONS ON MEANING

1. Quindlen's thesis (in pars. 8–9) is that abstraction from particular human beings to "issues" may distance us from problems and impede their solution — in this case, solving homelessness with homes.

2. The key is in paragraph 8: "The homeless" distances us from the problem suffered by particular people with particular needs.
3. Having a place to live makes you "somebody" (par. 2); it provides "certainty, stability, predictability, privacy" (4), and "pride of ownership" (7). Students' opinions about the importance of a home will vary. This question and the fourth writing suggestion provide good opportunities to discuss just what a home is, anyway: a house or an apartment? a room in a dorm? a heating grate?

QUESTIONS ON WRITING STRATEGY

1. Quindlen might have begun with a statement of her opinion (among other options), but the story of Ann draws the reader in and illustrates Quindlen's point. It also, perhaps even more important, reinforces Quindlen's argument that we should focus more on particular people with particular problems.
2. The examples bring Quindlen to earth and magnify the loss suffered by the homeless.
3. The author assumes that the reader has a home and feels strongly about it. Some students may not feel as strongly about having a home as Quindlen does. In paragraph 7, she addresses readers' likely assumption that shelters are better than the streets.
4. The second through final sentences enumerate examples and could be parallel simple sentences, but Quindlen varies their structures and complexity (notice the distribution of subordinate clauses), building to the brief, poignant fragment spoken by the mother.
5. She wants readers to agree that nothing short of homes will solve the problems of homeless people.

QUESTIONS ON LANGUAGE

1. It invests her opinion with passion and urgency.
2. Not only do our hearts reside in and take nourishment from our homes, but we can show heart by providing homes for those who lack them.
3. *Crux* is a Latin word meaning "cross." In English it is a critical point or essential feature.

ANNA QUINDLEN ON WRITING

Analyzing the differences between Quindlen's essay and a conventional news report (the second question for discussion) may engage students. To us, the myriad differences come down to "My God" (par. 9): Such a fervently personal exclamation would never appear in straight news, not even in feature writing. Other examples include statements of belief, such as "You are where you live" (par. 2) and "That [a home] is everything" (4), or personal details, such as the Irish grandfather (3) and the beloved hot-water heater (4).

SHARMAN APT RUSSELL

The Adored, Buzzing around Us

Sharman Apt Russell identifies herself as a pantheist and has said that, to her, religion is about bringing together her scientific and spiritual understandings of the natural world. Much of her writing, including "The Adored, Buzzing around Us," evokes a sense of this duality. Indeed, some readers may notice a certain religious quality to Russell's reflections on nature, particularly in her reference to God (par. 4) and in her subtle depiction of prayer in her conclusion, where she notes that "paying more attention to insects . . . usually requires getting down on my knees" (7). Even those who don't recognize or appreciate the author's religious reverence are sure to find a fresh perspective in her admiration for bugs and other unappealing elements of the natural environment.

A writing teacher herself, Russell has said that her goal is to help her students "feel more centered in who they are as writers and why they write." You might use this statement as a starting point for discussion: What does the writer mean by feeling "centered" in self and purpose? To what extent does her essay express Russell's own sense of centeredness?

QUESTIONS ON MEANING

1. Some students may pinpoint "They make us feel grateful for being on such an interesting planet" (par. 2) and "I live on such an interesting planet" (7) — as statements of Russell's main idea, but her thesis is much more focused and might be most clearly expressed in paragraph 6: "I have to get to know the parts of nature that make me wince and turn away. Because turning away is not really what good lovers do." The point of her metaphor is that all nature, not just the attractive parts, is worthy of love and that developing a connection with the natural world requires that we move beyond romanticized notions of beauty. Her purpose, then, is to persuade readers to find the glory in even the least appealing aspects of nature.
2. Russell admires beetles for their weirdness and fearsomeness (pars. 1, 4); their ubiquity (3); their variety, speed, and adaptiveness (4); their charisma (5); their ugliness (6); and their strength (7). Whether students share her fascination will vary.
3. The references to "the vanishing Siberian Tiger or your local threatened predator" (par. 3) are an allusion to species extinction. The glossed-over approach seems almost fatalistic, but Russell is appealing to readers to find hope and beauty where they can, rather than despair over something they can't easily control.

QUESTIONS ON WRITING STRATEGY

1. Russell's purpose is to get her readers to realign their view of the natural world and to recognize the value of denigrated or ignored species, such as beetles. Her appeal seems directed squarely at environmental activists, whom she assumes too often focus their efforts on "charis-

matic" (par. 2) animals and "gorgeous" (6) landscapes. Russell seems to believe that her readers are strongly invested in protecting the environment yet hostile to insects and anything "alien, brutal, and uncuddly" (6). Some students may take exception to such assumptions, while others will likely embrace them.

2. The author describes the strange features of three kinds of beetles: stink bugs (par. 1), tiger beetles (4), and North American rhinoceros beetles (7). Each example is both startling and admiring in its detail, helping to prove her point that insects are interesting and deserving of love.

3. In speaking to her readers directly in paragraph 2, Russell pulls them in and makes them complicit in her criticism of people who admire only the aesthetically pleasing and charismatic aspects of the natural world. She backs off from direct address in the rest of the essay to avoid alienating the very people she hopes to bring around to her point of view.

4. Russell compares the appeal of insects to that of "charismatic" animals and birds in paragraph 2, and returns briefly to the comparison in paragraphs 3 and 5, to emphasize that insects are just as wonderful and valuable as more conventionally adored creatures are — perhaps even more so.

QUESTIONS ON LANGUAGE

1. The label instantly evokes disgust. Russell opens with it both for its vividness and shock value and to establish the contrast between most people's perceptions of beetles and her own.

2. Russell's tone might best be characterized as awestruck and reverent — exactly the feelings she hopes to inspire in her readers.

3. The phrase underscores her point that to appreciate the less attractive aspects of nature, we have to "shift our attitude — and spatial perspective" (par. 3). By repeating and italicizing "In their way" (5), Russell emphasizes beetles' uniqueness and acknowledges that recognizing their charms doesn't come instinctively: The ability requires an adjustment in both how we look at the world and what we value.

4. On its surface, *charismatic* (from the Greek *kharisma*, for divine gift) refers to people who possess an innate quality that draws others toward them; Russell is using personification to characterize the appeal of certain animals. The word also, however, invokes that sect of Christianity that celebrates divine inspiration and healing, a fitting choice for an essay with spiritual and subtle religious overtones.

SHARMAN APT RUSSELL ON WRITING

Russell reminds us that the best research is born from genuine curiosity and that, when a writer is truly fascinated by something, writing about it doesn't feel like work. You might discuss with students how to adapt assignments to their own interests and thus how to shape their own "fruitful questions."

BRENT STAPLES

Black Men and Public Space

As Brent Staples demonstrates, the most gripping and convincing examples are often brief anecdotes. In this essay, examples of Staples's discovery — of the "alienation that comes of being ever the suspect" — take up most of the room. In addition, Staples gives examples of "tough guys" who died in street violence (par. 7) and precautions he takes to appear less threatening (11–12). His vivid opening paragraph, with its opening sentence pretending that he is a killer, deserves special scrutiny.

For collaborative work on this essay, we suggest focusing on just what public space is and what happens to us when we enter it. Students might try to define *public space* by coming up with examples and discovering what the examples have in common. How do they feel different in private and in public space? Once they have their examples and definitions, the groups could reassemble as a class to arrive at a generally accepted definition.

As an alternative, you could encourage students to explore their own feelings about public space. Are there places they feel more or less welcome, safe, at home? The "Journal Writing" topic after the essay gives students an opportunity to explore such questions. They might also find it helpful to generate a list of generalizations in small groups. What does it mean to be a student, a woman, a man, a member of a particular religious or ethnic group, and so on, in American public spaces? Working in small groups, students will probably feel freer to discuss their experiences; you might even consider dividing the groups along gender lines for those women and men who might be reluctant to speak up otherwise.

QUESTIONS ON MEANING

1. Students will state the author's purpose variously. Staples writes to communicate his experience as a black man of whom others are needlessly frightened. He writes to explain his discovery that, when mistaken for a criminal, it is wiser not to react with rage but to take precautions to appear less threatening. However the writer's purpose is put, this is personal experience and observation; we do not see Staples trying to predict the future or proposing any long-term solutions.
2. If we keep on reading, we find Staples acknowledging that women are often the victims of street violence, some of it perpetrated by young African American males. He believes, though, that reports have been exaggerated. He takes pains to make clear that he isn't dangerous. He considers himself not a tough guy but a "softy" who hates to cut up a raw chicken (par. 2); he has shrunk from street fights (6); his own brother and others have been killed in "episodes of bravado" (7).
3. By using it in this context, Staples gives the word *survivor* fresh connotations. Usually it suggests rugged strength, ability to endure, and so on, but here Staples helps us to understand that, in an area of gang warfare, knifings, and murders, timidity is a form of self-preservation.

QUESTIONS ON WRITING STRATEGY

1. Staples convinces by giving examples: anecdotes from his own experi-
    ence (pars. 1, 5, 8, 9) and that of another African American male (10).
2. The examples are set forth in detail too rich to seem a mere bare-bones
    list. The similar nature of all the examples lends the essay coherence
    and, to give it even more, Staples uses transitions skillfully. In nearly
    every paragraph, the opening sentence is transitional, and transitional
    phrases indicate time: "One day," "Another time," "a couple of summers
    ago."
3. Beginning with the scene of a near-empty street at night and a fright-
    ened woman fleeing him, Staples dramatizes his thesis and immediately
    sets forth a typical, recurrent situation.

QUESTIONS ON LANGUAGE

1. As we have seen, Staples's essay uses a narrative hook at the start and,
    to make the hook grab hard, the writer deliberately misleads us. The
    word *victim* leads us to take him for a self-confessed criminal. By the
    end of the paragraph, we doubt our impression, and in his second para-
    graph, Staples explains that he is harmless; he can hardly take a knife
    to a chicken. If we look back on the opening paragraph, we see the dis-
    crepancy between the word *victim* and reality. In truth, the fleeing
    woman is mistaken and fearful, a person on whom the innocent narra-
    tor has no designs. This discrepancy makes clear the writer's ironic atti-
    tude. As the essay proceeds, he expresses a mingling of anger, humor,
    and resignation.
2. We admire Staples's use of that fine old formal word *constitutionals*,
    "walks taken for health." Like the expression "robust constitution,"
    though, it seems a throwback to another era.
3. Students will have fun defining *dicey* ("risky, unpredictable"), recalling
    that shooting dice is, of course, a game of chance.

BRENT STAPLES ON WRITING

Staples provides a clear and enlightening illustration of how writing generates ideas, instead of simply recording them, as most inexperienced writers
seem to believe. His comparison of essay- and news-writing is related: The
work begins in the details, in the data, the observations, the feelings — in the
facts, as Staples says. The big picture depends on the details.

DAVID FOSTER WALLACE

This Is Water

"I want to author things that both restructure worlds and make living people feel stuff," David Foster Wallace once wrote. "This Is Water" might be one of the most world-altering and moving pieces of writing he ever produced — it is certainly the most accessible. Often described as a post-postmodernist, Wallace delighted in confounding his readers, forcing them to struggle through his self-conscious and tightly crafted diversions, which more often than not took over the body of his work. This speech has its diversions, as well, but they're relatively easy for a listener, or reader, to absorb. And we love "This Is Water" for its earnest and compelling advice to consciously seek out the good (or at least the tolerable) in any situation.

Wallace's suicide adds a deeply uncomfortable layer of complication for readers. For those who know the circumstances of the author's death (the victim of a long-running and severe depression, he took his own life), each of his casual references to suicide is a punch in the gut. It's worth noting that many of the emotional states Wallace describes in the speech — self-focused thinking, irritability, over-intellectualizing, loneliness, despair, and (of course) suicidal thoughts — are either causes or symptoms of clinical depression. Perceptive readers may remark that a common approach to talk therapy is to teach patients to recognize, and to consciously alter, automatic thoughts of the sort Wallace relates. Very few people were aware of the author's depression at the time he delivered his speech, but read with hindsight and a familiarity with the basics of cognitive therapy, it seems fairly clear that the speech represents Wallace's own effort to grapple with depression, to wrest some control over his debilitating perceptions. We encourage students to consider this possibility in the third writing topic, labeled "Critical Writing."

One way to begin discussion might be to ignore the suicide issue and focus on the journal prompt instead. What examples of irritating situations can students relate from their own experience? How much of the ensuing frustration was their own fault? How many are inspired to take Wallace's advice and cut other people — and themselves — some slack?

QUESTIONS ON MEANING

1. As with most commencement speeches, Wallace's purported purpose is to give advice to college graduates about to strike out on their own. The kernel of his advice is expressed most directly toward his conclusion, where he writes, "The really important kind of freedom involves attention, and awareness, and discipline, and effort, and being able truly to care about other people and to sacrifice for them, over and over, in myriad petty little unsexy ways, every day. That is real freedom. The alternative is unconsciousness, the default setting, the 'rat race' — the constant gnawing sense of having had and lost some infinite thing" (par. 14). Put succinctly, his main idea might be expressed as "You'll be a happier person if you make an effort to be consciously aware of your surroundings and look at the world through other people's eyes," or put even more simply, "Have empathy."

2. Wallace adheres to the philosophy (he calls it a cliché) that the goal of a liberal arts education is to teach students how to think. He extends the idea by asserting that "[l]earning how to think" (par. 5) enables adults to control their perceptions and to cope with life's difficulties.

3. Believing that one's self is "the absolute center of the universe" (par. 3) is apt to make a person miserable, as Wallace describes it, through frustration, irritation, and loneliness. Personal happiness, he suggests, can come only when selfishness is set aside in consideration of others. The point is a paradox: It seems contradictory but upon reflection makes perfect sense.

4. He's talking about general values and priorities, the mental hierarchies in which we "tap real meaning in life" (par. 13). Formal religion fits within Wallace's conception of worship, but he's more concerned with the worldly elements by which people set goals and define success — money, beauty, power, and intelligence. Aspiring to any of these, he warns, "will eat you alive" (13).

5. No. Acknowledging his (and presumably all college graduates') "tendency to overintellectualize stuff" (par. 5), Wallace insists that "banal platitudes can have life-or-death importance" (2) and defends each kind of intellectual shortcut as "express[ing] a great and terrible truth" (5). Taken as a group, he characterizes his "clichés," "platitudes," and so forth as "the truth with a whole lot of rhetorical bull pared away" (15).

QUESTIONS ON WRITING STRATEGY

1. Wallace was, of course, speaking to the 2005 graduating class of Kenyon College, a small liberal-arts college in central Ohio. He characterizes his listeners as young, inexperienced, intelligent, ambitious, and socially conscious and asserts that they "do not yet have any clue what 'day in, day out' really means" (par. 6). Wallace further assumes that his listeners, like he, possess a "natural, basic self-centeredness" (3) that will make them unhappy if they don't learn to master it. The middle-aged speaker attempts to connect with his young audience by adopting highly informal diction (see question 1 under "Language"), by making self-deprecating remarks, by promising that he's not going to lecture, by speaking to them in the second person, and by offering vivid (and highly amusing) images of the tedium and frustration they will soon have to endure.

2. Wallace's central example — a vivid illustration of a commute home from work rendered hellish by perception and attitude — begins in paragraph 7 and ends in paragraph 12.

3. Other examples can be found in the second half of paragraph 7, in both sentences of paragraph 9, in the middle of paragraph 11, and in the second sentence of paragraph 12. All of them relate what Wallace characterizes as the tedious and frustrating experience of trying to get home from work and put dinner on the table. Typical of Wallace's writing, these winding sentences (each one grammatically correct) string together multiple modifiers and compound clauses with a treadmill effect that leaves the reader both breathless and exhausted, much the way a harried commuter trying to get home might feel.

4. The anecdote sets up and exemplifies the central metaphor of Wallace's speech. Like the fish in the story, most of us are unaware of the most basic truths of our surroundings and our lives, and we take for granted those very things that have the power to sustain or destroy us. The

anecdote not only frames the speech by providing the introduction and conclusion but it also informs the title. The mantra "This Is Water," in Wallace's construction, translates to conscious awareness of one's internal responses to external stimuli.

5. The first pair of paragraphs contrasts Wallace's "automatic" agitated response to people in a grocery store with a calmer way of looking at things; the second contrasts his self-centered response to rush-hour traffic with "obviously different ways to think about these kinds of situations" (par. 11). His point is that, while we can't control such situations, we can control how we perceive and react to them, that it is "within [our] power to experience a crowded, loud, slow, consumer-hell-type situation as not only meaningful but sacred" (12).

QUESTIONS ON LANGUAGE

1. Wallace's diction is informal, intimate, and highly colloquial. Language of the sort Wallace uses is generally more natural in speaking than it would be in writing, so it makes sense that he would adopt it for a speech addressed to college students. Although the setting and Wallace's subject are both formal and serious, academic diction might have alienated or simply bored his audience, who one might presume were eager to be done with formal ceremonies and start celebrating their graduation.

2. The "default setting" Wallace describes is one of "basic self-centeredness," an ingrained tendency to "see and interpret everything through this lens of self" (par. 3). The metaphor, in invoking wiring and circuit boards, suggests that Wallace sees human beings as robots, or machines, programmed by some greater being and possessing little autonomous control. He insists, however, that with effort and discipline, we can override the "default," breaking free of the setting and reclaiming our humanity.

3. Students may appreciate the apparently deliberate redundancy of *banal platitude* (par. 2). Both words mean "unoriginal": Using them together underscores Wallace's assertion that he's not saying anything new.

DAVID FOSTER WALLACE ON WRITING

Wallace's philosophy may be eye-opening for student writers who focus on pleasing their audiences more than on challenging them. But it's true that readers appreciate having to do a little (or even a lot of) work. Though Wallace's techniques are unique and rather extreme, you might explore with students how to complicate their own prose without sacrificing clarity. They might, for instance, try playing with chronology, sentence length, or (relevant) digressions.

7
COMPARISON AND CONTRAST
Setting Things Side by Side

Many students dread the method of comparison and contrast, perhaps because of meeting it on essay examinations. We do our best to reassure them (in "The Method") that it is manageable with a little planning. The chapter offers extra help with outlining; we try to take some of the mystique out of it, and we urge the student not to feel a slave to a mere charting of letters and numerals. For a short paper, the formal outline — of the Roman numeral *I*, capital *A* variety — is surely more trouble than it's worth. But in writing any paper that compares and contrasts, a plan to follow, at least a rough plan, is especially useful.

Suzanne Britt's "Neat People vs. Sloppy People" is easy reading, but it makes sharp comments on human behavior. We've paired it with another humorous piece on human behavior, Dave Barry's "Batting Clean-Up and Striking Out." Both essays contrast neatniks and others, but they explain the differences differently.

Keeping up the humor, David Sedaris's essay, "Remembering My Childhood on the Continent of Africa," amusingly contrasts the writer's dull life in an American suburb with his partner's garishly textured life as the child of a nomadic diplomat. The three remaining essays in this chapter are more serious, though not somber. Bruce Catton's "Grant and Lee" remains a classic example of a method clearly serving a writer's purpose. And Fatema Mernissi's "Size 6: The Western Women's Harem" uses comparison to argue that the Muslim harem has its parallels among supposedly liberated Western women. Finally, George Chauncey demonstrates a half century's advancements in gay rights by contrasting the position of gays today with that prevailing fifty years ago.

For introducing the method of comparison and contrast, here's a lightweight illustration possibly worth reading to your class. At least it suggests that in comparing and contrasting, a writer has to consider a whole series of points. Craig Hosmer, a Republican and, at the time, representative from California's thirty-second district, introduced the following advice into the *Congressional Record* for October 1, 1974. (We found this item in *American Humor: An Interdisciplinary Newsletter*, Fall 1983, and offer it in a slightly abbreviated version, the better to illustrate comparison and contrast.)

How to Tell Republicans from Democrats

Republicans employ exterminators.
Democrats step on bugs.

Democrats name their children after popular sports figures, politicians, and entertainers.
Republican children are named after their parents or grandparents, according to where the money is.

Republicans tend to keep their shades drawn, although there is seldom any reason why they should.
Democrats ought to, but don't.

Republicans study the financial pages of the newspaper.
Democrats put them in the bottom of the bird cage.

Democrats buy most books that have been banned somewhere.
Republicans form censorship committees and read them as a group.

Democrats give their worn-out clothes to those less fortunate.
Republicans wear theirs.

Democrats raise Airedales, kids, and taxes.
Republicans raise dahlias, Dalmatians, and eyebrows.

Democrats eat the fish they catch.
Republicans hang them on the wall.

Republicans sleep in twin beds — some even in separate rooms.
That is why there are more Democrats.

SUZANNE BRITT

Neat People vs. Sloppy People

Whatever Suzanne Britt believes, she believes wholeheartedly. Then she merrily sets out to convince her readers that she's right. A danger in teaching this essay, perhaps, is that students without Britt's skill may be inspired to emulate her slapdash unreasonableness without quite achieving the desired effect. Some students, though, just might surprise you with the delightful writing they can produce with this essay as their inspiration.

Small groups can be useful for helping students through the brainstorming part of writing an essay. Students might appreciate having time to talk about the points of comparison they have come up with in preparing to write an essay for either of our first two writing suggestions. Group members can help each other expand their lists of comparative points and find the details that will bring these points to life.

QUESTIONS ON MEANING

1. Whoever said it failed to perceive Britt's humor.
2. Britt is hardly impartial. It's easy to see that her sympathies lie with sloppy people and that she considers herself one of them. Mostly, she writes to amuse and entertain.

3. "As always" means what it says. Yes, Britt is saying — with tongue only partially in cheek — the distinctions among people are moral.

QUESTIONS ON WRITING STRATEGY

1. Britt's tone is blunt, assured, and, of course, hyperbolic. The tone is established from the start: "Neat people are lazier and meaner than sloppy people." Words and phrases that illustrate the tone abound throughout the essay.
2. Britt finds no similarities at all between the two. Had she mentioned any, her essay would be less exaggerated and would therefore lose some of its force. Writers who aren't exaggerating might give short shrift to similarities, too, if they are obvious or irrelevant.
3. These broad statements are generalizations because they make conclusive assertions on the basis of some evidence — although, of course, Britt is deliberately exaggerating whatever evidence she has. By using so many generalizations, Britt compounds the outrageous nature of her essay. Her humor derives from her being unfair to neat people and finding no fault at all with their opposites.
4. Britt constantly clarifies her subjects by repeating *sloppy people* and *neat people*.
5. The examples do specify the kinds of behavior Britt has in mind, but they are themselves generalizations about the two kinds of people. They illustrate behavior but not particular persons.

QUESTIONS ON LANGUAGE

1. *The American Heritage Dictionary* tells us that *métier* is a word that began as the Latin *ministerium* ("occupation") and then became Vulgar Latin *misterium* and Old French *mestier* before assuming its present spelling and meaning ("specialty") in modern French and English.
2. The word is not to be understood literally, but humorously, as are *rectitude, stupendous* (par. 2), *excavation* (5), and *vicious* (9). Students may argue for one or two others that they perceive are not to be taken literally.

SUZANNE BRITT ON WRITING

Here are some responses to the questions for discussion.

1. Britt doesn't offer much specific advice for the student assigned to write about Guatemala. But the method she urges, it seems, is to study the subject long enough to discover some personal connection or interest in it.
2. Britt's first paragraph yields at least two metaphors ("you have to suck out all the marrow of whatever you do" and "My answer is rock bottom and hard") and a simile ("silence falls like prayers across the room"). More colorful still are the similes two paragraphs later, in which the student is advised to gather "your life around you as a mother hen gathers her brood, as a queen settles the folds in her purple robes." There's hyperbole, too, in the next paragraph: "an interminable afternoon in a biology lab."
3. What is the tone of Britt's remarks? Though she regards writing with humor and zest, and doesn't take it in grim earnest, clearly she deeply cares about it. In the end, she equates it with an act of faith.

DAVE BARRY

Batting Clean-Up and Striking Out

Dave Barry is one of America's best known and most prolific humorists, and his essay makes a perfect companion piece to Suzanne Britt's. Both writers rely on exaggeration and generalization to make readers laugh.

Students respond differently to humor based on stereotypes. While some will see this kind of humor as cathartic, others will be annoyed or even angered by it. The second through fourth writing suggestions all ask students to respond to Barry's use of stereotypes for their humorous potential. In addition, you might want to give students a chance to express their reactions in class. Encourage those who were offended by the essay to voice and clarify their objections; encourage those who enjoyed the essay to defend it.

QUESTIONS ON MEANING

1. Barry's purpose is to entertain and amuse. His humor is characterized by broad generalizations (such as the first sentence); tall tales (the "hormonal secretion" and the Pompeii example, par. 2); exaggeration ("clumps large enough to support agriculture," 2; "bacteria you could enter in a rodeo," 3); self-effacement ("an important project on the Etch-a-Sketch" and the pajamas anecdote, 4); and a tongue-in-cheek tone ("my specific family unit" and "Standard Male Cleaning Implements," 3; "a sensitive and caring kind of guy," 4; "human relationships or something," 8).
2. Barry is anything but objective. He is clearly writing from a male point of view, and he understands male behavior. However, his tone is far too facetious for the essay to be taken as a justification of boorish behavior. He makes as much fun of himself as of anyone else.
3. Barry seems to take the differences between the sexes as a given. He is less interested in reconciliation than in exploiting gender misunderstandings for their humorous potential.

QUESTIONS ON WRITING STRATEGY

1. A subject-by-subject organization would have undermined Barry's examples, which depend on the interaction of women and men to make their point.
2. From the first ironic sentence we know to take everything Barry says with a grain of salt.
3. The second half of Barry's thesis sentence is in paragraph 5: "The opposite side of the dirt coin, of course, is sports. This is an area where men tend to feel very sensitive and women tend to be extremely callous." Students (and teachers) may disagree over whether the divided thesis sentence helps or hurts. A single, early sentence might have tied the parts together, but it also would have stolen an element of surprise from the essay.
4. Barry effectively appropriates the force of Poe's story, giving his own anecdote an added dimension. The incongruity of Poe's horror story and Barry's domestic scene produces a comic effect.

5. He uses the phrase "the opposite side of the . . . coin."
6. This example is obviously invented. Its purpose is not to persuade but, like everything else in the essay, to amuse.

QUESTIONS ON LANGUAGE

1. Students sensitive to its connotation may object to Barry's use of *prattled* to describe the women's talk, even though he clearly intends it humorously. The word means "to talk idly or meaninglessly" and comes from a Dutch word, *praten*, with the same meaning.
2. The breathless, digressive nature of the sentence adds to the humor of the anecdote. It has the oral quality of someone gossiping on the telephone.
3. Again, the orality of the text is increased. We can hear the emphasis in Barry's voice, the near hysteria of "*during a World Series Game*" (par. 6), the sports-announcer tone of "Annual Fall Classic" (8).
4. By using *males*, Barry creates an anthropological distance between himself and his subject.

DAVE BARRY ON WRITING

Writing is a serious job for this humor writer, and students may be surprised at how difficult it can be for a funny man to wring a laugh from a reader. We appreciate Barry's observation that writing is, to quote Edison on genius, "one percent inspiration and ninety-nine percent perspiration." We also appreciate Barry's insistence that experience helps, a lesson that students may learn themselves as they gain more practice writing.

BRUCE CATTON

Grant and Lee: A Study in Contrasts

If ever that weary term *classic* applied to an essay, this is it. Where can you find a neater illustration of comparison and contrast? First Catton contrasts the two generals, then he compares them — gracefully moving from broad generalizations to specific evidence. Introducing the essay, you might remind students that they know a good deal about Grant and Lee already (or reveal that they need more knowledge). If your campus is far from Virginia, you may wish to acquaint the class with the connotations of *tidewater Virginia* (old family name, wealth, landowning, patrician). (See the third question on language.) A small group of students could research Virginia, the generals, and the Civil War and present their findings as a counterpoint to Catton's observations. (Note: If this sort of research is something you'd like to have students do fairly regularly, you might consider rotating the responsibility so that just one group works and reports on any given essay.)

QUESTIONS ON MEANING

1. Catton's central purpose is to explain how Grant and Lee stood for opposing social forces. Though he remarks in paragraph 13 that the two generals differed in personality, he doesn't expand on this observation. The qualities he cites (daring, resourcefulness, and so on) seem traits not of personality but of character.
2. Lee, an aristocrat from tidewater Virginia, believed in a leisure class of landowners responsible to their community and obliged to be models of strength and virtue. Grant, son of a frontier tanner, held with self-reliance, competition, and a society in which the most resourceful will rise. Lee's first loyalty was to his native soil; Grant's was to the nation. Lee's commitment was to the agrarian society of the past; Grant's, to an urban industrial future.
3. Both had "utter tenacity and fidelity," "daring and resourcefulness." Most important, both possessed the ability to turn quickly from war to peace. They made possible a reconciliation of North and South, for which all later Americans are indebted to them.
4. Each by nature was a warrior of "utter tenacity and fidelity" (par. 14), who fought for the ideals of his people (10–11).

QUESTIONS ON WRITING STRATEGY

1. *American Story* is a collection addressed to general readers with a special interest in American history. Catton doesn't assume a profound knowledge of the Civil War on their part, but he does assume that the campaigns of Petersburg, Second Manassas, Chancellorsville, and Vicksburg (in pars. 14–15) will be at least somewhat familiar to his readers.
2. Catton rounds out his essay by so doing; he stresses his point (made in his opening paragraph) that at Appomattox "a great new chapter" in American life began.
3. By arranging the essay to show that Grant and Lee, despite their profound differences of background and outlook, agreed on one essential, Catton saves his most important point for last. This structure makes the point more effectively than if Catton had begun by asserting that Grant and Lee were much alike and had then spent the body of his essay differentiating between them. Important points often stand out more when the reader is left with them.
4. Nearly every paragraph begins with a sentence containing some transition: sometimes no more than a word or phrase, such as "these men," "they," "each man," referring back to both Grant and Lee. Some transitions are explicitly comparative, such as "on the other hand" (par. 11). The most crucial sentence of transition is the one that opens paragraph 13: "Yet it was not all contrast, after all" — announcing the start of Catton's comparison.
5. The tone is sympathetic, admiring, and respectful. By imagining Lee with lance and banner, Catton hints that he finds the general's chivalric ideals a bit preposterous. But he is referring back to the point he makes in paragraph 5: Lee's way of life descended from "the age of knighthood." That he thinks its values outdated doesn't mean he finds them silly, nor that he mocks Lee for being their representative.
6. The classification broadens the significance of the comparison from two generals to the whole population. The analysis provides Catton with his points of comparison, his differences and similarities.

QUESTIONS ON LANGUAGE

1. Like most figures of speech, Catton's add vigor and concreteness to his prose. They include the metaphor of "two conflicting currents" (par. 3); the metaphor of an age "transplanted" (5); the metaphor of the "past that had settled into grooves" (8); the metaphors of the nation's expanding horizons and of the "dollars-and-cents stake" (9); the metaphor of Grant's seeing the Union as the ground under his feet (11); the personification of Grant as "the modern man emerging," the metaphor of the stage, and that of Lee as a knight with banner and lance (12); the metaphor of Grant and Lee as two battered boxers, each able to "remain on his feet and lift his two fists" (14).

2. *Poignant*, from the French verb *poindre* ("to sting"), means "sharply painful to the feelings; piercing or wounding." Clearly it is a stronger and more energetic word here than *touching, sad*, or *teary*. You might care to remind students (if you aren't tired of it) of Twain's remark about the right word being the lightning; the almost right word, the lightning bug.

3. Eastern Virginia's tidewater region, the low-lying coastal plain bisected by Chesapeake Bay, is so named because tidal water flows up its bays, inlets, and rivers. It is the area of the oldest colonial settlements (including Jamestown, Yorktown, and Williamsburg), where large plantations were established.

4. *Aristocratic* refers to a privileged class responsible for the well-being of the people it served as leaders.

5. Context will supply these meanings almost as well as a dictionary. This might be an opportune moment to point out that you don't expect students to interrupt their reading of an essay fourteen times to rummage through a dictionary. They usually can figure out the sense of words they don't know if they pay attention to other words in the neighborhood. Those they can't figure out they can circle and save up for a one-time trip to the dictionary.

BRUCE CATTON ON WRITING

In response to the questions: According to Jensen, concentration and getting up early in the morning made Catton the writer he was. And Catton the writer, it would seem, criticized his own work as unsparingly as Catton the editor criticized the work of others.

DAVID SEDARIS

Remembering My Childhood on the Continent of Africa

This essay is humorist David Sedaris's account of the exotic childhood and adolescent experiences of his partner Hugh — who grew up in various African outposts as the son of a US diplomat — as contrasted with Sedaris's far more mundane youth in suburban North Carolina. Students may initially have some trouble with Sedaris's subtle irony. You could begin discussion by asking class members whether they think Sedaris truly wishes he could have traded places with Hugh, whose youth, while "fascinating" in retrospect (par. 13), was in fact marked by some pretty gruesome and dangerous events. Sedaris admits that he can't acknowledge this fact because it means "I should have been happy with what I had" (21). Instead he retreats into fantasy, safely appropriating the stories he has heard from Hugh as memories of his own.

To pursue this question further, you could divide the class into small groups and have each group analyze the essay for evidence of Sedaris's clear awareness that Hugh's childhood was "not as glamorous as it sounds" (12). In reporting back their findings to the class, each group could consider what Sedaris seems to be suggesting about his own personality.

Sedaris's reading of *Me Talk Pretty One Day*, from which this essay comes, is available on audiotape and CD. Students may enjoy his distinctive delivery, familiar to anyone who has heard him on National Public Radio.

QUESTIONS ON MEANING

1. Sedaris contrasts his own "unspeakably dull" middle-class American childhood (par. 8) with the much more exotic and eventful childhood of his partner Hugh, who, as the son of a diplomat, grew up in various countries in Africa.
2. The thesis might seem to be that Sedaris's life was dull compared to Hugh's (par. 8) or that Sedaris makes up for his dull life by appropriating Hugh's (21). But hovering over all, just hinted, is the larger idea that Hugh's childhood, while much more exciting than Sedaris's and food for resentment and imagination, had terrible costs that Sedaris would not have wanted to pay.
3. Sedaris's envy is essentially ironic because many of Hugh's childhood experiences seem pretty lonely and harrowing, beginning with the field trip to the slaughterhouse. This is true even when Sedaris writes of something that one might indeed be envious of: For example, Hugh's family had servants, but they included guards with machetes (par. 11), suggesting that the family was always in danger. In paragraph 21 Sedaris notes that while he was longing for more exotic adventures as a child, Hugh ("[s]omeone unknown to me" at the time) was probably longing for something more normal.

QUESTIONS ON WRITING STRATEGY

1. Sedaris's point-by-point organization can be outlined as follows: comparison of field trips (pars. 1–7); of daily life (8); of access to popular culture, specifically movies and the circumstances of viewing them (9–10); of servants and security (11); of dangerous experiences (12–13); of meeting a celebrity (14); of Sedaris's ten-day visit with his senile grandmother and Hugh's two years living with strangers (15–19); and of vacations (20–21).
2. Transitions include "[w]hen I was in elementary school" (par. 7), "[w]hen I was seven years old" and "[w]hen he was seven years old" (8), "[u]nlike me" (10), "but" (11), and "[a]bout the same time" (16).
3. A monkey is a particularly exotic pet that many children might long to own. Hugh's monkey comes to represent for Sedaris everything that he envies about Hugh's childhood.

4. The opening conversation establishes the relationship between Sedaris and Hugh and particularly the fact that Hugh seems unfazed by his odd experiences. This opening also makes clear that Sedaris has had many such conversations with Hugh, on which he bases his knowledge of Hugh's experiences.
5. Sedaris narrates stories from his own life and from Hugh's to point up how different their experiences have been.

QUESTIONS ON LANGUAGE

1. The second and third, fourth and fifth, and sixth and seventh sentences in the paragraph are parallel in structure, which highlights the contrast that concludes each sentence. As Sedaris wittily puts it, "The verbs are the same, but [Hugh] definitely wins the prize when it comes to nouns and objects."
2. The term "petty thief" emphasizes the self-deprecating portrait that Sedaris has presented throughout. His use of Hugh's memories represents no "spiritual symbiosis" but is merely a way for Sedaris to live vicariously through the other man's experiences.
3. Almost any paragraph will provide examples of specific, concrete language. In paragraph 6 examples include "low-ceilinged concrete building," "small white piglet," "its dainty hooves clicking against the concrete floor," "class gathered in a circle," "turned from face to face," "drew a pistol from his back pocket, held it against the animal's temple, and shot the piglet, execution-style," "Blood-spattered, frightened children wept."
4. *Symbiosis*, from the Greek word for "living together," implies the intimate union of two dissimilar types.

DAVID SEDARIS ON WRITING

You might take a poll of the students in your class: How many have ever used a typewriter? Sedaris's animus against the computer and love of the typewriter probably grows quainter by the day, but we like what he says about the feel of writing, the sense "that you're actually building something."

FATEMA MERNISSI

Size 6: The Western Women's Harem

Mernissi, a Moroccan intellectual, comes to a rather startling conclusion in this essay. Discovering that she is overweight by American standards, she suggests that the invisibility imposed on women in Muslim cultures — being housebound in harems and completely veiled in public — has its counterpart in Western norms of female attractiveness: Western women who don't conform to an ideal of youthful beauty are ignored and devalued. Encourage students to discuss the extent to which the "norm is everywhere," as the saleswoman encountered by Mernissi says in paragraph 9. How often do television shows, movies, or fashion or cosmetics ads feature obviously mature or heavyset women?

If your classes are ethnically diverse, you could have students discuss how standards of attractiveness differ among cultures, not only internationally but within the United States as well.

QUESTIONS ON MEANING

1. Mernissi compares attitudes toward women in Western and Muslim cultures. She first states her thesis in paragraph 1 ("That distressing experience made me realize how the image of beauty in the West can hurt and humiliate a woman as much as the veil does when enforced by the state police in extremist nations such as Iran, Afghanistan, or Saudi Arabia"). She repeats it in paragraph 13 ("I realized for the first time that maybe 'size 6' is a more violent restriction imposed on women than is the Muslim veil"), elaborates on it in paragraph 14 ("Unlike the Muslim man, who uses space to establish male domination by excluding women from the public arena, the Western man manipulates time and light. He declares that in order to be beautiful, a woman must look fourteen years old"), repeats it in paragraph 15 ("This Western time-defined veil is even crazier than the space-defined one enforced by the ayatollahs"), and again elaborates on it in paragraph 17 ("Framing youth as beauty and condemning maturity is the weapon used against women in the West just as limiting access to public space is the weapon used in the East"). For Mernissi the objective is the same in both situations: "to make women feel unwelcome, inadequate, and ugly" (par. 17).
2. The saleswoman is initially superior and condescending. She later takes an interest in Mernissi's life and finally seems almost envious of a culture where size 6 is not the norm. Her change in attitude suggests the tyranny of size 6 for Western women.
3. Western attitudes are "more dangerous and cunning" because aging is inevitable ("that normal unfolding of the years," par. 15) and the Western stricture is "masked as an aesthetic choice" rather than "attacked directly" (16).

QUESTIONS ON WRITING STRATEGY

1. In paragraphs 6–7 Mernissi depicts herself as self-confident, impervious to attitudes about the way she looks within her own culture. It is only within Western culture that she feels humiliated by her physical attributes.
2. In paragraph 16 Mernissi first compares the Chinese custom of foot binding with the expectation that she shrink her hips (the transition here is "Similarly"). She then compares the month of fasting for the Muslim holy time of Ramadan with the perpetual dieting of the Western woman ("but").
3. The narrative (pars. 1–5, 8–13) draws readers into Mernissi's complex comparison and confronts them, as she was confronted, with the physical ideal imposed on Western women. She may have considered, too, that many of her readers might have had similarly humiliating experiences shopping for clothes.

QUESTIONS ON LANGUAGE

1. *Deviant* suggests not just a differing from the norm but also shamefulness, even immorality.
2. The veil is figurative in Western cultures, "wrapping [mature women] in shrouds of ugliness." In Muslim cultures, of course, it is literal, masking women in public.
3. Students may be unfamiliar with the sense of *generous* to mean "amply proportioned." Note that in context the word also has positive connotations.

GEORGE CHAUNCEY

The Legacy of Antigay Discrimination

In this first chapter from his book *Why Marriage? The History Shaping Today's Debate over Gay Equality,* historian George Chauncey contrasts gay life and rights today with the pervasive antigay discrimination of fifty years ago. How do students respond to Chauncey's examples of discrimination? We suspect that many will react with surprise, bearing out his assertion that the level of discrimination faced by gays and lesbians just fifty years ago "has virtually disappeared from popular memory" (par. 1).

This essay is somewhat unusual as an example of comparison and contrast because the contrast is one-sided: Today's situation receives nine sentences; the historical situation dominates. The second question under "Questions on Writing Strategy" asks students to consider why Chauncey structures the essay this way. Discussing this question in terms of audience can help students see how strongly content may be influenced by a writer's sense of readers' knowledge.

Chauncey's essay is an excellent example of an academic writer drawing on and formally citing sources, so you might want to assign it in conjunction with Chapter 3. Elsewhere in his book, Chauncey explains that this essay "is more extensively footnoted than the others, but it seemed important to provide documentation of the discriminatory measures it describes." Ask students why Chauncey thought this was important. Like the imbalance in the contrast, the documentation reflects Chauncey's awareness of audience, who might be skeptical of "a degree of policing and harassment that is almost unimaginable to us today" (par. 12).

Another point to discuss is how the history that Chauncey details in the essay "shapes today's debate over marriage" (par. 1). Few students would argue against homosexuals' rights to free speech, free press, free assembly, and the other rights Chauncey discusses. Why, then, has gay marriage become such a divisive issue? Could Chauncey be suggesting that in fifty years the right to same-sex marriage will be as much a given as those other rights are now?

QUESTIONS ON MEANING

1. Chauncey states his thesis in the first two sentences of paragraph 1.
2. Chauncey's purpose is to evaluate the treatment of homosexuals in American society, fifty years ago and today. In doing so, he is implicitly arguing for a continued expansion of gay and lesbian rights.
3. Chauncey means that discrimination was purposely practiced in many areas of American life and sanctioned by laws and official policies. Antigay discrimination wasn't just a practice of individuals.

QUESTIONS ON WRITING STRATEGY

1. The points of comparison are the portrayal of gays and lesbians in the media (pars. 3–4) and their rights to government jobs (5–6), free assembly (7–8), free speech and press (9), and "intimacy of their own choosing" (10–11).
2. Chauncey's point is that people are largely unaware of the systematic discrimination that gay men and lesbians faced fifty years ago, so he focuses more on the past than on the present. He assumes that readers know of the current rights he discusses, so he doesn't need to spend time illustrating the present situation. Beginning each paragraph "Fifty years ago" sufficiently summarizes the situation today.
3. The repetition of "Fifty years ago" at the beginning of nearly every paragraph clarifies the comparison, lends the essay coherence, and adds a note of forceful emphasis. Immediately after these sentences, transitions such as "instead," "in fact," and "for example" take readers into the historical situation.
4. The statistics help support Chauncey's claim that discrimination was widespread and systematic.
5. Chauncey opens each paragraph with a generalization about a particular type of antigay discrimination; he then supports that generalization with formally cited examples. By piling on example after example, he underscores just how serious and pervasive the discrimination was.

QUESTIONS ON LANGUAGE

1. Chauncey's tone is serious and controlled, but beneath the surface we can sense his anger and astonishment that such discrimination existed as recently as fifty years ago. Some words and phrases that suggest these attitudes include: "gay people were scorned and ridiculed, made to feel ashamed, afraid, and alone" (par. 2); "Hollywood films were *prohibited*" (3); "relentlessly attacked," "interrogated and coerced" (8); "a degree of policing and harassment that is almost unimaginable to us today" (12).
2. *Ferret out* alludes to hunting with ferrets, which were used to drive rabbits out of their burrows. Chauncey's word choice suggests that lesbians and gay men were treated as animals to be hunted down, rather than as people with civil rights.
3. He is signaling that he disagrees with the use of these phrases; he doesn't view homosexuals as immoral or as "deviants."
4. The word *lewd* offers a good illustration of how the definition of a word can change dramatically over time. In the twelfth century, the Old English *laewede* meant simply "not a member of the clergy." Because the clergy comprised most of the literate population at that time, the word came to mean "illiterate or uneducated." From there, *lewd* evolved to its present meaning of "obscene" or "preoccupied by sexual desire."

8
PROCESS ANALYSIS
Explaining Step by Step

This chapter provides a good sampling of process analyses, ranging from the directions in Linnea Saukko's "How to Poison the Earth" (albeit directions that are not to be followed) to the informative analyses in Gretel Ehrlich's "Chronicles of Ice," Jessica Mitford's "Behind the Formaldehyde Curtain," and Michael Pollan's "Corn's Conquest." In between, mixing both types, falls Firoozeh Dumas's personal reflections in "Sweet, Sour, and Resentful." The pair in this chapter is Saukko and Ehrlich. Both treat environmental processes — pollution in Saukko's case, global warming in Ehrlich's.

Incidentally, the opening of this chapter explains the *analysis* part of process analysis. We continue to introduce process analysis *before* analysis (Chap. 9) because we expect that many students find the former easier to understand. Process analysis thus becomes a way into analysis. But if you'd rather cover analysis itself first, nothing in the text discussion or essays will impede you.

LINNEA SAUKKO

How to Poison the Earth

It won't take students long to realize that Saukko's essay is an impassioned plea for sanity on the part of those whose actions are contributing to the pollution of the earth. Though it is mainly a directive process analysis, no one is expected to follow the directions. Clearly what the author hopes is just the reverse: that readers will make every effort to stop those who are already, and all too effectively, poisoning the earth. In this edition we pair Saukko's essay with another on the environment, Gretel Ehrlich's "Chronicles of Ice," which explains the formation of glaciers and the changes in them caused by global warming.

With Saukko's essay, students might be asked to do a little research into the issues — questioning why environmental destruction is permitted, whom it benefits, what its elimination might cost, and what its alternatives are. (The second writing suggestion can be helpful in this regard.) If students are themselves well informed about the issues, the discussion that results might be one of the liveliest of the year.

Saukko's technique — giving advice precisely opposite to what she really hopes will happen — is so effective that students may find themselves inspired to imitate her. While the method can be particularly forceful, duplicating her deadpan irony will not be so simple. You can give students practice at managing this tricky tone by asking them to work in pairs or threes to write a short how-to essay of their own. Have them consider carefully *why* Saukko's essay works so well and then try their own hands at giving advice in this backward way. (You may need to remind them that they will likely be more successful if they choose a subject they know a lot about.)

QUESTIONS ON MEANING

1. Saukko's purpose is to warn readers about threats to the future of our planet, and she has done her homework. She has taken the trouble to collect statistics and other information. She knows the names and strengths of the pollutants she mentions. She is familiar with the methods by which wastes are disposed of, oil wells are drilled, pesticides are applied, and bombs are tested. Her satire is all the more biting for being buttressed by facts.
2. Students will find the mechanisms explained succinctly in paragraphs 5–7.
3. Saukko mentions disposal of nuclear wastes and toxic chemicals through deep-well and shallow-well injection, the location of dumps and landfills where their poisons can spread, pesticide use, ocean dumping, industrial air pollution, and nuclear bomb testing as practices detrimental to the environment.

QUESTIONS ON WRITING STRATEGY

1. Clearly Saukko doesn't expect individual readers to carry out her instructions. Her point is that these dangerous exercises are already routine — practiced by corporations and by local, state, and federal governments on our behalf — and ought to be stopped.
2. Saukko introduces her essay effectively with some generalizations about poisoning the earth and then, starting with paragraph 2, moves more or less geographically, as water does, from land to ocean to air. The organization is effective because it corresponds with a natural order.
3. The people most likely to respond to this essay are those who share Saukko's concern about the future of the earth.
4. The tone is ironic, as almost every sentence demonstrates. Typically, satire depends on such irony to attack its subject.
5. Saukko uses the first-person plural *we* almost throughout, though she shifts to the imperative in paragraphs 7 and 8: "make sure" and "be sure."
6. The examples Saukko uses — nuclear wastes, PCB, DDT, nuclear fallout — are perhaps the most poisonous. Among the pollutants she doesn't mention, lead emissions from automobiles, carbon particles from smokestacks, and carbon dioxide from diverse sources come immediately to mind.

QUESTIONS ON LANGUAGE

1. All are dripping with irony.
2. One of the things students would do well to note about the word *nuclear* is its pronunciation. A number of people in the United States still speak of "nucular" war, "nucular" power, and the like, just because they've heard it wrong and never looked closely enough at the word to get it right.

LINNEA SAUKKO ON WRITING

Perhaps one of the reasons that Linnea Saukko's essay won a Bedford Prize for Student Writing was her feeling for the subject. Those writers who pick a subject about which they care passionately tend to write well. Students who know that are off to a running start.

GRETEL EHRLICH

Chronicles of Ice

In this lyrical essay, nature writer Gretel Ehrlich analyzes the life cycle of glaciers, making a larger point about their ecological importance and about the risks of letting them melt because of global warming. The essay is wonderful proof that science writing and process analysis need not be dry. In Ehrlich's hands, complex processes and geological terms become poetry.

We pair this essay with another piece on the environment, Linnea Saukko's "How to Poison the Earth." In recent years, Hurricane Katrina, Al Gore's *An Inconvenient Truth*, numerous scientific studies, and the popular media have brought global warming and other environmental issues to the forefront of public dialog. You might ask students how Ehrlich's and Saukko's essays differ from other things they have read or watched about the environment. Both writers use unique strategies to get readers' attention without sounding preachy: Ehrlich uses poetic imagery and philosophical musings and Saukko uses satire.

QUESTIONS ON MEANING

1. Industrialization brought with it the smokestacks of factories and the tailpipes of cars, whose emissions are largely responsible for the increasing carbon dioxide levels that contribute to rising temperatures.
2. Ehrlich compares glaciers to archivists and historians: They trap particles and oxygen bubbles that tell scientists "how living beings evolved, how weather vacillated, why plants and animals died" (par. 9). Thus when a glacier disappears, it is like losing a library full of valuable scientific information.
3. Before industrialization, people lived in communion with nature (pars. 13–14). Now they no longer feel a spiritual connection to the environ-

ment, and the lack of concern about how we develop it is destroying the "biological health of our planet" (15).

4. Ehrlich wants to instill in readers a greater appreciation for the awesomeness of nature and to warn of the dangers of global warming. She first mentions global warming offhandedly in paragraph 2, and her purpose becomes clear at the end of paragraph 8 and into paragraph 9.

5. Ehrlich's thesis accumulates over the course of the essay and might be stated thus: Human activity and unwillingness to consider its environmental costs are threatening the glaciers on which the planet's health — and thus human activity — depend.

QUESTIONS ON WRITING STRATEGY

1. The essay progresses from specific to general, as one particular glacier (pars. 1–3) leads Ehrlich to comment on the process by which all glaciers form (4–7) and then to reflect on the larger significance of both the process and the survival of glaciers (8–12). In the conclusion (13–16), Ehrlich expands her view even further, commenting on humans' changing relationship to the environment. The last paragraph neatly returns us to Perito Moreno, the specific glacier that triggered Ehrlich's musings.

2. Ehrlich uses process analysis to explain how glaciers form and decline (pars. 4–7). The explanation of how glaciers form and move conveys their awesome power. Ehrlich seems to want to instill in her audience the same respect and awe she feels upon seeing Perito Moreno, which will, she hopes, inspire readers to care about glaciers' survival.

3. Ehrlich's analysis of how a glacier forms and moves shows that she assumes a general audience. She explains the process carefully, using personification and analogy to convey complicated concepts. She also defines certain geologic terms, such as *firn* (par. 4) and *albedo effect* (10). She does, however, assume that her audience is well educated and somewhat knowledgeable about science, using terms such as *ablation* (7), *permafrost* (11), and *calving* (17) without defining them.

4. In detailing the consequences of warmer temperatures, Ehrlich describes a chain reaction that moves from fairly abstract problems to more concrete consequences that affect humans directly.

QUESTIONS ON LANGUAGE

1. Some examples: "lips, wombs, . . . gravelly elbows" (par. 1); "the glacier's snout" (2); "An icy cheekbone crumbles" (3); "They move like men on stilts" (5); "A glacier balances its gains and losses like a banker" (7); "A glacier is an archivist and historian" (8). The personification adds vividness to the essay and inspires readers to see glaciers as living creatures they should care about saving.

2. Ehrlich alludes to the biblical story of Adam and Eve, who disobeyed God, were expelled from Paradise, and descended into a state of innate sinfulness. Ehrlich suggests that the human activity affecting the glaciers is a continuation of that story.

3. This vocabulary list includes some technical terms from geology and zoology, including *accretes* (grows by addition), *limpets* (mollusks), *guanaco* (a small mammal related to the llama), and *calving* (the breaking off of a piece of a glacier or an iceberg). We define *ablation* in a footnote because it seems least likely to be recognized and is important to Ehrlich's analysis.

GRETEL EHRLICH ON WRITING

Ehrlich's statement may be difficult for some students to follow and appreciate, but we print it because it makes a strong point about surrendering one's ego while writing. Inexperienced writers are more likely to suffer anxiety and self-consciousness while composing. These feelings of "ego" (to use Ehrlich's word) can get in the way, at least during the early stages of the writing process.

FIROOZEH DUMAS

Sweet, Sour, and Resentful

Popular humorist Firoozeh Dumas has made it her mission to humanize Iranian people in the American consciousness, a mission that seems especially important in the context of political unrest and wars in the Middle East, nuclear proliferation, and terrorism.

Younger readers may not be familiar with the Iranian revolution to which Dumas refers or with the ensuing exodus of Iranian families to America and Americans' distrust of them in the 1970s and 1980s. We encourage students to research this background in the second writing suggestion, but you may also want to flesh out the basic outline provided in the gloss note on page 321: In the late 1970s, fundamentalist Muslims fostered political and religious unrest in the country, culminating in a coup and the exile of American-backed Shah Reza Pahlavi. In his place, revolutionaries installed Ayatollah Ruhollah Khomeini, who was determined to jettison Western influence and restructure Iranian culture and politics around strict interpretation of Islamic religious rule. In 1979, Khomeini supporters captured fifty-three Americans at the US embassy in Tehran, precipitating a hostage crisis that lasted 444 days and ended in a botched rescue attempt and embarrassment for the Carter administration; the hostages were released upon Ronald Reagan's inauguration in 1981. (During the same period, Iran was attacked by Iraq, leading to a brutal war that lasted until 1988.) Backlash against Iranians in the United States — the vast majority of whom had fled the violence and repression in their country — was severe and included general hostility, physical attacks, and demands for universal deportation.

If you assign Amy Tan's "Fish Cheeks" (p. 116), another short piece about a family tradition surrounding food, you might begin class discussion by inviting students to compare and contrast the two essays. Both writers, whose families immigrated to the United States in the wake of political unrest, explore the difficulty of keeping a tradition alive in their new country. Whereas Tan's difficulty stems from a desire to fit in with her American peers, Dumas's mother's difficulty is purely logistic. Nevertheless, the two essays make a similar point about the importance of maintaining family tradition and cultural ties. And although both writers make a similar point about the difficulty of adjusting to American life, Dumas states her thesis explicitly while Tan leaves it up to readers to work out the significance of her story.

QUESTIONS ON MEANING

1. The dinners provided an opportunity to orient recent Iranian immigrants to life in California; they also allowed the hosts to share "the hospitality that Iranians so cherish" (par. 3) as well as stay connected to their roots. For both the hosts and the guests, the elaborate and traditional Persian meals helped to maintain a sense of community; they also served as a bittersweet "reminder of the life [they] had left behind" (10).
2. "As I watched my mother experience the same draining routine week after week, I decided that tradition is good only if it brings joy to all involved. . . . Sometimes, even our most cherished beliefs must evolve" (par. 12).
3. Dumas wants to share a belief that she developed as a witness to her mother's exhaustion and resentment — the importance of adapting tradition and beliefs when circumstances demand it. To some extent, she is also relating the impetus behind her own assimilation into American culture.
4. Dumas suggests potluck, or requiring guests to contribute to the meals by bringing food with them. Based on the way Dumas characterizes her (traditional, diplomatic, judgmental of inadequate or lazy cooks, perfectionist, and controlling), we doubt her mother would have relinquished the role of hostess, no matter how much it strained her. However, Dumas does relate the process in the past tense, so it's possible that her mother did, indeed, scale back her efforts — or that the number of guests dwindled after the first wave of Iranian immigration in the late 1970s and early 1980s.

QUESTIONS ON WRITING STRATEGY

1. The introductory paragraphs establish the context behind the elaborate weekly meals: The guests who came to the author's parents' condo every weekend were reluctant immigrants, possibly even refugees, displaced from their "real home" (par. 1) by war. At the same time, the introduction indicates the parallels between Iranian culture and American culture to help make Iranians seem less "foreign" to readers — one of Dumas's overriding goals as a writer.
2. "Sweet, Sour, and Resentful" was, as the introduction to the essay indicates, first published in the now-defunct *Gourmet*, an upscale magazine for "foodies" (par. 5) that often featured complicated recipes and travel essays. Dumas could reasonably assume, then, that her readers held a strong interest in food and culture. Most readers of the magazine would have had some experience preparing elaborate dishes, hunting down elusive ingredients, and hosting large gatherings, so it's likely they could empathize with the difficulties and stresses the author's mother endured — if not, perhaps, her resentment.
3. Although Dumas identifies the "first step" as "preparing the herbs" (par. 6), the process actually began with her father taking phone calls and extending invitations to near strangers. Next came menu planning (on Mondays) and softening the neighbors with gifts of food (par. 4), followed by Tuesday shopping trips that usually ended in frustration. With all ingredients corralled, by midweek the author's parents began the simultaneous tasks of chopping by hand and frying herbs and onions (6); mixing, cooking, and rolling the contents of stuffed grape leaves (7); and preparing homemade yogurt and other side dishes (8). The guests would arrive on the weekends, at which time Dumas's mother cooked and

drained the rice. The meals would then be served "buffet-style" (10) and consumed in a matter of minutes (11). The final step was "fielding thank-you phone calls from . . . guests" (12) and extending more invitations. With several overlapping stages occurring over the course of a week, Dumas ensures coherence by providing clear time-markers and transitions throughout her analysis, then circling back to the first stage in her conclusion, implying that the process never ended.

4. By comparing bucolic local market days in Abadan with frustrating car-dependent shopping trips in California, Dumas harkens back to her introduction and underscores her point that adjusting to life in the United States was challenging and unpleasant for Iranian immigrants. At the same time, she emphasizes how much additional trouble her mother went to in order to give her guests a taste of home.

QUESTIONS ON LANGUAGE

1. Characteristically, Dumas's ironic tone in this essay borders on sarcasm but is nonetheless good-natured and appreciative. She tempers the implied criticism of her parents' and guests' behavior with several self-deprecating remarks, which is where most of her humor lies. You might ask students how the writer's attitude toward her parents would have come across without the mocking comments about her own abilities.

2. Dumas provides the Persian names for most of the dishes her mother prepared and served to guests every week. In doing so, she emphasizes the sense of home those meals provided for both her family and their guests. She ensures that American readers will understand the meaning by renaming each dish in an appositive phrase, such as "*fesenjan*, pomegranate stew with ground walnuts" (par. 4) or "*qormeh sabzi*, herb stew" (6).

3. In its literal sense, a "litmus test" is a chemical process that measures the pH level of a substance to determine where it falls within a range of base to acid; colloquially, the phrase refers to a basis for making a judgment. Dumas uses the term in its colloquial meaning, but we like the echo of "sweet" (base) and "sour" (acidic) with the title and the concept's effectiveness in evoking her mother's bitterness about performing her tasks.

4. *Locavore* — a combination of *local* and the Latin *vorare*, "to eat" — is a recent coinage and does not appear in all dictionaries. The word refers to a politically and environmentally motivated movement advocating a preference for organic, local foods, rather than those that have been processed or shipped long distances. Students may be interested to know that Michael Pollan (p. 337) and Barbara Kingsolver (p. 534) are both strong proponents of local eating.

FIROOZEH DUMAS ON WRITING

Many students may identify with Dumas's childhood memory of soaking up observations in a room full of adults. Fewer will relate to her experience of feeling almost intoxicated with the inspiration to write them down. One way to simulate the experience is to have students write for ten minutes from observation or from a prompt. Try having them write about their favorite Halloween costume or the first time they can remember feeling guilty. The only rule is to keep the pencil moving (or the fingers typing) until you call time.

JESSICA MITFORD

Behind the Formaldehyde Curtain

For that soporific class that sits and looks at you, here is a likely rouser. If Mitford can't get any response out of them, they're in a league with her Mr. Jones, and you might as well devote the rest of the course to silent study periods. Sometimes, it is true, a class confronted with this essay will just sit there like people in whose midst a large firecracker has been hurled, watching it sputter. Give them time to respond with five or ten minutes to freewrite about whatever Mitford's essay first inspires them to say. Then have them trade papers in groups of three or four, read the papers, and discuss their responses to each other. You can turn these smaller group discussions into a whole-class conversation whenever it seems appropriate.

Teaching Mitford's essay invites one possible danger: that someone in the class, having recently experienced the death of a loved one, will find Mitford's macabre humor cruel and offensive. We once received a painful letter from a student in Wenatchee, Washington, who complained bitterly about this "hideous" essay. "My husband was crushed in a logging accident," she wrote. "If Mitford also learned a little about grief, she would know that those people who view a body have an easier time with grief than those who don't. She wouldn't hate funeral directors. I guess Mitford would have had me view my husband's mangled body, but I'm glad the funeral director prepared his body for viewing."

How can you answer such a protest? Before assigning this essay for reading, you might ask the class whether anyone present has suffered a death in the family. At least warn students what to expect. Anyone recently bereaved might be given the option of skipping both Mitford's essay and the class discussion. If a student in mourning reads Mitford's essay anyway and protests its seeming callousness, you might see whether that student feels impelled to write a personal response to Mitford and her essay — as our correspondent did so effectively. The first and fourth writing suggestions may be helpful.

The painstaking legwork that Mitford did before she wrote *The American Way of Death* is documented in *Poison Penmanship: The Gentle Art of Muckraking* (1979). Much of her information came from professional journals, such as *Casket & Sunnyside, Mortuary Management,* and *Concept: The Journal of Creative Ideas for Cemeteries.* While laying stress on the value of such research, Mitford adds that a muckraker profits from sheer luck. A friend happened to recall a conversation with an undertaker when she was arranging for her brother-in-law's funeral. She had insisted on the cheapest redwood coffin available, but the undertaker objected. The deceased was too tall to fit into it; a costly coffin was required. When she continued to insist, the undertaker said, "Oh, all right, we'll use the redwood, but we'll have to cut off his feet." This grim example of high-pressure sales tactics supplied Mitford's book with one of its "more shining jewels."

When Mitford first showed her analysis of the embalming process (as a manuscript chapter for *The American Way of Death*) to her British and her American publishers, "it was met with instantaneous and thunderous disapproval from the editors on both sides of the Atlantic; this chapter is too revolting — it must go, they said." She insisted on keeping it, and lost the publishers. A year after Simon & Schuster brought out the book, she recalls, "those self-same embalming passages were chosen for inclusion in a college textbook on writing. Well! Of course I felt vindicated. The obvious moral is that although *some* editors can *sometimes* perform wonders in improving your work, in the last analysis your own judgment must prevail" (from *Poison Penmanship*, pp. 22–23).

QUESTIONS ON MEANING

1. In case anyone finds this essay repulsive and resents your assigning it, we suggest you begin by inviting reactions of all kinds. Let students kick the essay about, and, if they hate it, encourage them to say why. Almost certainly some will find it hilarious and will defend it as humor. Others will probably say that they didn't like it, that it's unpleasant, but that it tells truths we ought to know. You'll usually get more reactions if you are slow to advance your own. If the sense of the meeting should be vehemently against this essay, you may care to stick up for it (or you may want to skip on to the next selection in a hurry). But if, as is likely, most students are intrigued by it, they'll indicate this by their reactions, and your ensuing class discussion can ride on this momentum.
2. She speculates that perhaps undertakers keep it secret for fear that patrons, knowing what it is, wouldn't want it done (par. 6).
3. "To make the corpse presentable for viewing in a suitably costly container" (par. 2). Most of the usual obstacles to presentability are itemized in paragraphs 14–18: the effects of mutilation, emaciation, and disease.
4. If the subject was not dead, the undertaker will have killed him.
5. Her purpose is to attack the custom of embalming (and to chide the society that permits it). Mitford finds Americans "docile" and "ignorant" in tolerating such a procedure (par. 4). From her concluding paragraphs (23–27), we infer that she would urge Americans not to embalm, to admit the fact of death, and to bury the dead in closed coffins, as is done in much of the rest of the Western world.

QUESTIONS ON WRITING STRATEGY

1. Mitford's tone is cheerful scorn. Her verbs for the treatments inflicted on the corpse — "sprayed," "sliced," "pierced," "pickled," and so on — clearly show that she regards the process as ridiculous. The ironic phrase "suitably costly container" strongly hints that she regards morticians as racketeers.
2. She is determined to show that if we knew what embalming and restoration entailed — its every detail — we wouldn't stand for it.
3. The body becomes a character in her drama — whether it is that of an adult or a child.
4. Mitford's opening sentence indicates the start of a time sequence, and students should easily be able to find the ensuing time-markers. Her favorites are the small words "next" and "now," and most of the paragraphs about Mr. Jones contain one or the other.
5. Her audience is American general readers, whom she distinguishes from "funeral men" in paragraph 6.
6. The quotation in paragraph 3 suggests that embalming (and all it entails) may be illegal; the one in paragraph 10 suggests that dolling up

the corpse is more important to the mortician than possibly saving a life. Mr. Kriege (quoted in par. 22) makes the undertaker sound like a funeral football coach, in whose hands the corpse is a helpless ball. In offering these quotations, Mitford hangs the ethics and professional behavior of morticians by their own words and once more questions the desirability of embalming.

7. Mitford's passive verbs are to us very effective. They keep the focus on the grisly process, and they undermine her target actors, funeral directors.

8. The groups are "surgery" tools, tissue chemicals, restorative cosmetics and plasters, and props and stabilizers. The groups make the catalog of equipment and supplies more intelligible and reinforce Mitford's point about the pretentions and absurdities of the process.

QUESTIONS ON LANGUAGE

1. By alluding to the Prince of Denmark's speech with skull in hand (*Hamlet* 5.1), Mitford suggests that perhaps Yorick's "counterpart of today" is another luckless jester or clown. This theatrical allusion also enforces her metaphor of the drama that begins and the curtain that must be lifted.

2. Mitford delights in citing undertakers' euphemisms. The morticians, she implies, dislike plain words — in paragraph 20, she quotes one who warns against creating the impression "that the body is in a box" (which, of course, is fact). There seems an ironic discrepancy between the attitudes expressed in the last two sentences and Mitford's own view. A funeral, she implies, shouldn't be a "real pleasure" but an occasion for grief. Death isn't an opposing football team.

3. To the general reader, these brand names carry unpleasant connotations, and a lively class discussion may be devoted to unraveling what these are. Lyf-Lyk tint seems cutesy in its spelling, like some drugstore cosmetic item. Other brand names seem practical and unfeeling: Throop Foot Positioner, Armstrong Face Former and Denture Replacer. Porto-Lift and the Glide Easy casket carriage stress slickness and efficiency. Classic Beauty Ultra Metal Casket Bier seems absurdly grand. Mitford's purpose is to attack our sympathy and tolerance for the undertaker's art, and certainly these names rub us the wrong way.

4. "Dermasurgeon" (par. 8) is a euphemism Mitford especially relishes. Although it tries to dignify the mortician, Mitford points out how (unlike the surgeon he imitates) the embalmer acquired his training in a quick post–high-school course.

JESSICA MITFORD ON WRITING

Surprisingly often, authors are in total agreement when they discuss the art of writing. Mitford takes the common view that to write well, you have to care deeply about your subject. (We love that British phrase "besotted by.") Like so many writers, both amateur and professional, she knows that writing is hard work. Like George Orwell, muckraker Mitford sees writing as a valuable tool for righting the world's wrongs.

From what Mitford says about her research for *The American Way of Death*, students can learn how important it is to get the facts straight when doing an exposé. The author makes clear as well that in writing, as in most other activities, a sense of humor is a valuable asset.

MICHAEL POLLAN
Corn's Conquest

In just a few pages Pollan traces the ecological and biological processes of photosynthesis and carbon conversion, at the same time revealing that corn is a hidden ingredient in most of our food and showing what its ubiquity has done to human bodies. It sounds unreadable, but Pollan pulls it off wonderfully. In his hands what could be dry, impenetrable science turns amazing and engaging, even life altering.

In case some of your students resist science writing, you might start off by dividing the class into small groups to work on the first question on meaning. When they see clearly *why* Pollan goes through the trouble of explaining the intricacies of atomic weight, students will be able to relax and enjoy the ride.

When assigning Pollan's essay, you could also conduct an exercise to make his point concrete for students. Ask them to survey the nutrition labels on the packaged foods and drinks they have on hand, perhaps in a kitchen or desk drawer. Using Pollan's list of corn-derived additives in paragraphs 8 and 9, how many of their foods contain corn, and where does it appear in the list of ingredients? (The earlier it's listed, the higher its percentage of the total ingredients.) Students may be surprised to discover, in their own pantries, just how much corn they ingest daily.

QUESTIONS ON MEANING

1. Pollan's purpose is to inform. Specifically, he's writing to expose a few basic ecological and biological facts that will shock most readers, in service of nudging them to pay more attention to what they eat. We think he succeeds quite handily.

2. Pollan explains "the C-4 trick" in paragraphs 17–20. Put succinctly, corn absorbs an extra carbon atom during photosynthesis; the extra carbon makes *Zea Mays* much more energy efficient than most plants, which gives it a biological and caloric advantage in competition for air, water, and nutrients, rendering corn hardier and more likely to survive in less-than-ideal conditions. As a result, corn is one of the most abundant sources of food for animal and human consumption.

3. He is referring to cultural preferences for grains, or "staple food[s] of choice" (par. 21). "Wheat people" are those whose cultures rely on wheat — Europeans and Americans in particular. "Corn people," on the other hand, are those whose cultures privilege corn — primarily Mexicans, although Pollan posits that most Americans have unwittingly joined this group. The preferences are significant, not only for cuisine and cultural identity but also for the actual chemical composition of our bodies:

"Corn people," Pollan explains, have a noticeably higher ratio of carbon in their flesh and their bones, indicating a lack of variety in diet and nutrition (21).

4. The phrase brings to mind a mutant, monstrous plant or perhaps a human who has been altered to resemble corn. Both images effectively sum up Pollan's thesis: that corn has invaded our diets and changed our bodies in fundamental ways.

QUESTIONS ON WRITING STRATEGY

1. Pollan details two related processes — photosynthesis, or how a stalk of corn creates "life out of thin air" (pars. 16–19), and how the human body transforms corn and other nutrients into flesh and bone (15, 20–21). The latter process is directly affected by the former, in ways that Pollan suggests should be alarming or, at the very least, disconcerting.

2. Twinkies and "frankly synthetic coffee whiteners" (par. 4) come up three times in Pollan's essay: Specifically, he invokes the infamous cream-filled cakes and mystery powder in paragraphs 4, 6, and 11. Both are unapologetically chemical in origin — nobody pretends to believe that either is healthy or wholesome — and are typically considered unnatural, even a little frightening. Pollan mentions them repeatedly to emphasize that the origins of much of our food is synthetic, mysterious, and unnatural. Twinkies (and nondairy creamer), he seems to imply, should be the least of our worries because we *know* they're not real food.

3. One might presume that the information is so thoroughly synthesized that Pollan can't distinguish the original sources and that is pretty much the case: Although the information is highly surprising to general readers, most of it would be considered common knowledge in botanical and ecological circles. As a journalist writing for a general audience, Pollan provides a list of sources as a courtesy for readers who might wish to learn more or at least to confirm that his claims are based on science. Some students will be troubled and question why Pollan seems exempt from the very citation requirements to which they are held as writers; others won't care; and others might recognize that in-text citations are unnecessary.

4. Pollan classifies grocery-store offerings by their origins in the "industrial food chain" (par. 6) — whether they're animal, vegetable, mineral, chemical, or some combination. His point is both that determining those origins is increasingly difficult in a world of processed foods and that, with a little detective work, one discovers corn — his subject — is an element of nearly everything on display.

QUESTIONS ON LANGUAGE

1. Pollan masterfully combines formal, scientific language and technical terms with easy-going colloquial expressions and inventive figures of speech (we encourage students to analyze the last element in the writing suggestion labeled "Critical Writing"). Taken together, the writer's language choices clearly communicate the details of a complicated scientific process while making that process engaging and understandable, even for general readers with no background in science.

2. Pollan repeats the word so incessantly to drive home just how ubiquitous and inescapable corn is in our diets.

3. The incomprehensible vocabulary *is* Pollan's point. The vast majority of our food, he suggests, contains chemicals and synthetic ingredients that very few of us understand.

4. *Platonic* is a reference to the ancient Greek philosopher Plato (427?–347 BCE) and his philosophy of ideal forms that transcend practical reality. When lowercase, the word tends to mean *theoretical.* In either case, we thoroughly enjoy the image of "platonic peas" (par. 4) and Pollan's suggestion that the packaged, frozen vegetables are simultaneously perfect and unreal.

MICHAEL POLLAN ON WRITING

Pollan writes like dancers learn choreography: He takes it from the top before adding on. While students may have different processes for drafting, Pollan's is certainly worth a try. Students may find that going over past work each time they sit down to write makes for clearer theses and crisper sentences.

9
DIVISION OR ANALYSIS
Slicing into Parts

Division and classification have long been combined and confused in composition textbooks, so it is no wonder that some authors, some teachers, and many students cannot tell them apart. The true loser has seemed to be division. Indeed, some texts dispose of division as the mere servant of classification, the operation required to sort (divide) things into classes.

At the same time, freshman writing classes are absorbed in critical thinking, reading, and writing. Scholarly journals, textbooks, and teachers are inventing and experimenting with ways to teach these crucial skills. Yet all along we have had the means to introduce the skills through the Cinderella of the division and classification pair. Though generally treated, when treated at all, as a simple cutting operation, division is of course *analysis*. And what is analysis but the basis of criticism?

We have tried to rescue division/analysis and give it useful work in the composition course. We have, most noticeably, given the method its own chapter (and classification its own), in which we stress analytic thinking and discuss critical thinking. We have also made much more explicit the analytical underpinnings of the other methods of development, including (but not only) classification. (Two of these related methods — comparison-contrast and process analysis — continue to be covered before this chapter on the theory that they may be more familiar and accessible to students, even without explicit discussion of analysis. Of course, you may change the order of chapters if you see it differently.)

We now pair Judy Brady's provocative "I Want a Wife" with Christina Hoff Sommers's "Men — It's in Their Nature," an interesting (if indirect) rejoinder to what many see as Brady's unfair portrayal of men. "Vampires Never Die," a fascinating interpretation of legend and popular culture by Guillermo del Toro and Chuck Hogan, forms a bridge from simple division to critical analysis, illustrated by Bella DePaulo's "The Myth of Doomed Kids" and student Laila Ayad's "The Capricious Camera."

JUDY BRADY

I Want a Wife

In the late 1980s newspapers and magazines quoted an instantly famous remark attributed to the actress Joan Collins after her divorce from musician Peter Holm. Declaring that her bitter public divorce battle had soured her on remarrying, Collins is also said to have quipped, "I don't need a husband, I need a wife." But we suspect that the credit for originating this epigram belongs to Judy Brady.

Instructors who have taught this essay in earlier editions report that it's a trusty class-rouser, evoking lively comments and a few intense disputes. Does Brady overstate her case in "I Want a Wife"? Some students, reading her essay in the new millennium, may think so. Perhaps their skepticism indicates real advances in the status of women since Brady first wrote in 1972. Do wives today play roles as humble and exacting as the one Brady details here? Are men as well as women freer today to depart from prescribed patterns of behavior? Are women still as angry as Brady was? Note that similar questions are addressed in the third writing suggestion. Christina Hoff Sommers's "Men — It's in Their Nature" implicitly counters some of Brady's attitudes toward men, so the two essays together create an even stronger basis for discussion and writing.

Give students some time to consider the above questions by having them collaboratively update Brady's essay: What are the requirements of a wife these days? Students can replace "wife" with "husband," "girlfriend," or "boyfriend" if they prefer. You might ask a few groups to read their responses aloud to the class as a way to open discussion of Brady's essay.

QUESTIONS ON MEANING

1. The essay lists them all. In general, the duties of a wife seem to entail making life easy and comfortable for everyone in the family — except the wife herself.
2. What it all boils down to, in Brady's view, is that husbands shoulder whatever responsibilities they want to assume. All others they assign to their wives.
3. The thesis is implied: Wives are not persons but conveniences whose subservient roles have been fashioned by husbands.
4. Answers will vary. Are all men as demanding and insensitive as the composite male chauvinist Brady draws? Are there fewer who resemble him nowadays than there were in 1972, when the essay was first published? The class might like to consider the extent to which traditional roles have changed in the past decade.

QUESTIONS ON WRITING STRATEGY

1. Because the author's name clearly indicates that she is a woman, the title is a surefire attention-getter.

2. The first two paragraphs establish Brady's credentials, position her essay in the real world, and show from the outset that wishing for a wife is not uncommon — among men.
3. Brady's tone is sardonic.
4. Avoiding the pronoun, though a bit awkward here and there, contributes greatly to the irony of "I Want a Wife." It dehumanizes a wife; she is not a woman but a thing to be used.
5. The principle of analysis is determined by the thesis: The role of a wife can be divided into jobs that serve others, especially the husband. Other principles of analysis might be the jobs a wife does that require brainpower or the satisfactions of the role of wife — but these, of course, would produce entirely different essays.
6. Readers of *Ms.* have feminist leanings. To us, the essay's observations of husbands and wives remain fresh: "Supermom" is, after all, a recent coinage. However, not everyone will agree.
7. The groups of duties are nurse-governess (par. 3), maid (4), confidante (5), social planner (6), and sex object (7). Today, "bread winner" might get more play than Brady gives it (par. 3).

QUESTIONS ON LANGUAGE

1. It emphasizes the selfishness and the demanding tone of the words. The words themselves reduce a wife to the level of a possession.
2. You might be able to elicit a definition of *monogamy* by asking your class to list other words they know that contain *mono-* and to list what all the definitions have in common.
3. The essay's diction is appropriate, the words easy for any intelligent reader to understand. The repetition of "I want a wife" and the author's use of short sentences give the essay a staccato beat that underscores the anger behind it.

JUDY BRADY ON WRITING

Brady's essay is a perfect example of writing derived from the rhetorical situation. She went from "complaining" at a meeting of frustrated women to reading her essay in front of a crowd to, later, publishing it. Students should be made aware of their own opportunities to turn their private gripes into coherent and audience-appropriate public arguments, perhaps in the form of an opinion piece for the campus newspaper.

CHRISTINA HOFF SOMMERS

Men — It's in Their Nature

If Judy Brady's complaints about men don't raise vocal objections in your class, Christina Hoff Sommers's impassioned defense of them probably will. Asserting that males and females are inherently and biologically different and that no amount of social influence can change that, Sommers embraces stereotypes of male behavior in order to praise them. Depending on your students' politics and assumptions about gender difference, her argument might simultaneously anger and cheer the young men and women in your classroom.

You might begin discussion by asking for examples of "good" and "bad" masculinity, from TV shows, movies, books, and magazines — or of attempts to "resocialize" young boys. Is Sommers overstating her case? If not, what are the practical consequences of the stereotypes she cites — for instance, is "pathological" masculinity excused on the grounds that "men are just that way"? Many students will give examples from personal experience, which can segue into critical discussion of cultural assumptions. Does Sommers need more evidence? Different kinds of evidence? Are there factors that refute her claims? Where do students' own generalizations come from?

If your students don't catch it on their own, be sure to point out the cultural context implied in Sommers's last paragraphs. "Men — It's in Their Nature" was written in September 2003, just two years after 9/11 and the beginning of American fighting in Iraq and Afghanistan. Is it possible that Sommers's defense of men is, in fact, a defense of a controversial war?

QUESTIONS ON MEANING

1. Sommers's purpose is revealed in her concluding statement: ". . . traditional male traits such as aggression, competitiveness, risk taking, and stoicism — constrained by virtues of valor, honor, and self-sacrifice — are essential to the well-being and safety of our society" (par. 17). She means not only to defend stereotypically male characteristics as natural and unchangeable but also to emphasize their benefits.
2. As a conservative writer writing for a conservative publication, Sommers assumes that her readers share her values as well as her distrust of liberal and feminist agendas. Some students will fit this profile; others won't.
3. As Sommers sees it, "resocializing" involves devaluing masculine traits and "counterconditioning" (par. 8) boys in an overt attempt to "feminize" (14) them and "promote genuine equality between the sexes" by enforcing "sameness" (5). In contrast, according to Sommers "civilizing" boys is a matter of channeling their inborn tendencies toward personal and social good. The distinction is important because although Sommers acknowledges that traits such as aggression and insensitivity can be dangerous if not "constrained by morality" (12), she rejects the notion that masculinity in and of itself is a bad thing or that femininity is somehow superior.

QUESTIONS ON WRITING STRATEGY

1. Using instinctive behavioral traits and preferences as her principle of analysis, Sommers identifies several elements of maleness, among them "better spatial reasoning skills" (par. 6), risk taking, a preference for "action" and "competitive rough housing" (6), emotional distance, competitiveness, aggressiveness, insensitivity, an attraction to violence and destruction, focus, creativity, courage, and stoicism. Even the seemingly negative elements are, to Sommers, positive forces — as long as they are "constrained by virtues" (17).

2. For evidence, Sommers relies on a handful of anecdotes (see question 3, below); some examples; brief summaries of "decades of research in neuroscience, endocrinology, genetics, and developmental psychology" (par. 6), "[a] 2001 special issue of *Scientific American*" (8), and the "entire anthropological record" (9). She also draws on quotations and paraphrases of expert opinion, specifically of "anthropologist Lionel Tiger" (10), "social theorist Hannah Arendt" (12), and "[d]issident feminist Camille Paglia" (15). Students already inclined to agree with Sommers will probably find her evidence satisfactory; others may rightfully object that she could have offered more detail about the scientific research she glances at without elaboration.

3. Sommers provides four anecdotes: her son's experience with a "sensitivity exercise" at a "progressive-socialist kibbutz" in Israel (pars. 1–3); a North Carolina daycare "censured" for allowing toy soldiers (4); a Baltimore schoolteacher who gave dolls to a group of boys (7); and "Jimmy," an eleven-year-old who responded to a quilting assignment by portraying an incident of violence (7). The stories are meant both to amuse readers and to illustrate the futility of such efforts by highlighting their absurdity; most readers, after all, will recognize similar behaviors among young boys they have known and chuckle at the failed attempts to change them.

4. "In the face of what we know, it is altogether unreasonable to deny the biological basis for distinctive male and female preferences and abilities" (par. 9). Paragraphs 1–8 focus on establishing that boys will be boys, no matter what; paragraphs 10–17 consider the social and cultural implications of that observation.

5. Sommers offers brief point-by-point comparisons of men and women to argue that men are naturally aggressive, physical, and rational; while women are naturally nurturing, verbal, and emotional. Her point is that the differences are based in biology rather than in culture and that neither set of characteristics is superior to the other.

QUESTIONS ON LANGUAGE

1. Sommers is simultaneously disdainful and earnest. She dismisses gender reform efforts as wrongheaded and futile but is passionate in her defense of masculinity.

2. She is using the terms ironically. Sommers finds these concepts objectionable and uses the quotation marks to mark her disapproval and distance herself from them. Other instances include "find themselves" (par. 1), "haunting loneliness" (3), and "equity facilitator" (7).

3. From Greek words meaning "within" and "separate," *endocrinology* in biology is the study of ductless glands (such as the thyroid) and their secretions, specifically hormones.

CHRISTINA HOFF SOMMERS ON WRITING

Sommers's purpose in writing is, in part, to discredit other writers who she thinks disseminate inaccurate information. You might talk with students about scrutinizing their own writing and the sources they use. Competing voices on almost any topic are bound to yield inconsistencies, and students should be prepared to assess and present critically the information they find.

GUILLERMO DEL TORO AND CHUCK HOGAN

Vampires Never Die

Students may be surprised to discover that the creators of such pulp fiction as *Hell Boy*, *Blade II*, and *Prince of Thieves* are also capable of writing a poetic, sophisticated, and seriously academic literary analysis of a trend in popular culture. In just a few pages, del Toro and Hogan survey the complete history of vampire lore and offer a fresh take on what it reveals about the human condition, especially within contemporary culture. Some of their literary and philosophical allusions, as well as their unstated reliance on the psychological theories of Carl Jung, may wash over students, yet the analysis as a whole remains compelling and understandable. (We've glossed those allusions that seem most important to following the authors' ideas; others we leave to students to investigate if they're so inclined.) Fans of current vampire stories will surely be interested to learn of the legacy behind them and be intrigued by the idea that those stories could mean anything more than just good entertainment.

You may wish to begin class discussion with the question likely on many students' minds: Does popular culture, especially something as seemingly trivial as vampire fiction, merit academic study? Why, or why not? What can we learn from analyses such as del Toro and Hogan's? Or, as an alternative, you might consider encouraging students to find and share criticism of the authors' own literary and filmic productions. To what extent has their creative work been the subject of similar kinds of interpretation? And does "Vampires Never Die" make readers more — or less — inclined to read the authors' collaborative vampire novels for pleasure?

QUESTIONS ON MEANING

1. There's no question that "Vampires Never Die" serves as clever and well-conceived publicity for the authors' vampire trilogy. However, the authors also examine the larger cultural meanings of vampire stories in general, over time and across cultures. The essay is a sophisticated psychological analysis of one particular literary genre.

2. "Monsters, like angels, are invoked by our individual and collective needs. Today, much as during that gloomy summer in 1816, we feel the need to seek their cold embrace" (par. 7).

3. The authors posit that the concept of vampiric immortality fills a universal psychological and spiritual void. By tapping into deep-seated fears and desires, vampire stories both reassure us and "provide the possibility of mystery in our mundane . . . lives" (par. 16). The particulars of those fears and desires might change over time and across cultures, but the basic truths of death and sexuality do not. Vampires, say del Toro and Hogan, represent a powerful mixture of the two most profound aspects of human existence.

4. Students should be able to infer from the context that a social construct is any cultural moré, taboo, philosophy, or law designed to govern human conduct by repressing base urges. (The idea also refers to any cultural infusion of meaning onto abstractions, but the authors aren't using it that way.) The concept is important to del Toro and Hogan's

analysis because they see the vampire character as one released from the pressures of civilization, who allows human beings to reconnect vicarously with their primal instincts.

5. Although science appears to be rational and objective, new technologies can seem mysterious, even ominous to laypersons. Even those with a scientific mindset tend to embrace innovation and understanding as a faith in itself and, in so doing, to "experience fear and awe again, and to believe in the things [they] cannot see" (par. 15).

QUESTIONS ON WRITING STRATEGY

1. Writing for the *New York Times*, del Toro and Hogan assume an audience of well-educated readers with wide-ranging interests. At the same time, they assume a familiarity with popular culture, from classic novels to *American Idol*, and an immersion in communication technologies. Some students may object that several of the authors' allusions go above readers' heads, but other students will surely appreciate the apparent respect for their intelligence.

2. Their principle of analysis is the question of what makes vampires appeal across time and culture. The two basic elements identified by del Toro and Hogan are lust and death, introduced as "romantic hero" and "undead monster" (par. 4) and reiterated in the conclusion as "Eros and Thanatos fused together in archetypal embrace" (16). Subsets of those elements include primal fear (6), immortality (8), adaptability (10), uncertainty (13–14), superstition (15), and spirituality (16).

3. Their point is that the folklore taps into something deeply personal — yet primal and universal. That the first written story might have stemmed from deep-seated emotional, psychological, and sexual tensions is therefore highly significant (even if students don't recognize Jung's theory of the collective unconscious lurking behind the authors' assumptions).

4. The single word *forever* evokes immortality, both of vampires as individual characters and as a universal cultural need. Coming on the heels of a paragraph about faith and spirituality, it also echoes the concluding sentiment of Christian prayers: *Amen.*

5. The authors compare two eras "of great technical revolution" in paragraphs 13–15. Both in the early nineteenth century and now, people were confronted with "new gadgets . . . , various forms of communication . . . , and cutting-edge science" (par. 13). They name those new technologies in the case of the nineteenth century but leave it to readers to fill in the details for the twenty-first. In either case, such innovations were both liberating and disorienting, leaving us "still ultimately vulnerable to our fates and our nightmares" (15).

QUESTIONS ON LANGUAGE

1. For a definition of *mash-up*, students may need to turn to the Internet or to a recent dictionary of slang. The term, similar in meaning to *re-mix*, applies to the creative process that combines elements of multiple existing productions (songs, film clips, video clips, and the like) to create something new, a technique often used by avant-garde musicians and filmmakers. We find it interesting that del Toro and Hogan manage to apply a cutting-edge (and controversial) creative trend to "ancient myth" and folklore.

2. Traditionally, *twitter* means to chirp or speak excitedly, but the word also refers to the recent and fast-growing social networking application. The verb is especially effective, given that del Toro and Hogan are writing about the psychological effects of fast-paced technology and overwhelming torrents of communication.

3. *Alchemy* refers to medieval beliefs that an as-yet-undiscovered chemical process could transform base metals, lead in particular, into gold; the hope was that such transformations would form the foundation for an elixir for everlasting youth. The metaphor fits the vampire subject very well, both in the idea that commingling of blood would transform both biter and victim into something better and that the transformation would enable immortality; it also reinforced the suggestion that science is superstition (see par. 15). The authors return to the metaphor in the next paragraph (9).

GUILLERMO DEL TORO AND CHUCK HOGAN ON WRITING

Del Toro and Hogan provide valuable insight into their collaborative writing process. Their committal "bro-hug" and their banter during the interview indicate a rapport between the two men. Is a friendly relationship a prerequisite for the deep (and sometimes ruthless) revision del Toro and Hogan do? Students may want to discuss best practices for giving feedback and ways to approach suggested revisions with an open mind, especially if peer revision is part of your course.

BELLA DePAULO

The Myth of Doomed Kids

We excerpted this piece from *Singled Out* not only because the subject will be relevant to many students (especially those who were raised by a single parent or are single parents themselves) but also because Bella DePaulo so clearly models something students will be asked to do repeatedly in college and the workplace: close analysis of a published research study in service of a larger purpose.

Some discussion should certainly focus on DePaulo's interpretation of the data. Another writer might easily have drawn different conclusions from the same numbers, especially since the study she cites did, in fact, show a higher rate of drug abuse among children of single mothers than among children living with both parents, albeit a small difference — and many observers will consider the overall rates much more worrisome than DePaulo does. It may be worthwhile to address the slippery nature of statistics in general, reminding students of the adage that numbers can mean whatever you want them to. Ask your class to consider not only the numbers DePaulo presents but also the way she supports her analysis of the statistics with anecdotes, comparisons, and interpretation to make her own meaning.

QUESTIONS ON MEANING

1. As DePaulo's footnote makes clear, the Welfare Queen that Reagan described could not be found. The author begins with this character possibly for two reasons: The notorious Welfare Queen captures readers' attention, and the fiction gives DePaulo a vivid image to discredit in an analysis that might otherwise come across as abstract.
2. DePaulo comes closest to stating her thesis in paragraph 12: "There must be something wrong with my blather about all that emotional goodness that kids in nuclear families get that children living with just their moms do not." Of course, she means there *is* "something wrong": single parenthood does not harm children.
3. She suggests that two-parent households don't necessarily provide "double the money, time, love, and attention" (par. 12) that other kinds of families do. Sometimes such households are beset by "chaos, strife, and even abuse" (15). At the same time, nontraditional families can usually count on the support of other family members and unrelated adults.
4. The difference is small: 4.5 percent of teenagers living with both parents abuse drugs; whereas 5.7 percent of teenagers living with a single mother do.
5. She thinks they're nonsense.

QUESTIONS ON WRITING STRATEGY

1. The author was writing to reassure single parents who are worried about how their marital status might affect their children.
2. DePaulo analyzes the data from an academic study to discover the extent to which drug abuse (taken as an indicator of children's problems) is more prevalent among children of single mothers than among children in two-parent homes. She concludes that children of single parents aren't significantly disadvantaged.
3. The tables clearly display the data DePaulo is analyzing. The differences between the two tables help her make the point that the presence of others in children's lives *besides* parents affects the children's drug use.
4. DePaulo disputes the claim that children of single parents, especially single mothers, have more problems than children in two-parent homes do. In turn, she claims that single parenthood is not a negative factor in determining children's behavior.

QUESTIONS ON LANGUAGE

1. Examples of colloquial language include comments like "don't worry" and "it had better be good" (par. 3), "two is a magic number" (6), "think about it this way" (11), and "there must be something wrong with my blather" (12); phrases such as "knocked off its perch" (9); and casual vocabulary, particularly *mom* and *dad* (see question 2, below). Some students may like the irreverent tone for its accessibility; others may find that the tone verges on sarcasm and detracts from the seriousness of the argument.
2. *Mom* and *dad* evoke feelings of warmth and closeness, while *mother* and *father* sound almost clinical. In the midst of statistical analysis, the terms keep the focus on the dynamics of the family.
3. DePaulo means for readers to understand that the media reports about single mothers are "signifying nothing."

4.   Interestingly, after her second paragraph DePaulo uses few sophisticated words. In paragraph 2, she appears to mock the prevailing fears
about single parents and their children.

BELLA DePAULO ON WRITING

We like the distinction DePaulo makes between being "interested in" and
being "passionate about" a subject. The distinction for her and for many writers seems to lie in whether the writing involves discovery. As DePaulo proves,
it's possible to write well when you're merely interested, but it's fun when
you're passionate.

LAILA AYAD

The Capricious Camera

This documented student essay is complex in both its ideas and its
organization. It analyzes a photograph taken during the Nazi occupation of
Poland during World War II: an image of a young girl surrounded by soldiers.
Ayad makes two overlapping points — one about the Nazis' *Lebensborn*
experiment (the attempt to create a master race through breeding and adoption) and another about the ambiguities of photography.

Ayad assumes her readers will have some familiarity with the Nazi
agenda, so before you begin discussion you may want to explore what students know about Nazi Germany, its occupations, and the Holocaust.
Showing students photographs from the era could help them put Ayad's
analysis in context. Your library may even have the book by Clay and
Leapman that was Ayad's source.

QUESTIONS ON MEANING

1.   Ayad's dual theses are as follows: "It is not merely people of other persecuted races who can become victims in a racial war, but also those we
would least expect — the persecuting race itself" (par. 1); and "Unlike
hand-made art, which in its very purpose begs to be viewed through
various interpretations, photography, and particularly photojournalism,
. . . demands to be viewed alongside its agenda, for without this context,
it may never be fully understood" (par. 8). The two come together in the
final paragraph: "[E]ven if the original photographer saw the image as
artistic, subsequent events compel us to try to see the image of the
Polish girl with Nazis as journalism. In this endeavor, we must uncover
as much as possible about the surrounding context. As much as we
can, we need to know this girl's particular story."
2.   Ayad focuses on the Nazi *Lebensborn* experiment, in which "[c]hildren
who possessed strong Nordic or Aryan qualities were systematically
taken from their native countries, adopted by German parents (who

were paid by the Nazi regime), taught to forget their families and former lives, and raised to breed not only many children of their own but, above all, families that would uphold Nazi ideology" (par. 11). Thus the Nazis persecuted their own "race" as well as others.

3. Ayad seems to want to show both the limitations of and the opportunities in photojournalism. It must be viewed in context, but that analysis can be very revealing.

QUESTIONS ON WRITING STRATEGY

1. Ayad focuses extensively on the photograph to show the ways it can be interpreted out of context and to demonstrate that without context we cannot truly understand the image.

2. Ayad seems to assume a general familiarity with Nazi Germany: In paragraph 1, for example, she uses "Hitler," "Aryan," "anti-Semitism," and "Holocaust" without explanation. However, she does not assume familiarity with the *Lebensborn* program, which she explains in detail (pars. 1, 9–12).

3. The conclusion brings the essay full circle and (as noted in the answer to the first "Meaning" question) weaves together the essay's two threads. The last two sentences freeze the image of the girl in readers' minds, capturing the poignancy of her unknown fate.

4. Ayad uses description in paragraphs 2–6, giving readers the information they need to see the photograph as she does.

QUESTIONS ON LANGUAGE

1. Ayad is clearly moved by the girl's plight, as evident in language such as "overwhelming," "the magnitude and force of the oppressing men," "innocence and helplessness of the lone girl," "both cruel and terribly frightening," "menacing and unjust," "symbols of oppression, producing an eerily suffocating effect," "dramatic," "wistful and innocent," and "heads . . . hang in almost shameful disgrace."

2. The quotations from Hitler, Gunther, and Himmler chillingly prove the Nazis' racism and their goals of racial purification. The quotation from the Polish woman provides an eyewitness account of what happened to many children, including, perhaps, the girl in the photograph.

3. *Targeting* conveys a sinister intent, as in targeting prey.

4. *Aryan* originally referred to a Northern tribe that conquered much of Asia around 2000 BCE. German racialists began — some spuriously — to trace Northern Europeans back to these ancestors in the nineteenth century, and the Nazis found further reason to apply the term to themselves because of that people's idealization of conquest.

10
CLASSIFICATION
Sorting into Kinds

In our general comments on Chapter 9, we explain our reasons for divorcing the hoary pair of division and classification. Our reasons have mainly to do with salvaging division/analysis, but benefits accrue to classification, too. For one thing, it doesn't have to compete for attention (ours, yours, students'), so it's much clearer. For another, we can provide more illustrations.

The essays in this chapter range from humorous to serious, reflecting the classifications we find in the publications we read. Stephanie Ericsson and William Lutz look at the language of lies and obfuscation, respectively. Russell Baker contributes a well-known humorous piece of curmudgeonly confusion over our material possessions. Deborah Tannen examines the different conversational styles of men and women. And Dacher Keltner categorizes facial expressions in an academic study of nonverbal cues to people's emotions.

Troubleshooting: All our efforts to keep division/analysis and classification separate and equal are hampered by the inescapable fact that *divide* is sometimes taken to mean *classify*, as in "Divide the students into groups." You might want to point out this issue directly to students if you think the terminology will confuse them. We maintain that division/analysis treats a singular, whole, coherent subject (a camera, a theory, a poem), whereas classification treats a plural, numerous subject (cameras, theories, poems).

The confusion between division and classification may account for the tendency of some students to "classify" by taking a single item (say, the television show *Survivor*) and placing it in a category (say, reality shows). We'd explain that they haven't classified anything; they have just filed an item in a pigeonhole. If they'll remember that classification begins not with one thing but with several things, they may avoid much perplexity.

STEPHANIE ERICSSON
The Ways We Lie

Lying and being lied to are universal human experiences. This selection offers a thoughtful look at lying that should inspire lively class discussion. One way to begin work on the essay is to ask students to give their definitions of *lying*. Write the responses on the board, and invite students to challenge each other's definitions. What consensus does the class reach? What are the points of contention?

Ericsson admits that sometimes we lie for reasons that seem almost virtuous — to protect someone else's feelings, for example. How justifiable are the various kinds of lies she lists? Divide the class into five groups and have each group look closely at two sections of the essay, two kinds of lies. From what perspectives are these examples of unexcusable lies? Who would assert that they were necessary, valid, or reasonable manipulations of the truth? Once these points of view are established, ask each group to come up with a comprehensive definition of a *lie*. How do the groups' definitions differ depending on which sections the students were examining?

We pair Ericsson's essay with William Lutz's "The World of Doublespeak," a complementary examination of lies. Many of the questions raised about Ericsson's essay can be raised about Lutz's as well.

Some longer works on this topic are *Lying: Moral Choice in Public and Private Life*, by Sissela Bok (1978), and the title essay in *On Lies, Secrets, and Silence*, by Adrienne Rich (1979).

QUESTIONS ON MEANING

1. Ericsson's thesis, stated in paragraph 35, is that the lies we tell in everyday life, however seemingly unimportant and even necessary, cause us to lose our sensitivity to larger, more damaging lies.
2. No, it would not be possible to eliminate lies completely. Ericsson's experience (par. 4) supports this, as do the benefits of different lies, such as the sergeant's lie to help a soldier's family (9), the dismissal to help ration a parent's energy (31), the delusion to help us function despite the possibility of global disaster (33).
3. Eliminating lies might help us and others perceive reality clearly; it would be more just; and it would sharpen our awareness of the lies we are told.
4. The purpose is to examine the roles that lying plays in our lives and its effect of dulling our insistence on the truth.

QUESTIONS ON WRITING STRATEGY

1. She's not casting blame, since she's as much a liar as any of her readers. She puts herself eye-to-eye with her readers.
2. Answers will vary. The epigraphs could be judged on pithiness, wit, relation to the category following, and other criteria. Some of our favorites:

Cicero before paragraph 14, Freehill before 23, Wilde before 26, Hoffer before 32, Shaw before 35.

3. Ericsson begins by connecting delusion with the previous category, dismissal. Then she offers a definition, an example (alcoholics), and a continuation of her definition. She then suggests how common delusion is by referring to the examples of nuclear stockpiles and global warming, realities we ignore. She concludes by expanding on her definition.

4. Ericsson's message: As much as possible, tell yourself the truth and insist on it in others, or the "moral garbage" will become "invisible." Her conclusion is very effective, we think — it clearly shows the relation of the everyday lie to the Big Lie and urges that honesty begin where she has been showing lies begin, with each of us individually.

5. Answers will vary. Some of Ericsson's most pointed definitions are those of the white lie ("a vote of no confidence," par. 8), the stereotype ("a candy bar of misinformation instead of a balanced meal," 21), and delusion ("an adhesive to keep the status quo intact," 34). Some highly effective examples are the illustrations of groupthink with Pearl Harbor (24–25), out-and-out lies with her nephew's assertion that "murderers" broke the fence (26), and delusion with alcoholics (33).

QUESTIONS ON LANGUAGE

1. The internal disease of cancer (the lies we tell ourselves and others) affects our perception of the external garbage we're floating in (the lies told to us).

2. The tone, to us, seems more appropriate in the first passage than in the second. It may be strong to say that the Catholic Church was a "co-perpetrator" with Porter (par. 13), but its actions were deceitful and harmful. Ericsson's feelings about the "omission of Lilith from the Bible" (20) are a little harder to credit. The events she mentions are the subject of extensive scholarly inquiry and far from proved, and imputing contemporary motives to ancient people is ahistorical. (Still, the issue is a live one: Just in recent years, the church has condemned the elevation of the goddess by some of its members.)

3. Ericsson's most highly charged language seems to come in her discussion of religion: Note "pedophilia," the sexual abuse of children (par. 12), "co-perpetrator" (13) in her treatment of the Father Porter scandal, "misogynists" and "patriarchal" (20) in her inquiry into the suppression of Lilith.

4. The adult-children-of-alcoholics movement, as represented by groups like Al-Anon, may not be familiar to your class. The movement aims to empower, through support groups and literature dealing with shared problems, those whose parents were or are alcoholics.

STEPHANIE ERICSSON ON WRITING

We provide Ericsson's brief comments on writing-as-therapy because we like her idea about the "blank white page": It "will never contradict you, never ignore you, and never judge you." These could be encouraging words to students who are just beginning to experiment with journal writing, especially those (and there are many) who have trouble shaking their own internal censors or their sense of an audience besides themselves.

WILLIAM LUTZ

The World of Doublespeak

William Lutz is a leading figure in the campaign against the dishonest language that he (and others) call doublespeak. This essay, extracted from the first chapter of his book-length treatment of the subject, both defines the term and classifies its varieties. The many, many examples will leave students in no doubt about the meaning of doublespeak and should make it relatively easy for them to spot it.

One problem with doublespeak is that it often relies on multisyllabic words and complicated syntax. As a result, the most example-heavy parts of Lutz's essay may be difficult reading for some students. Lutz himself practices what he preaches, writing clearly and concisely, but you may want to warn students that some passages in the essay require patience.

Probably the best way to make this essay immediate and significant for students is to have them locate doublespeak in what they read and hear. Indeed, you may want to ask them to try the journal-writing assignment as soon as they've read the essay and to bring their examples to class. Even if each student contributes only one or two examples, you'll have a good collection. Working as a whole class or in small groups to sort their examples into Lutz's categories, students will be writing a continuation of the essay.

We pair Lutz's essay with the previous one, Stephanie Ericsson's "The Ways We Lie." Ericsson deals with explicit lies, Lutz with a more subtle form of deception, but both authors look at how we use language to avoid the truth. The fifth writing topic following each essay can be used as an assignment or to spark discussion.

QUESTIONS ON MEANING

1. Lutz's thesis might be stated briefly as follows: The four kinds of doublespeak all include language "that avoids or shifts responsibility, language that is at variance with its real or purported meaning" (the quotation is from par. 2). The thesis accumulates over paragraphs 2–3, with the addition of the intention to classify in paragraph 5.
2. Paragraph 4 offers the following questions: "Who is saying what to whom, under what conditions and circumstances, with what intent, and with what results?" These questions locate the motivation for dishonesty that would indicate doublespeak.
3. The greatest danger is that, as in Orwell's *Nineteen Eighty-Four*, doublespeak will lead to the "control of reality through language" (par. 23). Doublespeak "alter[s] our perception of reality and corrupt[s] our thinking. . . . [It] breeds suspicion, cynicism, distrust, and, ultimately, hostility" (22). It can "infect and eventually destroy the function of language" (23).
4. Lutz clearly assumes an educated reader, someone able to perceive the fundamental dishonesty in his examples. At the same time, his careful classification, scores of examples, and extensive discussion of the dangers indicate that he believes his reader probably is not sensitive to doublespeak and needs help to recognize it.

QUESTIONS ON WRITING STRATEGY

1. Lutz's principle of classification is the intention of doublespeakers. Those who use euphemisms are trying to "mislead or deceive" (par. 7) with inoffensive words. Those who use jargon seek to give their words "an air of profundity, authority, and prestige" (10). Those who use gobbledygook or bureaucratese are bent on "overwhelming the audience with words" (13). And those who use inflated language seek "to make the ordinary seem extraordinary; . . . to make the simple seem complex" (17).

2. Lutz begins by offering a definition of the category. Then he offers examples of euphemisms used to spare others' feelings or to avoid language regarded as taboo — euphemisms he finds acceptable. Finally, he contrasts these kinds of euphemism with three examples of euphemism used by government agencies to "mislead or deceive" — in which case it becomes doublespeak.

3. Greenspan's second comment is surprising because he acknowledges that he is deliberately unclear. With the quotation, Lutz shows that doublespeak is intentional.

4. Many of Lutz's examples are dated, and some students may at first think that doublespeak is an old, not a current, problem. The first writing suggestion, asking students to find current examples of their own, should help them see that doublespeak is no less a problem now than it was two decades ago.

5. Definition appears mainly in paragraphs 2 and 3 and in the explanations of each kind of doublespeak (pars. 5, 7, 9–10, 13, 17). Cause and effect also figures in the explanation of categories, as Lutz gives the intentions of doublespeakers, but mainly it develops the last section of the essay (20–23). The definition, of course, clarifies Lutz's subject and his categories. The cause and effect shows what is at stake with this dishonest language.

QUESTIONS ON LANGUAGE

1. Lutz's language provides a good foil to the quotations of doublespeak: He uses plain language and relatively simple syntax.

2. The words listed all have negative connotations, suggesting undesirable or even dangerous effects of doublespeak. More neutral language would not make Lutz's point as sharply. For just a few examples, see paragraph 1.

3. *Taboo* now refers to a prohibition against the use or practice of something. The word comes from the Tongan word *tabu*, an adjective meaning "set apart, consecrated to a special use or purpose." Captain Cook traveled to Tonga in 1777; his widely read narrative of his experiences, including an explanation of *tabu*, brought the term into common use in England.

WILLIAM LUTZ ON WRITING

Students may be encouraged to see recognizable behaviors, particularly procrastination, in a successful writer. Students aren't writing whole books for their classes, of course, but Lutz's advice, scaled down, should remind them that they needn't try to write an essay all at once, only a few paragraphs. The longer students wait to write a paper, the greater the chance they will have to do it in one sitting and will be daunted by the task.

The writer and humorist Fran Lebowitz once joked that being a writer was a bit like being a perpetual student . . . except you can't write a book the night before it is due. "I know," Lebowitz deadpanned, "because I tried twice."

RUSSELL BAKER

The Plot against People

In this essay, the well-known humorist Russell Baker makes a common use of classification — for humor. Baker takes a wry look at the universal human feeling that the material world is conspiring against us. Ask the class to come up with more examples of things that "have it in" for people.

Writing humor is difficult, as students who have tried can attest. Give students an opportunity to try their hands at a collaborative essay modeled on Baker's. What conspiracy theories can the class generate? (These might include the school's conspiracy to keep students from registering for any of the classes they most need, the local market's conspiracy to run out of Diet Coke when you most need one, and so on.) Make a list of ideas on the board, and have small groups of students write a short essay describing this conspiracy in detail. You might ask the groups to read their finished products.

Students who enjoy Baker's approach can be encouraged to look into some of his collections, such as *Poor Russell's Almanac* (1972) and *So This Is Depravity* (1980).

QUESTIONS ON MEANING

1. Baker's thesis is stated in paragraph 1. His larger meaning is that inanimate objects conspire to frustrate humans.
2. The reason may be that objects are doing humans a favor (par. 11) or that they are "incredibly stupid" (12).
3. He may also want to point out how ridiculous we are when we become infuriated with inanimate things.
4. By not working, thus "conditioning him never to expect anything of them" (par. 16).

QUESTIONS ON WRITING STRATEGY

1. Baker classifies objects by the ways they thwart human wishes. He might have included things that work for a while and then break, or even things that work fine; but his use of extreme cases adds to the essay's humor.
2. Baker begins by contrasting the category with the previous category. Next he provides two examples (pliers and keys) and then an additional

example (women's purses). Finally, he again contrasts things that break down with things that get lost, using the examples of a furnace and a woman's purse.

3. "[A]ny object capable of breaking down at the moment when it is most needed will do so" (par. 2); "A furnace . . . will invariably break down . . ." (10); "Thereafter, they never work again" (13). (Students will, of course, find others.) Hyperbole establishes Baker's comic tone of exasperation.

4. His pseudoscientific classification, with its dogmatic assertion of the three categories of objects, is a parody of intellectual authority. The pseudophilosophical discussion of spiritual "peace" in the conclusion reinforces the essay's mock-serious tone.

5. Baker's little stories (the cunning automobile of paragraph 3, or paragraph 8's climbing pliers) capture the reader's attention. Shared experiences provide a sense of recognition and help make the essay funny.

QUESTIONS ON LANGUAGE

1. The vocabulary words highlighted here all contribute to the essay's mock-serious tone. In general, the essay's diction is quite simple.

2. Clever, malicious, plotting. Its effect is to personify the automobile.

3. The general terms make the shared experiences more universal. Had Baker used *I*, he might have seemed more of a crank, less persuasive.

RUSSELL BAKER ON WRITING

What do lead pencils, Shakespeare, eternal quests, cave writing, dreaming, Luddites, and cornpone politicians have to do with computers? In Russell Baker's fertile mind, everything and nothing. In addition to enjoying the fun of the piece, students may be interested in noting how he cleverly shows a mind in the act of composition. Stream-of-consciousness writing has been used more often in confessions, but with some behind-the-scenes crafting, Baker demonstrates its humorous potential.

DEBORAH TANNEN

But What Do You Mean?

The linguist Deborah Tannen came to national prominence with *You Just Don't Understand*, a book about misunderstandings between men and women in conversation. Since then, she has continued to disseminate much of her research through the mass media, trying to help people solve the communication problems of daily life. Oliver Sacks, another intellectual who often addresses a general audience, wrote of *You Just Don't Understand*: "Deborah Tannen combines a novelist's ear for the way people speak with a rare power of original analysis. It is this that makes her an extraordinary sociolinguist, and it is this that makes her book such a fascinating look at that crucial social cement, conversation."

This is one essay that students should be able to apply easily to their own lives, although the men in your class may be more resistant than the women. The essay will certainly evoke a wide range of student response, which should lead to lively class discussion.

Here is an in-class exercise to test Tannen's theories: Ask students to bring in dialogs that illustrate conflict from novels, plays, or movie scripts, deleting characters' names and direct references to gender. Have students read the dialogs out loud and try to guess characters' genders, justifying their choices. Encourage students to look for instances of Tannen's seven categories of miscommunication in the dialogs. (A variation is to cross-cast the dialogs, with women reading men's lines and vice versa, and see if they are still believable.)

QUESTIONS ON MEANING

1. Tannen is pointing out the areas of communication in which misunderstandings between the sexes are most frequent. She seems to hope that a better understanding of how men's and women's communication styles differ will help eliminate such misunderstandings. A secondary purpose is to show women how their problems in the workplace may be linked to their style of communication.
2. Much of what we say is based on pure protocol, which serves as a kind of social cement. We're not so much communicating facts as establishing a rapport with the other person. This speech is often so automatic and predictable that we aren't even aware of what we're saying. (See also the journal prompt and first writing suggestion.)
3. "Many of the conversational rituals common among women are designed to take the other person's feelings into account, while many of the conversational rituals common among men are designed to maintain the one-up position, or at least avoid appearing one-down" (par. 2).
4. "Thank you" is not always used as an expression of gratitude, but is simply a ritual, "an automatic conversation starter and closer" (par. 15). An answer of "You're welcome" results in an imbalance between the speakers.

QUESTIONS ON WRITING STRATEGY

1. Tannen uses these characters as examples of the points she is making. She adds variety to the essay by referring to people alternately by their first names (real or fictitious) and by their functions ("a well-known columnist," par. 4; "[a] woman manager I know," 13). These characters are ciphers, empty vessels in the service of Tannen's argument, and as such do not need to be described in detail. Tannen reveals only what is relevant to her point. (See also question 4.)
2. Because the essay appeared in *Redbook,* a women's magazine, Tannen uses *you* to address women readers: "What's important is to be aware of how often you say you're sorry (and why), and to monitor your speech based on the reaction you get" (par. 9); "Although you may never enjoy verbal sparring, some women find it helpful to learn how to do it" (19). (Tannen takes a broader approach in *Talking from 9 to 5,* the book intended for a male *and* female audience from which this essay was excerpted.)
3. Tannen begins by redefining women's apologizing not as self-deprecation but as a "way of keeping both speakers on an equal footing." She then

offers an extended example of this redefinition. Next she expands on this through a brief dialog that reveals apologizing as "a mutual face-saving device." In paragraphs 6 and 7, she gives an example of a woman whose constant apologies may have limited perceptions of her competence. Finally, she poses a contrast: the negative response women may get if they don't use "ritual apologies."

4.   That the columnist is well known makes her apology all the more unexpected, less likely to be chalked up to insecurity.

5.   (1) *Apologies*: Women apologize more than men do. They see apology as a way of keeping both speakers on an equal footing, of sharing responsibility. Men take apologies at face value, seeing them as self-deprecating. (2) *Criticism*: Women tend to soften criticism more than men do. Men prefer "straight answers." (3) *Thank-yous*: Women say "thank you" more often, as a ritual. Men take "thank you," like "I'm sorry," more literally. (4) *Fighting*: Men see conversation as a battleground, stating their ideas and criticizing those of others in the strongest possible terms. Women often perceive this approach as a personal attack. (5) *Praise*: Women often assume that the absence of praise is the equivalent of criticism. For men, in contrast, praise is often implied when no criticism is given. Women who ask for criticism may really be asking for praise, but men will give them what they ask for. (6) *Complaints*: Women complain as a way of bonding with others. Men see these complaints as a call for a solution. (7) *Jokes*: "[T]he most common form of humor among men is razzing, teasing, and mock-hostile attacks, while among women it's self-mocking. Women often mistake men's teasing as genuinely hostile. Men often mistake women's mock self-deprecation as truly putting themselves down."

QUESTIONS ON LANGUAGE

1.   The humor here relies on exaggeration. It usually refers to finishing off a suffering animal.
2.   Tannen uses the metaphor of a gun: criticism as shooting.
3.   These verbs liven up the essay and inspire a strong visual or auditory impression. Other examples are "*leapt* into a critical response" (par. 10) and "*poke* holes" (17).
4.   Note Tannen's vocabulary of physical and verbal conflict: "contentious," "hedge," "sparring," "rebuttal," "retorted," as well as "disadvantage" (par. 2), "attack" (18), and "enemy" (19). You might discuss whether Tannen loads her case with such words, perhaps exaggerating the conflicts between genders.

DEBORAH TANNEN ON WRITING

Students may not be aware of the debate about the personal in scholarly writing, but many have probably been told at some time not to use *I* in their academic papers. Tannen suggests why and also argues in favor of the first person on scholarly grounds. Students in the natural and applied sciences may be more likely than others in the class to resist Tannen's argument, contending that they don't write about personal interactions. Uncovering resistance and getting a discussion going are of course the aims of the first follow-up question. For the second one, collaboration in small groups is ideal: Working together, students will find it easier to draft the third-person or first-person passage and then revise it, seeing firsthand what the differences are.

DACHER KELTNER
A Vocabulary of Smiles

Dacher Keltner may be relatively unknown, but the recent positive psychology movement is a growing force, especially on college campuses and daytime talk shows (Oprah Winfrey is a vocal supporter). At Harvard, for instance, Dr. Tal Ben-Shahar's "Popular Psychology" is the hands-down favorite course, always filled instantly at the start of the enrollment period. Indeed, the unprecedented success of Ben-Shahar's course and others like it, as well as of the pop-scholarly works of such esteemed psychologists as Martin Seligman, has caused many to question the field's academic rigor and appropriateness — a good starting point for discussion. Is there a science to happiness? Is it an emotion that can be learned and nurtured, or is it something that just happens? (Barbara Ehrenreich's "The Menace of Negative People," in Part Three of *The Bedford Reader*, offers a representative counterpoint to the optimism espoused by Keltner and his ilk.)

If any of your students have worked at McDonald's or at similar jobs — and almost certainly, they have — you might enlist their perspective on Keltner's framing device. Do "service industry" workers really feel as degraded, oppressed, and disconnected as Keltner says they do, or is he overstating his case? Or, has he, perhaps, managed to describe and explain an emotional state that people don't necessarily recognize when they feel it?

For students interested in learning more about emotional intelligence for the second writing topic (or simply for their own edification), the tenth anniversary edition of Daniel Goleman's *Emotional Intelligence: Why It Can Matter More Than IQ* (2006) would be an obvious starting point.

QUESTIONS ON MEANING

1. His goal is to "provide a coherent analysis of a category of behaviors" that at "first glance" don't seem to make sense (par. 3). By distinguishing Duchenne from non-Duchenne smiles, Keltner hopes to explain both why people smile when they're unhappy and how those false smiles affect human emotions and interactions.
2. An orbicularis oculi is a facial muscle, specifically the one around the eyes, that involuntarily scrunches when a person is truly happy; Keltner calls it the "happiness muscle" (par. 4). The presence or absence of activity of this muscle — Keltner's principle of classification — is what makes it possible to recognize a smile that denotes real happiness, as opposed to one that masks a negative emotion.
3. The table shows the correlation between types of smiles and types of emotions among recently widowed study participants who discussed their marital relationships. Keltner's analysis revealed that Duchenne, or sincere, smiles intensified positive feelings and diluted negative feelings; non-Duchenne smiles diluted positive feelings and intensified negative ones. The point is not only that each type of smile is self-fulfilling, but also that forced smiles (even if the effort is not conscious) cause emotional harm.

4. Keltner's thesis is most directly stated in paragraph 11, where he writes, "The Duchenne/non-Duchenne distinction is the first big distinction in a taxonomy of different smiles. One kind of smile . . . accompanies high spirits and goodwill. . . . [The other] kind of smile . . . reflects the attempt to mask some underlying negative state." Students may have difficulty recognizing the thesis *statement* without the modifiers and clarifications stripped away, but they should have no trouble identifying the thesis itself.

QUESTIONS ON WRITING STRATEGY

1. Most readers have had some experience at McDonald's or some other fast-food restaurant, either as employees or as customers. By relating the story, Keltner provides an entertaining example to which readers can readily relate, makes a potentially abstract concept concrete and understandable, and humanizes himself in the process.
2. Put simply, Duchenne smiles are sincere and non-Duchenne smiles are insincere. They can be distinguished by the activity (or lack thereof) of the orbicularis oculi muscle. Duchenne smiles, which tend to be brief and symmetrical, reflect and reinforce positive emotions; in contrast, non-Duchenne smiles, which vary in duration and tend to be asymmetrical, reflect and reinforce negative emotions.
3. Keltner's information is drawn from studies published in professional and scholarly journals in sociology and psychology. His own publications fall into this category; Keltner uses them because he wishes to distill the results of his academic and clinical research for a general audience. Since he is a leader in the field and is clearly knowledgeable about the work of other scholars, including his peers and collaborators, these sources strike us as more than appropriate.
4. A "service industry smile" is the false smile that low-grade workers plaster on their faces at their employers' insistence, despite their true feelings toward their customers or their jobs. Keltner devotes so much space (pars. 1–2) to explaining why employees are forced to adopt it, and how it turns them into "schizophrenics" (2), because it's an excellent, accessible example that allows him to both explain the category of the non-Duchenne smile and to outline its personal and social consequences before he even introduces the term.

QUESTIONS ON LANGUAGE

1. Although his language is mostly academic, sometimes downright scientific (pars. 6–10 especially), Keltner injects a wry humor throughout — either through his personal experiences or through brief asides (e.g., the baby [7]) — that is in keeping with his subject. His diction suggests that he assumes his readers to be educated and if not well-versed in scientific and psychological terminology, at least comfortable with new concepts and interested in his subject. Positive psychology is not universally accepted, especially in scholarly circles, so it's likely that although he was writing for a general audience, Keltner felt compelled to establish his authority through academic language.
2. Keltner is referring to Karl Marx's famous theory that modern capitalism is dehumanizing. Although students might not recognize the allusion, Keltner offers enough explanation and context for them to grasp

that fostering a "disconnect" (par. 2) between self and society has troubling psychological and sociological consequences.

3. *Morphologically* won't appear in dictionaries, but *morphology* will. The word refers both to biological structures and to linguistic structures — and thus perfectly reflects and explains Keltner's title.

11

CAUSE AND EFFECT

Asking Why

As you know, the matter of cause and effect can plunge a class into many complexities, and it can sometimes lead to fruitless wrangles. Still, many instructors find that this chapter leads to unusually satisfying results.

We start off with two complementary essays, Chitra Divakaruni's "Live Free and Starve" and student Marie Javdani's "*Plata o Plomo*: Silver or Lead" (Javdani's essay is documented), both examining effects of globalization. Then Helen Pilcher's "The New Witch Doctors: How Belief Can Kill" explains how fear influences people's health, and Charles Fishman's "The Squeeze" examines one small aspect of what the author has dubbed the "Wal-Mart effect." Finally, Chris Anderson's "The Rise and Fall of the Hit" probes the effects of new technology and media on the business of popular culture.

We have endeavored to clarify the difference between process analysis and cause-and-effect analysis, a frequent source of confusion for students. Process asks *how*; cause and effect asks *why*. Further, process deals with events that are repeated or repeatable or even just theoretically repeatable (like the creation of the Grand Canyon); cause and effect deals with singular events, one-time happenings.

Studying cause and effect can lead to a discussion of common errors in reasoning, as we indicate in this chapter when we touch on the fallacy of *post hoc*. If you wish to bring up logical fallacies, a few are listed, defined, and illustrated in Chapter 13, on argument and persuasion (pp. 554–56). Perhaps it is enough at this point merely to call students' attention to them. Cause and effect may be complicated enough without trying to tackle logical fallacies at the same time.

CHITRA DIVAKARUNI

Live Free and Starve

Both Chitra Divakaruni's "Live Free and Starve" and the essay we pair it with, Marie Javdani's "*Plata o Plomo*," tackle globalization — specifically, the effects that policies or actions in the United States can have on those in the developing world.

Divakaruni focuses on the drastically limited choices of child laborers: If they don't work, even under terrible conditions, they starve. Divakaruni argues that Americans should not try to stop child labor abroad without also taking responsibility for the terrible deprivation that sends children into labor in the first place. That "without also" is crucial for students to understand: Divakaruni may show the unintended consequences of a bill banning goods produced with child labor, but she certainly does not argue *for* child labor. For readers inclined to favor American action on unjust labor practices and similar issues of human rights around the world, Divakaruni's paragraph 5 presents a warning not to evaluate others' situations from a strictly American perspective. In the end, the author suggests the kinds of measures Americans would need to take if they really want to help child laborers.

We have previously included Divakaruni's essay in the argument chapter, and it could still be taught as an argument. It provides an excellent chance to discuss emotional appeals. Ask students to mark places in the essay where Divakaruni works to touch the emotions of readers, and then in class spend some time at the board noting the relevant passages. Small groups of students could each analyze one of the passages: What beliefs and values does Divakaruni appeal to? How accurate is she in gauging her readers' sympathies? Do the appeals work to strengthen her argument? (If you would like students to write on Divakaruni's emotional appeals, see the fourth writing suggestion.)

QUESTIONS ON MEANING

1. Divakaruni wants to make her readers think with greater complexity about the solutions available — or not available — for the problem of child labor in developing countries. The title alerts the readers that the author's perspective is perhaps unusual. The brief paragraph 2 makes it clear that she disagrees with the House's solution. Then in paragraph 4 she begins to explain why.
2. Divakaruni's thesis is stated in paragraph 8: "A bill like the one we've just passed is of no use unless it goes hand in hand with programs that will offer a new life to these newly released children."
3. Third World countries are the developing nations of Asia, Africa, and Latin America. The term comes from the Cold War: The first and second worlds were the non-Communist and Communist industrialized nations.
4. Divakaruni means that most Americans have already met their survival needs (for "bread," as she puts it) and thus can afford the relative luxury of seeking freedom and other needs at the top of the pyramid.
5. The children lack "food and clothing and medication," there are no schools for them, their governments can't provide these things, and ultimately no one takes responsibility for them.

QUESTIONS ON WRITING STRATEGY

1. The rhetorical questions expand on the opening (thesis) sentence. They push readers to think hard about the negative effects the legislation could have on child laborers and to consider their willingness to "shoulder the responsibility" for the children when they are jobless.

2. Divakaruni explains in this paragraph how child labor affects children. The first words ("It is true that child labor is a terrible thing") establish the idea of the paragraph, and the remainder concisely itemizes the effects.

3. In telling the detailed story of one child, Divakaruni grounds her essay in a specific case. She establishes her authority as an observer of child labor abroad, and an open-eyed and sympathetic observer at that. Though Nimai had a life that was "hardly a desirable existence for a child," he still was better off, Divakaruni contends, than the nonworking children in his village.

QUESTIONS ON LANGUAGE

1. The survival of the families is so borderline that caring for their own children could ruin them.

2. The words show compassion — "ribs sticking out," "hunger was too much to bear," "ate whatever they could find," "knew they'd be beaten for it."

3. *Blithe* has roots in Old Saxon, Middle Dutch, Old High German, and Old Norse. It earlier referred to the outward expression of a kindly feeling but has come to mean "heedless or careless, unaware of the full implications of an act."

CHITRA DIVAKARUNI ON WRITING

For Chitra Divakaruni, social activism broadens and sensitizes her and is thus a boon to her writing. Our questions prompt students to consider just what a writer gains from having her or his "preconceptions" challenged and from understanding the lives of others. The questions could open up a discussion of critical thinking, not just about others' ideas but about one's own as well.

MARIE JAVDANI

Plata o Plomo: Silver or Lead

Paired with the previous essay — Chitra Divakaruni's look at child labor in developing countries — this essay focuses on another problem that affects children in the third world: drug production and trafficking. In a good example of student research writing, Marie Javdani explores the plight of Colombian peasants caught between rebels who finance their cause through drug trafficking and government-condoned forces who battle the rebels. Extensive financial aid to the Colombian government from the United States has done little to stem the production and flow of drugs from the country, largely because of government corruption. Javdani argues that US money would be better spent drastically reducing US demand for drugs, which would, in turn, significantly decrease the profitability of the drug trade and thus improve the situation in places like Colombia.

Students may be surprised by the connection Javdani makes between young Americans' use of illegal drugs and the death of a young Colombian. Class discussion might focus on this connection, which brings the abstractions of globalization down to concrete cases. Do students accept the connection? Do they accept Javdani's conclusion that Americans have a responsibility to change their own behavior in order to help improve conditions in developing countries?

QUESTIONS ON MEANING

1. Javdani states her thesis at the end of paragraph 3, forecasting the organization of the essay. In paragraphs 4–7 she describes "what's happening in drug-source countries," in paragraphs 8–9 she covers "how the United States can and cannot help there," and in paragraphs 10–11 she makes a case for "what, instead, can be done at home."
2. Many peasants fear the government more than the rebels, in part because the rebels can provide protection from the government, whereas the government provides little protection from the rebels. Also, the peasants evidently receive money from the rebel drug lords to farm coca.
3. As Javdani writes in paragraph 8, money used to eradicate coca fields has "alienated peasants" and "escalated violence," and money intended to "help peasants establish alternative crops" and further legitimate police efforts has wound up helping arm paramilitary forces or simply disappearing. Javdani argues that greater efforts must be made to reduce the US market for drugs.

QUESTIONS ON WRITING STRATEGY

1. Students may have different thoughts about Javdani's intended audience, but in her final paragraph she clearly appeals to people her own age to recognize the extent to which their use of and tolerance for drug use in this country has harmful effects elsewhere. Javdani wrote the essay in a freshman writing class, so she may have had in mind an audience of her classmates.
2. Javdani's sympathies seem to lie with the Colombian peasants. For evidence, students might point to her opening description of Miguel and her discussion throughout of the Colombians' plight and the atrocities they face.
3. Javdani's extensive use of sources backs up her claims and gives her writing authority. The source citations are particularly effective in the detailed descriptions of the situation in Colombia.
4. The contrast Javdani sets up in her opening paragraphs is between a suburban teenager scoring drugs in the United States and a peasant boy facing execution because of his family's resistance to drug trafficking in Colombia. She creates a connection between the two that she returns to in her conclusion: It is the demand for drugs in the United States, typified by Eric, that endangers peasants in Colombia, typified by Miguel.

QUESTIONS ON LANGUAGE

1. The phrase "between a rock and a hard place" means being stuck between two equally bad choices with no alternative. The peasants can either work with the government and face torture and execution by the

rebel drug lords or work with the drug lords and face the same fate from government-condoned paramilitary forces.

2. Javdani writes that Eric lives in a "suburban paradise" and yet still faces the "stress of homework and ex-girlfriends"; obviously, she intends readers to see his life as not terribly stressful at all and certainly not an excuse to use drugs. Students should see immediately that Javdani has no sympathy for Eric.

3. The peasants are "traitors" to one side or the other no matter what their choice, so they are not literally traitors, and the "cooperation" the peasants are accused of is not voluntary but forced, so it is not literally cooperation.

4. *Guerilla* comes from the Spanish word for war, *guerra*, with the diminutive ending *-illa*; it might be translated literally as "small war." The word was coined in the early 1800s to describe the Spanish resistance movement against the French regime established by Napoleon Bonaparte. The Spanish word for "guerilla fighter" is *guerillero*, but in English *guerilla* has long referred to those who participate in guerilla warfare, as well as to the warfare itself.

MARIE JAVDANI ON WRITING

Having recently been one herself, Javdani offers much useful advice for student writers. We emphasize her counsel to care about one's topic because inexperienced writers, especially reluctant ones, often don't make the effort to find their own angle on a subject. We also like Javdani's warning that interest doesn't justify the speechifying of a soapbox orator: Moderation is the key.

HELEN PILCHER

The New Witch Doctors: How Belief Can Kill

Helen Pilcher's engaging survey of recent scientific research comes to a startling conclusion: Seeking medical help can make you sick. Implicitly comparing modern physicians with ominous witch doctors and medicine with voodoo, the author warns readers to be careful what they believe because "belief can kill."

You could begin discussion by asking students about the implied comparison that runs through Pilcher's essay. Is she, in fact, suggesting that modern medicine is no different than voodoo and that doctors are threats to human health? Or does she have a more subtle connection in mind?

Pilcher is one of several graduate-level scientists in *The Bedford Reader* who write for a general audience. Students who enjoy "The New Witch Doctors" may also want to check out Howard Markel's "Mary Ellen's Story" (p. 133), Bella DePaulo's "The Myth of Doomed Kids" (p. 379), Dacher Keltner's "A Vocabulary of Smiles" (p. 445), Barbara Kingsolver's "Rural Delivery"

(p. 534), and Barbara Ehrenreich's "The Menace of Negative People" (p. 634) — and ask themselves what it is about training in biology and medicine, in particular, that seems to make a writer so clearly attuned to readers' needs and interests.

QUESTIONS ON MEANING

1. Pilcher is writing mainly to inform readers about a developing scientific understanding of the relationship between belief and illness, or as her subtitle hints, to explain "how belief can kill." On a lesser scale, she aims to persuade readers, particularly medical practitioners, to be careful what they tell people who are or may become ill, on the theory that merely suggesting negative outcomes can bring those outcomes to fruition. On an informative level, she does quite well, but because she is so careful to stress that the relationship is not fully understood, some readers will be hesitant to accept her conclusions.

2. Pilcher hints at her thesis early in the essay, with "the curse has taken on a new form" (par. 8) and "[i]t seems modern witch doctors wear white coats and carry stethoscopes" (10). She clarifies the point in her conclusion, where she first says, "Despite the growing evidence that the nocebo effect is all too real, it is hard in this rational age to accept that people's beliefs can kill them" (28). Then she concludes with her thesis: "Perhaps when the biomedical basis of voodoo death is revealed in detail we will find it easier to accept that it is real — and that it can affect any one of us" (31).

3. Pilcher colorfully describes the nocebo effect as the placebo effect's "evil twin" (par. 12). While a placebo is a harmless, inert substance that seems able to cure illness through the power of suggestion, a nocebo (the word means "I will harm" [12]) is the opposite: It is a "dummy pill" (12) or harmful idea that has the potential to cause illness through the power of suggestion.

4. A self-fulfilling prophecy is an outcome that seems inevitable because it is directed by the expectation or prediction that it will happen. The idea neatly sums up Pilcher's point about voodoo and medicine: The mere suggestion of illness can make a person experience physical symptoms.

QUESTIONS ON WRITING STRATEGY

1. The story of Vance Vanders is entertaining, surprising, and thoroughly engaging — a hook practically guaranteed to grab readers' interest in a medical research topic that might otherwise seem dry or abstract. At the same time, the story's focus, a curse overcome by a clever and underhanded application of modern medicine, sets an ironic tone and establishes Pilcher's overarching analogy equating modern medicine with voodoo.

2. Pilcher's diction — a mix of scientific terminology and colloquial language — reveals that she is writing for educated readers who are interested in science (the essay originally appeared in *New Scientist*, a relatively academic science magazine aimed at a general readership). Presumably she counts doctors, patients, scientists, and study participants — but not people who believe in voodoo — among the potential members of that audience.

3. Pilcher's emphasis is on establishing the existence of the nocebo phenomenon and exploring its effects and "very real consequences" (par. 25). She doesn't dwell on causes, she explains, because they're not well understood: "We just don't know," she says (22).

4. The headings help Pilcher to organize her ideas and readers to follow them. The essay consists of three parts: the introductory anecdote, an overview of the research ("Voodoo Nouveau"), and a consideration of the implications of that knowledge ("Real Consequences").

5. The examples in boxes showcase more extreme instances of the nocebo effect and mass psychogenic illness. By pulling them out of the text itself, Pilcher is able to develop these particularly interesting cases in more narrative detail than she could in the body of the essay, where they might have read as unnecessary digressions. As an easily skimmed visual element, too, the boxes help capture the attention of a reader flipping through the pages of a magazine.

QUESTIONS ON LANGUAGE

1. As we point out in the introduction to Pilcher's essay, *voodoo* has occult connotations, ranging from sorcery to animal sacrifice to evil. How strongly students respond to it will depend on their backgrounds and assumptions. Pilcher seems to enjoy evoking the frightful associations, but in the end she uses the word in all seriousness, preferring its sense of faith and ritual, most significantly its links to curses and the powers of suggestion on those who believe.

2. Pilcher's humor in this essay is subtle, almost always taking the form of irony (in the introductory anecdote) and understatement, such as "It's not easy, after all, to get ethical approval for studies designed to make people feel worse" (par. 12). Far from undermining the author's credibility, the mild levity helps keep the science lively and interesting for non-specialists, without alienating trained scientists who might take the subject quite seriously.

3. Standard dictionary definitions of *dopamine* and *opioid* might not be of much help to students: The *American Heritage Dictionary, Second College Edition*, defines the former as "a monoamine neurotransmitter that is a carboxylated form of dopa and that is essential to normal nerve activity" and includes no entry for the latter. Both are brain chemicals that dull pain.

CHARLES FISHMAN

The Squeeze

Most of us love to hate Wal-Mart. Although many economists and social commentators repeatedly warn that the retail behemoth is destroying small retailers and exploiting workers, others point out that the store's trademark low prices have effectively improved the standard of living of working-class Americans by making necessities and luxuries alike more affordable. This excerpt from Fishman's book is especially interesting because it looks at an aspect of Wal-Mart that often escapes public notice: The megabusiness has the power to make — and to destroy — other businesses. As Fishman warns, the "Wal-Mart effect" reaches farther than even the most vocal opponents recognize.

Rather than bringing his gavel down on one side of the evil/wonderful dichotomy, Fishman has said that his goal in writing *The Wal-Mart Effect* was simply to present his findings evenhandedly and to put the conversation about the world's largest retailer on a more productive plane. "We need to understand the positive impact that Wal-Mart has, so we can preserve it," he said in an interview with his publisher. "And just as important, we need to understand all the negative impacts that Wal-Mart has, so we can find ways to encourage Wal-Mart to modify those negative effects, or insist through legislation that they be modified."

Students may be interested to know that Barbara Ehrenreich's *Nickel and Dimed* (2001) includes a lengthy and critical chapter about her undercover stint as a Wal-Mart associate. Other entries in the Wal-Mart debate include *The Wal-Mart Revolution: How Big-Box Stores Benefit Consumers, Workers, and the Economy* (2007), by Richard Vedder and Wendell Cox; *The Retail Revolution: How Wal-Mart Created a Brave New World of Business* (2009), by Nelson Lichtenstein; *The United States of Wal-Mart* (2005), by John Dicker; *Wal-Mart: The High Cost of Low Price* (2005), by Greg Spotts and Roger Greenwald; and *Wal-Mart, The Bully of Bentonville: How the High Cost of Everyday Low Prices Is Hurting America* (2007), by Anthony Bianco.

QUESTIONS ON MEANING

1. Fishman's relatively objective reportorial approach to telling the Vlasic story suggests that he wants to educate readers rather than express his opinion or spark outrage. As he explains his purpose in paragraph 20, the story "shows the impact of Wal-Mart's scale and power in what we all think is a market economy." If anything, he hopes to convince readers that we need to rethink the old laws of supply and demand because Wal-Mart has rendered them meaningless (a point implied in the book's subtitle and stated explicitly in its concluding chapter).

2. As one of Fishman's informants explains, Wal-Mart wanted to use the $2.97 gallon as a "'statement' item" (par. 3): The idea was to impress customers with an incredible value and demonstrate what Wal-Mart has to offer. Although executives knew that pickle profits would be minimal, their goal was to drive business and increase the volume of sales throughout the chain. The result was good for Wal-Mart: Customers bought the pickles in droves. But for the supplier, Wal-Mart's success came at a steep cost, sharply reducing their profits even as sales increased; worse, the gallon jars kept customers from buying Vlasic's more profitable products.

3. A "devastating success" is a deliberate oxymoron that might be summed up in the old saying, "Be careful what you wish for: You just might get it." The term describes a seemingly positive accomplishment that turns out to be damaging. In Vlasic's case, Wal-Mart helped the company dramatically increase pickle sales, yet Vlasic's profits dropped precipitously, leaving them no better off than they had been before they made the arrangement with Wal-Mart — and possibly much worse.

4. Fishman isn't really accusing Wal-Mart of deceptive business practices, although readers might certainly misinterpret him. He uses the word *lie*

to emphasize that Wal-Mart's price was a gimmick, rather than a true reflection of market conditions. His point is that the chain is so large, and has such power over its suppliers, that it has managed to exempt itself from the laws of supply and demand.

QUESTIONS ON WRITING STRATEGY

1. Fishman wrote this piece for an intelligent general audience, rather than for, say, economists or business leaders. (The book started as a cover story for *Fast Company*, a business magazine aimed at a popular readership.) His understanding of his audience can be seen in his storytelling approach, in his preference for colloquial language, and in his avoidance of economics and business jargon. He does seem to assume that his readers shop at Wal-Mart at least occasionally, and he takes for granted that they have at least a basic grasp of major economic principles, such as "market economy" and the "laws of supply, demand, and competition."

2. Given the author's purpose in explaining Wal-Mart's impact on the economy, cause-and-effect analysis is almost inevitable as the choice of method. The subject (Wal-Mart's effect) lends itself to the method perfectly.

3. A possible summary: A Wal-Mart buyer noticed the gallon jar of pickles and convinced Vlasic to experiment with selling it for a low price at a few stores. Both companies were shocked by the product's popularity and decided to try selling it even more cheaply on a national level. Sales were overwhelming, and Vlasic was forced to increase production, but profits fell as volume increased. Worse, customers started buying the gallon jars instead of (rather than in addition to) more profitable variations, putting Vlasic in a pickle.

4. Readers could easily argue that Fishman focuses too squarely on Wal-Mart's artificial price and ignores a host of possible mitigating factors. An academic economist, for example, would probably want to see a more nuanced consideration of both companies' business models, of market fluctuations, and of customers' buying habits. All the same, given Fishman's purpose and audience, the depth of his analysis seems sufficient.

5. As a reporter, Fishman naturally turns to narrative to make his point (he also chooses to focus the analysis on a single example). By presenting his analysis in the form of a story, he makes it more interesting and accessible for a general audience.

QUESTIONS ON LANGUAGE

1. Fishman compares pickles in a jar to reptiles in a dank aquarium. It's a wonderful metaphor evoking images of swamp creatures and sea monsters, and it grabs readers' attention by portraying a harmless consumer product as a lurking menace. Notice, too, that Fishman returns to the monster metaphor ever so subtly in other parts of the essay, describing the "story . . . floating in Vlasic's gallon jar" (par. 4), referring to "[w]hole fields of cucumbers . . . heading out the door" as though they were an advancing army of mutants (9), commenting that the "cannibalizing" (10) pickles "chewed up" Vlasic's profits (11), and repeating Young's comment that Wal-Mart "killed" the pickles (18) as though it were the victor in an epic battle.

2. In many ways, *abundance* captures the image Wal-Mart sought to create for itself. The word evokes a sense of plenty and of satisfaction. Each time Fishman repeats the word, however, his use becomes more ironic, ultimately implying that Wal-Mart's quantity comes closer to greed than to necessity.
3. Fishman's tone is simultaneously balanced and ironic — no small feat. He cultivates that sense of balance by relying on quotations from Wal-Mart insiders to tell the story, while he hovers in the background as the objective reporter. But at the same time, he weaves an understated story about the "devastating success" (par. 10) Wal-Mart inflicted on a supplier, leaving readers with what is ultimately a cautionary tale about the perils of victory.
4. Although Fishman uses *lockstep* to suggest obeisance, the word has military connotations: It originally referred to soldiers marching in tight formation and effectively evokes a sense of battle between Wal-Mart and Vlasic.

CHARLES FISHMAN ON WRITING

Fishman's description of his research methods might inspire some students and intimidate others. While students probably don't have the time to read thousands of pages or the resources to travel around the country, they can still adopt some of Fishman's strategies to delve deeper into their topics. Personal interviews, for instance, might reveal a different side to the story than could be derived from reading academic studies. Students might be surprised by how willing people are to talk to them about their research.

CHRIS ANDERSON

The Rise and Fall of the Hit

Chris Anderson's essay explains a major change in the way consumers relate to the popular culture of movies, television, and especially music. The blockbuster, Anderson claims, is virtually a thing of the past because the Internet and other technological innovations make it possible for businesses to respond to our individual interests and that kind of response is, in turn, what we now demand.

To good effect, we think, Anderson delays fully stating his thesis until near the end of the essay. He first establishes that change has occurred by providing sales figures and other statistics for the music business (pars. 1–4), and he offers explanations for the change, from file-sharing networks to failed marketing (5–10). Then he traces the rise of popular culture from the Industrial Revolution to the 1990s (11–20). Only in his final two paragraphs does he tie together "the rise and fall of the hit" by pointing to the Internet as the primary cause.

Undoubtedly, at least some of your students will have firsthand experience with the revolution Anderson describes. If they're old enough to remember when popular music was dominated by a few radio stations and record stores, ask them to discuss the differences between then and now. (Some of the writing topics after the essay could help get this conversation going.)

QUESTIONS ON MEANING

1. Anderson suggests his thesis in paragraph 5: "[T]he traditional model of marketing and selling music no longer works. . . . We are witnessing the end of an era." But he states the thesis fully only in the first few sentences of paragraph 21. Restated briefly, the thesis might read: The Internet has inverted the former top-down dissemination of popular culture so that people's individual interests, rather than corporations, determine what gets seen and heard.

2. Anderson is making the point that popular culture, as it was defined beginning in the late nineteenth century and until around the year 2000, resulted from technological advances that began in the Industrial Revolution: railroads, printing, photography, the phonograph, movies, and so on. The latest technological innovations — computers and the Internet — both intensify the consumption of popular culture and, almost paradoxically, return us to niches — now based on interests rather than on geography.

3. The "water-cooler effect" refers to workers gathering at the office water cooler to discuss "a shared cultural event." The "virtual" water cooler is of course online. Instead of bringing people together to discuss what the TV networks decided they should watch, it brings together people who share interests.

4. Anderson seems to want readers to recognize and also to feel excited and empowered by their ability to escape from "the tyranny of the top" (par. 21). As he writes in paragraph 5, "There has never been a better time to be an artist or a fan." In his final sentence he transfers the power to decide "who will win" from those "big players in the distribution system" to his readers ("You do"). His purpose is both to inform readers of their options and to encourage them to take advantage of them.

QUESTIONS ON WRITING STRATEGY

1. Anderson wants to make the point in his opening that pop music packaging and marketing reached an apotheosis with the huge sales of this 2000 release. As he goes on to show, the album's performance has not been equaled and may never be. NSync's success marked "the end of an era" (par. 5).

2. Anderson explains some causes for the decline in record sales in paragraphs 6–8: file-sharing networks, CD burning and trading, the ability to purchase single tracks online. Paragraphs 9 and 10 offer causes for the decline in rock radio ratings: market fragmentation and competition, homogeneity, and cell phones and iPods. Paragraphs 11–22 discuss technological developments that led to the expansion of mass popular culture — greater mobility, improved commercial printing technology, the invention of photography, the phonograph and movies. Finally, paragraphs 21 and 22 show how the Internet is changing the way culture is transmitted.

3. This question relates to the fourth question on meaning about Anderson's purpose: Anderson sees his audience as active participants in the changes he writes about.

4. Students should note Anderson's use of examples in paragraphs 1, 3, 6–8, 14–16, 18, and 19. In each case, the examples help clarify how and why the blockbuster increased or declined.

QUESTIONS ON LANGUAGE

1. Examples of words used to describe mass marketing: "all about looks and scripted personalities" and "The music itself . . . hardly mattered" (par. 1); "manufactured pop" (4); "a packaged act" (7); "cookie-cutter playlists" (9); "tyranny of the top" (21); and "monopoly" (22). The language suggests that Anderson sees such marketing as stifling, uncreative, and undemocratic.
2. The italics for *free* emphasize just how unbelievable (or "mind-blowing," as Anderson puts it) it was that the earliest broadcast media cost consumers nothing.
3. Some uses of *culture* or a variation: "limited the mixing of cultures" (par. 11); "vehicles for carrying common culture" (12); "hives of commerce," "powerful engine of new culture," and "mass media" (13); "the first great wave of pop culture" (14); "potent carriers of culture" (15); "gregarious" and "celebrity age" (16); "broadcast media" and "vehicle for stardom" (17); "television took over" (18); "a shared cultural event" (19); "the great American unifier" and "mainstream" (20). This language adds cohesion to Anderson's discussion, keeping clearly in the reader's mind the change he is describing.
4. On an à la carte restaurant menu (from French for "by the bill of fare"), each item is priced separately. Anderson uses *à la carte* figuratively to refer to the purchase of individual songs.

CHRIS ANDERSON ON WRITING

Anderson's thoughts on the diminished roles of "traditional gatekeepers" like himself are remarkable for not being self-protective: Evidently, he welcomes the upending of culture even at the risk of losing his own job. We hope students will find encouragement in Anderson's words and take advantage of the Internet's openness for their own self-expression.

12
DEFINITION
Tracing a Boundary

"When they come to definition," said the late Richard Beal, an author of textbooks, a director of composition, and our sage adviser, "most authors of rhetorically organized readers seem not to know what it is nor what to do about it."

Definition, he suggested, is not in itself a distinct and separate expository method, but a catchall name for a kind of explaining that involves whatever method or methods it can use. It would break with tradition, Beal said, to place definition last among methods of exposition. Then the instructor might use it to review all the rest.

We hope that this ordering of the book's contents proves useful to you. You will also find the book carefully distinguishing a short definition (the kind found in a dictionary), a stipulative definition (the kind that pins down an essential term in a paragraph or two), and extended definition (the kind found in whole essays).

All the essays in this chapter trace the shape of a definite territory and attempt to set forth its nature. In the paired selections, Gloria Naylor and Christine Leong demonstrate how words change meanings in different contexts: Each explores the alterations in a derogatory word for her race depending on who uses it. (As a bonus, Leong, a student, responds directly to Naylor — thus modeling a common writing assignment.) Thomas Sowell then questions the meaning of *needs*, maintaining that we overuse the word to our economic detriment. Barbara Kingsolver defines what *rural* means to people like her, who live far from urban centers. And Andrea Jones lyrically proposes a fresh understanding of human skin.

GLORIA NAYLOR
The Meanings of a Word

Focusing on the highly charged word *nigger*, Naylor maintains that context determines interpretation. Many students will disagree with this assertion, arguing that language carries its own meaning, so it might be useful to open up this issue right away. Students will certainly agree that saying something like "It was all my fault" means something completely different depending on whether uttered with sincerity or with sarcasm. Can students think of other instances when they have relied on inflection to convey meaning? Have they manipulated language — through exaggerations or half-truths, for example — for their own benefit? Stephanie Ericsson's "The Ways We Lie" (p. 408) provides another perspective on how we can (and often do) twist language to suit ourselves.

Part of Naylor's point, too, is that speech can be more precise (or more nuanced) than writing. How do writers overcome (or try to overcome) the limitations of written language? Students can explore the connections among tone, context, and meaning. Give groups fifteen or twenty minutes to look over essays they have already read this semester, in search of sentences, ideas, or passages that might be easily misinterpreted if read out of context. (It will be helpful if you read aloud a few examples as models. Promising examples appear in Anna Quindlen's "Homeless," Chap. 6, and Jessica Mitford's "Behind the Formaldehyde Curtain," Chap. 8.) Have students identify different interpretations for an isolated excerpt as well as interpretations for the excerpt when considered in the context of the entire selection. After each group explains its examples, the class will be better prepared for a discussion of writing strategies and/or Naylor's sense of the multiple meanings of language.

QUESTIONS ON MEANING

1. Written language, with less inflection and immediacy, doesn't offer the variety and richness of spoken language.
2. This was the first time it sounded offensive, so it was the first time she was shocked enough to really notice — "hear" — it.
3. They took a derogatory term and redefined it, gaining power from using it as a form both of praise and of informed condemnation rather than simply as a term of prejudice.
4. She wants to show how the meanings of a word change with the context in which it is used. (See the next question.)

QUESTIONS ON WRITING STRATEGY

1. Naylor holds that spoken language is richer and more powerful than written language and that the power of words derives from their context. The rest of the essay presents examples of these assertions in uses of *nigger*. To us, the opening is a bit flat and perhaps unnecessary: The assertions are well made through the examples. But some students may appreciate the initial overview.
2. Paragraphs 3, 14, and 15 discuss racist uses of the term: They sandwich nonracist uses, as the African American experience is sandwiched by racism. At the same time, the discussion of nonracist uses is longer, emphasizing the positive. The two definitions come together in paragraphs 14–15, in which Naylor sums up the nonracist uses and distinguishes them from the racist uses.
3. These last sentences make clear that despite the empowering use of the word within her family and community, her mother knows Naylor will face more uses of the word in a racist context. It also suggests a protective bond between Naylor and her mother.

4. They suggest how the word might be used in a sentence, so that the audience can get a sense of different inflections. Through them, Naylor tries to add a spoken component to written language.

QUESTIONS ON LANGUAGE

1. The old question is "Which came first, the chicken or the egg?" This debate helps Naylor show the circular ways that language and reality influence one another.
2. They identify, respectively, a sex-crazed woman and a person sexually interested in corpses. Both connote perversion, twistedness. Naylor uses the words to emphasize the unfamiliarity of *nigger*, but she implies with them just how venomous was the little boy's insult.
3. The religious connotations of mecca suggest a sense of reverence for a place that offers a retreat from daily strife. *Mecca* can be understood both in a religious sense (a spiritual center in Islam) and in a secular sense (a center for people who share a common interest). Describing the grandmother's house as a *mecca* identifies it as a safe and spiritual gathering place.

GLORIA NAYLOR ON WRITING

Naylor's remarks could fuel a discussion about the literary canon — what's included, what's excluded, who decides. Naylor turned a perceived disadvantage, a dearth of "approved" African American literature, into an advantage by deciding to help right the wrong herself. When she says she attempts to "articulate experiences that want articulating," she evokes many silenced forebears.

CHRISTINE LEONG

Being a Chink

Leong's essay is clearly modeled on Gloria Naylor's "The Meanings of a Word." Like Naylor, Leong explores the power to be gained from refusing to allow words, especially those originally intended as demeaning or offensive, to have fixed meanings. For students who resist the idea that language is flexible and that context often determines meaning, you might wish to consider some of the suggestions and questions we pose in the introduction to Naylor's essay.

Deborah Tannen's "But What Do You Mean?" (Chap. 10) is another interesting counterpart to this essay; both discuss ways that communication relies on mutual assumptions about the meanings of words. In clusters of three or four, students could brainstorm a list of groups that have "private" language. (Students may need to be reminded that groups may be defined not just by race, ethnicity, or gender, but also by age, occupation, marital status, education, hobby, and so on.) How does knowing the private language create a position of power for a speaker or a listener?

QUESTIONS ON MEANING

1. Leong explains *chink* in paragraph 10: a label that describes specific external characteristics but not internal ones.
2. For this group of friends, the word has become a way to comfort each other by acknowledging the way they have all had to deal with racism (par. 11).
3. Her purpose is the last one listed: Although her essay does both of the other things to some degree, Leong wants to show the reader how the flexible nature of language allows for power through redefining racist terms. You know this from the conjunction of her first and last paragraphs.

QUESTIONS ON WRITING STRATEGY

1. Both essays have an introduction on language and meaning, a story that starts "I remember the first time . . . ," and a conclusion that explains the power in co-opting racist terms. Leong places her experiences in the context of racist issues generally and of Naylor's reading of them specifically.
2. Leong builds suspense as she sifts through the trash. Ending with the envelope accomplishes several things: The envelope is both grouped with other forgotten rubbish and set apart by its racist inscription.
3. This example sets up the parallel between Naylor's family's redefinition of *nigger* and Leong's redefinition of *chink*, enhancing Leong's explanation of the way she and her friends dealt with the label and their reasons for doing so.
4. To make clear that they are consciously subverting the original meaning of *chink* and not misunderstanding it.
5. She assumes the slur is directed at her father and she is outraged on his behalf.

QUESTIONS ON LANGUAGE

1. Words like "imposed," "small," "weak," "insignificant," "paralyze," and "belittle" all suggest that racist language is debilitating.
2. This characterization of their use of *chink* suggests affection, gentleness, and mutual understanding, almost like a nickname — all of which are in contrast to racist uses.
3. Students should notice how careful Leong is with the language of labels: In terms of both race and gender, she is very politic, using "Caucasian" instead of "white," and "human" or "person" instead of "man." You might ask students how this care contributes to her essay's message.

CHRISTINE LEONG ON WRITING

Leong's insistence on the writer's personal involvement in writing is refreshing, especially coming from a student. Your students may be surprised by Leong's assertion that inspiration counts more than grammar and sense in reaching readers. With "Being a Chink" and her comments on writing — both not only correct but sensible — Leong makes a strong case for clarity informed by passion.

THOMAS SOWELL

"Needs"

In this essay the economist Thomas Sowell challenges readers to rethink their idea of the word *needs*. His point is that much of what some people claim they "need" from government is not needed at all but simply wanted. By asserting "rights" and "entitlements" based on supposed need, people — particularly politicians — ignore the inevitable trade-offs and jeopardize the economy and society as a whole. Sowell's underlying argument is that free markets in the private sector are more efficient than the government is at supplying what the citizenry can afford.

You might begin discussion by asking students: What is the bare minimum required for people to exist? To what extent are these requirements the responsibility of government?

QUESTIONS ON MEANING

1. Sowell defines needs in paragraph 7: "simply things we want — or that some of us want." The definition is distinctive in implying that the concept underlying the customary use of the word does not exist. Very little of what we claim we need is actually a need at all.
2. Essentially Sowell's underlying purpose is to convince readers that smaller government and reduced government spending on social programs benefit the economy and ultimately all citizens. This purpose is evident in paragraphs 12 and 16–20.
3. By "trade-offs" Sowell refers to the fact that we can never have everything we want and so we must forgo some things altogether or have less of our ideal. He believes that too many politicians, unwilling to face this reality, put certain services "on a pedestal," allowing constituents to see these services as "entitlements" (par. 8) even though funding them is not feasible (6).

QUESTIONS ON WRITING STRATEGY

1. With the opening anecdote, Sowell establishes that economists do not use the word *need* lightly and take issue with those who do. The anecdote supports his point that political discourse invokes "needs" far too often. Economists have a better grasp of the concept than politicians do, he implies.
2. The quotation marks highlight the misuse of the word. Sowell does not accept this use.

3. Sowell must concede that humans genuinely require food, but defining it as a "need" produces "[h]uge agricultural surpluses" and dangerous overconsumption. His old car provides a clear example of trade-offs and an opportunity to poke fun at government entitlements.
4. Fulfilling one "need" causes some other real need not to be met. Government wastefulness based on misconceived "needs" causes the economy and society to suffer.

QUESTIONS ON LANGUAGE

1. *Humbug* has the double meaning of "deception" and "nonsense," so the word well suits Sowell's purpose. The phrase "the higher humbug of politics" also has a nice ring.
2. *Entitlement*, a right or claim, has in government and politics become an adjective to describe programs, such as Social Security, that guarantee benefits.
3. *Rigid* emphasizes that *needs* and similar words used by politicians undermine flexible trade-offs and impede our thinking, creating "havoc in our policies."
4. Examples of informal language include "poor Mike" (par. 4), "good clean fun" (5), "keep body and soul together" (10), "knock you dead" (14), "old jalopy . . . messing up my life" (16), and "mushy" (18). "Trade-off" (12–15) is fairly informal as well. The effect is to appeal to average readers; Sowell presents himself as a regular guy rather than as a stuffy academic.

BARBARA KINGSOLVER

Rural Delivery

With Michael Pollan's *The Omnivore's Dilemma* (see p. 337), Barbara Kingsolver's *Animal, Vegetable, Miracle* has been credited with galvanizing the local-food movement, exposing the dangers of commercial agriculture and inspiring thousands to pay more attention to what they eat and where it comes from. Our food, both writers have argued, has physical, cultural, economic, and political consequences. In this excerpt from Kingsolver's book, the writer draws attention to a few of the political implications by asking readers to reconsider what the word *rural* (and by extension, *farmer*) means to them.

You may want to point out that Kingsolver defines largely by negation, explaining what rural people are *not* — "hick, redneck, hayseed, bumpkin" (par. 3) and so forth — to show them instead as she sees them. For Kingsolver, rural communities are not only sophisticated, cultured, and diverse but they are also essential to everybody else's survival, so we'd all better start showing more respect, both culturally and politically.

The vast majority (83%) of people in the United States live in urban or suburban areas, and many more relocate to densely populated areas every day. To engage your class in the topic before getting into the essay itself, you might begin discussion by focusing on students' own assumptions about rural living. What, if anything, do they know about it, and what have they heard? Would they ever willingly live "*so far from everything*" (par. 6)? Why, or why not?

QUESTIONS ON MEANING

1. Here is a possible summary: Rural communities are sparsely populated areas where farming dominates the landscape and the economy. They are characterized by a proud insularity, unacknowledged sophistication, a strong sense of community, cultural and political diversity, and a history of being exploited by urban dwellers — who would starve without them.
2. Yes and no. Kingsolver was not raised on a farm, but because her family did not live in town, others classified them as "farm" people (par. 1). As an adult, however, Kingsolver strongly identifies with farmers and does seem to count herself among them, even if she does not make a living from working the land. (She currently cultivates a small plot to feed her family, something we mention in the introduction to the essay, but which Kingsolver does not discuss in this excerpt.)
3. Paragraphs 9–11 expand Kingsolver's definition to the landscape and politics of the nation as a whole, highlighting the significance of her subject for readers in rural and urban areas alike.
4. Kingsolver's purpose goes well beyond defining *rural*. The essay is a tribute to the lives and cultures of rural Americans, farmers in particular. Kingsolver wants to share her vision with readers from all backgrounds and counter negative assumptions about rural life and politics. Most important, she wants readers to understand that the nation literally cannot survive without the contributions of its rural communities.

QUESTIONS ON WRITING STRATEGY

1. Opening with a depiction of a nonsensical "caste" system imposed by schoolmates draws readers in and shares an experience to which most can relate. Kingsolver's point is that distinctions between rural and urban are as arbitrary — and as relative — as were the distinctions between "farm" and "town" where she grew up.
2. Kingsolver covers quite a bit of ground in "Rural Delivery"; she maintains unity by ensuring that each paragraph includes a clear topic sentence related to the thesis. Kingsolver is also careful to mark transitions among her paragraphs and to repeat key words such as *farm*, *rural*, and *urban*.
3. Stipulative definitions in the essay include those of "farmer" (par. 1), "everything" (6), "Interior" (6), "Conservative" (7), and "insider" and "outsider" (8). With each definition, Kingsolver emphasizes that common assumptions about rural America are wrong.
4. During the 2000 presidential campaign, political commentators and newscasters began categorizing states as either Democratic (blue) or Republican (red), based on predicted election results. The labels have stuck in the popular consciousness and are still used to characterize whole regions by their supposed political leanings — even though, as Kingsolver asserts, such labels are grossly oversimplified and misleading. She considers the political divide at length because it has come to signify a country polarized by difference and because it parallels the

urban/rural "antipathy" that so concerns her. Ultimately, she hopes to bridge the gulf by questioning its existence.

QUESTIONS ON LANGUAGE

1. Berry is a well-known and respected writer who also happens to be a practicing farmer, so he lends authority to Kingsolver's arguments on two levels. The first quotation helps her to establish the importance of recognizing the politics of food; the second, which closes the essay, raises a dire warning of what will happen if the politics of food is not recognized and dealt with.
2. Kingsolver uses complex, formal words — such as *numinous* (par. 1), *bourgeoisie* (2), *symptomatic* (6), and *extractive* (9) — alongside colloquial expressions, including "Maybe you see where I'm going with this" (3) and "Okay, I'm exaggerating a little" (6). The informal language helps her connect with readers and build an earnest tone; the formal language expressly counters assumptions that rural people like Kingsolver are uneducated or unsophisticated.
3. Some readers will detect Marxist connotations in *bourgeoisie*, French for "middle class." By using that word in the same introductory paragraphs with *castes* (a reference to India) and *apartheid* (a reference to South Africa), Kingsolver strongly hints that her essay will emphasize political and class issues.

BARBARA KINGSOLVER ON WRITING

We don't often hear writers warning against cockiness, and it may not be your students' greatest writing problem. Still, Kingsolver's comments on the need for reverence toward the craft of writing seem valuable. Reverence instills the aspiration to do well and the patience to work through problems. Overconfidence, we assume Kingsolver means, can quiet the questioner within.

ANDREA JONES
Identity's Edge

Not many people would think to write an extended definition of *skin*, or to use it as an analogy for *identity*, but that's what Andrea Jones has done in "Identity's Edge" (and quite beautifully, too). The essay is meant to be poetic and evocative, not literal, so some readers may struggle with it, determined to find an obvious definition or a clear-cut meaning. If that should happen in your class, encourage students to enjoy Jones's piece for what it is: an impressionistic, philosophical reflection on the connections between body, self, and the world around us. Not every piece of writing has to be easily interpreted to be effective.

Students may be interested to know that Jones likely wrote this essay with an assigned subject. Along with several other short pieces, it appeared in a 2007 issue of *Orion* as part of a series of essays on skin.

QUESTIONS ON MEANING

1. On the surface, Jones's essay appears to be simply a definition of *skin*, but in fact she analyzes the organ to ponder the complexities of identity — both its formation, its protection of self, and its interplay with "*everything else*" (pars. 1, 6) in the world.

2. Careful self-examination, especially on a metaphysical level, can be disorienting and mind-altering. To think deeply about a physical characteristic most of us take for granted, Jones suggests, invites discomfort and anxiety.

3. *Dermatoglyphics* is the formal term for the "fluid patterns of whorls, arches, and loops" (par. 5) imprinted on a person's skin, particularly on fingertips but also on toes, palms, and soles of feet. As Jones explains, the word derives from the Greek *derma* and *glyphein* and translates to "skin carving" (5). She seems to prefer it because the word is both more exact and more evocative, its echo of the word *hieroglyphics* suggesting mysterious images with unknown (or only partially known) meanings.

4. "Your singular existence unfolds within it, but skin does not hold the universe at bay. Instead it marks the seam that joins your existence to *everything else*" (par. 6). Jones withholds her thesis statement until the end because she means for it to be a surprise.

QUESTIONS ON WRITING STRATEGY

1. Jones's essay is an analogy, an extended metaphor that uses something immediate and familiar (skin) to gain insight into something that is difficult to grasp (identity). This device, which encourages readers to apply their knowledge of the concrete subject to the writer's understanding of the abstract, allows Jones to define something complex with a minimum of words.

2. The second-person pronoun draws readers into the essay and makes each one an explicit part of Jones's definition, emphasizing their individual identities as well as their connections with others.

3. Jones's essay can be divided into its introduction (par. 1), a description of skin's appearance (2), consideration of skin's protective functions (3), contemplation of the sense of touch, both general and heightened (4, 5), and the summary/conclusion (6). Jones achieves unity by focusing each paragraph on a distinct subtopic related to skin, by starting each paragraph with a clearly stated topic sentence, and by imposing parallel structure at the sentence level, often from one paragraph to the next.

4. Fittingly, Jones's description of skin relies almost entirely on touch, with an emphasis on textures and physical sensations both pleasant and jarring. Together, her images create a dominant impression of something surprisingly complex, necessarily protective, and highly sensitive.

QUESTIONS ON LANGUAGE

1. The italics are for emphasis. The phrase is repeated in the introduction and in the conclusion, creating an effective framing device.

2. Additional examples: "heat, cold, pathogens, and the sharp edges of the world" (par. 3); "things that slash, nibble, pierce, abrade, infect, and sear" (6); "the colors of leaves in autumn, the smell of fresh-baked bread, the twining of bodies under the covers on a winter's night" (6). The parallelism creates both rhythm and a sense of unity — and calls attention to those elements that are deliberately not parallel, such as "the spark of pain when you bang your shin on the lowered door of the dishwasher." Overall, the effect is lyrical and poetic.

3. *Some metaphors*: "flimsy dermal bubble" (par. 1), "anatomical landscape" (2), "medley of textures" (2), "the sharp ache of snow" (4), "uniform carpet of bumps" (5). *Some similes*: "creases coalesce like knots on a pine board" (2), "think of the birthday suit as a membrane that separates" (6). *Some personifications*: "skin hugs the rim of a nostril" and "throws a seductive curl over the tragus" (2). Students' favorites will vary.

4. A *tragus* is that strange little piece of cartilage above the earlobe, connected to one's face. From the Greek, its literal translation is "goat."

13
ARGUMENT AND PERSUASION
Stating Opinions and Proposals

Argument and persuasion are often difficult for students to master, so the introduction to this chapter is more detailed than the others. We spell out the elements of argument, integrating the Toulmin method and the more traditional inductive and deductive reasoning. Then we cover the most common fallacies and (in the section headed "The Process") discuss possible structures for arguments. We also give emphasis to anticipating likely objections when conceiving and writing an argument.

This chapter's selections start with one piece that flies solo: "Too Much Pressure," by the student Colleen Wenke. Then we present three casebooks:

- Katha Pollitt and Charles Colson on gay marriage

- Peter F. Martin and Rodrigo Villagomez — both student writers — on steroids in sports

- Mark Krikorian, Edwidge Danticat, Linda Chavez, and Jay Nordlinger on the ongoing controversies over the status of immigrants (legal and not) in the United States. Within this foursome, Krikorian and Danticat form a pair discussing border protection and Chavez and Nordlinger form a pair tackling assimilation issues.

COLLEEN WENKE
Too Much Pressure

This student essay on the prevalence of cheating among today's students will likely strike close to home for most members of your class. As a prelude to discussion, you might have students in small groups list examples of cheating they have encountered among their peers in high school and college. What seem to be the most common forms of cheating? Is copying homework as bad as cribbing someone else's answers on a test? And what about those students who allow other students to copy their homework or who provide test questions or answers? Are they cheaters, too?

If you have a mix of younger and older students, you might ask if their experiences bear out the contention of the experts quoted by Wenke that cheating is more prevalent and acceptable among students now than it was in generations past. What percentage of high-school classmates do they think regularly cheated? Does the same hold true in college? What leads students to cheat? Does your class agree with Wenke that the pressure for grades is a primary cause? Or are there other reasons? Will any students admit to having cheated?

A larger question for discussion is what can be done to discourage cheating. If your college has guidelines for dealing with students caught cheating, this would be a good opportunity to discuss them in depth. It is also a good time to discuss plagiarism of published sources, though Wenke doesn't specifically mention it.

QUESTIONS ON MEANING

1. Wenke writes that students today who cheat are generally "college-bound overachievers . . . who are trying to juggle too many activities" (par. 6) and who are facing "too much competition" and "increased pressure to do well." Moreover, penalties for cheating are not strong enough to act as deterrents, particularly when students are more and more concerned about getting "the best grades so that they can get into the best schools and get the highest-paying jobs" (7). Increasingly, students believe that people who cheat are the ones who get ahead in life, so they find cheating "acceptable . . . as long as you don't get caught and you are getting As" (8). Thus, even students who would not normally cheat believe they must in order not to be at a disadvantage.
2. Wenke believes that cheating in school will carry over when today's students become business leaders and politicians: "In all likelihood they will not stop cheating once they get to the top" (par. 10).
3. Schools should put less emphasis on grades and more on the value of education for its own sake, on replenishing "the thirst for knowledge . . . in a student's mind" (par. 10).

QUESTIONS ON WRITING STRATEGY

1. Wenke's opening anecdote effectively conveys the pressure on students to resort to cheating in order to avoid bad grades. Her use of the pronoun *you* here suggests that she is writing at least in part to fellow students and that she wants other readers to experience firsthand the pressures students face.
2. Wenke uses sources to establish the extent to which students today actually do cheat (pars. 4, 8), to support the idea that much cheating results from the desire to get into good schools and then prosperous careers (7), and to establish that most students feel they have to cheat to compete (8–9). She also cites one writer's analysis of the causes of the increase in cheating in order to expand on his assertions (5).
3. Wenke's admission demonstrates her assertion that even those students who find cheating reprehensible feel compelled to do it at times to keep up with other students who cheat habitually. Students may differ over whether the admission enhances Wenke's ethical appeal. It makes her credible (she admits cheating) but also undermines her credibility (she has cheated).
4. Responses will vary. Some students, for instance, may think Wenke de-emphasizes the moral dimension of cheating.

QUESTIONS ON LANGUAGE

1. Examples of colloquial language include "a big fat F" (par. 1), "pull [a grade]" (2), "big deal" (3), "sucked into" (9), "in a jam" (9), and "cheat sheets" (9). Such language lends the essay the authenticity of a student's voice, although some readers may find it inconsistent with Wenke's generally more formal tone.
2. An oxymoron is a combination of contradictory words, often for poetic effect ("deafening silence," for example, or "sweet sorrow"). Wenke suggests that in the future no businessman will be honest — the two words will have become contradictory.
3. *Integrity*, from the Latin *integer*, "whole" or "complete," can refer to a state of being complete or undivided (as in the integrity of a geometric form) or to a condition that is sound or unimpaired (as in the integrity of a mechanical system). Wenke uses it in its more common sense of "adherence to a code of moral or ethical values."

KATHA POLLITT

What's Wrong with Gay Marriage?

Pollitt's essay is the first of a pair on marriage between homosexuals. She takes the "pro" position. Charles Colson, in the next essay, takes the "con." Though not directly, Pollitt in essence addresses Colson's main objections to same-sex marriage. In paragraphs 1, 2, 3, and 6 she presents opposing arguments and then refutes them. Even students who do not agree with her position should be able to learn a great deal from her model.

Students may have difficulty grasping Pollitt's conclusion about the separation of church and state. For all its religious trappings, she argues, marriage is ultimately a civil union — conferred by the government — and thus a civil right. If any man and woman can be married in the eyes of the government — no matter how ill suited — then, she asks, why should this status be denied to same-sex couples? Religious objections are irrelevant to Pollitt because religion does not figure in the civil relationship between marrying couples and the government.

One way to begin discussion might be to ask students to consider Pollitt's point in paragraph 6 that "people can live with civil unions but draw the line at marriage." What is it that makes marriage such a hot-button issue?

QUESTIONS ON MEANING

1. Pollitt first presents the argument that the fundamental purpose of marriage is procreation; this she attempts to refute by noting the fact that heterosexuals with no intention of having children are allowed to marry. Then she deals with George Gilder's claim that marriage must be a union of a man and a woman because marriage is "the way women domesticate men." She questions Gilder's premise but then says that

allowing same-sex marriage would in no way change the relationship between men and women in a heterosexual union. Finally, she presents the "argument from history" — "marriage has been around forever" — which she claims is false because marriage as currently defined does not have a particularly long history. Pollitt's implicit point here is that the concept of marriage has evolved and there is no reason it should not continue to do so.

2. Pollitt says that marriage "as we understand it" is "voluntary, monogamous, legally egalitarian, based on love, involving adults only" (par. 3); it is "love, commitment, stability" (4). Pollitt herself is not a proponent of marriage, believing that it reinforces unfairness in society and in relations between men and women.

3. Pollitt argues that the basic objection to same-sex marriage is really "religious prejudice" (par. 6) — that those who believe homosexuality to be a sin believe that same-sex marriage rewards sinful behavior.

4. Pollitt's thesis is stated at the end of paragraph 6: "People may think *marriage* is a word wholly owned by religion, but actually it's wholly owned by the state. . . . [T]wo men or two women should be able to marry, even if religions oppose it and it makes some heterosexuals, raised in those religions, uncomfortable."

QUESTIONS ON WRITING STRATEGY

1. The opening question brings to the essay a very human, somewhat grumbling voice, and it immediately establishes Pollitt's topic and viewpoint. The questions in paragraphs 2 and 5 ask readers to see that there is no affirmative answer — or that to answer affirmatively is to answer unreasonably.

2. The concessions make Pollitt sound reasonable. Still, once she makes each concession, she goes on to argue that the point conceded is not really significant.

3. The transitions make it clear where Pollitt is in her argument: Each one refers in some way to the preceding paragraph or paragraphs. (The one in par. 3 does so by asking a question that echoes par. 2's "How about: Marriage is the way women domesticate men.")

4. Some students may think that Pollitt includes the paragraph because it personalizes the essay or because it reduces the importance of marriage. Others may think that it weakens the argument because it shows that Pollitt doesn't value marriage anyway, so she wouldn't care about undermining it.

5. Pollitt identifies what she sees as the elements of the opposition to gay marriage — the subarguments to the main argument that it threatens traditional marriage.

QUESTIONS ON LANGUAGE

1. Examples of humorous language in paragraph 2 include the "husbandly failings" in various domestic crimes, "barbarian-adoption program," women "haven't been too successful at it anyway," "male-improvement project," and "heterosexual pothead with plans for murder and suicide." The language suggests that Pollitt doesn't take Gilder's argument seriously and underscores her rejection of it.

2. With the phrase "live in sin," Pollitt is adopting the language of social

conservatives for rhetorical purposes. She obviously would not agree with the characterization.

3. Putting "sacred" and "gay lifestyle" in quotation marks distances Pollitt from them: These are terms conservatives would use, but she would not.

4. The parallelism and repetition stress the contrast between the view of marriage as a solely religious institution and the reality of marriage as a government institution.

5. *Monogamous* comes from the Greek for "one" and "marriage." It originally meant being married to one person for life, but it now means being married to only one person at a time.

KATHA POLLITT ON WRITING

Pollitt's comments on poetry versus political prose might not have immediate utility for students, who after all might not write much poetry. But we include the comments because they point out an often-remarked difference that students may be unaware of.

Incidentally, students may think that Pollitt is disparaging nonfiction writing by implying that it makes a "statement" or has "only one level of meaning." Her work demonstrates that the political argument can have its own force, whether or not you agree with it.

CHARLES COLSON
Gay "Marriage": Societal Suicide

Colson's essay and the preceding one by Katha Pollitt form a pair on the issue of marriage between homosexuals. The arguments in the two essays cover opposing sides of similar points, so you'll probably want students to read and discuss the essays together.

In dealing with Colson's essay, students may have difficulty considering the effectiveness of the argument, particularly those who are opposed to same-sex marriage. Colson stresses his moral grounds for opposing gay marriage only in paragraph 8. For the most part he makes a sociological argument, linking gay marriage to an increasing "decoupling of marriage and procreation" that "would pull them completely apart, leading to an explosive increase in family collapse, out-of-wedlock births — and crime" (par. 4). His reasoning is deductive, and he offers statistics and expert opinion to back it up. In evaluating the argument, students will have to judge first whether the deduction holds up (see the first question on writing strategy). Do they agree that legalizing homosexual marriage would lead more heterosexuals to view marriage as no longer a requirement for having children and thus would increase single-parent households and societal problems?

QUESTIONS ON MEANING

1. Colson states his thesis in the final sentence of paragraph 4 and rephrases it in his concluding sentence.
2. Colson uses the example of Norway — where a rise in rates of out-of-wedlock births followed the legalization of same-sex marriage — to support the assertion (par. 6). He offers his own experience in prison ministry and the results of "[d]ozens of studies" to support the second (par. 5). We find the evidence for the first assertion shaky: It could illustrate the *post hoc* fallacy as much as a cause-and-effect relationship, and Norway is of course quite different from the United States. In paragraph 5 Colson might have bolstered his statistics by referring to their sources, but perhaps he did not see the need because, as he says at the start of paragraph 6, "Critics agree with this."
3. In paragraph 8 Colson makes a moral argument based on "[h]istory and tradition" that "[t]he family, led by a married mother and father, is the best available structure for both child rearing and cultural health." He also asserts in the final paragraph that marriage is "not a private institution designed solely for the individual gratification of its participants," though he doesn't really make a case for this point. You might ask students to consider the extent to which they can support this assertion.

QUESTIONS ON WRITING STRATEGY

1. Colson's claim is that gay marriage will cause family breakdown and societal problems. His assumption is that any form of marriage besides the traditional one will undermine the traditional one. His syllogism runs something like this: Any form of marriage besides the traditional one will lead to family breakdown and societal problems; gay marriage is not traditional; therefore, gay marriage will lead to family breakdown and societal problems.
2. With quotation marks Colson shows that he does not accept the word *marriage* when it is applied to same-sex couples.
3. The question provides an arresting opening, suggesting the worst-case scenario should same-sex unions become the law.
4. Paragraph 7 concedes an argument made by proponents of same-sex marriage: that heterosexuals themselves — including Christian heterosexuals — have weakened marriage. The concession supports Colson's reasonableness: He sees validity in the opponents' side. He then goes on to argue that the issue is not people's behavior but the institution of marriage.
5. The argument is based on cause and effect: Same-sex marriage will lead to a rise in single-parent households, which, in turn, will lead to an increasing number of children who pose a threat to themselves and society.

QUESTIONS ON LANGUAGE

1. "Lawlessness," "gleefully mocking," "egged them on," and "chaos" all have very negative connotations.
2. The words imply that same-sex marriage was forced on the people of Norway against their will. It is not clear if indeed it was.
3. Although *unorthodox* has come to be a fairly neutral word for action or belief that is not commonly accepted but not necessarily wrong,

etymologically its meaning is more like "not right or proper" (from the Greek *ortho*, "correct, right," and *doxa*, "opinion").

PETER F. MARTIN

Destroyed

Peter F. Martin wrote "Destroyed" as a sample column when he was hoping to get on the staff of the *Yale Daily News*. He figured he had "nothing to lose" for trying: "At worst," he thought, "the piece would be rejected, and I would be where I had been before I had written it." Of course that's not how things turned out: Ultimately he became a regular columnist for the paper, joined the staff of the undergraduate magazine, and continues to keep a blog at *peterfmartin.com*. Originally titled "Even More Than the Game, Drugs Destroy Athletes," Martin's first column is, we think, a good model of public argument written from strong personal conviction — and an inspiring example of the benefits to be gained by taking risks as a writer.

Martin tells us that "rereading this column now, a few years later, I see signs that this was my first one. . . . I can tell from the writing that I was trying very hard to impress readers (and my editors) with wordplay. At the same time, I was having fun with the piece. A couple of the lines are inside jokes I had with friends, or even with only myself, and they found their way into my draft because they made me smile. My editors must have liked them, because they stayed in." Martin's comment could provide an interesting starting point for class discussion: How might a sense of play and "having fun" with a piece of writing — which may not ever find an audience — contribute to its success?

We have paired this essay with "The Designer Player," which takes an unusual opposing view in favor of steroids. In that piece Rodrigo Villagomez, another student sportswriter with professional aspirations, holds that steroid use is an inevitable — and a positive — byproduct of sports as popular entertainment.

QUESTIONS ON MEANING

1. As Martin says, he agrees "to a point" (par. 5). Although he accuses steroid-using players of cheating and says that they "challenge the ideals of sports, passed down to us from the Greeks" (10), his sarcastic tone early in the essay suggests that he thinks such concerns are overblown and beside the point.
2. Martin has some concerns about the effect of steroids on sports overall, but his primary objection is that steroids threaten the health and the lives of the players themselves.
3. Martin states his thesis in his final paragraph: "Athletes — those who dope, who take steroids, who cheat — are victims of far more serious maladies than their sports."
4. Martin's concluding statement is complicated and will probably confuse some readers. It may take a second or third reading to catch that his

reference to "humans like the rest of us" harks back to earlier points about Greek athletes, who "more closely resembled real people" (par. 10) and who played "to honor the powers above" (7). On one level, Martin seems to suggest that steroids transform athletes into gods, but at the same time he is subtly invoking athletes' position as role models and reiterating his warning that steroids will kill them.

QUESTIONS ON WRITING STRATEGY

1. Martin intends these questions to get his readers to think about the nature and origin of rules governing sports. The questions suggest that definitions of *cheating* are somewhat arbitrary.
2. Martin's example — the premature death of the steroid-using baseball MVP Ken Caminiti — establishes his claim that steroids are dangerous to those who take them, that players "will pay the price with their own lives" (par. 11).
3. By placing his thesis at the end of the essay and acknowledging the prevailing view so strongly ("those who dope, who take steroids, who cheat"), Martin seems to acknowledge that his argument could be a tough sell. He is trying less to change people's minds than to spark some conversation and some reexamination of current assumptions.
4. Students should see that the entire argument is one of cause and effect, with steroid use being the cause and damage to sports and to players being the effects.

QUESTIONS ON LANGUAGE

1. Most students will catch on to Martin's point that the original Olympians competed naked. He is suggesting that any kind of sports equipment — even clothing — is to some extent a performance enhancer and that there are no clear lines to be drawn concerning what kinds of "objects, artifacts, or chemicals" exceed the limits of "fair play" (par. 7).
2. The prefix *extra-* means "outside or beyond." *Extra-human*, then, refers to items — tools, essentially — that enhance or adorn the body but are not part of it. The term is related to, but not quite the same in meaning as, both *inhuman* and *superhuman*, depending on a reader's perspective.
3. *Doping* is a slang term for injecting or ingesting steroids or other substances to enhance athletic performance. Students may be surprised to learn that the slang, and its current usage, dates back to 1900, or so *Merriam Webster Online* tells us.

PETER F. MARTIN ON WRITING

Martin's attention to audience is good practice for any writer. We love his message that audience is important no matter how small or large it might be. But like Martin, students may find that the more they keep their readers in mind, the more their readership will grow.

RODRIGO VILLAGOMEZ
The Designer Player

A baseball "fanatic" and a broadcast professional, student writer Rodrigo Villagomez writes here to come to the defense of athletes who have been "vilified" for using steroids. Basing his position on a point similar to that made by Colleen Wenke in "Too Much Pressure" (p. 564), Villagomez argues that players have no choice but to take performance enhancing drugs if they want to thrive in the highly competitive world of professional baseball. He takes that point further, though, insisting that steroids be credited for keeping the game relevant and successful as popular entertainment and urging readers to thank the players for using such supplements.

In assigning this essay, you'll probably want to make sure that students are aware of Villagomez's role as an experienced sports announcer striving for a broadcast career. Ask whether they think his background affects his perspective or how others might respond to it. (Villagomez brings this up himself in his comments on writing that follow the essay.)

We have paired "The Designer Player" with the preceding essay, "Destroyed," by Peter F. Martin, because the writers tackle similar claims yet reach opposing conclusions on the issue. Villagomez does not respond directly to Martin, but he does draw on some of the same examples and does explicitly reject many of the arguments Martin promotes. The "Connections" writing topic after Villagomez's essay encourages students to explore such similarities and contradictions.

QUESTIONS ON MEANING

1. Villagomez states his thesis at the end of his introduction: "Many believe that these drugs decrease the integrity of the players and ultimately the game itself. But if it were not for the small percentage of players who have recently been found to use steroids, baseball would not be enjoying the success it does today" (par. 1). In stating the major opposing view as part of his thesis statement, Villagomez makes clear that he assumes readers hold that opposing view.
2. Steroids help "build muscle mass" (par. 2) quickly and, combined with "an over-the-top workout schedule" (3), give batters more powerful swings (6). Villagomez also mentions medical applications for steroids, breast cancer treatment in particular, but doesn't elaborate (5). Students' views on these benefits will vary, of course.
3. Villagomez cites and immediately dismisses opponents' concerns about steroids: that they amount to cheating (par. 3), that "using is an attack on baseball's integrity" (4), and that they damage users' health (5). The only drawback he accepts as valid is that steroid-enhanced bulk alone can hurt a batter's swing (3).
4. Baseball players take steroids to improve their performance. As Villagomez sees it, they feel pressured to do this because paying fans expect ever "greater levels of strength and prowess" (par. 1) and demand to be entertained.

QUESTIONS ON WRITING STRATEGY

1. By emphasizing the business and entertainment aspects of professional baseball, and portraying players as cogs in a corporate machine, Villagomez is trying to reframe the terms of the debate over steroids.
2. The arrangement of opposing views presumably corresponds to Villagomez's sense of their importance, most (fair play and integrity) to least (players' health). Some students may have a different set of priorities (notice, for instance, that Peter F. Martin, in the preceding essay, considers health of paramount importance) or may have preferred that Villagomez build to the most important objection.
3. The seasons, and the players, that Villagomez discusses in paragraph 7 are widely considered the original catalyst for the ongoing controversy over steroids in baseball and other sports. The home-run competition between Mark McGwire and Sammy Sosa was treated as an epic battle by the media, and even casual fans got caught up in "the excitement of it all" (par. 7). Both players were later revealed to be steroid users — a revelation that for many observers ruined the fun and the game itself and sparked hours upon hours of angry commentary on talk radio. The example anchors Villagomez's argument that steroid-enhanced play excites fans and revives interest in the game and that accusations of foul play, not steroids themselves, are the real problem.
4. Paragraphs 1, 6, and 7 rely on cause and effect to trace a relationship between steroid use and the continuing popularity of professional baseball. As Villagomez sees it, steroids help make players more capable of hitting home runs, which gets fans excited, which makes the game popular. Without steroids, Villagomez believes, the game would be boring and fans would stop watching. (Conversely, without baseball's status as a lucrative entertainment vehicle, there would be no need for players to enhance their performance by taking steroids.)

QUESTIONS ON LANGUAGE

1. "Reluctant hero" suggests that professional baseball players are victims of their own success, that they didn't ask to be role models but are nonetheless looked up to by fans and held to unrealistic standards.
2. Villagomez's overall tone strikes us as both jaded and dismissive, as in "so why the big fuss over steroids?" (par. 2) or "Baseball has not been a fair game for years" (4). The tone does seem to suit Villagomez's argument, emphasizing both the pointlessness of "[a]rguing over the integrity of a product meant for entertainment" (8) and the author's somewhat ambivalent acceptance of a practice that makes that product more entertaining.
3. *Partake*, "to participate," is usually used in connection with festivities and indulgences and carries strong positive connotations. By using the word to refer to performance-enhancing drugs, Villagomez subtly signals his approval of, even admiration for, those who use steroids — and suggests that those who "choose not to" (par. 4) are depriving themselves.

RODRIGO VILLAGOMEZ ON WRITING

Villagomez found that his ethos, or credibility as a writer, was affected by his role as a sports announcer on his campus. His position both gave him the expertise to write about the topic he chose and caused his readers to criticize his opinion. You might discuss ethical appeals with students in terms of how their experiences and identities might affect their writing — and their readers' perception of it.

MARK KRIKORIAN

Safety through Immigration Control

Mark Krikorian's is the first essay in a four-selection casebook focusing on immigration issues. This essay pairs specifically with the following one by Edwidge Danticat: Danticat argues that overzealous immigration enforcement denies asylum to people who need it and at the same time adds to their suffering; Krikorian argues that strict enforcement is essential to protect the country from potential terrorists.

In teaching the Krikorian and Danticat essays together, you may want to help students see how different their argumentative strategies are on the surface: Danticat writes personally and relies for evidence on examples of detainees and their conditions, whereas Krikorian takes a more distanced, impersonal, and logical approach that cites research and expert opinions. At the same time, however, both rely heavily on emotional appeals — though of different kinds and for different effect. You might ask students to consider why the subject of immigration lends itself to emotional appeals on both sides of the issue.

QUESTIONS ON MEANING

1. A possible summary of Krikorian's thesis is stated in paragraph 5: "[K]eeping the terrorists out, or apprehending them after they get in, is indispensable to victory [over terrorism]."
2. Krikorian criticizes the 9/11 Commission for "devoting inordinate attention . . . to peripheral issues, such as who sent what memo to whom" (par. 1), when it should, he implies, be focused on immigration policy.
3. The United States must fight a battle on two fronts. The military's focus is on the enemy overseas, while civilian agencies — in particular those under the Department of Homeland Security — are responsible for focusing on the enemy on the home front. For attacks to be carried out on US soil, terrorists must get into the country; to fight terrorism, "immigration control is central."
4. As Krikorian states in paragraph 7, the immigration system should exercise more control over visas issued abroad, those people admitted into the country, and foreigners once they are in the country. He also makes the point that the focus should be people from around the world, not just those from the Middle East.

QUESTIONS ON WRITING STRATEGY

1. In his opening paragraph, Krikorian suggests that so-called experts do not take the link between national security and immigration control as seriously as they should, even denying that the bombings of 9/11 "can be attributed to the failure of our immigration laws." In the second paragraph he then says that "ordinary people," in contrast, recognize the "link between immigration and security." Thus he appeals to readers' common sense.

2. While Krikorian's argument is based on a rational appeal, the logic at the center of the argument is essentially deductive: We want to prevent terrorist attacks on US soil. Strict immigration control is essential to prevent terrorist attacks. Therefore, we need to institute strict immigration control. His ethical appeal is that of a reasonable person concerned for his country's security and open to solutions in addition to the one he proposes (par. 8). His emotional appeals include use of *our enemies* and *the enemy*, the commonsense appeal to "ordinary people" (2), the appeals to fear in "mass killings of civilians on American soil" (3) and "lack of effective immigration control leaves us naked" (8), and the appeal to the desire for safety in the equation of the Department of Homeland Security and the military (4).

3. Krikorian offers the evidence of expert opinions (pars. 3 and 7) and the results of a research study (6). The responses of students may depend on the degree to which they agree with Krikorian's claim.

4. In his concluding paragraph, Krikorian concedes that there is more to preventing domestic terrorist attacks than just ensuring effective immigration control, and he names other measures. He then goes on to restate the need for immigration control in strong terms.

QUESTIONS ON LANGUAGE

1. On carousels at carnivals and amusement parks, riders can sometimes earn a prize by grabbing a brass ring as they pass. *Brass ring* has come to be a general term for something highly desirable. Krikorian uses the phrase to mean, essentially, "top prize."

2. In battlefield and catastrophic medicine, the principle of triage involves dividing patients into three groups: those who will die anyway whether or not they receive medical attention, those who will survive anyway whether or not they receive medical attention, and those who will survive only if they receive immediate medical attention. This third group is given priority treatment. Krikorian uses the term in its more general sense, of establishing priorities to use limited resources where they can be most effective.

3. *Asymmetric* warfare and *fourth-generation warfare* are terms that were coined by military scholars to describe conflicts in which one side is not an established government but an army of rebels or guerrillas or terrorists working to disrupt a government.

4. *Naturalized citizens* are immigrants who have taken all the steps necessary to be admitted as citizens of a country; with a few exceptions (such as serving as president), they have the same rights as native-born citizens. *Naturalize* may come from the reference to plants that have established themselves in an area as if they were native.

EDWIDGE DANTICAT

Not Your Homeland

Edwidge Danticat's is the second essay focusing on issues of US immigration policy in the aftermath of September 11, 2001. An immigrant from Haiti, which for decades has been embroiled in violence, Danticat attempts to persuade readers that the national security of the United States does not require detaining Haitian asylum seekers in deplorable, sometimes fatal, conditions. These detainees are not terrorists and mean no harm to the United States, she says; in fact, they look upon the United States as a haven that will protect them.

The essay's headnote provides some background on the strife in Haiti that causes refugees to come to the United States. Many travel in small boats that are barely able to make the crossing. They are often intercepted by the Coast Guard before landing and are taken directly back to Haiti. Those who do make it ashore are considered illegal immigrants and can stay in the country only after proving that they face significant persecution in their home country. Failing such proof, they face deportation or the kind of detention that Danticat describes. US immigration authorities claim that most Haitians are fleeing poverty in their country, not persecution. Advocates for the Haitians point out that Cubans in similar circumstances are generally allowed to remain in the United States, and several independent panels have accused the Department of Homeland Security of failing to give asylum seekers a hearing as required by law.

Danticat's essay is an interesting example of an argument that depends almost entirely on emotional appeals: descriptions of a variety of detainees and their circumstances. (Students moved by the fate suffered by Danticat's uncle may be interested in her 2007 book, *Brother, I'm Dying*, which extends the story she tells in this essay and goes into great detail about the political unrest in Haiti and its personal and sociological consequences.) The essay that precedes this one, by Mark Krikorian, is also based significantly on emotional appeals, but in arguing for strict immigration enforcement he appeals to readers' concerns about possible terrorist attacks on US soil.

Danticat's and Krikorian's essays raise the issue of what justifies infringement on individual rights. Some of your students may believe that future terrorist attacks must be prevented at almost any cost, while others may think that the government has gone too far in singling out certain groups for scrutiny. You might divide students into discussion groups (the more balance in each group the better) so they can speak their minds and can hear one another's ideas.

QUESTIONS ON MEANING

1. In paragraph 11 Danticat refers to statements by former attorney general John Ashcroft that Pakistani and Palestinian terrorists are able to take refuge in Haiti. She thinks little of this justification because the government has offered no proof of the charge.
2. According to Danticat, most of those Haitians seeking asylum in the United States are fleeing their country to avoid being hurt or killed for

their political views or for crossing the gangs that control parts of the country. These conditions suggest that Haiti is a country where lawlessness, violence, and corruption prevail.

3. Danticat states her thesis in her final three sentences. A restatement of the first of the three might read, "The United States must figure out a way to make itself secure without harming those who seek refuge for their safety."

4. Clearly, Danticat wants readers both to feel sympathy for Haitian asylum seekers and to seek to change the policies that cause the Haitians' detention or deportation. Students will think that she has succeeded if they accept that the detainees mean no harm to the United States and suffer in their detention.

QUESTIONS ON WRITING STRATEGY

1. The essay is organized into four sections. Paragraphs 1 through 5 focus on the Haitian women and children held at the Comfort Suites, while paragraphs 6 through 10 focus on the Haitian men held in the Krome Detention Center. Paragraphs 11 and 12 consider the plight of a young Haitian man, and the final paragraphs tell the story of Danticat's uncle, who died while in detention. Each section provides examples of greater hardship than those in the previous section — the families held in a motel; the men held in a cold, dank prison; the young man deported back to likely death; Danticat's uncle actually dying in custody. The sections develop climactically to stress the injustice of the policies.

2. Danticat may assume that readers know something of the situation in Haiti: She doesn't spell it out, but at several points, she makes it plain that life there can be dangerous — for example, in the story of her uncle (pars. 15-16). Given the detail she provides about the circumstances of detention, she evidently assumes that readers know little or nothing about them.

3. Danticat's appeal is clearly emotional. She attempts to elicit sympathy for the people she writes about by describing their innocence, their initial hopefulness that the United States would take them in, and the hardships they face in detention: The women and children are crowded into their motel rooms, not allowed to leave; the men occupy cold cells, face arbitrary curfews, and sometimes suffer beatings. As for David Joseph and Danticat's uncle, both are also described as innocents who fled Haiti to save their lives; Joseph's deportation occurred despite an immigration judge's decision that he should be released, and the uncle, a priest, died while in custody.

4. Danticat writes about herself at several points: she describes her parents taking her to a Brooklyn detention center to meet Haitian asylum seekers who, in her father's words, "could have very well been us" (par. 5); she mentions meeting a detainee who came from a part of Haiti where she once lived (10); she says that she was denied access to her uncle for "security reasons" (16); and she refers again to her father's words (17). Interjecting herself shows that Danticat is not a disinterested bystander, but is affected directly by the policies she argues against.

5. The death of Danticat's uncle is especially poignant and pointless. The narrative covers his encounter with Haitian gang members, his hiding and eventual flight to the United States, his detention, and his death. She frames the narration with the date the police and UN forces attacked the gang that would threaten him and the date her uncle died while in

US detention. The fact that the two dates are only ten days apart amplifies the tragedy.

QUESTIONS ON LANGUAGE

1. A parable is a story that illustrates a moral. In this case, the parable equates the conditions in Haiti with mad dogs and the United States with the neighbor who should shelter the people escaping the dogs.
2. Alcatraz is a former maximum-security prison on an island in San Francisco Bay. Also known as "the Rock," it was notoriously Spartan and escape-proof. Alcatraz crossed with hell would be a decidedly terrible place to be incarcerated.
3. The quotation marks indicate that Danticat uses *peacekeepers* ironically. The UN forces have not kept the peace.
4. *Tangible* comes from the Latin *tangere*, "to touch," and literally means "capable of being perceived by touch." It has come to mean, as Danticat uses it, "capable of being realized by the mind."

EDWIDGE DANTICAT ON WRITING

Danticat's experience as a young immigrant using English will probably resonate with students who are also immigrants. In turn, their experiences should interest the native English speakers in the class, who may not have considered the challenges and rewards of adapting simultaneously to a new culture and its language.

LINDA CHAVEZ
Supporting Family Values

The third essay in a four-selection casebook focusing on controversies over immigration policy and attitudes in the United States, Linda Chavez's argument is the first of two that looks at issues of assimilation. Like Jay Nordlinger, whose essay follows hers, Chavez is a politically conservative writer concerned with Spanish-speaking immigrants to the United States, but unlike Nordlinger, she hails from a Spanish-speaking background and believes fully in immigrants' willingness and ability to adapt to American life and culture. Even more, Chavez suggests, that same group of immigrants so often vilified as lazy, uneducated, or criminal are in fact exemplars of virtue and should be honored, even rewarded, for their moral contributions to American society.

This essay is notable for using conservative ideals (family values) to argue for liberal policy (amnesty for illegal immigrants). Students may have some difficulty reconciling two points of view that would seem almost mutually exclusive, but we find it quite clever of Chavez to intertwine them in such a way that neither position can be easily refuted: As Chavez presents her argument, readers on either side of the conservative-liberal divide have little choice but to accept at least part of their opponents' way of thinking.

Although we have paired "Supporting Family Values" with Jay Nordlinger's "Bassackwards," note that Linda Chavez's essay also has strong thematic and argumentative ties with Edwidge Danticat's "Not Your Homeland," in which the author makes a strong emotional appeal for granting amnesty to a group of immigrant refugees.

QUESTIONS ON MEANING

1. Chavez opens her essay by noting it was prompted by a "new report out this week from the Pew Hispanic Center" (par. 1), but perceptive readers will notice from her remarks in the final two paragraphs that her argument was inspired as well by the ongoing conflict between efforts to aggressively identify and deport illegal immigrants and proposals to offer amnesty to illegal immigrants who meet certain criteria.

2. Although she mentions slight differences in family structure, education level, and income among illegal and legal immigrants, the only real distinction Chavez makes between the two groups is their legal status. Especially because so many immigrant families consist of both illegal and legal residents, Chavez suggests, the distinctions are practically meaningless.

3. Chavez's comparison of attitudes toward current Mexican and "other Latin American" immigrants with attitudes toward European immigrants of a century ago is a commonly used argument in favor of relaxed immigration controls. Her point is that a century of experience has shown that immigrants do assimilate into the larger culture over time and that fears of unfamiliar ethnic groups are unfounded. At the same time, because most of her readers are presumably of European heritage, Chavez subtly chides them for perpetuating the same hostilities that were once directed at their own ancestors — and reassures them that Spanish-speaking immigrants will, indeed, become an integral part of American culture if given the opportunity.

4. Chavez's purpose is revealed in the last two paragraphs: She is writing to argue in favor of "granting amnesty" to a qualified category of illegal immigrants. Her thesis might best be expressed in the penultimate sentence: "A better approach [to deportation] would allow those who have made their lives here, established families, bought homes, worked continuously and paid taxes to remain after paying fines, demonstrating English fluency, and proving they have no criminal record." By withholding her thesis and purpose until the end, Chavez acknowledges that her position will be difficult for readers to accept; she therefore fully makes her case before letting them in on what she wants them to believe.

QUESTIONS ON WRITING STRATEGY

1. Chavez characterizes opponents as unreasonable to the point of hysteria, referring to "hard-line immigration restrictionists," "alarm" (par. 2); "fear" (5); "worries [that] are no more rational today — or born out of actual evidence — than they were a hundred years ago" (6); and "popular but uninformed opinion" (8). In doing so, Chavez suggests that some readers may hold these views, yet she forces them to reexamine their

beliefs by portraying them as irrational. She seems to trust that most of her readers — "the rest of us" (2) — are reasonable people who can be persuaded to change their minds if presented with sufficient information.

2. Chavez states her main assumption in paragraph 2: "One of the chief social problems afflicting this country is the breakdown in the traditional family." Many readers, especially those of a conservative medium like *townhall.com*, will presumably share the writer's concern about family values; others will reject it outright. In either case, readers are likely to find Chavez's approach creative at the very least.

3. Chavez appeals to both reason and emotion. She is careful to base her argument on statistical evidence from a published report in paragraphs 1, 3, 6, 7, and 8, using the numbers to draw inferences about the character, values, and potential for success of undocumented Spanish-speaking immigrants, especially as they compare to legal immigrants and native-born families. But she appeals to emotion throughout, citing both family values and fears of cultural disintegration as she makes her case.

4. Chavez names three categories of American "households" in paragraph 3: native, legal, and illegal. As she explains, native families are the least likely to be "made up of two parents living with their own children," while a third of legal immigrant households and nearly half of all illegal immigrant households consist of traditional nuclear families. The point is central to her argument that immigrant families represent a positive influence on the rest of the country and should therefore be supported and encouraged, not broken apart by deportation or harassment.

QUESTIONS ON LANGUAGE

1. *Amnesty* is a political term for a government's pardon of illegal activities; in Chavez's case, it refers explicitly to ongoing proposals to grant legal status to illegal residents who have nonetheless established themselves successfully. The word comes from the same Latin and Greek roots as *amnesia*, or forgetting.

2. By "native" Chavez means those born in the United States and thus automatically granted citizenship. There are at least two layers of irony in her use of the term: First is the subtle reference to Native Americans, the peoples who were displaced with the first wave of European settlement in the fifteenth century; but Chavez also points out that nearly three-quarters of the children of illegal immigrants are "American-born" (par. 1) and thus citizens — a fact that complicates the issue of deportation, especially for readers with a strong interest in family values.

3. Most students will likely find Chavez's tone reasonable and levelheaded, even appealing. The diction is for the most part plain; Chavez avoids sarcasm and hectoring; and as she concludes she becomes somewhat informal, saying her evidence "should give pause to those who'd like to see all illegal immigrants rounded up and deported or their lives made so miserable they leave on their own."

LINDA CHAVEZ ON WRITING

Chavez's nostalgia for the old days of sentence diagramming might prompt students to reflect on their own grammatical education. How were they taught the rules? You might point out that understanding the rules is different from following them. Plenty of writers occasionally write "incorrect" sentences, but they do so on purpose and for a particular effect. Readers can tell the difference between intentional rule breaking and error.

JAY NORDLINGER

Bassackwards: Construction Spanish and Other Signs of the Times

Jay Nordlinger's is the final essay on US immigration policy and attitudes. A conservative writer with a strong sense of social justice and human rights, Nordlinger attempts to persuade readers that accommodating immigrants by learning to speak at least a little of their languages, while well-intentioned, ultimately hurts those immigrants and the nation as a whole.

We pair Nordlinger with Chavez before him because both writers are concerned with Spanish-speaking immigrants in particular and because, while both profess to support and respect those immigrants, the authors hold nearly opposite assumptions regarding immigrants' abilities, motivations, and influences on the larger American culture. Both essays come down to issues of assimilation versus acculturation, yet Nordlinger prefers the former while Chavez takes a strong interest in the possibilities of the latter. (Students may not recognize the distinction between the two concepts; for help explaining it, see number 4 under "Questions on Language," below.) The "Connections" writing suggestion encourages students to consider what *assimilation* means and whom it affects, and you could ask them to develop their ideas in class or, if you teach online, via a discussion group. Students' responses may depend as much on the diversity of their own communities (and classrooms) as on their politics.

QUESTIONS ON MEANING

1. Nordlinger believes that "the predominance of Hispanics" (par. 6) in particular fields, construction and maintenance especially, is the "obvious reason" (6) behind classes and books in Spanish for managers who need to communicate with their workers. He faults immigrants for failing to learn English but also employers and government representatives for "coddl[ing]" (1) Spanish speakers.
2. Nordlinger objects to the development on multiple grounds. For one, he says, it used to be that immigrants made an effort to learn enough English to get by (an assertion some readers might be quick to refute); he considers Spanish in the workplace "a gross act of separatism" (par. 14); he feels that "Survival Spanish" puts the onus of adjustment on people who are under no obligation to adjust; and most significant to Nordlinger, he believes that learning workplace Spanish to accommodate them insults immigrants' intelligence and oppresses them by hampering their ability to succeed in American work and life. Nordlinger makes it

quite clear that he would prefer that immigrants learn English.
3. By "we" Nordlinger means the nation as a whole — native citizens and immigrants alike. He doesn't say so directly, but he suggests throughout the essay that if immigrants reject "Americanization" the United States will lose its unity, becoming a fractured society of separate national identities.
4. Nordlinger is examining the implications of a recent trend — "Survival Spanish" classes for employers — to uncover its causes and to warn of the potential consequences for American culture. He hopes to spur his readers to rebel against the trend or, at the very least, to alarm them.

QUESTIONS ON WRITING STRATEGY

1. Nordlinger addresses readers in the second person in paragraphs 5–7, describing the books and classes available to employers and imagining how his readers (or their ancestors) would have approached language acquisition as new immigrants. The three paragraphs reveal that Nordlinger assumes his audience consists of English speakers and, more to the point, members of the managerial class.
2. Nordlinger focuses on the issue because it captures a significant part of his argument and because his correspondents' experiences and opinions reinforce his own. Presumably most of his readers — educated professionals — will have had similar experiences in their own workplaces but perhaps not given them much thought. Students may vary in evaluating the effectiveness of this extended example, but they should recognize that Nordlinger is portraying himself as a friend to those workers, someone with their best interests at heart.
3. Nordlinger gives multiple examples drawn from personal experience, published sources, and correspondence to demonstrate his knowledge of the issue. At the same time, he stresses throughout the essay that he respects the Spanish language and those who speak it. Some examples of Nordlinger's direct ethical appeals include his assertion that "[m]any Hispanics wrote of their frustration and resentment at having been shunted into Spanish-only classes" (16); his reference to a personal friendship with a Spanish-speaking janitor (21); his frustration in knowing that he will be accused "of being a jingo, boob, or xenophobe" (24); and his assurance that he likes "Spanish as much as the next guy — actually, considerably more" (26). How well he succeeds with individual readers will depend somewhat on their own perspectives on the issue, but he certainly makes the effort.
4. Nordlinger's evidence is almost entirely anecdotal, consisting of narrative examples from his own experience and those of *National Review* readers who have written to him to share their own stories.

QUESTIONS ON LANGUAGE

1. The phrase translates, "For Spanish, press 2." Callers to automated phone systems hear the phrase all the time, and most English speakers can figure out what it means, although they don't need to know its meaning in order to complete their call. Similarly, the translation isn't relevant to Nordlinger's purpose, as he suggests when he says, "We could talk about 'For English, press 1. *Para español, oprima el dos.*' But let's talk, instead, about Construction Spanish" (par. 2).

2. The phrase suggests a lost battle, a concept Nordlinger returns to in paragraph 13, when he calls himself "a veteran of the Spanish wars." As he portrays it, English-language acquisition is an element of an epic fight for the survival of American identity and culture.

3. Sarcastic elements begin with Nordlinger's title ("Bassackwards") and continue throughout the essay. Some examples: "they will not be reading *Don Quixote*" (par. 3); "We must put off such foolish questions" (4); "Hooray!" (7); "Not by encouraging their assimilation, that's for sure" (8); "(Really.)" (9); "That didn't go over terribly well" (15); and "Oh." (23). Such sarcastic moments express the writer's frustration with the situation he describes. They also add some humor to the essay and (assuming readers agree with it) strengthen the author's bond with his audience.

4. *Acculturation* is not quite a synonym of *assimilation*. While *assimilation* implies subsuming one's native culture to the dominant culture of a new country; *acculturation* refers both to the gradual absorption of the norms of any culture (including that to which a person is born), as well as to the mutual changing influences of multiple cultures upon each other.

MIXING THE METHODS

In this part of the book we provide an anthology, arranged alphabetically by author, of twelve works by very well-known writers. The collection has a dual purpose. First, we want to widen the tight focus of the previous ten chapters so that students see the methods as a kit of tools to be used *in combination* as the need arises. All twelve selections demonstrate just this flexibility in approach, narrating here, comparing there, analyzing a process for a couple of paragraphs, defining a term when helpful. The headnote to each selection lists the methods the author most relies on, pointing to specific paragraphs. And the introduction to Part Three gives students a list of questions — a kind of crib sheet of the methods — that they can use to explore or focus any subject.

The second goal of this anthology is to give you more leeway in your assignments. You can teach this part as a "mixing the methods" unit, of course, but you can also pluck out individual selections for any number of uses. If you want to show how a particular method works with other methods, you can point to, say, the cause and effect in Cisneros's "Only Daughter" or the description in White's "Once More to the Lake." If you're just seeking another example of a particular method, you can turn to, say, King's "I Have a Dream" for argument and persuasion or Orwell's "Shooting an Elephant" for narration. If you think students will respond to the thematic pairing of White's "Once More to the Lake" with Brad Manning's "Arm Wrestling with My Father" (in Chap. 5), you can assign them together.

We have highlighted the possible links in several ways. As we mentioned above, the headnote to each essay in this part itemizes the main methods used by the author. Among the writing suggestions for each selection in this part is at least one "Connections" topic that pulls in an essay from Part Two. For more general thematic links among selections, we provide a "Thematic Table of Contents" just after the book's main contents.

SANDRA CISNEROS
Only Daughter

This much-reprinted essay is sure to resonate with any students who have shared Cisneros's frustrations with a parent's lack of support for their interests and goals. For students who are children of immigrants, the essay may be especially affecting because cultural differences often exacerbate the normal parent-child conflicts.

Two possible approaches to discussing this essay: Focus on how your students define *success* and the degree to which their families contribute to that definition, directly or indirectly; or focus on how differences between parents and children nourish or thwart the children. For either approach, students will be drawing on their own experiences, so small groups may encourage freer discussion than a whole-class setting. Hearing their classmates' experiences and ideas will broaden students' own perspectives and prepare them for work on the first, second, and third writing suggestions.

QUESTIONS ON MEANING

1. Cisneros's main purpose is to show how being her father's only daughter and living with her father's indifference to her writing contributed to her choice of writing as a career.
2. Being the only daughter left Cisneros to herself (par. 3), allowed her to attend college (4), allowed her to major in English and "putter about" with writing (5), led her to seek her father's approval (7–8), and (she implies) led her to seek recognition (12).
3. All writers are "trying to woo" a public. Cisneros describes her father and the public as "uninterested in reading" and as those she is writing "about and for."
4. Cisneros had succeeded, finally, in impressing her father with her writing. She had won her "public" (par. 8).

QUESTIONS ON WRITING STRATEGY

1. Cisneros seems to be writing for an audience wider than Mexican Americans: She takes pains to explain the effects of being the only daughter in a Mexican American family, and she translates all the Spanish words she uses.
2. We can infer that Cisneros writes serious literature. The implicit contrast between her work and her father's reading material is particularly illuminating.
3. The opening definition establishes the range of formative experiences that Cisneros goes on to explain in more detail. To us, it is quite effective.
4. The incident was obviously crucial to Cisneros, as her last sentence makes clear. By recalling it in great detail, down to the "one black sock and a plastic urinal" in her father's bedroom (par. 18), she conveys both her own heightened awareness at the time and the suspense of eliciting her father's reaction.

QUESTIONS ON LANGUAGE

1. "Only daughter" expresses the specialness of being unique and perhaps the loneliness of being sisterless. "*Only* a daughter" retracts some of the specialness by implying that a daughter is not as good as a son.
2. Cisneros expresses some resentment in "As if he deserved a medal from the state" (par. 11). Her word "erased" to describe her feeling and her "tug at my father's sleeve" (12) convey the hurt she experienced and the urgency she brought to correcting her father.
3. *Philandering* has had an interesting history. Originally from the Greek word for a woman who loves her husband (*phil-*, "love," and *andr-*, "man"), it came to mean "loving" generally and now refers to the behavior of a man who has casual sexual affairs.

SANDRA CISNEROS ON WRITING

There's more evidence of the rhythmic possibilities for the bilingual writer in Cisneros's fiction than in "Only Daughter." Still, students might comment on how they're affected by the use of Spanish words in the essay. In class, bilingual students may offer their sense of how their versatility has affected their prose. How do they handle the issue of "translation" for an audience? How much are they required to translate?

JOAN DIDION

In Bed

Joan Didion is a novelist and essayist well known for her searching insights into many aspects of American life. Here she turns her gaze inward, examining migraines with medical detail and firsthand experience. Through her perspective, we view a migraine first as a shameful weakness, then as a debilitating barrier to normal life, and finally, in a Zen-like relationship, as a "friend." "In Bed" is a rich essay, and only if students read it carefully will they grasp the best part of what Didion provides.

The essay gives an opportunity to talk to students about control: Which parts of their lives do they have direct control over? What lies beyond their control? What can they gain from the latter? Does Didion gain the upper hand in her concession to the migraine's power, or has it defeated her?

Another approach is to ask students to discuss the essay in small groups: Provide them with some focus by asking that they list the annoyances and travails of life that are best met with the calm acceptance Didion exemplifies in the end of her essay. Examples could range from weather and traffic jams to disabilities such as migraines and the loss of loved ones.

For further reading, a good source of interviews with Didion and critical essays on her work is *Joan Didion: Essays and Conversations*, edited by Ellen G. Friedman (1984).

QUESTIONS ON MEANING

1. The main differences between migraines and ordinary headaches are that migraines are vascular headaches, preceded in most cases by an "aura," and sufferers apparently inherit a predisposition to migraine.
2. Didion explains her shame in the last sentence of paragraph 1 and the first sentence of paragraph 2. She must have been accused more than once of being a hypochondriac; her essay answers such accusations by outlining the very real medical and personal details of migraine.
3. That she is apparently a tense person with a "migraine personality" is expressed most directly in the final sentence of paragraph 6. Her perfectionism manifests itself in the way she approaches her writing.
4. Students' responses will vary. The idea is that Didion's relief from pain is so intense as to be euphoric.

QUESTIONS ON WRITING STRATEGY

1. Didion uses the first person whenever her description is subjective and the third person when she imparts objective information, switching from one to the other and back again several times in the essay.
2. Notable images of suffering appear in paragraphs 2 ("threw up in washrooms, stumbled home by instinct, . . . tried to freeze the pain in my right temple") and 5 ("an abrupt overpowering fatigue, a strokelike aphasia, and a crippling inability . . ."). The symptoms of migraine are overpowering, and the language describing them is just as strong. In paragraph 5 Didion also writes: "The actual headache, when it comes, brings with it chills, sweating, nausea, a debility that seems to stretch the very limits of endurance." "Stretch" is a wonderfully pain-filled verb in this context. The "pounding terror" in paragraph 8 and the final three sentences also provide sensuous details, all of which help make Didion's sense of pain and its aftermath come alive.
3. Didion exaggerates (with some humor) to convey that the pain of the migraine is terrible. Her amusing use of hyperbole helps to gain the empathy of "unafflicted" (para. 6) skeptics — who might well have come to the essay under the assumption that migraine is all in the sufferer's head — without alienating them.
4. The examples demonstrate the seriousness of her incapacitation and reasons it is "an ambiguous blessing" not to die of migraine.
5. The process analysis in paragraphs 3–4 broadens Didion's perspective to explain the known facts of migraine: We see that the author shares the malady with others, and we understand something of its physiology. Then, in paragraphs 7–8, the analysis shows how Didion copes personally with migraine, ending climactically with her ability to "count her blessings."

QUESTIONS ON LANGUAGE

1. We'd opt for colorful, and add that it is precise and accurate as well.
2. Perhaps the title led students to expect a different essay, but "In Bed" seems a good choice for summing up the helpless prostration caused by migraine.
3. "Circumnavigation" implies exploration and, in this case, deliberate indirection. "Guerilla war" suggests evasion, sneakiness, an unwillingness

(or inability) to fight openly. The "circuit breaker" halts the short circuits of resentments and anxieties that preceded the migraine.

4. *Contretemps* was originally a fencing term for a pass or thrust made at the wrong time. Its contemporary, general meaning is related: an unexpected or unfortunate event that disturbs things.

JOAN DIDION ON WRITING

Didion's comments on writing seem apt from a writer noted for observation. She has, however, been criticized for lacking a framework, for writing without a point. Do details as carefully selected and well written as Didion's make their own point, or does she have some other responsibility as a writer?

Students may be surprised at Didion's assertion about the relation between meaning ("the picture") and grammar, especially if they believe (as many students seem to) that grammar is somehow extrinsic to meaning, the frightening "rules" meant to be applied to already-expressed meaning.

BARBARA EHRENREICH

The Menace of Negative People

In this excerpt from *Bright-Sided: How the Relentless Promotion of Positive Thinking Has Undermined America* (2009), the prominent journalist and social critic Barbara Ehrenreich explores an intriguing subject that could engage students in lively debate. Thinking positively, Ehrenreich claims, helps neither the individual nor society. Quite the contrary, she argues — cultural pressure to put on a happy face, "no matter how you might actually be feeling" (par. 3), can have devastating consequences.

Ehrenreich wrote and published *Bright-Sided* in the midst of a deep recession, yet she barely alludes to the subject that was then on everyone's mind. Recognizing the timing could lead to an interesting discussion of Ehrenreich's purpose, aided by the fifth "Question on Meaning."

QUESTIONS ON MEANING

1. Ehrenreich's subtitle (and title, for that matter) suggests that she is muckraking. Her purpose is to expose the harmful social, cultural, and political consequences of what is generally considered constructive personal behavior. Furthermore, the word *relentless* implies that pressures to exude positivity amount to persecution against those who might think critically or express their concerns.

2. The essay's title is ironic: Ehrenreich does not view negative people as a menace, but her sources do. The self-help book *How Full Is Your Bucket?* and Gary S. Topchik, for instance, assert that "negative attitudes and behaviors" make coworkers uncomfortable and cost employers money (par. 4). Similarly, T. Harv Eker and J. P. Maroney warn that negative

people "suck the energy out of" friends, family members, coworkers, and businesses (5), while Jeffrey Gitomer and Judy Braley suggest that exposing oneself to unpleasant news stories causes depression (11–12, 14). Ehrenreich rejects these claims, arguing instead that "annoying . . . people might actually have something useful to say" (6).

3. "What has changed, in the last few years, is that the advice to at least act in a positive way has taken on a harsher edge. The penalty for non-conformity is going up, from the possibility of job loss and failure to social shunning and complete isolation" (par. 5). Ehrenreich offers examples of workers who have been fired for negative attitudes (4) and an instance of shunning (8); she also contemplates the causes and effects of isolation (6, 7).

4. Ehrenreich's thesis might be summarized as "the advice to be positive at all times is both misguided and dangerous."

5. "[T]he financial officer who keeps worrying about the bank's subprime mortgage exposure" is a reference to the housing-market collapse and credit meltdown caused by a rash of risky lending in the late 1990s and early 2000s; "the auto executive who questions the company's overin-vestment in SUVs and trucks" is a reference to the 2009 bankruptcy of General Motors. Ehrenreich is arguing that negative attitudes often reflect valid concerns and that dismissing them can be disastrous. She is further suggesting that pressures to be positive in the workplace are at least partly responsible for the global recession of the late 2000s.

QUESTIONS ON WRITING STRATEGY

1. Ehrenreich is writing for a general audience of Americans who, like her-self, may not be comfortable with the pressure to be positive at all times. Although it's likely that some of "the gurus" will read *Bright-Sided*, and although Ehrenreich would clearly like them to change their ways, she speaks of them in the third person and with disdain. She speaks of her readers, on the other hand, in the first and second person.

2. Ehrenreich quotes some of the advice given by self-appointed experts (pars. 3, 4, 5, 11, 12, and 14); she also gives an example of an anticom-plaining campaign (8) and quotes headlines from Web sites specializing in good news (13). She quotes these sources to demonstrate the nature of their advice and to highlight its absurdity; her intention is to show why the so-called experts are wrong by analyzing the implications of their suggestions.

3. The last sentence of the essay is Ehrenreich's somewhat sarcastic ver-sion of what the positive-thinking industry counsels. As she sees it, "to withdraw into one's own carefully constructed world of constant approval and affirmation, nice news, and smiling people" (par. 15) is not "positive" at all.

4. By contrasting the bad news presented through mainstream channels with the good news highlighted in upbeat blogs, Ehrenreich demon-strates that relying on the latter is a form of denial "suggestive of a deep helplessness at the core of positive thinking" (par. 14). This point sup-ports her larger claim that positive thinking can be both delusional and harmful.

5. Ehrenreich uses cause-and-effect analysis to characterize and debunk the advice offered by proponents of positive thinking. She concedes that being "nice" and cheerful can sometimes "improve your life in concrete, material ways" (par. 3), but her (qualified) approval ends there. She cau-

tions that "failing to generate positive vibes" (4) can get a person fired, that avoiding negative people can leave a person isolated and "cut off from reality" (6), and that a person reluctant or unable to act "in a positive way" is punished with ostracism (9). Her point is that embracing the ideal of positive thinking can have very negative outcomes.

QUESTIONS ON LANGUAGE

1. The word *cult* has ominous overtones. By referring to the positive-thinking movement as "the cult of cheerfulness," Ehrenreich suggests that its followers have given up control over their own thoughts and lives.
2. By adopting a tone that is both critical and levelheaded to make her case against positivity, Ehrenreich proves her point that negative people "might actually have something useful to say" (par. 6).
3. Notice that Ehrenreich uses several words with religious connotations: *Shunning, secular, dictum,* and *creed* in particular echo her implication in paragraph 4 that adherents of positive thinking have fallen victim to a cult (see question 1, above).

BARBARA EHRENREICH ON WRITING

Ehrenreich's comments on the media, particularly magazines, are thought provoking. Students should respond especially to what the author sees as the media's exclusive interest in upbeat stories. Some may agree that the media favor such stories or sugarcoat the more downbeat ones, but others may think the opposite: that the media stress bad news. You might ask students to bring in magazine articles or summaries of TV news items to support their views.

MARTIN LUTHER KING, JR.

I Have a Dream

Although King's speech was meant to be heard aloud, it remains impressive on the page, and it supplies a splendid illustration of a proposal that appeals to emotion. You will probably wish to point out, however, that some of its strategies are directed primarily toward listeners: the strong use of repetition, parallelism, and direct references to the audience.

Your students will better appreciate the power of this speech if they see or at least hear it as delivered by King in 1963. (One source for video of the speech: *youtube.com/watch?v=iEMXaTkUFA.*) Have students in small groups discuss the differences between reading and hearing this speech. Alternately, have a group of students listen to the speech and make a presentation to the rest of the class, playing certain brief selections and commenting on the differences in hearing versus reading.

If you do have students listen to the speech, you might encourage them to consider the textual differences in the spoken and printed versions. King revised the original text of his speech, no doubt after he had received many requests for a printable version. (Speakers often make such changes, either because a transcription from spoken delivery might contain elements that would transfer awkwardly to the page or because they want to make improvements.) The printed version of King's speech adds a few passages that were not part of his original delivery, including from "*Now* is the time" through "1963 is not an end, but a beginning" in paragraphs 4 and 5, and paragraphs 8 and 9 in their entirety. In our view, the new passages are wonderful: "to lift our nation from the quicksands of racial injustice to the solid rock of brotherhood" (4) and "You have been the veterans of creative suffering" (8) in particular. We don't believe that in making changes Dr. King lost the power of his spoken discourse; if anything, he strengthened it. Some students, however, may disagree.

QUESTIONS ON MEANING

1. The purpose is to inspire its hearers, despite their setbacks and disappointments, to go on working for civil rights.
2. African American people have yet to receive the freedom and the justice that the nation's founders guaranteed.
3. While King praises the rise of black activism, he believes it can advance its cause by nonviolent means, as he makes clear in this paragraph.
4. King recalls both early American history and the present occasion in his opening paragraph and in paragraphs 3 and 5.

QUESTIONS ON WRITING STRATEGY

1. Besides directly addressing his followers (in pars. 6–8), King employs parallelism in phrases such as "from the dark and desolate valley of segregation to the sunlit path of racial justice" (4). Still more impressively, he builds parallel structures by repeating phrases and clauses, lending them tremendous emphasis. This strategy informs much of the essay. In paragraph 2 there is a refrain ("One hundred years later"), and in paragraph 4 another ("*Now* is the time"). Most powerful of all are "I have a dream" (11–18) and "Let freedom ring" (20–27) — repeated again and again, at the start of each paragraph.
2. Paragraph 6.
3. Though he begins by recalling the past and its disappointments, he devotes by far the largest part of his speech to the future, in his extended description of his dream (pars. 10–27).
4. King's reasonableness is especially evident in his condemnation of bitterness and violence (par. 6). His personal authority — having been discriminated against and failing, having led demonstrations and achieving victories — combines with his rhetoric to give the speech its power.
5. In paragraph 2 the metaphors strengthen King's connection with the African Americans in his audience by showing his understanding of his race's hobbled, outcast state. In paragraph 4 the extended metaphor of the promissory note gives an argument by analogy, linking African American history to something concrete. The remaining metaphors in this paragraph intensify King's urgent appeal by contrasting what is with what could (and should) be.

QUESTIONS ON LANGUAGE

1. King uses concrete words in much of his imagery: the metaphors of "manacles" and "chains" (par. 2), that of the "check" (4), the visualization of the "governor's lips" (16). But for most of the speech his diction is largely abstract, as seems necessary to encompass two centuries of the past and the whole of the future.

2. King employs many figures, some biblical in connotation. Besides those noted in question 5 above and in the preceding question, they include "summer of . . . discontent" (5), an echo from Shakespeare ("Now is the winter of our discontent / Made glorious summer by this sun of York" — the opening lines of *Richard III*); "the palace of justice," "the cup of bitterness" (6); "justice rolls down like waters" and "righteousness like a mighty stream" (7); "storms of persecution" and "winds of police brutality" (8); "valley of despair" (9); the "heat of injustice and oppression" and the "oasis of freedom and justice" (13); the topographical references in paragraph 18; the "mountain of despair" and the "stone of hope" (19); and the "symphony of brotherhood" (19).

3. There seems freshness in King's application of *curvaceous* to California mountain peaks, instead of to (as in the usual cliché) Hollywood film goddesses.

MAXINE HONG KINGSTON

No Name Woman

Students are usually moved by Kingston's evocation of a haunting childhood story. Ask them to describe their own reactions to the tale of Kingston's aunt. Does it seem completely alien, from a world far away, or more immediate? Does it hold students' imaginations?

Kingston's books *The Woman Warrior* and *China Men* are sources of further mystery and understanding about Chinese and American culture. In addition, a number of films have depicted Chinese village life: *Ju Dou, Raise the Red Lantern,* and *To Live* are just a few available on DVD. Students who are interested in the films might consider writing a comparative paper on the role of women, for example, in Kingston's essay and in one of the films. How important is the medium to the message? What do the two media say in common? Another use of the films, given their complicated imagery, is to assign a collaborative paper. Interested students could watch one film together, discuss it, and prepare a comparison between it and Kingston's essay, addressing the questions above.

QUESTIONS ON MEANING

1. Kingston and her mother share the purpose of telling a riveting story. Kingston's purpose is also self-examination and an inquiry into Chinese cultural attitudes; her mother's is also to instill these cultural attitudes in her.

2. Her aunt's husband could not have been the child's father (par. 3). Kingston posits two possible fathers: a man who "commanded [the aunt] to be with him" (15), and a man she herself was drawn to (21).
3. It is meant to warn her against adultery and, by extension, sexuality.
4. Kingston is haunted by her Chinese heritage; she seeks "ancestral help" (par. 22). Her aunt is a powerful representative of that heritage, an example of its grip on women and their emotions. Her life and death are a profound "family secret" that transcends Kingston's own immediate family.

QUESTIONS ON WRITING STRATEGY

1. Kingston's family and other older Chinese would be unlikely to read the essay: Kingston does address Chinese Americans directly (par. 12), and her detailed descriptions of Chinese and Chinese American culture indicate that she is trying to explain them to other Americans. Older Chinese, and particularly her family, would be shocked that she is breaking the silence about her aunt. Chinese Americans would see themselves and their own "haunting" in her story. Other Americans might be enlightened about the complexity and power the Chinese heritage holds.
2. The story of the aunt is supposed to be kept secret by the mother. The mother's tale is supposed to be kept secret by Kingston but is instead examined minutely in this essay. Kingston's telling the secret of her aunt's story is an act of rebellion equivalent to her aunt's. Thus the opening line presages all the themes of the essay (and creates suspense as well).
3. The effect is to intensify the confusion of reality and truth and to show the subjective nature of memory and family history. Kingston creates this effect in passages such as "I want her fear to have lasted just as long as rape lasted" (par. 18), "I hope that the man my aunt loved appreciated a smooth brow" (25), and "She may have gone to the pigsty as a last act of responsibility" (44). You might want to draw students' attention to places where Kingston's different sources are intertwined — for example, "My mother spoke about the raid as if she had seen it, when she and my aunt, a daughter-in-law to a different household, should not have been living together at all" (19).
4. The details in paragraphs 15–18 tell a much bleaker story: "She obeyed him" (par. 16), "No one talked sex, ever" (18). The details in paragraphs 21–28 are those of a more romantic tale: "she often worked at herself in the mirror" (23), "my aunt combed individuality into her bob" (25), "she dreamed of a lover for the fifteen days of New Year's" (28). Kingston seems more caught up in the romantic version of the story, in her aunt's desire and need to rebel.
5. Her aunt might have been "commanded . . . to lie with" the father of her child (par. 15), or she might have "let dreams grow" and "offered us up for a charm that vanished" (21). The raid might have been organized by her rapist (16) or by villagers who were "speeding up the circling of events" (39). She might have killed her child because it was "a foreign growth that sickened her every day" (43) or because "Mothers who love their children take them along" (46). In the end, Kingston concludes that her aunt's suicide was caused by her feelings of imprisonment within the conventions of village life.

QUESTIONS ON LANGUAGE

1. Kingston's poetic language shows how deeply she responds to her Chinese heritage and its tales. Some striking phrases include "a protruding melon of a stomach" (par. 3), "the heavy, deep-rooted women were to maintain the past against the flood" (20), "women looked like great sea snails" (27), "violence could open up a black hole, a maelstrom that pulled in the sky" (37).
2. You might want to explain the "commensal" tradition (par. 19), in which food is shared by the generations of an extended family. The idea of food and its allocation is central to societies, like China's, where resources are stretched to their utmost. Kingston underscores this in paragraph 15, when she describes her ancestors as "people who hatch their own chicks and eat the embryos and the heads for delicacies and boil the feet in vinegar for party food, leaving only the gravel, eating even the gizzard lining."
3. Kingston blurs the distinction between history and her interpretation of it.

MAXINE HONG KINGSTON ON WRITING

In this interview, Kingston discloses a profound belief in the power of writing to generate writing, even to bring order and meaning to one's life. Some students may have had this experience of writing, and perhaps they can confirm Kingston's words for students who haven't. (Students often don't realize that the turmoil of writing can actually be productive.) Kingston also slips in a small warning: It's fine to let yourself go in drafting, but eventually the "intellectual" (Kingston seems to mean "critical") side must kick in for revision.

GEORGE ORWELL
Shooting an Elephant

Orwell's gripping narrative, told with vivid detail and an appealing self-effacement, tends to stick in the memory of anyone who studies it. Orwell's elegant prose may at first put some students off, but even they will soon enough be caught up in the narrator's tale.

Indelible as it is, the essay may strike students as remote from their concerns because it takes place in a country and a time far from their own. If you find this response, point out that the essay tells of doing what seems necessary, even what's wrong, to save face. Governments and their representatives everywhere, including our own, commit dubious actions for just this reason. The second writing suggestion can help students discover the relation between Orwell's experience and their own: Ask students to scour newspapers, TV news programs, or news blogs for examples of contemporary face-saving among public officials. In small groups, each student could present one such example for discussion of the perpetrator's likely motives as well as the effects of such behavior.

QUESTIONS ON MEANING

1. Orwell explains that he took his .44 Winchester with him because "the noise might be useful *in terrorem*" (par. 3). His borrowing the elephant rifle later (4) seems a wise precaution because the elephant had killed a man. As he explains in paragraph 5, the rifle was for self-defense only.
2. The answer is twofold. He had to save face — that was the more important reason. But, as he mentions in paragraph 9, his being a bad shot also influenced his behavior by injecting an element of fear.
3. He expresses the epiphany most clearly and vehemently in paragraph 7: "I perceived in this moment that when the white man turns tyrant it is his own freedom that he destroys." And so on to the end of the paragraph.
4. The coolie's death put the young Orwell "legally in the right." By the time he wrote "Shooting an Elephant," though, Orwell was no longer motivated by any need to save face. He had the courage to tell his story truthfully and unsparingly, awful as it was. It seems clear that the mature Orwell did not share his younger self's view of the coolie's death.
5. Orwell's purpose is clearly to show, through his experience of shooting the elephant, how the need to save face motivates — indeed, compels — the actions of himself and every other imperialist.

QUESTIONS ON WRITING STRATEGY

1. These paragraphs, because they reveal so much about the author's feelings toward his job and toward the Burmese who made it difficult, shed light on the complex motives that resulted in the unnecessary shooting. They also, perhaps, somewhat justify the author's behavior — to himself and to us.
2. He explains the circumstances best in his opening paragraphs. He had come to hate imperialism and all that it stood for. Still, because it was his job, he had to do "the dirty work of Empire." Adding to his misery was the abuse he and his English compatriots had to endure from the Burmese.
3. With hindsight, Orwell has a broader and deeper perspective on the events. At the time, he was bitter, embarrassed, and a little afraid. In retrospect, he can see his foolishness and the tyranny he helped to further.
4. The paragraphs seem to unfold almost in real time, and the details of the wounded elephant are excruciating. We understand, almost too plainly, Orwell's horror at his act.
5. The Burmese are portrayed as both detestable (spitting on European women, yelling "with hideous laughter," "sneering") and pitiable ("wretched prisoners huddling in the stinking cages," "gray, cowed faces," "scarred buttocks"). The contradiction makes Orwell's position "perplexing and upsetting."

QUESTIONS ON LANGUAGE

1. The term refers to the annual period during which a male elephant is most sexually aroused and is often violent.

2. Some examples: "chucked up my job" (par. 2), "had taken the wrong direction" (3), "rubbish van" (3), "had come suddenly upon him round the corner of the hut" (4), "I ought not to shoot him" (6), and various uses of *got*, such as "I had got to do it" (7), "I had got to shoot" (7), and "I had got to act quickly" (8).

3. *Sahib* is a title of respect from the Urdu use of the Arabic *cahib*, meaning "friend."

GEORGE ORWELL ON WRITING

This is a grim account of the writing process! "Writing a book is a horrible, exhausting struggle, like a long bout of some painful illness." But students who have suffered when writing even a brief paper may take heart from Orwell's account of his agonies.

Orwell's remark about the need to efface one's own personality (cited in the second discussion question) echoes similar advice given by T. S. Eliot in his familiar essay "Tradition and the Individual Talent" (1919). Blasting the Romantic poets' notion of writing as self-expression, Eliot finds the poet obligated to do something more interesting than vent personal emotions. He adds: "But, of course, only those who have personality and emotions to express know what it means to want to escape from these things."

Orwell here stresses the importance of writing both to achieve something readable and beautiful and — more important, because it affects the artistry of the finished work — writing to improve society.

FRANCINE PROSE

What Words Can Tell

Francine Prose's book *Reading like a Writer* holds that thoughtful reading is the key to good writing. This excerpt from Prose's best-selling writing guide both reinforces our own assumptions about the benefits of close reading and serves beautifully as a model of such reading. We hope students will be inspired by Prose's example to attempt similar analyses of both the fiction and the nonfiction included in *The Bedford Reader*. As Prose demonstrates, even a few sentences of a quality work reveal much meaning and have much to teach about the value of words.

Students who want to read "A Good Man Is Hard to Find" themselves can locate it in many venues. Flannery O'Connor's marvelous collection "*A Good Man Is Hard to Find" and Other Stories* is available in almost any library, and it can also be found online via the University of Central Florida at *pegasus.cc.ucf.edu/~surette/Goodman.html*. The critical writing topic following Prose's analysis invites students to read the story and then respond to Prose's interpretation of its opening paragraph. This topic could also spark class discussion as students share their responses to Prose and to the story itself.

QUESTIONS ON MEANING

1. Prose examines the paragraph to demonstrate just how informative and rewarding it can be to "slow down and read every word" (par. 2) of an enduring writer's work.
2. The author's thesis is stated in paragraph 3: "All the elements of good writing depend on the writer's skill in choosing one word instead of another. And what grabs and keeps our interest has everything to do with those choices."
3. Prose admires the passage for O'Connor's skill in establishing every character's personality, setting the tone, and foreshadowing the plot in a "highly concentrated . . . model of compression from which it would be hard to excise one word" (par. 12).

QUESTIONS ON WRITING STRATEGY

1. Prose's intended audience is made clear in the title of her book: *Reading like a Writer: A Guide for People Who Love Books and for Those Who Want to Write Them.* Her use of the language of literary criticism further suggests that she imagines her readers to be well educated, or at least somewhat experienced in reading literature.
2. Given that Prose has no qualms about including spoilers, she does seem to assume that most members of her audience have read O'Connor's short story. Yet she is careful to reprint the full passage under analysis and to alert readers to its connections with later plot developments. Even those who have never read "A Good Man Is Hard to Find" learn enough about it from Prose's essay to follow her examination of its introduction. (And we hope that those who have not yet had the pleasure of reading O'Connor's masterful story will be inspired by Prose's analysis to track it down for their own enjoyment.)
3. By giving a close reading of one short passage from a famous story, Prose proves her point that writers can learn a lot by reading the masters.
4. Prose ties her analysis together in paragraph 13: "Skimming just won't suffice" to "teach us about how to use the language."

QUESTIONS ON LANGUAGE

1. Figures of speech in the lead-in to Prose's analysis include her analogy of wiring to explain how readers need to relearn their approach to fiction (par. 1) and her similes comparing a writer's words to a composer's notes and an artist's paints (2). Each of these turns of phrase demonstrates the author's appreciation for colorful, meaningful writing and encourages her readers to think in creative terms.
2. The switch in address reflects Prose's switch in emphasis and purpose. The introductory paragraphs are meant as instruction for the readers who are the subject of Prose's lesson, so the second person is appropriate. In the analysis itself, however, Prose is more interested in the intricacies of reading and thinks of her audience (and herself) as the objects of O'Connor's efforts, hence the third-person *we*.
3. The allusions stress that Flannery O'Connor is part of a community of revered literary masters whose work continues to influence contemporary writers.

4. Notice that many of Prose's word choices — *psychic, archetypal, infan-tilizing, egocentrism, narcissism* — reveal her interest in the psychologi-cal school of literary criticism.

FRANCINE PROSE ON WRITING

Prose's statement about grammatical errors may puzzle those students who have been taught that errors are always wrong. Her point, we think, is that Philip Roth can get away with what might be considered a textbook error beause he knows what he's doing — the error is deliberate — and because his meaning is clear. What distinguishes his error from that of a less experienced writer is his control and clarity.

RICHARD RODRIGUEZ

Aria:
A Memoir of a Bilingual Childhood

Rodriguez, in sensuous detail, recalls from his childhood the pleasures and pains of growing up speaking Spanish in surroundings where English was the official language. Spanish was the family language; its use at home came to signify warmth and security, a way for the Rodriguez family to sepa-rate themselves from the difficulties encountered in the English-speaking world around them. Yet Rodriguez has come to feel that recent efforts to pro-vide bilingual education in the public schools for Spanish-speaking children are misguided. To prolong their dependence on Spanish, he insists, is to rel-egate them for an unnecessarily long time to the ranks of the disadvantaged.

Not all reviewers of *Hunger of Memory* sided with Rodriguez on this point. For a differing view of the book by a fellow Mexican American (like Rodriguez, the holder of a doctorate in English), see the attack in the *American Book Review* (May–June 1983) by Cordelia Candelaria. Although Candelaria thinks Rodriguez has a right to his opinions (he is against not only bilingual school-ing but also affirmative action), she objects to his being regarded as a spokesperson for Mexican Americans. She disputes, too, his assumption that good schooling inevitably leads to a loss of one's ethnic identity. Her own experience was otherwise: "My normal adolescent estrangement from family was never permanent."

Bilingual education continues to be controversial, of course. A writing suggestion encourages students to grapple with the issue and could be used as the basis of class discussion. You could also have students work in pairs or threes to locate another opinion on the subject to complement or refute Rodriguez's. What is the basis of this other perspective? How does it agree with or answer Rodriguez's claims? Have each group briefly explain its find-ings. Can the class as a whole come up with a sort of map of the debate?

QUESTIONS ON MEANING

1. Rodriguez objects to bilingual education in the schools for those children whose native language is not English. He introduces his view in paragraph 4, then returns to it in paragraphs 19–20 and 38–39. The author believes that by slowing down the Spanish-speaking child's assimilation into the cultural mainstream, bilingual education does a disservice.

2. In paragraphs 12 and 13 the author probes his ambivalent reactions. Though his parents always managed to understand and communicate necessary information, their son, in spite of himself, felt unsettled and occasionally embarrassed by their difficulties.

3. The author makes an important distinction between "sounds" and "words." For the child Rodriguez, the sounds of the Spanish language were synonymous with intimacy, with family, with home (pars. 8 and 14). Before he learned words in English, the gringos' sounds seemed to him exotic and polysyllabic, loud and confident, firm and clear, nasal and high (10). The sounds of Spanish constituted a private language. English was a public language. When he says he was a child longer than most, he means that for a longer time than most children he heard language in terms of sounds. His progress toward comprehending and using the words of public language was slow.

4. There was a somewhat troubling diminution of their togetherness. What Rodriguez doesn't acknowledge is that the loosening of family ties is an inevitable development in all families, regardless of their language. To the author, separation, language, and his growing inattention to "sounds" seem inextricably bound together.

5. The child Rodriguez was miserable over having to speak English. As an adult, the author was grateful to the nuns who had insisted that he learn English.

QUESTIONS ON WRITING STRATEGY

1. It offers the reader much necessary background: where and when the author's childhood experiences occurred, the facts that as a first-grader Rodriguez knew very little English and that his family included three siblings, two of them older than he was. Furthermore, "I remember," by promising a story at the outset, immediately captures the reader's interest.

2. It is hard to argue against what someone has learned through personal experience. The author's memories, therefore, strengthen his arguments against bilingual education. The autobiographical paragraphs in "Aria" do more, however. The insights they provide into the heart of a sensitive child lend the essay a touching, elegiac aura hard to forget.

3. In paragraph 1 the books brought home from school by his Spanish-speaking older siblings remain unread on the table. In paragraph 40, where Rodriguez writes about life in his house after he has learned English, the important detail about the schoolbooks is that, instead of remaining tightly closed, they are now being read. The child is fully Americanized, Rodriguez maintains, because he has mastered the English language.

4. Advocates of bilingual education — and their numbers are significant — would find much to criticize in "Aria." We think it would be hard even for them not to find much to praise as well.

5. English is "loud, booming," "high, nasal," "birdlike," "chirping" (par. 10). Spanish is embracing (14), "light and free," "fast," "twirling" (18), "tender" (33), "singsong" (37). The English sounds are unpleasant, the Spanish pleasant.

6. From his narrative, we know Rodriguez to be very sensitive, highly intelligent, thoughtful. His fairness might be questioned: He states but barely examines the opposing view. But since, as he says, bilingual education was well entrenched when he wrote, he might not have felt much obligation to present that side of the debate.

QUESTIONS ON LANGUAGE

1. Shy students might find it interesting that the word *diffident* came into Middle English from the Latin *dis-* ("not") and *fidere* ("to trust"). The present participle was *diffidens*. *Diffidere* literally meant "to mistrust." *Diffident* now means "lacking self-confidence; timid" (*The American Heritage Dictionary*).

2. For Rodriguez, Spanish was a private language and English was a public language. He insists that educators do a disservice to children whose native language is not English unless they oblige those children to learn English at the outset. To be unable to use the public language, Rodriguez maintains, is to be doubly disadvantaged.

3. He means that increasingly he was able to understand what he heard. He had always understood Spanish, of course. But it was even more important to his future that he hear English as *words*, not as interesting but useless sounds.

RICHARD RODRIGUEZ ON WRITING

Rodriguez is particularly adept at describing the conflicting feelings that writers sometimes experience when they look back over words they wrote long ago. In some cases he "cannot remember having written them." Some of his other words, conversely, "recall the very day they were composed" (par. 4).

The eloquent plea in the concluding paragraph deserves attention. The quality of a writer's audience, Rodriguez indicates, is tremendously important.

To stimulate class discussion about Rodriguez's comments, you may want to ask some of the following questions in addition to those that appear in the book:

1. For Rodriguez, what does writing have to do with *need*? (In a sense, Rodriguez wrote because he had to. "I began writing to stay alive — not as a job, but to stay alive" [par. 3]. For him, writing is serious business. His attitude supports what good teachers and good writers know: The best writing comes from those with something they are burning to say.)

2. What is "universality" in novels and essays? Describe in your own words the "paradox" that sometimes produces it. (Universality is that quality in literature that reaches out to every member of a diverse audience. The paradox, according to Rodriguez, is that writers who achieve universal appeal are generally those who are the most individual [par. 5]. Compare this statement with E. B. White's in "E. B. White on Writing" [p. 730], on the same subject.)

EDWARD SAID

Clashing Civilizations?

In this essay the late Arab American scholar Edward Said responds to British and American commentators who have made large claims of an irreparable divide between the West and the Islamic world. For Said, the idea of "clashing civilizations" not only grossly oversimplifies but also heightens the danger of terror. Terrorism, he argues, is not the work of Muslims as a group but of "a tiny band of crazed fanatics." Moreover, viewing Islam as a monolithic enemy ignores reality and does nothing to promote productive solutions to the conflicts that actually do exist.

You might begin discussion by asking students to think about the journal-writing prompt following the essay. What impression of Islam do the Western media generally portray? Is it the sort of image implied by those Said criticizes — that of a collective entity with a single anti-Western mindset? Are most non-Islamic Americans led to regard Islam broadly as "the enemy"?

QUESTIONS ON MEANING

1. Said is responding to Samuel P. Huntington's and Bernard Lewis's arguments that "Muslim rage" (par. 2) and the idea the Muslims are "convinced of the superiority of their culture, and obsessed with the inferiority of their power" (4) have resulted in a fundamental and unresolvable conflict between Islam and the West. Both arguments — originally published in the early 1990s — came to prominence after the 2001 terrorist attacks led many commentators and politicians to cast the Islamic world as essentially evil, out to destroy the West, and deserving of forcible response.
2. Said argues that Islam has no single face, that to see it and the West as monoliths pitted against each other is reductionist, unproductive, even dangerous.
3. Said's point in paragraph 6 is that no strict line exists between the West and Islam and, moreover, that the view of Islamic people as backward is belied by the technical sophistication of the September 11 terrorists.
4. Said states his thesis at the very end of the essay: It is easier to cast Islam in broad, negative, "bellicose" terms to gain support for anti-Muslim policies than it is to recognize Islam's complexity and its connections to the West.

QUESTIONS ON WRITING STRATEGY

1. Said uses Popeye and Bluto to represent what is for him an oversimplified, cartoonish image of the West and Islam engaged in violent conflict, with all virtue on the side of the West.
2. By comparing Bin Laden and his followers to violent American and Japanese cults, Said suggests that Islamic terrorists no more represent Islam than these cults represent the West or Asia.
3. Said uses quotation marks for "we" in paragraph 3; "West" in 5; "Western" in 6; and "West," "Islam," "ours," and "theirs" in 7. The quo-

tation marks indicate Said's own rejection of these labels when they are used to denote a deeply entrenched divide between the cultures.

4. Paragraph 2 takes apart the arguments of Huntington and Lewis to show their meanings and weaknesses. This paragraph is crucial to the rest of Said's argument because it specifies just what he finds objectionable.

5. Said uses this narrative example to point out that even strict and vocal proponents of Islam have adopted elements of Western culture.

QUESTIONS ON LANGUAGE

1. Said's language in referring to Huntington and others — "belligerent," "recklessly," "demagogy," "ignorance" (par. 2); "insidiously," "pontificated" (3); "unedifying" (6); "nihilistic," "bellicose" (7) — casts the anti-Islamic commentators in a negative light. The language may well backfire with some students.

2. Students may not know that *sic*, the Latin for "thus," indicates that a quotation is just as the original author wrote it. Writers often use *sic* to point to errors. Said uses it to question Huntington's claim that the civilizations of the world can be reduced to a vague "seven or eight" and thus to weaken Huntington's authority.

3. The parenthesis implies that Said is not using "big ideas" approvingly or even in its usual sense of large, difficult, even irresolvable issues but narrowly, as the terrorists themselves perceived their mission.

4. *Belligerent* and *bellicose* have the same root, *bellum*, the Latin for "war." They originally had a similar meaning, the first "engaged in war" and the second "inclined to provoke wars," but *belligerent* is more commonly used today to mean "hostile" or "combative."

JONATHAN SWIFT
A Modest Proposal

That Swift is being ironic in proposing this monstrous solution to the problems of Ireland usually dawns slowly on a few students. It will be a highly entertaining class wherein someone thinks Swift is serious. From Swift's essay a perfectly straightforward argument for Christian charity may be inferred. For a contemporary satiric essay that depends on irony, see Linnea Saukko's "How to Poison the Earth" (Chap. 8).

The irony of Swift's essay is masterful and inspiring. Students who would like to imitate Swift's tone would benefit from feedback on their attempts. Try assigning the class a single paragraph written in a tone of heavy irony. (You may wish to leave the subject up to students, or integrate this with the first writing suggestion.) Give students time in class to read their paragraphs aloud in small groups (it will help if every student in the group has a copy) and to discuss how they might revise their work to improve the tone and the point(s) they are making.

QUESTIONS ON MEANING

1. Swift is proposing that the Irish poor sell their year-old children to the rich for meat.
2. Swift is calling for charity and compassion. Some specific alternatives for relieving poverty are given in Swift's list of "other expedients," paragraph 29.
3. Swift's essay calls attention to both the plight of the poor in Ireland and the hard-heartedness of their oppressors.
4. Swift's image of the begging mothers and their children immediately arouses readers' sympathy and prepares them to react with horror against the "modest" proposal.
5. Objections should be obvious, unless one regards a human being as an animal to be butchered.

QUESTIONS ON WRITING STRATEGY

1. The author writes as a reasonable, kind, serious do-gooder, impatient with the failure of those in power to do anything about the problem.
2. Swift does this effectively by calling his proposal "modest," by citing authorities and experts to back him up (such as the "very knowing American," par. 9), by carefully listing the advantages of the proposal (21–28), by his concern that the flesh would spoil if exported (31), and by professing at the end that he doesn't stand to make a penny himself.
3. Probably not until paragraph 9.
4. Surely to our feelings. Most of the reasonable arguments are deliberately monstrous, although other convincing points appeal to reason in paragraph 29.
5. The process analysis makes us study the proposal in its every gruesome particular. It forces our noses into the proposal, and thus into the plight of the Irish poor, in a way mere generalities would not have. The cause and effect specifies the ways in which the proposal will achieve its goals, summarized in paragraph 33 as "advancing our trade, providing for infants, relieving the poor, and giving some pleasure to the rich."

QUESTIONS ON LANGUAGE

1. The words from breeding and butchery include "dam" (par. 4); "breed" (10); "carcass" (14); "flay" (15); "dressing them hot" (16); "mares in foal . . . ready to farrow" (26); "barreled beef . . . bacon" (27); and "customers for infants' flesh" (28).
2. Swift's vocabulary is extensive. When they read "A Modest Proposal," students might have to use their dictionaries more than they usually do when reading an essay. The exercise might increase their vocabularies.

JONATHAN SWIFT ON WRITING

Though dated, Swift's advice still makes sense. To be sure, when Swift set forth his fable of the spider and the bee in *The Battle of the Books*, he was writing in defense of the Roman classics, the study of which, needless to say, has been greatly curtailed since the early eighteenth century. Immediately after we quote his celebrated fable, we attempt to translate it into terms useful to the student, but we'll have to admit that our translation somewhat betrays the original. Still, Swift's advice to writers — don't just spin cobwebs out of your own entrails — can be taken as another argument for writers' paying attention to the world beyond their heads. You'll find comparable advice in the Writers on Writing feature by George Orwell (p. 671).

JOHN UPDIKE

Extreme Dinosaurs

We won't deny it: John Updike's "Extreme Dinosaurs" is difficult. Indeed, it's one of the most challenging selections in *The Bedford Reader*. We include it because the essay is evocative and beautifully written, loaded with wit and reverence for a topic that almost always captures the imagination. At the same time, it demonstrates that a writer who is not an expert in a subject can nonetheless learn enough about it to craft an authoritative and compelling essay, a point reinforced by the third "Suggestion for Writing."

Students may need to be reminded to slow down and take in Updike's essay one sentence, even one word, at a time. (We encourage this approach by asking them to summarize each paragraph, in the first "Question on Meaning.") Many of us tend to skim over scientific terms and words we don't immediately recognize, but read carefully and with patience, "Extreme Dinosaurs" reveals itself as an intriguing contemplation of the fate of humanity.

QUESTIONS ON MEANING

1. Possible summaries: (1) Dinosaurs have always seemed weird and mysterious, but recently discovered fossils raise even more questions. (2) Some dinosaurs share physical features with contemporary animals, such as lemurs and bats, but others had characteristics that seem to make no sense. (3) Modern creatures, especially humans, might well seem strange or senseless to dinosaurs. (4) Dinosaurs lived a thousand times longer than human beings have been in existence and twenty thousand times longer than human civilization. During dinosaurs' time on earth, the planet itself evolved, with continents shifting, mountains and oceans rising, and new plants and animals emerging. (5) Dinosaur bodies developed more weaponlike characteristics over time, but many of those physical features seem impractical. (6) Perhaps those physical features were for social and sexual purposes, rather than combat. (7) Although dinosaurs evolved, it's not clear that the evolutionary changes were improvements. (8) Just as dinosaurs became extinct, so can any modern species, including humans. (9) The smallest, least powerful of the dinosaurs evolved into birds and so are, in a sense, still with us today. New discoveries continue to bring new knowledge, and we have not yet learned everything there is to know about dinosaurs. (10) We tend to see the extinction of dinosaurs as one catastrophic event, but they died out over time, in numerous small ways. Evolution is a con-

tinuing process, and someday a new species will emerge to dominate the planet, leaving humans in the position dinosaurs are in today. (Updike's main point, it would seem, is that humans are not a model of evolutionary perfection and are no less vulnerable to extinction than dinosaurs were.)

2.　Part of Updike's purpose is explained in the headnote: He agreed to write about dinosaurs because to his mind it was "poignant and awesome that such creatures once existed as alive as you and [he] but are long since gone from the surface of the Earth." A larger purpose, then, would be to remind readers that human beings won't be around forever either, a point he underscores in his conclusion: Dinosaurs "were eventual losers, in a game of survival our own species is still playing . . ." (par. 10).

3.　Updike's explanations are educated guesses. He's not at all certain that his conclusions are correct. The same is true of paleontology: Although the experts have found numerous fossils and have been able to reconstruct the general appearance of some dinosaurs, much of their work is necessarily speculative. The challenge, as Updike puts it, is that "with dinosaurs we can't see them in action and tame them, as it were, with visual (and auditory and olfactory) witness" (par. 3). Most likely, we'll never fully understand what dinosaurs looked like or how they lived.

4.　Updike does seem to believe that evolution, as a process, is a scientific fact. He considers, for instance, the long-term changes in dinosaur features in paragraph 5 and the perpetuation of genes in paragraph 6, as well as the "adaptive puzzles" (par. 7) inherent to the study of dinosaurs; he even speculates that some dinosaurs "grew feathers and became birds, [and are] still singing and dipping all around us" (9). At the same time, Updike questions the idea that evolution is a process of adaptation and gradual improvement: "[B]iological features," he claims, don't "need to be efficient to be carried along" (7). He also points out that "[a]ll lifeforms, even . . . long-lasting ones . . . will eventually flunk some test posed by environmental conditions and meet extinction" (8).

QUESTIONS ON WRITING STRATEGY

1.　Presumably, older understandings of dinosaurs as "dragons, ogres, or giant victims of Noah's flood" (par. 1) demonstrate naïveté and a lack of scientific knowledge. What Updike is suggesting, though, is that our current knowledge is no more sophisticated or conclusive: "[T]he evidence seems stranger than any fable, and continues to get stranger" (1). The point previews an underlying idea of the essay as a whole: As sophisticated and modern as we may think we are, we actually know very little.

2.　The artwork established Updike's occasion for writing: *National Geographic* asked him to write an essay to introduce the images, which represent paleontologists' best understanding of what the dinosaurs may have looked like. The images themselves, however, help to bring the descriptions to life and give the writer some leeway to use striking language, such as "the *Mononykus*'s smug dependence on a single, stoutly clawed digit at the end of each minimal forearm" (par. 1). The essay does not need the images to make sense, but the drawings give it vibrancy and help readers to better visualize those dinosaurs that aren't depicted.

3.　In a sense, Updike seems to imagine his readers as "the American Protestant small-town middle class" he once described as his usual subject for writing (see the biographical note that precedes the essay). Because he was writing for *National Geographic*, Updike could reasonably assume that his readers would be interested in geography, archae-ology, and science in general. He also assumes that his audience is well educated (witness his extensive use of specialized vocabulary and his references to prehistoric times) yet familiar with popular culture (most notable in his references to the band Dire Straits [par. 2], to *Harry Potter* [6], and to Walt Disney's *Fantasia* [7]). We think he does an effective job of giving his readers credit for intelligence while also offering accessible examples to help ground his more esoteric ideas.

4. The overview of long-term changes to the earth's geology and life forms underscores Updike's point that everything evolves. It also emphasizes just how long dinosaurs existed, a "vast span of time [that] boggles the human mind" (par. 4).

5. The comparisons help Updike to explain that modern life forms — human beings included — don't necessarily represent an evolutionary improvement and to suggest that they, too, will someday cease to exist.

QUESTIONS ON LANGUAGE

1. Many of Updike's words are specialized terms from archeology and pale-ontology; others are simply difficult words that will be unfamiliar to stu-dents. Because Updike's purpose is to contemplate the implications of evolution and extinction — not to explain either in any technical detail — the scientific language does not necessarily keep a general audience from understanding the author's point.

2. Updike relies primarily on formal, sophisticated, and academic language through most of his essay, yet he frequently slips into everyday speech that any reader could understand. A few examples: "hot spots" (par. 1); "an oddity, all right," "ugh" (3); "flunk some test," "heavyweight cham-pion" (8); "could have peered into a second-story window" (9). The collo-quialisms inject a dose of wit and whimsy into what otherwise might become an overly academic essay; they also humanize the author and help readers follow his ideas.

3. Updike sometimes ascribes human thoughts and behaviors to dinosaurs. Most notably, he refers to "*Mononykus*'s smug dependence" (par. 1) and imagines "a well-armored, nicely specialized dino" asking of humans, "Whatever did this creature *do* to earn its place in the sun[?]" (3). He also describes some dinosaurs as trying "to make a daunting impression" (5) and mentions their "guileless enormity" (10). By con-necting dinosaurs and humans in this way, Updike not only makes the unknowable more vivid and real, he also reinforces his point that, from an evolutionary standpoint, the two species aren't so different.

4. Updike refers to a "stubby claw . . . probing after insects," to a dinosaur that "leaped on its prey, wrapped its long arms and three-fingered hands around it, and kicked it to death with sickle-shaped toenails" (par. 1); to "clinging," to "a skittery first step" (2); to a "mouth bristling" (3); to a cli-mate "warmer than today's, and wetter" (4); to "[b]utting matches" and "discreet pushing" (5); to "heat controls" (7); to "swift motion" (8); to small dinosaurs "scuttling for their lives underfoot" (9) — all descrip-tions of bodily sensations. He also refers to "music to dig by" (2), to "a trumpeting noisemaker" (6), to "singing . . . all around us" (9) — all descriptions of sound.

JOHN UPDIKE ON WRITING

Students would do well to take Updike's advice on first drafts and let inspiration run as far and as fast as it lasts. They may be cheered by Updike's advocacy of speed and his interrogation of "the whole idea of fineness and care in writing" (par. 2). Remind them that only a very experienced writer can afford to claim that revision might hurt a piece of writing (and most writers in *The Bedford Reader* take pains to make the opposite point).

E. B. WHITE

Once More to the Lake

Among White's essays, this is one of the most often reprinted. In July 1941 White made a pilgrimage back to the Belgrade Lakes, northwest of Augusta, Maine, together with his young son, Joel. "This place is as American as a drink of Coca Cola," he wrote to his wife, Katharine. "The white collar family having its annual liberty. I must say it seems sort of good" (*Letters of E. B. White*, 1976). After his return to civilization, White produced "Once More to the Lake" for a column he was then contributing to *Harper's* magazine. Too marvelous to be a reasonable model for most student writers, the essay can encourage them to believe that their own memories are worth recording and can interest others. "Once More to the Lake" exhibits a whole array of rhetorical methods, too: description, narration, exemplification, comparison and contrast, even process analysis.

Of course, it is White's description — of place, people, feelings — that is most inimitable, but students can try their hand in a small way at first. Give them a one-paragraph writing assignment — even with a word limit, if you desire — to describe a place that is highly familiar to them. Working in small groups, students can read aloud their paragraphs and get feedback on how they might revise them to make the images more vivid, the phrasing more precise, the details more developed. (This will work best if students bring copies of their paragraphs for the other members of their group.) Fine-tuning their own writing on this small scale should give students the confidence to undertake larger writing projects (like those in "Suggestions for Writing").

QUESTIONS ON MEANING

1. White senses that nothing essential at the lake has changed; besides, he sustains the illusion that his son is himself as a boy and that he has become his own father (par. 4 and later passages).
2. Once, inboard motors had made a sleepy sound; today, the outboards seem "petulant, irritable." A central detail: "this was the note that jarred, the one thing that would sometimes break the illusion and set the years moving."
3. White's son is engaged by the same attractions: the joy of getting up early and going off by himself in a boat (par. 4), the fun of learning tricks

with a motor (10). But the essay sets forth an insight that is White's alone, and the boy is not portrayed in any clear detail until the final paragraph.

4. White's purpose, made explicit in the final paragraph, is to set forth a theme: that although time at the lake seems to have stood still, time for the writer has been passing. He has aged and he will die like his father before him.

QUESTIONS ON WRITING STRATEGY

1. The repetitions help set forth the central theme of the essay. (In question 4 above we suggest one way of stating it.)
2. Beautifully arranged, this essay doesn't completely unfold its purpose until its final line. By a multitude of details, we have been lulled into accepting the illusion that time stands still. Suddenly, in one unforgettable image, White invokes reality. The feeling of donning an ice-cold bathing suit is a familiar sensation from childhood, but the cold of the suit also suggests the cold of the grave.
3. Young readers, we trust, will understand and appreciate it, too. Ask them. Students might not be greatly excited by White's slowly unfolding account at first, but most do warm to it.
4. The author's tone, sometimes gently humorous, in general is nostalgic, even dreamlike — as if he were viewing the lake and his early adventures there through a gentle haze.
5. White's images appeal to all five senses. They capture the smells of bedroom and wet woods (par. 2); the sight of a dragonfly, the boat, and its contents (5); the sounds of motors (10); the taste of donuts dipped in sugar (11); and the tactile sense of damp moss in the bait can (5), of the "soggy, icy" bathing trunks (13).
6. The comparison, notably between White's childhood experiences and his son's, contains the essay's theme of time and mortality.

QUESTIONS ON LANGUAGE

1. For the word *cultist* (par. 6), it might be worth pointing out that White apparently means an enthusiast for cleanliness.
2. The diction might sound exaggerated, but "unique" and "holy" describe the way the lake appears to White in memory.
3. White's description of a thunderstorm is only one of the essay's rich array of figurative language. The lake in early morning preserves "the stillness of the cathedral" (par. 2). Waves keep "chucking the rowboat under the chin" (5). In paragraph 10 a one-cylinder engine was like a wild animal "eating out of your hand," and a boat could approach a dock like a charging bull. In paragraph 11 a steamboat used to look like a Ubangi, and a drink of soda pop would backfire like an engine. In paragraph 12 the storm becomes a wild concert, and the generations are linked "in a strong indestructible chain." The essay ends in a splendid metaphor.

E. B. WHITE ON WRITING

For aspiring writers — probably every class has at least one or two — E. B. White's advice must be among the most encouraging in existence. To the discouraged seventeen-year-old who wrote to him, White simply said, "Write." What eager aspirants might fail to notice at first glance is White's confession that he wrote "half a million words" before trying to get any of them into print. This statement comes as a cool, refreshing breeze in a world where too many people try to get published before they are ready.

E. B. White isn't big on market tips, either. His whole point is that if you really care about what you write, if you really work at it until it's as good as it can be, someone will want to read it. Clearly, not every aspiring writer was born with a gift equal to White's. Still, we hope you agree that one of the most helpful things you can impress upon students is that their writing will be better if they care about what they're saying.

**THERE'S STRONG.
THEN THERE'S
ARMY STRONG.**

ARE YOU ARMY STRONG?

goarmy.com
©2006. Paid for by the United States Army. All rights reserved.

U.S.ARMY

ARMY STRONG.™

12

DEFINITION

Tracing a Boundary

◀ **Definition in an advertisement**

This army recruitment ad doesn't define *strong*. Instead, it invites viewers to work military service into their own personal definitions of the word. The ad is part of a campaign, launched in 2006, that features the slogan with diverse soldiers on Web sites and in magazines read by young adults. Who seem to be the intended viewers of such ads? What goals of the advertiser is the campaign meant to address? What desires and concerns in readers might the ad appeal to? Why is the ad image so stark, and what does each of its few elements contribute to the appeal? What does the text contribute? At the same time, what concerns in viewers does the ad ignore or even reject?

THE METHOD

As a rule, when we hear the word DEFINITION, we immediately think of a dictionary. In that helpful storehouse—a writer's best friend—we find the literal and specific meaning (or meanings) of a word. The dictionary supplies this information concisely: in a sentence, in a phrase, or even in a *synonym*—a single word that means the same thing ("**narrative** [năr-e-tĭv] *n.* 1: story . . .").

Stating such a definition is often a good way to begin an essay when basic terms may be in doubt. A short definition can clarify your subject to your reader, and perhaps help you limit what you have to say. If, for instance, you are writing a psychology paper about schizophrenia, you might offer a short definition at the outset, your subject and your key term.

In constructing a short definition, the usual procedure is to state the general class to which the subject belongs and then add any particular features that distinguish it. You could say: "Schizophrenia is a brain disease"—the general class—"whose symptoms include hallucinations, disorganized behavior, incoherence, and, often, withdrawal." Short definitions may be useful at *any* moment in an essay, whenever you introduce a technical term that readers may not know.

When a term is really central to your essay and likely to be misunderstood, a *stipulative definition* may be helpful. This fuller explanation stipulates, or specifies, the particular way you are using a term. The paragraph on pages 513–14, defining *TV addiction*, could be a stipulative definition in an essay on the causes and cures of the addiction.

In this chapter, we are mainly concerned with *extended definition*, a kind of expository writing that relies on a variety of other methods. Suppose you wanted to write an essay to make clear what *poetry* means. You would specify its elements—rhythm, IMAGES, and so on—by using DIVISION or ANALYSIS. You'd probably provide EXAMPLES of each element. You might COMPARE AND CONTRAST poetry with prose. You might discuss the EFFECT of poetry on the reader. (The poet Emily Dickinson once stated the effect that reading a poem had on her: "I feel as if the top of my head were taken off.") In fact, extended definition, unlike other methods of writing discussed in this book, is perhaps less a method in itself than the application of a variety of methods to clarify a purpose. Like DESCRIPTION, extended definition tries to *show* a reader its subject. It does so by establishing boundaries, for its writer tries to differentiate a subject from anything that might be confused with it.

When Gloria Naylor, in her essay in this chapter, seeks to define the freighted word *nigger*, she recalls her experiences of the word as an African American, recounting exactly what she heard in varying situations. Extended definition examines the nature of the subject, carefully summing up its chief characteristics and drawing boundaries around it, striving to answer the question "What makes this what it is, not something else?"

An extended definition can define a word (like *nigger*), a thing (a laser beam), a condition (schizophrenia), a concept (TV addiction), or a general phenomenon (the popularity of *YouTube*). Unlike a sentence definition, or any you would find in a standard dictionary, an extended definition takes room: at least a paragraph, often an entire essay. In having many methods of writing at your disposal, you have ample freedom and wide latitude.

Unlike a definition in a dictionary that sets forth the literal meaning of a word in an unimpassioned manner, some definitions imply biases. Samuel Johnson, the eighteenth-century English critic and dictionary maker, had asked the Earl of Chesterfield for financial help and been ignored. When later the earl tried to befriend him, Johnson replied with a scornful definition: "Is not a Patron, my Lord, one who looks with unconcern on a man struggling for life in the water, and, when he has reached the ground, encumbers him with help?" IRONY, a FIGURE OF SPEECH (metaphor), and a short definition have rarely been wielded with such crushing power. (*Encumbers*, by the way, is a wonderfully physical word in its context: It means "to burden with dead weight.")

THE PROCESS

Discovery of Meanings

The purpose of almost any extended definition is to explore a topic in its full complexity, to explain its meaning or sometimes to argue for (or against) a particular meaning. To discover this complexity, you may find it useful to ask yourself the following questions. To illustrate how the questions might work, at least in one instance, let's say you plan to write a paper defining *sexism*.[1]

1. *Is this subject unique, or are there others of its kind? If it resembles others, in what ways? How is it different?* As you can see, these last two questions invite you to COMPARE AND CONTRAST. Applied to the concept of sexism, these questions might prompt you to compare sexism with one or two other -isms, such as racism or ageism. Or the questions might remind

[1]The six questions that follow are freely adapted from those first stated by Richard E. Young, Alton L. Becker, and Kenneth L. Pike, who have applied insights from psychology and linguistics to the writing process. To investigate subjects in greater depth, their own six questions may be used in nine possible combinations, as they explain in detail in *Rhetoric: Discovery and Change* (1970).

Definition

you that sexists can be both women and men, leading you to note the differences.

2. *In what different forms does it occur, while keeping its own identity?* Specific examples might occur to you: a magazine story you read about a woman's experiences in the army and a girlfriend who is nastily suspicious of all men. Each form—the soldier and the girlfriend—might rate a description.

3. *When and where do we find it? Under what circumstances and in what situations?* Well, where have you been lately? At any parties where sexism reared its ugly head? In any classroom discussions? Consider other areas of your experience: Did you encounter any sexists while holding a job?

4. *What is it at the present moment?* Perhaps you might make the point that sexism was once considered an exclusively male preserve but is now an attribute of women as well. Or you could observe that many men have gone underground with their sexism, refraining from expressing it blatantly while still harboring negative attitudes about women. In either case, you might care to draw examples from life.

5. *What does it do? What are its functions and activities?* Sexists stereotype and sometimes act to exclude or oppress people of the opposite sex. These questions might also invite you to reply with a PROCESS ANALYSIS: You might show, for instance, how a sexist man you know, a personnel director who determines pay scales, systematically eliminates women from better-paying jobs.

6. *How is it put together? What parts make it up? What holds these parts together?* You could apply analysis to the various beliefs and assumptions that, all together, make up sexism. This question might work well in writing about an organization: the personnel director's company, for instance, with its unfair hiring and promotion policies.

Not all these questions will fit every subject under the sun, and some may lead nowhere, but you will usually find them well worth asking. They can make you aware of points to notice, remind you of facts you already know. They can also suggest interesting points you need to find out more about.

Methods of Development

The preceding questions will give you a good start on using whatever method or methods of writing can best answer the overall question "What is the nature of this subject?" You will probably find yourself making use of much that you have learned earlier from this book. A short definition like the one for *schizophrenia* on page 508 may be a good start for your essay, especially if you think your readers need a quick grounding in the subject. (But feel no duty to place a dictionaryish definition in the INTRODUCTION of every essay you write: The device is overused.) In explaining schizophrenia, if your readers already have at least a vague idea of the meaning of the term and need no short, formal definition of it, you could open your extended definition by DESCRIBING the experiences of a person who has the disease:

> On his twenty-fifth birthday, Michael sensed danger everywhere. The voices in his head argued loudly about whether he should step outside. He could see people walking by who he knew meant him harm—the trick would be to wait for a break in the traffic and make a run for it. But the arguing and another noise—a clanging like a streetcar bell—made it difficult to concentrate, and Michael paced restlessly most of the day.

You could proceed from this opening to explain how Michael's experiences illustrate some symptoms of schizophrenia. You could provide other examples of symptoms. You could, through process analysis, explain how the disease generally starts and progresses. You could use CAUSE AND EFFECT to explore the theories of why schizophrenia occurs—from abnormalities in the part of the brain that controls sensation to incompatibilities in the blood types or antibodies of a mother and her infant.

Thesis

Opening up your subject with questions and developing it with various methods are good ways to see what your subject has to offer, but they can also leave you with a welter of ideas and a blurred focus. As in description, when all your details build to a DOMINANT IMPRESSION, so in definition you want to center all your ideas and evidence about the subject on a single controlling idea, a THESIS. It's not essential to state this idea in a THESIS STATEMENT, although doing so can serve your readers. It is essential that the idea govern.

Here, from the essays in this chapter, are two thesis statements. Notice how each makes an assertion about the subject, and how we can detect the author's bias toward the subject.

> The people in my grandmother's living room took a word [*nigger*] that whites used to signify worthlessness or degradation and rendered it impotent. . . . Meeting the word head-on, they proved it had absolutely nothing to do with the way they were determined to live their lives.
> —Gloria Naylor, "The Meanings of a Word"

> The word *chink* may have been created to harm, ridicule, and humiliate, but for us [Chinese Americans] it may have done the exact opposite.
> —Christine Leong, "Being a Chink"

Evidence

Writing an extended definition, you are like a mapmaker charting a territory, taking in some of what lies within the boundaries and ignoring what
lies outside. The boundaries, of course, may be wide; and for this reason, the
writing of an extended definition sometimes tempts a writer to sweep across
a continent airily and to soar off into abstract clouds. Like any other method
of expository writing, though, definition will work only for the writer who
remembers the world of the senses and supports every generalization with concrete evidence.

There may be no finer illustration of the perils of definition than the scene,
in Charles Dickens's novel *Hard Times*, of the grim schoolroom of a teacher
named Gradgrind, who insists on facts but who completely ignores living
realities. When a girl whose father is a horse trainer is unable to define a
horse, Gradgrind blames her for not knowing what a horse is; and he praises
the definition of a horse supplied by a pet pupil: "Quadruped. Graminivorous.
Forty teeth, namely twenty-four grinders, four eye-teeth, and twelve incisive.
Sheds coat in the spring; in marshy countries, sheds hoofs, too. Hoofs hard,
but requiring to be shod with iron. Age known by marks in mouth." To anyone who didn't already know what a horse is, this list of facts would prove of
little help. In writing an extended definition, never lose sight of the reality
you are attempting to bound, even if its frontiers are as inclusive as those of
psychological burnout or *human rights*. Give your reader examples, narrate an
illustrative story, bring in specific description — in whatever method you use,
keep coming down to earth. Without your eyes on the world, you will define
no reality. You might define *animal husbandry* till the cows come home and
never make clear what it means.

FOCUS ON PARAGRAPH AND ESSAY UNITY

When drafting a definition, you may find yourself being pulled away from your
subject by the descriptions, examples, comparisons, and other methods you
use to specify meaning. Let yourself explore byways of your subject — doing
so will help you discover what you think. But in revising you'll need to direct
all paragraphs to your thesis and, within paragraphs, to direct all sentences to
the paragraph topic, generally expressed in a TOPIC SENTENCE. In other words,
you'll need to ensure the UNITY of your essay and its paragraphs.

Gloria Naylor's "The Meanings of a Word" (p. 517) opens with several
paragraphs of background to the definition of the word *nigger* as it was used in
Naylor's extended African American family. When Naylor focuses on defining,
she proceeds methodically. As shown in the following outline, the paragraphs
begin with topic sentences that state parts of the definition, which Naylor then

illustrates with examples. (Some parts of the definition require more than a single paragraph, but Naylor keeps the groups of paragraphs focused on a single idea.)

PARAGRAPH 6   In the singular, the word was always applied to . . .

PARAGRAPH 9   When used with a possessive adjective by a woman—"my nigger"— it became a term of . . .

PARAGRAPH 10   In the plural, it became a description of . . .

PARAGRAPH 11   A woman could never be a "nigger" in the singular . . .

PARAGRAPH 13   But if the word was used in a third-person reference or shortened . . . , it always involved . . .

CHECKLIST FOR REVISING A DEFINITION

✔ **MEANINGS**   Have you explored your subject fully, turning up both its obvious and its not-so-obvious meanings?

✔ **METHODS OF DEVELOPMENT**   Have you used an appropriate range of other methods to develop your subject?

✔ **THESIS**   Have you focused your definition and kept within that focus, drawing clear boundaries around your subject?

✔ **EVIDENCE**   Is your definition specific? Do examples, anecdotes, and concrete details both pin the subject down and make it vivid for readers?

✔ **UNITY**   Do all paragraphs focus on your thesis, and do individual paragraphs or group of paragraphs focus on parts of your definition?

DEFINITION IN PARAGRAPHS

Writing about Television

The paragraph below SUMMARIZES a definition of *TV addiction*. The paragraph was written for *The Bedford Reader* as an example of definition, but its opening question suggests a broader use than just illustration: In a full essay on the causes and cures of the addiction, the paragraph could serve as a stipulative definition of the essay's key term.

Who is addicted to TV? According to Marie Winn, author of *The Plug-in Drug: Television, Children, and Family Life*, TV addicts are similar to drug or alcohol addicts: They seek a more pleasurable

Definition of TV addiction

experience than they can get from normal life; they depend on the source of this pleasure; and their lives are damaged by their dependency. TV addicts, says Winn, use TV to screen out the real world of feelings, worries, demands. They watch compulsively—four, five, even six hours on a work day. And they reject (usually passively, sometimes actively) interaction with family or friends, diverting or productive work at hobbies or chores, and chances for change and growth.

Comparison with drug or alcohol addiction

Analysis of TV addicts' characteristics

Writing in an Academic Discipline

This paragraph from a biology textbook defines a term, *homology*, that is useful in explaining the evolution of different species from a common ancestor (the topic at this point in the textbook). The paragraph provides a brief definition, a more extensive one, and finally examples of the concept.

When the character traits found in any two species owe their resemblance to a common ancestry, taxonomists say the states are *homologous*, or are *homologues* of each other. *Homology* is defined as correspondence between two structures due to inheritance from a common ancestor. Homologous structures can be identical in appearance and can even be based on identical genes. However, such structures can diverge until they become very different in both appearance and function. Nevertheless, homologous structures usually retain certain basic features that betray a common ancestry. Consider the forelimbs of vertebrates. It is easy to make a detailed, bone-by-bone, muscle-by-muscle comparison of the forearm of a person and a monkey and to conclude that the forearms, as well as the various parts of the forearm, are homologous. The forelimb of a dog, however, shows marked differences from those of primates in both appearance and function. The forelimb is used for locomotion by dogs but for grasping and manipulation by people and monkeys. Even so, all of the bones can still be matched. The wing of a bird and the flipper of a seal are even more different from each other or from the human forearm, yet they too are constructed around bones that can be matched on a nearly perfect one-to-one basis.
—William K. Purves and Gordon H. Orians,
Life: The Science of Biology

Definition of homology *and related words*

Short definition

Refined definition

Examples:
• *Similar appearance, function, and structure*

• *Dissimilar appearance and function, but similar structure*

DEFINITION IN AN ESSAY EXAM

You might worry about essay exams—many students do—but take heart: Instructors who assign in-class timed essays don't expect prize-winning compositions. They do, however, expect students to demonstrate their knowledge and critical thinking about important concepts covered in lectures and assignments.

Preparation is key to success on an essay exam, and so is reading the questions carefully. Often you'll need to interpret the wording to figure out what kind of response is appropriate. Questions that ask *why*, for example, might call for CAUSE-AND-EFFECT ANALYSIS, while those that ask *how* might lead to a PROCESS ANALYSIS. Keep in mind that an essay you write for an in-class exam will necessarily be less polished than one you would write at home. Time constraints force you to make points quickly, and they limit your ability to tinker with organization, transitions, or even an introduction and a conclusion. That's fine—as long as you draft an accurate, detailed, and reasonably coherent answer to the question asked.

The midterm exam for Martin Ward's introductory American government class included multiple-choice questions, a short-answer section, and one short-essay question: "Explain the meaning of *civil liberties*, including an explanation of how civil liberties differ from civil rights." Ward quickly recognized that "explain the meaning of" called for a definition and that "differ" called for an element of COMPARISON AND CONTRAST. Following the advice of his teaching assistant in the exam review session, Ward quickly outlined the points he needed to cover before he started writing. Then he composed the following response.

Civil liberties are the freedoms that individuals have against state intrusion. Laws protecting civil liberties limit or prohibit government action. The US Constitution's Bill of Rights guarantees many of these liberties, including freedom of expression, freedom of religion, and freedom from unreasonable searches and seizures. Historically, the protection of civil liberties was established before the US Constitution in documents such as the English Magna Carta (1215). Since that time, free countries have defined themselves against authoritarian countries by their respect for—and legal protections of—these freedoms.

While most people agree that civil liberties are essential to a free state, there is some controversy surrounding their meaning. People don't always agree which rights are civil liberties.

Annotations (right margin):

Short definition of *civil liberties*

Examples

Brief history of the concept

Extended definition considers issues that complicate meaning:

Side tab: Definition

For example, the debate over abortion reflects a dispute over whether the Constitution protects privacy rights that include the right to have an abortion. There is also disagreement about what constitutes a violation of civil liberties. As the federal government has taken measures to protect the country from terrorism, many have questioned whether practices such as warrantless wiretapping violate privacy rights, speech rights, or the prohibition of unreasonable searches and seizures.

People often confuse civil liberties with civil rights. Civil liberties are freedoms from government intrusion protected primarily by the Bill of Rights. Civil rights, however, concern the equal treatment of individuals in society and are established mainly by the Equal Protection Clause of the Fourteenth Amendment. An example is the right of citizens to attend public schools regardless of their color or gender. Civil liberties and civil rights differ in another important way as well: While protections of civil liberties prohibit government action, the government must often act to protect civil rights, as in the creation of antidiscrimination laws.

Which rights are civil liberties?

What violates civil liberties?

Point-by-point contrast with civil rights

GLORIA NAYLOR

Gloria Naylor describes herself as "just a girl from Queens who can turn a sentence," but she is well known for bringing African American women vividly within the fold of American literature. She was born in 1950 in New York City and served for some years as a missionary for the Jehovah's Witnesses, working "for better world conditions." While in college, she made her living as a telephone operator. She graduated from Brooklyn College in 1981 and received an MA in African American literature from Yale University in 1983. While teaching at several universities and publishing numerous stories and essays, Naylor has written five interconnected novels: *The Women of Brewster Place* (1982), *Linden Hills* (1985), *Mama Day* (1988), *Bailey's Cafe* (1992), and *The Men of Brewster Place* (1998). *The Women of Brewster Place* won the American Book Award for best first novel. In 2004 Naylor published *Conversations with Gloria Naylor*, a collection of interviews with the author. A fictionalized memoir, *1996*, followed in 2005.

The Meanings of a Word

When she was in third grade, Naylor was stung by a word that seemed new. Only later did she realize that she'd been hearing the word all her life, but in an entirely different context. In "The Meanings of a Word," she uses definition to explore the varying meanings that context creates. The essay first appeared in the *New York Times* in 1986.

The essay following this one, Christine Leong's "Being a Chink," responds directly to Naylor and extends her point about context and meaning.

Language is the subject. It is the written form with which I've managed to keep the wolf away from the door and, in diaries, to keep my sanity. In spite of this, I consider the written word inferior to the spoken, and much of the frustration experienced by novelists is the awareness that whatever we manage to capture in even the most transcendent passages falls far short of the richness of life. Dialogue achieves its power in the dynamics of a fleeting moment of sight, sound, smell, and touch.

I'm not going to enter the debate here about whether it is language that shapes reality or vice versa. That battle is doomed to be waged whenever we seek intermittent reprieve from the chicken and egg dispute. I will simply take the position that the spoken word, like the written word, amounts to a nonsensical arrangement of sounds or letters without a consensus that assigns "meaning." And building from the meanings of what we hear, we order reality. Words themselves are innocuous; it is the consensus that gives them true power.

I remember the first time I heard the word *nigger*. In my third-grade class, our math tests were being passed down the rows, and as I handed the papers to a little boy in back of me, I remarked that once again he had received a much lower mark than I did. He snatched his test from me and spit out that word. Had he called me a nymphomaniac or a necrophiliac, I couldn't have been more puzzled. I didn't know what a nigger was, but I knew that whatever it meant, it was something he shouldn't have called me. This was verified when I raised my hand, and in a loud voice repeated what he had said and watched the teacher scold him for using a "bad" word. I was later to go home and ask the inevitable question that every black parent must face—"Mommy, what does *nigger* mean?"

And what exactly did it mean? Thinking back, I realize that this could not have been the first time the word was used in my presence. I was part of a large extended family that had migrated from the rural South after World War II and formed a close-knit network that gravitated around my maternal grandparents. Their ground-floor apartment in one of the buildings they owned in Harlem was a weekend mecca for my immediate family, along with countless aunts, uncles, and cousins who brought along assorted friends. It was a bustling and open house with assorted neighbors and tenants popping in and out to exchange bits of gossip, pick up an old quarrel, or referee the ongoing checkers game in which my grandmother cheated shamelessly. They were all there to let down their hair and put up their feet after a week of labor in the factories, laundries, and shipyards of New York.

Amid the clamor, which could reach deafening proportions—two or three conversations going on simultaneously, punctuated by the sound of a baby's crying somewhere in the back rooms or out on the street—there was still a rigid set of rules about what was said and how. Older children were sent out of the living room when it was time to get into the juicy details about "you-know-who" up on the third floor who had gone and gotten herself "p-r-e-g-n-a-n-t!" But my parents, knowing that I could spell well beyond my years, always demanded that I follow the others out to play. Beyond sexual misconduct and death, everything else was considered harmless for our young ears. And so among the anecdotes of the triumphs and disappointments in the various workings of their lives, the word *nigger* was used in my presence, but it was set within contexts and inflections that caused it to register in my mind as something else.

In the singular, the word was always applied to a man who had distin- 6
guished himself in some situation that brought their approval for his strength,
intelligence, or drive:

"Did Johnny *really* do that?" 7

"I'm telling you, that nigger pulled in $6,000 of overtime last year. Said he 8
got enough for a down payment on a house."

When used with a possessive adjective by a woman — "my nigger" — it be- 9
came a term of endearment for her husband or boyfriend. But it could be
more than just a term applied to a man. In their mouths it became the pure
essence of manhood — a disembodied force that channeled their past history
of struggle and present survival against the odds into a victorious statement
of being: "Yeah, that old foreman found out quick enough — you don't mess
with a nigger."

In the plural, it became a description of some group within the community 10
that had overstepped the bounds of decency as my family defined it. Parents
who neglected their children, a drunken couple who fought in public, people
who simply refused to look for work, those with excessively dirty mouths or
unkempt households were all "trifling niggers." This particular circle could
forgive hard times, unemployment, the occasional bout of depression — they
had gone through all of that themselves — but the unforgivable sin was a lack
of self-respect.

A woman could never be a "nigger" in the singular, with its connotation 11
of confirming worth. The noun *girl* was its closest equivalent in that sense,
but only when used in direct address and regardless of the gender doing the
addressing. *Girl* was a token of respect for a woman. The one-syllable word was
drawn out to sound like three in recognition of the extra ounce of wit, nerve,
or daring that the woman had shown in the situation under discussion.

"G-i-r-l, stop. You mean you said that to his face?" 12

But if the word was used in a third-person reference or shortened so that 13
it almost snapped out of the mouth, it always involved some element of communal disapproval. And age became an important factor in these exchanges.
It was only between individuals of the same generation, or from any older person to a younger (but never the other way around), that *girl* would be considered a compliment.

I don't agree with the argument that use of the word *nigger* at this social 14
stratum of the black community was an internalization of racism. The dynamics were the exact opposite: The people in my grandmother's living room took
a word that whites used to signify worthlessness or degradation and rendered
it impotent. Gathering there together, they transformed *nigger* to signify the
varied and complex human beings they knew themselves to be. If the word

was to disappear totally from the mouths of even the most liberal of white society, no one in that room was naive enough to believe it would disappear from white minds. Meeting the word head-on, they proved it had absolutely nothing to do with the way they were determined to live their lives.

So there must have been dozens of times that *nigger* was spoken in front   15
of me before I reached the third grade. But I didn't "hear" it until it was said by a small pair of lips that had already learned it could be a way to humiliate me. That was the word I went home and asked my mother about. And since she knew that I had to grow up in America, she took me in her lap and explained.

---

*For a reading quiz, sources on Gloria Naylor, and annotated links to further readings on the language of stereotypes, visit **bedfordstmartins.com/thebedfordreader**.*

Journal Writing

As Naylor shows, the language of stereotypes can be powerful and painful to encounter. In your journal, recall when you have experienced or witnessed this kind of labeling. What were your reactions? Keep in mind that race is but one object of stereotypes. Consider income, education, body type or other physical attributes, sexual preference, activities, or neighborhood, for just a few other characteristics. (To take your journal writing further, see "From Journal to Essay" on the next page.)

Questions on Meaning

1. Why does Naylor think that written language is inferior to spoken language (par. 1)?
2. In paragraph 15, Naylor says that although the word *nigger* had been used in her presence many times, she didn't really "hear" the word until a mean little boy said it. How do you explain this contradiction?
3. Naylor says that "[t]he people in my grandmother's living room . . . transformed *nigger*" (par. 14). How?
4. What is Naylor's primary PURPOSE in this essay?

Questions on Writing Strategy

1. In her first two paragraphs, Naylor discusses language in the ABSTRACT. How are these paragraphs connected to her stories about the word *nigger*? Why do

you think she begins the essay this way? Is this INTRODUCTION effective or not? Why?

2. Go through Naylor's essay and note which paragraphs discuss the racist uses of *nigger* and which discuss the nonracist uses. How do Naylor's organization and the space she devotes to each use help Naylor make her point? How does Naylor integrate the two definitions to achieve UNITY?

3. Look back at the last two sentences of Naylor's essay. What is the EFFECT of ending on this idea?

4. **OTHER METHODS** After each definition of the words *nigger* and *girl*, Naylor gives an EXAMPLE in the form of a quotation. These examples are in paragraphs 7–10 (for instance, "Yeah, that old foreman found out quick enough—you don't mess with a nigger" [9]) and paragraph 12 ("G-i-r-l, stop. You mean you said that to his face?"). What do such examples add to Naylor's definitions?

Questions on Language

1. What is "the chicken and egg dispute" (par. 2)? What does this dispute say about the relationship between language and reality?

2. What do the words *nymphomaniac* and *necrophiliac* CONNOTE in paragraph 3?

3. If you don't know the meanings of the following words, look them up in a dictionary: transcendent, dynamics (par. 1); intermittent, reprieve, consensus, innocuous (2); verified (3); gravitated, mecca (4); clamor, inflections (5); endearment, disembodied (9); unkempt, trifling (10); communal (13); stratum, internalization, degradation, rendered, impotent, naive (14).

Suggestions for Writing

1. **FROM JOURNAL TO ESSAY** Using as examples the experiences you wrote about in your journal entry, write an essay modeled on Naylor's in which you define "the meanings of a word" (or words). Do you find, too, that meaning varies with context? If so, make the variations clear.

2. Can you think of other labels that may be defined in more than one way? (These might include *smart, childish, old-fashioned, artistic, proud, attractive, heroic*, and so on.) Choose one such label, and write one paragraph for each possible definition. Be sure to explain the contexts for each definition and to give enough examples so that the meanings are clear.

3. Americans continually debate the use of the word *nigger*. Some have proposed banning the word entirely, while others argue that eliminating the word would erase its role in US history and its painful legacy. Two recent books explore the theoretical and practical issues of the word: Randall Kennedy, *Nigger: The Strange Career of a Troublesome Word* (2002), and Jabari Asim, *The N-Word: Who Can Say It, Who Shouldn't, and Why* (2007). Consult one or both of these books, and form your own opinion about how the word should be treated. Explain your position in an essay.

4. **CRITICAL WRITING** Naylor claims that words are "nonsensical . . . without a consensus that assigns 'meaning'" (par. 2). If so, how do we understand the meaning of a word like *nigger*, when Naylor has shown us that there is more than one

consensus about its meaning? Does Naylor contradict herself? Write an essay that either supports or refutes Naylor's claim about meaning and context. You will need to consider how she and you define *consensus*.

5. **CONNECTIONS** The next essay, Christine Leong's "Being a Chink," identifies a moment when Leong was first struck by the negative power of racist language. Write an essay that COMPARES AND CONTRASTS Naylor's and Leong's reactions to a derogatory label. How did the context help shape their reactions?

Gloria Naylor on Writing

Studying literature in college was somewhat disappointing for Gloria Naylor. "What I wanted to see," she told William Goldstein of *Publishers Weekly*, "were reflections of me and my existence and experience." Then, reading African American literature in graduate school, she discovered that "blacks have been writing in this country since this country has been writing and have a literary heritage of their own. Unfortunately, they haven't had encouragement or recognition for their efforts. . . . What had happened was that when black people wrote, it wasn't quite [considered] serious work — it was race work or protest work."

For Naylor this discovery was a turning point. "I wanted to become a writer because I felt that my presence as a black woman and my perspective as a woman in general had been underrepresented." Her work tries to "articulate experiences that want articulating — for those readers who reflect the subject matter, black readers, and for those who don't, basically white middle-class readers."

For Discussion

1. What does Naylor mean when she says that she tries to "articulate experiences that want articulating"?
2. Naylor is motivated to write by a consciousness of herself as an African American and a woman. How do you see this motivation driving her essay "The Meanings of a Word"?

CHRISTINE LEONG

Christine Leong was born in New York City in 1976 and attended Stuyvesant High School there, graduating in 1994. At the Stern School of Business at New York University, she majored in finance and information systems and interned at an investment firm. She graduated with a BS in 1998 and took a job in financial services. In her free time, Leong enjoys a good doughnut and cheering on the New York Yankees. "The one thing I couldn't live without," she says, "is music."

Being a Chink

Leong wrote this essay for her freshman composition class at NYU, and it was published in *Mercer Street, 1995–96,* a collection of NYU students' essays. As you'll see, Leong was inspired by Gloria Naylor's "The Meanings of a Word" (p. 517) to report her own experiences and to define a word that can be either hurtful or warm, depending on the speaker.

The power of language is something that people often underestimate. It is the one thing that allows people to communicate with each other, to be understood, to be heard. It gives us identity, personality, social status, and it also creates communities, defining both insiders and outsiders. Language has the ability to heal or to harm, to praise or belittle, to promote peace or even to glorify hate. But perhaps most important, language is the tool used to define us and differentiate us from the next person. Names and labels are what separate us from each other. Sometimes these things are innocuous, depending on the particular word and the context in which it is used. Often they serve to ridicule and humiliate.

I remember the first time I saw the word *chink.* I used to work over the summers at my father's Chinese restaurant, the Oriental, to earn a few extra dollars of spending money. It was a warm, sunny Friday morning, and I was busy performing my weekly task of cleaning out the storage area under the cash register at the front of the store. Armed with a large can of Pledge furniture polish and an old cloth, I started attacking the old oak shelves, sorting through junk mail that had accumulated over the last week, separating the bills and other important things that had to be set aside for later, before wiping each wooden panel clean. It was a pretty uneventful chore, that is, until I got to the bottom shelf, the last of three. I always hated cleaning this particular shelf because it required me to get down on my hands and knees behind the counter and reach all the way back into the compartment to dig out all the stuff that managed to get wedged against the wall.

After bending to scoop all the papers out of that third cubicle, I began 3 to sort through them haphazardly. A few old menus, a gum wrapper (I always wondered how little things like that got stuffed in there), some promotional flyers, two capless pens, a dusty scratch pad, and something that appeared to be a little white envelope. Nothing seemed unusual until I examined that last item more closely. It was an old MidLantic envelope from the bank across the street. I was just about to crumple it up and throw it into the trash can when I decided to check if there was any money left in it. Too lazy to deal with the actual "chore" of opening the envelope, I held it up to the light.

As the faint yellow glow from the antique light fixture above me shone 4 through the envelope, turning it transparent, my suspicion that it was empty was confirmed. However, what I found was more shocking than anything I could have imagined. There, outlined by the light, was the word *chink* written backwards. I quickly lowered my arm onto the cool, smooth surface of the counter and flipped the envelope onto its other side, refusing to believe what I had just read. On the back, in dark blue ink with a large circle drawn around it, was the word *CHINK* written in my father's handwriting.

Up until that moment, I hadn't known that my father knew such words, 5 and thinking again, perhaps he didn't know this one either. After all, it was a habit of his to write down English words he did not know when he heard them and look them up in the dictionary later that day, learning them and adding them to his vocabulary. My mind began spinning with all the possible reasons he had written this particular word down. I wondered if an angry patron who had come in earlier had called him that.

I was shocked at that possibility, but I was not surprised. Being one of only 6 two Asian families living and running a business in a small suburban town predominately inhabited by old Caucasian people was bound to breed some kind of discrimination, if not hatred. I know that my father might not have known exactly what the word *chink* meant, but he must have had a good idea, because he never came to ask me about it as he did with all the other slang words that couldn't be found in the dictionary. It's funny, though, I do not remember the first time I was called a *chink*. I only remember the pain and outrage I felt the first time I saw it in writing, perhaps the first time I discovered that someone had used that hateful word to degrade my father.

In her essay "The Meanings of a Word," Gloria Naylor examines the various meanings of the word *nigger*, definitions that have consensual meanings throughout society and others that vary according to how and when the word is used. In this piece, Naylor uses personal examples to describe how "[t]he

people in [her] grandmother's living room took a word that whites used to signify worthlessness or degradation and rendered it impotent," by transforming
nigger into a word signifying "the varied and complex human beings that they
knew themselves to be." Naylor goes on to add that although none of these
people were foolish enough to believe that the word *nigger* would magically
be erased from the minds of all humankind, they were convinced that their
"head-on" approach of dealing with the label that society had put on them
"proved [that] it had absolutely nothing to do with the way they were determined to live their lives."

It has been nearly eight years since that day I stumbled across the bank   8
envelope. Since then we have moved from that suburb in New Jersey to New
York City, where the Asian population is much larger, and the word *chink*,
although still heard, is either heard less frequently or in a rather "harmless"
manner between myself and fellow Chinese (Asian) teenage friends. I do not
remember how it happened exactly. I just know that we have been calling
each other *chink* for quite a long while now. The word has never been used to
belittle or degrade, but rather as a term of endearment, a loving insult between
friends, almost but not quite exactly the way *nigger* is sometimes used among
black people. It is a practice that we still engage in today, and although we
know that there are times when the use of the word *chink* is very inappropriate, it is an accepted term within our circle.

Do not misunderstand us, we are all intelligent Asian youths, all graduat-   9
ing from New York City's top high school, all college students, and we know
what the word *chink* truly means. We know, because over the years we have
heard it countless times, from strangers on the streets and in stores, from fellow students and peers, and in some instances even from teachers, although it
might not have been meant for us to hear.

So you see, even though we may use the term *chink* rather casually, it is   10
only used that way amongst ourselves because we know that when we say
it to each other it is truly without malice or harmful intent. I do not think
that any of us knows exactly why we do it, but perhaps it is our own way, like
the characters in Naylor's piece, of dealing with a label that can never be
removed. It is not determined by who we are on the inside, or what we are
capable of accomplishing, but instead by what we look like—the shape of
our eyes, the color of our skin, the texture of our hair, and our delicate features. Perhaps we intentionally misuse the word as a symbol of our overcoming the stereotypes that American society has imposed upon us, a way of
showing that although others have tried to make us feel small, weak, and
insignificant, we are the opposite. We are strong, we are determined, we are
the voices of the future, and we refuse to let a simple word paralyze us, belittle
us, or control us.

The word *chink* may have been created to harm, ridicule, and humiliate,   11
but for us it may have done the exact opposite. In some ways it has helped us
find a certain comfort in each other, each of us knowing what the other has
gone through, a common thread of racism binding us all together, a strange
union born from the word *chink* that was used against us, and a shared goal of
perseverance.

> For a reading quiz and annotated links to further readings on the language of stereo-
> types, visit **bedfordstmartins.com/thebedfordreader**.

Journal Writing

Although children often assume they will be protected by their parents, Leong presents a situation in which she felt the need to protect her father. Can you identify with
Leong's feelings? Have you ever felt particularly angry or defensive on behalf of a
parent? In your journal, explore why and what happened as a result. (To take your
journal writing further, see "From Journal to Essay" on the facing page.)

Questions on Meaning

1. In paragraph 9 Leong says that she and her friends "know what the word *chink*
   truly means." Where in her essay does she explain this "true" meaning?
2. What has the word *chink* come to mean when Leong and her friends use it? Where
   in the essay does Leong explain this?
3. One might argue that the THESIS of Leong's essay is that language is not absolute.
   Is her PURPOSE, then, to propose a new DEFINITION for a word, to teach the reader
   something about how labels work, or to explain how adapting a racist term can
   be a form of gaining power? How do you know?

Questions on Writing Strategy

1. Look carefully at Gloria Naylor's essay "The Meanings of a Word" (p. 517). What
   structural similarities do you notice between it and Leong's? Why do you think
   Leong adapts these features of Naylor's essay?
2. In paragraph 3 Leong details all the forgotten items she finds under the counter.
   What is the EFFECT of ending with the "old MidLantic envelope from the bank
   across the street"?
3. What is the main purpose of the extended example from Naylor's essay in paragraph 7?

4. Why is Leong so careful to explain that she and her friends are all intelligent and educated (par. 9)?
5. **OTHER METHODS** Leong suggests CAUSE AND EFFECT when she expresses shock and disbelief at seeing the word *chink* in writing (par. 4). Why does Leong react so strongly to the writing on the envelope?

Questions on Language

1. In paragraph 10 Leong explains that she and her friends are "dealing with a label that can never be removed." What other words does she use in this paragraph to suggest the potential helplessness of being permanently labeled?
2. What do the CONNOTATIONS of "term of endearment" (par. 8) indicate about the way Leong and her friends have redefined *chink*?
3. Make sure you know the meanings of the following words: status, belittle, innocuous (par. 1); cubicle, haphazardly (3); Caucasian, degrade (6); consensual (7); malice (10); perseverance (11).

Suggestions for Writing

1. **FROM JOURNAL TO ESSAY** Write an essay that explores why and how children might feel compelled to act like parents toward their own parents. Is this a shift that comes with age? with specific circumstances? out of the blue? Make some GENERALIZATIONS about this process, using as EVIDENCE the personal recollections from your journal entry.
2. As Leong explains in her INTRODUCTION, not all labels are intended to be hurtful. Often they are shorthand ways for our families and friends to identify us, perhaps reflecting something about our appearance ("Red," "Slim") or our interests ("Sport," "Chef"). What do your family or friends call you? Write several paragraphs giving a careful definition of this label. Where did it come from? Why is it appropriate (or not)?
3. Research the history of Chinese Americans. When and why did the initial wave of immigration occur? What forces have led to other patterns of immigration over the years? Have Chinese Americans faced different kinds of discrimination than other immigrants have? In an essay, answer these or other questions that occur to you.
4. **CRITICAL WRITING** In her opening paragraph Leong says that "language is the tool used to define us." But she goes on to explain how she and her friends *refuse* to be defined by racist language. Does this apparent contradiction weaken her essay? Why, or why not? (To answer this question, consider the purpose of Leong's essay; see "Meaning" question 3.)
5. **CONNECTIONS** Both Leong and Gloria Naylor, in "The Meanings of a Word" (p. 517), show that racist language can be taken over by those against whom it is directed. They also show that for groups or communities to redefine, and thus to own, these racist slurs can be empowering. Do you find their ARGUMENTS convincing, or do these redefinitions reveal what Naylor denies—namely, "an internalization of racism" (par. 14)? In an essay, explain your opinion on this issue, using as evidence passages from Naylor's and Leong's essays as well as insights and EXAMPLES from your own observations and experience.

Christine Leong on Writing

For *The Bedford Reader,* Christine Leong commented on the difficulties of writing and the rewards that can ensue.

Writing is something that comes easily for many people, but unfortunately I am not one of them. For me the writing process is one of the hardest and quite possibly is *the* most nerve-wracking thing that I have ever experienced. I can't even begin to count all the hours I have spent throughout the course of my life staring at a blank computer screen, trying desperately to come up with the right combination of words to express my thoughts and feelings, and although after many hours of frustration I eventually end up with something, I am never happy with it because I am undoubtedly my own worst critic. Perhaps my mentality of "it's not good enough yet" stems from my belief that writing can never really be completed; to me it has no beginning and no end but is rather a small representation of who I am at a given moment in time, and I believe that the more things I experience in life, the more I am able to contribute to my writing. Thus, whatever I write always has the potential of being better; there's always room for improvement via more revisions, greater insight, and about a hundred more drafts.

I used to believe that writing always had to make sense, but since then I have learned that there are many things in this life that do not adhere to this "rule." I now realize that writing doesn't necessarily have to be grammatically correct or even sensible, and the only thing that really matters is that whatever is written is truly inspired. Passion comes through very clearly in a writer's words, and the more emotion that goes into a piece, the more impact it will ultimately have on the reader. In recent years I have learned that there are no real writing guidelines, and that writing is much like any other art form: It can be abstract or it can follow more traditional "themes." However, in order for a piece of writing to be effective, in the sense that it can differentiate itself from any other writing sample and hopefully have some significance to the reader, I believe that it has to come from within.

The majority of what I write about, and that which I feel is worth reading, is inspired by actual experiences that I have had. For example, "Being a Chink" began as an assignment in a freshman writing workshop class in college. When first presented with the task of writing it, I was at a complete loss for words and had absolutely no clue where to start. However, after reading Gloria Naylor's "The Meanings of a Word," I was reminded of one of the most traumatic and memorable events in my life. The piece triggered a very strong memory, and before long I found myself writing down anything that came into my head, letting my thoughts and emotions flow freely in the form of words without thinking about whether or not they made any kind of sense. Many hours later I discovered that I had written the basic structure of what would eventually be my final product. I must honestly say that I can't really recall the actual process of writing "Being a Chink"; it was just an essay that seemed to take on a life and form of its own. Perhaps that, along with its universal theme, is what makes it such a strong piece. It not only is a recollection from my adolescence but is something that defines the very essence of the person that I have become since then.

In retrospect, I now realize that writing "Being a Chink" was not only about completing an essay and fulfilling a writing requirement; it was also about the acknowledgment of my own growth as a person. In many ways, without my initially being aware of it, the piece has helped me come to terms with one of the most controversial issues that I have ever been faced with.

For Discussion

1. Does Leong's characterization of writing as "nerve-wracking" ring bells with you? How do you overcome writer's block?
2. What do you think about Leong's statement that "writing doesn't necessarily have to be grammatically correct or even sensible, and the only thing that really matters is that whatever is written is truly inspired"? In your experience with writing, what are the roles of correctness, sense, and inspiration? What matters most to you? What matters most to readers?

THOMAS SOWELL

Thomas Sowell has been called "perhaps the leading black scholar among conservatives." His support for free markets and corresponding disdain for government regulations and social programs has endeared him to those on the right of center, while his logic and clarity have earned him respect from those on the left. Born in North Carolina in 1930, Sowell attended a segregated high school and went on to earn three degrees in economics: a BA from Harvard College (1958), an MA from Columbia University (1959), and a PhD from the University of Chicago (1968). He has taught at Cornell University, the University of California at Los Angeles, Amherst College, and other schools; served as an economist in government and business; and since 1980 has been affiliated with the Hoover Institution at Stanford University. Sowell writes a syndicated newspaper column and has published over three dozen books on economics, education, and race, including *Affirmative Action around the World: An Empirical Study* (2004), *Black Rednecks and White Liberals* (2005), and *The Housing Boom and Bust* (2009). His latest book is *Intellectuals and Society* (2010), a critique of how the "intelligentsia" influence public opinion and government policy.

"Needs"

What do we really need? In this essay from his collection *Is Reality Optional?* (1993), Sowell says that most of our genuine needs are already met; what we think we need is only what we want. Failing to make this distinction, Sowell believes, hurts us all.

1   A group of UCLA economists were having lunch together one day at the faculty club. One of them, named Mike, got up to get himself some more coffee. Being a decent sort, he asked:

2   "Does anybody else here need coffee?"

3   "Need?!" another economist cried out in astonishment and outrage.

4   The other economists around the table also pounced on this unfortunate word, while poor Mike retreated to the coffee maker, like someone who felt lucky to escape with his life.

5   Partly this was good clean fun—or what passes for good clean fun among economists. But partly it was a very serious issue.

6   Someone is always talking about what we "need"—more child care centers, more medical research, more housing, more environmental protection. The list goes on and on. All the things we "need" would add up to far more than the gross national product. Obviously we cannot and will not get all the things we "need."

Why call them "needs" then? We obviously get along without them, sim- 7
ply because we have no choice. These "needs" are simply things we want—or
that some of us want. Given that we cannot possibly have all the things we
want, we have to make trade-offs. That is what economics is all about.

Words like *needs, rights,* or *entitlements* try to put some things on a pedes- 8
tal, so that they don't have to face the reality of trade-offs. This is part of the
higher humbug of politics.

Surely some things are really needs, you might say. If that is true, food 9
must be one of those needs, since we would die without it. Huge agricultural
surpluses are one result of this kind of mushy thinking.

There is obviously some amount of food that is urgently required to keep 10
body and soul together. But the average American already takes in far more
food than is necessary to sustain life—and in fact so much food as to make his
lifespan shorter than it would be at a lower weight.

Like virtually everything else, food beyond some point ceases to be as 11
urgently demanded and even ceases to be a benefit. When it reaches the point
of being positively harmful, it can hardly be called a "need." That is why rigid
words like *need* spread so much confusion in our thinking and havoc in our
policies.

Prices force us into trade-offs, which is one of many reasons why the mar- 12
ketplace operates so much more efficiently than political allocation according
to "need," "entitlement," "priorities" or other such rigid notions.

The real issue is almost never whether we should have nothing at all or 13
some unlimited amount, or even some fixed amount of a particular good. The
real issue is what kind of trade-off makes sense. That usually means having
some of many things but not all we want of anything.

Prices tell us what the terms of the trade-offs are. Do we "need" more cloth- 14
ing? At some prices we do and at other prices we can get along with what we
have. I happen to own three suits. But if clothing prices were one-tenth of
what they are, I might have a wardrobe that would knock you dead.

My daughter used to make snide remarks about an old car that I drove 15
for eight years. She stopped only when I told her that I could easily afford
to get a new car, just by not paying her tuition. That's what trade-offs are all
about.

If the government were giving out cars to those who "needed" them, I 16
could have written an application that would have brought tears to your eyes.
I could have gone on talk shows and worked up public sympathy over the ways
my old jalopy was messing up my life—even threatening my life because the
brakes failed completely twice.

If the taxpayers were paying for it, I would have "needed" a new car. But, 17
since it was my money that was being spent, I had a brake job instead.

Politicians take advantage of our mushy thinking by promising to meet   18
our "need" or by giving us a "right" or "entitlement" to this or that. But let's
go back to square one. Politicians don't manufacture anything except hot air.
Every "need" they meet takes away from some other "need" somewhere else.

Every job the government creates is supported by resources taken out of   19
the private sector, where those same resources could have created another
job—or maybe two other jobs, given the wastefulness of government.

"Needs" are a dangerous concept. Mike the economist suffered only a   20
momentary embarrassment from using the word. Our whole economy and society
suffer much more from the mindless policies based on such misconceptions.

> For a reading quiz, sources on Thomas Sowell, and annotated links to further readings
> on the concepts of wants and needs in economics, visit **bedfordstmartins.com/
> thebedfordreader**.

Journal Writing

How would you define your own personal needs? In your journal, write about what you
require for a comfortable and fulfilled life. (To take your journal writing further, see
"From Journal to Essay" on the next page.)

Questions on Meaning

1. How does Sowell define the customary use of *needs*? What is distinctive about this
   definition?
2. What would you say is Sowell's underlying PURPOSE in offering his definition?
3. What does Sowell mean when he talks about "trade-offs" (pars. 12–15)?

Questions on Writing Strategy

1. Why do you think Sowell begins his essay with the story of Mike and the other
   UCLA economists? How does this story support his point about *needs*?
2. Why does Sowell put quotation marks around *need* in his title and throughout
   the essay?
3. What is Sowell's reason for writing about food in paragraphs 9–11 and his old car
   in paragraphs 15–17? Do you think these EXAMPLES help clarify his point?
4. **OTHER METHODS** How does Sowell use CAUSE AND EFFECT in paragraphs 18–20?

Questions on Language

1. Check a dictionary for the meanings of *humbug* (par. 8). Why do you think Sowell chose to use this word?
2. If you don't know the meanings of *allocation* and *entitlement* (par. 12), look them up in a dictionary.
3. Sowell refers to *need* as a "rigid" word (par. 11). What is his point in using this adjective?
4. Point to some examples of informal language in the essay. What is the EFFECT of such language?

Suggestions for Writing

1. **FROM JOURNAL TO ESSAY** Based on your journal writing, compose an essay in which you define your own needs. Which needs do you share with most other people, and which are particular to yourself? What trade-offs must you make among your needs?
2. Because government cannot provide everything we think we need, Sowell says, we have to establish priorities for allocating public funds. Write an essay that lays out what you believe should be the priorities in government spending. What must government provide, and what should it not be responsible for?
3. **CRITICAL WRITING** Write an essay in which you ANALYZE the UNITY of Sowell's essay. What methods does Sowell use to create unity? Does he digress at all?
4. **CONNECTIONS** Consider Sowell's essay in COMPARISON with Anna Quindlen's "Homeless" (p. 216), which focuses on the need for a home, and Chitra Divakaruni's "Live Free and Starve" (p. 466), which questions the need for laws banning child labor. Using all three works as examples, write your definition of *need*.

BARBARA KINGSOLVER

A writer of fiction, poetry, and nonfiction and a self-described "human rights activist," Barbara Kingsolver was born in Annapolis, Maryland, in 1955 and grew up in eastern Kentucky. She studied biology at DePauw University (BA, 1977) and the University of Arizona (MS, 1981) and worked in the field as a researcher and technical writer. A full-time writer since 1985, Kingsolver has published a variety of well-received books including the novels *The Bean Trees* (1988), *The Poisonwood Bible* (1998), and *The Lacuna* (2009); the essay collections *High Tide in Tucson* (1995) and *Small Wonder* (2002); a poetry collection in English and Spanish, *Another America/Otra America* (1990); and the observational memoir *Animal, Vegetable, Miracle: A Year of Food Life* (2007). In 2000, Kingsolver won the National Humanities Medal for service through the arts.

Rural Delivery

In *Animal, Vegetable, Miracle,* Kingsolver records and reflects on a year-long project to eat nothing but locally produced organic food. Having uprooted themselves from Tucson, Arizona, she and her family settled on a small farm in Appalachia and began raising poultry and planting, harvesting, and preserving their own fruits and vegetables, calling on nearby farmers and merchants for beef, pork, and sundries. In this excerpt from the book, Kingsolver explores the labels and assumptions too often used to define a small yet significant group of Americans.

I grew up among farmers. In my school system we were all born to our rank, as inescapably as Hindus, the castes[1] being only two: "farm" and "town." Though my father worked in town, we did not live there, and so by the numinous but unyielding rules of high school, I was "farmer." It might seem astonishing that a rural-urban distinction like this could be made in a county that boasted, in its entirety, exactly two stoplights, one hardware store, no beer joints (the county was dry), and fewer residents than an average Caribbean cruise ship. After I went away to school, I remained in more or less constant marvel over the fact that my so-called small liberal arts college, with an enrollment of about 2,000, was 25% larger than my hometown.

And yet, even in a community as rural as that, we still had our self-identified bourgeoisie, categorically distinguished from our rustics. We of the

---

[1] Traditional Indian Hindu society groups people into five social classes, or castes: intellectuals, rulers, merchants, laborers, and "untouchables." The classes are assigned at birth and, because they are based on heredity, can never be changed. — EDS.

latter tribe could be identified by our shoes (sometimes muddy, if we had to cover rough country to get to the school bus), our clothes (less frequently updated), or just the bare fact of a Rural Free Delivery mailing address. I spent my childhood in awe of the storybook addresses of some of my classmates, like "14 Locust Street." In retrospect I'm unsure of how fact-based the distinction really was: Most of us "farm" kids were well-scrubbed and occasionally even stylish. Nevertheless, the line of apartheid was unimpeachably drawn. Little socializing across this line was allowed except during special events forced on us by adults, such as the French Club Dinner, and mixed-caste dating was unthinkable except to the tragic romantics.

Why should this have been? How did the leafy, sidewalked blocks behind 3 the newspaper office confer on their residents a different sense of self than did the homes couched among cow pastures and tobacco fields? The townie shine would have dimmed quickly (I now realize) if the merchants' confident offspring were catapulted suddenly into Philadelphia or Louisville. "Urban" is relative. But the bottom line is that it matters. The antipathy in our culture between the urban and nonurban is so durable, it has its own vocabulary: (A) city slicker, tenderfoot; (B) hick, redneck, hayseed, bumpkin, rube, yokel, clodhopper, hoecake, hillbilly, Dogpatch, Daisy Mae, farmer's daughter, from the provinces, something out of *Deliverance*.[2] Maybe you see where I'm going with this. The list is lopsided. I don't think there's much doubt, on either side, as to which class is winning the culture wars.

Most rural people of my acquaintance would not gladly give up their status. 4 Like other minorities, we've managed to turn several of the aforementioned slurs into celebrated cultural identifiers (for use by insiders only). In my own life I've had ample opportunity to reinvent myself as a city person — to *pass*, as it were — but I've remained tacitly rural-identified in my psyche, even while living in some of the world's major cities. It's probably this dual citizenship that has sensitized me to my nation's urban-rural antipathy, and how it affects people in both camps. Rural concerns are less covered by the mainstream media, and often considered intrinsically comic. Corruption in city governments is reported as grim news everywhere; from small towns (or Tennessee) it is fodder for talk-show jokes. Thomas Hardy[3] wrote about the sort of people who milked cows, but writers who do so in the modern era will be dismissed as marginal. The policy of our nation is made in cities, controlled largely by urban voters who aren't well informed about the changes on the face of our land, and the men and women who work it.

---

[2] James Dickey's 1970 novel, made into a film in 1972, in which city residents taking a river-rafting trip in backcountry Georgia are hunted and tortured by locals. — EDS.
[3] English novelist (1840–1928). — EDS.

Those changes can be mapped on worry lines: As the years have gone by,   5
as farms have gone out of business, America has given an ever-smaller cut
of each food dollar (now less than 19%) to its farmers. The psychic divide
between rural and urban people is surely a part of the problem. "Eaters must
understand," Wendell Berry[4] writes, "that eating takes place inescapably in the
world, that it is inescapably an agricultural act, and that how we eat determines,
to a considerable extent, how the world is used." Eaters *must*, he claims, but it
sure looks like most eaters *don't*. If they did, how would we frame the sentence
suggested by today's food-buying habits, directed toward today's farmers? "Let
them eat dirt" is hardly overstating it. The urban US middle class appears
more specifically concerned about exploited Asian factory workers.

Symptomatic of this rural-urban identity crisis is our eager embrace of a   6
recently imposed divide: the Red States and the Blue States. That color map
comes to us with the suggestion that both coasts are populated by educated
civil libertarians, while the vast middle and south are crisscrossed with the
studded tracks of ATVs leaving a trail of flying beer cans and rebel yells. Okay,
I'm exaggerating a little. But I certainly sense a bit of that when urban friends
ask me how I can stand living here, "*so far from everything?*" (When I hear this
question over the phone, I'm usually looking out the window at a forest, a running creek, and a vegetable garden, thinking: Define *everything*.) Otherwise
sensitive coastal-dwelling folk may refer to the whole chunk of our continent
lying between the Cascades and the Hudson River as "the Interior." I gather
this is now a common designation. It's hard for me to see the usefulness of
lumping Minneapolis, Atlanta, my little hometown in Kentucky, Yellowstone
Park, and so forth, into a single category that does not include New York
and California. "Going into the Interior" sounds like an endeavor that might
require machetes to hack through the tangled vines.

In fact, the politics of rural regions are no more predictable than those   7
in cities. "Conservative" is a reasonable position for a farmer who can lose
home and livelihood all in one year by taking a risk on a new crop. But that's
conservative as in, "eager to conserve what we have, reluctant to change the
rules overnight," and unrelated to how the term is currently (often incompre-
hensibly) applied in party politics. The farm county where I grew up had so
few Republicans, they all registered Democrat so they could vote in the only
local primary. My earliest understanding of radical, class-conscious politics
came from miners' strikes in one of the most rural parts of my state, and of our
nation.

---

[4] American farmer and writer, born in 1934. —Eds.

The only useful generalization I'd hazard about rural politics is that they   8
tend to break on the line of "insider" vs. "outsider." When my country neighbors sit down with a new social group, the first question they ask one another
is not "What do you do?" but rather, "Who are your people?" Commonly
we will spend more than the first ten minutes of a new acquaintance tracing
how our families might be related. If not by blood, then by marriage. Failing
that, by identifying someone significant we have known in common. Only
after this ritual of familial placing does the conversation comfortably move
on to other subjects. I am blessed with an ancestor who was the physician
in this county from about 1910 into the 1940s. From older people I'll often
hear of some memorably dire birth or farm accident to which my great-uncle
was called; lucky for me he was skilled and Hippocratic.[5] But even a criminal
ancestor will get you insider status, among the forgiving. Not so lucky are
those who move here with no identifiable family ties. Such a dark horse is
likely to remain "the new fellow" for the rest of his natural life, even if he
arrived in his prime and lives to be a hundred.

The country tradition of mistrusting outsiders may be unfairly applied, but   9
it's not hard to understand. For much of US history, rural regions have been
treated essentially as colonial property of the cities. The carpetbaggers of the
reconstruction era[6] were not the first or the last opportunists to capitalize on
an extractive economy. When urban-headquartered companies come to the
country with a big plan—whether their game is coal, timber, or industrial
agriculture—the plan is to take out the good stuff, ship it to the population
centers, make a fortune, and leave behind a mess.

Given this history, one might expect the so-called Red States to vote con-   10
sistently for candidates supporting working-class values. In fact, our nation in
almost every region is divided in a near dead heat between two parties that
apparently don't distinguish themselves clearly along class lines. If every state
were visually represented with the exact blend of red and blue it earned in
recent elections, we'd have ourselves a big purple country. The tidy divide is
a media just-so story.

Our uneasy relationship between heartland and coasts, farm and factory,   11
country and town, is certainly real. But it is both more rudimentary and more
subtle than most political analysts make it out to be. It's about loyalties, perceived communities, and the things each side understands to be important

[5] A reference to the Hippocratic Oath of doctors to practice ethically. The oath is generally attributed to the ancient Greek doctor Hippocrates.—Eds.

[6] After the Civil War, many northern politicians and businessmen went to the South in
search of opportunity. Some had luggage made of heavy tapestry—hence the derisive name
carpetbaggers.—Eds.

because of the ground, literally, upon which we stand. Wendell Berry summed it up much better than "blue and red" in one line of dialogue from his novel *Jayber Crow*, which is peopled by farmers struggling to survive on what the modern, mostly urban market will pay for food. After watching nearly all the farms in the county go bankrupt, one of these men comments: "I've wished sometimes that the sons of bitches would starve. And now I'm getting afraid they actually will."

*For a reading quiz, sources on Barbara Kingsolver, and annotated links to further readings on farming, visit **bedfordstmartins.com/thebedfordreader**.*

Journal Writing

Where did you grow up? Is the area considered rural, urban, or something in between? Take a few minutes to characterize your hometown in your journal. Consider its physical attributes (landscape, buildings, roads, and such) as well as its culture and politics. (To take your journal writing further, see "From Journal to Essay" on the facing page.)

Questions on Meaning

1. In your own words, SUMMARIZE Kingsolver's definition of *rural*.
2. Kingsolver writes in her introduction (par. 1) that "by the numinous but unyielding rules of high school, I was 'farmer.'" What does she mean? Does she, in fact, consider herself a farmer? Explain your answer.
3. How do paragraphs 9–11 contribute to Kingsolver's definition?
4. What would you say is Kingsolver's PURPOSE in this essay?

Questions on Writing Strategy

1. Why do you suppose Kingsolver opens the essay as she does? What point does she make by discussing her childhood identity?
2. How does Kingsolver maintain UNITY in her essay?
3. "Rural Delivery" is a model of an *extended* definition, yet the essay also includes several *stipulative* definitions. Locate at least two of these. What do they contribute to Kingsolver's meaning?
4. **OTHER METHODS** Paragraphs 6–10 develop a binary, or two-part, CLASSIFICATION. Why do you think Kingsolver considers "Red States" and "Blue States" at such length? To what is she ALLUDING?

Questions on Language

1. Kingsolver twice quotes Wendell Berry in her essay. Why? What is the EFFECT of these quotations?
2. Find some examples of both formal and informal DICTION in the essay. What is the effect of Kingsolver's word choice?
3. Be sure you know the meanings of the following words, checking a dictionary if necessary: castes, numinous (par. 1); bourgeoisie, categorically, latter, apartheid, unimpeachably (2); confer, catapulted, antipathy (3); tacitly, psyche, intrinsically (4); symptomatic, civil libertarians, endeavor (6); colonial, capitalize, extractive (9); rudimentary (11).

Suggestions for Writing

1. **FROM JOURNAL TO ESSAY** How do outsiders view the place where you grew up? Building on your journal entry and using Kingsolver's essay as a model, write an essay of your own that COMPARES AND CONTRASTS your perception of your hometown with the perception of it by people who don't live there. What ASSUMPTIONS do others make, and how accurate are they? Are there any misconceptions you would like to correct, or do you share outsiders' assessment of the area? Why?
2. According to the National Institute of Food and Agriculture, 17% of Americans live in rural areas and fewer than 2% farm for a living. Research a current issue with family farms in the United States: Timely topics include competition with agribusiness, federal regulations and subsidies, financial stability, and opportunities. Then write an essay that presents your findings.
3. **CRITICAL WRITING** Based on this essay, ANALYZE Kingsolver's view of the state of national politics. In what ways has the political climate changed in recent years, according to the writer? How meaningful does she find the distinction between "red" and "blue" states? How does she portray conservative and liberal philosophies, as well as disagreements among political parties? Which groups does Kingsolver consider most powerful and which most disadvantaged? Why? What problems does she identify, and what solutions, if any, does she propose?
4. **CONNECTIONS** Kingsolver writes in paragraph 4 that "[l]ike other minorities," rural people have "managed to turn several . . . slurs into celebrated cultural identifiers (for use by insiders only)" — an effort similar to those discussed in detail by Gloria Naylor in "The Meanings of a Word" (p. 517) and by Christine Leong in "Being a Chink" (p. 523). Where those two writers tackle issues of race, however, Kingsolver bases her idea of what constitutes a *minority* on culture and geography. How might Naylor and Leong respond to Kingsolver's use of the word *minority* to characterize herself? Are slurs aimed at cultural or geographic identity of the same caliber as those aimed at race? In an essay, bring these three writers together, considering what they have in common as well as what they do not.

Barbara Kingsolver on Writing

"People think it's sort of funny," Barbara Kingsolver says, "that I went to graduate school as a biologist and then became a writer." In a 1996 interview with Robin Epstein of *The Progressive* magazine, Kingsolver explains that the processes of science and writing are very similar. "What I learned [in science] is how to formulate or identify a new question that hasn't been asked before, and then to set about solving it, to do original research to find the way to an answer. And that's what I do when I write a book."

Asked if she ever has doubts about her "abilities as a writer," Kingsolver replies, "I still have them. Beginning a book is really hard. I'm trying to begin one now and I just keep throwing stuff away and thinking, 'Can I do this? I don't think I'm smart enough.' You have to have a reverence for the undertaking. And I think reverence implies a certain lack of self-esteem. . . . You feel daunted and unworthy. But in this age of glorifying the individual and self-esteem, I think there's something healthy about being daunted. Cockiness doesn't lend itself to good writing. It really doesn't."

For Discussion

1. Many writers, including experienced ones, often feel hampered by a lack of confidence in their abilities. How then could an excess of confidence harm a writer's work?
2. What parallels does Kingsolver see between scientific inquiry and writing? Are her insights about writing potentially helpful to nonscientists?

ANDREA JONES

Andrea Jones was born in Colorado and grew up enjoying camping and horse-back riding. After graduating from the University of Colorado, she worked for a year as a horse trainer before obtaining a master's degree in literary research from Lancaster University in England. Jones eventually earned a PhD in interdisciplinary studies from Capella University in Minneapolis, Minnesota, writing her dissertation on nonscientists' perspectives on science. She continues to write on the environment, natural history, and science; her articles have been published in the *Christian Science Monitor, Orion,* and *Camas,* among other periodicals. Jones is self-employed as a professional indexer and freelance writer. She lives in rural Colorado where she spends plenty of time outdoors and volunteers for a hospice, a museum, and the National Weather Service.

Identity's Edge

"Identity's Edge," first published in *Orion* magazine in 2007, takes a close, lyrical look at the largest organ of the human body. Jones muses that, more than just a protective membrane, skin is our gateway to the world and everything in it.

Stretched over a singular arrangement of muscle, bone, and memory, skin 1 is the membrane that distinguishes self from world. Inside its margins: you. Beyond its flexy surface: *everything else.* Pause to consider this for long, and you may be inclined to sit very, very still. To call attention to yourself seems risky, even insane. There should be more than this flimsy dermal bubble separating the vastness of the cosmos from the throb of blood and consciousness that is you.

Your skin marks the tangible, visible, and sensory edge of the anatomical 2 landscape you claim as your own. From fingerprints to facial features, the thin topcoat of your body carries the nuances of form, texture, and tone that make you identifiable as an individual. Think about the variability of your skin, the medley of textures that play across your body's convolutions: smooth, lined, shiny, baggy, tight, freckled, scarred, goose-pimply, plump. Here, skin hugs the rim of a nostril. There, it throws a seductive curl over the tragus of the ear. It cups your heels with thickened pads. On your knuckles, creases coalesce like knots on a pine board.

Your skin's position at the body's outer edge obligates it with protective 3 functions. It guards the tender tissues of your interior from heat, cold, pathogens, and the sharp edges of the world. But to be alive—to be human— you must let certain things in. Lest you explode from the weight of your waste, loneliness, and bad ideas, you must also let some things out. Your skin, accordingly, is shot with holes—pores, nostrils, auditory canals, ducts, the ins and outs of the digestive tract, sockets for eyes.

Skin is the edge to which nerves run their finest feelers. What you reg-   4
ister at your body's fringe is the dazzling sensory display that we corral under the term "touch": the sloppy glide of a dog's tongue, the sharp ache of snow trapped between wrist and mitten cuff, the scabrous rub of sand beneath your feet, the spark of pain when you bang your shin on the lowered door of the dishwasher, cool fingers on a fevered forehead, a kiss. At its best, sensation is a shared gift, touch and feel echoing and bouncing between bodies.

Over most of the body, the structures that house the peripheral nerves are   5
arranged in a uniform carpet of bumps, like the taste buds scattered across your tongue. At the body's extremities, however, a more refined sense of touch is called for. The meandering ridges and furrows that grace your palms and soles show where touch receptors are packed together as tightly and efficiently as possible. These fluid patterns of whorls, arches, and loops are popularly called fingerprints, but they also swirl across the soles of your feet and are more for-mally referred to as *dermatoglyphics*, from the Greek roots *derma* and *glyphein*: skin carving. Your dermatoglyphics reflect a biological investment in height-ened sensitivity where you most commonly make contact with the world.

It is convenient to think of the human birthday suit as a membrane that   6
separates, preserving the boundary between self and not-self. But from the moment your parental gametes linked their half-strands of DNA to form the zygote that would develop into you, everything you now claim as yourself has been derived from matter and information imported across your body's external membrane. The world may be full of things that slash, nibble, pierce, abrade, infect, and sear, but it is also replete with oxygen, sunlight, chocolate, laughter, the colors of leaves in autumn, the smell of fresh-baked bread, the twining of bodies under the covers on a winter's night. Skin differentiates but does not isolate. Your singular existence unfolds within it, but skin does not hold the universe at bay. Instead it marks the seam that joins your existence to *everything else*.

For a reading quiz, sources on Andrea Jones, and annotated links to further readings on the human body, visit **bedfordstmartins.com/thebedfordreader**.

Journal Writing

Jones writes about a physical and metaphorical relationship between skin and identity, between "you" and "*everything else*" (par. 1). Of course, other elements have led to your becoming a unique person with certain abilities, likes and dislikes, quirks, and so forth. In your journal explore the most important aspects of your personal history that have influenced who you are today. (To take your journal writing further, see "From Journal to Essay" on the next page.)

Questions on Meaning

1. What exactly does Jones define in this essay? Does she write merely to contemplate the features of human skin, or does she seem to have a larger PURPOSE in mind?
2. Why does Jones say, "To call attention to yourself seems risky, even insane" (par. 1)? What does she mean?
3. What are *dermatoglyphics* (par. 5)? Why does Jones prefer that word to *fingerprints*?
4. Where does Jones state her THESIS? What is it? Why doesn't she include it in her introduction?

Questions on Writing Strategy

1. Explain how Jones uses concrete images to explain an abstract concept. What makes her analogy effective as a definition? (See *Abstract and concrete* as well as *Analogy* in Useful Terms.)
2. This definition essay is unusual in that the writer addresses her AUDIENCE in the second person (*you*). What is the EFFECT of this pronoun on you as a reader?
3. Analyze the organization of "Identity's Edge." What does Jones discuss in each of her paragraphs? How does she create UNITY among them?
4. **OTHER METHODS** In addition to using DIVISION OR ANALYSIS to break skin down into its component parts and functions, Jones's definition relies on DESCRIPTION, drawing on sense impressions to give a vivid picture. Which senses does Jones invoke? What is the DOMINANT IMPRESSION created by her imagery?

Questions on Language

1. Why do you suppose Jones italicizes "everything else" in paragraphs 1 and 6?
2. Jones often strings together series of adjectives, nouns, or phrases, such as "smooth, lined, shiny, baggy, tight, freckled, scarred, goose-pimply, plump" (par. 2) and "pores, nostrils, auditory canals, ducts, the ins and outs of the digestive tract, sockets for eyes" (3). Find at least three additional examples. What is the EFFECT of this construction?
3. Point out some of the FIGURES OF SPEECH Jones uses in this essay. What metaphors, similes, or personifications do you find particularly fresh or inventive?

4. Consult a dictionary if you don't know the meaning of any of the following words: membrane, dermal (par. 1); tangible, anatomical, nuances, convolutions, tragus, coalesce (2); obligates, pathogens, lest, auditory (3); scabrous (4); peripheral, receptors, whorls (5); gametes, zygote, abrade, sear, replete, twining (6).

Suggestions for Writing

1. **FROM JOURNAL TO ESSAY** Based on your journal writing, compose an essay in which you contemplate and explain your sense of identity. How do you define yourself? What distinguishes you from and connects you to "*everything else*" in the world? What has made you who you are?

2. Using Jones's essay as a model, write an essay of your own that defines another part of the human body—*heart*, for example, or *brain* or *eyes* or *hair*. As Jones does, consider not only the physical aspects of your subject but also any symbolic meanings that occur to you.

3. **CRITICAL WRITING** Write an essay in which you analyze Jones's use of language in this essay or a portion of it. How would you characterize her DICTION? What are some especially creative uses of language? What overall effect does Jones create based on the language she uses?

4. **CONNECTIONS** Like Jones, several other writers in this book find connections among skin, identity, and one's interactions with the world. (See, for instance, Maya Angelou's "Champion of the World" on p. 110, Brent Staples's "Black Men and Public Space" on p. 226, and Martin Luther King's "I Have a Dream" on p. 643.) Unlike Jones, however, those writers focus on the effects of skin color. Why do you suppose Jones omits color from her examination of skin and its meanings? How do the other writers' observations complicate her definition?

ADDITIONAL WRITING TOPICS
Definition

1. Write an essay in which you define an institution, trend, phenomenon, or abstraction as specifically and concretely as possible. Following are some suggestions designed to stimulate ideas. Before you begin, limit your subject.

Responsibility	Sportsmanship
Fun	Leadership
Sorrow	Leisure
Unethical behavior	Originality
The environment	Character
Education	Imagination
Progress	Democracy
Advertising	A smile
Happiness	A classic (of music, literature, art, or film)
Fads	Dieting
Feminism	Meditation
Marriage	Friendship

2. In a brief essay, define one of the following. In each instance, you have a choice of something good or something bad to talk about.

A good or bad boss
A good or bad parent
A good or bad host
A good or bad TV newscaster
A good or bad physician
A good or bad nurse
A good or bad minister, priest, rabbi, or imam
A good or bad roommate
A good or bad driver
A good or bad disk jockey

3. In a paragraph, define one of the following slang expressions for someone who has never heard the term: *bling, sick, hook up, wack, dis, cred, wicked, poser, wimp, loser, quack, chill, sweet.*

13

ARGUMENT AND PERSUASION

Stating Opinions and Proposals

◀ **Argument and persuasion in an image**

Adbusters Media Foundation, an activist group "concerned about the erosion of our physical and cultural environments by commercial forces," launched its Corporate America flag in 1999. This version appeared in a full-page advertisement in the *New York Times*. Replacing the American flag's stars with well-known corporate logos, the image adapts a symbol that many Americans revere to make a strong argument about the United States. What is the argument? How do you respond to the image: Are you offended? persuaded? amused? Why? Whatever your view, do you understand why others might think differently?

THE METHOD

Practically every day, we try to persuade ourselves or someone else. We usually attempt such persuasion without being aware that we follow any special method at all. Often, we'll state an *opinion:* We'll tell someone our own way of viewing things. We say to a friend, "I'm starting to like Senator Clark. Look at all she's done to help people with disabilities. Look at her voting record on toxic waste." And, having stated these opinions, we might go on to make a *proposal,* to recommend that some action be taken. Addressing our friend, we might suggest, "Hey, Senator Clark is talking on campus at four-thirty. Want to come with me and listen to her?"

Sometimes you try to convince yourself that a certain way of interpreting things is right. You even set forth an opinion in writing—as in a letter to a friend who has asked, "Now that you're at New Age College, how do you like the place?" You may write a letter of protest to a landlord who wants to raise your rent, pointing out that the bathroom hot water faucet doesn't work. As a concerned citizen, you may wish to speak your mind in an occasional letter to a newspaper or to your elected representatives.

In many professions, one is expected to persuade people in writing. Before arguing a case in court, a lawyer prepares briefs setting forth all the points in favor of his or her side. Businesspeople regularly put in writing their ideas for new products and ventures, for improvements in cost control and job efficiency. Researchers write proposals for grants to obtain money to support their work. Scientists write and publish papers to persuade the scientific community that their findings are valid, often stating hypotheses, or tentative opinions.

Even if you never produce a single persuasive work (which is very unlikely), you will certainly encounter such works directed at you. In truth, we live our lives under a steady rain of opinions and proposals. Organizations that work for causes campaign with posters and direct mail, all hoping that we will see things their way. Moreover, we are bombarded with proposals from people who wish us to act. Religious leaders urge us to lead more virtuous lives. Advertisers urge us to rush right out and buy the large economy size.

Small wonder, then, that argument and persuasion—and CRITICAL THINK-ING about argument and persuasion—may be among the most useful skills a college student can acquire. Time and again, your instructors will ask you to criticize or to state opinions, either in class or in writing. You may be asked to state your view of anything from the electoral college to animal rights. You may be asked to judge the desirability or undesirability of compulsory testing for drugs or the revision of existing immigration laws. On an examination in, say, sociology, you may be asked, "Suggest three practical approaches to the most pressing needs of disadvantaged people in urban areas." Critically read-ing other people's arguments and composing your own, you will find, helps you discover what you think, refine it, and share what you believe.

Is there a difference between argument and persuasion? It is, admittedly, not always clear. Strictly speaking, PERSUASION aims to influence readers' actions, or their support for an action, by engaging their beliefs and feelings, while ARGUMENT aims to win readers' agreement with an assertion or claim by engaging their powers of reasoning. But most effective persuasion or argument contains elements of both methods; hence the confusion. In this book we tend to use the terms interchangeably.

One other point: We tend to talk here about *writing* argument and per-suasion, but most of what we say has to do with *reading* them as well. When we discuss your need, as a writer, to support your claims, we are also discussing your need, as a reader, to question the support other authors provide for their claims. In reading arguments critically, you apply the critical-thinking skills we discussed in Chapter 1 — ANALYSIS, INFERENCE, SYNTHESIS, EVALUATION — to a particular kind of writing.

Transaction between Writer and Reader

Unlike some television advertisers, responsible writers of argument and persuasion do not try to storm people's minds. In writing a paper for a course, you persuade by gentler means: by sharing your view with readers willing to consider it. You'll want to learn how to express your view clearly and vigor-ously. But to be fair and persuasive, it is important to understand your readers' views as well.

In stating your opinion, you present the truth as you see it: "The immi-gration laws discourage employers from hiring nonnative workers" or "The immigration laws protect legal aliens." To persuade your readers that your view makes sense, you need not begin by proclaiming that, by Heaven, your view is absolutely right and should prevail. Instead, you might begin by trying to state what your readers probably think, as best you can infer it. You don't con-sider views that differ from your own merely to flatter your readers. You do so to correct your own view and make it more accurate. Regarded in this light, argument and persuasion aren't cynical ways to pull other people's strings. Writer and reader become two sensible people trying to find a common ground. This view will relieve you, whenever you have to state your opinions in writing, of the terrible obligation to be one hundred percent right at all times.

Elements of Argument

The British philosopher Stephen Toulmin has proposed a useful division of argument into three parts. Adapted to the terminology of this book, they are *claims*, *evidence*, and *assumptions*.

Claims and Thesis Statements

A CLAIM is an assertion that requires support. It is what an argument tries to convince readers to accept. The central claim—the main point—is almost always stated explicitly in a THESIS STATEMENT like one of the following:

A CLAIM ABOUT REALITY   The war on drugs is not winnable because it cannot eradicate demand or the supply to meet it.

A CLAIM OF VALUE   Drug abuse is a personal matter that should not be subject to law.

A CLAIM FOR A COURSE OF ACTION   The United States must intensify its efforts to reduce production of heroin in Afghanistan.

Usually, but not always, you'll state your thesis at the beginning of your essay, making a play for readers' attention and clueing them in to your purpose. But if you think readers may have difficulty accepting your thesis until they've heard some or all of your argument, then you might save the thesis statement for the middle or end.

The essays in this chapter provide a variety of thesis statements as models. Here are three examples:

Today there is more pressure placed on students to do well [in school]. . . . This new pressure is what is causing the increase in cheating.
—Colleen Wenke, "Too Much Pressure"

Athletes—those who dope, who take steroids, who cheat—are victims of far more serious maladies than their sports.
—Peter F. Martin, "Destroyed"

[T]hose of us who are refugees and exiles must live with the double menace of being both possible victims and suspects, sometimes with fatal consequences. Will America ever learn again how to protect itself without sacrificing a great many innocent lives? So that my uncle did not die in vain, I truly hope so.   —Edwidge Danticat, "Not Your Homeland"

Evidence

A claim is nothing without the EVIDENCE to make it believable and convincing. Toulmin calls evidence *data* or *grounds*, using terms that convey how specific and fundamental it is. Depending on your subject, your evidence may include facts, statistics (facts expressed in numbers), expert opinions, examples, and reported experience. These kinds of evidence should meet certain criteria:

- *Accuracy:* Facts, examples, and opinions are taken from reliable sources and presented without error or distortion.
- *Representation:* Evidence reflects reality, neither slanting nor exaggerating it.
- *Relevance:* Evidence is directly applicable to the claims, reflecting current thinking by recognized experts.
- *Adequacy:* Evidence is sufficient to support the claims entirely, not just in part.

To strengthen the support for your claims, you can also make appeals to readers either directly or indirectly, in the way you present your argument.

- Make a RATIONAL APPEAL by relying on sound reasoning and marshaling evidence that meets the criteria above. See pages 552–56 for more on reasoning.
- Make an ETHICAL APPEAL by showing readers that you are a well-informed person of goodwill, good sense, and good moral character — and, therefore, to be believed. Strengthen the appeal by collecting ample evidence, reasoning carefully, demonstrating respect for opposing views, using an appropriate emotional appeal (see below), and minding your TONE (see pp. 558–59).
- Make an EMOTIONAL APPEAL by acknowledging what you know of readers' sympathies and beliefs and by showing how your argument relates to them. An example in this chapter appears in Colleen Wenke's "Too Much Pressure," when Wenke appeals to readers' sense of fairness (or unfairness) by pointing out that many future leaders may gain their positions by cheating in school. Carefully used, an emotional appeal can stir readers to constructive belief and action by engaging their feelings as well as their minds. Be careful, though, that your emotional appeal is appropriate for your argument. "Do you really want to deprive your children of what's best for them?" asks a pitch for a certain learn-to-read program, appealing to pride or shame while neglecting to provide evidence that the program works.

Assumptions

The third element of argument, the ASSUMPTION, is in Toulmin's conception the connective tissue between grounds, or evidence, and claims: An assumption explains why the evidence leads to and justifies the claim. Called a *warrant* by Toulmin, an assumption is usually a belief, a principle, or an inference whose truth the writer takes for granted. Here is how an assumption might figure in an argument for one of the claims given earlier:

> CLAIM   The United States must intensify its efforts to reduce the production of heroin in Afghanistan.
>
> EVIDENCE   Afghanistan is the world's largest heroin producer and the dominant supplier to the United States.
>
> ASSUMPTION   The United States can and should reduce the production of heroin in other countries when its own citizens are affected.

As important as they are, the assumptions underlying an argument are not always stated. As we will see in the discussion of deductive reasoning, which begins on the next page, unstated assumptions can sometimes pitch an argument into trouble.

Reasoning

When we argue rationally, we reason—that is, we make statements that lead to a conclusion. Two reliable methods of reasoning date back to the Greek philosopher Aristotle, who identified the complementary process of INDUCTIVE REASONING (induction) and DEDUCTIVE REASONING (deduction). In *Zen and the Art of Motorcycle Maintenance*, Robert M. Pirsig gives examples of both processes:

> If the cycle goes over a bump and the engine misfires, and then goes over another bump and the engine misfires, and then goes over another bump and the engine misfires, and then goes over a long smooth stretch of road and there is no misfiring, and then goes over a fourth bump and the engine misfires again, one can logically conclude that the misfiring is caused by the bumps. That is induction: reasoning from particular experiences to general truths.
>
> Deductive inferences do the reverse. They start with general knowledge and predict a specific observation. For example if, from reading the hierarchy of facts about the machine, the mechanic knows the horn of the cycle is powered exclusively by electricity from the battery, then he can logically infer that if the battery is dead the horn will not work. That is deduction.

Inductive Reasoning

In inductive reasoning, the method of the sciences, we collect bits of evidence on which to base a GENERALIZATION, the claim of the argument. The assumption linking evidence and claim is that what is true for some circumstances is true for others as well. For instance, you might interview a hundred representative students about their attitudes toward changing the school's honor code. You find that 65% of your interviewees believe that the code should remain as it is, 15% believe that the code should be toughened, 10% believe that it should be loosened, and 10% have no opinion. You then assume that these statistics can be applied to the student body as a whole and make a claim against changing the code because 65% of students don't want change.

The more evidence you have, the more trustworthy your claim will be, but it would never be airtight unless you interviewed every student on campus. Since such thoroughness is almost always impractical if not impossible, you assume in an *inductive leap* that the results can be generalized. The smaller the leap—the more evidence you have—the better.

Deductive Reasoning

Deductive reasoning works the opposite of inductive reasoning: It moves from a general statement to particular cases. The basis of deduction is the SYL-LOGISM, a three-step form of reasoning practiced by Aristotle:

> All men are mortal.
>
> Socrates is a man.
>
> Therefore, Socrates is mortal.

The first statement, called a *major premise,* is an assumption: a fact, principle, or inference that you believe to be true. The second statement, or *minor premise,* is the evidence—the new information about a particular member of the larger group named in the major premise. The third statement, or *conclusion,* is the claim that follows inevitably from the premises. If the premises are true, then the conclusion must be true. Following is another example of a syllogism. You may recognize it from the discussion of assumptions on pages 551–52, only here the statements are simplified and arranged differently:

> MAJOR PREMISE (ASSUMPTION)   The United States can and should reduce heroin production when its own citizens are affected.
>
> MINOR PREMISE (EVIDENCE)   The dominant producer of heroin for the US market is Afghanistan.
>
> CONCLUSION (THESIS)   The United States can and should reduce heroin production in Afghanistan.

Problems with deductive reasoning start in the premises. In 1633, Scipio Chiaramonti, professor of philosophy at the University of Pisa, came up with this untrustworthy syllogism: "Animals, which move, have limbs and muscles. The earth has no limbs and muscles. Hence, the earth does not move." This is bad deductive reasoning, and its flaw is to assume that all things need limbs and muscles to move—ignoring raindrops, rivers, and many other moving things.

When they're spelled out like Chiaramonti's, bad syllogisms are pretty easy to spot. But many deductive arguments are not spelled out. Instead, one of the premises goes unstated, as in this statement: "Mayor Perkins was humiliated in his recent bid for reelection, winning only 2,000 out of 5,000 votes." The unstated assumption here, the major premise, is "Winning only two-fifths of the votes humiliates a candidate." (The rest of the syllogism: "Mayor Perkins received only two-fifths of the votes. Thus, Mayor Perkins was humiliated.")

The unstated premise isn't necessarily a problem in argument—in fact, it's quite common. But it *is* a problem when it's wrong or unfounded. For instance, in the statement "She shouldn't be elected mayor because her husband has bad ideas on how to run the city," the unstated assumption is that the candidate cannot form ideas independently of her husband. This is a possibility, perhaps, but it requires its own discussion and proof, not concealment behind other assertions.

Here's another argument with an unstated assumption, this one adapted from a magazine advertisement: "Scientists have no proof, just statistical correlations, linking smoking and heart disease, so you needn't worry about the connection." Now, the fact that this ad was placed by a cigarette manufacturer would tip off any reasonably alert reader to beware of bias in the claim. To discover the slant, we need to examine the unstated assumption, which runs something like this: "Since they are not proof, statistical correlations are worthless as guides to behavior." It is true that statistical correlations are not scientific proof, by which we generally mean repeated results obtained under controlled laboratory conditions—the kind of conditions to which human beings cannot ethically be subjected. But statistical correlations *can* establish connections and in fact inform much of our healthful behavior, such as getting physical exercise, avoiding fatty foods, brushing our teeth, and not driving while intoxicated. The advertiser's unstated premise isn't valid, so neither is the argument.

Logical Fallacies

In arguments we read and hear, we often meet logical FALLACIES: errors in reasoning that lead to wrong conclusions. From the time you start thinking about your proposition or claim and planning your paper, you'll need to watch out for them. To help you recognize logical fallacies when you see them or hear them, and so guard against them when you write, here is a list of the most common.

- **Non sequitur** (from the Latin, "it does not follow"): stating a conclusion that doesn't follow from one or both premises.

  I've lived in this town a long time — why, my grandfather was the first mayor — so I'm against putting fluoride in the drinking water.

- **Oversimplification:** supplying neat and easy explanations for large and complicated phenomena.

  No wonder drug abuse is out of control. Look at how the courts have hobbled police officers.

  Oversimplified solutions are also popular:

  All these teenage kids that get in trouble with the law — why, they ought to put them in work camps. That would straighten them out!

  (See also p. 459.)

- **Hasty generalization:** leaping to a generalization from inadequate or faulty evidence. The most familiar hasty generalization is the stereotype:

  Men aren't sensitive enough to be day-care providers.

  Women are too emotional to fight in combat.

- **Either/or reasoning:** assuming that a reality may be divided into only two parts or extremes; assuming that a given problem has only one of two possible solutions.

  What's to be done about the trade imbalance with Asia? Either we ban all Asian imports, or American industry will collapse.

  Obviously, either/or reasoning is a kind of extreme oversimplification.

- **Argument from doubtful or unidentified authority:**

  Uncle Oswald says that we ought to imprison all sex offenders for life.

  According to reliable sources, my opponent is lying.

- **Argument ad hominem** (from the Latin, "to the man"): attacking a person's views by attacking his or her character.

  Mayor Burns is divorced and estranged from his family. How can we listen to his pleas for a city nursing home?

- **Begging the question:** taking for granted from the start what you set out to demonstrate. When you reason in a *logical* way, you state that because something is true, then, as a result, some other truth follows. When you beg the question, however, you repeat that what is true is true. For instance:

  Dogs are a menace to people because they are dangerous.

This statement proves nothing, because the idea that dogs are dangerous is already assumed in the statement that they are a menace. Beggars of questions often just repeat what they already believe, only in different words. This fallacy sometimes takes the form of arguing in a circle, or demonstrating a premise by a conclusion and a conclusion by a premise:

I am in college because that is the right thing to do. Going to college is the right thing to do because it is expected of me.

- **Post hoc, ergo propter hoc** (from the Latin, "after this, therefore because of this"), or *post hoc* for short: assuming that because B follows A, B was caused by A.

Ever since the city suspended height restrictions on skyscrapers, the city budget has been balanced.

(See also p. 459.)

- **False analogy:** the claim of persuasive likeness when no significant likeness exists. An ANALOGY asserts that because two things are comparable in some respects, they are comparable in other respects as well. Analogies cannot serve as evidence in a rational argument because the differences always outweigh the similarities; but analogies can reinforce such arguments *if* the subjects are indeed similar in some ways. If they aren't, the analogy is false. Many observers see the "war on drugs" as a false and damaging analogy because warfare aims for clear victory over a specific, organized enemy, whereas the complete eradication of illegal drugs is probably unrealistic and, in any event, the "enemy" isn't well defined: the drugs themselves? users? sellers? producers? the producing nations? (These critics urge approaching drugs as a social problem to be skillfully managed and reduced.)

THE PROCESS

Finding a Subject

Your way into a subject will probably vary depending on whether you're writing an argument that supports an opinion or one that proposes. In stating an opinion, you set forth and support a claim—a truth you believe. You may find such a truth by thinking and feeling, by reading, by talking to your instructors or fellow students, by listening to a discussion of some problem or controversy. Before you run with a subject, take a minute to weigh it: Is this something about which reasonable people disagree? Arguments go nowhere when they start with ideas that are generally accepted (pets should not have to endure physical abuse from their owners) or are beyond the pale (pet own-ers should be able to hurt their animals if they want).

In stating a proposal, you already have an opinion in mind, and from there, you go on to urge an action or a solution to a problem. Usually, these two statements will take place within the same piece of writing: You will first set forth a view ("The campus honor code is unfair to first offenders"), provide the evidence to support it, and then make your proposal as a remedy ("The campus honor code should be revised to give more latitude to first offenders").

Whatever your subject, resist the temptation to make it big. If you have two weeks to prepare, an argument about the litter problem in your town is probably manageable: In that time you could conduct your own visual research and talk to town officials. But an argument about the litter problem in your town compared with that in similar-sized towns across the state would surely demand more time than you have.

Organizing

There's no one right way to organize an argument because so much depends on how your readers will greet your claim and your evidence. Below we give some ideas for different situations.

Introduction

In your opening paragraph or two, draw readers in by connecting them to your subject if possible, showing its significance, and providing any needed background. End the introduction with your thesis statement if you think readers will entertain it before they've seen the evidence. Put the thesis state-ment later, in the middle or even at the end of the essay, if you think readers need to see some or all of the evidence in order to be open to the idea.

Body

The body of the essay develops and defends the points that support your thesis. Generally, start with your least important point and build in a crescendo to your strongest point. However, if you think readers may resist your ideas, con-sider starting strong and then offering the more minor points as reinforcement.

For every point you make, give the evidence that supports it. The methods of development can help here, providing many options for injecting evidence. Say you were arguing for or against further reductions in welfare funding. You might give EXAMPLES of wasteful spending, or of neighborhoods where welfare funds are still needed. You might spell out the CAUSES of social problems that call for welfare funds, or foresee the likely EFFECTS of cutting welfare programs or of keeping them. You could use NARRATION to tell a pointed story; you could use DESCRIPTION to portray certain welfare recipients and their neighborhoods.

Response to Objections

Part of the body of the essay, but separated here for emphasis, a response to probable objections is crucial to effective argument. If you are arguing fairly, you should be able to face potential criticisms fairly and give your critics due credit, reasoning with them, not dismissing them. This is the strategy Linda Chavez uses later in this chapter in "Supporting Family Values" by conceding, more than once, that arguments against immigration have some merit ("But the greater concern for some opponents," "It is true that," and so on) before she points out what she sees as their logical flaws. As Chavez does, you can tackle possible objections throughout your essay, as they pertain to your points. You can also field objections near the end of the essay, an approach that allows you to draw on all of your evidence. But if you think that readers' own opposing views may stiffen their resistance to your argument, you may want to address those views very early, before developing your own points.

Conclusion

The conclusion gives you a chance to gather your points, restate your thesis in a fresh way, and leave readers with a compelling final idea. In an essay with a strong emotional component, you may want to end with an appeal to readers' feelings. But even in a mostly rational argument, try to involve readers in some way, showing why they should care or what they can do.

FOCUS ON TONE

Readers are most likely to be persuaded by an argument when they sense a writer who is reasonable, trustworthy, and sincere. Sound reasoning, strong evidence, and acknowledgment of opposing views do much to convey these attributes, but so does TONE, the attitude implied by choice of words and sentence structures.

Generally, you should try for a tone of moderation in your view of your subject and a tone of respectfulness and goodwill toward readers and opponents.

- State opinions and facts calmly:

  OVEREXCITED   One clueless administrator was quoted in the newspaper as saying she thought many students who claim learning disabilities are faking their difficulties to obtain special treatment! Has she never heard of dyslexia, attention-deficit disorders, and other well-established disabilities?

CALM   Particularly worrisome was one administrator's statement, quoted in the newspaper, that many students who claim learning disabilities may be "faking" their difficulties to obtain special treatment.

- Replace arrogance with deference and sarcasm with plain speaking:

ARROGANT   I happen to know that many students would rather party or just bury their heads in the sand than get involved in a serious, worthy campaign against the school's unjust learning-disabled policies.

DEFERENTIAL   Time pressures and lack of information about the issues may be what prevents students from joining the campaign against the school's unjust learning-disabled policies.

SARCASTIC   Of course, the administration knows even without meeting students what is best for every one of them.

PLAIN   The administration should agree to meet with each learning-disabled student to learn about his or her needs.

- Choose words whose CONNOTATIONS convey reasonableness rather than anger, hostility, or another negative emotion:

HOSTILE   The administration <u>coerced</u> some students into dropping their lawsuits. [*Coerced* implies the use of threats or even violence.]

REASONABLE   The administration <u>convinced</u> some students to drop their lawsuits. [*Convinced* implies the use of reason.]

*For exercises on language, visit Exercise Central at **bedfordstmartins.com/ thebedfordreader**.*

CHECKLIST FOR REVISING AN ARGUMENT OR PERSUASION

✔ **AUDIENCE** Have you taken account of your readers' probable views? Have you reasoned with readers, not attacked them? Are your emotional appeals appropriate to readers' likely feelings? Do you acknowledge opposing views?

✔ **THESIS** Does your argument have a thesis, a claim about how your subject is or should be? Is the thesis narrow enough to argue convincingly in the space and time available? Is it stated clearly? Is it reasonable?

✔ **EVIDENCE** Is your thesis well supported with facts, statistics, expert opinions, and examples? Is your evidence accurate, representative, relevant, and ample?

Argument and Persuasion

> ✔ **ASSUMPTIONS** Have you made sound connections between your evidence and your thesis and other claims?
>
> ✔ **LOGICAL FALLACIES** Have you avoided common errors in reasoning, such as oversimplifying or begging the question? (See pp. 554–56 for a list of fallacies.)
>
> ✔ **STRUCTURE** Does your organization lead readers through your argument step by step, building to your strongest ideas and frequently connecting your evidence to your central claim?
>
> ✔ **TONE** Is the tone of your argument reasonable and respectful?

ARGUMENT AND PERSUASION IN PARAGRAPHS

Writing about Television

This self-contained paragraph, written for *The Bedford Reader*, argues that TV news aims for entertainment at the expense of serious coverage of events and issues. The argument here could serve a number of different purposes in full essays: For instance, in a paper claiming that television is our least reliable source of news, the paragraph would give one cause of unreliability; or in an essay analyzing television news, the paragraph would examine one element.

Television news has a serious failing: It's show business. Unlike a newspaper, its every image has to entertain the average beer drinker. To score high ratings and win advertisers, the visual medium favors the spectacular: riots, tornados, air crashes. Now that satellite transmission invites live coverage, newscasters go for the fast-breaking story at the expense of thoughtful analysis. "The more you can get data out instantly," says media critic Jeff Greenfield, "the more you rely on instant data to define the news." TV zooms in on people who make news, but, to avoid boredom, won't let them argue or explain. (How can they, in speeches limited to fifteen seconds?) In 2010, as Congress prepared for a historic vote on health-care reform, President Obama held a press conference to explain the bill. His lengthy remarks were clipped to twenty seconds on one news broadcast, and then an anchorwoman digested the opposition to a single line: "Republicans tonight were critical of the president's proposal." During the last two presidential elections, the candidates sometimes deliberately packaged bad news so that it could not be distilled to a sound bite on the evening news — and thus would not make the evening news at all. Americans who rely on television for their news (one-third, according to recent polls) exist on a starvation diet.

Margin annotations:

Topic sentence: the claim

Evidence:
• Expert opinion

• Facts and examples

• Statistic

Writing in an Academic Discipline

Taken from a textbook on public relations, the following paragraph argues that lobbyists (who work to persuade public officials in behalf of a cause) are not slick manipulators but something else. The paragraph falls in the textbook's section on lobbying as a form of public relations, and its purpose is to correct a mistaken definition.

Although the public stereotypes a lobbyist as a fast-talking person twisting an elected official's arm to get special concessions, the reality is quite different. Today's lobbyist, who may be fully employed by one industry or represent a variety of clients, is often a quiet-spoken, well-educated man or woman armed with statistics and research reports. Robert Gray, former head of Hill and Knowlton's Washington office and a public affairs expert for thirty years, adds, "Lobbying is no longer a booze and buddies business. It's presenting honest facts and convincing Congress that your side has more merit than the other." He rejects lobbying as being simply "influence peddling and button-holing" top administration officials. Although the public has the perception that lobbying is done only by big business, Gray correctly points out that a variety of special interests also do it. These may include such groups as the Sierra Club, Mothers Against Drunk Driving, the National Association of Social Workers, the American Civil Liberties Union, and the American Federation of Labor. Even the American Society of Plastic and Reconstructive Surgeons hired a Washington public relations firm in their battle against restrictions on breast implants. Lobbying, quite literally, is an activity in which widely diverse groups and organizations engage as an exercise of free speech and representation in the marketplace of ideas. Lobbyists often balance each other and work toward legislative compromises that benefit not only their self-interests but society as a whole.

> Topic sentence: the claim

> Evidence:
> • Expert opinion

> • Facts and examples

—Dennis L. Wilcox, Phillip H. Ault, and Warren K. Agee,
Public Relations: Strategies and Tactics

ARGUMENT AND PERSUASION IN A PROPOSAL

In many courses and occupations, you'll be expected to write proposals that identify specific problems or related sets of problems and argue for reasonable solutions. A proposal addresses clearly defined readers who are in a position to take action or approve an action. It addresses those readers' unique needs and concerns, anticipating objections and offering evidence to demonstrate the benefits of the solution.

As a member of Corden University's Green Student Group, Amelia Jones knew that some nearby schools had recently instituted green policies and programs. Eager to see her own campus improve its environmental standing, she researched possible changes and also the attitudes toward change on the part of students, faculty, and administrators. The following paragraphs come from her longer proposal that the university adopt an environmental initiative similar to those that had proven successful elsewhere. Before this section, Jones opened with an overview of environmental problems on campus. After this section, she explained the potential solutions in greater detail, suggested steps for implementing them, and outlined the anticipated costs.

These problems of waste, costliness, and irresponsibility need not dominate the university's environmental profile. By adopting an environmental initiative like that at other schools, the university can achieve practical benefits for itself and its students while behaving ethically in its community and on earth. Such an initiative calls for simple changes in energy use, food procurement and disposal, and educational programs.

Transition from discussion of problems

Solution: environmental initiative

Elements of the solution:

Reducing energy use would not only reduce carbon emissions but also save money. Based on the Accounting Office's most recent report on campus utility costs, lowering the average temperature in all campus buildings from 72 to 68 degrees and installing more efficient light bulbs and water lines could save the university almost $2 million per year. Other measures, such as campuswide recycling and composting and switching to hybrid fleet vehicles, all have potential to cut costs significantly by reducing money spent on waste disposal and on fuel.

Reducing energy use to lower carbon emissions and costs

Of course, the practical benefits of a greener campus go beyond merely saving money. If Dining Services could obtain even thirty percent of its produce, dairy, and meat from local farmers, it would reduce the carbon emissions caused by shipping such products while it also strengthened ties with the local community. In addition, Dining Services could coordinate with the newly established Campus Food Bank and the Green Student Group to donate excess food and to compost unused produce, thereby reducing the amount of waste generated by the student dining halls.

Shopping locally to reduce carbon emissions and improve community ties

Food donation and composting to reduce waste

Many prospective students would find the greening of our campus appealing both ethically and academically. An interdisciplinary environmental initiative would allow the environmental studies and engineering programs to offer hands-on practice as students design new green roofs for dorms or install solar-powered recycling bins. Students could have the option to devote their senior projects to implementing new parts of the environmental initiative. At the same time, the initiative could earn the school additional funding by attracting sustainability grants from public agencies and private foundations.

Integrating academic programs to attract students, provide practical student projects, and possibly increase funding

Some administrators and alumni who oppose environmental actions argue that our campus accounts for a barely measurable percentage of the country's greenhouse emissions. They also claim that such actions are outside the traditional mission of the school and that diverting funds to them from other programs would be unacceptable. But cost would be an issue only for the first years of an environmental initiative, because many of the projects will pay for themselves over time by reducing operational costs, attracting more students, and attracting more funding. Moreover, higher education has a higher calling: In the face of the projected large-scale effects of global warming, what "mission" is more important than conservation and moderation? These actions go beyond any simple costs-and-benefits analysis. They are the responsible course — and the right course.

Acknowledgment of objections

Response to objections

COLLEEN WENKE

Colleen Wenke was born in 1979 and grew up in Queens, New York. After graduating from Boston College in 2001 with a degree in psychology, she moved back to New York City and took a job at a real estate investment and development firm, where she is now a vice president. She received an MA in real estate from New York University and is active in professional organizations such as the New York Building Congress and Young Real Estate Professional Women in Construction. An avid traveler, Wenke spent a semester at the University of New South Wales in Sydney, Australia, and she has taken trips to Europe and Southeast Asia. She is also an enthusiast of extreme sports, such as skydiving, rappelling, white-water rafting, and scuba diving.

Too Much Pressure

Why do students cheat in school? In this argument written when she was a college freshman, Wenke explores several answers to the question, finding one especially compelling. "Too Much Pressure" was published in the 1998 edition of *Fresh Ink,* a collection of work by students in Boston College's first-year writing course.

Wenke's essay follows MLA style for documenting sources, as discussed on pages 73–86. The text does not have the parenthetical citations normally found in MLA style because Wenke names source authors in her sentences and the sources—two Web documents and a television program—did not have numbered pages she could cite.

You hear the clock ticking in your head, and your teacher keeps erasing, in ten-minute decrements, the time you have left to complete the test. You do not remember anything from the last month of class. You probably should have studied more, watched less television, and spent less time on the phone. All the "should haves" are not important now. You need to finish the test and get out of here. The thought of a big fat F and a "See me" on the top of your midterm scares you. You remember the small piece of paper you have hidden in your pocket just in case. For a fleeting moment you think about what will happen if you are caught; then you slip the paper from your pocket onto the desktop. You transfer all the required information onto the test in time. You smile in anticipation of the A you are going to get. You think of how easy it was to cheat. All that matters is getting the grade.

Cheating is taking work done by somebody else, be it a friend or someone you do not know, and writing your name on it and saying it is your work. Any time I walked through my high school cafeteria or the hallways, I saw people

564

cheating. It came in many forms, from copying homework to giving out copies of the exam. Students even wrote the answers to a Scantron exam down
the sides of number-2 pencils and gave the pencils to their friends. My history teacher freshman year had a name for these students: "cafeteria scholars."
These were the students who pulled 90s by knowing what the test questions
were before they got to the classroom. Their friends who had taken the exam
earlier in the day would tell them the questions and answers during lunch. The
teachers knew that these things went on, yet nobody seemed to do anything
about them. I thought this was the way school went. The people who were
cheating were doing the best in all of my classes. I would study for hours and
still pull Bs. They would pull As.

I remember conversations over the dinner table with my parents on the   3
subject of cheating. My parents were disgusted at the apathetic views my
brothers and I held. We really didn't think it was a big deal to copy homework.
I thought everyone cheated, probably even my parents and teachers when
they were my age. But my parents swore that they had never cheated. Did I
believe them? Not really. I thought that they were giving us the "it was so
much better when we were growing up" speech.

I soon learned differently. In the article "When the Ends Justify the   4
Means," written by Robin Stansbury, a reporter for the Connecticut newspaper *The Courant*, I found that my parents were telling the truth. Stansbury
reports that "cheating in school has probably been around since the first exam
was given." But he goes on to say, "State and national statistics show cheating
among high-school students has risen dramatically during the past fifty years."
Reading this upset me and made me think about what had caused this increase.
I hoped this was not a reflection of moral decline in the people who would
soon be running my country. I blamed our school system for not instilling the
proper values in its students. I figured that the dramatic change in the role of
the family over the past generation, from two-parent homes with a working
father and a mother who stayed at home and watched her children to families
which have only a single parent or in which both parents work outside the
home, meant schools needed to include moral standards in the curriculum. I
believed schools were not fulfilling their role and therefore were producing
students who do not know the difference between right and wrong.

An article written by Robert L. Maginnis, a policy analyst in the Cul-   5
tural Studies Project at the Family Research Council, indicates my hypothesis
had some truth to it. Maginnis states that "the erosion of values is traceable
largely to changes in institutions which have traditionally been responsible for
imparting them to our youth." He defines "these key institutions [to] include
family, school, church, media and government." I agree with Maginnis, but I
can't accept these factors as the only sources in the increase of cheating in the

classroom. The facts seem contradictory. If my parents' generation had such high morals and wouldn't cheat, wouldn't they teach their children the same? My parents had taught me that cheating was wrong, yet I seemed to accept it.

There is a new "class" of cheaters today. In the past, as one would expect,   6 the students who cheated were the ones who could not pass or did not do the work. They were the lazy students. But today the majority of the students who admit to cheating are college-bound overachievers. The students who are trying to juggle too many activities are resorting to compromising their integrity for a good grade. There is too much competition between students, which leads to increased pressure to do well. Cheating becomes a way to get the edge over the other students in the class. In addition, penalties for getting caught are mild. If you were caught cheating at my high school, you received a zero for the test. Your parents were not called, and you were not suspended. True, a zero would hurt your grade severely if all grades for each quarter counted. But there was a loophole in the system: Each quarter the lowest grade was dropped. If the zero grade was dropped, it made no difference; the average was not affected. Students who cheated on all the tests but only got caught once still received good grades.

A main difference between school today and school when my parents were   7 enrolled is that we are now very goal-oriented and will compromise our values to achieve these goals. Stansbury sees this compromise of values and reports in his article that "cheating is a daily occurrence in high school. . . . What this says is that many of our students today do not have much internal integrity." Stansbury argues that students "want a goal, and how to get the goal is somewhat irrelevant." Today there is more pressure placed on students to do well. They are expected to receive good grades, play a sport, and volunteer if they are to be looked at by a good college. With a B tainting your transcript, a college might not look at you. This new pressure is what is causing the increase in cheating. Maginnis agrees with Stansbury and goes further, reporting, "A national survey found a shift in motivation away from altruism and toward concern with making money and getting power and status." Like Stansbury, Maginnis says that "students are finding it easier to rationalize lying or cheating in pursuit of their goals." And what goals are these students pursuing? They want the best grades so that they can get into the best schools and get the highest-paying jobs. Starting in the classroom, we are sending the message that it is acceptable to cheat as long as you do not get caught and you do the best.

Dean Morton, a broadcaster for *Good Morning America*, reported that   8 according to a national survey conducted in 1997 by *Who's Who in American High School Students*, as many as ninety-eight percent of students who participated in the survey admitted to cheating. The segment of the show was even entitled "Guess What? Cheaters Do Prosper." Like Stansbury and Maginnis, this survey also concluded that it is now the common belief among students that cheaters are getting ahead in life. Stansbury interviewed several high-school students in his article and discovered that many of them feel cheaters do get ahead in the classroom: "In high school, the cheaters always win. They don't get caught and they are the ones getting 100 on the exams when the noncheaters are getting 80s and 90s. Cheaters do win." We are sending a message to our youth that it is acceptable to cheat as long as you don't get caught and you are getting As. In this kind of society, morals take a back seat to how much you earn and how prosperous you are.

Students who would not usually cheat get sucked into believing it is the only way to get ahead in school: If the cheaters are doing better than they are and not getting caught, then they had better try it. Stansbury proposes that there is such an enormous increase in cheating because more students are joining in: "They see others cheating and they think they are being unfairly disadvantaged." He adds that the "only way many of them feel they can keep in the game, to get into the right schools, is to cheat." In high school I always felt at a disadvantage, because everybody else was cheating and doing better than I was, even if only by a few points. My friends felt the same way, that copying work or cheating was the only way to keep up with the rest of the class. It frustrated me, because the cheaters were not earning their grades. But there were plenty of times when I was in a jam and copied homework from friends. Thinking about this now, I wonder what allowed me to push aside my conviction that cheating was wrong. I wasn't bringing in cheat sheets and didn't know the questions to tests before I got there, but I was cheating nonetheless. 9

How should we respond to the huge increase in cheating over the past generation? We need to step back and look at the broader picture. We are creating a society in which people feel it is acceptable to cheat. This attitude will not stop in the classroom, but will carry on into the business world. Those who are cheating are the ones getting the grades and getting into the best schools. They are the "smart" ones. They in turn are the ones who will be running our country. They will become the heads of businesses and presidents of big corporations. Are these the people we want to have the power? In all likelihood they will not stop cheating once they get to the top. They become the people we idolize and aspire to be like. Because they are powerful, we consider them clever, highly respectable people. I do not hold any respect for a dishonest cheater. The phrase "honest businessman" will truly be an oxymoron. I am scared to think of the consequences of having cheaters rule our country. Is our society teaching that this is the only way to get ahead in life? Does obtaining status and power make you good? Schools are drifting away from emphasizing 10 learning and are emphasizing the grade instead. When the thirst for knowledge is replenished in a student's mind, the desire for the grade without the work will dissolve. Only then will cheating decline.

Works Cited

Maginnis, Robert L. "Cheating Scandal Points to Moral Decline." *Family Research Council*. Family Research Council, 1994. Web. 3 May 1997.

Morton, Dean. "Guess What? Cheaters Do Prosper." *Good Morning America*. ABC. WCVB, Boston. 16 Apr. 1997. Television.

Stansbury, Robin. "Cheating in Connecticut's Classrooms: When the Ends Justify the Means." *Courant.com*. Hartford Courant 2 Mar. 1997. Web. 2 May 1997.

For a reading quiz and annotated links to further readings on cheating in school, visit **bedfordstmartins.com/thebedfordreader.**

Journal Writing

Do you agree with Wenke that most students think cheating is acceptable? In your journal, write down your views of how common cheating is in your school and what students' attitudes are toward it. (To take your journal writing further, see "From Journal to Essay" on the facing page.)

Questions on Meaning

1. What reasons does Wenke suggest for the increase in cheating among students?
2. What does Wenke see as a possible negative consequence of cheating among students today?
3. What solution does Wenke offer for the problem of student cheating?

Questions on Writing Strategy

1. How effective do you find Wenke's opening paragraph? What does it suggest to you about her intended AUDIENCE?
2. Wenke cites several outside sources in the course of her essay. What do these sources contribute to her argument?

3. What is the EFFECT of Wenke's admission that she herself copied homework from friends in high school (par. 9)? Does this admission add to or detract from Wenke's ethical appeal? Why?

4. **OTHER METHODS**   Wenke's argument is based largely on CAUSE AND EFFECT ANALY-SIS. Does her analysis seem sound to you? Do you think she overemphasizes some causes or overlooks others? Explain.

Questions on Language

1. Find examples of COLLOQUIAL EXPRESSIONS in Wenke's essay. What is the effect of such language? Does it strike you as appropriate for her argument?

2. What does Wenke mean when she says, "The phrase 'honest businessman' will truly be an oxymoron" (par. 10)? What is an *oxymoron*?

3. Use a dictionary if necessary to help you define any of the following words: decre-ments (par. 1); apathetic (3); hypothesis (5); integrity (6); altruism, rationalize (7); replenished (10).

Suggestions for Writing

1. **FROM JOURNAL TO ESSAY**   Based on your journal entry, write an essay in which you analyze the problem of student cheating at your school. Who does it? Why? What do others think about it? What does the school do about it? If cheating is uncommon at your school, analyze why.

2. Wenke refers to the intense pressure students are under today to get good grades as well as to participate in sports and other extracurricular activities. Besides cheat-ing, what are some other consequences of the pressure faced by contemporary students—including positive consequences, if you think there are any? Drawing on your own experiences as well as the experiences of people you know, write an essay about what happens to students when they feel they are under pressure to excel.

3. Wenke wrote her essay in 1998. Has the problem of student cheating improved or worsened since then? Research the problem in several studies published since 1998—the more recent the better. Then write an essay in which you explain the current trend in cheating and what you think causes it.

4. **CRITICAL WRITING**   In an essay, EVALUATE Wenke's argument. How well does she convince you of the extent of the problem of student cheating and of its causes? How well do you think she develops her proposed solutions?

5. **CONNECTIONS**   In "The Ways We Lie" (p. 408), Stephanie Ericsson categorizes the kinds of lies people tell in everyday life. In what sense is cheating a form of lying? Which of Ericsson's categories might it belong to? On the scale of lying, how bad is cheating? Are cheaters likely to lie in other ways as well?

KATHA POLLITT

Katha Pollitt is a poet and an essayist. Her poetry has been praised for its "serious charm" and "spare delicacy" in capturing thought and feeling. Her essays have contained strong and convincing commentary on such topics as surrogate motherhood and women in the media. Pollitt was born in New York City in 1949 and earned a BA from Radcliffe College in 1972. Her verse began appearing in the 1970s in such magazines as *The New Yorker* and *The Atlantic Monthly;* it was collected in the book *Antarctic Traveler* (1982), which won the National Book Critics Circle award in 1983. Pollitt has received several other awards as well, including a grant from the National Endowment for the Arts and a Guggenheim fellowship. Her essays and criticism have appeared in *Mother Jones,* the *New York Times, The New Yorker,* and *The Nation,* where she currently writes a regular column. Her books include *Reasonable Creatures: Essays on Women and Feminism* (1994), *Subject to Debate: Sense and Dissent on Women, Politics, and Culture* (2001), and *Learning to Drive and Other Life Stories* (2007). Pollitt lives in New York City.

What's Wrong with Gay Marriage?

In her *Nation* column Pollitt regularly takes on controversial topics from a fresh, unabashedly liberal perspective. In this 2003 essay she counters arguments against marriage between homosexuals, including those posed by Charles Colson in the next essay, "Gay 'Marriage': Societal Suicide" (p. 576).

Both Pollitt and Colson refer to the 2003 decision of the Massachusetts Supreme Judicial Court that gays and lesbians cannot be denied the right to marry under the state constitution. The decision still stands, despite considerable political and judicial wrangling over it. As of mid-2010 the District of Columbia and four more states—Connecticut, Iowa, Vermont, and New Hampshire—had legalized gay marriage, while thirty-one states had passed legislation either defining marriage as a heterosexual union or banning same-sex unions. The legal landscape can change quickly, though; and with court challenges from both sides, one or more cases will eventually be heard by the US Supreme Court, whose ruling could require a uniform approach to same-sex marriage across the nation.

Will someone please explain to me how permitting gays and lesbians 1
to marry threatens the institution of marriage? Now that the Massachusetts

Supreme Court has declared gay marriage a constitutional right, opponents really have to get their arguments in line. The most popular theory, advanced by David Blankenhorn, Jean Bethke Elshtain and other social conservatives, is that under the tulle and orange blossom, marriage is all about procreation. There's some truth to this as a practical matter—couples often live together and tie the knot only when baby's on the way. But whether or not marriage is the best framework for child rearing, having children isn't a marital requirement. As many have pointed out, the law permits marriage to the infertile, the elderly, the impotent and those with no wish to procreate; it allows married couples to use birth control, to get sterilized, to be celibate. There's something creepily authoritarian and insulting about reducing marriage to procreation, as if intimacy mattered less than biological fitness. It's not a view that anyone outside a right-wing think tank, a Catholic marriage tribunal or an ultra-Orthodox rabbi's court is likely to find persuasive.

So scratch procreation. How about: Marriage is the way women domes-   2
ticate men. This theory, a favorite of right-wing writer George Gilder, has some statistical support—married men are much less likely than singles to kill people, crash the car, take drugs, commit suicide—although it overlooks such husbandly failings as domestic violence, child abuse, infidelity and abandonment. If a man rapes his wife instead of his date, it probably won't show up on a police blotter, but has civilization moved forward? Of course, this view of marriage as a barbarian-adoption program doesn't explain why women should undertake it—as is obvious from the state of the world, they haven't been too successful at it anyway. Nor does it explain why marriage should be restricted to heterosexual couples. The gay men and lesbians who want to marry don't impinge on the male-improvement project one way or the other. Surely not even Gilder believes that a heterosexual pothead with plans for murder and suicide would be reformed by marrying a lesbian?

What about the argument from history? According to this, marriage has   3
been around forever and has stood the test of time. Actually, though, marriage as we understand it—voluntary, monogamous, legally egalitarian, based on love, involving adults only—is a pretty recent phenomenon. For much of human history, polygyny was the rule—read your Old Testament—and in much of Africa and the Muslim world, it still is. Arranged marriages, forced marriages, child marriages, marriages predicated on the subjugation of women—gay marriage is like a fairy-tale romance compared with most chapters of the history of wedlock.

The trouble with these and other arguments against gay marriage is that   4
they overlook how loose, flexible, individualized and easily dissolved the bonds of marriage already are. Virtually any man and woman can marry, no matter how ill assorted or little acquainted. An eighty-year-old can marry an

eighteen-year-old; a john can marry a prostitute; two terminally ill patients can marry each other from their hospital beds. You can get married by proxy, like medieval royalty, and not see each other in the flesh for years. Whatever may have been the case in the past, what undergirds marriage in most people's minds today is not some sociobiological theory about reproduction or male socialization. Nor is it the enormous bundle of privileges society awards to married people. It's love, commitment, stability.

Speaking just for myself, I don't like marriage. I prefer the old-fashioned ideal of monogamous free love, not that it worked out particularly well in my case. As a social mechanism, moreover, marriage seems to me a deeply unfair way of distributing social goods like health insurance and retirement checks, things everyone needs. Why should one's marital status determine how much you pay the doctor, or whether you eat cat food in old age, or whether a child gets a government check if a parent dies? It's outrageous that, for example, a working wife who pays Social Security all her life gets no more back from the system than if she had married a male worker earning the same amount and stayed home. Still, as long as marriage is here, how can it be right to deny it to those who want it? In fact, you would think that, given how many hetero-sexuals are happy to live in sin, social conservatives would welcome maritally minded gays with open arms. Gays already have the baby—they can adopt in many states, and lesbians can give birth in all of them—so why deprive them of the marital bathwater?

At bottom, the objections to gay marriage are based on religious preju-dice: The marriage of man and woman is "sacred," and opening it to same-sexers violates its sacral nature. That is why so many people can live with civil unions but draw the line at marriage—spiritual union. In fact, polls show a striking correlation of religiosity, especially evangelical Protestantism, with opposition to gay marriage and with belief in homosexuality as a choice, the famous "gay lifestyle." For these people gay marriage is wrong because it lets gays and lesbians avoid turning themselves into the straights God wants them to be. As a matter of law, however, marriage is not about Adam and Eve versus Adam and Steve. It's not about what God blesses; it's about what the govern-ment permits. People may think *marriage* is a word wholly owned by religion, but actually it's wholly owned by the state. No matter how big your church wedding, you still have to get a marriage license from city hall. And just as divorced people can marry even if the Catholic Church considers it bigamy, and Muslim and Mormon men can marry only one woman even if their holy books tell them they can wed all the girls in Apartment 3G, two men or two women should be able to marry, even if religions oppose it and it makes some heterosexuals, raised in those religions, uncomfortable.

Gay marriage—it's not about sex, it's about separation of church and state.

*For a reading quiz, sources on Katha Pollitt, and annotated links to further readings on same-sex marriage, visit **bedfordstmartins.com/thebedfordreader**.*

Journal Writing

Write in your journal about your thoughts on marriage—not necessarily who should be allowed to marry or what you see as the ideal marriage, but rather why you think people marry. What do they hope to gain? What do they give up? How is being married different from simply living together as a couple? Base your entry on your observations and experiences. (To take your journal writing further, see "From Journal to Essay" on the next page.)

Questions on Meaning

1. What three arguments against same-sex marriage does Pollitt summarize in her first three paragraphs, and how does she refute each argument?
2. What, according to Pollitt, is the common understanding of what marriage is? What is Pollitt's own attitude toward marriage?
3. What does Pollitt believe to be the most basic reason why people object to same-sex marriage?
4. What is Pollitt's THESIS, and where does she state it directly?

Questions on Writing Strategy

1. What is the EFFECT of Pollitt's opening her essay with the question that she does? of her asking several questions in paragraphs 2 and 5?
2. Why, in paragraphs 1 and 2, does Pollitt admit "some truth" to the point that "marriage is all about procreation" and admit "some statistical support" for the point that "[m]arriage is the way women domesticate men"? How do these concessions affect her argument?
3. ANALYZE Pollitt's TRANSITIONS between paragraphs 1 and 2, 2 and 3, 3 and 4, and 5 and 6. How do they work?
4. Why do you think Pollitt spends a paragraph on her own negative views of marriage? Does this paragraph strengthen or weaken Pollitt's argument?
5. **OTHER METHODS**   How does Pollitt use DIVISION or ANALYSIS to structure her argument?

Questions on Language

1. Some of the language in paragraph 2 is deliberately humorous. Point to EXAMPLES of humor in the paragraph. Why do you think Pollitt chose to use such language at this point in the essay?

2. In the second-to-last sentence of paragraph 5, why does Pollitt use the phrase "live in sin" rather than, say, "live together without being married"? Does she believe such living situations are sinful?
3. What is Pollitt's point in putting some words in paragraph 6 in quotation marks?
4. Notice the PARALLELISM and repetition in the passage beginning "As a matter of law" in the middle of paragraph 6. What is the effect of the writing here?
5. Consult a dictionary if you are unsure of the meaning of any of the following: tulle, procreation, celibate, authoritarian (par. 1); impinge (2); monogamous, egalitarian, polygyny, subjugation (3); proxy, undergirds (4).

Suggestions for Writing

1. **FROM JOURNAL TO ESSAY**   Using your journal writing as a starting point, write an essay that presents a detailed view of the function of marriage in contemporary society. Refer to specific examples from your experience as appropriate. If you wish, use your observations and reflections to make a point about same-sex marriage.
2. Pollitt writes in paragraph 3 that "marriage as we understand it . . . is a pretty recent phenomenon." Research the history of marriage, beginning with its earliest forms and including marriage in non-Western cultures. Use your research in an essay to amplify or dispute Pollitt's CLAIM.
3. **CRITICAL WRITING**   Write an essay in which you analyze Pollitt's TONE in the essay. How does she present herself and her attitudes toward others (gays, women, men, opponents of gay marriage)? How do you respond to her tone?
4. **CONNECTIONS**   The next essay, by Charles Colson, argues against same-sex marriage. Write an essay in which you evaluate both Pollitt's and Colson's arguments for their EVIDENCE, reasonableness, fairness, response to opposing views, tone, and overall success. Be as OBJECTIVE as possible: Imagine yourself (if you aren't in fact) undecided on the issue of same-sex marriage.

Katha Pollitt on Writing

Katha Pollitt began writing early. "I started writing poetry when I was in about sixth grade," she told Ruth Coniff of *The Progressive* magazine in 1994. "I used to come home from school and go up to my room and sit on my bed and write my poems. And I was writing angry letters to the newspaper. . . . I recently came across a letter I had written when I was twelve years old to the *New York Times*. It was about some complicated legal case involving someone who was accused of being a spy, but I have absolutely no memory of writing this letter or of what this case was. It was actually like something I would write today. I thought, . . . have I been doing this for that long?"

Coniff observed that Pollitt's poetry is not political and asked why. "Well," Pollitt replied, "I was always a two-track writer. I always wrote poetry and prose. . . . I have to say that I see poetry and political writing as different endeavors. What I want in a poem is not an argument, it's not a statement, it has to do with language. I'm looking for a kind of energized, fresh, alive perception. . . . To me it's much more interesting to read that than to read a poem with whose politics I would agree, but that doesn't have a lot of depth of language and imagination in it. . . . What I like about poetry is the verbal concentration and levels of meaning. A poem with only one level of meaning is not a very interesting poem."

For Discussion

1. What are your earliest memories of writing? When have you written on your own (that is, not for a school assignment)? What moves you to write?
2. Explore Pollitt's ideas about poetry by looking at Joyce Carol Oates's "Edward Hopper's *Nighthawks*, 1942" (p. 194). How does the poem illustrate "verbal concentration and levels of meaning"?

CHARLES COLSON

Born in Boston in 1931, Charles Colson graduated from Brown University in 1953 and earned a law degree from George Washington University. He served in the US Marine Corps and was a partner in a law firm before rising to national prominence—and notoriety—as special counsel to President Richard Nixon during the Watergate scandal that caused Nixon to resign. Colson ended up serving seven months in prison for his involvement in the scandal. After his release in 1974, he founded Prison Fellowship Ministries, an outreach group that provides support both for prisoners and for victims of crime. Colson's many books include the autobiographies *Born Again* (1976) and *Life Sentence* (1979) as well as *Kingdoms in Conflict: An Insider's Challenging View of Politics, Power, and the Pulpit* (1987), *Why America Doesn't Work* (1991), *Justice That Restores* (2001), and *God and Government: An Insider's View on the Boundaries between Faith and Politics* (2007). Colson is a contributing editor of *Christianity Today* magazine and a commentator on the radio program *BreakPoint,* which takes a Christian perspective on current issues. In 1993 he received the Templeton Prize for Progress in Religion and donated the substantial prize money to Prison Fellowship Ministries.

Gay "Marriage": Societal Suicide

Written with Anne Morse for *Christianity Today* in 2004, this essay presents a case against same-sex marriage and thus counters the preceding essay, Katha Pollitt's "What's Wrong with Gay Marriage?" For a summary of the legal status of gay marriage as of this writing, see the headnote to Pollitt's essay on page 570.

Is America witnessing the end of marriage? The Supreme Judicial Court 1 of Massachusetts has ordered that the state issue marriage licenses to same-sex couples. (By late March, the Massachusetts legislature voted to recognize same-sex civil unions instead.) An unprecedented period of municipal lawlessness has followed, with officials in California, New York, Oregon, and New Mexico gleefully mocking their state constitutions and laws. The result: Thousands of gays rushed to these municipalities to "marry," while much of the news media egged them on.

In the midst of the chaos, President Bush announced his support for a 2 Federal Marriage Amendment, which assures that this contentious issue will be debated in every quarter of American life. It should be, because the consequences of having "gay marriage" forced on us by judicial (or mayoral) fiat will fall on all Americans—not just those who embrace it.

As a supporter of the amendment, I'm well aware of the critical arguments. 3 As the president noted, "After more than two centuries of American jurisprudence, and millennia of human experience, a few judges and local authorities are presuming to change the most fundamental institution of civilization. Their action has created confusion on an issue that requires clarity."

He's right. Here's the clarity: Marriage is the traditional building block 4 of human society, intended both to unite couples and bring children into the world. Tragically, the sexual revolution led to the decoupling of marriage and procreation; same-sex "marriage" would pull them completely apart, leading to an explosive increase in family collapse, out-of-wedlock births—and crime.

How do we know this? In nearly thirty years of prison ministry, I've wit- 5 nessed the disastrous consequences of family breakdown—in the lives of thousands of delinquents. Dozens of studies now confirm the evidence I've seen with my own eyes. Boys who grow up without fathers are at least twice as likely as other boys to end up in prison. Sixty percent of rapists and 72% of adolescent murderers never knew or lived with their fathers. Even in the toughest inner-city neighborhoods, just 10% of kids from intact families get into trouble, but 90% of those from broken families do. Girls raised without a father in the home are five times more likely to become mothers while still adolescents. Children from broken homes have more academic and behavioral problems at school and are nearly twice as likely to drop out of high school.

Critics agree with this but claim gay "marriage" will not weaken hetero- 6 sexual marriage. The evidence says they're wrong. Stanley Kurtz of the Hoover Institution writes: "It follows that once marriage is redefined to accommodate same-sex couples, that change cannot help but lock in and reinforce the very cultural separation between marriage and parenthood that makes gay marriage conceivable to begin with." He cites Norway, where courts imposed same-sex "marriage" in 1993—a time when Norwegians enjoyed a low out-of-wedlock birth rate. After the imposition of same-sex "marriage," Norway's out-of-wedlock birth rate shot up as the link between marriage and childbearing was broken and cohabitation became the norm.

Gay "marriage" supporters argue that most family tragedies occur because 7 of broken *heterosexual* marriages—including those of many Christians. They are right. We ought to accept our share of the blame, repent, and clean up our own house. But the fact that we have badly served the institution of marriage is not a reflection on the institution itself; it is a reflection on us.

As we debate the wisdom of legalizing gay "marriage," we must remem- 8 ber that, like it or not, there is a natural moral order for the family. History and tradition—and the teachings of Jews, Muslims, and Christians—support the overwhelming empirical evidence: The family, led by a married mother and father, is the best available structure for both child rearing and cultural health. This is why, although some people will always pair off in unorthodox ways, society as a whole must never legitimize any form of marriage other than that of one man and one woman, united with the intention of permanency and the nurturing of children.

Marriage is not a private institution designed solely for the individual grat-   9
ification of its participants. If we fail to enact a Federal Marriage Amend-ment, we can expect, not just more family breakdown, but also more criminals behind bars and more chaos in our streets.

---

*For a reading quiz, sources on Charles Colson, and annotated links to further readings on same-sex marriage, visit **bedfordstmartins.com/thebedfordreader**.*

Journal Writing

In paragraph 5 Colson makes a number of claims about the effect on children of being raised by single parents, particularly single mothers. Write in your journal about friends and family members — or the children of friends and family members — who have been raised by a single parent. (If you were raised by a single parent, consider yourself as well.) What have been the effects? (To take your journal writing further, see "From Journal to Essay" on the facing page.)

Questions on Meaning

1. What is Colson's THESIS? Where does he state it directly?
2. What evidence does Colson present to link same-sex marriage to an increase in out-of-wedlock births? to link single-parent households to increases in crime, early parenthood, and other problems of young people? How effective do you find this evidence?
3. What other argument does Colson make against same-sex marriage?

Questions on Writing Strategy

1. ANALYZE the reasoning in Colson's argument. What are its CLAIM and ASSUMP-TION? What is the DEDUCTIVE SYLLOGISM?
2. Why does Colson use quotation marks around *marriage* when referring to same-sex unions?

3. What is the EFFECT of the question with which Colson opens his essay?
4. What is the purpose of paragraph 7? Why do you think Colson includes it?
5. **OTHER METHODS**   What role does CAUSE AND EFFECT play in the essay?

Questions on Language

1. How do the words Colson uses in paragraphs 1 and 2 reinforce his opinion of recent moves to legitimate same-sex marriage?
2. Why do you think Colson uses the words *imposed* and *imposition* in the last two sentences of paragraph 6?
3. Consult a dictionary if you are unsure of the meaning of any of the following: unprecedented, gleefully (par. 1); millennia (3); decoupling, procreation (4); intact (5); unorthodox (8).

Suggestions for Writing

1. **FROM JOURNAL TO ESSAY**   Using your journal entry as a starting point, write an essay in which you explain what you think are the effects on children of being raised in single-parent households. From what you have seen, do such children fit the patterns described by Colson? If your observations do not coincide with Colson's, how do you account for the differences? (You may want to expand your thinking by reading Bella DePaulo's "The Myth of Doomed Kids," which also addresses the effects on children of being raised in single-parent households. See p. 379.)
2. Research the current status of same-sex marriage in the United States, including both state laws and constitutional amendments and the proposed amendment to the US Constitution. Then write an essay in which you discuss your findings and predict what you believe will be the future of legally recognized unions between same-sex couples.
3. **CRITICAL WRITING**   Write an essay in which you examine the TONE of Colson's essay. How does the author present himself, his issue, and his opponents? How reasonable do you find his language?
4. **CONNECTIONS**   In the previous essay, Katha Pollitt addresses many of the arguments raised by opponents of same-sex marriage, including those of Colson. Draw on Pollitt's and Colson's essays as you see fit to argue your own views on same-sex marriage.

PETER F. MARTIN

Peter F. Martin was born and raised in New York City, where he attended Hunter College High School. As an undergraduate at Yale University, he wrote a sports column for the *Yale Daily News* and later became an opinion editor for the newspaper. He was also a writer, a photographer, and an editor for the *Yale Globalist*, a quarterly undergraduate magazine of international affairs. For the *Globalist*, Martin traveled widely, photographing in Tanzania and India and reporting on foreign investment in Venezuela and on water contamination in an Illinois coal-mining town. He graduated in 2010 and plans to become a teacher.

Destroyed

"Destroyed" (editors' title) was the first of twenty-five sports columns Martin wrote for the *Yale Daily News* during his sophomore year. Satirizing the fans and news anchors who demonize steroid-using athletes as "sinners" who ruin their sports, Martin urges his readers to reconsider and recognize such players as the victims of dangerous drugs.

In the essay following this one, "The Designer Player," Rodrigo Villagomez shares Martin's criticism of the media hype but argues a much different position on the place of steroids in professional sports.

Last week I had to write a paper for Introduction to Psychology about mind enhancers, drugs currently in development that would help brains work more quickly and more sharply, effectively making users smarter. I wondered if such drugs might help me finish the assignment. In our papers we were asked to explain the benefits and risks of these drugs, and to weigh in on the question posed: Are mind enhancers "cheating"? As a sports fan, I drew the obvious connection.

"Brain Doping?" I titled my piece. I've heard a lot about cheating. I've thought about it some. And I know it's bad. Athletes out there, stop cheating. Cheating ruins the game. Stop.

If only it were so easy. Performance-enhancing drugs, those nasty chemicals that athletes are guzzling down, rubbing in, and shooting up, are here to stay. They've made their way into almost every professional sport, and even created a new sport in the process. Now we all get to guess who's doping and who's clean. Head to Vegas and you can drop money on your guesses. Just make sure you cover the spread,[1] because it's not enough to say slammin' Sammy Sosa's been hitting the juice. You've got to call him out, naming which drugs he's taken and when. This is the new sport, replacing the old times when people simply sat and watched.

But in all the hubbub, some voices are drowned out. We hear the shouts 4 of enraged fans, their sports mercilessly torn from purer eras, when the babes playing in the street and in the fields could look up to their athletes, those stoic giants, noble and morally firm. Writers, too, cry out from all corners. In this modern age they are joined by "anchors," suits behind a desk with rigid spines and pomade hair, crafted smiles on wax figurines. The wails are always the same. Players—sinners!—have brutally violated the games. The punishments must be swift and harsh. These criminals must be found, they must be confronted, and they must be forced out. Sports, remember, is a world of purity, of natural cleanliness. Syringes don't belong here.

I agree with the rhetoric, at least to a point. The world of sports is not for 5 cheaters. I used to be the kid in gym class who ticked off the others by trying to enforce the rules. I don't get along well with anarchists. Or cheaters. But there are other voices out there, muffled under the deafening glow of ESPN neon and the invisible radiation of 24-hour sportstalk radio, and they're asking: Who's cheating?

Or really, what's cheating? Is it cheating to inject anabolic steroids into 6 your buttocks, or, better yet, have a teammate do it for you? (Sharing is caring!) Yeah, sure, when everyone's outlawing the stuff. But why is it against the rules in the first place? Why can't Gaylord Perry throw his spitter? Why can't bats be stuffed with cork? These rules come from somewhere, I guess.

And it all goes back to purity. Sport, after all, isn't just entertainment. 7 The original Olympians, heroes of sport around the world, saw nothing light-hearted or comical in their competition. Under the mountain of the gods they played, besting one another in competitions of strength and skill to honor the powers above. Zeus, one can imagine, was no fan of artificial enhancers. He liked athletes natural, apparently so much so that even clothing was off-limits. From this history we receive the spirit of sport: Competition is to be played fairly and naturally, without help from extra-human objects, artifacts, or chemicals that can be manufactured, bought, and sold. Nothing but grass and human flesh on any field where fair play is to be found.

---

[1] A gambler on the outcome of a sports game "covers the spread" by betting on the difference in the teams' scores, not just who will win or lose. —Eds.

So here we find ourselves today. The fields, once clean, are soaked in juice. Baseball players, bicyclists, and track athletes are among the most egregious violators—or at least the most visible. The Olympics, in their modern-day incarnation, have lost luster as a result of the doping scandals across sports. And no one seems ready or able to stop the abuse.

But there's another problem to doping, one not seen on the field. As new   9 anti-steroid messages illustrate visually with limbs falling off bodies, steroids are wildly destructive to their users. Though they may feel like magic to an athlete recovering from an injury or simply looking for easy strength, their longer-term effects are undeniable and devastating. Ken Caminiti, the whistle-blower for the steroid problem in major league baseball, died three years ago of a heart attack, at age forty-one, and only eight years after winning baseball's Most Valuable Player award. He had taken steroids during his MVP season, and for several years after. It is the players, much more than the games, that we must protect.

Steroids and other performance enhancers are a true threat to sports.   10 They challenge the ideals of sports, passed down to us from the Greeks and more recently from earlier decades of professional competition, when athletes more closely resembled real people. But more important than the games are the athletes themselves, whose physical health is threatened. Sports fans and commentators bemoan their beautiful games lost to artificial enhancers, charging the players with destroying competition by cheating. But what about the players?

Athletes—those who dope, who take steroids, who cheat—are victims   11 of far more serious maladies than their sports. They will pay the price with their own lives, not too many years after they retire. Meanwhile, the only offense to us, the fans, is uncertainty: We must wonder which records and stats are "natural" and should be free from scrutiny and asterisks. I charge the sports-loving world to take a different look at steroid use (or abuse). Sinners? Athletes are as free as other people to make mistakes and suffer the conse-quences; in short, they are humans like the rest of us. Or at least they were before they started juicing.

For a reading quiz and annotated links to further readings on steroid use in sports, visit **bedfordstmartins.com/thebedfordreader**.

Journal Writing

How do you respond to Martin's concerns about steroid use among athletes? What do you think about performance-enhancing drugs in professional sports? in the Olympics? at the college level? Does using steroids constitute "cheating," for example, or is it on a par with athlete-friendly advanced technologies such as drag-reducing swimsuits and laser eye surgery? Does it matter that steroids might harm the health of athletes who take them? How important to you is "natural" ability in competition? Reflect on these issues in your journal. (To take your journal writing further, see "From Journal to Essay" on the next page.)

Questions on Meaning

1. Does Martin agree with the fans and writers who argue that steroids destroy the "purity" of sport? How can you tell?
2. On what grounds does Martin object to steroid use among elite athletes?
3. What is Martin's THESIS, and where does he state it?
4. In his conclusion, Martin writes, "Athletes are as free as other people to make mistakes and suffer the consequences; in short, they are humans like the rest of us. Or at least they were before they started juicing" (par. 11). What does he mean? Is he saying that athletes have a right to use steroids no matter the risks, or is he suggesting something else?

Questions on Writing Strategy

1. In paragraph 6 Martin asks a series of questions. What is the purpose of these questions, and what is their EFFECT?
2. Identify Martin's use of a specific EXAMPLE in paragraph 9. What does it contribute to his argument?
3. Consider the placement and wording of Martin's thesis. Why do you think Martin might have chosen this placement and wording?
4. **OTHER METHODS** How does Martin's essay use CAUSE AND EFFECT?

Questions on Language

1. In paragraph 7 Martin says, "Zeus, one can imagine, was no fan of artificial enhancers. He liked athletes natural, apparently so much so that even clothing was off-limits." What is he talking about? What are the implications of this reference?
2. What does Martin mean by "extra-human" (par. 7)? What are some CONNOTATIONS of the term?
3. Be sure you are familiar with the following words, checking a dictionary if necessary: enhancers (par. 1); doping (2); hubbub, stoic, wails (4); rhetoric, anarchists (5); anabolic (6); egregious, incarnation (8); bemoan (10).

Suggestions for Writing

1. **FROM JOURNAL TO ESSAY**   Based on your journal entry, draft an essay in which you explain your position on steroid use in sports. Are performance-enhancing drugs acceptable, or do you think they should be banned? Why? As you write, imagine an audience that may not entirely agree with you. Try to make a convincing case for your own viewpoint.
2. Martin suggests that, for a variety of reasons, sports have been ruined—they're no longer as good as they once were. Write an essay in which you offer your view of this idea, arguing for or against some recent change in a particular sport. If you generally support the change, offer specific EXAMPLES and speculate about the benefits. If you generally disapprove, challenge supporters with examples that counter their arguments.
3. **CRITICAL WRITING**   In an essay, ANALYZE the image that Martin presents of himself, his ETHICAL APPEAL. Consider specific examples of his language and TONE, along with what he says about himself and his attitude toward sports. How do you respond to this appeal?
4. **CONNECTIONS**   While Martin comments that "[s]port, after all, isn't just entertainment" (par. 7), Rodrigo Villagomez, in the next essay, takes the opposite view as the basis for his argument in favor of steroids. In an essay of your own, examine both writers' ASSUMPTIONS regarding the purpose and function of sports, both professional and amateur. Which of those assumptions come closest to your own?

Peter F. Martin on Writing

For *The Bedford Reader,* Peter F. Martin reflected on the importance of writing for an audience.

When I began doing journalism, I became hyperaware of the need to keep people reading. Newspapers and magazines make a difference only when people choose to read what's inside them, so a journalist's job is to produce something people will want to read. There's no reason writers shouldn't keep the same standard through all writing forms, even when the only reader will be a teacher or a friend. When I write, I hope to craft something meaningful. That isn't to say I don't write lighthearted pieces or use humor, but I want readers to take something away from my pieces. . . .

Ideally, readers won't pick up on the editing an article has undergone. The average reader is interested in the final product, not a marked-up draft with revisions and author's notes. I almost always write for a specific audience, keeping my imagined reader in mind. And for the most part, I write for my readers, not for myself. But I always enjoy the challenge of crafting a thought into words—and I still get excited when I know others will be able to read what I've written. That's the only way writing of any kind makes a difference.

For Discussion

1. In what ways does Martin think all forms of writing should adhere to the standards of journalistic writing?
2. Do you agree with Martin's position that writing makes a difference only when it is read by others?

RODRIGO VILLAGOMEZ

Rodrigo Villagomez is a blogger, podcaster, and social-media journalist. Born in 1976, he graduated from high school in Stockton, California, in 1994, joined the US Army as a musician, and served ten years in Afghanistan and Korea as well as stateside. In 2005, Villagomez returned to Stockton to pursue a career in sports broadcasting. He worked for Citadel Broadcasting, where he held various positions ranging from promotions assistant to producer to on-air talent. At the same time, he attended San Joaquin Delta College and reported on campus sports for the college's newspaper, radio station, and television network. Villagomez earned degrees in liberal arts and sciences (AA, 2007) and communications (AA, 2009). He is currently the owner of, and a play-by-play announcer for, Valley Sports Network, an online broadcast service that covers high school and semiprofessional sports in the San Joaquin Valley.

The Designer Player

With many professional athletes bringing home multimillion-dollar salaries and many fans paying hundreds to sit in the stands, some might say that professional sports are simply one aspect of the high-stakes entertainment industry. In this essay, Villagomez argues that athletes' status as entertainers justifies the use of steroids, a view that opposes him to Peter F. Martin in the previous essay, "Destroyed." Villagomez first published "The Designer Player" in the 2006 issue of *Delta Winds*, a collection of student essays from courses at San Joaquin Delta College. He revised and edited it for *The Bedford Reader*.

Villagomez conducted research to support his argument, so he acknowledges his sources both in the text of his essay and in a Works Cited list at the end. In accordance with MLA style, he includes page numbers for sources that have them but not for unpaginated online documents.

Baseball is a multibillion-dollar entertainment industry. The modern age of American sports has seen to it that we no longer look at baseball as just "America's pastime." We must now see it as another corporation striving to produce a product that will be consumed by the populace. It is a corporation that produces the reluctant hero, a man who begrudgingly accepts the title "role model." These players are under intense pressure to be continually on top of their game. They are driven by relentless fans to achieve greater levels of strength and prowess. Because of this pressure, more professional baseball players are turning to performance-enhancing drugs, specifically steroids, to aid them in their quest for greatness. Many believe that these drugs decrease the integrity of the players and ultimately the game itself. But if it were not for the small percentage of players who have recently been found to use steroids, baseball would not be enjoying the success it does today. We should be thanking these players for keeping the game popular.

Let's first look at the clinical definition of a steroid. A steroid is "any group of organic compounds belonging to the general class of biochemicals called lipids, which are easily soluble in organic solvents and slightly soluble in water" (Dempsey). The sportswriter Dayn Perry explains that steroids build muscle mass and that the physical conditioning of players, combined with the ingestion of the hormone testosterone, accelerates the muscle building. There are a million other supplements out there designed to do the same thing, so why the big fuss over steroids?

Most people have a problem with steroids because of the speed with which users obtain results. But it is not the drug alone that causes enhanced play. In fact, by using steroids, a batter could be hurting his swing. Being big and bulky and able to hit the ball out of the park is great, but not being able to move those humongous arms around quickly enough to hit a 90 mph fastball is counterproductive. To be a better hitter, the player must combine an over-the-top workout schedule with the drugs. If it were possible to become the world's greatest baseball player by simply using steroids and doing nothing else, don't you think that everyone would be doing so?

The main opponents against the use of steroids are those who say that using is an attack on baseball's integrity. Every player who takes the drug damages the credibility of the sport, and this is unfair to those who choose not to partake. These opponents should wake up. Long before the media brought the issue of steroids to the forefront, the drugs were being injected, rubbed, or swallowed in locker rooms. In his tell-all book, *Juiced*, Jose Canseco claims that many of his fellow teammates joined him in using steroids and that he personally injected most of them, beginning as early as 1985 (4). In 2002, Ken Caminiti, a retired third baseman and National League MVP, told *Sports Illustrated*, "It's no secret what's going on in baseball. At least half the guys are using. They talk about it. They joke about it with each other" (qtd. in Verducci). In reality, the so-called integrity of the game has been lost for years. Pitchers have always found ways to doctor the ball so that their pitches have extra movement. Batters have used lighter or corked bats to achieve a faster swing. Pete Rose was caught betting on his team while he was a manager. Baseball has not been a fair game for years.

Another of the major arguments of those opposed to using steroids is the   5
health risk factor. Steroid use has been linked to liver, prostate, and even tes-
ticular cancers as well as to heart disease. According to epidemiologist Charles
Yesalis, however, "We know steroids can be used with a reasonable measure
of safety. We know this because they're used in medicine all the time, just
not to enhance body image or improve athletic performance" (qtd. in Perry).
Steroids are also used in the treatment of breast cancer. In response to the fear
of long-term effects from the continued use of steroids, Yesalis has this to say:
"We've had thousands upon thousands [of long-term studies] done on tobacco,
cocaine, you name it . . . but for as much as you see and hear about anabolic
steroids, [we] haven't taken that step" (qtd. in Perry). The truth is that we hear
all the time from modern medicine that we can get cancer in ways we never
thought about. Remember when standing in front of the microwave could give
us cancer? Or now we hear that talking on a cell phone might be damaging to
our health. Living is unhealthy. We all do things that are not good for our bodies, be it smoking or drinking or whatever. These players are no more ruining
their bodies than those people who have to have a smoke break every thirty
minutes; in fact, using a natural hormone to increase muscle mass is arguably
healthier.

Baseball fans love home runs. Ever since the days of Babe Ruth, the loyal   6
fan has loved to see the sheer beauty of a baseball leaving the stadium. The
home run is a display of strength; it is poetry in motion. So is it any wonder
that players continually strive to increase the power of their swing? Nobody
wants to be known just as the one who could consistently get on base or the
one with the stellar batting average. They all want to be the one who gets
noticed by both the press and the fans for home runs. Without the ever-present
chance that sluggers can take it deep when they step up to the plate, the game
might get a little boring. In fact baseball itself has been making changes in the
game to help encourage home-run production: Many ballparks have changed
the dimensions of their outfields, moving the fences in to make it easier to
hit the ball out. Just look at steroids as a baseball player's attempt at trying to
move the wall in a little closer.

The recent batch of steroid allegations is not the first case of performance-   7
enhancing drugs in baseball causing a stir. During the 1998 season Mark
McGwire broke Roger Maris's long-standing record of sixty-one home runs
in a single season. This new record could not have come at a better time for
baseball, as most fans still held on to disappointing memories of the 1994 players' strike and a season cut short. McGwire's assault on the record revitalized
the game and gave people a reason to watch again. That joy was carried into
the very next season, when both McGwire and Sammy Sosa embarked on a

head-to-head battle to break McGwire's record. After the excitement died down, controversy ignited when accusations were made that McGwire was taking androstendione, a substance equal to the over-the-counter supplement hydroxycut. Most fans did not care whether Mark McGwire was hitting his home runs with help or not. We just loved the excitement of it all—until the vilification of the supplement he used forced us to feel guilty for enjoying the show.

Above all, we must remember baseball is a game. It is intended for the en-   8
tertainment of the crowd. There are of course fanatics (like myself) who hang on every swing and every throw, but most are casual fans who watch their favorite team when possible. Arguing over the integrity of a product meant for entertainment is futile. We as a society should not look to baseball to produce our perfect example of humanity. These people put themselves on stage every night in order to show us things we are not capable of, things that we want to do but can't. For three hours or so we get to escape into a world that is filled with strength and agility. Does it matter how our modern-day gladiators achieve their greatness? I certainly think not. Fans should not be let down because their favorite players used steroids to make them watch. They should thank them. Without those players, there might not even be a game to watch.

Works Cited

Canseco, Jose. *Juiced: Wild Times, Rampant 'Roids, Smash Hits, and How Baseball Got Big.* New York: HarperCollins, 2005. Print.

Dempsey, Mary E. "Steroid." *AccessScience.* McGraw-Hill, 2010. Web. 14 Feb. 2010.

Perry, Dayn. "The Problem of Steroid Use in Major League Baseball Is Exaggerated." *Opposing Viewpoints Resource Center.* Thomson Gale, 2005. Web. 15 Feb. 2010.

Verducci, Tom. "Totally Juiced." *Sports Illustrated* 3 Jun. 2002: 34+. *MasterFILE Premier.* Web. 17 Feb. 2010.

For a reading quiz and annotated links to further readings on steroid use in sports, visit **bedfordstmartins.com/thebedfordreader**.

Journal Writing

Villagomez suggests that athletes take steroids partly because fans and teammates encourage them to do so, a dynamic similar to the peer pressure teenagers and college students often cite as the reason for tobacco, drug, or alcohol use. Have you ever felt pressured to use a substance that you knew you shouldn't or that you flat out didn't want to? What did you do? Discuss the incident in your journal. (To take your journal writing further, see "From Journal to Essay" below.)

Questions on Meaning

1. What is Villagomez's THESIS, and where does he state it? What does the thesis suggest may be Villagomez's ASSUMPTIONS about his readers' attitudes toward steroids in sports?
2. What does Villagomez see as the primary benefits of steroids? Do you agree or disagree with his assessment? Why?
3. What drawbacks associated with steroids does Villagomez cite? Does he accept these as valid concerns?
4. According to Villagomez, why do some baseball players use steroids?

Questions on Writing Strategy

1. Why do you think Villagomez opens his argument as he does? What is the EFFECT of this opening?
2. In what order does Villagomez present opposing views (pars. 3–5)? Do you think this arrangement is effective, or would you prefer another? Why?
3. Why, in an essay written in 2006, does Villagomez devote an entire paragraph to the 1998 and 1999 baseball seasons? How is the old EXAMPLE central to his point?
4. **OTHER METHODS**   Where in the essay does Villagomez use CAUSE AND EFFECT, and how does it help further his argument?

Questions on Language

1. In paragraph 1 Villagomez refers to professional baseball as "a corporation that produces the reluctant hero." What does the phrase "reluctant hero" suggest?
2. How would you characterize Villagomez's TONE in this essay? Is it appropriate for his argument? Why, or why not?
3. Check a dictionary if you are unfamiliar with the meanings of any of the following words: populace, prowess, enhancing (par. 1); partake (4); prostate, epidemiologist (5); allegations, revitalized, vilification (7); futile, agility (8).

Suggestions for Writing

1. **FROM JOURNAL TO ESSAY**   What should people do when they are pressured to engage in potentially harmful activities? Using your journal entry as a spring-

board for ideas, write an essay that proposes a solution to the problem of peer pressure. Alternatively, write an essay that argues that peer pressure does (or does not) justify a person's choices, whether good or bad.

2. Villagomez mentions several times that baseball is a business with billions of dollars at stake. How do you feel about the astronomical figures offered to baseball players and other professional athletes? Are individual contracts worth millions of dollars a year fair or outrageous? Why? Write an essay that argues for or against the high salaries paid to professional athletes, using specific EXAMPLES to support your claims.

3. **CRITICAL WRITING**   Some of Villagomez's argument relies on EVIDENCE from published sources. Write an essay in which you discuss how effective, or ineffective, you find this evidence to be and explore what else, if anything, Villagomez might have brought in to support his claims.

4. **CONNECTIONS**   Rodrigo Villagomez and Peter F. Martin, in the previous essay, each consider a similar set of points about steroid use in sports, yet they come to nearly opposite conclusions. At the same time, both writers invoke the example of baseball player Ken Caminiti to further their arguments, but for very different reasons and to very different effects. How can that be? In an essay of your own, examine how each writer develops his argument, paying particular attention to reasoning and watching for any logical FALLACIES. Which argument do you find more persuasive, and why?

Rodrigo Villagomez on Writing

Rodrigo Villagomez tells *The Bedford Reader* that he wrote "The Designer Player" because he "found it disturbing . . . that the media were making such an issue" out of steroid use among professional athletes "when it was their fault in the first place" that players feel pressured to do whatever it takes to deliver excitement to fans. All the same, his position got a strong response from readers who noted his role as a play-by-play announcer for college sports: "Many people found my opinion on the topic disturbing. Parents . . . criticized me for encouraging their children to take steroids so they can be sports superstars."

Villagomez maintains that advocating for steroid use among nonprofessional athletes was never his intention, but he also understands that facing criticism is an inevitable part of voicing an opinion on a contentious issue: "When writing about a controversial topic, I always have to remember that no matter what my opinion, someone is going to disagree with me, especially when I take the less popular stance."

For Discussion

1. Why would Villagomez's role as a sports broadcaster make a difference to his readers?
2. Villagomez says that he chose to write about steroids in part because of the media's focus on the issue at the time. How important is context in terms of the relevance of an argument?

MARK KRIKORIAN

Mark Krikorian is executive director of the Center for Immigration Studies, a research organization that advocates stricter US immigration policy and enforcement. He was born in 1961 in New Haven, Connecticut, received a BA in 1982 from Georgetown University, and received an MA in 1984 from the Fletcher School of Law and Diplomacy at Tufts University. He has served as an editor at the *Winchester* (Virginia) *Star* and the monthly newsletter of the Federation for Immigration Reform. In addition to his work at the Center for Immigration Studies, Krikorian frequently testifies before Congress and writes for the *National Review Online*. He published his first book, *The New Case against Immigration—Both Legal and Illegal*, in 2008.

Safety through Immigration Control

In this essay first published in the *Providence Journal* in 2004, Krikorian argues that the relatively open borders of the United States are an invitation to terrorists for whom "the brass ring . . . is mass killings of civilians on American soil." The only way to stop them, Krikorian insists, is to restrict immigration tightly and to enforce the rules.

For another view of the effects of strict immigration policies, see the next essay, Edwidge Danticat's "Not Your Homeland."

Supporters of high immigration have tried to de-link immigration control from security. A week after the September 11, 2001, hijackings, the head of the American Immigration Lawyers Association said, "I don't think [9/11] can be attributed to the failure of our immigration laws." Even the 9/11 Commission[1]—which in January held hearings on the immigration failures that had contributed to the attacks—is devoting inordinate attention, as we saw the other week, to peripheral issues, such as who sent what memo to whom.   1

While ordinary people don't need hearings to know there's a link between immigration and security, a fuller understanding of the issue is necessary if we are to fix what needs to be fixed and reduce the likelihood of future attacks.   2

---

[1] The National Commission on Terrorist Attacks upon the United States was created in 2002 by Congress and the president to investigate the circumstances of the attacks on September 11, 2001. —Eds.

Deputy Defense Secretary Paul Wolfowitz said in October 2002:   3

> Sixty years ago, when we said, "home front," we were referring to citizens
> back home, doing their part to support the war front.[2] Since last September,
> however, the home front has become a battlefront, every bit as real as any
> we've known before.

The reality of the home front isn't confined to the threat posed by Islamic terrorism. No enemy, whatever his ideology, has any hope of defeating America's
armies in the field, and must therefore resort to what scholars call "asymmetric" or "fourth-generation" warfare: terrorism and related tactics, which we
saw before 9/11 in the Mideast and East Africa, and which we are now seeing
in Iraq. But the brass ring of such a strategy is mass killings of civilians on
American soil.

Our objective on the home front is different from that faced by the mili-   4
tary, because the goal is defensive: to block and disrupt the enemy's ability
to carry out attacks on our territory. This will then allow offensive forces,
if needed, to find, pin down and kill the enemy overseas. So the burden of
homeland defense is not borne by our armed forces but by agencies seen as
civilian entities — mainly, the Department of Homeland Security. And of the
DHS's many responsibilities, immigration control is central. The reason is
elementary: No matter the weapon or delivery system — hijacked airliners,
shipping containers, suitcase nukes, anthrax spores — terrorists are needed to
carry out the attacks. And those terrorists have to enter and operate in the
United States. In a very real sense, the primary weapons of our enemies are
not the inanimate objects at all but, rather, the terrorists themselves, especially in the case of suicide attackers.

Thus, keeping the terrorists out, or apprehending them after they get in,   5
is indispensable to victory. In the words of the administration's July 2002
"National Strategy for Homeland Security":

> Our great power leaves these enemies with few conventional options for
> doing us harm. One such option is to take advantage of our freedom and
> openness by secretly inserting terrorists into our country to attack our home-
> land. Homeland security seeks to deny this avenue of attack to our enemies
> and thus to provide a secure foundation for America's global engagement.

Our enemies have repeatedly exercised this option of inserting terrorists   6
by exploiting weaknesses in our immigration system. A Center for Immigration Studies analysis found that nearly every element of the immigration sys-

---

[2] Wolfowitz refers to World War II. — Eds.

tem has been penetrated by the enemy. Of the forty-eight al-Qaida[3] operatives who have committed terrorist acts here since 1993 (including the 9/11 hijackers), a third were here on various temporary visas, another third were legal residents or naturalized citizens, a fourth were illegal aliens, and the rest had pending asylum applications. Nearly half of the total had, at some point or another, violated immigration laws.

An immigration system designed for homeland security, therefore, needs   7
to apply to all stages in the process: issuing visas overseas, screening people at the borders and airports, and enforcing the rules inside the country. Nor can we focus all our efforts on Mideasterners and ignore people from elsewhere; that may make sense in the short term—as triage, if you will—but in the longer term we need comprehensive improvements, because al-Qaida is adapting. The FBI has warned local law enforcement that al-Qaida is already exploring the use of Chechen terrorists,[4] people with Russian passports who won't draw our attention if we're focusing mainly on Saudis and Egyptians.

None of this is to say that there are no other weapons against domestic   8
terrorist attacks. We certainly need more effective international coordination, improved intelligence gathering and distribution, and special military operations. But in the end, the lack of effective immigration control leaves us naked in the face of the enemy.

*For a reading quiz, sources on Mark Krikorian, and annotated links to further readings on immigration and border control, visit **bedfordstmartins.com/thebedfordreader**.*

Journal Writing

Throughout this essay, Krikorian refers to "our enemies" and "the enemy." What does the word *enemy* mean to you? In your journal, write about whom you consider to be your personal enemies and the enemies of the United States or another country with which you identify. (To take your journal writing further, see "From Journal to Essay" on the next page.)

[3] Al-Qaida (also spelled al-Qaeda or al-Qa'ida) is the international terrorist organization responsible for the 9/11 attacks as well as many other acts of violence around the world. —Eds.
[4] Chechnya is a republic of Russia. Its battles for independence from Russia have included acts of terrorism. —Eds.

Questions on Meaning

1. How would you summarize Krikorian's THESIS? Where does he state it?
2. In what ways is Krikorian critical of the 9/11 Commission?
3. What is Krikorian's point in paragraph 4? What are the objectives of homeland defense?
4. How does Krikorian say the immigration system should protect homeland security?

Questions on Writing Strategy

1. Why might Krikorian have chosen to open his essay as he does? What is the EFFECT of his first two paragraphs?
2. Identify the primary APPEALS Krikorian makes in the essay. Do you find them effective?
3. What kinds of EVIDENCE does Krikorian offer to support his claim? Is his evidence convincing? Why, or why not?
4. What is notable about Krikorian's concluding paragraph?

Questions on Language

1. In paragraph 3 Krikorian writes that "the brass ring of [terrorism] is mass killings of civilians on American soil." What does he mean by "brass ring"? What is the source of this term?
2. In paragraph 6 Krikorian uses the term *triage* to refer to immigration control efforts that may be useful in the short term. What is the meaning of *triage*, and how is he using the word here?
3. Do some research about "asymmetric" and "fourth-generation" warfare (par. 3). To what do these terms refer specifically?
4. If you are unfamiliar with the following words, check a dictionary for their meanings: peripheral (par. 1); ideology (3); anthrax, inanimate (4); visas, naturalized citizens, pending, asylum (6).

Suggestions for Writing

1. **FROM JOURNAL TO ESSAY**   Using your journal entry as a starting point, write an essay in which you offer a multifaceted DEFINITION of the word *enemy*. How do you use the term? How do you regard other people's use of it? What are some of the benefits and drawbacks of defining others as enemies? Have your thoughts about the concept of "the enemy" evolved over time?
2. Write an essay in which you present your view on an aspect of US immigration policy or practice that you have strong opinions about—for example, amnesty for illegal immigrants, treatment of asylum seekers, or restrictions on immigration since 9/11. Before beginning your draft, do some research to support your position and also to explore opposing views so that you answer them squarely and fairly.
3. **CRITICAL WRITING**   How does Krikorian develop the subject of immigration control? What specific examples does he give? Based on his essay, how well do you understand the policies and laws of immigration control of the Department of

Homeland Security? What questions would you like to ask Krikorian, if any, and why?

4. **CONNECTIONS**   In the next essay Edwidge Danticat writes about what she sees as the unwarranted detention and mistreatment of Haitians seeking asylum in the United States. Write an essay in which you COMPARE AND CONTRAST the ways Krikorian and Danticat present their cases. Which argument do you find more effective? Why?

EDWIDGE DANTICAT

Edwidge Danticat was born in Port-au-Prince, Haiti, in 1969. When she was a child, her parents emigrated to find work in New York, leaving her to be raised by an aunt and uncle until she too emigrated at the age of twelve. She went to school in Brooklyn, New York, and then enrolled in Barnard College, intending to study nursing. However, a love of reading and writing inspired her to change her major to French literature. After graduation in 1990, Danticat pursued an MFA at Brown University (1993). Her first novel, which she began writing as a teenager and completed as her thesis at Brown, was *Breath, Eyes, Memory* (1994). Her books since then include the novels *The Farming of Bones* (1998) and *The Dew Breaker* (2004); the memoirs *After the Dance: A Walk through Carnival in Haiti* (2002) and *Brother, I'm Dying* (2007); and the story collection *Krik? Krak!* (1995)—the latter two both finalists for the National Book Award. Danticat was awarded a MacArthur Foundation fellowship, popularly known as "the genius grant," in 2009.

Not Your Homeland

Danticat's birthplace, the Caribbean island of Haiti, is the poorest country in the Americas. When its people suffered the devastating earthquake of 2010, they had already endured decades of social and political upheaval, including violent conflicts between the government and rebels that prompted intervention in 2004 by the United States and the United Nations. Fearing for their lives, many Haitians have sought asylum in the United States, some entering legally, many not. In this 2005 essay from *The Nation,* Danticat reports on the conditions she observed in US detention centers, where thousands of would-be immigrants have been held as possible security threats. Surely, she argues, US security does not demand the treatment suffered by the detainees.

From the outside, it looks like any other South Florida hotel. There is a   1
pool, green grass and tall palms bordering the parking lot. An ordinary guest may not even be aware that his or her stopover for the night is indeed a prison, a holding facility for women and children who have fled their countries, in haste, in desperation, hoping for a better life.

A year and four months after September 11, 2001, I visited, along with   2
some friends, a Comfort Suites hotel in Miami where several Haitian women

and children were jailed. One of the people we met there was a three-year-old girl who had been asking for a single thing for weeks. The little girl wanted to sit under one of those tall palm trees in the hotel courtyard, feel the sunshine on her face and touch the green grass with her feet. Tearfully, her mother said she could not grant her that. Nor could she even dream of it for herself.

We also met a little boy who was wearing one of the gray adult-size T-shirts 3 all the detainees in the hotel wore. There was no uniform small enough for him, so the little boy didn't have pants. We met a pretty young woman who told us that she'd lost a lot of weight, not only because of the sorrow that plagued her constrained life—a life in which she was forbidden even to stand in the hotel hallway—but also because she couldn't bring herself to eat. The food she was fed would neither "stay up nor down," she said. Either she vomited it or it gave her diarrhea.

The women in that hotel also told us how six of them must live together 4 in one room, how some of them were forced to sleep on the floor when there wasn't enough space on the beds or couches. They told us how they missed their own clothes and seeing their children play in the sun, how they had perhaps been wrong about America. Maybe it no longer had any room for them. Maybe it had mistaken them for criminals or terrorists.

Once we were quickly ushered out of the hotel, my mind returned to the 5 Krome Detention Center in Miami, which we had visited earlier that day. Even before setting foot on its premises, Krome had always seemed like a strange myth to me, a cross between Alcatraz and hell. I'd imagined it as something like the Brooklyn Navy Yard detention center, where my parents had taken me on Sunday afternoons in the early 1980s, when I was a teenager in New York, to visit with Haitian asylum seekers we did not know but feared we might, people who, as my father used to say, "could have very well been us."

Krome's silent despair became tangible when a group of Haitian men in 6 identical dark-blue uniforms walked into a barbed wire courtyard to address our delegation that morning. "My name is . . . ," they began. "I came on the July boat." Or, "I came on the December boat." Or the most famous one of all, the October 29, 2002, boat, the landing of which was broadcast live on CNN and other national television outlets.

As if suddenly empowered by this brief opportunity to break their silence, 7 the men spoke in clear, loud voices, some inventing parables to explain their circumstances. One man told the story of a mad dog that forced a person to seek shelter at a neighbor's house. "If mad dogs are chasing you, shouldn't your neighbor shelter you?" he asked.

One man asked us to tell the world that the detainees were sometimes 8 beaten. He told us of a friend who had his back broken by a guard and was deported before he could get medical attention. They said that the rooms they slept in were so cold that they shivered all night long. They spoke of arbitrary curfews, how they were woken up at 6 AM and forced to go back to those cold rooms by 6 PM.

One man said, "If I had a bullet, I'd have shot myself already. I'm not a   9
criminal. I'm not used to prison."

I met an older man who came from Bel Air, the same area in Port-au-   10
Prince where I spent the first twelve years of my life. His eyes were red. He couldn't stop crying. His mother had died the week before, he said, and he was heartbroken that he couldn't attend her funeral.

Two months after that visit, then Attorney General John Ashcroft vetoed   11
an immigration judge's decision to release an eighteen-year-old Haitian boy named David Joseph, whom we'd met at Krome that day. Ashcroft argued that Joseph had to remain in custody because he posed a threat to national security. He further stated that Haiti harbors Pakistani and Palestinian terrorists, but the government could offer no proof for this charge in response to a Freedom of Information Act request from the Florida Immigration Advocacy Center. The truth was that, like many of the other refugees we had seen that day, David Joseph had fled his home not because he wanted to harm the United States but because it was impossible for him to live in his own country. Scorned by their neighbors for their parents' political views, he and his brother had been stoned and burned, their father severely beaten. Had he not fled, he would have been killed.

In November 2004 David Joseph was deported after two years in detention,   12
even though the area in Haiti where he was from had recently been devastated by a season of tropical storms that resulted in three thousand deaths and left a quarter-million people homeless. He also had no family to return to, since no one knew, least of all him, whether any of his relatives were alive or dead.

In the fall of 2004 I too suffered a devastating loss in a way I had never   13
expected or imagined.

On Sunday, October 24, 2004, United Nations troops and Haitian police   14
forces launched an antigang operation in Bel Air, where my eighty-one-year-old uncle, Joseph Danticat, had been living for fifty years. During the operation the UN "peacekeepers," accompanied by the Haitian police, used the roof of my uncle's three-story house, school and church compound to fire at the gangs. When the forces left Bel Air the gang members came to my uncle's home, told him that fifteen of their friends had been killed and said he had to pay for the burials or die. Knowing he'd never be able to produce the kind of money they were seeking, my uncle asked for a few minutes to make a phone call, grabbed some important papers and fled to a nearby house.

My uncle hid under a neighbor's bed for three days as the gang members 15
searched for him. When they were not able to find him, they ransacked his
home and church and set his office on fire. A few days later a family member
helped him escape the neighborhood, and on October 29, 2004, he took a
plane to Miami, just as he had done many times for more than thirty years.
He had a valid multiple-entry visa. But when immigration officials at Miami
International Airport asked how long he would be staying in the United
States, he explained that he would be killed if he returned to Haiti and that
he wanted "temporary" asylum. He was immediately arrested and taken to
Krome, where medicine he had brought with him from Haiti for an inflamed
prostate and high blood pressure was taken away from him. On November 3,
2004, while still in the custody of the Krome Detention Center, and thus the
Department of Homeland Security, he died at a nearby hospital.

As my uncle lay dying in a hospital bed in a ward reserved for hardened 16
criminals, my repeated requests to visit him were denied by Department of
Homeland Security and Krome officials for what I was told were "security
reasons." In other words, my uncle was treated like a criminal when his only
offense was thinking that he could find shelter in the United States.

Before this tragedy struck our family, I had not quite heeded my father's 17
warning and never truly believed that the asylum seekers we visited so often
could really include one so close to us. However, nothing proves more than
what happened to my uncle, an elderly man of the cloth, that we all live with
a certain level of risk in post–9/11 America. Still, those of us who are refugees
and exiles must live with the double menace of being both possible victims
and suspects, sometimes with fatal consequences. Will America ever learn
again how to protect itself without sacrificing a great many innocent lives? So
that my uncle did not die in vain, I truly hope so.

*For a reading quiz, sources on Edwidge Danticat, and annotated links to further readings
on immigration and border control, visit* **bedfordstmartins.com/thebedfordreader.**

Journal Writing

Write about a time when you were punished unjustifiably, when you were innocent of
what you were punished for. What were the circumstances, and what was the punishment? How did the situation make you feel about whoever punished you? about

yourself? about others involved, such as anyone who may have gotten you into trouble to begin with? (To take your journal writing further, see "From Journal to Essay" below.)

Questions on Meaning

1. What does Danticat point to as the US government's justification for detaining and deporting Haitian asylum seekers? What does she think of this justification? How do you know?
2. What, according to Danticat, leads most Haitians who seek asylum in the United States to do so?
3. Where in the essay does Danticat state her THESIS? How would you restate it?
4. How do you suppose Danticat hoped readers would respond to this essay? What is her PURPOSE? What is your response, and why?

Questions on Writing Strategy

1. How is Danticat's essay organized? What is the effect of this organization?
2. What assumptions does Danticat make about her AUDIENCE'S familiarity with the situation in Haiti and the plight of Haitian refugees in the United States?
3. How does Danticat try to elicit sympathy for the people she writes about? What kinds of details does she offer about them? How would you describe the primary APPEAL of her argument?
4. Where in the essay does Danticat write about herself? What is the point of her doing so?
5. **OTHER METHODS** Danticat uses NARRATION in paragraphs 14–15, framing the story with two dates. Why is the story important? What does the date frame contribute to it?

Questions on Language

1. In paragraph 7 Danticat quotes a detainee's parable for his situation. What is a *parable*? What does this parable mean?
2. Danticat says that she imagined the Krome Detention Center as "a cross between Alcatraz and hell" (par. 5). What does she mean?
3. In paragraph 14 Danticat puts the word *peacekeepers* in quotation marks. Why?
4. If you are unfamiliar with any of the following words, check a dictionary for their meanings: constrained (par. 3); asylum (5); tangible (6); arbitrary (8); devastating (13); ransacked (15).

Suggestions for Writing

1. **FROM JOURNAL TO ESSAY** Based on your journal entry, write an essay in which you narrate your experience (or, perhaps, experiences) with being punished unjustifiably. As you plan and draft your essay, try to draw a larger point about the results of unjustifiable punishment in general.

2. In her final paragraph Danticat writes that "we all live with a certain level of risk in post–9/11 America." How has the continued threat of terrorist attacks affected your life and the lives of others you know? How has this threat affected the country more generally? Do you and other people feel safer now than in the months immediately following 9/11? Why, or why not? Write an essay in which you detail your view of the aftereffects of 9/11.

3. Research how US immigration officials determine which would-be immigrants to the United States will be denied entrance, based on country of origin and other factors. In an essay, explain these policies and evaluate their fairness as you see it.

4. **CRITICAL WRITING**   Evaluate Danticat's TONE in this essay. What contributes to this tone, and to what extent does it serve her purpose in writing? How might a different tone have changed your response to the essay?

5. **CONNECTIONS**   In the preceding essay, Mark Krikorian defends the immigration policies of the Department of Homeland Security, writing that "the lack of effective immigration control leaves us naked in the face of the enemy." Write an essay in which you consider how Danticat might respond to Krikorian and how Krikorian might respond to Danticat. Could they come to any common ground, or are their viewpoints too far opposed to reach any sort of agreement?

Edwidge Danticat on Writing

In an interview upon the publication of her novel *Breath, Eyes, Memory,* Edwidge Danticat explained why she chose to write in English when she first arrived in the United States from Haiti.

I came to the United States at an interesting time in my life, at twelve years old, on the cusp of adolescence. I think if we had moved to Spain, I probably would have written in Spanish. My primary language was Haitian Creole, which at the time that I was in school in Haiti was not taught in a consistent written form. My instruction was done in French, which I only spoke in school and not at home. When I came here I was completely between languages. It's not unusual for me to run into young people, for example, who have been here for a year and stutter through both their primary language and English because the new language is settling into them in a very obvious way. I came to English at a time when I was not adept enough at French to write creatively in French and did not know how to write in Creole because it had not been taught to me in school, so my writing in English was as much an act of personal translation as it was an act of creative collaboration with the new place I was in. My writing in English is a consequence of my migration, in the same way that immigrant children speaking to each other in English is a consequence of their migration.

For Discussion

1. How would using the language of her new country be "an act of creative collaboration" for a recent immigrant?
2. If you have immigrated to the United States, to what extent does Danticat's experience ring true to you? Did you also speak English to other immigrants as a way of adapting to your new culture?

LINDA CHAVEZ

An outspoken voice on issues of civil rights and affirmative action, Linda Chavez was born in 1947 in Albuquerque, New Mexico, to a Spanish American family long established in the Southwest. She graduated from the University of Colorado (BA, 1970) and did graduate work at the University of California, Los Angeles, and at the University of Maryland. She has held a number of government positions, including director of the White House Office of Public Liaison under President Ronald Reagan and chair of the National Commission on Migrant Education under President George H. W. Bush. She has published three books: *Out of the Barrio: Toward a New Politics of Hispanic Assimilation* (1991), which argues against affirmative action and bilingual education; *An Unlikely Conservative: The Transformation of an Ex-Liberal (Or How I Became the Most Hated Hispanic in America)* (2002); and *Betrayal: How Union Bosses Shake Down Their Members and Corrupt American Politics* (with Daniel Gray, 2004). Chavez currently chairs the Center for Equal Opportunity, a public-policy research organization. She also writes a syndicated newspaper column, hosts a syndicated radio show, and is a political analyst for Fox News.

Supporting Family Values

In this piece written in 2009 for *townhall.com*, a conservative news and information Web site, Chavez makes an unusual case in favor of immigration, legal or not. Presenting evidence that challenges the stereotype of immigrants as unstable and unable to adapt to life in the United States, she argues that established American citizens should be taking life lessons from their newest neighbors.

For another view on the assimilation of immigrants to the United States, see the following essay, Jay Nordlinger's "Bassackwards: Construction Spanish and Other Signs of the Times."

A new report out this week from the Pew Hispanic Center confirms what many observers already suspected about the illegal immigrant population in the United States: It is made up increasingly of intact families and their American-born children. Nearly half of illegal immigrant households consist of two-parent families with children, and 73% of these children were born here and are therefore US citizens.

"Supporting Family Values" from *townhall.com*, Friday, April 17, 2009. Reprinted by permission of Linda Chavez and Creators Syndicate, Inc.

The hard-line immigration restrictionists will, no doubt, find more cause   2
for alarm in these numbers. But they should represent hope to the rest of us.
One of the chief social problems afflicting this country is the breakdown in the
traditional family. But among immigrants, the two-parent household is alive
and well.

Only 21% of native households are made up of two parents living with   3
their own children. Among legal immigrants, the percentage of such households jumps to 35%. But among the illegal population, 47% of households
consist of a mother, a father and their children.

Age accounts for the major difference in household composition between   4
the native and foreign-born populations: Immigrants, especially illegal immigrants, tend to be younger, while the native population includes large numbers
of older Americans whose children have already left home. But out-of-wedlock
births and divorce, which are more common among the native born—especially blacks, but also Hispanics and whites—also mean that even young native
households with children are more likely to be headed by single women than
immigrant households are.

But the greater concern for some opponents of immigration—legal and   5
illegal—is the fear that these newcomers will never fully adapt, won't learn
English, will remain poor and uneducated, and transform the United States
into a replica of Mexico or some other Latin American country. The same
fears led Americans of the mid-nineteenth century to fear German and Irish
immigrants, and in the early twentieth century to fear Italians, Jews, Poles,
and others from Eastern and Southern Europe.

Such worries are no more rational today—or born out of actual evi-   6
dence—than they were a hundred years ago. It is true that Hispanic immigrants today take awhile to catch up with the native born just as their European
predecessors did, and illegal immigrants never fully do so in terms of education
or earnings. But there is still some room for optimism in the Pew Hispanic
report. Nearly half of illegal immigrants between the ages of 18 and 24 who have
graduated from high school attend college. A surprising 25% of illegal immigrant adults have at least some college, with 15% having completed college.

And although earnings among illegal immigrants are lower than among
either the native population or legal immigrants, they are far from destitute.   7
The median household income for illegal immigrants was $36,000 in 2007
compared with $50,000 for native-born households. And illegal immigrant
males have much higher labor force participation rates than the native born,
94% compared with 83% for US-born males.

The inflow of illegal immigrants has slowed substantially since the peak,   8
which occurred during the economic boom of the late 1990s, not in recent
years, contrary to popular but uninformed opinion. The Pew Hispanic Center
estimates there are nearly 12 million illegal immigrants living in the United

States now, a number that has stabilized over the last few years as a result both of better border enforcement and the declining job market. As a result, there might never be a better time to grapple with what to do about this population than right now.

The fact that so many illegal immigrants are intertwined with American citizens or legal residents, either as spouses or parents, should give pause to those who'd like to see all illegal immigrants rounded up and deported or their lives made so miserable they leave on their own. A better approach would allow those who have made their lives here, established families, bought homes, worked continuously and paid taxes to remain after paying fines, demonstrating English fluency and proving they have no criminal record. Such an approach is as much about supporting family values as it is granting amnesty.

*For a reading quiz, sources on Linda Chavez, and annotated links to further readings on immigration and assimilation, visit **bedfordstmartins.com/thebedfordreader**.*

Journal Writing

How do you feel about illegal immigrants? Are they criminals who should be punished? victims of circumstance who should be helped? something in between? In your journal, explore your thoughts on illegal immigration. Why do you feel as you do? (To take your journal writing further, see "From Journal to Essay" on the next page.)

Questions on Meaning

1. What seems to have prompted Chavez's essay? How can you tell?
2. What distinctions, if any, does Chavez make between legal and illegal immigrants? Are such distinctions important to her?
3. What is Chavez's point in paragraphs 5 and 6, and how does this point fit into her larger argument?
4. At what point does Chavez reveal her PURPOSE in writing? Why do you suppose she chose not to state her THESIS in the introduction?

Questions on Writing Strategy

1. How does Chavez characterize those who hold opposing views? What does this characterization suggest about how she imagines her AUDIENCE?
2. On what underlying ASSUMPTION does Chavez base her argument? Is that assumption reasonable?

3. As a whole, is Chavez's essay an example of appeal to emotion or reasoned argument or both? Give EVIDENCE to support your answer.
4. **OTHER METHODS**   Where and how does Chavez use CLASSIFICATION to support her argument?

Questions on Language

1. Consult a dictionary if you are unsure of the meaning of any of the following: restrictionists (par. 2); wedlock (4); replica (5); predecessors (6); destitute, median (7); stabilized, grapple (8); intertwined, amnesty (9).
2. What does Chavez mean by "native" households and populations? Do you detect any IRONY in her use of the word?
3. How would you describe Chavez's TONE in this essay?

Suggestions for Writing

1. **FROM JOURNAL TO ESSAY**   Based on your journal entry, draft an essay in which you respond directly to Chavez, explaining why you agree or disagree with her position. If you wish, write your essay as a letter to the editor of *townhall.com*, the online journal in which Chavez's essay was published. (See pp. 463–65 for an example of a letter to the editor.)
2. Identify a current controversy over national policy—Social Security benefits for the wealthy, the right to carry a concealed weapon, government funding for private schools, and so on. Read newspaper and weekly magazine editorials, letters to the editor, and other statements on the subject of the controversy. You could also discuss the issue with your friends and family. Based on your research, write a CLASSIFICATION essay in which you group people according to their stand on the issue. Try to be as objective as possible.
3. **CRITICAL WRITING**   Write an essay in which you ANALYZE the main CLAIMS of Chavez's argument. What EVIDENCE does she provide to back up these claims? Do you find the evidence adequate? (You may wish to track down and examine the source Chavez cites in her introduction: Published by the Pew Hispanic Center on April 14, 2009, its title is *A Portrait of Unauthorized Immigrants in the United States*.)
4. **CONNECTIONS**   In the following essay Jay Nordlinger takes a different view of assimilation among Spanish-speaking immigrants. Write an essay in which you COMPARE AND CONTRAST Chavez's and Nordlinger's arguments. Where do they agree? Where do they disagree? In your view, whose case is stronger? Why?

Linda Chavez on Writing

To Linda Chavez, telling writers they don't need to know the rules of grammar is like "telling aerospace engineers they don't need to learn the laws of physics." In a 2002 article for *The Enterprise*, Chavez writes about her affection for the lost art of diagramming sentences—using a branching structure to identify sentence parts and map their relationships. She fondly recalls her years in elementary school, then called "grammar school," when learning "where to place a modifier and whether to use an adverb or adjective" was an essential part of the curriculum. Abandoning grammar instruction, she writes, is leaving students scrambled.

Chavez criticizes recent classroom practices of emphasizing creativity over accuracy in composition: "For years now, schools have been teaching students to 'express' themselves, without worrying about transmitting the finer points of grammar and syntax. . . . But effective communication always entails understanding the rules. There are no short-cuts to good writing." According to Chavez, self-expression and grammar are not at odds with each other at all. As she sees it, a solid grasp of grammar is what allows a writer to clearly communicate meaning. In her own writing, Chavez follows the adage of her childhood teacher: "If you can't diagram it, don't write it."

For Discussion

1. Why do you think grammar may not be taught the same way it once was? Are there advantages to writing freely without worrying about form?
2. Why does Chavez draw the comparison between a writer without knowledge of grammar and an aerospace engineer without knowledge of physics?

JAY NORDLINGER

Jay Nordlinger is a political journalist and a classical music enthusiast. Born in 1963 in Ypsilanti, Michigan, he grew up in nearby Ann Arbor and graduated from the University of Michigan in 1985. Nordlinger is a music critic for *The New Criterion;* at the same time, he is managing editor of the conservative magazine *National Review,* for which he writes opinion pieces on a wide range of topics as well as a regular online column. In 2000 he took a brief hiatus to write speeches for George W. Bush during the presidential campaign. Nordlinger often writes about human rights in Cuba and China because, in his own words, "so few others do," and in 2001 he was awarded the Eric Breindel Journalism Award for "bearing witness to the evils of totalitarianism." His recent book, *Here, There, and Everywhere* (2007), collects many of his eclectic articles.

Bassackwards: Construction Spanish and Other Signs of the Times

According to the Pew Hispanic Center, 79% of the nearly 5.5 million Spanish-speaking immigrants who arrived in the United States between 2000 and 2008 came speaking English "less than very well." Nordlinger has a problem with that, but not for the reasons you might expect. In this 2007 essay from the *National Review,* he makes an impassioned plea for speedy English-language acquisition among all American newcomers.

America, of course, has always been a place of many languages, along with our common tongue, English. German, its cousin Yiddish, Chinese, Italian, Polish—they have all been spoken here, especially in homes and community centers. But Spanish in today's America is something else: a language coddled, bowed to, enshrined.

We could talk about "bilingual education," which too often turns out to be monolingual education, and in the wrong tongue. We could talk about Spanish-language election ballots. We could talk about "For English, press 1. *Para español, oprima el dos.*" But let's talk, instead, about Construction Spanish.

Classes in—shall we call it "Con. Span."?—have sprouted up all over America. These are classes designed to teach contractors, supervisors, and other bosses in the construction business how to speak to their Hispanic workers. The bosses aren't learning Spanish, exactly; they will not be reading *Don*

610

Quixote.[1] This is a specialized language: *casco* for hard hat; *montacarga* for fork-lift; *pistola de clavos* for nail gun.

But wouldn't it be better, for all concerned, if the workers learned "hard   4
hat," "forklift," and "nail gun"? We must put off such foolish questions, for the moment.

Construction Spanish is an example of what has been called "Survival   5
Spanish," or "Command Spanish"—bits of Spanish acquired for a specific pur-pose. You can get trained in Restaurant Spanish, Fireman Spanish, or Health Care Spanish. And this last Spanish has sub-branches, such as Dental Spanish and Physical Therapy Spanish. Also, you can buy books and tapes that tell you how to converse with your gardener or maid, if that is your need.

But Construction Spanish has loomed especially large lately, for an obvi-   6
ous reason: the predominance of Hispanics in that field. Go into a Lowe's or Home Depot—stores that sell building materials—and you will see signs in Spanish (quite naturally). And you can buy any number of glossaries or hand-books. My favorite is *Spanish on the Job,* for its ad copy:

> No previous knowledge of Spanish is necessary. All words are phonetically
> spelled out to assure correct pronunciation. Trust me, yelling in English isn't
> going to help.

Let me yell, just a little bit. The old deal was, you came to America and   7
you assimilated into the culture. You presumably wanted to, otherwise you wouldn't have immigrated. You retained your mother tongue, of course, and you figured your children would know it, and you hoped your grandchildren would be interested (although that was no guarantee). But you were in Amer-ica, and America included English. Hooray!

And what of now? Forgetting an immigrant mindset, what is the general   8
American mindset? An article published in the *Washington Post* a few years ago shed some light. It concerned a Northern Virginia county, Fairfax, which had trained 450 of its employees in Spanish. A Fairfax official explained, "As we saw the changing demographics of the county, we said, 'How are we responding to the needs of new residents of the county?'" Not by encouraging their assimilation, that's for sure.

Hispanic immigrants had joined the sanitation department, so an assistant   9
superintendent there took Spanish for Garbage Workers. (Really.) He said, "In our type of business, it's something we're gonna have to learn." It was not too long ago that immigrants thought English was something they had to learn. They did not expect their employers or supervisors to take Survival Polish or Survival Serbian; they saw to it that they acquired some Survival English.

---

[1] A classic novel by the Spanish writer Miguel de Cervantes (1547–1616).—Eds.

The *Post*'s reporter found one person, a middle-aged "supervisor on build-   10
ing projects in downtown Washington," who was not too happy about the new
order. He acknowledged to the reporter that he wished his workers would simply learn English. But they were not—so he enrolled in Construction Spanish.
"I'm not saying I like what's happening," he said. "But I figure I can't fight it."

Which is a near-perfect expression of cultural defeatism.   11

There is always a tug between the pragmatic and the idealistic, or the   12
short term and the long term. You want assimilation and acculturation; but
you also want to do business in the here and now, in whatever language. You
want to be considerate of the immigrant, who has enough challenges, without
a new language; but you are not pleased to see him trapped in a linguistic
ghetto—barrio-ization, some people have called it.

I consider myself a veteran of the Spanish wars, although I participated   13
in the most minor of ways. Years ago, I was working at a firm in Washington,
DC. We were told that, when we wanted boxes thrown away, we had to mark
them "BASURA." *Basura* is the Spanish word for *trash*. And all of our janitors
were Hispanic.

Everything in my traditional-American soul rebelled at writing "BASURA,"   14
thinking it a gross act of separatism, and probably an insult to the workers.
"Why don't we write 'TRASH'?" I asked. "We're in America, and we don't want
anyone walled off. We want them to join the American family. How will they
ever rise in our society if they don't learn English? In Guatemala, we would
write 'BASURA.' But here we write 'TRASH.'"

That didn't go over terribly well, and I made no headway. But I took to   15
writing "BASURA/TRASH" on my boxes to be thrown out. That was my pathetic
little stand: a word, a slash, and another word. But I liked it.

A while back, I wrote about this experience in a *National Review Online*   16
column, and the subject provoked a ton of mail. I seemed to have touched
some national nerve. Many Hispanics wrote of their frustration and resentment at having been shunted into Spanish-only classes, or "bilingual" classes
that were the usual Spanish-preservation rackets. And a former manager of
custodial crews in Phoenix wrote the following:

> I once spent a few months trying to convince people in the corporate offices
> of a major insurance company that my employees didn't need orders in Span-
> ish. They may have been willing to do menial labor, but that didn't mean
> that they were stupid, and it was condescending to think they couldn't learn
> a simple five-letter word in the English language.

Namely, "trash."

Another correspondent added a twist, saying, "Here in Chicago, the big   17
offices distribute stickers to be placed on garbage items. They read, 'GARBAGE/
BASURA/SMIECI,'" laying it out in English, Spanish, and Polish.

Still another reader contributed this: 18

An acquaintance once told me that, years ago, when he was preparing for a
job that involved supervising an office cleaning crew, the guy he was replacing suggested that he come in a half-hour early each day of the following
week so he could learn enough Spanish to deal with the crew. The new guy
replied: "I've got a better idea: Why don't you have them come in a half-hour
early each day to learn enough English to deal with me?"

A stirring protest against the ass-backwardness of contemporary American
life.

At that Washington firm, a young janitor and I became friends, and I   19
learned that he had no dictionary: no English-Spanish, Spanish-English dictionary. I got him one. That night, he left me a note that contained one word:
"Grasias." Mainly because of the misspelling, I'm sure, it was one of the most
touching notes I had ever received.

Yet I am under no illusion that everyone who comes to America is dying   20
to melt into the pot. Is aching to bear out the national motto, *E pluribus
unum*. Years before I worked at the Washington firm, I worked at a public golf
course in Michigan, and we had many leagues, one of which was "the Korean
League." I was appalled at this, mortified for those good Americans of Korean
origin who played every Wednesday afternoon.

So, brimming with idealism, I said to the leader of the group, "We should 21
call it the Korean-American League or something else, right? Because you are
fellow Americans, and it's not right to call it the Korean League." He looked
at me blankly and said, "No, we're Koreans." Oh.

In any case, I tried—and so should all Americans, I dare say (native and   22
immigrant alike). Of course, when you talk as I have, in this piece, someone
always accuses you of being a jingo, boob, or xenophobe. People who can't
find their way to the toilet in any European capital will paint you as a foe of
languages. Will say that you're "afraid of the Other."

This even happened to S. I. Hayakawa, the famed linguist and politician.   23
He was the fellow who founded US English, the lobbying group. Hayakawa
liked to say, "Bilingualism for the individual is fine, but not for a country." I
imagine he spoke more languages than most people have toes. Yet that did not
spare him the usual accusations.

I assure the reader that I like Spanish as much as the next guy—actually,   24
considerably more. And Con. Span., Dental Span., and all the rest of the
Spans. are hardly the worst threat we face. Moreover, I trust that Americanization will sometime kick in, for the masses of newly arrived Hispanics. But if
it doesn't, we will lose a lot—all of us will.

*For a reading quiz, sources on Jay Nordlinger, and annotated links to further readings on immigration and assimilation, visit **bedfordstmartins.com/thebedfordreader**.*

Journal Writing

Think of a situation in which you had to learn a new procedure, custom, or language. You may have had a lot of help, as in a training program or with a guide or mentor, or you may have had to go it alone. In your journal write down what you recall most vividly about adjusting to the new situation. (To take your journal writing further, see "From Journal to Essay" on the facing page.)

Questions on Meaning

1. What, according to Nordlinger, explains the emergence of specialized Spanish-language instruction for "contractors, supervisors, and other bosses" (par. 3)? Whom does he blame for the development?
2. Why does Nordlinger object to classes in "Survival" or "Command" Spanish? What alternatives would he prefer, and why?
3. Explain the implications of Nordlinger's concluding sentences: ". . . I trust that Americanization will sometime kick in, for the masses of newly arrived Hispanics. But if it doesn't, we will lose a lot—all of us will." Whom does he mean by "we"? What do "all of us" stand to lose?
4. What would you say is Nordlinger's PURPOSE in this essay?

Questions on Writing Strategy

1. Where in the essay does Nordlinger use the second-PERSON *you* to address his readers? What do these paragraphs reveal about his intended AUDIENCE?
2. Why does Nordlinger devote so much attention to a personal battle over labeling boxes *basura* versus *trash*? Do you find this strategy effective for his argument? Why, or why not?
3. What is Nordlinger's ETHICAL APPEAL? What steps does he take to portray himself as knowledgeable and reasonable? Does he succeed?
4. **OTHER METHODS**   How does Nordlinger use EXAMPLE and NARRATION to support his argument?

Questions on Language

1. Although Nordlinger provides English translations for most of the Spanish words and phrases he cites in his essay, he does not do so for "*Para español, oprima el*

dos" (par. 2). Based on the context, what do you think this sentence means? Why doesn't Nordlinger translate it?

2. In paragraph 11 Nordlinger refers to a building supervisor's reluctant willingness to learn Spanish as "cultural defeatism." What does this phrase suggest?

3. At what points in his essay does Nordlinger adopt a sarcastic TONE? What does his use of sarcasm contribute to (or take away from) his argument? (For a definition of *sarcasm*, see *Irony* in Useful Terms.)

4. Look up any of the following words whose meanings you are unsure of: coddled, enshrined (par. 1); bilingual, monolingual (2); acquired (5); loomed, predominance, phonetically (6); demographics (8); pragmatic, acculturation, linguistic (12); separatism (14); shunted, rackets (16); brimming (21); jingo, xenophobe (22).

Suggestions for Writing

1. **FROM JOURNAL TO ESSAY**   Starting with the experience you wrote about in your journal, compose an essay that describes the challenges of adapting to a new situation. As you write, consider who you think should take responsibility for helping newcomers orient themselves and learn the ropes — the newcomers alone, those already comfortable with things the way they are, or both? How might people experienced with a situation benefit from helping others adapt to it? Or what might newcomers gain from self-reliance?

2. Do some research on the English-only movement and the opposition to it, beginning with the stated agenda of US English, the lobbying group Nordlinger mentions in paragraph 23 (you can find information at *usenglish.org*). Focus on an issue that interests you. For example, should English be the official language of the United States? Should government forms, or public signage, be printed in multiple languages? Should schoolchildren be taught in English or in their native languages or in both? Should fluency in English be required of immigrants seeking citizenship? Write an essay in which you give background information on one such issue and support your own view in a well-reasoned argument.

3. **CRITICAL WRITING**   Write an essay examining the organization of Nordlinger's essay. What does Nordlinger accomplish in each paragraph? How effectively does he use TRANSITIONS to move from one idea to the next?

4. **CONNECTIONS**   Nordlinger acknowledges that not "everyone who comes to America is dying to melt into the pot" (par. 20), yet he and Linda Chavez, in the previous essay, both stress the need for immigrants to assimilate to American culture. What does it mean to be "American" in a country as diverse as the United States? Is the idea of American culture as a "melting pot" still valid? In an essay, define, defend, or dispute the concept of assimilation. To what extent should recent immigrants be expected to trade ethnic or national identity for a new American identity? What might such an identity encompass, and how could it be obtained? What is gained, or lost, when immigrants become "Americanized"?

ADDITIONAL WRITING TOPICS

Argument and Persuasion

1. Write a persuasive essay in which you express a deeply felt opinion. In it, address a particular person or audience. For instance, you might direct your essay

   To a friend unwilling to attend a ballet performance (or a wrestling match) with you on the grounds that such an event is a waste of time

   To a teacher who asserts that more term papers, and longer ones, are necessary for students to master academic writing

   To a developer who plans to tear down a historic house

   To someone who sees no purpose in studying a foreign language

   To a high-school class whose members don't want to go to college

   To an older generation skeptical of the value of current popular music

   To an atheist who asserts that religion just distracts us from the here and now

   To the members of a library board who want to ban a book you love

2. Write a letter to your campus newspaper or a city newspaper in which you argue for or against a certain cause or view. You may wish to object to a particular feature or editorial in the paper. Send your letter and see if it is published.

3. Write a short letter to your congressional or state representative, arguing in favor of (or against) the passage of some pending legislation. See a news magazine or a newspaper for a worthwhile bill to write about. Or else write in favor of some continuing cause: for instance, requiring (or not requiring) cars to reduce exhaust emissions, reducing (or increasing) military spending, providing (or reducing) aid to the arts, expanding (or reducing) government loans to college students.

4. Write an essay arguing that something you believe strongly about should be changed, removed, abolished, enforced, repeated, revised, reinstated, or reconsidered. Be sure to propose some plan for carrying out whatever suggestions you make. Possible topics, listed to start you thinking, are these:

   Gun laws

   Graduation requirements

   ROTC programs in schools and colleges

   Movie ratings (G, PG, PG-13, R, NC-17, X)

   School prayer

   Fraternities and sororities

   Dress codes in primary and secondary schools

MIXING THE METHODS

Everywhere in this book, we have tried to prove how flexible the methods of development are. All the preceding essays offer superb examples of DESCRIPTION or CLASSIFICATION or DEFINITION or ARGUMENT, but every one also illustrates other methods, too—description in PROCESS ANALYSIS, ANALYSIS and NARRATION in COMPARISON, EXAMPLES and CAUSE AND EFFECT in argument.

In this part of the book, we take this point even further by abandoning the individual methods. Instead, we offer a collection of twelve essays, many of them considered classics, all of them by well-known writers. The selections range widely in their subjects and approaches, but they share a significant feature: All the authors draw on whatever methods of development, at whatever length, will help them achieve their PURPOSES with readers. (To show how the writers combine methods, we have highlighted the most significant ones in the note preceding each essay.)

You have already begun to command the methods by focusing on them individually, making each a part of your kit of writing tools. Now, when you face a writing assignment, you can consider whether and how each method may help you sharpen your focus, develop your ideas, and achieve your aim. Indeed, as we noted in Chapter 2, one way to approach a subject is to apply each method to it, one by one. The following list distills the discussion on pages 38–39 to a set of questions that you can ask about any subject:

1. *Narration:* Can you tell a story about the subject?
2. *Description:* Can you use your senses to illuminate the subject?
3. *Example:* Can you point to instances that will make the subject concrete and specific?
4. *Comparison and contrast:* Will setting the subject alongside another generate useful information?
5. *Process analysis:* Will a step-by-step explanation of how the subject works add to the reader's understanding?
6. *Division or analysis:* Can slicing the subject into its parts produce a clearer vision of it?
7. *Classification:* Is it worthwhile to sort the subject into kinds or groups?
8. *Cause and effect:* Does it add to the subject to ask why it happened or what its results are?
9. *Definition:* Can you trace a boundary that will clarify the meaning of the subject?
10. *Argument and persuasion:* Can you back up an opinion or make a proposal about the subject?

Rarely will every one of these questions produce fruit for a given essay, but inevitably two or three or four will. Try the whole list when you're stuck at the beginning of an assignment or when you're snagged in the middle of a draft. You'll find the questions are as good at removing obstacles as they are at generating ideas.

SANDRA CISNEROS

Born in 1954 in Chicago, Sandra Cisneros attended Loyola University, where she received a BA in 1976. Two years later, she earned an MFA from the University of Iowa Writers' Workshop. While at Iowa, she embraced her Chicano heritage in her writing, turning to her childhood for inspiration. Most of her published work deals explicitly with issues of ethnic heritage, poverty, and personal identity. She is the author of two novels, *The House on Mango Street* (1984), for which she won the American Book Award, and *Caramelo* (2003); a collection of short stories, *Woman Hollering Creek* (1991); and four books of poetry, including *My Wicked, Wicked Ways* (1987) and *Loose Woman* (1994). Cisneros has received numerous awards, including two from the National Endowment for the Arts, a Lannan Foundation Literary Award, the Texas Medal of the Arts, and a MacArthur Fellowship. She is currently working on a collection of fiction, a children's book, and a book about writing.

Only Daughter

Growing up, Cisneros faced expectations placed on girls by both American society and her Mexican American culture. Her father had little interest in reading, and his only ambition for his daughter was marriage, yet he proved to be the main reason that she became a writer. In this essay from a 1990 *Glamour* magazine, Cisneros explains why.

"Only Daughter" mixes several methods of development to show the difficult yet fruitful bond between daughter and father:

Narration (Chap. 4): paragraphs 9–12, 15–22
Description (Chap. 5): paragraphs 7, 13, 16–21
Cause and effect (Chap. 11): paragraphs 3, 5, 7, 8
Definition (Chap. 12): paragraphs 1–2

Once, several years ago, when I was just starting out my writing career, I was 1
asked to write my own contributor's note for an anthology I was part of. I wrote: "I am the only daughter in a family of six sons. *That* explains everything."

Well, I've thought about that ever since, and yes, it explains a lot to me, 2
but for the reader's sake I should have written: "I am the only daughter in a *Mexican* family of six sons." Or even: "I am the only daughter of a Mexican father and a Mexican-American mother." Or: "I am the only daughter of a working-class family of nine." All of these had everything to do with who I am today.

I was/am the only daughter and *only* a daughter. Being an only daughter in 3
a family of six sons forced me by circumstance to spend a lot of time by myself

because my brothers felt it beneath them to play with a *girl* in public. But that aloneness, that loneliness, was good for a would-be writer—it allowed me time to think and think, to imagine, to read and prepare myself.

Being only a daughter for my father meant my destiny would lead me to become someone's wife. That's what he believed. But when I was in fifth grade and shared my plans for college with him, I was sure he understood. I remember my father saying, *"Que bueno, mi'ja,* that's good." That meant a lot to me, especially since my brothers thought the idea hilarious. What I didn't realize was that my father thought college was good for girls—for finding a husband. After four years in college and two more in graduate school, and still no husband, my father shakes his head even now and says I wasted all that education.

In retrospect, I'm lucky my father believed daughters were meant for husbands. It meant it didn't matter if I majored in something silly like English. After all, I'd find a nice professional eventually, right? This allowed me the liberty to putter about embroidering my little poems and stories without my father interrupting with so much as a "What's that you're writing?"

But the truth is, I wanted him to interrupt. I wanted my father to understand what it was I was scribbling, to introduce me as "My only daughter, the writer." Not as "This is my only daughter. She teaches." *El maestra*—teacher. Not even *profesora.*

In a sense, everything I have ever written has been for him, to win his approval even though I know my father can't read English words, even though my father's only reading includes the brown-ink *Esto* sports magazines from Mexico City and the bloody *¡Alarma!* magazines that feature yet another sighting of *La Virgen de Guadalupe* on a tortilla or a wife's revenge on her philandering husband by bashing his skull in with a *molcajete* (a kitchen mortar made of volcanic rock). Or the *fotonovelas,* the little picture paperbacks with tragedy and trauma erupting from the characters' mouths in bubbles.

My father represents, then, the public majority. A public who is uninterested in reading, and yet one whom I am writing about and for, and privately trying to woo.

When we were growing up in Chicago, we moved a lot because of my father. He suffered periodic bouts of nostalgia. Then we'd have to let go our flat, store the furniture with mother's relatives, load the station wagon with baggage and bologna sandwiches, and head south. To Mexico City.

We came back, of course. To yet another Chicago flat, another Chicago neighborhood, another Catholic school. Each time, my father would seek out the parish priest in order to get a tuition break, and complain or boast: "I have seven sons."

He meant *siete hijos,* seven children, but he translated it as "sons." "I have seven sons." To anyone who would listen. The Sears Roebuck employee who sold us the washing machine. The short-order cook where my father ate his ham-and-eggs breakfasts. "I have seven sons." As if he deserved a medal from the state.

My papa. He didn't mean anything by that mistranslation, I'm sure. But somehow I could feel myself being erased. I'd tug my father's sleeve and whisper: "Not seven sons. Six! and *one daughter*." 12

When my oldest brother graduated from medical school, he fulfilled my father's dream that we study hard and use this — our heads, instead of this — our hands. Even now my father's hands are thick and yellow, stubbed by a history of hammer and nails and twine and coils and springs. "Use this," my father said, tapping his head, "and not this," showing us those hands. He always looked tired when he said it. 13

Wasn't college an investment? And hadn't I spent all those years in college? And if I didn't marry, what was it all for? Why would anyone go to college and then choose to be poor? Especially someone who had always been poor. 14

Last year, after ten years of writing professionally, the financial rewards started to trickle in. My second National Endowment for the Arts Fellowship. A guest professorship at the University of California, Berkeley. My book, which sold to a major New York publishing house. 15

At Christmas, I flew home to Chicago. The house was throbbing, same as always; hot *tamales* and sweet *tamales* hissing in my mother's pressure cooker, and everybody — mother, six brothers, wives, babies, aunts, cousins — talking too loud and at the same time, like in a Fellini[1] film, because that's just how we are. 16

I went upstairs to my father's room. One of my stories had just been translated into Spanish and published in an anthology of Chicano writing, and I wanted to show it to him. Ever since he recovered from a stroke two years ago, my father likes to spend his leisure hours horizontally. And that's how I found him, watching a Pedro Infante movie on Galavision and eating rice pudding. 17

There was a glass filmed with milk on the bedside table. There were several vials of pills and balled Kleenex. And on the floor, one black sock and a plastic urinal that I didn't want to look at but looked at anyway. Pedro Infante was about to burst into song, and my father was laughing. 18

I'm not sure if it was because my story was translated into Spanish, or because it was published in Mexico, or perhaps because the story dealt with Tepeyac, the *colonia* my father was raised in, but at any rate, my father punched the mute button on his remote control and read my story. 19

---

[1]Federico Fellini (1920–93), an Italian, directed *La Strada*, *La Dolce Vita*, *Satyricon*, and other movies. — EDS.

I sat on the bed next to my father and waited. He read it very slowly. As   20
if he were reading each line over and over. He laughed at all the right places
and read lines he liked out loud. He pointed and asked questions: "Is this So-
and-so?" "Yes," I said. He kept reading.

When he was finally finished, after what seemed like hours, my father   21
looked up and asked: "Where can we get more copies of this for the relatives?"

Of all the wonderful things that happened to me last year, that was the   22
most wonderful.

*For a reading quiz, sources on Sandra Cisneros, and annotated links to further readings
on parent-child relationships, visit **bedfordstmartins.com/thebedfordreader**.*

Journal Writing

Cisneros's father thinks of success primarily in terms of financial rewards. Do you
agree? In your journal, consider the meaning of *success*, focusing on these questions:
Whom in your own life do you consider to be successful, and why? Where do your
ideas of success come from — your parents? your friends? your schooling? the media?
(To take your journal writing further, see "From Journal to Essay" on the next page.)

Questions on Meaning

1. What do you take to be Cisneros's main PURPOSE in this essay?
2. Cisneros writes, "I am the only daughter in a family of six sons. *That* explains
   everything" (par. 1). What does it explain in this essay?
3. What are some of the parallels Cisneros draws between her father and "the public
   majority" (par. 8)?
4. Why do you think her father's appreciation of her story was, for Cisneros, "the
   most wonderful" thing that happened to her in a year that was already good?

Questions on Writing Strategy

1. Does Cisneros seem to be writing mainly for other Mexican Americans or for a
   wider AUDIENCE? Cite passages from the essay to support your answer.
2. What can you INFER about Cisneros's stories and poems from the information
   about her education (par. 4), the details about her father's reading (7–8), and the
   list of her successes (15)?

3. **MIXED METHODS**   Cisneros's INTRODUCTION (pars. 1–2) gives a DEFINITION of the author. How effective is this introduction for setting up the essay that follows?
4. **MIXED METHODS**   Perhaps a third of Cisneros's essay is devoted to a NARRATIVE and DESCRIPTION of a Christmas visit home (pars. 16–22). Why do you think Cisneros relates this incident in so much detail? What do we gain from knowing what was cooking, what her father was watching on TV, or what questions he asked as he read Cisneros's story?

Questions on Language

1. What are the contrasting ideas in Cisneros's paired phrases "the only daughter and *only* a daughter" (par. 3)?
2. How do Cisneros's words convey her feeling about her father's translation of *siete hijos* as "seven sons" (pars. 11–12)?
3. Consult a dictionary if you need help in defining the following: retrospect, putter (par. 5); philandering, mortar (7); woo (8).

Suggestions for Writing

1. **FROM JOURNAL TO ESSAY**   Write an extended definition of *success* that also examines the sources of your definition, as you explored them in your journal. (The sources could be negative as well as positive—that is, your own ideas may have formed in reaction *against* others' ideas as well as in agreement *with* them.) Be sure your essay has a clear THESIS and plenty of EXAMPLES to make your definition precise.
2. Cisneros writes of differences from her father that frustrated her but that also motivated her to achieve. In a narrative and descriptive essay, relate some aspect of a relationship with a parent or other figure of authority that you found troubling or even maddening at the time but that now seems to have shaped you in positive ways. Did a parent (or someone else) push you to study when you wanted to play sports or hang out with your friends? make you attend religious services when they seemed unimportant? refuse to acknowledge accomplishments you were proud of? try to direct you onto a path you didn't care to take?
3. **CRITICAL WRITING**   Cisneros attributes many of her father's attitudes to his Mexican heritage. As an extension of the previous assignment, consider whether Cisneros's experiences are particular to Mexican American families or are common in all families, whatever their ethnicity. Are conflicts between children and their parents inevitable, do you think? Why, or why not?
4. **CONNECTIONS**   Cisneros's essay is one of several in this book that explore the experience of growing away from one's parents; other essays include Amy Tan's "Fish Cheeks" (p. 116), Brad Manning's "Arm Wrestling with My Father" (p. 163), Sarah Vowell's "Shooting Dad" (p. 171), Firoozeh Dumas's "Sweet, Sour, and Resentful" (p. 320), Maxine Hong Kingston's "No Name Woman" (p. 649), and Richard Rodriguez's "Aria" (p. 681). Looking at one or two of these essays along with Cisneros's, compare and contrast the authors' relations with their parents. How are the parents themselves and the authors' feelings similar or different? Use quotations or paraphrases from the essays as evidence for your ideas.

5. **CONNECTIONS**   The authors highlighted in the previous question all use dialog to make the interactions with their parents vivid. Try your hand at using dialog in a brief narrative that recalls a significant incident between yourself and a parent. Then write briefly about your experience using dialog: How easy or difficult was it to remember who said what? How easy or difficult was it to make the speakers sound like themselves?

Sandra Cisneros on Writing

A bilingual author, Sandra Cisneros writes primarily in English. Yet Spanish influences her English sentences, and she frequently uses Spanish words in her prose. She spoke with Feroza Jussawalla and Reed Way Dasenbrock about how Spanish affects her writing:

"What it does is change the rhythm of my writing. I think that incorporating the Spanish, for me, allows me to create new expressions in English — to say things that have never been said before. And I get to do that by translating literally. I love calling stories by Spanish expressions. I have this story called 'Salvador, Late or Early.' It's a nice title. It means 'sooner or later,' *tarde o temprano,* which literally translates as 'late or early.' All of a sudden something happens to the English, something really new is happening, a new spice is added to the English language."

In some of her work, Cisneros uses Spanish and then offers a translation for English readers. At other times, she thinks complete translation is unnecessary: "See, sometimes, you don't have to say the whole thing. Now I'm learning how you can say something in English so that you know the person is saying it in Spanish. I like that. You can say a phrase in Spanish, and you can choose not to translate it, but you can make it understood through the context. 'And then my *abuelita* called me a *sin verguenza* and cried because I am without shame,' you see? Just in the sentence you can weave it in. To me it's really fun to be doing that; to me it's like I've uncovered this whole mother lode that I haven't tapped into. All the *expresiones* in Spanish when translated make English wonderful."

That said, Cisneros believes that "[t]he readers who are going to like my stories the best and catch all the subtexts and all the subtleties, that even my editor can't catch, are Chicanas. When there are Chicanas in the audience, and they laugh, they are laughing at stuff that we talk about among ourselves. And there's no way that my editor at Random House is ever going to get those jokes." This seems particularly true, she finds, when she's making use of Mexican and Southwestern myths and legends about which the general public might not be aware. "That's why I say the real ones who are going to get it are the Latinos, the Chicanos. They're going to get it in that they're going to understand the myth and how I've revised it. When I talked to someone at *Interview* magazine, I had to explain to him what I was doing with *la llorona,* *La Malinche,* and the Virgin of Guadalupe in the story ['Woman Hollering Creek']. But he said, 'Hey, I didn't know that, but I still got the story.' You can get it at some other level. He reminded me, 'Sandra, if you're from Ireland, you're going to get a lot more out of Joyce than if you're not, but just because you're not Irish doesn't mean you're not going to get it at another level.'"

For Discussion

1. In the passages quoted here, Sandra Cisneros is talking about her fiction writing. Do her thoughts about Spanish apply to the kind of English she uses when she writes a nonfiction piece like "Only Daughter"?
2. In "Only Daughter," Sandra Cisneros writes of her father: "In a sense, everything I have ever written has been for him, to win his approval, even though I know my father can't read English words. . . ." How does this square with her claim that Chicana readers are her best readers?
3. Who is the reader who would best understand your essays?

JOAN DIDION

A writer whose fame is fourfold—as novelist, essayist, journalist, and screen-writer—Joan Didion was born in 1934 in California, where her family had lived for five generations. After graduation from the University of California, Berkeley, she spent a few years in New York, working as a feature editor for the fashion magazine *Vogue*. She gained wide notice in the 1960s and 1970s with the publication of the essay collections *Slouching Towards Bethlehem* (1968) and *The White Album* (1979) and the novels *River Run* (1963), *Play It as It Lays* (1971), and *A Book of Common Prayer* (1977). *Salvador* (1983), her book-length essay based on a visit to war-torn El Salvador, and *Miami* (1987), a study of Cuban exiles in Florida, also received close attention. With her late husband, John Gregory Dunne, Didion coauthored a number of screenplays, notably for *A Star Is Born* (1976), *True Confessions* (1981), and *Up Close and Personal* (1996). Her latest books are *The Last Thing He Wanted* (1996), a novel; *Political Fictions* (2001) and *Fixed Ideas: America Since 9.11* (2003), both critiques of US politics; *Where I Was From* (2003), a memoir and an assessment of Didion's native California; and *The Year of Magical Thinking* (2005), a memoir of life after Dunne's sudden death that was adapted into an acclaimed Broadway play.

In Bed

In this essay from *The White Album,* Didion explains migraine headaches in general and her own in particular. Any migraine sufferer will recognize the pain and debility she describes. Even nonsufferers are likely to wince under the spell of Didion's vivid, sensuous prose.

Didion draws on half a dozen methods of development to give a full picture of migraine:

Narration (Chap. 4): paragraphs 1–2, 7–8
Description (Chap. 5): paragraphs 1–2, 7–8
Example (Chap. 6): paragraphs 2–3, 5, 7
Process analysis (Chap. 8): paragraphs 3–5, 7–8
Cause and effect (Chap. 11): paragraph 6
Definition (Chap. 12): paragraph 3

Three, four, sometimes five times a month, I spend the day in bed with a   1
migraine headache, insensible to the world around me. Almost every day of
every month, between these attacks, I feel the sudden irrational irritation and
flush of blood into the cerebral arteries which tell me that migraine is on its
way, and I take certain drugs to avert its arrival. If I did not take the drugs,
I would be able to function perhaps one day in four. The physiological error

called migraine is, in brief, central to the given of my life. When I was fifteen, sixteen, even twenty-five, I used to think that I could rid myself of this error by simply denying it, character over chemistry. "Do you have headaches *sometimes? frequently? never?*" the application forms would demand. "Check one." Wary of the trap, wanting whatever it was that the successful circumnavigation of that particular form could bring (a job, a scholarship, the respect of mankind and the grace of God), I would check one. "*Sometimes,*" I would lie. That in fact I spent one or two days a week almost unconscious with pain seemed a shameful secret, evidence not merely of some chemical inferiority but of all my bad attitudes, unpleasant tempers, wrongthink.

For I had no brain tumor, no eyestrain, no high blood pressure, nothing   2
wrong with me at all: I simply had migraine headaches, and migraine headaches were, as everyone who did not have them knew, imaginary. I fought migraine then, ignored the warnings sent, went to school and later to work in spite of it, sat through lectures in Middle English and presentations to advertisers with involuntary tears running down the right side of my face, threw up in washrooms, stumbled home by instinct, emptied ice trays onto my bed and tried to freeze the pain in my right temple, wished only for a neurosurgeon who would do a lobotomy on house call, and cursed my imagination.

It was a long time before I began thinking mechanistically enough to   3
accept migraine for what it was: something with which I would be living, the way some people live with diabetes. Migraine is something more than the fancy of a neurotic imagination. It is an essentially hereditary complex of symptoms, the most frequently noted but by no means the most unpleasant of which is a vascular headache of blinding severity, suffered by a surprising number of women, a fair number of men (Thomas Jefferson had migraine, and so did Ulysses S. Grant, the day he accepted Lee's surrender), and by some unfortunate children as young as two years old. (I had my first when I was eight. It came on during a fire drill at the Columbia School in Colorado Springs, Colorado. I was taken first home and then to the infirmary at Peterson Field, where my father was stationed. The Air Corps doctor prescribed an enema.) Almost anything can trigger a specific attack of migraine: stress, allergy, fatigue, an abrupt change in barometric pressure, a contretemps over a parking ticket. A flashing light. A fire drill. One inherits, of course, only the predisposition. In other words I spent yesterday in bed with a headache not merely because of my bad attitudes, unpleasant tempers and wrongthink, but because both my grandmothers had migraine, my father has migraine and my mother has migraine.

No one knows precisely what it is that is inherited. The chemistry of   4
migraine, however, seems to have some connection with the nerve hormone named serotonin, which is naturally present in the brain. The amount of sero-

tonin in the blood falls sharply at the onset of migraine, and one migraine drug, Methysergide, or Sansert, seems to have some effect on serotonin. Methysergide is a derivative of lysergic acid (in fact Sandoz Pharmaceuticals first synthesized LSD-25 while looking for a migraine cure), and its use is hemmed about with so many contraindications and side effects that most doctors prescribe it only in the most incapacitating cases. Methysergide, when it is prescribed, is taken daily, as a preventive; another preventive which works for some people is old-fashioned ergotamine tartrate, which helps to constrict the swelling blood vessels during the "aura," the period which in most cases precedes the actual headache.

Once an attack is under way, however, no drug touches it. Migraine gives   5
some people mild hallucinations, temporarily blinds others, shows up not only as a headache but as a gastrointestinal disturbance, a painful sensitivity to all sensory stimuli, an abrupt overpowering fatigue, a strokelike aphasia, and a crippling inability to make even the most routine connections. When I am in a migraine aura (for some people the aura lasts fifteen minutes, for others several hours), I will drive through red lights, lose the house keys, spill whatever I am holding, lose the ability to focus my eyes or frame coherent sentences, and generally give the appearance of being on drugs, or drunk. The actual headache, when it comes, brings with it chills, sweating, nausea, a debility that seems to stretch the very limits of endurance. That no one dies of migraine seems, to someone deep into an attack, an ambiguous blessing.

My husband also has migraine, which is unfortunate for him but fortu-   6
nate for me: Perhaps nothing so tends to prolong an attack as the accusing eye of someone who has never had a headache. "Why not take a couple of aspirin," the unafflicted will say from the doorway, or "I'd have a headache, too, spending a beautiful day like this inside with all the shades drawn." All of us who have migraine suffer not only from the attacks themselves but from this common conviction that we are perversely refusing to cure ourselves by taking a couple of aspirin, that we are making ourselves sick, that we "bring it on ourselves." And in the most immediate sense, the sense of why we have a headache this Tuesday and not last Thursday, of course we often do. There certainly is what doctors call a "migraine personality," and that personality tends to be ambitious, inward, intolerant of error, rather rigidly organized, perfectionist. "You don't look like a migraine personality," a doctor once said to me. "Your hair's messy. But I suppose you're a compulsive housekeeper." Actually my house is kept even more negligently than my hair, but the doctor was right nonetheless: Perfectionism can also take the form of spending most of a week writing and rewriting and not writing a single paragraph.

But not all perfectionists have migraine, and not all migrainous people   7
have migraine personalities. We do not escape heredity. I have tried in most

of the available ways to escape my own migrainous heredity (at one point I learned to give myself two daily injections of histamine with a hypodermic needle, even though the needle so frightened me that I had to close my eyes when I did it), but I still have migraine. And I have learned now to live with it, learned when to expect it, how to outwit it, even how to regard it, when it does come, as more friend than lodger. We have reached a certain understanding, my migraine and I. It never comes when I am in real trouble. Tell me that my house is burned down, my husband has left me, that there is gunfighting in the streets and panic in the banks, and I will not respond by getting a headache. It comes instead when I am fighting not an open but a guerrilla war with my own life, during weeks of small household confusions, lost laundry, unhappy help, canceled appointments, on days when the telephone rings too much and I get no work done and the wind is coming up. On days like that my friend comes uninvited.

And once it comes, now that I am wise in its ways, I no longer fight it.   8
I lie down and let it happen. At first every small apprehension is magnified, every anxiety a pounding terror. Then the pain comes, and I concentrate only on that. Right there is the usefulness of migraine, there in that imposed yoga, the concentration on the pain. For when the pain recedes, ten or twelve hours later, everything goes with it, all the hidden resentments, all the vain anxieties. The migraine has acted as a circuit breaker, and the fuses have emerged intact. There is a pleasant convalescent euphoria. I open the windows and feel the air, eat gratefully, sleep well. I notice the particular nature of a flower in a glass on the stair landing. I count my blessings.

For a reading quiz, sources on Joan Didion, and annotated links to further readings on migraine headaches and their sufferers, visit bedfordstmartins.com/thebedfordreader.

Journal Writing

Write a passage of OBJECTIVE DESCRIPTION about an illness you know intimately, even a cold. Or, if you prefer, pick an unwelcome mood you know: the blues, for instance, or an irresistible desire to giggle during a solemn ceremony. Then, on the same subject, write a second passage — this time, a SUBJECTIVE DESCRIPTION of the same malady or mood. (To take your journal writing further, see "From Journal to Essay" on the facing page.)

Questions on Meaning

1. According to the author, how do migraines differ from ordinary headaches? What are their distinctive traits?
2. What once made Didion ashamed to admit that she suffered from migraines? How does her former sense of shame help to explain her reason for writing?
3. While imparting facts about migraine, what does Didion simultaneously reveal about her own personality?
4. Sum up in your own words the tremendous experience that Didion describes in the final paragraph.

Questions on Writing Strategy

1. Didion's essay mixes subjective description based on personal experience with objective information based on medical knowledge. How does she signal her transitions from subjective to objective and from objective back to subjective?
2. Point to a few examples of sensuous detail in Didion's writing. What do such IMAGES contribute to her essay's EFFECT?
3. In paragraph 2 Didion declares that she "wished only for a neurosurgeon who would do a lobotomy on house call"; later (par. 5) she remarks, "That no one dies of migraine seems, to someone deep into an attack, an ambiguous blessing." Does she mean for readers to take her literally? How do you know? (See *hyperbole* under *Figures of speech* in Useful Terms.)
4. **MIXED METHODS**   In paragraph 5 the author uses strings of EXAMPLES. What is the effect of these examples? What GENERALIZATION do they support?
5. **MIXED METHODS**   What do Didion's two uses of PROCESS ANALYSIS (pars. 3–5 and 7–8) contribute to her essay?

Questions on Language

1. How would you characterize Didion's word choice: colorful, utilitarian, flowery, careless, or lyrical? Support your answer with examples.
2. In the title of Didion's essay, what arrests you? Is this title a teaser, having little to do with the essay, or does it fit?
3. Speaking in paragraph 1 of the "circumnavigation" of an application form, Didion employs a metaphor. In paragraph 7 she introduces another—"a guerrilla war." In paragraph 8 she uses a simile—"The migraine has acted as a circuit breaker." Comment on the aptness of these FIGURES OF SPEECH.
4. Consult a dictionary if you need help in defining the following: vascular, contretemps, predisposition (par. 3); synthesized, contraindications, aura (4); aphasia (5).

Suggestions for Writing

1. **FROM JOURNAL TO ESSAY**   Expand your journal entry into a full descriptive essay, blending objective and subjective description as you see fit to explain your illness or mood, to convey the way it makes you feel, and to show how it affects your life.

2. Didion mentions "the accusing eye" (par. 6) she endures from those who don't suffer migraine. Write an essay in which you express and defend something about yourself that other people don't seem to understand. It could be a disability, a need for solitude, a habit, a hobby or interest that others find odd or dull. Explain the reactions you receive and how you respond to and cope with them.

3. **CRITICAL WRITING**   Write an essay examining Didion's TONE. Are there passages in which she seems self-pitying? courageous? determined? resigned? triumphant? What is the overall tone of the essay? Is it effective? Why?

4. **CONNECTIONS**   COMPARE Didion's essay to Nancy Mairs's "Disability" (p. 13). Mairs and Didion describe how multiple sclerosis and migraine, respectively, affect their lives. What is the PURPOSE of each essay? What do Mairs and Didion want us to understand about them and their lives? How does each want us to respond?

5. **CONNECTIONS**   Both Joan Didion's "In Bed" and David Foster Wallace's "This Is Water" (p. 233) examine how the writers choose to respond to annoyances. Write an essay that considers the extent to which attitude affects a person's ability to cope with frustration, using these two essays and your own experience for examples and EVIDENCE.

Joan Didion on Writing

In "Why I Write," an essay published by the *New York Times Book Review*, adapted from her Regents' Lecture at the University of California at Berkeley, Joan Didion writes, "I stole the title for this talk, from George Orwell [see pp. 663 and 671]. One reason I stole it was that I like the sound of the words: Why I Write. There you have three short unambiguous words that share a sound, and the sound they share is this:

I

I

I

In many ways writing is the act of saying *I*, of imposing oneself upon other people, of saying *listen to me, see it my way, change your mind.* . . ."

Didion's "way," though, comes not from notions of how the world works or should work but from its observable details. She writes, "I am not in the least an intellectual, which is not to say that when I hear the word 'intellectual' I reach for my gun, but only to say that I do not think in abstracts. During the years when I was an undergraduate at Berkeley I tried, with a kind of hopeless late-adolescent energy, to buy some temporary visa into the world of ideas, to forge for myself a mind that could deal with the abstract. . . . In short, I tried to think. I failed. My attention veered inexorably back to the specific, to the tangible, to what was generally considered, by everyone I knew then and for that matter have known since, the peripheral. I would try to contemplate the Hegelian dialectic and would find myself concentrating instead on the flowering pear tree outside my window and the particular way the petals fell on my floor."

Later in the essay, Didion writes, "During those years I was traveling on what I knew to be a very shaky passport, forged papers: I knew that I was no legitimate resident in any world of ideas. I knew I couldn't think. All I knew then was what I wasn't, and it took me some years to discover what I was.

"Which was a writer.

"By which I mean not a 'good' writer or a 'bad' writer but simply a writer, a person whose most absorbed and passionate hours are spent arranging words on pieces of paper. Had my credentials been in order I would never have become a writer. Had I been blessed with even limited access to my own mind there would have been no reason to write. I write entirely to find out what I'm thinking, what I'm looking at, what I see, and what it means. What I want and what I fear. . . . *What is going on in these pictures in my mind?*"

In the essay, Didion emphasizes that these mental pictures have a grammar. "Grammar is a piano I play by ear, since I seem to have been out of school the year the rules were mentioned. All I know about grammar is its infinite power. To shift the structure of a sentence alters the meaning of that sentence, as definitely and inflexibly as the position of a camera alters the meaning of the object photographed. Many people know about camera angles now, but not so many know about sentences. The arrangement of the words matters, and the arrangement you want can be found in the picture in your mind. The picture dictates the arrangement. The picture dictates whether this will be a sentence with or without clauses, a sentence that ends hard or a dying-fall sentence, long or short, active or passive. The picture tells you how to arrange the words and the arrangement of the words tells you, or tells me, what's going on in the picture."

For Discussion

1. What is Didion's definition of thinking? Do you agree with it?
2. To what extent does Didion's writing support her remarks about how and why she writes?
3. What does Didion mean when she says that grammar has "infinite power"? Power to do what?

BARBARA EHRENREICH

Born in 1941 in Butte, Montana, Barbara Ehrenreich is an essayist and investigative journalist known for sharp political and social criticism. After graduating from Reed College, she received a PhD in biology from Rockefeller University and taught briefly while becoming an activist and a writer. She has contributed to dozens of periodicals, among them *The New Republic, Mother Jones, Time,* and *The Atlantic Monthly.* She currently writes a column for *The Progressive* and keeps a blog at *barbaraehrenreich.com.* Her many books include *Poverty in the American Dream: Women and Children First* (1983), *Fear of Falling: The Inner Life of the Middle Class* (1989), *Blood Rites: Origins and History of the Passions of War* (1997), *Nickel and Dimed: On (Not) Getting By in America* (2001), *Dancing in the Streets: A History of Collective Joy* (2006), and, most recently, *Bright-Sided: How the Relentless Promotion of Positive Thinking Has Undermined America* (2009). The recipient of numerous grants and awards, Ehrenreich is also a fellow at the New York Institute for the Humanities and a scholar at the Institute for Policy Studies.

The Menace of Negative People

Why shouldn't we complain? In this excerpt from *Bright-Sided*, Ehrenreich challenges conventional wisdom about keeping a positive attitude—that cheerfulness leads to success, for instance, or that employees should always be upbeat. With typical clarity and force, she argues instead that negativity can be a positive personality trait.

Ehrenreich uses footnotes to provide source citations for the books, Web sites, and personal interviews she refers to and quotes. She does not follow any widely used documentation system (such as MLA or Chicago) but nonetheless provides clear information about each source.

"The Menace of Negative People" mainly examines a series of examples to argue against a particular way of looking at the world. But Ehrenreich draws on several other methods as well to develop the essay:

Example (Chap. 6): throughout
Comparison and contrast (Chap. 7): paragraphs 12–14
Process analysis (Chap. 8): paragraphs 5, 8
Division or analysis (Chap. 9): paragraphs 14–15
Cause and effect (Chap. 11): paragraphs 3, 4, 6–7, 9
Definition (Chap. 12): paragraphs 1–2

Americans are a "positive" people. This is our reputation as well as our self-image. We smile a lot and are often baffled when people from other cultures do not return the favor. In the well-worn stereotype, we are upbeat, cheerful, optimistic, and shallow, while foreigners are likely to be subtle, world-weary, and possibly decadent. American expatriate writers like Henry James and James Baldwin wrestled with and occasionally reinforced this stereotype, which I once encountered in the 1980s in the form of a remark by Soviet émigré poet Joseph Brodsky to the effect that the problem with Americans is that they have "never known suffering." (Apparently he didn't know who had invented the blues.) Whether we Americans see it as an embarrassment or a point of pride, being positive — in affect, in mood, in outlook — seems to be engrained in our national character. . . .

Like a perpetually flashing neon sign in the background, like an inescapable jingle, the injunction to be positive is so ubiquitous that it's impossible to identify a single source. Oprah routinely trumpets the triumph of attitude over circumstance. A Google search for "positive thinking" turns up 1.92 million entries. At the Learning Annex, which offers how-to classes in cities like New York and Los Angeles, you'll find a smorgasbord of workshops on how to succeed in life by overcoming pessimism, accessing your inner powers, and harnessing the power of thought. A whole coaching industry has grown up since the mid-1990s, heavily marketed on the Internet, to help people improve their attitudes and hence, supposedly, their lives. For a fee on a par with what a therapist might receive, an unlicensed career or life coach can help you defeat the "negative self-talk" — that is, pessimistic thoughts — that impedes your progress. . . .

The promise of positivity is that it will improve your life in concrete, material ways. In one simple, practical sense, this is probably true. If you are "nice," people will be more inclined to like you than if you are chronically grumpy, critical, and out of sorts. Much of the behavioral advice offered by [self-help] gurus, on their Web sites and in their books, is innocuous. "Smile," advises one success-oriented positive-thinking site. "Greet coworkers." The rewards for exuding a positive manner are all the greater in a culture that expects no less. Where cheerfulness is the norm, crankiness can seem perverse. Who would want to date or hire a "negative" person? What could be wrong with him or her? The trick, if you want to get ahead, is to simulate a positive outlook, no matter how you might actually be feeling. . . .

Hardly anyone needs to be reminded of the importance of interpersonal skills. Most of us work with people, on people, and around people. We have become the emotional wallpaper in other people's lives, less individuals with our own quirks and needs than dependable sources of smiles and optimism. "Ninety-nine out of every 100 people report that they want to be around more positive people," asserts the 2004 self-help book *How Full Is Your Bucket?*

Positive Strategies for Work and Life.[1] The choice seems obvious—critical and challenging people or smiling yes-sayers? And the more entrenched the cult of cheerfulness becomes, the more advisable it is to conform, because your coworkers will expect nothing less. According to human resources consultant Gary S. Topchik, "the Bureau of Labor Statistics estimates that US companies lose $3 billion a year to the effects of negative attitudes and behaviors at work" through, among other things, lateness, rudeness, errors, and high turnover.[2] Except in clear-cut cases of racial, gender, age, or religious discrimination, Americans can be fired for anything, such as failing to generate positive vibes. A computer technician in Minneapolis told me he lost one job for uttering a stray remark that was never identified for him but taken as evidence of sarcasm and a "negative attitude." Julie, a reader of my Web site who lives in Austin, Texas, wrote to tell me of her experience working at a call center for Home Depot:

> I worked there for about a month when my boss pulled me into a small room and told me I "obviously wasn't happy enough to be there." Sure, I was sleep deprived from working five other jobs to pay for private health insurance that topped $300 a month and student loans that kicked in at $410 a month, but I can't recall saying anything to anyone outside the lines of "I'm happy to have a job." Plus, I didn't realize anyone had to be happy to work in a call center. . . .

What has changed, in the last few years, is that the advice to at least act   5
in a positive way has taken on a harsher edge. The penalty for nonconformity is going up, from the possibility of job loss and failure to social shunning and complete isolation. In his 2005 best seller, *Secrets of the Millionaire Mind,* T. Harv Eker, founder of Peak Potentials Training, advises that negative people have to go, even, presumably, the ones that you live with: "Identify a situation or a person who is a downer in your life. Remove yourself from that situation or association. If it's family, choose to be around them less."[3] In fact, this advice has become a staple of the self-help literature, of both the secular and Christian varieties. "GET RID OF NEGATIVE PEOPLE IN YOUR LIFE," writes motivational speaker and coach Jeffrey Gitomer. "They waste your time and bring you down. If you can't get rid of them (like a spouse or a boss), reduce your time with them."[4] And if that isn't clear enough, J. P.

---

[1] Tom Rath and Donald O. Clifton, *How Full Is Your Bucket? Positive Strategies for Work and Life* (New York: Gallup Press, 2004), 47.
[2] Quoted on the American Management Association's Web site, http://www.amanet.org/books/book.cfm?isbn=9780814405826.
[3] T. Harv Eker, *Secrets of the Millionaire Mind: Mastering the Inner Game of Wealth* (New York: HarperBusiness, 2005), 101.
[4] Jeffrey Gitomer, *Little Gold Book of YES!* (Upper Saddle River: FT Press, 2007), 138.

Maroney, a motivational speaker who styles himself "the Pitbull of Business," announces:

> Negative People SUCK!
>   That may sound harsh, but the fact is that negative people do suck. They suck the energy out of positive people like you and me. They suck the energy and life out of a good company, a good team, a good relationship. . . . Avoid them at all cost. If you have to cut ties with people you've known for a long time because they're actually a negative drain on you, then so be it. Trust me, you're better off without them.[5]

What would it mean in practice to eliminate all the "negative people"   6
from one's life? It might be a good move to separate from a chronically carping spouse, but it is not so easy to abandon the whiny toddler, the colicky infant, or the sullen teenager. And at the workplace, while it's probably advisable to detect and terminate those who show signs of becoming mass killers, there are other annoying people who might actually have something useful to say: the financial officer who keeps worrying about the bank's subprime mortgage exposure or the auto executive who questions the company's overinvestment in SUVs and trucks. Purge everyone who "brings you down," and you risk being very lonely or, what is worse, cut off from reality. The challenge of family life, or group life of any kind, is to keep gauging the moods of others, accommodating to their insights, and offering comfort when needed.

But in the world of positive thinking other people are not there to be nur-   7
tured or to provide unwelcome reality checks. They are there only to nourish, praise, and affirm. Harsh as this dictum sounds, many ordinary people adopt it as their creed, displaying wall plaques or bumper stickers showing the word "Whining" with a cancel sign through it. There seems to be a massive empathy deficit, which people respond to by withdrawing their own. No one has the time or patience for anyone else's problems.

In mid-2006, a Kansas City pastor put the growing ban on "negativity"   8
into practice, announcing that his church would now be "complaint free." Also, there would be no criticizing, gossiping, or sarcasm. To reprogram the congregation, the Reverend Will Bowen distributed purple silicone bracelets that were to be worn as reminders. The goal? Twenty-one complaint-free days, after which the complaining habit would presumably be broken. If the wearer broke down and complained about something, then the bracelet was to be transferred to the other wrist. This bold attack on negativity brought Bowen a spread in *People* magazine and a spot on the *Oprah Winfrey Show*. Within a few months, his church had given out 4.5 million purple bracelets

[5]http://guruknowledge.Org/articles/255/l/The-Power-of-Negative-Thinking/The-Power-of-Negative-Thinking.html.

to people in over eighty countries. He envisions a complaint-free world and boasts that his bracelets have been distributed within schools, prisons, and homeless shelters. There is no word yet on how successful they have been in the latter two settings.

So the claim that acting in a positive way leads to success becomes self- 9 fulfilling, at least in the negative sense that not doing so can lead to more profound forms of failure, such as rejection by employers or even one's fellow worshipers. When the gurus advise dropping "negative" people, they are also issuing a warning: Smile and be agreeable, go with the flow—or prepare to be ostracized.

It is not enough, though, to cull the negative people from one's imme- 10 diate circle of contacts; information about the larger human world must be carefully censored. All the motivators and gurus of positivity agree that it is a mistake to read newspapers or watch the news. An article from an online dating magazine offers, among various tips for developing a positive attitude: "Step 5: Stop Watching the News. Murder. Rape. Fraud. War. Daily news is often filled with nothing but negative stories and when you make reading such material a part of your daily lifestyle, you begin to be directly affected by that environmental factor."

Jeffrey Gitomer goes further, advising a retreat into one's personal efforts 11 to achieve positive thinking: "All news is negative. Constant exposure to neg- ative news can't possibly have a positive impact on your life. The Internet will give you all the news you need in about a minute and a half. That will free up time that you can devote to yourself and your positive attitude."[6]

Why is all news "negative"? Judy Braley, identified as an author and attor- 12 ney, attributes the excess of bad news to the inadequate spread of positive thinking among the world's population:

> The great majority of the population of this world does not live life from the space of a positive attitude. In fact, I believe the majority of the population of this world lives from a place of pain, and that people who live from pain only know how to spread more negativity and pain. For me, this explains many of the atrocities of our world and the reason why we are bombarded with negativity all the time.[7]

. . . For those who need more than the ninety-second daily updates per- 13 mitted by Gitomer, there are at least two Web sites offering nothing but "posi- tive news." One of them, *Good News Blog*, explains that "with ample media attention going out to the cruel, the horrible, the perverted, the twisted, it is

---

[6]Gitomer, *Little Gold Book*, 45.
[7]Judy Braley, "Creating a Positive Attitude," http://ezinearticles.com/?Creating-a-Positive-Attitude&id=759618.

easy to become convinced that human beings are going down the drain. *Good News* [is] going to show site visitors that bad news is news simply because it *is* rare and unique." Among this site's recent top news stories were "Adoptee Reunited with Mother via Webcam Reality Show," "Students Help Nurse Rescued Horses Back to Good Health," and "Parrot Saves Girl's Life with Warning." At *happynews.com*, there was a surprising abundance of international stories, although not a word about Darfur, Congo, Gaza, Iraq, or Afghanistan. Instead, in a sampling of a day's offerings, I found "Seven-Month-Old from Nepal Receives Life-Saving Surgery," "100th Anniversary of the US-Canada Boundary Waters Treaty," "Many Americans Making Selfless Resolutions," and "Childhood Sweethearts Attempt Romantic Adventure."

This retreat from the real drama and tragedy of human events is suggestive of a deep helplessness at the core of positive thinking. Why not follow the news? Because, as [one life coach] told me, "You can't do anything about it." Braley similarly dismisses reports of disasters: "That's negative news that can cause you emotional sadness, but that you can't do anything about." The possibilities of contributing to relief funds, joining an antiwar movement, or lobbying for more humane government policies are not even considered. But at the very least there seems to be an acknowledgment here that no amount of attitude adjustment can make good news out of headlines beginning with "Civilian casualties mount . . ." or "Famine spreads . . ." 14

Of course, if the powers of mind were truly "infinite," one would not have to eliminate negative people from one's life either; one could, for example, simply choose to interpret their behavior in a positive way — maybe he's criticizing me for my own good, maybe she's being sullen because she likes me so much and I haven't been attentive, and so on. The advice that you must change your environment — for example, by eliminating negative people and news — is an admission that there may in fact be a "real world" out there that is utterly unaffected by our wishes. In the face of this terrifying possibility, the only "positive" response is to withdraw into one's own carefully constructed world of constant approval and affirmation, nice news, and smiling people. 15

*For a reading quiz, sources on Barbara Ehrenreich, and annotated links to further readings on positive thinking, visit **bedfordstmartins.com/thebedfordreader**.*

Journal Writing

Do you agree with Ehrenreich that acting positive despite your true feelings is a self-defeating practice? Or do you try to follow self-help writers' advice to be consistently cheerful and upbeat? Why? If you've ever had to hide your emotions, how did the effort affect you and those around you? (To take your journal writing further, see "From Journal to Essay" on the facing page.)

Questions on Meaning

1. This essay is excerpted from a book entitled *Bright-Sided: How the Relentless Promotion of Positive Thinking Has Undermined America.* How might the subtitle reveal Ehrenreich's PURPOSE in writing about this subject? What do you think her purpose is?
2. How are negative people a "menace"? Whom or what do they threaten?
3. In what ways, according to Ehrenreich, are the personal costs of negativity higher today than in the past?
4. Ehrenreich's THESIS develops over the course of the essay. What is it?
5. What point does Ehrenreich make with the examples of a financial officer and an auto executive in paragraph 6? To what recent events does she ALLUDE here? Why are they significant to her main idea?

Questions on Writing Strategy

1. For whom does Ehrenreich seem to be writing? The "gurus" who promote positive thinking? their clients? someone else? What EVIDENCE in the essay supports your answer?
2. Where in the essay does Ehrenreich cite the opinions of experts on positive thinking? What does this strategy contribute to the essay?
3. Explain the IRONY of Ehrenreich's conclusion.
4. **MIXED METHODS** What does Ehrenreich COMPARE AND CONTRAST in paragraphs 10–14? What purpose does the comparison serve?
5. **MIXED METHODS** Explain how Ehrenreich uses CAUSE AND EFFECT to build her critique of the positive-thinking movement.

Questions on Language

1. What does the phrase "the cult of cheerfulness" (par. 4) suggest about Ehrenreich's attitude toward her subject? What are the CONNOTATIONS of the word *cult*?
2. How does Ehrenreich's TONE reinforce, or undermine, her point?
3. If any of the following words are unfamiliar, be sure to look them up in a dictionary: expatriate, émigré (par. 1); injunction, ubiquitous, smorgasbord (2); innocuous, exuding, simulate (3); entrenched (4); shunning, staple, secular (5); carping, colicky, purge (6); dictum, creed, empathy (7); ostracized (9); cull (10); lobbying, humane (14); affirmation (15).

Suggestions for Writing

1. **FROM JOURNAL TO ESSAY**   Working from your journal entry, write an essay that responds to Ehrenreich's argument against adopting a positive attitude. Whether you agree with it or not, consider what is gained and what is lost—and for whom—when people push themselves to be pleasant.

2. Ehrenreich questions the usefulness of one piece of advice common in self-help literature: "Be positive." Using her essay as a model, write an essay of your own in which you reveal the problems with another oft-repeated suggestion, such as "Be yourself," "Treat others the way you'd like to be treated," or "Don't sweat the small stuff." As Ehrenreich does, present a wide range of examples to suggest various aspects of your subject, and explain why readers should not necessarily follow the advice they've been given.

3. **CRITICAL WRITING**   Respond to Ehrenreich's assertion that "retreat from the real drama and tragedy of human events is suggestive of a deep helplessness at the core of positive thinking" (par. 14). How well does Ehrenreich support this claim? In an essay, ANALYZE and EVALUATE Ehrenreich's criticism, looking in particular at her evidence, her reasoning, and whether and how she considers possible opposing arguments.

4. **CONNECTIONS**   Read or reread Dacher Keltner's "A Vocabulary of Smiles" (p. 445). Taken together, what do Ehrenreich's and Keltner's essays reveal about the importance (or unimportance) of happiness in our culture? Write an essay that considers whether happiness is a function of circumstance (as Ehrenreich suggests) or of attitude (as Keltner seems to believe). Why would some Americans feel a need to pretend that they're happy when they're not?

5. **CONNECTIONS**   Joan Didion, in "In Bed" (p. 627), writes that her tendency for migraines "seemed . . . evidence . . . of all my bad attitudes, unpleasant tempers, wrongthink" (par. 1); she also suggests that she has learned to find the good in her headaches. In an essay, consider how Didion's experience supports or contradicts Ehrenreich's stance against positive thinking.

Barbara Ehrenreich on Writing

The printed word, in the view of Barbara Ehrenreich, should be a powerful instrument for reform. In an article in *Mother Jones*, though, she complains about a tacit censorship in American magazines that has sometimes prevented her from fulfilling her purpose as a writer. Ehrenreich recalls the difficulties she had in trying to persuade the editor of a national magazine to assign her a story on the plight of Third World women refugees. "Sorry," said the editor, "Third World women have never done anything for me."

Ehrenreich infers that writers who write for such magazines must follow a rule: "You must learn not to stray from your assigned sociodemographic stereotype." She observes, "As a woman, I am generally asked to write on 'women's topics,' such as cooking, divorce, how to succeed in business, diet fads, and the return of the bustle. These are all fine topics and give great scope to my talents, but when I ask, in faltering tones, for an assignment . . . on the trade deficit, I am likely to be told that *anyone* (Bill, Gerry, Bob) could cover that, whereas my 'voice' is *essential* for the aerobic toothbrushing story. This is not, strictly speaking, 'censorship'—just a division of labor in which white men cover politics, foreign policy, and the economy, and the rest of us cover what's left over, such as the bustle."

Over the years Ehrenreich has had many manuscripts rejected by editors who comment, "too angry," "too depressing," and "Where's the bright side?" She agrees with writer Herbert Gold, who once deduced that the American media want only "happy stories about happy people with happy problems." She concludes, "You can write about anything—death squads, AIDS . . .—so long as you make it 'upbeat.'" Despite such discouragements, Ehrenreich continues her battle to "disturb the stupor induced by six straight pages of Calvin Klein ads."

For Discussion

1. Is Ehrenreich right about "a tacit censorship in American magazines"? Check a recent issue of a magazine that prints signed articles. How many of the articles *not* on "women's topics" are written by women? How many are written by men?
2. To what extent do you agree with Ehrenreich—and with Herbert Gold—that the American media are interested only in "upbeat" stories?

MARTIN LUTHER KING, JR.

Martin Luther King, Jr. (1929–68), was born in Atlanta, the son of a Baptist minister, and was himself ordained in the same denomination. Stepping to the forefront of the civil rights movement in 1955, King led African Americans in a boycott of segregated city buses in Montgomery, Alabama; became the first president of the Southern Christian Leadership Conference; and staged sit-ins and mass marches that helped bring about the Civil Rights Act passed by Congress in 1964 and the Voting Rights Act of 1965. He received the Nobel Peace Prize in 1964. While King preached "nonviolent resistance," he was himself the target of violence. He was stabbed in New York, pelted with stones in Chicago; his home in Montgomery was bombed; and ultimately he was assassinated in Memphis by a sniper. On his tombstone near Atlanta's Ebenezer Baptist Church are these words from the spiritual he quotes at the conclusion of "I Have a Dream": "Free at last, free at last, thank God almighty, I'm free at last." Martin Luther King's birthday, January 15, is now a national holiday.

I Have a Dream

In Washington, DC, on August 28, 1963, King's campaign of nonviolent resistance reached its historic climax. On that date, commemorating the centennial of Lincoln's Emancipation Proclamation freeing the slaves, King led a march of 200,000 persons, black and white, from the Washington Monument to the Lincoln Memorial. Before this throng, and to millions who watched on television, he delivered an unforgettable speech. (We reprint a version that King prepared for print publication.)

Intended to inspire and motivate its audience, King's speech is a model of a certain kind of persuasion. To make his point, King draws on a number of methods:

Narration (Chap. 4): paragraphs 1–2
Description (Chap. 5): paragraphs 2, 4
Example (Chap. 6): paragraphs 6–9, 12–16, 21–22
Comparison and contrast (Chap. 7): paragraphs 3–4, 6
Cause and effect (Chap. 11): paragraphs 5, 7, 19
Argument and persuasion (Chap. 13): throughout

Five score years ago, a great American, in whose symbolic shadow we stand, signed the Emancipation Proclamation. This momentous decree came as a great beacon light of hope to millions of Negro slaves who had been seared in the flames of withering injustice. It came as a joyous daybreak to end the long night of captivity.

But one hundred years later, we must face the tragic fact that the Negro is 2 still not free. One hundred years later, the life of the Negro is still sadly crippled by the manacles of segregation and the chains of discrimination. One hundred years later, the Negro lives on a lonely island of poverty in the midst of a vast ocean of material prosperity. One hundred years later, the Negro is still languishing in the corners of American society and finds himself in exile in his own land. So we have come here today to dramatize an appalling condition.

In a sense we have come to our nation's capital to cash a check. When 3 the architects of our republic wrote the magnificent words of the Constitution and the Declaration of Independence, they were signing a promissory note to which every American was to fall heir. This note was a promise that all men would be guaranteed the unalienable rights of life, liberty, and the pursuit of happiness.

It is obvious today that America has defaulted on this promissory note 4 insofar as her citizens of color are concerned. Instead of honoring this sacred obligation, America has given the Negro people a bad check; a check which has come back marked "insufficient funds." But we refuse to believe that the bank of justice is bankrupt. We refuse to believe that there are insufficient funds in the great vaults of opportunity of this nation. So we have come to cash this check—a check that will give us upon demand the riches of freedom and the security of justice. We have also come to this hallowed spot to remind America of the fierce urgency of *now*. This is no time to engage in the luxury of cooling off or to take the tranquilizing drugs of gradualism. *Now* is the time to make real the promises of Democracy. *Now* is the time to rise from the dark and desolate valley of segregation to the sunlit path of racial justice. *Now* is the time to open the doors of opportunity to all of God's children. *Now* is the time to lift our nation from the quicksands of racial injustice to the solid rock of brotherhood.

It would be fatal for the nation to overlook the urgency of the moment 5 and to underestimate the determination of the Negro. This sweltering summer of the Negro's legitimate discontent will not pass until there is an invigorating autumn of freedom and equality; 1963 is not an end, but a beginning. Those who hope that the Negro needed to blow off steam and will now be content will have a rude awakening if the nation returns to business as usual. There will be neither rest nor tranquillity in America until the Negro is granted his citizenship rights. The whirlwinds of revolt will continue to shake the foundations of our nation until the bright day of justice emerges.

But there is something that I must say to my people who stand on the 6 warm threshold which leads into the palace of justice. In the process of gaining our rightful place we must not be guilty of wrongful deeds. Let us not seek to satisfy our thirst for freedom by drinking from the cup of bitterness and hatred. We must forever conduct our struggle on the high plane of dignity and discipline. We must not allow our creative protest to degenerate into physical violence. Again and again we must rise to the majestic heights of meeting physical force with soul force. The marvelous new militancy which has engulfed the Negro community must not lead us to a distrust of all white people, for many of our white brothers, as evidenced by their presence here today, have come to realize that their destiny is tied up with our destiny and their freedom is inextricably bound to our freedom. We cannot walk alone.

And as we walk, we must make the pledge that we shall march ahead. We cannot turn back. There are those who are asking the devotees of civil rights, "When will you be satisfied?" We can never be satisfied as long as the Negro is the victim of the unspeakable horrors of police brutality. We can never be satisfied as long as our bodies, heavy with the fatigue of travel, cannot gain lodging in the motels of the highways and the hotels of the cities. We cannot be satisfied as long as the Negro's basic mobility is from a smaller ghetto to a larger one. We can never be satisfied as long as a Negro in Mississippi cannot vote and a Negro in New York believes he has nothing for which to vote. No, no, we are not satisfied, and we will not be satisfied until justice rolls down like waters and righteousness like a mighty stream. 7

I am not unmindful that some of you have come here out of great trials and tribulations. Some of you have come fresh from narrow jail cells. Some of you have come from areas where your quest for freedom left you battered by the storms of persecution and staggered by the winds of police brutality. You have been the veterans of creative suffering. Continue to work with the faith that unearned suffering is redemptive. 8

Go back to Mississippi, go back to Alabama, go back to South Carolina, go back to Georgia, go back to Louisiana, go back to the slums and ghettos of our northern cities, knowing that somehow this situation can and will be changed. Let us not wallow in the valley of despair. 9

I say to you today, my friends, that in spite of the difficulties and frustra-tions of the moment I still have a dream. It is a dream deeply rooted in the American dream. 10

I have a dream that one day this nation will rise up and live out the true meaning of its creed: "We hold these truths to be self-evident; that all men are created equal." 11

I have a dream that one day on the red hills of Georgia the sons of former slaves and the sons of former slaveowners will be able to sit down together at the table of brotherhood. 12

I have a dream that one day even the state of Mississippi, a desert state sweltering with the heat of injustice and oppression, will be transformed into an oasis of freedom and justice. 13

I have a dream that my four little children will one day live in a nation   14
where they will not be judged by the color of their skin but by the content of
their character.

I have a dream today.   15

I have a dream that one day the state of Alabama, whose governor's lips   16
are presently dripping with the words of interposition and nullification, will
be transformed into a situation where little black boys and black girls will be
able to join hands with little white boys and white girls and walk together as
sisters and brothers.

I have a dream today.   17

I have a dream that one day every valley shall be exalted, every hill   18
and mountain shall be made low, the rough places will be made plain, and
the crooked places will be made straight, and the glory of the Lord shall be
revealed, and all flesh shall see it together.

This is our hope. This is the faith with which I return to the South. With   19
this faith we will be able to hew out of the mountain of despair a stone of hope.
With this faith we will be able to transform the jangling discords of our nation
into a beautiful symphony of brotherhood. With this faith we will be able to
work together, to pray together, to struggle together, to go to jail together, to
stand up for freedom together, knowing that we will be free one day.

This will be the day when all of God's children will be able to sing with   20
new meaning

> My country, 'tis of thee,
> Sweet land of liberty,
>   Of thee I sing:
> Land where my fathers died,
> Land of the pilgrims' pride,
> From every mountainside
>   Let freedom ring.

And if America is to be a great nation this must become true. So let free-   21
dom ring from the prodigious hilltops of New Hampshire. Let freedom ring
from the mighty mountains of New York. Let freedom ring from the height-
ening Alleghenies of Pennsylvania!

Let freedom ring from the snowcapped Rockies of Colorado!   22

Let freedom ring from the curvaceous peaks of California!   23

But not only that; let freedom ring from Stone Mountain of Georgia!   24

Let freedom ring from Lookout Mountain of Tennessee!   25

Let freedom ring from every hill and molehill of Mississippi. From every   26
mountainside, let freedom ring.

When we let freedom ring, when we let it ring from every village and   27
every hamlet, from every state and every city, we will be able to speed up that

day when all of God's children, black men and white men, Jews and Gentiles, Protestants and Catholics, will be able to join hands and sing in the words of the old Negro spiritual, "Free at last! free at last! thank God almighty, we are free at last!"

For a reading quiz, sources on Martin Luther King, Jr., and annotated links to further readings on the civil rights movement in the United States, visit ***bedfordstmartins.com/ thebedfordreader.***

Journal Writing

Do you think we have moved closer to fulfilling King's dream in the decades since he gave this famous speech? In your journal, explore why or why not. (To take your journal writing further, see "From Journal to Essay" on the next page.)

Questions on Meaning

1. What is the apparent PURPOSE of this speech?
2. What THESIS does King develop in his first four paragraphs?
3. What does King mean by the "marvelous new militancy which has engulfed the Negro community" (par. 6)? Does this contradict King's nonviolent philosophy?
4. In what passages of his speech does King notice events of history? Where does he acknowledge the historic occasion on which he is speaking?

Questions on Writing Strategy

1. What indicates that King's words were meant primarily for an AUDIENCE of listeners, and only secondarily for a reading audience? To hear these indications, try reading the speech aloud. What uses of PARALLELISM do you notice?
2. Where in the speech does King acknowledge that not all of his listeners are African American?
3. How much EMPHASIS does King place on the past? How much does he place on the future?
4. **MIXED METHODS**   Analyze the ETHICAL APPEAL of King's ARGUMENT (see p. 551). Where in the speech, for instance, does he present himself as reasonable despite his passion? To what extent does his personal authority lend power to his words?
5. **MIXED METHODS**   The DESCRIPTION in paragraphs 2 and 4 depends on metaphor, a FIGURE OF SPEECH in which one thing is said to be another thing. How do the metaphors in these paragraphs work for King's purpose?

Questions on Language

1. In general, is the language of King's speech ABSTRACT or CONCRETE? How is this level appropriate to his message and to the span of history with which he deals?
2. Point to memorable figures of speech besides those examined in the "Mixed Methods" question on the preceding page.
3. Define momentous (par. 1); manacles, languishing (2); promissory note, unalienable (3); defaulted, hallowed, gradualism (4); inextricably (6); mobility, ghetto (7); tribulations, redemptive (8); interposition, nullification (16); prodigious (21); curvaceous (23); hamlet (27).

Suggestions for Writing

1. **FROM JOURNAL TO ESSAY**   Use your journal entry to write an essay that explains your sense of how well the United States has progressed toward realizing King's dream. You may choose to focus on America as a whole or on your particular community, but you should use specific EVIDENCE to support your opinion.
2. Propose some course of action in a situation that you consider an injustice. Racial injustice is one possible area, or unfairness to any minority, or to women, children, the elderly, ex-convicts, the disabled, the poor. If possible, narrow your subject to a particular incident or a local situation on which you can write knowledgeably.
3. **CRITICAL WRITING**   What can you INFER from this speech about King's own attitudes toward oppression and injustice? Does he follow his own injunction not "to satisfy our thirst for freedom by drinking from the cup of bitterness and hatred" (par. 6)? Explain your answer, using evidence from the speech.
4. **CONNECTIONS**   King's "I Have a Dream" and Linda Chavez's "Supporting Family Values" (p. 605) both seek to influence readers, either to cause them to act or to change their views. Yet the two authors take very different approaches to achieve their purposes. COMPARE AND CONTRAST the authors' persuasive strategies, considering especially their effectiveness for the situation each writes about and the audience each addresses.
5. **CONNECTIONS**   King's speech was delivered in 1963. Brent Staples's essay "Black Men and Public Space" (p. 226) was first published in 1986. In an essay, explore the changes, if any, that are evident in the ASSUMPTIONS the authors make about their audiences' attitudes, about race in general, and about racism.

MAXINE HONG KINGSTON

Maxine Hong Kingston grew up caught between two complex and very different cultures: the China of her parents and the America of her surroundings. In her first two books, *The Woman Warrior: Memoirs of a Girlhood among Ghosts* (1976) and *China Men* (1980), Kingston combines Chinese myth and history with family tales to create a dreamlike world that shifts between reality and fantasy. Born in 1940 in Stockton, California, Kingston was the first American-born child of a scholar and a medical practitioner who became laundry workers in this country. After graduating from the University of California at Berkeley (BA, 1962), Kingston taught English at California and Hawaii high schools, at the University of Hawaii, and for many years at UC Berkeley. She has contributed essays, poems, and stories to *The New Yorker,* the *New York Times Magazine, Ms.,* and other periodicals. Other books by Kingston include a collection of essays, *Hawaii One Summer* (1987); a novel, *Tripmaster Monkey: His Fake Book* (1989); a collection of lectures and verse, *To Be a Poet* (2002); and a blend of fiction and nonfiction, *The Fifth Book of Peace* (2003). Most recently, Kingston edited *Veterans of War, Veterans of Peace* (2006), a collection of essays written in workshops she holds for military veterans.

No Name Woman

"No Name Woman" is part of *The Woman Warrior.* Like much of Kingston's writing, it blends the "talk-stories" of Kingston's elders, her own vivid imaginings, and the reality of her experience—this time to discover why her Chinese aunt drowned herself in the family well.

Kingston develops "No Name Woman" with four main methods, all intertwined: In the context of narrating her own experiences, she seeks the causes of her aunt's suicide by comparing various narratives of it, and she employs description to make the narratives concrete and vivid. The main uses of these methods appear below:

Narration (Chap. 4): paragraphs 1–8, 14, 16–20, 23, 28–30, 34–35, 37–46
Description (Chap. 5): paragraphs 4–8, 21, 23–27, 31, 37, 40–46
Comparison and contrast (Chap. 7): paragraphs 15–18, 20–24, 27–28, 31
Cause and effect (Chap. 11): paragraphs 10–11, 15–18, 21–25, 29–31, 33–39, 44–48

"You must not tell anyone," my mother said, "what I am about to tell 1
you. In China your father had a sister who killed herself. She jumped into the family well. We say that your father has all brothers because it is as if she had never been born.

"In 1924 just a few days after our village celebrated seventeen hurry-up   2
weddings—to make sure that every young man who went 'out on the road'
would responsibly come home—your father and his brothers and your grandfather and his brothers and your aunt's new husband sailed for America, the
Gold Mountain. It was your grandfather's last trip. Those lucky enough to get
contracts waved good-bye from the decks. They fed and guarded the stow-
aways and helped them off in Cuba, New York, Bali, Hawaii. 'We'll meet in
California next year,' they said. All of them sent money home.

"I remember looking at your aunt one day when she and I were dressing; I   3
had not noticed before that she had such a protruding melon of a stomach. But
I did not think, 'She's pregnant,' until she began to look like other pregnant
women, her shirt pulling and the white tops of her black pants showing. She
could not have been pregnant, you see, because her husband had been gone
for years. No one said anything. We did not discuss it. In early summer she was
ready to have the child, long after the time when it could have been possible.

"The village had also been counting. On the night the baby was to be born   4
the villagers raided our house. Some were crying. Like a great saw, teeth strung
with lights, files of people walked zigzag across our land, tearing the rice. Their
lanterns doubled in the disturbed black water, which drained away through the
broken bunds. As the villagers closed in, we could see that some of them, probably men and women we knew well, wore white masks. The people with long
hair hung it over their faces. Women with short hair made it stand up on end.
Some had tied white bands around their foreheads, arms, and legs.

"At first they threw mud and rocks at the house. Then they threw eggs   5
and began slaughtering our stock. We could hear the animals scream their
deaths—the roosters, the pigs, a last great roar from the ox. Familiar wild
heads flared in our night windows; the villagers encircled us. Some of the faces
stopped to peer at us, their eyes rushing like searchlights. The hands flattened
against the panes, framed heads, and left red prints.

"The villagers broke in the front and the back doors at the same time,   6
even though we had not locked the doors against them. Their knives dripped
with the blood of our animals. They smeared blood on the doors and walls.
One woman swung a chicken, whose throat she had slit, splattering blood in
red arcs about her. We stood together in the middle of our house, in the family hall with the pictures and tables of the ancestors around us, and looked
straight ahead.

"At that time the house had only two wings. When the men came back,   7
we would build two more to enclose our courtyard and a third one to begin a
second courtyard. The villagers pushed through both wings, even your grandparents' rooms, to find your aunt's, which was also mine until the men returned.
From this room a new wing for one of the younger families would grow. They

ripped up her clothes and shoes and broke her combs, grinding them under-foot. They tore her work from the loom. They scattered the cooking fire and rolled the new weaving in it. We could hear them in the kitchen breaking our bowls and banging the pots. They overturned the great waist-high earthen-ware jugs; duck eggs, pickled fruits, vegetables burst out and mixed in acrid torrents. The old woman from the next field swept a broom through the air and loosed the spirits-of-the-broom over our heads. 'Pig.' 'Ghost.' 'Pig,' they sobbed and scolded while they ruined our house.

"When they left, they took sugar and oranges to bless themselves. They 8 cut pieces from the dead animals. Some of them took bowls that were not bro-ken and clothes that were not torn. Afterward we swept up the rice and sewed it back up into sacks. But the smells from the spilled preserves lasted. Your aunt gave birth in the pigsty that night. The next morning when I went up for the water, I found her and the baby plugging up the family well.

"Don't let your father know that I told you. He denies her. Now that you 9 have started to menstruate, what happened to her could happen to you. Don't humiliate us. You wouldn't like to be forgotten as if you had never been born. The villagers are watchful."

Whenever she had to warn us about life, my mother told stories that ran 10 like this one, a story to grow up on. She tested our strength to establish reali-ties. Those in the emigrant generations who could not reassert brute survival died young and far from home. Those of us in the first American generations have had to figure out how the invisible world the emigrants built around our childhoods fit in solid America.

The emigrants confused the gods by diverting their curses, misleading 11 them with crooked streets and false names. They must try to confuse their off-spring as well, who, I suppose, threaten them in similar ways—always trying to get things straight, always trying to name the unspeakable. The Chinese I know hide their names; sojourners take new names when their lives change and guard their real names with silence.

Chinese-Americans, when you try to understand what things in you are 12 Chinese, how do you separate what is peculiar to childhood, to poverty, insan-ities, one family, your mother who marked your growing with stories, from what is Chinese? What is Chinese tradition and what is the movies?

If I want to learn what clothes my aunt wore, whether flashy or ordinary, I 13 would have to begin, "Remember Father's drowned-in-the-well sister?" I can-not ask that. My mother has told me once and for all the useful parts. She will add nothing unless powered by Necessity, a riverbank that guides her life. She plants vegetable gardens rather than lawns; she carries the odd-shaped toma-toes home from the fields and eats food left for the gods.

Whenever we did frivolous things, we used up energy; we flew high kites. 14 We children came up off the ground over the melting cones our parents brought home from work and the American movie on New Year's Day—*Oh, You Beautiful Doll* with Betty Grable one year, and *She Wore a Yellow Ribbon* with John Wayne another year. After the one carnival ride each, we paid in guilt; our tired father counted his change on the dark walk home.

Adultery is extravagance. Could people who hatch their own chicks and 15 eat the embryos and the heads for delicacies and boil the feet in vinegar for party food, leaving only the gravel, eating even the gizzard lining—could such people engender a prodigal aunt? To be a woman, to have a daughter in starvation time was a waste enough. My aunt could not have been the lone romantic who gave up everything for sex. Women in the old China did not choose. Some man had commanded her to lie with him and be his secret evil. I wonder whether he masked himself when he joined the raid on her family.

Perhaps she encountered him in the fields or on the mountain where the 16 daughters-in-law collected fuel. Or perhaps he first noticed her in the marketplace. He was not a stranger because the village housed no strangers. She had to have dealings with him other than sex. Perhaps he worked an adjoining field, or he sold her the cloth for the dress she sewed and wore. His demand must have surprised, then terrified her. She obeyed him; she always did as she was told.

When the family found a young man in the next village to be her husband, 17 she stood tractably beside the best rooster, his proxy, and promised before they met that she would be his forever. She was lucky that he was her age and she would be the first wife, an advantage secure now. The night she first saw him, he had sex with her. Then he left for America. She had almost forgotten what he looked like. When she tried to envision him, she only saw the black and white face in the group photograph the men had had taken before leaving.

The other man was not, after all, much different from her husband. They 18 both gave orders: she followed. "If you tell your family, I'll beat you. I'll kill you. Be here again next week." No one talked sex, ever. And she might have separated the rapes from the rest of living if only she did not have to buy her oil from him or gather wood in the same forest. I want her fear to have lasted just as long as rape lasted so that the fear could have been contained. No drawn-out fear. But women at sex hazarded birth and hence lifetimes. The fear did not stop but permeated everywhere. She told the man, "I think I'm pregnant." He organized the raid against her.

On nights when my mother and father talked about their life back home, 19 sometimes they mentioned an "outcast table" whose business they still seemed to be settling, their voices tight. In a commensal tradition, where food is precious, the powerful older people made wrongdoers eat alone. Instead of letting them start separate new lives like the Japanese, who could become samurais and geishas, the Chinese family, faces averted but eyes glowering sideways, hung on to the offenders and fed them leftovers. My aunt must have lived in the same house as my parents and eaten at an outcast table. My mother spoke about the raid as if she had seen it, when she and my aunt, a daughter-in-law to a different household, should not have been living together at all. Daughters-in-law lived with their husbands' parents, not their own; a synonym for marriage in Chinese is "taking a daughter-in-law." Her husband's parents could have sold her, mortgaged her, stoned her. But they had sent her back to her own mother and father, a mysterious act hinting at disgraces not told me. Perhaps they had thrown her out to deflect the avengers.

20 She was the only daughter; her four brothers went with her father, husband, and uncles "out on the road" and for some years became western men. When the goods were divided among the family, three of the brothers took land, and the youngest, my father, chose an education. After my grandparents gave their daughter away to her husband's family, they had dispensed all the adventure and all the property. They expected her alone to keep the traditional ways, which her brothers, now among the barbarians, could fumble without detection. The heavy, deep-rooted women were to maintain the past against the flood, safe for returning. But the rare urge west had fixed upon our family, and so my aunt crossed boundaries not delineated in space.

21 The work of preservation demands that the feelings playing about in one's guts not be turned into action. Just watch their passing like cherry blossoms. But perhaps my aunt, my forerunner, caught in a slow life, let dreams grow and fade and after some months or years went toward what persisted. Fear at the enormities of the forbidden kept her desires delicate, wire and bone. She looked at a man because she liked the way the hair was tucked behind his ears, or she liked the question-mark line of a long torso curving at the shoulder and straight at the hip. For warm eyes or a soft voice or a slow walk — that's all — a few hairs, a line, a brightness, a sound, a pace, she gave up family. She offered us up for a charm that vanished with tiredness, a pigtail that didn't toss when the wind died. Why, the wrong lighting could erase the dearest thing about him.

22 It could very well have been, however, that my aunt did not take subtle enjoyment of her friend, but, a wild woman, kept rollicking company. Imagining her free with sex doesn't fit, though. I don't know any women like that, or men either. Unless I see her life branching into mine, she gives me no ancestral help.

23 To sustain her being in love, she often worked at herself in the mirror, guessing at the colors and shapes that would interest him, changing them frequently in order to hit on the right combination. She wanted him to look back.

On a farm near the sea, a woman who tended her appearance reaped a   24
reputation for eccentricity. All the married women blunt-cut their hair in
flaps about their ears or pulled it back in tight buns. No nonsense. Neither
style blew easily into heart-catching tangles. And at their weddings they displayed themselves in their long hair for the last time. "It brushed the backs of
my knees," my mother tells me. "It was braided, and even so, it brushed the
backs of my knees."

At the mirror my aunt combed individuality into her bob. A bun could   25
have been contrived to escape into black streamers blowing in the wind or
in quiet wisps about her face, but only the older women in our picture album
wear buns. She brushed her hair back from her forehead, tucking the flaps
behind her ears. She looped a piece of thread, knotted into a circle between
her index fingers and thumbs, and ran the double strand across her forehead.
When she closed her fingers as if she were making a pair of shadow geese
bite, the string twisted together catching the little hairs. Then she pulled the
thread away from her skin, ripping the hairs out neatly, her eyes watering from
the needles of pain. Opening her fingers, she cleaned the thread, then rolled
it along her hairline and the tops of her eyebrows. My mother did the same
to me and my sisters and herself. I used to believe that the expression "caught
by the short hairs" meant a captive held with a depilatory string. It especially
hurt at the temples, but my mother said we were lucky we didn't have to have
our feet bound when we were seven. Sisters used to sit on their beds and cry
together, she said, as their mothers or their slave removed the bandages for a
few minutes each night and let the blood gush back into their veins. I hope
that the man my aunt loved appreciated a smooth brow, that he wasn't just a
tits-and-ass man.

Once my aunt found a freckle on her chin, at a spot that the almanac said   26
predestined her for unhappiness. She dug it out with a hot needle and washed
the wound with peroxide.

More attention to her looks than these pullings of hairs and pickings at   27
spots would have caused gossip among the villagers. They owned work clothes
and good clothes, and they wore good clothes for feasting the new seasons.
But since a woman combing her hair hexes beginnings, my aunt rarely found
an occasion to look her best. Women looked like great sea snails—the corded
wood, babies, and laundry they carried were the whorls on their backs. The
Chinese did not admire a bent back; goddesses and warriors stood straight.
Still there must have been a marvelous freeing of beauty when a worker laid
down her burden and stretched and arched.

Such commonplace loveliness, however, was not enough for my aunt.   28
She dreamed of a lover for the fifteen days of New Year's, the time for families

to exchange visits, money, and food. She plied her secret comb. And sure enough she cursed the year, the family, the village, and herself.

Even as her hair lured her imminent lover, many other men looked at her. Uncles, cousins, nephews, brothers would have looked, too, had they been home between journeys. Perhaps they had already been restraining their curiosity, and they left, fearful that their glances, like a field of nesting birds, might be startled and caught. Poverty hurt, and that was their first reason for leaving. But another, final reason for leaving the crowded house was the never-said.

She may have been unusually beloved, the precious only daughter, spoiled and mirror gazing because of the affection the family lavished on her. When her husband left, they welcomed the chance to take her back from the in-laws; she could live like the little daughter for just a while longer. There are stories that my grandfather was different from other people, "crazy ever since the little Jap bayoneted him in the head." He used to put his naked penis on the dinner table, laughing. And one day he brought home a baby girl, wrapped up inside his brown western-style greatcoat. He had traded one of his sons, probably my father, the youngest, for her. My grandmother made him trade back. When he finally got a daughter of his own, he doted on her. They must have all loved her, except perhaps my father, the only brother who never went back to China, having once been traded for a girl.

Brothers and sisters, newly men and women, had to efface their sexual color and present plain miens. Disturbing hair and eyes, a smile like no other, threatened the ideal of five generations living under one roof. To focus blurs, people shouted face to face and yelled from room to room. The immigrants I know have loud voices, unmodulated to American tones even after years away from the village where they called their friendships out across the fields. I have not been able to stop my mother's screams in public libraries or over telephones. Walking erect (knees straight, toes pointed forward, not pigeon-toed, which is Chinese-feminine) and speaking in an inaudible voice, I have tried to turn myself American-feminine. Chinese communication was loud, public. Only sick people had to whisper. But at the dinner table, where the family members came nearest one another, no one could talk, not the outcasts nor any eaters. Every word that falls from the mouth is a coin lost. Silently they gave and accepted food with both hands. A preoccupied child who took his bowl with one hand got a sideways glare. A complete moment of total attention is due everyone alike. Children and lovers have no singularity here, but my aunt used a secret voice, a separate attentiveness.

She kept the man's name to herself throughout her labor and dying; she did not accuse him that he be punished with her. To save her inseminator's name she gave silent birth.

29

30

31

32

He may have been somebody in her own household, but intercourse with 33 a man outside the family would have been no less abhorrent. All the village were kinsmen, and the titles shouted in loud country voices never let kinship be forgotten. Any man within visiting distance would have been neutralized as a lover—"brother," "younger brother," "older brother"—one hundred and fifteen relationship titles. Parents researched birth charts probably not so much to assure good fortune as to circumvent incest in a population that has but one hundred surnames. Everybody has eight million relatives. How useless then sexual mannerisms, how dangerous.

As if it came from an atavism deeper than fear, I used to add "brother" 34 silently to boys' names. It hexed the boys, who would or would not ask me to dance, and made them less scary and as familiar and deserving of benevolence as girls.

But, of course, I hexed myself also—no dates. I should have stood up, 35 both arms waving, and shouted out across libraries, "Hey, you! Love me back." I had no idea, though, how to make attraction selective, how to control its direction and magnitude. If I made myself American-pretty so that the five or six Chinese boys in the class fell in love with me, everyone else—the Caucasian, Negro, and Japanese boys—would too. Sisterliness, dignified and honorable, made much more sense.

Attraction eludes control so stubbornly that whole societies designed to 36 organize relationships among people cannot keep order, not even when they bind people to one another from childhood and raise them together. Among the very poor and the wealthy, brothers married their adopted sisters, like doves. Our family allowed some romance, paying adult brides' prices and providing dowries so that their sons and daughters could marry strangers. Marriage promises to turn strangers into friendly relatives—a nation of siblings.

In the village structure, spirits shimmered among the live creatures, bal- 37 anced and held in equilibrium by time and land. But one human being flaring up into violence could open up a black hole, a maelstrom that pulled in the sky. The frightened villagers, who depended on one another to maintain the real, went to my aunt to show her a personal, physical representation of the break she made in the "roundness." Misallying couples snapped off the future, which was to be embodied in true offspring. The villagers punished her for acting as if she could have a private life, secret and apart from them.

If my aunt had betrayed the family at a time of large grain yields and peace, 38 when many boys were born, and wings were being built on many houses, perhaps she might have escaped such severe punishment. But the men—hungry, greedy, tired of planting in dry soil, cuckolded—had been forced to leave the village in order to send food-money home. There were ghost plagues, bandit plagues, wars with the Japanese, floods. My Chinese brother and sister had died of an unknown sickness. Adultery, perhaps only a mistake during good times, became a crime when the village needed food.

The round moon cakes and round doorways, the round tables of gradu-   39
ated size that fit one roundness inside another, round windows and rice bowls—these talismans had lost their power to warn this family of the law: A family must be whole, faithfully keeping the descent line by having sons to feed the old and the dead who in turn look after the family. The villagers came to show my aunt and lover-in-hiding a broken house. The villagers were speeding up the circling of events because she was too shortsighted to see that her infidelity had already harmed the village, that waves of consequences would return unpredictably, sometimes in disguise, as now, to hurt her. This roundness had to be made coin-sized so that she would see its circumference: punish her at the birth of her baby. Awaken her to the inexorable. People who refused fatalism because they could invent small resources insisted on culpability. Deny accidents and wrest fault from the stars.

After the villagers left, their lanterns now scattering in various directions   40
toward home, the family broke their silence and cursed her. "Aiaa, we're going to die. Death is coming. Death is coming. Look what you've done. You've killed us. Ghost! Dead Ghost! Ghost! You've never been born." She ran out into the fields, far enough from the house so that she could no longer hear their voices, and pressed herself against the earth, her own land no more. When she felt the birth coming, she thought that she had been hurt. Her body seized together. "They've hurt me too much," she thought. "This is gall, and it will kill me." With forehead and knees against the earth, her body convulsed and then relaxed. She turned on her back, lay on the ground. The black well of sky and stars went out and out and out forever; her body and her complexity seemed to disappear. She was one of the stars, a bright dot in blackness, with-out home, without a companion, in eternal cold and silence. An agoraphobia rose in her, speeding higher and higher, bigger and bigger; she would not be able to contain it; there would be no end to fear.

Flayed, unprotected against space, she felt pain return, focusing her body.   41
This pain chilled her—a cold, steady kind of surface pain. Inside, spasmodically, the other pain, the pain of the child, heated her. For hours she lay on the ground, alternately body and space. Sometimes a vision of normal comfort obliterated reality: She saw the family in the evening gambling at the dinner table, the young people massaging their elders' backs. She saw them congratulating one another, high joy on the mornings the rice shoots came up. When these pictures burst, the stars drew out further apart. Black space opened.

She got to her feet to fight better and remembered that old-fashioned   42
women gave birth in their pigsties to fool the jealous, pain-dealing gods, who do not snatch piglets. Before the next spasms could stop her, she ran to the

pigsty, each step a rushing out into emptiness. She climbed over the fence and knelt in the dirt. It was good to have a fence enclosing her, a tribal person alone.

Laboring, this woman who had carried her child as a foreign growth that   43 sickened her every day, expelled it at last. She reached down to touch the hot, wet, moving mass, surely smaller than anything human, and could feel that it was human after all—fingers, toes, nails, nose. She pulled it up on to her belly, and it lay curled there, butt in the air, feet precisely tucked one under the other. She opened her loose shirt and buttoned the child inside. After resting, it squirmed and thrashed and she pushed it up to her breast. It turned its head this way and that until it found her nipple. There, it made little snuffling noises. She clenched her teeth at its preciousness, lovely as a young calf, a piglet, a little dog.

She may have gone to the pigsty as a last act of responsibility: She would   44 protect this child as she had protected its father. It would look after her soul, leaving supplies on her grave. But how would this tiny child without family find her grave when there would be no marker for her anywhere, neither in the earth nor the family hall? No one would give her a family hall name. She had taken the child with her into the wastes. At its birth the two of them had felt the same raw pain of separation, a wound that only the family pressing tight could close. A child with no descent line would not soften her life but only trail after her, ghostlike, begging her to give it purpose. At dawn the villagers on their way to the fields would stand around the fence and look.

Full of milk, the little ghost slept. When it awoke, she hardened her breasts   45 against the milk that crying loosens. Toward morning she picked up the baby and walked to the well.

Carrying the baby to the well shows loving. Otherwise abandon it. Turn   46 its face into the mud. Mothers who love their children take them along. It was probably a girl; there is some hope of forgiveness for boys.

"Don't tell anyone you had an aunt. Your father does not want to hear her   47 name. She has never been born." I have believed that sex was unspeakable and words so strong and fathers so frail that "aunt" would do my father mysterious harm. I have thought that my family, having settled among immigrants who had also been their neighbors in the ancestral land, needed to clean their name, and a wrong word would incite the kinspeople even here. But there is more to this silence: They want me to participate in her punishment. And I have.

In the twenty years since I heard this story I have not asked for details   48 nor said my aunt's name; I do not know it. People who comfort the dead can also chase after them to hurt them further—a reverse ancestor worship. The real punishment was not the raid swiftly inflicted by the villagers, but the family's deliberately forgetting her. Her betrayal so maddened them, they saw to it that she would suffer forever, even after death. Always hungry, always needing, she would have to beg food from other ghosts, snatch and steal it from those whose living descendants give them gifts. She would have to fight the ghosts massed at crossroads for the buns a few thoughtful citizens leave to decoy her away from village and home so that the ancestral spirits could feast unharassed. At peace, they could act like gods, not ghosts, their descent lines providing them with paper suits and dresses, spirit money, paper houses, paper automobiles, chicken, meat, and rice into eternity—essences delivered up in smoke and flames, steam and incense rising from each rice bowl. In an attempt to make the Chinese care for people outside the family, Chairman Mao encourages us now to give our paper replicas to the spirits of outstanding soldiers and workers, no matter whose ancestors they may be. My aunt remains forever hungry. Goods are not distributed evenly among the dead.

My aunt haunts me—her ghost drawn to me because now, after fifty years   49
of neglect, I alone devote pages of paper to her, though not origamied into houses and clothes. I do not think she always means me well. I am telling on her, and she was a spite suicide, drowning herself in the drinking water. The Chinese are always very frightened of the drowned one, whose weeping ghost, wet hair hanging and skin bloated, waits silently by the water to pull down a substitute.

For a reading quiz, sources on Maxine Hong Kingston, and annotated links to further readings on Chinese culture and on Chinese American culture, visit **bedfordstmartins.com/thebedfordreader**.

Journal Writing

Most of us have heard family stories that left lasting impressions—ghost stories like Kingston's, biographies of ancestors, explanations for traditions, family superstitions, and so on. Write in your journal about a family story you remember vividly from your childhood. (To take your journal writing further, see "From Journal to Essay" on the next page.)

Questions on Meaning

1. What PURPOSE does Kingston have in telling her aunt's story? How does this differ from her mother's purpose in relating the tale?

2. According to Kingston, who could have been the father of her aunt's child? Who could not?
3. Kingston says that her mother told stories "to warn us about life." What warning does this story provide?
4. Why is Kingston so fascinated by her aunt's life and death?

Questions on Writing Strategy

1. Whom does Kingston seem to include in her AUDIENCE: her family and other older Chinese? second-generation Chinese Americans like herself? other Americans? How might she expect each of these groups to respond to her essay?
2. Why is Kingston's opening line—her mother's "You must not tell anyone"—especially fitting for this essay? What secrets are being told? Why does Kingston divulge them?
3. As Kingston tells her tale of her aunt, some events are based on her mother's story or her knowledge of Chinese customs, and some are wholly imaginary. What is the EFFECT of blending these several threads of reality, perception, and imagination?
4. **MIXED METHODS** Examine the details in the two contrasting NARRATIVES of how Kingston's aunt became pregnant: one in paragraphs 15–18 and the other in paragraphs 21–28. How do the details create different realities? Which version does Kingston seem more committed to? Why?
5. **MIXED METHODS** Kingston COMPARES AND CONTRASTS various versions of her aunt's story, trying to find the CAUSES that led her aunt to drown in the well. In the end, what causes does Kingston seem to accept?

Questions on Language

1. How does Kingston's language—lyrical, poetic, full of FIGURES OF SPEECH and other IMAGES—reveal her relationship to her Chinese heritage? Find phrases that are especially striking.
2. Look up any of these words you do not know: bunds (par. 4); acrid (7); frivolous (14); tractably, proxy (17); hazarded (18); commensal (19); delineated (20); depilatory (25); plied (28); miens (31); abhorrent, circumvent (33); atavism (34); maelstrom (37); talismans, inexorable, fatalism, culpability (39); gall, agoraphobia (40); spasmodically (41).
3. Sometimes Kingston indicates that she is reconstructing or imagining events through verbs like "would have" and words like "maybe" and "perhaps" ("Perhaps she encountered him in the fields," par. 16). Other times she presents obviously imaginary events as if they actually happened ("Once my aunt found a freckle on her chin," 26). What effect does Kingston achieve with these apparent inconsistencies?

Suggestions for Writing

1. **FROM JOURNAL TO ESSAY** Develop the family story from your journal into a narrative essay. Build in the context of the story as well: Who told it to you? What

purpose did he or she have in telling it to you? How does it illustrate your family's beliefs and values?

2. Write an essay explaining the role of ancestors in Chinese family and religious life, supplementing what Kingston says with research in the library or on the Web or (if you are Chinese American) drawing on your own experiences.

3. **CRITICAL WRITING** ANALYZE the ideas about gender roles revealed in "No Name Woman," both in China and in the Chinese American culture Kingston grew up in. How have these ideas affected Kingston? Do you perceive any semblance of them in contemporary American culture?

4. **CONNECTIONS** Both Kingston and Gloria Naylor, in "The Meanings of a Word" (p. 517), examine communication within their families. Relate an incident or incidents from your own childhood that portray something about the communication within your family. You might want to focus on the language of communication, such as the words used to discuss (or not discuss) a taboo topic, the special family meanings for familiar words, a misunderstanding between you and an adult about something the adult said. Use dialog and as much CONCRETE detail as you can to clarify your experience and its significance.

5. **CONNECTIONS** Amy Tan in "Fish Cheeks" (p. 116) and Christine Leong in "Being a Chink" (p. 523) also write about relationships between parents and children in Chinese American families. In an essay, analyze what these two essays along with Kingston's suggest about the experiences of the children of Chinese immigrants to the United States.

Maxine Hong Kingston on Writing

In an interview with Jean W. Ross published in *Contemporary Authors* in 1984, Maxine Hong Kingston discusses the writing and revising of *The Woman Warrior*. Ross asks Kingston to clarify an earlier statement that she had "no idea how people who don't write endure their lives." Kingston replies: "When I said that, I was thinking about how words and stories create order. Some of the things that happen to us in life seem to have no meaning, but when you write them down you find the meanings for them; or, as you translate life into words, you force a meaning. Meaning is intrinsic in words and stories."

Ross then asks if Kingston used an outline and planned to blend fact with legend in *The Woman Warrior*. "Oh no, no," Kingston answers. "What I have at the beginning of a book is not an outline. I have no idea of how stories will end or where the beginning will lead. Sometimes I draw pictures. I draw a blob and then I have a little arrow and it goes to this other blob, if you want to call that an outline. It's hardly even words; it's like a doodle. Then when it turns into words, I find the words lead me to various scenes and stories which I don't know about until I get there. I don't see the order until very late in the writing and sometimes the ending just comes. I just run up against it. All of a sudden the book's over and I didn't know it would be over."

A question from Ross about whether her emotions enter her writing leads Kingston to talk about revision. "Well, when I first set something down I feel the emotions I write about. But when I do a second draft, third draft, ninth draft, then I don't feel very emotional. The rewriting is very intellectual; all my education and reading and intellect are involved. The mechanics of sentences, how one phrase or word goes with another one—all that happens in later drafts. There's a very emotional first draft and a very technical last draft."

For Discussion

1. Do you agree with Kingston that when you write things down you find their meaning? Give examples of when the writing process has or hasn't clarified an experience for you.
2. Kingston doodles as a way to discover her material. How do you discover what you have to say?
3. What does Kingston mean by "[t]he mechanics of sentences"? Do you consider this element as you revise?

GEORGE ORWELL

George Orwell was the pen name of Eric Blair (1903–50), born in Bengal, India, the son of an English civil servant. After attending Eton on a scholarship, he joined the British police in Burma, where he acquired a distrust for the methods of the empire. Then followed years of tramping, odd jobs, and near-starvation — recalled in *Down and Out in Paris and London* (1933). From living on the fringe of society and from reporting on English miners and factory workers, Orwell deepened his sympathy with underdogs. Severely wounded while fighting in the Spanish civil war, he wrote a memoir, *Homage to Catalonia* (1938), voicing disillusionment with Loyalists who, he claimed, sought not to free Spain but to exterminate their political enemies. A socialist by conviction, Orwell kept pointing to the dangers of a collective state run by totalitarians. In *Animal Farm* (1945), he satirized Soviet bureaucracy; and in his famous novel *Nineteen Eighty-Four* (1949), he foresaw a regimented England whose government perverts truth and spies on citizens by two-way television. (The motto of the state and its leader: Big Brother Is Watching You.)

Shooting an Elephant

Orwell wrote compellingly of his five years as a police officer in Burma, a southeast Asian country (now known as Myanmar) that the British began colonizing in the early 1800s and ruled until 1947. In this selection from *Shooting an Elephant and Other Essays* (1950), Orwell combines personal experience and piercing insight to expose both an oppressive government and himself as the government's hireling.

"Shooting an Elephant" is foremost a narrative, but Orwell uses description, example, and cause and effect as well to develop and give significance to his tale.

Narration (Chap. 4): throughout
Description (Chap. 5): paragraphs 2, 4–12
Example (Chap. 6): paragraphs 1–2, 4, 14
Cause and effect (Chap. 11): paragraphs 1–2, 6–7

In Moulmein, in Lower Burma, I was hated by large numbers of people — 1
the only time in my life that I have been important enough for this to happen
to me. I was subdivisional police officer of the town, and in an aimless, petty
kind of way anti-European feeling was very bitter. No one had the guts to raise
a riot, but if a European woman went through the bazaars alone somebody
would probably spit betel juice over her dress. As a police officer I was an obvious target and was baited whenever it seemed safe to do so. When a nimble

Burman tripped me up on the football field and the referee (another Burman) looked the other way, the crowd yelled with hideous laughter. This happened more than once. In the end the sneering yellow faces of young men that met me everywhere, the insults hooted after me when I was at a safe distance, got badly on my nerves. The young Buddhist priests were the worst of all. There were several thousands of them in the town and none of them seemed to have anything to do except stand on street corners and jeer at Europeans.

All this was perplexing and upsetting. For at that time I had already made   2
up my mind that imperialism was an evil thing and the sooner I chucked up my job and got out of it the better. Theoretically—and secretly, of course—I was all for the Burmese and all against the oppressors, the British. As for the job I was doing, I hated it more bitterly than I can perhaps make clear. In a job like that you see the dirty work of Empire at close quarters. The wretched pris-oners huddling in the stinking cages of the lockups, the grey, cowed faces of the long-term convicts, the scarred buttocks of the men who had been flogged with bamboos—all these oppressed me with an intolerable sense of guilt. But I could get nothing into perspective. I was young and ill-educated and I had had to think out my problems in the utter silence that is imposed on every Englishman in the East. I did not even know that the British Empire is dying, still less did I know that it is a great deal better than the younger empires that are going to supplant it. All I knew was that I was stuck between my hatred of the empire I served and my rage against the evil-spirited little beasts who tried to make my job impossible. With one part of my mind I thought of the Brit-ish Raj[1] as an unbreakable tyranny, as something clamped down, in *saecula saeculorum*,[2] upon the will of prostrate peoples; with another part I thought that the greatest joy in the world would be to drive a bayonet into a Buddhist priest's guts. Feelings like these are the normal by-products of imperialism; ask any Anglo-Indian official, if you can catch him off duty.

One day something happened which in a roundabout way was enlighten-   3
ing. It was a tiny incident in itself, but it gave me a better glimpse than I had had before of the real nature of imperialism—the real motives for which des-potic governments act. Early one morning the subinspector at a police station the other end of town rang me up on the phone and said that an elephant was ravaging the bazaar. Would I please come and do something about it? I did not know what I could do, but I wanted to see what was happening and I got on to a pony and started out. I took my rifle, an old .44 Winchester and much too small to kill an elephant, but I thought the noise might be useful

---

[1] British imperial government. *Raj* in Hindi means "reign," a word similar to *rajah*, "ruler."— EDS.

[2] Latin, "world without end."—EDS.

in terrorem.[3] Various Burmans stopped me on the way and told me about the elephant's doings. It was not, of course, a wild elephant, but a tame one which had gone "must." It had been chained up, as tame elephants always are when their attack of "must" is due, but on the previous night it had broken its chain and escaped. Its mahout,[4] the only person who could manage it when it was in that state, had set out in pursuit, but had taken the wrong direction and was now twelve hours' journey away, and in the morning the elephant had suddenly reappeared in the town. The Burmese population had no weapons and were quite helpless against it. It had already destroyed somebody's bamboo hut, killed a cow and raided some fruit stalls and devoured the stock; also it had met the municipal rubbish van and, when the driver jumped out and took to his heels, had turned the van over and inflicted violences upon it.

The Burmese subinspector and some Indian constables were waiting for   4
me in the quarter where the elephant had been seen. It was a very poor quarter, a labyrinth of squalid bamboo huts, thatched with palmleaf, winding all over a steep hillside. I remember that it was a cloudy, stuffy morning at the beginning of the rains. We began questioning the people as to where the elephant had gone and, as usual, failed to get any definite information. That is invariably the case in the East; a story always sounds clear enough at a distance, but the nearer you get to the scene of events the vaguer it becomes. Some of the people said that the elephant had gone in one direction, some said that he had gone in another, some professed not even to have heard of any elephant. I had almost made up my mind that the whole story was a pack of lies, when we heard yells a little distance away. There was a loud, scandalized cry of "Go away, child! Go away this instant!" and an old woman with a switch in her hand came round the corner of a hut, violently shooing away a crowd of naked children. Some more women followed, clicking their tongues and exclaiming; evidently there was something that the children ought not to have seen. I rounded the hut and saw a man's dead body sprawling in the mud. He was an Indian, a black Dravidian coolie, almost naked, and he could not have been dead many minutes. The people said that the elephant had come suddenly upon him round the corner of the hut, caught him with its trunk, put its foot on his back and ground him into the earth. This was the rainy season and the ground was soft, and his face had scored a trench a foot deep and a couple of yards long. He was lying on his belly with arms crucified and head sharply twisted to one side. His face was coated with mud, the eyes wide open, the teeth bared and grinning with an expression of unendurable agony. (Never tell me, by the way, that the dead look peaceful. Most of the corpses I

---

[3]Latin, "to give warning." — EDS.
[4]Keeper or groom, a servant of the elephant's owner. — EDS.

have seen looked devilish.) The friction of the great beast's foot had stripped the skin from his back as neatly as one skins a rabbit. As soon as I saw the dead man I sent an orderly to a friend's house nearby to borrow an elephant rifle. I had already sent back the pony, not wanting it to go mad with fright and throw me if it smelled the elephant.

The orderly came back in a few minutes with a rifle and five cartridges, and meanwhile some Burmans had arrived and told us that the elephant was in the paddy fields below, only a few hundred yards away. As I started forward practically the whole population of the quarter flocked out of the houses and followed me. They had seen the rifle and were all shouting excitedly that I was going to shoot the elephant. They had not shown much interest in the elephant when he was merely ravaging their homes, but it was different now that he was going to be shot. It was a bit of fun to them, as it would be to an English crowd; besides they wanted the meat. It made me vaguely uneasy. I had no intention of shooting the elephant—I had merely sent for the rifle to defend myself if necessary—and it is always unnerving to have a crowd following you. I marched down the hill, looking and feeling a fool, with the rifle over my shoulder and an ever-growing army of people jostling at my heels. At the bottom, when you got away from the huts, there was a metalled road and beyond that a miry waste of paddy fields a thousand yards across, not yet ploughed but soggy from the first rains and dotted with coarse grass. The elephant was standing eight yards from the road, his left side towards us. He took not the slightest notice of the crowd's approach. He was tearing up bunches of grass, beating them against his knees to clean them and stuffing them into his mouth.

I had halted on the road. As soon as I saw the elephant I knew with perfect certainty that I ought not to shoot him. It is a serious matter to shoot a working elephant—it is comparable to destroying a huge and costly piece of machinery—and obviously one ought not to do it if it can possibly be avoided. And at that distance, peacefully eating, the elephant looked no more dangerous than a cow. I thought then and I think now that his attack of "must" was already passing off; in which case he would merely wander harmlessly about until the mahout came back and caught him. Moreover, I did not in the least want to shoot him. I decided that I would watch him for a little while to make sure that he did not turn savage again, and then go home.

But at that moment, I glanced round at the crowd that had followed me. It was an immense crowd, two thousand at the least and growing every minute. It blocked the road for a long distance on either side. I looked at the sea of yellow faces above the garish clothes—faces all happy and excited over this bit of fun, all certain that the elephant was going to be shot. They were watching me as they would watch a conjuror about to perform a trick. They did not like me, but with the magical rifle in my hands I was momentarily worth watching. And suddenly I realized that I should have to shoot the elephant after all. The people expected it of me and I had got to do it; I could feel their two thousand wills pressing me forward, irresistibly. And it was at this moment, as I stood there with the rifle in my hands, that I first grasped the hollowness, the futility of the white man's dominion in the East. Here was I, the white man with his gun, standing in front of the unarmed native crowd—seemingly the leading actor of the piece; but in reality I was only an absurd puppet pushed to and fro by the will of those yellow faces behind. I perceived in this moment that when the white man turns tyrant it is his own freedom that he destroys. He becomes a sort of hollow, posing dummy, the conventionalized figure of a sahib. For it is the condition of his rule that he shall spend his life in trying to impress the "natives," and so in every crisis he has got to do what the "natives" expect of him. He wears a mask, and his face grows to fit it. I had got to shoot the elephant. I had committed myself to doing it when I sent for the rifle. A sahib has got to act like a sahib; he has got to appear resolute, to know his own mind and do definite things. To come all that way, rifle in hand, with two thousand people marching at my heels, and then to trail feebly away, having done nothing—no, that was impossible. The crowd would laugh at me. And my whole life, every white man's life in the East, was one long struggle not to be laughed at.

But I did not want to shoot the elephant. I watched him beating his bunch   8
of grass against his knees, with that preoccupied grandmotherly air that elephants have. It seemed to me that it would be murder to shoot him. At that age I was not squeamish about killing animals, but I had never shot an elephant and never wanted to. (Somehow it always seems worse to kill a *large* animal.) Besides, there was the beast's owner to be considered. Alive, the elephant was worth at least a hundred pounds; dead, he would only be worth the value of his tusks, five pounds, possibly. But I had got to act quickly. I turned to some experienced-looking Burmans who had been there when we arrived, and asked them how the elephant had been behaving. They all said the same thing: He took no notice of you if you left him alone, but he might charge if you went too close to him.

It was perfectly clear to me what I ought to do. I ought to walk up to within,   9
say, twenty-five yards of the elephant and test his behavior. If he charged, I could shoot; if he took no notice of me, it would be safe to leave him until the mahout came back. But also I knew that I was going to do no such thing. I was a poor shot with a rifle and the ground was soft mud into which one would sink at every step. If the elephant charged and I missed him, I should have about as much chance as a toad under a steamroller. But even then I was not thinking particularly of my own skin, only of the watchful yellow

faces behind. For at that moment, with the crowd watching me, I was not afraid in the ordinary sense, as I would have been if I had been alone. A white man mustn't be frightened in front of "natives"; and so, in general, he isn't frightened. The sole thought in my mind was that if anything went wrong those two thousand Burmans would see me pursued, caught, trampled on, and reduced to a grinning corpse like that Indian up the hill. And if that happened it was quite probable that some of them would laugh. That would never do. There was only one alternative. I shoved the cartridges into the magazine and lay down on the road to get a better aim.

The crowd grew very still, and a deep, low, happy sigh, as of people who   10
see the theater curtain go up at last, breathed from innumerable throats. They were going to have their bit of fun after all. The rifle was a beautiful German thing with cross-hair sights. I did not then know that in shooting an elephant one would shoot to cut an imaginary bar running from ear-hole to ear-hole. I ought, therefore, as the elephant was sideways on, to have aimed straight at his ear-hole; actually I aimed several inches in front of this, thinking the brain would be further forward.

When I pulled the trigger I did not hear the bang or feel the kick—one   11
never does when a shot goes home—but I heard the devilish roar of glee that went up from the crowd. In that instant, in too short a time, one would have thought, even for the bullet to get there, a mysterious, terrible change had come over the elephant. He neither stirred nor fell, but every line of his body had altered. He looked suddenly stricken, shrunken, immensely old, as though the frightful impact of the bullet had paralyzed him without knocking him down. At last, after what seemed a long time—it might have been five seconds, I dare say—he sagged flabbily to his knees. His mouth slobbered. An enormous senility seemed to have settled upon him. One could have imagined him thousands of years old. I fired again into the same spot. At the second shot he did not collapse but climbed with desperate slowness to his feet and stood weakly upright, with legs sagging and head drooping. I fired a third time. That was the shot that did for him. You could see the agony of it jolt his whole body and knock the last remnant of strength from his legs. But in falling he seemed for a moment to rise, for as his hind legs collapsed beneath him he seemed to tower upward like a huge rock toppling, his trunk reaching sky-wards like a tree. He trumpeted, for the first and only time. And then down he came, his belly towards me, with a crash that seemed to shake the ground even where I lay.

I got up. The Burmans were already racing past me across the mud. It was   12
obvious that the elephant would never rise again, but he was not dead. He was breathing very rhythmically with long rattling gasps, his great mound of

a side painfully rising and falling. His mouth was wide open. I could see far down into caverns of pale pink throat. I waited a long time for him to die, but his breathing did not weaken. Finally I fired my two remaining shots into the spot where I thought his heart must be. The thick blood welled out of him like red velvet, but still he did not die. His body did not even jerk when the shots hit him, the tortured breathing continued without a pause. He was dying, very slowly and in great agony, but in some world remote from me where not even a bullet could damage him further. I felt I had got to put an end to that dreadful noise. It seemed dreadful to see the great beast lying there, powerless to move and yet powerless to die, and not even to be able to finish him. I sent back for my small rifle and poured shot after shot into his heart and down his throat. They seemed to make no impression. The tortured gasps continued as steadily as the ticking of a clock.

In the end I could not stand it any longer and went away. I heard later   13
that it took him half an hour to die. Burmans were bringing dahs and baskets even before I left, and I was told they had stripped his body almost to the bones by the afternoon.

Afterwards, of course, there were endless discussions about the shooting of   14
the elephant. The owner was furious, but he was only an Indian and could do nothing. Besides, legally I had done the right thing, for a mad elephant has to be killed, like a mad dog, if its owner fails to control it. Among the Europeans opinion was divided. The older men said I was right, the younger men said it was a damn shame to shoot an elephant for killing a coolie, because the elephant was worth more than any damn Coringhee coolie. And afterwards I was very glad that the coolie had been killed; it put me legally in the right and it gave me sufficient pretext for shooting the elephant. I often wondered whether any of the others grasped that I had done it solely to avoid looking a fool.

For a reading quiz, sources on George Orwell, and annotated links to further readings on British imperial rule in Burma, visit bedfordstmartins.com/thebedfordreader.

Journal Writing

How do you respond to Orwell's decision to shoot the elephant even though he believed it unnecessary to do so? Do you have any sympathy for his action? Recall a time when you acted against your better judgment in order to save face in front of others. Write as honestly as you can about what motivated you and what mistakes you made. (To take your journal writing further, see "From Journal to Essay" below.)

Questions on Meaning

1. How would you answer the exasperated student who, after reading this essay, exploded, "Why didn't Orwell just leave his gun at home?"
2. Why did Orwell shoot the elephant?
3. Describe the epiphany that Orwell experiences in the course of the event he writes about. (An *epiphany* is a sudden realization of a truth.)
4. In the last paragraph of his essay, Orwell says he was "glad that the coolie had been killed." How do you account for this remark?
5. What is the PURPOSE of this essay?

Questions on Writing Strategy

1. In addition to serving as an INTRODUCTION to Orwell's essay, what function is performed by paragraphs 1 and 2?
2. From what circumstances does the IRONY of Orwell's essay spring?
3. What does "Shooting an Elephant" gain from having been written years after the events it recounts?
4. **MIXED METHODS**   What does the blend of NARRATION and DESCRIPTION in paragraphs 11–12 contribute to the story? How does it further Orwell's purpose?
5. **MIXED METHODS**   How do the EXAMPLES in paragraphs 1 and 2 illustrate Orwell's conflict about his work as a police officer in Burma?

Questions on Language

1. What do you understand by Orwell's statement that the elephant had "gone 'must'" (par. 3)? Look up *must* or its variant *musth* in your dictionary.
2. What examples of English (as opposed to American) usage do you find in Orwell's essay?
3. Define, if necessary, bazaars, betel (par. 1); intolerable, supplant, prostrate (2); despotic (3); labyrinth, squalid, invariably (4); dominion, sahib (7); magazine (9); innumerable (10); senility (11).

Suggestions for Writing

1. **FROM JOURNAL TO ESSAY**   Write a narrative essay from your journal entry. Tell the story of your action, and consider what the results were, what you might have done differently, and what you learned from the experience.
2. With what examples of governmental face-saving are you familiar? If none leaps to mind, read a newspaper or watch the news on television to catch public officials in the act of covering themselves. (Not only national government but also local or student government may provide examples.) In an essay, ANALYZE two

or three examples: What do you think was really going on that needed covering? Did the officials succeed in saving face, or did their efforts fail? Were the efforts harmful in any way?

3. **CRITICAL WRITING**   Orwell is honest with himself and his readers in acknowledging his mistakes as a government official. Write an essay that examines the degree to which confession may, or may not, erase blameworthiness for misdeeds. Does Orwell remain just as guilty as he would have been if he had not taken responsibility for his actions? Why, or why not? Feel free to supplement your analysis of Orwell's case with examples from your own life or from the news.

4. **CONNECTIONS**   Read William Lutz's "The World of Doublespeak" (p. 418), which CLASSIFIES language that deliberately conceals or misleads. In an essay, examine which of Lutz's categories of doublespeak seem to arise from the motives Orwell describes in paragraph 7: the need "to impress," to do what is expected of one, "to appear resolute," "not to be laughed at." Use specific examples from Lutz's essay — or from your own experience — to support your ideas.

5. **CONNECTIONS**   Like "Shooting an Elephant," Maya Angelou's "Champion of the World" (p. 110) also blends narration and description. COMPARE AND CONTRAST the two essays, not on their purposes, which are vastly different, but on this blending. What senses do the authors rely on? How do they keep their narratives moving? How much of themselves do they inject into their essays?

George Orwell on Writing

George Orwell explains the motives for his own writing in the essay "Why I Write" (1946), from which we reprint the following excerpts.

What I have most wanted to do throughout the past ten years is to make political writing into an art. My starting point is always a feeling of partisanship, a sense of injustice. When I sit down to write a book, I do not say to myself, "I am going to produce a work of art." I write it because there is some lie that I want to expose, some fact to which I want to draw attention, and my initial concern is to get a hearing. But I could not do the work of writing a book, or even a long magazine article, if it were not also an esthetic experience. Anyone who cares to examine my work will see that even when it is downright propaganda it contains much that a full-time politician would consider irrelevant. I am not able, and I do not want, completely to abandon the worldview that I acquired in childhood. So long as I remain alive and well I shall continue to feel strongly about prose style, to love the surface of the earth, and to take a pleasure in solid objects and scraps of useless information. It is no use trying to suppress that side of myself. The job is to reconcile my ingrained likes and dislikes with the essentially public, nonindividual activities that this age forces on all of us.

It is not easy. It raises problems of construction and of language, and it raises in a new way the problem of truthfulness. Let me give just one example of the cruder kind of difficulty that arises. My book about the Spanish civil war, *Homage to Catalonia*, is, of course, a frankly political book, but in the main it is written with a certain detachment and regard for form. I did try very hard in it to tell the whole truth without violating my literary instincts. But among other things it contains a long chapter, full of newspaper quotations and the like, defending the Trotskyists who were accused of plotting with Franco. Clearly such a chapter, which after a year or two would lose its interest for any ordinary reader, must ruin the book. A critic whom I respect read me a lecture about it. "Why did you put in all that stuff?" he said. "You've turned what might have been a good book into journalism." What he said was true, but I could not have done otherwise. I happened to know, what very few people in England had been allowed to know, that innocent men were being falsely accused. If I had not been angry about that I should never have written the book.

In one form or another this problem comes up again. The problem of language is subtler and would take too long to discuss. I will only say that of late years I have tried to write less picturesquely and more exactly. In any case I find that by the time you have perfected any style of writing, you have always outgrown it. *Animal Farm* was the first book in which I tried, with full consciousness of what I was doing, to fuse political purpose and artistic purpose into the whole. . . .

Looking back through the last page or two, I see that I have made it appear as though my motives in writing were wholly public-spirited. I don't want to leave that as the final impression. All writers are vain, selfish, and lazy, and at the very bottom of their motives there lies a mystery. Writing a book is a horrible, exhausting struggle, like a long bout of some painful illness. One would never undertake such a thing if one were not driven on by some demon whom one can neither resist nor understand. For all one knows that demon is simply the same instinct that makes a baby squall for attention. And yet it is also true that one can write nothing readable unless one constantly struggles to efface one's own personality. Good prose is like a windowpane. I cannot say with certainty which of my motives are the strongest, but I know which of them deserve to be followed. And looking back through my work, I see that it is invariably where I lacked a *political* purpose that I wrote lifeless books and was betrayed into purple passages, sentences without meaning, decorative adjectives, and humbug generally.

For Discussion

1. What does Orwell mean by his "political purpose" in writing? by his "artistic purpose"? How did he sometimes find it hard to fulfill both purposes?
2. Think about Orwell's remark that "one can write nothing readable unless one constantly struggles to efface one's own personality." From your own experience, have you found any truth in this observation, or any reason to think otherwise?

FRANCINE PROSE

Francine Prose is the author of more than twelve novels as well as a children's book, several short-story collections, and works of nonfiction, such as *Gluttony* (2003) and *Caravaggio: Painter of Miracles* (2005). She was born in Brooklyn, New York, and graduated from Radcliffe College in 1968. She has received Guggenheim and Fulbright fellowships and has served as a judge for literary prizes. Prose's novel *Blue Angel* (2001), a satire set on a college campus, was nominated for the National Book Award. *A Changed Man* (2005), her novel about a reformed neo-Nazi, won the Dayton Literary Peace Award. From 2007 to 2009 Prose served as president of PEN American Center, the US branch of an international literary organization. She lives in New York and teaches writing at Bard College.

What Words Can Tell

"What Words Can Tell" (editors' title) comes from Prose's book *Reading like a Writer: A Guide for People Who Love Books and for Those Who Want to Write Them* (2006). In this excerpt, Prose gives a detailed reading of the opening paragraph of "A Good Man Is Hard to Find," a short story by the southern American writer Flannery O'Connor (1925–64). In the story a family on vacation intersects the path of an escaped convict, known only as The Misfit. Prose's analysis of O'Connor's words is a model of close attention illuminating a written work.

The primary methods of development Prose uses are example and division or analysis, but she also draws on several other methods:

Description (Chap. 5): paragraphs 7–11
Example (Chap. 6): paragraphs 4–12
Comparison and contrast (Chap. 7): paragraphs 2, 6–7, 11
Process analysis (Chap. 8): paragraphs 3–4
Division or analysis (Chap. 9): paragraphs 5–12
Cause and effect (Chap. 11): paragraphs 7, 12
Argument and persuasion (Chap. 13): paragraphs 2, 12–13

Part of a reader's job is to find out why certain writers endure. This may 1
require some rewiring, unhooking the connection that makes you think you
have to have an *opinion* about the book and reconnecting that wire to whatever terminal lets you see reading as something that might move or delight
you. . . .

With so much reading ahead of you, the temptation might be to speed   2
up. But in fact it's essential to slow down and read every word. Because one
important thing that can be learned by reading slowly is the seemingly obvious but oddly underappreciated fact that language is the medium we use in
much the same way a composer uses notes, the way a painter uses paint. I realize it may seem obvious, but it's surprising how easily we lose sight of the fact
that words are the raw material out of which literature is crafted.

Every page was once a blank page, just as every word that appears on   3
it now was not always there, but instead reflects the final result of countless
large and small deliberations. All the elements of good writing depend on the
writer's skill in choosing one word instead of another. And what grabs and
keeps our interest has everything to do with those choices.

One way to compel yourself to slow down and stop at every word is to ask   4
yourself what sort of information each word—each word choice—is conveying. Reading with that question in mind, let's consider the wealth of information provided by the first paragraph of Flannery O'Connor's "A Good Man Is
Hard to Find":

> The grandmother didn't want to go to Florida. She wanted to visit some
> of her connections in east Tennessee and she was seizing at every chance to
> change Bailey's mind. Bailey was the son she lived with, her only boy. He
> was sitting on the edge of his chair at the table, bent over the orange sports
> section of the *Journal*. "Now look here, Bailey," she said, "see here, read
> this," and she stood with one hand on her thin hip and the other rattling the
> newspaper at his bald head. "Here this fellow that calls himself The Misfit
> is aloose from the Federal Pen and headed toward Florida and you read here
> what it says he did to these people. Just you read it. I wouldn't take my chil-
> dren in any direction with a criminal like that aloose in it. I couldn't answer
> to my conscience if I did."

The first simple declarative sentence could hardly be more plain: subject,   5
verb, infinitive, preposition. There is not one adjective or adverb to distract us
from the central fact. But how much is contained in these eight little words!

Here, as in the openings of many stories and novels, we are confronted   6
by one important choice that a writer of fiction needs to make: the question
of what to call her characters. Joe, Joe Smith, Mr. Smith? Not, in this case,
Grandma or Grandma Smith (no one in this story has a last name) or, let's
say, Ethel or Ethel Smith or Mrs. Smith, or any of the myriad terms of address
that might have established different degrees of psychic distance and sympathy between the reader and the old woman.

Calling her "the grandmother" at once reduces her to her role in the fam-   7
ily, as does the fact that her daughter-in-law is never called anything but "the

children's mother." At the same time, the title gives her (like The Misfit) an archetypal, mythic role that elevates her and keeps us from getting too chummy with this woman whose name we never learn, even as the writer is preparing our hearts to break at the critical moment to which the grandmother's whole life and the events of the story have led her.

The grandmother didn't want to go to Florida. The first sentence is a refusal,   8
which, in its very simplicity, emphasizes the force with which the old woman is digging in her heels. It's a concentrated act of negative will, which we will come to understand in all its tragic folly—that is, the foolishness of attempting to exert one's will when fate or destiny (or as O'Connor would argue, God) has other plans for us. And finally, the no-nonsense austerity of the sentence's construction gives it a kind of authority that—like *Moby-Dick's*[1] first sentence, "Call me Ishmael"—makes us feel that the author is in control, an authority that draws us farther into the story.

The first part of the second sentence—"She wanted to visit some of her   9
connections in east Tennessee"—locates us in geography, that is, in the South. And that one word, *connections* (as opposed to *relatives* or *family* or *people*), reveals the grandmother's sense of her own faded gentility, of having come down in the world, a semi-deluded self-image that, like the illusions of many other O'Connor characters, will contribute to the character's downfall.

The sentence's second half—"she was seizing at every chance to change   10
Bailey's mind"—seizes our own attention more strongly than it would have had O'Connor written, say, "*taking* every chance." The verb quietly but succinctly telegraphs both the grandmother's fierceness and the passivity of Bailey, "the son she lived with, her only boy," two phrases that convey their domestic situation as well as the infantilizing dominance and the simultaneous tenderness that the grandmother feels toward her son. That word *boy* will take on tragic resonance later. "Bailey Boy!" the old woman will cry after her son is killed by The Misfit, who is already about to make his appearance in the newspaper that the grandmother is "rattling" at her boy's bald head. Meanwhile, the paradox of a bald, presumably middle-aged boy leads us to make certain accurate conclusions about the family constellation.

The Misfit is "aloose"—here we find one of those words by which O'Con-   11
nor conveys the rhythm and flavor of a local dialect without subjecting us to the annoying apostrophes, dropped g's, the shootin' and talkin' and cussin', and the bad grammar with which other authors attempt to transcribe regional speech. The final sentences of the paragraph—"I wouldn't take my children in any direction with a criminal like that aloose in it. I couldn't answer to

[1] A novel by the American writer Herman Melville (1819–91).—Eds.

my conscience if I did"—encapsulate the hilarious and maddening quality of the grandmother's manipulativeness. She'll use *anything*, even an imagined encounter with an escaped criminal, to divert the family vacation from Florida to east Tennessee. And her apparently unlikely fantasy of encountering The Misfit may cause us to reflect on the peculiar egocentrism and narcissism of those people who are constantly convinced that, however minuscule the odds, the stray bullet will somehow find *them*. Meanwhile, again because of word choice, the final sentence is already alluding to those questions of conscience, morality, the spirit and soul that will reveal themselves as being at the heart of O'Connor's story.

Given the size of the country, we think, they can't *possibly* run into the   12
criminal about whom the grandmother has warned them. And yet we may recall Chekhov's[2] remark that the gun we see onstage in an early scene should probably go off by the play's end. So what *is* going to happen? This short passage has already ushered us into a world that is realistic but at the same time beyond the reach of ordinary logic, and into a narrative that we will follow from this introduction as inexorably as the grandmother is destined to meet a fate that (we *do* suspect) will involve The Misfit. Pared and edited down, highly concentrated, a model of compression from which it would be hard to excise one word, this single passage achieves all this, or more, since there will be additional subtleties and complexities obvious only to each individual reader.

Skimming just won't suffice if we hope to extract one fraction, such as   13
the fraction above, of what a writer's words can teach us about how to use the language.

---

*For a reading quiz, sources on Francine Prose, and annotated links to further readings on the skill of close reading, visit **bedfordstmartins.com/thebedfordreader.***

Journal Writing

Prose's book *Reading like a Writer* holds that careful reading like that she demonstrates in this excerpt can teach the skills of effective writing. How convinced are you of this connection between reading and writing? Is it reasonable to expect student writers to

---

[2]Anton Chekhov (1860–1904), Russian writer of plays and stories. —EDS.

follow the example set by professionals? In your journal, consider what you've learned about writing from your reading. How, if at all, have you tried to adopt another writer's techniques, and how successful was the effort? (To take your journal writing further, see "From Journal to Essay" on the next page.)

Questions on Meaning

1. To what end does Prose examine the first paragraph of Flannery O'Connor's short story? What is her PURPOSE?
2. What is Prose's THESIS?
3. Why is Prose so impressed by the introductory paragraph of "A Good Man Is Hard to Find"?

Questions on Writing Strategy

1. For whom is Prose writing? What clues in the text reveal how she imagines her AUDIENCE?
2. To what extent does Prose ASSUME that her readers are familiar with Flannery O'Connor's "A Good Man Is Hard to Find"? How does she ensure that readers can follow her ANALYSIS even if they haven't read the story?
3. **MIXED METHODS**   How does Prose use a single extended EXAMPLE to make a point about reading and writing?
4. **MIXED METHODS**   Prose relies on DIVISION or ANALYSIS to illuminate O'Connor's writing. How does she reassemble the parts to reach a conclusion about a broader subject?

Questions on Language

1. Identify two FIGURES OF SPEECH in Prose's first three paragraphs and explain what they contribute to her essay.
2. Why do you suppose the author switches from the second person (*you*) in her introduction to the first-person plural (*we*) in her examination of O'Connor's paragraph? What is the EFFECT of this shift?
3. What are the implications of Prose's ALLUSIONS to Herman Melville's *Moby-Dick* (par. 8) and Anton Chekhov's axiom about guns appearing onstage (12)?
4. Check a dictionary if any of the following words are unfamiliar to you: deliberations (par. 3); conveying (4); declarative (5); myriad, psychic (6); archetypal (7); austerity (8); gentility (9); succinctly, telegraphs, infantilizing, resonance, constellation (10); transcribe, encapsulate, egocentrism, narcissism, minuscule (11); inexorably, excise (12).

Suggestions for Writing

1. **FROM JOURNAL TO ESSAY**   Building on the comments you made in your journal, write an essay for an audience of novice writers that explains what, if anything, they can learn about writing from reading.

2. Read Shirley Jackson's short story "The Lottery" (p. 139) or one of the works of creative nonfiction in this book, such as Maya Angelou's "Champion of the World" (p. 110), Sharman Apt Russell's "The Adored, Buzzing around Us" (p. 221), David Sedaris's "Remembering My Childhood on the Continent of Africa" (p. 274), Andrea Jones's "Identity's Edge" (p. 541), Maxine Hong Kingston's "No Name Woman" (p. 649), George Orwell's "Shooting an Elephant" (p. 663), or E. B. White's "Once More to the Lake" (p. 723). Following Prose's analysis as a model, do a close reading of a short passage from the story or essay. (You may choose the first paragraph, as Prose does, or any brief passage that conveys a lot of meaning, but be sure to select an excerpt that has enough substance to support an analysis.) Explain your interpretation in a brief essay.

3. **CRITICAL WRITING** Locate a copy of Flannery O'Connor's short story "A Good Man Is Hard to Find" and read it for yourself. Then write an essay that responds to Prose's analysis of the first paragraph. Do you agree with her analysis, or do you read the paragraph differently? Why?

4. **CONNECTIONS** While Prose examines a paragraph from Flannery O'Connor's story to discover the author's strategies, Guillermo del Toro and Chuck Hogan, in their essay "Vampires Never Die" (p. 372), take a close look at vampire stories over time to examine the cultural trends they reveal. The writers of both selections, in other words, assume that works of fiction carry meanings beyond mere entertainment. What do you think of this approach to literature? Using "What Words Can Tell" and "Vampires Never Die" as examples, write an essay that considers both what is gained by analyzing works of fiction and what, if anything, may be lost.

5. **CONNECTIONS** In her essay "But What Do You Mean?" (p. 435), Deborah Tannen looks at some of the ways in which men and women communicate. In a brief essay, consider how Tannen's discussion of gender differences might add another layer of meaning to the grandmother's words in the passage from "A Good Man Is Hard to Find."

Francine Prose on Writing

On the Web site *Barnes & Noble Book Clubs* ("Where Readers and Writers Meet"), Francine Prose was asked by a reader about an apparent contradiction in her book *Reading like a Writer:* She stresses the importance of correct grammar in writing, and yet she admiringly quotes an ungrammatical passage by the noted American fiction writer Philip Roth. "The problem with so many grammatical mistakes," Prose responds, "is that they call attention to themselves. You know that something is wrong with the sentence even if you don't know precisely what it is. And it's distracting. The whole point of grammar is clarity—to help us to write, and to understand, as clearly and comprehensively as possible." As for Philip Roth's errors, Prose explains, "Never—not for a moment—are we confused about what Roth means, nor do we feel he's making a mistake or that he's not in control of the language."

For Discussion

1. Why does Prose accept Roth's grammatical errors but disapprove of those made by others?
2. In what way does grammar "help us to write, and to understand, as clearly and comprehensively as possible"? Have you had the experience of reading someone else's writing and not being able to understand it at first—finding it "distracting"—because of grammatical errors? Or has your writing been misunderstood because of such errors?

RICHARD RODRIGUEZ

The son of Spanish-speaking Mexican Americans, Richard Rodriguez was born in 1944 in San Francisco. After graduation from Stanford in 1967, he earned an MA from Columbia, studied at the Warburg Institute in London, and received a PhD in English literature from the University of California at Berkeley. He once taught but now devotes himself to writing and lecturing. In 1982 Rodriguez published *Hunger of Memory,* a widely discussed book of autobiographical essays. His *Mexico's Children* (1991) is a study of Mexicans in America, and *Days of Obligation: An Argument with My Mexican Father* (1992) is a memoir. His latest book is *Brown* (2002), in which he explores color and race in American society. Rodriguez's essays have appeared in *The American Scholar, Change,* and many other magazines. His on-air essays for PBS's *NewsHour with Jim Lehrer* won him the George Foster Peabody Award in 1997. Rodriguez is currently an editor at Pacific News Service and a contributing editor for *US News & World Report, Harper's,* and the *Los Angeles Times.*

Aria: A Memoir of a Bilingual Childhood

"Aria: A Memoir of a Bilingual Childhood" is taken from *Hunger of Memory.* First published in *The American Scholar* in 1981, this poignant memoir sets forth the author's views of bilingual education. To the child Rodriguez, Spanish was a private language, English a public one. The boy would not have learned faster and better if his teachers had allowed him the use of his native language in school. Since Rodriguez wrote this essay, bilingual education has remained controversial, and in recent years it has lost ground. The No Child Left Behind Act of 2001 eliminated requirements that schools give English-language learners access to their first languages and emphasized students' accountability for learning and testing in English.

Rodriguez uses four main methods of development to serve a fifth, argument. The argument is pervasive but most explicit in the paragraphs listed below.

Narration (Chap. 4): paragraphs 1–3, 5–9, 13, 16–18, 21, 23–37
Description (Chap. 5): paragraphs 7–11, 13, 16–18, 21, 23–29
Comparison and contrast (Chap. 7): paragraphs 10–11, 14, 22, 29–30, 33–35, 38–40
Cause and effect (Chap. 11): paragraphs 12, 15, 18–20, 28–32, 36, 38–40
Argument and persuasion (Chap. 13): paragraphs 4, 19–20, 38–39

I remember, to start with, that day in Sacramento, in a California now 1
nearly thirty years past, when I first entered a classroom—able to understand
about fifty stray English words. The third of four children, I had been preceded
by my older brother and sister to a neighborhood Roman Catholic school. But

neither of them had revealed very much about their classroom experiences. They left each morning and returned each afternoon, always together, speaking Spanish as they climbed the five steps to the porch. And their mysterious books, wrapped in brown shopping-bag paper, remained on the table next to the door, closed firmly behind them.

An accident of geography sent me to a school where all my classmates were white and many were the children of doctors and lawyers and business executives. On that first day of school, my classmates must certainly have been uneasy to find themselves apart from their families, in the first institution of their lives. But I was astonished. I was fated to be the "problem student" in class. 2

The nun said, in a friendly but oddly impersonal voice: "Boys and girls, this is Richard Rodriguez." (I heard her sound it out: *Rich-heard Road-ree-guess*.) It was the first time I had heard anyone say my name in English. "Richard," the nun repeated more slowly, writing my name down in her book. Quickly I turned to see my mother's face dissolve in a watery blur behind the pebbled-glass door. 3

Now, many years later, I hear of something called "bilingual education"— a scheme proposed in the late 1960s by Hispanic-American social activists, later endorsed by a congressional vote. It is a program that seeks to permit non–English-speaking children (many from lower-class homes) to use their "family language" as the language of school. Such, at least, is the aim its supporters announce. I hear them, and am forced to say no: It is not possible for a child, any child, ever to use his family's language in school. Not to understand this is to misunderstand the public uses of schooling and to trivialize the nature of intimate life. 4

Memory teaches me what I know of these matters. The boy reminds the adult. I was a bilingual child, but of a certain kind: "socially disadvantaged," the son of working-class parents, both Mexican immigrants. 5

In the early years of my boyhood, my parents coped very well in America. My father had steady work. My mother managed at home. They were nobody's victims. When we moved to a house many blocks from the Mexican-American section of town, they were not intimidated by those two or three neighbors who initially tried to make us unwelcome. ("Keep your brats away from my sidewalk!") But despite all they achieved, or perhaps because they had so much to achieve, they lacked any deep feeling of ease, of belonging in public. They regarded the people at work or in crowds as being very distant from us. Those were the others, *los gringos*. That term was interchangeable in their speech with another, even more telling: *los americanos*. 6

I grew up in a house where the only regular guests were my relations. On a   7
certain day, enormous families of relatives would visit us, and there would be
so many people that the noise and the bodies would spill out to the backyard
and onto the front porch. Then for weeks no one would come. (If the doorbell
rang, it was usually a salesman.) Our house stood apart—gaudy yellow in a
row of white bungalows. We were the people with the noisy dog, the people
who raised chickens. We were the foreigners on the block. A few neighbors
would smile and wave at us. We waved back. But until I was seven years old, I
did not know the name of the old couple living next door or the names of the
kids living across the street.

In public, my father and mother spoke a hesitant, accented, and not al-   8
ways grammatical English. And then they would have to strain, their bodies
tense, to catch the sense of what was rapidly said by *los gringos*. At home, they
returned to Spanish. The language of their Mexican past sounded in counterpoint to the English spoken in public. The words would come quickly, with
ease. Conveyed through those sounds was the pleasing, soothing, consoling
reminder that one was at home.

During those years when I was first learning to speak, my mother and   9
father addressed me only in Spanish; in Spanish I learned to reply. By contrast, English (*inglés*) was the language I came to associate with gringos, rarely
heard in the house. I learned my first words of English overhearing my parents
speaking to strangers. At six years of age, I knew just enough words for my
mother to trust me on errands to stores one block away—but no more.

I was then a listening child, careful to hear the very different sounds of   10
Spanish and English. Wide-eyed with hearing, I'd listen to sounds more than
to words. First, there were English (gringo) sounds. So many words still were
unknown to me that when the butcher or the lady at the drugstore said something, exotic polysyllabic sounds would bloom in the midst of their sentences.
Often the speech of people in public seemed to me very loud, booming with
confidence. The man behind the counter would literally ask, "What can I do
for you?" But by being so firm and clear, the sound of his voice said that he was
a gringo; he belonged in public society. There were also the high, nasal notes
of middle-class American speech—which I rarely am conscious of hearing
today because I hear them so often, but could not stop hearing when I was a
boy. Crowds at Safeway or at bus stops were noisy with the birdlike sounds of
los gringos. I'd move away from them all—all the chirping chatter above me.

My own sounds I was unable to hear, but I knew that I spoke English   11
poorly. My words could not extend to form complete thoughts. And the words
I did speak I didn't know well enough to make distinct sounds. (Listeners
would usually lower their heads to hear better what I was trying to say.) But

it was one thing for *me* to speak English with difficulty; it was more troubling to hear my parents speaking in public: their high-whining vowels and guttural consonants; their sentences that got stuck with "eh" and "ah" sounds; the confused syntax; the hesitant rhythm of sounds so different from the way gringos spoke. I'd notice, moreover, that my parents' voices were softer than those of gringos we would meet.

I am tempted to say now that none of this mattered. (In adulthood I am embarrassed by childhood fears.) And, in a way, it didn't matter very much that my parents could not speak English with ease. Their linguistic difficulties had no serious consequences. My mother and father made themselves understood at the county hospital clinic and at government offices. And yet, in another way, it mattered very much. It was unsettling to hear my parents struggle with English. Hearing them, I'd grow nervous, and my clutching trust in their protection and power would be weakened. 12

There were many times like the night at a brightly lit gasoline station (a blaring white memory) when I stood uneasily hearing my father talk to a teenage attendant. I do not recall what they were saying, but I cannot forget the sounds my father made as he spoke. At one point his words slid together to form one long word—sounds as confused as the threads of blue and green oil in the puddle next to my shoes. His voice rushed through what he had left to say. Toward the end, he reached falsetto notes, appealing to his listener's understanding. I looked away at the lights of passing automobiles. I tried not to hear any more. But I heard only too well the attendant's reply, his calm, easy tones. Shortly afterward, headed for home, I shivered when my father put his hand on my shoulder. The very first chance that I got, I evaded his grasp and ran on ahead into the dark, skipping with feigned boyish exuberance. 13

But then there was Spanish: *español,* the language rarely heard away from the house; *español,* the language which seemed to me therefore a private language, my family's language. To hear its sounds was to feel myself specially recognized as one of the family, apart from *los otros.* A simple remark, an inconsequential comment could convey that assurance. My parents would say something to me and I would feel embraced by the sounds of their words. Those sounds said: *I am speaking with ease in Spanish. I am addressing you in words I never use with los gringos. I recognize you as someone special, close, like no one outside. You belong with us. In the family. Ricardo.* 14

At the age of six, well past the time when most middle-class children no longer notice the difference between sounds uttered at home and words spoken in public, I had a different experience. I lived in a world compounded of sounds. I was a child longer than most. I lived in a magical world, surrounded by sounds both pleasing and fearful. I shared with my family a language enchantingly private—different from that used in the city around us. 15

Just opening or closing the screen door behind me was an important expe-   16
rience. I'd rarely leave home all alone or without feeling reluctance. Walking
down the sidewalk, under the canopy of tall trees, I'd warily notice the (suddenly) silent neighborhood kids who stood warily watching me. Nervously, I'd
arrive at the grocery store to hear there the sounds of the gringo, reminding
me that in this so-big world I was a foreigner. But if leaving home was never
routine, neither was coming back. Walking toward our house, climbing the
steps from the sidewalk, in summer when the front door was open, I'd hear
voices beyond the screen door talking in Spanish. For a second or two I'd
stay, linger there listening. Smiling, I'd hear my mother call out, saying in
Spanish, "Is that you, Richard?" Those were her words, but all the while her
sounds would assure me: *You are home now. Come close inside. With us.* "*Sí,*"
I'd reply.

Once more inside the house, I would resume my place in the family. The   17
sounds would grow harder to hear. Once more at home, I would grow less conscious of them. It required, however, no more than the blurt of the doorbell
to alert me all over again to listen to sounds. The house would turn instantly
quiet while my mother went to the door. I'd hear her hard English sounds.
I'd wait to hear her voice turn to soft-sounding Spanish, which assured me,
as surely as did the clicking tongue of the lock on the door, that the stranger
was gone.

Plainly it is not healthy to hear such sounds so often. It is not healthy   18
to distinguish public from private sounds so easily. I remained cloistered by
sounds, timid and shy in public, too dependent on the voices at home. I
remember many nights when my father would come back from work, and I'd
hear him call out to my mother in Spanish, sounding relieved. In Spanish,
his voice would sound the light and free notes that he never could manage
in English. Some nights I'd jump up just hearing his voice. My brother and
I would come running into the room where he was with our mother. Our
laughing (so deep was the pleasure!) became screaming. Like others who feel
the pain of public alienation, we transformed the knowledge of our public
separateness into a consoling reminder of our intimacy. Excited, our voices
joined in a celebration of sounds. *We are speaking now the way we never speak
out in public—we are together,* the sounds told me. Some nights no one seemed
willing to loosen the hold that sounds had on us. At dinner we invented new
words that sounded Spanish, but made sense only to us. We pieced together
new words by taking, say, an English verb and giving it Spanish endings. My
mother's instructions at bedtime would be lacquered with mock-urgent tones.
Or a word like *sí,* sounded in several notes, would convey added measures of
feeling. Tongues lingered around the edges of words, especially fat vowels, and
we happily sounded that military drum roll, the twirling roar of the Spanish *r.*

Family language, my family's sounds: the voices of my parents and sisters and brother. Their voices insisting: *You belong here. We are family members. Related. Special to one another. Listen!* Voices singing and sighing, rising and straining, then surging, teeming with pleasure which burst syllables into fragments of laughter. At times it seemed there was steady quiet only when, from another room, the rustling whispers of my parents faded and I edged closer to sleep.

Supporters of bilingual education imply today that students like me miss a great deal by not being taught in their family's language. What they seem not to recognize is that, as a socially disadvantaged child, I regarded Spanish as a private language. It was a ghetto language that deepened and strengthened my feeling of separateness. What I needed to learn in school was that I had the right, and the obligation, to speak the public language. The odd truth is that my first-grade classmates could have become bilingual, in the conventional sense of the word, more easily than I. Had they been taught early (as upper-middle-class children often are taught) a "second language" like Spanish or French, they could have regarded it simply as another public language. In my case, such bilingualism could not have been so quickly achieved. What I did not believe was that I could speak a single public language. **19**

Without question, it would have pleased me to have heard my teachers address me in Spanish when I entered the classroom. I would have felt much less afraid. I would have imagined that my instructors were somehow "related" to me; I would indeed have heard their Spanish as my family's language. I would have trusted them and responded with ease. But I would have delayed—postponed for how long?—having to learn the language of public society. I would have evaded—and for how long?—learning the great lesson of school: that I had a public identity. **20**

Fortunately, my teachers were unsentimental about their responsibility. What they understood was that I needed to speak public English. So their voices would search me out, asking me questions. Each time I heard them I'd look up in surprise to see a nun's face frowning at me. I'd mumble, not really meaning to answer. The nun would persist. "Richard, stand up. Don't look at the floor. Speak up. Speak to the entire class, not just to me!" But I couldn't believe English could be my language to use. (In part, I did not want to believe it.) I continued to mumble. I resisted the teacher's demands. (Did I somehow suspect that once I learned this public language my family life would be changed?) Silent, waiting for the bell to sound, I remained dazed, diffident, afraid. **21**

Because I wrongly imagined that English was intrinsically a public language and Spanish was intrinsically private, I easily noted the difference between classroom language and the language at home. At school, words were directed **22** to a general audience of listeners. ("Boys and girls . . .") Words were meaningfully ordered. And the point was not self-expression alone, but to make oneself understood by many others. The teacher quizzed: "Boys and girls, why do we use that word in this sentence? Could we think of a better word to use there? Would the sentence change its meaning if the words were differently arranged? Isn't there a better way of saying much the same thing?" (I couldn't say. I wouldn't try to say.)

Three months passed. Five. A half year. Unsmiling, ever watchful, my   23
teachers noted my silence. They began to connect my behavior with the slow progress my brother and sisters were making. Until, one Saturday morning, three nuns arrived at the house to talk to our parents. Stiffly they sat on the blue living-room sofa. From the doorway of another room, spying on the visitors, I noted the incongruity, the clash of two worlds, the faces and voices of school intruding upon the familiar setting of home. I overheard one voice gently wondering, "Do your children speak only Spanish at home, Mrs. Rodriguez?" While another voice added, "That Richard especially seems so timid and shy."

That Rich-heard!   24

With great tact, the visitors continued, "Is it possible for you and your   25
husband to encourage your children to practice their English when they are home?" Of course my parents complied. What would they not do for their children's well-being? And how could they question the Church's authority which those women represented? In an instant they agreed to give up the language (the sounds) which had revealed and accentuated our family's closeness. The moment after the visitors left, the change was observed. "*Ahora,* speak to us only *en inglés,*" my father and mother told us.

At first, it seemed a kind of game. After dinner each night, the family   26
gathered together to practice "our" English. It was still then *inglés,* a language foreign to us, so we felt drawn to it as strangers. Laughing, we would try to define words we could not pronounce. We played with strange English sounds, often overanglicizing our pronunciations. And we filled the smiling gaps of our sentences with familiar Spanish sounds. But that was cheating, somebody shouted, and everyone laughed.

In school, meanwhile, like my brother and sisters, I was required to attend   27
a daily tutoring session. I needed a full year of this special work. I also needed my teachers to keep my attention from straying in class by calling out, *"Rich-heard"* — their English voices slowly loosening the ties to my other name, with its three notes, *Ri-car-do.* Most of all, I needed to hear my mother and father speak to me in a moment of seriousness in "broken" — suddenly heartbreaking — English. This scene was inevitable. One Saturday morning I entered

the kitchen where my parents were talking, but I did not realize that they were talking in Spanish until, the moment they saw me, their voices changed and they began speaking English. The gringo sounds they uttered startled me. Pushed me away. In that moment of trivial misunderstanding and profound insight, I felt my throat twisted by unsounded grief. I simply turned and left the room. But I had no place to escape to where I could grieve in Spanish. My brother and sisters were speaking English in another part of the house.

Again and again in the days following, as I grew increasingly angry, I was obliged to hear my mother and father encouraging me: "Speak to us *en inglés.*" Only then did I determine to learn classroom English. Thus, sometime afterward it happened: One day in school, I raised my hand to volunteer an answer to a question. I spoke out in a loud voice and I did not think it remarkable when the entire class understood. That day I moved very far from being the disadvantaged child I had been only days earlier. Taken hold at last was the belief, the calming assurance, that I *belonged* in public.   28

Shortly after, I stopped hearing the high, troubling sounds of *los gringos.* A more and more confident speaker of English, I didn't listen to how strangers sounded when they talked to me. With so many English-speaking people around me, I no longer heard American accents. Conversations quickened. Listening to persons whose voices sounded eccentrically pitched, I might note their sounds for a few seconds, but then I'd concentrate on what they were saying. Now when I heard someone's tone of voice—angry or questioning or sarcastic or happy or sad—I didn't distinguish it from the words it expressed. Sound and word were thus tightly wedded. At the end of each day I was often bemused, and always relieved, to realize how "soundless," though crowded with words, my day in public had been. An eight-year-old boy, I finally came to accept what had been technically true since my birth: I was an American citizen.   29

But diminished by then was the special feeling of closeness at home. Gone was the desperate, urgent, intense feeling of being at home among those with whom I felt intimate. Our family remained a loving family, but one greatly changed. We were no longer so close, no longer bound tightly together by the knowledge of our separateness from *los gringos.* Neither my older brother nor my sisters rushed home after school anymore. Nor did I. When I arrived home, often there would be neighborhood kids in the house. Or the house would be empty of sounds.   30

Following the dramatic Americanization of their children, even my parents grew more publicly confident—especially my mother. First she learned the names of all the people on the block. Then she decided we needed to have a telephone in our house. My father, for his part, continued to use the word *gringo,* but it was no longer charged with bitterness or distrust. Stripped of   31 any emotional content, the word simply became a name for those Americans not of Hispanic descent. Hearing him, sometimes, I wasn't sure if he was pronouncing the Spanish word *gringo,* or saying gringo in English.

There was a new silence at home. As we children learned more and more   32
English, we shared fewer and fewer words with our parents. Sentences needed to be spoken slowly when one of us addressed our mother or father. Often the parent wouldn't understand. The child would need to repeat himself. Still the parent misunderstood. The young voice, frustrated, would end up saying, "Never mind" — the subject was closed. Dinners would be noisy with the clinking of knives and forks against dishes. My mother would smile softly between her remarks; my father, at the other end of the table, would chew and chew his food while he stared over the heads of his children.

My mother! My father! After English became my primary language, I no   33
longer knew what words to use in addressing my parents. The old Spanish words (those tender accents of sound) I had earlier used — *mamá* and *papá* — I couldn't use anymore. They would have been all-too-painful reminders of how much had changed in my life. On the other hand, the words I heard neighborhood kids call their parents seemed equally unsatisfactory. "Mother" and "father," "ma," "pa," "dad," "pop" (how I hated the all-American sound of that last word) — all these I felt were unsuitable terms of address for *my* parents. As a result, I never used them at home. Whenever I'd speak to my parents, I would try to get their attention by looking at them. In public conversations, I'd refer to them as my "parents" or my "mother" and "father."

My mother and father, for their part, responded differently, as their chil-   34
dren spoke to them less. My mother grew restless, seemed troubled and anxious at the scarceness of words exchanged in the house. She would question me about my day when I came home from school. She smiled at my small talk. She pried at the edges of my sentences to get me to say something more. ("What . . . ?") She'd join conversations she overheard, but her intrusions often stopped her children's talking. By contrast, my father seemed to grow reconciled to the new quiet. Though his English somewhat improved, he tended more and more to retire into silence. At dinner he spoke very little. One night his children and even his wife helplessly giggled at his garbled English pronunciation of the Catholic "Grace Before Meals." Thereafter he made his wife recite the prayer at the start of each meal, even on formal occasions when there were guests in the house.

Hers became the public voice of the family. On official business it was she,   35
not my father, who would usually talk to strangers on the phone or in stores. We children grew so accustomed to his silence that years later we would routinely refer to his "shyness." (My mother often tried to explain: Both of his parents died when he was eight. He was raised by an uncle who treated

him as little more than a menial servant. He was never encouraged to speak. He grew up alone—a man of few words.) But I realized my father was not shy whenever I'd watch him speaking Spanish with relatives. Using Spanish, he was quickly effusive. Especially when talking with other men, his voice would spark, flicker, flare alive with varied sounds. In Spanish he expressed ideas and feelings he rarely revealed when speaking English. With firm Spanish sounds he conveyed a confidence and authority that English would never allow him.

The silence at home, however, was not simply the result of fewer words 36 passing between parents and children. More profound for me was the silence created by my inattention to sounds. At about the time I no longer bothered to listen with care to the sounds of English in public, I grew careless about listening to the sounds made by the family when they spoke. Most of the time I would hear someone speaking at home and didn't distinguish his sounds from the words people uttered in public. I didn't even pay much attention to my parents' accented and ungrammatical speech—at least not at home. Only when I was with them in public would I become alert to their accents. But even then their sounds caused me less and less concern. For I was growing increasingly confident of my own public identity.

I would have been happier about my public success had I not recalled, 37 sometimes, what it had been like earlier, when my family conveyed its intimacy through a set of conveniently private sounds. Sometimes in public, hearing a stranger, I'd hark back to my lost past. A Mexican farm worker approached me one day downtown. He wanted directions to some place. "*Hijito*, . . ." he said. And his voice stirred old longings. Another time I was standing beside my mother in the visiting room of a Carmelite convent, before the dense screen which rendered the nuns shadowy figures. I heard several of them speaking Spanish in their busy, singsong, overlapping voices, assuring my mother that, yes, yes, we were remembered, all our family was remembered, in their prayers. Those voices echoed faraway family sounds. Another day a dark-faced old woman touched my shoulder lightly to steady herself as she boarded a bus. She murmured something to me I couldn't quite comprehend. Her Spanish voice came near, like the face of a never-before-seen relative in the instant before I was kissed. That voice, like so many of the Spanish voices I'd hear in public, recalled the golden age of my childhood.

Bilingual educators say today that children lose a degree of "individuality" 38 by becoming assimilated into public society. (Bilingual schooling is a program popularized in the seventies, that decade when middle-class "ethnics" began to resist the process of assimilation—the "American melting pot.") But the bilingualists oversimplify when they scorn the value and necessity of assimilation. They do not seem to realize that a person is individualized in two ways. So they do not realize that, while one suffers a diminished sense of *private* individuality by being assimilated into public society, such assimilation makes possible the achievement of *public* individuality.

Simplistically again, the bilingualists insist that a student should be re-   39
minded of his difference from others in mass society, of his "heritage." But they equate mere separateness with individuality. The fact is that only in private — with intimates — is separateness from the crowd a prerequisite for individuality; an intimate "tells" me that I am unique, unlike all others, apart from the crowd. In public, by contrast, full individuality is achieved, paradoxically, by those who are able to consider themselves members of the crowd. Thus it happened for me. Only when I was able to think of myself as an American, no longer an alien in gringo society, could I seek the rights and opportunities necessary for full public individuality. The social and political advantages I enjoy as a man began on the day I came to believe that my name is indeed *Rich-heard Road-ree-guess*. It is true that my public society today is often impersonal; in fact, my public society is usually mass society. But despite the anonymity of the crowd, and despite the fact that the individuality I achieve in public is often tenuous — because it depends on my being one in a crowd — I celebrate the day I acquired my new name. Those middle-class ethnics who scorn assimilation seem to me filled with decadent self-pity, obsessed by the burden of public life. Dangerously, they romanticize public separateness and trivialize the dilemma of those who are truly socially disadvantaged.

If I rehearse here the changes in my private life after my Americanization,   40
it is finally to emphasize a public gain. The loss implies the gain. The house I returned to each afternoon was quiet. Intimate sounds no longer greeted me at the door. Inside there were other noises. The telephone rang. Neighborhood kids ran past the door of the bedroom where I was reading my schoolbooks — covered with brown shopping-bag paper. Once I learned the public language, it would never again be easy for me to hear intimate family voices. More and more of my day was spent hearing words, not sounds. But that may only be a way of saying that on the day I raised my hand in class and spoke loudly to an entire roomful of faces, my childhood started to end.

*For a reading quiz, sources on Richard Rodriguez, and annotated links to further readings on bilingual education, visit **bedfordstmartins.com/thebedfordreader**.*

Journal Writing

Rodriguez remembers thinking as a child, "We are speaking now the way we never speak out in public—we are together" (par. 18). In your journal, write about any aspect of language spoken by you and your family when you were a child—language different from what you heard in public. Perhaps, like Rodriguez's family, your family spoke a language other than the dominant one in the larger culture. Or perhaps your private language consisted of a special vocabulary, inside jokes, ALLUSIONS, particular tones of voice, or other differences. (To take your journal writing further, see "From Journal to Essay" on the next page.)

Questions on Meaning

1. Rodriguez's essay is both memoir and ARGUMENT. What is the thrust of the author's argument?
2. How did the child Rodriguez react when, in his presence, his parents had to struggle to make themselves understood by *"los gringos"*?
3. What does the author mean when he says, "I was a child longer than most" (par. 15)?
4. According to the author, what impact did the Rodriguez children's use of English have on relationships within the family?
5. Contrast the child Rodriguez's view of the nuns who insisted he speak English with his adult view.

Questions on Writing Strategy

1. How effective an INTRODUCTION is Rodriguez's first paragraph?
2. Several times in his essay Rodriguez shifts from memoir to argument and back again. What is the overall EFFECT of these shifts? Do they strengthen or weaken the author's stance against bilingual education?
3. Twice in his essay (in pars. 1 and 40) the author mentions schoolbooks wrapped in shopping-bag paper. How does the use of this detail enhance his argument?
4. What AUDIENCE probably would not like this essay? Why would they not like it?
5. **MIXED METHODS**   Examine how Rodriguez uses DESCRIPTION to COMPARE AND CONTRAST the sounds of Spanish and English (pars. 10, 11, 13, 14, 18, 33, 37). What sounds does he evoke? What are the differences among them?
6. **MIXED METHODS**   Rodriguez's essay is an argument supported mainly by personal NARRATIVE—Rodriguez's own experience. What kind of ETHICAL APPEAL (p. 551) does the narrative make? What can we INFER about Rodriguez's personality, intellect, fairness, and trustworthiness?

Questions on Language

1. Consult the dictionary if you need help defining these words: counterpoint (par. 8); polysyllabic (10); guttural, syntax (11); falsetto, exuberance (13); incon-

sequential (14); cloistered, lacquered (18); diffident (21); intrinsically (22); incongruity (23); bemused (29); effusive (35); assimilated (38); paradoxically, tenuous, decadent (39).

2. In Rodriguez's essay, how do the words *public* and *private* relate to the issue of bilingual education? What important distinction does the author make between *individuality* and *separateness* (par. 39)?

3. What exactly does the author mean when he says, "More and more of my day was spent hearing words, not sounds" (par. 40)?

Suggestions for Writing

1. **FROM JOURNAL TO ESSAY**   Expanding on your journal entry, write an essay DEFINING the distinctive quality of the language spoken in your home when you were a child. What effect, if any, did this language have on you when you went out into public? Does it influence your memories of childhood? Do you revert to this private language when you are with your family?

2. Bilingual education is a controversial issue with EVIDENCE and strong feelings on both sides. In a page or so of preliminary writing, respond to Rodriguez's essay with your own gut feelings on the issue. Then do some library research to extend, support, or refute your views. In a well-reasoned and well-supported essay, give your opinion on whether or not public schools should teach children in their "family language."

3. **CRITICAL WRITING**   In his argument against bilingual education, Rodriguez offers no data from studies, no testimony from education experts, indeed no evidence at all except his personal experience. In an essay, ANALYZE and EVALUATE this evidence: How convincing do you find it? Is it adequate to support the argument? (In your essay consider Rodriguez's ethical appeal, the topic of the sixth question on writing strategy.)

4. **CONNECTIONS**   Jay Nordlinger, in "Bassackwards: Construction Spanish and Other Signs of the Times" (p. 610), also writes about language education, and like Rodriguez he believes that Spanish speakers in the United States should learn English for public interactions. But while Rodriguez examines grade-school education from his experience as a Spanish-speaking child, Nordlinger focuses on continuing education from the perspective of an English-speaking adult. Imagine a conversation between Rodriguez and Nordlinger. On what points would they agree, and where might they disagree? In an essay, COMPARE their arguments for assimilation, considering how each writer's point of view affects his position on the issue.

5. **CONNECTIONS**   In "Arm Wrestling with My Father" (p. 163), Brad Manning writes about the effect of his father's silence on his growth into adulthood. In an essay, compare and contrast the experiences of Rodriguez and Manning, focusing on the two writers' views of how communication (whether verbal or nonverbal) fuels both intimacy and distance within families.

Richard Rodriguez on Writing

For *The Bedford Reader,* Richard Rodriguez described the writing of "Aria."

From grammar school to college, my teachers offered perennial encouragement: "Write about what you know." Every year I would respond with the student's complaint: "I have nothing to write about . . . I haven't done anything." (Writers, real writers, I thought, lived in New York or Paris; they smoked on the back jackets of library books, their chores done.)

Stories die for not being told. My story got told because I had received an education; my teachers had given me the skill of stringing words together in a coherent line. But it was not until I was a man that I felt any need to write my story. A few years ago I left graduate school, quit teaching for political reasons (to protest affirmative action). But after leaving the classroom, as the months passed, I grew desperate to talk to serious people about serious things. In the great journals of the world, I noticed, there was conversation of a sort, glamorous company of a sort, and I determined to join it. I began writing to stay alive—not as a job, but to stay alive.

Even as you see my essay now, in cool printer's type, I look at some pages and cannot remember having written them. Or else I can remember earlier versions—unused incident, character, description (rooms, faces)—crumbled and discarded. Flung from possibility. They hit the wastebasket, those pages, and yet, defying gravity with a scratchy, starchy resilience, tried to reopen themselves. Then they fell silent. I read certain other sentences now and they recall the very day they were composed—the afternoon of rain or the telephone call that was to come a few moments after, the house, the room where these sentences were composed, the pattern of the rug, the wastebasket. (In all there were about thirty or forty versions that preceded this final "Aria.") I tried to describe my experiences exactly, at once to discover myself and to reveal myself. Always I had to write against the fear I felt that no one would be able to understand what I was saying.

As a reader, I have been struck by the way those novels and essays that are most particular, most particularly about one other life and time (Hannibal, Missouri; one summer; a slave; the loveliness of a muddy river) most fully achieve universality and call to be cherished. It is a paradox apparently: The more a writer unearths the detail that makes a life singular, the more a reader is led to feel a kind of sharing. Perhaps the reason we are able to respond to the life that is so different is because we all, each of us, think privately that we are different from one another. And the more closely we examine another life in its misery or wisdom or foolishness, the more it seems we take some version of ourselves.

It is, in any case, finally you that I end up having to trust not to laugh, not to snicker. Even as you regard me in these lines, I try to imagine your face as you read. You who read "Aria," especially those of you with your theme-divining yellow felt pen poised in your hand, you for whom this essay is yet another assignment, please do not forget that it is my life I am handing you in these pages — memories that are as personal for me as family photographs in an old cigar box.

For Discussion

1. What seems to be Rodriguez's attitude toward his AUDIENCE when he writes? Do you think he writes chiefly for his readers, or for himself? Defend your answer.
2. Rodriguez tells us what he said when, as a student, he was told, "Write about what you know." What do you think he would say now?

EDWARD SAID

Edward Said was born in Jerusalem in 1935 and educated at Victoria College in Cairo, Egypt. As a boy he attended boarding school in Massachusetts, and then he went to Princeton and Harvard universities, taking a PhD from Harvard in 1964. Until his death in 2003, Said was professor of English and comparative literature at Columbia University. He wrote much literary criticism during his life, but his fame and notoriety came from his political writing. His book *Orientalism* (1978) was nominated for the National Book Critics Circle Award, translated into thirty-six languages, and acclaimed for its unblinkered view of the ideology and racism behind Western attitudes toward Islam. But that work and others also brought Said virulent attacks in print, occasional death threats, and, for his support of the Palestinian cause, the label "professor of terror." In his lifetime Said received many awards, including the Picasso Medal (1994), the Spinoza Prize (1999), and the Lannan Foundation Lifetime Achievement Award (2001). His memoir, *Out of Place* (1999), received *The New Yorker*'s award for nonfiction. An accomplished pianist, Said also wrote frequently on music and was music critic for *The Nation*.

Clashing Civilizations?

Just after the terrorist attacks of September 11, 2001, Said published an essay, "We All Swim Together," in *New Statesman*. This excerpt from the essay takes strong issue with the view that the West and Islam are definable, inevitably opposed "civilizations." To Said, such concepts are not only misleading but also dangerous.

Said's essay is overall an argument against a certain comparison, classification, and definition, developed by other methods as well:

Narration (Chap. 4): paragraphs 1, 6
Example (Chap. 6): paragraphs 3, 4, 6
Comparison and contrast (Chap. 7): paragraphs 2–4, 6–7
Division or analysis (Chap. 9): paragraphs 2–7
Classification (Chap. 10): paragraphs 1–3, 6–7
Cause and effect (Chap. 11): paragraphs 1, 3–7
Definition (Chap. 12): paragraphs 5–7
Argument and persuasion (Chap. 13): throughout

Samuel Huntington's article "The Clash of Civilizations?" appeared in the summer 1993 issue of *Foreign Affairs*, where it immediately attracted a surprising amount of attention and reaction. Because the article was intended to supply Americans with an original thesis about "a new phase" in world politics after the end of the Cold War, Huntington's terms of argument

1

seemed compellingly large, bold, even visionary. "It is my hypothesis," he wrote,

> that . . . the great divisions among humankind and the dominating source of conflict will be cultural. Nation-states will remain the most powerful actors in world affairs, but the principal conflicts of global politics will occur between nations and groups of different civilizations. The clash of civilizations will dominate global politics. The fault lines between civilizations will be the battle lines of the future.

Most of the argument in the pages that followed relied on a vague notion of something Huntington called "civilization identity" and "the interactions among seven or eight [sic] major civilizations," of which the conflict between two of them, Islam and the West, gets the lion's share of his attention. In this belligerent kind of thought, he relies heavily on a 1990 article by the veteran orientalist Bernard Lewis, whose ideological colors are manifest in its title, "The Roots of Muslim Rage." In both articles, the personification of enormous entities called "the West" and "Islam" is recklessly affirmed, as if hugely complicated matters such as identity and culture existed in a cartoonlike world where Popeye and Bluto bash each other mercilessly, with one always more virtuous pugilist getting the upper hand over his adversary. Certainly neither Huntington nor Lewis has much time to spare for the internal dynamics and plurality of every civilization; or for considering that the major contest in most modern cultures concerns the definition or interpretation of each culture; or for the unattractive possibility that a great deal of demagogy and downright ignorance is involved in presuming to speak for a whole religion or civilization. No, the West is the West, and Islam is Islam.

The basic model of west versus the rest (the Cold War opposition reformulated) is what has persisted, often insidiously and implicitly, in discussion since the terrible events of September 11. The carefully planned and horrendous, pathologically motivated suicide attack and mass slaughter by a small group of deranged militants has been turned into proof of Huntington's thesis. Instead of seeing it for what it is—the capture of big ideas (I use the word loosely) by a tiny band of crazed fanatics for criminal purposes—international luminaries from the former Pakistani prime minister Benazir Bhutto to the Italian prime minister, Silvio Berlusconi, have pontificated about Islam's troubles and, in the latter's case, have used Huntington's ideas to rant on about the West's superiority, how "we" have Mozart and Michelangelo and they don't.

But why not instead see parallels, admittedly less spectacular in their destructiveness, to Osama Bin Laden and his followers in such cults as the Branch Davidians, or the disciples of the Reverend Jim Jones in Guyana, or the Japanese Aum Shinrikyo? Even *The Economist*, in its issue of September

22–28, 2001, couldn't resist reaching for the vast generalization, praising Huntington extravagantly for his "cruel and sweeping, but nonetheless acute" observations about Islam. "Today," the journal says, Huntington writes that "the world's billion or so Muslims are 'convinced of the superiority of their culture, and obsessed with the inferiority of their power.'" Did he canvass one hundred Indonesians, two hundred Moroccans, five hundred Egyptians and fifty Bosnians? Even if he did, what sort of sample is that?

Uncountable are the editorials in every American and European news-   5
paper and magazine of note adding to this vocabulary of gigantism and apoc-
alypse, each use of which is plainly designed to inflame the reader's indignant passion as a member of the "West," and what we need to do. Churchillian rhetoric[1] is used inappropriately by self-appointed combatants in the West's, and especially America's, war against its haters, despoilers, destroyers, with scant attention to complex histories that defy such reductiveness and have seeped from one territory into another, overriding the boundaries that are supposed to separate us all into divided armed camps.

This is the problem with unedifying labels such as *Islam* and *the West*:   6
They mislead and confuse the mind, which is trying to make sense of a disor-
derly reality that won't be pigeonholed. I remember interrupting a man who, after a lecture I had given at a West Bank[2] university in 1994, rose from the audience and started to attack my ideas as "Western," as opposed to the strict Islamic ones he espoused. "Why are you wearing a suit and tie?" was the first retort that came to mind. "They're Western, too." He sat down with an embarrassed smile on his face, but I recalled the incident when information on the September 11 terrorists started to come in: how they had mastered all the technical details required to inflict their homicidal evil on the World Trade Center, the Pentagon and the aircraft they had commandeered. Where does one draw the line between "Western" technology and, as Berlusconi declared, "Islam's" inability to be a part of "modernity"?

One cannot easily do so. How finally inadequate are the labels, general-   7
izations and cultural assertions. At some level, for instance, primitive passions and sophisticated know-how converge in ways that give the lie to a fortified boundary not only between "West" and "Islam," but also between past and present, us and them, to say nothing of the very concepts of identity and nationality about which there is unending debate. A unilateral decision made to undertake crusades, to oppose their evil with our good, to extirpate terror-

---

[1] A statesman and gifted orator, Winston Churchill (1874–1965) was British prime minis-
ter during World War II, when his stirring speeches fortified his embattled nation's resolve to fight the Germans. —Eds.

[2] Disputed territory adjacent to Israel, controlled partly by Israel and partly by the Palestinian Authority. —Eds.

ism and, in Paul Wolfowitz's[3] nihilistic vocabulary, to end nations entirely, doesn't make the supposed entities any easier to see; rather, it speaks to how much simpler it is to make bellicose statements for the purpose of mobilizing collective passions than to reflect, examine, sort out what it is we are dealing with in reality, the interconnectedness of innumerable lives, "ours" as well as "theirs."

*For a reading quiz, sources on Edward Said, and annotated links to further readings on Western views of Islam, visit **bedfordstmartins.com/thebedfordreader**.*

Journal Writing

Write in your journal about the images of Islam that you see in the US media. Based on news reports and other media presentations, what view would an average American have of Islam? (To take your journal writing further, see "From Journal to Essay" on the next page.)

Questions on Meaning

1. SUMMARIZE the views to which Said responds. How were these views affected by the events of September 11, 2001?
2. Summarize Said's ARGUMENT in response to Huntington's and others' views on the West and Islam.
3. What is Said's point in paragraph 6?
4. What is Said's THESIS? Where does he state it?

Questions on Writing Strategy

1. What is Said's point in referring to Popeye and Bluto in paragraph 2?
2. Why does Said compare Osama Bin Laden and his followers to "such cults as the Branch Davidians, or the disciples of the Reverend Jim Jones in Guyana, or the Japanese Aum Shinrikyo" (par. 4)?
3. Look for places where Said puts words in quotation marks though not actually quoting anyone in particular. What do the quotation marks signify?
4. **MIXED METHODS**   What does Said use DIVISION or ANALYSIS for in paragraph 2? What PURPOSE does this paragraph serve in Said's argument?

---

[3]Deputy secretary of defense (2001–05) under President George W. Bush. —EDS.

5. **MIXED METHODS**   How does Said's EXAMPLE and NARRATION about the West Bank man who challenged him contribute to his point in paragraph 6?

Questions on Language

1. What words does Said use to characterize the attitude of those he is criticizing? What is the EFFECT of his language? How do you respond to it?
2. In quoting Huntington in paragraph 2, what does Said intend by the use of *sic* in brackets?
3. In paragraph 3 Said refers to the September 11 terrorist attack as "the capture of big ideas (I use the word loosely) by a tiny band of crazed fanatics for criminal purposes." What does he mean by the sentence in parentheses?
4. Consult a dictionary if you are unsure of the meaning of any of the following: visionary (par. 1); belligerent, personification, pugilist, plurality, demagogy (2); insidiously, luminaries, pontificated (3); gigantism, apocalypse, reductiveness (5); unedifying (6); unilateral, extirpate, nihilistic, bellicose, mobilizing (7).

Suggestions for Writing

1. **FROM JOURNAL TO ESSAY**   Based on your journal entry, write an essay in which you analyze images of Islam presented by the US media. (You may want to supplement your current knowledge with research among news magazines and television and radio news and talk shows.) EVALUATE the accuracy of these images.
2. Do you think that there is an inevitable "clash of civilizations" between Islam and the West? Write an essay in which you respond to the view of Samuel P. Huntington, Bernard Lewis, and others quoted by Said.
3. **CRITICAL WRITING**   Write an essay in which you analyze the TONE of Said's essay. Does the tone reinforce Said's argument? Is it effective? Why, or why not?
4. **CONNECTIONS**   Throughout his essay Said suggests that Western culture is not necessarily superior to Islamic culture, asking why we are reluctant to examine the less flattering parallels between the two. Write an essay in which you examine Fatema Mernissi's "Size 6: The Western Women's Harem" (p. 282) as a response to Said's implied challenge.
5. **CONNECTIONS**   Mark Krikorian, in "Safety through Immigration Control" (p. 593), writes about the threat of Islamic terrorism since September 11, 2001. In an essay bring Krikorian and Said face to face. What would Said have to say about Krikorian's assumptions? How might Krikorian respond?

JONATHAN SWIFT

Jonathan Swift (1667–1745), the son of English parents who had settled in Ireland, divided his energies among literature, politics, and the Church of England. Dissatisfied with the quiet life of an Anglican parish priest, Swift spent much of his time in London hobnobbing with writers and producing pamphlets in support of the Tory Party. In 1713 Queen Anne rewarded his political services with an assignment the London-loving Swift didn't want: to supervise St. Patrick's Cathedral in Dublin. There, as Dean Swift, he ended his days—beloved by the Irish, whose interests he defended against the English government. Although Swift's chief works include the remarkable satires *The Battle of the Books* and *A Tale of a Tub* (both 1704) and scores of fine poems, he is best remembered for *Gulliver's Travels* (1726), an account of four imaginary voyages. This classic is always abridged when it is given to children because of its frank descriptions of human filth and viciousness. In *Gulliver's Travels,* Swift pays tribute to the reasoning portion of "that animal called man," and delivers a stinging rebuke to the rest of him.

A Modest Proposal

Three consecutive years of drought and sparse crops had worked hardship upon the Irish when Swift wrote this ferocious essay in the summer of 1729. At the time, there were said to be thirty-five thousand wandering beggars in the country: Whole families had quit their farms and had taken to the roads. Large landowners, of English ancestry, preferred to ignore their tenants' sufferings and lived abroad to dodge taxes and payment of church duties. Swift had no special fondness for the Irish, but he hated the inhumanity he witnessed.

Although printed as a pamphlet in Dublin, Swift's essay is clearly meant for English readers as well as Irish ones. When circulated, the pamphlet caused a sensation in both Ireland and England and had to be reprinted seven times in the same year. Swift is an expert with plain, vigorous English prose, and "A Modest Proposal" is a masterpiece of SATIRE and IRONY. (If you are uncertain what Swift argues for, see the discussion of these devices in Useful Terms.)

"A Modest Proposal" is an argument developed chiefly by process analysis and cause and effect. These two methods mix with notable uses of description, example, and comparison and contrast.

Description (Chap. 5): paragraphs 1–2, 19
Example (Chap. 6): paragraphs 1–2, 6, 10, 14, 18, 32
Comparison and contrast (Chap. 7): paragraph 17
Process analysis (Chap. 8): paragraphs 4, 6–7, 10–17
Cause and effect (Chap. 11): paragraphs 4–5, 13, 21–29, 31, 33
Argument and persuasion (Chap. 13): throughout

For Preventing the Children of Poor People in Ireland
from Being a Burden to Their Parents or Country,
and for Making Them Beneficial to the Public

It is a melancholy object to those who walk through this great town[1] or   1
travel in the country, when they see the streets, the roads, and cabin doors,
crowded with beggars of the female sex, followed by three, four, or six children,
all in rags and importuning every passenger for an alms. These mothers, instead
of being able to work for their honest livelihood, are forced to employ all their
time in strolling to beg sustenance for their helpless infants, who, as they grow
up, either turn thieves for want of work, or leave their dear native country to
fight for the Pretender in Spain, or sell themselves to the Barbados.[2]

I think it is agreed by all parties that this prodigious number of children   2
in the arms, or on the backs, or at the heels of their mothers, and frequently
of their fathers, is in the present deplorable state of the kingdom a very great
additional grievance; and therefore whoever could find out a fair, cheap, and
easy method of making these children sound, useful members of the commonwealth would deserve so well of the public as to have his statue set up for a
preserver of the nation.

But my intention is very far from being confined to provide only for the   3
children of professed beggars; it is of a much greater extent, and shall take in
the whole number of infants at a certain age who are born of parents in effect
as little able to support them as those who demand our charity in the streets.

As to my own part, having turned my thoughts for many years upon this   4
important subject, and maturely weighed the several schemes of other projectors,[3] I have always found them grossly mistaken in their computation. It
is true, a child just dropped from its dam may be supported by her milk for a
solar year, with little other nourishment; at most not above the value of two
shillings, which the mother may certainly get, or the value in scraps, by her
lawful occupation of begging; and it is exactly at one year that I propose to
provide for them in such a manner as instead of being a charge upon their parents or the parish, or wanting food and raiment for the rest of their lives, they
shall on the contrary contribute to the feeding, and partly to the clothing, of
many thousands.

---

[1] Dublin. — EDS.
[2] The Pretender was James Stuart, exiled in Spain; in 1718 many Irishmen had joined
an army seeking to restore him to the English throne. Others wishing to emigrate had signed
papers as indentured servants, agreeing to work for a number of years in the Barbados or other
British colonies in exchange for their ocean passage. — EDS.
[3] Planners. — EDS.

There is likewise another great advantage in my scheme, that it will pre- 5
vent those voluntary abortions, and that horrid practice of women murdering
their bastard children, alas, too frequent among us, sacrificing the poor innocent babes, I doubt, more to avoid the expense than the shame, which would
move tears and pity in the most savage and inhuman breast.

The number of souls in this kingdom being usually reckoned one million 6
and a half, of these I calculate there may be about two hundred thousand
couples whose wives are breeders; from which number I subtract thirty thousand
couples who are able to maintain their own children, although I apprehend
there cannot be so many under the present distress of the kingdom; but this
being granted, there will remain an hundred and seventy thousand breeders.
I again subtract fifty thousand for those women who miscarry, or whose children die by accident or disease within the year. There only remain an hundred
and twenty thousand children of poor parents annually born. The question
therefore is, how this number shall be reared and provided for, which, as I
have already said, under the present situation of affairs, is utterly impossible by
all the methods hitherto proposed. For we can neither employ them in handi-
craft or agriculture; we neither build houses (I mean in the country) nor cul-
tivate land. They can very seldom pick up a livelihood stealing till they arrive
at six years old, except where they are of towardly parts;[4] although I confess
they learn the rudiments much earlier, during which time they can however
be looked upon only as probationers, as I have been informed by a principal
gentleman in the country of Cavan, who protested to me that he never knew
above one or two instances under the age of six, even in a part of the kingdom
so renowned for the quickest proficiency in that art.

I am assured by our merchants that a boy or a girl before twelve years old 7
is no salable commodity; and even when they come to this age they will not
yield above three pounds, or three pounds and half a crown at most on the
Exchange; which cannot turn to account either to the parents or the kingdom,
the charge of nutriment and rags having been at least four times that value.

I shall now therefore humbly propose my own thoughts, which I hope will 8
not be liable to the least objection.

I have been assured by a very knowing American of my acquaintance in 9
London, that a young healthy child well nursed is at a year old a most delicious,
nourishing, and wholesome food, whether stewed, roasted, baked, or boiled;
and I make no doubt that it will equally serve in a fricassee or a ragout.[5]

I do therefore humbly offer it to public consideration that of the hundred 10
and twenty thousand children, already computed, twenty thousand may be

---

[4]Teachable wits, innate abilities. —Eds.
[5]Stew. —Eds.

reserved for breed, whereof only one fourth part to be males, which is more than we allow to sheep, black cattle, or swine; and my reason is that these children are seldom the fruits of marriage, a circumstance not much regarded by our savages, therefore one male will be sufficient to serve four females. That the remaining hundred thousand may at a year old be offered in sale to the persons of quality and fortune through the kingdom, always advising the mother to let them suck plentifully in the last month, so as to render them plump and fat for a good table. A child will make two dishes at an entertainment for friends; and when the family dines alone, the fore or hind quarter will make a reasonable dish, and seasoned with a little pepper or salt will be very good boiled on the fourth day, especially in winter.

I have reckoned upon a medium that a child just born will weigh twelve   11
pounds, and in a solar year if tolerably nursed increaseth to twenty-eight pounds.

I grant this food will be somewhat dear, and therefore very proper for   12
landlords, who, as they have already devoured most of the parents, seem to have the best title to the children.

Infant's flesh will be in season throughout the year, but more plentiful in   13
March, and a little before and after. For we are told by a grave author, an eminent French physician,[6] that fish being a prolific diet, there are more children born in Roman Catholic countries about nine months after Lent than at any other season; therefore, reckoning a year after Lent, the markets will be more glutted than usual, because the number of popish infants is at least three to one in this kingdom; and therefore it will have one other collateral advantage, by lessening the number of Papists among us.

I have already computed the charge of nursing a beggar's child (in which   14
list I reckon all cottagers, laborers, and four-fifths of the farmers) to be about two shillings per annum, rags included; and I believe no gentleman would repine to give ten shillings for the carcass of a good fat child, which, as I have said, will make four dishes of excellent nutritive meat, when he hath only some particular friend or his own family to dine with him. Thus the squire will learn to be a good landlord, and grow people among the tenants; the mother will have eight shillings net profit, and be fit for work till she produces another child.

Those who are more thrifty (as I must confess the times require) may flay   15
the carcass; the skin of which artificially[7] dressed will make admirable gloves for ladies, and summer boots for fine gentlemen.

---

[6]Swift's favorite French writer, François Rabelais, sixteenth-century author; not "grave" at all, but a broad humorist. — EDS.

[7]With art or craft. — EDS.

As to our city of Dublin, shambles[8] may be appointed for this purpose in   16
the most convenient parts of it, and butchers we may be assured will not be
wanting; although I rather recommend buying the children alive, and dressing
them hot from the knife as we do roasting pigs.

A very worthy person, a true lover of his country, and whose virtues I   17
highly esteem, was lately pleased in discoursing on this matter to offer a refinement upon my scheme. He said that many gentlemen of his kingdom, having
of late destroyed their deer, he conceived that the want of venison might be
well supplied by the bodies of young lads and maidens, not exceeding fourteen
years of age nor under twelve, so great a number of both sexes in every county
being now ready to starve for want of work and service; and these to be disposed of by their parents, if alive, or otherwise by their nearest relations. But
with due deference to so excellent a friend and so deserving a patriot, I cannot
be altogether in his sentiments; for as to the males, my American acquaintance assured me from frequent experience that their flesh was generally tough
and lean, like that of our schoolboys, by continual exercise, and their taste
disagreeable; and to fatten them would not answer the charge. Then as to
the females, it would, I think with humble submission, be a loss to the public,
because they soon would become breeders themselves; and besides, it is not
improbable that some scrupulous people might be apt to censure such a practice (although indeed very unjustly) as a little bordering upon cruelty; which,
I confess, hath always been with me the strongest objection against any
project, how well soever intended.

But in order to justify my friend, he confessed that this expedient was put   18
into his head by the famous Psalmanazar,[9] a native of the island Formosa, who
came from thence to London above twenty years ago, and in conversation
told my friend that in his country when any young person happened to be
put to death, the executioner sold the carcass to persons of quality as a prime
dainty; and that in his time the body of a plump girl of fifteen, who was crucified for an attempt to poison the emperor, was sold to his Imperial Majesty's
prime minister of state, and other great mandarins of the court, in joints from
the gibbet, at four hundred crowns. Neither indeed can I deny that if the same
use were made of several plump young girls in this town, who without one
single groat to their fortunes cannot stir abroad without a chair, and appear at
the playhouse and assemblies in foreign fineries which they never will pay for,
the kingdom would not be the worse.

---

[8]Butcher shops or slaughterhouses. —EDS.

[9]Georges Psalmanazar—a Frenchman who pretended to be Japanese, the author of a completely imaginary *Description of the Isle Formosa* (1705)—had become a well-known figure in
gullible London society. —EDS.

Some persons of a desponding spirit are in great concern about that vast   19
number of poor people who are aged, diseased, or maimed, and I have been
desired to employ my thoughts what course may be taken to ease the nation
of so grievous an encumbrance. But I am not in the least pain upon that matter, because it is very well known that they are every day dying and rotting by
cold and famine, and filth and vermin, as fast as can be reasonably expected.
And as to the younger laborers, they are now in almost as hopeful a condition.
They cannot get work, and consequently pine away for want of nourishment
to a degree that if any time they are accidentally hired to common labor, they
have not strength to perform it; and thus the country and themselves are happily delivered from the evils to come.

I have too long digressed, and therefore shall return to my subject. I think   20
the advantages by the proposal which I have made are obvious and many, as
well as of the highest importance.

For first, as I have already observed, it would greatly lessen the number of   21
Papists, with whom we are yearly overrun, being the principal breeders of the
nation as well as our most dangerous enemies; and who stay at home on purpose to deliver the kingdom to the Pretender, hoping to take their advantage
by the absence of so many good Protestants, who have chosen rather to leave
their country than to stay at home and pay tithes against their conscience to
an Episcopal curate.

Secondly, the poorer tenants will have something valuable of their own,   22
which by law may be made liable to distress,[10] and help to pay their landlord's
rent, their corn and cattle being already seized and money a thing unknown.

Thirdly, whereas the maintenance of an hundred thousand children,   23
from two years old and upwards, cannot be computed at less than ten shillings
a piece per annum, the nation's stock will be thereby increased fifty thousand
pounds per annum, besides the profit of a new dish introduced to the tables
of all gentlemen of fortune in the kingdom who have any refinement in taste.
And the money will circulate among ourselves, the goods being entirely of our
own growth and manufacture.

Fourthly, the constant breeders, besides the gain of eight shillings sterling   24
per annum by the sale of their children, will be rid of the charge of maintaining them after the first year.

Fifthly, this food would likewise bring great custom to taverns, where the   25
vintners will certainly be so prudent as to procure the best receipts for dressing
it to perfection, and consequently have their houses frequented by all the fine
gentlemen, who justly value themselves upon their knowledge in good eating;

---

[10]Subject to seizure by creditors. — EDS.

and a skillful cook, who understands how to oblige his guests, will contrive to make it as expensive as they please.

Sixthly, this would be a great inducement to marriage, which all wise nations have either encouraged by rewards or enforced by laws and penalties. It would increase the care and tenderness of mothers toward their children, when they were sure of a settlement for life to the poor babes, provided in some sort by the public, to their annual profit instead of expense. We should see an honest emulation among the married women, which of them could bring the fattest child to the market. Men would become as fond of their wives during the time of their pregnancy as they are now of their mares in foal, their cows in calf, or sows when they are ready to farrow; nor offer to beat or kick them (as is too frequent a practice) for fear of a miscarriage.   26

Many other advantages might be enumerated. For instance, the addition of some thousand carcasses in our exportation of barreled beef, the propagation of swine's flesh, and improvements in the art of making good bacon, so much wanted among us by the great destruction of pigs, too frequent at our tables, which are no way comparable in taste or magnificence to a well-grown, fat, yearling child, which roasted whole will make a considerable figure at a lord mayor's feast or any other public entertainment. But this and many others I omit, being studious of brevity.   27

Supposing that one thousand families in this city would be constant customers for infants' flesh, besides others who might have it at merry meetings, particularly weddings and christenings, I compute that Dublin would take off annually about twenty thousand carcasses, and the rest of the kingdom (where probably they will be sold somewhat cheaper) the remaining eighty thousand.   28

I can think of no one objection that will possibly be raised against this proposal, unless it should be urged that the number of people will be thereby much lessened in the kingdom. This I freely own, and it was indeed one principal design in offering it to the world. I desire the reader will observe, that I calculate my remedy for this one individual kingdom of Ireland and for no other that ever was, is, or I think ever can be upon earth. Therefore let no man talk to me of other expedients: of taxing our absentees at five shillings a pound: of using neither clothes nor household furniture except what is of our own growth and manufacture: of utterly rejecting the materials and instruments that promote foreign luxury: of curing the expensiveness of pride, vanity, idleness, and gaming in our women: of introducing a vein of parsimony, prudence, and temperance: of learning to love our country, in the want of which we differ even from Laplanders and the inhabitants of Topinamboo:[11]   29

[11] A district of Brazil. —EDS.

of quitting our animosities and factions, nor acting any longer like the Jews, who were murdering one another at the very moment their city was taken: [12] of being a little cautious not to sell our country and conscience for nothing: of teaching landlords to have at least one degree of mercy toward their tenants: lastly, of putting a spirit of honesty, industry, and skill into our shopkeepers; who, if a resolution could now be taken to buy only our native goods, would immediately unite to cheat and exact upon us in the price, the measure, and the goodness, nor could ever yet be brought to make one fair proposal of just dealing, though often and earnestly invited to it.

Therefore I repeat, let no man talk to me of these and the like expedients, till he hath at least some glimpse of hope that there will ever be some hearty and sincere attempt to put them in practice.

But as to myself, having been wearied out for many years with offering vain, idle, visionary thoughts, and at length utterly despairing of success, I fortunately fell upon this proposal, which, as it is wholly new, so it hath something solid and real, of no expense and little trouble, full in our own power, and whereby we can incur no danger in disobliging England. For this kind of commodity will not bear exportation, the flesh being of too tender a consistence to admit a long continuance in salt, although perhaps I could name a country which would be glad to eat up our whole nation without it.

After all, I am not so violently bent upon my own opinion as to reject any offer proposed by wise men, which shall be found equally innocent, cheap, easy, and effectual. But before something of that kind shall be advanced in contradiction to my scheme, and offering a better, I desire the author or authors will be pleased maturely to consider two points. First, as things now stand, how they will be able to find food and raiment for an hundred thousand useless mouths and backs. And secondly, there being a round million of creatures in human figure throughout this kingdom, whose sole subsistence put into a common stock would leave them in debt two millions of pounds sterling, adding those who are beggars by profession to the bulk of farmers, cottagers, and laborers, with their wives and children who are beggars in effect; I desire those politicians who dislike my overture, and may perhaps be so bold to attempt an answer, that they will first ask the parents of these mortals whether they would not at this day think it a great happiness to have been sold for food at a year old in this manner I prescribe, and thereby have avoided such a perpetual scene of misfortunes as they have since gone through by the oppression of landlords, the impossibility of paying rent without money or trade, the want of common sustenance, with neither house nor clothes to cover them from the

---

[12] During the Roman siege of Jerusalem (AD 70), prominent Jews were executed on the charge of being in league with the enemy. — Eds.

inclemencies of the weather, and the most inevitable prospect of entailing the like or greater miseries upon their breed forever.

I profess, in the sincerity of my heart, that I have not the least personal 33 interest in endeavoring to promote this necessary work, having no other motive than the public good of my country, by advancing our trade, providing for infants, relieving the poor, and giving some pleasure to the rich. I have no children by which I can propose to get a single penny; the youngest being nine years old, and my wife past childbearing.

For a reading quiz, sources on Jonathan Swift, and annotated links to further readings on eighteenth-century Ireland, visit *bedfordstmartins.com/thebedfordreader*.

Journal Writing

Swift's proposal is aimed at a serious social problem of his day. In your journal, consider a contemporary problem that—like the poverty and starvation Swift describes—seems to require drastic action. For instance, do you believe that a particular group of people is neglected, mistreated, or victimized? Turn to the news media for ideas if no problem comes immediately to mind. (To take your journal writing further, see "From Journal to Essay" on the next page.)

Questions on Meaning

1. On the surface, what is Swift proposing?
2. Beneath his IRONY, what is Swift's argument?
3. What do you take to be the PURPOSE of Swift's essay?
4. How does the introductory paragraph serve Swift's purpose?
5. Comment on the statement "I can think of no one objection that will possibly be raised against this proposal" (par. 29). What objections can you think of?

Questions on Writing Strategy

1. Describe the mask of the personage through whom Swift writes.
2. By what means does the writer attest to his reasonableness?
3. At what point in the essay did it become clear to you that the proposal isn't modest but horrible?
4. **MIXED METHODS** As an ARGUMENT, does "A Modest Proposal" appeal primarily to reason or to emotion? (See p. 551 for a discussion of the distinction.)

5. **MIXED METHODS**   What does Swift's argument gain by his careful attention to PROCESS ANALYSIS and to CAUSE AND EFFECT?

Questions on Language

1. How does Swift's choice of words enforce the monstrousness of his proposal? Note especially words from the vocabulary of breeding and butchery.
2. Consult your dictionary for the meanings of any of the following words not yet in your vocabulary: importuning, sustenance (par. 1); prodigious, commonwealth (2); computation, raiment (4); apprehend, rudiments, probationers (6); nutriment (7); fricassee (9); repine (14); flay (15); scrupulous, censure (17); mandarins (18); desponding, encumbrance (19); per annum (23); vintners (25); emulation, foal, farrow (26); expedients, parsimony, animosities (29); disobliging, consistence (31); overture, inclemencies (32).

Suggestions for Writing

1. **FROM JOURNAL TO ESSAY**   Write an essay in which you propose a solution to the problem raised in your journal. Your essay may be either of the following:
   a. A straight argument, giving EVIDENCE, in which you set forth possible solutions to the problem.
   b. An ironic proposal in the manner of Swift. If you do this one, find a device other than cannibalism to eliminate the victims or their problems. You don't want to imitate Swift too closely; he is probably inimitable.
2. In an encyclopedia, look into what has happened in Ireland since Swift wrote. Choose a specific contemporary aspect of Irish-English relations, research it in books and periodicals, and write a report on it.
3. **CRITICAL WRITING**   Choose several examples of irony in "A Modest Proposal" that you find particularly effective. In a brief essay, ANALYZE Swift's use of irony. Do your examples of irony depend on understating, overstating, or saying the opposite of what is meant? How do they improve on literal statements? What is the value of irony in argument?
4. **CONNECTIONS**   Read Jessica Mitford's "Behind the Formaldehyde Curtain" (p. 326) alongside "A Modest Proposal," and analyze the use of irony and humor in these two essays. How heavily does each author depend on irony and humor to make his or her argument? Do these elements strengthen both authors' arguments? What evidence does each offer that would also work in a more straightforward argument?
5. **CONNECTIONS**   Analyze the ways Swift and Martin Luther King, Jr., in "I Have a Dream" (p. 643), create sympathy for the oppressed groups they are concerned about. Concentrate not only on what they say but also on the words they use and their TONE. Then write a process analysis explaining techniques for portraying oppression so as to win the reader's sympathy. Use quotations or PARAPHRASES from Swift's and King's essays as EXAMPLES. If you can think of other techniques that neither author uses, by all means include and illustrate them as well.

Jonathan Swift on Writing

Although surely one of the most inventive writers in English literature, Swift voiced his contempt for writers of his day who bragged of their newness and originality. In *The Battle of the Books*, he compares such a self-professed original to a spider who "spins and spits wholly from himself, and scorns to own any obligation or assistance from without." Swift has the fable-writer Aesop praise that writer who, like a bee gathering nectar, draws from many sources.

> Erect your schemes with as much method and skill as you please; yet if the materials be nothing but dirt, spun out of your own entrails (the guts of modern brains), the edifice will conclude at last in a cobweb. . . . As for us Ancients, we are content, with the bee, to pretend to nothing of our own beyond our wings and our voice, that is to say, our flights and our language. For the rest, whatever we have got has been by infinite labor and search and ranging through every corner of nature; the difference is, that, instead of dirt and poison, we have rather chosen to fill our hives with honey and wax, thus furnishing mankind with the two noblest of things, which are sweetness and light.

Swift's advice for a writer would seem to be: Don't just invent things out of thin air; read the best writers of the past. Observe and converse. Do legwork.

Interestingly, when in *Gulliver's Travels* Swift portrays his ideal beings, the Houyhnhnms, a race of noble and intelligent horses, he includes no writers at all in their society. "The Houyhnhnms have no letters," Gulliver observes, "and consequently their knowledge is all traditional." Still, "in poetry they must be allowed to excel all other mortals; wherein the justness of their description are indeed inimitable." (Those very traits—striking comparisons and detailed descriptions—make much of Swift's own writing memorable.)

In his great book, in "A Modest Proposal," and in virtually all he wrote, Swift's purpose was forthright and evident. He declared in "Verses on the Death of Dr. Swift,"

> As with a moral view designed
> To cure the vices of mankind:
> Yet malice never was his aim;
> He lashed the vice but spared the name.
> No individual could resent,
> Where thousands equally were meant.
> His satire points at no defect
> But what all mortals may correct.

For Discussion

1. Try applying Swift's parable of the spider and the bee to our own day. How much truth is left in it?
2. Reread thoughtfully the quotation from Swift's poem. According to the poet, what faults or abuses can a satiric writer fall into? How may these be avoided?
3. What do you take to be Swift's main PURPOSE as a writer? In your own words, SUMMARIZE it.

JOHN UPDIKE

The esteemed and widely popular writer John Updike published about eighty books of fiction, poetry, and essays, all of them distinctively lyrical and evocative. He was born in 1932 in Shillington, Pennsylvania, grew up in that small town, and carried it with him into his writing. "My subject," he once said, "is the American Protestant small-town middle class." Updike graduated from Harvard University (BA, 1954) and attended art school in England. He worked for a couple of years at *The New Yorker* and subsequently published many of his short stories and book reviews in that magazine. His awards include the Pulitzer Prize, the National Book Award, the American Book Award, and the Howells Medal of the American Academy and the Institute of Arts and Letters, of which he was also a member. Updike's twenty-four novels, for which he is best known, include the linked stories *Rabbit, Run* (1960), *Rabbit Redux* (1971), *Rabbit Is Rich* (1981), and *Rabbit at Rest* (1990); his last novel was *The Widows of Eastwick* (2008). He died in 2009.

Extreme Dinosaurs

Updike wrote "Extreme Dinosaurs" in 2007 at the request of *National Geographic Magazine,* whose editors were looking for an essay to introduce a gallery of illustrations depicting "bizarre dinosaurs." (We include four of the images here.) Although he was intimidated by the prospect of writing about paleontology for a well-known science magazine, Updike accepted the challenge because dinosaurs fascinated him and because he found it "poignant and awesome that such creatures once existed as alive as you and I but are long since gone from the surface of the Earth." What does a novelist do when assigned to write about a scientific subject he doesn't fully understand? Read on.

Updike relies most heavily on example and description but draws on a number of other methods to ponder the evolution and extinction of dinosaurs, as well as how history might repeat itself:

Description (Chap. 5): paragraphs 1, 2, 5, 6, 7
Example (Chap. 6): throughout
Comparison and contrast (Chap. 7): paragraphs 3, 8, 10
Process analysis (Chap. 8): paragraphs 4–5, 9, 10
Division or analysis (Chap. 9): paragraphs 1, 3, 5
Cause and effect (Chap. 11): paragraphs 6, 7

Before the nineteenth century, when dinosaur bones turned up they were taken as evidence of dragons, ogres, or giant victims of Noah's Flood. After two centuries of paleontological harvest, the evidence seems stranger than any fable, and continues to get stranger. Dozens of new species emerge each year; China and Argentina are hot spots lately for startling new finds. Contemplating the bizarre specimens recently come to light, one cannot but wonder what on earth Nature was thinking of. What advantage was conferred, say, by the ungainly eight-foot-long arms and huge triple claws of *Deinocheirus*? Or, speaking of arms, by *Mononykus*'s smug dependence on a single, stoutly clawed digit at the end of each minimal forearm? Guesses can be hazarded: The latter found a single stubby claw just the thing for probing after insects; the former stripped the leaves and bark from trees in awesome bulk. A carnivorous cousin, *Deinonychus*, about the size of a man, leaped on its prey, wrapped its long arms and three-fingered hands around it, and kicked it to the death with sickle-shaped toenails.

Mononykus

Styracosaurus

Tiny *Epidendrosaurus* boasted a hugely elongated third finger that served, 2 presumably, a clinging, arboreal lifestyle, like that of today's aye-aye, a lemur that possesses the same curious trait. With the membrane they support, the elongated digits of bats and pterosaurs enable flight, and perhaps *Epidendrosaurus* was taking a skittery first step in that direction. But what do we make of such apparently inutile extremes of morphology as the elaborate skull frills of ceratopsians like *Styracosaurus* or the horizontally protruding front teeth of *Masiakasaurus knopfleri,* a late Cretaceous oddity recently uncovered in Madagascar by excavators who named the beast after Mark Knopfler, the lead singer of the group Dire Straits, their favorite music to dig by?

Masiakasaurus is an oddity, all right, its mouth bristling with those slightly   3
hooked, forward-poking teeth; but, then, odd too are an elephant's trunk and
tusks, and an elk's antler rack, and a peacock's tail. A difficulty with dinosaurs
is that we can't see them in action and tame them, as it were, with visual
(and auditory and olfactory) witness. How weird might a human body look
to them? That thin and featherless skin, that dish-flat face, that flaccid erectitude, those feeble, clawless five digits at the end of each limb, that ghastly
utter lack of a tail—*ugh*. Whatever did this creature *do* to earn its place in the
sun, a well-armored, nicely specialized dino might ask.

Dinosaurs dominated the planet's land surface from some 200 million years   4
ago until their abrupt disappearance, 135 million years later. The vast span of
time boggles the human mind, which took its present, *Homo sapiens* form less
than 200,000 years ago and began to leave written records and organize cities
less than 10,000 years in the past. When the first dinosaurs—small, lightweight, bipedal, and carnivorous—appeared in the Triassic, the first of three
periods in the Mesozoic geologic era, the Earth held one giant continent,
Pangaea; during their Jurassic heyday Pangaea split into two parts, Laurasia
and Gondwana; and by the late Cretaceous the continents had something like
their present shapes, though all were reduced in size by the higher seas, and
India was still an island heading for a Himalaya-producing crash with Asia.
The world was becoming the one we know: The Andes and the Rockies were
rising; flowering plants had appeared, and with them, bees. The Mesozoic climate, generally, was warmer than today's, and wetter, generating lush growths
of ferns and cycads and forests of evergreens, ginkgoes, and tree ferns close to
the poles; plant-eating dinosaurs grew huge, and carnivorous predators kept
pace. It was a planetary summertime, and the living was easy.

Not *that* easy: Throughout their long day on earth, there was an intensifi-   5
cation of boniness and spikiness, as if the struggle for survival became grimmer.
And yet the defensive or attacking advantage of skull frills and back plates is
not self-evident. The solid-domed skull of *Pachycephalosaurus*, the largest of
the bone-headed dinosaurs, seems made for butting—but for butting what?
The skull would do little good against a big predator like *Tyrannosaurus rex*,
which had the whole rest of *Pachycephalosaurus*'s unprotected body to bite
down on. Butting matches amid males of the same species were unlikely,
since the bone, though ten inches thick, was not shock-absorbent. The skulls
of some pachycephalosaurs, moreover, were flat and thin, and some tall and
ridged—bad designs for contact sport. Maybe they were just used for discreet
pushing. Or to make a daunting impression.

An even more impractical design shaped the skull of the pachycephalo-   6
saurid *Dracorex hogwartsia*—an intricate sunburst of spiky horns and knobs,

Parasaurolophus

without a dome. Only one such skull has been unearthed; it is on display, with the playful name derived from Harry Potter's school of witchcraft and wizardry, in Indianapolis's Children's Museum. Duck-billed *Parasaurolophus walkeri,* another late Cretaceous plant-eater, sported a spectacular pipelike structure, sweeping back from its skull, that was once theorized to act as a snorkel in swimming. But the tubular crest had no hole for gathering air. It may have served as a trumpeting noisemaker, for herd communication, or supported a bright flap of skin beguiling to a *Parasaurolophus* of the opposite gender. Sexual success and herd acceptance perpetuate genes as much as combative prowess and food-gathering ability.

Dinosaurs have always presented adaptive puzzles. How did huge herbi-   7
vores like *Brachiosaurus, Apatosaurus,* and *Diplodocus* get enough daily food into their tiny mouths to fill their cavernous guts? Of the two familiar dinosaurs whose life-and-death struggle was memorably animated in Walt Disney's 1940 *Fantasia* (though in fact they never met in the corridors of time, failing to overlap by fully 75 million years), *T. rex* had puzzlingly tiny arms and *Stegosaurus* carried on its back a double row of huge bony plates negligible as defensive armor and problematic as heat controls. Not that biological features need to be efficient to be carried along. Some Darwinian purists don't even like the word "adaptive," as carrying a taint of implied teleology, of purposeful self-improvement. All that is certain is that dinosaur skeletons demonstrate the viability, for a time, of certain dimensions and conformations. Yet even

Darwin, on the last page of *The Origin of Species*, in summing up his theory as "Natural Selection, entailing Divergence of Character and the Extinction of less-improved forms," lets fall a shadow of value judgment with the "less-improved."

In what sense are living forms improvements over the dinosaurs? All life-forms, even such long-lasting ones as blue-green algae and horseshoe crabs and crocodiles, will eventually flunk some test posed by environmental conditions and meet extinction. One can safely say that no dinosaur was as intelligent as *Homo sapiens*, or even as chimpanzees. And none that are known, not even a heavyweight champion like *Argentinosaurus*, was as big as a blue whale. One can believe that none was as beautiful in swift motion as a cheetah or an antelope, or as impressive to our mammalian aesthetic sense as a tiger. But beyond this it is hard to talk of improvement, especially since for all its fine qualities *Homo sapiens* is befouling the environment like no fauna before it.

The dinosaurs in their long reign filled every niche several times over, and the smallest of them—the little light-boned theropods scuttling for their lives underfoot—grew feathers and became birds, still singing and dipping all around us. It is an amazing end to an amazing evolutionary story—*Deinonychus* into dove. Other surprises certainly lurk within the still unfolding saga of the dinosaurs. In Inner Mongolia, so recently that the bones were revealed to the world just this past spring, a giant birdlike dinosaur, *Gigantoraptor*, has been discovered. It clearly belongs among the oviraptorosaurs of the late Cretaceous—ninety-pound weaklings with toothless beaks—but weighed in at one-and-a-half tons and could have peered into a second-story window. While many of its fellow theropods—for example, six-foot, large-eyed, big-brained *Troodon*—were evolving toward nimbleness and intelligence, *Gigantoraptor* opted for brute size. But what did it eat, with its enormous toothless beak? Did its claw-tipped arms bear feathers, as did those of smaller oviraptorosaurs?

The new specimens that emerge as tangles of bones embedded in sedimentary rock are island peaks of a submerged continent where evolutionary currents surged back and forth. Our telescoped perspective gives an impression of a violent struggle as anatomical ploys, some of them seemingly grotesque, were desperately tried and eventually discarded. The dinosaurs as a group saw myriad extinctions, and the final extinction, at the end of the Mesozoic, looks to have been the work of an asteroid. They continue to live in the awareness of their human successors on the throne of earthly dominance. They fascinate children as well as paleontologists. My second son, I well remember, collected the plastic dinosaur miniatures that came in cereal boxes, and communed with them in his room. He loved them—their amiable grotesquerie, their

Gigantoraptor

guileless enormity, their unassuming small brains. They were eventual losers, in a game of survival our own species is still playing, but new varieties keep emerging from the rocks underfoot to amuse and amaze us.

*For a reading quiz, sources on John Updike, and annotated links to further readings on dinosaurs and on evolution, visit **bedfordstmartins.com/thebedfordreader**.*

Journal Writing

Updike writes, in paragraph 8, that "for all its fine qualities *Homo sapiens* is befouling the environment like no fauna before it." How do you respond to this statement? Do you believe that human beings are destroying the environment? Could humanity be contributing to its own eventual extinction? Write a journal entry in which you consider these questions. (To take your journal writing further, see "From Journal to Essay" on the facing page.)

Questions on Meaning

1. Write a one- or two-sentence summary of each of Updike's paragraphs. In your own words, what is his overall point?
2. Beyond contemplating the strangeness of dinosaurs, what other PURPOSE might Updike have had for writing this essay?
3. Throughout his essay, Updike describes dinosaur appendages, such as spikes and crowns, and considers what their uses may have been (see, for instance, pars. 1, 5, and 6). How certain is the writer of his conclusions? How do his explanations reflect a basic truth about paleontology?
4. To what extent does Updike accept the theory of evolution? How can you tell?

Questions on Writing Strategy

1. Why does Updike open his essay with examples of what people two hundred years ago interpreted dinosaur bones to mean?
2. What is the purpose of the visual images described by Updike? Does each seem necessary?
3. How does Updike seem to imagine his AUDIENCE? How reasonable are his ASSUMPTIONS about his readers?
4. **MIXED METHODS**   How does PROCESS ANALYSIS serve Updike in paragraphs 4–5? Why does he explain changes to the earth in such detail?
5. **MIXED METHODS**   Why does Updike COMPARE AND CONTRAST dinosaurs and current-day animals in paragraphs 3, 8, and 10?

Questions on Language

1. Updike uses specialized vocabulary and difficult words throughout this essay. Consult a dictionary to define the following words: paleontological, conferred, digit, carnivorous, sickle (par. 1); elongated, arboreal, membrane, inutile, morphology, ceratopsians, Cretaceous (2); auditory, olfactory, flaccid, erectitude, armored (3); bipedal, Triassic, Mesozoic, geologic, Jurassic, cycads, ginkgoes (4); predator, pachycephalosaurs (5); dome, crest, beguiling, perpetuate, prowess (6); adaptive, herbivores, teleology, conformations (7); aesthetic, fauna (8); theropods, oviraptorosaurs (9); sedimentary, telescoped, anatomical, ploys, myriad, communed, amiable, grotesquerie, guileless (10). Must you know the meanings of all of Updike's words to understand his essay?
2. How would you characterize Updike's prevailing DICTION? Why does he also use COLLOQUIAL EXPRESSIONS? Find at least three examples of everyday speech and explain their EFFECT.
3. How does Updike use personification to enliven his subject? (For a definition of *personification*, see *Figures of speech* in Useful Terms.)

4. Much of Updike's description relies on visual IMAGES, but he does appeal to other senses as well. Point to language that evokes bodily sensation and sound.

Suggestions for Writing

1. **FROM JOURNAL TO ESSAY** Based on your journal entry, write an essay that examines the problem of global warming. To what extent are human beings responsible for changes in the environment? Are changing temperatures and air currents part of a natural cycle that we can't control? What, if anything, can be done about the situation? How do you envision the future of the planet, and of humanity?

2. At a library or online at *ngm.nationalgeographic.com/2007/12-bizarre-dinosaurs*, locate the full collection of "extreme dinosaur" illustrations commissioned by *National Geographic* for its December 2007 issue. Choose two or three images and write your own DESCRIPTION of the creatures, using Updike's essay for inspiration.

3. **CRITICAL WRITING** Research the work of John Updike, looking for reviews of his books as well as interviews with him. (A good starting point would be his interview with Jamie Shreeve of *National Geographic* at *ngm.national geographic.com/2007/12-bizarre-dinosaurs*.) In an essay, consider Updike's achievements as a writer. In particular, examine what might have qualified him to write a nonfiction essay about dinosaurs for a highly esteemed science publication.

4. **CONNECTIONS** Updike remarks in paragraph 8 that "*Homo sapiens* is befouling the environment like no fauna before it." Gretel Ehrlich makes a similar point in "Chronicles of Ice" (p. 313), in which she details some of the effects of global warming. Drawing on these two writers' observations and concerns for EVIDENCE, write an essay comparing environmental changes in the Mesozoic era and today. What similarities and differences do you find most striking? What conclusions can you draw from them?

5. **CONNECTIONS** In "The Capricious Camera" (p. 387), Laila Ayad describes a photograph of a young girl and attempts to interpret its historical meanings. Using Updike's and Ayad's essays for examples, write an essay of your own in which you discuss how writers can create meaning through DESCRIPTION and ANALYSIS of visual images.

John Updike on Writing

A famously meticulous writer, John Updike nonetheless claimed to write quickly. Fairly early in his career, in 1967, he explained to Charles Thomas Samuels of *The Paris Review* just what's to be gained from speed.

"There may be some reason," he said, "to question the whole idea of fineness and care in writing. Maybe something can get into sloppy writing that would elude careful writing. I'm not terribly careful myself, actually. I write fairly rapidly if I get going, and don't change much, and have never been one for making outlines or taking out whole paragraphs or agonizing much. If a thing goes, it goes for me, and if it doesn't go, I eventually stop and get off."

Updike was asked what "gets into sloppy writing that eludes more careful prose."

"It comes down to what is language," Updike replied. "Up to now, until this age of mass literacy, language has been something spoken. In utterance there's a minimum of slowness. In trying to treat words as chisel strokes, you run the risk of losing the quality of utterance, the rhythm of utterance, the happiness. A phrase out of Mark Twain — he describes a raft hitting a bridge and says that it 'went all to smash and scatteration like a box of matches struck by lightning.' The beauty of 'scatteration' could only have occurred to a talkative man, a man who had been brought up among people who were talking and who loved to talk himself. I'm aware myself of a certain dryness of this reservoir, this backlog of spoken talk. A Rumanian once said to me that Americans are always telling stories. I'm not sure this is as true as it once was. Where we once used to spin yarns, now we sit in front of the TV and receive pictures. I'm not sure the younger generation even knows how to gossip. But, as for a writer, if he has something to tell, he should perhaps type it almost as fast as he could talk it. We must look to the organic world, not the inorganic world, for metaphors; and just as the organic world has periods of repose and periods of great speed and exercise, so I think the writer's process should be organically varied. But there's a kind of tautness that you should feel within yourself no matter how slow or fast you're spinning out the reel."

For Discussion

1. To what extent do you think Updike's ideas about feeling "a kind of tautness" while composing apply to academic as well as to fiction writing? What might *you* gain by writing fast?

2. What might be the advantage to a writer — any kind of writer — of talk? Do you agree with Updike that to "sit in front of the TV and receive pictures" rather than "gossip" could deprive a writer of essential experience? Why, or why not?

E. B. WHITE

Elwyn Brooks White (1899–1985) for half a century was a regular contributor to *The New Yorker,* and his essays, editorials, anonymous features for "The Talk of the Town," and fillers helped build the magazine a reputation for wit and good writing. If as a child you read *Charlotte's Web* (1952), you have met E. B. White before. The book reflects some of his own life on a farm in North Brooklin, Maine. His *Letters* were collected in 1976, his *Essays* in 1977, and his *Poems and Sketches* in 1981. On July 4, 1963, President Kennedy named White in the first group of Americans to receive the Presidential Medal of Freedom, with a citation that called him "an essayist whose concise comment . . . has revealed to yet another age the vigor of the English sentence."

Once More to the Lake

"Once More to the Lake" first appeared in *Harper's* magazine in 1941. Perhaps if a duller writer had written the essay, or an essay with the same title, we wouldn't much care about it, for at first its subject seems as personal and ordinary as a letter home. White's loving and exact portrayal, however, brings this lakeside camp to life for us. In the end, the writer arrives at an awareness that shocks him—shocks us, too, with a familiar sensory detail.

"Once More to the Lake" is a stunning mixture of description and narration, but it is also more. To make his observations and emotions clear and immediate, White relies extensively on several other methods of development as well.

Narration (Chap. 4): throughout
Description (Chap. 5): throughout
Example (Chap. 6): paragraphs 2, 7–8, 11, 12
Comparison and contrast (Chap. 7): paragraphs 4–7, 9–10, 11–12
Process analysis (Chap. 8): paragraphs 9, 10, 12

August 1941

One summer, along about 1904, my father rented a camp on a lake in Maine and took us all there for the month of August. We all got ringworm from some kittens and had to rub Pond's Extract on our arms and legs night and morning, and my father rolled over in a canoe with all his clothes on; but outside of that the vacation was a success and from then on none of us ever thought there was any place in the world like that lake in Maine. We returned summer after summer—always on August 1 for one month. I have since become a salt-water man, but sometimes in summer there are days when the restlessness of the tides and the fearful cold of the sea water and the incessant wind that blows across the afternoon and into the evening make me wish for the placidity of a lake in the woods. A few weeks ago this feeling got so strong I bought myself a couple of bass hooks and a spinner and returned to the lake where we used to go, for a week's fishing and to revisit old haunts.

I took along my son, who had never had any fresh water up his nose and   2
who had seen lily pads only from train windows. On the journey over to the lake I began to wonder what it would be like. I wondered how time would have marred this unique, this holy spot—the coves and streams, the hills that the sun set behind, the camps and the paths behind the camps. I was sure that the tarred road would have found it out, and I wondered in what other ways it would be desolated. It is strange how much you can remember about places like that once you allow your mind to return into the grooves that lead back. You remember one thing, and that suddenly reminds you of another thing. I guess I remembered clearest of all the early mornings, when the lake was cool and motionless, remembered how the bedroom smelled of the lumber it was made of and of the wet woods whose scent entered through the screen. The partitions in the camp were thin and did not extend clear to the top of the rooms, and as I was always the first up I would dress softly so as not to wake the others, and sneak out into the sweet outdoors and start out in the canoe, keeping close along the shore in the long shadows of the pines. I remembered being very careful never to rub my paddle against the gunwale for fear of disturbing the stillness of the cathedral.

The lake had never been what you would call a wild lake. There were   3
cottages sprinkled around the shores, and it was in farming country although the shores of the lake were quite heavily wooded. Some of the cottages were owned by nearby farmers, and you would live at the shore and eat your meals at the farmhouse. That's what our family did. But although it wasn't wild, it was a fairly large and undisturbed lake and there were places in it that, to a child at least, seemed infinitely remote and primeval.

I was right about the tar: It led to within half a mile of the shore. But when   4
I got back there, with my boy, and we settled into a camp near a farmhouse and into the kind of summertime I had known, I could tell that it was going to be pretty much the same as it had been before—I knew it, lying in bed the first morning smelling the bedroom and hearing the boy sneak quietly out and go off along the shore in a boat. I began to sustain the illusion that he was I, and therefore, by simple transposition, that I was my father. This sensation persisted, kept cropping up all the time we were there. It was not an entirely new feeling, but in this setting it grew much stronger. I seemed to be living a dual existence. I would be in the middle of some simple act, I would be picking

up a bait box or laying down a table fork, or I would be saying something and suddenly it would be not I but my father who was saying the words or making the gesture. It gave me a creepy sensation.

We went fishing the first morning. I felt the same damp moss covering the worms in the bait can, and saw the dragonfly alight on the tip of my rod as it hovered a few inches from the surface of the water. It was the arrival of this fly that convinced me beyond any doubt that everything was as it always had been, that the years were a mirage and that there had been no years. The small waves were the same, chucking the rowboat under the chin as we fished at anchor, and the boat was the same boat, the same color green and the ribs broken in the same places, and under the floorboards the same fresh water leavings and debris—the dead hellgrammite, the wisps of moss, the rusty discarded fishhook, the dried blood from yesterday's catch. We stared silently at the tips of our rods, at the dragonflies that came and went. I lowered the tip of mine into the water, tentatively, pensively dislodging the fly, which darted two feet away, poised, darted two feet back, and came to rest again a little farther up the rod. There had been no years between the ducking of this dragonfly and the other one—the one that was part of memory. I looked at the boy, who was silently watching his fly, and it was my hands that held his rod, my eyes watching. I felt dizzy and didn't know which rod I was at the end of.

We caught two bass, hauling them in briskly as though they were mackerel, pulling them over the side of the boat in a businesslike manner without any landing net, and stunning them with a blow on the back of the head. When we got back for a swim before lunch, the lake was exactly where we had left it, the same number of inches from the dock, and there was only the merest suggestion of a breeze. This seemed an utterly enchanted sea, this lake you could leave to its own devices for a few hours and come back to, and find that it had not stirred, this constant and trustworthy body of water. In the shallows, the dark, water-soaked sticks and twigs, smooth and old, were undulating in clusters on the bottom against the clean ribbed sand, and the track of the mussel was plain. A school of minnows swam by, each minnow with its small individual shadow, doubling the attendance, so clear and sharp in the sunlight. Some of the other campers were in swimming, along the shore, one of them with a cake of soap, and the water felt thin and clear and unsubstantial. Over the years there had been this person with the cake of soap, this cultist, and here he was. There had been no years.

Up to the farmhouse to dinner through the teeming dusty field, the road under our sneakers was only a two-track road. The middle track was missing, the one with the marks of the hooves and the splotches of dried, flaky manure. There had always been three tracks to choose from in choosing which track to walk in; now the choice was narrowed down to two. For a moment I missed terribly the middle alternative. But the way led past the tennis court, and something about the way it lay there in the sun reassured me; the tape had loosened along the backline, the alleys were green with plantains and other weeds, and the net (installed in June and removed in September) sagged in the dry noon, and the whole place steamed with midday heat and hunger and emptiness. There was a choice of pie for dessert, and one was blueberry and one was apple, and the waitresses were the same country girls, there having been no passage of time, only the illusion of it as in a dropped curtain—the waitresses were still fifteen; their hair had been washed, that was the only difference—they had been to the movies and seen the pretty girls with the clean hair.

Summertime, oh, summertime, pattern of life indelible, the fade-proof   8
lake, the woods unshatterable, the pasture with the sweetfern and the juniper forever and ever, summer without end; this was the background, and the life along the shore was the design, the cottages with their innocent and tranquil design, their tiny docks with the flagpole and the American flag floating against the white clouds in the blue sky, the little paths over the roots of the trees leading from camp to camp and the paths leading back to the outhouses and the can of lime for sprinkling, and at the souvenir counters at the store the miniature birchbark canoes and the postcards that showed things looking a little better than they looked. This was the American family at play, escaping the city heat, wondering whether the newcomers in the camp at the head of the cove were "common" or "nice," wondering whether it was true that the people who drove up for Sunday dinner at the farmhouse were turned away because there wasn't enough chicken.

It seemed to me, as I kept remembering all this, that those times and those   9
summers had been infinitely precious and worth saving. There had been jollity and peace and goodness. The arriving (at the beginning of August) had been so big a business in itself, at the railway station the farm wagon drawn up, the first smell of the pine-laden air, the first glimpse of the smiling farmer, and the great importance of the trunks and your father's enormous authority in such matters, and the feel of the wagon under you for the long ten-mile haul, and at the top of the last long hill catching the first view of the lake after eleven months of not seeing this cherished body of water. The shouts and cries of the other campers when they saw you, and the trunks to be unpacked, to give up their rich burden. (Arriving was less exciting nowadays, when you sneaked up in your car and parked it under a tree near the camp and took out the bags and in five minutes it was all over, no fuss, no loud wonderful fuss about trunks.)

Peace and goodness and jollity. The only thing that was wrong now,   10
really, was the sound of the place, an unfamiliar nervous sound of the out-

board motors. This was the note that jarred, the one thing that would sometimes break the illusion and set the years moving. In those other summertimes
all motors were inboard; and when they were at a little distance, the noise
they made was a sedative, an ingredient of summer sleep. They were one-
cylinder and two-cylinder engines, and some were make-and-break and some
were jump-spark, but they all made a sleepy sound across the lake. The one-
lungers throbbed and fluttered, and the twin-cylinder ones purred and purred,
and that was a quiet sound, too. But now the campers all had outboards. In the
daytime, in the hot mornings, these motors made a petulant irritable sound;
at night in the still evening when the afterglow lit the water, they whined
about one's ears like mosquitoes. My boy loved our rented outboard, and his
great desire was to achieve single-handed mastery over it, and authority, and
he soon learned the trick of choking it a little (but not too much), and the
adjustment of the needle valve. Watching him I would remember the things
you could do with the old one-cylinder engine with the heavy flywheel, how
you could have it eating out of your hand if you got really close to it spiritually.
Motorboats in those days didn't have clutches, and you would make a landing
by shutting off the motor at the proper time and coasting in with a dead rud-
der. But there was a way of reversing them, if you learned the trick, by cutting
the switch and putting it on again exactly on the final dying revolution of the
flywheel, so that it would kick back against compression and begin reversing.
Approaching a dock in a strong following breeze, it was difficult to slow up
sufficiently by the ordinary coasting method, and if a boy felt he had complete
mastery over his motor, he was tempted to keep it running beyond its time
and then reverse it a few feet from the dock. It took a cool nerve, because if
you threw the switch a twentieth of a second too soon you would catch the flywheel when it still had speed enough to go up past center, and the boat would
leap ahead, charging bull-fashion at the dock.

   We had a good week at the camp. The bass were biting well and the sun   11
shone endlessly, day after day. We would be tired at night and lie down in
the accumulated heat of the little bedrooms after the long hot day and the
breeze would stir almost imperceptibly outside and the smell of the swamp
drift in through the rusty screens. Sleep would come easily and in the morning the red squirrel would be on the roof, tapping out his gay routine. I kept
remembering everything, lying in bed in the mornings — the small steamboat
that had a long rounded stern like the lip of a Ubangi, and how quietly she
ran on the moonlight sails, when the older boys played their mandolins and
the girls sang and we ate doughnuts dipped in sugar, and how sweet the music
was on the water in the shining night, and what it had felt like to think about
girls then. After breakfast we would go up to the store and the things were in
the same place — the minnows in a bottle, the plugs and spinners disarranged

and pawed over by the youngsters from the boys' camp, the Fig Newtons and the Beeman's gum. Outside, the road was tarred and cars stood in front of the store. Inside, all was just as it had always been, except there was more Coca-Cola and not so much Moxie and root beer and birch beer and sarsaparilla. We would walk out with a bottle of pop apiece and sometimes the pop would backfire up our noses and hurt. We explored the streams, quietly, where the turtles slid off the sunny logs and dug their way into the soft bottom; and we lay on the town wharf and fed worms to the tame bass. Everywhere we went I had trouble making out which was I, the one walking at my side, the one walking in my pants.

One afternoon while we were at the lake a thunderstorm came up. It was   12
like the revival of an old melodrama that I had seen long ago with childish awe. The second-act climax of the drama of the electrical disturbance over a lake in America had not changed in any important respect. This was the big scene, still the big scene. The whole thing was so familiar, the first feeling of oppression and heat and a general air around camp of not wanting to go very far away. In midafternoon (it was all the same) a curious darkening of the sky, and a lull in everything that had made life tick; and then the way the boats suddenly swung the other way at their moorings with the coming of a breeze out of the new quarter, and the premonitory rumble. Then the kettle drum, then the snare, then the bass drum and cymbals, then crackling light against the dark, and the gods grinning and licking their chops in the hills. Afterward the calm, the rain steadily rustling in the calm lake, the return of light and hope and spirits, and the campers running out in joy and relief to go swimming in the rain, their bright cries perpetuating the deathless joke about how they were getting simply drenched, and the children screaming with delight at the new sensation of bathing in the rain, and the joke about getting drenched linking the generations in a strong indestructible chain. And the comedian who waded in carrying an umbrella.

When the others went swimming my son said he was going in, too. He   13
pulled his dripping trunks from the line where they had hung all through the shower and wrung them out. Languidly, and with no thought of going in, I watched him, his hard little body, skinny and bare, saw him wince slightly as he pulled up around his vitals the small, soggy, icy garment. As he buckled the swollen belt, suddenly my groin felt the chill of death.

*For a reading quiz, sources on E. B. White, and annotated links to further readings on vacation memories and on fatherhood, visit **bedfordstmartins.com/thebedfordreader**.*

Journal Writing

White strongly evokes the lake camp as a place that was important to him as a child. What place or places were most important to you as a child? In your journal, jot down some memories. (To take your journal writing further, see "From Journal to Essay" on the next page.)

Questions on Meaning

1. How do you account for the distortions that creep into the author's sense of time?
2. What does the discussion of inboard and outboard motors (par. 10) have to do with the author's divided sense of time?
3. To what degree does White make us aware of his son's impression of this trip to the lake?
4. What do you take to be White's main PURPOSE in the essay? At what point do you become aware of it?

Questions on Writing Strategy

1. In paragraph 4 the author first introduces his confused feeling that he has gone back in time to his own childhood, an idea that he repeats and expands throughout his account. What is the function of these repetitions?
2. Try to describe the impact of the essay's final paragraph. By what means is it achieved?
3. To what extent is this essay written to appeal to any but middle-aged readers? Is it comprehensible to anyone whose vacations were never spent at a Maine summer cottage?
4. What is the TONE of White's essay?
5. **MIXED METHODS**   White's DESCRIPTION depends on many IMAGES that are not FIGURES OF SPEECH but literal translations of sensory impressions. Locate four such images.
6. **MIXED METHODS**   Within White's description and NARRATION of his visit to the lake, what purpose is served by the COMPARISON AND CONTRAST between the lake now and when he was a boy?

Questions on Language

1. Be sure you know the meanings of the following words: incessant, placidity (par. 1); gunwale (2); primeval (3); transposition (4); hellgrammite (5); undulating, cultist (6); indelible, tranquil (8); petulant (10); imperceptibly (11); premonitory (12); languidly (13).
2. Comment on White's DICTION in his reference to the lake as "this unique, this holy spot" (par. 2).
3. Explain what White is describing in the sentence that begins, "Then the kettle drum" (par. 12). Where else does the author use figures of speech?

Suggestions for Writing

1. **FROM JOURNAL TO ESSAY**   Choose one of the places suggested by your journal entry, and write an essay describing the place now, revisiting it as an adult. (If you haven't visited the place since childhood, you can imagine what seeing it now would be like.) Your description should draw on your childhood memories, making them as vivid as possible for the reader, but you should also consider how your POINT OF VIEW toward the place differs now.

2. In a descriptive paragraph about a real or imagined place, try to appeal to each of your reader's five senses.

3. **CRITICAL WRITING**   While on the vacation he describes, White wrote to his wife, Katharine, "This place is as American as a drink of Coca-Cola. The white collar family having its annual liberty." Obviously, not everyone has a chance at the lakeside summers White enjoyed. To what extent, if at all, does White's privileged point of view deprive his essay of universal meaning and significance? Write an essay answering this question. Back up your ideas with EVIDENCE from White's essay.

4. **CONNECTIONS**   In White's "Once More to the Lake" and Brad Manning's "Arm Wrestling with My Father" (p. 163), the writers reveal a changing sense of what it means to be a father. Write an essay that examines the similarities and differences in their definitions of fatherhood. How does a changing idea of what it means to be a son connect with this redefinition of fatherhood?

5. **CONNECTIONS**   White's essay is full of images that place readers in an important setting of his childhood. David Sedaris, in "Remembering My Childhood on the Continent of Africa" (p. 274), also uses vivid images to evoke childhood, both his own and Hugh's. After reading these two essays, write an essay of your own ANALYZING four or five images from each that strike you as especially evocative. What sense impression does each image draw on? What does each one tell you about the author's feelings?

E. B. White on Writing

"You asked me about writing—how I did it," E. B. White replied to a seventeen-year-old who had written to him, wanting to become a professional writer but feeling discouraged. "There is no trick to it. If you like to write and want to write, you write, no matter where you are or what else you are doing or whether anyone pays any heed. I must have written half a million words (mostly in my journal) before I had anything published, save for a couple of short items in *St. Nicholas*.[1] If you want to write about feelings, about the end of the summer, about growing, write about it. A great deal of writing is not

---

[1] A magazine for children, popular early in the twentieth century. —EDS.

'plotted'—most of my essays have no plot structure, they are a ramble in the woods, or a ramble in the basement of my mind. You ask, 'Who cares?' Everybody cares. You say, 'It's been written before.' Everything has been written before. . . . Henry Thoreau, who wrote *Walden*, said, 'I learned this at least by my experiment: that if one advances confidently in the direction of his dreams and endeavors to live the life which he has imagined, he will meet with a success unexpected in common hours.' The sentence, after more than a hundred years, is still alive. So, advance confidently."

In trying to characterize his own writing, White was modest in his claims. To his brother Stanley Hart White, he once remarked, "I discovered a long time ago that writing of the small things of the day, the trivial matters of the heart, the inconsequential but near things of this living, was the only kind of creative work which I could accomplish with any sincerity or grace. As a reporter, I was a flop, because I always came back laden not with facts about the case, but with a mind full of the little difficulties and amusements I had encountered in my travels. Not till *The New Yorker* came along did I ever find any means of expressing those impertinences and irrelevancies. Thus yesterday, setting out to get a story on how police horses are trained, I ended by writing a story entitled 'How Police Horses Are Trained' which never even mentions a police horse, but has to do entirely with my own absurd adventures at police headquarters. The rewards of such endeavor are not that I have acquired an audience or a following, as you suggest (fame of any kind being a Pyrrhic victory[2]), but that sometimes in writing of myself—which is the only subject anyone knows intimately—I have occasionally had the exquisite thrill of putting my finger on a little capsule of truth, and heard it give the faint squeak of mortality under my pressure, an antic sound."

For Discussion

1. Sometimes young writers are counseled to study the market and then try to write something that will sell. How would you expect E. B. White to have reacted to such advice?
2. What, exactly, does White mean when he says, "Everything has been written before"? How might an aspiring writer take this remark as encouragement?
3. What interesting distinction does White make between reporting and essay writing?

[2] A victory won at great cost. The Greek king Pyrrhus defeated the Romans in 279 BC but exclaimed afterward, "One more such victory and I am lost."—EDS.

USEFUL TERMS

Abstract and concrete Two kinds of language. *Abstract* words refer to ideas, conditions, and qualities we cannot directly perceive: *truth, love, courage, evil, poverty, progressive*. *Concrete* words indicate things we can know with our senses: *tree, chair, bird, pen, motorcycle, perfume, thunderclap*. Concrete words lend vigor and clarity to writing, for they help a reader to picture things. See IMAGE.

　　Writers of expository and argumentative essays tend to shift back and forth from one kind of language to the other. They often begin a paragraph with a general statement full of abstract words ("There is *hope* for the *future* of *motoring*"). Then they usually go on to give examples and present evidence in sentences full of concrete words ("Inventor *Jones* claims his *car* will go from *Fresno* to *Los Angeles* on a *gallon* of *peanut oil*"). Inexperienced writers often use too many abstract words and not enough concrete ones. See also pages 44–45.

Academic writing The kind of writing generally undertaken by scholars and students, in which a writer responds to another's work or uses multiple sources to develop and support an original idea. Typically based on one or more TEXTS, all academic writing calls on a writer's CRITICAL THINKING, READING, AND WRITING and shares the common goal of using reading and writing to build and exchange knowledge. See Chapter 3.

Active voice The form of the verb when the sentence subject is the actor: *Trees* [subject] *shed* [active verb] *their leaves in autumn*. Contrast PASSIVE VOICE.

Allude, allusion   To refer to a person, place, or thing believed to be common knowledge (*allude*), or the act or result of doing so (*allusion*). An allusion may point to a famous event, a familiar saying, a noted personality, a well-known story or song. Usually brief, an allusion is a space-saving way to convey much meaning. For example, the statement "The game was Coach Johnson's Waterloo" informs the reader that, like Napoleon meeting defeat in a celebrated battle, the coach led a confrontation resulting in his downfall and that of his team. If the writer is also showing Johnson's character, the allusion might further tell us that the coach is a man of Napoleonic ambition and pride. To make an effective allusion, you have to ensure that it will be clear to your audience. Not every reader, for example, would understand an allusion to a neighbor, to a seventeenth-century Russian harpsichordist, or to a little-known stock-car driver.

Analogy   An extended comparison based on the like features of two unlike things: one familiar or easily understood, the other unfamiliar, abstract, or complicated. For instance, most people know at least vaguely how the human eye works: The pupil adjusts to admit light, which registers as an image on the retina at the back of the eye. You might use this familiar information to explain something less familiar to many people, such as how a camera works: The aperture (like the pupil) adjusts to admit light, which registers as an image on the film (like the retina) at the back of the camera. Analogies are especially helpful for explaining technical information in a way that is nontechnical, more easily grasped. For example, the spacecraft *Voyager 2* transmitted spectacular pictures of Saturn to Earth. To explain the difficulty of their achievement, NASA scientists compared their feat to a golfer sinking a putt from five hundred miles away. Because it can make abstract ideas vivid and memorable, analogy is also a favorite device of philosophers, politicians, and preachers. In his celebrated speech "I Have a Dream" (p. 643), Martin Luther King, Jr., draws a remarkable analogy to express the anger and disappointment of African Americans that, one hundred years after Lincoln's Emancipation Proclamation, their full freedom has yet to be achieved. "It is obvious today," declares King, "that America has defaulted on this promissory note"; and he compares the Founding Fathers' written guarantee—of the rights of life, liberty, and the pursuit of happiness—to a bad check returned for insufficient funds.

Analogy is similar to the method of COMPARISON AND CONTRAST. Both identify the distinctive features of two things and then set the features side by side. But a comparison explains two obviously similar things—two Civil War generals, two responses to a mess—and considers both their differences and their similarities. An analogy yokes two apparently unlike things (eye and camera, spaceflight and golf, guaranteed human rights and bad checks) and focuses only on their major similarities. Analogy is thus an extended *metaphor*, the FIGURE OF SPEECH that declares one thing to be another—even though it isn't, in a strictly literal sense—for the purpose of making us aware of similarity: "Hope," writes the poet Emily Dickinson, "is the thing with feathers / That perches in the soul."

In an ARGUMENT, analogy can make readers more receptive to a point or inspire them, but it can't prove anything because in the end the subjects are dissimilar. A false analogy is a logical FALLACY that claims a fundamental likeness when none exists. See page 556.

Analyze, analysis   To separate a subject into its parts (*analyze*), or the act or result of doing so (*analysis*, also called *division*). Analysis is a key skill in CRITICAL THINK-

ING, READING, AND WRITING; see page 18. It is also considered a method of development; see Chapter 9.

Anecdote   A brief NARRATIVE, or retelling of a story or event. Anecdotes have many uses: as essay openers or closers, as examples, as sheer entertainment. See Chapter 4.

Appeals   Resources writers draw on to connect with and persuade readers:

- A **rational appeal** asks readers to use their intellects and their powers of reasoning. It relies on established conventions of logic and evidence.
- An **emotional appeal** asks readers to respond out of their beliefs, values, or feelings. It inspires, affirms, frightens, angers.
- An **ethical appeal** asks readers to look favorably on the writer. It stresses the writer's intelligence, competence, fairness, morality, and other qualities desirable in a trustworthy debater or teacher.

See also page 551.

Argument   A mode of writing intended to win readers' agreement with an assertion by engaging their powers of reasoning. Argument often overlaps PERSUASION. See Chapter 13.

Assume, assumption   To take something for granted (*assume*), or a belief or opinion taken for granted (*assumption*). Whether stated or unstated, assumptions influence a writer's choices of subject, viewpoint, EVIDENCE, and even language. See also pages 19 and 551–52.

Audience   A writer's readers. Having in mind a particular audience helps the writer in choosing strategies. Imagine, for instance, that you are writing two reviews of a new movie, one for the students who read the campus newspaper, the other for amateur and professional filmmakers who read *Millimeter*. For the first audience, you might write about the actors, the plot, and especially dramatic scenes. You might judge the picture and urge your readers to see it—or to avoid it. Writing for *Millimeter*, you might discuss special effects, shooting techniques, problems in editing and in mixing picture and sound. In this review, you might use more specialized and technical terms. Obviously, an awareness of the interests and knowledge of your readers, in each case, would help you decide how to write. If you told readers of the campus paper too much about filming techniques, you would lose most of them. If you told *Millimeter*'s readers the film's plot in detail, probably you would put them to sleep.

You can increase your awareness of your audience by asking yourself a few questions before you begin to write. Who are to be your readers? What is their age level? background? education? Where do they live? What are their beliefs and attitudes? What interests them? What, if anything, sets them apart from most people? How familiar are they with your subject? Knowing your audience can help you write so that your readers will not only understand you better but care more deeply about what you say.

Cause and effect   A method of development in which a writer ANALYZES reasons for an action, event, or decision, or analyzes its consequences. See Chapter 11. See also EFFECT.

Chronological order   The arrangement of events as they occurred or occur in time, first to last. Most NARRATION and PROCESS ANALYSIS use chronological order.

Claim   The proposition that an ARGUMENT demonstrates, generally expressed in a THESIS STATEMENT. See page 550.

Classification   A method of development in which a writer sorts out plural things (contact sports, college students, kinds of music) into categories. See Chapter 10.

Cliché   A worn-out, trite expression that a writer employs thoughtlessly. Although at one time the expression may have been colorful, from heavy use it has lost its luster. It is now "old as the hills." In conversation, most of us sometimes use clichés, but in writing they "stick out like sore thumbs." Alert writers, when they revise, replace a cliché with a fresh, concrete expression. Writers who have trouble recognizing clichés should be suspicious of any phrase they've heard before and should try to read more widely. Their problem is that, so many expressions being new to them, they do not know which ones are full of moths.

Coherence   The clear connection of the parts in effective writing so that the reader can easily follow the flow of ideas between sentences, paragraphs, and larger divisions, and can see how they relate successively to one another.

In making your essay coherent, you may find certain devices useful. TRANSITIONS, for instance, can bridge ideas. Reminders of points you have stated earlier are helpful to a reader who may have forgotten them — as readers tend to do sometimes, particularly if your essay is long. However, a coherent essay is not one merely pasted together with transitions and reminders. It derives its coherence from the clear relationship between its THESIS (or central idea) and all its parts. See also pages 43 and 250–51.

Colloquial expressions   Words and phrases occurring primarily in speech and in informal writing that seeks a relaxed, conversational tone. "My favorite chow is a burger and a shake" or "This math exam has me wired" may be acceptable in talking to a roommate, in corresponding with a friend, or in writing a humorous essay for general readers. Such choices of words, however, would be out of place in formal writing — in, say, a laboratory report or a letter to your senator. Contractions (*let's, don't, we'll*) and abbreviated words (*photo, sales rep, ad*) are the shorthand of spoken language. Good writers use such expressions with an awareness that they produce an effect of casualness.

Comparison and contrast   Two methods of development usually found together. Using them, a writer examines the similarities and differences between two things to reveal their natures. See Chapter 7.

Conclusion   The sentences or paragraphs that bring an essay to a satisfying and logical end. A conclusion is purposefully crafted to give a sense of unity and completeness to the whole essay. The best conclusions evolve naturally out of what has gone before and convince the reader that the essay is indeed at an end, not that the writer has run out of steam.

Conclusions vary in type and length depending on the nature and scope of the essay. A long research paper may require several paragraphs of summary to review and emphasize the main points. A short essay, however, may benefit from a few brief closing sentences.

In concluding an essay, beware of diminishing the impact of your writing by finishing on a weak note. Don't apologize for what you have or have not written, or cram in a final detail that would have been better placed elsewhere.

Although there are no set formulas for closing, the following list presents several options:

- Restate the thesis of your essay, and perhaps your main points.
- Mention the broader implications or significance of your topic.
- Give a final example that pulls all the parts of your discussion together.
- Offer a prediction.
- End with the most important point as the culmination of your essay's development.
- Suggest how the reader can apply the information you have just imparted.
- End with a bit of drama or flourish. Tell an ANECDOTE, offer an appropriate quotation, ask a question, make a final insightful remark. Keep in mind, however, that an ending shouldn't sound false and gimmicky. It truly has to conclude.

Concrete   See ABSTRACT AND CONCRETE.

Connotation and denotation   Two types of meanings most words have. *Denotation* is the explicit, literal, dictionary definition of a word. *Connotation* refers to a word's implied meaning, resonant with associations. The denotation of *blood* is "the fluid that circulates in the vascular system." The connotations of *blood* range from *life force* to *gore* to *family bond*. A doctor might use the word *blood* for its denotation, and a mystery writer might rely on the word's connotations to heighten a scene.

Because people have different experiences, they bring to the same word different associations. A conservative's emotional response to the word *welfare* is not likely to be the same as a liberal's. And referring to your senator as a *diplomat* evokes a different response, from the senator and from others, than would *baby-kisser, political hack,* or even *politician*. The effective use of words involves knowing both what they mean literally and what they are likely to suggest.

Critical thinking, reading, and writing   A group of interlocking skills that are essential for college work and beyond. Each seeks the meaning beneath the surface of a statement, poem, editorial, picture, advertisement, Web site, or other TEXT. Using ANALYSIS, INFERENCE, SYNTHESIS, and often EVALUATION, the critical thinker, reader, and writer separates this text into its elements in order to see and judge meanings, relations, and ASSUMPTIONS that might otherwise remain buried. See also pages 9–12, 16–31, 353–54, 548–49.

Data   A name for EVIDENCE favored by philosopher Stephen Toulmin in his conception of ARGUMENT. See pages 550–51.

Deductive reasoning, deduction   The method of reasoning from the general to the particular: From information about what we already know, we deduce what we need or want to know. See Chapter 13, pages 553–54.

Definition   A statement of the literal and specific meaning or meanings of a word or a method of developing an essay. In the latter, the writer usually explains the nature of a word, a thing, a concept, or a phenomenon. Such a definition may employ NARRATION, DESCRIPTION, or any other method. See Chapter 12.

Denotation   See CONNOTATION AND DENOTATION.

Description   A mode of writing that conveys the evidence of the senses: sight, hearing, touch, taste, smell. See Chapter 5.

Diction   The choice of words. Every written or spoken statement contains diction of some kind. To describe certain aspects of diction, the following terms may be useful:

- **Standard English:** the common American language, words, and grammatical forms that are used and expected in school, business, and other sites.
- **Nonstandard English:** words and grammatical forms such as *theirselves* and *ain't* that are used mainly by people who speak a dialect other than standard English.
- **Dialect:** a variety of English based on differences in geography, education, or social background. Dialect is usually spoken but may be written. Maya Angelou's essay in Chapter 4 transcribes the words of dialect speakers ("'He gone whip him till that white boy call him Momma' ").
- **Slang:** certain words in highly informal speech or writing, or in the speech of a particular group—for example, *blow off, dis, dweeb.*
- **Colloquial expressions:** words and phrases from conversation. See COLLO-QUIAL EXPRESSIONS for examples.
- **Regional terms:** words heard in a certain locality, such as *spritzing* for "raining" in Pennsylvania Dutch country.
- **Technical terms:** words and phrases that form the vocabulary of a particular discipline (*monocotyledon* from botany), occupation (*drawplate* from die-making), or avocation (*interval training* from running). See also JARGON.
- **Archaisms:** old-fashioned expressions, once common but now used to suggest an earlier style, such as *ere* and *forsooth.*
- **Obsolete diction:** words that have passed out of use (such as the verb *werien,* "to protect or defend," and the noun *isetnesses,* "agreements"). *Obsolete* may also refer to certain meanings of words no longer current (*fond* for foolish, *clipping* for hugging or embracing).
- **Pretentious diction:** use of words more numerous and elaborate than necessary, such as *institution of higher learning* for college, and *partake of solid nourishment* for eat.

Archaic, obsolete, and pretentious diction usually have no place in good writing unless for ironic or humorous effect: the journalist and critic H. L. Mencken delighted in the hifalutin use of *tonsorial studio* instead of barber shop. Still, any diction may be the right diction for a certain occasion: The choice of words depends on a writer's PURPOSE and AUDIENCE.

Discovery   The stage of the writing process before the first draft. It may include deciding on a topic, narrowing the topic, creating or finding ideas, doing reading and other research, defining PURPOSE and AUDIENCE, planning and arranging material. Discovery may follow from daydreaming or meditation, reading, or perhaps carefully ransacking memory. In practice, though, it usually involves considerable writing and is aided by the act of writing. The operations of discovery—reading, research, further idea creation, and refinement of subject, purpose, and audience—may all continue well into drafting as well. See also pages 37–39.

Division   See ANALYZE, ANALYSIS.

Dominant impression   The main idea a writer conveys about a subject through DESCRIPTION—that an elephant is gigantic, for example, or an experience scary. See also Chapter 5.

Drafting   The stage of the writing process during which a writer expresses ideas in complete sentences, links them, and arranges them in a sequence. See also pages 40–41, 51–53.

Editing   The final stage of the writing process, during which a writer corrects errors and improves stylistic matters by, for example, using the ACTIVE VOICE and reworking sentences to achieve PARALLEL STRUCTURE. Contrast with REVISION. And see pages 44–50 and 56–57.

Effect   The result of an event or action, usually considered together with CAUSE as a method of development. See the discussion of cause and effect in Chapter 11. In discussing writing, the term *effect* also refers to the impression a word, a sentence, a paragraph, or an entire work makes on the reader: how convincing it is, whether it elicits an emotional response, what associations it conjures up, and so on.

Emotional appeal   See APPEALS.

Emphasis   The stress or special importance given to a certain point or element to make it stand out. A skillful writer draws attention to what is most important in a sentence, a paragraph, or an essay by controlling emphasis in any of the following ways:

- **Proportion:** Important ideas are given greater coverage than minor points.
- **Position:** The beginnings and ends of sentences, paragraphs, and larger divisions are the strongest positions. Placing key ideas in these spots helps draw attention to their importance. The end is the stronger position, for what stands last stands out. A sentence in which less important details precede the main point is called a **periodic sentence:** "Having disguised himself as a guard and walked through the courtyard to the side gate, the prisoner made his escape." A sentence in which the main point precedes less important details is a **loose sentence:** "Autumn is orange: gourds in baskets at roadside stands, the harvest moon hanging like a pumpkin, and oak leaves flashing like goldfish."
- **Repetition:** Careful repetition of key words or phrases can give them greater importance. (Careless repetition, however, can cause boredom.)
- **Mechanical devices:** Italics (underlining), capital letters, and exclamation points can make words or sentences stand out. Writers sometimes fall back on these devices, however, after failing to show significance by other means. Italics and exclamation points can be useful in reporting speech, but excessive use sounds exaggerated or bombastic.

For additional ways to emphasize ideas at the sentence level, see pages 46–47.

Essay   A short nonfiction composition on one central theme or subject in which the writer may offer personal views. Essays are sometimes classified as either formal or informal. In general, a **formal essay** is one whose DICTION is that of the written language (not colloquial speech), serious in TONE, and usually focused on a subject the writer believes is important. (For example, see Bruce Catton's "Grant and Lee.") An **informal essay,** in contrast, is more likely to admit COLLOQUIAL EXPRESSIONS; the writer's tone tends to be lighter, perhaps humorous, and the subject is likely to be personal, sometimes even trivial. (See Dave Barry's "Batting Clean-Up and Striking Out.") These distinctions, however, are rough ones: An essay such as Judy Brady's "I Want a Wife" uses colloquial language and speaks of personal experience, but its tone is serious and its subject important.

Ethical appeal   See APPEALS.

Euphemism   The use of inoffensive language in place of language that readers or listeners may find hurtful, distasteful, frightening, or otherwise objectionable—for instance, a police officer's announcing that someone *passed on* rather than *died*, or a politician's calling for *revenue enhancement* rather than *taxation*. Writers sometimes use euphemism out of consideration for readers' feelings, but just as often they use it to deceive readers or shirk responsibility. (For more on euphemism, see William Lutz's "The World of Doublespeak" in Chap. 10.)

Evaluate, evaluation   To judge the merits of something (*evaluate*) or the act or result of doing so (*evaluation*). Evaluation is often part of CRITICAL THINKING, READING, AND WRITING. In evaluating a work of writing, you base your judgment on your ANALYSIS of it and your sense of its quality or value. See also pages 19–20, 30–31, 67–70.

Evidence   The details that support an argument or an explanation, including facts, examples, and expert opinions. A writer's opinions and GENERALIZATIONS must rest upon evidence. See pages 550–51.

Example   Also called **exemplification** or **illustration**, a method of development in which the writer provides instances of a general idea. See Chapter 6. An *example* is a verbal illustration.

Exposition   The mode of prose writing that explains (or exposes) its subject. Its function is to inform, to instruct, or to set forth ideas: the major trade routes in the Middle East, how to make a dulcimer, why the United States consumes more energy than it needs. Exposition may call various methods to its service: EXAMPLE, COMPARISON AND CONTRAST, PROCESS ANALYSIS, and so on. Most college writing is at least partly exposition, and so are most of the essays in this book.

Fallacies   Errors in reasoning. See pages 554–56 for a list and examples.

Figures of speech   Expressions that depart from the literal meanings of words for the sake of emphasis or vividness. To say "She's a jewel" doesn't mean that the subject of praise is literally a kind of shining stone; the statement makes sense because its CONNOTATIONS come to mind: rare, priceless, worth cherishing. Some figures of speech involve comparisons of two objects apparently unlike:

- A **simile** (from the Latin, "likeness") states the comparison directly, usually connecting the two things using *like, as,* or *than:* "The moon is like a snowball," "He's as lazy as a cat full of cream," "My feet are flatter than flyswatters."
- A **metaphor** (from the Greek, "transfer") declares one thing to *be* another: "A mighty fortress is our God," "The sheep were bolls of cotton on the hill." (A **dead metaphor** is a word or phrase that, originally a figure of speech, has come to be literal through common usage: "the *hands* of a clock.")
- **Personification** is a simile or metaphor that assigns human traits to inanimate objects or abstractions: "A stoop-shouldered refrigerator hummed quietly to itself," "The solution to the math problem sat there winking at me."

Other figures of speech consist of deliberate misrepresentations:

- **Hyperbole** (from the Greek, "throwing beyond") is a conscious exaggeration: "I'm so hungry I could eat a saddle," "I'd wait for you a thousand years."
- The opposite of hyperbole, **understatement**, creates an ironic or humorous effect: "I accepted the ride. At the moment, I didn't feel like walking across the Mojave Desert."
- A **paradox** (from the Greek, "conflicting with expectation") is a seemingly self-contradictory statement that, on reflection, makes sense: "Children are the

poor person's wealth" (wealth can be monetary, or it can be spiritual). *Paradox* may also refer to a situation that is inexplicable or contradictory, such as the restriction of one group's rights in order to secure the rights of another group.

Flashback   A technique of NARRATION in which the sequence of events is interrupted to recall an earlier period.

Focus   The narrowing of a subject to make it manageable. Beginning with a general subject, you concentrate on a certain aspect of it. For instance, you may select crafts as a general subject, then decide your main interest lies in weaving. You could focus your essay still further by narrowing it to operating a hand loom. You also focus your writing according to who will read it (AUDIENCE) or what you want it to achieve (PURPOSE).

General and specific   Terms that describe the relative number of instances or objects included in the group signified by a word. *General* words name a group or class (*flowers*); *specific* words limit the class by naming its individual members (*rose, violet, dahlia, marigold*). Words may be arranged in a series from more general to more specific: *clothes, pants, jeans, Levis.* The word *cat* is more specific than *animal*, but less specific than *tiger cat*, or *Garfield*. See also ABSTRACT AND CONCRETE and pages 158–59.

Generalization   A statement about a class based on an examination of some of its members: "Lions are fierce." The more members examined and the more representative they are of the class, the sturdier the generalization. The statement "Solar heat saves home owners money" would be challenged by home owners who have yet to recover their installation costs. "Solar heat can save home owners money in the long run" would be a sounder generalization. Insufficient or nonrepresentative EVIDENCE often leads to a hasty generalization, such as "All freshmen hate their roommates" or "Men never express their feelings." Words such as *all, every, only, never,* and *always* have to be used with care: "Some men don't express their feelings" is more credible. Making a trustworthy generalization involves the use of INDUCTIVE REASONING (discussed on pp. 552–53).

Genre   The category into which a piece of writing fits. Shaped by PURPOSE, AUDIENCE, and context, genres range from broad types (such as fiction and nonfiction) to general groups (novel, essay) to narrower groups (science fiction novel, personal narrative) to specific document formats (steampunk graphic novel, post on a retail workers' community forum) — and they tend to overlap. The genres of college writing vary widely. Examples appear on pages 107–09 (case study), 161–62 (field observation), 209–10 (job-application letter), 253–54 (review), 307 (lab report), 359 (annotated bibliography), 407 (résumé), 464–65 (letter to the editor), 515–16 (essay exam), and 562–63 (proposal).

Most readers are instinctively aware of individual genres and the characteristics that distinguish them, and they expect writers to follow the genre's conventions for POINT OF VIEW, structure and organization, types of EVIDENCE, language, TONE, length, appearance, and so forth. Consider, for instance, your daily newspaper: As a reader, you expect the news articles to be objective statements of fact, with none of the reporters' personal thoughts and little rhetorical flourish; but when you turn to the op-ed page or your favorite columnist, such opinions and clever turns of phrase are precisely what you're looking for. Similar expectations exist for every kind of writing, and good writers make a point of knowing what they are. See also pages 11, 22, 36, and 41–42 and the individual chapter introductions in Part Two.

Grounds   A name for EVIDENCE favored by philosopher Stephen Toulmin in his conception of ARGUMENT. See page 550.

Hyperbole   See FIGURES OF SPEECH.

Illustration   Another name for EXAMPLE. See Chapter 6.

Image   A word or word sequence that evokes a sensory experience. Whether literal ("We picked two red apples") or figurative ("His cheeks looked like two red apples, buffed and shining"), an image appeals to the reader's memory of seeing, hearing, smelling, touching, or tasting. Images add concreteness to fiction—"The farm looked as tiny and still as a seashell, with the little knob of a house surrounded by its curved furrows of tomato plants" (Eudora Welty in a short story, "The Whistle")—and are an important element in poetry. But writers of essays, too, use images to bring ideas down to earth. See also FIGURES OF SPEECH.

Inductive reasoning, induction   The process of reasoning to a conclusion about an entire class by examining some of its members. See pages 552–53.

Infer, inference   To draw a conclusion (*infer*), or the act or result of doing so (*inference*). In CRITICAL THINKING, READING, AND WRITING, inference is the means to understanding a writer's meaning, ASSUMPTIONS, PURPOSE, fairness, and other attributes. See also pages 19 and 28–30.

Introduction   The opening of a written work. Often it states the writer's subject, narrows it, and communicates the writer's main idea (THESIS). Introductions vary in length, depending on their purposes. A research paper may need several paragraphs to set forth its central idea and its plan of organization; a brief, informal essay may need only a sentence or two for an introduction. Whether long or short, good introductions tell readers no more than they need to know when they begin reading. Here are a few possible ways to open an essay effectively:

- State your central idea, or thesis, perhaps showing why you care about it.
- Present startling facts about your subject.
- Tell an illustrative ANECDOTE.
- Give background information that will help your reader understand your subject, or see why it is important.
- Begin with an arresting quotation.
- Ask a challenging question. (In your essay, you'll go on to answer it.)

Irony   A manner of speaking or writing that does not directly state a discrepancy, but implies one. **Verbal irony** is the intentional use of words to suggest a meaning other than literal: "What a mansion!" (said of a shack); "There's nothing like sunshine" (said on a foggy morning). (For more examples, see the essays by Jessica Mitford, Linnea Saukko, and Judy Brady.) If irony is delivered contemptuously with an intent to hurt, we call it **sarcasm:** "Oh, you're a real friend!" (said to someone who refuses to lend the speaker the coins to operate a clothes dryer). With **situational irony,** the circumstances themselves are incongruous, run contrary to expectations, or twist fate: Juliet regains consciousness only to find that Romeo, believing her dead, has stabbed himself. See also SATIRE.

Jargon   Strictly speaking, the special vocabulary of a trade or profession. The term has also come to mean inflated, vague, meaningless language of any kind. It is characterized by wordiness, ABSTRACTIONS galore, pretentious DICTION, and needlessly complicated word order. Whenever you meet a sentence that obviously could express its idea in fewer words and shorter ones, chances are that it is jargon. For instance: "The motivating force compelling her to opt continually for the most labor-intensive mode of operation in performing her functions was consistently observed to be the single constant and regular factor in her behavior patterns." Translation: "She did everything the hard way." (For more on such jargon, see William Lutz's "The World of Doublespeak" in Chap. 10.)

Journal   A record of one's thoughts, kept daily or at least regularly. Keeping a journal faithfully can help a writer gain confidence and develop ideas. See also page 37.

Metaphor   See FIGURES OF SPEECH.

Narration   The mode of writing that tells a story. See Chapter 4.

Narrator   The teller of a story, usually either in the first PERSON (*I*) or in the third (*he, she, it, they*). See pages 100–01.

Nonstandard English   See DICTION.

Objective and subjective   Kinds of writing that differ in emphasis. In *objective* writing, the emphasis falls on the topic; in *subjective* writing, it falls on the writer's view of the topic. Objective writing occurs in factual journalism, science reports, certain PROCESS ANALYSES (such as recipes, directions, and instructions), and logical arguments in which the writer attempts to downplay personal feelings and opinions. Subjective writing sets forth the writer's feelings, opinions, and interpretations. It occurs in friendly letters, journals, bylined feature stories and columns in newspapers, personal essays, and ARGUMENTS that appeal to emotion. Few essays, however, contain one kind of writing exclusive of the other.

Paradox   See FIGURES OF SPEECH.

Paragraph   A group of closely related sentences that develop a central idea. In an essay, a paragraph is the most important unit of thought because it is both self-contained and part of the larger whole. Paragraphs separate long and involved ideas into smaller parts that are more manageable for the writer and easier for the reader to take in. Good paragraphs, like good essays, possess UNITY and COHERENCE. The central idea is usually stated in a TOPIC SENTENCE, often found at the beginning of the paragraph that relates directly to the essay's THESIS. All other sentences in the paragraph relate to this topic sentence, defining it, explaining it, illustrating it, providing it with evidence and support. If you meet a unified and coherent paragraph that has no topic sentence, it will contain a central idea that no sentence in it explicitly states, but that every sentence in it clearly implies. See also pages 250–51 (paragraph coherence), 403–04 (paragraph development), and 512–13 (paragraph unity).

Parallelism, parallel structure   A habit of good writers: keeping ideas of equal importance in similar grammatical form. A writer may place nouns side by side (*"Trees* and *streams* are my weekend tonic") or in a series ("Give me *wind, sea,* and *stars*"). Phrases, too, may be arranged in parallel structure (*"Out of my bed, into my shoes, up to my classroom*—that's my life"); or clauses ("Ask not what your country can do for you; ask what you can do for your country").

Parallelism may be found not only in single sentences but in larger units as well. A paragraph might read: "Rhythm is everywhere. It throbs in the rain forests of Brazil. It vibrates ballroom floors in Vienna. It snaps its fingers on street corners in Chicago." In a whole essay, parallelism may be the principle used to arrange ideas in a balanced or harmonious structure. See the famous speech given by Martin

Luther King, Jr. (p. 643), in which paragraphs 11–18 all begin with the words "I have a dream" and describe an imagined future. Not only does such a parallel structure organize ideas, but it also lends them force. See also page 47.

Paraphrase   Putting another writer's thoughts into your own words. In writing a research paper or an essay containing EVIDENCE gathered from your reading, you will find it necessary to paraphrase—unless you are using another writer's very words with quotation marks around them—and to acknowledge your sources. Contrast SUMMARY. And see pages 65–66.

Passive voice   The form of the verb when the sentence subject is acted upon: *The report* [subject] *was published* [passive verb] *anonymously*. Contrast ACTIVE VOICE.

Person   A grammatical distinction made between the speaker, the one spoken to, and the one spoken about. In the first person (*I, we*), the subject is speaking. In the second person (*you*), the subject is being spoken to. In the third person (*he, she, it*), the subject is being spoken about. The point of view of an essay or work of fiction is often specified according to person: "This short story is told from a first-person point of view." See POINT OF VIEW.

Personification   See FIGURES OF SPEECH.

Persuasion   A mode of writing intended to influence people's actions by engaging their beliefs and feelings. Persuasion often overlaps ARGUMENT. See Chapter 13.

Plagiarism   The use of someone else's ideas or words as if they were your own, without acknowledging the original author. See pages 71–73.

Point of view   In an essay, the physical position or the mental angle from which a writer beholds a subject. On the subject of starlings, the following three writers would likely have different points of view: An ornithologist might write OBJEC-TIVELY about the introduction of these birds into North America, a farmer might advise other farmers how to prevent the birds from eating seed, and a bird-watcher might SUBJECTIVELY describe a first glad sighting of an unusual species. Whether objective or subjective, point of view also encompasses a writer's biases and ASSUMPTIONS about a subject. For instance, the scientist, farmer, and bird-watcher would likely all have different perspectives on starlings' reputation as nuisances: Although such perspectives may or may not be expressed directly, they would likely influence each writer's approach to the subject. See also PERSON.

Premise   A proposition or ASSUMPTION that leads to a conclusion. See pages 553–54 for examples.

Process analysis   A method of development that most often explains step by step how something is done or how to do something. See Chapter 8.

Purpose   A writer's reason for trying to convey a particular idea (THESIS) about a particular subject to a particular AUDIENCE of readers. Though it may emerge gradually during the writing process, in the end purpose should govern every element of a piece of writing.

   In trying to define the purpose of an essay you read, ask yourself, "Why did the writer write this?" or "What was this writer trying to achieve?" Even though you cannot know the writer's intentions with absolute certainty, an effective essay will make some purpose clear.

Rational appeal   See APPEALS.

Revision   The stage of the writing process during which a writer "re-sees" a draft from the viewpoint of a reader. Revision usually involves rethinking fundamental

matters such as PURPOSE and organization as well as rewriting to ensure COHER-
ENCE and UNITY. See pages 41–43, 53–57. See also EDITING.

Rhetoric   The study (and the art) of using language effectively. *Rhetoric* also has a
negative CONNOTATION of empty or pretentious language meant to waffle, stall,
or even deceive. This is the meaning in "The president had nothing substantial
to say about taxes, just the usual rhetoric."

Rhetorical question   A question posed for effect, one that requires no answer. Instead,
it often provokes thought, lends emphasis to a point, asserts or denies something
without making a direct statement, launches further discussion, introduces an
opinion, or leads the reader where the writer intends. Sometimes a writer throws
one in to introduce variety in a paragraph full of declarative sentences. The following questions are rhetorical: "When will the United States learn that sending
people into space does not feed them on the earth?" "Shall I compare thee to a
summer's day?" "What is the point of making money if you've no one but yourself
to spend it on?" Both reader and writer know what the answers are supposed to
be. (1) Someday, if the United States ever wises up. (2) Yes. (3) None.

Sarcasm   See IRONY.

Satire   A form of writing that employs wit to attack folly. Unlike most comedy, the
purpose of satire is not merely to entertain, but to bring about enlightenment —
even reform. Usually, satire employs irony — as in Linnea Saukko's "How to
Poison the Earth" and Jonathan Swift's "A Modest Proposal." See also IRONY.

Scene   In a NARRATION, an event retold in detail to re-create an experience. See
Chapter 4.

Sentimentality   A quality sometimes found in writing that fails to communicate.
Such writing calls for an extreme emotional response on the part of an AUDIENCE,
although its writer fails to supply adequate reason for any such reaction. A sentimental writer delights in waxing teary over certain objects: great-grandmother's
portrait, the first stick of chewing gum baby chewed (now a shapeless wad), an
empty popcorn box saved from the World Series of 1996. Sentimental writing
usually results when writers shut their eyes to the actual world, preferring to
snuffle the sweet scents of remembrance.

Signal phrase   Words used to introduce a quotation, PARAPHRASE, or SUMMARY,
often including the source author's name and generally telling readers how the
source material should be interpreted: "Nelson argues that the legislation will
backfire." See also pages 66–67.

Simile   See FIGURES OF SPEECH.

Slang   See DICTION.

Specific   See GENERAL AND SPECIFIC.

Standard English   See DICTION.

Strategy   Whatever means a writer employs to write effectively. The methods set
forth in this book are strategies; but so are narrowing a subject, organizing ideas
clearly, using TRANSITIONS, writing with an awareness of your reader, and other
effective writing practices.

Style   The distinctive manner in which a writer writes. Style may be seen especially
in the writer's choice of words and sentence structures. Two writers may write on
the same subject, even express similar ideas, but it is style that gives each writer's
work a personality.

Subjective   See OBJECTIVE AND SUBJECTIVE.

Summarize, summary   To condense a work (essay, movie, news story) to its essence (*summarize*), or the act or result of doing so (*summary*). Summarizing a piece of writing in one's own words is an effective way to understand it. (See p. 17.) Summarizing (and acknowledging) others' writing in your own text is a good way to support your ideas. (See pp. 64–65.) Contrast PARAPHRASE.

Suspense   Often an element in NARRATION: the pleasurable expectation or anxiety we feel that keeps us reading a story. In an exciting mystery story, suspense is constant: How will it all turn out? Will the detective get to the scene in time to prevent another murder? But there can be suspense in less melodramatic accounts as well.

Syllogism   A three-step form of reasoning that employs DEDUCTION. See page 553 for an illustration.

Symbol   A visible object or action that suggests further meaning. The flag suggests country, the crown suggests royalty—these are conventional symbols familiar to us. Life abounds in such clear-cut symbols. Football teams use dolphins and rams for easy identification; married couples symbolize their union with a ring.

In writing, symbols usually do not have such a one-to-one correspondence, but evoke a whole constellation of associations. In Herman Melville's *Moby-Dick*, the whale suggests more than the large mammal it is. It hints at evil, obsession, and the untamable forces of nature. Such a symbol carries meanings too complex or elusive to be neatly defined.

Although more common in fiction and poetry, symbols can be used to good purpose in nonfiction because they often communicate an idea in a compact and concrete way.

Synthesize, synthesis   To link elements into a whole (*synthesize*), or the act or result of doing so (*synthesis*). In CRITICAL THINKING, READING, AND WRITING, synthesis is the key step during which you use your own perspective to reassemble a work you have ANALYZED or to connect the work with others. (See pp. 19 and 30.) Synthesis is a hallmark of ACADEMIC WRITING in which you respond to others' work or use multiple sources to support your ideas. (See pp. 63–64, 70–71.)

Text   Any creation—written, visual, auditory, physical, or experiential—that can be interpreted or used as a source for writing. The starting point for most ACADEMIC WRITING, texts include written documents such as essays, articles, and books, of course, but also photographs, paintings, advertisements, Web sites, performances, musical scores, experiments, conversations, lectures, field observations, interviews, dreams, jokes—anything that invites a response, sparks an idea, or lends itself to CRITICAL READING, THINKING, AND WRITING. See pages 62–64.

Thesis   The central idea in a work of writing, to which everything else in the work refers. In some way, each sentence and PARAGRAPH in an effective essay serves to support the thesis and to make it clear and explicit to readers. Good writers, while writing, often set down a **thesis statement** or **thesis sentence** to help them define their purpose. They also often include this statement in their essay as a promise and a guide to readers. See also pages 20, 39–40, 42, and 356.

Tone   The way a writer expresses his or her regard for subject, AUDIENCE, or self. Through word choice, sentence structures, and what is actually said, the writer conveys an attitude and sets a prevailing spirit. Tone in writing varies as greatly as tone of voice varies in conversation. It can be serious, distant, flippant, angry, enthusiastic, sincere, sympathetic. Whatever tone a writer chooses, usually it informs an entire essay and helps a reader decide how to respond. For works of strong tone, see the essays by Maya Angelou, Jessica Mitford, Judy Brady, Russell Baker, Edwidge Danticat, and Martin Luther King, Jr. See also pages 558–59.

Topic sentence   The statement of the central idea in a PARAGRAPH, usually asserting one aspect of an essay's THESIS. Often the topic sentence will appear at (or near) the beginning of the paragraph, announcing the idea and beginning its development. Because all other sentences in the paragraph explain and support this central idea, the topic sentence is a way to create UNITY.

Transitions   Words, phrases, sentences, or even paragraphs that relate ideas. In moving from one topic to the next, a writer has to bring the reader along by showing how the ideas are developing, what bearing a new thought or detail has on an earlier discussion, or why a new topic is being introduced. A clear purpose, strong ideas, and logical development certainly aid COHERENCE, but to ensure that the reader is following along, good writers provide signals, or transitions.

To bridge sentences or paragraphs and to point out relationships within them, you can use some of the following devices of transition:

- Repeat or restate words or phrases to produce an echo in the reader's mind.
- Use PARALLEL STRUCTURES to produce a rhythm that moves the reader forward.
- Use pronouns to refer back to nouns in earlier passages.
- Use transitional words and phrases. These may indicate a relationship of time (*right away, later, soon, meanwhile, in a few minutes, that night*), proximity (*beside, close to, distant from, nearby, facing*), effect (*therefore, for this reason, as a result, consequently*), comparison (*similarly, in the same way, likewise*), or contrast (*yet, but, nevertheless, however, despite*). Some words and phrases of transition simply add on: *besides, too, also, moreover, in addition to, second, last, in the end.*

Understatement   See FIGURES OF SPEECH.

Unity   The quality of good writing in which all parts relate to the THESIS. In a unified essay, all words, sentences, and PARAGRAPHS support the single central idea. Your first step in achieving unity is to state your thesis; your next step is to organize your thoughts so that they make your thesis clear. See also pages 512–13.

Voice   In writing, the sense of the author's character, personality, and attitude that comes through the words. See TONE.

Warrant   The name for ASSUMPTION favored by philosopher Stephen Toulmin in his conception of ARGUMENT. See pages 551–52.

Acknowledgments

Chris Anderson. "The Rise and Fall of the Hit" from the book *The Long Tail: Why the Future of Business Is Selling Less of More* by Chris Anderson. Copyright © 2006 by Chris Anderson. Reprinted by permission of Hyperion. All rights reserved.

Maya Angelou. "Champion of the World" from *I Know Why the Caged Bird Sings* by Maya Angelou. Copyright © 1969 and renewed 1997 by Maya Angelou. Reprinted by permission of Random House, Inc. "Maya Angelou on Writing" excerpted from Sheila Weller, "Work in Progress/Maya Angelou," from *Intellectual Digest*, June 1973. Reprinted by permission of Sheila Weller.

Barbara Lazear Ascher. "On Compassion," from *The Habit of Loving* by Barbara Ascher. Copyright © 1986, 1987, 1989 by Barbara Lazear Ascher. Used by permission of Random House, Inc. "Barbara Lazear Ascher on Writing" from Gale Group. *Contemporary Authors Online*. Copyright © Gale, a part of Cengage Learning, Inc. Reprinted by permission. *www.cengage.com/permissions*

Laila Ayad, "The Capricious Camera." Reprinted by permission of the author.

Russell Baker. "The Plot against People" from the *New York Times*, June 18, 1968. Copyright © June 18, 1968, by The New York Times. All rights reserved. Used by permission and protected by the Copyright Laws of the United States. The printing, copying, redistribution, or retransmission of the Material without express written permission is prohibited. "Russell Baker on Writing" from "Computer Fallout" in the *New York Times Magazine*, October 11, 1987. Copyright © 1987 by Russell Baker. Reprinted by permission of Don Congdon Associates, Inc.

Dave Barry. "Batting Clean-Up and Striking Out" from *Dave Barry's Greatest Hits* by Dave Barry. Copyright © 1988 by Dave Barry. Reprinted by permission of Crown Publishers, a division of Random House, Inc. "Dave Barry on Writing" from Gale Group. *Contemporary Authors Online*. Copyright © Gale, a part of Cengage Learning, Inc. Reprinted by permission. *www.cengage.com/permissions*

Judy Brady. "I Want a Wife." Copyright © 1970 by Judy Brady. Reprinted by permission of the author. "Judy Brady on Writing" from a September 5, 2007, interview with Judy Brady.

Suzanne Britt. "Neat People vs. Sloppy People" from *Show and Tell*, 1982. Reprinted by permission of the author. "Suzanne Britt on Writing." Reprinted by permission of the author.

Bruce Catton. "Grant and Lee: A Study in Contrasts." Copyright © 1956 by United States Capitol Historical Society. All rights reserved. Reprinted by permission. "Bruce Catton on Writing" excerpted from Oliver Jensen's introduction to Bruce Catton's *America*. Copyright © 1979.

George Chauncey. "The Legacy of Antigay Discrimination" from *Why Marriage? The History Shaping Today's Debate over Gay Equality*. Copyright © 2005 George Chauncey. Reprinted by permission of Basic Books, a member of the Perseus Books Group.

Linda Chavez. "Supporting Family Values" from *townhall.com*, Friday, April 17, 2009. Reprinted by permission of Linda Chavez and Creators Syndicate, Inc. "Linda Chavez on Writing" from *The Enterprise*, February 11, 2002.

Sandra Cisneros. "Only Daughter." Copyright © 1990 by Sandra Cisneros. First published in *Glamour*, November 1990. Reprinted by permission of Susan Bergholz Literary Services, New York, NY, and Lamy, NM. All rights reserved. "Sandra Cisneros on Writing" excerpted from *Interviews with Writers of the Post-Colonial World*, edited by Feroza Jussawalla and Reed Way Dasenbrock. Copyright © 1992 by the University Press of Mississippi. Reprinted by permission.

Charles Colson with Anne Morse. "Gay 'Marriage': Societal Suicide" from *Christianity Today*, June 2004, as found at *http://www.christianitytoday.com/ct/2004/006/8.72.html*. Reprinted by permission of Dr. Charles Colson.

Edwidge Danticat. "Not Your Homeland." Reprinted with permission from the September 25, 2005, issue of *The Nation*. For subscription information, call 1-800-333-8536. Portions of each week's *Nation* magazine can be accessed at *http://www.thenation.com*. "Edwidge Danticat on Writing" excerpted from an "Author Q&A" with Edwidge Danticat. Copyright © 1998. Reprinted by permission of Edwidge Danticat and Aragi Inc.

Guillermo del Toro and Chuck Hogan. "Why Vampires Never Die" from the *New York Times*. Copyright © July 13, 2009, by The New York Times. All rights reserved. Used by permission and

Marie Javdani. "*Plata o Plomo*: Silver or Lead." Reprinted with the permission of the author.

Andrea Jones. "Identity's Edge" from *Orion*, January/February 2007. Reprinted by permission of the author.

Dacher Keltner. "A Vocabulary of Smiles" from *Born to Be Good: The Science of Meaningful Life* by Dacher Keltner. Copyright © 2009 by Dacher Keltner. Reprinted by permission of W. W. Norton & Company, Inc.

Martin Luther King, Jr. "I Have a Dream." Reprinted by arrangement with the Heirs to the Estate of Martin Luther King, Jr., c/o Writers House as agent for the proprietor, New York, NY. Copyright 1963 Dr. Martin Luther King, Jr.; copyright renewed 1991 Coretta Scott King.

Barbara Kingsolver. "Rural Delivery" excerpted from "Life in a Red State" (pp. 205–10) from *Animal, Vegetable, Miracle* by Barbara Kingsolver, Steven L. Hopp, and Camille Kingsolver. Copyright © 2007 by Barbara Kingsolver, Steven L. Hopp, and Camille Kingsolver. Reprinted by permission of HarperCollins Publishers. "Barbara Kingsolver on Writing." Reprinted by permission from The Progressive, 409 E. Main Street, Madison, WI 53703. *www.progressive.com*

Maxine Hong Kingston. "No Name Woman" from *The Woman Warrior* by Maxine Hong Kingston. Copyright © 1975, 1976 by Maxine Hong Kingston. Reprinted by permission of Alfred A. Knopf, a division of Random House, Inc. "Maxine Hong Kingston on Writing" from Gale Group, *Contemporary Authors Online*. Copyright © Gale, a part of Cengage Learning, Inc. Reprinted by permission. *www.cengage.com/permissions*

Mark Krikorian. "Safety through Immigration Control," op-ed, *The Providence Journal*, April 24, 2004, p. B-06. Reprinted by permission of the Center for Immigration Studies, 1522 K Street, NW, Suite 820, Washington, DC 20005-1202.

Christine Leong. "Being a Chink" and "Christine Leong on Writing," copyright © 1996 by Bedford Books. Reprinted by permission of the author.

William Lutz. "The World of Doublespeak" from *Doublespeak* (New York: HarperCollins, 1989). Copyright © 1989 by Blonde Bear, Inc. Reprinted by permission of the Jean V. Naggar Literary Agency. "William Lutz on Writing" excerpted from transcript of *Booknotes* (C-Span, December 31, 1989), *http://www.booknotes.org/transcriptarchive*. Reprinted by permission of C-Span.

Nancy Mairs. "Disability" excerpted from *Carnal Acts: Essays* by Nancy Mairs. Copyright © 1990 by Beacon Press. Reproduced with the permission of Beacon Press in the format Textbook via Copyright Clearance Center.

Brad Manning. "Arm Wrestling with My Father." Reprinted with the permission of the author.

Howard Markel. "Mary Ellen's Story" (editors' title) from "The Child Who Put a Face on Abuse" from the *New York Times*. Copyright © December 15, 2009, by The New York Times. All rights reserved. Used by permission and protected by the Copyright Laws of the United States. The printing, copying, redistribution, or retransmission of the Material without express written permission is prohibited. "Howard Markel on Writing" from *Contemporary Authors Online*, Thomson Gale 2005.

Peter F. Martin. "Destroyed" from "Even More Than the Game, Drugs Destroy Athletes," *Yale Daily News*, September 25, 2007. Copyright 2007 Yale Daily News Publishing Company, Inc. All rights reserved. Reprinted with permission. "Peter F. Martin on Writing" published courtesy of the author.

Fatema Mernissi. "Size 6: The Western Women's Harem" from *Scheherazade Goes West: Different Cultures, Different Harems* by Fatema Mernissi. Copyright © 2001 by Fatema Mernissi. All rights reserved. Reprinted by permission of Pocket Books, a division of Simon & Schuster, Inc.

Jessica Mitford. "Behind the Formaldehyde Curtain" from *The American Way of Death* by Jessica Mitford, pp. 66–77. Reprinted by permission of the Estate of Jessica Mitford. Copyright © 1963, 1978 by Jessica Mitford. All rights reserved. "Jessica Mitford on Writing" excerpted from *Poison Penmanship: The Gentle Art of Muckraking* (New York: Alfred A. Knopf, 1979). Copyright 1979 by Jessica Mitford. Reprinted by permission of the Estate of Jessica Mitford. All rights reserved.

Gloria Naylor. "The Meaning of a Word" (editors' title), originally "A Word's Meaning Can Often Depend on Who Says It," from *The New York Times Magazine*, February 20, 1986. Copyright by Gloria Naylor. Reprinted by permission of SLL/Sterling Lord Literistic, Inc. "Gloria Naylor on Writing" excerpted from William Goldstein, "A Talk with Gloria Naylor," from *Publishers Weekly*, September 9, 1983. Copyright © 1983 by Publishers Weekly.

Jay Nordlinger. "Bassackwards: Construction Spanish and Other Signs of the Times" from *The National Review*, January 29, 2007. Copyright © 2007 by National Review, Inc., 215 Lexington Avenue, New York, NY 10016. Reprinted by permission.

Joyce Carol Oates. "Edward Hopper's *Nighthawks*, 1942," from *The Time Traveler* by Joyce Carol Oates. Copyright © 1983, 1984, 1985, 1986, 1987, 1988, 1989 by The Ontario Review, Inc. Reprinted by permission of Dutton, a division of Penguin Group (USA) Inc. "Joyce Carol Oates on Writing" from *Introspection: American Poets on One of Their Own Poems*, by Robert Pack and Jay Parini. Copyright © University Press of New England, Lebanon, NH. Reprinted by permission.

George Orwell. "Shooting an Elephant" from *Shooting an Elephant and Other Essays* by George Orwell. Copyright 1950 by Sonia Brownell Orwell and renewed © 1978 by Sonia Pitt-Rivers. Reprinted by permission of Houghton Mifflin Harcourt Publishing Company. "George Orwell on Writing" excerpted from "Why I Write" from *Such, Such Were the Joys* by George Orwell. Copyright 1953 by Sonia Brownell Orwell and renewed 1981 by Mrs. George K. Perutz, Mrs. Miriam Gross, and Dr. Michael Dickson, executors of the Estate of Sonia Brownell Orwell. Reprinted by permission of Houghton Mifflin Harcourt Publishing Company.

Bradley Philbert. "Good" from *Knightscapes* (2008) and "Bradley Philbert on Writing." Reprinted by permission of the author.

Helen Pilcher. "The New Witch Doctors: How Belief Can Kill You" from *New Scientist*, May 16, 2009. Copyright © New Scientist Magazine. Reprinted by permission of New Scientist.

Michael Pollan. "Corn's Conquest" from *The Omnivore's Dilemma* by Michael Pollan. Copyright © 2006 by Michael Pollan. Reprinted by permission of The Penguin Press, a division of Penguin Group (USA) Inc. "Michael Pollan on Writing" from Pamela Demory, " 'It's All Storytelling': An Interview with Michael Pollan" from *Writing on the Edge*, Volume 17.1, Fall 2006. Copyright © 2006 The Regents of the University of California. Reprinted by permission of the author.

Katha Pollitt. "What's Wrong with Gay Marriage?" (editors' title), originally "Adam and Steve—Together at Last," from *The Nation*, December 15, 2003. Copyright © 2003 by Katha Pollitt. Reprinted by permission of the author. "Katha Pollitt on Writing" excerpted from Ruth Conniff, "An Interview with Katha Pollitt," *The Progressive* 58:12 (December 1994). This piece was originally written for the Progressive Media Project, 409 E. Main Street, Madison, WI 53703. *www.progressivemediaproject.com*

Francine Prose. "What Words Can Tell" (editors' title) excerpted from pp. 15–19 of *Reading like a Writer* by Francine Prose. Copyright © 2006 by Francine Prose. Reprinted by permission of HarperCollins Publishers.

Anna Quindlen. "Homeless" and "In the Beginning," from *Living Out Loud* by Anna Quindlen. Copyright © 1987 by Anna Quindlen. Reprinted by permission of Random House, Inc.

Richard Rodriguez. "Aria: A Memoir of a Bilingual Childhood." Copyright © 1980 by Richard Rodriguez. Originally appeared in *The American Scholar*. Reprinted by permission of Georges Borchardt, Inc., on behalf of the author.

Sharman Apt Russell. "The Adored, Buzzing Around Us," *Orion* Magazine, March/April 2009. Reprinted by permission of the author. "Sharman Apt Russell on Writing" from an interview conducted by Susan J. Tweit. Copyright 2009 Susan J. Tweit. Reprinted by permission of Story Circle Book Reviews (*www.storycirclebookreviews.org*).

Edward Said. "Clashing Civilization?" excerpted from "We All Swim Together" in *The New Statesman* 14, October 15, 2001. Copyright © 2010 New Statesman Ltd. All rights reserved.

Linnea Saukko. "How to Poison the Earth." Reprinted by permission of the author.

David Sedaris. "Remembering My Childhood on the Continent of Africa" and "David Sedaris on Writing" (originally "Nutcracker.com") from *Me Talk Pretty One Day* by David Sedaris. Copyright © 2000 by David Sedaris. Reprinted by permission of Little, Brown and Company.

Visual Images

Nighthawks (full painting and detail), 1942, painting by Edward Hopper, American, 1882–1967. Oil on canvas, 84.1 × 152.4 cm, Friends of American Art Collection, 1942.51, The Art Institute of Chicago. Photography © The Art Institute of Chicago.

Low-Energy Drinks, cartoon by Glen Le Lievre. Copyright © Glen Le Lievre/The New Yorker Collection/*www.cartoonbank.com*.

American Gothic, 1930, painting by Grant Wood, American, 1891–1942. Oil on beaver board, 30 11/16 × 25 11/16 in. (78 × 65.3 cm) unframed, Friends of American Art Collection, 1930.934, The Art Institute of Chicago. Art © Figge Art Museum, successors to the Estate of Nan Wood Graham/Licensed by VAGA, New York, NY. Photography © The Art Institute of Chicago.

Rural Rehabilitation Client, photograph by Ben Shahn. Copyright © CORBIS.

Workers Making Cabbage Patch Dolls, photograph by Wall McNamee. Copyright © Wally McNamee/CORBIS.

Deconstructing Lunch, cartoon by Roz Chast. Copyright © Roz Chast/The New Yorker Collection/*www.cartoonbank.com*.

Mounted Nazi Troops on the Lookout for Likely Polish Children, photograph from *Master Race: The Lebensborn Experiment in Nazi Germany* by Catrine Clay and Michael Leapman, published by Hodder and Stoughton.

Please Recycle. Ridge Meadows Recycling Society @ RMRecycling.org.

Smile Quiz. Reprinted by permission of Dacher Keltner.

Im txtng while drvng, cartoon by Mike Luckovich. Reprinted by permission of Mike Luckovich and Creators Syndicate. All rights reserved.

There's Strong. Courtesy of the US Army.

Corporate America Flag. Courtesy of Adbusters Media Foundation.

Mononykus. Pixeldust Studios.

Styracosaurus. Renegade 9/National Geographic Stock.

Parasaurolophus. Pixeldust Studios.

Gigantoraptor. Pixeldust Studios.

INDEX